Probation, Parole, and Community Corrections

Fifth Edition

Dean John Champion
Texas A & M International University

PEARSON

Prentice
Hall

Upper Saddle River, New Jersey 07458

Library of Congress Cataloging-in-Publication Data

Champion, Dean J.
  Probation, parole, and community corrections / by Dean J.
Champion.—5th ed.
      p. cm.
  Includes bibliographical references and indexes.
  ISBN 0-13-182984-X
  1. Probation—United States. 2.   Parole–United States.
I. Title.

  HV9304.C463 2005
  364.6'3'0973--dc22

                                                    2004011351

Executive Editor: Frank Mortimer, Jr.
Associate Editor: Sarah Holle
Production Editor: Linda Duarte, Pine Tree Composition
Production Liaison: Barbara Marttine Cappuccio
Director of Manufacturing and Production: Bruce Johnson
Managing Editor: Mary Carnis
Manufacturing Buyer: Cathleen Petersen
Creative Director: Cheryl Asherman
Cover Design Coordinator: Miguel Ortiz
Cover Designer: Marianne Frasco
Cover Image: Spencer Grant, PhotoEdit
Editorial Assistant: Barbara Rosenberg
Marketing Manager: Tim Peyton
Formatting and Interior Design: Pine Tree Composition
Printing and Binding: Courier Westford

Chapter Opening Photo Credits

p. 1 A. Ramey, PhotoEdit; **p. 31** Al Dodge; **p. 76** Michael Newman, PhotoEdit; **p. 127** Robert Harbison; **p. 313** Mikael Karlsson, Arresting Images; **p. 382** Mikael Karlsson, Arresting Images; **p. 429** Les Stone, Corbis/Sygma; **p. 471** Andrew Lichtenstein, Aurora & Quanta Product; **p. 503** Gary Wagner, Gary Wagner Photography; **p. 615** David J. Sams, Stock Boston.

Pearson Education, Ltd., *London*
Pearson Education Australia Pty. Limited, *Sydney*
Pearson Education Singapore, Pte. Ltd.
Pearson Education North Asia Ltd., *Hong Kong*
Pearson Education Canada, Ltd., *Toronto*
Pearson Education de Mexico, S.A. de C.V.
Pearson Education—Japan, *Tokyo*
Pearson Education Malaysia, Pte. Ltd.
Pearson Education, Upper Saddle River, *New Jersey*

1 0 9 8 7 6 5 4 3 2
ISBN 0-13-182984-X

Contents

Chapter 3

Sentencing and the Presentence Investigation Report: Background, Preparation, and Functions

76

Chapter 4

Probation and Probationers: History, Philosophy, Goals, and Functions

127

Chapter 5

Programs for Probationers

170

Chapter 6

Jails and Prisons

235

Chapter 7

Parole and Parolees

283

Chapter 11

Theories of Offender Treatment   471

Chapter 12

Offender Supervision: Types of Offenders
and Special Supervisory Considerations   503

Chapter 13

Juvenile Probation and Parole   543

Chapter 14

Evaluating Programs: Balancing Service Delivery and Recidivism Considerations

615

Preface

Probation, Parole, and Community Corrections, fifth edition, is about adults and juveniles who have been convicted of criminal offenses or adjudicated as delinquent and punished. Judges may sentence offenders to incarceration in prison or jail for a definite period, or they may suspend the sentence, subject to the offender's compliance with certain conditions. Judges may also sentence offenders to incarceration for a fixed period of years, but offenders may serve only a portion of that time. Parole boards, the court, or others may authorize the early release of offenders, again subject to certain conditions.

Some adult and juvenile offenders are permitted by the courts to remain free in their communities, provided that they comply with certain conditions. Other offenders are granted early release from incarceration under similar provisions. These offenders will be supervised by officers and agencies as provided by law. This book is also about the personnel and agencies who monitor these offenders.

The distinction between probation and parole is not clear-cut. *Probation* applies to a class of programs for those offenders sentenced to incarceration but who have had their incarcerative sentences conditionally suspended. *Parole* applies to those programs for offenders who have been incarcerated but have been released prior to serving the full term of their incarceration. Therefore, *parolees* are convicted or adjudicated offenders who have been incarcerated but have been released before their sentences have been fully served. *Probationers* are convicted or adjudicated offenders who are ordered to serve conditional sentences in the community in lieu of incarceration.

In both instances, parolees and probationers are supervised by parole and probation officers. But there are other classes of offenders whose activities are monitored by these officers as well. Sometimes, offenders are granted diversion by the court. *Diversion* is a pretrial alternative whereby offenders may avoid a formal criminal prosecution. If offenders successfully comply with the conditions of their diversion, then criminal charges against them are either dropped or reduced in seriousness when they complete their diversionary programs.

Distinguishing clearly between probation and parole is difficult for at least two reasons. First, there are many probation and parole programs, and most of them overlap. Thus, the clients of a specific program may be comprised of both probationers and parolees. Second, there are many different kinds of probationers and parolees to be supervised. There is disagreement among professionals about which programs are most effective for different types of offenders. Furthermore, there are disagreements about the philosophical objectives of probation and parole programs. This book describes the objectives of probation and parole and whether these objectives are achieved. Understanding these philosophies will be achieved through an examination of the history of parole and probation in the United States. Besides describing probation and parole programs, various classes of offenders are portrayed. Some of these are called special-needs offenders, who may be mentally ill, have HIV/AIDS, be gang members, have drug/alcohol dependencies, or have other disabilities. Additionally, several problems associated with the selection and training of probation and parole officers are highlighted, including their relationships with different types of offender-clients.

Juvenile offenders pose special problems for those assigned to supervise them. A profile of juvenile offenders is also presented, together with a discussion of several controversial issues associated with processing juveniles. The juvenile justice system is gradually changing, acquiring several characteristics that are making it less distinct compared with the criminal justice system. Larger numbers of juveniles are being processed as adult offenders, either through statutes or recommendations from prosecutors and juvenile judges. Since 1966, juveniles have been granted certain constitutional rights equivalent to those of adult offenders. Some of these rights will be described, and the influence of these rights upon juvenile probation and parole programs will be examined.

One premise of this book is that all components of the criminal and juvenile justice systems are interrelated to varying degrees. While experts contend that these systems are better described as loosely related processes, each component has an impact on each of the other components. Police discretion influences the disposition of adult and juvenile offenders. In turn, the courts influence police discretion and affect prisons and jails through particular sentencing practices. Prison and jail problems such as overcrowding often overburden probation and parole officers with excessive offender caseloads. Varying offender caseloads influence the quality of officer-offender interaction and the ultimate effectiveness of probation and parole programs. Ineffective probation and parole programs may increase the number of repeat offenders who come to the attention of police when they commit new crimes. Thus, probation and parole programs do not exist in a vacuum, unaffected by other agencies and organizations.

Probation and parole policy decisions are sometimes politically motivated. However, economic considerations and limited human resources also play important parts in shaping correctional priorities. The influence of political and economic considerations on probation and parole programs as well as officer effectiveness will be described. Important questions pertain to whether our programming is effective: Does a particular program meet the needs of certain offenders? How do we know whether an intervention is successful or unsuccessful? Therefore, one chapter is devoted to program evaluation and examining the criteria we apply in determining program effectiveness. Effectiveness of programs is often measured according to recidivism rates. Recidivism is conceptualized in several different ways. This concept is examined in great detail, and its relation to program effectiveness is extensively described.

Underlying all intervention programs are theories or structured explanations of delinquency and crime. Why do we have delinquents and criminals? What explanations are provided to explain their behavior? Many theories of delinquency and adult criminality are examined. These are largely biological, psychological, and sociological theories. Not all theories are equally utilized in criminological research, since some of them are more popular than others. Some theories have been largely abandoned, because they lack the predictive utility necessary to be of use to criminal justice professionals who establish and operate programs for probationers and parolees. Various criteria are examined that enable us to evaluate which theories seem best for understanding the behaviors of offenders. Knowing about their motives for committing crimes or delinquent offenses enables us to structure programs that are seemingly effective in modifying or eliminating those events that led to criminality and delinquency initially. Therefore, evaluative criteria are examined that allow us to assess the value of different theories that drive our programming efforts.

The book has the following features that add to its value as a teaching tool.

- Questions for review at chapter ends to facilitate group discussion and class assignments.
- A comprehensive glossary is provided so that students can look up unfamiliar words. All key words that are boldfaced in each chapter are listed in a general glossary.
- Comprehensive, up-to-date references are included for those students who wish to do additional reading and learn more about the different subjects presented.
- Each chapter includes suggested readings.
- All chapters are summarized, highlighting the major points.
- Persons who work in probation and parole services are profiled in personality highlights. Students should find these personality highlights of interest, since these have been written by practitioners in the field who work with either adult or juvenile probationers and parolees, or who work in other parts of the criminal justice system.
- For instructors who use this book, an Instructor's Manual is provided, which includes a test bank. The Instructor's Manual includes chapter synopses, key objectives of each chapter, and true-false, multiple-choice, and short-answer essay questions for use in examination preparation.
- While every effort has been made to include the most up-to-date information in various tables and literature discussed throughout the text, there is always continuous updating of information by the U.S. government and other data sources. There is always at least a one-year delay between the time information is compiled and reported by any federal or state agency. Thus, in late 2003 the most current information available about probationers and parolees was for 2002. By the time this book was published, more time elapsed and new information was generated. Positively, trends and descriptive information reported, even the research literature and contemporary findings, remain fairly stable over time. Few surprises are encountered across years about innovative programming and theories. But if students desire the most current information available, such as mid-year government reports or documents, this information may be accessed easily via the Internet websites provided at chapter ends. It is also true that some websites on the Internet are active and functional when the book is published, but some of these websites are discontinued after a time. In the event that one or more websites do not respond when you attempt to access them, general searches for similar websites will yield productive results through Yahoo or some other search engine.

The author wishes to acknowledge the following persons who have reviewed the manuscript in its various editions and have given their comments about how this edition could be improved. I am grateful for their suggestions and note that any possible factual mistakes are my own. Lee Ayers-Schlosser, Southern Oregon University, Ashland, OR; Terry Campbell, Western Illinois University, Macomb, IL; Michael Grabowski, Santa Rosa Junior College, Santa Rosa, CA; Craig W. Laker, Tri-State University, Angola, IN; Jeffrey Ross, University of Baltimore, Baltimore, MD. I encourage anyone using this book to contact me for additional examination information and for other ancillary materials I will be pleased to provide upon request in different software formats on diskette. I want to thank Frank Mortimer, my Prentice Hall editor, as well as my production editor, Linda Duarte, for the hard work that has gone into developing this project from beginning to end.

Also I would like to thank Sarah Holle, my Associate Editor, for her prodigious efforts in coordinating the review process, assembling and researching photos for inclusion, and many other endless forms of assistance rendered to me as this edition has progressed to completion. I would be remiss if I failed to mention John Yarley and Steve Helba, who were editors at Merrill Publishing Company in Columbus, Ohio, when the first edition of this book was published in 1990. As an untested author of criminal justice books at that time, I appreciate their confidence in my ability to write in this field and the strong support they provided. This book was subsequently acquired by Macmillan and fell under the editorship of Chris Cardone, who continued to support the second edition. When Prentice Hall acquired Macmillan in the mid-1990s, other editors continued to assist me. I want to thank successive editors Robin Baliszewski, Neil Marquardt, and Kim Davies, all of whom were very supportive of this book and its subsequent editions. My current editor, Frank Mortimer, has also been supportive of this and other of my projects. Many thanks to you, Frank.

Dean John Champion
Department of Social Sciences
Texas A & M International University
5201 University Blvd.
Laredo, TX 78041
E-mail: dchampion@tamiu.edu

CHAPTER I | *Criminal Justice System Components: Locating Probation and Parole*

Chapter Outline

As the result of reading this chapter, the following objectives will be realized:

1. Providing a brief overview and description of the components of the criminal justice system.
2. Distinguishing between probation and parole and specifying those agencies and organizations within these categories.
3. Describing traditional offender categorizations including property offenders and violent offenders, first offenders, recidivists, and career criminals.
4. Describing the *Uniform Crime Reports* and the *National Crime Victimization Survey* and their weaknesses and strengths.
5. Describing prosecutorial decision making and the plea bargaining process.
6. Examining judicial discretion in the sentencing process and some of the factors that impact the sentencing decision.

INTRODUCTION

• *Fuller was an Oregon parolee who had his parole transferred to Idaho, which was closer to his family. Under an interstate compact agreement, Idaho parole authorities assumed supervision of Fuller through one of their district offices. Fuller signed an Idaho parole agreement form and was thereafter expected to abide by Idaho parole program conditions. These conditions included a waiver of Fuller's Fourth Amendment rights and an agreement to submit to tests for controlled substances. Subsequently Fuller allegedly violated several conditions of his parole program, and his supervising officer, an Idaho parole officer, reported these violations to Oregon. Oregon parole authorities issued an order suspending Fuller's supervision and directing Idaho officials to take Fuller into custody. However, the Oregon order could only be served in Oregon, not Idaho. A short time later when Fuller appeared in an Idaho parole office for his regularly scheduled visit, a urine sample collected from him tested positive for methamphetamines. Idaho parole officers and police then searched Fuller's automobile, where they found a quantity of drugs under the front seat of his vehicle. Idaho authorities arrested Fuller and charged him with possession of a controlled substance. Fuller moved to suppress the drug evidence against him, contending that the Oregon order terminated his Idaho parole program, and thus the Idaho paroling authority no longer had the right to search his person or possessions, including his automobile. An Idaho court of appeals agreed with Fuller, but the Idaho Supreme Court reversed their ruling and held that despite Oregon's order, Fuller was still under Idaho parole supervisory authority under the parole agreement he had signed when he initially entered Idaho. Thus, Idaho parole officers had the authority to conduct warrantless searches and seizures of Fuller and his property. The discovered drug evidence was admissible against Fuller in a subsequent Idaho criminal action. [State v. Fuller, 2002].*

• *Smith was placed on a term of probation in Indiana for child molestation. Some of his probation conditions were that he must notify his probation officer of any dating, intimate, or sexual relationship; that he not participate in any activities involving children under the age of 18; that he should not view sexually explicit adult material of any kind; and that he should not use a computer or access any online computer service at any location. Smith appealed, contending that these conditions were unconstitutional. On review, the Indiana Court of Appeals agreed in part. The court evaluates claims on the basis of three criteria: (1) the purpose to be served by probation; (2) the extent to which constitutional rights enjoyed by law-abiding citizens should be enjoyed by probationers; and (3) the legitimate needs of law enforcement. In Smith's case, barring him from encounters with children under 18 was permissible. Further, advising his probation officer about his dating, intimate, or sexual relationships with adults was not prohibited; rather, Smith only needed to report such experiences. Although this dating brought Smith into contact with a girlfriend's child, this fact alone could not bar such dating. The condition preventing Smith from viewing or possessing pornographic material was also reasonable. However, the court noted that a blanket prohibition on "pornography" was unclear and unconstitutionally vague. Thus, it remanded the case to the trial court with instructions to set forth explicitly what it meant by pornographic materials. Restrictions regarding computer access were also reasonable, since the computer and Internet make it easy for Smith to access pornographic sites. Generally, however, Smith's appeal was rejected. [Smith v. State, 2002].*

• *Demarce was convicted in Arizona of sexual assault. At his sentencing hearing and under a previous plea agreement, Demarce received a sentence of probation from the judge, together with several special conditions. However, the judge departed from the contemplated plea agreement and imposed lifetime probation on Demarce. Demarce objected and attempted to refuse probation in exchange for statutory incarceration less time served, which would be substantially less than lifetime probation and less onerous, considering the rights relinquished by probationers. The Arizona Supreme Court upheld the right of the judge to impose lifetime probation on Demarce, noting that accepting a plea agreement may result in a more severe sentence than that contemplated between one's defense counsel and the prosecutor. Furthermore, Arizona law permits lifetime probation for certain types of felony offenses, at the sentencing judge's discretion. Demarce could have rejected the plea agreement initially, but he did not have a right to withdraw from the plea agreement once the sentence had been imposed. In sum, Demarce did not have the right to reject probation and elect incarceration for a lesser term after finding that the probation conditions were simply too onerous. [Demarce v. Willrich, 2002].*

• *McAllister was convicted in Delaware of several drug offenses and placed on probation. One probation condition was that McAllister submit to warrantless searches of his premises at any time by probation officers. Subsequently probation officers received a tip from an informant that McAllister was secreting a large quantity of illegal drugs on his premises, and that he kept these drugs in a locked room. Probation officers entered McAllister's premises and asked McAllister about the locked room. McAllister admitted that he sometimes slept in a padlocked room and that he had a key. When probation officers asked him for the key to the room, he attempted to flee but was quickly apprehended. The key was recovered from McAllister's person and a search of the locked room was conducted which yielded a large quantity of drugs. McAllister was charged with a new offense of possession of illegal drugs, but attempted to suppress the evidence, contending that the warrantless search by probation officers was illegal and not based on probable cause. The court upheld the legality of the warrantless search by probation officers, noting that they were authorized to conduct such searches. Furthermore, the furtive actions of McAllister gave them considerable justification to detain him while they searched his premises thoroughly. The court held that the evidence against McAllister was properly and legally seized by probation officers within the scope of their authority under the probation agreement. [McAllister v. State, 2002].*

These cases indicate that probation and parole are both conditional sentences and releases from incarceration, either immediately following conviction for a crime or after a period of incarceration in a prison or jail. The conditions imposed relate to behavioral requirements and involve agreements between the state and probationers/parolees based upon mutual trust. The reward for probationers/parolees is freedom, which is either limited or completely unrestricted. The penalties for violating this trust involve loss of freedom through incarceration or more restrictive forms of probation/parole supervision. This book is about all types of programs involving convicted offenders, and where such programs include diverse conditions of supervised release. These programs are almost always operated in communities and are designed to supervise offender behaviors more or less intensively. These are broadly labeled probation, parole, or community corrections.

This chapter is an overview of the **criminal justice system.** Probation and parole are identified in relation to various criminal justice system components. The first part of this chapter defines crime and distinguishes between several types of crime. Different offense categories are listed by which offenders are classified. Two popular crime information sources are described. These are the *Uniform Crime Reports (UCR)* and the *National Crime Victimization Survey (NCVS).* Several criticisms of these information sources are listed. Additional descriptions are provided for both traditional offenders and special-needs offenders. These classifications include first offenders and recidivists, drug/alcohol dependent offenders, offenders who are mentally and/or physically challenged, and those with HIV/AIDS and other communicable diseases. Major components of the criminal justice system are identified and described, including law enforcement, prosecutorial decision making, courts and court processing, and corrections. When a crime is committed and someone is charged with committing it, the criminal justice system processes the offender through a series of established stages. The final part of the chapter looks at probation and parole. Probation and parole are defined as essentially different programs, although there are many similarities among these programs for convicted offenders.

AN OVERVIEW OF THE CRIMINAL JUSTICE SYSTEM

The criminal justice system consists of **law enforcement,** the **courts,** and **corrections.** Law enforcement officers attempt to control crime and apprehend criminals. The courts determine a defendant's guilt or innocence and sentence convicted offenders. Corrections punishes, manages, and rehabilitates those who have been sentenced. Ideally, this is how things are supposed to work. In actual practice, however, the criminal justice system is seriously flawed. Many criminals are never caught. Many of those criminals who are apprehended never go to trial. Many of those whose cases go to trial are acquitted even though they are guilty of the offenses charged. Many convicted offenders are never incarcerated. Many incarcerated offenders are never rehabilitated. They leave prisons and jails only to resume their criminal activity. Considerable responsibility is given to corrections personnel. Much is expected of those working directly with offenders. Not only are they expected to provide inmates with food, shelter, and basic living requirements, but they are also supposed to rehabilitate them and make them suitable for return to society as law-abiding citizens. As we will see in later chapters, corrections falls far short of this goal. But we will also see that it is not necessarily the fault of corrections for the low incidence of **offender rehabilitation.** Besides institutional corrections, such as prisons and jails, personnel who work in **probation, parole,** and **community corrections** are heavily involved with offender supervision and operate programs designed to rehabilitate or reintegrate offender-clients. These personnel are also expected to accomplish the difficult task of supervising and offering different forms of assistance to their clients with the express purpose of making them law-abiding citizens. Again, it will be disclosed that **probation officers (POs)** and **parole officers (POs)** often fail to achieve their personal and departmental objectives. However, the reasons for their client failures are often beyond their direct control.

Entry into the criminal justice system begins with the commission of a crime, followed by the **arrest** of one or more suspected perpetrators of that crime (McKean and Raphael, 2002). Assuming **offenders** have been identified and apprehended, their movement through the criminal justice system is similar for both state and federal processing. Persons suspected of committing crimes are arrested, booked, and charged with one or more offenses. If there are successful **prosecutions** of **defendants** by **prosecutors,** they are found guilty and sentenced by judges. Probation is one **sentencing** option imposed by judges in lieu of incarceration. **Probationers** are allowed to remain free in their communities, although they must abide by certain probation conditions for a period of time. Another option is parole. Parole is an **early release** from prison or jail, permitting convicted offenders the opportunity of living in their communities, again with parole program restrictions and conditions. Convicted offenders who have served some time in jail or prison before earning early release are called **parolees.**

This book describes what happens to offenders who are either sentenced to probation or granted parole after serving a portion of their sentence in prison. In both situations, these offenders must obey several program conditions. Otherwise, their probation or parole may be revoked or cancelled. A **parole revocation** means that parolees may be returned to prison for some or all of the remainder of their original sentences. For probationers, a **probation revocation** may mean incarceration, or it may mean a more intensive form of supervision by probation by program officials. Enforcing the conditions of probation and parole are probation and parole officers (POs). The designation, PO, is used to refer either to probation or parole officers throughout this text. Offenders are required to report to their POs regularly and to comply with other rules and regulations. Thus, a second major goal of this book is to describe the personnel and programs that manage probationers and parolees.

Figure 1.1 is a diagram of the criminal justice system, showing the commission of a crime which leads to an arrest. Other phases of offender processing are also depicted. Figure 1.1 also shows that if offenders are juveniles, they are sent to the juvenile justice system.

POs often collaborate with community agencies that provide special services for offenders. For example, in the state of Washington, a program has been established to treat **sex offenders.** It is called the Special Sex Offender Sentencing Alternative (SSOSA) (Starzyk and Marshall, 2003). Probation officers assist community **corrections officers** with their supervisory chores in overseeing large numbers of sex offenders. Some of these offenders were **recidivists,** meaning that they had been convicted of one or more previous crimes (McKay, 2002). Some amount of **recidivism** is a part of all probation and parole programs, regardless of how carefully they are established and how closely offenders are supervised. **Recidivism rates** were lower for those sex offenders who participated in the community treatment and were under the close supervision of both

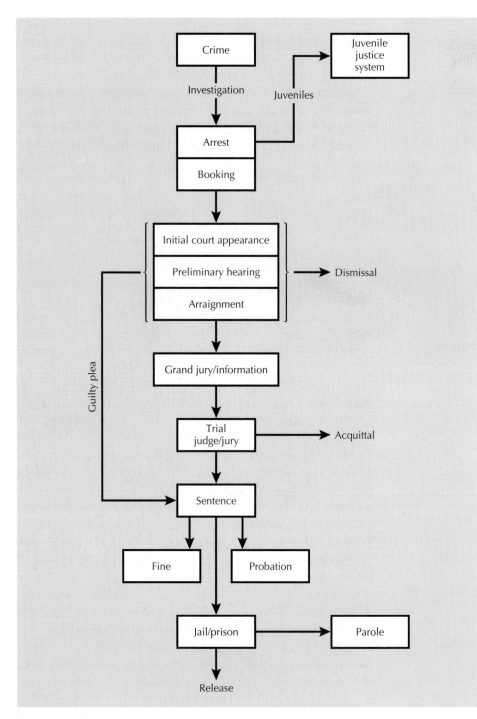

FIGURE 1.1   An overview of the criminal justice process.

probation and community agency personnel. The SSOSA program has had similar results in other cities throughout the state. Thus, depending on the **jurisdiction,** POs may be assigned to supervise (1) adult probationers and/or parolees; (2) juvenile probationers and/or parolees; and/or (3) offenders with special needs. While POs perform many other duties, their primary responsibility is the management and supervision of nonincarcerated offenders (Frost, 2002).

All probationers and parolees are a part of corrections. Corrections is the aggregate of programs, services, facilities, and organizations responsible for the management of people who have been accused or convicted of criminal offenses. This book focuses largely upon the nonincarcerative dimension of corrections, although some attention will be given to jails or prisons, where offenders may receive treatment or assistance for their needs or problems. More often than not, inmates of prisons or jails are influenced by those they associate with while confined. These associations may not be positive or therapeutic. In fact, the **criminogenic environment** of prisons and jails and social interactions with other inmates often lead to and explain probation or parole program failures.

TYPES OF OFFENSES

Crimes are violations of the law by people held accountable by the law. Two general categories of crime are felonies and misdemeanors.

Felonies and Misdemeanors

Felonies.   A **felony** is a major crime which carries potentially severe penalties of one or more years in prison or jail and **fines.** Fines are monetary assessments that accompany a conviction for one or more crimes. Fines are prescribed by statute. Usually, statutory penalties are associated with all felonies and include both fines and/or incarceration in a state or federal prison for one or more years. Felonies include arson, murder, rape, burglary, robbery, vehicular theft, and aggravated assault. In recent years, stalking behavior, where persons follow others with the intent of harming or annoying them, has been promoted to a serious felony (Maxey, 2002). Both misdemeanor and felony convictions mean that offenders acquire criminal records. Some jurisdictions have a third class of crimes. A certain type of minor offense may be known as a **summary offense.** These are petty crimes and ordinarily carry penalties of fines only. Also, convictions for these petty offenses will not result in a criminal record. Examples of summary offenses are speeding or dumping litter from an automobile on a public highway.

Misdemeanors.   A **misdemeanor** is a minor or petty offense. Misdemeanor offenses carry less severe penalties than major crimes or felonies. Misdemeanor offenses may result in fines and/or incarceration for less than one year. A **misdemeanant** is someone who commits a misdemeanor and may be incarcerated in a local jail. Examples of misdemeanors include making a false financial statement to obtain credit, prostitution, shoplifting, and criminal trespass.

Violent and Property Crimes

Violent crimes are characterized by extreme physical force, including murder or homicide, forcible rape, child sexual abuse, assault and battery by means of a dangerous weapon, robbery, and arson (Steck et al., 2002). Sometimes these offenses are referred to as **crimes of violence,** or **crimes against the person,** because victims are directly affected emotionally and physically by the crime. Nonviolent offenses include crimes such as burglary, vehicular theft, embezzlement, fraud, forgery, and larceny. These are often referred to as **crimes against property,** and although persons are indirectly victimized or affected by such offenses, their lives and physical well-being are not directly jeopardized by such acts. Two sources that report crime in the United States are the *Uniform Crime Reports* and the *National Crime Victimization Survey.*

The *Uniform Crime Reports* and the *National Crime Victimization Survey*

The Uniform Crime Reports (UCR).   The *Uniform Crime Reports (UCR)* is published annually by the **Federal Bureau of Investigation (FBI).** This publication includes statistics about the number and kinds of crimes reported in the United States annually by over 15,000 law enforcement agencies. The *UCR* is the official compendium of crime statistics for the United States. The *UCR* is compiled by gathering information about twenty-nine types of crime from reporting law enforcement agencies. Crime information is requested from all rural and urban law enforcement agencies and is subsequently reported to the Federal Bureau of Investigation (FBI). The FBI has established a **crime classification index. Index offenses** include eight serious types of crime used by the FBI to measure crime trends. These are arson, murder and non-negligent manslaughter, aggravated assault, robbery, motor vehicle theft, forcible rape, larceny-theft, and burglary (Hensley, Koscheski, and Tewksbury, 2002). Information is also compiled about twenty-one less serious offenses ranging from forgery and counterfeiting to curfew violations and runaways. Index offense information is presented in the *UCR* for each state, city, county, and township that has submitted crime information during the most recent year. The *UCR* is published annually by the U.S. Government Printing Office.

Criticisms of the UCR.   Although the *UCR* publishes the most current crime figures available from reporting law enforcement agencies, this information is inaccurate in several respects. First, when criminals are questioned about other crimes they have committed, there are discrepancies between *UCR* figures and **self-reported information.** Many criminals are not caught for many of the crimes they have committed. Therefore, there is considerably more crime committed annually than is disclosed by official estimates published in the *UCR.* Second, not all law enforcement agencies report crimes in uniform ways. For instance, North Dakota has no forcible rape category for this type of sex crime. This doesn't mean that rape doesn't occur in that state. Rather, North Dakota classifies forcible rape as "gross sexual imposition." Third, more aggressive enforcement of certain laws in different jurisdictions may lead to more arrests, although there are few convictions. Further, not all law enforcement agencies report their crime figures consistently. Also, many crimes are never reported to the police. Finally, when a crime report is submitted to the *UCR,* only the most serious offense is often reported. Thus, if someone robs a convenience store, shoots and kills the clerk, injures customers, and steals a car before being captured by police, the police department will report only the most serious offense, or "murder or non-negligent manslaughter" as the most serious offense rather than all of the other offenses the perpetrator committed. Thus, there is good reason for experts to believe that the *UCR* greatly underestimates the amount of crime committed in the United States (Kautt, 2002).

The National Crime Victimization Survey (NCVS).   The limitations of the *UCR* and other official documents measuring the amount of crime in the United

States have caused some persons to draw comparisons between the *UCR* and the *National Crime Victimization Survey (NCVS),* which is conducted annually by the United States Bureau of the Census. The *NCVS* is a random survey of approximately 60,000 dwellings, about 127,000 persons age 12 and over, and approximately 50,000 businesses. Smaller samples of persons from these original figures form the database from which annual crime estimates are compiled. Carefully worded questions lead people to report incidents that can be classified as crimes. This material is statistically manipulated in such a way so as to make it comparable with *UCR* statistics. This material is usually referred to as **victimization data.**

The *NCVS* distinguishes between **victimizations** and **incidents.** A victimization is the basic measure of the occurrence of a crime and is a specific criminal act that affects a single victim. An incident is a specific criminal act involving one or more victims. However, the *NCVS* has certain persistent problems similar to the *UCR.* Some crime victims cannot remember when or where the offense against them occurred. Other victims are reluctant to report a rape, particularly if the rapist is known to them, such as a family member or close friend. Often, crimes are committed in the workplace, where employees steal goods from their employers. Much **white-collar crime,** or crime conducted in the course of one's occupation, is handled internally and not reported, sometimes because those involved don't believe the crimes are serious enough to warrant police intrusion. Nonreporting is also related to victim fear, feelings of helplessness or apathy, the perceived powerlessness of police, and fear of the authorities themselves. The poor are especially reluctant to report crime because they fear reprisals from the criminals who are often known to them. Also, police may detect evidence of other crimes or statutory violations such as health code infractions, illegal aliens, and overcrowded apartment dwellings. Regardless of these shortcomings, the *UCR* and *NCVS* are better than no information. Researchers find many uses for the information from both sources (Lynch, 2002).

In recent years, summary statistical information in the *Uniform Crime Reports* and other official sources has gradually been replaced by the **National Incident-Based Reporting System (NIBRS).** This system involves the collection of incident-level data for a broad range of offenses. Thus, a more accurate picture of the amount of crime committed in the United States can be gleaned from an examination of NIBRS figures.

CLASSIFYING OFFENDERS

Distinguishing between different types of offenders is fairly easy, particularly if we classify them strictly on the basis of the crimes they have committed. However, some burglars are more violent or dangerous than others. Some rapists are more aggressive than other rapists. Some murderers are more dangerous than other murderers. Prisons and jails must place their inmates according to the most appropriate form of supervision. Various classification schemes have been devised and are used by prison and jail officials to determine which **level of custody** is most appropriate for each inmate. Corrections officials want to know which inmates should be isolated from other inmates and which ones should be permitted to associate with other inmates under more general supervision. Some inmates may pose physical threats either to themselves or to other inmates. Aggressive and violent prisoners can exploit, injure, or kill weaker inmates. Some inmates are suicide risks. Yet other inmates have mental illnesses or suffer from poor social adjustment (Craissati, McClurg, and Browne, 2002).

Probation and parole agencies also have a vested interest in classifying offenders accurately. Different probation programs target particular types of offenders, although the effectiveness of classification is sometimes questionable. Some offenders may be impaired mentally or physically. Some may have personality disorders or poor self-concepts. Yet other offenders may have serious alcohol or drug dependencies. Thus, various treatment programs are designed to meet specific offender needs, such as narcotics addiction. These classification problems are pervasive for both adult and juvenile offenders. Several additional offender classifications have been developed for probation and parole programs. These traditional offender classifications include first offenders and recidivists or career criminals.

Traditional Offender Categorizations

Besides violent and property offenders, two additional classifications include (1) first offenders and (2) recidivists and career criminals.

First Offenders.   **First offenders** are those who commit one or more crimes but have no previous history of criminal behavior. There is nothing especially unique about first offenders. They may commit violent crimes or **property crimes.** First offenders may be male or female. They may be old or young. They may or may not have records as juvenile **delinquents.** No useful blanket generalizations can be made about first offenders other than the fact they have no previous criminal history. First offenders who commit only the offense for which they were apprehended and prosecuted and are unlikely to commit future crimes are called **situational offenders.** Situational offenders may commit serious crimes or petty offenses. The situation itself creates the unique conditions leading to the criminal act. An argument between husband and wife over something trivial may lead to the death of one of the spouses. An argument between a convenience store clerk and a customer may lead to a serious altercation, even death. Serious financial pressures or setbacks may prompt situational offenders to commit embezzlement.

Often, first offenders are given special treatment by different components of the criminal justice system. Prosecutors are inclined to give first offenders another chance by either diverting them from the criminal justice system entirely or downgrading the seriousness of their instant offense. These persons are frequently good candidates for community treatment programs. If they have not become deeply entrenched in criminal activity, there is a good chance that one or more programs can reach them and help them to become more law-abiding. Probation departments also target first offenders as most eligible for their programs. Knowing an offender's criminal history can indicate much about whether their participation in these community programs will be worthwhile and/or successful (Peck and Voas, 2002).

Recidivists.   Besides first offenders and situational criminals, some offenders are recidivists who continue to commit new offenses. Even after they have been apprehended, prosecuted, and incarcerated, many offenders continue their criminal activity when released. Drug or narcotics addiction contributes signifi-

BOX 1.1

Should the following persons receive prison or probation for their crimes?

• *John L. is a television station equipment assistant manager working in Los Angeles. In January 2002 John L.'s wife gave birth to a baby boy, although the birth had complications. John L.'s wife had to be hospitalized for an extended period. John L. also gambled at a casino in a Los Angeles suburb. Between his gambling losses, which were substantial, and his wife's protracted hospitalization and care, John L. did not have enough money to pay for their necessities. One day in July 2002 during the noon hour, John L. entered a Los Angeles bank with a note which he gave to the teller. The note read, "I have a gun and will use it if you don't do what I say. Give me all of your money. Say nothing to anyone." The teller gave John L. all of her money, including some marked bills which she kept in a separate compartment in her cash drawer. John L. fled, but he was in police custody by 5:00 p.m. Security cameras in the bank clearly identified him as the robber. When he was taken into custody, he broke down and cried. He claimed that he wasn't thinking clearly and became desperate over not having enough money. He never had a weapon, and this was his first offense. But prosecutors charged him with robbery, a major felony, and he was convicted in June 2003. A presentence investigation report was prepared for the court by a probation officer. Should John L. be imprisoned or placed on probation?*

• *Dale M. is a Nebraska offender who has been convicted of at least six felonies in other states. These felonies were all nonviolent burglaries. At no time did anyone suffer injuries during Dale M.'s crimes. Dale M. was apprehended in Lincoln in November 2002 by local police after setting off a silent alarm in a closed convenience store. Police apprehended Dale M. exiting the store through a rear door a few minutes later. Dale M. had a box full of cigarettes, some six-packs of beer, and a small amount of cash. The prosecutor charged Dale M. with burglary*

and larceny, crimes that could result in substantial imprisonment upon conviction. A presentence investigation report disclosed the six prior felony convictions for burglary. When asked why he burglarized the store, Dale M. replied, "I was out of beer and cigarettes." He showed little remorse at his sentencing hearing. The burglary and larceny were the only crimes Dale M. had committed in Nebraska, and thus he was considered a first offender. As the judge, would you sentence Dale M. to incarceration or place him on probation?

• *Kyle B. is a Las Vegas, Nevada resident. He has been convicted before of several violent offenses, including several muggings of tourists. In February 2003 Kyle B. was arrested for attempting to steal jewelry from a Las Vegas casino gift shop. The jewelry was worth $12,000. A Las Vegas prosecutor charged him with attempted grand theft, a crime punishable by a term of years in prison. In negotiations with the prosecutor's office, Kyle B. identified three other men who were stealing on a regular basis from casino gift shops up and down the Las Vegas strip. His information led to the arrest of these men, all of whom were awaiting trial at the time of this writing. Because of his cooperation and valuable information provided to police, the prosecutor recommended leniency to the judge on Kyle B.'s behalf. Given Kyle B.'s prior history of violent crime convictions, how lenient would you be as the judge? Would you sentence Kyle B. to a prison term or place him on probation?*

• *Martha Q. is a convicted shoplifter in Oklahoma. She has three prior shoplifting convictions. She has served short jail sentences for two of these convictions. Martha Q. was on probation in 2003 when she shoplifted an expensive coat from a department store in Oklahoma City. She was apprehended once again and charged with theft. This time the possible punishment included a prison sentence of up to four years. Martha Q.'s attorney argued that Martha Q. was*

(continued)

BOX 1.1 (Continued)

mentally impaired and that she was despondent when she committed her most recent theft. Nevertheless, the jury returned a guilty verdict. Martha appeared before the judge at her sentencing hearing. As the judge, would you incarcerate Martha Q. or put her on probation?

• James R. is a first offender who was convicted of participating in the robbery of a convenience store in New York in January 2003. James R. has no prior record and was the driver of the car. Two other accomplices robbed the store at gunpoint while James R. waited in the car. The robbery was planned a few nights earlier in a bar where James R. and his two friends were drinking. James R. agreed to drive the car for his friends, but he claims he was drunk when he made this agreement. Someone noticed James R.'s license plate as his car sped away from the crime scene, and he and his associates were apprehended the following day. James R. immediately confessed to his role in the robbery, although he continually denied that he did anything but drive the car. Under a New York felony robbery law, James R. is facing considerable prison time for his role in the crime. However, he cooperated fully with police officers

and investigating detectives and furnished valuable information which led to the arrests of the two other suspects. James R. faced a sentencing hearing in May 2003. If you were the judge, would you put James R. in jail or on probation?

• John L. received a three-year sentence of probation.

• Dale M. received a two-year term of probation and a suspended prison sentence of five years pursuant to a plea agreement.

• Kyle B. was placed on intensive supervised probation, requiring home confinement with electronic monitoring, for a period of four years.

• Martha Q. received a prison sentence of three years for the theft and for being an habitual offender. She would be parole eligible after serving two years in prison.

• First-offender James R. was given three years' probation for his role in the robbery pursuant to a plea agreement, where he agreed to testify against his associates.

cantly to recidivism rates (McKean and Raphael, 2002). Sometimes these persons are called **persistent offenders, persistent felony offenders, habitual offenders, repeat offenders,** or **chronic offenders.** Many programs devised by probation and parole departments are not particularly effective for helping hardcore recidivists. Some offenders will continue to reoffend no matter how carefully certain community programs are designed (Southern Methodist University, 2002).

Career Criminals.   **Career criminals** are offenders who earn their living from the crimes they commit (Eggleston and Laub, 2002). Their criminal activity is a craft, involving expertise and special training. Career criminals are those who have reached a stage of criminality where they view crime as an occupation or profession. Many of these offenders are more bothersome than dangerous. They frequently commit petty offenses involving theft, burglary, and vandalism. When they are punished, they are often overpenalized. This is the result of legislation where repeat offenders are subject to harsher penalties, even life imprisonment without the possibility of parole, if they are convicted of numerous petty crimes and are nonviolent toward others. Understandably, it is difficult for probation and parole officials to tailor programs that will rehabilitate or cure career criminals from their patterns of criminal activity.

CRIMINAL JUSTICE SYSTEM COMPONENTS

The primary components of the criminal justice system include (1) law enforcement; (2) prosecutorial decision making; (3) courts and judges; and (4) corrections.

Law Enforcement

All law enforcement agencies vest their officers with arrest powers. Police officers have the authority to make arrests whenever law violations occur within their jurisdictions. These arrest powers include apprehending anyone suspected of committing crimes. Offenses justifying arrests may range from traffic violations to first-degree murder, forcible rape, or kidnapping. Law enforcement officers are empowered to enforce the laws and statutes of their jurisdictions. Primarily an investigative body, the FBI has arrest powers involving violations of over 200 federal laws. FBI agents observe all appropriate jurisdictional boundaries associated with their position. These agents do not issue traffic citations or monitor speeders on interstate highways. Accordingly, state troopers seldom investigate and arrest counterfeiters or conspirators in interstate gambling or drug trafficking.

Arrest and Booking.   An arrest means taking a crime suspect into custody. Ordinarily, police officers make arrests of those suspected of committing crimes. Once defendants have been taken into custody, they are booked. **Booking** is an administrative procedure that furnishes personal background information of offenders for law enforcement officials. Booking includes compiling a file for defendants, including their name, address, telephone number, age, place of employment, relatives, and other personal data. The extensiveness of the booking procedure varies among jurisdictions. In some jurisdictions, the suspect may be photographed and fingerprinted, while in others, defendants may answer a few personal, descriptive questions.

Bail.   When defendants are arrested, a decision is made by prosecutors whether these persons will be brought to trial at some future date. If there is a trial, most defendants can obtain temporary release from detention. Criminal defendants may be **released on their own recognizance (ROR). Bail** is only available to those entitled to bail. Those not entitled to bail include suspects likely to flee the jurisdiction if released temporarily, as well as those who pose a danger to others or themselves. Bail is a surety to procure the release of those under arrest and to assure that they will appear later to face criminal charges in court. Bail is ordinarily specified at the time criminal suspects are brought before a judge or magistrate in an **initial appearance.** An initial appearance involves a preliminary specification of criminal charges against the defendant. Presiding judges may specify bail or they require defendants to be held until a **preliminary hearing** or **preliminary examination** can be convened for the purpose of establishing **probable cause.** At the conclusion of preliminary hearings, bail may be ordered or suspects may be released on their own recognizance (ROR).

In the federal system, U.S. Probation Officers perform various **pretrial services.** These services include conducting investigations of certain persons who have been charged with federal crimes (Henning and Klesges, 2002).

 **BOX 1.2**

Ken Clark
Law Enforcement Officer and Field Training Officer, Field Services/ Patrol Division, Coral Springs Police Department, Coral Springs, Florida

Statistics:

A.S. (criminal justice), Columbus State Community College; B.A. (organizational management), Warner Southern College; M.A. (criminal justice management and administration), University of Alaska-Fairbanks

Background:

As a teen, I believed that I wanted a career in public service. I joined the military after graduating from high school. During my two years of active duty, I had the opportunity to look at several careers and checked out the professions that caught my interest. I took advantage of any college courses that I could take that would help me with a bachelor's degree down the road. After two years of service, I joined the National Guard to complete my eight-year tour of duty. Then I began my police academy at Columbus, Ohio and went to college full time. After completing the academy and my two-year degree, I wanted to get back down to Florida to start my career in law enforcement. I was hired by the Polk County Sheriff's Office, where I gained extremely valuable experience. I started in the Patrol Division and after two years became a Field Training Officer (FTO). I really enjoyed working with new officers and being able to share the knowledge that I had picked up in my brief career along with making sure the trainees had what it takes to make it on their own. I found that being an FTO was very rewarding, especially when one of the folks I trained would come up to me a year or two down the road and tell me that they really enjoyed their training experience with me and that they learned a lot from our time together. Besides going over the required material that all new trainees need to learn, I had three things that I tried to embed in each one of them. The first was to stay alert

and stay alive; you can never get complacent in the job. The second ideal was to always maintain your command bearing on the job. When an officer arrives on a scene, one of two things is going to happen immediately. The subject(s) that you make contact with are going to size you up and determine if they can try to get something over on you or if they are going to cooperate with you. An officer's ability to display a command presence and professionalism is required at all times. The third thing that I stressed was to always try to be calm, cool, and collected. If you can keep your head about you when everything else is going to hell real quick, an officer has the best chance to complete any situation safely and successfully.

In 1992 Hurricane Andrew destroyed thousands of homes and an enormous amount of property in Miami-Dade County. My National Guard unit was activated and we spent five weeks in the hardest-hit areas providing assistance to the Miami Police Department and the Miami-Dade County Sheriff's Office. This was one of the most rewarding periods in my military and law enforcement career. I was able to put my law enforcement training into effect with my fellow National Guardsmen by training them on how to make a proper traffic stop, conducting a field interview, and proper methods for searching suspects and handcuffing procedures. My unit worked side by side with the local law enforcement agencies to help prevent looting and to enforce the curfew that was in place until the local municipalities and the county were functional with their regular services.

After four years in the Patrol Division of the Sheriff's Office, I interviewed and was selected to be a detective within the Major Crimes Bureau. My first assignment was working in the Sexual Abuse and Family Exploitation Unit (S.A.F.E.). While working in this unit, I mainly worked sex and physical abuse crimes on children and adults. While in the S.A.F.E. Unit, I was able to become a member of the Florida Sex Crimes Investigators Association. I have to admit that working with children who were sexually and physically abused by adults was very difficult at times, but when I was able to get a child molester to give me a full confession about his or her crimes, there was no better feeling in the world than to place my handcuffs on that individual and eventually see that person go to prison for many years. During my time as a detective, I was selected to become a Detective Training Instructor. After a rigorous course of instruction, I had the opportunity to train new detectives that were assigned to the Major Crimes Bureau. I was then transferred to the Homicide Division, where I worked some of the most intense and tedious investigations of my career. I was also exposed to some of the best training and classes in advanced investigations that I could ever ask for. It is so important to get the proper training and to become familiar with the current techniques and technologies that are available within the law enforcement field. While assigned to the Major Crimes Division, I was able to finish my bachelor's degree in Organizational Management. During my time as a Major Crimes Detective, I had the great fortune of working with several other investigators from different agencies along with working on cases with the Federal Bureau of Investigation, the Florida Department of Law Enforcement, and even NASA.

In 1998 I left the Polk County Sheriff's Office to try my hand in the private sector. For two years I worked with a private firm and was promoted within my first year to area manager. This promotion required me to relocate to Ft. Lauderdale, Florida. The job required many hours, dealing with approximately 15 employees, but the pay was great. Unfortunately the company I was with found itself in financial difficulty and like so many others in the corporate world, I was downsized. I had never been unemployed before, and I quickly realized that it sucked. And so in June 2000 I was hired by the Coral Springs Police Department, which is located in the Northwest area of Broward County, Florida. Coral Springs is a city with a population of 130,000. It is more of a suburban community with many higher income residents. The police department is one of the best departments that I have had the pleasure to be affiliated with. The culture and reputation that the department has developed over the years is that of respect and professionalism, and the pay scale isn't that bad either. Since my hire date, I have been assigned to the Field Services/Patrol Division. As a patrol officer, I prefer to work the midnight shift. Working midnights allows me to deal with different types of calls for service than an officer working the day shift, and it also allows me to be more proactive in searching for criminal activity.

As I stated earlier, I think it is very important to get all the training you can. I am currently a Field Training Officer, a member of the Field Force Unit, Honor Guard, and work with civilians who attend the Coral Springs Citizen's Police Academy. It is my goal to be as active as I can be within the department along with having the quality time with my family. I am completing my master's degree in Criminal Justice Management and Administration and wish to excel through the ranks within the police department into a management position in the future. There are still many goals to accomplish within my law enforcement career and I'm looking forward to every one of them.

Work Experience:

Working in law enforcement has its many benefits, but it can have some negative aspects as well. As professional law enforcement officers, we have sworn an oath to protect others and to enforce the law. Sometimes the job we do can be very dangerous

(continued)

BOX 1.2 (*Continued*)

and that is why not everyone is cut out for this profession. Back in 1993 one of my trainees from approximately one year earlier was hired on in a major city in Hillsborough County, Florida. As I was driving to work one morning, I heard on the radio that two officers had been involved in a chase of four suspects who had stolen a car. While pursuing one of the suspects on foot through a dark city alley, the suspect had ambushed the two officers with an SKS sub-machine gun. Both officers were critically wounded. The story on the radio advised that one of the officers wounded had just joined the police department about six months ago. Right then and there, I had a sick feeling in my gut and knew that it was my former trainee whom I had developed a close relationship with. I quickly called our dispatch center to ascertain if they knew the identity of the down officers, and sure enough, it was my friend. A call was given out over the radio for people to donate blood for the two officers who were attacked, and the request for blood donations was met with an overwhelming response. Thank God, both officers survived and the suspects were arrested and sentenced. My former trainee and friend still works with the police department, but his partner had to retire due to his serious wounds.

Another incident involved me. While I was assigned to the Patrol Division with Polk County, I was working a special detail in a very economically depressed area known for its drug trafficking. While on foot patrol, I observed a subject who I did not recognize and it was apparent that he did not want me to see him. I decided to make contact with him and observed a large bulge in his right front pants pocket. I asked him if he had any identification, and he said, "No." I then asked him what was in his front pocket, and he replied, "My wallet." I then asked him if he was sure about not having any identification. He then stated, "It's not a wallet, it's a gun." Well, needless to say, my alertness jumped about five levels and I secured the concealed firearm from him. As I was placing him in custody, I received an elbow in my face with extreme force and quickness. The fight was

on. I immediately called for backup and began a short foot chase in order to catch him. I was able to tackle him and wrestle him to the ground. He then attempted to pull my 9mm firearm from my duty holster. I deployed my expandable baton and tried to strike him in the thigh area. He deflected the blow with his right hand. Then I tried to strike him in the upper shoulder area, and when contact was made, he must have moved, because I hit him square on the head with little effectiveness. After several minutes of fighting with him and keeping him away from my firearm, I placed him in a full bear hug and slammed him to the street. While on top of him, I attempted to get my handcuffs on him, but he continued to resist. To reinforce the fact that he didn't want to be arrested, he kneed me in the groin several times and attempted to impale one of his bloody fingers into my eye. Well, this really pissed me off, and so I grabbed him by the ears and head-butted him with everything I had. Fortunately this was sufficient to reinforce the strike he had received earlier with my baton, and I was able to cuff him. At this point, 12 minutes after I called for backup, I could hear the backup responding. They eventually took the suspect away to the hospital. They also took me to the hospital for multiple cuts and abrasions and to check out my eye. During this incident, the suspect and I became blood brothers (an exchange of blood-borne pathogens), and I had to go through the turmoil of getting a search warrant for the suspect's person, in order to draw blood to determine if he had any sexually transmitted disease, such as AIDS/HIV. Luckily, I was not infected with anything, and the guy I fought received 32 years in prison. Now, some of you might say that's a long sentence, but the thing I learned later was that he was on probation for second-degree murder. I also learned that while he was in prison for the murder charge, his girlfriend, who lived in the area I was patrolling that night, had been cheating on him. He was walking to his girlfriend's place to kill her with the gun I took off of him. You never know who or what type of person you will run into on this job. I could probably write for hours about other stories and investigations I have worked on, but I thought I would just share a couple of these incidents.

Advice to Students:

I would first like to commend you for taking the class that allows you to read some of the Personality Highlights of professionals from many different areas of the criminal justice field. If you're reading this, then you are truly on the right course to achieve your personal goal, education, and career choice. Education is so important for today's law enforcement professionals. Most police or county agencies will not look at an individ-

ual without at least a two-year degree. And so keep up the good work on obtaining your education. I have tried to be very open about my background and experiences, because I want people thinking about a career in criminal justice to understand some of the things that a person can go through and achieve. If you feel that the best-educated and professional people should be our law enforcement officers, then I encourage you to be one of those people. The job is not always full of excitement, and it can be very frustrating at times. However, if you truly want to make a positive impact on the community you serve and belong to a growing brotherhood/sisterhood of dedicated professionals, then welcome aboard and be safe!

Recommendations are often made by these federal officers to U.S. Magistrates regarding an offender's bail eligibility. U.S. Magistrates want to know whether a defendant poses a flight risk or poses a danger to others if freed on bail. Federal probation officers furnish the court with important information about the nature of the charges against defendants. These officers work closely with the U.S. Attorney's Office and determine whether to recommend bail.

Prosecutorial Decision Making

Prosecutions.   After suspects have been arrested and booked for alleged violations of the law, a prosecutor examines their cases and the evidence against them and determines whether these suspects should be prosecuted. Not all arrests for serious crimes result in prosecutions. Furthermore, not all prosecutions result in convictions. A prosecution is the carrying forth of criminal proceedings against a person culminating in a trial or other final disposition, such as a guilty plea in lieu of trial. Prosecutors make these decisions and they are influenced by a consideration of factors such as the adequacy of evidence, whether there are eyewitnesses, and the seriousness of the crime.

Screening and Prioritizing Cases.   The prosecuting attorney screens cases and determines which ones have the highest probability for conviction. **Screening cases** involves determining the priority to be given particular kinds of cases such as murder or vehicular theft. Some cases lack merit or have insufficient evidence to sustain a criminal conviction. In other instances, there may be so many criminal cases to prosecute, that not all of them can be prosecuted. Thus, prosecutors must prioritize their cases and prosecute only the most serious ones. Prosecutors also decide whether certain cases should be dropped.

Prosecutors act as negotiators between defendants, their attorneys, and judges. Prosecutors attempt to work out mutually advantageous arrangements between the state and defendants. The role of a **defense counsel** is to secure for clients the best possible outcome, preferably an acquittal. The stage is set for

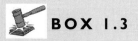 **BOX 1.3**

PERSONALITY HIGHLIGHT

John W. Erickson, Jr.
Career Law Clerk, U.S. District Court, District of Alaska

Statistics:

B.A. (criminal justice), University of Alaska-Fairbanks; J.D., J. Reuben Clark Law School, Brigham Young University; M.A. (criminal justice administration), University of Alaska-Fairbanks

Work History:

I am currently employed as a Career Law Clerk for the U.S. District Court, District of Alaska, where I serve as District Judge Ralph R. Beistline's top legal advisor and staff attorney. My primary duties include conducting legal research, preparing bench memos, drafting orders and opinions, verifying citations, communicating with counsel regarding case management and procedural requirements, and assisting the judge during courtroom proceedings.

I am also assigned to the 168th Air Refueling Squadron, Alaska Air National Guard, as a KC-135R Navigator, where I perform duties necessary to accomplish air refueling, training, and other assigned missions. Prior to this assignment, I served as the 168th Air Refueling Wing's Deputy Staff Judge Advocate, and was previously enlisted as a KC-135D/E Boom Operator.

Background:

I became interested in the criminal justice field while working as a State Park Maintainer in Hamden, Connecticut. It was there where I decided to become a Park Ranger and Manager. After receiving some advice from my employer, I enrolled at the University of Alaska at Fairbanks (UAF), with the goal of getting a B.S. in Forestry Management. However, after one chemistry class, I determined a B.S. was not in my future. Nevertheless, an introduction to justice course caught my attention.

My first job in the criminal justice system was that of a Security Officer at UAF. I enjoyed the work and took pride in the fact that, for a time, I held the record for the most parking tickets issued in a single day. . . I was young. That summer I returned to Connecticut where I was hired as a Seasonal Park Patrolman for the Department of Environmental Protection. In conjunction with that job, I attended a course at the Connecticut Municipal Police Academy, where I received my commission. I was 19 years old.

At the conclusion of my term as a patrolman, I returned to Alaska and the UAF Security Department, where I became a supervisor. Taking a deeper interest in the law, I took a number of upper-division law classes, e.g., criminal law and criminal procedure, and enrolled in some public speaking and debate courses in order to acquire some advocacy skills. In my senior year, I was hired as the Ombudsman for the Associated Students of the University of Alaska, where I worked until I graduated from UAF. Although I had planned on becoming an Alaska State Trooper, I withdrew my application in order to do mission work for my church. Upon my return from the mission field, I decided to take the Law School Admission Test (LSAT); and subsequently, I applied to a number of law schools. Fortunately, I was able to attend my first choice.

At the conclusion of law school, I was hired as a law clerk to the Honorable Ralph R. Beistline, then an Alaska Superior Court Judge. Following my clerkship, I was hired by a large law firm in Anchorage, where I practiced insurance and aviation law. Inundated with insurance and bad faith claims, I realized that I had lost sight of my goals and dreams. As a result, I took a pay cut and became an Assistant District Attorney for the State of Alaska, which has been by far the best job I have had to date. But for the fact that I was personally invited to clerk for newly appointed U.S. District Judge Ralph R. Beistline, I would still be there today.

Work Experience:

Of the many jobs I have held, I enjoyed being an Assistant District Attorney most of all. The work was interesting, and without fail, it always kept me busy. Moreover, it provided me with ample opportunities to gain invaluable courtroom experience by doing that which I love best, to argue cases.

As a prosecutor, I took advantage of every opportunity that I had to work with local law enforcement, e.g., ride-alongs, training. I encourage all to do the same. The more I knew about the work performed by law enforcement, the more successful I was in the courtroom. Moreover, I found that getting to know the police officers with whom I worked made my job that much more enjoyable and/or rewarding.

If there was a downside to my prosecutorial experience, it was handling domestic violence cases. In the State of Alaska, where domestic violence is high, family disputes and/or matters encompassed a greater part of my day and a large volume of my work. As a result, I was sometimes left to wonder whether I was doing criminal or family law. In conjunction with the same, and even though I am a proponent for victims' rights, I dreaded calls from victims who chose to recant their earlier testimony, and subsequently, became angry, sometimes irate, due to the fact that I refused to drop any and/or all assault charges against their assailant(s). Nevertheless, the good experiences far outweighed the bad.

Advice to Students:

For those specifically interested in practicing law, I suggest you increase your writing and speaking skills. Never turn down an opportunity to do either, and learn to network in the process. More importantly, follow your dreams! Learn to be happy with what you have and where you are in life. Don't be easily dissuaded by those who think they have your best interests in mind. Only you know what is best for you. Once you have decided what that is, stick to your guns. I am living proof that you can do anything that you set your mind to. Stay focused. Listen to those who have gone before you. There is no sense in reinventing the wheel. If others have already been there, done that, etc., learn from their experiences and move on. By doing so you will increase your knowledge in a minimal amount of time.

negotiations. Prosecutors want guilty pleas from defendants. Defendants, who may or may not be guilty of the offenses alleged, weigh the alternatives. Considering the strength of the evidence and other factors, defendants, after consulting with their attorneys, may decide to plead guilty, provided the government makes adequate concessions. Sentences resulting from trial convictions are often more severe than those imposed as the result of plea-bargained convictions for the same offenses.

Plea Bargaining.   Over 90 percent of all felony convictions in the United States are obtained prior to trial through **plea bargaining.** Plea bargaining is a preconviction agreement between the defendant and the state whereby the defendant pleads guilty with the expectation of either a reduction in the charges, a promise of sentencing leniency, or some other governmental concession short of the maximum penalties that could be imposed under the law. Plea bargaining is not exclusively an American phenomenon. It is found in many other countries, such as Canada (Ma, 2002). Plea bargaining is largely at the discretion of prosecutors who use this tool as a means of regulating case flow, managing case backlogs, and facilitating case completion. Without plea bargaining, in most jurisdictions the criminal justice system would probably be seriously impaired and grind to a halt. This is because almost every case would be subject to more lengthy trials and the costs and personpower involved would be prohibitive.

Four types of plea bargaining are described as follows. The first type is **implicit plea bargaining,** where defendants plead guilty with the expectation that they will receive more lenient sentences than if they were to go to trial and be found guilty by a jury. Generally, plea bargaining results in greater leniency in sentencing compared with a sentence derived from a jury finding of guilty at the conclusion of a **criminal trial.** A second type is **sentence recommendation plea bargaining,** where the prosecutor proposes a sentence in exchange for a guilty plea. A third type is **charge reduction plea bargaining,** where the prosecutor downgrades charges in exchange for a guilty plea. This is sometimes called **overcharging.** A fourth type of plea bargaining is **judicial plea bargaining,** where the judge makes a plea offer to a defendant, such that if the defendant pleads guilty, the judge will impose a specific lenient sentence. Sentence recommendation bargaining and charge reduction bargaining are probably the most frequently used in plea negotiating.

Prosecutors do not have the authority to grant probation to any criminal defendant in exchange for a guilty plea. Prosecutors can only recommend probation to judges. Judges are the ultimate arbiters, and they decide whether to approve or disapprove any plea agreement. The plea bargaining process is important to any criminal defendant entering into negotiations with government prosecutors. Several constitutional rights are waived by defendants, and they acquire a criminal record. In the present context, plea bargaining is any offer or recommendation of sentencing leniency in exchange for a guilty plea from a defendant (Greenwood Press, 2002).

Informations, Indictments, and Presentments.   If prosecutors persist in a prosecution against certain defendants, they have several options for commencing criminal proceedings. Prosecutors may file an **information,** or a formal criminal charge against a defendant. In about half of all states, a **grand jury** convenes and may issue an **indictment** or **presentment** against criminal suspects. Indictments and presentments are also charges stemming from grand jury consideration of evidence against the accused. Indictments are charges against criminal suspects brought by the grand jury at the request of prosecutors. Presentments are criminal charges against the accused where the grand jury has acted on its own authority. These actions simply specify that sufficient evidence exists to establish probable cause, that a crime has been committed and the accused committed it. A **true bill** indicates that the grand jury has found sufficient evidence to establish probable cause that the accused committed a crime. No true bills issue from grand jury action and indicate that insufficient evidence exists to establish probable cause. If a **no true bill** or **no bill** is issued, suspects are most often freed from further criminal prosecutions.

Arraignments.   Trials are preceded by an **arraignment.** An arraignment is an formal proceeding where the finalized list of charges is furnished criminal defendants. Arraignments also are held for the purposes of entering a plea (e.g., guilty, not guilty, guilty but mentally ill), and determining a trial date. In a worst-case scenario, suppose a criminal defendant pleads not guilty to a criminal charge. When this happens, a trial date is established and a trial is scheduled where one's guilt or innocence can be determined by a judge or jury.

Courts and Judges

Court Dockets and Judicial Workloads.   In many federal district courts as well as state criminal courts, court calendars are glutted with cases. About 85 percent of these cases are civil, and they consume considerable court time. The remainder of the cases are criminal. The courtroom is the place where a defendant's guilt is ultimately determined. It functions as a public forum for the airing of all relevant information and evidence in the case. The government presents its evidence against the accused, and the defense counters with its own evidence. Witnesses are called to testify both for and against the accused, and defendants have the right to cross-examine their accusers and to offer testimony and evidence in their own behalf. The courtroom is also the place where the sufficiency of evidence against the accused is tested. The prosecution carries the burden of proof against the accused and must establish one's guilt **beyond a reasonable doubt.**

Speedy Trials and Case Processing.   All defendants are entitled to a **jury trial** in any criminal proceeding as a matter of right, if the charges are serious and could result in incarceration for a period of six months or more. This applies to either misdemeanors or felonies. A jury is an objective, impartial body of persons who convene to hear the case against the accused and make a determination of guilt or innocence on the basis of the factual evidence presented. Despite speedy trial measures, streamlined case processing, and other court reforms, most state and federal judges are overworked and their dockets are glutted with case backlogs (McKean and Raphael, 2002). Therefore, judges encourage prosecutors to work out arrangements with defendants, if possible, so that the number of trials can be at least minimized.

Sentencing and Implications for Convicted Offenders.   Defendants who are found not guilty are acquitted and freed from the criminal justice system. When defendants are found guilty, an appeals process exists at both the state and federal levels whereby these defendants may appeal the verdict and request a new trial. In the meantime, convicted offenders are sentenced. Several options are available to judges in sentencing criminal defendants. For example, first offenders may receive light sentences and not be incarcerated. However, convicted offenders with prior records will probably receive harsher sentences. Judges may sentence offenders to incarceration in a local jail or regional prison for a specified period of time. If the judge sentences convicted offenders to some non-incarcerative punishment, defendants may be placed on probation for a prescribed period (King et al., 2002).

Probation is a sentence involving a conditional suspension of incarceration, usually with several behavioral provisions or conditions. These conditions are often prescribed by law. Although this is not an exhaustive list, these conditions include (1) not associating with other known criminals, (2) refraining from committing future criminal acts, (3) obtaining and maintaining employment, and/or (4) participating in appropriate medical or counseling programs and therapy. Also, in many cases, judges must sentence convicted offenders to prison according to prescribed statutes. These are mandatory statutory provisions that bind judges and restrict their discretionary powers.

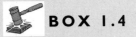 **BOX 1.4**

Brandy "BC" Thompson Franson, Esq.
Assistant Professor of Justice Administration, Southwest State University, Marshall, Minnesota

Statistics:

J.D., University of South Dakota Law School, Vermillion, South Dakota; B.A. (government), College of Saint Benedict, St. Joseph, Missouri.

Work History and Experiences:

During my legal career, I worked as a law clerk for a district court judge, as *pro bono publico* for legal aid services, and as a prosecuting attorney for the Lyon County Attorney's Office. I spent five years working as a prosecutor and I can say that it was both an interesting and challenging job. With all of the television shows about the courts, I believe that the public gets an impractical idea of the criminal justice system. Although criminal attorneys tend to go to court more often than other attorneys, on the average, they spend more time with paper work and returning telephone calls than actually arguing cases and defending their clients.

During my career as a prosecutor, my duties included the prosecution of juvenile and adult crimes (misdemeanors to felonies), plus representing the state social service agency in cases involving the welfare of children. Due to the diversity of people you deal with in criminal law, one of the most important skills you can possess is communication. Communication is not just telling someone something, but actually conveying an idea or successfully getting information from someone about a specific event. This sharing of information is critical because of the amount of information in each type of case. You have to communicate with many different people, for example: law enforcement officers (from patrol officers to special agents), witnesses (from laypersons to experts in various fields), victims (children and adults), probation officers, social workers, *guardians ad litem,* reporters, the pub-

lic, and other attorneys, not to mention the judges, court personnel and, in trial, the jurors. You have to give, receive, retain, and organize this information in a way that benefits your case.

The plea bargaining process is another interesting area of criminal law. Plea bargaining generally means that the original charge is either reduced to a lesser offense or the punishment for the original charge is reduced. For example, one could be charged with burglary and end up pleading guilty to theft (a lesser degree offense), which would in turn result in lesser punishment. On the other hand, one could simply be given a plea offer where the punishment is equal to that of a theft offense but still be pleading guilty to the burglary charge. The deciding factor in the plea bargaining process is usually the strength of the prosecutor's case (the evidence).

Every good prosecutor knows that you rarely get to try a "slam-dunk" case—the case where all of the witnesses are strong and convincing, where the cops did everything by the book, and where the defendant was caught on videotape. The shoplifting case against Winona Ryder would be that type of case: the evidence was good, reliable, and convincing (and yes, there was a videotape). There are many reasons that plea offers are made. For instance, if the state has a strong case against the defendant, it is likely that the defendant will plead or accept a plea bargain rather than risk the chance of being convicted of the original, more serious, charge. If the state has a relatively weak case, the state is more likely to make a plea offer that is a significant reduction in punishment from the original charge to induce the defendant to plead. When this occurs, the defendant is likely to accept the plea offer rather than risk a jury trial and a possible conviction on the original charge. It is usually the cases that are neither the "slam-dunk" nor the extremely weak that are tried. Often when a case goes to trial, it is because the state and the defendant cannot reach an agreement.

Whenever a prosecutor looks at making a plea offer, he or she must consider not only the strength of the evidence that supports the crime but the defendant's criminal history, other similar case outcomes (this can include sentencing guidelines), and if applicable, the wishes of the victim(s).

When a defendant has an extensive criminal history (many prior offenses), it is difficult to give a plea offer that is a significant reduction in punishment. When an offer can only reduce a punishment by a few months in prison, the defendant is more likely to believe that there is nothing to lose

by going to trial. The chance that a jury might acquit is worth the risk, because the sentence after a conviction will not be much different from the sentence offered by the plea bargain. It is important to remember that one cannot be punished for exercising one's right to trial, so the judge cannot impose a harsher sentence simply because a jury convicted you, versus you having entered a plea of guilty to the original charge. The only time this is modified is through the plea bargaining process, and that agreement still needs the approval of a judge, for he or she is the guardian of justice within the system.

Advice to Students:

For those of you interested in a career in the criminal justice field, any type of internship you can get within the system will be highly beneficial to your career. For those of you who go on to law school, I highly recommend that you clerk for a judge; it is a valuable experience, plus it gives you a unique view of the justice system.

Generally, however, convicted offenders collectively fall under the supervision of corrections.

Corrections

The last component of the criminal justice system is corrections. Corrections includes all of the agencies, organizations, and personnel who deal with convicted offenders after court processing and convictions. Typically, corrections are associated with **jails** and **prisons.** Jails are typically short-term confinement facilities operated by cities and county governments. They are usually used for persons enduring short-term confinement for misdemeanor offenses or for persons charged with more serious offenses who are awaiting trial. Prisons are long-term facilities that are more self-contained and house inmates serving sentences of one or more years. While prisons and jails are important features of the corrections system, they are hardly the dominant components of it. By 2003, approximately 7 million adults were under some form of correctional supervision in the United States. There were over 1 million prison inmates and about 750,000 jail inmates (Glaze, 2003).

Jail and Prison Overcrowding.   Frequently, there is little room in many prisons and jails to house new convicted offenders. This is **overcrowding.** By 2003, 30 states were under court order to decrease their prison inmate populations to

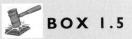

BOX 1.5

PERSONALITY
HIGHLIGHT

Judge William F. Todd, Jr.
Judge of State Court of Rockdale County, Georgia

Statistics:

B.A. (psychology), University of Georgia; J.D., University of Georgia
School of Law

Present and Former Positions, Honors:

Chief Assistant District Attorney, Ogeechee Judicial Circuit, 1979–1981; Chief Assistant District Attorney, Rockdale Judicial Circuit, 1983–1993; Judge, State Court of Rockdale County, 1993 to present; member, past chairman, Georgia County and Municipal Probation Advisory Council; faculty member, National Judicial College, 2002 to present; Georgia Governor's Zero Tolerance Task Force; NHTSA "Gold Standards" region IV DUI Advisory Council; expert advisor to National Highway Traffic Safety Administration (NHTSA) 2nd Edition DUI Sentencing Guide, 2002; National MADD (Mothers Against Drunk Driving) Child Endangerment Panel member, 2003; National Commission Against Drunk Driving, Finalist Award, 2001; National Association of State Judicial Educators Hardcore Drunk Driving Judicial Education Summit member, 2002; past speaker at American Probation and Parole Association national convention, Phoenix, AZ; teacher and speaker at numerous judicial, law enforcement, and public seminars.

Background:

The only son of a career Navy father, I grew up in seaports around the country with my parents and five sisters. I learned to work hard at an early age, working at gas stations, grocery stores, and a local mineral refinery. I earned my way through the University of Georgia, eventually becoming a lawyer and a prosecuting trial attorney as Chief Assistant District Attorney for 12 years. My decision to go into criminal law as a prosecutor resulted from having worked in defense of criminals in the Georgia prison system while in law school. This eye-opening experience left me disillusioned of the Perry Mason image I had conjured for myself.

Twice in my career I had brief stints as a criminal defense attorney—a position that posed both moral and professional conflicts in my conscience—and ultimately led me to choose fulfillment in public service over the potential attainment of wealth as a private attorney. While believing deeply in the constitutional rights of accused persons, I personally favored being in a position of protecting the rights of accused persons and victims of crimes at the same time, as a prosecutor. Later in my career, I faced a crisis—whether to become a defense attorney, stay a prosecutor, or run for an elected judgeship. I chose the latter. I have been elected to three four-year terms as State Court Judge of Rockdale County, a suburban community of metropolitan Atlanta.

Upon my first election, my goal was to be the best judge I could be. I worked for months, designing and implementing innovative programs in DUI and domestic violence sentencing, and in probation supervision. I devised a pretrial diversion program that is now used in many courts throughout Georgia, a DUI sentencing program that has been studied, endorsed, and used as a model across the country by MADD, NHTSA, and other courts, and have studied, taught, and lectured on the varied uses of probation in altering criminal behavior.

Interesting Experiences:

I have tried many serious cases as a prosecutor (e.g., murder, cocaine trafficking, rape, child molestation, armed robbery, burglary), but the most interesting case involved a murder where the defendant claimed he killed the victim with a shotgun because he was scared of a pit bull dog that the victim had standing beside him when shot. The defendant alleged that he thought the victim was going to sic the dog on him. The dog looked mean, according to the defendant, but the dog was actually very gentle. To prove this, I had a dog handler keep the dog in the jury room just a few feet away from the courtroom until I dramatically went out and got him and led him toward the jury box, where he proceeded to lick several of the jurors while wagging his tail profusely! I put my face next to the dog and told the handler to tell the dog to "get" me, which caused the dog to lick my face also. The defendant was subsequently convicted of murder.

When I became a judge, I had the experience of sentencing Howard Rollins, the actor who played Detective Tibbs in the television show, *In the Heat of the Night,* which was filmed in the Rockdale-Newton County area. Mr. Rollins was charged with DUI. I sentenced him and put him in jail for several weeks. Then he received another DUI. There was considerable publicity, and I found that both the proceedings and I were widely discussed on a weekly basis in such tabloids as *The Star* and *National Inquirer.* I even got to meet Carroll O'Connor, who came to court to speak on Mr. Rollins' behalf.

Once I had a physically impaired defendant named Steve who went on a hunger strike. He refused to do anything to defend himself at his trial for shoplifting. He sat in his wheelchair in the courtroom, bearded, long-haired, skinny, and pale, three weeks into his fast, refusing to participate in the trial or to be represented by counsel while the state paraded witness after witness against him. I remembered this defendant from my days as a prosecutor. He had a tattoo on his arm that said "Born to Loose" (I always wondered if he had meant the tattoo to read "Born to Lose" or "Born Too Loose"). He

had a serious drinking problem, which had been the primary cause of his lifetime of crime, including the current offense. I finally got tired of watching this tragedy play out, and I sent the jury to the jury room. I told him that if he would admit to having a drinking problem, I would help him. He looked at me and said, "Yes, I do have a drinking problem." I told him that if he pleaded guilty, I would sentence him to an alcohol treatment facility called the Rockdale House. To my amazement, he agreed. A few months later, I stopped by the Rockdale House to check up on his progress. I saw a strong, tanned, clean-shaven young man standing around the front door and I asked, "Have you seen Steve?" He replied, "Don't you recognize me, Judge Todd? I'm Steve." He finished the program and worked for a while as a Rockdale House staff member helping other alcoholics.

Insights:

I realized early on in my judicial career that there were so many things that a judge could do by understanding probation law and using flexibility and innovation in shaping probation conditions to rehabilitate criminals and change criminal and substance abuse behavior. Domestic violence and crimes involving alcohol or drugs particularly lend themselves to the types of control and counseling methods available through current technological advances and treatment alternatives.

Random breath and drug tests are very important. I use house arrest and electronic monitoring with breath testing equipment to enforce "no alcohol" conditions. We have a new work release facility that is an effective alternative to jail, allowing the probationer to work, while also ensuring sobriety during the evening hours. Jail time or the threat of it is very important in deterring future criminal behavior. It is very important to promptly sanction probationers for violation of probation conditions. I use professional drug and alcohol evaluators in the courtroom to make recommendations for substance abuse treatment for the persons I sentence. I sentence defendants in cases involving violence to long-term group counseling programs that are tailored to their

(*continued*)

BOX 1.5 (*Continued*)

particular problem. Alcoholics Anonymous or Narcotics Anonymous meetings, Victim Impact Panel attendance, mental health counseling, together with fines, restitution, and community service, are staple arrows in my judicial quiver.

I have found that private companies offer greater flexibility, better supervision, and more innovative technologies at lower cost to the government compared with traditional public probation offices. I have used a company called BI, Inc. for over ten years for precisely this reason. In addition to probation supervision services, BI, Inc. offers domestic violence counseling, conflict resolution classes, and electronic monitoring at a low cost to the probationer. In many rural areas of Georgia, the public sector does not offer the counseling and electronic monitoring services made available by private probation companies; thus, private probation fills an important need in the criminal justice system.

I have had more "ups" than "downs" in my judicial experience. The political side of the job is not fun. I have had three contested elections that drained much of my energy. However, I drew several insights from each election that improved the job I do. In the most recent election, I received almost 70 percent of the vote; but I still work very hard every day, because I realize that no job is ever secure, and that every person (and voter) is important—even those persons whom I sentence. I try to give my best in every case and every situation. I have had fun being on the cutting edge of criminal justice innovations. Many people call me to serve my fellow men through my ideas. Through some of my efforts, Utah now has a private probation system to supervise DUI offenders. I get a lot of satisfaction from that. NHTSA conducted a 1998 study of my DUI sentencing program (using a combination of punishment and structured probation), which showed that it was twice as effective in preventing recidivism than a comparative program that used more traditional sentencing (e.g., jail, fines, and community service). This study has caused me to receive considerable favorable attention.

How Technology Supports Outcomes:

I use BI, Inc.'s Sobrietor to monitor the sobriety of repeat DUI offenders. This enables me to place persons on probation and set curfew hours for them, monitored by the Sobrietor that also ensures their sobriety. Violations are strictly enforced, and court hearings are promptly scheduled when such program violations occur. The flexibility of electronic monitoring allows a probationer's schedule to be modified in accordance with work hours and also allows monitoring to be done even at long distances from the court. Sobriety tends to reduce recidivism.

Advice to Students:

Try to keep a good humor and perspective on your job. You cannot save the world and there will always be setbacks. You are dealing with human beings, and to be human is to fail occasionally. However, you have to give your very best to each case, because that case may become your greatest success. You never know. Treat every person with dignity, always return your telephone messages, and don't be afraid to approach the judge with your questions and problems.

comply with health and safety standards as well as other factors (Pastore and Maguire, 2003). Among other states, Texas, Tennessee, and Louisiana have been targeted for rehabilitative reforms by the courts. **Prison overcrowding** and **jail overcrowding** are primarily responsible for the large increase in the number of nonincarcerated offenders currently under some form of correctional supervision. Overcrowding in jails or prisons occurs whenever the operating capacity of any jail or prison is exceeded by the number of inmates it is intended to accommodate (Kury and Smartt, 2002). Many judges have reported that prison overcrowding is a significant factor in their sentencing decisions whether to incarcerate convicted offenders. One increasingly important factor affecting prison populations in both state and federal facilities is the growing population of non-citizen felony offenders (Cohn et al., 2002).

Judicial Discretion in Sentencing Offenders.   Judges frequently have considerable latitude in sentencing criminal offenders. Besides sentencing offenders to incarceration, judges may impose other sentences, including **community service,** restitution, and even probation (Nellis, 2002). In 2002, the probation and parolee population exceeded 6 million. Among the factors considered by trial judges when sentencing offenders are: (1) the nature and circumstances of the offense and the history and characteristics of the defendant; (2) the need for the sentence imposed to reflect the seriousness of the offense, to promote respect for the law, to afford adequate **deterrence** to criminal conduct, and to protect the public from further crimes of the defendant; (3) the kinds of educational or training services, medical care, or other correctional treatment which might be appropriate for any particular defendant; (4) the kinds of sentences available; and (5) the need to avoid unwarranted sentence disparities among defendants with similar records who have been found guilty of similar conduct. Some critics of judicial discretion say that judges have too much unregulated power, and that this often results in questionable decision making such as excessive leniency for violent offenders and sending nonserious juveniles to criminal courts for processing (Bowen et al., 2002). Numerous sentencing reforms have been dedicated to controlling judicial discretion at all levels, although no sentencing scheme seems to work perfectly.

The Availability of Community Services and Facilities.   Many citizens equate corrections with punishment involving incarceration. In reality, a majority of convicted offenders are never incarcerated. Rather, they are permitted the freedom of living in their communities under some form of **alternative sentencing** or **creative sentencing.** Alternative sentencing involves some form of community service, some degree of restitution to victims of crimes, becoming actively involved in educational or vocational training programs, or becoming affiliated with some other productive activity. Two goals of alternative sentencing are enabling offenders to avoid the criminal label of imprisonment and allowing convicts to participate in rehabilitative and reintegrative community programs. Community programs are designed to provide convicted offenders with needed services and therapy while they remain free in their communities. Alternative sentencing is also intended to reduce jail and prison overcrowding and reduce correctional operating costs (Bowen et al., 2002).

PROBATION AND PAROLE DISTINGUISHED

Probation is considered a front-end sentence, whereby judges impose conditional sentences in lieu of incarceration. In most cases, probationers do not serve time in either jail or prison. Rather, they must comply with an extensive list of probation program conditions as specified by the court. Probationers remain free within the jurisdiction of sentencing judges while on probation. If probationers violate one or more conditions of their probation orders while on probation, judges decide whether to revoke or terminate their probation programs.

In contrast, parole is early release from prison or jail by a **parole board**. Most states have parole boards that convene to determine whether inmates should be released short of serving their full sentences. Since almost all jails and prisons in the United States are overcrowded, any mechanism that might reduce such overcrowding is viewed favorably, particularly by state legislatures. Parole is one such mechanism. Parole differs from probation in that parolees have spent a period of time in a jail or prison. Another feature of parole is that parole boards have jurisdiction over parolees and decide whether they should be released short of serving their full incarcerative terms.

SUMMARY

The major components of the criminal justice system include law enforcement, prosecution and the courts, and corrections. Probation and parole are integral features of corrections, which includes all organizations and personnel who manage offenders who have been convicted of crimes. Probation is a conditional sentence imposed by a judge in lieu of incarceration, while parole is conditional early release from prison granted by a parole board.

The entire criminal justice process starts whenever a crime is committed and someone is arrested and charged with a crime. Crimes are violations of the law by persons held accountable under the law. They may be distinguished as either misdemeanors or felonies, and they may involve property or violence. Official sources of crime statistics in the United States are the *Uniform Crime Reports (UCS)* and the *National Crime Victimization Survey (NCVS)*. Both of these sources are flawed in various respects. Both official sources are considered underestimates of the actual amount of crime committed in the United States annually. When persons are arrested for a crime, they are booked. Prosecutors decide whether to prosecute defendants. Prosecutors prioritize cases if their caseloads are particularly large. Over 90 percent of all criminal defendants enter guilty pleas to criminal charges in exchange for sentencing leniency. This process is known as plea bargaining. For other defendants, trials are held where juries or judges determine their guilt or innocence. If defendants are convicted through trial, judges must sentence offenders to some type of punishment. All sentences are a type of punishment, although the punishment does not always involve incarceration. Probation is a punishment, although it is a nonincarcerative alternative. Probationers must comply with numerous probation program conditions and behavioral restrictions.

Judges decide whether to place offenders on probation or send them to jails or prisons. Sentencing offenders depends upon the seriousness of their offenses and their prior records. Jails are short-term facilities intended to house minor offenders and pretrial detainees. Prisons are long-term and self-contained facilities designed to accommodate more serious offenders for longer time periods. Depending upon the type of crime they have committed, offenders are classified in different ways to determine their level of custody and/or the nature of their treatment or assistance. Some offenders are first offenders, while others may be recidivists or career criminals. Those offenders with prior criminal records usually receive harsher treatment from judges when sentenced. Some offenders are designated as special needs criminals. They may have AIDS or some other communicable illness. They may be handicapped in some respect, or psychologically or mentally impaired. Some offenders may have drug or alcohol dependencies and require special treatment or counseling. Other offenders may be sex offenders and child sexual abusers requiring extraordinary therapy.

Corrections is expected to accommodate all types of offenders. Depending upon how offenders are sentenced, different corrections agencies or institutions will be responsible for offender supervision. Those sentenced by judges to probation are supervised by probation agencies and probation officers, while parole officers and agencies supervise those who have been paroled from either state or federal penitentiaries by parole boards. Community-based corrections are intended to assist both probationers and parolees in various ways in order to enhance the likelihood that they will complete their respective probation or parole programs successfully. The long-term goal of these agencies and organizations is to cause their clients to become law-abiding so that they will refrain from future criminal activity.

QUESTIONS FOR REVIEW

1. What is the *Uniform Crime Reports (UCR)?* What are some general criticisms of it? What can you say about its accuracy relative to general crime and crime trends in the United States?

2. What is the *National Crime Victimization Survey (NCVS)?* How does it differ from the *UCR?* Explain. What are some general criticisms of the *NCVS?*

3. What are the major components of the criminal justice system? Which part of the system deals with convicted offenders? What are the functions of these components relative to convicted offenders?

4. What is a crime? What are some major differences between felonies and misdemeanors? What are some differences between property crimes and violent crimes? How do these types of crimes differ from summary offenses?

5. What are index offenses? What is their usefulness regarding crime in the United States and crime trends?

6. What is the difference between a victimization and an incident?

7. Who are situational offenders? How do they differ from career criminals and recidivists?

8. What are some of the criteria used by prosecutors for prioritizing cases? How is plea bargaining used in this process? What are four types of plea bargaining and what are their characteristics?

9. What is meant by judicial discretion in sentencing? How do judges influence the sentencing process? What are some of the factors that influence judicial sentencing decisions?

10. What are indictments? What are the implications for defendants of no true bills and true bills?

SUGGESTED READINGS

Felson, Marcus (2002). *Crime and Everyday Life 3/e.* Thousand Oaks, CA: Sage.

Kellough, Gail and Scot Wortley (2002). "Remand for Plea: Bail Decisions and Plea Bargaining and Commensurate Decisions." *The British Journal of Criminology* *42:* 186–210.

Rodriguez, Nancy (2003). *Persistent Offender Law: Racial Disparity, Patterned Offenses, and Unintended Effects.* New York: LFB Scholarly Publishing LLG.

Sgarzi, Judith and Jack McDevitt (2003). *Victimology: A Study of Victims and Their Roles.* Upper Saddle River, NJ: Prentice Hall.

Spohn, Cassia C. (2002). *How Do Judges Decide? The Search for Fairness and Justice in Punishment.* Thousand Oaks, CA: Sage.

Starzyk, Katherine B. and William L. Marshall (2003). "Childhood, Family, and Personalogical Risk Factors for Sexual Offending." *Aggression and Violent Behavior 8:* 93–105.

Strang, Heather (2002). *Victim Participation in Restorative Justice.* New York: Oxford Univ. Press.

Temkin, Jennifer (2003). *Rape and the Legal Process.* New York: Oxford Univ. Press.

INTERNET CONNECTIONS

American Bar Association
http://www.abanet.org/crimjust/links.html

Criminal justice links
http://www.lawguru.com/ilawlib/96.htm

Federal Judicial Center
http://www.fjc.gov

History of Federal Bureau of Prisons
http://www.bop.gov/lpapg/pahist.html

Legal Resource Center
http://www.crimelynx.com/research.html

National Institute of Justice
http://www.ojp.usdoj.gov/NIJ

State court links
http://www.doc.state.co.us/links

State criminal justice links
http://www.statesnews.org/other_resources/law_and_justice.htm

U.S. Department of Justice
http://www.usdoj.gov/02organizations/02_1.html

Vera Institute of Justice
http://www.vera.org

CHAPTER 2. | *An Overview of Community Corrections: Types, Goals, and Functions*

Chapter Outline

Chapter Objectives

As the result of reading this chapter, the following objectives will be realized:

1. Examining the meaning of community corrections.
2. Discussing the origination of community corrections acts as well as the general nature of community corrections programs today.
3. Highlighting the features, goals, and functions of community corrections programs.
5. Discussing selected issues in community corrections, including public resistance to them.
6. Describing the NIMBY syndrome.
7. Defining home confinement, its goals, functions, and effectiveness.
8. Profiling home confinement clients and their potential for program success, as well as discussing selected issues related to home confinement.
9. Identifying and describing electronic monitoring systems, their characteristics, and variations.
10. Comparing and contrasting the relative effectiveness of home confinement and electronic monitoring as viable alternatives to incarceration or more intensive supervised probation programs.
11. Examining day reporting programs and other types of community sanctions.

• *Brown was convicted of a felony in Florida and placed on probation with the special condition of home confinement or detention. Another condition was that Brown was to report to a community agency and do a certain number of hours of community service. A probation officer subsequently went to Brown's residence at 2:00 a.m. and knocked on the door. No one answered. The next day, the probation officer checked with the community agency and determined that Brown had performed no community service for them. The probation officer asked the judge to revoke Brown's probation program. An order was issued by the judge revoking Brown's probation program for the two violations: curfew violation and failure to perform the required community service hours. Brown appealed, alleging that she was at her residence at the time when the probation officer knocked, but that she was not awakened by the knocking. Given the latitude of searches of probationer's premises by probation officers, there was nothing to prevent the probation officer from intruding into Brown's home forcefully to determine her whereabouts. The probation officer had not done so. Furthermore, Brown had duly reported to the community agency to perform community service, but the community agency rejected her for such service. Under these circumstances, the appellate court reversed the order to revoke Brown's probation. The evidence was insufficient to establish that Brown was not at home, merely because no one answered the door. Further, Brown's rejection for volunteer work by the community agency was beyond her control. Thus, her failure to complete the required service hours could not be attributed to her* [Brown v. State,*2002].*

• *Peacock was a defendant in a Florida criminal action and sought to be released on bond pending trial. The judge ordered Peacock released on bond, but Peacock was ordered to be electronically monitored upon release on bond. Subsequently a jailer advised Peacock that he was free to leave the jail and Peacock left. Shortly thereafter, Peacock and his attorney contacted an electronic monitoring agency and requested that Peacock should be electronically monitored. The agency outfitted Peacock with an electronic monitor, an ankle bracelet, but did not connect it to their base computer system.*

Subsequently Peacock was arrested for failure to be electronically monitored and returned to jail after a judge revoked the order for his release. On appeal, it was determined that Peacock did what he had been told by the jailer by leaving the jail. Furthermore, Peacock and his attorney made substantial effort to comply with the judicial order for electronic monitoring. In fact, Peacock was in the process of getting connected to the electronic monitoring system at the time of his emergency bond revocation hearing. The order revoking Peacock's bond was reversed [Peacock v. State, 2001].

• *Kremer was convicted of a crime in a U.S. district court and sentenced to prison. After serving a portion of his sentence, Kremer was sentenced to supervised release, the federal equivalent of parole. While on supervised release, Kremer violated one or more conditions of his supervised release program and was brought back before the judge for resentencing. The judge extended the amount of supervised release time for Kremer. Further, the judge imposed house arrest as an additional supervised release condition. Kremer appealed, but the appellate court upheld the judge's decision. A U.S. district court is permitted to extend a term of supervised release if less than the maximum authorized term was previously imposed. Furthermore, a district court is authorized to modify, reduce, or enlarge the conditions of supervised release [United States v. Kremer, 2002].*

• *Martin was convicted of a crime in Indiana and served a fixed amount of time in home detention as a condition of his probation. Subsequently Martin violated one or more conditions of his probation and revocation of probation was sought. Martin asked to have the time served in home detention counted against his maximum sentence, but the court refused to grant this request. An appellate court reversed the trial court, however, and held that Martin was entitled to credit for the time served on home detention as a condition of his probation. [Martin v. State, 2002]. Brattain was a convicted Indiana offender who was also sentenced to home detention as a condition of probation. Following one or more probation violations, Brattain's probation was revoked. Brattain requested that the time served on home detention be credited toward the maximum sentence of incarceration imposed, but the court refused to grant this request. Brattain appealed, but the ruling of the trial court was upheld. In this case, there was no evidence or documentation presented to show how much time had been spent by Brattain on home detention as a probation condition. Thus Brattain was not entitled to credit for time served. Whether home detention is documented makes the important difference between whether offenders receive or do not receive credit for time served in home detention against their maximum sentences if their probation programs are subsequently revoked for one or more program violations [Brattain v. State, 2002].*

• *Stevens was convicted of a crime in Florida and sentenced to probation. She was ordered to perform a specified number of community service hours at a water treatment plant. A log book was provided Stevens with instructions to have someone at the water treatment plant initial the log book indicating that the community service hours had been performed. Subsequently Stevens' probation officer was given a log book by Stevens showing that 24 community service hours had been completed. The log book contained two sets of initials, including one set, "B.J." Upon checking with the water treatment plant record-keeper, the probation officer determined that no one at that water treatment plant had those initials. Stevens was charged with falsifying her log book, although she explained that she had performed the additional community service hours at another water treatment plant located in the same city. The record-keeper of the first water treatment plant said that no one at her plant had those initials, and that although she wasn't sure, she didn't think anyone at the other plant had those initials either. On this basis, the probation officer testified at Stevens' revocation hearing that Stevens had falsified her records and her probation program was revoked. Stevens appealed and the appellate court reversed the trial court, reinstating Stevens' probation program. It held that no direct evidence of record falsification had ever been presented, and that while hearsay evidence may be admissible at revocation hearings, such evidence alone cannot support a probation violation. The record-keeper's testimony only established that the record-keeper at the first plant did not know anyone at the other plant with the initials B.J. It did not establish that no one at the second plant had those same initials [Stevens v. State, 2002].*

INTRODUCTION

These scenarios involve probationers and parolees under different types of supervision within their own communities in various jurisdictions. These probationers and parolees or clients are supervised within their own communities. The broad categorical term for such supervision is community corrections. Since the mid-1970s, increasing numbers of jurisdictions have relied upon community corrections as an alternative to incarceration, believing that many offenders can be effectively monitored and supervised within their own communities. The successfulness of community corrections has been firmly established. Most jurisdictions have discovered that community corrections not only eases prison and jail overcrowding, but the cost of supervising offenders in their own communities is but a fraction of the cost of imprisonment.

This chapter is organized as follows. First, community corrections is defined and contrasted with intermediate punishments. An historical context of the development and philosophy of community corrections is provided. Several characteristics of community-based corrections programs will be described. Various goals and functions of community corrections programs will be presented. Community corrections clients are also profiled. Next, an overview of different types of community corrections programs is presented. Three kinds of community-based correctional programs include home confinement, electronic monitoring, and day reporting. Each of these types of programs is described, including their functions and goals, advantages and disadvantages, and primary features.

The chapter concludes with a discussion of selected community-based correctional issues. These issues relate to public opposition toward community-based corrections programs; the privatization of community-based correctional programs; and whether community-based corrections are true punishments. Some persons have been critical of community-based corrections because they have involved net-widening, or drawing in certain clients who would not be subject to any type of supervision if these programs did not exist. Other issues pertain to the management and operations of community-based corrections, the quality of service delivery, and staff training and education.

COMMUNITY CORRECTIONS AND INTERMEDIATE PUNISHMENTS

Community-based corrections is the broad array of correctional programs established at the community level that provide alternatives to incarceration (Marion, 2002). These community-based programs are intended to continue one's punishment, but in the context of the community rather than in a prison or jail. Another term that is often used synonymously with community corrections is **intermediate punishments.** Intermediate punishments include any community-based programs that are somewhere between standard probation and incarceration. The conceptual confusion between community corrections and intermediate punishments is easily explained. This author conducted a content analysis of over 600 articles and books extracted from the *Criminal Justice Abstracts* in 2001. These articles and books were selected according to the key words "community corrections" and "intermediate punishments." An inspection of the abstracts of these articles and books disclosed a remarkably high number of similarities.

Let's examine a few articles that focused on "intermediate punishments" or "intermediate sanctions." For instance, Karol Lucken (1997) examined intermediate punishments as including home confinement and day reporting programs. Henry Sontheimer and Traci Duncan (1997) investigated intermediate sanctions in Pennsylvania, and these included community service, restitution, house arrest/electronic monitoring, residential work release, intensive supervision, and other programs. David Rasmussen and Bruce Benson (1994) examined various intermediate punishment programs in Florida, including day fines, shock incarceration, **intensive probation supervision (IPS),** electronic monitoring, house arrest, and day reporting. A fourth source, an article by Kevin Courtright, Bruce Berg, and Robert Mutchnick (1997:19), indicated among other things that "if offenders who would have been sentenced to standard probation are now being sentenced to an intermediate punishment program, e.g., house arrest, intensive supervision, or electronic monitoring . . . then net widening would have occurred."

Next, let's examine several articles that focused on "community corrections" or "community-based corrections" or "community-based sanctions." Research reported by Jody Sundt and her associates (1998:25) investigated public opinions about different types of sanctions to be imposed on fictitious criminals with specific types of criminal histories. Sundt et al. reported that "given the community-based options, respondents preferred sentencing offenders to halfway houses or house arrest . . . rather than strict probation." In an essay describing Michigan's Community Corrections Act (CCA), Patricia Clark (1995:68) has noted that "since the implementation of Michigan's CCA, community service work, electronic monitoring, day reporting, employment, and drug testing and treatment programs have been initiated and expanded in most communities in the state." And in a definitive study of community corrections conducted by Robert Sigler and David Lamb (1995:7), types of community corrections included the following: regular probation; intensive probation; shock probation; work release; electronic monitoring; house arrest; halfway house; victim restitution and fines; and community service.

What is clear is that the differences between community-based corrections and intermediate punishments are unclear (Kleinig and Smith, 2002). The primary reason for this lack of clarity is that virtually all intermediate punishments are community-based sanctions. All intermediate punishment programs are located in communities, where offenders are permitted various freedoms to work at jobs, attend school, and/or participate in different forms of individual or group therapy. All intermediate punishment programs have behavioral conditions. Virtually every intermediate punishment program is administered by a probation or parole agency or by a private organization. All intermediate punishment clients are under some form of supervision by these agencies or organizations. The intensity of such supervision varies according to the agency and program requirements.

Some states, such as Florida, have a program known as **community control.** According to Florida officials, community control is not intensive supervised probation or parole. Rather, it is home confinement, often coupled with **electronic monitoring.** However, Florida clouds the picture by describing how community control involves frequent face-to-face contacts between probationers and parolees and their supervisors; that curfews are strictly enforced; and that probation and parole officers have deliberately low caseloads of 20 or fewer clients so as to allow officers to supervise offenders closely or intensively. This description of community control sounds a lot like intensive supervised probation/parole, and it has all of the identifying characteristics of community corrections.

A fine line is sometimes drawn between programs that offer offenders community freedoms but require them to be monitored frequently and intensively (e.g., repeated drug and alcohol testing through urinalysis, curfew checks, unannounced but frequent inspections of one's residence), and programs that place offenders in designated locations, such as their homes or halfway houses. But the simple fact is that **professionals** themselves obscure the differences between community-based programs by lumping together any and all programs that involve client freedom but some form of community supervision, regardless of its nature or intensity.

In this book, community corrections consists of any community-based program designed to supervise convicted offenders in lieu of incarceration, either at the city, county, state or federal level; that provides various services to client/offenders; that monitors and furthers client/offender behaviors related to sentencing conditions; that heightens client/offender responsibility and accountability regarding the payment of fines, victim compensation, community service, and restitution orders; and that provides for a continuation of punishment through more controlled supervision and greater accountability (Lin-Ruey, 1997).

Various community-based correctional alternatives include programs such as intensive probation or parole supervision, home confinement, electronic surveillance or monitoring, narcotics and drug deterrence, work furlough programs or work release, study release, day reporting centers, and probationer violation and restitution residential centers (Israel and Dawes, 2002). Also included under the community corrections umbrella are programs such as diversion, **pretrial release** and pre-parole. Community corrections programs can also be distinguished according to the controlling authority. Community-based correctional programs may be community-run (locally operated, but lacking state funding and other external support); community-placed (programs that are located in communities but do not network with any community agency); and community-based (programs that are locally operated but are also financially supplemented from outside sources; programs that network with other community agencies and the criminal justice system).

The term may also refer to any of several different programs designed to closely control or monitor offender behaviors. Since there are several possible meanings of intermediate punishments, the term is widely applied, correctly or incorrectly, to a variety of community-based offender programs involving nonincarcerative sanctions. Major distinguishing features of intermediate punishments are the high degree of offender monitoring and control of offender behaviors by program staff. Other characteristics of intermediate punishments include curfews, where offenders must observe time guidelines and be at particular places at particular times and frequent monitoring and contact with program officials. The amount and type of frequent monitoring or contact varies with the program, although daily visits by probation officers at an offender's workplace or home are not unusual (Kleinig and Smith, 2002).

One semantic problem is that the intensive supervision refers to different levels of monitoring or officer-offender contact, depending on the jurisdiction. Intermediate punishments are intended for prison- or jail-bound offenders. Therefore, offenders who are probably going to receive probation anyway are considered the least likely candidates for these more intensively supervised programs. However, judges often assign these low-risk probation-bound offenders to intermediate punishment programs anyway. This practice tends to defeat the goals of such programs, because the programs target offenders who would otherwise occupy valuable prison or jail space unnecessarily. Cluttering these intensive supervision programs with offenders who don't need close supervision is a waste of money, time, and personnel. When this occurs, it is referred to as **net-widening** (Spooner et al., 2001). Offenders are given considerable freedom of movement within their communities, although it is believed that such intensive monitoring and control fosters a high degree of compliance with program requirements. It is also suspected that this intensive supervision deters offenders from committing new crimes.

THE COMMUNITY CORRECTIONS ACT

A **community corrections act** is the enabling medium by which jurisdictions establish local community corrections agencies, facilities, and programs. A generic definition of a community corrections act is a statewide mechanism through which funds are granted to local units of government to plan, develop and deliver correctional sanctions and services at the local level. The overall purpose of this mechanism is to provide local sentencing options in lieu of imprisonment in state institutions (Kleinig and Smith, 2002).

The aim of community corrections acts is to make it possible to divert certain prison-bound offenders into local, city- or county-level programs where they can receive treatment and assistance rather than imprisonment. Usually, those offenders who are eligible or otherwise qualify for community corrections programs are low-risk nonviolent, nondangerous offenders. Community corrections acts also target those incarcerated offenders who pose little or no risk to the public if released into the community under close parole supervision. Thus, community corrections acts function to alleviate prison and jail overcrowding by diverting certain jail- or prison-bound offenders to community programs.

For instance, Wisconsin implemented a community corrections act in the early 1990s. This act was designed to provide alternatives to both incarceration and new prison construction by encouraging local communities to provide appropriate community sanctions for adult and juvenile offenders. At the time Wisconsin implemented its community-based programs, there were 196,000 crimes committed in the state annually, largely by recidivists (Mitchell, 1999). Wisconsin community corrections currently utilizes a variety of programs as a part of its community corrections, including home confinement, day reporting centers, halfway houses, electronic monitoring, and intensive supervised probation and parole to supervise its 68,000 offenders. Under present fiscal allocations, the annual cost of these community-based programs to the state averages $1,500 per offender (Camp and Camp, 2003).

In 2002, there were over 200,000 offenders on probation in Ohio, with about 60,000 of these involved in community corrections programs (Pastore and Maguire, 2003). Targeted offenders include nonviolent clients who participate in both residential and nonresidential placement options. These placement options include work release and halfway house programs, intensive supervised probation, day reporting centers, home confinement, community service, and standard probation. Personnel conduct urinalyses of clients as well as other forms of behavioral monitoring. Ohio programming staff look for the following resident/client traits:

1. A demonstrated willingness to comply with program rules and regulations.
2. A motivation to work on individual treatment plans as described by program staff.
3. A target population pool consisting primarily of nonviolent offenders, including but not limited to misdemeanants, probation eligible felony offenders, and parolees who are amenable to community sanctions (Latessa, Travis, and Holsinger, 1997:2–10).

THE PHILOSOPHY AND HISTORY OF COMMUNITY CORRECTIONS

The philosophy of community corrections is to provide certain types of offenders with a rehabilitative and reintegrative milieu, where their personal abilities and skills are improved, and where their chances for recidivism are minimized (Nijboer et al., 2002). The primary purpose of community-based correctional programs is to assist probationers in becoming reintegrated into their communities, although parolees are assisted by such programs as well. It is not so much the case that probationers compared with parolees have lost touch with their communities through incarceration, but rather they have the opportunity of avoiding confinement and remaining within their communities to perform productive work to support themselves and others and to repay victims for losses suffered.

A secondary purpose of community-based programs is to help alleviate prison and jail overcrowding by accepting those offenders who are not dangerous and pose the least risk to society. Of course, the difficulty here is attempting to sort those most dangerous offenders from those least dangerous. Assessments of offender risk are not infallible, and often, persons predicted to be dangerous may never commit future violent offenses or harm others. At the same time, some risk instruments may suggest that certain offenders will be nonviolent and not dangerous, although the offender will turn out to be dangerous. These two types of offenders are called **false positives** and **false negatives** (Poletiek, 2002). False positives are offenders considered dangerous based on independent criteria such as their prior institutional conduct or prior record of offending, although they do not pose a danger to others. False negatives are offenders believed to be nonviolent on the basis of independent criteria, such as **risk assessment instruments** and psychological evaluations, although they turn out to be dangerous by subsequently harming others and committing violent offenses (Bickle et al., 2002). In order to reduce the risks posed by false negatives and improve the likelihood of releasing false positives, community corrections acts generally provide that (1) states should continue to house violent offenders in secure facilities; (2) judges and prosecutors need a variety of punishments; and (3) local communities cannot develop these programs without additional funding from such legislatures.

California was one of the first states to implement a community corrections program. California's **Probation Subsidy Program** was implemented in

1965. This program provided local communities with supplemental resources to manage larger numbers of probationers more closely. A part of this subsidization provided for **community residential centers** where probationers could check in and receive counseling, employment assistance, and other forms of guidance or supervision. Soon, other states, such as Colorado and Oregon, established their own community-based programs to assist probationers and others (Lauen, 1997). However, it took at least another decade for large-scale philosophical shifts to occur among different U.S. jurisdictions so that community corrections could be implemented more widely.

Community-based programs are geared to assist offenders by providing nonsecure lodging, vocational/educational training, job assistance, and a limited amount of psychological counseling. Such programs perform rehabilitative and reintegrative functions. One of the first official acknowledgments of the need for community-based programs as a possible front-end solution to prison and jail overcrowding was the 1967 **President's Commission on Law Enforcement and Administration of Justice.** Subsequently, the National Advisory Commission on Criminal Justice Standards and Goals as well as the Law Enforcement Assistance Administration encouraged the establishment of community-based programs as alternatives to incarceration in 1973 and provided extensive financial sponsorship for such programs (Clear and Dammer, 2000).

The growing use of community-based programs has occurred for at least three reasons. First, the 1967 President's Commission on Law Enforcement and Administration of Justice indicated that community-based monitoring of offenders is much cheaper than incarceration. The **Law Enforcement Assistance Administration (LEAA)** provided considerable funding for experiments in community-based programming. Second, since incarceration has been unable to offer the public any convincing evidence that large numbers of inmates emerge rehabilitated, community corrections programs will not be any worse. Community-based correctional programs are perhaps the major form of offender management today. Offender management, control, and punishment are key functions of community corrections.

Another important reason for community-based correctional programs is that prisons are increasingly considered destructive for both offenders and society (Marion, 2002). Many inmates who are confined in prisons for several years become accustomed to an alien lifestyle unlike anything occurring within their communities. There is physical separation from an offender's family unit and friends. Inmates are subject to demeaning experiences and treatment not designed to equip offenders with the necessary skills to cope with life on the outside when they are eventually released.

CHARACTERISTICS, GOALS, AND FUNCTIONS OF COMMUNITY CORRECTIONS PROGRAMS

Community-based programs vary in size and scope among communities although they share certain characteristics such as the following:

1. Community-based program administrators have the authority to oversee offender behaviors and enforce compliance with their probation conditions.

2. These programs have job referral and placement services where paraprofessionals or others act as liaisons with various community agencies and organizations to facilitate offender job placement.

3. Administrators of these programs are available on-premises on a 24-hour basis for emergency situations and spontaneous assistance for offenders who may need help.

4. One or more large homes or buildings located within the residential section of the community with space to accommodate between 20 and 30 residents are provided within walking distance of work settings and social services.

5. A professional and paraprofessional staff "on call" for medical, social, or psychological emergencies.

6. A system is in place for heightening staff accountability to the court concerning offender progress (Lauen, 1997).

Community-based corrections is not intended to free thousands of violent felons into communities. Rather, these programs advocate the continued use of incarceration for violent offenders. However, a portion of prison-bound offenders might benefit by becoming involved in community-based correctional programming (Stephens, 2002). Community-based corrections seeks to preserve offender attachments with their communities by diverting them from incarceration and housing them in local neighborhoods. Thus, there is a strong reintegrative objective that drives such community programming. One of the major obstacles for implementing community-based corrections on a large scale is community opposition because of fear and a lack of understanding about how such programming is operated (Kramer and Ulmer, 2002).

Citizens are entitled to believe that freeing dangerous felons into their communities certainly poses some degree of risk to public safety. There is also the view that offenders who remain free also remain unpunished. But community-based corrections are replete with the characteristics associated with punishment. All community-based correctional programs are considered to be continuations of punishments for offenders. For instance, offender/clients must pay restitution to victims, perform public service, pay fines and maintenance fees, adhere to stringent rules and curfews, put up with unannounced searches of their premises by POs, and they must comply with other seemingly unreasonable behavioral restrictions and limitations. Indeed, some offenders have opted for imprisonment instead of probation or parole, since they regard probation or parole as a substantial intrusion on their privacy. They would rather serve out their time and be free of the criminal justice system entirely rather than be subjected to all of the rules and regulations associated with community-based corrections programs (Marion, 2002).

The Goals of Community-Based Corrections

The goals of community corrections programs include (1) facilitating offender reintegration; (2) fostering offender rehabilitation; (3) providing an alternative range of offender punishments; and (4) heightening offender accountability.

Facilitating Offender Reintegration.   It is considered advantageous for both offenders and correctional personnel to supervise as many offenders in their communities as possible. One reason is that continued community involvement means continuous and hopefully positive contact with one's family and close friends (Gooding, 2001). Also, there is a broader range of social and psychological services available to offenders compared with their opportunities for personal growth and development while in prison or jail. Convicted offenders who remain free in their communities can help with community-based correctional programming operating costs, work at jobs to support themselves and their families, and take advantage of vocational/technical and educational programs available through local colleges and universities. Some offenders require closer monitoring than others. Therefore, it is imperative that community-based correctional programs devise effective screening mechanisms for their clients in order to diagnose their needs accurately. Offender reintegration is therefore an important objective of community-based correctional programs in most states. Also, community-based corrections is becoming increasingly popular in other countries, such as Canada, Germany, Australia, and Italy (U.S. General Accounting Office, 2001).

Fostering Offender Rehabilitation.   A major goal of any community-based correctional program is rehabilitation. Rehabilitation occurs when community correctional clients, offenders, participate in vocational, educational, and/or counseling programs that are intended to improve their coping skills (Allen et al., 2002). These programs are particularly beneficial for first-time nonviolent offenders. Several jurisdictions disclose that they have much lower rates of recidivism among community-based correctional clientele compared with offenders who have been incarcerated. In a program in a large urban probation department, officials operate a program known as SAFE-T. SAFE-T adopts cognitive-behavioral approaches that target contemporary youth culture. While SAFE-T is oriented toward more youthful offenders, it has promise also for young adults. Clients are exposed to four-month series of 32 group sessions. These sessions are led by probation officers who have been intensively trained in group work methods and exposed to urban youth culture. Clients are guided in establishing personal responsibility and learning how to cope with others who may be involved in drugs, alcohol, or illicit activities. Low recidivism rates have been reported (Fals, 2003).

Providing an Alternative Range of Offender Punishments.   The range of punishments is vast within community-based corrections. Programs are tailored to fit clients from all age groups, including those with diverse needs and special problems, such as addictions to drugs or alcohol, learning disabilities, or vocational/educational deficiencies. Community centers are created under community corrections acts to assist clients in filling out job applications or overcoming illiteracy. Individual and group counseling are offered to different clients in need of such assistance. The private sector has become increasingly involved in the treatment of community-based correctional clients, and program expansion and diversification has occurred in many cities and communities (Haulard, 2001).

Heightening Offender Accountability.   One of the primary reasons that traditional unsupervised probation has been unsuccessful in rehabilitating offenders is that all too often, probationers are completely unsupervised. They may be permitted simply to fill out a one-page report of their work activities and submit these to probation offices by mail. This means absolutely no direct supervision of these offenders occurs. This condition exists whenever there are large numbers of offenders on probation and relatively few probation officers available to supervise them. One aim of community-based corrections, therefore, is to provide substantial supervision and services to those in need. Substance abusers comprise a class of clients requiring special assistance and intervention. Often these offenders have committed crimes in the past to acquire the drugs they need to satisfy their addictions. With appropriate intervention and accountability mechanisms established, many of these offenders can overcome their addictions and accept responsibility for their actions. Over time, they learn to cope and overcome their substance dependencies to the extent that they can perform full-time jobs and support their dependents. Heightening offender accountability is a key goal of community-based correctional programs, both in the United States and elsewhere, such as Australia and Canada (Bottoms, Gelsthorpe, and Rex, 2001).

The Functions of Community-Based Corrections

Community-based corrections performs the following functions: (1) client monitoring and supervision to ensure program compliance; (2) ensuring public safety; (3) employment assistance; (4) individual and group counseling; (5) educational training and literacy services; (6) networking with other community agencies and businesses; and (7) alleviating jail and prison overcrowding.

Client Monitoring and Supervision to Ensure Program Compliance. When offenders are sentenced to a community corrections program, it is expected that they will comply with all program conditions. The nature of their supervision is more or less intense in order to ensure program compliance. Victim compensation, restitution, and/or community service are often crucial program components. Public safety is enhanced to the extent that program requirements are enforced by community-based correctional personnel. Measures must be established to ensure that offenders comply with court orders and participate in designated programs. This is especially important for those clients with substance abuse problems and dependencies and who need special drugs to aid them in their withdrawal process (Utting and Vennard, 2000).

Ensuring Public Safety. Community-based corrections is greatly concerned with the matter of public safety. Clients selected for inclusion in these community-based programs are carefully screened so that those likely to pose the most risk or danger to others are excluded. The supervisory safeguards, such as curfew, and drug/alcohol abuse checks, are intensive (Bottoms, Gelsthorpe, and Rex, 2001). Offender-clients are selected primarily on the basis of their low-risk profile and the prospect that they will complete their programs successfully.

Employment Assistance. An important objective of community corrections is to provide offender-clients with job assistance. Many of these clients do not know how to fill out job application forms. Other clients do not know how to interview properly with prospective employers. Minimal assistance from staff of community-based corrections agencies can do much to aid offenders in securing employment and avoiding further trouble with the law.

Individual and Group Counseling. Many offender-clients who become involved in community corrections programs have drug or alcohol dependencies. Often, these offenders have difficulty getting along with others and coping with societal expectations. These offenders have certain social, psychological, and

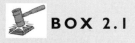
BOX 2.1

Joe Peterson
Career Corrections Agent, Field Services Division, Minnesota Department of Corrections

Statistics:

B.S. (criminal justice major, sociology minor), Moorhead State University

Background:

I am currently based in Park Rapids, Minnesota and am responsible for the supervision of adult offenders living in Hubbard County who are either on probation or parole status. I have been with the Minnesota Department of Corrections in my current capacity for approximately six years, and I have been employed in the field as a probation and parole agent for a total of ten years. I graduated from Moorhead State University in 1993 with a degree in criminal justice. Upon entering college I decided on a major in mass communications with an emphasis on public relations. I recall making the decision to change career directions as I walked across campus one beautiful spring day during my freshman year. The thought of working in the mass communication field and being confined to an office building for 40+ hours a week was not attractive. This did not mean that I was longing for a career in forestry, but rather a field where I could dictate my own schedule during a workweek and not be bound to an office.

One of my first thoughts for a career choice was that of law enforcement; however, I did not necessarily want to work as a police officer. I was introduced to the profession of probation and parole through literature obtained from the Criminal Justice Department. It seemed to be a perfect fit; I would be able to work with people, have the ability to work with the community, and the freedom to develop my own work schedule. I have never regretted the change in majors since gaining employment in the field of corrections. I do find it somewhat ironic that even though I left mass communications and public relations, I now find myself performing communication in mass and relaying information to the public on a daily basis.

Unique Work:

The work that is done by a probation or parole agent follows specific guidelines and policies, and it can be riddled with emotion. Early in my career I would come home after a busy day and complain to my wife that I was exhausted. She found this hard to believe, since I hadn't performed any physical labor. It did not take long to figure out that an agent can expend a great deal of emotional energy each day in dealing with manipulative offenders, offering assistance to victims, and answering questions posed by curious citizens.

One of the frustrations I have faced is that of being able to see the fruits of my labor. I imagine that carpenters, for example, enjoy the work they do for a number of reasons, with one being the ability to actually see on a daily basis what has been accomplished. In the field of corrections, success often comes in small increments that develop over weeks, months, or even years. It is very satisfying to see an offender achieve positive change in his/her life, and while it would be ideal to see this type of change on a daily basis, the reality is that destructive or anti-social traits, beliefs, and values are not easily torn apart and rebuilt.

A Challenging Case:

One of my most difficult cases involved the supervision of a female sex offender. I took over supervision of this person from an agent who transferred out of the office. This offender was very needy, dealing with alcohol

(continued)

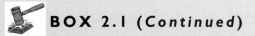

BOX 2.1 (Continued)

addiction and a chaotic home life. She was also trying to deal with the deaths of two of her own children. They had passed away approximately five years earlier, with the cause of death labeled as SIDS. There were rumors that she had possibly killed her children by either shaking or smothering them. Investigations had been done in the past, but there was no solid evidence to warrant charges.

During the course of probation, she was provided with chemical dependency treatment, individual counseling, and sex offender programming. This offender would make some small positive strides, but soon thereafter, she would self-destruct. She committed a number of probation violations relating to the use of alcohol and/or narcotics. The sentencing judge gave her a number of chances to make positive changes in her life; however, the violations mounted. Finally, she committed a new offense concerning check forgery, and my recommendation was that she be sent to prison. The sentencing judge agreed.

She was held in prison for a number of months and then released back into the community, this time on parole supervision under my direction. She was again provided with services in the community to pick up where treatment programming in the prison ended. She again made some progress, completing a lengthy term of individual counseling pertaining mainly to both her offending and past abuse issues. Unfortunately, she began a relationship with a male sex offender who was very manipulative, and she became pregnant. The therapist and I met with both of them to discuss the ramifications and consequences of the situation. On the day that she gave birth, I again notified the social services office, and a deputy and child protection specialist took the infant from her at the hospital. In my mind I knew it was the proper thing to do, but my heart was telling me different.

She did well in light of the situation; however, as one could expect based on her past behavior, she did return to destructive patterns. She again committed an offense relative to check forgery. She was placed in custody for a parole violation and eventually returned to prison for approximately three months of consequence time. After completion of the three-month sentence, she was re-

leased into the community under my supervision, and again services were in place for her needs. She lived with her mother and was somewhat isolated due to the rural area and her lack of a driver's license. During this time, I had received information from law enforcement that new evidence had been uncovered regarding the deaths of her two children. The evidence was so compelling that a criminal complaint was filed by the Attorney General's Office alleging two counts of murder. She was taken into custody and held pending trial.

She did eventually accept a plea agreement whereby she admitted to smothering both of her children and was given one life sentence. I recall the sentencing judge telling her that he hoped she would be able to deal in a positive manner with the demons that had been haunting her. After hearing those words, I immediately knew at least one of the reasons why she had never been able to make a positive adjustment in the community. She was carrying an extraordinary amount of guilt. It was impossible for her to accept praise or acknowledge accomplishments knowing that she had taken the life from two small, innocent children. I found myself questioning my own skills: Why wasn't I able to figure this out? Was there something I should have done differently? Am I at fault? While it had to be heartbreaking to have her newborn baby taken from her arms, I knew then that I had done the right thing by notifying social services of the birth. That child is now safe and being reared by a caring family. Doing the right thing in this line of work can oftentimes conflict with emotions of the heart.

Advice to Students:

I would say that anyone who is considering a career as a probation or parole officer should be a "people person." This does not mean that you should befriend every offender who comes through the office door, but rather you should treat every offender with respect within the boundaries of a professional relationship. It is important to be fair, firm, and consistent, while at the same time being conscious of the individual needs and risks that offenders present.

physical needs that must be treated, either through individual or group counseling (Utting and Vennard, 2000). Many community corrections agencies have established such counseling programs for these offenders.

Educational Training and Literacy Services.   It is surprising for some citizens to learn that many offenders cannot read or write. Thus, whenever they are released, either on probation or parole, they find it difficult to find and retain good jobs in the workplace. Most jobs require minimal reading and writing skills. A significant proportion of offenders lack these basic skills. Community-based correctional programming is increasingly offering educational experiences to offenders who are illiterate or do not have reading levels commensurate with the jobs they are seeking to provide for themselves and their families. Greater use is being made of needs instrumentation for the purpose of screening program-eligible offenders and determining which needs they have and how best those needs can be met (Haulard, 2001).

Networking with Other Community Agencies and Businesses.   An important function of community corrections is to network with various community agencies and businesses to match offender-clients with needed treatments and services. Community corrections agencies may not have a full range of offender services. Cooperative endeavors are necessary if certain offenders are to receive the type of treatment they need most. Sometimes, the networking performed by community corrections enables offender-clients to obtain vocational and educational training, or perhaps group or individual counseling. Networking with businesses enables community corrections personnel to determine job availability. Thus, community corrections offers a valuable job placement service for those offenders who have difficulty finding work (Marion, 2002).

Alleviating Jail and Prison Overcrowding.   Community-based corrections alleviates some amount of jail and prison overcrowding. In New York, for instance, it costs about $45,000 per prisoner per year for prison housing. In contrast, community-based offender monitoring which offers more intensive offender supervision but less than full incarceration, costs the state about $5,500 per prisoner (Camp and Camp, 2003).

SELECTED ISSUES IN COMMUNITY CORRECTIONS

Several important issues relating to community-based correctional programs include: (1) public resistance to locating community programs in communities; (2) punishment and public safety versus offender rehabilitation and reintegration; (3) net-widening; (4) the privatization of community-based corrections agencies; and (5) services delivery.

Public Resistance to Locating Community Programs in Communities (The NIMBY Syndrome: "Not In My Back Yard")

Some amount of community resistance is encountered whenever any community plans to establish a community corrections facility in a neighborhood. From the standpoint of community corrections personnel, they desire locations for their facilities which are near city centers or within walking distance of schools, hospitals, counseling centers, and workplaces. Corrections personnel believe that neighborhood milieus are an integral feature of the therapy required for more complete offender rehabilitation and reintegration. Locating community-based services within communities is critical, therefore, since offenders can experience the freedoms and responsibilities associated with their probation and parole programs.

The view from citizens is quite different. Some citizens, especially those whose homes are located near these community-based centers and services, believe that they are endangered by the presence of convicted felons roaming about freely near them and their children. Some citizens believe that their property values are adversely affected, and that they will have difficulty selling their property if they decide to move. After all, who wants to live near a home which houses numerous convicted felons? This is a fairly typical community reaction and stems largely from the fact that most persons don't understand what community-based corrections is all about and how it is intended to operate (Hubbard, 1998). It is such a typical reaction that it has been given a name. Corrections personnel call it the **NIMBY syndrome.** NIMBY is an acronym meaning "Not In My Back Yard." The NIMBY syndrome means that although many citizens believe in correctional rehabilitation and that community corrections are an essential part of one's rehabilitation and reintegration into neighborhood life, these same citizens would prefer that such corrections agencies or operations should not be located in their own neighborhoods. The NIMBY syndrome has been investigated in various locations, including Canada (U.S. Office of Justice Programs, 1998).

Benzvy-Miller (1990) says that communities tend to manifest the NIMBY syndrome for at least three reasons: (1) They fear crime and expect that close proximity to offenders will expose them to greater risk; (2) they have attitudes and perceptions about offenders that have little to do with reality; and (3) they are afraid that a group home will somehow taint the neighborhood and cause property values to decline. These attitudes and the problems they generate can be overcome by educating the public and increasing their awareness of what these programs are all about and how offenders are supervised or monitored. However, educating the public about community-based corrections is a long and sometimes difficult process (Hubbard, 1998).

Punishment and Public Safety versus Offender Rehabilitation and Reintegration

Public safety is a perennial issue raised whenever community corrections seeks to establish agencies within neighborhoods. There is substantial evidence that the general public has an intense fear of crime, and that this fear of crime has led them to oppose the idea of community corrections programming for dangerous felons. Residents are repelled by the idea that they will have convicted felons roaming freely among them. At the same time, corrections officials cite the need to place certain offenders into communities where they can learn to function normally in law-abiding ways. Offenders need community experience, while community residents need to feel safe. Thus, public safety is often at odds with the **rehabilitative ideal** of community corrections programs. The cost of treating and supervising offenders in their communities is considerably less than incarcerating offenders in jails or prisons. This is a largely undisputed fact

(Wilson and Petersilia, 2002). However, there is considerable disagreement over whether permitting some offenders to remain in their communities either unsupervised or supervised is the functional equivalent of punishment. The dilemma is deciding whether it is therapeutic for offenders to remain within their communities where their reintegration and rehabilitation may be maximized, or whether their freedom places law-abiding citizens at risk. Both of these views are valid.

LaMont Flanagan reduces the dilemma over whether community corrections is a punishment to an issue of dollars and cents. Regarding public safety, Flanagan says that community corrections programs seek to preserve public safety by screening prospective clients and including only those most likely to succeed. He believes that imprisonment should be reserved only for the most violent offenders who pose the greatest danger to public safety (Flanagan, 1997). Furthermore, Flanagan says that the bulk of current jail and prison inmates are largely nonviolent offenders who are capable of becoming safely reintegrated into their communities under some form of monitoring or close supervision. He believes that their remediation should be a key correctional priority.

Many offenders derive numerous rehabilitative benefits from community-based programs. Proof of community-based programming effectiveness is manifested by lower recidivism rates among community corrections clientele, which is also a gauge of supervisory effectiveness of correctional staff. It is also manifested by the increasing number of countries throughout the world who are developing community-based correctional programming for a portion of their criminal populations. Researchers in the United States and elsewhere declare that how offenders are supervised makes a significant difference in their potential for recidivism (Oldfield and Oldfield, 2002). For instance, community-based correctional personnel may supervise their clients as enforcers, treating their clients in ways similar to police officer–offender encounters. Such a supervisory style emphasizes rules and punitiveness. Another supervisory style is pro-social, where problem solving and empathy are key supervisory tactics in relation to offender/clients. Studies of this pro-social approach to offender supervision suggest that offender/clients respond more positively and perceive their supervisors as supportive rather than punitive. The result is that recidivism rates among those supervised in pro-social ways are up to 50 percent less than offenders who are supervised punitively (Trotter, 1996).

Net-Widening

Net-widening occurs whenever offender/clients are included in community programs simply because those programs exist. If the programs did not exist, then these offender/clients would probably be placed on probation. Thus, the mere existence of a community-based correctional program raises questions about who should be included in the program. The clear intent of most community-based correctional programs is to encompass jail- or prison-bound offenders who might benefit more from community treatment rather than incarceration. Decisions about which offenders should be placed in community-based programs and which offenders should be incarcerated are most often made by judges. Judges are influenced by probation officers who often make sentencing recommendations.

Community-based correctional programs often screen prospective clients and determine their eligibility. Some of the criteria used in the screening process include whether the community agency can provide the right type of assistance for particular offenders; whether certain offenders have undesirable behaviors, habits, or prior records; and whether certain offenders are considered amenable to various treatment strategies. If community corrections officers determine that certain offenders are ineligible for their programs, then they can refuse to admit them.

Most community-based corrections agencies have a strong vested interest in including offenders in their programs who are the most likely to be successful in their compliance with program requirements and program completion. Often, the most nonviolent offenders are selected as clients. They have behavioral histories of compliance with authority. They are considered the best risks. When these offenders are included in community programs and more serious offenders are excluded, a self-serving selection process is set in motion where the programming outcomes for certain clients are highly predictable. Some corrections professionals refer to this process as **creaming,** as in skimming the cream from fresh milk. Applied to those considered eligible for community-based programs, creaming means that only those who show the greatest promise of being successful in their programs will be included in those programs. When these offender/clients eventually succeed and complete their program requirements successfully, program supervisors are not especially surprised. In fact, they may be delighted. This usually means that these same successful offender/clients will leave their programs and be the least likely to reoffend compared with more serious offenders who were barred from community corrections programs initially in the screening process. Thus, low recidivism rates among such offender/clients is quite predictable. Low recidivism rates are the most direct indication of the program's success as a rehabilitative medium. Most community corrections agencies depend upon state or federal resources to defray their operating costs, so a program with low recidivism rates will most likely continue to be funded. This is a somewhat cynical view, although it is based largely on political reality (Wilson and Petersilia, 2002).

Privatization of Community-Based Correctional Agencies

Some proportion of the chronic overcrowding problems of jails and prisons has been alleviated through community-based correctional programs. Through community corrections acts, many communities have established programs to accommodate jail- or prison-bound offenders. Thus, some scarce prison and jail space has been made available for more serious offenders through various types of community programming. However, the public sector has been unable to provide necessary rehabilitative services for large numbers of offenders. Increasingly, the private sector has made a concerted effort to establish itself as a legitimate alternative to public community corrections (Chang and Thompkins, 2002).

The **privatization** of corrections, or the intrusion of private industry into community programs and the administration of jail and prison systems, is succeeding in furthering the public relations image of corrections by suggesting greater control of prisons and offender programs by the private sector (Mitchell, 1999). In 2002, for example, private corporations supervised at least 50,000 inmates in over 150 prisons, while over 250 privately operated jails and detention facilities accommodated over 75,000 prisoners (Camp and Camp, 2003).

At least five reasons have been given for why privately run community-based treatment programs would be regarded as a progressive solution to present-day jail and prison overcrowding. These reasons include:

1. Privatization would break the traditional treatment–custody link and the resulting corruption from overconcern with custody and control. A greater incentive would exist to make rehabilitation work if the profit motive were present, since profits are ordinarily related to program effectiveness.

2. Privatization would result in more, not less, accountability if program rehabilitation objectives fail. Systems linking payment or contract renewal to the quality and effectiveness of services provided would make private vendors more accountable and responsive.

3. The infusion of private interests into corrections would promote experimentation with new ideas and strategies for offender treatment and rehabilitation. Under existing management schemes, the routinization of policy is commonplace, with little or no innovation.

4. The introduction of business into offender rehabilitation may enhance the political acceptability of correctional treatment. In short, the public relations dimension of corrections would be enhanced and greater community acceptance would ensue.

5. Privatization is consistent with capitalist philosophy, and this basic compatibility would make sense since it offers businesses the chance to make money from corrections (Cullen, 1986:13–15).

Major criticisms of privatization of both institutional and community corrections are that (1) private enterprise removes control of offenders from professional corrections personnel; (2) it creates accountability issues for the courts; (3) private enterprise would encourage more prisons and community-based facilities to warehouse larger numbers of offenders because of the profit motive; (4) private enterprise would lead to a downgrading of supervisory quality by reducing the standards by which personnel are trained to monitor dangerous offenders; and (5) it is unconstitutional for private enterprise to sanction state and federal offenders.

Pro-privatization arguments are that (1) private agencies can respond more quickly to problems of financing than legislatures and other political organizations; (2) private enterprise can make initial capital investments in facility construction, thus saving the states billions of dollars; (3) private enterprise can decrease the amount of government liability arising from lawsuits brought by clients against program administrators and staff; (4) private enterprises can operate more efficiently and at less cost than public agencies; and (5) private enterprise staff are usually drawn from public sector correctional positions where they have already been professionally trained.

The fact is that there is no constitutional prohibition against using private enterprise as an option to publicly operated correctional facilities, either institutionally or within the community. Under the theory of **agency,** the government may direct private corporations to establish different types of correctional facilities, as long as these facilities are in compliance with state and federal guidelines. Thus, the government vests private corporations with the authority to supervise offenders, both juvenile and adult, under different conditions and for varying periods. All privately operated correctional programs are subject to the same mechanisms of accountability, control, and regulation as publicly operated facilities (Chang and Thompkins, 2002).

A major difference between private and public correctional facilities is their relative cost effectiveness. Private enterprise is able to compete more vigorously with public facilities in providing a broad range of services to offender/clients. A comparative study of privately and publicly operated correctional organizations in Louisiana, for instance, disclosed that compared with state operated facilities, private correctional agencies were able to operate in more cost-effective ways; reported fewer critical incidents; provided safer work environments for employees and safer living environments for offenders; judiciously and effectively used inmate disciplinary actions to maintain order; deployed fewer security personnel while achieving higher safety levels; had proportionately more offenders complete their basic education, literacy, and vocational training courses; and equaled or surpassed the number of offender screenings for community corrections placements (Archambeault and Deis, 1996). Similar findings about privatization have been disclosed for other state jurisdictions, such as Florida, Washington, and Wisconsin (Blomberg and Waldo, 2002). The use of privately operated correctional programs in other countries has also resulted in positive outcomes compared with publicly operated agencies and organizations.

Services Delivery

Delivering the appropriate services for offenders is often a difficult task for community corrections agencies (Cocozza and Stainbrook, 1998). Assessments of offender-clients are frequently superficial, largely because of understaffing or underfunding. Sometimes, offenders have several types of problems that are difficult to diagnose and treat. Historically, services delivery has been deficient in many community corrections programs, where supervisory chores and offender accountability have been regarded as primary goals (Dillingham et al., 1999).

One way to insure that services delivery is offender-relevant and appropriate is to individualize the needs of specific offenders. For instance, many persons are placed in probation and parole programs who have undiagnosed mental illnesses or suffer from other mental or physical impairments (Byrne, Byrne, and Howells, 2001). Appropriate diagnostic procedures must be in place in order for community corrections personnel to determine each offender's needs. If any particular agency is not equipped to deal with certain offender needs, then the agency should be in a position to network with other community agencies to make sure that the necessary services are provided in a timely manner. For instance, Texas has a Special Needs Parole Program that provides for an early parole review for special health needs offenders who require 24-hour skilled nursing care and supervision. Although inmates considered for Special Needs Parole are at a higher risk of recidivating and have committed more severe offenses than regular parole cases, the parole board approves them at a higher rate for early release to particular community-based programs where they can obtain necessary mental health services. Improved screening, referral, and review processes increase the program's use without increasing public safety risks (Texas Criminal Justice Policy Council, 2000). An additional feature of this program is that those offenders with significant medical problems and who represent little or no threat to public safety are detected and diverted from prison to more cost-effective community programs for appropriate treatment.

Many offender/clients released to community-based correctional programs have substance abuse problems and dependencies. Often, substance abuse led to their convictions, and when they are released into the community under some form of supervision, they are unable to refrain from substance abuse without strong intervention and assistance from appropriate community agencies (McKean and Raphael, 2002). Many of these offenders pose substantial supervision problems for POs and other supervisors, who must monitor their progress. Any effective community-based treatment and rehabilitation program must be prepared to cope directly or indirectly with substance abusers, since they pose more significant problems for supervisory agencies than any other class of offenders.

HOME CONFINEMENT PROGRAMS

There are many types of community-based correctional programs. One of the most frequently used programs is home confinement, also known as house arrest or **home incarceration.**

Home Confinement Defined

Home confinement or **house arrest** is a community-based program consisting of confining offenders to their residences for mandatory incarceration during evening hours, curfews, and/or on weekends (Gowen, 2001). Home confinement is a sentence imposed by the court. Offenders may leave their residences for medical reasons or employment. Additionally, they may be required to perform community service or pay victim restitution and/or supervisory fees.

Home confinement is not new. St. Paul the Apostle was detained under house arrest in biblical times. In the 1600s, Galileo, the astronomer, was forced to live out the last eight years of his life under house arrest. In 1917, Czar Nicholas II of Russia was detained under house arrest until his death. And during Czar Nicholas II's reign, Lenin was placed under house arrest for a limited period (Meachum, 1986:102). St. Louis was the first city in the United States to use home confinement in 1971. St. Louis officials originally limited its use to juvenile offenders, although home confinement became more widespread over the next several decades in many other jurisdictions (Stalans, Seng, and Yarnold, 2001).

The Early Uses of Home Confinement

Florida was the first state to officially use home confinement on a statewide basis (Voss et al., 2002). Offenders are confined to their own homes, instead of prison, where they are allowed to serve their sentences. The cost of home confinement is only about $10 per day compared with about $50 per day in operating costs for imprisonment (Camp and Camp, 2003). Florida statutes regard community control as a form of intensive supervised custody in the community, including surveillance on weekends and holidays, administered by officers with restricted caseloads. It is an individualized program in which the freedom of an offender is restricted within the community, home, or noninstitutional residential placement and specific sanctions imposed and enforced. Community control officers work irregular hours and at nights to help ensure that offenders stay in their homes except while working at paid employment to support themselves and dependents.

In Florida, community controllees or offenders eligible for the house arrest program include low-risk, prison-bound criminals. They are expected to comply with the following program requirements:

1. Contribute from 150 to 200 hours of free labor to various public service projects during periods ranging from six months to one year.
2. Pay a monthly maintenance fee of $30 to $50 to help defray program operating costs and officer salaries.
3. Compile and maintain daily logs accounting for their activities; these logs are reviewed regularly by officers for accuracy and honesty.
4. Pay restitution to crime victims from a portion of salaries earned through employment.
5. Remain gainfully employed to support themselves and their dependents.
6. Participate in vocational/technical or other educational courses or seminars which are individualized according to each offender's needs.
7. Observe a nightly curfew and remain confined to their premises during late evening hours and on weekends, with the exception of court-approved absences for health-related reasons or other purposes.
8. Submit to monitoring by officials 28 times per month either at home or at work.
9. Maintain court-required contacts with neighbors, friends, landlords, spouses, teachers, police, and/or creditors (Ansay and Benveneste, 1999).

The record of successes through home incarceration in Florida has been impressive. By 2002, over 14,000 offenders were under house arrest and intensive supervision by probation officers (Camp and Camp, 2003). There have been relatively few program failures. Most of these failures are persons who have committed technical program violations, such as violating curfew. Under Florida's home confinement program, **community control house arrest,** offenders eligible for home confinement fall into three categories: (1) those found guilty of nonforcible felonies; (2) probationers charged with technical or misdemeanor violations; and (3) parolees charged with technical or misdemeanor violations. The basic conditions for home confinement cases include:

1. Report to home confinement officer at least four times a week, or if employed part-time, report daily.
2. Perform at least 140 hours of public service work, without pay, as directed by the home confinement officer.
3. Remain confined to residence except for approved employment, public service work, or other special activities approved by the home confinement officer.
4. Make monthly restitution payments for a specified total amount.
5. Submit to and pay for urinalysis, breathalyzer, or blood specimen tests at any time as requested by the home confinement officer or other professional staff to determine possible use of alcohol, drugs, or other controlled substances.
6. Maintain an hourly account of all activities in a daily log to be submitted to the home confinement officer upon request.

7. Participate in self-improvement programs as determined by the court or home confinement officer.

8. Promptly and truthfully answer all inquiries of the court or home confinement officer, and allow the officer to visit the home, employer, or elsewhere.

9. For sex offenders, the court requires, as a special condition of home confinement, the release of treatment information to the home confinement officer or the court (Florida Advisory Council, 1994).

House arrest programs such as Florida's are increasingly common, especially in those states with prison overcrowding problems. Home confinement programs for both juveniles and adults have been established and are proliferating in both federal and state jurisdictions (Ulmer, 2001). Additional conditions are usually imposed, including substance abuse counseling and treatment, victim compensation, and community service. Figure 2.1 is an example of a standard home confinement agreement form used by various jurisdictions.

Some Examples of Home Confinement in Action.   Conventional home confinement systems usually require offenders to wear bracelets or anklets which emit electronic signals. This is electronic monitoring and will be discussed in greater detail in the following section. Offenders must remain in their homes during evening hours, and they are permitted leave from their dwellings only for medical or work-related purposes. The electronic bracelets or anklets worn by home confinement clients are capable of detecting whether clients move out of range of their home monitoring stations, which are semi-permanent fixtures in their dwellings. POs may conduct random visits to one's dwelling at times when the offender must be at home. Voice verification may be effected by telephone. Also, POs may conduct drive-bys with electronic receptors to make an unobtrusive check to see if the offender is on his/her premises at particular times. In some instances, video cameras are installed in one's home and are activated from some central location as another means of verifying the offender's whereabouts. In 2000 there were 11 companies manufacturing and distributing wrist/ankle electronic surveillance products. Targeted for inclusion in home confinement programs are carefully selected nonviolent offenders who have either been removed or diverted from high-cost incarcerative facilities (Bowers, 2000:106).

In another instance, the Dane County Sheriff's Office in Wisconsin uses SpeakerID. SpeakerID permits the sheriff's department to confine certain nonviolent offenders to their homes. The SpeakerID program started by supervising 8 to 12 offenders, and in 1998 it was supervising between 30 to 35 offenders. Two staff members at the jail run the program and monitor offenders. SpeakerID uses voice verification for persons sentenced to home confinement. These persons are telephoned at random times, and their voices are compared with digitalized recordings previously made of offender's vocal patterns. Such voice verification is about 97 percent accurate. If SpeakerID does not get a successful match or an answer on the first call, then the number is automatically redialed for authentication. After a maximum of four unsuccessful attempts, the sheriff's office is notified of a possible violation, and a deputy goes to the offender's residence for a face-to-face visit. If the offender is not there, this is grounds for terminating one's program and returning the offender to jail (Listug, 1996:85). Eligibility requirements for the home confinement program include being nonviolent, employed, and having a relatively stable family environment. If the offender has

HOME CONFINEMENT PROGRAM PARTICIPANT AGREEMENT

1. I _____ have been placed in the Home Confinement Program. I agree to comply with all program rules set forth in this agreement, and the instructions of my probation officer. Failure to comply with this Agreement or any instructions of my officer will be considered a violation of my supervision and may result in an adverse action. I agree to call my officer immediately if I have any questions about these rules or if I experience any problems with the monitoring equipment.

2. I will remain at my approved residence at all times, except for employment and other activities approved in advance by my probation or pretrial services officer. Regularly occurring activities are provided for in my written weekly schedule which remains in effect until modified by my officer. I must obtain my officer's advance permission for any special activities (such as doctor's appointments) that are not included in my written schedule.

3. I shall not deviate from my approved schedule except in an emergency. I shall first try to get the permission of my officer. If this is not possible, I must call my officer as soon as I am able to do so. If I call during non-business hours, I will leave a message on my officer's answering machine, including my name, the date, the time, a brief description of the emergency, and my location or destination. I agree to provide proof of the emergency as requested by my officer.

4. While under home confinement supervision, I agree to wear a non-removable ankle bracelet which will be attached by my officer.

5. I agree to provide and maintain a telephone, with modular telephone connectors, at my residence and maintain telephone and electrical service there at my own expense.

6. On the line to which the monitoring equipment is connected, I agree to not have party lines, telephone answering machines, cordless telephones, "call forwarding," "Caller ID," "call waiting," and other devices and services that may interfere with the proper functioning of the electronic monitoring equipment.

7. I agree to allow a monitoring device (receiver/dialer) to be connected to the telephone and the telephone outlet at my residence.

8. I acknowledge receipt of receiver/dialer number _____, and transmitter number _____. I understand that I will be held responsible for damage, other than normal wear, to the equipment. I also understand that if I do not return the equipment, or do not return it in good condition, I may be charged for replacement or the repair of the equipment and I agree to pay these costs. I understand that I may be subject to felony prosecution if I fail to return my monitoring equipment.

9. I agree to not move, disconnect, or tamper with the monitoring device (receiver/dialer).

10. I agree to not remove or tamper with the ankle bracelet (transmitter) except in a life-threatening emergency or with the prior permission of my officer.

11. I agree to allow authorized personnel to inspect and maintain the ankle transmitter and receiver/dialer.

12. I agree to return the receiver/dialer and transmitter to my officer upon demand.

13. I agree that I will not make any changes in the telephone equipment or services at any residence without prior approval of my officer.

14. I agree to provide copies of my monthly telephone bill when requested by my officer.

15. I agree to notify my officer immediately if I lose electrical power at my residence, if I have to remove the ankle bracelet because of an emergency, or if I experience any problems with the monitoring equipment. During non-business hours, I agree to call my officer and leave a message on his/her answering machine including my name, the date, the time, and the nature of my problem. If there is a power problem, I agree that I will call and leave another message when the power is restored. I also agree to notify my officer of any problems with my telephone service as soon as I am able to do so.

16. I agree that I will not attempt to use my telephone when the Receiver/Dialer's "Phone Busy" or "Phone Indicator" light is on.

17. I understand that my officer will use telephone calls and personal visits to monitor my compliance with my approved schedule. If I fail to answer the telephone or door when I am supposed to be at home, my officer will conclude that I am absent, and in violation of my curfew restrictions.

18. I understand that my officer must be able to contact me at work at any time. If I do not have a job with a fixed location (as in construction work) my officer must be able to locate me by calling my employer and promptly obtaining my work location. I also understand that jobs that do not meet these requirements are not permitted while I am under home confinement supervision. I understand that all job changes must be approved in advance by my officer.

19. I agree to refrain from the excessive use of alcohol or any use of controlled substances unless the controlled substance is prescribed by a licensed medical practitioner.

20. I understand that I will be required to undergo periodic, unscheduled urine collection and testing.

21. I agree to comply with all other conditions of my release and supervision as imposed by the court or parole board.

22. I understand and agree that all telephone calls from the monitoring connector to my residence will be tape-recorded by the monitoring contractor.

23. I understand that I may be ordered to pay all or part of the daily cost of my electronic monitoring. If so ordered, I agree, as directed by my officer, to pay _____ per day directly to the monitoring service.

24. Additional Rules (As needed)

I acknowledge that I have received a copy of these rules and that they have been explained to me. I understand that I must comply with these rules until _____, or until otherwise notified by my probation/parole officer. I further understand that any violations of these rules will also constitute a violation of supervision and may cause immediate adverse action.

_____   _____

FIGURE 2.1 Home Confinement Agreement.

formerly been in prison or jail, then prior institutional good conduct is considered together with these other qualifying characteristics.

The Goals of Home Confinement Programs

The goals of home confinement programs include the following:

1. To continue the offender's punishment while permitting the offender to live in his/her dwelling under general or close supervision.
2. To enable offenders to perform jobs in their communities to support themselves and their families.
3. To reduce jail and prison overcrowding.
4. To maximize public safety by ensuring that only the most qualified clients enter home confinement programs and are properly supervised.
5. To reduce the costs of offender supervision.
6. To promote rehabilitation and reintegration by permitting offenders to live under appropriate supervision within their communities.

Jeffrey Ulmer (2001) has described several advantages and disadvantages of home confinement or house arrest. Among the advantages are: (1) It is cost effective; (2) it has social benefits; (3) it is responsive to local citizen and offender needs; and (4) it is easily implemented and is timely in view of jail and prison overcrowding. Some of the disadvantages of home confinement are: (1) House arrest may actually widen the net of social control; (2) it may narrow the net of social control by not being a sufficiently severe sentence; (3) it focuses primarily upon offender surveillance; (4) it is intrusive and possibly illegal; (5) race and class bias may enter into participant selection; and (6) it may compromise public safety. Some of these advantages and disadvantages will be addressed at length below as issues concerning home confinement where electronic monitoring is also used.

A Profile of Home Confinement Clients

No precise figures exist for describing home confinement clientele. Unofficial estimates for 2002 show that approximately 65,000 offenders were in home confinement programs and supervised generally by probation departments (Camp and Camp, 2003). An examination of the screening procedures and eligibility requirements of different home confinement programs currently operating among the states suggests that most home confinement clients are first offenders and nonviolent. They tend to have close family ties, are married and live with their spouses, and are employed full time. They do not have drug or alcohol dependencies. Compared with clients in other types of probation and parole programs, home confinement clients tend to have higher amounts of education and vocational skills. They also tend to be older, age 30 or over (Ulmer, 2001).

Selected Issues in Home Confinement

Because home confinement means permitting some misdemeanants and felons the opportunity of living in personal dwellings within their communities, this type of programming is not seen by the public as particularly punitive. As a result, several issues have been raised about whether home confinement is a viable punishment option and should be used. These issues include but are not limited to the following: (1) Home confinement may not be much of a punishment; (2) is home confinement constitutional?; (3) public safety versus offender needs for community reintegration; and (4) home confinement may not be much of a crime deterrent.

Home Confinement May Not Be Much of a Punishment.

The public tends to view offenders confined to their homes as more of a luxury than a punishment. It may even lead some persons to contemplate committing crimes, since they might reason that being confined to one's home isn't that bad of a punishment. However, the experiences of home confinement clients who have been confined to their homes for a period of weeks or months suggest that home confinement is very much a punishment.

One reason home confinement is perceived as less than true punishment compared with incarceration in a jail or prison is that the courts do not equate time served at home with time served in prison. In 1990 an Illinois defendant, Ramos, was confined to his parents' home for several weeks under house arrest while awaiting trial for a crime. He was not permitted to leave the premises except to work or receive medical treatment. Later he was convicted of the crime and asked the court to apply the time he spent at home toward the time he would have to serve in prison. The court denied his request, holding that his home confinement did not amount to custody (*People v. Ramos,* 1990). Subsequent court decisions have been consistent with the Ramos ruling. Several federal cases have held that the amount of time offenders spend in house arrest cannot be counted against jail or prison time to be served (*United States v. Cannon,* 2002; *United States v. Hager,* 2002; *United States v. Kremer,* 2002). However, some state courts, such as Indiana, have ruled that the time spent by an offender under house arrest may apply toward the fulfillment of their sentence of probation (*Martin v. State,* 2002).

Also, when offenders leave their residences without permission while under home confinement, they are not charged with escaping from prison; rather, they are guilty of a technical program violation. Brown, a convicted Florida offender, was sentenced to house arrest. At some point, he failed to report to his supervising probation officer. The officer claimed this was the equivalent of an "escape" and sought to have him prosecuted as an escapee. A Florida court disagreed, indicating that unauthorized departures from community residences are not the same as unauthorized departures from halfway houses, mental health facilities and hospitals, and failures to return from furloughs or work release (*Brown v. State,* 2002). Thus, if the courts are unwilling to consider home confinement to be the equivalent of incarceration in a prison or jail, why should the public feel differently?

Is Home Confinement Constitutional?

Some scholars have argued that home confinement is unconstitutional because it involves various warrantless intrusions into one's premises by POs at any time for supervisory purposes. But this argument has no legal merit. State legislatures, the U.S. Congress, and the U.S. Supreme Court determine what is or is not constitutional. Thus far, home confinement has not been declared unconstitutional by the U.S. Supreme Court. Home confinement is simply one of several approved community corrections alternatives specified under every state community corrections act. The intent of the act is to provide alternative community punishments in lieu of incarceration in jails or prisons. A reduction in jail and prison inmate populations is sought, and more than a few offenders, particularly the least serious ones, have often been diverted to some type of community corrections punishment. Offenders diverted to community corrections programs should be those who are determined to be in need of more restrictive monitoring or supervision compared with standard probationers or standard parolees.

Perhaps the most compelling argument that overcomes the constitutionality issue is that any sentence of home confinement is strictly voluntary. Judges give offenders a choice—they can accept home confinement and its accompanying conditions and restrictions, or they can go to jail or prison. Any criminal court judge contemplating using home confinement as a punishment for any particular offender must determine whether that offender agrees in writing with the program conditions. The Fourth Amendment issue of illegal search and seizure has also been raised. Some offenders believe that one's residence is a sacred place and that random curfew checks and travel restrictions are unreasonable. If offenders do not wish to enter home confinement programs with those restrictions, then they can choose jail or prison. It is up to them, not the courts. Since those offenders who accept the program conditions waive certain constitutional rights, then the Fourth Amendment issue becomes irrelevant.

In virtually every jurisdiction, the appellate courts have held that there is no fundamental right to receive probation or any other community-based sentence (*Speth v. State,* 1999). Granting probation of any kind is within the discretion of the trial court, and offenders who are sentenced to probation must declare their objections to any probation condition when they are sentenced. If any defendant finds any probation condition objectionable, then the court has the discretion to withdraw the probationary sentence and impose an incarcerative one. Convicted offenders who receive sentences of probation are considered to have waived any issues and rights regarding any conditions imposed on appeal later. In the Alabama case of *Ford v. State* (1999), for instance, Ford was a convicted offender who was sentenced to a prison term, but who was subsequently ordered by the court to serve a term of probation, with conditions, in lieu of incarceration. However, Ford objected to the stringent probationary terms and declared that he would rather serve his time in jail. An Alabama appellate court held that because Ford did not accept the judge's offer of probation, the judge cannot order probation unless Ford indicates that he is willing to accept it. In this case, Ford was sentenced to prison for the duration of his original sentence.

Public Safety versus Offender Needs for Community Reintegration.   In any community corrections program, corrections staff consider public safety to be a primary consideration. This is why eligibility requirements are strict and why such careful screening of potential home confinement candidates occurs. If offenders are first-timers without prior records, and if their conviction offenses are nonviolent, they are considered for inclusion. But the absence of a prior record is no guarantee that an offender will automatically qualify. Predictions are made, usually on the basis of sound criteria, about one's success chances.

There are obvious problems with placing convicted felons in home confinement programs. They have the freedom to leave their dwellings and roam about their communities freely. Only detection by a PO can result in terminating one's program. Home confinement does not control offender behaviors. Rather, it is a less expensive alternative to incarceration, and only the most eligible offenders are given an opportunity to participate in such programs (Marciniak, 2000). The therapeutic value of home confinement and avoiding the criminal taint of incarceration are believed essential to an offender's rehabilitation and reintegration. Public safety is enhanced through the sound application of strenuous selection criteria. However, no selection criteria are foolproof.

Home Confinement May Not Be Much of a Crime Deterrent.   Does home confinement function as a crime deterrent? No. It isn't supposed to be a crime deterrent. The main function of home confinement is to enable POs to maintain a high degree of supervisory control over an offender's whereabouts. No home confinement program can claim that house arrest deters crime from occurring (Ulmer, 2001). However, there are several controls that deter those on home confinement programs from violating their program requirements, such as drug or alcohol abuse and curfew.

ELECTRONIC MONITORING PROGRAMS

Frequently accompanying home confinement is electronic monitoring (Finn and Muirhead-Steves, 2002). Primarily designed for low-risk, petty offenders, particularly misdemeanants and first-offender felons, electronic monitoring is a growing alternative to incarceration in prison or jail. Several manufacturers, such as GOSSlink, BI Inc., and Controlec, Inc., produce tamper-resistant wrist and ankle bracelets that emit electronic signals which are often connected to telephone devices and are relayed to central computers in police stations or probation departments.

Electronic Monitoring Defined

Electronic monitoring (EM) is the use of telemetry devices to verify that offenders are at specified locations during particular times. Electronic devices such as wristlets or anklets are fastened to offenders and must not be removed by them during the course of their sentence. The sanction for tampering with an offender's telemetry device is strong, consisting of a revocation of privileges and return to prison or jail. In 2002 it was reported in a survey of over 90 percent of all U.S. jurisdictions that over 28,000 clients were under some form of EM supervision (Camp and Camp, 2003). However, independent sources report that in 2002 there were over 1,700 EM programs operating in the United States, with 115,000 EM units being used (Finn and Muirhead-Steves, 2002; Newburn, 2002). The average cost of EM per offender per day nationally in 2002 was about $10, with a cost variation ranging from $5 to $25 depending upon the jurisdiction (Camp and Camp, 2003). This is a fraction of the expense of maintaining inmates under jail or prison supervision.

Early Uses of Electronic Monitoring

The first commercial use of EM devices occurred in 1964 as an alternative to incarcerating mental patients and certain parolees. In subsequent years, EM was extended to include monitoring office work, employee testing for security clearances, and many other applications (Vollum and Hale, 2002). The feasibility of using electronic devices to monitor probationers was investigated by various researchers during the 1960s and 1970s, although New Mexico officially sanctioned its use for criminal offenders in 1983.

New Mexico Second Judicial District Judge Jack Love implemented a pilot project in 1983 to electronically monitor persons convicted of drunk driving and various white collar offenses. The New Mexico Supreme Court examined the program and approved it subject to the voluntary consent and participation

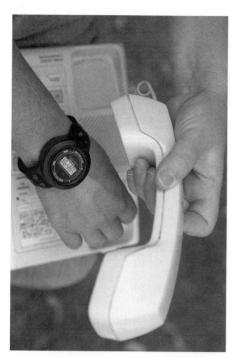

FIGURE 2.2 Electronic wristlet verifies offender location at particular times.
Courtesy of A. Ramey, PhotoEdit.

 **BOX 2.2**

 **PERSONALITY HIGHLIGHT**

Wayne L. Ellis
Program Administrator, Electronic Monitoring Home Detention, Grant County Community Corrections, Marion, Indiana

Statistics:

B.S., *summa cum laude* (sociology, psychology, social work), Indiana Wesleyan University; Instructor, Indiana Department of Correction; Licensed Probation Officer; Law Enforcement Officer (retired); Colonel (retired), USAR

Background:

As a young man, I had a personal ambition to become an FBI agent. Shortly before my senior year in high school, I discovered one of the prerequisites was a bachelor's degree. Due to our socioeconomic level and the Vietnam war, the path I anticipated following changed. Four years after entering the U.S. Army as a private, I returned to the real world a more mature individual. My experience within a structured environment during those critical years laid the foundation for my future. Over the next few years, our family enjoyed success within the insurance industry until one morning when I literally asked myself, "Is this what you want to do the rest of your life?" My response was, "No." I took a significant reduction in pay and followed the desire to make a difference in the lives of people. The next 20 years as a law enforcement officer I enjoyed a variety of responsibilities within our department. I served as a patrolman, uniformed sergeant, juvenile investigator, lieutenant of investigations, Director of the Police Athletic League, and Director of Training. In 1975, while working full time and raising a family, I began my college career. As only the third police officer from a department of 68 to pursue and complete a college degree, opportunities inside and outside of the criminal

(continued)

BOX 2.2 (Continued)

justice arena presented themselves as retirement neared. One such offer was an opportunity to become program administrator for a home detention program that was in its infancy. Ironically, the offer came from the Director of Correctional Services who, a decade earlier, had completed an internship with me when I was a uniformed patrol officer. Accepting the position has been personally gratifying. Working with prosecutors, defense attorneys, the courts and court services to provide a complex structured environment has been professionally rewarding. Using a combination of the latest technology, treatment, and accountability has provided an alternative to jail, serves justice, saves taxpayers money, and has produced tangible results that will significantly affect future generations.

Work Experience:

I've been extremely fortunate to have worked within the three major components of the criminal justice system: law enforcement, courts, and corrections. As a law enforcement officer, I saw the pain and discomfort of a victim, and often that was the impetus for my pursuit of the perpetrator. My focus at that time was to arrest the bad guy or right the wrong. As a probation officer, I better understand and appreciate the tremendous responsibilities placed on prosecutors, defense attorneys, and jurors and judges in the pursuit of justice. As a member of the community corrections staff since 1993, I see first-hand the hardships faced by defendants, spouses, and their children. We observe how someone's actions can cause consequences far beyond that immediate moment. We see them in a correctional setting when they are no longer angry beyond control, under the influence of alcohol or drugs. They often seem just like us.

One of my earliest experiences with the criminal justice system came while in the U.S. Army. After returning from Vietnam in 1970, I was assigned as a basic training company commander at Fort Campbell, Kentucky. A new group of recruits had ar-

rived, and among them were five men from the Black Panther Party in Detroit, Michigan. As a result of their most recent encounter with the law, a judge had provided them with two options: prison or the U.S. Army. There are many parallels between how these young men were sanctioned and how we seek to sanction offenders today with our electronic monitoring home detention program. In both cases, offenders are provided an alternative to incarceration. Many come with baggage or hardships that would still be present if they executed their sentence in a jail setting. However, an alternative gives them the opportunity—perhaps for the last time—to regroup, assess where they are in life, and go forward with a new purpose and perhaps a new attitude, a different set of values and beliefs. All five young men from Detroit responded to the challenge and successfully completed basic training. One became a squad leader and was promoted at the end of training.

This positive rehabilitation is evident within our program as well. Fortunately, we're augmented by a counseling staff that assesses each offender and follows up with court-ordered or voluntary treatment programs. Program guidelines require electronic confinement to the interior of the home except when traveling to and from approved locations. Alcohol and drug testing are routine, and adult visitors are limited to two nonfelons. The transition process is just that, a process. We extract negative influences and then fill the vacuum in their life with positive influences. Often offenders will write us and express their gratitude for our services and share their life-changing experiences. One such person successfully completed a one-year sentence and six months later returned complaining. He commented that we had messed up his life because now he just went to work and then home. We chuckled and congratulated him. Three years later when he was on his death bed at a local hospital, he asked for us because he sensed that we cared for him beyond just drawing a paycheck. Another young mother with three children wrote, "Thanks for treat-

BOX 2.2 (Continued)

ing me as a person, not a number. You helped me realize that people can make mistakes but also can correct those mistakes and make their life different for the future."

It's important to find success and a sense of accomplishment in your work, but you must be willing to accept that occasional positive drug screen, noncompliance or rearrest by an ex-participant. As a sports enthusiast, I'm reminded that a baseball player doesn't quit after striking out. He keeps swinging the bat in order to find success. Our work is demanding, but occasionally something happens that brings you a big smile. We have precious little time to impact their lives, and so we quickly develop a level of respect and sincerity. Participants complete an evaluation of our program and staff once they've finished. Over 98 percent of them encourage us to continue doing exactly what we're doing. They may complain as we work with them, but experience has taught us that it's important to establish parameters, provide opportunities, and hold them accountable. Also, we hope for but do not expect that sudden, instantaneous life-changing experience just because we've crossed paths.

Advice to Students:

Generally speaking, I would encourage each student to examine your heart when selecting a career or profession. Look beyond the immediate need to pay off a student loan and find work that you will enjoy going to each day. Serve, serve, serve and resist the natural urge to aggressively pursue upward mobility. Demonstrate a good work ethic, and opportunities will come to you. You're not a clone, and so occasionally think outside of the box and be creative. Those specifically interested in the criminal justice system should consider an internship or any part-time or full-time position to initially get your foot in the door. Once inside, you'll develop a reputation and know when a vacancy occurs, and then wait for the appropriate timing to go with your heart.

Finally, we don't throw the glass away because the water in it may be dirty. Our challenge is to clean up the glass and fill it with good water. You will impact individual lives and family structures in a greater measure than you realize. To an offender, a minor success may be the first positive step to a new future and a source of pride.

If you believe for every drop of rain a flower grows.

If you believe when life gives you lemons, you make lemonade.

If you believe for every adverse situation, something positive springs forth.

If you believe in the potential power of dynamite even though the fuse may be wet.

If you believe people are inherently good but make poor choices.

We need you! I believe you'll be a great addition to our criminal justice work force.

of offenders as a condition of their probation and as long as their privacy, dignity, and families were protected. Offenders were required to wear anklets or wristlets that emitted electronic signals that could be intercepted by probation officers conducting surveillance operations (Houk, 1984).

Following the New Mexico experiment, other jurisdictions commenced using a variety of EM systems for supervising parolees, probationers, inmates of jails and prisons, and pretrial releasees. Both praised and condemned by criminal justice practitioners, EM seems to be the most promising cost-effective solution to the problems of prison overcrowding and the management of **probation officer caseloads** (Bonta, Capretta-Wallace, and Rooney, 2000). Until the advent of EM devices, the idea of confining convicted offenders to their homes as a punishment was simply unworkable, unless a jurisdiction was willing to pay for the continuous monitoring services of a probation officer. In 1983 an electronic device was used to monitor low-risk offenders in New Mexico. In the next few years, experiments with EM devices were tried in Florida, California, and Kentucky (Schmidt, 1998).

The use of EM is presently global. Successful EM programs have been reported in England, Canada, and the Netherlands (Bonta, Capretta-Wallace, and Rooney, 2000; Richardson, 1999; Spaans and Verwers, 1997; Whitfield, 1997). For instance, a study of EM was conducted in Greater Manchester, Norfolk, and Berkshire, UK. Approximately 375 offenders were placed on EM with curfew orders in 1996 and investigated for nearly two years. These were compared with 2,400 offenders who were given community service orders, and 2,900 offenders who were placed on probation without any type of EM. Recidivism rates were lowest among those who were electronically monitored, with a recidivism rate of only 18 percent (Mortimer and May, 1997). Those most likely to receive EM were convicted of nonviolent offenses, including theft, burglary, and driving without a license.

Similarly successful results have been reported in Canada where numerous offenders have been placed on EM accompanied by various community-based treatments. Offender recidivism was far lower in electronically monitored programs compared with those programs where EM was not used (Bonta, Capretta-Wallace, and Rooney, 2000). In the Canadian study, a control sample of inmates receiving treatment without the EM condition was compared with a matched sample of electronically monitored offenders. Rehabilitative services were more effectively delivered under EM conditions. Subsequently, jurisdictions such as Boston have experimented with EM with substance abuse treatment of female offenders (Johnston, 2001).

Types of Electronic Monitoring Systems

There are four general categories of EM equipment. Two of these categories include devices that use telephones at the monitoring location, while the remaining two categories include radio signal-emitting systems where radio signals are received either by portable or stationary units.

Continuous Signaling Devices. **Continuous signaling devices** use a miniature transmitter strapped to the offender. The transmitter broadcasts an encoded signal that is picked up by a receiver-dialer in the offender's home. The signal is relayed to a central receiver over telephone lines.

Programmed Contact Devices. **Programmed contact devices** are similar to the continuous signal units, except that a central computer calls at random times to verify that offenders are where they are supposed to be. Offenders answer the telephone and their voices are verified by computer.

Cellular Telephone Devices. **Cellular telephone devices** are apparatuses worn by offenders. They emit a radio signal that is received by a local area monitor. Such systems can monitor as many as 25 offenders simultaneously.

Continuous Signaling Transmitters. **Continuous signaling transmitters** are also worn by the offender and emit a continuous electronic signal. Portable receiver units are used by probation officers so they may drive by an offender's home and verify the offender's presence. Drive-by checks by POs are not only useful for detecting an offender's presence at his or her dwelling, but also whether the offender is attending prescribed counseling sessions or meetings, such as Alcoholics Anonymous or at one's workplace (Schmidt, 1998:11).

EM systems may be either passive or active. In passive systems, offenders have to answer a telephone and speak to a PO or insert the transmitter into the home monitoring device to verify one's presence. Some passive systems emit signals so that if offenders move out of range (150 to 500 yards away from the home monitoring device), an alarm sounds and the central monitoring center is alerted. Active systems emit electronic signals on a continuous basis and can be tracked by POs or by global positioning system technology. Victims may be protected from offenders as well, since these devices can be programmed to alert POs if offenders enter a specified range around the victim.

Home monitoring systems have the capability of reporting tampering or the loss of electrical power. They have memory retention capability so all saved messages can be restored after power outages. Sufficient battery backup power is provided for up to 48 hours. Mechanisms are waterproofed to protect against pests and infestation. And internal antennae are installed to prevent offender tampering. Electronic transmitters worn on the wrist or ankle are light and manageable, no larger than a pack of cigarettes. They are shockproof and waterproof, thus allowing offenders to bathe or swim without damaging the system's internal components. They are also tamperproof and cannot be removed except by special devices in the possession of POs. Any tampering is easily detected, since these EM devices are often composed of shiny black plastic. POs are equipped with field monitoring devices and can track an offender's whereabouts anywhere in public (National Law Enforcement and Corrections Technology Center, 1999:3).

Electronic Monitoring with Home Confinement

In many jurisdictions, EM is used together with home confinement (Marion, 2002). One of the greatest benefits of using both of these supervisory methods is that client reintegration and rehabilitation are facilitated. A study of 261 probationers and parolees was conducted over several years, and data were compiled from a Family Environment Scale and the Beck Depression Inventory. These are personality assessment devices to measure a client's responsiveness to community-based treatment programming. The most significant factor contributing to an offender's positive reintegration with his or her community was electronically monitored house arrest which tended to facilitate one's integration and personal improvement (Enos, Holman, and Carroll, 1999).

An Example of Electronic Monitoring in Action.   The U.S. Probation Office for the Southern District of Mississippi experimented with EM beginning in 1994 (Gowen, 1995). The selection criteria for federal offenders included the following: no history of violence, mental illness, and no severe substance abuse history. Subsequently, the federal EM program began to include more serious types of offenders, including substance abusers who tested positive for alcohol or drugs, and irresponsible offenders, who often failed to report, failed to complete community service, or made false statements to their POs. Candidates for EM placement did exhibit good work histories, however, including relatively stable home environments. Increasing numbers of pretrial defendants and post-sentence non-violent offenders were added to the list of program-eligible clientele. For all clients, an approved daily activity schedule was established, which permitted offenders to be "out of range" for certain periods during the day for work purposes or hospital or counseling visits (Gowen, 1995:11). Arrangements were made with the EM manufacturer and supplier for daily facsimile reports of offender departures from, and arrivals to, the residence. This high-precision information made it possible to detect minor violations, such as missing one's curfew.

Interestingly, program personnel found that when offender/clients began wearing electronic wristlets or anklets, an "incredible deterrent effect" was observed (Gowen, 1995:11). The bracelet, which transmitted an electronic signal for reception by a home monitoring unit, served as a constant reminder to offenders to comply with specified program requirements. Face-to-face visits on an irregular basis and at random times further increased offender compliance with program specifications. Some EM clients were also placed in home confinement. The federal EM program exhibited a 92 percent success rate, with only 8 percent of the offenders recidivating.

Arguments For and Against Electronic Monitoring

Arguments favoring the use of EM are: (1) EM assists offenders in avoiding the criminogenic atmosphere of prisons or jails and helps reintegrate them into their communities; (2) EM permits offenders to retain jobs and support families; (3) EM assists probation officers in their monitoring activities and has potential for easing their caseload responsibilities; (4) EM gives judges and other officials considerable flexibility in sentencing offenders; (5) EM has the potential of reducing recidivism rates more than existing probationary alternatives; (6) EM is potentially useful for decreasing jail and prison populations; (7) EM is more cost-effective in relation to incarceration; and (8) EM allows for pretrial release monitoring as well as for special treatment cases such as substance abusers, the mentally retarded, women who are pregnant, and juveniles (Marion, 2002; Newburn, 2002).

Arguments against EM include: (1) Some potential exists for race, ethnic, or socioeconomic bias by requiring offenders to have telephones or to pay for expensive monitoring equipment and/or fees (ironically, some jurisdictions report that many offenders enjoy better living conditions in jail or prison custody compared with their residences outside of prison); (2) public safety may be compromised through the failure of these programs to guarantee that offenders will go straight and not endanger citizens by committing new offenses while free in the community; (3) EM may be too coercive, and it may be unrealistic for officials to expect full offender compliance with such a stringent system; (4) little consistent information exists about the impact of electronic monitoring on recidivism rates compared with other probationary alternatives; (5) persons frequently selected for participation are persons who probably don't need to be monitored anyway; (6) technological problems exist making electronic monitoring somewhat unreliable; (7) EM may result in widening the net by being prescribed for offenders who otherwise would receive less costly standard probation; (8) EM raises right to privacy, civil liberties, and other constitutional issues such as Fourth Amendment search and seizure concerns; (9) much of the public interprets this option as going easy on offenders and perceives electronic monitoring as a nonpunitive alternative; and (10) the costs of electronic monitoring may be more than published estimates (Finn and Muirhead-Steves, 2002).

A Profile of Electronic Monitoring Clients

It is difficult to articulate specific criteria that are applicable to all electronically monitored clients. Some clients are juveniles, while others are awaiting trial. Many are probationers where electronic monitoring has been specified as a condition of their probation. Others are parolees who are placed under an electronic monitoring program for short periods following their early release. Some offenders have been convicted of domestic-violence related crime and may require greater supervision that EM provides (Ames and Dunham, 2002).

However, EM isn't for all offenders. Ordinarily, those considered for electronic monitoring have been charged with or convicted of minor, nonviolent offenses—property offenders (e.g., burglars, larcenists and thieves, automobile thieves, shoplifters, embezzlers). Prospective clients include those who have no prior records. Some offenders might be nonviolent, but they may be chronic offenders with lengthy criminal histories. Thus, if there is a great likelihood that certain prospective clients might reoffend, then they would be barred from participating in an electronic monitoring program (Ulmer, 2001).

Selected Issues in Electronic Monitoring

Invariably, electronic monitoring has generated considerable controversy since its inception in the 1960s. Any attempt to employ electronic means in offender supervision is going to raise one or more issues about the suitability and/or legality of these devices. Electronic monitoring is no exception. Some of the more important issues are described here. The following list is fairly thorough although not comprehensive: (1) the ethics of electronic monitoring; (2) the constitutionality of electronic monitoring and client rights; (3) punishment versus rehabilitation and reintegration; (4) the public safety issue; (5) deterrence; and (6) privatization and net-widening.

The Ethics of Electronic Monitoring.   One criticism of EM is the potential for the ultimate political control of the public. Is EM ethical? One response is to consider the fundamental purpose or intent of EM. Is EM intentionally designed to snoop on private citizens? No. Is EM intentionally designed to invade one's privacy? No. Is EM intentionally designed to assist POs in verifying an offender's whereabouts? Yes. Is EM capable of detecting program violations in lieu of direct PO supervision? Yes.

Perhaps the ethics of EM becomes more relevant or focused if we theoretically project what the limits of electronic monitoring might be in some future context. Some critics might be justified, therefore, in contending that if we use electronic monitoring for a limited purpose today (e.g., to verify an offender's whereabouts), what other uses might be made of electronic monitoring in future years (e.g., intruding into bedrooms to detect criminal sexual acts or other possible criminal behaviors)? Presently, EM equipment is placed in convenient areas, such as kitchens or living rooms. Video-capable EM equipment is also presently limited to verifying one's identity and whether drug or alcohol program violations have occurred. No one has suggested that cameras be placed in one's bedroom or bathroom to be activated at the whim of an equipment operator. If there is an issue to be raised here, then it would be the reasonableness issue.

One extreme extrapolation of the use of EM has been suggested by Toombs (1995). Given present-day technology and the existence of numerous satellite surveillance systems, it may be possible to surgically implant electronic transponders in offenders. Such transponders could be implanted in ways that would make their removal difficult. Furthermore, any attempt to remove an implanted transponder would trigger an alarm and immediately immobilize the offender. A satellite surveillance system could be significantly less costly than present prison operations. Such a system would permit community-based programs to use EM in the design of individualized treatment programs to maximize various types of assistance for offenders so that they can live acceptably in society (Johnston, 2001). However, there are strong ethical objections to such monitoring methods that involve physically intrusive procedures such as surgical implants. Less intrusive methods, such as the use of electronic pulse emission by wristlets and anklets worn by offenders and tracked by Global Positioning Satellites, or transmissions of an offender's whereabouts over either telephone lines or wireless networks, even the Internet, are being devised (Frost, 2002). Preferred EM methods aim toward supervising low-risk offenders who are least likely to reoffend.

The Constitutionality of Electronic Monitoring and Client Rights.   Certain legal issues about EM are presently unresolved, although the constitutionality of EM has never been successfully challenged. Many of the same legal arguments raised regarding the constitutionality of home confinement are also raised about EM. But like home confinement, offenders who are placed in EM programs must agree to abide by all EM program conditions. If any particular offender doesn't want to be placed in an EM program, then the judge can impose incarceration in a jail or prison. The consensual nature of offender participation in such programs undermines virtually all constitutional challenges that might be raised. Perhaps the most compelling constitutional issue relates to whether EM discriminates against particular offenders who do not have permanent dwellings or telephones. However, the range of EM options is such that discrimination is not a factor. Anyone can be outfitted with some type of EM device to suit the circumstance. POs can conduct drive-bys or checks with handheld EM equipment to verify an offender's whereabouts without actually using telephonic equipment.

Punishment versus Rehabilitation and Reintegration.   Another criticism is that home confinement and electronic monitoring are not really punishments at all, because offenders are not assigned to hard time behind jail or prison walls (Batchelder and Pippert, 2002). The average length of time offenders are placed on electronic monitoring is about 80 days. Thus, critics might claim that less than 3 months is insufficient time to accomplish any significant reintegration or rehabilitation. But the overwhelming evidence supports EM as a rehabilitative and reintegrative tool (Gowen, 2000, 2001).

The Public Safety Issue.   Whenever offenders are placed on EM and/or home confinement, they are free to commit new crimes if they wish to do so. They are not incapacitated; therefore, they pose possible risks to public safety. The press plays a significant role in the use of EM as well, since it publishes stories about high-profile offenders who may be placed on EM for various reasons. Therefore, many citizens may feel that EM is not really a punishment at all; rather, it is just a slap on the wrist (Payne and Gainey, 2003). However, the criteria used for selecting offenders as EM clients are very strenuous. For example, the Nevada

County Probation Department uses electronic monitoring with home confinement as a means of providing an alternative incarceration site besides jail. Participants are eligible for electronic monitoring if they meet the following criteria:

1. Participants must be assessed as low-risk offenders.
2. Participants must exhibit good conduct while in jail.
3. Participants must be physically and mentally capable of caring for themselves or be in circumstances where another person can provide their needed care.
4. Participants must have a verifiable local address as well as a telephone and electricity at their home location.
5. Participants must have no less than 10 days and no more than 90 days to serve in jail.
6. Participants must pay an administrative fee of $10 per day while being monitored.
7. Participants cannot have any holds or warrants from other jurisdictions while on the program.
8. Participants must wear an electronic anklet and have a field monitoring device placed in their home.
9. Participants must have the support and cooperation of family members.
10. Participants must seek and maintain employment while on the program.
11. Participants must participate in any specified rehabilitative programs while on the program.
12. Participants must volunteer to participate in the program (Latimer, Curran, and Tepper, 1992).

Although violent felons are generally rejected as potential candidates for community corrections programs such as EM, there are instances where EM has been used to monitor their behaviors. The Georgia Board of Pardons and Paroles used EM on a sample of paroled violent felons, for instance, in 1995. Subsequently, a follow-up assessment of EM was done to determine whether it was an effective deterrent to recidivism. While EM was found to have no direct effect on the likelihood of recommitment to prison or time until failure when relevant demographic and criminal history variables were controlled, it was found that those on EM remained in their communities longer than those not on EM. Specific categories of offenders were also investigated, including sex offenders. Sex offenders on EM were far less likely to return to prison than sex offenders not on EM. While the study results suggested that EM was only incidental to program failure, there was at least some indication that it could be used successfully in future years with additional behavioral controls and supervision (Finn and Muirhead-Steves, 2002).

Deterrence.   Despite the sophistication of our technology, it can be beaten. POs have found that some offenders have installed call forwarding systems so that when the computers dial their telephone numbers automatically, the calls may be forwarded electronically to cell telephones elsewhere. Also, some offenders have devised tape-recorded messages so that electronic voice verifications are deceived about the offender's actual whereabouts. Some offenders may convert their homes into a criminal base of operations, conducting fencing operations, fraud, illegal drug exchanges, and other criminal activity without attracting suspicion from the POs who supervise them. Thus, there is some question as to whether EM deters persons from committing crimes. But we must remember the primary objective of EM. It is not a behavior control mechanism; it is a means of determining an offender's whereabouts at particular times. Thus, although deterrence from criminal activity is desirable, it is not the primary objective of EM.

Privatization and Net-Widening.   EM is susceptible to privatization by outside interests. Companies that manufacture EM equipment and the wristlets and anklets worn by offenders already are involved to a great degree in the implementation and operation of home confinement programs in various jurisdictions. They train probation officers and others in the use of EM equipment, and they offer instruction to police departments and probation agencies on related matters of **offender control.** Thus, it is conceivably a short step to complete involvement by private interests in this growing nonincarcerative alternative.

Another concern is the potential EM has for net widening (Payne and Gainey, 1999). Some officials have said that judges and others may use these options increasingly for larger numbers of offenders who would otherwise be diverted to standard probation involving minimal contact with probation officers. In order for home confinement and EM to be maximally effective at reducing jail and prison overcrowding and not result in the feared net-widening, only jail- or prison-bound offenders should be considered for participation in these programs. EM supervision has interested other countries in recent years, and this supervisory method is growing (Albrecht, 2002).

DAY REPORTING CENTERS

For many furloughees and work/study releasees, community residences or centers are established to facilitate their work or educational placement and assist them in other needs they might have. These are known as **day reporting centers** (Brunet, 2002). Sometimes called invisible jails, day reporting centers are a hybrid of intensive probation supervision, house arrest, and early release. They are facilities where offenders spend their days being supervised and receiving services (Martin, Lurigio, and Olson, 2003:24). Day reporting is a highly structured non-residential program utilizing supervision, sanctions, and services coordinated from a central focus. In 2002 there were approximately 150 day reporting centers in the United States (Camp and Camp, 2003). Unofficial estimates from 90 percent of the reporting state and federal jurisdictions surveyed for 2002 indicate that approximately 15,000 offenders were under some form of day reporting center supervision (Camp and Camp, 2003).

Day reporting centers are conveniently located in the midst of various preparole releasees living within the community (Marion, 2002). Sometimes they are operated in conjunction with other programs, such as intensive probation supervision (Martin, Lurigio, and Olson, 2003). These centers handle the daily activities and provide minimum supervision for participating work and study releasees and furloughees. Many of these offender-clients have special conditions associated with their work/study release or furlough programs, such as restitution to victims, payment of program costs and supervisory fees. Also, clients must be checked to determine if they are involved in drug or alcohol abuse. Day reporting centers assist authorities in providing these services and offender monitoring.

Another function of day reporting centers is to assist clients in job placement and completing job applications. In some instances, these programs provide some educational and vocational opportunities to prepare them for better-paying jobs.

Several guidelines for operating day reporting centers have been established. These include the following:

1. Sign a contract with participants spelling out expectations about home, work, schooling, financial matters, drug tests, counseling, community service, and restitution.
2. Notify the police department in the offender's hometown.
3. Set a curfew; 9:00 P.M. is frequent.
4. Require an advance copy of the participant's daily itinerary points.
5. Perform spot-checks of the participant's home, job, other itinerary points.
6. Institute proper urinalysis procedures—this is crucial; twice a week is typical.
7. Schedule telephone checks more heavily on Thursday, Friday, and Saturday nights.
8. Establish services—addiction education, parenting, and transition skills are popular topics (Schmitz, Wassenberg, and Patterson, 2000).

Day reporting center clients should have the following characteristics:

1. Good candidates for day reporting centers include those convicted of drug offenses, larceny, driving while intoxicated, breaking and entering of commercial buildings, and similar charges; Massachusetts excludes sex offenders and, for the most part, violent offenders.
2. Offenders without an identified victim.
3. Those with a home to go to (check).
4. And, typically, inmates within six months of release.

Three Examples of Day Reporting Centers In Action

Example 1.   Liz Marie Marciniak (2000) has provided a detailed description of a day reporting center established in Southeastern North Carolina as the result of monies supplied through the 1994 North Carolina Structured Sentencing Act. In North Carolina, day reporting center programs are a special condition of probation. That is, judges may sentence offenders to probation with the special condition that they attend day reporting centers and participate in prescribed programming. Marciniak obtained a sample of 1,026 cases where day reporting had been included in probationary sentences as a special condition. The North Carolina Day Reporting Center program was set up as follows:

1. A four-phase program lasting 12 months.
2. Clients must check in between one to six times per week, depending upon the special conditions of their probation programs.
3. Clients must be employed or engaged in a concentrated job search while in the program.
4. Day reporting center staff assess clients for substance abuse problems, educational/vocational, and mental health needs, and appropriate referrals are made to other community agencies or organizations.

5. The day reporting center offers GED classes, literacy training, adult basic skills, parenting, Alcoholics Anonymous, Narcotics Anonymous, drug education, and individual counseling.

6. All clients must develop and submit daily itineraries to their case managers.

7. All clients must submit to random drug tests at the center.

8. The center operates on a three-strikes system, so that once a client accrues three strikes, he or she is terminated from the program (strikes include missed or late appointments, swearing, assaulting a case manager, positive drug screens, and technical or legal violations of one's probation conditions).

9. All clients are under intensive supervised probation.

10. All clients must observe a curfew from 7:00 P.M. to 7:00 A.M.

11. All clients must have contact with their probation officer five times per week.

12. All clients must submit to warrantless searches of their residences.

13. All clients must submit to random drug tests at their residences.

14. All clients must perform community service as specified in their probation orders.

15. All clients must work or attend school.

About half of all offenders supervised by the day reporting program were sentenced to the program by a judge. The other half were sent to the program as a way of intensifying their regular probation programs, usually for committing technical program violations. Marciniak concluded as the result of her study that those who participated in the day reporting program had many rehabilitative advantages compared with other probationers not involved in the program. One interesting result of Marciniak's research about day reporting centers was that the clients did not differ in their recidivism rates compared with other probationers not involved in day reporting. However, she observed that individual clients who did participate in day reporting were able to earn their GED degrees, have substance abuse counseling, literacy courses, and take anger management classes. Thus, recidivism rate comparisons, at least in Marciniak's view, do not give us a full and accurate portrayal of the benefits of day reporting programs for involved clients.

Example 2.   The Northern Utah Day Reporting Center (NUDRC) was opened in Ogden, Utah in 1996 (Williams and Turnage, 2001:2). The NUDRC is operated by the Utah Department of Corrections and contracted with the Valley Mental Health of Salt Lake City to provide treatment services. Two full-time and two part-time therapists were hired to provide treatment. Also, there was a program specialist, two probation/parole agents, and two correctional officers. A psychiatrist and a registered nurse were also available to provide psychotropic medication evaluation and management.

Offenders are referred to the NUDRC by probation or parole agents in the community. Most referrals, however, are parolees. When offenders are accepted into the program, they meet with a therapist for a psychosocial assessment and then are prescribed treatment programming based on the assessment and the conditions of their probation or parole agreements. Treatment possibilities include classes or group meetings for substance abuse, cognitive restructuring, anger management, domestic violence, mental health and parenting skills. Treatment is cognitive-behavioral and transtheoretical, relapse prevention, rational-emotive, and other models on an individualized basis, depending upon offender needs. Successful program completion occurs over an 18-week period, where offenders meet with their therapists and are routinely evaluated. The total offender population at the NUDRC ranges from 100 to 200 clients.

Program characteristics include:

1. Established as recently as two or three years ago by a local agency.
2. Accepts primarily male offenders who are on probation or have violated the conditions of probation, abuse alcohol and other drugs, and pose a low risk to the community.
3. Focuses on providing treatment and needed services to offenders and reducing jail or prison overcrowding.
4. Operates five days per week and has a program duration of about five months.
5. Serves fewer than 100 offenders at any given time, with exceptions.
6. Maintains a strict level of surveillance and requires frequent contact with offenders.
7. Directs successful offenders through distinct phases with increasingly less stringent requirements.
8. Frequent tests of offenders for drug use.
9. Provides numerous services on-site to address each offender's employment, education, and counseling needs.
10. Requires offenders to perform community service.
11. Employs one line-staff member for about every seven offenders.
12. Costs approximately $10 per day per offender.

A sample of 92 participants was obtained, ranging in age from 17 to 54, with an average age of 31. Sixty-eight percent were male offenders, and most were white. About 40 percent were single, and a majority had completed high school. A majority (54 percent) were property offenders and considered low-risk. Almost all offenders had some substance-abuse–related problem when they entered the program. Offenders were classified according to race, gender, marital status, number of children, educational attainment, current offense(s), and psychiatric diagnosis at the time of their acceptance into the program. Of the 92 offenders studied, 62 had no post-discharge problems within at least a year of completing the NUDRC program. There were 20 reincarcerations, although some of these were for brief periods of 24 hours or less. About 78 percent of all persons studied remained out of prisons or jails. This is a recidivism rate of only 22 percent. This is seen as encouraging, since most of these clients are more serious parolees (Williams and Turnage, 2001:3).

Example 3.   The Vigo County (Indiana) Day Reporting Center (VCDRC) was opened for adult offenders in 1996 by the Indiana Department of Corrections (Roy and Grimes, 2002:46). The goals of the VCDRC are to (1) help illiterate clients learn to read and write; (2) assist clients lacking a high school diploma to get a GED; (3) to help unemployed clients get jobs; and (4) to keep misdemeanants out of institutions. Program rules require that all clients must report to the VCDRC five days a week (Monday through Friday) and attend any class and/or treatment outlined by the program manager. Random drug tests are conducted, and alcohol-sensor tests are also used. Two types of training are mandatory for all clients: (1) anger management and (2) cognitive behavior modification.

The following range of services is provided: alcohol/drug counseling; AA/NA meetings; GED training; life skills training; and job skills training. Violations of rules (either technical or drug-testing) are recorded by case managers and reviewed to determine whether offending clients should remain in the program. Intake information is obtained initially about each client's educational level and drug/alcohol related problems. During a study of 164 clients from 1997 to 2001, it was found that about 91 percent were white, 78 percent were male, and age range was from 18 to 68, with a mean age of 29. Nearly 60 percent of all clients were married. Most of those married clients had one or more children. Most clients were employed throughout the duration of the program. About two-thirds (65 percent) of all clients were convicted felons, and most had histories of drug/alcohol abuse. Depending upon the seriousness of their offense, clients remained in the VCDRC from 60 days to 360 days, with an average of about 120 days.

About 69 percent of all clients successfully completed the VCDRC program. This is a 31 percent recidivism rate, which is marginally acceptable. Those who did not complete the program either absconded or had their programs revoked for one or more program violations. It is significant that most program failures occurred among those offenders with longer sentence lengths. This suggests that crime seriousness, which directly influences sentence lengths, must be considered cautiously when selecting potential clients for inclusion in day reporting programs generally. Also, younger offenders had higher failure rates compared with older offenders. One additional feature of the VCDRC program is the required anger management course. Although this course was a required element, not all participants were able to become involved in it. This was due to the fact that it was only offered once during the year, at a particular time, and thus some clients were excluded. Some of these excluded offenders were among those who failed to complete the program successfully. This is a staffing issue, but one which must be addressed in future years as day reporting programs are increasingly used (Roy and Grimes, 2002:49).

SUMMARY

Community corrections refers to any community-based correctional program designed to supervise convicted offenders in lieu of incarceration, including payment of fines, victim compensation and restitution, and community service. Community corrections involves any type of intermediate punishment, ranging somewhere between standard probation and incarceration. Such programs involve halfway houses, day reporting centers, work release, study release, furloughs, home confinement, electronic monitoring, and intensive supervised probation. These community-based programs are located in neighborhoods and provide a rehabilitative and reintegrative milieu for offender-clients. These facilities also function as a continuation of punishment.

Community corrections are established largely through community corrections acts. These acts fund service agencies at the local level and are intended to divert jail- or prison-bound offenders. These community-based corrections programs attempt to facilitate offender reintegration into society, offender rehabilitation, heighten offender accountability, and provide a range of nonincarcerative punishments. Functions of community corrections are to monitor and supervise offender-clients to ensure program compliance (e.g., victim compensation; restitution; community service orders); ensure public safety; offer job placement and employment assistance; provide individual and group counseling; provide educational training and literacy services; network with other agencies to maximize services to offender-clients; and to alleviate jail and prison overcrowding.

Major issues of community corrections concern the controversy of locating community corrections programs within communities, thereby posing a potential risk to citizens. Some persons believe that community corrections is not punishment at all. There is a struggle between meeting offender needs with reintegrative programs and ensuring public safety. Possible net-widening may occur, simply because community programs have been established. Growing privatization of community corrections suggests that large-scale use of incarceration as a punishment may occur as privatization of these programs expands. Many community corrections programs are underequipped and understaffed. Many staff of these agencies have not been trained adequately to deal with diverse populations of offenders. Special needs offenders pose unique problems that are sometimes difficult to resolve. The growth of community corrections as well as the rise of professionalization of staff suggests that these programs are becoming more effective at meeting the needs of growing numbers of offender-clients.

Home confinement is an intermediate punishment consisting of confining offenders to their residences for mandatory incarceration during evening hours, curfews, and/or on weekends. Home confinement as a punishment was first used in St. Louis, Missouri in 1971. It was adopted statewide in Florida in 1983. Offenders on home confinement may be assigned to community service, may be required to pay maintenance fees of the program, and may be required to pay restitution to victims. Other requirements may include participation in vocational/educational courses, observance of curfews, submit to random drug and alcohol checks, and maintain other court-required contacts. The goals of home confinement programs are to reduce jail and prison overcrowding, reduce offender costs, foster rehabilitation and reintegration among offender-clients, ensure public safety, and to continue one's punishment under nonincarcerative conditions.

Often used in conjunction with home confinement is electronic monitoring. Electronic monitoring is the use of telemetry devices to verify that offenders are at specified locations during particular times. Electronic monitoring was first used in New Mexico to monitor the behaviors of those convicted of drunk driving. Various forms of electronic monitoring include continuous signaling devices, programmed contact devices, cellular telephone devices, and continuous signaling transmitters. Most persons on electronic monitoring pose little or no risk to public safety. They are often first offenders and are nonviolent. Many of the same issues that are associated with home confinement also apply to electronic monitoring. These issues pertain to the ethics of electronic monitoring, certain possible constitutional rights violations, the punishment versus rehabilitation or reintegration issue, the concern for public safety, the crime deterrence issue, and the issue of privatization and possible net-widening.

Day reporting centers are also used as mechanisms for supervising low-risk and nonviolent offenders. Support services are made available through such programs, and most research about the successfulness of day reporting clientele has been favorable. Day reporting is regarded as an important rehabilitative and reintegrative tool when clients are properly screened and supervised, and when they receive appropriate therapies and treatments.

QUESTIONS FOR REVIEW

1. What is meant by community-based corrections? What is a community corrections act and what is it intended to accomplish?

2. What are the major goals and functions of community corrections programs?

3. In what sense is there a conflict between ensuring public safety and providing a community environment to promote offender therapy and reintegration?

4. What is the general philosophy of community corrections? What are three major issues concerning community-based corrections? How important are these issues relative to developing community-based correctional programs?

5. What is home confinement? What types of offenders qualify for home confinement programming? What are some general criticisms of home confinement?

6. What is meant by net-widening? How can net-widening occur under electronic monitoring? What is meant by creaming? How does creaming influence community-based program effectiveness?

7. What are some constitutional issues raised about the use of electronic monitoring? How does one's voluntariness to become involved in electronic monitoring programs influence the credibility of these constitutional issues?

8. What are four types of electronic monitoring systems? What do you think is the effectiveness of each relative to offender supervision? In what ways does electronic monitoring prevent or deter crime?

9. What are day reporting centers? What are two examples of day reporting centers? What are some of their key characteristics?

10. What are some general characteristics of day reporting center clients? What types of offenders seem best-suited for day reporting center assignments?

SUGGESTED READINGS

Finn, Mary A. and Suzanne Muirhead-Steves (2002). "The Effectiveness of Electronic Monitoring with Violent Male Parolees." *Justice Quarterly* 18:293–312.

Haapanen, Rudy and Lee Britton (2002). "Drug Testing for Youthful Offenders on Parole: An Experimental Evaluation." *Criminology and Public Policy* 1:217–244.

Karp, David R. and Todd R. Clear (2002). *What is Community Justice? Case Studies of Restorative Justice and Community Supervision.* Thousand Oaks, CA: Sage.

McGrath, Robert J., Georgia Cumming, and John Holt (2002). "Collaboration among Sex Offender Treatment Providers and Probation and Parole Officers: The Beliefs and Behaviors of Treatment Providers." *Sexual Abuse: A Journal of Research and Treatment* 14:49–65.

Payne, Brian K. and Randy R. Gainey (2003). "The Influence of Demographic Factors on the Experience of House Arrest." *Federal Probation* 66:64–74.

Roy, Sudipto (2002). "Adult Offenders in a Day Reporting Center—A Preliminary Study." *Federal Probation* 66:44–50.

Vollum, Scott and Chris Hale (2002). "Electronic Monitoring: A Research Review." *Corrections Compendium* 27:1–4, 23–27.

INTERNET CONNECTIONS

American Community Corrections Institute
http://www.accilifeskills.com/

American Correctional Association:
Past, Present, and Future
http://www.corrections.com/ACA/
pastpresentfuture/history.htm

American Probation and Parole Association
http://www.appa-net.org

BI Incorporated
http://www.bi.com

Center for Community Corrections
http://www.communitycorrectionsworiks
.org/aboutus

Center for Restorative Justice
http://www.ssw.che/.umn.edu/rjp

Citizen Probation
http://www.citizenprobation.com/

Fairfax County Pre-Release Center
http://www.g2.to/fairfax/departments/
prc/prc

Federal Prison Consultants
http://www.federalprisonconsultants.com

Home Confinement Program
http://thwp.uscourts.gov/homeconfinement
.html

International Community Corrections
Association
http://www.iccaweb.org

National Institute on Drug Abuse
http://www.nida.nih.gov

New York Corrections History Society
http://www.correctionshistory.org

New York State Probation Officer's
Association
http://www.nyspoa.com/

Probation agency links
http://www.cppca.org/link

Probation and parole sites
http://www.angelfire.com/md/ribit/states

CHAPTER 3 | *Sentencing and the Presentence Investigation Report: Background, Preparation, and Functions*

Chapter Outline

Chapter Objectives
Introduction
The Sentencing Process: Types of Sentencing Systems and Sentencing Issues
The Role of Probation Officers in Sentencing
Presentence Investigation (PSI) Reports: Interstate Variations

The Sentencing Hearing
Aggravating and Mitigating Circumstances
A Presentence Investigation Report from Wisconsin
Changing Responsibilities of Probation Officers Resulting from Sentencing Reforms and Trends

Summary
Questions for Review
Suggested Readings
Internet Connections
Appendix: Sample Federal Presentence Investigation Report

Chapter Objectives

As the result of reading this chapter, the following objectives will be realized:

1. Describing various types of sentencing systems and their functions.
2. Examining the roles of parole boards and good-credit accumulation relative to different types of sentencing.
3. Examining several sentencing issues, including jail overcrowding, the ineffectiveness of rehabilitation, and predicting dangerousness of prospective probationers.
4. Describing the roles of probation officers in the sentencing process.
5. Describing presentence investigation reports and other relevant documents used by judges in imposing sentences and evaluating offender risk.
6. Examining the functions of presentence investigation reports and their contents, including victim impact statements.
7. Explaining and describing the purposes of sentencing hearings.
8. Describing aggravating and mitigating circumstances as sentencing considerations.
9. Illustrating several types of presentence investigation reports from various states and the federal government.

• *Buford and Smith were Kentucky defendants who were placed under house arrest as a pretrial condition following their arraignment for separate crimes. Subsequently, they were convicted and sentenced to various terms of years. Both appealed, arguing that they should have received credit against their sentences for the time they spent under house arrest. An appellate court disagreed and ruled that they were not entitled to credit against their individual sentences for time spent under house arrest while awaiting trial [Buford v. Commonwealth, 2001; Smith v. Commonwealth, 2001].*

• *Torrance was a Texas offender who was sentenced to a term of years for a crime. A presentence investigation report was filed in his case and relied upon by the judge in imposing his sentence. At no time did Torrance actually read his presentence investigation report. However, following his sentence he appealed, contending that the sentence should be set aside because he was not permitted to read his presentence investigation report for accuracy, nor was he permitted to comment on it. The appellate court denied his appeal, noting that either the defendant or his attorney were entitled to read the presentence investigation report. In the present case, Torrance's attorney had read the report prior to sentencing and raised no objections to it. Thus, the requirements of the law were fulfilled. Because Torrance's attorney had read the report, Torrance was not entitled to look at or review it for accuracy [Torrance v. State, 2001].*

• *Taylor was a federal defendant convicted of conspiracy to distribute cocaine. He was sentenced to a term of confinement. Later Taylor appealed his sentencing, contending that the judge had improperly relied upon incorrect drug amounts listed in the presentence investigation report, which Taylor later read. Taylor disputed the drug amount that had been stated by the federal probation officer who had completed the presentence investigation report. However, the probation officer was not present at the time of sentencing to testify as to the source of the information relied upon to determine the quantity of drugs stated in the report. Since the quantity of drugs is a critical issue and one that would have significant bearing on the harshness of Taylor's sentence, an appellate court set aside Taylor's sentence. The appellate court noted that the government had failed to carry its burden of proof in demonstrating that the drug amounts relied upon in the presentence investigation report came from information that was independent from the information provided by Taylor [United States v. Taylor, 2001].*

- *Melendez was a federal offender sentenced to a period of years under a plea agreement and the filing of a presentence investigation report prior to sentencing. Because Melendez had committed the crime with others, the presentence investigation report included statements about the conduct and circumstances associated with others who had committed the crime with Melendez. Included in those statements was factual information that another defendant had used a weapon. Melendez objected to the inclusion of such statements in his own presentence investigation report, since he thought such a statement might prejudice the judge against him and draw a harsher sentence. Nevertheless, the judge permitted the statements to remain in his report and Melendez was sentenced according to the U.S. sentencing guidelines according to his offense characteristics. On appeal, the appellate court upheld Melendez's sentence and rejected his appeal, noting that Melendez had not contested the factual accuracy of the statements. Furthermore the sentencing judge indicated his clear understanding that the statements about the other defendants in no way pertained to Melendez and that his sentence was unaffected accordingly. Melendez's sentence was upheld [*United States v. Melendez, *2002*].*

- *Music was convicted in a U.S. district court of possession of child pornography. As a first offender, he was placed on probation with the conditions that he regularly submit to a polygraph (lie detector) test, as well as a penile plethysmograph test. The latter test involves a device attached to the penis to determine one's response to sexually oriented material and whether one's sexual urges can be controlled. Music objected to these conditions as invalid and unreliable and sought relief from a higher court. He argued that neither polygraph or plethysmograph test results are admissible in court against defendants; therefore, they are not sufficiently reliable as conditions of one's supervised release. The Fourth Circuit Court of Appeals disagreed. Although these tests are inadmissible for purposes of criminal convictions, their use as supervised release program conditions is valid to the extent that they provide probation officers with potential program revocation information. The test of reliability of these procedures is not as high as evidentiary standards in criminal court, and therefore they do have some program value. If one or both of these tests lead to a future recommendation to terminate Music's supervised release program at a later date, he would have the opportunity to challenge their validity for that purpose at that time [*United States v. Music, *2002*].*

- *Glavic was an Ohio offender convicted of a crime. In a plea bargain agreement between the prosecutor, Glavic, and his counsel, a two-year term of imprisonment for the crime was agreed upon, and the trial court moved directly to the sentencing phase upon receiving the plea bargain agreement and the contemplated punishment. During the questioning by the judge prior to sentencing, Glavic's attorney stated that upon conferring with his client, they would waive the presentence investigation report and proceed accordingly. Glavic was sentenced to two years. Later, Glavic appealed, alleging that he was entitled to a presentence investigation report prior to being sentenced. He contended that his counsel was ineffective because he had failed to make a request of the court for a presentence investigation report. The appellate court examined the record and found no evidence that the defendant had made a demand for a presentence investigation report prior to sentencing. Glavic's two-year sentence without the presentence investigation report was upheld [*State v. Glavic, *2001*].*

- *Buchanan was a Texas offender who was sentenced to a period of years under community supervision following his conviction for a crime. Buchanan requested a presentence investigation from the court but the court refused to order one prepared. Buchanan appealed, alleging that his community supervision sentence was unreasonable and illegal since he had requested a presentence investigation report and was denied one by the judge. In Texas, unless requested by the defendant, judges are not required to direct a probation officer to prepare a presentence investigation report for an offender if (1) the punishment is to be assessed by a jury; (2) the defendant is convicted of or enters a plea of guilty or nolo contendere to capital murder; (3) the only available punishment is imprisonment; or (4) the judge is informed that a plea agreement exists, under which the offender agrees to a punishment of imprisonment, and the judge intends to follow the agreement. In this case, the judge erred when he failed to order a presentence investigation report upon request from Buchanan. However, the same judge presided at Buchanan's trial, was very familiar with Buchanan, the circumstances surrounding the crime's commission, and the terms of Buchanan's community supervision; and Buchanan could point to no information that was unavailable to the court that would have been included in the presentence investigation report had one been prepared. The appellate court ruled this error on the part of the trial judge as harmless error and upheld Buchanan's community supervision sentence [Buchanan v. State, 2001].*

INTRODUCTION

Decisions by judges about the types of sentences to be imposed are not always clear-cut. Every trial is different from the next and sentencing offenders is not as easy as it appears. This chapter is about the sentencing process. Sentencing is a major concern of those who advocate justice reforms. The federal government and most states have passed new sentencing legislation in response to criticisms that present sentencing practices are discriminatory according to gender, race or ethnic background, and/or socioeconomic status. Four different types of sentencing schemes will be described, including indeterminate, determinate, presumptive or guidelines-based, and mandatory sentencing. Several important sentencing issues are examined.

In most major felony cases and in some minor misdemeanor cases, judges request probation officers to prepare **presentence investigations** of convicted offenders who are about to be sentenced. These reports are called **presentence investigation reports (PSIs).** These PSIs are described, including their functions, contents, and preparation. Probation officers have many duties and responsibilities. Among these responsibilities is a duty to the court to conduct investigations into the backgrounds of convicted offenders and determine relevant information about them. This information is eventually delivered to judges in a report that becomes useful in determining the most appropriate sentence. Besides the probation officer's observations, factual information is acquired about an offender's family, educational background, and family relations. If there are persons who have been victimized by the offender, sometimes PSIs will contain **victim impact statements** to set forth the nature of injuries or damage sustained. These statements are helpful to judges when considering if there are any circumstances that might warrant harsher penalties. Sometimes PSIs are privately prepared. Additionally, they may contain statements from offenders about their version of events. All of this material will be described and explained.

The next section of the chapter will describe the sentencing hearing. An important part of the sentencing hearing is the opportunity for judges to weigh any aggravating or mitigating circumstances that might heighten or lessen the severity of one's sentence. Both sides speak out on behalf of or against the convicted offender in order to persuade the judge to be lenient or severe in the sentence imposed. Both state and federal jurisdictions have identified specific factors that are considered either aggravating or mitigating. These factors are statutory and must be considered by the sentencing authority. Several of these factors will be listed and described. Whenever PSI reports are prepared for the court, it is the probation officer's responsibility to identify both aggravating and mitigating circumstances for judges and include them in their PSI reports. The chapter concludes with a discussion of the changing responsibilities of probation officers resulting from various sentencing reforms.

THE SENTENCING PROCESS: TYPES OF SENTENCING SYSTEMS AND SENTENCING ISSUES

Functions of Sentencing

The **Sentencing Reform Act of 1984** restated a number of sentencing objectives that have guided sentencing judges in their leniency or harshness toward convicted defendants. Some of these objectives have been made explicit by various states and local jurisdictions in past years, while others have been implicitly incorporated into prevailing sentencing guidelines (Taha, 2001). Some of the more important functions of sentencing are (1) to promote respect for the law, (2) to reflect the seriousness of the offense, (3) to provide just punishment for the offense, (4) to deter the defendant from future criminal conduct, (5) to protect the public from the convicted offender, and (6) to provide the convicted defendant with education and/or vocational training or other rehabilitative relief. The purposes of sentencing include punishment or retribution, deterrence, custodial monitoring or incapacitation, and rehabilitation.

To Promote Respect for the Law.   When offenders are sentenced, judges send a message to the criminal community. If the sentence is too lenient, then the message is that offending will not be punished harshly. Therefore, many offenders may engage in further criminal conduct believing that even if they are subsequently apprehended, they will not be punished severely. Most judges attempt to impose sentences that are fair or equitable. They may use legislated standards of punishment, such as fines and prescribed terms of incarceration. Or they may impose less stringent sentences than the maximums prescribed by law. Their ultimate aim is to promote respect for the law. Their intended message is that if the law is violated, violators will be sanctioned. Ideally, this view promotes respect for the law and functions as a deterrent to would-be criminals.

To Reflect the Seriousness of the Offense.   One objective of sentencing is to match the sentence with the seriousness of the offense. More serious crimes deserve harsher punishments. Violent criminals are usually punished more severely than property offenders, because violent crimes often result in serious bodily injury or death. Property can be replaced while life cannot. Thus, punishments should be proportional to the seriousness of the crime. Some observers believe, however, that regardless of the punishment, no sanction is a definite deterrent to future offending. Nevertheless, most judges tend to impose sentences that reflect a crime's seriousness—the more serious the offense, the harsher the penalty (Kautt, 2002).

To Provide Just Punishment for the Offense.   In recent years, sentencing policies in most jurisdictions in the United States have shifted to the reflect the **justice model,** which is a legitimatization of the power of the state to administer sanctions. The justice model emphasizes punishment as a primary objective of sentencing, an abolition of parole, an abandonment of the rehabilitative ideal, and determinate sentencing (Erez and Laster, 2000).

To Deter Future Criminal Conduct.   Not only is sentencing designed as a punishment to fit the crime, but it is also designed to function as a deterrent to future criminal offending. At least two major actions have been designed to equate offense seriousness with harsher penalties. The most significant legislation has been the establishment of habitual offender or repeat offender laws, whereby those convicted of three or more felonies are sentenced to life imprisonment. California has a "Three Strikes and You're Out!" law where repeat offenders are sentenced to life-without-parole terms. This get-tough action was designed to deter violent recidivists, such as robbers and murderers (Kempker, 2003:2). The thinking is that if repeat violent offenders have not learned their lesson by the time they are convicted of their third violent offense, then they should be locked up permanently.

To Protect the Public from Convicted Offenders.   Incarcerating convicted offenders is the most direct way of protecting the public from them. If they are locked up, they cannot perpetrate crimes against citizens. Longer sentences generally mean longer periods where criminals cannot victimize others. Some persons believe that all criminals should be locked up for some period of time, in order to insulate a vulnerable public from their criminal activities (Aguirre and Baker, 2000).

To Provide Education and Vocational Training and/or Other Rehabilitative Relief.   This is the rehabilitative function of sentencing. Rehabilitation has always been a fundamental goal of sentencing. A prevailing belief is that some attempt should be made to reform criminals while they are incarcerated. We should not merely warehouse offenders. Rather, educational and vocational programs should be offered in order to help those who are interested in helping themselves. It is better to provide some services for those who will use these services productively rather than to withhold all rehabilitative services because of those who will never be rehabilitated (Glaeser and Sacerdote, 2000).

Types of Sentencing

During the last several decades, sentencing practices in most states have undergone transformation. Experts disagree about the number and types of sentencing systems currently used by the states (Stinchcomb and Hippensteel, 2001). Furthermore, new sentencing schemes continue to be proposed in contrast to existing ones. The following types of sentencing schemes are used in most jurisdictions: (1) indeterminate sentencing, (2) determinate sentencing, (3) presumptive sentencing, and (4) mandatory sentencing.

Indeterminate Sentencing.   The most frequently used sentencing for many years was **indeterminate sentencing.** Indeterminate sentencing occurs where the court sets either explicit (according to statute) or implicit upper and lower limits on the amount of time to be served by the offender, and where the actual release date from prison is determined by a parole board (Lynett and Rogers, 2000). The judge may sentence an offender to "one to ten years," or "not more than five years," and a parole board determines when the offender may be released within the limits of those time intervals. In the "one to ten year" scenario, an inmate may be released early by a parole board after serving at least one year of the sentence. The parole board may release the inmate after two or three years. Early release is often based upon an inmate's institutional behavior. Good behavior is rewarded by early release, while bad conduct may result in an inmate having to serve the entire 10-year sentence. At the end of the 10-year sentence, however, the jurisdiction must release the inmate since all of the sentence will have been served (Connelly and Williams, 2000).

Determinate Sentencing.   **Determinate sentencing** is a fixed term of incarceration that must be served in full, less any good time earned while in prison. **Good time** is the reduction in the amount of time incarcerated amounting to a certain number of days per month for each month served. If inmates obey the rules and stay out of trouble, they accumulate good time credit which accelerates their release from incarceration. In states using determinate sentencing, parole boards have no discretion in determining an inmate's early release (Mears and Field, 2000). In 2002 there were 17 states that used determinate sentencing. A total of 24 states used both indeterminate and determinate sentencing in 2002 (Camp and Camp, 2003).

Three types of good time credit can be accumulated by inmates to influence their early release chances (Payne and Gainey, 2000). These are (1) **statutory good time,** where inmates acquire good time by serving time without problems or incidents; (2) **earned good time,** where inmates acquire good time by good behavior, participation in education, self-improvement programs, or work programs; and (3) **meritorious good time,** where good-time credit is earned by exceptional acts or service. Inmates may earn all three types of good time during their imprisonment. For example, Nebraska authorizes statutory good time of 7.5 days per month, up to 1/2 maximum term reduction; earned days: 7.5 days per month served; total of 15 days per month per 30 days served. In North Dakota, 5 days of statutory good time are allowed per month; up to 2 additional days per month may be granted for extraordinary acts by inmates; 5 days per month of earned good time (given for performance at work, school, treatment programs); all must comply to earn good time; all inmates are given the highest possible amount of good time to be earned upon entrance; if they become noncompliant with programming, they receive an "incident report" (write-up), and the Adjustment Committee sanctions loss of good time.

Several variations on good-time accumulation are as follows. New Hampshire adds 150 days to one's minimum sentence; these days are reduced by earning 12-1/2 days per month for exemplary conduct; failure to earn this good time means the inmate must serve additional time beyond the minimum sentence. In Ohio, one day of statutory good time per month up to a total sentence reduction of 3 percent may be accumulated, while one day per month of earned good time can be accumulated (Proctor and Pease, 2000). The Federal Bureau of Prisons permits up to 54 days per year of statutory good time. Actually, 54 days a year is approximately 15 percent of one's sentence. This fits the federal sentencing model where offenders are expected to serve at least 85 percent of their sentences before becoming eligible for parole. The federal government has encouraged individual states to adopt **truth-in-sentencing provisions** whereby incarcerated offenders must serve most of their original sentences before being considered eligible for parole. Various states have adopted these truth-in-sentencing provisions in their sentencing schemes in exchange for federal grant monies for correctional improvements (Wang et al., 2000).

Presumptive Sentencing.   **Presumptive sentencing** or **guidelines-based sentencing** is a specific sentence, usually expressed as a range of months, for each and every offense or offense class (Feather and Souter, 2002). The sentence must be imposed in all unexceptional cases, but when there are mitigating or aggravating circumstances, judges are permitted some latitude in shortening or lengthening sentences within specific boundaries. An example of the sentencing grids used by states with guidelines-based or presumptive sentencing schemes is the **Minnesota sentencing grid** shown in Figure 3.1.

Presumptive sentencing has the following aims: (1) to establish penalties commensurate with harm caused by the criminal activity; (2) to produce a fairer system of justice; (3) to reduce the typical severity of penalties; (4) to incarcerate only the most serious offenders; (5) to reduce discretionary power of judges

Presumptive Sentence Lengths in Months

Italicized numbers within the grid denote the range within which a judge may sentence without the sentence being deemed a departure.

Offenders with nonimprisonment felony sentences are subject to jail time according to law.

Criminal History Score

Severity Levels of Conviction Offense		0	1	2	3	4	5	6 or more
Sale of a Simulated Controlled Substance	I	12*	12*	12*	13	15	17	19 *18–20*
Theft-Related Crimes ($2500 or less) *Check Forgery ($200–$2500)*	II	12*	12*	13	15	17	19	21 *20–22*
Theft Crimes ($2500 or less)	III	12*	13	15	17	19 *18–20*	22 *21–23*	25 *24–26*
Nonresidential Burglary Theft Crimes (over $2500)	IV	12*	15	18	21	25 *24–26*	32 *30–34*	41 *37–45*
Residential Burglary Simple Robbery	V	18	23	27	30 *29–31*	38 *36–40*	46 *43–49*	54 *50–58*
Criminal Sexual Conduct 2nd Degree (a) & (b)	VI	21	26	30	34 *33–35*	44 *42–46*	54 *50–58*	65 *60–70*
Aggravated Robbery	VII	48 *44–52*	58 *54–62*	68 *64–72*	78 *74–82*	88 *84–92*	98 *94–102*	108 *104–112*
Criminal Sexual Conduct, 1st Degree *Assault, 1st Degree*	VIII	86 *81–91*	98 *93–103*	110 *105–115*	122 *117–127*	134 *129–139*	146 *141–151*	158 *153–163*
Murder, 3rd Degree *Murder, 2nd Degree (felony murder)*	IX	150 *144–156*	165 *159–171*	180 *174–186*	195 *189–201*	210 *204–216*	225 *219–231*	240 *234–246*
Murder, 2nd Degree (with intent)	X	306 *299–313*	326 *319–333*	346 *339–353*	366 *359–373*	386 *379–393*	406 *399–413*	426 *419–433*

First-degree murder is excluded from the guidelines by law and continues to have a mandatory life sentence. At the discretion of the judge, up to a year in jail and/or other nonjail sanctions can be imposed as conditions of probation.

FIGURE 3.1   Minnesota Sentencing Guidelines Grid.

and parole authorities; (6) to allow special sentences for offenders where the circumstances are clearly exceptional; (7) to eliminate early release procedures for inmates, and (8) to make participation in treatment or rehabilitative programs completely voluntary by inmates with no effect on their terms of incarceration (Koons-Witt, 2002; Steffensmeier et al., 2001).

By 2002, 95 percent of the states had reformed their sentencing laws so that an offender's parole eligibility was either eliminated or made more difficult (U.S. Sentencing Commission, 2003). Accompanying these reforms were changes relating to modifying the amount of good time inmates can earn and how good time should be calculated. Therefore, while the certainty of incarceration has increased under determinate sentencing, the sentences served are often shorter compared with what they might have been under indeterminate sentencing. Presumptive sentencing has become increasingly popular in other countries such as England (Roberts, 2002).

Mandatory Sentencing.   **Mandatory sentencing** is the imposition of an incarcerative sentence of a specified length, for certain crimes or certain categories of offenders, and where no option of probation, suspended sentence, or immediate parole eligibility exists (Tonry, 1999). California, Hawaii, Illinois, Kentucky, and Michigan are a few of the many states that have enacted mandatory sentencing provisions for certain offenses. As has been previously stated, Michigan imposes a two-year additional sentence of **flat time** (where offenders must serve the full two years without relief from parole) if they use a dangerous weapon during the commission of a felony (Roberts, Nuffield, and Hann, 2000). In Kentucky, those convicted of being habitual offenders are sentenced to life without parole in prison for violating Kentucky's Habitual Offender Statute. Florida has a similar provision (Kovandzic, 2001). Usually, mandatory sentences including life imprisonment are prescribed for those who use dangerous weapons during the commission of a crime, habitual offenders with three or more prior felony convictions, and major drug dealers. These laws are also known as "three-strikes-and-you're-out" laws in some jurisdictions, meaning that if the offender is convicted of a third felony, a mandatory term of life imprisonment may be charged (Auerbahn, 2002). But some critics question whether any significant deterrent value obtains from such mandatory sentencing laws, since attorneys and judges find numerous ways to circumvent them to suit their own purposes (Boswell et al., 2002). One factor working against strict application of these mandatory sentence statutes is the fact that their enforcement would exacerbate already overcrowded prisons and jails (Florida Department of Corrections, 1999).

Sentencing Issues

This section examines briefly some of the major sentencing issues that continue to plague most jurisdictions. Issues are usually questions that need to be addressed and are not, as yet, resolved. Issues also involve factors that must be considered when sentencing offenders. While a discussion of all sentencing issues that might be included here is beyond the scope of this book, several important issues have been selected here. These are (1) whether convicted offenders should be placed on probation or incarcerated, (2) the fact of jail and prison overcrowding, (3) the ineffectiveness of rehabilitation, and (4) offender needs and public safety.

Probation or Incarceration?   Should offenders be placed on probation or in jail or prison? This is often a difficult judicial decision. Probation officers might recommend probation to judges when filing a PSI report for some convicted offender, although the court may disregard this recommendation. The just-deserts philosophy is a dominant theme in U.S. corrections today, and judges appear to be influenced by this philosophy as reflected in the sentences they impose. Generally, their interest is in matching sentences to the seriousness of the offense.

Jail and Prison Overcrowding.   Jail and prison overcrowding conditions influence judicial discretion in sentencing offenders. Judges have many sentencing options, including incarceration or a non-jail/prison penalty such as fines, probation, community service, restitution to victims, halfway houses, treatment, or some combination of these. It is precisely because of this broad range of discretionary options associated with the judicial role as well as the independence of other actors in the criminal justice system that has led to jail and prison overcrowding becoming the most pressing problem facing the criminal justice system today.

　　As we have seen, there have been drastic changes in the sentencing policies of most states and the federal government (Harris, Petersen, and Rapoza, 2001). As increasing numbers of jurisdictions adopt tougher sentencing policies and implement sentencing schemes that will keep offenders behind bars for longer periods, present jail and prison overcrowding conditions are exacerbated by these policies. In many instances, judges have no choice but to impose incarceration for specified durations on convicted offenders. Often, they have little latitude to depart from whatever sentences are required under the law. When the **U.S. sentencing guidelines** were implemented in 1987, for instance, the discretion of federal court judges to impose probation as an alternative to incarceration was drastically curtailed (Conaboy, 1997). The pre-guidelines use of probation applied to over 60 percent of all convicted federal offenders. In the post-guidelines aftermath, less than 15 percent of all convicted federal offenders are granted probation at the discretion of federal judges. This automatically means greater use of existing federal prison space by larger numbers of convicted offenders sentenced to incarcerative terms.

The Ineffectiveness of Rehabilitation.   The failure of incarceration or various nonincarcerative alternatives to rehabilitate large numbers of offenders for long periods may not necessarily be the fault of those particular programs but rather the nature of clients served by those programs. It is generally acknowledged that jail and prison do not rehabilitate (Bickle et al., 2002). While most prisons and some jails have one or more programs designed to assist inmates to develop new vocational skills and to counsel them, the effectiveness of these programs is questionable. Understaffing is a chronic problem often attributable to the lack of funding for such programs. Also, the equipment used in prison technical education programs is often outdated. If inmates earn an educational certificate, it often bears the name of the prison facility where the degree or accomplishment was acknowledged. Thus, employers are deterred from hiring such persons with prison records. Further, many of these institutions are principally concerned with the custody and control of their inmate populations, and rehabilitation is a remote consideration for them (McMahon and Pence, 2003).

　　One important reason that rehabilitation is less effective in prison and jail settings is that they are chronically overcrowded. In some instances, the overcrowding level in certain prisons approaches the cruel and unusual punishment level, where court intervention is required. Thus, there may be an extensive array of vocational and educational programs within different prison settings, but overcrowding means that not all inmates can take advantage of these services. Further, the effectiveness of services delivery is adversely impacted because too many inmates in classes interfere with learning potential and teacher performance (New Zealand Department of Corrections, 2001).

Offender Needs and Public Safety.   As the courts move voluntarily or involuntarily toward the greater use of **felony probation,** judicial concern is increasingly focused upon determining which offenders should be incarcerated and which ones should not be imprisoned. Therefore, in recent years several investigators have attempted to devise prediction schemes which would permit judges and other officials to predict a convicted defendant's **dangerousness.** Obviously, this concern is directed toward the preservation of public safety and minimizing public risks possibly arising from placing violent and dangerous offenders on probation rather than imprisoning them (Barbee, Eosemberg, and Gunter, 2002).

 **BOX 3.1**

 **PERSONALITY HIGHLIGHT**

Carla E. Bass
Judicial District Manager, North Carolina Department of Correction, Division of Community Corrections, Kinston, North Carolina

Statistics:
B.S.W. (social work), East Carolina University

Background:

Currently, I am Judicial District Manager with Community Corrections in Kinston, North Carolina. In July 1979 I began my employment with the North Carolina Department of Correction as a parole officer under the Pre-Release and Aftercare Program. I worked for 10 years as a parole officer covering up to five rural counties in the eastern part of the state. In 1989 I was promoted to a Unit Supervisor supervising a parole unit at a new facility known as the Driving While Impaired (DWI) Treatment Facility in Goldsboro, North Carolina. This was a new concept at the time of combining parole supervision within a treatment program. Inmates were paroled into the DWI facility and participated in a 28-day treatment program. Now as I look back, I realize that I was in on the innovations in North Carolina of collaborating the supervision of offenders with their treatment needs. There were many trials and errors during this time while we combined the philosophies of control and treatment. I gained a lot of knowledge and experience from this time in Goldsboro which has prepared me for working as a manager in the community corrections field. In 1996 I was offered a position as a Chief Probation/Parole Officer III in Kinston, North Carolina. I worked in this position until 1998 when I was promoted to be the Judicial District Manager position in Kinston, North Carolina. As a manager, I am responsible for a Judicial District made up of 35 employees in Greene and Lenoir Counties. These are rural counties located in the eastern part of North Carolina, and they are only about 65 miles from the coast.

BOX 3.1 (Continued)

From a very early age I knew that I wanted to work in a field which was a part of the helping professions. I obtained my bachelor's degree in social work from East Carolina University in Greenville, North Carolina, in 1978. My plans were to work with the elderly in the social work field. However, my last semester at college changed all that. I had to complete an internship, and one of my professors advised me that he had placed me with a Probation/ Parole Office as I had requested to stay in my home area if possible. This internship was instrumental in my decision to change the direction of my career. I was placed to work under the supervision of a female officer who was one of the first women officers hired in the eastern part of North Carolina. She also had about 20 years' experience in working in the helping professions. The home contacts I made with her on offenders and working on the investigations made me realize that corrections was the field I wanted to be a part of. This internship also made me think back on my childhood and an experience my family reminded me of. In the early 1960s in North Carolina, inmates from the Department of Transportation were responsible for clearing the roadside ditches. One summer when the ditches in front of my family's residence were being cleared by the inmates, I would stand in front of our home and watch them work and would try to talk to them. When my family would pass by the State Camp where the inmates were housed, my parents said that I would always ask questions about the camp and the types of people who were there. From an early age, I have had a fascination and interest in the criminal population. I wanted to know what had happened to make these people turn to a life of crime, since they looked just like most of us.

After graduating from college, I tried for about a year to get hired with the Department of Correction as a Probation/Parole Officer. Finally, my persistence paid off, and I was hired as a parole officer. I was ready to get out and change this world, even though I had lived a sheltered and protected life. An-

other obstacle for me was that I was 23 years old and so young when I started in this field. As I look back now, with all my experience gained through the years, I realize how innocent and naive I was. But I had a desire to help people and a determination to do the best job that I could.

Experiences:

One of the very first offenders that I paroled had been involved in a bank robbery in the community with two other offenders. There was only one teller working in the bank at the time, and she was murdered during the robbery. The offender I paroled had basically been the lookout and the person with the getaway car for the other two. After hearing so much about what had occurred during the robbery, I was apprehensive about supervising this man. During the time, I worked very closely with the local police department in the community in sharing information about his activities. Community policing is a vital part of working in community corrections. I eventually had to obtain a parole warrant for this man's arrest for technical violations of parole. The local police department actually served the warrant and arrested him for the violation. During the 1970s and 1980s in North Carolina, most of the arresting on probation/ parole violations was handled by local law enforcement. This offender was actually paroled again and made it successfully off parole the second time.

When I was hired as a parole officer in 1979, no probation/parole officer in North Carolina carried a firearm as a part of their official duties. When interviewed for my first position, I inquired about being firearm-certified and was advised that no officer in North Carolina would be firearm-certified. Times and the world we live in have changed all of that. In 1986 the Intensive Supervision Program began in North Carolina, and the first officers with probation/ parole were firearm-certified. In response to the high crime rate and increase in violence in the mid-1990s, firearm-certified officers

(continued)

BOX 3.1 (Continued)

have increased in North Carolina. Now approximately two-thirds of caseload-carrying officers in North Carolina are firearm-certified.

Working in community corrections is an awesome responsibility and a demanding job. Offenders are under supervision 24 hours a day, seven days a week, and problems arise at all hours of the day and night. This job deals with people with problems and who often have values about life that differ from our own. It is a stressful job dealing with offenders, other agencies, and the court system. Community corrections is a vital part of the criminal justice system, and it deals with public safety first and foremost. When listening to the local news and you hear of a serious crime being committed, you tend to hold your breath and wonder, is that someone on our caseload? Success in this job is not readily seen or measured. However, it is gratifying when months or years later, former offenders that you supervised call you or stop by to see you to let you know that they appreciated everything that you did for them, or they tell you about their successes.

One successful case that comes to mind was an offender married to a friend I grew up with. The offender developed a drug addiction involving cocaine and heroin. He was eventually caught for selling drugs and received an active sentence. He was released on parole supervision with the condition of attending treatment. The mental health counselor and I worked together on setting his appointments and following up on his progress. He continued to use drugs and one afternoon I followed him to the residence of a known drug user. After he went inside the residence, he refused to come out. I had to request a warrant for his arrest. He was arrested and his family called me very upset over arresting him, as he was trying to get clean. He returned to prison on the violation and served the remainder of his sentence. This second time in incarceration helped him get his life together, and he

remained drug-free. Due to his years of drug abuse, he developed medical problems and died at the age of 45, but he was drug-free and leading a law-abiding life. His wife later told me that she thought all of the persistence in enforcing the terms of parole and insisting that he remain in treatment is what helped him beat the drug habit.

My work in community corrections has always been a challenge for me. No two days of work are exactly the same, and each day holds new challenges. I often miss the direct contact with the offenders we supervise and truly believe that I have a calling for working with the criminal population. I have advanced up the ranks and now have the opportunity to mentor and lay the foundation and philosophy for the supervision of offenders in the district. Work as a probation/parole officer is either a career that you enjoy or the field that is not for you. There is no middle ground in this line of work. Having a great mentor in this field is also an advantage for working in this field. My mentor who taught me a lot about probation and working with people was my former supervisor, Chester Wiggins. He truly knew policy and procedure in community corrections and was one of the first to recognize the need to also help the victims of crime. I have about five years until I reach full retirement age in my present job. However, due to my love and interest in community corrections, I will continue to volunteer in some capacity in this field.

Advice to Students:

If you are considering a career in the community corrections field, try to volunteer at an agency or observe the work of the staff. I would also encourage anyone to visit a courtroom and see the criminal justice system and how it works. Talk with professionals in the criminal justice field and learn the advantages and disadvantages of working in this field. Be prepared to work with a population that can be dangerous.

Most states have laws permitting officials to detain criminal defendants on the basis of the defendant's perceived dangerousness. The legal test used is called the dangerous-tendency test, which is the propensity of a person to inflict injury (Black, 1990:394; *Frazier v. Stone,* 1974). Dangerousness is interpreted differently depending upon the particular jurisdiction. In twenty-one states, for example, dangerousness is defined as a history of prior criminal involvement (Champion, 1994). This history may include a prior conviction, probation or parole status at the time of arrest, or a pending charge when the defendant is arrested. In seven states, the type of crime with which the offender is charged defines dangerousness (e.g., a violent crime such as aggravated assault, robbery, homicide). And in twenty-three states, judicial discretion determines dangerousness. However, many offenders, even those convicted of numerous offenses, are nonviolent and not dangerous. These types of offenders are often overincarcerated, even when they would otherwise function normally within their own communities under close supervision as an alternative to confinement in a jail or prison.

THE ROLE OF PROBATION OFFICERS IN SENTENCING

Probation officers are closely connected with the sentencing process, regardless of the type of sentencing scheme used by any particular jurisdiction (Hunt et al., 2001). Different aspects of their roles relative to sentencing are listed and described below.

1. POs prepare presentence investigation reports at the request of judges. Probation officers play a fundamental role in sentencing. At the request of judges, probation officers prepare presentence investigation reports or PSIs for various convicted offenders. While a more comprehensive definition will be provided in the following section, it is sufficient for now to know that PSI reports are more or less extensive compilations of situational and personal details about offenders, their crimes, crime victims, and any other relevant information yielded during the investigative process.

2. POs classify and categorize offenders. Before sentences are imposed or sentence lengths are contemplated, probation officers do some preliminary categorizing of their offender-clients. Different classification schemes are used depending upon the jurisdiction.

3. POs recommend sentences for convicted offenders. Besides preparing PSI reports, POs also make recommendations to judges about the sentences they believe are warranted under the circumstances associated with given offenses. In several states, POs are guided by presumptive sentencing guidelines or guidelines-based sentencing schemes. Using a numerical system, they can weigh various factors and generate a score. Usually associated with this score are various incarcerative lengths, expressed in either years or months. The power of PO sentence recommendations should not be underestimated. Many POs either look for information in their investigations of offenders that confirms or justifies their sentence recommendations or for information that might lead to a modification or rejection of their recommendations. Their own work dispositions determine which investigative mode they tend to follow.

4. Probation officers work closely with courts to determine the best supervisory arrangement for probationer-clients. When offenders are sentenced to

probation, POs may or may not supervise them closely. Usually, the greater the likelihood that an offender will recidivate, the more supervision will be directed toward that offender (D'Anca, 2001).

5. Probation officers are a resource for information about any extralegal factors that might impact either positively or adversely on the sentencing decision. Thus, judges may rely heavily on probation officer reports to decide whether offenders are socially situated so that they can comply with different probation conditions. If judges want to impose restitution in particular cases, will offenders be able to repay the victims for damages inflicted? The PO has a fairly good sense of whether certain offenders will be able to comply with this and other probation conditions. POs also work with atypical offenders, including transgendered and transsexual individuals. Because reintegration into society may be difficult for some of these persons, POs can assist the court in recommending appropriate treatment interventions and other strategies potentially useful in their rehabilitation (Poole, Whittle, and Stephens, 2002).

PRESENTENCE INVESTIGATION (PSI) REPORTS: INTERSTATE VARIATIONS

Whether a conviction is obtained through plea bargaining or a trial, a presentence investigation (PSI) is often conducted on instructions from the court. The result is a presentence investigation report. This investigation is sometimes waived in the case of negotiated guilty pleas, because an agreement has been reached between all parties concerning the case disposition and nature of sentence to be imposed (Walklate, 2002).

When requested by federal district judges, PSIs are usually prepared within a 60-day period from the time judges make their requests. While there is no standard PSI format among states, most PSIs contain similar information. A presentence investigation report is a document prepared, usually by a probation agency or officer, which provides background information on the convicted offender including name, age, present address, occupation (if any), potential for employment, the crime(s) involved, relevant circumstances associated with the crime, family data, evidence of prior record (if any), marital status, and other relevant data. Although it was much more informally prepared contrasted with contemporary PSIs, **John Augustus** has been credited with drafting the first one in 1841 (Administrative Office of U.S. Courts, 1997). It has been estimated that there are over 1.5 million PSI reports prepared by probation officers annually in the United States (Pastore and Maguire, 2003).

PSIs are written summaries of information obtained by the probation officer through interviews with the defendant and an investigation of the defendant's background. An alternative definition is that PSI reports are narrative summaries of an offender's criminal and non-criminal history, used to aid a judge in determining the most appropriate decision as to the offender's sentence for a crime. These documents are often partially structured in that they require probation officers to fill in standard information about defendants. PSIs also contain summaries or accounts in narrative form highlighting certain information about defendants and containing sentencing recommendations from probation officers. In some instances, space is available for the defendant's personal account of the crime and why it was committed (Koons-Witt, 2002).

In most felony convictions in local, state, and federal trial courts, a presentence investigation is conducted. The purpose of this investigation is to assist the judge in determining the most appropriate punishment or sentence for the convicted defendant. This investigation is usually made by a probation officer attached to the court and consists of a check of all relevant background information about a convicted defendant. Similar investigations are conducted for all juvenile offenders as well (Norman and Wadman, 2000).

A presentence report is prepared from the facts revealed from the investigation. This report varies considerably in focus and scope from jurisdiction to jurisdiction, but it should contain at least the following items:

1. A complete description of the situation surrounding the criminal activity
2. The offender's educational background
3. The offender's employment history
4. The offender's social history
5. The residence history of the offender
6. The offender's medical history
7. Information about the environment to which the offender will return
8. Information about any resources available to assist the offender
9. The probation officer's view of the offender's motivations and ambitions
10. A full description of the offender's criminal record
11. A recommendation from the probation officer as to the sentence disposition (Black, 1990:1184).

An informal component of many PSIs is the **narrative** prepared by the probation officer. In many instances, judges are persuaded to deal more leniently or harshly with offenders, depending upon how these narratives have been prepared. Probation officers exercise considerable discretion to influence the favorableness or unfavorableness of these reports for offenders. One important factor is the probation officer's judgment of the degree of public risk posed by the offender if placed on probation. Thus, probation officers must attempt to predict an offender's future behavior. This is one of the most difficult tasks associated with probation work. Assessments of offender risk to the public will be examined later in this chapter. A sample PSI report is illustrated in this chapter appendix.

The PSI report is an informational document prepared by a probation officer which contains the following personal data about convicted offenders, the conviction offense(s), and other relevant data:

1. Name
2. Address
3. Prior record including offenses and dates
4. Date and place of birth
5. Crime(s) or conviction offense and date of offense
6. Offender's version of conviction offense
7. Offender's employment history
8. Offender's known addiction to or dependency on drugs or alcohol or controlled substances of any kind
9. Statutory penalties for the conviction offense

10. Marital status
11. Personal and family data
12. Name of spouse and children, if any
13. Educational history
14. Any special vocational training or specialized work experience
15. Mental and/or emotional stability
16. Military service, if any, and disposition
17. Financial condition including assets and liabilities
18. Probation officer's personal evaluation of offender
19. Sentencing data
20. Alternative plans made by defendant if placed on probation
21. Physical description
22. Prosecution version of conviction offense
23. Victim impact statement prepared by victim, if any
24. Codefendant information, if codefendant is involved
25. Recommendation from probation officer about sentencing
26. Name of prosecutor
27. Name of defense attorney
28. Presiding judge
29. Jurisdiction where offense occurred
30. Case docket number and other identifying numbers (e.g., Social Security, driver's license, etc.)
31. Plea
32. Disposition or sentence
33. Location of probation or custody

The Administrative Office of the United States Courts uses standardized PSIs including five core categories that must be addressed in the body of the report. These are: (1) the offense, including the prosecution version, the defendant's version, statements of witnesses, codefendant information, and a victim impact statement; (2) prior record, including juvenile adjudications and adult offenses; (3) personal and family data, including parents and siblings, marital status, education, health, physical and mental condition, and financial assets and liabilities; (4) evaluation, including the probation officer's assessment, parole guideline data, sentencing data, and any special sentencing provisions; and (5) recommendation, including the rationale for the recommendation and voluntary surrender or whether the offender should be transported to the correctional institution on his own or should be transported by U.S. marshals. Under existing federal sentencing guidelines implemented in November, 1987, PSIs have not been eliminated. Rather, they now include material besides that listed above regarding an offender's **acceptance of responsibility** for the crime. Judges select sentences for offenders from a sentencing table and may lessen or enhance the severity of their sentences, based on probation officer recommendations, offender acknowledgment of wrongdoing or acceptance of responsibility, or other criteria (U.S. Sentencing Commission, 2003).

Judges frequently treat the PSI in a way similar to how they treat plea bargain agreements. They may concur with probation officer sentencing recom-

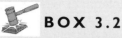 **BOX 3.2**

Sharon B. Lawrence
Senior Probation Officer
Adult Probation Services
Lake County, IL

Statistics:

Bachelor of Social Work, Andrews University; Masters of Social Work, University of Illinois

Work History and Experience:

I have had the privilege of being a probation officer, in various capacities, in Lake County, Illinois, since 1980. After spending eight fascinating years in Juvenile Intake, I transferred to the adult system in 1988. I was reared in Westchester, Illinois, which is a suburb of Chicago. I attended Andrews University in Berrien Springs, Michigan, graduating in 1979 with a BSW. I earned an MSW from the University of Illinois in 1986.

My interest in the field of corrections began early in my college career. I was able to engage in numerous types of volunteer work, including meeting with inmates at the State Prison of Southern Michigan, through an organization called Twin Cities Opportunity. During the last quarter of my senior year, I had the good fortune of doing a full-time field placement with Adult Probation in Berrien County, Michigan. This was by far the most valuable part of my four years of college. I still hold in highest esteem the gentleman who patiently supervised me throughout that term. To this day, I can honestly say that he was the hardest-working, most dedicated probation officer I have ever met. He taught me the importance of reaching out to victims and of writing very thorough presentence investigation reports.

The responsibilities of probation officers have certain basic duties, such as monitoring compliance with court orders; brokering services; and reporting back to the courts. The most effective probation officers are those who view their work as truly their profession, not merely the means to a paycheck.

Advice to Students:

As early as possible in your college career, by all means volunteer with agencies that have some connection with the criminal justice field. It will be beneficial on general principles, and it should help you determine whether or not this is your calling. If there is any doubt, for your sake and for the sake of the profession, please do not hesitate to change your occupational plans. If you have the opportunity to do an internship or field placement, take full advantage of it. Don't just bide your time until you have put in the minimum requirement of hours. Be there as many hours as you can, and learn as much as possible. Please do not, even for a fleeting moment, view it as "free labor." The agency where you are placed is doing you a favor. You are indebted to that agency, and not vice versa. The staff will invest much time and energy in training you before you will make tangible contributions to that organization. With the right attitude, you can make it a most enjoyable and valuable experience.

mendations, or they may ignore the recommendations made in these reports. However, since most convictions occur through plea bargaining, the only connection a judge usually has with the defendant before sentencing is through the PSI report. In federal district courts, judges may decide not to order PSIs if they feel there is sufficient information about the convicted offender to "enable the meaningful exercise of sentencing discretion, and the court explains this finding on the record" (18 U.S.C., Rule 32(c)(1), 2004). If the defendant wishes, the PSI and report may be waived, with court permission.

The Confidentiality of PSI Reports

The general public is usually excluded from seeing the contents of PSI reports. They serve numerous purposes. Their functions and uses will be discussed later in this section. It is imperative that confidentiality be maintained concerning these reports. Often they contain the results of tests or examinations, psychiatric or otherwise. Probation officers contact one's former employers and work associates and include a summary of interview information as a part of the narrative. Ordinarily, only those court officials and others working closely on a particular case have a right to examine the contents of these reports. All types of information are included in these documents. Convicted offenders are entitled to some degree of privacy relative to a PSI report's contents.

The federal government requires the disclosure of the contents of PSIs to convicted offenders, their attorneys, and to attorneys for the government at least ten days prior to actual sentencing (18 U.S.C., Sec. 3552(d), 2004). At state and local levels, this practice varies, and the PSI report may or may not be disclosed to the offender. Under 18 U.S.C., Fed. R. Cr. Proc. 32(c)(3)(B) (2004), some information in the PSI may be withheld from the defendant. The report may contain confidential information such as a psychiatric evaluation or a sentencing recommendation. The presiding judge determines those portions of the PSI report to be disclosed to offenders and their counsels. Anything disclosed to defendants must also be made available to the prosecutors. Some federal courts have interpreted these provisions to mean that convicted offenders should have greatly restricted access to these PSI reports. Indeed, many federal prisoners have filed petitions under the **Freedom of Information Act (FOIA)** in order to read their own PSI reports in some judicial districts. This Act makes it possible for private citizens to examine certain public documents containing information about them, including IRS information or information compiled by any other government agency, criminal or otherwise. This is a drastic way of gaining access to a document that may or may not contain erroneous information about the offender, the circumstances of the offense, and other relevant information. Some persons believe that the post-sentence disclosure of PSI reports to prisoners ought to be converted into a routine function rather than as a right to be enjoyed only after exhausting the provisions of the FOIA.

At least one state, California, permits an examination by the public of any PSI report filed by any state probation office for up to ten days following its filing with the court. Under exceptional circumstances, however, even California courts may bar certain information from public scrutiny if a proper argument can be made for its exclusion. Usually, a good argument would be potential danger to one or more persons who have made statements or declarations in the report. Further, some witnesses or information-givers do so only under the condition that they will remain anonymous. This anonymity guarantee must be protected by the court. But as has been previously indicated, most jurisdictions maintain a high level of confidentiality regarding PSI documents and their contents.

The Preparation of PSI Reports

Most PSI reports are prepared by probation officers at the direction of criminal court judges. There are several different approaches to PSI report preparation. In about half of the states, PSI report preparation is mandatory for all felony offense convictions (Pastore and Maguire, 2003). Other factors may prompt PSI report preparation in some states, such as when incarceration of a year or longer is a possible sentence; when the offender is under 21 or 18 years of age; and when the defendant is a first offender. In several states, statutes provide for mandatory PSI report preparation in any felony case where probation is a possible consideration. When probation is not a consideration, then the PSI report preparation is sometimes optional or discretionary with particular judges. Finally, PSI reports may be wholly discretionary with the presiding judge. Some variations in state policies regarding the preparation of PSI reports include the following:

New Jersey

PSI report = required in all felony cases; suggested in misdemeanor cases involving one or more years incarceration

Connecticut

PSI report = mandatory for any case where incarceration is one or more years

Pennsylvania

PSI report = mandatory for any case where incarceration is one or more years

District of Columbia

PSI report = required unless offenders waive their right to one with court permission

California

PSI report = mandatory for all felony convictions; discretionary for misdemeanor cases

Arizona

PSI report = mandatory for anyone where incarceration is a year or more; may be ordered in other cases

Texas

PSI report = totally discretionary with the judge (Administrative Office of U.S. Courts, 1997).

How Long Does It Take to Prepare a PSI Report?   There is no standard length of time that can be given for PSI report completion. Interstate variations are such that some PSI reports are quite short and can be completed in a few hours, while others are very long and take several days to complete. The fact is that a large proportion of a PO's time is consumed with PSI report preparation (Norman and Wadman, 2000). If we factor in the investigative time it takes for POs to verify an offender's prior employment, compile educational records, conduct interviews with family members, obtain victim and/or witness information, analyze court records, review police reports of the arrest and crime details, and many other types of necessary and relevant information, this activity is only the preliminary step in the process of PSI report preparation. Officers must still sit down and prepare these reports. Most probation agencies do not have adequate secretarial staff where such information can be dictated and subsequently transcribed and converted into a written report. Most often POs must write their own reports. Thus, knowing how to type or use a word processor and computer is an essential PO skill. If interested persons want to become POs, they should know basic typing skills. Without such training, they will be at a considerable disadvantage and unable to perform their jobs properly (Geer et al., 2001).

Functions and Uses of PSI Reports

Although no standard format exists among the states for PSI report preparation, many PSIs are patterned after those used by the Administrative Office of the United States Courts in the Appendix of this chapter. The PSI report was adopted formally by the Administrative Office of the United States Courts in 1943. Since then, the PSI has been revised several times. The 1984 version reflects changes in correctional law that have occurred in recent decades. Prior to 1943, informal reports about offenders were often prepared for judges by court personnel. Probably the earliest informal PSI was prepared in 1841 by John Augustus, the father of probation in the United States (Conrad, 1987).

Although the U.S. Probation Office represents federal interests and not necessarily those of individual states, their PSI report functions have much in common with the general functions of PSI reports among the states. The PSI report for the U.S. District Courts and the U.S. Probation Office serves at least five important functions. These include:

1. To aid the court in determining the appropriate sentence for offenders.
2. To aid probation officers in their supervisory efforts during probation or parole.
3. To assist the Federal Bureau of Prisons and any state prison facility in the classification, institutional programming, and release planning for inmates.
4. To furnish the U.S. Parole Commission and other parole agencies with information about the offender pertinent to a parole decision.
5. To serve as a source of information for research (Administrative Office of U.S. Courts, 1997).

Providing information for offender sentencing is the primary function of a PSI. It continues to be an important function, since judges want to be fair and impose sentences fitting the crime. If there are mitigating or aggravating circumstances that should be considered, these factors appear in the report submitted to the judge. Aiding POs in their supervisory efforts is an important report objective because proper rehabilitative programs can be individualized for different offenders. If vocational training or medical help is needed, the report suggests this. If the offender has a history of mental illness, psychological counseling or medical treatment may be appropriate and recommended. This information is also helpful to ancillary personnel who work in community-based probation programs and supervise offenders with special problems such as drug or alcohol dependencies. PSIs assist prisons and other detention facilities in their efforts to classify inmates appropriately. Inmates with special problems or who are handicapped physically or mentally may be diverted to special prison facilities or housing where their needs can be addressed by professionals. Inmates with diseases or viruses such as AIDS can be isolated from others for health purposes (Strickland, 2002).

The fourth function of federal PSIs is crucial in influencing an inmate's parole chances. In those jurisdictions where parole boards determine an inmate's early release potential, PSIs are often consulted as background data. Decisions about early release are often contingent upon the recommendation of the probation officer contained in the report. Finally, criminologists and others are interested in studying those sentenced to various terms of incarceration or probation. Background characteristics, socioeconomic information, and other relevant data assist researchers in developing explanations for criminal conduct. Also, research efforts of criminologists and those interested in criminal justice may be helpful in affecting the future design of prisons or jails. Special needs areas can be identified and programs devised that will assist offenders with their various problems. Since most inmates will eventually be paroled, research through an examination of PSIs may help corrections professionals devise more effective adaptation and reintegration mechanisms, permitting inmates to make a smoother transition back into their respective communities.

A General Summary of PSI Report Functions Among the States.   One function of the PSI is to provide the sentencing judge with an adequate analysis of the offender's background and prospects for rehabilitation. Ideally, this enables judges to be fairer in the sentencing process. A reasonably complete PSI report assists judge in dispensing more equitable sentences consistent with the justice model. Logically, with more factual and background information about offenses and offenders, judges can make more informed sentencing decisions, and sentencing disparities can be minimized among offenders convicted of similar offenses (Norman and Wadman, 2000).

If offenders are placed on probation, the PSI permits probation officers to determine offender needs more clearly and to be more helpful in assisting offenders in locating jobs or completing applications for vocational/educational training. Thus, a second function of PSIs is to assist probation officers in their officer/client planning. Such planning may involve community service, restitution to crime victims, assignment to community-based corrections agencies, house arrest/electronic monitoring, or some other nonincarcerative alternative.

Probation officers are expected to assess the offender's dangerousness and public risk. This assessment is a vital part of the narrative and the recommendation prepared by these officers. Probation officers have considerable influence in the sentencing disposition of offenders (Norman and Wadman, 2000). Thus, a third function of PSIs is to classify and categorize offenders into various risk categories. These risk assessments frequently determine the level of custody or supervision imposed by judges in sentencing. Offenders considered extremely dangerous to the public are seldom granted probation. Rather, they are committed to medium- and maximum-security prisons or other facilities, and for longer periods of incarceration. Their offenses and prior records are also primary determinants of length and severity of the sentence imposed.

For incarcerated offenders, a PSI report is of value to parole boards in determining one's early release and the conditions accompanying the granting of parole. This fact underscores both the short-term and the long-term relevance and importance of PSI reports for influencing an offender's chances at securing freedom from the criminal justice system. Offenders may be prison inmates for many years. When they appear before parole boards 15, 20, or even 30 years after they have been incarcerated for their crimes, the parole boards refer to their PSI reports that were originally prepared at the time of their sentencing. These "ancient" documents contain important information about the offender's earlier circumstances. Even though much of this material is badly dated, parole boards consider it in their early-release decision making.

A fourth function of PSIs is to permit probation officers or other supervisory authorities greater monitoring capability over offenders sentenced to some form of probation. The report contains background information, personal habits, and names of acquaintances of the offender. Should it become necessary to apprehend probationers for any probation violation or new crime alleged, the PSI also functions as a locating device. A fifth function of PSIs is to provide research material for scholars to conduct investigations of crime patterns, parole board decision making, judicial sentencing trends, and other related phenomena. This function is unrelated to offender sentencing decisions, and it is closely tied to academic interests in the criminal justice process.

Criticisms of PSI Report Preparation.   PSIs have been criticized in recent years because of the subjectivity inherent in their preparation. Probation officers consider both factual background information as well as their personal impressions of offenders (Meredith and Paquette, 2001). Some probation officers rely heavily on statistical data about offenders when making recommendations about possible public risks offenders may pose. Overpredicting antisocial behavior has occurred, where misinterpretations of technical terminology have been made by probation officers. In some jurisdictions, PO supervisors encourage them not to oversimplify the background of offenders when preparing PSI reports. This is especially difficult where officers have heavy caseloads and severe time limitations.

Investigations of probation officer behaviors in PSI preparation have disclosed diverse perspectives ranging from rehabilitative to legalistic. A dilemma exists for many probation officers when preparing PSIs. They must balance quantitative data (e.g., arrest reports, probation records, juvenile adjudications) with qualitative data (e.g., alcohol adjustment, social history, substance abuse). A basic requirement for probation officers is that they possess a reasonable understanding of human nature in their report preparations. Many officers lack sufficient understanding about different types of offenders, and they are inclined to rely on group norms for making decisions about individual offenders (Raynor and Honess, 1998). Thus, it is difficult to avoid subjective decision making that may have adverse consequences for convicted offenders, both at the time of sentencing and later when parole boards consider them for early release.

Not all PSIs contain officer assessments of an offender's risk. Those reports that do contain such assessments are founded on many different criteria that are peculiar to each probation officer. In federal district courts currently as well as in those states (e.g., Minnesota, Florida, Arizona, California, Washington) that have adopted sentencing guidelines, PSIs are declining in their importance and relevance, since sentencing decisions by judges are increasingly perfunctory as sentencing tables are consulted. Their value continues, however, as evidence of mitigating or aggravating circumstances about the offense and offender may decrease or increase the harshness of sentences imposed.

The Defendant's Sentencing Memorandum

The Administrative Office of the United States Courts (Probation Division) has recommended the inclusion of the offender's version of the offense (Administrative Office of U.S. Courts, 1997). These statements are often called the **defendant's sentencing memorandum.** Although not specifically required under the 1987 federal sentencing guidelines, it is important that if such a statement is prepared, it should be prepared with assistance of defense counsel and attached to the PSI report filed by the probation officer. Often, these memorandums contain material judges regard as mitigating, and the sentence imposed may be reduced in severity accordingly. Again, these memorandums are not required by law, although the offender's acceptance of responsibility weighs heavily in affecting the sentence federal judges impose.

Whether a PSI report contains the defendant's version of the offense should be determined on the basis of the best interests of the offender. This is why the assistance of counsel is important. If offenders decide to appeal the conviction later, a written statement prepared by them about their version of the offense could be used by the court to impeach them and cause the appeal to fail.

The Inclusion of Victim Impact Statements

In some jurisdictions, victims of crimes are required to submit their own versions of the offense as a victim impact statement (VIS) (Gillis, 2002b). The victim impact statement is a statement made by the victim and addressed to the judge for consideration in sentencing. It includes a description of the harm inflicted on the victim in terms of financial, social, psychological, and physical consequences of the crime. It also includes a statement concerning the victim's feelings about the crime, the offender, and a proposed sentence (Myers and Arbuthnot, 1999). Although the federal government and states have no statutes currently requiring victims to file such statements with the court prior to sentencing, proponents of victim compensation regard victim impact statements as an increasingly important part of the sentencing process. This is seen as a form of victim participation in sentencing, and a victim impact statement is given similar weight compared with the offender's version of events. Usually, these victim impact statements are not required. They pertain exclusively to the direct effects of the crime and are regarded as aggravating circumstances just as the offender's **sentencing memorandum** serves as a basis for mitigating circumstances. While victim participation in sentencing raises certain ethical, moral, and legal questions, indications are that victim impact statements are used with increasing frequency and appended to PSI reports in various jurisdictions (Meredith and Paquette, 2001).

Victim impact statements usually take two forms. One is as an attachment to a PSI report. The victim or victims create a written account of how the crime and offender influenced them, usually adversely. The second is in the form of a speech or verbal declaration. This is ordinarily a prepared document read by one or more victims at the time offenders are sentenced. The admission of victim impact statements in either written or verbal form at the time of sentencing or in PSI reports is controversial. Some experts feel that these statements are inflammatory and detract from objective sentencing considerations. Obviously prejudicial, victim impact statements may intensify sentencing disparities in certain jurisdictions with sentencing schemes that rely more heavily on subjective judicial impressions compared with those jurisdictions where more objective sentencing criteria are used, such as mandatory sentencing procedures or guidelines-based sentencing schemes (*Booth v. Maryland,* 1987). Proponents of victim impact statements believe that such statements personalize the sentencing process by showing that actual persons were harmed by certain offender conduct. Also, victim's rights advocates contend that victims have a moral right to influence one's punishment (Walklate, 2002). While this controversy continues, it is increasingly the case that victims are exerting greater influence and have growing input in sentencing decisions in most jurisdictions.

Privatizing PSI Report Preparation

The Private Preparation of PSI Reports.   Sometimes PSIs are prepared by private corporations or individuals. Criminological Diagnostic Consultants, Inc., Riverside, California, founded by brothers William and Robert Bosic, is a corporation that prepares privately commissioned PSIs for defense attorneys and others (Kulis, 1983:11). William Bosic is a former prison counselor and probation officer, while his brother, Robert, is a retired police officer. Their claim is, "we don't do anything different from the probation department; we just do it better." While the average cost of a government-prepared PSI averages about $250, privately prepared PSIs cost from $200 to $2,000 or more. The cost depends on the PSI contents, and whether psychiatric evaluations of offenders are made. The amount of investigative detail required in particular cases influences preparation costs as well. Increasing numbers of PSIs are being prepared privately, often by ex-probation officers or others closely related to corrections. The quality of private PSI report preparation varies greatly. Some private agencies prepare quite elaborate and sophisticated reports for clients able to afford them.

Many jurisdictions now accept privately prepared sentencing memorandums to accompany the official PSI. These private sector PSIs are often prepared by former probation officers or criminal justice consultants. Defendant's sentencing memorandums contain similar PSI information, especially the defendant's version of what happened, and any mitigating factors that would lessen sentencing severity. This independently prepared report serves to make the official PSI more objective and to clarify or resolve facts that may be in dispute.

THE SENTENCING HEARING

Under Rule 32 of the Federal **Rules of Criminal Procedure** (18 U.S.C., 2004), the contents of a PSI must be disclosed to defendants and their counsels, although some information is exempt from disclosure. Mental or psychological reports, interviews with family members or a personalized account of the defendant's marital problems, and certain personal observations by the probation officer and court are potentially excludable from PSIs.

In most jurisdictions a **sentencing hearing** is held where defendants and their attorneys can respond to the contents of the PSI report (Atkins, 1996). Also, an increasing number of jurisdictions are permitting crime victims to attend sentencing hearings and provide victim impact statements either orally, in writing, or both. Evidence suggests a general increase in citizen involvement at other stages of the criminal justice process as well (Meredith and Paquette, 2001). Of course, many jurisdictions do not allow victims to participate in the sentencing

BOX 3.3

VICTIM HELPS VICTIMIZER IN PAROLE BID

• *Jon Buice.* It happened on July 4, 1991. Several men were leaving a gay bar in Houston, Texas. Suddenly, they were attacked by 10 high school students who had traveled to Houston that evening in search of gay men to assault. Ray Hill, John Broussard, and a third man were subsequently beaten by Jon Buice and nine other students from Conroe McCullough High School in The Woodlands, a Houston suburb. Hill and Broussard both received beatings. Broussard suffered a broken rib, crushed testicles, and two stab wounds that eventually caused his death. Hill was badly beaten. The third man was able to escape and report the incident to police, who investigated. Buice was arrested and identified by Hill as one of his attackers. Of the ten attackers, five received prison time, with two others going to prison following probation violations. Buice received a 45-year prison term for his role in Broussard's murder.

• Although Hill assisted police in identifying Buice, he did not especially like seeing 17-year-old high schooler Buice receive such a lengthy sentence, even though Hill's friend, Broussard, had been killed. During the years, Hill visited Buice in prison and assisted him in different ways. Hill encouraged Buice to finish his high school education and seek to acquire vocational skills. In 2003 Buice had served 12 years in prison and became parole eligible. Hill has lobbied extensively in his behalf. When Buice appears before the Texas Parole Board, Hill plans to speak in favor of Buice's early release. This is a rare event, when a crime victim speaks in favor of the potential release of someone who victimized him. [Adapted from the Associated Press, "Activist Working to Free Man He Helped to Convict." July 7, 2003.]

process. The nature of victim participation varies among jurisdictions, although often their participation consists of an objective delineation of the personal and psychological effects of the crime and the financial costs incurred.

Sentencing hearings also permit offenders and their attorneys to comment on the PSI report and append to it additional informational material which may mitigate the circumstances of the conviction offense. The role of defense attorneys is important particularly at this stage because they can work with the probation officer who prepared the report as well as the victims, and they can make timely legal attacks on erroneous information presented to the judge. In addition to considering the contents of a PSI, the oral and written reports furnished by victims and the offenders themselves, and attorney arguments both from the prosecution and defense, judges use their best judgment in arriving at the most equitable sentence for offenders. Judges consider mitigating and aggravating circumstances surrounding the offense, the age, psychological and physical condition, and social/educational background of the offender, and the minimum and maximum statutory penalties of incarceration and/or fines accompanying the crime in arriving at a decision. Judges also take into account both **aggravating circumstances** and **mitigating circumstances.**

AGGRAVATING AND MITIGATING CIRCUMSTANCES

Aggravating Circumstances

Aggravating circumstances are those factors that increase the severity of punishment. Some of the factors considered by judges to be aggravating include:

1. Whether the crime involved death or serious bodily injury to one or more victims.
2. Whether the crime was committed while the offender was out on bail facing other criminal charges.
3. Whether the offender was on probation, parole, or work release at the time the crime was committed.
4. Whether the offender was a recidivist and had committed several previous offenses for which he or she had been punished.
5. Whether the offender was the leader in the commission of the offense involving two or more offenders.
6. Whether the offense involved more than one victim and/or was a violent or nonviolent crime.
7. Whether the offender treated the victim(s) with extreme cruelty during the commission of the offense.
8. Whether the offender used a dangerous weapon in the commission of the crime and the risk to human life was high (Coyne and Entzeroth, 2001).

If the convicted defendant has one or more aggravating circumstances accompanying the crime committed, the judge is likely to intensify the punishment prescribed. In simple terms, this means a longer sentence, incarceration in lieu of probation, or a sentence to be served in a maximum security prison rather than a minimum- or medium-security prison facility. Mitigating circumstances may cause the judge to be lenient with the defendant and prescribe probation rather than confinement in a jail or prison. A sentence of a year or less may be imposed rather than a five-year term.

Mitigating Circumstances

Mitigating factors are those circumstances considered by the sentencing judge to lessen the crime's severity (Schwartz and Isser, 2001). Some of the more frequently cited mitigating factors in the commission of crimes might be the following:

1. The offender did not cause serious bodily injury by his or her conduct during the commission of the crime.
2. The convicted defendant did not contemplate that his/her criminal conduct would inflict serious bodily injury on anyone.
3. The offender acted under duress or extreme provocation.
4. The offender's conduct was possibly justified under the circumstances.
5. The offender was suffering from mental incapacitation or physical condition which significantly reduced his/her culpability in the offense.
6. The offender cooperated with authorities in apprehending other participants in the crime or in making restitution to the victims for losses suffered.

7. The offender committed the crime through motivation to provide necessities for himself/herself or his or her family.

8. The offender did not have a previous criminal record (Wilson, 1997).

If a convicted defendant has one or more mitigating circumstances associated with the crime committed, the sentencing judge may lessen the severity of the sentence imposed. In view of the current trend toward greater use of felony probation, first offenders and nonviolent criminals are likely to be considered prime candidates for alternative sentencing that does not involve incarceration. But recidivists, especially those who have committed a number of violent acts and show every likelihood of continuing their criminal behavior, are likely candidates for punishment enhancement (e.g., longer, more severe sentences and/or fines). These circumstances are usually outlined in PSI reports.

A PRESENTENCE INVESTIGATION REPORT FROM THE STATE OF WISCONSIN

Several states, such as North Dakota, provide previously printed forms for PSI report preparation. Probation officers must fill in the blanks on these forms, with explicit information required. However, a growing number of states are using a more free-flowing format for their PSI reports. As long as specific information is included, there is great variation in how such PSI reports are formatted.

The following material presents a rather detailed PSI report from the State of Wisconsin. Wisconsin authorizes general PSI preparations without adhering to a fixed PSI format. Thus, there are some components of Wisconsin PSI reports that may not be applicable for particular offenders. The intent of Wisconsin officials is to individualize these reports to fit offender characteristics, needs, and sentence recommendations. The Wisconsin Department of Corrections states that the purpose of any PSI is a careful study of how the individual's personal characteristics, environmental factors, and behavioral patterns have interacted to produce the present situation. The agent must comply with confidentiality laws when securing and disclosing medical, psychiatric, psychological, and educational information. Courts may order PSI reports following conviction and prior to imposition of sentence for felony cases. Investigation due dates are usually set by the court.

STATE OF WISCONSIN

Department of Corrections

PRESENTENCE INVESTIGATION

Date

August 10, 1996

Name and DOB

John Ming
November 20, 1962

PRESENT OFFENSE

Description of Offense

Attempted Sexual Assault. Offense date is November 3, 1995. This offense involves an incident in which a 29-year-old nude woman's body was discovered on a rural road. The body had been decapitated, and the woman's head and articles of bloody clothing were discovered on another road three miles away. It was discovered that the woman, in an intoxicated condition, had accompanied some men from a tavern who reportedly took the woman to their apartment, forced her to engage in sexual intercourse, then at least one of the men attacked the woman with a kitchen knife, cut her throat, then decapitated her. Four men were eventually charged in the offense, including the defendant, Mu Chou (life sentence), Bok Suk Kim (life sentence), and Raymond Phu (10 years). Mr. Ming admits that he resides at the apartment where the offense occurred, but denies any involvement in or knowledge of the offense until his arrest two weeks later. He was not released on bond. Rationale: "I never see girl, I don't know about it."

Offender's Version

The subject is a 34 year-old Chinese National male, first offender, who is currently confined in the Briggs Unit facing a 10-year sentence in Madison County for one count of Attempted Sexual Assault. The subject states that on or about November 3, 1995 during an unknown time he allegedly committed the offense of Attempted Sexual Assault on a 29-year-old female, but he denies the Attempted Sexual Assault and any knowledge of the woman's murder or decapitation. He admits to occasional marijuana use at age 27; admits to three prior arrests resulting in a two-year probationary term for DWI. He states that he left the apartment for an unknown period of time, and when he returned, his friends and the woman were gone. He admits that there was blood on the floor and in the bedroom where the woman was allegedly raped by the other men.

Victim's Statement

Not applicable

PRIOR RECORD

Juvenile Record

No record of juvenile arrests

Adult Record

Three prior arrests for DWI; sentenced to two years probation; claims completed.

Pending Charges

One detainer warrant from U.S. Immigration "Hold"

Correctional Experience

Good jail report from Madison County Jail from jail authorities

Offender's Explanation of Record

Claims no contact with father, mother, or two siblings; claims single; residence unstable; education claims high school completed; employment claims "laborer"; home stability poor due to lack of contact with family; admits to experimental use of marijuana at age 27; current offense of Attempted Sexual Assaulting a 29-year-old female and allegedly cutting her head off, subject denies; speaks little English.

PERSONAL HISTORY

Academic/Vocational Skills

Subject states he completed 12 years of school in China. Subject worked as "laborer" but did not elaborate on what "laborer" did.

Employment

Worked as "laborer" at various jobs in different states; would not disclose which establishments employed him. No information is forthcoming about subject's past educational level or occupations in his native country of China. He had been in English classes in Indiana for about a year prior to coming to Wisconsin. While in Wisconsin, the subject worked in a few different jobs. He bussed tables in a restaurant, worked in a furniture factory, and did some janitorial work. He then moved to Madison where he worked for the ABC Packing Company as a meat cutter.

Financial Management

Has given no indication of ability to manage financial affairs.

Marital/Alternate Family Relationships

Has not seen family for many years.

Companions

Has no close associates presently. Admits to knowing other men who were convicted of woman's murder only because they were also Oriental and in the tavern when he was there. He admits to being drunk when he left tavern but denies any involvement in woman's murder.

Emotional Health

See attached Psychiatric Evaluation.

Physical Health

Transferred to mental health unit at Briggs for psychiatric and psychological evaluation. Subject was referred because he was mute, refused to eat, and exhibited unusual behavior. Subject appeared detached, withdrawn, in distress, and depressed. His blood pressure was low, he had lost much weight, and he appeared to be dehydrated. He would give no information to medical staff. He would sit in one place on his bunk for seven or eight hours at a time. At that time he stated that he was very nervous and scared. He had been making statements that he needed to stay in prison because he would not have anything on the outside now. He flooded his cell on one occasion and became quite unresponsive. His physical and mental condition deteriorated further. He lost 26 pounds of weight because he was not eating. He was transferred to the medical unit for acute care. When received, the subject was on Haldol C, 15 mgs., TID, and Cogentin, 2 mgs, BID. The subject may have been a suicide risk and was placed on suicide precaution status. The subject began to eat on the second day of his admission. The subject is being treated for a positive TB test with INH. The file reflects no other medical problems at this time.

Mental Ability

The subject is now a 34-year old, frail-looking Chinese male who was dressed in a disheveled Department of Corrections white uniform. He looked undernourished. He was mute and had poor eye contact. He was able to answer one question by head movement at one time. His mood seemed depressed to euthymic. He had an inappropriate smile at some part of his evaluation. There was no indication that subject had delusions or hallucinations, although he reportedly has history of having fairly loose delusions and grandiose delusions in the past. The rest of his mental status examination was not tested because of his uncooperativeness and because he remained mute.

Chemical Usage

Subject admitted to using marijuana and drinking beer. Presently on prescribed medications as indicated.

Sexual Behavior

Convicted of Attempted Sexual Assault, subject denies. Has no close friends or acquaintances.

Military

None

Religion

Born into Buddhist faith; now is nondenominational.

Leisure Activities

None determined.

Residential History
Taipei, Taiwan 1962–1985
Lafayette, Indiana 1985–1986
Madison, Wisconsin 1986–present

SUMMARY AND CONCLUSIONS

Agent's Impressions

Ming is a Line Class I inmate, unassigned due to his mental health status. He needs recreational therapy. He does not attend any educational, vocational, or character development programs due to his mental status. He is not a gang member. Ming is receiving INH for TB prevention. Ming denies any mental health treatment in society and denies suicide attempts. Ming has been diagnosed with Schizoeffective Disorder, Bipolar Type Rule out Bipolar Disorder, Mixed with Psychotic Features, Rule Out Schizophrenia, Chronic, Catatonic Type with Acute Exacerbation. Alcohol use in remission. Addicted to Cannabis, in remission due to incarceration. Interviews with Ming indicate that he is unwilling or unable to relate any new information to this officer about his present offense. Ming maintains he is not guilty and claimed he did not know any details about the present offense until he was arrested. Ming claims he does not know if he was ever physically or sexually assaulted and has never been married and has no children. Ming claims he cannot remember if he engaged in sex with prostitutes. Due to the subject's past probation for DWI, it appears he may need monitoring in the area of alcohol usage. He may also benefit from psychological counseling.

Restitution Information

Not applicable

Recommendation

Recommend that Ming be confined in mental unit at Briggs until such time as his eating behavior is stabilized. Recommend Ming for psychological counseling. Statutory punishment of ten years should be imposed. Ming must accept responsibility for his actions, since this officer interviewed two other persons convicted of the murder and they give consistent accounts of Ming's involvement in the female victim's murder and decapitation. Both subjects accused Ming of committing the decapitation and joking about it later. Other than mental problems contained in psychiatric evaluation, there are no outstanding mitigating circumstances that would cause this officer to recommend sentencing leniency or a shorter incarcerative term at this time.

1. Confinement is necessary to protect the public from further criminal activity.

2. The subject is in need of correctional treatment that can most effectively be provided through confinement.

3. Nonconfinement would unduly depreciate the seriousness of the instant offense.

Probation is not recommended.

John J. Beecher, Probation Officer, Madison County

PSYCHIATRIC EVALUATION
WISCONSIN DEPARTMENT OF CORRECTIONS

Name: John Ming

Wdoj#:   47324568

Date: July 15, 1996

Examiner: Dominique Daws, M.D.

SOURCE OF INFORMATION:

Patient and WDOC Records.

PERTINENT MEDICAL HISTORY:

The patient's chart indicates that he has tuberculosis Class II and he is currently taking medication for this. He has no allergies to medications.

PERTINENT PSYCHIATRIC AND LEGAL HISTORY:

Reports in patient's brown chart indicated that he has a history of psychiatric hospitalizations and was given the diagnoses of Psychotic Disorder, NOS, Alcohol Abuse, and Cannabis Abuse. During that hospitalization, he was given Ativan 1 mg po hs prn for his complaint of having difficulty with his sleeping. He was also treated with other psychotropic medications prior to his discharge. His final diagnosis was Schizophrenia, Chronic, Undifferentiated Type, Alcohol Abuse, and Cannabis Abuse. His previous records also indicated that he had experienced delusional thinking such as thinking that he has special powers and special knowledge of prediction of the future, and he had worldwide powerful activities. His mental status on his psychiatric hospitalization indicated that he made a statement that he went with too many gods in the war, saw them and talked to them, went with them anywhere, and that they told him things about the CIA and the life of Americans and that the American religions were always at odds with his religion. Social History done at Briggs indicated that patient reported being arrested one time in Indianapolis, Indiana, for not having any money for a bus ticket. He reportedly spent a week in jail and a friend paid the fine and got him out. He was also arrested once in Lafayette, Indiana, for driving while intoxicated. He was released and was told to appear in court, which he did not do and which led to his being arrested later for failure to appear. He reportedly paid a fine and as a result was discharged. The patient is reportedly serving a ten-year sentence for murder.

FAMILY HISTORY:

There is no available information about the patient's family or history of medical or psychiatric illness at this time.

SOCIAL HISTORY:

This information is obtained from the social history compiled during the patient's hospitalization at Briggs. The patient was reportedly born in Taipei, Taiwan, and his family all reside in Taipei. He reportedly went to school there. He was not married. He came to the United States in 1985 as a refugee, is staying in Indiana for one year, and worked in a factory in Madison, Wisconsin, for three years prior to his present incarceration. For additional Social History, please read Social History in the brown chart.

MENTAL STATUS EXAMINATION:

The patient is a 34-year-old, frail-looking Chinese male who was dressed in a disheveled white WDOC uniform. He looked undernourished. He was mute and he had poor eye contact. He was able to answer one question by head movement at one time. There were no indications that patient had delusions or hallucinations. The rest of his mental status examination was not tested because of his uncooperativeness and his remaining mute.

SUMMARY OF POSITIVE FINDINGS AND TARGET SYMPTOMS:

This 34-year-old male reportedly came to the United States as a refugee in 1985 and has been living with friends in Madison prior to his incarceration. He reportedly is serving a ten-year sentence for murder. His records indicated that he has a history of delusions and hallucinations and was hospitalized at a mental hospital with a diagnosis of Undifferentiated Schizophrenia, Alcohol Abuse and Cannabis Abuse. He reportedly was observed to have unusual behavior at Briggs, remaining mute and not making eye contact with anyone and was observed looking at his wall while in his cell. He also started refusing to eat, causing him to lose weight. The patient was transferred to the medical unit at Briggs electively mute and not eating although he started eating the next day. The patient at this time remains mute although he started to answer by moving his head. It is possible that this patient has a Schizoaffective Disorder and a possible Bipolar Disorder in addition to his history of Alcohol and Cannabis Abuse.

DIAGNOSIS:

Axis I:	295.70 Schizoaffective Disorder, Bipolar Type
	Rule Out Bipolar Disorder, Mixed with Psychotic Features 296.64
	Rule Out Schizophrenia, Chronic, Catatonic Type with Acute Exacerbation 295.24
	305.00 Alcohol Abuse, in remission due to incarceration
	305.20 Cannabis Abuse, in remission due to incarceration
Axis II:	799.90 Deferred
Axis III:	Tuberculosis Class II
Axis IV:	Severe (incarceration and no family support)
Axis V:	Current GAF: 20 Highest GAF Past Year: 0

PROGNOSIS:

Poor.

_____

Dominique Daws, MD

RECOMMENDATIONS:

It is recommended that Inmate Ming be kept in acute care until he is stabilized. He should do well on a dorm unit once he has achieved some remission.

PROGNOSIS:

Guarded.

_____   _____
Raul Hastings, ACP III   William G. Fraley, Ph.D.
Staff Psychologist   Supervising Psychologist

REASON FOR REFERRAL:

Inmate Ming was informed that the contents of this report would be shared with the appropriate treating personnel and the evaluation was completed following inmate's tacit consent.

This inmate is a thin, frail, 34-year-old Chinese male who understands English better than he can speak it. Records indicate that he has been hospitalized before. His travel card indicates that he is serving time for Rape. He allegedly cut off the victim's head. There is some question as to whether he might have been charged with the crime and did not actually participate in the decapitation. This was a gang-rape situation. Inmate Ming has been electively mute since his admission to Briggs. He will look at this examiner; however, he makes no verbal response. Records indicate that he has experienced delusional thinking in the past. He has verbalized special powers, special knowledge, and has been able to predict the future. He has been diagnosed as Psychotic Disorder, NOS, Schizoaffective Disorder, Depressed, and Schizoaffective Disorder, Bipolar Type. There has also been some question as to whether he may be a catatonic schizophrenic.

MENTAL STATUS:

Inmate Ming cannot be interviewed or tested at this time because of his refusal to talk. He does not appear to be attending to hallucinations. He appears flat, withdrawn, depressed, detached, and medicated.

PSYCHOMETRICS:

Not applicable.

This is a real PSI and psychiatric evaluation of an offender who is currently incarcerated in another state. The names of the offender, accomplices, probation officers, and physicians were changed for reasons of confidentiality.

CHANGING RESPONSIBILITIES OF PROBATION OFFICERS RESULTING FROM SENTENCING REFORMS AND TRENDS

We have already seen how the probation officer role has changed somewhat as the result of changing from one type of sentencing scheme to another (Wilson and Petersilia, 2002). Under the previous indeterminate sentencing scheme used by the federal district courts, for example, the U.S. Probation Office used to have its probation officers collect diverse information about prospective probationers and present this information in a subsequent sentencing hearing. Probation officers embellished their reports frequently with personal observations and judgments. They also recommended sentences to federal district court judges, based upon their own impressions of each case. However, the U.S. sentencing guidelines caused considerable changes in the PO role. Now, probation officers must learn to add and subtract points from one's **offense seriousness score** according to whether a drug transaction occurred within a specified distance of a school, whether the offender used a dangerous weapon during the commission of the crime, and/or whether offenders accepted responsibility for their actions. In drug cases, amounts of drugs must be factored into an increasingly complex formula to determine where an offender's case might be categorized. Fortunately, much of this calculating has been computerized to make it easier for POs to determine one's offense level and crime seriousness.

Ellen Steury (1989:95-96) illustrates the complexity of score determination under the new federal sentencing guidelines with an hypothetical example. She suggests the following:

A hypothetical offense situation might be helpful in portraying the mechanics of the guidelines. Consider the case of a defendant convicted of armed robbery, where the facts are as follows: (1) the robbery offense; (2) was carefully planned; (3) $23,000 was stolen; (4) the robber pointed a gun at the teller; (5) no injuries occurred; (6) the offender had three previous felony convictions, of which two carried terms of imprisonment longer than 13 months and one carried a term of probation; (7) the offender had been out of prison six months at the time of committing the instant offense, but was not under legal sentence at the time of the offense; (8) had no other currently pending charges; (9) confessed to the crime, wholly cooperated with law enforcement authorities, and offered restitution. In the ordinary case, this fact situation would require the court to sentence the offender to a term of imprisonment between 57 months (4 years, 9 months) and 71 months (5 years, 11 months). In the hypothetical situation detailed above, each of the items would carry the following values:

1. The robbery itself carries a base level score of 18.
2. The "more than minimal planning" does not affect the sentence in the case of robbery, but it does (inexplicably) in other offenses such as burglary, property damage or destruction, embezzlement, and aggravated assault.
3. The amount of money taken increases the base level by two points.
4. Brandishing a firearm increases the base level by another three points.
5. The fact that no victim injuries occurred avoids other possible level increases, which would otherwise be calculated on the basis of the degree of the injury.
6. The criminal history score totals nine points, comprised of three points for each sentence of imprisonment longer than thirteen months, and one point for the sentence of probation; while the recency of the latest imprisonment incurs two additional points.
7. The absence of other pending charges avoids a possible score increase.
8. The confession, coupled with the cooperation and the volunteered restitution, might persuade the court to conclude that the offender had "accepted responsibility" for the crime, which could result in decreasing the offense level score by two points.

In the above example, the offense points sum to 21, and the criminal history points sum to 9. The sentencing range associated with offense level 21 and the criminal history score of 9 (Category IV) is 57 to 71 months. Defendants so sentenced, or the government, could appeal by claiming that the guidelines had been incorrectly applied (18 U.S.C., Sec. 3742(a)(2) and Sec. 3742(b)(2), 2004). An appellate court would review the case.

If the sentencing court in its wisdom believed that the offender deserved less than 57 months or more than 71 months, a departure from the guidelines would be allowable, provided a written justification from the judge accompanied the departure. In such cases, defendants (if the sentence were longer than the maximum specified by the guidelines) or the government (if the sentence were shorter than the minimum specified by the guidelines) could appeal for a review of the stated reasons given by the judge for the departure (18 U.S.C., Sec. 3742(a)(3)(A) and Sec. 3742(b)(3)(A), 2004) (Steury, 1989:95-96).

Frank Marshall, a federal PO with the U.S. Probation Office in Philadelphia in 1989, has observed several significant changes in PO work as the result of the federal sentencing guidelines that went into effect in November, 1987. He notes that the U.S. Parole Commission was to be abolished in 1992, that all parolees would be placed under the supervision of the U.S. Probation Office, and that a new term, supervised release, would replace terms such as parole and special parole. Marshall also indicates that POs will acquire more sentencing responsibilities with the sentencing change. Federal district court judges will increasingly rely on PO work for determining appropriate sentences of offenders. At the same time, fewer convicted offenders will be eligible for probation or diversion (Marshall, 1989:153-164). In the few years following the sentencing guidelines, for example, federal sentencing patterns shifted so that probation as a sentence was imposed about 10 to 12 percent of the time in the post-guidelines period compared with 60 to 65 percent probation sentences in the pre-guidelines period (Champion, 1994). In short, the federal sentencing guidelines have drastically reduced the number of persons eligible for and receiving probation. The work of federal POs is not substantially reduced, however, since they now supervise parolees under supervised release and their PSI report preparation has become more complex.

SUMMARY

Sentencing is a crucial stage in offender processing. Sentencing is intended to promote respect for the law, reflect the seriousness of the offense, provide just punishment for the crime(s), deter future criminal conduct, protect the public from convicted offenders, and provide education and vocational training for convicted offenders. Many factors are considered in determining the appropriateness of the sentences convicted criminals receive. Much depends on the type of sentencing scheme used by any particular jurisdiction. Four major sentencing schemes include indeterminate sentencing, determinate sentencing, presumptive or guidelines-based sentencing, and mandatory sentencing. Indeterminate sentencing involves a judge imposing a term of years and where parole boards determine one's early release from jail or prison. Determinate sentencing also involves a sentence imposed by the judge, but offenders are released according to the amount of good time they accumulate while confined. Good time credit may be accrued by inmates. The different types of good time that may be acquired include statutory, earned, or meritorious.

Parole boards are not involved in the early release of inmates sentenced under determinate sentencing. Guidelines-based or presumptive sentencing involves utilizing established sentencing ranges, usually expressed in numbers of months, which fit particular crimes and are associated with offenders with particular criminal histories. Judges are obligated to stay within approved guidelines in the sentences they impose, although they may depart from these guidelines whenever they furnish a written rationale for doing so. Mandatory sentences must be served in their entirety despite the judge's beliefs or feelings. One goal of sentencing reform and generating different sentencing schemes is to yield an equitable punishment proportional to the offense committed, and to remove from the sentencing equation all extralegal factors, including one's age, socioeconomic status, gender, race, or ethnicity.

The role of probation officers has become increasingly varied and complex. Probation officers must classify and categorize offenders and prepare presentence investigation reports about them at the direction of criminal court judges. These reports contain recommended sentences for offenders. Judges may either consider or disregard such recommendations. However, most judges seem to take such recommendations seriously. Probation officers also work closely with the courts to ensure that the best supervisory arrangement for offenders is provided if probation is used as a sentencing option.

The presentence investigation report or PSI is an important document. It contains many bits of information, including a summary of the offense and circumstances about it, the offender's background, and the impact of the offense on victims, if any. PSI reports are confidential court documents, although designated persons are permitted to see them at various times in different jurisdictions. Whether reports are prepared is contingent upon prevailing statutes in given jurisdictions as well as the discretion of sentencing judges.

PSI reports may be privately prepared for the court by certain offenders who desire them, whether or not judges order POs to prepare such reports. These private PSI reports provide additional data for the court prior to formal sentencing. Private PSI reports are usually favorable to convicted offenders and are intended to positively influence judicial sentencing decisions. PSI reports perform several important functions, including assisting judges in imposing the most appropriate sentences for offenders; subsequently assisting POs in their supervisory efforts with probationer-clients; assisting prison officials in their decision making about inmate classification; assisting parole boards in determining whether to release inmates short of serving their full terms of incarceration; and serving as a source for research. Offenders may append to the PSI report a defendant's sentencing memorandum, which is their version of events as well as any exculpatory information that might mitigate their sentences. These memorandums are also intended to show whether the offender accepts responsibility for the crime(s) he/she committed.

Offenders who are about to be sentenced usually have a sentencing hearing. These hearings are important because they provide an opportunity for both victims and offenders to make statements favoring their respective positions. Victim impact statements reflect how the conduct of the offender influenced the lives of victims. Offenders themselves can furnish the court with positive information in an attempt to persuade sentencing judges to be lenient. Defendants' sentencing memorandums are used to detail the offender's version of the crime and why it was committed. Also considered are reports submitted by probation officers.

Influencing one's sentence is the presence of various aggravating and mitigating circumstances. Aggravating circumstances intensify the severity of one's sentence. These include whether serious bodily injury or death occurred as the result of the offense; whether the offender was on probation or parole when the offense was committed; whether there was more than one victim; whether the offender played a major leadership role in the crime's commission; whether a weapon was used; and whether there was extreme cruelty against victims during the crime. Mitigating circumstances are those that lessen the seriousness of the offense. Such circumstances include whether the crime was committed by a first-time offender; whether the offender was mentally ill or under the influence of alcohol or drugs prior to the offense's commission; whether the offender cooperated with authorities in capturing others who committed the crime; whether there was duress or some other factor that induced the offender to commit the crime; and whether the criminal act did not result in serious bodily injury or death to anyone. These factors are given variable weight by individual judges who use these circumstances to decide the most appropriate punishment for each offender.

QUESTIONS FOR REVIEW

1. What are four functions of sentencing? Are these functions realized in view of the different types of sentencing schemes which have evolved over time? Why or why not?

2. Differentiate between indeterminate and determinate sentencing. Under each sentencing scheme, how do offenders gain early release from jail or prison? What are good-time credits? What are three examples of good-time credits and how are they used to shorten one's sentence?

3. What is mandatory sentencing? What are some examples of mandatory sentences? What are guidelines-based or presumptive sentences? Why are so many mandatory-sentence related schemes, such as habitual offender laws or repeat offender laws, seldom used by the various states?

4. What are three sentencing issues? How does the need for offender rehabilitation conflict with the need for community or public safety?

5. What is the role of probation officers in the sentencing process?

6. What is a presentence investigation? Who prepares this report? Are such reports always prepared for all offenders? Under what circumstances are PSIs usually prepared?

7. What information is usually provided in a PSI? What are the general functions of PSI reports?

8. What is a victim impact statement? What is the influence of victim impact statements on sentencing decisions by judges?

9. What is the defendant's sentencing memorandum? Why is accepting responsibility so important in the sentencing process?

10. What are four aggravating and four mitigating circumstances? What weight is given to these circumstances by judges when sentencing offenders?

SUGGESTED READINGS

Barbrey, J.W. and Keith E. Clement (2001). "An Investigation into the Hybridization of State Sentencing Schemes." *American Jails* 15:27–37.

Oldfield, Mark (2002). "What Works and the Conjunctural Politics of Probation: Effectiveness, Managerialism, and Neo-Liberalism." *British Journal of Community Justice* 1:79–97.

Ulrich, Thomas E. (2002). "Pretrial Diversion in the Federal Court System." *Federal Probation* 66:30–37.

Wright, Ronald F. (2002). "Counting the Cost of Sentencing in North Carolina, 1980–2000." In Michael Tonry (ed.) *Crime and Justice: A Review of Research, Vol. 29.* Chicago: University of Chicago Press.

INTERNET CONNECTIONS

Bureau of Justice Statistics
http://www.ojp.usdoj.gov/bjs/correct.htm

Bureau of Justice Statistics Courts and Sentencing Statistics
http://www.ojp.usdoj.gov/bjs/stsent.htm

Coalition for Federal Sentencing Reform
http://www.mn.sentencing.org

National Association of Pretrial Services
http://www.napsa.org

National Criminal Justice Reference Service
http://www.ncjrs.org

Punishment and Sentencing
http://www.uaa.alaska.edu/just/just110/courts4.html

Sentencing Advisory Panel
http://www.sentencing-advisory-panel
.gov.uk/

U.S. Probation Department of Southern
District of Ohio
http://www.ohsp.uscourts.gov/pdfs/psi.pdf

Sentencing Project
http://www.sentencingproject.org/

U.S. Sentencing Commission
http://www.ussc.gov/

U.S. Courts
http://www.flmp.uscourts.gov/Presentence/
presentence

Vera Institute of Justice Projects: State
Sentencing and Corrections Program
http://www.vera.org/project/project1_1
.asp?section_id=26

APPENDIX 3.1

SAMPLE FEDERAL PRESENTENCE INVESTIGATION REPORT

IN THE UNITED STATES DISTRICT COURT
FOR THE NORTHERN DISTRICT OF OHIO

UNITED STATES OF AMERICA)		
)		
)		
v.)		Docket No. 03-00014-01
)		
Michael Mali)		

PRESENTENCE REPORT

<u>Prepared for:</u>	The Honorable Kelly G. Green United States District Judge
<u>Prepared by:</u>	Craig T. Doe United States Probation Officer (216) 633-6226
<u>Sentencing Date:</u>	September 15, 2003 at 9:00 a.m.
<u>Offense:</u>	<u>Count One:</u> Conspiracy to Violate Federal Narcotics Laws (18 U.S.C. 846) 10 years to life/ $4,000,000 fine
<u>Release Status:</u>	Detained without bail since 6/19/02
<u>Identifying Data:</u>	
Date of Birth:	March 19, 1969
Age:	34
Race:	Black
Sex:	Male
Social Security Number:	881-22-4444
Address:	24 Apple Street Breaker Bay, Maryland 10012

SS#:	333-33-3333
FBI#:	102-631-476
USM#:	03-214670-1
Other ID#:	Not applicable.

Education:	11th grade
Dependents:	Two
Citizenship:	U.S.

| Aliases: | None. |

| Detainers: | None. |

| Codefendants: | Sammy Maples - CR 03-00015-1 |
| | John Smith - CR 03-00016-1 |

Assistant U.S. Attorney	Defense Counsel
Mr. Robert Prosecutor	Mr. Arthur Goodfellow
U.S. Courthouse	113 Main Street
Breaker Bay, Maryland	Breaker Bay, Maryland
(216) 333-3333	(216) 444-4444

Date report prepared: August 21, 2003
Revised September 3, 2003

Part A. The Offense

Charge(s) and Conviction(s)

1. Michael Mali, Sammy Maples, and John Smith were named in a two-count indictment returned by the Eastern District of Maryland grand jury on November 1, 2002. Count one charges that from December 1998 until June 19, 2001 the defendants conspired to violate the federal narcotics laws, in violation of 18 U.S.C. 846. Count two charges that on June 19, 2001, the defendants possessed with intent to distribute 500 grams or more of heroin, in violation of 18 U.S.C. §§ 812, 841(a)(1), 841(b)(1)(B) and 18 U.S.C. § 2.

2. On July 20, 2003, Michael Mali, Sammy Maples, and John Smith pled guilty to count one and are scheduled to be sentenced on September 30, 2003. All of the above defendants have pled guilty in accordance with the terms of written plea agreements which require a plea of guilty to count one in return for the dismissal of count two in the original indictment.

3. The assistant U.S. attorney has filed a motion pursuant to 18 U.S.C. § 3553(e) and U.S.S.G. § 5K1.1, advising that the defendants have provided substantial assistance to the Government. Accordingly, the Government will recommend a sentence below the mandatory minimum sentence and applicable guideline range.

The Offense Conduct

4. This case was initiated by the Drug Enforcement Administration in early January 1999 upon the receipt of information from a confidential informant that Michael Mali and Sammy Maples were involved in the distribution of multiple-ounce quantities of heroin from an apartment located in the Breaker Bay, Maryland housing project. Subsequent investigation revealed that Mali and Maples were regularly distributing heroin to John Smith. After several months of investigation and surveillance, drug enforcement agents learned that Smith

regularly purchased heroin from Mali and Maples, and sold the heroin to Leon Williams, who would travel to the Breaker Bay area each month from Bodega Bay, Maryland, a small community approximately 200 miles south of Breaker Bay. Williams gave Smith the money to purchase heroin, but generally waited in a parked car near the housing project while Kent conducted the heroin transaction inside apartment 4J in the housing project. Mali and Maples relied on a number of heroin sources, including two unidentified Asian males, and on at least two occasions, John Smith.

5. According to information provided by a confidential informant and testimony presented at Leon Williams's trial, sometime in September 2002, Mali met Smith in November 1998 while they were being held by local police authorities on unrelated drug charges. While in custody, Mali told Smith that he sold small quantities of heroin in Breaker Bay and relied on various suppliers. Mali complained that his suppliers were unreliable and frequently provided him with heroin of poor quality. Smith, although cautious and somewhat suspicious of Mali, revealed that he might be aware of other suppliers whom Mali might use once he was released from custody and ready to resume his drug distribution operation. The two exchanged telephone numbers and agreed to discuss Smith's suppliers in the future. Several days later, Mali was released from custody and shortly thereafter resumed his heroin distribution operation with his partner Sammy Maples.

6. In early December 1998 Mali contacted Smith by telephone and discussed the possibility of obtaining ten ounces of heroin. After several weeks of negotiations, Smith agreed to meet with Mali at Mali's apartment, accompanied by an unidentified Hispanic male. Prior to entering the apartment building in late January 1999, Smith was observed handling a package, which investigators later learned contained 300 grams of heroin, to the Hispanic male. Once inside the apartment, Mali tested a small sample of the heroin, and agreed to purchase the package of heroin for $70,000. Mali gave Smith the $70,000 in cash, and in turn, Smith directed the Hispanic male to give Mali the package of heroin. A short time later, Smith and his companion were observed leaving Mali's apartment.

7. Later that afternoon, Federal agents observed Leon Williams driving a 1998 Porsche in the vicinity of the housing project. Williams parked the vehicle nearby and was observed carrying a brown duffle bag as he entered the housing project where he proceeded to Mali's apartment. According to the confidential informant, once inside the apartment, Williams spoke briefly to Mali and Maples, and Mali and Williams proceeded to a back bedroom where Mali was known to weigh and package drugs. A few moments later, Williams and Mali returned to the living room of the apartment and Mali was carrying the brown duffle bag that Williams had brought to the apartment. Mali then emptied the duffle bag that contained a large sum of U.S. currency, bound in $50, $20, and $10 denominations. Mali assured Williams that he would find the heroin to be of high quality and agreed to provide additional quantities of heroin to Williams whenever his out-of-town buyer needed them. A short time later, Williams left the apartment and returned to the vehicle.

8. For over a year, agents maintained surveillance on Mali's apartment, and on many occasions, the agents monitored Smith's arrival at Mali's apartment followed by the arrival of Williams. On each occasion, Williams would remain outside, sitting in the 1998 Porsche, while Smith entered Mali's apartment. Smith would deliver a large duffle bag to the apartment and return a short time later carrying a small package under his arm. On June 14, 2001 an undercover agent of the Drug Enforcement Administration posing as a drug purchaser met with Mali in the vicinity of the housing project to negotiate the purchase of ten grams of heroin. Mali told the undercover agent that he expected to receive a shipment of heroin the following day and that, while he anticipated transacting a large heroin deal with another out-of-town customer, he would be able to sell the undercover agent ten grams of heroin from the shipment for $7,000.

9. For the next two days, Federal agents maintained 24-hour surveillance on the housing project and Mali's residence. On June 19, 2001 the agents observed Smith when he arrived at Mali's residence carrying a shopping bag. Smith arrived at the apartment with the shopping bag and had a gun which was visible in his waistband. Smith remained in Mali's apartment and a short time later, Williams arrived. Williams was carrying a blue gym bag. Shortly thereafter the agents entered the apartment and the defendants scattered. The agents observed Maples, Williams, and Smith seated in a back bedroom of the apartment, and they were all placed under arrest without incident. Other Federal agents, who were positioned outside of the apartment building, observed Mali as he jumped out of the apartment's kitchen window and landed in a patch of bushes on the

ground below, where he was placed under arrest. At the time of Mali's arrest, a loaded .38 caliber revolver was found in the bushes near the spot where Mali landed. In addition, other agents proceeded to the parked Porsche. Agents recovered a .357 magnum revolver from Williams' waistband. Williams told agents that he had driven to Breaker Bay from Bodega Bay and had visited some friends.

10. The agents searched Mali's apartment and recovered a large quantity of suspected heroin from the toilet that the defendants attempted to destroy. The agents safeguarded the seized narcotics using plastic bags. The following day, the bags were reopened and the water/heroin solution was drained into plastic bottles for laboratory submission. According to the results of a later laboratory report, the agents recovered an additional 725.12 grams of 20 percent pure heroin. In addition, the agents recovered an additional 55.4 grams of 20 percent pure heroin from the top of the refrigerator in the kitchen, and heroin residue from a table in the bedroom, along with an Ohaus triple beam scale, a strainer, and other drug-related paraphernalia. Moreover, the agents seized $1,032,160 in cash bundles of U.S. currency from the blue gym bag that the agents had previously observed being carried by Williams, and $16,870 from Williams' jacket pockets.

11. The agents then proceeded to apartment 6J where, according to confidential informant information, Mali was believed to store narcotics proceeds and other property. The apartment was occupied by Michael Mali's mother, Carol Mali, who consented to the search of the apartment. Agents recovered an additional $13,000 in cash and jewelry, later appraised to be valued at $50,000.

12. All of the participants in the offense shared equally important functions in this loosely organized heroin distribution operation. Defendant John Smith was the supplier for the June transactions. Michael Mali and Sammy Maples were the brokers, while Williams was a buyer, who authorities believe operated a street-level heroin distribution operation in Bodega Bay, Maryland, and he frequently traveled to Breaker Bay to purchase heroin. A total of 1,090.52 grams (or slightly more than one kilogram) of heroin was distributed during the course of this offense, which has an estimated wholesale value of $350,000.

Victim Impact

13. There were no victims in this offense.

Adjustment for Obstruction of Justice

14. Although Mali attempted to flee prior to his arrest, he was apprehended almost immediately. The probation officer has no other information to suggest that the defendant impeded or obstructed justice.

Adjustment for Acceptance of Responsibility

15. During an interview with drug enforcement officials shortly after his arrest, and later during an interview with the probation officer, Mali readily admitted his involvement in this offense. In substance, Mali acknowledged that he had participated in this conspiracy to distribute heroin and takes full responsibility for his conduct.

Offense Level Computation

16. The 2003 edition of the *Guidelines Manual* has been used in this case.

17. Base Offense Level: The guideline for 18 U.S.C. 846 is found in U.S.S.G. § 2D1.4. That section provides that the base offense level for a narcotics conspiracy shall be the same as if the object of the conspiracy or attempt had been completed. In this case, the defendant conspired to distribute 1,090.52 grams of heroin. In accordance with the provisions found in U.S.S.G. § 2D1.1(a)(3)(c)(6), the base offense level is 32.   <u>32</u>

18. Specific Offense Characteristics: Pursuant to the provision in U.S.S.G. § 2D1.1(b)(1) because the agents retrieved a loaded .38 caliber revolver in the bushes where the defendant was arrested, the offense level is increased by two levels.   <u>+2</u>

19. Victim Related Adjustments: None   <u>0</u>

20. Adjustment for Role in the Offense: None   <u>0</u>

21. Adjustment for Obstruction of Justice: None   <u>0</u>

22. Adjustment for Acceptance of Responsibility: The defendant has shown recognition of responsibility for the offense and a reduction of two levels for Acceptance of Responsibility is applicable under U.S.S.G. § 3E1.1.   <u>−2</u>

23. Total Offense Level: <u>32</u>

Chapter Four Enhancements

24. Career Criminal Provision: In accordance with the provisions found in U.S.S.G. § 4B1.1, because the defendant was at least 18 years old at the time of the instant offense, and the defendant had at least two prior felony controlled substance convictions as detailed below, Mali is a career criminal and the adjusted offense level is 37.   <u>37</u>

25. Adjustment for Acceptance of Responsibility: The defendant has shown recognition of responsibility for the offense and a reduction of two levels for Acceptance of Responsibility is applicable under U.S.S.G. § 3E1.1.   <u>−2</u>

26. Total Offense Level: <u>35</u>

Part B. The Defendant's Criminal History

Juvenile Adjudications

27. None

Adult Criminal Convictions

	Date of Arrest	Conviction/ Court	Date Sentence Imposed/Disp.	Guidelines/ Points
28.	3/2/89	Criminal sale of controlled substance, Class D Felony, Breaker Bay Superior Court, Breaker Bay, MD Dkt. #86541	9/23/89, 5 years probation	4A1.1(c)

<u>1</u>

The defendant was represented by counsel. Mali was arrested, along with Sidney Reynolds, after Breaker Bay police officers observed them selling a quantity of heroin to a third individual not arrested. At the time of arrest, the police recovered 20 glassine envelopes of heroin which, according to a later laboratory report, had a total net weight of three grams. Mali was represented by counsel and subsequently pled guilty as noted above, although during his interview with the Breaker Bay county probation officer, he denied his guilt in the offense, stating that he pled guilty in return for the assurance that he would be placed on probation supervision. According to local county probation records, Mali successfully completed probation supervision and was given an early discharge from that supervision on September 27, 1990.

| 29. | 4/4/91 | Criminal sale of controlled substance, Class C Felony, Breaker Bay Superior Court, Breaker Bay, MD Dkt. # 869215 | 10/24/91, 2 to 4 years imprisonment, paroled 8/4/92, parole revoked 2/27/93, returned to custody. | 4A1.1(a) | 3 |

The defendant was represented by counsel. Police officers observed the defendant passing glassine envelopes to others in exchange for money. At the time of his arrest, police officers recovered 55 glassine envelopes containing 2.5 grams of heroin and 16 glassine envelopes containing 26 grams of cocaine, marked "Freeze," wrapped to Mali's arm. Mali failed to return to court as scheduled on July 26, 1990, and a bench warrant was issued for his arrest. The defendant was subsequently returned to court when he was arrested on a new un-related charge. During his interview with the probation officer, Mali freely acknowledged possession of the narcotics, although he explained that the drugs were for his own personal use. Mali was arrested on the below-listed charges shortly after his release on parole. According to State parole officials, the defendant's parole was violated and he was returned to state custody. His sentence ran to expiration.

| 30. | 4/14/94 | Criminal possession of marijuana, 5th degree, Class B Misd., Breaker Bay Criminal Court, Breaker Bay, MD Dkt. # 245678 | 9/27/94 7 days imprisonment | 4A1.1(a) | 1 |

The defendant was represented by counsel. Mali was arrested and originally charged with assault, resisting arrest and criminal possession of marijuana, while at liberty on bail in connection with the above-mentioned offense.

| 31. | 8/19/97 | Robbery, 3rd degree, Class E Felony, Breaker Bay Superior Court, Breaker Bay, MD Dkt. # 258769 | 2/27/98 18 months probation | | 3 |

The defendant was represented by counsel. Mali was arrested by Breaker Bay Transit police officers after he snatched a gold chain from a victim's neck. According to the victim, who sustained minor injuries, the defendant approached him at gunpoint and demanded that he remove the gold chain. When the victim resisted, Mali snatched the chain and fled, but was apprehended when he ran into two transit officers who were standing nearby. Officers determined that Mali was intoxicated on the basis of a urinalysis test conducted later. No firearm was recovered from Mali, and Mali said he didn't have a firearm; rather, he pointed a cell phone at the victim pretending that it was a gun. Mali was placed on probation for 18 months.

Criminal History Computation

32. The criminal convictions above result in a subtotal criminal history score of 8.

33. At the time when the instant offense was committed, Mali was on probation supervision. In accordance with the provisions of U.S.S.G. § 4A1.1(d), two points are added.

34. The instant offense was committed less than two years following Mali's previous conviction. As such, pursuant to U.S.S.G. § 4B1.1, one point is added.

35. The total criminal history score is 11, and according to the sentencing table found in chapter 5, part A, 10 to 12 criminal history points establish a criminal history category of V; however, the defendant's criminal history category is enhanced to a VI because he is considered a career criminal.

36. As detailed above, the defendant has three prior felony convictions involving controlled substances and a crime of violence, and as such pursuant to the provisions found in U.S.S.G. § 4B1.1, Mali is a career criminal and his criminal history category must be a VI.

Part C. Offender Characteristics

Personal and Family Data

37. Michael Mali was born on March 19, 1969, in Breaker Bay, Maryland, to the union of Carlos and Carol Mali, nee Hewson. His parents were never married and seldom lived together making it necessary for his mother to obtain public assistance for financial support. According to the defendant, his father died in 1987 following a massive heart attack. Prior to his death, the father collected public assistance for financial support and had difficulty maintaining employment. Michael has one brother, David Mali, age 43, who was reared by his maternal grandmother in Washington, DC. David was previously convicted of narcotics charges in the District of Columbia in May, 1988, and sentenced to 30 months imprisonment. At the present time, David is serving a three-year term of supervised release in this district and is living with their mother, age 67, at the Breaker Bay public housing development in an apartment where the defendant was arrested in the instant offense.

38. The defendant was reared by his paternal grandmother, Claudia Mali, now age 75, who has resided at the Breaker Bay housing project at 1430 Bird Avenue for the past 30 years. According to the defendant, he has a good relationship with his mother and brother, David, although he acknowledged that he has not seen them in several months primarily because his mother abuses alcohol and is difficult to talk to when she is intoxicated.

39. According to the defendant's grandmother, she assumed responsibility for Michael when he was approximately 12 years old because of the frequent fights and discord in the mother's residence which is located in a nearby building within the same housing project. Michael was a quiet child and was frequently neglected by his mother who never provided a positive living environment for Michael and frequently allowed him to miss school. The defendant's mother has a reported history of narcotics abuse and was frequently hospitalized and treated for alcohol and narcotics abuse. The grandmother explained that she was employed as a laundry worker prior to her retirement eight years ago and now collects Social Security insurance and retirement benefits for financial support. She explained that she has always felt that Michael had the potential for positive contributions to the community but was frequently sidetracked by his friends.

40. The defendant has never been married, but from 1992–1994 maintained a long-term relationship with his former girlfriend, Jackie Smith, now age 27. This union produced one child, Chanel Mali, now age 5, who currently resides with Smith's mother in an apartment at the Breaker Bay housing project. Several attempts to contact Ms. Smith have been unsuccessful.

41. Simultaneously from 1990 until the present, Mali has maintained an ongoing relationship with Mary Santeangelo, now age 26. The union has produced one child, Cynthia Mali, who was born on October 1, 1993. Mali states that for approximately four months prior to his arrest, he was residing in a third-floor apartment in a three-family house in Bodega Bay, Maryland, which he shared with Ms. Santeangelo that rented for $500 a month. Mali states that after his arrest, Ms. Santeangelo lost the apartment because she was unable to pay the rent and now resides with her mother in an apartment on the lower west side of Breaker Bay. Attempts

to contact Ms. Santeangelo have proven negative in that she has failed to appear at the probation office for several scheduled interviews. The defendant has elected to reside with his grandmother upon his release from custody.

Physical Condition

42. Michael Mali is 5'7" tall and weighs 170 pounds. He has brown eyes and brown hair, and at the time of our interview, he wore a mustache and goatee. The defendant states that he is in good general health, but noted that he was hospitalized in April 1990 and treated for a gunshot wound to the arm, which he states he received from a stray 9mm hollowpoint round fired by his co-defendant, Sammy Maples, at someone else in a dispute. While medical records have been requested and are awaited, the defendant states that the bullet broke his arm and he still has bullet fragments in his arm. In addition, Mali noted that he was hospitalized in 1993 after he received a stab wound on his left arm during an argument with his then girlfriend, Jackie Smith.

Mental and Emotional Health

43. The defendant states that he has never been seen by a psychiatrist and describes his overall mental and emotional health as good. We have no documented evidence to suggest otherwise. During our interview, the defendant communicated effectively, but his demeanor is street-wise and tough.

Substance Abuse

44. The defendant states that prior to his arrest he drank alcohol almost every day; however, he does not believe that he is in need of alcohol treatment. The defendant revealed that he has smoked marijuana regularly since 1984 and from 1986–1989, he inhaled cocaine and smoked crack cocaine. According to Mali, prior to his state incarceration, he spent approximately $200 a day to support his cocaine addiction, but has been relatively drug-free since his release from state custody. While in State custody, Mali completed the Network Substance Abuse Program. He attended an out-patient treatment program for a brief period after he tested positive for cocaine in January 1995. At the time of his arrest in this offense, a urine specimen collected from the defendant by a pretrial services officer tested positive for marijuana and opiates.

Educational and Vocational Skills

45. Mali attended Breaker Bay High School from September 1983 until October 1986, when he was discharged in the first semester of the 12th grade at age 17. According to school officials, the defendant had a poor scholastic record, but had an average attendance record and attitude. According to State corrections records, the defendant was administered the BETA IQ test in November 1984 and scored 93. The defendant enrolled in adult education programming and a pre-GED course in July 1994 until December 1995, but was discharged from the program due to disciplinary action. While in the program he was characterized as an average student, according to available academic reports.

Employment Record

46. Mali states that he was briefly employed by messenger services prior to his state prison terms. While under probation supervision, Mali was gainfully employed for a messenger service, was a waiter, and later a cook, until approximately February 1994. Mali was also employed as a porter and dishwasher, earning $6.00 an hour, with Caroline's at Breaker Bay Sea Port from October 2, 1991 until he resigned in February, 1992. According to a representative from Caroline's, Mali was a reliable and good worker, and he would be considered for rehire.

47. Mali candidly admitted that during significant periods of employment, he sold marijuana, cocaine, and heroin to support himself. Mali asserts that he has earned as much as $18,000 a day from his narcotics

activities. While such claims cannot be directly verified, the Government seized approximately $13,000 in cash and $5,500 in jewelry from the apartment of the defendant's mother on the day of the defendant's arrest. Mali states that he used the money to enjoy the "fast life," which included the purchase of a 2001 Audi 5000, also recently seized by the Government.

Financial Condition: Ability to Pay

48. The defendant prepared a signed financial statement, wherein he reported no assets or liabilities. His counsel has been appointed by the court, and a recent credit bureau inquiry reveals that the defendant has never established credit. Mali has no known sources of income and upon his release he will be financially dependent upon others.

Part D: Sentencing Options

Custody

49. Statutory Provisions: The minimum term of imprisonment for this offense, a Class A felony, is ten years and the maximum term of imprisonment is life, pursuant to 18 U.S.C. 846 and 841(b)(1)(A).

50. Guideline Provisions: Based upon a total offense level of 35 and a criminal history category of VI, the guideline imprisonment range is 292 to 365 months.

Impact of Plea Agreement

51. Under the plea agreement, Mali has entered a guilty plea to count one, the conspiracy count, in return for the dismissal of all other counts. Pursuant to U.S.S.G. § 3D1.2(d), counts involving the same transaction are grouped together into a single group. All of the substantive counts in this offense pertain to the same transactions. Accordingly a conviction on the additional counts would not affect the offense level or any other guideline calculation.

Supervised Release

52. Statutory Provisions: If a term of imprisonment is imposed, a term of supervised release of five years must also be imposed, pursuant to 18 U.S.C. 3583(b)(2).

53. Guideline Provisions: The guideline range for a term of supervised release is at least five years, pursuant to U.S.S.G. § 5B1.1(b)(1).

Probation

54. Statutory Provisions: The defendant is ineligible for probation, pursuant to 18 U.S.C. 846 and 841(b)(1)(A).

55. Guideline Provisions: The defendant is ineligible for probation, pursuant to U.S.S.G. § 5B1.1(b)(1).

Fines

56. Statutory Provisions: The maximum fine for this offense is $4,000,000, pursuant to 18 U.S.C. 846 and 841(b)(1)(A).

57. A special assessment of $50 is mandatory, pursuant to 18 U.S.C. 3013.

58. Guideline Provisions: Pursuant to U.S.S.G. § 5E1.2(c)(3), the minimum fine for this offense is $20,000 and the maximum fine is $4,000,000.

59. Subject to the defendant's ability to pay, the court shall impose an additional fine amount that is at least sufficient to pay the costs to the Government of any imprisonment, probation, or supervised release, pursuant to U.S.S.G. § 5E1.2(i). The most recent advisory from the Administrative Office of the U.S. Court suggests that a monthly cost of $1,210.05 be used for imprisonment, a monthly cost of $91.66 for supervision, and a monthly cost of $938.44 for community confinement.

Restitution

60. Restitution is not an issue in this case.

Denial of Federal Benefits

61. Statutory Provisions: Pursuant to 18 U.S.C. 862, upon a second conviction for possession of a controlled substance a defendant may be declared ineligible for any or all Federal benefits for up to five years as determined by the court.

62. Guideline Provisions: Pursuant to U.S.S.G. § 5F1.6, the court may deny eligibility for certain Federal benefits of any individual convicted of distribution or possession of a controlled substance.

Part E. Factors that May Warrant Departure

63. The assistant U.S. attorney has filed a motion pursuant to 18 U.S.C. § 3553(e) and U.S.S.G. § 5K1.1, advising that the defendant has provided substantial assistance to the Government. Accordingly, the Government will recommend a sentence below the mandatory minimum sentence and applicable guideline range.

Respectfully submitted,

Frank D. Gilbert
Chief Probation Officer

By

_____

John W. Phillips
U.S. Probation Officer

Reviewed and Approved:

_____

William Hackett
Supervising U.S. Probation Officer

SENTENCING RECOMMENDATION

United States v. Michael Mali,
U.S. District Court, Eastern District

Custody

Statutory maximum:	10 years to life
Guideline range:	292 to 365 months
Recommendation:	180 months

Fine

Statutory maximum:	$4,000,000
Guideline range:	$20,000 to $4,000,000
Recommendation:	$0

Supervised Release

Statutory maximum:	5 years
Guideline range:	At least 5 years
Recommended sentence:	5 years

Probation

Statutory term:	Ineligible
Guideline term:	Ineligible
Recommended term:	Not applicable

Restitution

Statutory provisions:	Not applicable
Guideline provisions:	Not applicable
Recommended sentence:	Not applicable

Special Assessment

Statutory provisions:	$50
Guideline provisions:	$50
Recommended sentence:	$50

Justification:

We have been advised by the assistant U.S. attorney, who has filed a motion for downward departure in this case, that Mali entered into a cooperation agreement shortly after his arrest. In addition to his testimony at the trial of another defendant, Mali has reportedly provided substantial and extraordinary cooperation relative to organized crime figures, over and beyond the scope of the instant offense. While the Government has filed a motion for downward departure, the conduct in this offense, coupled with the defendant's prior criminal record, would have otherwise supported a sentence near the higher end of the guideline range. Mali has an extensive criminal record, which includes two prior drug-related convictions. At the age of 34, Mali has a limited employment record and, by his own admission, has primarily supported himself through lucrative narcotics trafficking. He has a history of violence and appears to be extremely street-wise and tough. As such, his overall prognosis for rehabilitation is extremely poor, he poses a risk for recidivism, and a sentence of 15 years imprisonment appears appropriate for the protection of the community.

The mandatory five-year statutory term of supervised release is recommended in this case with a special condition requiring drug testing and treatment in view of the defendant's history of drug and alcohol abuse. While the defendant is subject to the provision of Federal benefit denial, in view of his expected prison sentence, these provisions will expire prior to his release from custody. The defendant does not have the ability to pay a fine at this time. No fine is recommended and therefore, the fine payment should be waived by the court. Although the court may deny Federal benefits to the defendant for up to five years, denial of such benefits is not recommended. Unless the defendant were to receive less than a five-year sentence in this case, the period of ineligibility would expire while he is incarcerated.

Voluntary Surrender

The defendant has been detained without bail since his arrest. In light of his conviction and expected lengthy prison sentence, Mali is not eligible for voluntary surrender in accordance with the provisions found in 18 U.S.C. 3143(a)(2).

Recommendation

It is respectfully recommended that sentence in this case be imposed as follows:

Pursuant to the Sentencing Reform Act of 1984, it is the judgment of the court that the defendant, Michael Mali, is hereby committed to the custody of the Bureau of Prisons to be imprisoned for a term of 180 months.

Upon release from imprisonment, the defendant shall be placed on supervised release for a term of five years. Within 72 hours of release from the custody of the Bureau of Prisons, the defendant shall report in person to the probation office in the district to which the defendant is released.

While on supervised release, the defendant shall not commit another Federal, state, or local crime. The defendant shall be prohibited from possessing a firearm or other dangerous device, and he shall not possess a controlled substance. In addition, the defendant shall comply with the standard conditions of supervised release as recommended by the United States Sentencing Commission. The defendant shall also comply with the following special conditions of supervised release: The defendant shall participate in a program of testing and treatment for drug and alcohol abuse, as directed by the probation officer, until such time as the defendant is released from the program by the probation officer.

THE COURT FINDS that the defendant does not have the ability to pay a fine.

IT IS ORDERED that the defendant pay a special assessment in the amount of $50 for Count one which shall be due immediately.

Respectfully submitted,

Frank D. Gilbert
Chief Probation Officer

By

_____

John W. Phillips
U.S. Probation Officer

Reviewed and Approved:

_____

William Hackett
Supervising U.S. Probation Officer

Date: September 12, 2000

ADDENDUM TO THE PRESENTENCE REPORT

The probation officer certifies that the presentence report, including any revision thereof, has been disclosed to the defendant, his attorney, and counsel for the Government, and that the content of the Addendum has been communicated to counsel. The Addendum fairly states any objections they have made.

Objections

By the Government

The Government has no objections.

By the Defendant

The defense attorney has no objections.

CERTIFIED BY

Frank D. Gilbert
Chief Probation Officer

By

_____

John W. Phillips
U.S. Probation Officer

Reviewed and Approved

_____

William Hackett
Supervising U.S. Probation Officer

Probation and Probationers: History, Philosophy, Goals, and Functions

Chapter Outline

Chapter Objectives

As the result of reading this chapter, the following objectives will be realized:

1. Defining probation and distinguishing it from parole.
2. Describing the historical development of probation and the various persons instrumental in its origination and evolution in the United States.
3. Examining and describing the philosophy and functions of probation.
4. Describing several popular models that have been used as patterns for probation programs.
5. Describing probationers and their sociodemographic characteristics.
6. Distinguishing between first offenders and recidivists and how they are treated for probation consideration.
7. Describing pretrial diversion, the conditions under which it is used in various jurisdictions, and its history and functions.
8. Examining alternative dispute resolution, its definition and functions.
9. Describing victim-offender reconciliation projects and their functions.
10. Describing judicial discretion in sentencing decision making.

DO ANY OF THESE CASES DESERVE PROBATION?

• *John M. was a popular newscaster at a local midwestern television station. At 57 he was a grandfather with four grandchildren. He had two sons and two daughters. He was a familiar face at many local events, including the state fair. Local citizens were shocked when John M. was arrested for child sexual abuse. It seems that John M. had abused his own daughters when they were in their early teens, forcing them at different times to fondle his genitals. Neither of his daughters said anything to his wife at the time. However, as they married and moved away from John M.'s home, the daughters got together later and compared histories with their father. They decided to tell their mother about what he had done. She found out and was quite upset. She confronted John M. with this information and he admitted it, professing never to do it again. Subsequently, one daughter visited John M.'s home in the summer of 2002. She brought her family with her, including her own 10-year-old daughter. During their weekend stay, the 10-year-old girl told her mother about some things John M. had done with her, touching her in bad places. When this news reached John M.'s wife, she didn't confront John M. She called the police. They arrested John M. for child molestation and took him to jail. In the meantime, they conducted a thorough search of his residence, including his personal computer. They determined that he had catalogued numerous sites offering child pornography. He had downloaded and printed about two dozen photos showing young children in lewd poses. These items were confiscated. At his trial, John M. was contrite, and numerous persons testified on his behalf. Nevertheless, the jury convicted him. At his sentencing hearing in February 2003, John M. appealed to the judge for leniency and a sentence of probation, vowing never to engage in that behavior again. He produced evidence from a psychiatrist, showing that he had undergone considerable counseling. Other information disclosed that he, himself, had been abused by his own father as a child. The parish priest appealed to the judge for leniency for John M. With a broad array of punishments at his disposal, what should the judge do?*

• *Ellen K., 43, was the daughter of a prominent principal who had recently retired at a Catholic elementary school in 2002. Ellen K.'s mother, Melba K., the retired principal,* *was a respected member of the small community in Nebraska. Ellen K. worked as the secretary-treasurer of school funds and managed three school checking accounts. She continued to do her clerical and financial work for the school. The new principal, Mary G., worked hard to do a good job, coordinating teacher's schedules, planning school events, and other educational activities. After working at the school for eight months, Mary G. was approached by an eighth-grader, Tommy T., who had won an essay contest. The cash award was a $250 check from the state. Tommy T. and his mother asked Mary G. about the check and when Tommy T. was supposed to receive it. Mary G. asked Ellen K. about the check, and Ellen K. replied that the state never sent it to the school, but that she, Ellen K., would "look into it." A few weeks passed and Mary G. became suspicious. She asked Ellen K. to bring in the school financial records the following day, including bank deposits and other financial materials. Ellen K. called in sick the following day, which was a Friday, and the following Monday she resigned from the school, saying that she didn't know what happened to the school financial records. Mary G. went to the bank and subsequently retrieved copies of checks and deposit slips covering the time Mary G. had been principal. It seems that Ellen K. had been writing checks to various local businesses to purchase personal items, although she wrote on the checks that these were presents or gifts for various students who were ill or hospitalized for different reasons. Also, most deposit slips had cash withheld. Ellen K. made it a practice to have the bank give her some cash back from most deposits. In one of the three checking accounts, a state check for $250 made out to Tommy T. was found, $50 of which had been deposited. The back of the check showed a forged signature of Tommy T. and an Ellen K. endorsement. Ellen K. had kept $200. Mary G. determined that over an eight-month period, Ellen K. had embezzled almost $30,000 from the school by keeping various amounts of cash from weekly deposits. Furthermore, some of the account items showed that Melba K. had endorsed some of the checks under Ellen K.'s signature. The Catholic Church was advised of these irregularities through their local priest. Since Ellen K. had resigned, it was decided to not press the matter further. Mary G., the principal, was told simply to "forget it." However, Ellen K. continued to attend the church. When asked by parishioners why she no longer worked at the school, she made up stories about Mary G. driving her away. Subsequently, church members began to shun Mary G. However, when Mary G. became aware of Ellen K.'s allegations, she contacted the local FBI office and gave copies of the school financial records to them. The incriminating item drawing FBI involvement was the check issued to Tommy T., which was a state-issued item, but which also was funded from a federal writing grant. The FBI later arrested Ellen K., who promptly confessed. She told of how she and her mother had been "doing the cash thing at the school for years." While Ellen K.'s mother was never an FBI target, Ellen K. was charged with forgery. She and her attorney entered into a plea agreement with federal prosecutors. Since Ellen K. and her mother had embezzled many thousands of dollars from the school over several years, what sort of punishment should the district court judge impose? Was Ellen K. eligible for probation, which her attorney requested?*

• Coincidentally in the same Nebraska community where Ellen K. lived, another woman, Wilma B., 35, worked at a local car dealership as the bookkeeper. During a surprise audit, it was discovered that she had embezzled at least $30,000 over an 18-month period. When confronted with the evidence against her, Wilma B. confessed. The state prosecuted her on embezzlement charges. Her attorney met with state prosecutors and proposed a plea agreement which would grant her a period of probation. Should Wilma B. be granted probation instead of a prison sentence?

• Eddie L., 56, is a small-time Maryland burglar and thief who has over 35 arrests and nearly 30 convictions in various states. He has served time in prison for short periods, as well as several jail sentences. Since recently moving to Maryland in January 2003, Eddie L. was caught shoplifting in a Baltimore home appliance store. Also,

his fingerprints matched those found at a recent burglary of a residential dwelling, where money and jewelry were taken. On the basis of the evidence against him, Eddie L. consulted with his court-appointed attorney and entered into a plea agreement with prosecutors. He would plead guilty to the shoplifting charges and a plea of "no contest" in the burglary in exchange for a recommendation of leniency from the district attorney. At Eddie L.'s sentencing hearing, the prosecutor presented the plea agreement to the judge with a recommendation for leniency for Eddie L. A presentence investigation had also been prepared, which detailed some of Eddie L.'s crimes in other states. The report also included information to the effect that Eddie was addicted to drugs and had an alcohol dependency. As the judge with this information, what type of sentence would you impose on Eddie L.? Is probation deserved in this case?

• *Jack C., 23, is a drug dealer who has never been arrested. He makes his living selling crack cocaine to various addicts in Miami, Florida. Jack C. is also a college student who attends a local university. He is working on a business degree. He lives in a nice apartment and drives a new car. In December 2002, Jack C. was busted by an undercover narcotics officer who bought some crack cocaine from Jack C. A search of Jack C.'s apartment did not turn up additional crack cocaine, although over $40,000 in cash was found in a closet. It was apparent to police that Jack C. kept his drugs elsewhere, although they were never discovered. Jack C.'s arrest came about as the result of a tip from an informant, who claimed that Jack C. was a good crack connection who had been dealing for at least two years. When Jack C. was arrested and the story reached the newspapers, his fellow students and professors were surprised. They had no idea Jack C. had supported himself in this manner. In all other respects, Jack C. seemed to be an above average, good-looking college student. He was well-liked by his fellow students and was not associated with drugs on the university campus. A presentence investigation disclosed some of Jack C.'s drug involvement, although it was difficult for the probation officer to ascertain all of the details concerning Jack C.'s drug transactions. Jack C. retained a private criminal attorney to represent him. The attorney approached the government and offered that Jack C. would plead guilty to one count of possession of crack cocaine under one gram in exchange for two years of probation. The defense counsel cited Jack C.'s lack of a criminal record to beef up his probation request. What should happen to Jack C.?*

WHAT HAPPENED?

• *John M. received 15 years in prison for his conviction on the child molestation charges.*

• *Ellen K. received a sentence of 3 years of probation, including 180 days of home confinement with electronic monitoring. It was also agreed that she should never work in a position that allowed her access to company funds.*

• *Wilma B.'s proposed probationary sentence was rejected by the judge, who sentenced her to 3 years in prison.*

• *Eddie L. received 3 years probation, the first year of which would be intensive supervised probation. This would include weekly face-to-face visits with the probation officer, random drug/alcohol checks, and a curfew. Eddie L. should find steady work and file a monthly report with the probation department.*

• *Jack C. was permitted to plead guilty to one count of simple possession of crack cocaine. The drug court judge approved a plea agreement entitling Jack C. to a probationary term of 2 years.*

INTRODUCTION

The above scenarios are some of the many types of cases that come before judges throughout the United States every day. Each case is decided on its own merits. Different jurisdictions are involved and there are numerous variations in sentences imposed for seemingly similar offenses. One thread common to all cases above is that in each situation, the presiding judge had a decision to make. Should the offender receive probation?

This chapter is about probation in the United States. The first section defines probation and places it in an historical context. Probation is unique to the United States and its origins date to the 1830s. Besides describing the historical antecedents of probation and its emergence throughout the nation, the philosophy of probation will be presented. Next, various models that practitioners use for dealing with probationers will be described. These models are orientations that influence the types of treatments or programs designed for probationers. These models also reflect the nature of political sentiment at particular points in our history, ranging from primarily treatment-centered and rehabilitation-oriented to more justice-oriented, due-process frames of reference for guiding PO and probation agency thinking and practice. Several important functions of probation are also presented. The chapter next profiles probationers, including first offenders and recidivists.

The final part of the chapter examines several pretrial options available to prosecutors whenever low-level, nonserious types of offenders have committed crimes. It is not always feasible to pursue criminal charges against certain defendants, especially when such cases can be resolved through less stigmatized civil proceedings. Thus, two options are presented, including pretrial diversion and alternative dispute resolution. Both of these options require court approval, although they often result in satisfactory resolutions of disputes between complainants and offenders. In recent years, restorative justice has been used to describe a slightly different civil dispute resolution option available to prosecutors and the courts. This process will be described. The chapter concludes with a brief discussion of judicial discretion in probation decision making.

PROBATION DEFINED

Probation is releasing convicted offenders into the community under a conditional suspended sentence, avoiding imprisonment, showing good behavior, under the supervision of a probation officer (Black, 1990:1202). The word, probation, derives from the Latin usage, *probatio*. **Probatio** means a period of proving or trial and forgiveness. Thus, offenders who prove themselves during the trial period by complying with the conditions of their probation are forgiven and released from further involvement with the criminal justice system. Their criminal records may not be expunged or forgotten, but at the very least, they avoid incarceration. Some states such as California authorize expungement of criminal records under certain conditions after a probation program has been successfully completed.

Probation is applied among the states in many different ways. In some states, probation is granted for particular crimes, whereas in other states, the same type of offense might draw prison or jail time. In order to understand the nature and reasons for this variation in when probation is imposed, we must examine interstate variation of criminal statutes as well as federal criminal laws. Every state or federal criminal statute carries statutory sanctions. These sanctions always provide for the *possibility* of incarceration and/or a fine, depending upon the seriousness of the offense. In Tennessee, for instance, a convicted shoplifter is punished by a fine of *not more than* three hundred dollars ($300) or imprisonment for *not more than* six (6) months, or both (T.C.A., 39-3-1124, 2004). A conviction for violating a federal criminal law, such as the willful destruction of United States government property not exceeding the sum of $100, is punishable by a fine of *not more than* $1,000 or by imprisonment for *not more than* one year, or both (18 U.S.C. Sec. 1361, 2004). If United States government property damage exceeds $100, the punishment escalates to a fine of *not more than* $10,000 or imprisonment for *not more than* ten years, or both (18 U.S.C., Sec. 1361, 2004).

The important phrase in these statutes is *not more than.* Judges have the discretionary power to sentence offenders to the maximum penalties provided by law (e.g., whatever maximum penalties are provided in each criminal statute). Or judges may decide to impose no penalties. A third option is that they may impose a portion of the maximum sentence prescribed by the particular criminal statute. Sometimes, a judge may declare, "You are hereby sentenced to six months in the county jail and ordered to pay a $500 fine—the six-month sentence is suspended upon the payment of a $500 fine and court costs." Or the judge may say, "You are sentenced to four years in prison, but the four-year sentence is suspended and I order you placed on probation for four years." All judges have diverse sentencing options.

In the federal system, until November, 1987, federal judges were encouraged to refrain from incarcerating convicted offenders. In fact, 18 U.S.C., Sec. 3582 (2004) says that "recognizing that imprisonment is not an appropriate means of promoting correction and rehabilitation," the court (judge) should consider any relevant policy statements by the Sentencing Commission and recommend an appropriate sentence for the defendant. Furthermore, 18 U.S.C., Sec. 3651 (2004) provides that judges may grant probation for any offense not punishable by death or life imprisonment, when they are satisfied that the ends of justice and the best interest of the public as well as the defendant will be served. Within this same section, the period of probation is limited to five years, regardless of more excessive penalties associated with the original sentence and fine. Several states have followed these federal guidelines in writing their own sentencing provisions and guidelines.

However, in November, 1987, new federal sentencing guidelines were established. These presumptive guidelines were intended to establish greater uniformity and consistency among federal judges and the sentences they impose. Furthermore, these guidelines severely restrict a federal judge's sentencing options. Because of these new sentencing guidelines, every federal criminal statute has been modified (U.S. Sentencing Commission, 2003).

The public is ambivalent about probation and who should receive it. Popular opinion views probation as a nonsentence, no punishment, or excessive leniency. Even experts disagree about how and when probation should be used (Arthur, 2000). The word, probation, is sometimes used to indicate a legal disposition, a measure of leniency, a punitive measure, an administrative process, and a treatment method. Probation is the supervised release of offenders into the community in lieu of incarceration subject to conditions (Black, 1990:1202).

THE HISTORY OF PROBATION IN THE UNITED STATES

Many American laws and judicial procedures in the United States have been influenced by early British common law and judicial customs. Also, evidence shows a distinct British influence on United States prison architecture and design as well as other corrections-related phenomena (Wilson and Petersilia, 2002).

Judicial Reprieves and Releases on an Offender's Recognizance

During the late 1700s and early 1800s, English judges increasingly exercised their discretion in numerous criminal cases by granting convicted offenders **judicial reprieves.** Under English common law, judicial reprieves suspended the incarcerative sentences of convicted offenders. These were demonstrations of judicial leniency, especially in those cases where offenders had no prior records, had committed minor offenses, and where the punishments were deemed excessive by the courts. Judges believed that in certain cases, incarceration would serve no useful purpose. While no accurate records are available about how many convicted offenders actually received judicial reprieves in English courts during this period, the practice of granting judicial reprieves was adopted by some judges in the United States (Stastny and Tyrnauer, 1982).

Judges in Massachusetts courts during the early 1800s typically used their discretionary powers to suspend incarcerative sentences of particular offenders. Jail and prison overcrowding no doubt influenced their interest in devising options to incarceration. One of the more innovative judges of that period was Boston Municipal Judge Peter Oxenbridge Thatcher. Judge Thatcher used judicial leniency when sentencing offenders. He also sentenced some offenders to be released on their own recognizance (ROR), either before or after their criminal charges had been adjudicated. Thatcher's decision to release convicted offenders on their own recognizance amounted to an indefinite suspension of their incarcerative sentences. Thatcher believed that such sentences would encourage convicted offenders to practice good behavior and refrain from committing new crimes.

While judicial reprieves and suspensions of incarcerative sentences for indefinite periods continued throughout the nineteenth century, the United States Supreme Court declared this practice unconstitutional in 1916. The Supreme Court believed that such discretion among judges infringed the "separation of powers" principle by contravening the powers of the legislative and executive branches to write laws and ensure their enforcement. However, during the 1830s when releases on an offender's own recognizance and judicial reprieves flourished, the stage was set for the work of another Boston correctional pioneer.

John Augustus, the Father of Probation in the United States

Many court practices in the United States have been inherited from England, but there are many exceptions. In corrections, probation is one of those exceptions. Probation in the United States was conceived in 1841 by the successful cobbler, or shoemaker, and philanthropist, John Augustus, although historical references to this phenomenon may be found in writings as early as 422–437 B.C. Also the actions of Judge Thatcher have been regarded by some scholars as probation, since he sentenced convicted offenders to release on their own recognizance instead of jail. However, John Augustus is most often credited with pioneering probation in the United States, although no statutes existed at the time to label it or dictate how it should be conducted (Conrad, 1987).

The Temperance Movement against alcohol provided the right climate for using probation (Behr, 1996). Augustus attempted to rehabilitate alcoholics and to assist those arrested for alcohol-related offenses. Appearing in a Boston municipal court one morning to observe offenders charged and sentenced for various crimes, Augustus intervened on behalf of a man charged with being a "common drunkard" (Augustus, 1852). Instead of placing the convicted offender in the **Boston House of Corrections,** Augustus volunteered to supervise the man for a three-week period and personally guaranteed his reappearance later. Knowing Augustus's reputation for philanthropy and trusting his motives, the judge agreed with this proposal. When Augustus returned three weeks later with the drunkard, the judge was so impressed with the man's improved behavior that he fined him only one cent and court costs, which were less than $4.00. The judge also suspended the six-month jail term. Between 1841 and 1859, the year Augustus died, nearly 2,000 men and women were spared incarceration because of Augustus's intervention and supervision.

Augustus attracted several other philanthropic volunteers to perform similar probation services. These volunteers worked with juvenile offenders as well as with adults. However, few records were kept about the dispositions of juveniles. Thus, the precise number of those who benefited from the work of Augustus and his volunteers is unknown. In all likelihood, several thousand youths probably were supervised effectively as informal probationers.

The Ideal-Real Dilemma: Philosophies in Conflict

Probation was a true correctional innovation in 1841. Before Augustus's work, offenders convicted of criminal offenses were either fined, imprisoned, or both. Between 1790 and 1817, sentences in United States courts had to be served in their entirety (Bottomley, 1984). Federal prisoners increased beyond the government's capacity to confine them, and overcrowding became a critical correctional issue. Today jail and prison overcrowding is the greatest problem confronting corrections. After 1817, prison systems began releasing some prisoners early before serving their full terms. These early release decisions were often made informally by prison administrators, with court approval. Thus, the informal use of parole in the United States technically preceded the informal use of probation by several decades.

Presently, the **get-tough movement** is pressing for a return to sentencing policies that were practiced in the early 1800s, where convicted offenders had to serve their full incarcerative terms. The get-tough movement is not a specific association of persons with a defined membership list who band together for the purpose of creating harsher punishments for criminal offenders. Rather, the term is used to characterize a general philosophy meaning tougher criminal laws, longer imprisonment lengths for convicted offenders, greater fines, and closer supervision of those who are placed on either probation or parole (Ruefle and Reynolds, 1995).

Prison and jail overcrowding continue to frustrate efforts by judges and others to incarcerate larger numbers of convicted offenders for their full sentences. Court-ordered prison and jail inmate population reductions shorten the actual amount of time served by inmates. Logistical considerations regarding where convicted offenders may be housed often conflict with the philosophy of just-deserts and punishment. Furthermore, the constitutional rights of inmates must be preserved. These include the right to prison and jail environments that ensure inmate health and safety. While no constitutional provisions exist that require prison and jail administrators to provide comfortable quarters for inmates, penal authorities are obligated to insure that their incarcerative environments are not "cruel and unusual" and in violation of the Eighth Amendment (Faulkner, 2002).

Public Reaction to Probation

Many citizens believe that probation actually means coddling offenders and causes them not to take their punishment seriously (Arthur, 2000). In the 1840s, Augustus himself was criticized by the press, politicians, and especially jailers. The livelihood of jailers was based on the cost of care and inmate accommodations, including provisions for food and clothing. Jailer income was based on the numbers of prisoners housed in jails. The greater the occupancy, the greater the jailer's income. Under such a system of jailer rewards, some jailers embezzled funds intended for inmate food and clothing for their own use. While it is unknown how much embezzlement occurred among jailers while this arrangement thrived, it is known that more than a few jailers profited from large inmate populations.

Augustus's philanthropy indirectly decreased profiteering among those jailers embezzling funds allocated for inmate care. The lack of an effective system of accountability for these funds explains why the Boston House of Corrections, as well as other Massachusetts jails of that period, was described as a rat-infested hellhole to be avoided if at all possible (Lindner and Savarese, 1984). But Augustus could not save everyone from incarceration. In fact, that was not his intention. He only wanted to rescue those he felt worthy of rehabilitation. Therefore, he screened offenders by asking them questions and engaging in informal background checks of their acquaintances and personal habits. Particularly, he limited his generosity to first offenders or those never before convicted of a criminal offense. By his own account, only one offender out of nearly 2,000 ever violated his trust (Probation Association, 1939). Pre-sentence investigations (PSIs) are now routinely conducted in all United States courts where defendants have been convicted of felonies or less serious crimes where they may be incarcerated.

When Augustus died in 1859, probation did not die with him. Various prisoners' and children's aid societies, many religiously based, continued to volunteer their services to courts in the supervision of convicted offenders on a probationary basis. Another philanthropist, **Rufus R. Cook,** continued Augustus's work as well, particularly assisting juvenile offenders through the Boston Children's Aid Society in 1860 (Timasheff, 1941:10). **Benjamin C. Clark,** a philanthropist and volunteer probation officer, assisted in probation work with court permission throughout the 1860s.

Massachusetts became the first state to pass a probation statute in 1878, since Augustus's probation activity originated in Boston. This statute authorized the mayor of Boston to hire the first probation officer, Captain Savage, a former police officer. He was supervised by the Superintendent of Police. Thus, probation was given official recognition, although it was based on political patronage. Several other states passed similar statutes before 1900. In 1901, New York enacted a statutory probation provision similar to that of Massachusetts. Between 1886 and 1900, a number of "settlements" were established, primarily in impoverished parts of cities, for the purposes of assisting the poor and improving the lot of the disadvantaged. These settlements were "experimental efforts to aid in the solution of the social and industrial problems . . . engendered by the modern conditions of life in a great city," and they were to figure prominently in the development and use of probation during that period (Lindner, 1992a, 1992c).

In 1893, **James Bronson Reynolds,** an early prison reformer, was appointed headworker of the **University Settlement,** a private facility in New York operated to provide assistance and job referral services to community residents. When New York passed the probation statute in 1901, Reynolds seized this opportunity to involve the University Settlement in probation work. Interestingly, the statute itself prohibited compensation for persons performing "probation officer" chores. Probation work was to be simply another facet of the full-time work they did.

For example, many early probation officers worked as police officers, deputies, or clerks in district attorney's offices. The statute also provided that "private citizens would serve as probation officers without cost to the city or county" (Lindner, 1992b, 1992c). Thus, the voluntary and privately operated University Settlement project was ideally suited to experiments with future probationers. Besides, Reynolds was a member of several political committees including the Executive Committee of the Prison Association of New York, and his connections directly benefited the University Settlement as a new probation facility. Despite political opposition to Reynolds and the program he attempted, volunteers are widely used today in various capacities by both publicly and privately operated agencies and programs that serve the needs of probationers. Volunteers work in halfway houses, provide foster care for dependent youths, and perform a large number of services that assist POs in the performance of their jobs. Without volunteers, the work of POs would be considerably more burdensome.

By 1922, twenty-two states had provided for probation in their corrections systems. During the late 1800s and early 1900s, federal district judges were also releasing certain offenders on their own recognizance following the pattern of Massachusetts and other states, often utilizing the services of various state probation officers to supervise offenders. The federal government implemented probation formally through a bill sponsored by the Judicial Committee of the House of Representatives on March 4, 1925. The United States Attorney General was given control of probation officers through another bill in 1930. The Federal Juvenile Delinquency Act was passed on June 16, 1938, so that probation could apply to juveniles as well as to adults, although "general probation" for both juveniles and adults had already been created technically through the 1925 and 1930 acts (Timasheff, 1941:64-66). Thus, all states had juvenile probation programs by 1927, and by 1957, all states had statutes authorizing the use of probation as a sanction for adults where appropriate. Figure 4.1 summarizes the major developments influencing the evolution of probation in the United States.

Today probation operates very differently from the way it was originally conducted in 1841. Also, dramatic changes have occurred in the forms of probation used and approved by the court. Among other things, technological developments have spawned several different kinds of offender management systems compared with the traditional probation officer/client face-to-face relation.

Year	Event
1791	Passage of Bill of Rights
1817	New York passes first good-time statute
1824	New York House of Refuge is founded
1830	Judge Peter Oxenbridge Thatcher in Boston introduces release on one's own recognizance
1836	Massachusetts passes first recognizance with monetary sureties law
1841	John Augustus introduces probation in the United States in Boston
1863	Gaylord Hubbell, warden of the State Correctional Facility at Ossining, New York (Sing Sing), visits Ireland and is influenced by Walter Crofton's ticket of leave or mark system; later led to good-time credits earned by prisoners for early release
1869	Elmira Reformatory established in New York, with early release dates set by the board of managers
1870	Establishment of the National Prison Association (later the American Correctional Association), emphasizing indeterminate sentencing and early release
1876	Zebulon Brockway releases inmates on parole from Elmira Reformatory
1878	First probation law passed by Massachusetts
1899	Illinois passes first juvenile court act, creating special juvenile courts
1906	Work release originates in Vermont through informal sheriff action
1913	Huber Law or first work release statute originates in Wisconsin
1916	U.S. Supreme Court declares that sentences cannot be indefinitely suspended by courts; rather, this right is a legislative right
1918	Furlough program begun in Mississippi
1932	44 states have parole mechanisms
1954	All states have parole mechanisms
1965	Prisoner Rehabilitation Act passed by Congress applicable to federal prisoners
1967	*Mempa v. Rhay* case decided involving probationer; court-appointed counsel must be appointed for probationers who are in jeopardy of having their probation programs revoked; any indigent must be represented by counsel at any stage where substantial rights of accused may be affected
1972	*Morrissey v. Brewer,* U.S. Supreme Court case involving parolee; declared parolees entitled to minimum due process rights before parole programs are revoked; also required two-stage hearings for parole revocations, to determine if allegations are true and what punishment(s) should be imposed
1973	*Gagnon v. Scarpelli,* U.S. Supreme Court case involving probationer, equated probation revocation with parole revocation; entitled to a two-stage hearing before probation is revoked

(continued)

FIGURE 4.1 Developments Influencing the Growth and Change of Probation in the United States. (compiled by author)

Year	Event
1976	Maine abolishes parole
1983	*Bearden v. Georgia,* U.S. Supreme Court case declaring that probationers who were indigent and could not pay fines could not have their probation programs revoked solely on that basis
1984	Sentencing Reform Act passed; created U.S. Sentencing Guidelines, implemented in 1987; federal probation use reduced from 65 percent to 10 percent as the result of newly implemented presumptive guidelines
1985	*Black v. Romano,* U.S. Supreme Court case declaring that judges are not obligated to consider options other than incarceration for probationers whose programs are revoked
1987	*Board of Pardons v. Allen,* U.S. Supreme Court declared that parolee was entitled to statement of reasons for parole denial from parole board
1998	*Pennsylvania Board of Probation and Parole v. Scott,* U.S. Supreme Court declares Fourth Amendment right not applicable in parole revocation proceedings, where parole officer enters one's premises without a warrant and seizes incriminating evidence which is later used in parole revocation action

FIGURE 4.1 (CONTINUED)

THE PHILOSOPHY OF PROBATION

Probation in the 2000s has undergone significant changes in its general conception and implementation. Presently there are diverse opinions among experts about how probation should be reconceptualized and reorganized (Arthur, 2000; Johnson, 2000). One observer suggests that the reason for these disagreements and confusion is a general lack of understanding about what probation does and for whom. Even though probation supervises two-thirds of all convicted felons in the United States, it receives little publicity or financial support (Burt et al., 2000).

The idea of proving, or trial, or forgiveness implied by probation says much about its underlying philosophy. The primary aim of probation is to give offenders an opportunity to prove themselves by remaining law-abiding. Avoiding jail or prison is a powerful incentive to refrain from committing new crimes. Helping to promote probation as a viable alternative to imprisonment are various societal views about the rehabilitative value of prisons and jails. One belief is that incarceration does not deter crime. In fact, locking up offenders only makes matters worse, according to some observers (Wilson and Petersilia, 2002). Newly confined offenders learn more about crime from more experienced hard-core prisoners. Also, new prison and jail construction is costly. Higher taxes are required to pay for this construction. Probation is far less expensive. Some forms of probation, such as electronic monitoring and home confinement, are both effective and cheap client management tools. This thinking minimizes the importance of rehabilitation as an important aim of incarceration. Offender punishment, containment, and control should be the priorities of incarceration. While it may be true that some rehabilitation may occur among some offenders, this is an unintended fringe benefit.

However, more than a few observers question whether incarceration should be applied to all criminals, although the art of differentiating those who deserve incarceration from those who don't is imperfect. Many offenders are imprisoned for minor crimes, and a significant proportion of these persons will never reoffend. Many convicted offenders are placed on probation as well, but we know that a substantial number of these clients continue to commit new crimes. Inmates themselves have appraised incarceration and probation accordingly. Some inmates have reported that they would rather do more time in prison than have to adhere to a probation program with strings attached (Hofer et al., 1999). At the same time, some inmates believe that probation should not be granted to certain offenders, while incarceration should be rejected as a sanction for other criminals.

For guidance about the general philosophy of probation, we can examine the original intent of its pioneer, John Augustus. Augustus wanted to reform offenders. He wanted to rehabilitate common drunks and petty thieves. Thus, **rehabilitation** was and continues to be a strong philosophical aim of probation. But over time, probation has changed from the way Augustus originally viewed it. Let's look at how Augustus supervised his probationers. First, he stood their bail in the Boston Municipal Court. Second, he took them to his home or other place of shelter, fed them, and generally looked after them. He may have even provided them with job leads and other services through his many friendships as well as his political and philanthropic connections. In short, he provided his probationers with fairly intensive supervision and personalized assistance, financial and otherwise. He supervised approximately 100 probationers a year between 1841 and 1859. We know that he kept detailed records of their progress. In this respect, he compiled what are now called pre-sentence investigations, although he usually made extensive notes about offenders and their progress after they had been convicted. He showed great interest in their progress, and no doubt many of these probationers were emotionally affected by his kindness and generosity. According to his own assessment of his performance, rehabilitation and reformation were occurring at a significant rate among his clients.

But this oversimplifies the philosophy of probation. It has many overtones. For example, John Augustus's goal was **behavioral reform.** Much of his philanthropy was directed toward those offenders with drinking problems. He believed that some offenders would change from drunkenness and intemperance to sobriety and honesty, if they could avoid the stigma of imprisonment. Several religious principles guided his belief, as well as the views of the Temperance Society to which he belonged.

The major difficulty with pinning down a specific philosophy of probation is that among the public and professionals, there are diverse impressions of what probation is or should be. But the word that recurs most often is rehabilitation. Regardless of the form of rehabilitation prescribed by the court when offenders are sentenced, probation appears beneficial by diverting offenders from incarceration (Farrall et al., 2002).

Present-day probation has become streamlined and bureaucratic. While there are exceptions among probation officers, relatively few take interest in their clients to the extent that they feed and clothe them and look after their other personal needs. No probation officers sit in municipal courtrooms waiting for the right kinds of offenders who will be responsive to personalized attention and care. No probation officers eagerly approach judges with bail bonds and assume personal responsibility for a probationer's conduct, even if for brief periods.

Today, probation officers define their work in terms of client caseloads and officer/client ratios. Much paperwork is required for each case, and this consumes over half of a probation officer's time on the job. If we have strayed far from Augustus's original meaning of what probation supervision is and how it should be conducted, it is probably because of bureaucratic expediency. There are too many probationers and too few probation officers. It is hardly unexpected that the public has gradually become disenchanted with the rehabilitative ideal probation originally promised.

BOX 4.1

PERSONALITY HIGHLIGHT

Michael Murray
Firearms and Arrest Techniques, Senior Probation/Parole Officer, District 5, Probation and Parole Field and Community Corrections, Twin Falls, Idaho

Statistics:

B.A. (criminal justice), Boise State University

Background:

My background is somewhat traditional working class. I was raised in Idaho. My roots are Irish and Scot. My father was a railroad brakeman and my mother was a career registered nurse. I grew up in a rough-and-tumble family in a classic 1960s setting when it was OK to wander uptown alone or with a friend when you were 7 years old and watch a Steve McQueen movie. However, we would also tend late at night to linger outside the bars (I guess there was a supervision problem then) and watch the intoxicated unfortunates coming out. At a very young age I witnessed first-hand many of the social problems that I initially viewed with curiosity and sometimes as entertainment. I was too young to connect these incidents with alcoholism, drug addiction, mental illness, and poverty. Yes, I even learned about pedophilia and child molesters who were more an object of ridicule than fear. Later on, my brother gravitated to becoming a fireman while my sisters pursued more traditional forms of social work. For some reason, I had a yen from age 12 to go into law enforcement. I recall shortly after my high school

graduation thinking of applying for a big city police department and actually acquiring the application. Fortunately, I didn't and instead pursued criminal justice at Boise State University where I graduated with a B.A. in 1979. I went to work in adult corrections in 1981, and I found that probation and parole suited my nature more than traditional law enforcement.

Work Experience:

My entire 20 years have been in the field working on the street. My career almost ended abruptly when after two weeks on the job I disregarded everything I learned in the academy and handcuffed an individual wearing a back brace in the front. The back brace turned out to be a ploy, and at the first opportunity he bolted. You can see by my picture that I am built for anything but speed. Being a slow news day in Idaho, I found myself in the position of having to explain my mistake over and over to reporters. I later got a call that SWAT had recovered the escapee and the offending brace a few hundred miles away, but my handcuffs were lost forever. My superiors, though

BOX 4.1 (*Continued*)

unimpressed, did not consider it sufficient to end my career. In Idaho we partner very well with other law enforcement agencies, and as a result I have had the benefit of wide exposure to all kinds of law enforcement situations. Some have been exciting, while others have been downright scary. We work with a dangerous and unpredictable population. Often we come into their lives when we are the least welcomed.

In the 20 or so years I have been doing this, I have accumulated my share of war stories. As I write this, it has only been a few weeks since several shots were fired from the road at our main probation office. Home visits require a great deal of care, as you never know what type of situation you are walking into. Similarly, house searches can also be dangerous. We have encountered methamphetamine labs as well as booby traps. On the rehabilitative side, heavy emphasis is placed on cognitive change programs, and most officers are familiar with the inner workings of rehabilitative programs. You also work closely with the courts, prosecutors, and judges. Each has their own unique personality. This is in addition to the various types of offenders and their families. The job also has other rewards. I remember those individuals in years past who were assigned to my caseload who have achieved a good deal of success in life. A couple of individuals who come to mind are one gentleman who later worked in the Antarctic. Another was a budding writer who had a story to tell and ultimately published her work. Several other people are too numerous to

mention and talk about here, but they have put much back into their communities. I take no credit for their success, but privately I share a good feeling about my little contribution.

Advice to Students:

Knowledge builds professionalism, and you must motivate yourself to continue your education throughout your career. You must learn to be adaptable. The past 20 years I have considered to be the Golden Age of Probation and Parole and Corrections, and the only constant that can be counted on is that the winds of change are always blowing. New administrators bring new philosophies, and to survive burnout, you must be constantly learning. New techniques and practices are always being developed and tested. Secondly, while there are numerous career opportunities in probation, parole, and corrections, do not forget why you came into this field. It is public service. No more and no less. Do not allow politics and disappointment to sway you from why you entered this field in the first place. If you lose sight of this, you will affect far more people's lives than just your own. You also need to make a decision if probation and parole is the field you sincerely wish to become a part of, or if more traditional forms of law enforcement are more to your liking. They are worlds apart, believe me. Finally, this is a high-stress occupation, and you need to make a good life plan and exercise program and stick with it in order to beat the odds. There is a reason why we get to retire early.

The rehabilitative aim of probation has not been abandoned. Rather, it has been rearranged in a rapidly growing list of correctional priorities. One dominant, contemporary philosophical aim of probation is offender control. If we can't rehabilitate offenders, at least we can devise more effective ways of managing them while they are on probation. As a result, the development of several alternative punishments, each connected directly with increased offender supervision and control, has occurred. The community is most frequently used for managing growing offender populations. Many community corrections programs have been established to accommodate different types of offenders.

Observers generally agree that the future of probation is closely connected with the effectiveness of community corrections. And the key to effective community corrections is effective client management through more intensive supervised release (Bowen et al., 2002). However, investigators have found that in some jurisdictions, those who are placed under intensive supervision in their communities do not pose any greater risk to the public than those who have served prison terms and are subsequently paroled. According to some authorities, probation serves several purposes.

1. Probation keeps those convicted of petty crimes from the criminogenic environment of jails and prisons. Prisons are viewed as colleges of crime where inmates are not rehabilitated but rather learn more effective criminal techniques.

2. Probation helps offenders avoid the stigma of the criminal label. Some authorities believe that once offenders have been labeled as delinquent or criminal, they will act out these roles by committing subsequent offenses.

3. Probation allows offenders to integrate more easily with noncriminals. Offenders may hold jobs, earn a living for their families and themselves, and develop more positive self-concepts and conforming behaviors not likely acquired if incarcerated.

4. Probation is a practical means by which to ease the problems of prison and jail overcrowding. Greater use of probation is a major **front-end solution** to jail and prison overcrowding. Thus, probation serves the purely logistical function of enabling correctional institutions to more effectively manage smaller inmate populations (Johnson, 2000; Munson and Ygnacio, 2000).

MODELS FOR DEALING WITH CRIMINAL OFFENDERS

Those who supervise offenders either on probation or parole operate from a variety of different offender management assumptions. Depending upon the assumptions made about offenders and the programs used to manage them, different supervisory styles and approaches may have different client outcomes. For instance, some probation officers are more law enforcement-oriented than others. Some officers believe that their roles should be as educators or enablers. Assisting clients in finding jobs or locating housing may be more important to some officers than whether a client commits a technical program infraction, such as committing a curfew violation or failing a drug test. Therefore, we should acquire an understanding of probation officer work ideologies in order to determine which ideologies seem most effective at reducing client recidivism rates (Wilson and Petersilia, 2002). Several models are presented below. These represent different ways of approaching the officer/client relationship. These models are: (1) the treatment or medical model; (2) the rehabilitation model; (3) the justice/due process model; (4) the just-deserts model; and (5) the community model.

The Treatment or Medical Model

Despite the religious, moral, and philanthropic interests that influenced the early practice of probation, its current rehabilitative nature derives from the **treatment model** of treating criminals. Also known as the **medical model,** this model considers criminal behavior as an illness to be remedied. The custodial approach of incarcerating criminals does not treat the illness; rather, it separates the ill from the well. When released from incarceration, the ill continue to be ill and are likely to commit further crimes. The nonincarcerative alternative, probation, permits rehabilitation to occur, through treatment programs and therapeutic services not otherwise available to offenders under conditions of confinement. Additionally, rehabilitative measures within prison and jail settings have been taken through the creation and use of vocational/technical, educational, and counseling programs as parallels to the treatment received by nonincarcerated probationers (Stevens et al., 2002).

Some observers claim the fundamental flaw of the treatment model is that offenders are treated as objects (Craissati, McClurg, and Browne, 2002). But selectively applying probation to some offenders and not to others leads to more fundamental criticisms justifiably associated with inequitable treatment on the basis of gender, race/ethnic status, socioeconomic differences, and other factors.

The Rehabilitation Model

Closely related to the treatment or medical model is the **rehabilitation model.** This model stresses rehabilitation and reform (Stinchcomb and Hippensteel, 2001). Although rehabilitation may be traced to William Penn's work in correctional reform, the most significant support for the rehabilitation orientation came from Zebulon Brockway's Elmira Reformatory in 1876. Eventually, federal recognition of rehabilitation as a major correctional objective occurred when the Federal Bureau of Prisons was established on May 14, 1930. Although the first federal penitentiary was built in 1895 in Leavenworth, Kansas, it took 35 more years for an official federal prison policy to be devised. The original mandate of the Bureau of Prisons called for rehabilitating federal prisoners through vocational and educational training, as well as the traditional individualized psychological counseling that was associated with the treatment model. In later years, encounter groups, group therapy, and other strategies were incorporated into federal prison operations and policy as alternative rehabilitative methods (Roberts, 1997).

Between 1950 and 1966, over 100 prison riots occurred in federal facilities. These incidents were sufficient for officials to reconsider the rehabilitation model and define it as ineffective for reforming prisoners. There were other weaknesses of this model as well. Similar to the treatment model that preceded it, the rehabilitation model stresses "individual" treatment or reform, and as a result, inmate sanctions have often been individualized. This means that those who have committed similar offenses of equal severity might receive radically different rehabilitation or punishment. The inequity of this individualized system is apparent, and in many jurisdictions, such inequities in the application of sanctions have been associated with race, ethnicity, gender, or socioeconomic status (Bowen et al., 2002).

The 1960s and 1970s are regarded as the **Progressive Era,** where rehabilitation was stressed by liberals for both incarcerated and nonincarcerated offenders. However, rising crime rates and the recidivism of probationers and parolees stimulated a public backlash against social reform programs. Studies conducted in the 1970s disclosed the apparent lack of success of rehabilitation programs, including probation. While some critics contend that these studies are inconclusive and misleading, one result was the general condemnation of rehabilitation and specific probation alternatives. Despite these criticisms, rehabilitation continues to be a strong correctional goal (Skotnicki, 2000).

The Justice/Due Process Model

While the rehabilitation ideal has not been abandoned, it has been supplemented by an alternative known as the justice or **due process model** (Schwartz, 1999). The justice model is not intended to replace the rehabilitative model, but rather to enhance it. Probation practices in the United States have been influenced by the justice model in recent years through the imposition of more equitable sentences and fairness. Sentencing reforms have been undertaken to eliminate sentencing disparities attributable to race/ethnic background, gender, or socioeconomic status. The justice model applied to probation stresses fair and equitable treatment. Probably the most important reason citizens oppose the use of probation is that they do not define probation as punishment. In response to this criticism, several justice-oriented writers (von Hirsch, 1992) have proposed the following:

1. Probation is a penal sanction whose main characteristic is punitive.
2. Probation should be a sentence, not a substitute for a real sentence threatened after future offenses.
3. Probation should be a part of a single graduated range of penal sanctions available for all levels of crime except for the most serious felonies.
4. The severity of the probation sentence should be determined by the quality and quantity of conditions (e.g., restitution or community service).
5. Neither the length of term nor any condition should be subject to change during the sentence, unless the conditions are violated.
6. Conditions should be justified in terms of seriousness of offense.
7. Where conditions are violated, courts should assess additive penalties through show-cause hearings.

The Just-Deserts Model

The **just-deserts model** or **deserts model** emphasizes equating punishment with the severity of the crime. In this respect, Beccaria's ideas are evident in the development of just-deserts as a punishment orientation. Offenders should get what they deserve. Therefore, retribution is an important component. Just-deserts dismisses rehabilitation as a major correctional aim. If rehabilitation occurs during the punishment process, this is not undesirable, but it is also not essential (Miller, 1996). Applying the just-deserts philosophy, offenders sentenced to prison would be placed in custody levels fitting the seriousness of their crimes. Petty offenders who commit theft or burglary might be sentenced to minimum-security facilities with few guards and fences. Accordingly, robbers, rapists, and murderers would be placed in maximum-security prisons under close supervision. If offenders are sentenced to probation, their level of supervision would be adjusted to fit the seriousness of their offenses. The more serious the offense, the more intensive the supervision.

The just-deserts model has emerged in recent years as a popular alternative to the rehabilitation model, which influenced correctional programs for many decades. Penal and sentencing reforms among jurisdictions are currently consistent with the just-deserts approach. Public pressure for applying the just-deserts orientation in judicial sentencing, including greater severity of penalties imposed, has stimulated the get-tough movement (McLennan, 1999).

The Community Model

The **community model** is a relatively new concept based on the correctional goal of offender reintegration into the community (Balboni and McDevitt, 2001). Sometimes called the reintegration model, the community model stresses offender adaptation to the community by participating in one or more programs that are a part of community-based corrections. More judges are using community-based corrections because they are in place within the community and because they offer a front-end solution to prison and jail overcrowding. Often, offenders are accommodated in large homes where curfews and other rules are imposed. Food, clothing, and employment assistance are provided. Sometimes, counselors and psychiatrists are on call to assist their clients with serious adjustment or coping problems if they occur (Lehman, 2001). Some community interventions are geared to assisting battered women to understand abusive behaviors and the influence of spousal abuse on their offending behaviors (Ferraro, 2003; Holt et al., 2003).

The primary strengths of the community model are that offenders are able to reestablish associations with their families and they have the opportunity to work at jobs where a portion of their wages earned can be used for victim restitution, payment of fines, and defrayment of program maintenance costs. Furthermore, offenders may participate in psychological therapy or educational and vocational programs designed to improve their work and/or social skills. POs often function as brokers, locating important and necessary community services for their offender/clients. POs also provide a means whereby offenders can obtain employment.

The community model uses citizen involvement in offender reintegration. Often, paraprofessionals may assist probation officers in their paperwork. Community volunteers also assist offenders by performing cleaning and kitchen work. Occasionally, important community officials may be members of boards of directors of these community-based services, further integrating the community with the correctional program. However, the presence of community celebrities is sometimes purely symbolic, where they are figureheads exclusively and seldom become actively involved in these programs. Nevertheless, these healthy liaisons with community residents generally increase community acceptance of offenders and offender programs. With such community support, offenders have a better chance of adapting to community life. In recent years, operators of community-based offender programs have been keenly aware of the importance of cultivating links with the community, especially with community leaders (Wilson and Petersilia, 2002).

FUNCTIONS OF PROBATION

The functions of probation are closely connected with its underlying philosophy. Within the rehabilitation context, the primary functions of probation are (1) crime control, (2) community reintegration, (3) rehabilitation, (4) punishment, and (5) deterrence.

Crime Control

Crime control as a probation function stems directly from the fact that probationers are often supervised more or less closely by their POs (Wilson and Petersilia, 2002). Jurisdictions with large numbers of probationers have difficulty supervising these offenders closely. This is because there simply aren't enough POs to do the job of supervision properly. In many cases, probationers either mail in a form to the probation office weekly or monthly. This form is usually a checklist where the offenders report any law infractions, their most recent employment record, and other factual information. They may also pay pre-established fees to defray a portion of their probation costs and maintenance. Of course, much of this information is self-reported and subjective. It is difficult, if not impossible, to verify the veracity of these self-report statements without some alternative supervisory scheme. Most of the time, probation agencies simply do not have the resources to conduct checks of this self-reported information. If offenders are rearrested within the jurisdiction supervising them, this is often how they come to the attention of probation offices again (McDonald, 2002).

Precisely how much crime control occurs as the result of probation is unknown. When offenders are outside the immediate presence of probation officers, they may or may not engage in undetected criminal activity. Standard probation offers little by way of true crime control, since there is minimal contact between offenders and their probation officers. However, it is believed that even standard probation offers some measure of crime control by extending to probationers a degree of trust as well as minimal behavioral restrictions. It would be wrong to believe that no monitoring occurs under standard probation supervision. Probation officers are obligated to make periodic checks of workplaces and conversations with an offender's employer disclose much about how offenders are managing their time. But again, limited probation department resources confine these checks to so much cursory and superficial activity. Placing offenders on probation and requiring them to comply with certain conditions succeeds to some extent as a method of crime control (Small and Torres, 2001).

In some jurisdictions, a "broken windows" approach has been taken by POs to crime control among probationers. The broken windows approach was originally suggested by criminologists George Kelling and James Wilson. It suggested that one of the many signs of social disorder was broken windows. If we fix signs of social disorder (broken windows), we will fix small problems before they become big ones. In the probation context, the broken windows approach suggests greater PO involvement at the community level, where POs will have a better chance of staying in closer touch with their offender-clients. One of the critical components of effective PO work is the enforcement of all program conditions, including various technical requirements (e.g., curfew, drug/alcohol checks). When violations are detected, they should be reported, and appropriate sanctions should be imposed. In short, this means more proactive PO work, where POs enter clients' neighborhoods more frequently, supervise offenders more in the community rather than in probation offices, and enforce violation warrants (Arola and Lawrence, 2000:33).

Community Reintegration

One obvious benefit for offenders receiving probation is that they avoid the criminogenic environment of incarceration. This is because they remain in their communities and benefit from **community reintegration.** Offenders on probation usually maintain jobs, live with and support their families, engage in vocational/technical training or other educational programs, receive counseling, and lead otherwise normal lives (Fabelo, 2002). While minimum-security prisons and some jails do afford prisoners opportunities to learn skills and participate in programs designed to rehabilitate them, there is nothing about prisons and jails that comes close to the therapeutic value of remaining free within the community (Ryan, Davis, and Yang, 2001).

Rehabilitation

One benefit of probation is that it permits offenders to remain in their communities, work at jobs, support their families, make restitution to victims, and perform other useful services (Bowen et al., 2002). In addition, offenders avoid the criminogenic influence of jail or prison environments. It is most difficult to make the transformation from prison life to community living, especially if an inmate has been incarcerated for several years. Prison life is highly regulated, and the nature of confinement bears no relation to life on the outside. The community reintegration function of probation is most closely associated with its rehabilitative aim (Logan, Williams, and Leukefeld, 2001).

Punishment

Is probation a punishment? Those on probation think it is. There are many behavioral conditions accompanying probation orders. Any violation can lead to having one's probation program revoked and the offender may be incarcerated in a jail or prison as a result. Filing a late monthly report is a technical violation. Being absent from work without a legitimate excuse might also be a violation of an offender's probation terms. Other sanctions may be imposed as a part of standard probation, although they do not involve direct or frequent contact with the probation officer. For example, the judge may order the convicted offender to make restitution to victims, to pay for damages and medical bills sustained through whatever crime was committed. However, restitution is effective only to the extent that it is enforceable (Gillis, 2002a:3). Public service of a particular type may be required, and others may be asked to report on the offender's work quality in the service performed. And, of course, the offender may be fined. A portion of an offender's wages may be garnished by the court regularly during the term of probation as payment toward the fine assessed. The offender must sustain regular employment in order to meet these court-imposed fine obligations and community service. These are punishments and place virtually all probationers at risk of losing their freedom for violating one or more conditions of their probation programs (Bond-Maupin and Maupin, 2002).

Deterrence

Does probation deter criminals from committing new crimes? Not much. Because of the low degree of offender control associated with standard probation supervision, which often means no supervision at all, recidivism rates are higher than those associated with offenders in more intensively supervised intermediate punishment programs. Observers disagree about the deterrent effect probation serves (Palmer, Holmes, and Hollin, 2002). Although no national standard exists about what is a respectable or successful recidivism level, 30 percent has been defined by various researchers as a cutting point, where more successful probation programs have recidivism rates below 30 percent. Thus, the deterrent value of probation may vary according to the standard by which deterrence is measured. Traditional probation programs have recidivism rates of about 65 percent, meaning that only 35 percent of the probationers do not commit new crimes (Maxwell and Gray, 2000).

A PROFILE OF PROBATIONERS

The profile of probationers in the United States changes annually. Each year, the probation population includes increasing numbers of felony offenders (Glaze, 2003). At the beginning of 2003, there were 3,995,165 adults on probation in the United States. This is a 26.6 percent increase since 1995. The average annual increase in probationers was 3.1 percent. Several states with the largest numbers of probationers include Texas (434,493), California (358,121), Florida (294,281), and Ohio (211,237). Table 4.1 shows a distribution of the number of adults on probation at the end of 2002.

Some of the characteristics of persons on probation in the United States are illustrated in Table 4.2. Table 4.2 shows a comparison of probationers for the years 1995, 2000, and 2002. Approximately 77 percent of all probationers were male in 2002. Between 1995 and 2002, the proportion of female probationers increased from 21 percent to 23 percent. The racial distribution of probationers hasn't changed much during this same period. White probationers increased to 55 percent in 2002 from 53 percent in 1995, while black probationers remained steady at 31 percent for the same time interval. The proportion of Hispanic probationers declined slightly from 14 percent to 12 percent between 1995–2002.

Table 4.2 also shows that proportionately greater numbers of probationers are entering probation programs without serving any jail time first. In 2002, 60 percent of all probationers entered probation without incarceration, up from 48 percent in 1995. There were proportionately about the same successful completions of probation programs in 2002 (62 percent), compared with a successful completion of 62 percent in 1995. About 14 percent of all probationers were returned to incarceration in 2002 compared with 21 percent in 1995 for various program violations. About half (50 percent) of all probationers in 2002 were on probation for felony convictions. Less frequent use was made of split sentencing in 2002, where offenders sentenced to probation were also obligated to do some jail time. About 9 percent of all probationers received split sentences in 2002 compared with 15 percent in 1995. There were fewer suspended sentences (22 percent) in 2002 compared with 26 percent suspended sentences in 1995 (Glaze, 2003:4).

FIRST OFFENDERS AND RECIDIVISTS

Probation decision making is solely at the discretion of criminal court judges. Judges receive sentencing assistance from probation officers, who are frequently directed to prepare background investigations or PSI reports of convicted offenders. These reports summarize the basic information relating to the offense. To the extent that judges must impose specific sentences in particular cases under mandatory sentencing laws, their hands are tied. For instance, if an offender uses a firearm during the commission of an offense in Michigan,

TABLE 4.1

Adults on probation, 2002

Region and jurisdiction	Probation population, 1/1/02	2002 Entries	Exits	Probation population, 12/31/02	Percent change, 2002	Number on probation per 100,000 adult residents, 12/31/02
U.S. total	3,931,731	2,129,084	2,064,506	3,995,165	1.6%	1,854
Federal	31,562	14,349	14,266	31,326	−0.7%	15
State	3,900,169	2,114,735	2,050,240	3,963,839	1.6	1,840
Northeast	591,948	219,382	204,493	606,944	2.5%	1,469
Connecticut	49,352	23,572	21,940	50,984	3.3	1,947
Maine	8,939	6,669	6,162	9,446	5.7	957
Massachusetts	44,119	40,855	40,961	44,013	−0.2	890
New Hampshire[a,b]	3,665	1,466	1,429	3,702	1.0	387
New Jersey	132,846	43,711	42,374	134,290	1.1	2,062
New York	193,074	41,114	36,146	198,042	2.6	1,358
Pennsylvania[b]	125,928	50,137	45,279	130,786	3.9	1,388
Rhode Island	24,759	6,721	5,566	25,914	4.7	3,168
Vermont	9,266	5,137	4,636	9,767	5.4	2,091
Midwest	907,701	579,072	556,463	930,108	2.5%	1,915
Illinois	141,508	61,329	61,293	141,544	0.0	1,506
Indiana	104,116	90,705	88,234	106,587	2.4	2,325
Iowa	22,061	16,603	15,275	23,389	6.0	1,057
Kansas	15,250	23,366	23,399	15,217	−0.2	758
Michigan[a,b]	170,967	124,702	121,570	173,940	1.7	2,330
Minnesota[b]	120,720	57,236	57,318	120,638	−0.1	3,237
Missouri	55,767	23,395	24,578	54,584	−2.1	1,289
Nebraska	20,847	15,625	17,302	19,170	−8.0	1,493
North Dakota	2,970	2,049	1,820	3,199	7.7	669
Ohio[a,b]	195,213	133,991	117,924	211,237	8.2	2,469
South Dakota	4,462	3,511	3,014	4,959	11.1	886
Wisconsin[c]	53,820	26,560	24,736	55,644	3.4	1,369
South	1,619,937	918,777	910,572	1,625,536	0.3%	2,105
Alabama	40,627	16,767	17,696	39,697	−2.3	1,181
Arkansas	28,119	9,056	9,182	27,993	−0.4	1,384
Delaware	19,995	14,638	14,432	20,201	1.0	3,328
District of Columbia[a]	9,663	6,790	7,334	9,389	−2.8	2,032
Florida[a,b]	292,842	258,077	254,333	294,281	0.5	2,283
Georgia[b,d]	360,037	193,915	187,067	366,885	—	—
Kentucky	22,794	13,978	11,916	24,856	9.0	804
Louisiana	35,744	13,268	12,693	36,319	1.6	1,110
Maryland	80,708	42,588	41,314	81,982	1.6	2,010
Mississippi	15,435	8,141	6,943	16,633	7.8	794
North Carolina	110,676	61,122	58,898	112,900	2.0	1,790
Oklahoma[a,b]	30,269	14,364	15,925	28,708	−5.2	1,105
South Carolina	44,399	13,433	16,224	41,608	−6.3	1,353
Tennessee	40,889	25,643	22,974	42,988	5.1	982
Texas	443,682	193,867	203,056	434,493	−2.1	2,758
Virginia	37,882	30,148	27,671	40,359	6.5	730
West Virginia[b]	6,176	2,983	2,915	6,244	1.1	446

(continued)

TABLE 4.1   (CONTINUED)

Region and jurisdiction	Probation population, 1/1/02	2002 Entries	2002 Exits	Probation population, 12/31/02	Percent change, 2002	Number on probation per 100,000 adult residents, 12/31/02
West	780,583	397,504	378,712	801,251	2.6%	1,658
Alaska	4,803	913	767	4,949	3.0	1,095
Arizona[a]	63,073	41,849	38,705	66,217	5.0	1,652
California[a]	350,768	171,400	164,047	358,121	2.1	1,388
Colorado[a,b]	55,218	33,164	31,190	58,986	6.8	1,748
Hawaii	15,581	6,404	5,213	16,772	7.6	1,780
Idaho[e]	35,670	25,292	29,601	31,361	−12.1	3,263
Montana	6,248	3,598	3,147	6,699	7.2	987
Nevada	12,416	4,750	4,876	12,290	−1.0	762
New Mexico	10,263	9,112	7,749	11,626	13.3	865
Oregon	46,063	17,002	17,304	45,761	−0.7	1,724
Utah	10,292	5,215	4,832	10,675	3.7	671
Washington[a,b]	165,711	76,358	68,953	173,198	4.5	3,819
Wyoming	4,477	2,447	2,328	4,596	2.7	1,246

Note: Because of incomplete data, the population for some jurisdictions on December 31, 2002, does not equal the population on January 1, 2002, plus entries, minus exits.
—Not calculated.
[a]All data were estimated.
[b]Data for entries and exits were estimated for nonreporting agencies.
[c]Data are for year ending November 30, 2002.
[d]Counts include private agency cases and may overstate the number under supervision.
[e]Counts include estimates for misdemeanors based on admissions.
Source: Lauren E. Glaze, *Probation and Parole in the United States, 2002*. Washington, DC: U.S. Department of Justice, 2003:3.

TABLE 4.2

Characteristics of adults on probation, 1995, 2000, and 2002

Characteristic of adults on probation	1995	2000	2002
Total	100%	100%	100%
Gender			
Male	79%	78%	77%
Female	21	22	23
Race			
White	53%	54%	55%
Black	31	31	31
Hispanic	14	13	12
American Indian/Alaska Native	1	1	1
Asian/Pacific Islander[a]	—	1	1

(continued)

TABLE 4.2   (CONTINUED)

Characteristic of adults on probation	1995	2000	2002
Status of probation			
Direct imposition	48%	56%	60%
Split sentence	15	11	9
Sentence suspended	26	25	22
Imposition suspended	6	7	9
Other	4	1	1
Status of supervision			
Active	79%	76%	75%
Inactive	8	9	10
Absconded	9	9	11
Supervised out of State	2	3	2
Other	2	3	2
Type of offense			
Felony	54%	52%	50%
Misdemeanor	44	46	49
Other infractions	2	2	1
Most serious offense			
Sexual assault	**	**	2%
Domestic violence	**	**	7
Other assault	**	**	10
Burglary	**	**	8
Larceny/theft	**	**	13
Fraud	**	**	5
Drug law violations	**	24	24
Driving while intoxicated	16	18	17
Minor traffic offenses	**	6	6
Other	84	52	8
Adults entering probation			
Without incarceration	72%	79%	83%
With incarceration	13	16	14
Other types	15	5	2
Adults leaving probation			
Successful completions	62%	60%	62%
Returned to incarceration	21	15	14
With new sentence	5	3	3
With the same sentence	13	8	6
Unknown	3	4	4
Absconder[b]	**	3	3
Other unsuccessful[b]	**	11	13
Death	1	1	—
Other	16	11	9

Note: For every characteristic there were persons of unknown status or type. Detail may not sum to total because of rounding.
**Not available.
—Less than 0.5%.
[a]Includes Native Hawaiians.
[b]In 1995 absconder and other unsuccessful were reported among "other."
Source: Lauren E. Glaze, *Probation and Parole in the United States, 2002.* Washington, DC: U.S. Department of Justice, 2003:4.

Michigan criminal court judges must impose a two-year additional sentence for using a firearm during the commission of a felony. This mandatory punishment, which must be served after one's original sentence for the conviction offense is imposed, is intended as a deterrent against the use of dangerous weapons by criminals (Myers, 2001). It doesn't always work.

Because of the diversity of offenders, their crimes, their prior records or criminal histories, their ages, family stability, work record, and a host of other factors, judges attempt to develop and apply a consistent set of sentencing standards to cover each convicted offender. Thus, some individuality in sentencing occurs. Where such individualization occurs, extralegal factors often function to influence judicial decision making. These factors include race or ethnicity, gender, age, socioeconomic status, and demeanor/attitude. Many offenders are habitual offenders and chronic recidivists. Judges tend to impose harsher sentences on such persons because of their offending chronicity (Spohn and Holleran, 2002). Those with extensive prior records of offending, especially those previously convicted of violent offenses, are less likely to be considered for probation (Cohn et al., 2002).

Other factors are considered as well, and judges are virtually powerless to do anything about them. For example, if a state has a jail or prison overcrowding problem, then this overcrowding might obligate judges to impose nonincarcerative sentences, such as probation, more often than incarcerative sentences. But in many jurisdictions, judges are ignorant of the overcrowding conditions of their jails and prisons, and they may impose jail or prison terms for convicted offenders, only to find out later that the convicted offenders were released because there were no jail or prison accommodations for them (Wilson and Petersilia, 2002).

Most probationers share the following characteristics:

1. Probationers tend to be **first time offenders** or low-risk offenders.
2. More property offenders than violent offenders are considered for probation.
3. More convicted females are considered for probation than convicted males.
4. Not having a history of drug or alcohol use or abuse is considered as a positive factor in granting probation.
5. If there are no physical injuries resulting from the convicted offender's actions, and/or if no weapons were used to commit the crime, the chances for probation are greater.

CIVIL MECHANISMS IN LIEU OF PROBATION

Increasingly, because of the large volume of offenders being arrested for various crimes, prosecutors are faced with burgeoning numbers of criminal cases. Many of these cases involve petty offenses, although even the least serious crimes consume valuable court time. Thus, not every criminal case can be prosecuted, even if prosecutors had the personpower to initiate such prosecutions. There simply aren't enough courts and judges to handle the great volume of criminal cases. Two alternative solutions chosen by prosecutors in a growing number of jurisdictions are to target certain low-level criminal cases for alternative dispute resolution, where a civil court or other authorized body meets with victims and offenders to work out a civil remedy; and diversion, where a criminal case is temporarily suspended from the criminal justice system while offenders must engage in constructive, remedial work or programs and resolve their disputes with victims (Lemon, 2001). Consider the following scenarios:

- *Two men leave a strip club intoxicated and attempt to locate their car. Unable to find it, they see a car with keys left in the ignition. They get in the car and drive home. Police officers investigating a report of a stolen car later that evening spot the car in one of the men's driveways. The man admits to taking the car but says he was drunk at the time. He intended to return it to the car parking lot after he sobered up and retrieve his own car. He and his friend are arrested for vehicular theft.*

- *A man is staying in an out-of-town motel attending a professional conference. Someone knocks on his door and he answers. It is a young woman dressed in a miniskirt and halter top. She asks if he'd like some company. He allows her into his room and she asks for a drink. The man offers her $50 for some sex. The woman produces a badge and identifies herself as an undercover vice officer. The man is arrested for soliciting. He is a respected professor from an out-of-state university.*

- *It is Christmas time and a young woman passes an unlocked car in a Toys 'R' Us parking lot. There are wrapped gifts in the back seat of the car. She opens the door and takes some of the gifts. Shortly thereafter she is arrested by police for theft. The woman has no criminal record and is recently divorced. She has little money and two small children at home. Her idea to steal the gifts was an on-the-spot decision, and she had no idea what she had taken. She assumed the gifts might be for children.*

- *A man is in a K-Mart where he is shopping. He passes the jewelry section and notices a diamond ring with a price tag lying on the floor. He picks it up and pockets it. He leaves the store subsequently with his other purchases but a store employee and police officer arrest him shortly thereafter for theft. The man is a local radio personality and has no criminal record. He is ashamed for what he did and said that he doesn't know why he pocketed the $700 ring.*

- *An elderly man is driving on a highway when a teenager cuts him off while changing lanes. Angered by being cut off, the man speeds up and rams the rear end of the teenager's vehicle. The teenager's car goes out of control and scrapes the highway guard rail. The elderly man is arrested by the highway patrol down the road for assault with a vehicle and leaving the scene of an accident.*

- *A bank teller is running short of $5 bills in her cash drawer and goes to the head teller for 100 $5 bills wrapped in cash bands. The head teller mistakenly gives her two packs of $5 bills instead of one pack. The bank teller notices the extra cash but says nothing. Later that day, she pockets the extra pack of bills. When the tellers balance at the end of the day, the bank teller checks in her cash drawer with the vault teller, while the head teller is $500 short. The following day, the bank teller is arrested by police officers because the erroneous cash exchange was videotaped. The tape shows the bank teller slipping the extra bills into her purse. She breaks down and cries, telling authorities that she has been behind in her monthly payments on credit cards and "didn't think the bank would miss the money." It is her first offense.*

None of these cases excites prosecutors. Two drunks driving off in a vehicle where the owner left the keys in the ignition, a professor offering an undercover officer money for sex in his hotel room, a woman taking gifts from an unlocked car, a man pocketing a ring off the floor from a department store, an elderly man with a temporary case of road rage, and a bank teller pocketing some $5 bills are bothersome cases for most prosecutors. Sure, they are crimes. Justice says that people should pay for the crimes they commit. But should each and every one of these cases be prosecuted to the fullest extent of the law? Should we hold trials for all of these cases and attempt to imprison these offenders? For many prosecutors, the idea of a civil resolution of some or all of these cases seems like a reasonable alternative, especially under the different circumstances of the individual scenarios above. Thus, prosecutors may opt for diversion or alternative dispute resolution. Both of these procedures effectively remove a case from the criminal justice system, at least temporarily, while one or more civil remedies are sought.

Civil procedure and criminal procedure involve two separate systems. The most common portrayal of civil procedure is *Judge Judy* on television. This popular program resolves disputes between parties within certain monetary limits, with Judge Judy in action as the impartial arbiter. Civil wrongs or **torts** are commonly settled in civil actions. In all civil actions, damages are sought, not criminal convictions. The person who had his car stolen from the strip club would like to have his car returned undamaged. The professor who offered the undercover female officer money for sex would prefer discrete counseling or therapy and the incident forgotten. The Toys 'R' Us customer whose gifts were stolen would like them returned undamaged. K-Mart would like it's $700 ring returned. The teenager whose car was damaged by the elderly driver would like his car repaired. The bank wants $500 restitution.

Many of these solutions are restorative in nature, where stolen or damaged property is restored. But in the process, the perpetrators should be held accountable for their actions with some type of punishment. They must do something besides pay for damages to show their contrition, and they must accept responsibility for whatever they did. In recent years, this process has become known as **restorative justice,** which is every action that is primarily oriented toward doing justice by repairing the harm that has been caused by a crime (Dzur and Wertheimer, 2002). Restorative justice usually means a face-to-face confrontation between the victim and perpetrator, where a mutually agreeable restorative solution is proposed and agreed upon. A key feature of restorative justice is equity, where all parties not only agree upon the proposed solution, but offender accountability is also heightened. The offender needs to know that whatever was done has serious consequences. A victim suffered either through injuries or property loss (Tomkins et al., 2002). The offender must realize the consequences of whatever was done and accept responsibility for those consequences. Restorative justice has had modest success where it has been implemented, although some evidence suggests that it doesn't work under all victim-offender scenarios (Karp, 2003:34). Two types of programs similar to restorative justice are presented in the next section. These are alternative dispute resolution and diversion.

Any victim can seek damages in a civil court as a remedy for being victimized. In an increasing number of cases, however, those who allegedly offend against victims may be prosecuted as criminals in the criminal justice system. But in numerous instances, the offenses alleged are petty or minor. Even though the criminal justice system might define certain conduct as criminal, that conduct might be redefined as a civil wrong. If conduct that could be defined as criminal is actually reinterpreted as a civil wrong or a tort, then civil mechanisms can be brought into action to resolve or mediate disputes between victims and offenders. Besides pursuing cases against offenders in civil actions, victims can seek compensation through other means, such as alternative dispute resolution (Umbreit, Coates, and Vos, 2002b).

ALTERNATIVE DISPUTE RESOLUTION

In cases involving minor criminal offenses, one option increasingly used by the prosecution is **alternative dispute resolution (ADR).** ADR is a community-based, informal dispute settlement between offenders and their victims (Braithwaite, 2002). Most often targeted for participation in these programs are misdemeanants. A growing number of ADR programs are being implemented throughout the nation. With its early roots in the Midwest, **victim-offender reconciliation** or ADR programs now exist in over 100 U.S. jurisdictions, 54 in Norway, 40 in France, 25 in Canada, 25 in Germany, 18 in England, 20 in Finland, and eight in Belgium (Holterman, 2001).

In growing circles, ADR is also known as restorative justice (Braithwaite, 2002). ADR involves the direct participation of the victim and offender, with the aim of mutual accommodation for both parties (Strang, 2002). The emphasis of ADR is upon restitution rather than punishment. There are small costs associated with it compared with trials, and criminal **stigmatization** is avoided. However, it is sometimes difficult to decide which cases are best arbitrated through ADR and which should be formally resolved through trial. This should not be interpreted as meaning that juveniles are excluded from ADR. There are specific programs in various jurisdictions especially tailored for juvenile offenders (Doelling, Hartmann, and Traulsen, 2002). In a growing number of jurisdictions, many criminal cases are being diverted from the criminal justice system through ADR. ADR is a relatively new phenomenon, but it is recognized increasingly as a means whereby differences between criminals and their victims can be resolved through a conciliation, mediation, or arbitration process (Karp, 2003). **Restitution** or **victim compensation** also makes such programs easier for victims to accept.

The Dispute Settlement Center, Durham, North Carolina.   A good example of ADR is the Dispute Settlement Center of Durham (DSCD), which was established in North Carolina in 1983 (McGillis, 1998:2). Originally, the DSCD received financial assistance from the Orange County Dispute Settlement Center, the Human Relations Commission of the City of Durham, and Hassle House, a local drop-in center for youths. Michael Wendt was hired as the first DSCD director in March 1983. By 1988, the DSCD was a full-time operation with a board of directors.

Early activities of the DSCD included training staff members in the art of **mediation.** Mediation is the process of working out amicable and mutually satisfactory agreements between offenders and victims in disputes. Training was conducted by attorneys affiliated with the North Carolina division of the American Bar Association. A balanced pool of mediators was selected to represent a cross-section of the gender, racial, and ethnic composition of the community. A total of 38 volunteers were trained in the first mediator pool for the DSCD. In 1990 an office building was constructed to accommodate all DSCD activities.

Presently, the DSCD considers numerous minor criminal cases that have been referred by the Durham County District Court. Referrals come from a daily review of new arrest warrants issued at the court clerk's office. Some of the cases heard by the DSCD include bad-check writing, divorce and family mediation, drive-by shooting injuries, landlord-tenant disputes, traffic and parking complaints, workplace mediation, school mediation, shoplifting cases, petty theft, burglary, and criminal trespass. Some of the cases excluded from DSCD action include domestic violence, child abuse, alcohol and drug abuse, and incidents involving serious and untreated mental illness.

Criminal matters are usually referred to the DSCD with a letter from the court, which says "A warrant has been sworn out against you by _____ alleging that you committed the criminal offense of _____. You can avoid having to appear in criminal court by submitting this matter to mediation." Respondents are provided with a specific hearing time and informed that they may reschedule if necessary, as long as the revised time occurs prior to the court date set for the case. The letter closes by saying, "If you choose not to appear at the Dispute Settlement Center or mediation is not successful, you must be in Criminal Court at [specific time and place]" (McGillis, 1998:8-9).

The process of mediation involves two mediators, the victim, and the perpetrator. Ground rules are established where neither party may interrupt the other while speaking. Complainants are then asked to describe the problem from their perspective. Respondents are asked to respond to complainants' comments and to indicate their views regarding the dispute. Mediators focus on having the parties clearly state their positions and on exploring common perspectives and areas of disagreement.

If the mediation session does not appear to be working out, mediators may meet with each party individually to discuss their particular perceptions and possible solutions. Such private meetings with individual participants may disclose evidence or information which one of the parties feels uncomfortable about sharing among all present. Mediators may also ask each party to consider further steps. If and when disputants reach an agreement, the terms are written down and signed by both parties. The agreement has the legal status of a written contract and is enforceable. About 90 percent of all mediations result in such agreements. If the case was originally referred by the district attorney's office, the parties also sign a letter stating that, "As a result of mediation, an agreement has been reached. We, the undersigned, request that all pending criminal charges in the above case be dismissed." The letter is signed by the complainant, the respondent, and the two mediators who handled the case.

In 1998 there were 24 community dispute settlement centers throughout North Carolina. Over 16,000 disputes have been satisfactorily resolved without further criminal prosecution. About 50 percent of these disputes were originally referred by the criminal court. Presently, the DSCD receives its funding from state appropriations and the Administrative Office of the U.S. Courts. The impact of volunteer mediators should not be underestimated. In 1995, for example, the average mediator spent 460 hours performing board service; 450 hours mediating disputes; 132 hours performing clerical and other support functions; 83 hours facilitating groups; 65 hours conducting training sessions; 40 hours of fundraising; and 10 hours engaging in community outreach (McGillis, 1998:10).

Not all DSCD cases are successfully resolved. In fact, in some isolated instances, there have been lethal consequences. For instance, a name-calling incident involving two students at a local high school escalated to a beating of one

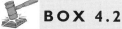 **BOX 4.2**

Jack Fulda
Chief Operating Officer, AmeriCare Communities
Muncie, Indiana

Statistics:

B.A. (sociology and corrections), Anderson University; M.P.A. (public administration), John Jay College of Criminal Justice; M.A. (administration of criminal justice), SUNY, Albany

Background and Work Experience:

I actually began my career in criminal justice as a means of getting married while still a student at Anderson University. I joined the local police department and spent the next five and one-half years working in most areas of the department. During this time, I applied for and received a federal fellowship to earn a master's degree at the John Jay College of Criminal Justice. I left the police department in 1971 to accept a position with Indiana University as an associate director for the Center for Criminal Justice Training. While working at the university, I was contacted by the Public Safety Director in St. Petersburg, Florida, and asked to become the Director of Training and Personnel for the St. Petersburg, Florida, Public Safety Agency. In this position, I was responsible for all police and fire training, as well as personnel policies and procedures for an agency of over 1,000 people. I left this position in 1974 to return to the Midwest to teach criminal justice at Anderson University.

I spent thirteen years at the university teaching both sociology and criminal justice courses and chairing the Department of Sociology, Social Work, and Criminal Justice for the last seven years of my tenure at the university. In 1986, I founded a company with a former colleague from the police department. That year, I read an article about the electronic monitoring of criminal offenders in a criminal justice publication. I secured the necessary financing to purchase EM equipment and started one of the first electronic monitoring service companies in

the United States. The company was ultimately purchased in 1990 by BI Incorporated, and I remained on for the next four years as the corporate vice president for monitoring services.

I left the company in 2002 after receiving an offer to become chief operating officer for a company providing services to our nation's seniors. At 60 years of age, this was a difficult decision, especially with 36 years of experience in criminal justice, but I can attest that the years of experience in both the public and private sector have provided me with the background needed to be successful in this new and exciting opportunity. While those I now work with are very different from those I worked with in criminal justice, the very same interpersonal skills and servant heart are still required for success.

Advice to Students:

Criminal Justice has been a rewarding experience for me and has provided unusual opportunities to serve others, through both the public and private sectors. The one thing I have learned is that criminal justice, like so many other career paths, demands people with sound interpersonal skills and a servant heart. The technical aspects of any career choice can be taught, but it is the intangibles in a person's life that are the most important and spell the difference between success and failure. As you embark on a career path, you need to ask yourself the question, "Why am I entering this particular field and what do I believe I can offer those being served by the agencies that
(continued)

BOX 4.2 (Continued)

comprise the system?" If you believe that you have what it takes to serve, the criminal justice field can be a very rewarding career choice and one that will bring a great deal of personal and professional satisfaction. You may never achieve the financial rewards found in some other careers, but you will experience the satisfaction that comes with knowing that you are performing a vital role in our society and one that demands that only the best apply.

I applaud those who have made a decision to enter the criminal justice field, whether that decision takes you to a public agency or to a private company providing criminal justice services. I thoroughly en-joyed both my public service career and my private sector experience and recognize that there is room for both to operate together in today's society.

This is an exciting time to be consider-ing a career in criminal justice. It is also a unique point in history that offers tremen-dous challenges for creating and applying programmatic and technological solutions to the problems of crime in our society. It does require the best that we have to offer as a society, and I believe that those who enter this field will be the ones who have incredi-ble opportunities to make a difference and to place their unique imprint on the system of criminal justice.

---

of the students by friends of the other student. Subsequently, some of the students in one of the groups engaged in a drive-by shooting of an innocent pedestrian while attempting to kill another student. Warrants were sworn out for attempted murder against several students believed to be involved in the drive-by shooting. However, police were unable to positively ID the gunman. The prosecutor feared that the case might be dropped for lack of evidence, and therefore, he referred the case to the DSCD for mediation between the two student groups. Fifteen students and 30 parents agreed to participate in mediation. Student peer mediators ensured that all involved in the shooting participated in the mediation hearing. After one hour, the two groups apologized to each other. Parents of 11 out of 13 students who had sworn out warrants against other students agreed to have their cases dismissed. The parties signed forms requesting dismissals and the cases were dismissed by the criminal court judge. The parents of two other students persisted in their complaints, however, and took their cases to court. But when the parties reached court, the judge dismissed the two cases since the two larger groups of students had reconciled.

The DSCD conducted a survey of all disputants who had been served by the center several years after it started operating. About 88 percent of all disputes had resulted in agreements. Between 85 to 95 percent of all disputants indicated that they were satisfied with the results from DSCD mediation. The primary result of the DSCD program was that it illustrated how an energetic and creative mediation program can provide a wide range of rehabilitative services to the community. While the DSCD was not 100 percent successful, it is clear that numerous cases that otherwise would have consumed valuable criminal court time were resolved through civil means, and to most everyone's satisfaction. Mediation is a growing world phenomenon found in many countries outside the United States. Regardless of where it is used, discretion will be required to ensure that the right parties are involved in dispute resolution (Holterman, 2001).

Victim-Offender Reconciliation Projects.   Another version of alternative dispute resolution is victim-offender reconciliation. Victim-offender reconciliation is a specific form of conflict resolution between the victim and the offender. Face-to-face encounter is the essence of this process (Shichor and Sechrest, 1998). Elkhart County, Indiana, has been the site of the **Victim-Offender Reconciliation Project (VORP)** since 1987. The primary aims of VORPs are to (1) make offenders accountable for their wrongs against victims, (2) reduce recidivism among participating offenders, and (3) heighten responsibility of offenders through victim compensation and repayment for damages inflicted (Poulson and Elton, 2002).

Officially, VORP was established in Kitchener, Ontario, in 1974 and was subsequently replicated as PACT or Prisoner and Community Together in northern Indiana near Elkhart. Subsequent replications in various jurisdictions have created different varieties of ADR, each variety spawning embellishments, additions, or program deletions deemed more or less important by the particular jurisdiction. The Genessee County (Batavia), New York, Sheriff's Department established a VORP in 1983, followed by programs in Valparaiso, Indiana, Quincy, Massachusetts, and Minneapolis, Minnesota, in 1985. In Quincy, for instance, the program was named EARN-IT and was operated through the Probation Department. More than 25 different states have one or another version of VORP (Umbreit, Coates, and Vos, 2002a).

Pretrial Diversion

Pretrial diversion is a procedure whereby criminal defendants are diverted to either a community-based agency for treatment or assigned to a counselor for social and/or psychiatric assistance (Harris and Lo, 2002). Pretrial diversion may involve education, job training, counseling, or some type of psychological or physical therapy. Diversion is the official halting or suspension of legal proceedings against a criminal defendant or juvenile after a recorded justice system entry, and possible referral of that person to a treatment or care program administered by a nonjustice agency or private agency. Technically, diversion is not true probation in that the alleged offender has not been convicted of a crime. The thrust of diversion is toward an informal administrative effort to determine (1) whether nonjudicial processing is warranted, (2) whether treatment is warranted, (3) if treatment is warranted, which one to use, and (4) whether charges against the defendant should be dropped or reinstated (Harris and Lo, 2002; Swaminath et al., 2002).

Diversion is intended for first offenders who have not committed serious crimes (King et al., 2002). It is similar to probation because offenders must comply with specific conditions established by the court. Successful completion of those conditions usually leads to a dismissal of charges against the defendant. A **totality of circumstances** assessment of each offender's crime is made by the prosecutor and the court, and a decision about diversion is made. Each case is considered on its own merits. Those charged with driving while intoxicated may be diverted to attend Alcoholics Anonymous meetings or special classes for drunk drivers as a part of their diversion. Often, diverted defendants must pay monthly fees or **user fees** during the diversion period to help defray expenses incurred by the public or private agencies who monitor them.

Unconditional and Conditional Diversion.   **Diversion** in the United States includes one or more behavioral conditions and prescribes involvement in treatment programs such as Alcoholics Anonymous, driver's training schools, and/or individual or group psychological counseling. However, a **diversion program** may simply specify that offenders known as **divertees** should be law-abiding and submit monthly reports and user fees for the duration of their diversion terms. When an offender is placed in such a program, it is called a **unconditional diversion program.** Unconditional diversion programs place no restrictions on a divertee's behavior, and there are no formal controls operating through which divertee behaviors can be monitored.

A **conditional diversion program** involves some behavioral monitoring by probation officers or personnel affiliated with local probation departments in cities or counties. The degree of monitoring depends on the conditions of the diversion program and the special needs of divertees. For the least monitored divertees, monthly contact with the probation department by letter or telephone may be all that is required, together with the payment of a monthly maintenance fee that may range from $10 to $100 or more. Divertees are often required to submit a statement regularly (usually monthly or weekly) indicating their present successful employment, family support, and other pertinent data.

The History and Philosophy of Diversion. Diversion originated in the United States through the early juvenile courts in Chicago and New York in the late 1800s. There were concerted efforts by religious groups and reformers to keep children from imprisonment of any kind, since children over eight years of age were considered eligible for adult court processing. Cook County, Illinois, implemented a diversion program for youthful offenders in 1899 (Doeren and Hageman, 1982:23). The underlying philosophy of diversion is community reintegration and rehabilitation, where offenders avoid the stigma of incarceration and the public notoriety accompanying appearances and trials. In most state courts where diversion is condoned, diversion does not entirely remove offenders from court processing, since the court usually must approve prosecutorial recommendations for diversion in each case. Since these approvals are often conducted in less publicized hearings, a divertee's crimes are less likely to be scrutinized publicly. When an offender completes his or her diversion program successfully, one of two things happens. First, the offender's arrest record pertaining to that offense is erased through an **expungement** and the prosecution is terminated. If this event doesn't occur, then the second optional result is a downgrading of the original criminal charge to a lesser offense and a resulting conviction. For instance, a first offender charged with felony theft may have his or her offense downgraded to misdemeanor theft following the successful completion of the diversion program. Either way for offenders who are permitted diversion, their diversion programs are win-win situations.

Functions of Diversion

Some of the more important functions are:

1. To permit divertees the opportunity of remaining in their communities where they can receive needed assistance or treatment, depending upon the nature of the crimes charged.

2. To permit divertees the opportunity to make restitution to their victims where monetary damages were suffered and property destroyed.

3. To permit divertees the opportunity of remaining free in their communities to support themselves and their families, and to avoid the stigma of incarceration.

4. To help divertees avoid the stigma of a criminal conviction.

5. To assist corrections officials in reducing prison and jail overcrowding by diverting less serious cases to nonincarcerative alternatives.

6. To save the courts the time, trouble, and expense of formally processing less serious cases and streamlining case dispositions through informal case handling.

7. To make it possible for divertees to participate in self-help, educational, or vocational programs.

8. To preserve the dignity and integrity of divertees by helping them avoid further contact with the criminal justice system and assisting them to be more responsible adults capable of managing their own lives.

9. To preserve the family unit and enhance family solidarity and continuity.

This list highlights the rehabilitative nature of diversion. Presently, it is unknown about how much diversion affects the court system and court caseloads. Accurate estimates of those placed on diversion are difficult to determine, primarily because of the potential for record expungements. Once these criminal records or arrest warrants for various charges have been expunged, the media and official agencies usually cannot access them. Literally, they cease to exist.

Criteria Influencing Pretrial Diversion.   Who qualifies for pretrial diversion? First, it helps to be a first offender. First offenders who are charged with petty crimes are the most likely candidates for diversion programs. Those barred from such programs might include the following: (1) those with prior drug offense convictions, former drug offense divertees, and/or who traffic in drugs; (2) those convicted of a felony within the previous five-year period; (3) those whose current offense involves violence; and (4) those who are past or present probation or parole violators (Maxwell and Morris, 2002).

Other relevant criteria used by different jurisdictions for deciding which offenders deserve to be included in diversion programs are (1) the age of the offender; (2) the residency, employment and familial status of the offender; (3) the prior record of the offender; (4) the seriousness of the offense; (5) aggravating or mitigating circumstances associated with the commission of the offense (Harrell et al., 2002).

Criticisms of Diversion.   Not everyone favors using diversion as a means of removing those charged with crimes from the criminal justice system, even on a temporary basis. They believe that diversion is too lenient on criminals. Critics of diversion generally focus on the nonpunitive nature of diversion conditions, which are often no conditions.

Other criticisms include that diversion is an inappropriate punishment for criminals and that it does not deal effectively with offenders. Furthermore, some critics allege that diversion leads to net-widening. Another criticism is that diversion excludes female offenders. Some observers think that diversion resolves an offender's case without the benefit of due process. For instance, whenever a prosecutor examines a case, the evidence against the defendant, and other pertinent circumstances, an offer of diversion may be made. If the offer is accepted, this is a tacit admission by the defendant that he/she is guilty of the offense(s) alleged. If the offer of diversion is rejected, then prosecutors can always exercise their option to pursue criminal charges against the defendant later in court. Thus, diversion assumes guilt without a trial.

However, supporters of diversion say that diversion greatly reduces offender recidivism when applied appropriately. For instance, a sample of first-time offenders was placed on diversion in Vanderburgh County, Indiana, during the mid-1990s. A sample of 243 divertees was studied. The recidivism rate for those who successfully completed their diversion programs was only 9 percent, while those who did not successfully complete their programs had 39 percent recidivism (Walsh et al., 1997). Those favoring diversion also counter by arguing that diversion enables divertees to avoid the stigma and criminogenic atmosphere of prisons and jails. Furthermore, there does not appear to be any gender discrimination that applies to diversion program in any jurisdiction. Males appear equally likely to receive diversion compared with females. The idea that guilt is assumed without the benefit of a criminal trial is difficult to overcome. This is precisely what prosecutors assume. However, the benefit of freedom to live within the community without restriction, and the fact that participation in diversion is strictly voluntary, outweighs the argument that one's right to due process is somehow jeopardized. If someone charged with a crime really wants to fight it in court, then they can exercise their constitutional rights and have a trial in the matter (Maxwell and Morris, 2002).

JUDICIAL DISCRETION AND THE PROBATION DECISION

Criminal court judges play a pivotal role in the sentencing process. They decide which sentences to impose, and they determine the severity or leniency of those sentences. Most judges have a variety of sentencing options, ranging from probation to incarceration. They can even impose some incarceration interspersed with some probation.

Judges are guided in their sentencing decisions by the different standards of the jurisdictions of their criminal courts. Probation officers assist them by preparing PSI reports about offenders who are awaiting sentencing for different types of crimes. Probation officers frequently append their own sentencing recommendations to these PSI reports, although judges are only obligated to consider them. No judge is bound by the contents of PSIs. However, if judges are in jurisdictions with sentencing guidelines or presumptive sentencing schemes, these schemes provide for particular sentencing ranges, usually expressed in months, which function as guides for judges to follow. Again, there is no hard-and-fast rule obligating judges to follow these guidelines, no matter how binding they may appear. The only constraints upon judges are mandatory sentencing provisions. If cases come before them where particular sentences are mandated, they must impose these sentences. For instance, if a repeat offender is convicted of being an habitual offender, many state statutes provide for mandatory terms of life without parole. Therefore, judges have no discretion in these cases and must impose life-without-parole terms.

But under most sentencing scenarios, judges have considerable latitude in the sentences they impose. Judges may impose probation. They may also impose probation with special conditions. These special conditions are appended to probation orders issued by the sentencing judge. These special conditions are not uncommonly applied. Probationers must comply with all of these conditions or they are subject to having their probation programs revoked. They may be placed in a jail or prison for the duration of their sentences. While most states by law suggest conditions to be imposed on new probationers, judges generally have complete discretion to accept, modify, or reject these conditions (Klinenberg, 2001).

In Texas, for instance, judges may impose some of the following special conditions of probation on offenders:

1. Probationer shall not open a checking account.
2. Probationer must attend basic education or vocational training as directed by the supervising probation officer.
3. Probationer must notify any prospective employer regarding criminal history, if position of financial responsibility is involved.
4. Probationer shall be assigned to the highest level of supervision or supervision case load until appropriate level of supervision is further established by objective assessment instrument and supervision case classification.
5. Probationer shall comply with any other condition specified herein (e.g., no controlled substances).
6. Probationer shall participate in a mental health/mental retardation treatment or counseling program as directed by the supervising probation officer.
7. Probationer shall make restitution payments as required by supervising probation officer in an amount to be set by the court. By the 10th of each month, payments (cashier's check or money order) shall be paid to the Texas Department of Criminal Justice Probation Division, Capital Station, Texas, 78711.
8. Probationer shall submit to substance (alcohol/narcotics) treatment program, which may include urinalysis monitoring, attendance at scheduled counseling sessions, driving restrictions, or related requirements as directed by supervising probation officer.
9. Probationer shall not contact victim(s).
10. Probationer shall not enter the specified county without prior written judicial approval.

Judges circle the appropriate special conditions above and attach these to the probation order. The probationer must agree with these conditions and other program requirements and sign the form. If the prospective probationer refuses to sign the form, then probation will be denied. Judges cannot force offenders into probation programs against their wishes.

Probation conditions are usually classified as general or specific. General conditions are imposed on all probationers, while specific conditions are only applied to certain probationers. Judges usually use a previously adopted set of standard probation conditions that include the following: (1) Make periodic reports to their probation officer; (2) notify the officer about changes in employment or residence; (3) obtain permission for out-of-state travel; (4) refrain from possessing firearms; (5) not associate with known criminals; and (6) obey the law (Hemmens, 1999:16).

Original sentencing judges or their courts maintain jurisdiction over all probationers for the duration of their probationary terms. If any probationer violates one or more program conditions and these violations are detected, the information is transmitted to the court. The judge considers the evidence in a special hearing before the court and decides what to do. The judge may intensify a probationer's supervision or place the offender under home confinement with electronic monitoring. The judge may require probation officers to make frequent checks of the offender's premises and test the offender for drugs, alcohol, or other substances that may be prohibited.

Judges are responsive to what the public wants and they attempt to impose sentences that fit the particular offense. But those most directly involved in the enforcement of conditions of a probationer's program are probation officers. These officers are the primary link between the court and their probationer-clients. As far as the court is concerned, probation officers should stress the following in their supervisory responsibilities:

1. The public wants probation to deliver public safety.
2. Probation can both raise public safety and help probationers become law-abiding citizens.
3. Probation needs to enforce probation orders and help offenders.
4. The idea, "get tough on probationers" doesn't need to lead to more imprisonment; in fact, it could lead to an increase in general deterrence (Evans, 1999:30).

Recommendations from judges to probation officers include the following admonitions:

1. Public safety comes first.
2. Probation officers should spend more time supervising offenders who pose the greatest risk to public safety.
3. Probation officers should be assigned to supervise specific geographical areas rather than being randomly assigned to offenders.
4. Permissive practices should be abandoned, and in their place a response that is certain and incorporates graduated sanctions to deal with technical violations.
5. Probation should encourage involvement of other agencies, organizations, and interest groups in offender treatment.
6. Program performance should be used as the measure for the allocation of resources (Evans, 1999:31).

Although probation officers are given a great deal of supervisory responsibility over sentenced offenders on probation, their initial input through PSI report preparation in certain jurisdictions is mixed. For example, a study was conducted of PSI report preparation for 468 persons convicted of sexual assault in Sacramento County, California, during the period, 1992–1994 (Kingsnorth et al., 1999). Probation officers were excluded entirely from sentencing decisions in 23 percent of the cases which were plea bargained. Furthermore, probation officers made more severe sentencing recommendations than those contemplated by plea agreements in 29 percent of these cases, and the judges ignored their PSI reports and recommendations in all cases. Even though probation officers relied upon the same sentencing criteria as prosecutors and judges in all of their recommendations, they were nevertheless viewed negatively by defense attorneys who perceived them as agents of the state. Thus, judicial discretion may operate to the probation officer's disadvantage in some cases. Part of the problem is the growing bureaucratization of probation services and a general breakdown in communication between judges and probation agencies (Edwards and Hensley, 2001; Senjo, 2001).

Judges have broad discretion, therefore, in promoting offender accountability. Judges may impose restitution orders or community service as a means of heightening offender responsibilities. In some jurisdictions, restitution to victims by offenders is mandated by legislative statute. In Pennsylvania, for instance, judges must impose restitution on probationers whenever damages are easy to quantify. Some experiments have shown that whenever restitution orders are imposed, they operate in ways to minimize one's likelihood of being rearrested. Also influential in heightening offender accountability are the facts that many offenders are married, employed, and older.

Judicial discretion and the special conditions of probation they impose are valid so long as they (1) do not violate the constitution, (2) are reasonable, (3) are unambiguous, and (4) are intended to promote the rehabilitation of the offender and/or the protection of society (Hemmens, 1999:17). In recent years, the job of sentencing offenders has become less perfunctory. Judges are increasingly exercising what some persons term **therapeutic jurisprudence,** which attempts to combine a "rights" perspective—focusing on justice, rights, and equality issues—with an "ethic of care" perspective—focusing on care, interdependence, and response to need (Senjo and Leip, 2001). Thus, judging and sentencing offenders is increasingly becoming a collaborative enterprise between the court and community. Sentencing judges attempt to create appropriate dispositional outcomes, including securing treatment and social services for offenders who are sentenced (Edwards and Hensley, 2001). This is where the special conditions of probation can come into play and influence the offender's life chances significantly. The public seems to desire a more involved and responsive judiciary. Thus, the judiciary is gradually being transformed into a process removed somewhat from the traditional one followed for so many decades. A comparison of the traditional process with the transformed court process is shown below:

Traditional Process	**Transformed Process**
■ Dispute resolution	■ Problem-solving dispute avoidance
■ Legal outcome	■ Therapeutic outcome
■ Adversarial process	■ Collaborative process
■ Claim- or case-oriented	■ People-oriented
■ Rights-based	■ Interest- or needs-based
■ Emphasis placed on adjudication	■ Emphasis placed on postadjudication and alternative dispute resolution
■ Interpretation and application of law	■ Interpretation and application of social science
■ Judge as arbiter	■ Judge as coach
■ Backward looking	■ Forward looking
■ Precedent-based	■ Planning-based
■ Few participants and stakeholders	■ Wide range of participants and stakeholders
■ Individualistic	■ Interdependent
■ Legalistic	■ Common-sensical
■ Formal	■ Informal
■ Efficient	■ Effective

Thus, the orientation underlying therapeutic jurisprudence directs the judge's attention beyond the specific dispute before the court and toward the needs and circumstances of the individuals involved in the dispute (Rottman and Casey, 1999:14; Warren, 1998). All participants in the process of creating safer communities, including judges and probation officers, must stay focused on their areas of influence, ensure ongoing interagency training needs to become the norm, and continue a focus on policy development built upon reliable research. Many criminal justice organizations, including the courts and probation departments, are partnering increasingly with other criminal justice organizations in a greater effort to create safer communities and more law-abiding probationer-clients (Klinenberg, 2001).

SUMMARY

Probation derives from the word, *probatio,* which means a period of proving or trial and forgiveness. It was formally recognized by statute in Massachusetts in 1878 although a Massachusetts reformer, John Augustus, is credited with introducing it in the United States in 1841 as part of his philanthropy and temperance beliefs. Prior to the work of Augustus, judges issued judicial reprieves, where sentences imposed on offenders were suspended according to judicial discretion. Today the guiding philosophy of probation is rehabilitation, although some question whether rehabilitation actually occurs.

Several models for dealing with criminal offenders sentenced to probation were described. These include the traditional or treatment model, which conceptualizes crime as a disease which can be treated like an illness or physical ailment. Also known as the medical model, this offender view uses community services as rehabilitative mediums to improve offender skills and remedy their weaknesses which contributed to or caused their crimes initially. The rehabilitation model focuses upon equipping probationers with vocational and educational skills in order to qualify them for jobs that will induce more law-abiding behavior. The justice/due process model focuses on equitable sentences and fairness. The just-deserts model is intended to mete out punishment in direct proportion to the seriousness of the offense committed. The community model stresses reintegration into the community as a therapeutic endeavor designed to encourage probationers to participate in constructive community programs, including individual and/or group counseling, and treatments for various addictions, such as substance abuse.

Several functions of probation were examined. These functions closely parallel the models used to describe how offenders may be treated by professionals. The general functions of probation include crime control, community reintegration, punishment, public safety, and deterrence or prevention. It is difficult to profile probationers throughout the United States, because they cut across and represent virtually every offender category. However, about half of all probationers are on probation for felony offenses. About 20 percent of all probationers are female, although females make up about 7 percent of the inmate population of jails and prisons. A majority of probationers are white, with about a third of all probationers being black. About 12 percent of all probationers are Hispanic. Nearly 4 million persons were on probation in 2003.

The average length of probation for most offenders varies between 24 and 36 months, although those convicted of the most serious crimes have the longest probation lengths. The use of probation is also contingent upon the nature of the sentencing scheme in any jurisdiction. Guidelines-based sentencing schemes and mandatory sentencing procedures restrict judicial options in sentencing considerably. Nevertheless, most jurisdictions throughout the United States report greater use of probation annually.

Those most likely placed on probation include first-time offenders, particularly those convicted of nonviolent crimes. Currently, probation refers to any conditional nonincarcerative sentence imposed by judges for a criminal conviction. Probation differs from parole in that probationers do not ordinarily serve time in either a prison or jail, whereas parolees are former inmates of such institutions who have been released early by parole boards. Judges control probationers, whereas parolees are dependent upon parole board discretion for their early release from incarceration. Not everyone agrees that probation is a suitable punishment for criminal offenders. Many regard probation as nothing more than a wrist-slap for serious wrongdoing. However, proponents of probation argue that it prevents persons from succumbing to the criminogenic influence of prisons and jails. The stigma of being labeled as a criminal may compel some persons to commit new crimes. Probation means avoiding this criminal label to some extent. Probation also alleviates prison and jail overcrowding. Also, probation permits offenders to remain in their communities and become reintegrated to do lawful and useful activities. Opponents of probation argue that it gives criminals the attitude that they will not really be punished if they commit crimes.

Before criminal cases are prosecuted, prosecutors, judges, and offenders sometimes enter into agreements to have their cases disposed of through civil mechanisms. An umbrella term, restorative justice, has been used to depict any action that is primarily oriented toward doing justice by repairing the harm that has been caused by a crime. One civil mechanism involving offender mediation with one or more victims is alternative dispute resolution (ADR). ADR is a community-based, informal dispute settlement process. Usually targeted for involvement in such programs are misdemeanants, although low-level nonviolent felons may become involved in the ADR process, depending upon the circumstances. Also used are various victim-offender reconciliation projects (VORPs), where mediation is used. These projects are increasingly common methods for reducing case backlogs in prosecutors' offices.

Another option available to prosecutors is pretrial diversion. Diversion is a temporary suspension of a case from the criminal justice process while offenders are diverted to community-based agencies for treatment and/or supervision for a period of time. Once this process is completed, one's criminal record may be either downgraded to a lesser offense or completely expunged. Several functions of pretrial diversion were examined. These include permitting offenders to remain free in their communities in order to support their families; to make restitution to victims; to perform community service and pay fines; to reduce prison and jail overcrowding; and to reduce the glut of more serious criminal court cases.

At the hub of any pre-conviction action is the criminal court judge. Criminal court judges have broad discretionary powers and can impose any one of several different punishments. Judges may impose probation for offenders who are considered good candidates for such programs. These offenders are usually low-risk, nonviolent offenders with no prior criminal records.

Increasing numbers of offenders have substance abuse problems or mental illnesses, and judges can prescribe special conditions of probation in order for these persons to receive appropriate treatment from community-based agencies. Increasingly, the judiciary is moving toward greater collaboration with community agencies and organizations to deliver sentences that not only preserve public safety, but tend to hold offenders accountable to their victims in restorative ways.

QUESTIONS FOR REVIEW

1. What does probation mean? Where and when did it originate in the United States? What was the influence of John Augustus in the practice of probation in the United States?

2. What were judicial reprieves? In what sense did judicial reprieves precede the use of probation in the United States?

3. What are some differences between the justice and community models for dealing with offenders? How does the justice model reflect the get-tough philosophy of an increasingly skeptical public? In what way does the just-deserts model influence offender treatment?

4. What are the major functions of probation? What is the general philosophy of probation? Do you think this philosophy is being realized today? Why or why not?

5. What are some of the sociodemographic characteristics of probationers in the United States today?

6. What is meant by alternative dispute resolution? What are some of its functions?

7. What is pretrial diversion? What are some of the purposes of pretrial diversion? Why is it important to reduce stigmatization by granting offenders pretrial diversion?

8. What are two important optional consequences for those who successfully complete their diversionary programs?

9. What is a victim–offender reconciliation project and what are some of its characteristics?

10. What is the nature of judicial discretion in probation decision making? What are some of the special conditions probation judges may impose on offenders during the sentencing process?

SUGGESTED READINGS

Chappell, Richard A. (2002). "Looking Back at Federal Probation." *Federal Probation* 66:3–10.

Elm, Donna Lee (2003). "Limits on the Search Waiver Term." *APPA Perspectives* 27:42–45.

Frost, Gregory A. (2002). "Florida's Innovative Use of GPS for Community Corrections." *Journal of Offender Monitoring* 15:6–13.

Martin, Ginger (2003). "The Effectiveness of Community-Based Sanctions in Reducing Recidivism." *Corrections Today* 65:26–36.

Viano, Emilio C. (2000). "Restorative Justice for Offenders: A Return to American Traditions." *Corrections Today* 62:132–138.

Waters, Kathy L. (2003). "Probation, Parole, and Community Corrections: A Difficult Topic to Understand?" *Corrections Today* 66:16.

INTERNET CONNECTIONS

Abuse of Judicial Discretion
*http://www.constitution.org/abus/discretion/
judicial/judicial_discretion.htm*

American Arbitration Association
http://www.adr.org/index2.1.jsp

Association of Pretrial Professionals of
Florida
http://www.appf.org/

Colorado Council of Mediators
http://www.coloradomediation.org/

CPR Institute for Dispute Resolution
http://www.cpradr.org/homel.htm

Grundy County Probation Department
http://www.grundyco.com/probation.htm

History of American Probation and Parole
Association
*http://www.appa-net.org/about%20appa/
history.htm*

Massachusetts Council on Family Mediation
*http://www.divorcenet.com/ma-mediators
.html*

Montana Mediation Association
http://www.mtmediation.org/

National Association for Community
Mediation
http://www.nafcm.org/

National Association of Pretrial Services
Agencies
http://www.napsa.org/

National Association of Probation
Executives
http://www.napchome.org/

Pretrial Procedures
*http://www.uaa.alaska.edu/just/just110/
courts2.html*

Pretrial Services Resource Center
http://www.pretrial.org/

Probation philosophy
*http://www.appa-net.org/about%20appa/
probatio.htm*

CHAPTER 5 | *Programs for Probationers*

Chapter Outline

As the result of reading this chapter, the following objectives will be realized:

1. Describing standard probation programs, including their weaknesses and strengths.
2. Understanding several intensive supervised probation programs, including programs from Georgia, Idaho, and South Carolina, and several local jurisdictions.
3. Describing shock probation and split sentencing, including the philosophy and objectives of these sentencing alternatives.
4. Assessing the effectiveness of split sentencing and shock probation as related to client successes.
5. Understanding the weaknesses, strengths, functions and goals of boot camps as youth-oriented measures to improve accountability and discipline.
6. Describing the characteristics of female probationers and parolees.
7. Examining various programs for female inmates and community clients.
8. Describing the probation revocation process and highlighting various landmark U.S. Supreme Court cases that have influenced this process.
9. Describing interstate variations in probation revocation.

DO ANY OF THESE PERSONS QUALIFY FOR PROBATION?

• *Fryman was a California offender convicted of being under the influence of cocaine and possession of cocaine (People v. Fryman, 2002). In a presentence investigation report provided by the probation officer, it was disclosed that Fryman had nine prior felonies. The judge asked Fryman if it was true that he was convicted of nine prior felonies, and Fryman admitted these convictions in court at his sentencing hearing. At the time of Fryman's convictions for the drug charges, a drug treatment program had been established in various California jurisdictions, including Fryman's. The California statute pertaining to certain drug offenses, including Fryman's, makes probation the mandatory sentence for certain nonviolent drug possession offenses. Specifically, the court may not impose incarceration as an additional condition of probation. With Fryman's admission to nine prior felony convictions, should Fryman be incarcerated on the basis of these aggravating factors or should he be placed on probation? What would you do if you were the judge?*

• *Bruce G. was a California offender convicted of committing lewd and lascivious acts upon a child under the age of 14 (People v. Bruce G., 2002). California sex offenders who commit sex acts with children under age 14 are considered ineligible for probation unless the court makes five specific findings: (1) the defendant is the victim's natural parent; (2) a grant of probation to the defendant would be in the best interests of the child; (3) the defendant is amenable to treatment; (4) that the defendant is removed from the household of the victim; and (5) there is no threat of physical harm to the child victim if probation is granted. In the present case, the trial court declared Bruce G. ineligible for probation and sentenced him to prison. Bruce G. appealed. If you were a member of the appeals court, what decision would you make about the judge's sentence?*

• *Brown was a California offender convicted of vandalizing his wife's car after being involved in a domestic disturbance (People v. Brown, 2001). The judge ordered Brown placed on probation subject to the condition that he enroll in an anger management course and receive treatment to control himself. Brown claimed that he didn't need such treatment and refused to accept that probation condition. The trial judge sentenced Brown to six months in jail as an alternative to probation. Brown appealed, claiming that the judge abused his discretion when sentencing him to six months in jail, and that Brown was entitled to regular probation without special conditions. An appeals court heard Brown's case. If you were a member of the appeals court, how would you decide concerning the allegation that the judge abused his discretion when sentencing Brown to six months in jail?*

• *Tousignant was an Arizona offender convicted of solicitation to possess narcotics, his second drug conviction* (State v. Tousignant, *2002). The judge placed Tousignant on mandatory probation under conditions specified by the Arizona Drug Medicalization Prevention and Control Act. Subsequently Tousignant violated several conditions of his probation by failing to report to his probation officer and not participating in a prescribed drug program. The judge decided to resentence Tousignant to probation with other conditions, but Tousignant indicated that he wished to reject probation. The court accepted Tousignant's request to refuse probation and terminated his probation program as unsuccessfully completed. Tousignant was released from custody. The prosecution objected, contending that Tousignant should have received at least a 60-day jail term. If you were an appellate court member, how would you decide this matter? Should Tousignant have the right to refuse probation and be released?*

• *Cunningham was a federal offender convicted of defrauding a financial institution* (United States v. Cunningham, *2002). Pursuant to a plea agreement between the U.S. Attorney's Office and Cunningham, Cunningham entered a guilty plea to the charges, which included a provision to make restitution. At the time of sentencing, the judge imposed a term of supervised release on probation for Cunningham, which had not been mentioned in the plea agreement Cunningham had signed. Cunningham appealed the supervised release term of probation to a higher court. If you were a member of the appellate court, would you approve probation for Cunningham?*

WHAT HAPPENED?

• *Fryman was placed on probation in an appropriate drug treatment program. The court rejected the prosecution's argument that a lengthy prison term was justified in this case because of Fryman's nine prior felony convictions.*

• *The California appeals court reversed the judge's sentence, holding that the judge erred when he considered Bruce G. ineligible for probation. It was subsequently determined that the judge was misinformed about his discretionary authority and wrongfully imprisoned Bruce G. Bruce G. was placed on probation since the five specific findings existed in his case.*

• *The California appeals court sided with the judge in this case and held that since Brown had a right to refuse probation and undergo a sentence of incarceration instead, the judge had not abused his discretion. Moreover, the sentencing court was not relying solely on the prosecutor's recommendation, but on its own view of the seriousness of the crime in question and the sentence the crime deserved. Given the degree of violence evidenced by the defendant and his refusal to accept help with regard to his obvious violent tendencies, the court could not say that the sentence of six months was an abuse of judicial discretion.*

• *The Arizona Court of Appeals vacated the order of the trial judge, holding that any person who has been placed on probation and found to be in violation of probation shall have new conditions of probation established by the court. The court shall select additional conditions as it deems necessary, including intensified drug treatment, community service, intensive probation, home arrest, or any other such sanctions short of incarceration. A probation violator is not permitted simply to reject probation, nor is the trial court authorized to terminate the probation if unsuccessful.*

- *In Cunningham's case, the supervised release probation order had to be vacated. The original plea agreement failed to make any provisions for a probation program or any other type of supervised release for Cunningham. Because the government did not draft a broader waiver concerning the defendant's rights under the plea agreement, it was bound by the language contained in the agreement that it did draft, which excluded any type of supervised release or probation.*

INTRODUCTION

This chapter begins with an examination of **standard probation programs** and **intensive supervised probation programs (ISP)** as alternatives to incarceration. After a determination of guilt in criminal court, some convicted offenders are sentenced to probation for a period of years. Several probation programs will be featured. We have already described the history, philosophy, and functions of probation. In this chapter we will explore several popular probation options, including specific programs of intensive supervised probation. Several state programs will be featured, including Georgia, Idaho, and South Carolina. Other local programs will be described.

The final part of this chapter examines shock probation, split sentencing, and boot camps as increasingly used probation variations and options. The goals and effectiveness of shock probation will be presented. Boot camps will be described, including some of the more popular models developed in various states. Boot camp participants will be profiled. The effectiveness of boot camps will be discussed, together with several criticisms of it. The costs of these nonincarcerative options will be compared with the costs of incarceration, and several trends in diversion and probation will be described.

STANDARD PROBATION

Standard probation supervision in many jurisdictions is essentially no supervision at all. When offenders are convicted of one or more crimes, judges sentence a portion of these convicted offenders to a probation program in lieu of incarceration. These programs may or may not have conditions. Prospective probationers are required to sign a form outlining the conditions of their probation. Compliance with the probation program conditions is monitored closely by POs. However, these officers are often so overworked and understaffed that they cannot possibly oversee all of the activities of their probationer/clients. The caseloads or numbers of offenders POs are assigned to supervise vary among jurisdictions. Offender caseloads may be as high as 2,000 in some cities or counties, while in others, the caseloads may be 30 or fewer. Caseloads vary according to the type of program, the number of offenders, and the number of probation officers who are available. In many instances, hardcore recidivists, sex offenders, and other dangerous types of persons are placed on probation because of serious jail and prison overcrowding problems in more than a few jurisdictions (Stalans et al., 2001).

Standard probation is considered by many critics to be the most ineffective probationary form. Often, probationers may contact their probation officers by telephone and avoid face-to-face visits. Additionally, the requirements of their probationary programs are often less stringent compared with more intensive probation programs. The caseloads of POs in some jurisdictions are so high that officers cannot devote special attention to those offenders in the greatest need of special attention. This is the great failing of standard probation. There are no easy solutions to this problem. The probation department can only do so much in view of its staffing problems and varying clientele. And there is no relief in sight. The chances are that this probation form is growing rather than declining, despite high recidivism rates among standard probationers (Johnson, 2001).

Another problem with probation is that often those in administrative positions in probation departments attach greater importance to those things that enhance paper-processing, office efficiency, and career development rather than to those things that directly affect probationers. For instance, a study of the Massachusetts probation system was conducted. It involved a mail survey that yielded 500 responses. These responses were supplemented with interviews and field efforts involving 60 different criminal courts and more than 400 individuals. The resulting report addressed at least 60 different improvements in Massachusetts probation programs. But a more selective list of those improvements receiving the greatest priority and attention is significant, not because of what is included, but rather, what is excluded. The list of eleven priority concerns is as follows:

1. The review and redefinition of the overall mission of probation.
2. Career advancement opportunities for all personnel.
3. Greater emphasis on affirmative action.
4. Adjustments in the staffing level in some courts.
5. Increased training opportunities.
6. Substantially improved physical facilities.
7. Immediate attention to computerizing the central file.
8. Formation of citizen advisory groups.
9. Substantially improved social services for offenders.
10. Specific attention to the unique needs of the various trial court departments.
11. An immediate and forceful public education campaign to enlist support for improved social services from all branches of government and the general public (Spangenberg et al., 1987).

All but one of these improvement recommendations has to do with office policy, office efficiency, office work, office environment, public relations with the community, and office relations with courts. It is unclear about what is meant by "improved social services for offenders." Ideally, probation offices exist to supervise offenders. Many probation departments act as brokers between the agency and various community businesses, to identify potential workplaces where probationer-clients might find and maintain employment. Probationer assistance has always been a mission of probation departments. However, most of these key priorities are unrelated directly to assisting probationers, except for improving their social activities, whatever they may be. This may be one reason why some observers have declared that probation is in trouble (Cohn et al., 2002).

Federal and State Probation Orders

Standard probation among the states is quite diverse, although the conditions of probation share many of the same characteristics. The U.S. Probation Department oversees adult probationers as well as certain juveniles who have been sentenced by U.S. Magistrates or federal district court judges for federal crimes. As the result of the U.S. Sentencing Guidelines, the use of probation in the federal system since 1987 has been drastically reduced. In the preguideline period prior to 1987, probation was granted by federal district court judges about 65 percent of the time. Today the proportion of federal offenders who are granted probation is about 10–15 percent (U.S. Department of Justice, 2003). Below are some examples of standard probation orders. Figure 5.1 shows a U.S. district court probation form indicating specific standard conditions of probation. A reading of these conditions will disclose that federal standard probation and supervised release is geared toward crime control and heightening offender accountability. Besides paying fines and restitution, federal offenders must report periodically to the probation office. Probationers cannot possess firearms. They cannot leave their jurisdictions without permission from the federal court. Probationers must work at jobs unless otherwise involved in educational or vocational programs or undergoing psychological counseling for mental health or substance abuse problems. They must refrain from excessive use of alcohol, and they are forbidden from taking illegal drugs. Even their associations with others and the places they may visit are restricted. Probationers must make their dwellings available at any time for a PO's inspection and search for contraband. Also note in Figure 5.1 that space has been provided for judges to add special conditions of probation, which may include various community-based sanctions, including home confinement, electronic monitoring, day reporting, and other activities which are deemed necessary for an offender's rehabilitation and reintegration.

The conditions of standard probation for prospective Florida probationers are fairly standard for most other state standard probation programs. Under Florida probation guidelines supplied to judges, the following conditions do not require oral pronouncement in court by a judge. Rather, they are prepared in written form and a copy is submitted to the offender for his/her consent and signature. These conditions are as follows:

1. Probationer must report to the probation supervisor as directed.
2. Probationer must permit supervisors to visit him or her at his or her home or elsewhere.
3. Probationer must work faithfully at suitable employment insofar as may be possible.
4. Probationer must remain within a specified place.
5. Probationer must make reparation or restitution to the aggrieved party for the damage or loss caused by his or her offense in an amount to be determined by the court.
6. Probationer must make payment of the debt due and owing to a county or municipal detention facility for medical care, treatment, hospitalization, or transportation received by the probationer while in that detention facility.
7. Probationer must support his or her legal dependents to the best of his or her ability.

PROB 7A
(Rev. 10/89)   **Conditions of Probation and Supervised Release**

UNITED STATES DISTRICT COURT
FOR THE

_____

Name _____   Docket No. _____

Address _____

Under the terms of your sentence, you have been placed on probation/supervised release (strike one) by the Honorable _____ , United States District Judge for the District of _____ . Your term of supervision is for a period of _____ , commencing _____ .

While on probation/supervised release (strike one) you shall not commit another Federal, state, or local crime and shall not illegally possess a controlled substance. Revocation of probation and supervised release is mandatory for possession of a controlled substance.

CHECK IF APPROPRIATE:

☐ As a condition of supervision, you are instructed to pay a fine in the amount of _____ ; it shall be paid in the following manner _____ .

☐ As a condition of supervision, you are instructed to pay restitution in the amount of _____ to _____ ; it shall be paid in the following manner _____ .

☐ The defendant shall not possess a firearm or destructive device. Probation must be revoked for possession of a firearm.

☐ The defendant shall report in person to the probation office in the district to which the defendant is released within 72 hours of release from the custody of the Bureau of Prisons.

☐ The defendant shall report in person to the probation office in the district of release within 72 hours of release from the custody of the Bureau of Prisons.

It is the order of the Court that you shall comply with the following standard conditions:

(1)   You shall not leave the judicial district without permission of the Court or probation officer;

(2)   You shall report to the probation officer as directed by the Court or probation officer, and shall submit a truthful and complete written report within the first five days of each month;

(3)   You shall answer truthfully all inquiries by the probation officer and follow the instructions of the probation officer;

FIGURE 5.1   U.S. District Court conditions of probation and supervised release.

Source: Administrative Office of the U.S. Courts, 1997:21.

8. Probationer must make payment of debt due and owing to the state subject to modification based on change in circumstances.

9. Probationer must pay any application fee assessed and attorney's fees and costs assessed subject to modification based on change of circumstances.

10. Probationer must not associate with persons engaged in criminal activities.

(4)   You shall support your dependents and meet other family responsibilities;

(5)   You shall work regularly at a lawful occupation unless excused by the probation officer for schooling, training, or other acceptable reasons;

(6)   You shall notify the probation officer within 72 hours of any change in residence or employment;

(7)   You shall refrain from excessive use of alcohol and shall not purchase, possess, use, distribute, or administer any narcotic or other controlled substance, or any paraphernalia related to such substances, except as prescribed by a physician;

(8)   You shall not frequent places where controlled substances are illegally sold, used, distributed, or administered;

(9)   You shall not associate with any persons engaged in criminal activity, and shall not associate with any person convicted of a felony unless granted permission to do so by the probation officer;

(10)   You shall permit a probation officer to visit you at any time at home or elsewhere, and shall permit confiscation of any contraband observed in plain view by the probation officer;

(11)   You shall notify the probation officer within 72 hours of being arrested or questioned by a law enforcement officer;

(12)   You shall not enter into any agreement to act as an informer or a special agent of a law enforcement agency without the permission of the Court;

(13)   As directed by the probation officer, you shall notify third parties of risks that may be occasioned by your criminal record or personal history or characteristics, and shall permit the probation officer to make such notifications and to confirm your compliance with such notification requirement.

The special conditions ordered by the Court are as follows:

Upon a finding of violation of probation or supervised release, I understand that the Court may (1) revoke supervision or (2) extend the term of supervision and/or modify the conditions of supervision.

These conditions have been read to me. I fully understand the conditions, and have been provided a copy of them.

(Signed) _____   _____
                    Defendant   Date

_____   _____
U.S. Probation Officer/Designated Witness   Date

FIGURE 5.1   (Continued).

11. Probationer must submit to random testing as directed by the correctional probation officer or the professional staff of the treatment center where he or she is receiving treatment to determine the presence of alcohol or use of alcohol or controlled substances.

12. Probationer is prohibited from possessing, carrying, or owning any firearm unless authorized by the court and consented to by the probation officer.

13. Probationer is prohibited from using any intoxicants to excess or possessing any drugs or narcotics unless prescribed by a physician. The proba-

tioner shall not knowingly visit places where intoxicants, drugs, or other dangerous substances are unlawfully sold, dispensed, or used.

14. Probationer will attend an HIV/AIDS awareness program consisting of a class of not less than two hours or more than four hours in length, the cost of which shall be paid by the offender, if such a program is available in the county of the offender's residence.

15. Probationer shall pay not more than $1 per month during the term of probation to a nonprofit organization established for the sole purpose of supplementing the rehabilitative efforts of the Department of Corrections.

Florida also imposes certain special conditions of probation similar to the federal standard probation conditions. These are as follows:

1. Probationer is required to be intensively supervised and under probation officer surveillance.

2. Probationer is required to maintain specified contact with the probation officer.

3. Probationer shall be confined to an agreed-upon residence during hours away from employment and public service activities.

4. Probationer shall perform mandatory public service.

5. Probationer shall be supervised by means of an electronic monitoring device.

6. Probationer placed on electronic monitoring shall be monitored 24 hours a day.

7. Probationers placed on electronic monitoring will be subject to investigation and supervision by a probation officer 24 hours a day.

8. The court shall receive a diagnosis and evaluation of any probationer for appropriate community treatment (Florida Department of Corrections, 2003).

In the Florida Department of Corrections, for instance, several different types of public service or community service are prescribed. These include: (1) maintenance work on any property or building owned or leased by any state, county, or municipality or any nonprofit organization or agency; (2) maintenance work on any state-owned, county-owned, or municipally owned road or highway; (3) landscaping or maintenance work in any state, county, or municipal park or recreational area; (4) work in any state, county, or municipal hospital or any developmental services institution or other nonprofit organization or agency. For Florida offenders convicted of drug crimes, they may be required to pay a fine ranging from $500 to $10,000; perform at least 100 hours of public service; submit to routine and random drug testing; and participate, at their own expense, in some appropriate self-help group, such as Narcotics Anonymous, Alcoholics Anonymous, or Cocaine Anonymous, if available. In 2001, the Florida Department of Corrections reported that 145,098 offenders were on probation, with 107,078 or 81 percent on standard probation. The remainder of nonincarcerated clients were under other forms of supervision, such as community control, pretrial intervention, or post-prison release (Florida Department of Corrections, 2003:1).

Figure 5.2 shows a monthly supervision report used by the U.S. Probation Office that must be completed by all probationers under federal supervision. The form is quite detailed and takes probationers time to complete. It contains information about their residence and contact data, employment, vehicle(s) owned or operated, finances (including checking accounts), spousal information (if applicable), and a host of other questions. These have to do with whether the probationer was arrested or contacted by the police for any reason; any pending charges against the probationer; any arrests of household members during the past month; drug/alcohol possession or use; whether the probationer left the jurisdiction at any time, and the reason(s) for such departures, if any; fines assessed and their payment; community service work performed; and mental health, alcohol, or drug aftercare compliance, if ordered by the court. The probationer must sign this form, certifying its authenticity. Any false statements may subject the probationer

PROB 8
(Rev. 09/00)

U.S. PROBATION OFFICE
MONTHLY SUPERVISION REPORT FOR THE MONTH OF _____, 20 _____.

Name	Court Name (if different):

PART A: RESIDENCE (If new address, attach copy of lease/purchase agreement)

Street Address, Apt. Number:	Own or Rent?	Home Phone:	Cellular Phone:	Pager:
City, State, Zip Code:		Persons Living With You:		
Secondary Residence	Own or Rent?	Did you move during the month? ☐ Yes ☐ No		
Mailing Address (if different):	E-Mail Address	If yes, date moved: _____ Reason for Moving:		

PART B: EMPLOYMENT (If unemployed, list source of support under Part D.)

Name, Address, Phone No. of Employer:	Name of Immediate Supervisor:	Is your employer aware of your criminal status: ☐ Yes ☐ No
	How many days of work did you miss? _____ Why?	
	Position Held:	Gross Wages:	Normal Work Hours:
Did you change jobs? ☐ Yes ☐ No Were you terminated? ☐ Yes ☐ No	If changed jobs or terminated, state when and why:	

PART C: VEHICLES (List all vehicles owned or driven by you)

1. Year/Make/Model/Color:	Mileage:	Tag Number:	Owner:
		Vehicle I.D.#:	
2. Year/Make/Model/Color:	Mileage:	Tag Number:	Owner:
		Vehicle I.D.#:	

PART D: MONTHLY FINANCIAL STATEMENT

Net Earnings from Employment: (Attach Proof of Earnings) _____	Do you rent or have access to: a post office box? ☐ Yes ☐ No a safe deposit box? ☐ Yes ☐ No
Other Cash Inflows: _____	a storage space? ☐ Yes ☐ No
TOTAL MONTHLY CASH INFLOWS: _____	Name and Address of Location: Box No. or Space
TOTAL MONTHLY CASH OUTFLOWS: _____	

Do you have checking account(s)? ☐ Yes ☐ No Bank Name: _____ Account No: _____ Balance: _____ Do you have savings account(s)? ☐ Yes ☐ No Bank Name: _____ Account No: _____ Balance: _____ Attach a complete listing of all other financial account information, if you have multiple accounts.	Does your spouse, significant other, or dependant have a checking or savings account that you enjoy the benefits of or make occasional contributions toward? ☐ Yes ☐ No Bank Name: _____ Account No: _____ Balance: _____

List all expenditures over $500 (including e.g., goods, services, or gambling losses)			
Date	Amount	Method of Payment	Description of Item
_____	_____	_____	_____
_____	_____	_____	_____
_____	_____	_____	_____

FIGURE 5.2 U.S. Probation Office Monthly Supervision Report.

PART E: COMPLIANCE WITH CONDITIONS OF SUPERVISION DURING THE PAST MONTH	
Were you questioned by any law enforcement officers? □ Yes □ No If yes, date: _____ Agency: _____ Reason: _____	Were you arrested or named as a defendant in any criminal case? □ Yes □ No If yes, when and where? _____ Charges: _____ Disposition: _____

(Attach copy of citation, receipt, charges, disposition, etc.)

Were any pending charges disposed of during the month? □ Yes □ No If yes, date: _____ Court: _____ Disposition: _____	Was anyone in your household arrested or questioned by law enforcement? □ Yes □ No If yes, whom? _____ Reason: _____ Disposition: _____
Do you have any contact with anyone having a criminal record? □ Yes □ No If yes, whom? _____	Do you possess or have access to a firearm? □ Yes □ No If yes, why? _____
Did you possess or use any illegal drugs? □ Yes □ No If yes, type of drug: _____	Did you travel outside the district without permission? □ Yes □ No If yes, when and where? _____

Do you have a special assessment, restitution, or fine? □ Yes □ No If yes, amount paid during the month:		
Special Assessment: _____	Restitution: _____	Fine: _____

NOTE: ALL PAYMENTS TO BE MADE BY MONEY ORDER (POSTAL OR BANK) OR CASHIER'S CHECK ONLY.

Do you have community service work to perform? □ Yes □ No Number of hours completed this month: _____ Number of hours missed: _____ Balance of hours remaining: _____	Do you have drug, alcohol, or mental health aftercare? □ Yes □ No If yes, did you miss any sessions during this month? □ Yes □ No Did you fail to respond to phone recorder instructions? □ Yes □ No If yes, why? _____
WARNING: ANY FALSE STATEMENTS MAY RESULT IN REVOCATION OF PROBATION, SUPERVISED RELEASE, OR PAROLE, IN ADDITION TO 5 YEARS IMPRISONMENT, A $250,000 FINE, OR BOTH. **(18 U.S.C. § 1001)**	I CERTIFY THAT ALL INFORMATION FURNISHED IS COMPLETE AND CORRECT. _____ _____ SIGNATURE DATE
REMARKS: _____ _____ U.S. Probation Officer Date	**RECEIVED** _____Mail _____OC _____HC _____CC **RETURN TO:**

FIGURE 5.2 *(Continued)*

to a revocation proceeding later. This document is frequently the only contact the U.S. Probation Office has with some of its probationer-clients.

One of the major problems with standard probation is high offender recidivism. Most jurisdictions throughout the United States report recidivism rates of 60 percent or higher for offenders who are placed on standard probation. Some attempt has been made to reduce these high recidivism rates by establishing programs that involve much more intensive offender monitoring and supervision. These programs are categorically called intensive supervised probation (ISP) programs.

INTENSIVE SUPERVISED PROBATION (ISP)

An intensive supervised probation (ISP) program or an intensive probation supervision (IPS) program is an increasingly common method of supervising offenders who require closer monitoring. Also known as traditional probation, ISP is a type of intermediate punishment, since it is somewhere between standard probation and incarceration. One short-range goal of intermediate punishments is to reduce prison and jail overcrowding. There is government endorsement of this ISP program goal as well as support within the professional community (Bond-Maupin and Maupin, 2002). Other types of intermediate punishments include electronic monitoring, home incarceration, **community-based supervision,** and **community-based corrections** (Maloney, Bazemore, and Hudson, 2001). Offenders are assigned probation officers who arrange frequent contacts with their clients on a face-to-face basis. These contacts may be weekly, a few times a week, or daily. ISP is a special form of traditional probation where the intensity of offender monitoring is greatly increased and the conditions of probation are considerably more stringent. The logic is that the greater amount of contact between the probationer and PO will function as an incentive for greater offender compliance with program requirements. Known in some circles as smart sentencing, ISP often involves greater client/officer contact, which may mean that POs are more frequently accessible to clients if they are experiencing personal or financial difficulties, social stresses, or other problems (Johnson, 2001).

There is considerable variation in ISP programs among jurisdictions, since probation officer caseloads vary. These caseloads depend on the financial resources of the jurisdiction and local definitions of the maximum number of clients probation officers must supervise. ISP in many jurisdictions limits the number of offender-clients to 30 per probation officer. In some jurisdictions, the maximum number of offenders supervised may be limited to 15 or 20 (Camp and Camp, 2003). Also influencing one's caseload is the nature of supervisory technology used. In Florida, for example, CrimeTrax is used as an advanced method of tracking offenders through the use of global positioning satellite (GPS) technology. Using this method of tracking offenders, Florida POs can locate particular offenders on particular streets at certain times of the day or night. While GPS isn't yet foolproof, it does provide a futuristic supervisory option which is likely to be adopted by more jurisdictions in future years. Thousands of staff hours may be saved by GPS tracking (Frost, 2002).

Another feature of ISP programs is that they are often established and implemented at the county level rather than at the state level. Thus, within any particular state, there may be wide variations in ISP programming from county to county. More than a few states continue to operate standardized ISP programs, however. Georgia was one of the first states to implement ISP in 1982. Georgia's ISP program, as well as the programs of several other jurisdictions, are featured in a subsequent section of this chapter.

ISP programs have received mixed reactions among the public. One problem is that many of these programs, their objectives, and the ways they are being implemented are misunderstood by community residents and interpreted in the most unfavorable light. Despite the fact that these programs monitor probationers more closely than standard probation supervision and are tougher on offenders, many citizens believe that offender freedom in the community is not an acceptable punishment. There is no standard definition for ISP, although all ISP programs feature small offender caseload sizes. "Intensive" is a relative term, but

the basic idea is to increase the intensity of supervision for designated probationers in order to satisfy public demand for applying a just punishment. Some
persons distinguish between standard probation and intensive surveillance coupled with substantial community service and/or restitution. But probably the
best way of conceptualizing what ISP means is to identify ISP program components which have been operationalized in several states (Harris and Lo, 2002).

Three Conceptual Models of ISP

Before examining several state ISP programs, three conceptual models of ISP
will be described. These models will help to explain not only interstate variations in ISP programs but also their individual rationales. These include (1) the
justice model; (2) the limited risk control model; and (3) the traditional,
treatment-oriented model. Table 5.1 contrasts these three models and highlights
several of their important features.

TABLE 5.1

The Justice, Limited Risk Control, and Traditional Treatment-Oriented Models Compared by Intensive Supervised Probation Factors.

Program Elements	JM	LRCM	TTOM
1. Recommended caseload	"low"	10	"low"
2. Daily contact with probation officer. . .	Yes	No	No
3. Weekly contact with probation officer. . .	No	Yes	20 times per month, variable
4. Community service. . .	Yes	Optional	Yes
5. Restitution. . .	Yes	Optional	Yes
6. Field visits. . .	Yes	Yes	Optional
7. Probation fees. . .	Yes	Yes	Optional
8. Curfew. . .	Yes	Optional	Yes
9. Shock probation. . .	Optional	No	Yes
10. Offender volunteers for program. . .	No	No	Yes
11. Periodic committee review of offender progress. . .	No	Yes	Yes
12. Use of risk assessment devices. . .	No	Yes	Optional
13. Minimum time in ISP.	6 mo.	Individual, but 90 days minimum	12 mo.
14. Normal program length. . .	6–36 mo.	Variable	18 mo.
15. House arrest. . .	Optional	No	Optional
16. Fines. . .	Optional	Optional	Yes
17. Counseling. . .	No	Probably	Probably
18. Voc/Rehab Training.	No	Probably	Probably

JM = Justice Model; LRCM = Limited Risk Control Model; and TTOM = Traditional, Treatment-Oriented Model.
[Source: James M. Byrne. "The Control Controversy: A Preliminary Examination of Intensive Supervision Programs in the United States." *Federal Probation* **50**:4–16, 1986.] [public domain]

The Justice Model.   The justice model makes no pretense of being anything other than punishment-centered, but not to the point of being unfair to offenders. The penalty should fit the crime committed, and the offender should receive his just deserts. This model emphasizes (a) daily contact between offenders and probation officers, (b) community service orders, and/or (c) restitution. No counseling is required, nor is any participation in any specific rehabilitative program (Maxwell and Gray, 2000).

The Limited Risk Control Model.   The **limited risk control model** is based on anticipated future criminal conduct and uses risk assessment devices to place offenders within an effective control range. This model fits a presumptive sentencing format specifying ranges of penalties or varying control levels depending upon risk assessment scores (Karp, 2001). Thus, judges would rely on predictions of probable future criminal conduct and sentence offenders to one of three degrees of community supervision (e.g., minimum, regular, and intensive). Compared with the justice model, the limited risk control model appears more flexible and provides for periodic reassessments of predicted offender behaviors and corresponding adjustments of degrees of community supervision.

The Traditional, Treatment-Oriented Model.   The **traditional treatment-oriented model** stresses traditional rehabilitative measures that seek to reintegrate the offender into the community through extensive assistance. While this model may include elements of the justice and limited risk control models, its primary aim is long-term change in offender behavior. Therefore, this model includes strategies such as developing individual offender plans for life in the community such as work, study, or community service, full-time employment and/or vocational training, and/or using community sponsors or other support personnel to provide assistance and direction for offenders (Bowen et al., 2002).

No states currently use the justice model exclusively. States using the limited risk control model include Oregon and Massachusetts. Several other states have initiated ISP programs as well. Georgia created an ISP program in 1982. Two other state programs were commenced in Idaho and South Carolina in 1984. The Georgia, Idaho, and South Carolina plans are being featured here because (1) they represent three different approaches to the problem of managing probationers, and (2) other states have incorporated many of the elements of these programs into their own ISP programs (Petersilia, 1998). Several local ISP programs are also reviewed.

The Georgia ISP Program

In the 1970s Georgia had the highest per capita incarceration rate in the United States (Erwin, 1986:17). Because of prison overcrowding and the spill-over effect into Georgia's jails to house their prison overflow, Georgia was desperate to devise a workable probation program. After spending much money on feasibility studies and considering alternatives to incarceration, Georgia's ISP was put into effect in 1982.

Georgia Program Elements.   The **Georgia Intensive Supervision Probation Program (GISPP)** has established several punitive intensive probation conditions that parallel the justice model. Three phases of the program were outlined

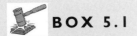

BOX 5.1

Brett M. Judd

Senior Probation and Parole Officer, Idaho Department of Corrections, Community Correction

Statistics:

B.A. (social work, sociology), Idaho State University; NRA police handgun and shotgun, tactical handgun firearms instructor; Glock firearms instructor and armorer; Master Facilitator for A Framework for Breaking Barriers, through Gordon Graham and Company

Background:

I entered college with the intent of obtaining a degree in psychology and entering practice as a youth and family counselor. I changed to social work after seeing the need for a more global intervention focus not offered in the psychology field. I have come to understand that you cannot change an individual's behavior without work on the entire social system associated with that individual.

While completing my degree, I worked with at-risk youth in a special school setting. We implemented global theories as the whole family of the student entered counseling and received intervention to change the social system and upbringing of the child. The educational focus was not based on the hard-line instruction of fact, but rather the understanding of the process. I remember a day when I entered the 14–18 year-old class to hear the teacher working through fractions using partial cans of beer as the fractional medium. During the instructional day, we would engage the students in open discussion groups. These were topic driven, based on the individual needs of students. During this time I realized the importance of the individual and that every case is different. This has been a great benefit to me as a probation officer.

Idaho changed the direction of juvenile intervention in the mid-1990s. It has become much more punitive and less corrections based. I was graduating from college and needed a job. I was contemplating continuing on with my schooling and either entering into a master's of counseling program or the Police Academy. That is when I read an announcement for Adult Probation. It described a merging of both law enforcement and social work. The job description fit in with my desires. I chose to test and nine months later was hired.

Work Experiences:

Much of the time, the work is uneventful. I lead behavioral change and self-analysis groups in the county jail and in the office. This is a very rewarding part of the job. I get the chance to interact with individuals in a way that would not be expected from a probation officer. We work on ways to change and dismantle the barriers that keep them involved in self-destructive behavior. There is a great satisfaction at knowing I have had a hand in helping someone move away from criminal behaviors.

Shortly after being hired I had the opportunity to obtain my firearms certification and training. This is very rewarding and has been a major part of my career. Officer safety is a serious topic and I believe that we often allow ourselves to become complacent in the area. Many of the people we work with would not consider violence in their interactions, but there have been occasions when tactical skills have been an asset. This also helps keep my focus balanced so that I do not become too one-sided in my approach. Probation work is a strange blend of both law enforcement and social work. We have to be flexible enough to move between both fields. In one arrest where weapons were drawn and drugs and manufacturing materials were located, I was still able to engage

BOX 5.1 (Continued)

my offender in a civil and counseling manner after controlling the situation. Without building the rapport prior to the event or being able to shift roles when needed, the current relationship I have with this individual would not be possible. After spending time in the penitentiary, this individual is out and doing very well.

Advice to Students:

If you are considering a career in probation, keep an open mind. The work can be very rewarding and you can see great change in the lives of those you work with. A professor I had in school taught me a lesson that I will always remember. He said that for many of us, the difference between the criminal and the non-criminal is about two minutes. He meant that if we truly analyze our own lives, we would find behaviors that are currently or were not in keeping

with the law at times in our life, e.g., drinking at a party and driving home. Understanding that I am no different from the offender has helped me to deal more equitably with someone during the changes probation is to create.

Also, come to understand addiction. Most of the offenders under supervision are on for a substance abuse-related problem. However, addiction is deeper than drugs and alcohol. Hyrum Smith of Franklin Covey teaches that addiction is any "compulsive behavior with short-term benefits and long-term destruction." This includes the way we spend money, deal with relationships, and console our emotions with food. Understanding this has also been a great asset to me as I help others to create changes in their lives. In reality, we all have addictions and must work to overcome them.

according to the level of control, Phase I being the most intensive supervision and Phase III being the least intensive. These standards include:

1. Five face-to-face contacts per week in Phase I (decreasing to two face-to-face contacts per week in Phase III).
2. 132 hours of mandatory community service.
3. Mandatory curfew.
4. Mandatory employment.
5. Weekly check of local arrest records.
6. Automatic notification of arrest elsewhere via State Crime Information Network listings.
7. Routine alcohol and drug screens.
8. Assignment of one probation officer and one surveillance officer to 25 probationers or one probation officer and two surveillance officers to 40 probationers (surveillance officers have corrections backgrounds or law enforcement training and make home visits, check arrest records, and perform drug/alcohol tests among other duties).
9. Probation officer determines individualized treatment (e.g., counseling, vocational/educational training) for offender.
10. Probation officer is liaison between court and offender and reports to court regularly on offender's progress from personal and surveillance observations and records.

The Successfulness of the Georgia ISP Program.   The successfulness of the GISPP thus far has been demonstrated by low recidivism rates among offenders under ISP (recidivism rates are almost always used as measures of probation program effectiveness). Compared with paroled offenders and others supervised by standard probation practices, the GISPP participants had systematically lower recidivism rates depending upon their risk classification. Classifications of risk consisted of low risk, medium risk, high risk, and maximum risk. Reconvictions for these groups were 25 percent, 16 percent, 28 percent, and 26 percent respectively compared with parolees who had considerably higher reconviction rates for all risk groupings.

The Idaho ISP Program

The **Idaho Intensive Supervised Probation Program** was launched as a pilot project in 1982 (Brown, 1992:7). Initially, a team consisting of one PO and two surveillance officers closely supervised a small group of low-risk offenders who normally would have been sent to prison. The program was quite successful. In October, 1984, Idaho established a state-wide ISP program with legislative approval. This step was seen as a major element in the get-tough-on-crime posture taken by the state.

Elements of the Idaho ISP Program.   When implemented in 1984, the ISP program operated in teams, consisting of two POs and a Section Supervisor responsible for supervising a maximum of 25 high-risk clients. This team was required to work evenings and in shifts. POs carried firearms while performing their duties. The court-referred clientele for these POs and supervisors consisted of felony probationers or parolees who were classified at a maximum level of supervision. All clients had lengthy criminal records of violent crimes and in need of intensive supervision. Clients were obligated to stay in their programs for four to six months and had to complete two major phases of supervision.

The first phase consisted of seven face-to-face visits per week, four of which occurred in the clients' homes. Phase II reduced the number of face-to-face contacts with clients per week to four. Both phases included random, day or night checks for possible curfew violations, drug and/or alcohol abuse, and any other possible program violation. Probationers who violated one or more program conditions received either verbal warnings or informal staff hearings, where several additional program conditions might be imposed, including community service. Perhaps those probationers in Phase II would be returned to Phase I.

Idaho ISP Program Effectiveness.   Between 1984 and 1992, the Idaho Department of Corrections has processed 2,487 clients. About 63 percent of these probationers have completed the program successfully. During 1992, 179 clients were under ISP of one form or another. The overall rate of technical violations, such as curfew violations, drinking, and unauthorized travel, was only about 28 percent, while the rate of new felonies charged was only 1.3 percent (Brown, 1992:7-8). The major result of this ISP program has been a drastic reduction in new convictions for felonies among successful program participants.

The South Carolina ISP Program

In order to ease prison overcrowding in South Carolina, a legislative mandate was given in 1984 to establish an ISP program for state-wide use. The South Carolina Department of Probation, Parole, and Pardon Services (DPPPS) was responsible for the **South Carolina Intensive Supervised Probation Program** implementation. The primary aims of the ISP program were to heighten surveillance of participants, increase PO/client contact, and increase offender accountability. Like Idaho, South Carolina started its ISP program as a pilot or experimental project. Their program goal was to involve 336 probationers during the first year of operation. By 1991, 13,356 offenders had been processed through the ISP program. During that year, South Carolina was supervising 1,589 probationers and 480 parolees (Cavanaugh, 1992:1,5). By 2002 over 30,000 offenders had been processed through the South Carolina ISP program (South Carolina Department of Corrections, 2003).

South Carolina ISP Program Elements.   Offenders placed in South Carolina ISP programs must pay a $10 per week supervision fee. Supervision fees are not particularly unusual in many ISP programs. Clients are supervised by specialized POs known as intensive agents with caseloads of no more than 35 offenders at any given time. Weekly face-to-face contacts with offenders are mandatory, together with visits to neighbors, friends, employers, and service providers of probationers. POs in the South Carolina program act as liaisons between the private sector and their clients, lining up job possibilities. Thus, POs do some employment counseling when necessary.

Offender Classification for Participation.   Each offender is classified according to risk and needs. Then POs tailor individual program requirements to fit these offender needs. The level of supervision over particular offenders is influenced by their particular risk level determined through risk assessment. The goal of DPPPS POs is to provide offenders with the proper balance of control and assistance. Thus, the ISP program is also supplemented with curfews, electronic monitoring, and house arrest or home incarceration elements for certain high-risk offenders. Offenders sentenced to home incarceration are in a program known as ISP Home Detention and confined to their homes from 10:00 P.M. to 6:00 A.M. excepting authorized leaves from home by their supervising POs. Offenders are subject to random visits from POs, day or night. Clients must work or seek employment, undergo medical, psychiatric or mental health counseling or other rehabilitative treatment, attend religious services, or perform community service work (Cavanaugh, 1992:5-6).

The length of their stay in this ISP program varies from three to six months. Electronic monitoring is used to supplement this program. Offenders are placed on electronic monitoring and must wear an electronic wristlet or anklet for the first 30 days. After successfully completing the first 30-day period of ISP, they are taken off electronic monitoring and subject to a 60-day period of simple voice verification. Such verification occurs by telephone means, where POs call offenders at particular times to verify their whereabouts. Offenders give requested information over the telephone, and electronic devices verify whether the voice pattern transmitted matches that of the offender being called.

Like POs in the Idaho program, POs in the DPPPS work in shifts, in order that offenders can be checked both day and night. Thus, there are First and Second Shift Surveillance Teams. The DPPPS also uses paraprofessionals in Operation Specialist capacities. These persons assist POs in performing surveillance work, particularly in the larger counties throughout the state (Cavanaugh, 1992:6).

Effectiveness of the South Carolina ISP Program.   The ISP program in South Carolina appears successful. Less than 10 percent of the probationers who have participated in the South Carolina ISP program have had their programs revoked due to new offenses rather than for technical program violations. Using the arbitrary 30 percent recidivism standard for determining whether a program is successful, the South Carolina ISP program is successful for both its probationers as well as its parolees.

Criticisms of the Georgia, Idaho, and South Carolina ISP Programs

A general criticism leveled at any ISP program is that it does not achieve its stated goals. Some observers say that victims are ignored in probation decision making. Yet others say that ISP programs contribute to net-widening, by bringing certain offenders under the ISP program umbrella who really do not need to be intensively supervised (Maxwell and Gray, 2000). Simultaneously, an equally vocal aggregate of critics praises ISP for alleviating prison inmate overcrowding and providing a meaningful option to incarceration (Lemov, 1992:134). Among the ISP program components in certain jurisdictions that have drawn criticism have been supervision fees (Mills, 1992:10). These costs are normally incurred by probationer-clients. But even this particular issue is hotly debated. The controversy over ISP programs will likely remain unresolved for many years.

Regardless of their disputed effectiveness, the fact is that different ISP programs have been developed and used in other states. For example, several elements of the Georgia model have been adopted by Colorado, Nevada, Oregon, and Washington. These states have not copied Georgia precisely in their probation guidelines, but their newly developed programs resemble the Georgia program to a high degree.

The Georgia program has been both praised and criticized. First, it has demonstrated low rates of recidivism. Convicted criminals who participate in the program do not commit new offenses with great frequency. The ISP program has alleviated some prison overcrowding by diverting a large number of offenders to probationary status rather than incarceration. The most important criticism of Georgia's program credibility pertains to those selected for inclusion in it. Fewer than 30 percent of the offenders placed on ISP in Georgia consist of maximum-risk cases. Thus, most Georgia ISP probationers are those least likely to recidivate anyway (Petersilia, 1999a). Also, the division of labor between probation officers and surveillance officers has not been as clear as originally intended. Surveillance officers perform many of the same functions as standard probation officers. Therefore, it is difficult to formulate a clear caseload picture for regular Georgia probation officer functions.

Another criticism is that Georgia handpicks its clients for ISP involvement. The selection process deliberately includes low- to medium-risk offenders with the greatest potential to succeed. Deliberately excluded are the most serious offenders with the least success likelihood. In fact, some researchers have said the current composition of ISP clients consists of persons who would have been diverted from prison anyway (Petersilia, 1999b). In order for ISP programs to be effective, more high-risk offenders ought to be targeted for inclusion rather than those most likely to succeed (Dickey and Wagner, 1990).

The Idaho and South Carolina ISP programs exhibit relatively low rates of recidivism for their participating offenders. Compared with the Georgia program, these programs rely fairly heavily on the use of risk assessment instruments for recruiting clients and determining their level of intensive supervision. The South Carolina program element involving the payment of a $10 per week supervision fee is only a token amount, but it nevertheless is regarded by staff as heightening offender accountability and serves as a reminder that they are paying for their crimes, even if the payment is hardly excessive. POs in both Idaho and South Carolina perform functions as liaisons when they unite their clients with receptive employers. Further, the integrated use of home confinement and electronic monitoring, together with frequent face-to-face visits and checks by supervising POs, means that offender control is heightened.

Other ISP Programs

The Delaware and Virginia ISP Programs.   The Bureau of Community Custody and Supervision for Delaware has established several programs for offenders requiring more intensive supervision. This Bureau seeks to (1) promote public safety through effective supervision of offenders placed in the community; (2) provide supervision, programs, and treatment services that promote long-term, self-sufficient, law-abiding behavior by offenders; and (3) support efforts to make victims whole (Delaware Department of Corrections, 2003:1).

Actually, Delaware has several supervision levels—Levels I, II, and III—for its offenders assigned to the community. Level I is for first-time offenders who pose little or no risk to the community of reoffending or harming others. They are required to pay a fine, make restitution, and attend a first offenders program. Offenders are monitored during their participation in designated programs, such as anger management and individual/group counseling, and progress reports are made routinely to the court. An advanced supervision level, Level II, requires systematic contacts with probation officers based on risk/needs assessments. Level II probation officers serve in traditional counseling roles.

Level III is the Delaware ISP program. The officer–client ratio is 1:25, purposely low so that POs can closely supervise adult offenders for the purpose of crime control. Supervision is frequent and intense. Recommendations are made periodically by the POs about whether to move cases upward or downward in terms of Level III behavioral requirements and client progress. For those offenders who are unable to comply fully with the Level III requirements, a 4th level, Level IV, is a house arrest program, where offenders are restricted to an approved residence in which specific sanctions are imposed. Electronic monitoring is used as well. Day reporting centers are located in strategic places throughout the community, and community work programs are operated where offenders can perform various types of labor for nonprofit organizations in order to satisfy special conditions of supervision or to be relieved of court-ordered fines or assessments. The Delaware ISP program, reflecting behavioral requirements consistent with those found in Georgia, South Carolina, New Jersey, and Idaho, appears successful with a recidivism rate of less than 20 percent (Delaware Department of Corrections, 2003).

The Virginia ISP program is similar to that of Delaware, but without the different supervisory levels. Most program requirements are in place similar to those of Georgia, South Carolina, and Idaho. Virginia ISP involves enhanced surveillance of offenders through increased contacts with offenders and in the community. Services provided to offenders include random urinalyses, home electronic monitoring or telephonic monitoring, curfews, treatment agency referrals and follow-ups, employment, and home checks. Upon completion of ISP, offenders are returned to conventional probation supervision. Virginia initiated its program in 1985 and it is available statewide. Interestingly, unlike Georgia and several other state programs, eligibility for the Virginia program deliberately includes high-risk offenders who require supervision, which is more stringent than conventional supervision. These high-risk offenders include community corrections' facilities graduates, predatory sex offenders, and hate group members. The recidivism rate for the Virginia program is less than 30 percent (Virginia Department of Corrections, 2004:1).

The Stearns County, Minnesota, ISP Program.   Stearns County, Minnesota established an ISP program in 1997 through its Adult Supervision Unit (ASU). The purpose of the ASU is to supervise adult offenders placed on probation or supervised release. Only offenders who are classified as either medium- or high-level risk or needs are managed by this unit. Caseloads of POs consist of a mixture of adult felony, gross misdemeanor, and misdemeanor probationers, as well as those offenders on supervised release from a state correctional facility. Contact standards involve frequent face-to-face field visits as well as frequent office visits. POs also work with offender-clients to devise case plans and make referrals to local treatment programs based on court requirements. These programs include substance abuse intervention, ranging from educational programs to inpatient treatment; domestic abuse education; anger management; mental health interventions; referrals for financial assistance; and education on financial management. A cognitive intervention component is included as well (County of Stearns, 2003).

All offender-clients take a risk/needs assessment inventory. Those having high scores on this inventory are required to report every month for supervision. Those with lower scores report on a quarterly basis. All offenders complete a monthly report to notify staff of any changes in their residence or employment. POs meet individually with each offender to review case plans, discuss any issues, and make necessary referrals to community-based programs based on each offender's needs.

The ISP nature of the Stearns County program is accomplished through group meetings, required individual sessions with therapists, and regular individual contact with POs at homes and workplaces. The program relies heavily on field contact. Program participants are required to be in an approved outpatient treatment program. All offenders convicted of a sexual or sex-related offense are assigned to the Sex Offender Program (SOP). SOP employs a specialized approach. Three elements of this approach are (1) sex offender-specific treatment to help offenders learn to develop internal controls; (2) probation supervision and monitoring to exert control over offenders; and (3) polygraph examinations to obtain complete sexual history information and monitor a participant's fantasies or behaviorally specific access to victims.

Community service work (CSW) holds both adult and juvenile offenders accountable for their crimes by having them spend a specified number of hours serving the community or crime victims through uncompensated work in lieu of a fine, local correctional fees, restitution, or jail. CSW may also be ordered as a condition of probation by the court. Eligibility requirements are that participants must admit to having committed an eligible offense in Stearns County. Eligible offenses include certain felony, gross misdemeanor, or misdemeanor crimes, other than crimes against the person. The ISP program is designed to provide an alternative for repeat DUI offenders, which combines ISP with chemical dependency treatment. It enhances public safety through the use of frequent, random supervision, drug testing and monitoring techniques. Electronic monitoring and house arrest are also used for specified intervals. Participants must transition through five phases of progressively diminishing levels of supervision and programming. Completion of the full ISP program takes from 12 to 20 months.

A unique element of the Stearns County ISP program is the services available to the female offender population in the county. These services include family planning centers; battered women's self-help and support groups; sexual abuse support groups; shelters for abused and pregnant women; family counseling and parenting; in-patient and out-patient chemical dependency treatment; chemical dependency halfway house care; individual counseling on gender-specific issues; health care; adult basic education; employment and job training; day care; post-secondary education; and gender-specific programming for at-risk females. Recidivism rates associated with the Stearns County program have been 25 percent less among participating offenders (County of Stearns, 2003).

The Cook County, Illinois, ISP Program.   The Adult Probation Department (APD) of Cook County, Illinois started an ISP program in 1984 as a prison diversionary program for high-risk offenders convicted of serious felonies. The program stresses increased surveillance and intervention. Probationers placed under ISP are required to comply with rigorous conditions that include frequent reporting, curfews, drug testing, and community service, as well as any other special conditions deemed important by the court. The APD conducts eligibility screenings on cases recommended for ISP. An ISP officer begins the screening process by determining a defendant's suitability for the program. This process includes conducting a social history investigation, reviewing the conditions of ISP with the defendant, obtaining a full criminal history and making a field visit to the defendant's residence to discuss the program with family members and/or other individuals living with the defendant. Once a case is accepted, an ISP officer meets again with the probationer to develop a supervision strategy that addresses court mandates and other probationer needs. Officers work in pairs with reduced caseloads, with each two-person team supervising between 30 and 40 cases. Officers carry firearms while in the field.

Probationers sentenced to ISP are supervised in accordance with three phases that are similar to the Idaho and Georgia requirements. The term of ISP shall not be less than 12 months and no longer than 24 months. All offenders must complete 130 hours of community service and are subject to random drug tests and weekly arrest record checks. Less serious violations that do not involve new criminal charges may be addressed through a progressive disciplinary process that does not involve court hearings. When successfully completing the ISP program, offenders serve the remainder of their sentences on standard probation. The recidivism rate for this program is 22 percent (Cook County Circuit Court, 2003:3).

In 1997 an administrative sanctions protocol (ASP) was devised. This protocol permits POs to respond quickly to violations of one or more probation conditions. Examples of violations eligible for ASP include missing a probation appointment; testing positive for drug use; failing to comply with community service mandates; failing to make payments toward court-mandated monies as scheduled; and/or failing to comply with treatment mandates or other special conditions. Sanctions may be imposed by POs that include increased reporting; increased performance of community service hours; substance abuse evaluations and treatment; random drug testing; establishment of curfews; participation in an educational/vocational program; and/or referral to any service that may be beneficial to the probationer. However, POs cannot mandate more jail time, impose monetary sanctions, or alter the length of probation.

The Douglas County, Kansas, ISP Program.   ISP in Douglas County, Kansas, targets adults convicted of nonviolent felonies, including drug offenses. The program excludes persons with long criminal histories and those with histories of aggressively assaultive sexually deviant behavior. When accepted into the ISP program, each offender is required to enter into an intensive supervised plan that may include vocational, educational, and psychological, or alcohol or drug treatment. The intensity of supervision ranges from jail work release and house arrest to frequent and unannounced contacts at one's home or workplace. ISP officers and surveillance officers make random curfew and drug/alcohol checks during evening and weekend hours. Offenders are supervised based on a risk/needs scoring instrument, which determines the appropriate supervisory level. Through intensive supervision and counseling, POs monitor the daily activities of offenders and provide them with opportunities to prepare themselves to remain law-abiding and contributing community members.

Offenders must make regular restitution payments to victims and pay court costs. Additional fees may be paid by some offenders in the form of reimbursements to help defray program costs. Others are given the opportunity to pay off court-ordered costs by participating in a community service work program. Resource specialists are on duty to assist with job development for unemployed offenders. Services include job training and placement, GED development, post-secondary information and assistance with budgeting. Anger management classes are also offered. These classes consist of an 8-week course, which meets once per week and addresses ways of managing anger appropriately. The community service component may involve an adopt-a-highway program, an adopt-a-park program, assistance with July 4th displays, county fair assistance, the American Cancer Society volunteer work, and United Way assistance. A graffiti removal project has also been established to keep the community free of offensive and gang-related graffiti. Community citizens act as volunteers to assist in helping offenders in different activities. The recidivism rate of this ISP program is under 25 percent (Douglas County Court, 2003).

The Arizona ISP Program.   Arizona implemented an ISP program during the early 1990s and authorizes its probation offices to operate ISP programs depending upon staff availability and caseloads (Arizona Department of Corrections, 2004:1). Chief adult POs of each county initiate ISP programs with the approval of the presiding county judge of the superior court. ISP teams are appointed, consisting of one adult PO and one surveillance officer, or one adult PO and two surveillance officers. Two-person ISP teams supervise no more than 25 clients at one time, while three-person ISP teams supervise no more than 40 persons at one time. ISP officers may serve warrants on, make arrests of, and bring before the court any persons who have violated the terms of their ISP programs.

All persons accepted into the ISP program have secure and complete identification records maintained by POs. These include written statements of probation orders from the superior court judge. Close supervision is exercised over all clients. This supervision includes visual contact with each probationer at least four times per week and weekly contact with the probationer's employer. Information is obtained and assembled about the conduct of persons sentenced to ISP, including weekly arrest records, and the information is reported to the court. A report is made to the court any time the offender engages in behavior inconsistent with the requirements of the ISP program. POs monitor the payment of restitution and probation fees and bring into court any probationer who fails to pay restitution or fines. POs perform all other responsibilities required by the terms and conditions of the court. Supervisory conditions of the Arizona ISP program are similar to the Georgia, Idaho, and South Carolina programs. Recidivism rates for ISP clients are 25 percent or less (Arizona Department of Corrections, 2004:6).

It is apparent from the discussions of these various state and local programs that ISP is designed as a diversionary measure, keeping offenders from prison or jail, while at the same time providing them with meaningful and close supervision to monitor their conduct. For instance, the Greene County, Ohio, Common Pleas Court has implemented an ISP program that includes surveillance and upholding the strict conditions of probation in order to restrain offenders in their communities and help deter future criminal conduct (Greene County Criminal Court, 2003).

Running throughout these various programs are case plans and their development, which are designed to assist in rehabilitating offenders, enabling them to uphold their responsibilities and become law-abiding citizens. Most of these ISP programs use home confinement and/or electronic monitoring to assist POs in their supervisory tasks. While these methods of supervision are not foolproof, they do provide some measure of crime control with the threat of revoking one's program if one or more program conditions are violated. These programs also reflect the tendency of probation departments to work with high-risk or more serious offenders, including those with serious drug or alcohol problems. Intensive treatment programs are usually established, and close ties with community agencies are established to network in effective ways to ensure fulfillment of each offender's needs. Specialized caseloads are critical as well, as POs attempt to utilize their limited resources in the best ways possible. But ISP programming is expensive. Of the more than 4 million probationers in the United States in 2002, only about 6 or 7 percent were on some form of ISP. And the durations of these programs are relatively short, ranging from 6 to 24 months. Do ISP programs generally have better success at rehabilitating offenders? According to recidivism figures reported by these different agencies and departments, they have considerable promise. But again, their implementation is greatly hampered by scarce resources. There is simply not enough money to operate these programs on a more widespread scale in most U.S. jurisdictions.

SHOCK PROBATION AND SPLIT SENTENCING

Shock Probation

Shock probation, also referred to as **split sentencing** or **shock parole,** first appeared as a federal split sentencing provision in 1958, although the California legislature had authorized a bill permitting judges to impose a combination of incarceration and probation for the same offender in the early 1920s (New York State Division of Parole, 1998). The term, shock probation, was later coined by Ohio in 1964. Ohio was the first state to use shock probation. It has been characterized as a brief application of the rigors of imprisonment (in Ohio, 90–130 days served) that will deter criminal behavior and not impede the readjustment of the individual upon release. Shock probation has been used increasingly in other states in recent years. In more than a few jurisdictions, problem drinkers, DWI cases, and drug abusers have been targeted for **shock probation programs** (Burns and Vito, 1995).

Some persons have wondered whether shock probation is an appropriate term, since offenders sentenced to shock probation are actually incarcerated in a jail or prison for a short period, primarily for shock value. Shock probation stems from the fact that judges initially sentence offenders to lengthy terms of incarceration, usually in a jail. After offenders have been in jail for short interval (e.g., 30, 60, 90, or 120 days), they are brought before the judge where they are sentenced to probation. This type of sentence shocks and surprises these offenders, since they didn't expect to receive probation. Offenders who have been resentenced under these circumstances are **shock probationers.** The shock of incarceration is supposed to be a deterrent against further offending. It is anticipated that recidivism rates among shock probationers will be low.

Split Sentencing Distinguished from Shock Probation.   There is a difference between split sentencing and shock probation (Burns and Vito, 1995). Split sentencing means that the judge imposes a **combination sentence,** a portion of which includes incarceration and a portion of which includes probation. Thus, the judge may sentence the offender up to one year, with a maximum incarceration of six months. The remainder of the sentence is to be served on probation. Violating one or more conditions of probation may result in reincarceration, however.

Split Sentencing

Most states have authorized the use of one of three general types of either split sentencing or shock probation by judges in the sentencing of low-risk offenders. These types include (1) the California scheme, where jail is attached as a condition of probation, (2) the federal scheme under the 1987 sentencing guidelines, where supervised release of up to five years may follow sentences of imprisonment of more than one year (the length of supervised release varies according to the crime classification and ranges from one year for misdemeanors to five years), and (3) the Ohio scheme, where a judge resentences offenders within a 130-day incarcerative period to a probationary sentence. Other states, including Texas, have similar systems, although incarcerative periods are often longer than 130 days before resentencing to probation is considered (Burns and Vito, 1995).

Other terms used to describe these phenomena are **mixed sentence, intermittent confinement,** and **jail as a condition of probation.** A mixed sentence is imposed by a judge whenever an offender has committed two or more offenses. The judge imposes a separate sentence for each offense. One sentence may involve probation, while the other may involve incarceration. The judge decides whether the two sentences are to be served concurrently or consecutively. The intermittent sentence is imposed whenever the offender is sentenced to a term requiring partial confinement. Perhaps the offender must serve weekends in jail. A curfew may be imposed. In all other respects, the nature of intermittent sentencing is much like probation. Finally, jail as a condition of probation is an option whereby the judge imposes a fixed jail term to be served prior to the offender's completion of a sentence of probation.

The Philosophy and Objectives of Shock Probation

Shock Probation and Deterrence.   Deterrence is one of shock probation's primary themes. Another prominent philosophical objective is reintegration. Confining offenders to jail for brief periods and obligating them to serve their remaining months on probationary status enables them to be employed, support themselves and their families, and otherwise be productive citizens in their communities. The freedom shock probation permits offenders to receive specialized attention and to participate in programs designed to deal with their problems. Ideally, exposure to jail should be sufficiently traumatic to cause offenders to want to refrain from further criminal activity.

Shock Probation and Rehabilitation.   Consistent with the philosophy of shock probation and split sentencing generally are community reintegration and rehabilitation. A brief exposure to incarceration followed by release into the community permits offenders to hold jobs, support themselves and their families, pay restitution to victims, perform various public services, and/or participate in therapeutic or educational programs designed to help them with their special problems.

Shock Probation and Creative Sentencing.   Judges are permitted greater flexibility in the punishments they impose for low-risk offenders. Short-term incarceration is one form of creative sentencing.

Shock Probation as a Punishment.   The confinement phase of shock probation is considered a punishment. Low-risk offenders who have never been incarcerated are able to understand what it is like to be locked up without the freedoms to which they have become accustomed while living in their communities.

Shock Probation and Offender Needs.   Short-term confinement in a jail enables judges to determine appropriate services and therapies needed by offenders. Jail reports often disclose certain offender needs that must be addressed through community agencies. Judges can configure a suitable probationary punishment which includes programs that directly address particular offender needs.

Shock Probation and Offender Accountability.   Shock probation heightens offender awareness of the seriousness of their crimes. For many low-risk of-fenders, spending three or four months in jail is a sufficiently punishing experi-ence to cause them to reflect on the seriousness of the crimes they committed and to accept responsibility for their actions.

Shock Probation and Community Safety.   There is some question as to whether short-term incarceration ensures community safety. Eventually, shock probationers will be placed on probation within their communities. However, short-term incarceration seems to satisfy the public's demand for punitiveness where the law has been violated.

The Effectiveness of Shock Probation

Is shock probation effective? The answer to this question depends on what is expected from shock probation. If shock probation is expected to deter offend-ers from future offending, then it appears to be modestly successful in those ju-risdictions where it has been used (New York State Division of Parole, 1998; U.S. General Accounting Office, 1998). Recidivism rates among shock proba-tioners tend to be fairly low, averaging under 30 percent. Perhaps this is due primarily to the fact that low-risk, nonviolent offenders are most often selected as targets of shock probation sentences (Burns and Vito, 1995). Thus, those least likely to re-offend are included in the broad class of shock probationers and re-ceive this special sanction.

If shock probation is expected to alleviate prison and jail overcrowding, the results are mixed. Some professionals have observed that shock probation is one viable alternative to alleviating prison overcrowding (Vito, Holmes, and Wilson, 1985). This is because most offenders sentenced to shock probation will serve brief terms of confinement, usually in county jails. Thus, they will not occupy valuable long-term prison space which should be reserved for more serious or dangerous offenders (South Carolina State Reorganization Commis-sion, 1991, 1992). Nevertheless, shock probationers do occupy some jail space, even if their periods of confinement are relatively short. The high turnover among jail inmates suggests that shock probation has only an imperceptible ef-fect on jail overcrowding.

One dimension of shock probation is that in recent years, the public has become increasingly aware of it and convicted offenders often ask for it from judges during their sentencing hearings. Thus the shock value of shock proba-tion is diminished significantly. In one instance, which is fairly typical, Bran-don Brumett, 23, was convicted in Covington, Kentucky, in January 2001 of second-degree manslaughter and three counts of second-degree assault. He had driven his automobile under the influence of alcohol and crossed the median on an interstate highway, crashing head-on into another vehicle. One of his pas-sengers was killed, with several others sustaining critical injuries. Brumett was held for 14 months in jail. When he stood facing the judge during his sentenc-ing, he said, "These past 14 months have scared me to death. If you can bless me with shock probation, you will never see me in the court system again." The judge sentenced Brumett to 10 years in prison (Crowley, 2003:1-3). If these types of offender expectations become more widespread, it is likely that shock probation will lose most if not all of its deterrent value.

FIGURE 5.3 General Patrick H. Brady Boot Camp Correctional Facility.

BOOT CAMPS

Closely related to shock probation is **shock incarceration** or **boot camps.** In the case of shock incarceration or boot camps, convicted offenders are jailed or otherwise confined, but their confinement resembles military boot camp training. Shock probation involved sentencing offenders to a plain jail term, with no participation in any military-like programs. In contrast, shock incarceration or boot camp programs do provide military-like regimentation and regulation of inmate behavior.

Boot Camps Defined

Boot camps are highly regimented, military-like, short-term correctional programs (90–180 days) where offenders are provided with strict discipline, physical training, and hard labor resembling some aspects of military basic training; when successfully completed, boot camps provide for transfers of participants to community-based facilities for nonsecure supervision. By 1998, boot camps had been formally established in most of the states (Benda, 2002).

Boot camps were officially established in 1983 by the Georgia Department of Corrections Special Alternative Incarceration (SAI), although the general idea for boot camps originated sometime earlier in late 1970s, also in Georgia. The usual length of incarceration in boot camps varies from three to six months. During this period, boot camp participants engage in marching, work, and classes that are believed useful in one's rehabilitation. Usually, youthful offenders are targeted by these programs (Benda, Toombs, and Peacock, 2002).

The Rationale for Boot Camps.   Boot camps were established as an alternative to long-term, traditional incarceration. Austin, Jones, and Bolyard outline a brief rationale for boot camps:

1. A substantial number of youthful first-time offenders now incarcerated will respond to a short but intensive period of confinement followed by a longer period of intensive community supervision.

2. These youthful offenders will benefit from a military-type atmosphere that instills a sense of self-discipline and physical conditioning that was lacking in their lives.

3. These same youths need exposure to relevant educational, vocational training, drug treatment, and general counseling services to develop more positive and law-abiding values and become better prepared to secure legitimate future employment.

4. The costs involved will be less than a traditional criminal justice sanction that imprisons the offender for a substantially longer period of time (Austin, Jones, and Bolyard, 1993:1).

Goals of Boot Camps

Boot camps have several general goals. These goals include: (1) rehabilitation/ reintegration; (2) discipline; (3) deterrence; (4) ease prison/jail overcrowding; and (5) vocational, educational, and rehabilitative services.

To Provide Rehabilitation and Reintegration.   Boot camp programs are designed to improve one's sense of purpose, self-discipline, self-control, and self-confidence through physical conditioning, educational programs, and social skills training, all within the framework of strict military discipline (Lutze and Murphy, 1999). The time youthful offenders spend in boot camps is not especially lengthy. The emphasis upon discipline and educational skills is calculated to provide structure for participants which was lacking in their previous family and social environment. Thus, there are both rehabilitative and reintegrative objectives sought by most boot camp programs.

To Provide Discipline.   Boot camps are intended to improve one's discipline (Gover, MacKenzie, and Styve, 2000). Many youthful offenders find it difficult to accept authority and often refuse to learn in traditional classroom or treatment environments. Within the context of a boot camp program, however, there are incentives to become involved in program activities. Most boot camp programs also include educational elements pertaining to literacy, academic and vocational education, intensive value clarification, and resocialization (Benda, 2002).

To Promote Deterrence.   Being thrust into a military-like atmosphere is a frightening experience for many boot camp clients. It is believed that a highly regimented boot camp experience will cause most participants to lead more law-abiding lives when they successfully complete their programs. However, there have been numerous boot camp failures. These failures have caused some observers to regard boot camp programs with some amount of skepticism. It has been recommended, for instance, that more selective criteria should be used to include those clients most amenable to change under military-like boot camp conditions. Furthermore, post-release follow-ups should be conducted to gauge program effectiveness. In some instances, boot camp staff have appeared to be overzealous in exercising their authority over youthful offenders. Thus, several ethical questions have been generated about how much control these authorities should have and how that control should be applied, especially where youthful offenders are involved (Hemmens and Stohr, 2000).

To Ease Prison and Jail Overcrowding.   Boot camps are believed to have a long-term impact on jail and prison overcrowding (Benda, 2002). One primary purpose of boot camps is to divert prison-bound youthful offenders to a structured environment where they can learn discipline and become rehabilitated. Compared with the population of jail and prison inmates, the total number of boot camp clientele accounts for only a small fraction of these populations, however. Thus, it is doubtful whether boot camps seriously ease prison or jail overcrowding to a significant degree (Benda, Toombs, and Peacock, 2002).

To Provide Vocational and Rehabilitative Services.   Most boot camp programs offer educational and/or vocational training to clients. Rehabilitative services might include drug abuse intervention counseling, mental health services, and sex offender therapy (Fabelo, 2002).

A Profile of Boot Camp Clientele

Who can participate in boot camps or shock incarceration programs? Participants may or may not be able to enter or withdraw from boot camps voluntarily. It depends on the particular program. Most boot camp participants are prison-bound youthful offenders convicted of less serious, nonviolent crimes, and who have never been previously incarcerated. Depending upon the program, there are some exceptions (Benda, 2002). Participants may either be referred to these programs by judges or corrections departments or they may volunteer. They may or may not be accepted, and if they complete their programs successfully, they may or may not be released under supervision into their communities.

Boot Camp Programs

While boot camp programs share certain features, there are obviously different program components among these boot camps to make them fairly distinctive from the others. It is interesting to note which features are included or excluded from one program to the next.

Jail Boot Camps

Jail boot camps are short-term programs for jail inmates serving short sentences of less than one year. In 2002 there were 20 jail boot camp programs operating in U.S. jails involving 3,004 inmates (Camp and Camp, 2003). In Washoe County, Nevada, for instance, a jail boot camp was established in May 1995. A wide range of ages was represented, with no explicit minimum or maximum age restrictions. The main goals of the Washoe program were to instill in

 **BOX 5.2**

Elkhorn Correctional Facility Boot Camp.
The Elkhorn Correctional Facility Boot Camp is located in Fresno County, California. Program elements include the following:

1. Military model followed, with military drill
2. Discipline
3. Physical training, conditioning, and discipline
4. Acquiring fundamental academic skills through educational coursework
5. Participants range in age from 14 to 18
6. 5 1/2-month in-custody program
7. Assessments conducted regularly by on-site school staff, mental health staff, substance abuse staff, and boot camp staff to determine each cadet's expected level of achievement
8. Individual needs and skills assessed, including families of cadets; family involvement is mandatory and serves to strengthen cadet's home improvement and parent's communication skills
9. Six-week victim awareness course confronts cadets with actual crime victim's accounts of their victimization and the impact of crime through restorative justice model
10. Drug awareness/education programming
11. Intensive gang redirection efforts and job preparedness courses
12. Aftercare supervision includes intensive face-to-face supervision ranging from 6 to 12 months, together with electronic monitoring, drug testing, individual and family counseling, and community service experiences
13. Follow-up shows 13 percent recidivism rate, measured by either rearrests or convictions for new offenses, based on 533 post-commitment juvenile offenders.

The Sheffield Boot Camp.
The Texas Youth Commission Sheffield Boot Camp is a 64-bed facility for male juvenile offenders who were committed to the agency's care by a juvenile court. Youths are subjected to a 90-day military-style program and referred to as cadets. The staff are responsible for daily living services. Military-style uniforms are provided. Cadets learn military-style courtesy, drill, and ceremony.

1. Military model, militaristic chain of command
2. Youths range in age from 14 to 20 years of age, committed to facility by juvenile court
3. Based on elements of correctional therapy, education, work, and discipline training
4. Youths must have mental and physical capacity and be amenable to treatment
5. Youths are initially placed in orientation platoon, where military courtesy is taught; eventually move up to first platoon, which is the Honor Platoon; failure to maintain the expectations of each platoon phase may result in demotion to more restrictive platoon for remedial training; platoons consist of 16 cadets and are assigned to teams of four; cooperative effort is expected in all group activities
6. Regimen: 16-hour day begins at breakfast at 5:00 A.M., when cadets attend to personal hygiene, police area and stand inspection; cadets move in a military manner, marching in formation to all scheduled activities; daytime activities include educational classes, physical training (road marches), and community service; cadets may become eligible to participate in 4-H Club activities, such as raising and caring for rabbits, goats, and peacocks; each new platoon level earns cadets more privileges
7. Services provided include medical, vocational, physical, social (drug and alcohol counseling); coping and life skills programs; school administration promotes goals of fostering skills and attitudes in reflection (thinking about

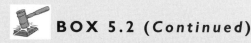

BOX 5.2 (Continued)

thinking) so that they are capable of thinking critically, creatively and affirmatively to help them function independently as well as cooperatively

8. Participants required to practice good grooming and personal hygiene habits; structured activities designed to prepare them for successful reintegration into society

9. Program activities are mandatory

10. Recidivism of 27 percent.

The Sergeant Henry Johnson Youth Leadership Academy (YLA).
The Sergeant Henry Johnson Youth Leadership Academy established in New York has the following program features:

1. Targets high-risk male juvenile delinquents from New York City

2. Judges control inmate selection process, according to broad statutory criteria

3. Program features physical training, drill and ceremony, hard labor, and treatment, particularly in early stages

4. Six months of residential care followed by post-residential day treatment in the City Challenge (CCh) program for the remainder of the youth's placement in state custody

5. Quasi-military orientation

6. Strong values orientation, featuring leadership (what it is like to be a leader), skill development (distinguishing between right and wrong), and academic education in the transition from YLA to CCh

7. Medical treatment or other individual treatment provided for both youths and family members

8. Graduated sequence of transitional programming linked with family and other potential support systems

9. Values promoted include self-discipline and personal accountability; affiliation and teamwork, with ability to form trust relationships; self-esteem and personal competence; and self-worth, valuing

self and others, enough to consider the consequences of behavior

10. Curriculum includes "Magic Within," a cognitively oriented program designed to help youths understand how what they value and what they believe about themselves influence what they perceive to be their options and how they ultimately choose to behave

11. Follow-up includes six home visits and psychosocial evaluations of family circumstances

12. Broker services provided through other community-based agencies, after-school programming, foster care certification, and access to special education programs

13. Recidivism rate of 20 percent

Mount Carmel Youth Ranch.
Mount Carmel Youth Ranch, located in Powell, Wyoming, includes the following characteristics:

1. Alcohol/drug/cigarette usage and awareness

2. Year-round program featuring wilderness experiences

3. Camp psychologist counseling sessions for emotionally troubled youth, characterized by poor peer choices, academic underachievement, anger problems, rebelliousness and defiance, low self-esteem, and impulsive behavior

4. At-risk boys and girls range in age from 12 to 17

5. Program includes physical training, hard work, and education experiences

6. Participants perform various tasks on a 40,000-acre cattle ranch

7. Job placement and counseling services

8. Christian principles are imparted in special educational sessions

9. Parental involvement required to deal with divorce problems, adoption issues, peer/sibling conflicts, and depression

10. Recidivism of 18 percent

Sources: California Department of Corrections (2003); Mount Carmel Youth Ranch (2003); New York State Division of Criminal Justice Services (2002); Texas Youth Commission, (2003:1-3).

inmates a positive attitude by stressing academic achievement, coping skills, anger and money management, and good work habits. The intent was to inspire the inmate to succeed in society after he leaves jail (Radli, 1997:87). Six basic objectives were sought: (1) inmates will develop good work habits and skills; (2) inmates will no longer sit idle while they are held in jail; (3) members will partially repay the community for the cost of their incarceration; (4) members will become more self-sufficient; (5) members will adjust more smoothly back into society; and (6) the recidivism rate will be reduced.

Known as the Highly Intensive Supervision, Training, and Education Program (HISTEP), the Washoe County program was implemented through the Washoe County Sheriff's Office and involved 452 inmates. Five levels were incorporated in the program. Levels I and II ran for six weeks. During these weeks, inmates were introduced to the military way of life. Physical training, inspections, and educational classes were conducted in somewhat of a shock environment, breaking inmates out of the traditional general inmate population mold. Various tests were administered to determine their educational and personality maturity levels. Skills classes were taught, emphasizing anger management, communication, building self-esteem, decision making, parenting techniques, and financial management. Core values were taught also. These core values were a sense of responsibility, pride, and acceptable behavior in various real-life situations. Level III initiated members to the fundamentals of seeking employment, writing resumes, exploring employment resources, and learning interviewing techniques. This level lasted eight weeks. Levels IV and V included work at the jail at a jail industry job. The inmates received a small hourly wage, part of which was used to support the program. Work furloughs were made available to certain inmates who would reside within the jail during evening hours but would work at a job outside the jail during the day. Again, jail inmate wages would be divided into offsetting program costs, establishing a small inmate savings account, and commissary items. Levels IV and V lasted eight weeks. Thus, the program was designed for inmates to leave the jail with a job skill, a job, and money in the bank (Radli, 1997:87-88).

Washoe County Jail officials have conducted a follow-up of the number of inmates who went through the program during the period May 1995 through August 1996. Of the 452 entering the HISTEP program, 30 percent or 138 completed it. Of the successful jail boot camp inmates who completed the program, the recidivism rate was only 11 percent. Considering substantially higher rates of recidivism associated with standard probation and parole programs and other community-based or intermediate punishments, the 11 percent recidivism figure was interpreted by Washoe officials as a very positive indicator of their HISTEP program success (Radli, 1997:90). It is not possible to generalize Washoe County's HISTEP success rate to other jurisdictions with substantial accuracy, although this program does seem to be typical of other jail boot camp programs presently operating in other jurisdictions (Wood and Grasmick, 1999).

The Effectiveness of Boot Camps

Are boot camps or shock incarceration programs successful? Programs with recidivism rates of 30 percent or less are considered successful by many criminal justice professionals. If we use this standard as a measure of boot camp effectiveness, there seems to be considerable support in the literature for their effectiveness. For instance, a Louisiana IMPACT (Intensive Motivational Program of Alternative Correctional Treatment) program reported that during the first six months of community supervision following boot camp participation, between 7 to 14 percent of the boot camp clients recidivated compared with from 12 to 23 percent of the boot camp dropouts or those who failed to complete the program. A New York Rikers Boot Camp has reported recidivism rates of 23 percent among its graduates. However, a 38 percent recidivism rate was reported by a Georgia SAI (Special Alternative Incarceration) program (Grossi, 1997). Recidivism rates generally continue to be low among boot camp participants (Benda, Toombs, and Peacock, 2002).

The simple fact is that because most of these boot camp programs were established during the late 1980s and 1990s, there hasn't been much evaluation research about boot camp program effectiveness. One study of boot camp effectiveness was conducted by Albright et al. (1996). Albright and her associates investigated boot camps in Cleveland, Ohio, Denver, Colorado, and Mobile, Alabama, during the 1990–1995 period. The findings were disappointing. Recidivism figures were about the same for boot camp participants compared with youthful offenders who participated in traditional probation programs, averaging between 65–70 percent. However, the cost-effectiveness of the boot camp programs was considerably lower when compared with youths housed in secure confinement. For instance, residential services for boot camp youths averaged $54 per day compared with $139 per day for those in secure confinement and who did not participate in boot camp programming. Thus, boot camp programming and aftercare were substantially cheaper than institutional confinement. However, the cost of supervising youths on standard probation averaged about $2 per day. Their rates of recidivism were only about 10 percent higher, on the average, compared with boot camp participants. Therefore, boot camp youths had somewhat lower rates of recidivism compared with standard probationers, although the boot camp costs were 27 times as high ($54 compared with $2). Similar results have been found in studies of other boot camps, such as the Los Angeles County Juvenile Drug Treatment Boot Camp in 1999 (Zhang, 2000).

It is difficult to draw clear conclusions from these preliminary investigations of boot camp costs. In 2002 there were between 50 and 100 different boot camps operating in the United States. Little evaluation research has been made available about them and whether they are effective. There are major differences among these boot camps in the clientele selected for inclusion, however. Some boot camps are designated for those with substance abuse problems, while other programs are intended for those with disciplinary problems and who are relatively drug-free. Different selection criteria exist, therefore, and all programs are operated in different ways. The general impression we might draw from existing literature about boot camps is that they appear to be reasonably successful for those who complete programming requirements (Benda, Toombs, and Peacock, 2002). This would suggest that more rigorous criteria ought to be used when targeting participants for boot camp involvement.

FEMALE PROBATIONERS AND PAROLEES: A PROFILE

In 2002, females accounted for 23 percent of all probationers and 14 percent of all parolees (Glaze, 2003:4, 6). Women were most represented proportionately in various property offense categories, such as fraud (40 percent) and larceny

(24 percent). Overall, women made up about 25 percent of all probationers convicted of property offenses. On the average, women are sentenced to probation more often than men. But this is likely attributable to the fact that male and female offenders have different offending patterns. Males are involved to a greater degree in violent offending, while females are involved to a greater degree in more passive offending, such as fraud and burglary (Harrison and Beck, 2003:10). Another explanation for these sentencing differences is that judges have tended to be more paternalistic toward female offenders in the past. In recent years, however, presumptive or guidelines-based sentencing schemes used by different states and the federal government have caused male–female sentencing differentials to narrow. Generally, the rate of female offending and incarceration has increased both dramatically and systematically since the early 1980s. This does not necessarily mean that there is a new breed or a more dangerous female offender in society—rather, more women are being subject to less lenient treatment by a more equitable criminal justice system. Some observers have labeled this phenomenon gender parity (Festervan, 2003).

Regarding parole, women tended to be distributed in ways similar to their conviction patterns. This proportion is similar to the proportionate distribution of women incarcerated in federal and state prisons. With a few exceptions, female parolee distributions by conviction offense were similar to their original conviction offense patterns. The female failure rate while on probation or parole is approximately the same as it is for male probationers and parolees, about 65 percent (Pastore and Maguire, 2003).

Special Programs and Services for Female Offenders

In 1992, the American Correctional Association formulated a National Correctional Policy on Female Offender Services (Festervan, 2003). This policy is as follows.

> *Introduction*: Correctional systems must develop service delivery systems for accused and adjudicated female offenders that are comparable to those provided to males. Additional services must also be provided to meet the unique needs of the female offender population.

> *Statement*: Correctional systems must be guided by the principle of parity. Female offenders must receive the equivalent range of services available to other offenders, including opportunities for individualized programming and services that recognize the unique needs of this population. The services should:

> 1. Assure access to a range of alternatives to incarceration, including pretrial and post-trial diversion, probation, restitution, treatment for substance abuse, halfway houses, and parole services.
> 2. Provide acceptable conditions of confinement, including appropriately trained staff and sound operating procedures that address this population's needs in such areas as clothing, personal property, hygiene, exercise, recreation, and visitation with children and family.
> 3. Provide access to a full range of work and programs designed to expand economic and social roles of women, with emphasis on education; career counseling and exploration of nontraditional as well as traditional vocational training; relevant life skills, including parenting and social and economic assertiveness; and pre-release and work/education release programs.

4. Facilitate the maintenance and strengthening of family ties, particularly those between parent and child.

5. Deliver appropriate programs and services, including medical, dental, and mental health programs, services to pregnant women, substance abuse programs, child and family services, and provide access to legal services.

6. Provide access to release programs that include aid in establishing homes, economic stability, and sound family relationships.

Criticisms of Women's Prison and Community Programming

One criticism of programs for female probationers and parolees is that they are often placed in programs designed for male offenders without any consideration given to their special needs (Shearer, 2003:46). For instance, the incidence of female substance abuse has escalated greatly in recent years. The needs of female substance abusers differ greatly from their male counterparts and different treatments are often required. For instance, compared with male offenders, far more female offenders have histories of physical, psychological, and sexual abuse at higher rates. They are simply more likely to use drugs and alcohol as coping mechanisms for these traumatic events. These differences require basic differences in treatment therapies for male and female offenders.

Male programs often stress anger management courses in order for male offenders to subdue their anger and get along with others in the community. However, females have greater difficulty expressing anger in any form. Women tend to be more responsive to programming that includes techniques for reducing feelings of guilt and self-blame, and that foster self-esteem and self-awareness. Also, male programs seldom address parenting issues. Females are more receptive to parenting training. Such training has been positively correlated with assisting in the recovery from alcohol and drug addictions among women. Additionally, while both male and female offenders tend to come from families where drugs and alcohol have been abused, there is little focus on family dynamics or issues in male-oriented programs, whereas female offenders could profit from such programming and emphasis. Furthermore, most of the services and educational/vocational training offered to offenders is male-oriented, with little effort made to provide female offenders with similar opportunities. Thus, most women leaving prison do not have marketable skills so that they can survive well in their communities (Shearer, 2003:47-48). Similar observations have been made subsequently about women offenders by others (Sharp and Muraskin, 2003).

Descriptions of prison life for women are not particularly pleasant. Many imprisoned women report that their experiences are considerably harsher than they believed were warranted, given the crimes they committed. Further, there continue to be inequities in women's prisons compared with those for men. These inequities pertain to more limited programming and services, fewer opportunities for acquiring vocational and educational skills, although there have been improvements in medical care, prison classification systems, and efforts at rehabilitation (Pogrebin and Dodge, 2001).

It is generally acknowledged that women's prisons and programming for women in community-based correctional programs have not compared favorably with programs and facilities for men (Dalley, 2002). For instance, programs for female offenders have been poorer in quality, quantity, variability, and availability in both the United States and Canada. Despite these inequities, courts generally declare that men and women in prisons do not have to be treated equally, and that separate can be equal when men's and women's prisons are compared. There are exceptions, however. In 1979, the case of *Glover v. Johnson* (1979) involved the Michigan Department of Corrections and the issue of equal programming for female inmates. A class action suit was filed on behalf of all Michigan female prison inmates to the effect that their constitutional rights were violated because they were being denied educational and vocational rehabilitation opportunities that were then being provided male inmates only. Among other things, the Michigan Department of Corrections was ordered to provide the following to its incarcerated women: (1) two-year college programming, (2) paralegal training and access to attorneys to remedy past inadequacies in law library facilities, (3) equal wages for female inmates, (4) access to programming at camps previously available only to male inmates, (5) enhanced vocational offerings, (6) apprenticeship opportunities, and (7) prison industries that previously existed only at men's facilities (American Correctional Association, 1993:32). Several similar cases in other jurisdictions have been settled without court action (Connecticut, California, Wisconsin, and Idaho).

The *Glover* case is like the tip of an iceberg when it comes to disclosing various problems associated with women's prisons and other corrections institutions for women (Hyde, Brumfield, and Nagel, 2000). The following are criticisms that have been leveled against women's correctional facilities in the last few decades. Some of these criticisms have been remedied in selected jurisdictions.

1. No adequate classification system exists for female prisoners. Women from widely different backgrounds with diverse criminal histories are celled with one another in most women's prisons. This is conducive to greater criminalization during the incarceration period. Further, most women's prisons have only medium-security custody, rather than a wider variety of custody levels to accommodate female offenders of differing seriousness and dangerousness. Better classification methods should be devised. In recent years, the Female Offender Critical Intervention Inventory has been devised. This is a gender-specific needs inventory for female offenders that shows promise of working well to identify needs specific to female offenders (Shearer, 2003:48-49).

2. Most women's prisons are remotely located; thus, many female prisoners are deprived of immediate contact with out-of-prison educational or vocational services that might be available through study or work release.

3. Women who give birth to babies while incarcerated are deprived of valuable parent–child contact. Some observers contend this is a serious deprivation for newborn infants.

4. Women have less extensive vocational and educational programming in the prison setting.

5. Women have less access to legal services; in the past, law libraries in women's facilities were lacking or nonexistent; recent remedies have included provisions for either legal services or more adequate libraries in women's institutions.

6. Women have special medical needs, and women's prisons do not adequately provide for meeting these needs.

7. Mental health treatment services and programs for women are inferior to those provided for men in men's facilities.

8. Training programs that are provided women do not permit them to live independently and earn decent livings when released on parole (Culliver, 1993:407).

Because of the rather unique role of women as caregivers for their children, many corrections professionals rule the imprisonment of women differently from the imprisonment of men. For various reasons, female imprisonment is opposed on moral, ethical, and religious grounds (Landry, 2001). Legally, these arguments are often unconvincing. In an attempt to at least address some of the unique problems confronting female offenders when they are incarcerated or when they participate in community-based programs, some observers have advocated the following as recommendations:

1. Institute training programs that would enable imprisoned women to become literate.

2. Provide female offenders with programs that do not center on traditional gender roles—programs that will lead to more economic independence and self-sufficiency.

3. Establish programs that would engender more positive self-esteem for imprisoned women and enhance their assertiveness and communication and interpersonal skills.

4. Establish more programs that would allow imprisoned mothers to interact more with their children and assist them in overcoming feelings of guilt and shame for having deserted their children. In addition, visitation areas for mothers and children should be altered to minimize the effect of a prison-type environment.

5. An alternative to mother-and-child interaction behind prison bars would be to allow imprisoned mothers to spend more time with their children outside of the prison.

6. Provide imprisoned mothers with training to improve parenting skills.

7. Establish more programs to treat drug-addicted female offenders.

8. Establish a community partnership program to provide imprisoned women with employment opportunities.

9. Establish a better classification system for incarcerated women—one that would not permit the less-hardened offender to be juxtaposed with the hardened female offender.

10. Provide in-service training (sensitivity awareness) to assist staff members (wardens, correctional officers) in understanding the nature and needs of incarcerated women (Culliver, 1993:409-410).

Other observers have recommended the establishment and provision for an environment which would allow all pregnant inmates the opportunity to rear their newborn infants for a period of one year and provide counseling regarding available parental services, foster care, guardianship, and other relevant activities pending their eventual release (Miller, 2001).

Responses to Criticisms about the Lack of Programs for Female Offenders

In recent years there have been vast improvements in programming for female offenders in almost every jurisdiction. Some of these programs have been offered on a statewide basis, while others have been implemented locally, usually at the county level. Several of these programs are described below.

The Program for Female Offenders, Inc. (PFO). Some women's facilities have cottages on prison grounds where inmates with infants can accomplish some of these objectives. One of these is the **Program for Female Offenders, Inc. (PFO).** The PFO was established in 1974 as the result of jail overcrowding in Allegheny County, Pennsylvania (Festervan, 2003). The PFO is a work-release facility operated as a nonprofit agency by the county. It is designed to accommodate up to 36 women and space for six preschool children. It was originally created to reduce jail overcrowding, but because of escalating rates of female offending and jail incarceration, the overcrowding problem persists.

When the PFO was established, the Allegheny County Jail was small. Only twelve women were housed there. Nevertheless, agency founders worked out an agreement with jail authorities so that female jail prisoners could be transferred to PFO by court order. Inmate-clients would be guilty of prison breach if they left PFO without permission. While at PFO, the women would participate in training, volunteering in the community, and learning how to spend their leisure time with the help of a role modeling and parent education program for mothers and children. The program is based on freedom reached by attaining levels of responsibility. In the mid-1980s, a much larger work-release facility was constructed in Allegheny County. Currently, over 300 women per year are served by PFO. PFO authorities reserve the right to screen potential candidates for work release (Arnold, 1992:38). The successfulness of the program is demonstrated by its low 3.5 percent recidivism rate in the community program and only a 17 percent recidivism rate at the residential facility.

The Women in Community Services Lifeskills Program (WICS). More women are being convicted of drug offenses annually (Griffin and Armstrong, 2003). Three-fourths of all women inmates are in need of substance abuse treatment, although only 30 percent of all incarcerated women have conviction offenses involving drugs (Grabarek, Bourke, and Van Hasselt, 2002). Most offenders had dropped out of high school or had not received the GED. Most had been unable to hold a job for longer than six months. Presently, most of the 170 surveyed institutions offer vocational and educational courses for these women. Two-thirds offer college courses and 70 have pre-release programs. Most facilities have institutional work assignments, and about half have parenting programs (Festervan, 2003). These policy changes involve increased opportunities for women to work and/or participate in vocational and educational programming originally available only to male inmates. Major changes have occurred in classification, visitation, and housing. Clothing policy changes have also been effected. Many of these changes have been occasioned by the parity issue, where women's facilities are brought more in line with men's facilities. In most instances, this has meant improved services delivery to women's prisons. Most prison and community correctional policy changes have benefited women generally (Bednar, 2003).

During the late 1970s, the **Women in Community Services Lifeskills Program (WICS)** was established in selected jurisdictions to meet some of the needs of incarcerated women or women who were attempting to make the transition from institutional life to community living on parole (Hale, 2001:33). The WICS program responded to the facts that 57 percent of all female inmates in state prisons had histories of sexual and/or physical abuse. Furthermore, only 36 percent of these women had some education or employable skills. About 75 percent of these women had drug and/or alcohol dependencies, while 50 percent had at least one other family member serving time in prison for various crimes.

The WICS program responded by using a women-centered learning model to both train and support female offenders through promoting self-sufficiency and economic independence. Program participants were provided with a comprehensive set of services, including job readiness, personal empowerment, support services, and life management skills that would prepare them for their successful return to the community. WICS currently operates programs for female offenders in Portland, Oregon, Memphis, Tennessee, and Dallas, Texas (Hale, 2001:34).

The WICS program is delivered in a 12-week curriculum offered within two months' of a female inmate's release from prison. Classes include comprehensive skills management, job readiness, and assorted workshops on various vocational and educational skills. Drug and alcohol education programs are also featured. Each female offender is encouraged to set goals for herself about who she is, what she needs, and what she wants. A core feature of WICS is the use of volunteers who donate hundreds of hours assisting female offenders in different ways (e.g., teaching, counseling, mentoring). Each offender is taught about alternative lifestyles that are law-abiding and conventional. The WICS Lifeskills program's primary purpose is to help women in prison create visions for their lives and gain skills to achieve them. There is some positive benefit accruing to these female offenders from program participation. Women who graduate from the WICS program have a 13 percent lower rate of recidivism compared with female offenders who do not participate (Hale, 2001:37). The overall rate of recidivism among WICS participants is only 29 percent.

The Early Head Start Program.   The Washington Department of Correction (WDOC) has partnered with the **Early Head Start Program** to provide intensive parenting classes before and after birth for imprisoned pregnant women. A child care center was established in 1999 at the Washington Corrections Center for Women in Gig Harbor, and up to 20 mothers and their children occupy one wing of the 90-bed residential unit at the minimum-security compound of the prison, which also has medium- and maximum-security units (Kauffman, 2001:63). Other inmates at the prison who receive special training in childcare and parenting may serve as caregivers for the women involved in the parenting program. Inmate mothers may keep their babies for up to 18 months before being transferred to one of two prerelease centers, where they may remain confined for an additional 18 months. This reintegrative process has had successful results. There is no official name for this women's parenting program in the WDOC, although it has reduced female inmate recidivism among participating inmate mothers by 25 percent. A similar program has been established in the Nebraska Correctional Center for Women, which opened its nursery doors in 1994 (Kauffman, 2001:63).

The Women's Network.   In Maricopa County, Arizona, a program known as the **Women's Network (WN)** was implemented in the early 1990s (Griffin and Armstrong, 2003:220). Officially known as the Women's Treatment, Services, and Supervision Network, the program was simply abbreviated as the Women's Network. The WN focuses upon female probationers with substance abuse problems. Program assessors typically meet with female volunteers who wish to enter the program when released from jails after serving short jail terms. In order to be eligible for acceptance into the WN, a woman had to be on probation (or would be placed on probation after her release from jail), self-identified as having a substance abuse problem, living in Maricopa County, and not diagnosed as having any mental disorders. A portion of these women were convicted for dealing drugs, although most of those who dealt drugs were also drug users. Thus a key program goal was to educate female offenders about drug use and its short- and long-term consequences, and to assist them in developing strategies for avoiding drug use in the future. Besides individual and group counseling, participants received educational courses and instruction. Furthermore, they were tested for drugs and/or alcohol at random times during their program involvement. Over the course of the program, 95 percent of the participants shifted from using drugs to not using drugs. Key experiences in observed behavioral changes were changes in employment status, living situation, relationship status, and whether these women were living with a significant other. Many of these women obtained employment during the course of the program. Also, several women detached themselves from abusive relationships or entered more stable relations. During the late 1990s and into the early 2000s, recidivism rates among participants were less than 25 percent, suggesting a successful program experience.

The Community Education Centers (CEC).   In Denver, Colorado and Newark, New Jersey, **Community Education Centers (CEC)** has established several programs to meet the needs of female offenders with substance abuse problems. Those targeted for involvement in CEC have often exhibited prior experiences of physical and sexual abuse, post-traumatic depression, and drug or alcohol abuse. The CEC is designed to prevent relapse and to address these various issues associated with female offenders. At the Denver site, CEC operates Tooley Hall, which is a cognitively based residential treatment program for women with substance abuse problems. It features vocational and educational courses designed to equip women with productive life skills prior to their reintegration into society.

Relapse prevention is facilitated through individual and group counseling, and increasing female education and employment functioning, equipping women with management strategies, and achieving healthy relationships with others. A Pathways to Change program is also offered which seeks to promote effective community reintegration. When women arrive at these CEC centers, they spend their first ten days undergoing a comprehensive assessment to determine their needs. The intake assessment consists of a clinical interview and testing to determine treatment needs, substance abuse, mental health, trauma history, family needs, and vocational issues. This is followed by monthly assessments which are used to evaluate progress in the treatment program. Mental health counseling is provided by qualified therapists. Courses in anger management, cognitive restructuring, and women's issues are offered. Aftercare services are also provided, which include ongoing drug/alcohol treatment, post-release analyses, applied cognitive restructuring for residents without family groups, and peer mentoring. A six-week resident/family group therapy session is conducted to assess various reintegration issues (Community Education Centers, 2003:1-2).

The Female Offender Regimented Treatment Program (FORT).   The Oklahoma Department of Corrections (ODOC) established the **Female Offender Regimented Treatment Program (FORT)** in 1984 (Camp and Sandhu, 2003:1). The goals of FORT were to (1) reduce the term of incarceration of improvable offenders through regimented discipline and thus to reduce prison overcrowding and costs; and (2) to reduce the rate of recidivism of program participants. Targeted for inclusion in the FORT program were first-offender women in the ODOC who were believed to be responsive to disciplinary programs such as FORT, particularly those with substance-abuse problems. The age range for FORT participants was from 18 to 32, with an average age in the early 20s. The program elements were similar to boot camps operated for men and included education, training in parenting, substance abuse counseling, exercise, drilling, strict military discipline, and self-esteem enhancing experiences. The recidivism rate of FORT participants compared with equivalent groups of female nonparticipants was about 34 percent. Thus, the boot camp experience for female offenders is considered marginally successful, at least in Oklahoma.

Other Programs for Women.   A variety of other programs have been established for women by different jurisdictions. It is beyond the scope of this text to cover them all. One program developed by the California Department of Alcohol and Drug Programs (CDADP) is the Female Offender Treatment Program (FOTP). This is a community residential treatment program for the California Institution for Women (CIW) called Forever Free. Forever Free caters to those women paroled into various California counties. In 2003, participating counties included Los Angeles, Riverside, Orange, and San Bernardino. The program is funded by federal money from a Substance Abuse Prevention and Treatment Block Grant. The program design is for six months of continuous treatment upon release from the CIW. The treatment capacity is 35 beds throughout the four counties. Residential individual and group counseling are provided, together with educational programming stressing addictions to alcohol and drugs. Medical staff are available 24/7 to provide necessary treatments as appropriate (California Department of Alcohol and Drug Programs, 2003:1).

Another program that is gender-specific to women is operated by the Taycheedah Correctional Institution (TCI) in Wisconsin. The TCI had a population of 600 women in 2003 (Taycheedah Correctional Institution, 2003). This maximum-security institution has a wide variety of programming, including industries, vocational, academic, psychological services, and health services. The industries programming includes screen printing, embroidery and computer recycling, and Badger Industries, which refurbishes used computers that are either donated or sold at low cost to non-profit agencies. Vocational programs include office assistant courses. Academic programs offer the G.E.D., college correspondence courses, personal self-development classes, financial management, personal self-fulfillment, skills for the workplace, cognitive group intervention, and a literature circle. Alcohol and drug abuse counseling are also offered on an individual basis for those female offenders with such needs. TCI also offers anger redirection, wellness and health issues courses, cognitive intervention programming, victims of childhood abuse courses, sex offender treatment, as well as Alcoholics Anonymous and Narcotics Anonymous groups.

Victim empathy programming is also featured. Psychological counseling is provided for those women with various diagnosed personality disorders. The TCI has a recidivism rate of less than 30 percent, which is considered modestly successful (Taycheedah Correctional Institution, 2003:2-3).

Alabama offers Aid to Inmate Mothers (AID), which is a network of services and programs for incarcerated mothers. Prison classes offered include parenting, anger management, domestic violence education, self-esteem courses, rape survival and support groups, and creative writing. A monthly visitation program is featured that enables mothers to reunite with their children. These are 3-hour visits where mothers and children can maintain or rebuild their relationships (AIM, Inc., 2003:1). Another prison program for inmate mothers is MILK, or Mothers Inside Loving Kids. This program is operated at the Fluvanna Correctional Center for Women in Virginia (Virginia Department of Corrections, 2002). Children are permitted to reunite with their imprisoned mothers at Fluvanna for 2 hours per week. Eventually inmate mothers can have their children visit for up to 5 hours at a time, six times a year. Friendships between mothers and children are encouraged. Women who have abused their children in past years are barred from participating. About 35 to 40 inmates participate in the program. Mothers are assisted in different ways to grow closer to their children and instill such values as honesty, respect for authority, friendliness, and personal courage.

The Thurston County, Washington Jail operates a program for women called the Turning Point Female Offender Program (TPFOP). The mission of the TPFOP is to provide information on life skills, resources, self-awareness, and health goal structures including steps to recovery from co-dependence; self care; boundaries; communication skills; healthy risk-taking; strategies for finding employment; issues related to chemical dependency; community resources; characteristics of health and unhealthy relationships; and sexuality education. The TPFOP has a low recidivism rate, less than 30 percent (Thurston County Corrections Facility, 2003:2).

The C.H.A.M.P. (Canine Helpers Allow More Possibilities) program assists female inmates in training dogs for special purposes, such as training seeing-eye dogs for the blind (Wittenauer, 2003). The Florida Department of Corrections operates several substance abuse programs tailored for female offenders who are about to enter their communities on supervised release (Florida Department of Corrections, 2000:1). These programs are designed for relapse prevention, drug abuse education, and comprehensive therapeutic community intervention. Mental health disorders are also covered in this substance-abuse treatment therapy for those women manifesting such symptoms. Finally, in New York the Women's Prison Association and Home (WPA) exists to provide programs through which women can acquire skills needed to end their involvement in the criminal justice system and to make positive, healthy choices for themselves and their families. The WPA features a transitional residential program where women can live in the community under supervision from six to 18 months (Block, 2003:1).

THE PROBATION REVOCATION PROCESS

What if probationers violate one or more conditions of their probation? First, the program violation must be detected. Second, if it is detected, the detector, usually the PO, must decide whether to report it. Third, if it is reported, it may or may not be serious enough to warrant a hearing by a judge. Fourth, if it is serious enough to warrant a hearing by a judge, it may or may not result in the termination of the probationer's program. Fifth, if the probationer's probation program is terminated, it may or may not result in prison or jail confinement. This means that a judge could resentence the probationer to a different type of probation program involving more intensive supervised probation, perhaps a program involving home confinement and/or electronic monitoring. The probationer may even be directed to participate in some form of mediation if the violation involved property loss or physical injury to others. Therefore, the probation revocation process, whenever it is initiated, may lead anywhere (Barbee, Eosemberg, and Gunter, 2002). Largely because of the

 **BOX 5.3**

DEFENDANT'S RIGHTS AT PROBATION REVOCATION HEARINGS

You have a right to a hearing on the motion or request to revoke your probation, and, at least, the following rights at that probation revocation hearing:

1. To be informed, in writing, of the manner in which it is claimed that you have violated your probation.

2. The right to be represented by a lawyer. If you cannot afford a lawyer, one will be appointed for you.

3. The right to confront and cross-examine the witnesses against you in court.

4. The right to know the evidence against you, in general terms, before the hearing.

5. The right to present witnesses or documentary evidence on your behalf.

6. The right to compulsory process, that is the right to ask the clerk of the court to issue subpoenas to compel the attendance of witnesses you want at your hearing, and to require them to bring documents or things necessary to your defense.

7. The right to a written statement by the judge as to the evidence relied on and the reasons for revoking your probation if it is revoked.

Normally, your hearing will be before the judge who heard your criminal case(s).

You are not entitled to a jury trial on a probation revocation matter. Just because a motion to revoke your probation has been filed, it is not presumed by the judge that you have violated your probation. The State has the burden of proving that you have violated the terms of your probation. While you may testify at the hearing if you desire, you cannot be forced to testify and incriminate yourself.

If your probation is not revoked, you would be continued on probation, with or without a change in the conditions of your probation. The term of your probation may be lengthened.

If your probation is revoked by the court, you have the right to present evidence and argument to the court or alternatives to placing you in jail or the penitentiary. You could be placed back on probation, with or without a sentence being imposed.

I acknowledge receipt of a copy of this statement, and I further state that I have read my rights or they have been read to me, and I understand my rights at a probation revocation hearing.

Date: _____

Defendant: _____

potential for a loss of liberty associated with any probation revocation hearing (i.e., being incarcerated in a jail or prison as one possible consequence), probationers have several important rights which must be observed. It is customary for each jurisdiction to provide probationers with a list of their rights prior to any revocation proceeding. Box 5.3 is an example of a defendant's rights at probation revocation hearings. These rights are generalizable to virtually every jurisdiction.

Technically, any probation program violation is regarded seriously whenever it is detected (Gray, 2001). If the PO determines that the probationer violated curfew by one or more minutes, this is a curfew violation and could be reported. If the probationer were to test positive for drugs or alcohol, this type of program violation is regarded as serious and could be reported. Much discretionary power rests with the PO and his or her relationship with the particular probationer/client. Usually, an attempt is made to determine why the program violation occurred (Paulsen and del Carmen, 2000). Notes maintained by the PO indicate whether or not the offense has occurred before, and if so, how often. In reality, POs prioritize probation program requirements and treat their seriousness on a graduated scale known only to them. Reporting a probationer for a technical program violation involves a certain amount of paperwork and a subsequent court appearance. Thus, this is a time-consuming process and one which POs often seek to avoid. Therefore, only the most serious program violations are often considered for formal action, such as committing new crimes or being visibly impaired from chronic substance or alcohol abuse (Barbee, Eosemberg, and Gunter, 2002).

Interestingly, POs know much about their probationer/clients and whether they will complete their probation programs successfully. For instance, probationers with less education and a record of numerous prior arrests are more likely to fail in their probation programs. Less education would mean that certain offenders had not completed high school. Offenders with a history of substance abuse and who were under- or unemployed preceding their instant conviction offenses are also more likely to fail during the period of their probation. Those POs who take greater interest in their clients might likely refer them to certain community services where some or all of their needs can be addressed. But high PO caseloads in many jurisdictions often mean that POs can spend very little or no time face-to-face with their clients.

Whether formal probation revocation proceedings will occur involves a great deal of PO discretion. However, there are certain factors or events which are beyond a PO's direct control. For instance, a probationer may be arrested for and charged with a crime. The probationer may be carrying a concealed weapon and the weapon is discovered by police officers or detectives who are interviewing witnesses at a crime scene. The probationer may get in an automobile accident while driving a car he or she is not supposed to be driving. Official reports filed by different law enforcement agencies cannot be ignored. The fact that a person is on probation is a matter of public record. When a probationer gets into any type of trouble with a law enforcement agency of any kind, there is bound to be a report made of that trouble to the court with jurisdiction over that probationer. Figure 5.4 illustrates a detailed form from North Carolina used whenever a probationer is alleged to have committed one or more probation program violations.

Under current law in every U.S. jurisdiction, probationers are entitled to a hearing before the judge if their probation is in jeopardy. Thus, if a PO is

BOX 5.4

PERSONALITY HIGHLIGHT

Victor R. Herrera
Hearing Officer, Juvenile Parole Board of the State of New Mexico

Statistics:

B.S. (sociology/anthropology), University of New Mexico Highlands

Background:

I obtained a bachelor's degree in sociology/anthropology with an emphasis in criminology from the University of New Mexico Highlands in 1999. During my freshman year, I was undecided on my major and thought about studying in the fields of business and education. While completing my core curriculum, I registered for some classes in the fields of criminology and sociology and found them to be very interesting. My older brother, Daniel Herrera Jr., also graduated from New Mexico Highlands in 1994 with the same degree. He advised me how interesting criminology and sociology were. He was killed in a car accident soon after starting to work for a treatment facility working with kids, which he enjoyed very much. I took his appreciated and important advice and decided to major in sociology/criminology. Also I was very interested in working with troubled adolescents and helping to provide them with the proper skills and needs to survive in everyday life. It was also my duty to continue providing the services my brother started with troubled youth of today's society.

Work Experience:

During my senior year in college, I was required to do an internship. I chose to work in the field of juvenile probation/parole. I was assigned to the Juvenile Probation/Parole Office in Raton, New Mexico, which at the time was supervised by Larry Pompeo. I was really nervous and excited to start my internship and also ready to take on the challenges of what I was about to face. Every day was a learning experience which consisted of meeting with clients, paperwork, court, and learning the juvenile probation/parole rules and regulations of the State of New Mexico. When it was time to actually take on my own caseload, I got to experience the life of a probation/parole officer. This is when I decided that this is what I would like to do upon graduation.

After graduation from college, I was fortunate to obtain a full-time position as a juvenile probation/parole officer with the same office where I completed my internship. I was very excited about the job and it was also nice to start off my career working in an office with so many experienced and great people. The people in this office were not only co-workers, but they were also my friends. I was assigned to work with clients in the community and also given the duty to work inside a juvenile facility, the New Mexico Boy's School, as the on-site juvenile probation/parole officer. During my employment, I got to experience both sides of life as a probation officer as well as life inside a juvenile correctional facility. It was very interesting to work with troubled adolescents from around the state and from different cultural backgrounds. For instance, some kids you deal with are easy-going and not difficult to deal with, while others are very rebellious and hard to control. You have to be very patient and try to deal with each child's individual needs. At the facility, I was also in charge of working as a liaison with the New Mexico Boy's School and the Juvenile Parole Board. I would help

BOX 5.4 (Continued)

provide facility information to the Parole Board on clients who had been placed on the parole agenda and were ready to experience the period of their parole. This also gave me some experience about their lives after they left the facility and became integrated back into their communities. Some kids did well and never came back, but some would violate their parole conditions and return to the facility where they would face new charges or technical parole violations. As time went by, I really enjoyed the parole aspect of my job, which is a very important part of a troubled youth's life after being incarcerated in a facility for a period of their young lives. I was then hired as hearing officer for the Juvenile Parole Board in Albuquerque, New Mexico in December 2002. This job consists of providing information to the Juvenile Parole Board membership about juveniles who are committed to a juvenile correctional facility; conducting special hearings/interviews on juveniles who are currently incarcerated; and compiling, summarizing, and entering data containing hearings/interview information. This job is really exciting because you get to encourage the juveniles, both boys and girls, to do well and give them advice on what it's going to take for them to succeed on parole in the future. The majority of the kids listen and try to learn from their experiences and mistakes, but you also have a few who will probably never change their negative ways. You have to understand that most of the children come from gangs, drug-infested families, or broken homes. Most of them have no one to talk with or to seek advice from. And so when you sit down and talk with them one-on-one, they listen and respect the advice you give them. Some kids just don't have a family to talk to about things that are bothering them, and they are too embarrassed to discuss these issues with their friends. It's sad, but you have to understand that you're not going to save all the children you work with, but you at least need to give it a try.

Advice to Students:

My advice to students is that if you feel that you want to work in the field of probation/parole, you must be ready to face a variety of different challenges. Every day presents different obstacles which will keep you on your toes and alert. You have to understand that you cannot and will not save all of the children you work with, and so you must be able to accept the feeling of failure. These cases will help you get stronger and enable you to prepare for future cases down the road. You must have the mentality that you can make a difference in children's lives and be willing to provide more time to your job other than a 40-hour work week. Students should also be aware that there are many areas in the fields of criminology, sociology, and probation/parole that work together and that can give you the experience to start a career changing children's lives.

charged with committing either a technical probation program violation (e.g., curfew violation, frequenting a place where alcoholic beverages are served) or a crime, then the matter of revoking one's probation is referred to the original sentencing court for further action (Jermstad and del Carmen, 2002).

The court must conduct a two-stage proceeding. Allegations against the probationer must be heard by the judge. Supporting evidentiary information must be presented to show the probationer's guilt relating to the charges filed. The probationer is permitted to introduce exculpatory information on his/her own behalf and to offer supporting testimony. All of this evidence is heard in the first stage of a two-stage revocation process. Therefore, the first stage of a

STATE OF NORTH CAROLINA

File No.
Co. Of Hearing

_____ County_____   Seat of Court

NOTE: (This form is not to be used for structured sentencing offenses.)

In The General Court Of Justice
☐ District ☐ Superior Court Division

STATE VERSUS

Name Of Defendant

ORDER ON VIOLATION
OF PROBATION
OR ON MOTION TO MODIFY

Attorney For State

☐ Def. Found Not Indigent   ☐ Def. Waived Attorney

Attorney For Defendant

☐ Appointed ☐ Retained

☐ **AND COMMITMENT ON SPECIAL PROBATION**

G.S. 15A-1344, 15A-1345

The defendant was placed on probation pursuant to the following Judgment Suspending Sentence:

Date Of Judgment Suspending Sentence

☐ Superior Court
☐ District Court

Name Of County And File No. (County Of Original Conviction)

This matter is before the Court upon: (check one option)

☐ 1. review under G.S. 15A-1342(b) or (d). After reasonable notice to the defendant, the Court ☐ finds ☐ does not find that termination of probation is warranted by the defendant's conduct and the ends of justice.

☐ 2. a motion to modify the conditions of the defendant's probation for good cause without charge of violation. After notice and hearing, or upon the consent of the State and the defendant, the Court ☐ finds ☐ does not find that good cause has been shown to modify the original Judgment Suspending Sentence.

☐ 3. charge(s) of violation. After considering the record contained in the files numbered above, together with the evidence presented by the parties and the statements made on behalf of the State and the defendant, the Court finds that the defendant is charged with having violated specified conditions of the defendant's probation as alleged in the Violation Report or Notice

Upon due notice or waiver of notice, a hearing was held before the Court and:

☐ 1. the defendant admitted or the Court is reasonably satisfied in the exercise of its discretion that the defendant has violated each of the conditions of probation set forth in

☐ a. paragraphs _____ in the Violation Report or Notice of Hearing dated _____.
☐ b. the attached sheet.

The defendant violated each condition willfully and without valid excuse; and each violation occurred at a time prior to the expiration or termination of the period of the defendant's probation.

☐ 2. by the evidence presented, the Court is not reasonably satisfied that the defendant has violated any of the conditions of the defendant's probation except those found above, if any.

ORDER

It is ORDERED that:

☐ 1. the original Judgment is modified as set forth below and, except as specifically so modified, shall remain in full force and effect.

☐ 2. the original Judgment is not modified, but remains in full force and effect.

☐ 3. the defendant's limited driving privilege is REVOKED; the defendant shall surrender all copies of that privilege to the Clerk of Superior Court for transmittal/notification to the Division of Motor Vehicles.

☐ 4. the defendant's probation is terminated.

☐ 5. all charges of probation violation in this case, which are not specifically found above, are dismissed.

☐ 6. the disposition of this matter is continued until _____.

SPECIAL PROBATION/ACTIVE SENTENCE

☐ As a condition of special probation, the defendant shall ☐ serve an active term of _____ ☐ days ☐ months in the custody of the ☐ N.C. DOC. ☐ Sheriff of this County. ☐ submit to IMPACT imprisonment per attached AOC-CR-302, Page Two. ☐ pay jail ☐ work release recommended. **(NOTE:** This term shall **NOT** be reduced by jail or treatment time, good time, gain time or parole.)

The defendant shall report in a sober condition to begin serving this term on:

Day	Date	Hour	☐ AM ☐ PM	and shall remain in custody until:	Day	Date	Hour	☐ AM ☐ PM

☐ The defendant shall again report in a sober condition to continue serving this term on the same day of the week for the next _____ consecutive weeks, and shall remain in custody during the same hours each week.

MODIFIED MONETARY CONDITIONS

The "Monetary Conditions" in the Judgment Suspending Sentence are modified to read as follows: Pay to Clerk of Superior Court ☐ $ _____ on or before _____

☐ the "Modified Amount Due" shown below, plus the monthly probation supervision fee set by law ☐ pursuant to a schedule determined by the probation officer ☐ at the rate of $ _____ per _____, beginning on _____ and continuing on the same day of each _____ thereafter until paid in full.

☐ Other:

Balance On Original Obligation*	Arrearage On Probation Fee	Attorney Fee This Proceeding	Modified Amount Due
$	$	$	$

*Equals "Total Amount Due" as shown on original Judgment, less all payments made to date, and adjusted to reflect any modifications on Side

AOC-CR-316, Rev. 9/02   Material opposite unmarked squares is to be disregarded as surplusage.
© 2002 Administrative Office of the Courts

FIGURE 5.4 North Carolina Probation Revocation Form. (3 pages)

probation revocation hearing is to determine the guilt or innocence of the accused relating to the probation program violation, whatever it may be. If the judge determines that there is no basis for the allegations, then the matter is concluded. The probationer remains on his/her probation program. However, if the judge determines that the probationer is guilty of the allegations, then a second stage is conducted. This second stage may be conducted in court after a recess. During this second stage of the two-stage process, the judge determines what the penalty should be for violating the particular program requirement(s).

OTHER MODIFICATIONS OF PROBATION

☐ 1. The defendant's term of probation is extended for a period of _____ , from _____ to _____ .

☐ 2. The defendant's assignment to the Intensive Probation Supervision Program is terminated and the defendant is continued on supervised probation.

☐ 3. The defendant is transferred to ☐ unsupervised ☐ supervised probation.

☐ 4. The defendant is allowed until _____ to comply with the following condition(s)

☐ 5. The special conditions of probation identified below, as numbered and set out in the Judgment Suspending Sentence, are modified as follows: *(state number of each condition to be modified and set out modification.)*

☐ 6. The defendant shall also comply with the following additional special conditions of probation which the Court finds are reasonably related to the defendant's rehabilitation:
   ☐ complete _____ hours of community service during the first _____ days of probation, as directed by the community service coordinator, and pay the fee prescribed by G.S. 143B-475.1(b).
   ☐ Other: *(set out conditions)*

☐ 7. Comply with the Additional Conditions of Probation which are set forth on AOC-CR-302, Page Two, attached.

CONTEMPT

NOTE: *This Contempt section applies to a defendant <u>sentenced</u> on or after May 1, 1994. [G.S. 5A-11(a)(9a) and 15A-1344.]*

Upon due notice or waiver of notice, a hearing was held before the Court and the defendant is found guilty of contempt beyond a reasonable doubt.
It is ORDERED that the defendant for willful contempt:
   ☐ a. be imprisoned for _____ days in the custody of the sheriff.
   ☐ b. pay a fine of _____ .
   ☐ c. Other: _____

AWARD OF FEE TO COUNSEL FOR DEFENDANT

☐ A hearing was held in open court in the presence of the defendant at which time a fee, including expenses, was awarded the defendant's appointed counsel or assigned public defender in this proceeding.

ORDER OF COMMITMENT/APPEAL ENTRIES

☐ 1. It is ORDERED that the Clerk deliver <u>two</u> certified copies of this Order and Commitment to the sheriff or other qualified officer and that the officer cause the defendant to be delivered with these copies to the custody of the agency named on the reverse to serve the sentence imposed or until the defendant shall have complied with the conditions of release pending appeal.

☐ 2. The defendant gives notice of appeal from the judgment of the District Court to the Superior Court. The current pretrial release order is modified as follows:

☐ 3. The defendant gives notice of appeal from the judgment of the Superior Court to the Appellate Division. Appeal entries and any conditions of post conviction release are set forth on form AOC-CR-350.

SIGNATURE OF JUDGE

Date	Name Of Presiding Judge (Type Or Print)	Signature Of Presiding Judge

CERTIFICATION

I certify that this Order and the attachment(s) marked below is a true and complete copy of the original which is on file in this case.
   ☐ 1. Appellate Entries (AOC-CR-350)
   ☐ 2. Additional Conditions Of Probation (AOC-CR-302, Page Two)
   ☐ 3. Judgment Suspending Sentence *(Check only if a term of imprisonment is imposed as a new condition of special probation.)*

Date Of Certification	Date Certified Copies Delivered To Sheriff	Signature And Seal
		☐ Deputy CSC ☐ Assistant CSC ☐ Clerk Of Superior Court

(NOTE: *Defendant signs the following statement in all cases of supervised probation except where probation is terminated or is not modified.)*
I have received a copy of this Order which contains modifications of my probation and I agree to them. I understand that no person who supervises me or for whom I work while performing community or reparation service is liable to me for any loss or damage which I may sustain unless my injury is caused by that person's gross negligence or intentional wrongdoing. I understand that my probation may be

Date Signed	Signature Of Defendant	Witnessed By

NOTE: *Send a Certified Copy to the Clerk of Superior Court of the County of Original Conviction, if Different.*

AOC-CR-316, Side Two, Rev. 9/02
©2002 Administrative Office of the Courts   Material opposite unmarked squares is to be disregarded as surplusage.

FIGURE 5.4   *(Continued)*

Judges are encouraged to avoid incarcerating probationers if it is reasonable to do so under particular circumstances. Judges may determine that even though the probationer has violated one or more program conditions based on the evidence presented, that the probationer should be permitted to continue in his/her probation program for its duration (del Carmen et al., 2000; Podkopacz and Feld, 2002). Or judges may decide to impose additional conditions to one's program as sanctions or penalties. The offender may be required to make restitution to victims, pay a fine, or enter into mediation with one or more other parties. Or the offender may be placed in home confinement and/or

STATE VERSUS	File No.
Name Of Defendant	

ADDITIONAL CONDITIONS OF PROBATION - G.S. 15A-1343(b1)

NOTE: *Use this page in conjunction with AOC-CR-302, "Judgment Suspending Sentence"; AOC-CR-310, "Impaired Driving Judgment Suspending Sentence"; or AOC-CR-316, "Order On Charge Of Violation Of Probation Or On Motion To Modify".*

In addition to complying with the regular and any special conditions of probation set forth in the "Judgment Suspending Sentence" entered in the above case(s), the defendant shall also comply with the following special conditions of probation and conditions of special probation, which the Court finds are reasonably related to the defendant's rehabilitation.

☐ Be assigned to the INTENSIVE PROBATION SUPERVISION PROGRAM for a period of not less than six months, obey all rules, regulations and directions of the program until discharged, and

1. Submit at reasonable times to warrantless searches by a probation officer of the defendant's person, and of the defendant's vehicle and premises while the defendant is present, for the following purposes which are reasonably related to the defendant's probation supervision:
☐ stolen goods   ☐ controlled substances   ☐ contraband   ☐ _____

2. Not use, possess or control any illegal drug or controlled substance unless it has been prescribed for the defendant by a licensed physician and is in the original container with the prescription number affixed on it; not knowingly associate with any known or previously convicted users, possessors or sellers of any illegal drugs or controlled substances; and not knowingly be present at or frequent any place where illegal drugs or controlled substances are sold, kept or used.

3. Supply a breath, urine and/or blood specimen for analysis of the possible presence of a prohibited drug or alcohol, when instructed by the defendant's probation officer.

4. Complete not less than _____ hours or more than _____ hours of community or reparation service, as determined by the defendant's probation officer, and under the direction of the community service coordinator and pay the fee prescribed by G.S. 143B-475.1(b) ☐ within _____ days of this Judgment and before beginning service.

5. Participate in any evaluation, counseling, treatment or education program as directed by the defendant's probation officer, faithfully keep all scheduled appointments, and abide by all rules, regulations and directions of each program.

6. Not be away from the defendant's place of residence between the hours of _____ p.m. and _____ a.m. unless authorized in writing by the defendant's probation officer.

7. Not leave the defendant's county of residence without prior approval of the defendant's probation officer.

8. Other:

☐ Submit as directed by the defendant's probation officer to a medical evaluation by a physician approved by the officer and, if certified to be medically fit for participation in the Intensive Motivation Program of Alternative Correctional Treatment (IMPACT), further submit, as ordered by the officer, on the date and at the place specified, to imprisonment in a facility for youthful offenders for a period of 90 days from that date, and abide by all rules and regulations as provided in conjunction with the IMPACT program, provided:

a. at the end of this 90 day period, the defendant shall continue to submit to imprisonment for an additional period of 30 days if required to do so as provided in those rules and regulations, and

b. If, within _____ days from the date of this Judgment, the defendant is not certified to be medically fit for program participation or for any other reason is not ordered to submit to imprisonment as provided above then ☐ the defendant shall reappear before the Court as directed by the probation officer for a hearing to determine what modifications, if any, should be made to this Judgment.
☐ Other:

☐ *(Use this option when placing defendant under house arrest as a special condition of supervised probation in any case, or as a condition of supervised special probation upon conviction of DWI under G.S. 20-138.1 and imposition of Level One or Level Two imprisonment. In DWI cases, check the block at the end of this option, see G.S. 20-179(g) and (h), and designate days of imprisonment and house arrest accordingly.)* Be assigned to the Electronic House Arrest Program for a period of _____ days, submit to electronic monitoring and abide by all rules, regulations and directions of the program until discharged ☐ and before being assigned, serve a term of imprisonment of _____ days in the custody of the sheriff of this county.

☐ Other Conditions:

Date	Name Of Presiding Judge (Type Or Print)	Signature Of Presiding Judge

AOC-CR-302, Page Two, Rev. 7/2000
© 2000 Administrative Office of the Courts   Material opposite unmarked squares to be disregarded as surplusage.

FIGURE 5.4 *(Continued)*

electronic monitoring. Or the offender may be required to have more frequent face-to-face visits with the PO in an intensive supervision scenario. If the program violation is serious enough, the judge has the authority to terminate one's probation program and order the probationer incarcerated. These are the options available to judges.

Figure 5.4 illustrates virtually every option available to North Carolina judges whenever they conduct probation revocation hearings. In the first part of the form, the judge indicates whether sufficient evidence has been presented to support the allegations against the probationer. Several judicial options are indicated, including orders to modify the existing probationary sentence and its accompanying conditions. This form affects those on intensive supervised probation as well. Penalties include additional monetary assessments, fines, and a host of other conditions. The probationer must sign this form except when probation is terminated or there is no modification of one's probation program. Below are some leading cases relating to probation revocation. The next section also contains several common scenarios involving probationers and how different state jurisdictions have concluded these revocation actions.

Special Circumstances: Mandatory Federal Probation Revocation

Federal district court judges have been exposed to numerous changes in sentencing laws during the 1980s and 1990s. The Sentencing Reform Act of 1984 led to the promulgation of U.S. sentencing guidelines which went into effect in October 1987 (Tonry, 2001). Federal district court judges were obligated to follow these guidelines as closely as possible, although they have been allowed to engage in upward or downward departures from these guidelines in sentencing certain offenders, provided that they furnish a written rationale for doing so (Petersilia, 2001).

In 1994, Congress passed the Violent Crime and Law Enforcement Act (VCCA) which further affected federal judges and the sentences they imposed. Of particular interest were changes in sentencing regulations that pertained to revoking the probation programs of federal offenders. In the pre-VCCA period (pre-September 1994), federal district court judges could revoke a federal probationer's probation program, but the revocation sentence must fall within the guideline range available for the original sentence. However, in the post-VCCA period, a revocation sentence could be any sentence that the court could have imposed at the time of the original sentence. For example, if a probationer had originally been sentenced to 12 months of probation resulting from a recommendation from the federal prosecutor for a downward guideline departure, a subsequent revocation sentence from the court could be for a 24-month probationary sentence or even imprisonment, absent a renewal motion from the federal prosecutor. Under the post-VCCA sentencing scheme, a federal judge could impose any sentence that could have been imposed at the original sentencing date, regardless of prosecutorial recommendations.

Under a new post-VCCA provision, a revocation sentence resulting from drug possession must result in a term of imprisonment. This is a new mandatory sentence. Although it is mandatory, the court may determine that the revoked probationer may benefit from drug treatment as an alternative to incarceration. This is a very narrow option which is contained in the new post-VCCA provisions. However, if the mandatory incarcerative term is imposed, it must be at least one third of the maximum guideline provision for the original offense. Thus, if the original sentence had an upper guideline of 30 months, then the term of incarceration which the court must impose would be 10 months, absent any consideration given to one's amenability to drug treatment (Adair, 2000).

LANDMARK CASES AND SPECIAL ISSUES

In this section we will examine several U.S. Supreme Court cases which have affected probationers and the conditions under which judges may revoke their probation programs. Several cases are highlighted which have had national significance and application. Other cases are described at the state level, where individual state supreme or appellate courts have ruled in particular probation revocation matters. The issues described in each of the following scenarios are generally applicable among the states, with very few and limited exceptions.

Landmark Cases

Mempa v. Rhay (1967).   Jerry Mempa was convicted of "joyriding" in a stolen vehicle on June 17, 1959. He was placed on probation for two years by a Spokane, Washington judge. Several months later, Mempa was involved in a burglary on September 15, 1959. The county prosecutor in Spokane moved to have Mempa's probation revoked. Mempa admitted participating in the burglary. At his probation revocation hearing, the sole testimony about his involvement in the burglary came from his probation officer. Mempa was not represented by counsel, was not asked if he wanted counsel, and was not given an opportunity to offer statements in his own behalf. Furthermore, there was no cross-examination of the probation officer about his statements. The court revoked Mempa's probation and sentenced him to ten years in the Washington State Penitentiary.

Six years later in 1965, Mempa filed a writ of **habeas corpus,** alleging that he had been denied a right to counsel at the revocation hearing. The Washington Supreme Court denied his petition, but the U. S. Supreme Court elected to hear it on appeal. The U. S. Supreme Court overturned the Washington decision and ruled in Mempa's favor. Specifically, the U. S. Supreme Court said Mempa was entitled to an attorney but was denied one. While the Court did not question Washington authority to defer sentencing in the probation matter, it said that any indigent (including Mempa) is entitled at every stage of a criminal proceeding to be represented by court-appointed counsel, where "substantial rights of a criminal accused may be affected." Thus, the U. S. Supreme Court considered a probation revocation hearing to be a "critical stage" that falls within the due process provisions of the Fourteenth Amendment. In subsequent years, several courts also applied this decision to parole revocation hearings.

Gagnon v. Scarpelli (1973).   Gerald Scarpelli pled guilty to a charge of robbery in July, 1965 in a Wisconsin court. He was sentenced to 15 years in prison. But the judge suspended this sentence on August 5, 1965 and placed Scarpelli on probation for a period of 7 years. The next day, August 6, Scarpelli was arrested and charged with burglary. His probation was revoked without a hearing and he was placed in the Wisconsin State Reformatory to serve his 15-year term. About three years later, Scarpelli was paroled. Shortly before his parole, he filed a habeas corpus petition, alleging that his probation revocation was invoked without a hearing and without benefit of counsel. Thus, this constituted a denial of due process. Following his parole, the U. S. Supreme Court acted on his original habeas corpus petition and ruled in his favor. Specifically, the U. S. Supreme Court said that Scarpelli was denied his right to due process because no revocation hearing was held and he was not represented by court-appointed counsel within the indigent claim.

Bearden v. Georgia (1983).   Bearden's probation was revoked by Georgia authorities because he failed to pay a fine and make restitution to his victim as required by the court. He claimed he was indigent, but the court rejected his claim as a valid explanation for his conduct. The U.S. Supreme Court disagreed. It ruled that probation may not be revoked in the case of indigent probationers who have failed to pay their fines or make restitution. They further suggested alternatives for restitution and punishments that were more compatible with the abilities and economic resources of indigent probationers such as community service. In short, the probationer should not be penalized where a reasonable effort has been made to pay court-ordered fines and restitution. The states have ruled similarly in more recent cases (People v. Bouyer, 2002; *United States v. Jones*, 2002).

Offender indigence does not automatically entitle them to immunity from restitution orders. In a 1993 case, *United States v. Bachsian* (1993), Bachsian was convicted of theft. He was required to pay restitution for the merchandise still in his possession under the Victim Witness Protection Act. Bachsian claimed, however, that he was indigent and unable to make restitution. The 9th Circuit Court of Appeals declared in Bachsian's case that it was not improper to impose restitution orders on an offender at the time of sentencing, even if the offender was unable to pay restitution then. In this instance, records indicated that Bachsian was considered by the court as having a future ability to pay, based on a presentence investigation report. Eventually, Bachsian would become financially able and in a position to make restitution to his victim. His restitution orders were upheld. Also, bankruptcy does not discharge an offender's obligation to make restitution, although the amount and rate of restitution payments may be affected (United States v. Leigh, 2002).

Black v. Romano (1985).   A probationer had his probation revoked by the sentencing judge because of alleged program violations. The defendant had left the scene of an automobile accident, a felony in the jurisdiction where the alleged offense occurred. The judge gave reasons for the revocation decision, but did not indicate that he had considered any option other than incarceration. The U.S. Supreme Court ruled that judges are not generally obligated to consider alternatives to incarceration before they revoke an offender's probation and place him in jail or prison.

Clearly, probationers and parolees have obtained substantial rights in recent years. U. S. Supreme Court decisions have provided them with several important constitutional rights that invalidate the arbitrary and capricious revocation of their probation or parole programs by judges or parole boards. The two-stage hearing is extremely important to probationers and parolees, in that it permits ample airing of the allegations against offender, cross-examinations by counsel, and testimony from individual offenders.

Special Issues

Probationers who are acquitted of other crimes while on probation must be represented by counsel at subsequent probation revocation proceedings. Furthermore, judges may not use evidence from their trial acquittals against them to enhance the punishment in a probation revocation proceeding. Gibbs was a Delaware probationer (Gibbs v. State, 2000). During his probationary term, he was arrested and charged with a crime. He was subsequently acquitted. In a unilateral action, the original sentencing judge ordered Gibbs' probation program revoked. The judge did not allow Gibbs to be represented by counsel, nor did he permit Gibbs to offer testimony in his own behalf. The judge summarily revoked Gibbs' parole, citing as evidence some of the information from the trial where Gibbs was acquitted. Furthermore, the judge declared that on the basis of the **preponderance of evidence,** he found that Gibbs had indeed violated one or more of his probation program conditions. Gibbs appealed, arguing that he was entitled to counsel and that he should be permitted to give testimony in his own behalf. A Delaware appellate court agreed and overturned the judge's revocation order. Probationers are entitled to counsel in their probation revocation proceedings.

Statements made to a PO while being interrogated, not in custody, are admissible in court for the purpose of supporting new criminal charges. In Minnesota v. Murphy (1984), Murphy, a probationer, was serving a three-year probation term for criminal sexual conduct. One of Murphy's probation conditions was that he was to report regularly to his PO and answer all questions truthfully. Another condition was that he seek sexual therapy and counseling. During one of these counseling sessions, Murphy confessed to one of his counselors that he had committed a rape and murder in 1974. The counselor told his probation officer, who, in turn, interrogated Murphy at his residence. Murphy admitted the crime (responding truthfully) after extensive interviewing and interrogation by the PO. The PO gave this incriminating information to police who arrested Murphy later and charged him with the 1974 rape and murder. Murphy claimed later that the PO had not advised him of his Miranda rights (e.g., right to an attorney, right to terminate questioning at any point, right against making self-incriminating statements) and thus, his confession should not be admitted later in court against him. As a general rule, criminal suspects who are the targets of a police investigation must be advised of their Miranda rights if undergoing an interrogation, whether they are in custody. A similar rule pertains to probationers. It might be argued, for instance, that the fact of their probation is a form of "custody." Thus, all probationers (and parolees) might be considered "in custody" during the their program terms. However, "custody" implies being unable to leave the presence of the interrogator. When suspects conclude their interrogation, they may or may not be permitted to leave. If they leave, they are not considered to be in custody. Otherwise, they are in custody. Murphy was not in custody, however. In Murphy's case, he was not in custody. Also, he was not compelled to answer the PO's questions. Obviously, this is a complex case involving seemingly conflicting obligations and constitutional rights.

Search and seizure grounds are less stringent for POs who intend to search their client's homes for illegal contraband. Monteiro was convicted on four counts of mail fraud and was placed on a period of supervised release (United States v. Monteiro, 2001). One condition of his supervised release program was that Monteiro's person, residence, and vehicle were subject to search and seizure upon demand by any law enforcement officer. Monteiro objected to this condition but his objection was rejected by the court. Monteiro later appealed to the 7th Circuit Court where his case was heard. Monteiro claimed that this condition was invalid since it was overly broad. The court rejected his claim and held that given the life pattern of Monteiro, including his commission of fraudulent use of a credit device, the search condition was reasonably related to the goals of rehabilitation and protection of the public. However, the court held that the "seizure" provision was invalid and directed the case back to the district court where a limiting instruction could be crafted and restated as a special condition of supervised release.

In another case, Bonner was a convicted offender in Indiana who objected to the condition that a probation officer could search Bonner's person, residence, and vehicle at any time without warrant (Bonner v. State, 2002). Bonner objected to this condition as unreasonable and in violation of his constitutional privacy rights. The court held that probation is a criminal sanction wherein a convicted defendant specifically agrees to accept the conditions of supervision in lieu of imprisonment. Thus, restrictions on the probationer's conduct are permissible to ensure that probation serves as a period of genuine rehabilitation and the public is not harmed by the probationer's conduct in the community. The only limitation is that the conditions must demonstrate a reasonable relation to the treatment of the accused the protection of the public. When Bonner claimed that that probation condition was unduly intrusive upon a constitutional right, the following three factors must be balanced: (1) the purpose sought to be served by probation; (2) the extent to which the constitutional right in question should be afforded probationers; and (3) the legitimate needs of law enforcement. Although the condition to search in this case did not include "reasonableness," its absence did not render the condition overbroad and unconstitutional. Nor could the court say that the condition was improper. A warrantless search condition is an invaluable aid in rehabilitation. Moreover, the supervision and monitoring of probationers helps to facilitate the probation system's overall goal of genuine rehabilitation. Further, a warrantless search condition was also helpful in protecting the public from Bonner's possible further illegal activities.

Conditions of probation/parole, including victim restitution payments, are legitimate; however, whenever restitution is imposed, it must relate reasonably to the original conviction offense. Torpen was convicted of a property crime in Wisconsin (State v. Torpen, 2001). Torpen had a prior criminal record. When Torpen was sentenced to probation, the judge included a restitution order for Torpen to pay for his previous, unrelated offenses. Torpen objected and appealed. The Wisconsin appellate court threw out the judge's restitution order as a condition of Torpen's probation, holding that it did not reasonably relate to Torpen's present conviction offense. It is improper for judges to impose restitution in relation to previous unrelated crimes as a condition of Torpen's probation for the present conviction offense.

In an Alaska case, Mahan was convicted of cruelty to animals and animal neglect (Mahan v. State, 2002). One of her probation conditions was the payment of restitution to an animal care organization for the expenses incurred in taking care of her animals. Mahan appealed, claiming that her restitution payments should be reduced by the amount of charitable contributions received by the animal care organization as the result of the publicity surrounding her conviction. The appellate court disagreed and held that people who donated money did not intend for their donations to reduce Mahan's restitution obligations. Restitution serves two goals: (1) it restores victims and (2) makes defendants pay the expenses they have caused by their criminal conduct. The second goal would not be served if Mahan received credit for money that crime victims received from sympathetic members of the community.

Judges who impose probation in lieu of mandatory sentences for particular offenses may have their probation judgments declared invalid. In a New

York case, a plea bargain was worked out between the state and a defendant, Hipp (People v. Hipp, 1993). Hipp was determined by the court to be addicted to gambling. The nature of the conviction offense and the gambling addiction compel the Court under mandatory sentencing to prescribe a jail term as well as accompanying therapy for the addiction. In this instance, the judge simply accepted a plea agreement, accepting the defendant's guilty plea in exchange for a term of probation. The New York Court of Appeals overruled the judge in this case, indicating that New York statutes do not authorize a trial court to ignore clearly expressed and unequivocal mandatory sentencing provisions of the New York Penal Law. However, in Florida, a judge imposed probation on an offender convicted under an Habitual Offender Statute (McKnight v. State, 1993). McKnight, was convicted of being an habitual felony offender. Ordinarily, this conviction carries a mandatory life-without-parole penalty. However, the judge in McKnight's case imposed probation. While the Florida Court of Appeals did not like the judge's decision, they upheld it anyway, supporting the general principle of judicial discretion.

Probationers may be barred from using computers if computers were involved in their conviction offenses. Sofsky pleaded guilty to receiving Internet images of child pornography (United States v. Sofsky, 2002). Sofsky was sentenced to confinement followed by a three-year term of supervised release, subject to the following conditions: (1) Sofsky must participate in a mental health treatment program; (2) Sofsky must permit a search of his premises for possible contraband or evidence of a violation of a condition of his probation; (3) Sofsky may not have access to any computer, the Internet, or bulletin board systems at any time; and (4) Sofsky must not view, purchase, or possess child pornographic materials. Sofsky appealed his access to the Internet, contending that it violated his free speech right. In this case, Sofsky's condition barring him from access to the Internet was declared invalid. The court said that probation officers could monitor Sofsky's computer use in alternative ways, including unannounced inspections, an examination of material on his hard drive, or removable disks. The government could also check on Sofsky by means of a sting operation, whereby they would send Sofsky messages from time to time, offering child pornography materials.

In another case, Wardle was an Idaho probationer convicted of battery (State v. Wardle, 2002). Among other probation conditions, Wardle was prohibited from possessing or using a computer in his home or workplace. The court based its computer prohibition on the fact that Wardle used his computer to show the victim various pornographic images. Wardle challenged the order, contending that it was unfairly broad and violated his constitutional rights. An appellate court upheld the computer ban in Wardle's case, since that condition reasonably related to the prevention of further criminal activity on his part.

Probation officers are forbidden from creating their own rules for their probationer-clients in addition to those imposed by the sentencing judge. In the Massachusetts case of Commonwealth v. MacDonald (2000), MacDonald was placed on probation in relation to a felony conviction. Among other requirements, MacDonald was ordered by the sentencing judge to "stay away" from Cynthia Evans. He was also ordered to submit to counseling for drug and alcohol abuse. However, when he arrived at the probation office, the PO advised MacDonald that MacDonald was to have "no contact" with Evans. Subse-

IN THE SUPREME COURT, STATE OF WYOMING

2003 WY 64

APRIL TERM, A.D. 2003

May 23, 2003

IVAN LEE SWEETS,

    Appellant
    (Defendant) ,

    v.

THE STATE OF WYOMING,

    Appellee
    (Plaintiff) .

No. 02-92

Appeal from the District Court of Sweetwater County
The Honorable Jere Ryckman, Judge

Representing Appellant:
> Kenneth M. Koski, State Public Defender; Donna D. Domonkos, Appellate Counsel; and Tina N. Kerin, Senior Assistant Appellate Counsel

Representing Appellee:
> Hoke MacMillan, Attorney General; Paul S. Rehurek, Deputy Attorney General; D. Michael Pauling, Senior Assistant Attorney General; and Ericka S. Cook, Assistant Attorney General

Before HILL, C.J., and GOLDEN, LEHMAN, and VOIGT, JJ., and BURKE, D.J.

> *NOTICE: This opinion is subject to formal revision before publication in Pacific Reporter Third. Readers are requested to notify the Clerk of the Supreme Court, Supreme Court Building, Cheyenne, Wyoming 82002, of any typographical or other formal errors so that correction may be made before final publication in the permanent volume.*

FIGURE 5.5   Appeal of Probation Revocation by Ivan Lee Sweets Before the Wyoming Supreme Court.

quently, MacDonald sent a letter to Evans regarding an upcoming care and protection hearing concerning their two minor children. The PO considered this to be a violation of the "no contact" order he had issued and moved to revoke MacDonald's probation. The judge revoked MacDonald's probation program and he appealed. An appellate court overturned the revocation, saying that the PO illegally added the "no contact" provision and that that this differed significantly from the "stay away" provision contemplated by the judge. POs cannot write new rules for their clients.

BURKE, District Judge.

[¶1]   Appellant Ivan Sweets (Sweets) appeals a district court's order that revoked his probation and imposed the underlying two-to-four-year prison sentence. Sweets alleges that he was denied due process because he was not given notice of allegations upon which the district court based its decision. We find that Sweets' admission to one of the allegations in the petition conclusively established a probation violation, and that the district court did not abuse its discretion in revoking probation. We affirm.

ISSUES

[¶2]   Sweets presents the following issue for review:

> Whether the district court erred in revoking [Sweets'] probation and violated his right to due process by revoking [his] probation based upon allegations of which [he] had no notice[.]

The State phrases the issue as follows:

> Whether the district court abused its discretion when it revoked [Sweets'] probation after [he] admitted an allegation in the petition for revocation.

FACTS

[¶3]   On May 17, 2000, Sweets pleaded guilty to a charge of delivery of cocaine in violation of Wyo. Stat. Ann. § 35-7-1031(a)(i) (LexisNexis 2001). Pursuant to a plea agreement, a prison term of two to four years was suspended, and Sweets was placed on supervised probation for four years. The district court set forth terms of probation, including conditions that Sweets abide by the law and not consume, possess, purchase, or sell any illegal controlled substance.

[¶4]   On November 7, 2001, the State filed a petition to revoke Sweets' probation. The petition alleged the following probation violations: Sweets failed to report to his probation agent; he failed to attend Criminal Thinking Group; he refused to report to a specified location to provide a urine sample; his urine tested positive for cocaine on three occasions; he failed to obtain a substance abuse evaluation; and he refused and failed to apply for, enroll in, and complete the Intensive Supervision Program (ISP).

[¶5]   On November 19, 2001, the district court advised Sweets of his rights in accordance with W.R.Cr.P. 39(a)(3). On December 14, 2001, Sweets appeared with his attorney and

FIGURE 5.5   *(Continued)*

Defendants may or may not refuse probation if the court imposes probation as a sentence, depending on the jurisdiction. In a case reported elsewhere in the text, Brown was a California defendant convicted of vandalizing his wife's car (People v. Brown, 2001). The judge imposed a sentence of probation, but Brown refused it, claiming that the probation conditions were too onerous. Brown settled for a six-month jail sentence instead. Brown's refusal of probation was upheld by a higher court.

denied the allegations of the petition.

[¶6]   After several continuances, a final hearing on the petition was held on February 27, 2002. Prior to any testimony being presented, Sweets admitted to having violated his probation by using cocaine. The hearing proceeded on the remaining allegations of the petition.

[¶7]   The State presented the testimony of the probation agent currently assigned to Sweets. The agent's testimony was based upon her limited recollection of the written notes made by a previous agent. At the conclusion of the agent's testimony, the district court concluded that the evidence did not support a finding that Sweets had violated his probation for failing to report, for failing to attend Criminal Thinking Group, for refusing to provide a urine sample, or for failing to obtain a substance abuse evaluation. After Sweets testified and counsel presented argument, the district court further concluded that the State failed to demonstrate that Sweets had failed to participate in ISP.

[¶8]   The district court determined that Sweets admitted an allegation in the petition and that the admitted conduct violated terms of probation. The district court revoked probation and sentenced Sweets to the state penitentiary to serve the two-to-four-year sentence. This appeal followed.

STANDARD OF REVIEW

[¶9]   A district court's decision to revoke probation and impose a sentence is discretionary and will not be disturbed unless the record shows a clear abuse of discretion. *Mapp v. State*, 929 P.2d 1222, 1225 (Wyo. 1996); *Kupec v. State*, 835 P.2d 359, 362 (Wyo. 1992). Judicial discretion is a composite of many things, among which are conclusions drawn from objective criteria; it means a sound judgment exercised with regard to what is right under the circumstances and without doing so arbitrarily or capriciously. *Vaughn v. State*, 962 P.2d 149, 151 (Wyo. 1998). "Upon review, all that is necessary to uphold a district court's decision to revoke probation is evidence that it made a conscientious judgment, after hearing the facts, that a condition of probation had been violated." *Krow v. State*, 840 P.2d 261, 264 (Wyo. 1992).

DISCUSSION

[¶10]   Sweets argues that the district court's decision to revoke probation was based upon information of which he had no notice, thereby violating his right to due process. A probation revocation proceeding consists of two distinct phases. The first part, the adjudicatory phase, requires the district court to determine by a preponderance of the evidence whether a condition of probation was violated. W.R.Cr.P. 39(a)(5). The

FIGURE 5.5   *(Continued)*

However, in Demarce v. Willrich (2002), also reported elsewhere in this text, the Arizona defendant refused probation and opted for a jail sentence instead, under conditions similar to Brown's. In the *Demarce* case, an appellate court held that the defendant did not have the right to reject probation and elect incarceration for a lesser term after finding that the probation conditions were too onerous. Thus, it depends on the particular state jurisdiction whether defendants may reject probation if they don't like its conditions.

second, dispositional phase, is triggered only upon a finding that a condition of probation was violated. *Mapp*, 929 P.2d at 1226.

[¶11] Due process requires that a defendant be given written notice of the claimed violations of probation. *Shaw v. State*, 998 P.2d 965, 967 (Wyo. 2000). In probation revocation proceedings, notice pertains to the charges regarding a violation of the conditions of probation, not to matters discussed during a dispositional phase. W.R.Cr.P. 39(a)(4); *Gailey v. State*, 882 P.2d 888, 892 (Wyo. 1994). Sweets does not claim that he did not receive a copy of the petition or that the petition did not set forth an alleged violation based upon cocaine use. Sweets' concern about notice seems to be directed at the dispositional phase and is not, in actuality, a due process argument. In addressing Sweets' concerns, we will consider whether the district court abused its discretion in revoking Sweets' probation.

[¶12] Sweets concedes that he admitted using cocaine, but asserts that because none of the other allegations of the petition were established, the district court erred in revoking his probation. He contends that three positive urinalyses, standing alone, would not have prompted Probation and Parole to petition to revoke his probation and should not result in revocation. However, Sweets was advised before he admitted the allegation that *any* violation of his probation could result in revocation and imposition of the suspended prison sentence. Additionally, we reject the notion that illicit drug use is not conduct sufficiently serious to prompt revocation proceedings.

[¶13] Sweets' admission that he violated a condition of probation conclusively established the violation. *Mapp*, 929 P.2d at 1226. Once a violation is established, the district court considers an appropriate disposition. *Id.*

[¶14] Sweets asserts that remarks by the district court demonstrate that its decision to revoke was based upon violations other than his admitted use of cocaine. At the revocation hearing the district court commented:

> Mr. Sweets, let me finish here. You know what got you here this last time, it wasn't the probation violations. It was delivery of cocaine. You know, that was a felony for which you were facing, you know, a lot of years in prison, and as a third-time offender, you got a tremendous break when you got probation this time. You were facing up to 20 years in prison and a $25,000 fine, and after having gone to the penitentiary twice, you got a two-to-four-year suspended sentence, and for the past two years, probation has not aided you in any way, because we now have another -- you're still dinking around with cocaine six months ago, and who knows how many other

FIGURE 5.5   *(Continued)*

Sentences of probation cannot be served simultaneously with sentences of incarceration. If a judge imposes incarceration for an offender for Offense A, and if that same judge imposes probation for the same offender for Offense B, both the incarcerative sentence and the probationary sentence cannot be served concurrently (United States v. Swan, 2002). Generally, sentences of both incarceration and probation must be served consecutively in most jurisdictions.

> times because you did not go to your probation agent and you were not getting UAs.
>
> I don't know if there were more. I guess I can't assume that there were, but I do know that you did use cocaine on three times. You don't grow that in your own home. You're dealing with drug dealers. Those are people you're not supposed to be associating with. You haven't cut off your previous ties to your – your drug life.
>
> This Court is revoking your probation and sending you to the State penitentiary, there to serve your two-to-four-year prison sentence.

[¶15]   Sweets claims that he did not receive notice that associating with "drug dealers" was a claimed violation. However, the district court did not find a violation of probation terms based on association with drug dealers. The above-quoted comments were made during the dispositional phase and explain the district court's disposition, not its findings as to the violations established.

[¶16]   In the dispositional phase, the district court must deliberate not only upon the violation, but also the reasons the conditions were originally imposed and the circumstances surrounding the violation. After consideration of all these factors, the district court must then determine the appropriate consequences of the probationer's violation. *Mapp*, 929 P.2d at 1226. The record reveals thoughtful consideration by the district court, and we find no abuse of discretion in the imposition of a prison term. Sweets was placed on probation for a drug crime, so abstinence from illegal drugs would appear to be critical to successful probation. In considering the circumstances surrounding the violation, the district court inferred that Sweets still had ties to the drug world.

[¶17]   Sweets contends that the district court failed to consider intensive supervised probation as an alternative to prison. However, the record demonstrates that the district court did consider probation and concluded that it had not aided him in any way. By referring to Sweets' continued drug use and his failure to report to his agent during the time the revocation was pending, the district court explained why continued probation was not appropriate.

CONCLUSION

[¶18]   Sweets' admitted use of cocaine was a violation of his probation, and the district court did not abuse its discretion by revoking probation. The order revoking Sweets' probation and imposing sentence is affirmed.

FIGURE 5.5   (*Continued*)

Appeals of Probation Revocation Actions.   Appeals of any probation revocation decision may be made by a probationer. These appeals may be for any legitimate reason, such as not considering pertinent evidence, errors of facts presented and relied upon during the revocation proceeding, or perceived inequities because of extralegal factors, such as race/ethnicity, gender, socioeconomic status, or age. If probationers believe that any of their due process rights were violated, they are entitled to appeal. All of the cases cited above as examples of state or federal probation revocation actions are the results of appeals initiated by probationers who believed they had one or more appealable issues. The outcomes of most appeals filed by probationers who have had their probation programs revoked are unsuccessful. Figure 5.5 shows an actual appeal filed with and decided by the Wyoming Supreme Court by probationer Ivan Lee Sweets in May 2003.

SUMMARY

When offenders are convicted of crimes, they may receive probation in lieu of incarceration. The most common form of probation is standard probation. Offenders are expected to comply with a list of behavioral requirements. Ordinarily, some form of reporting to probation agencies is specified so that probationers can have contact with their POs at regular intervals. Some offenders require closer supervision. Increasing the amount of contact between probationers and their supervising officers is intensive supervised probation. Intensive supervised probation refers to a wide range of nonincarcerative programs exerting variable control over probationers. Intensive supervision means different things depending upon the jurisdiction. Most corrections professionals consider intensive supervision to mean frequent face-to-face contact with probationers. Thus, intensive supervision means to supervise probationers more closely than standard probationers. Often, intensive supervision is accompanied by home confinement and electronic monitoring, as well as other program conditions.

Unpopular with the general public, probation of any kind is designed to reintegrate offenders into their respective communities and assist jail and prison officials with their overcrowding problems. Intensive supervised probation programs in current use among the states are based on one or more correctional philosophies stressing contrasting orientations toward how offenders on probation ought to be controlled. The justice model is most punitive and emphasizes penalties for offenders that fit the crimes they committed. The limited-risk control model is founded on the idea that an offender's degree of risk to the public can be measured and that the intensity of supervision imposed should vary with the severity of the offense. The treatment-oriented model is most closely aligned with the rehabilitative ideal of corrections and emphasizes community reintegration, community service, restitution, curfew, and home confinement alternatives.

Most intensive supervised probation programs are characterized with low probation officer caseloads and frequent face-to-face contact with probationers either at home or at work. Many of these programs include counseling or some form of vocational/educational training and/or restitution/public service. Three programs are the Georgia ISP program, the Idaho ISP program, and the South Carolina ISP program. These programs have similar elements and characteristics and are designed for low-risk nonviolent offenders. Georgia handpicks its probationers, and thus, only the most eligible offenders are included. This biases the program in such a way so as to maximize its success for clients. The Idaho ISP program uses teams of two POs and a supervisor who work in shifts to monitor offender conduct. South Carolina's ISP program utilizes specialized POs who have training specific to different offender needs. Offenders must also pay a regular, nominal program maintenance fee.

Another incarcerative alternative is shock probation. Shock probation, also known as split sentencing, involves a short period of incarceration followed by participation in a probation program. Mixed sentences, intermittent sentences, and jail as a condition of probation are also considered variations of split sentencing and shock probation. Shock probation was pioneered in Ohio, although it is currently used in many other states as a sanction. The philosophy of shock probation is that offenders will be shocked into the realization that their crimes are serious and that incarceration is undesirable. Shock incarceration is sometimes known as a boot camp experience. Boot camp goals are multifaceted, emphasizing self-discipline, self-awareness, and various educational and vocational skills. Boot camps are aimed primarily at more youthful offenders, although older offenders are not excluded by most programs. Most states have either developed or are in the process of developing boot camp programs. Boot camp graduates tend to have low recidivism rates compared with standard probationers. Some boot camps are operated by county jails. These are known as jail boot camps. They have been instrumental in upgrading one's social and vocational skills as well as preparing participants for entering the work force and supporting their families.

Approximately 20 to 25 percent of all probationers are women. Until the last few decades, female offenders have had limited access to the variety of rehabilitative programs available to men under similar circumstances. Such programming limitations have also been apparent when distinguishing between men's and women's prisons. However, the U.S. Supreme Court case of Glover v. Johnson stressed great equity in women's programming in prison settings. Stemming from this decision was a concerted effort by all corrections departments throughout the United States to provide more equitable services to female offenders, whether they were institutional inmates or community clients on probation or parole.

Major changes have occurred over the last several decades concerning women's programming in community corrections and in prisons or jails. The Program for Female Offenders, Inc. was established during the 1970s to meet the needs of growing numbers of inmate mothers and to impart to them various parenting skills and practical child care knowledge. The Women in Community Services Lifeskills Program was also established during the 1970s to focus upon treatments for female offenders who were victims of spousal abuse or who had drug/alcohol dependencies. The aims of such programming were to give female offenders greater personal empowerment, job readiness, and life management skills. Other programs were subsequently established for women in many jurisdictions. These programs have emphasized different types of problems associated with female offenders, and they have focused upon more sophisticated programming relative to substance-abuse education, vocational/educational training, parenting, anger management, and life skills experiences. Some boot camp programs have been established especially for those female offenders in need of greater discipline and structure in their lives. For the most part, these programs have been extremely beneficial in achieving parity with comparable programming for male offenders under similar circumstances.

When one or more probation program requirements are violated, POs initiate action against probationers. Some program requirements are more important than others, and thus, in certain instances no action is taken. However, where new crimes are alleged or drug or alcohol dependencies are detected, some probationers are in jeopardy of having their probation programs revoked by their original sentencing judges. The probation revocation process is a formal, two-stage proceeding. The first stage determines one's guilt or innocence relating to the allegations of program violations. If judges find that probationers have indeed violated one or more probationary terms, then they must decide the punishment to impose. This occurs in the second phase of the proceeding. Punishment may be a simple return to one's probation program. In other instances, it may be a resentence to more intensive supervised probation. In yet other instances, some probationers may be placed in jails or prisons for a period of time. Several landmark cases have been decided by the U.S. Supreme Court to govern the probation revocation process. Since a liberty interest is involved in the probation revocation process, probationers who are in jeopardy of having their probation programs revoked have certain rights. These rights vary according to different state jurisdictions, although the U.S. Supreme Court has vested probationers throughout the United States with several basic rights regardless of their individual state standards. These cases include Mempa v. Rhay, Gagnon v. Scarpelli, Morrissey v. Brewer, Black v. Romano, and Bearden v. Georgia.

QUESTIONS FOR REVIEW

1. What is standard probation? How does it differ from intensive supervised probation? Why is intensive supervised probation used so infrequently in the United States, despite its successfulness as an effective supervisory tool for offenders in the community?

2. What are some general conditions of standard probation contained in state and federal probation orders? How are these conditions regarded as punishments?

3. Differentiate between the Georgia and South Carolina intensive supervised probation models. How are participants selected for each program?

4. What are three correctional models which have influenced intensive supervised probation programs in recent years? How does each model modify or shape existing probation programs?

5. What are three other types of ISP programs for probationers in other jurisdictions? What are their major features or components? What is the general successfulness of these programs using offender recidivism as the measure of program effectiveness?

6. What is shock probation and what is its philosophy? Has shock probation achieved its general objectives? Why or why not? How does shock probation differ from an intermittent sentence? What are the general functions and goals of shock probation?

7. What are boot camps? What are their goals? What are the characteristics of three different boot camps? What are some of the characteristics of boot camp clientele? What types of offenders seem most suitable for boot camp experiences? What is a jail boot camp?

8. What are some general characteristics of female probationers and parolees? What are some criticisms of female programming in prison institutions and within community corrections? What is the significance of the case of Glover v. Johnson, and what long-term effect did it have in remedying inequities in programming for female offenders?

9. What are three major programs for women, either in prison institutions or in community corrections? What types of problems do these programs seem to address?

10. What rights do probationers have when they are subject to having their probation programs revoked? What are three major U.S. Supreme Court cases which have influenced the probation revocation process? What rights did they bestow upon all probationers? To what extent is there uniformity in probation revocation actions among the states?

SUGGESTED READINGS

Eadie, Tina, and Charlott Knight (2002). "Domestic Violence Programs: Reflections on the Shift from Independent to Statutory Provision." *Howard Journal of Criminal Justice* 41: 167–181.

Gillis, John W. (2002). *Ordering Restitution to the Crime Victim.* Washington, DC: U.S. Department of Justice.

Hook, Melissa and Anne Seymour (2003). "Offender Reentry Requires Attention to Victim Safety."*APPA Perspectives* 27: 24–29.

Karp, David R. (2003). "Does Community Justice Work? Evaluating Vermont's Reparative Probation." *APPA Perspectives* 27: 32–37.

Sachwald, Judith (2003). "Opening Windows to Effective Intervention: Proactive Community Supervision." *APPA Perspectives* 27: 22–24.

INTERNET CONNECTIONS

Boot Camps
http://www.boot-camps-info.com/

Boot Camps for Struggling Teens
http://www.juvenile-boot-camps.com

Colorado Judicial Department Probation Program
http://www.courts.state.co.us/panda/ statrep/ar2000/probnarr.pdf

Crawford County Intensive Supervised Probation
http://www.crawfordcocpcourt.org/ ISProbation.htm

Department of Probation and Court Services
http://www.co.mchenry.il.us/CountyDpt/ CourtServ/CSerAdult.asp

Michigan 36th District Court Probation Programs
http://www.36thdistrictcourt.org/probation-programs.html

Thunder Road Probation Program
http://www.thunder-road.org/programs_ acp.html

U.S. Parole Commission
http://www.usdoj.gov/uspc/releasetxt.htm

CHAPTER 6 | *Jails and Prisons*

Chapter Outline

Chapter Objectives

As the result of reading this chapter, the following objectives will be realized:

1. Describing jails, their early origins, and their major characteristics and primary functions.
2. Profiling jail inmates.
3. Describing prisons, their historical origins, and their major characteristics and functions.
4. Identifying several inmate classification systems and their characteristics.
5. Describing the sociodemographic characteristics of prison inmates.
6. Describing some general contrasts between jails and prisons.
7. Understanding several important jail and prison issues, including overcrowding; violence and inmate discipline; jail and prison design and control; rehabilitative prison programs; and privatization.
8. Understanding the role of prisons and jails in the probation and parole decision-making process.

• What Can Be Done about Jail Violence? *Jails are designed to hold inmates for short periods of incarceration, such as periods of less than one year. We know that at least some jails hold prisoners for longer terms, however. Jails are supposed to be safe havens for those housed there. However, many of the nation's jails are becoming increasingly violent as the types of jail occupants become more diverse and gang-affiliated. For instance, at San Antonio, Texas's Dominguez State Jail, some prisoners have become victims of violence from other inmates. In the hospital at the jail, a Mexican American in his late 20s was lying on a gurney. His forehead was swollen and red. His right eyebrow was puffy and criss-crossed with three dozen black stitches. His eyelid closed by swelling. His nose and lips were red and inflamed. The evening before, he had been assaulted by three assailants in his pod, or residential unit, which housed 54 others during evening hours. Apparently, three men from another pod illegally entered this man's pod and pummeled him severely. There is some evidence to indicate that the man knew his attackers, but he was unwilling to name those who beat him. The major reason was a fear of being killed for informing on them.*

The Dominguez State Jail is headed by Warden Harry Kinker. Kinker said that the assailants who beat the inmate were in the man's pod illegally and that the pods should be locked during evening hours. The incident looked to Kinker like gang-related violence. In almost all of the 105 prisons in Texas today, there are inmate gangs. These gangs pose an immense problem related to inmate control and behavior. Warden Kinker interviewed the man who was beaten and determined that the violence against him was gang-related. Kinker says that much of the violence in jails such as his are attributable to the fact that many of the inmates share large dormitory-like pods with at least 50 or more other inmates. It is virtually impossible to guard against every single contingency that might occur, involving inmate-on-inmate violence. Add to that the fact that gang presence is pervasive and you have a very volatile situation that can trigger violent acts at any time. There is also violence attributable to racial differences among inmates. Gangs tend to group along racial lines. Their conflicts with one another for jail dominance are notorious. Jail policies and procedures are maintained to a degree, usually by awarding good-time credits to those offenders who behave well. But the presence of a small segment of violent offenders, often from state prison overflow, does little to prevent violence from occurring. What should jail officials do to make their jails safer for

*nonviolent inmates? Should there be closed-circuit cameras in all areas of jails to moni-
tor inmate conduct? What do you think? [Source: Adapted from Dick J. Reavis and the
Associated Press. "Limiting Violence in Jail is Tricky." August 18, 2001].*

• The Texas Prison System and the Mentally Ill. *Numerous federal lawsuits have been
filed by or on behalf of mentally ill inmates in both state and federal prisons. Some of
these lawsuits date back to 1980, when a federal district court judge ruled that the
Texas prison system was unconstitutional on various grounds. During December 2001, a
psychologist hired to evaluate Texas inmates being held in solitary confinement issued
a report which has stimulated a re-examination of these lawsuits.*

*The report issued from an order from U.S. District Court Judge William Wayne Jus-
tice, the same judge who declared the Texas prison system unconstitutional in 1980.
Justice ordered that a psychologist should be hired to evaluate those maintained in solitary confinement and determine their mental condition or stability. Specifically, Justice
wanted to know about the presence of seriously mentally ill prisoners being held in administrative segregation (solitary confinement) by the Texas prison system. The psychologist subsequently visited various prisons in Texas and interviewed prisoners in
isolation, conducting detailed interviews as needed. He also talked with security officers
to determine if they had any concerns about any of the offenders regarding their mental
illness. Based on the report filed by the psychologist, it may be that steps will be taken
to move mentally ill prisoners to places more appropriate to their mental condition.
Should mentally ill prisoners be placed in administrative segregation or solitary confinement? Should we expand the number of hospitals for mentally ill inmates? What do
you think? [Source: Adapted from the Associated Press. "Fed Court Gets Report on Mentally Ill Inmates." December 5, 2001].*

• Long Distance Dads. *In the Algoa Correctional Center near Jefferson City, Missouri, a
12-week program called Long Distance Dads has been established. The program was
started in January 2001 at two other Missouri prisons and is designed to help inmates
develop skills to become more involved and supportive fathers. Long Distance Dads is
modeled after a similar program in Pennsylvania. It emphasizes self-discipline, the psychological development of fathers and children, and how to deal with the challenges of
being an incarcerated father. John Kerr, a psychologist at Algoa, said, "We wanted to
have some kind of model and method so these men could reach out and make contact
with their families." One of the inmates Kerr assists is Odell Bailey, an inmate convicted
of robbery and kidnapping. Bailey has been involved in the Long Distance Dads program and likes it. Bailey, 49, says, "It gave me the skills to listen to what's happening in
the world. I'm ready to go out there and be a father. It's a scary deal, but I am ready."
Bailey had 11 more months to serve in prison before his release on parole.*

*Nearly 7,000 inmates in various Missouri prisons have children under the age of
18. Through June 2001, 38 inmates have successfully completed the Long Distance Dads
program. Pennsylvania's Long Distance Dads program has been operating since 1996.
Various states such as Missouri have copied it. Officials in North Carolina and at
Riker's Island in New York City have also expressed an interest in using the program's
manual, most of which was written by other prison inmates. Other states are trying similar strategies at making their inmate-parents more responsible adults. The Virginia Department of Corrections and Women in Transition, a nonprofit organization, has been
assisting inmates to create 15-minute videotapes with messages for their children as a
way to be with them on Father's Day. John Kerr says that the Long Distance Dads program at Algoa Correctional Center has caused many inmates to understand for the first
time in their lives the significance of Father's Day. What do you think about the Long
Distance Dads program? Should it be applied in other jurisdictions? What other types of
interventions would you regard as helpful for assisting young men with children to assume greater responsibility for them? [Source: Adapted from the Paul Sloca and the Associated Press, "Dads Behind Bars Learn to Improve." June 17, 2001].*

• Hawaiian Inmates in Arizona. *Arizona prisons accommodate about 1,100 Hawaiian inmates per year. Corrections Corporation of America (CCA), a private firm, operates various prisons throughout the United States on a "for profit" basis. Increasingly, states and the federal government are turning to privatization in order to solve the growing problem of institutional overcrowding. One site housing at least 1,100 Hawaiian inmates is the Florence, Arizona prison operated by CCA. Hawaii pays CCA about $17 million per year to house these inmates. This is relatively cheap, considering what Hawaiian prison officials must spend to accommodate their prisoners in Hawaiian institutions. As the state contract was about to expire with CCA, Hawaiian officials flew to Florence, Arizona, to conduct an inspection of the prison system. In recent months, two Hawaiian prisoners died while in CCA custody. These deaths were unrelated to CCA negligence, however. One inmate died of natural causes, while the other inmate died of a drug overdose when he swallowed a package of drugs in an attempt to smuggle them into the facility. Despite the nature of these deaths, CCA has been criticized anyway.*

According to the monitoring team sent to inspect the Florence prison, there was widespread drug use among inmates. Furthermore, the inspection team did not tour the entire prison because of what they perceived to be a hostile environment. The hostile environment was attributable to gang activity and menacing prisoners. Gang presence in prisons throughout the United States is pervasive. No one denies that. Can it be prevented or controlled? Probably not. Attempts are made to break up gang members by segregating them or shipping them to different prisons within various states. But somehow, gangs persist. Furthermore, almost every prison has drug problems. Inmates get drugs smuggled into them by different means, often by corrupt prison correctional officers. Thus, drug use among inmates is extremely difficult to control or eliminate. Despite the hostility encountered by the Hawaiian inspection team, the CCA contract was renewed. CCA authorities indicated that they are establishing new drug treatment programs and counseling sessions. Further, they plan to establish educational and various rehabilitative programs in future years. Typical inmate complaints are that they lack educational, sex offender and drug treatment programs, or opportunities to work at prison jobs (Prendergast et al., 2002). Hawaii has been sending some of its inmates to mainland prisons and jails since 1995. Most of the inmates they send to the mainland are "problem prisoners" that many systems reject. One Hawaiian prison official said, "We send them to Arizona because Arizona accepts them. We didn't have too many alternatives. We know these were problem inmates." What do you think of prison privatization? Should it be minimized? How can we accommodate growing numbers of offenders who deserve to be incarcerated without privatization? What do you think? [Source: Adapted from the Associated Press, July 1, 2001].

INTRODUCTION

This chapter is about jails and prisons. Jails in the United States are one of the most maligned and forgotten components of the criminal justice system. In the first section, a brief history of jails in the United States will be presented. Jail inmates will also be profiled. Typically, jails are city- or county-funded and operated facilities designed to confine offenders serving short sentences as well as those awaiting trial. Jails are an integral feature of U.S. corrections. In contrast, prisons are intended as long-term custodial facilities for more serious offenders. The second section of this chapter presents a brief history of prisons in the United States and discusses their characteristics and functions. In past years, we could distinguish clearly between prisons and jails in terms of whether convicted offenders had committed felonies or misdemeanors. Misdemeanants were usually sent to jails, while convicted felons were sent to prisons. This is no longer the case, since overcrowding of prisons has caused prison officials to negotiate with smaller jails to accommodate some of their inmate overflow. These inmates housed in local jails are contract prisoners. Both state and federal governments have contracted with many local jails as a means of housing a certain proportion of their offender populations. This contracting has directly aggravated existing jail overcrowding. Prison inmates will be profiled and compared with jail inmates.

The last section of the chapter will present and discuss several important issues relevant for both jails and prisons. These issues include the overcrowding problem, the problem of inmate violence and discipline, the design and control of jails and prisons, vocational and educational programs for inmates, and privatization. It is important to understand some of the functions and culture of jails and prisons, since inmate conduct is one determinant of early release decisions by parole boards. Also, inmate conduct is important for those offenders experiencing shock probation. Shock probation prescribes one to four months of incarceration, whereupon judges remove offenders from jails and resentence them to probation. However, inmates who behave poorly while confined for these short terms may not be resentenced to probation. Judges exercise discretion and are influenced by inmate conduct. They must decide whether to continue incarcerating offenders or resentence them to probation after one or more months of confinement. Thus, jails and prisons play an important role in probation and parole programs.

JAILS AND JAIL CHARACTERISTICS

In 2002, there were over 14 million admissions to and from U.S. jails, with a jail population of 665,475 (Harrison and Karberg, 2003). This is a jail population increase of 31 percent since 1995. In turn, this increase has created serious overcrowding problems in city and county jails in most jurisdictions. Jail overcrowding has been directly or indirectly responsible for numerous inmate deaths and extensive violence, much offender litigation challenging among other things the constitutionality of the nature of their confinement and treatment, and administrative and/or supervisory problems of immense proportions (Tonry, 2001). How did jails reach this stage and acquire these problems? A brief history of jails in the United States explains several contemporary jail problems.

The term, **jail,** is derived from old English term, **gaol** (also pronounced "jail"), which originated in 1166 A.D. through a declaration by Henry II of England. Henry II established gaols as a part of the Assize or Constitution of Clarendon (American Correctional Association, 1983:3). Gaols were locally administered and operated, and they housed many of society's misfits. Paupers or vagrants, drunkards, thieves, murderers, debtors, highwaymen, trespassers, orphan children, prostitutes, and others made up early gaol populations. Since the Church of England was powerful and influential, many religious dissidents were housed in these gaols as a punishment for their dissent. This practice continued for several centuries.

Local control over the administration and operation of jails by **shire-reeves** in England was a practice continued by the American colonists in later years. Most jails in the United States today are locally controlled and operated similar to their English predecessors. Thus, political influence upon jails and jail conditions is strong. In fact, changing jail conditions from one year to the next are often linked to local political shifts through elections and new administrative appointments. Also, the fact that local officials controlled jails and jail operations meant that no single administrative style typified these facilities. Each county (shire) was responsible for establishing jails and managing them according to their individual discretion. Current U.S. jail operations in most jurisdictions are characterized by this same individuality of style.

Originally, jails were designed as holding facilities for persons accused of crimes. Alleged law violators were held until court convened, when their guilt or innocence could be determined. Today, pre-trial detainees make up a significant proportion of the U.S. jail population. Shire- reeves made their living through reimbursements from taxes collected in the form of fees for each inmate housed on a daily basis. For instance, the reeve would receive a fixed fee, perhaps 50 or 75 cents per day for each inmate held in the jail. Therefore, more prisoners meant more money for reeves and their assistants. Such a reimbursement scheme was easily susceptible to corruption, and much of the money intended for inmate food and shelter was pocketed by selfish reeves. Quite logically, the quality of inmate food and shelter was very substandard, and jails became notorious because of widespread malnutrition, disease, and death among prisoners.

Workhouses

Deplorable jail conditions continued into the sixteenth century, when workhouses were established largely in response to mercantile demands for cheap labor. A typical **workhouse** in the mid-sixteenth century was the **Bridewell Workhouse** established in 1557. This London facility housed many of the city's vagrants and general riffraff. Jail and workhouse sheriffs and administrators quickly capitalized on the cheap labor these facilities generated, and additional profits were envisioned. Thus, it became commonplace for sheriffs and other officials to "hire out" their inmates to perform skilled and semi-skilled tasks for various merchants. While the manifest functions of workhouses and prisoner labor were supposed to improve the moral and social fiber of prisoners and train them to perform useful skills when they were eventually released, profits from inmate labor were often pocketed by corrupt jail and workhouse officials. Workhouses were also established in other countries such as Italy and the Netherlands during the same period (Spruit et al., 1998). In the United States, workhouses were prevalent well into the 1800s and existed to house disreputable persons, such as prostitutes and drunkards.

Jails were commonplace throughout the colonies. Sheriffs were appointed to supervise jail inmates, and the fee system continued to be used to finance these facilities. All types of people were confined together in jails, regardless of their gender or age. Orphans, prostitutes, drunkards, thieves, and robbers were often contained in large, dormitory-style rooms with hay and blankets for beds. Jails were great melting pots of humanity, with little or no regard for inmate treatment, health, or rehabilitation. Even today, jails are characterized similarly (Kerle, 1998).

The Walnut Street Jail

The Pennsylvania legislature authorized in 1790 the renovation of a facility originally constructed on Walnut Street in 1776, a two-acre structure initially designed to house the overflow resulting from overcrowding of the High Street Jail.

The **Walnut Street Jail** was both a workhouse and a place of incarceration for all types of offenders. But the 1790 renovation was the first of several innovations in U.S. corrections. Specifically, the Walnut Street Jail was innovative because (1) it separated the most serious prisoners from others in 16 large solitary cells, (2) it separated other prisoners according to their offense seriousness, and (3) it separated prisoners according to gender. Besides these innovations, the Walnut Street Jail assigned inmates to different types of productive labor according to their gender and conviction offense. Women made clothing and performed washing and mending chores. Skilled inmates worked as carpenters, shoemaking, and other crafts. Unskilled prisoners beat hemp or jute for ship caulking. With the exception of women, prisoners received a daily wage for their labor which was applied to defray the cost of their maintenance. The Quakers and other religious groups provided regular instruction for most offenders. The Walnut Street Jail concept was widely imitated by officials from other states during the next several decades. Many prisons were modeled after the Walnut Street Jail for housing and managing long-term prisoners (Okun, 1997).

The Quakers in Pennsylvania were a strong influence in jail reforms. In 1787 they established the **Philadelphia Society for Alleviating the Miseries of Public Prisons.** This society was made up of many prominent Philadelphia citizens, philanthropists and religious reformers who believed prison and jail conditions ought to be changed and replaced with a more humane environment. Members of this Society visited each jail and prison daily, bringing food, clothing, and religious instruction to inmates. Some of these members were educators who sought to assist prisoners in acquiring basic skills such as reading and writing. Although their intrusion into prison and jail life was frequently resented and opposed by local authorities and sheriffs, their presence was significant and brought the deplorable conditions of confinement to the attention of politicians (Rowe, 1989).

Subsequent Jail Developments

Information about the early growth of jails in the United States is sketchy. One reason is that there were many inmate facilities established during the 1800s and early 1900s serving many functions and operating under different labels. Sheriffs' homes were used as jails in some jurisdictions, while workhouses, farms, barns, small houses, and other types of facilities served similar purposes in others. Thus, depending on who did the counting, some facilities would be labeled as jails and some would not. Limiting jail definitions only to locally operated short-term facilities for inmates excluded also those state-operated jails in jurisdictions such as Alaska, Delaware, and Rhode Island. Another reason for inadequate jail statistics and information was that there was little interest in jail populations. Another problem was that it was difficult to transmit information from jails and jail inmates to any central location during that period of time. Often, local records were not maintained, and many sheriff's departments were not inclined to share information about their prisoners with others. Streamlined communications systems did not exist, and information was compiled very slowly, if at all. State governments expressed little or no interest in the affairs of jails within their borders, since these were largely local enterprises funded with local funds. Even if there had been a strong interest in jail information among corrections professionals and others, it would have been quite difficult to acquire.

The U.S. Census Bureau began to compile information about jails in 1880 (Cahalan and Parsons, 1986:73). At ten-year intervals following 1880, general jail information was systematically obtained about race, nativity, gender, and age. Originally, the U.S. Census Bureau presented data separately for county jails, city prisons, workhouses, houses of correction, and leased county prisoners (Cahalan and Parsons, 1986:73). But in 1923, these figures were combined to reflect more accurately what we now describe as jail statistics. A special report was prepared by the U.S. Census Bureau entitled *Prisoners 1923*. And in that same year, Joseph Fishman, a federal prison inspector, published a book, *Crucible of Crime,* describing living conditions of many U.S. jails (Cahalan and Parsons, 1986:73). Comparisons with 1880 base figures show the jail population of the United States to be 18,686 in 1880 and almost doubling to 33,093 by 1890.

Most reports about jail conditions in the United States have been largely unfavorable. The 1923 report by Fishman was based on his visits to and observations of 1500 jails, describing the conditions he saw as horrible. More recent reports suggest these conditions have not changed dramatically since Fishman made his early observations. It was not until 1972 that national survey data about jails became available. Exceptions include the years 1910, 1923, and 1933, where jail inmate characteristics were listed according to several offense categories. A majority of jail inmates each of those years had committed petty offenses such as vagrancy, public drunkenness, and minor property crimes (Cahalan and Parsons, 1986:86). Even since 1972, jail data have not been regularly and consistently compiled (Kerle, 1998).

There are several reasons for many of the continuing jail problems in the United States. While some of these persistent problems will be examined in-depth later in this chapter, it is sufficient for the present to understand that (1) most of the U.S. jails today were built before 1970, and many were built five decades or more before that; (2) local control of jails often results in erratic policies that shift with each political election, thus forcing jail guards and other personnel to adapt to constantly changing conditions and jail operations; and (3) jail funding is a low-priority budget item in most jurisdictions, and with limited operating funds, the quality of services and personnel jails provide and attract is considerably lower compared with state and federal prison standards and personnel (Kerle, 1998).

The Number of Jails in the United States

No one knows the exact number of jails in the United States at any given time. One reason is that observers disagree about how jails ought to be defined. Some people count only locally operated and funded, short-term incarceration facilities as jails, while other people include state-operated jails in their figures. In remote territories such as Alaska, World War II–era Quonset huts may be used to house offenders on a short-term basis. Work release centers, farms for low-risk inmates, and other facilities may be included or excluded from the jail definition. Sometimes, a **lock-up** (drunk tank, holding tank) might be counted as a jail, although such a facility exists primarily to hold those charged with public drunkenness or other minor offenses for up to 48 hours (Tartaro, 1999). These are not jails in the formal sense, but rather, they are simple holding tanks or facilities. The American Jail Association suggests that to qualify as a bonafide jail, the facility must hold inmates for 72 hours or longer, not 48 hours (Kerle, 1998). One of the more accurate estimates of the number of jails in the United States is 3,365, reported by the U.S. **Department of Justice** jail census in 1999 (U.S. Department of Justice, 2001).

FUNCTIONS OF JAILS

John Irwin (1985) says that jails are more likely to receive, process, and confine mostly detached and disreputable persons rather than true criminals. He says that many noncriminals are arrested simply because they are offensive and not because they have committed crimes. Irwin worked as a caseworker in several county jails in San Francisco, California, during the early 1980s, and he based his conclusions on personal observations as well as conversations and interviews with county pretrial release and **public defender** personnel.

Jails were originally conceived as short-term holding facilities for inmates serving short sentences as well as for those awaiting trial. The general and most basic function of jails is security. In the last twenty years, however, jails have changed considerably in response to public policy and practicality. Presently, jails perform a myriad of functions, some of which are unrelated to their original historical purpose (Kerle, 1998). The following functions characterize a majority of jails in the United States:

Jails Hold Indigents, Vagrants, and the Mentally Ill.   Jails are generally ill-equipped to handle those with mental or physical disorders. Often, physicians are available only on an on-call basis from local clinics in communities, and no rehabilitative programs or activities exist. More than a few of these inmates have communicable diseases, such as HIV/AIDS or tuberculosis (Krebs, 2002; Valette, 2002).

Jails Hold Pretrial Detainees.   Offenders arrested for various crimes who cannot afford or are denied bail are housed in jails until their trial. For most defendants awaiting trial, their period of **pretrial detention** is fairly short. **Pretrial detainees** may be held in jail without bail if they pose an escape risk or are considered dangerous. Such action is sometimes known as **preventive detention.**

Jails House Witnesses in Protective Custody.   Material witnesses to crimes in key cases may be housed in jails until trials can be held, if it appears that their lives are in danger or their safety is threatened. Some witnesses may be reluctant to testify, and thus prosecutors may wish to guarantee their subsequent appearance by placing them in protective custody. Often, jails are designed so that special accommodations are provided these witnesses, and they do not ordinarily associate with offenders.

Jails House Convicted Offenders Awaiting Sentencing.   Convicted offenders awaiting sentencing are usually held in local jail facilities. These offenders may be federal, state, or local prisoners. When these offenders are housed in local jails, the jurisdiction is ordinarily reimbursed for offender expenses from state or federal funds.

Jails House Persons Serving Short-Term Sentences.   Jails were never designed to accommodate offenders for lengthy incarcerative periods beyond one year. Prisons were constructed and intended for that type of long-term inmate confinement. Many offenders still serve relatively short terms in jails, but increasing numbers of inmates are incarcerated for periods exceeding the one-year standard.

Jails House Some Juvenile Offenders.   Because of the **jail removal initiative,** most juveniles have been diverted from jails for processing. However, annually some juveniles are incarcerated in jails for short periods, until their identity can be verified (Austin, Johnson, and Gregoriou, 2000). Many juveniles have fake IDs and lie to police about who they are and where they live. Some juveniles appear to be much older than they really are. Thus, jail authorities may not know that they are incarcerating juveniles if their fake IDs say otherwise and they appear to be adults. In those cases where juveniles are held in jails for brief periods, they are usually segregated from adult offenders, unless jail conditions do not permit such segregation (Alarid and Cromwell, 2002). Despite the jail removal initiative and efforts from various vested interest groups to remove juveniles from adult jails, their numbers have increased over the years. For instance, there were 5,900 juveniles held in adult jails in 1995. In 2002 there were over 10,000 (Harrison and Beck, 2003). One reason for this is that more jurisdictions are getting tough with youthful offenders and changing laws so that incarceration of younger youths in adult facilities is approved.

Jails Hold Prisoners Wanted by Other States on Detainer Warrants.   Jails must often accommodate prisoners wanted by other jurisdictions in other states. **Detainer warrants** are notices of criminal charges or unserved sentences pending against prisoners. Even though these types of prisoners will eventually be moved to other jurisdictions when authorities from those jurisdictions take them into custody, detainees take up space and time when initially booked and processed.

Jails Hold Probation and Parole Violators.   If probationers or parolees violate one or more of their program conditions, they are subject to arrest and incarceration until authorities can determine what to do about their program violations. Often, sentencing judges will return probation program violators back out on the streets after finding that their program violations were not especially serious. Parole boards may release a certain proportion of parolees for similar reasons. Nevertheless, these persons take up valuable jail space while they are confined, even if the periods of confinement are brief.

Jails Hold Contract Prisoners from Other Jurisdictions.   More than a few jails in Texas, Virginia, Oregon, Washington, and other states work out agreements with state and federal prison systems to house a certain portion of their inmate population overflows. Many jurisdictions have serious inmate overcrowding problems. Thus, the existence of available jail space to accommodate some of this overflow is appealing to these state and federal jurisdictions. In effect, the state or federal government pays the county jail, wherever it is located, to house a certain number of prisoners for a specified period. These prisoners are known as contract prisoners. For instance, Hawaii has exported a large number of its state prisoners to Texas jails to be held for periods of one or more years. This transportation of inmates from Hawaii to the mainland has caused the families of many inmates to complain, since it is prohibitive to visit incarcerated relatives on a regular basis. However, prisoners have no right to determine where they are housed, as long as their accommodations are not cruel and unusual. Furthermore, family members of inmates have no legal rights in this decision making.

Jails Operate Community-Based Programs and Jail Boot Camps.   Increasingly, some of the larger jails are offering some inmates an opportunity to improve their employability by taking vocational and educational training at nearby schools. In more than a few jurisdictions, educational training is a mandatory part of one's incarceration experience (Glover, 2002). Some of these jails operate jail boot camps, which give inmates an opportunity to participate in counseling and self-help programs. Some of these programs are aimed at meeting their needs. If certain inmates are alcohol or substance abusers, they are permitted to join local Alcoholics Anonymous or Narcotics Anonymous groups for brief periods. The Los Angeles County Jail, for instance, operates a Community Transition Unit that enhances inmate participation in educational, vocational, and other life skills training programs to assist with their successful reintegration into the community (Parker, 2002).

Jails Hold Mentally Ill Inmates Pending Their Removal to Mental Health Facilities.   No one knows for sure how many mentally ill inmates pass through jails or prisons annually (Jacoby, 2002). The mentally ill pose supervisory and medical problems for jail staff, because often, their specific illnesses are undiagnosed and there is inadequate medical assistance available on the jail premises to treat them (Walters et al., 2002). Furthermore, some of the more serious mentally ill inmates may injure themselves or other inmates by committing acts of violence. No official estimates are available, although some observers have indicated that jails hold as many as 600,000 mentally ill persons annually (Lurigio, 2000). One major reason for larger numbers of mentally ill persons winding up in jails is massive deinstitutionalization of the mentally ill. In 1955, for example, there were 559,000 patients in state mental hospitals. In 1999, there were less than 60,000 patients in these same hospitals (Torrey, 1999:12). Theoretically, at least, patients who were discharged were supposed to receive out-patient follow-up care and services in their communities. But such care and services occurred in only a fraction of these cases. In recent years, this problem has received significant media attention as well as government recognition, and growing numbers of mentally ill offenders currently housed in jails and prisons are being discharged to appropriate medical and mental health centers for treatment rather than punishment (Farrell and Edson, 2003).

A PROFILE OF JAIL INMATES

In 2002, there were 665,475 jail inmates in the United States, with 88.4 percent of all jail inmates male, 43.8 percent white, 39.8 percent black, and 14.7 percent Hispanic (Harrison and Karberg, 2003:1, 8). The nation's jail population has increased over 40 percent since 1990. The number of female arrestees has climbed slowly since 1995 from 10.2 percent to 11.6 percent in 2002. Figures for all minorities other than blacks or Hispanics have remained fairly constant during the 1990s and into the early 2000s, with all non-black, non-Hispanic minorities making up about 1.6 percent of the jail population during the period 1995–2002. Some observers believe that selective law enforcement and racial profiling have contributed to the disproportionately large number of black jail inmates over the years, although the percentage of black jail inmates has decreased from 43.5 percent in 1995 to 39.8 percent in 2002 (Harrison and Karberg, 2003:8). About 60 percent of all jail inmates were unconvicted. At midyear 2002, it was estimated that about 93 percent of all available jail space in the United States was occupied. Some of the types of occupants in U.S. jails are described below.

Drunks, Vagrants, and Juveniles. Many sorts of persons are processed through jails daily. In recent years, virtually every large U.S. city has experienced an escalation in the number of homeless persons, or those without any means of support and nowhere to stay except on city streets, in doorways or public parks. Police officers may bring loiterers and vagrants to jail and hold them temporarily until they can establish their identity and account for their conduct. These arrests and detentions most often result in releases several hours later. Drunk drivers are taken to jails by police officers every evening, and they are released in the morning, after they have sobered up. Some juveniles whose identities are unknown may be held in separate areas of jails for brief periods until they can be reunited with their families or guardians.

Pretrial Detainees and Petty Offenders. Many jail inmates are held for the purpose of awaiting trial on assorted criminal charges. Other inmates are held for periods of less than a year for petty offense convictions.

BOX 6.1

PERSONALITY HIGHLIGHT

Patsy Phillips Horvath
Chief Jail Administrator (Captain, retired), Jones County Jail, Laurel, MS

Statistics:

A.A. (corrections, Jones County Junior College); continuing education courses, Mississippi Department of Corrections and Federal Bureau of Prisons.

Background:

I am the retired Chief Jail Administrator (Captain) for the Jones County Jail in Laurel, Mississippi. I began my career in corrections in 1980, when I was the first female hired by the Sheriff's Department to serve in an enforcement capacity. I am a high school graduate and earned an A.A. degree in corrections from Jones County Junior College. During my career in corrections, I attended training and continuing education classes sponsored by the Mississippi Department of Corrections and the Federal Bureau of Prisons. I retired in 2000 after 20 years of service.

During my tenure at the Jones County Jail, I advanced through the ranks from correctional officer, to sergeant, lieutenant, and finally, captain. My career has many memorable moments, some good and some not so good. I started in the old jail, which is still

standing next to the main courthouse. The old jail was a dilapidated building, without air conditioning or proper ventilation that was finally ordered closed by the U.S. Department of Justice in the early 1990s. While there, correctional officers had to be on their best guard because inmates were housed 30 per cell. The cells were nicknamed "cages." Other inmates were housed separately, but these inmates were high-risk and had mental disabilities. The old jail was not modernized and had few amenities. Meals had to be catered to the jail because the kitchen suffered from damage and disrepair due to a lack of funding over the years. It was more cost-effective to cater the meals rather than remodel and modernize the existing kitchen. That may sound hard to believe but that is the case in many jails across America today. To be a correctional officer at that facility

BOX 6.1 (Continued)

required a lot of nerve, together with an even temperament and a lot of patience.

Experiences:

In 1995 the new jail facility was opened. This facility can house up to 200 inmates. We housed county, state, federal, and private institution inmates. I worked in conjunction with the Federal Bureau of Investigation, the U.S. Marshals Service, and the Mississippi Department of Corrections. Private institutions also used our facility when transporting prisoners across the country. Moving to the new jail alleviated a lot of problems that I had experienced at the old jail, but at the same time, it created new challenges for me. The new jail is so much larger and modernized that training for current and new correctional officers had to be streamlined to meet the requirements of the new jail. The training consisted of updated records-keeping, computer training, operating the central control room (the "Central Nervous System" of the jail), safety training, and public relations. The new jail required more from correctional officers and made the job more demanding while at the same time creating a better work environment.

There was a public outcry when the funds for the new jail were appropriated. Many people assume that once an inmate is taken to jail that that is the end of any problems. That is a common misconception. Inmates are human beings and have to be treated accordingly. Inmates experience health and emotional problems, family crises, and conflict with other inmates, together with a seemingly endless list of other problems. A phrase that always applied to corrections is, "The worse you make it on the inmates, the worse you make it on the guards." I always explained this to new correctional officers. For a jail or correctional facility to function properly, the primary focus should be the inmate, regardless of whether that inmate is there serving county time or if he/she is awaiting transfer to a state or federal institution. Punishment is the reason for incar-

ceration, but reform is a goal that is just as important, because the majority of inmates are eventually going to be released. For that reason, reforming is paramount to incarceration. We implemented programs such as the GED completion or the learning of trades while serving on work crews. However, even if an inmate did not perform any tasks or jobs while incarcerated, he/she would adjust better if they felt like they mattered. I observed this over and over again throughout my career. Former inmates have approached me in public places and thanked me for treating them like they mattered. My response was that I always tried to treat people the way that I would want them to treat me.

I enjoyed my career very much. I would have to say that the highlight was seeing the new jail finally come into existence and being able to work there for five years. The most negative aspect would be the continuing lack of funding by politicians. As mentioned earlier, a lack of funds was always a problem, because many people feel that inmates do not matter, and so the funding should be used elsewhere. Corrections has always taken a back seat to other law enforcement activities. This needs to be remedied. Although a correctional facility is the final destination for many inmates, life's problems and dilemmas do not cease. A correctional facility is just as important as any other part of our judicial system.

Advice to Students:

My advice to any student seeking a job or career in corrections is to consider that not everyone is cut out to be in corrections or law enforcement in general. If you do decide to enter corrections, pursue your education. Education will prepare you and make you a better person and officer. When I entered corrections, education was not emphasized as it is today. I observed that when education and training are gained, the job tasks are handled better and more diligently. Good luck and God bless.

Shock Probationers and Prison Inmate Overflow. Scarce jail space must be found for a certain number of jail inmates who are known as shock probationers. These are persons who have been sentenced by judges to long prison terms. However, the judge's intention is to hold these persons in jails for periods ranging from 30 to 120 days. Then, these persons will be brought back before the judge and resentenced to probation. The judge merely wishes to scare these persons by incarcerating them for brief periods. The belief is that the shock value of short-term incarceration will act as a deterrent to further offending. Despite this noble crime prevention objective, shock probationers take up valuable jail space and are not considered particularly serious. However, another contingent of jail inmates consists of more serious offenders from various state and federal jurisdictions. State and federal prisons with overcrowding problems will contract with jail authorities to house a certain number of prisoners, thus reducing a certain amount of prison overcrowding. These **contract prisoners** are usually held for periods of one year or longer in designated jails with sufficient space to accommodate them. They take up scarce jail space on a long-term basis.

Contract prisoners are usually held in special cell blocks or on designated floors of jails. Further, they are supervised more closely than other jail inmates, because they constitute a general inmate class that is considered more dangerous. Contract prisoners cost jails more to supervise, therefore, although this cost is offset by state and federal government funds that are allocated to particular counties where jail space is used. In 2002 there were over 50,000 contract prisoners being housed in U.S. jails (Camp and Camp, 2003).

Work Releasees and the Mentally Ill. Jail services also include managing a certain portion of offenders on work release programs in those jurisdictions that have them. Jail inmates sentenced to work release programs are low-risk and nonviolent offenders. Psychologically disturbed inmates may prove bothersome or disruptive to other inmates. These people pose additional problems to jail staff, because in especially small jail facilities, there are no separate facilities for segregating these from serious offenders (Midkiff, 2000:49). Often, local jail facilities are ill-equipped to meet the special needs of mentally ill offenders or those who may be retarded. In 2002 about a fourth of all U.S. jails had no psychological or health staff (Camp and Camp, 2003).

Probationers and Parolees. A small proportion of jail inmates consists of probationers and parolees who have violated one or more conditions of their programs and are awaiting hearings to determine their dispositions and whether their programs should be revoked. About 5,000 jail inmates were probation or parole violators in 2002 (Pastore and Maguire, 2003). About a fourth of these offenders (1,250) were being held in jails for allegedly committing new crimes.

PRISONS, PRISON HISTORY, AND PRISON CHARACTERISTICS

Prisons Defined

Prisons are state or federally funded and operated institutions that house convicted offenders under continuous custody on a long-term basis. Compared with jails, prisons are completely self-contained and self-sufficient. In 2002, there were 1,440,655 inmates in both federal and state penitentiaries (Harrison and Beck, 2003:1). State prisons were operating at between 1 percent and 17 percent above their operating capacity. The Federal Bureau of Prisons was operating at 33 percent above its operating capacity. Erving Goffman (1961) has described a prison as a **total institution,** because it is an environmental reality of absolute dominance over prisoner's lives. These self-contained facilities have recreational yards, workout rooms, auditoriums for viewing feature films, and small stores for purchases of toiletries and other goods (O'Connor, 2000).

The Development and Growth of U.S. Prisons.   Early English and Scottish penal methods were very influential on the subsequent growth and development of U.S. prisons (American Correctional Association, 1983; Hughes, 1987). Most English and Scottish prisons that existed to house criminals and others often had operational policies that were influenced by economic or mercantile interests as well as those of the Church. **John Howard** (1726–1790), an influential English prison reformer, criticized the manner and circumstances under which prisoners were administered and housed. Howard had been a county squire and later, in 1773, he was the sheriff of Bedfordshire. He conducted regular inspections of gaol facilities and found that prisoners were routinely exploited by gaolers, since gaolers had no regular income other than that extracted from prisoners through their labor. Howard visited other countries to inspect their prison systems. He was impressed with the Maison de Force (House of Enforcement) of Ghent, where prisoners were treated humanely. They were clothed, lodged separately from others during evening hours, and well-fed. He thought that these ideas could be used as models for British prisons and gaols. He succeeded in convincing British authorities that certain reforms should be undertaken (Richardson and Galaway, 1995). In 1779, the Penitentiary Act was passed.

The Penitentiary Act provided that new facilities should be created, where prisoners could work productively at hard labor rather than suffer the usual punishment of **banishment.** Prisoners were to be well-fed, clothed, and housed in isolated sanitary cells. They were to be given opportunities to learn useful skills and trades. Fees for their maintenance were abolished, rigorous inspections were conducted regularly, and balanced diets and improved hygiene were to be strictly observed. Howard believed that prisoners should be given a hearty work regimen. Through hard work, prisoners would realize the seriousness and consequences of their crimes. Thus, work was a type of penance. The new word, penitentiary, was originated and was synonymous with reform and punishment. Presently, penitentiaries in the United States are regarded as punishment-centered rather than reform-oriented, as significant philosophical shifts have occurred in American corrections (Braithwaite, 2001).

State Prisons.   The first state prison was established in Simsbury, Connecticut in 1773. This prison was actually an underground copper mine that was converted into a confinement facility for convicted felons. It was eventually made into a permanent prison in 1790. Prisoners were shackled about the ankles, worked long hours, and received particularly harsh sentences for minor offenses. Burglary and counterfeiting were punishable in Simsbury by imprisonment not exceeding ten years, while a second offense meant life imprisonment (American Correctional Association, 1983:26–27).

Actually, the Walnut Street Jail was the first true American prison that attempted to correct offenders. Compared with the Simsbury, Connecticut

FIGURE 6.1   Men's Correctional
Unit, North Dakota State Penitentiary.

underground prison, a strictly punishment-centered facility, the Walnut Street
Jail operated according to rehabilitation model. A signer of the Declaration of
Independence, Dr. Benjamin Rush (1745–1813), was both a physician and a
humanitarian. He believed that punishment should reform offenders and prevent them from committing future crimes. He also believed that they should be
removed temporarily from society until they became remorseful. Rush believed that prisoners should exercise regularly and eat wholesome foods.
Thus, he encouraged prisoners to grow gardens where they could produce
their own goods. Prisoner-produced goods were so successful at one point that
produce and other materials manufactured or grown by inmates were marketed to the general public. Therefore, he pioneered the first prison industry,
where prisoners could market goods for profit and use some of this income to
defray prison operating expenses. Some of Rush's ideas were incorporated into
the operation of the Walnut Street Jail, and eventually, the pattern of discipline and offender treatment practiced there became known popularly as the
Pennsylvania System. Although the Walnut Street Jail Pennsylvania System
became a model used by many other jurisdictions (American Correctional Association, 1983:31).

Auburn State Penitentiary.   New York correctional authorities developed a
new type of prison in 1816, the **Auburn State Penitentiary,** designed according
to **tiers,** where inmates were housed on several different levels. The **tier system**
became a common feature of subsequent U.S. prison construction, and today,
most prisons are architecturally structured according to tiers. The term **penitentiary,** is used to designate an institution that not only segregates offenders
from society but also from each other. The original connotation of penitentiary
was a place where prisoners could think, reflect, and repent of their misdeeds
and possibly undergo reformation (Spiegel and Spiegel, 1998). Today, the
words *prison* and *penitentiary* are used interchangeably, since virtually every
prison has facilities for isolating prisoners from one another according to various levels of custody and control. Thus, each state has devised different names

for facilities designed to house its most dangerous offenders. Examples include Kentucky State Penitentiary, California State Prison at San Quentin, New Jersey State Prison, North Dakota Penitentiary, and Maine State Prison.

At the Auburn State Penitentiary, prisoners were housed in solitary cells during evening hours. This was the beginning of what is presently known as **solitary confinement.** Another innovation at Auburn was that inmates were allowed to work together and eat their meals with one another during daylight hours. This was known as the **congregate system** (American Correctional Association, 1983). Auburn Penitentiary also provided for divisions among prisoners according to the nature of their offenses. The different tiers conveniently housed inmates in different offense categories, with more serious offenders housed on one tier and less serious offenders housed on another. Certain tiers were reserved for the most unruly offenders who could not conform their conduct to prison policies. The most dangerous inmates were kept in solitary confinement for long periods as punishment. These periods ranged from a few days to a few months, depending upon the prison rule violated. Therefore, Auburn Penitentiary is significant historically because it provided for the minimum-, medium-, and maximum-security designations by which modern penitentiaries are known.

Prisoners were provided with different uniforms as well, to set them apart from one another. The stereotypical striped uniform of prison inmates was a novelty at Auburn that was widely copied as well. Over half of all state prisons patterned their structures after the Auburn system during the next half century, including the style of prison dress and manner of separating offenders according to their crime seriousness (American Correctional Association, 1983:49–54). Striped prison uniforms for prisoners continued until the 1950s when they became outmoded.

Other Prison Developments.   Between 1816 and 1900, many other state prisons were established. One of the first successful prisons was constructed in Cherry Hill, Pennsylvania in the early 1830s. This prison was considered successful because it was the first to offer a continuing internal program of treatment and other forms of assistance to inmates (Johnston, 1973). The first state penitentiary in Ohio was opened in Columbus in 1834. The largest state prison of that time period was established in Jackson, Michigan, in 1839. By 1999, this State Prison of Southern Michigan had been torn down and rebuilt. It houses 615 male inmates. Another large state prison was built in Parchman, Mississippi, in 1900. In 2002, it housed 4,900 inmates. Louisiana claims one of the largest and oldest state prisons, however, being built in 1866 with a capacity of 4,750 inmates. In 2002, the Louisiana State Penitentiary in Angola housed 5,125 males (American Correctional Association, 2003).

The American Correctional Association and Elmira Reformatory.   In 1870 the **American Correctional Association (ACA)** was established and Rutherford B. Hayes, a future U.S. president, was selected to head that organization. The goals of the ACA were to formulate a national correctional philosophy, to develop sound correctional policies and standards, to offer expertise to all interested jurisdictions in the design and operation of correctional facilities, and to assist in the training of correctional officers. The ACA was originally called the National Prison Association, then the American Prison Association, and finally and more generally, the American Correctional Association.

The United States was entering a new era of correctional reform with the establishment of the ACA. Six years later, the Elmira State Reformatory in Elmira, New York was constructed. **Elmira Reformatory** experimented with certain new rehabilitative philosophies espoused by various penologists including its first superintendent, Zebulon Brockway (1827–1920). Brockway was critical of the harsh methods employed by the establishments he headed, and he envisioned better and more effective treatments for prisoners (Eggleston, 1989). He had his chance in 1876 when he was selected to head Elmira Reformatory. Elmira was considered the new penology and used the latest scientific information in its correctional methods. Penologists from Scotland and Ireland, **Captain Alexander Maconochie** and **Sir Walter Crofton,** were instrumental in bringing about changes in European correctional methods during the period when Elmira was established in the early 1870s. These men influenced U.S. corrections by introducing the **mark system,** where prisoners could accumulate **tickets-of-leave,** which would enable them to be released early from their lengthy incarcerative sentences. Through hard work and industry, prisoners could shorten their original sentences which earlier had to be served in their entirety (Clay, 2001).

Elmira was truly a reformatory and used a military model comparable to contemporary boot camps. Prisoners performed useful labor and participated in educational or vocational activities, where their productivity and good conduct could earn them shorter sentences. Elmira inmates were trained in close-order drill, wore military uniforms, and paraded about with wooden rifles. Authorities regarded this as a way of instilling discipline in inmates and reforming them. Historians credit Elmira Reformatory with individualizing prisoner treatment and the use of indeterminate sentencing directly suited for parole actions. Elmira Reformatory was widely imitated by other state prison systems (Rafter, 1997).

THE FUNCTIONS OF PRISONS

The functions served by prisons are closely connected with the overall goals of corrections. Broadly stated, correctional goals include deterrence, rehabilitation, societal protection, offender reintegration, just-deserts, justice and due process, and retribution or punishment. The goals of prisons are listed and described below.

Prisons Provide Societal Protection

Locking up dangerous offenders or those who are persistent nonviolent offenders means that society will be protected from them for variable time periods. It is not possible at present to lock up all offenders who deserve to be incarcerated. Space limitations are such that we would require at least four or five times the number of existing prisons to incarcerate all convicted felons and misdemeanants. Thus, the criminal justice system attempts to incarcerate those most in need of incarceration. This is one method of crime control (Wortley et al., 2002).

Prisons Punish Offenders

Restricting one's freedoms, confining inmates in cells, and obligating them to follow rigid behavioral codes while confined is regarded as punishment for criminal conduct (Dunbabin, 2002). The fact of incarceration is a punishment compared with the greater freedoms enjoyed by probationers and parolees.

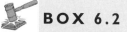

BOX 6.2

Ginger Winings
PAIII, Unit Supervisor, Chico, California Parole

Statistics:

B.S. (business administration, economics), Portland State University

Background:

Pure curiosity led me to a career in corrections! With my double major in business administration and economics out of Portland (Oregon) State University, I was quite happy with my commission sales job in Bakersfield, California. One day the California Department of Corrections (CDC) was holding a recruiting seminar for correctional officers at the local community college and I happened to attend. What the recruiters were saying made pretty good sense to me, and besides, they didn't look so tough! I hadn't grown up "wanting to go to prison" and even though I anticipated disapproval from family and friends and I knew the hiring process would take about a year and half to complete, I applied anyway. A year and a half passed quickly and I found myself a correctional officer with CDC until, as I fondly say, "I paroled to Bakersfield, California." The trip to parole, like the trip to the institution, was not planned. But based on my belief that one should be open to opportunities regardless of their value at the time, I signed up for the Parole Agent Exam. Bear in mind that at the time, I had no idea what a parole agent was and even less of an idea of what they did, but I met the minimum qualifications. That's about as green as you can get! Little did I know I was about to embark on the most irritating, agitating, aggravating, rewarding career one could ever imagine.

After the Parole Agent Academy, I was thrown into a rural caseload in the middle of the Mojave Desert, not your most sought-after of available positions. My on-the-job training consisted of a day with another pa-

role agent who had been working "The Desert" prior to my arrival. Kern County, California, is one of the largest counties in the world, and it stretches over miles and miles of desert, with small towns scattered here and there. I became another "desert rat" from the Bakersfield office. My area stretched 100 miles in one direction, 70 miles in another, and 90 miles in a third. In addition to small towns, my territory included both Edwards Air Force Base where the Space Shuttle lands, and China Lake Naval Weapons Center. I did a lot of driving. I got to drive up dry creek beds, across desert lakes that appear after a torrential rain, and across Edwards Air Force Base. The desert provides many remarkable and memorable moments. The desert in full bloom, the desert at sunset, a Space Shuttle loaded, sitting on its mother ship waiting for transport, and a Stealth Fighter flying so close to the ground that it seems as though you can reach up and touch it.

After I had worked in the desert for a while, CDC offered the Parole Agent II Exam. Again I took the exam and was fortunate enough to be ranked in a reachable position on the list. I had little interest in doing anything other than Parole Agent I work and expressed this thought to the Parole Agent II in my Unit. His reply was, "Ginger, someday you are going to get tired of going over fences!" Shortly afterward, I promoted to a Parole Agent II in a Community Correctional Facility (CCF), a prison operated by a private company or a municipality contracted by CDC. I became the liaison between the two and the only CDC employee at the Susanville,

(continued)

BOX 6.2 (Continued)

California facility. I was responsible for enforcing departmental policy and creating a balance between CDC and the contractor. I later transferred from the Bakersfield area to work in the Shafter CCF. From there I promoted to a Parole Agent III and supervised four CCFs, once again driving long distances.

The Parole Division of CDC relinquished control of the CCFs to the Institutions Division, and I opted to stay with Parole. I transferred to the Visalia Parole Office as a Unit Supervisor. After about a year, the District Administrator for the Chico Office called me and asked if I would be interested in transferring to Chico. I said "No" as I was quite happy where I was. She asked me what it would take to get me to transfer. I rattled off something knowing full well the State would not go for it. The following day she called and said, "OK!" That is an abridged version of how I became the Supervisor of the Chico Parole Unit.

Experiences:

In parole, we interface with families, the community, law enforcement, and governmental agencies to insure the safety and security of the community while facilitating the successful integration of parolees and civil addicts into mainstream society. My time in the Institution gave me valuable insight into understanding criminal behavior.

As a field agent I spent time making home calls, anti-narcotic testing, developing programs, interfacing with the community, families, law enforcement, monitoring behavior, encouraging acceptable behavior, and completing the never-ending paperwork that goes with the job. Often a parole agent is the only positive influence in a parolee's life. Sometimes I had to make decisions for them that they either could not or would not make for themselves. While I was not responsible for the parolee's or civil addict's behavior, I was responsible for the structure for the choice they made.

As a supervisor I have combined my training and experience to work with the staff that works for me. In my mind one of the most important functions I perform is to train parole agents to make effective independent decisions. I accomplish this with on-going training at the Unit level and teaching at the Parole Academy. For a parole agent, the two most important things to remember are: (1) look out for your own safety and you will do it better than anyone else; cover your authority; and (2) know your department policy and the legal limitations of your classification. They will keep you and your department out of trouble.

The downside of parole is far outweighed by the upside. You can find yourself entrenched in the job and forget that you only work with a small population, a sub-culture of our society. There is endless paperwork, most of which is time-sensitive, and there is never enough time to do all you want to do. However, the upside is an independent work environment, parolee's stories, the adrenaline rush of going into an unknown, and in the elation of being instrumental in the success of a parolee or civil addict. Continuing your work-related education and keeping your life in balance are essential.

In this "people business" communication skills, in addition to firm, fair, and consistent supervision administered with respect, are your greatest assets. No two parolees or civil addicts are alike, no two situations are the same, and there is no such thing as a routine home call.

Stories:

Soon after CDC opened a new prison in Northern California, inmates discovered a flaw in the construction—the doors were not secure. As a result we had to move inmates from one housing unit and yard to another so that the flaw could be fixed. When it was time to move the Administrative Segregation Unit, it was an understandably intense time, since most inmates are in Ad Seg because they had trouble on the yard. The yard was closed except for those inmates

BOX 6.2 (Continued)

who were rolled up and moving, gunners were posted, officers were on the yard with small groups of inmates to monitor, and the sergeant was giving orders. I had my group, and a couple of them were discussing the slow and somewhat unassuming movement of another inmate. One referred to an inmate by his AKA and said, "You know he had better hurry up." The other said, "Ah, don't worry about it," to which the first replied, "No, he'd better get moving." The other inmate said, "Nah, he'll get going; he's just slow." Still worried, the first inmate replied, "That sergeant is getting mad and he is going to be in big trouble if he doesn't hurry up." The other inmate replied, "Ah, don't worry about it; I'm telling you he's just slow—why it takes him an hour and a half just to watch *60 Minutes.*" With the exception of being slow, the moves went fine.

Not too long after I started as a Field Agent, I had a parolee in my office for an initial interview. During the course of the interview, he told me that he was a second-striker, and he wasn't going back. I asked him how he got his strikes. He said he caught his significant other in bed with another man, and so he shot 'em. I asked him if he killed them, to which he replied, "Well no, if I had killed 'em, I wouldn't have

taught 'em anything!" To my knowledge, he never went back.

I was on my way to conduct a home visit 20 miles from nowhere with a parolee who had been transferred from another county to my area. It was dark but I found the place and made my initial contact. He was tall, really tall; buffed, I mean really buffed; tattooed pretty much all over the area I could see. He was somewhat forbidding to say the least. As we talked he made the statement in a non-threatening manner, "You know, a lot of people are afraid of me." I replied, "Well, I'll betcha one thing." He asked, "What's that?" I said, "I betcha I can run scared faster than you can mad!" I had no trouble with him, nor did he violate his parole while on my caseload.

Advice to Students:

I would say to anyone embarking on this profession the following. Develop your sense of humor; some days it's all you've got. Create potential opportunities for yourself, even if you think you won't need them. The people you least expect to teach you will. Don't let your "can't do's" get in the way of your "can do's." Bad news will always beat you home.

Prisons Rehabilitate Offenders

Few criminal justice scholars accept the idea that prisons rehabilitate inmates. Little support exists for the view that imprisonment does much of a rehabilitative nature for anyone confined. Nevertheless, many prisons have vocational and educational programs, psychological counselors, drug dependency programming and counseling, and an array of services available to inmates in order that they might improve their skills, education, and self-concept (King et al., 2002). Prisons also have libraries for inmate self-improvement. More often than not, prisons also socialize inmates in adverse ways, so that they might emerge from prisons later as better criminals who have learned ways of avoiding detection when committing future crimes (Dear et al., 2002). One growing problem in prisons that often interferes with rehabilitative efforts of institutional programming is the greater cultural diversity of inmates and the lack of suitable interventions to fit different inmate needs (Winfree, Newbold, and Tubb, 2002).

Prisons Reintegrate Offenders

It might be argued that moving offenders from higher security levels, where they are more closely supervised, to lower security levels, where they are less closely supervised, helps them understand that conformity with institutional rules is rewarded. As prisoners near their release dates, they may be permitted unescorted leaves, known as furloughs or work/study release where they may participate in work or educational programs and visit with their families during the week or on weekends. These experiences are considered reintegrative. Most prisons have such programs, but they are presumably aimed at certain offenders who are believed to no longer pose a threat to society. Prisons also provide parenting services and courses to younger inmates with children.

While a lot of work has been done to foster more effective parenting for inmate mothers, inmate fathers are increasingly receiving this same type of parenting training (Boswell and Wedge, 2002; Nurse, 2002). In Fairfax County, Virginia, for instance, the Fairfax County Responsible Fatherhood Program (FRFP) was launched in 2002. The objectives of the FRFP are to:

1. Promote responsible fatherhood both during and upon release from incarceration
2. Encourage fathers to get involved in their children's lives
3. Teach parenting skills
4. Provide an understanding of child development and the role that fathers play in it
5. Define responsible fatherhood
6. Promote emotional, moral, spiritual, and financial responsibility for children
7. Teach the value of positive communication between parents
8. Teach methods of minimizing parental conflict

The FRFP has clients meet during a 10-week program. Participants meet once a week for 90 minutes. The curriculum covers statistics about fatherhood and parenting, understanding child development, co-parenting, responsible manhood, conflict resolution, and moving on. Findings suggest that there are individual benefits, relationship benefits, and social benefits. Interestingly the vast majority of participants have jumped at the chance to rekindle relationships with their children and reestablish family stability (Robbers, 2003:31).

INMATE CLASSIFICATION SYSTEMS

Religious movements are credited with establishing early prisoner classification systems in the eighteenth century (American Correctional Association, 1983:194). The Walnut Street Jail in 1790 in Philadelphia attempted to segregate prisoners according to age, gender, and offense seriousness. Subsequent efforts were made by penal authorities to classify and separate inmates according to various criteria in many state and federal prison facilities. Adequate classification schemes for prisoners have yet to be devised (California Department of Corrections, 1998). Classification schemes are based largely on psychological, behavioral, and sociodemographic criteria. Until the late 1990s, classification instruments were primarily targeted at male rather than female offenders (Figueira-McDonough et al., 2002). The use of psychological characteristics as predictors of risk or dangerousness and subsequent custody assignments for prisoners was stimulated by research during the period, 1910–1920 (American Correctional Association, 1983:196).

No single scheme for classifying offenders is foolproof, although several instruments have been used more frequently than others for inmate classification and placement (Schram and Morash, 2002). The Megargee Inmate Typology presumes to measure inmate adjustment to prison life (Megargee and Carbonell, 1985). Several items were selected from the Minnesota Multiphasic Personality Inventory (MMPI), a psychological assessment device, to define ten prisoner types and to predict an inmate's inclination to violate prison rules or act aggressively against others. Basically a psychological tool, the Megargee Inmate Typology has been adopted by various state prison systems for purposes of classifying prisoners into different custody levels. The predictive utility of this instrument is questionable, however. One problem Megargee himself detected was that prisoner classification types based on his index scores change drastically during a one-year period. For some observers, this finding has caused serious questions about the reliability of Megargee's scale. For other observers, however, inmate score changes on Megargee's scale indicate behavioral change, possibly improvement. Thus, reclassifications are conducted of most prison inmates at regular intervals to chart their behavioral progress.

Besides Megargee, other professionals have devised useful inmate classification criteria that have been particularly fruitful. For example, Holt (1996) found that inmate misconduct is correlated with being affiliated with street gangs. Other criteria have been used in different research throughout each of the state and federal systems with varying results (Dowdy, Lacy, and Unnithan, 2002). One's prior record of offending, age, unemployment history, and race have functioned as both legal and extralegal criteria and have been associated with program failures or successes under different research conditions (Wood and May, 2003). The present generation of objective prison classification systems must be capable of more than simple risk assessment. Systems must be able to identify the needs of an increasingly diverse population with changing characteristics to provide appropriate programs, services, and treatment opportunities, and prepare offenders for re-entry into their communities. Presently the focus of risk assessment development is upon identifying high-risk, disruptive offenders in order to foster more effective correctional planning and monitoring, as well as promoting safer environments for staff and inmates (Brown, 2000:138).

One thing is certain about risk instruments and inmate classifications resulting from applications of these instruments. Exactly how prison inmates are initially classified and housed will directly influence their parole chances. Inmates classified as maximum security may not deserve this classification, since it means that the inmate is considered dangerous. Inmate opportunities for personal development and rehabilitation are limited by these classifications. However, inmates who are classified as minimum security have a wide variety of prison benefits and programs (Waters and Megathlin, 2002). They are neither supervised as closely nor considered dangerous. When minimum security inmates face parole boards, their custody levels are assets. When maximum security inmates face parole boards, their classification is a liability. An example of a prison risk assessment instrument to determine an inmate's placement or security level is the one used by the Alaska Department of Corrections and is illustrated in Figure 6.2.

STATE OF ALASKA DEPARTMENT OF CORRECTIONS

Security Designation Form for Long-Term Sentenced Prisoners

(1) _____   (3) _____
      Institution   Designation Staff Member

(2) _____   (4) _____
      Date   Supt. Signature (exception case only)

SECTION A   IDENTIFYING DATA

(1) _____
Prisoner's Name   Last   First   Middle Initial

(2) _____
      Date of Birth

(3) Type of Case: Regular _____   Exception _____   (4) OBSCIS _____

(5) Separatees: _____

_____

SECTION B   SECURITY SCORING

1. Type of Detainer:

| 0 = None | 3 = Class C Felony | 7 = Unclassified or | |
| 1 = Misdemeanor | 5 = Class B Felony | Class A Felony | [ ] 1 |

2. Severity of Current Offense:

| 1 = Misdemeanor | 3 = Class C Felony | 7 = Unclassified | |
| | 5 = Class B Felony | or Class A Felony | [ ] 2 |

3. Time to Firm Release Date:

0 = 0–12 months	3 = 60–83 months		
1 = 13–59 months	5 = 84 + months	_____	[ ] 3
		Firm Release Date	

4. Type of Prior Convictions:

| 0 = None | 1 = Misdemeanor | 3 = Felony | [ ] 4 |

5. History of Escapes or Attempted Escapes:

	None	+15 Years	10–15 Years	5–10 Years	−5 Years	
Minor	0	1	1	2	3	
Serious	0	4	5	6	7	[ ] 5

6. History of Violent Behavior:

	None	+15 Years	10–15 Years	5–10 Years	−5 Years	
Minor	0	1	1	2	3	
Serious	0	4	5	6	7	[ ] 6

FIGURE 6.2 Alaska Long-Term Prisoner Classification Form.
Courtesy of the Alaska Department of Corrections, 2003.

7. SECURITY TOTAL   [ ] 7

8. Security Level:
   Minimum = 0–6 points   Medium = 7–13 points   Maximum = 14–36 points

9. Designated Custody Level:
   Community/Minimum   Medium   Close   Maximum
           0 – 6   7 – 13   14 – 25   26 – 36

10. Designation Staff Comments:

_____

_____

_____

SECTION C	MANAGEMENT CONSIDERATION	
1. Release Plans	5. Special Treatment	9. Residence
2. Medical	6. Ethnic/Cultural	10. Restitution Center
3. Psychiatric	Consideration	11. Contract Misdemeanant
4. Education	7. Overcrowding	Housing
	8. Judicial Recommendation	

FIGURE 6.2   (Continued).

All prisons in the United States have classifications that differentiate be-tween prisoners and cause them to be placed under various levels of custody or security. One of the main purposes for the initial inmate classification is to iden-tify those likely to engage in assaultive or aggressive disciplinary infractions. Pris-oners are eventually channeled into one of several fixed custody levels known as (1) **minimum-security,** (2) **medium-security,** and (3) **maximum-security.**

Minimum-Security Classification

Minimum-security prisons are facilities designed to house low-risk, nonviolent first-offenders. These institutions are also established to accommodate those serving short-term sentences. Sometimes, minimum-security institutions func-tion as intermediate housing for those prisoners leaving more heavily moni-tored facilities on their way toward parole or eventual freedom. Minimum-security housing is often of a dormitory-like quality, with grounds and physical plant features resembling a university campus more than a prison. Those as-signed to minimum-security facilities are trusted to comply with whatever rules are in force (Simons, Wertele, and Heil, 2002).

Administrators place greater trust in inmates in minimum-security institu-tions, and these sites are believed to be most likely to promote greater self-confidence and self-esteem among prisoners. The rehabilitative value of minimum-security inmates is high. Also, family visits are less restricted. The emphasis of minimum-security classification is definitely upon prisoner reinte-gration into society.

Medium-Security Classification

Seventy percent of all state and federal prisons in the United States are medium- and minimum-security institutions. The American Correctional Association (2000) says that a majority of state and federal prison facilities are designed to accommodate medium- and minimum-security inmates. As of 2002, of all U.S. penitentiaries, all but the one in Atlanta, Georgia were classified as medium-security (American Correctional Association, 2003). Medium-security facilities at both state and federal levels offer inmates opportunities for work release, furloughs, and other types of programs (Wogan and MacKenzie, 2002).

Maximum-Security Classification

Thirty percent of all U.S. prisons are exclusively maximum-security institutions. Ordinarily, those sentenced to serve time in maximum-security facilities are considered among the most dangerous, high-risk offenders (Walters et al., 2002). Maximum-security prisons are characterized by many stringent rules and restrictions, and inmates are isolated from one another for long periods in single-cell accommodations. Closed-circuit television monitors often permit correctional officers to observe prisoners in their cells or in work areas which are limited. Visitation privileges are minimal. Most often, no efforts are made by officials to rehabilitate inmates.

An example of one of the most memorable maximum-security penitentiaries ever constructed was the federal prison at Alcatraz in San Francisco Bay. Alcatraz was constructed in 1934 but closed in 1963 because of poor sanitation and the great expense of prisoner maintenance. During the period Alcatraz was operated, Alcatraz held over 1,500 prisoners, including Al Capone and Robert "Birdman" Stroud. In maximum-security prisons, inmate isolation and control are stressed, and close monitoring by guards either directly or through closed-circuit television reduces prisoner misconduct significantly (Jacoby, 2002).

Maxi-Maxi, Admin Max, and Super Max Prisons

Prisons such as the federal penitentiary at Marion, Illinois, are considered maxi-maxi prisons. The Marion facility accommodated only 568 inmates in 1999, and those incarcerated at Marion are considered the very worst prisoners (American Correctional Association, 2000). Marion inmates are the most violence-prone, inclined to escape whenever the opportunity arises, and extremely dangerous. Two correctional officers were killed by prisoners in the Control Unit. When the riot was contained, Marion officials ordered a **lockdown,** where all prisoners were placed in solitary confinement and severe restrictions were imposed. For Marion inmates, lockdown meant confinement in isolation for 23 1/2 hours per day, with 1/2 hour for exercise. Privileges were extremely limited. Subsequently Marion was closed temporarily for repairs and updating (Kurki and Morris, 2001).

Prisons with the highest levels of security and inmate supervision are designated as **maxi-maxi.** Sometimes these prisons are known as **super max** facilities. It is believed that maxi-maxi, admin max, and super max all refer to essentially the same types of facilities with equivalent levels of the highest supervision and custody for the most dangerous offenders (Abramsky, 2002; Camp et al., 2003).

An example of a super max facility is the Federal Administrative Maximum Penitentiary in Florence, Colorado. This facility, designated as an **admin max,** is designed to house 700 of the federal government's most violent offenders. Correctional officers carry weapons and have access to tear gas. The facility supports the use of deadly force against inmates if it should become necessary. Cell furniture includes a concrete sleeping platform with a pad, a wall-mounted writing surface and shelf, a stainless steel "combi unit" (water closet, lavatory, and drinking fountain), and a small, stainless steel mirror. Strategically placed security vestibules provide additional circulation control and allow portions of the facility to be sealed off at will (Coid, 2001).

It is apparent that there are many types of prisons ranging from minimum-security, honor farm-type facilities to maxi-maxi penitentiaries. A low degree of violence is associated with minimum-security facilities. This is because inmates tend to be less dangerous and pose the least risk to the safety of correctional officers and others. Each prison setting with its peculiar inmate profile means that wardens or superintendents will be presented with different kinds of problems to resolve.

The Importance of Classification for Prisoners

Whether prisoners realize it or not, their classification when they enter prison has substantial influence on their early-release eligibility. Other factors, such as institutional conduct, not getting into fights with other inmates, avoiding disruptive behavior, controlling anger, participating in self-help programs, enrolling in counseling and other available prison services, all combine to influence parole board decision making when it comes time to decide whether any particular inmate should be released.

Paroling authorities consider it significant, for instance, if an inmate enters prison and is placed in maximum-security or medium-security custody, and if that same inmate eventually works his/her way down to minimum-security custody. What this means is that the inmate has earned a level-of-custody reduction through good behavior. Parole boards are not going to grant parole easily to an inmate who has been placed in maximum-security custody and has remained there for several years. Furthermore, if an inmate advances to a higher custody level, such as moving from minimum-security to medium-security, this is evidence of poor conduct. The inmate may have a bad attitude, reject authority or any type of helpful intervention, or engage in disruptive behavior. Thus, it is definitely to an inmate's advantage to do the right types of things that will earn him/her level-of-custody reductions.

In Nevada, for instance, a parole-eligible inmate faced the parole board. He was a young man in his mid-twenties. His record indicated that he lacked a high school education. He had been unemployed and on drugs at the time of his arrest for a property offense. He had served two years of a six-year term. The parole board asked him, "Well, why should we release you now? Have you worked on your GED? Have you done anything to correct your drug problem?" The inmate answered, condemning himself to further confinement. He said, "No, I haven't done any of that. I don't like education. I hate teachers. I don't think I've got a drug problem. I've been in this place for a few years and I don't do drugs. But I'm just not interested in those different things they say we can get involved in. I just hate authority." The Nevada Parole Board rejected his parole application. In this case, his own attitude about self-improvement was sufficient to cause the parole board to turn him down on his early-release request. Perhaps if he had obtained a GED or participated in drug therapy and counseling, the parole board may have granted him early release on that occasion.

In another case, the North Dakota Parole Board heard the early-release request from a young black inmate who was serving a four-year sentence for aggravated assault. He had assaulted his girlfriend. He had served two years and faced the parole board. One parole board member observed, "Lionel, it looks like you got into some trouble over the last few months. You've been in some fights. Got into some trouble. What about that?" Lionel looked at the parole board and said, "Listen, when some dude calls me a nigger, I'm not going to let it go. I'll fight him. That's what he wants, and that's what he's going to get from me." "Well," the parole board member further queried, "Why should we let you out now? You've served less than two years of a four-year sentence. Have you taken any anger management classes? You know that you are going to face that sort of thing no matter where you go. Are you always going to fight? What do you have to say about that?" Lionel told the parole board, "No, I haven't taken any anger management. I can control myself. It's just that these dudes are going to do anything they can to f____ me. They don't like me and they are going to try to get me into trouble by starting fights. The guards come along, they see two dudes fightin', and what do they do? They write both of us up. It ain't fair. No, I don't think I can walk away from that. But I think I can control my anger. About my parole, I think I deserve a 'cut' in my sentence. I know other guys who have got out early, and they're worse than me. I just think I deserve a 'cut.'" The parole board turned down Lionel for early release. When they advised him of their negative decision, he threw a pencil at one of the parole board members and cussed them out. He said he'd "max out" his time or serve his sentence in its entirety if it meant that he wouldn't have to put up with being called a nigger by some whitey in the 'block (North Dakota Parole Board, 2003).

There are many self-help options available to most prisoners in most prisons in both the state and federal systems. They have to assist in their own defense, however. This means that they can't simply sit and wait for a parole board to grant them early release. They can do things to speed up the early-release process. One of these things is to earn a lower level of custody by following institutional rules and not causing trouble (Gido, 1998). Some inmates are incapable of understanding this, however.

A PROFILE OF PRISONERS IN U.S. PRISONS

Considerable diversity exists among prisoners in state and federal institutions. These differences include the nature and seriousness of their conviction offenses, age, and psychological or medical problems (Clayton, 2003). In order to cope more effectively with meeting the needs of such diverse offenders, prisons have established different confinement facilities and levels of custody, depending upon how each prisoner is classified. Between 1980 and 2002, a majority of states increased their number of sentenced prisoners by over 500 percent (Harrison and Beck, 2003:2). Overall, state and federal prisoner populations in-

---

TABLE 6.1

Change in the State and Federal Prison Populations, 1980–2002

Year	No. of Inmates	Annual Percent Change	Total Percent Change Since 1980
1980	329,821	—	—
1981	369,930	12.2%	12.2%
1982	413,606	11.9	25.5
1983	436,855	5.6	32.5
1984	482,002	5.8	40.1
1985	502,752	8.8	52.4
1986	546,378	8.5	65.4
1987	585,292	7.3	77.5
1988	631,990	8.0	91.6
1989	712,967	12.8	116.2
1990	773,124	8.4	134.4
1991	824,133	6.6	149.9
1992	883,593	7.2	167.9
1993	932,074	5.4	182.6
1994	1,016,691	9.0	208.2
1995	1,585,586	5.6	380.7
1996	1,646,020	3.8	399.0
1997	1,743,643	5.9	428.6
1998	1,816,931	4.2	450.8
1999	1,890,837	4.1	473.2
2000	1,937,482	2.5	487.4
2001	1,961,247	1.2	494.6
2002	2,033,331	3.6	516.4

Source: Paige M. Harrison and Allen J. Beck. *Prisoners in 2002.* Washington, DC: U.S. Department of Justice, Bureau of Justice Statistics, 2003:2.

---

creased by 516 percent between 1980 and 2002. Generally, the average increase in the federal and state prison inmate population was about 5 percent per year. This information is shown in Table 6.1.

A survey of state prison inmates was conducted in 2002 by the **Bureau of Justice Statistics** and compared with 1995 figures. The percentage of white prison inmates increased slightly from 33.5 percent in 1995 to 34.2 percent in 2002. The percentage of black inmates decreased from 45.7 percent in 1995 to 45.1 percent in 2002. Asian, Native American, and Pacific Islander inmates declined from 3.2 percent in 1995 to 2.6 percent in 2002. There was a small increase in the percentage of Hispanic inmates from 1995 to 2002, from 17.6 percent in 1995 to 18.1 percent in 2002 (Harrison and Beck, 2003:9). There are also record numbers of elderly offenders (older than 55) in state and federal prisons annually (Kempker, 2003:1).

In 2002 6.8 percent of all state and federal prisoners were female (Harrison and Beck, 2003:1). Females have been incarcerated at increasing rates since the mid-1990s. For instance, between 1995–2002, the average annual percentage of female inmates increased 5.2 percent, outpacing male incarcerations, which rose an average of 3.5 percent for the same period. Between 1995 and 2002, the female inmate population increased by 41 percent, while the male inmate population increased by 27 percent for the same period. The more rapid rise in female incarceration is mostly attributable to more property-related convictions among women than among men. For instance, there was a 22.3 percent rise in the female state and federal inmate population between 1995–2002 for property offenses, whereas there was actually a slight decline in male property offenders in state and federal facilities for the same period. The largest gains for male commitments were for violent crimes (a 63.9 percent increase between 1995 and 2002). Female commitments for violent crimes increased 48.6 percent during the same period. There were similar proportions

TABLE 6.2

Sentenced Prisoners under the Jurisdiction of State or Federal Correctional Authorities, Yearend 1995, 2001, and 2002

Region and Jurisdiction	Sentenced Prisoners			Percent Change, 1995–02	Percent Change, 2001–02	Incarceration Rate, 2002[a]
	2002	2001	1995			
U.S. total	1,380,370	1,345,217	1,085,022	27.2%	2.6%	476
Federal	143,040	136,509	83,663	71.0	4.8	49
State	1,237,330	1,208,708	1,001,359	23.6	2.4	427
Northeast	165,783	163,635	155,030	6.9%	1.3%	304
Connecticut	14,082	13,276	10,419	35.2	6.1	405
Maine	1,817	1,641	1,326	37.0	10.7	141
Massachusetts[b]	8,947	9,355	10,427	−14.2	−4.4	234
New Hampshire	2,451	2,392	2,015	21.6	2.5	192
New Jersey[c]	27,891	28,142	27,066	3.0	−0.9	322
New York	67,065	67,533	68,486	−2.1	−0.7	346
Pennsylvania	40,164	38,057	32,410	23.9	5.5	325
Rhode Island	2,045	1,926	1,833	11.6	6.2	191
Vermont	1,321	1,313	1,048	26.0	0.6	214
Midwest	244,226	239,948	192,177	27.1%	1.8%	373
Illinois[c]	42,693	44,348	37,658	13.4	−3.7	336
Indiana	21,542	20,883	16,046	34.3	3.2	348
Iowa[c]	8,398	7,962	5,906	42.2	5.5	284
Kansas[c]	8,935	8,577	7,054	26.7	4.2	327
Michigan	50,591	48,849	41,112	23.1	3.6	501
Minnesota	7,129	6,606	4,846	47.1	7.9	141
Missouri	30,080	28,736	19,134	57.2	4.7	529
Nebraska	3,972	3,865	3,006	32.1	2.8	228
North Dakota	1,025	1,027	544	88.4	−0.2	161
Ohio[c]	45,646	45,281	44,663	2.2	0.8	398
South Dakota	2,891	2,781	1,871	54.5	4.0	378
Wisconsin	21,324	21,033	10,337	–	1.4	391

(continued)

TABLE 6.2   (CONTINUED)

Region and Jurisdiction	Sentenced Prisoners 2002	Sentenced Prisoners 2001	Sentenced Prisoners 1995	Percent Change, 1995–02	Percent Change, 2001–02	Incarceration Rate, 2002[a]
South	552,795	539,774	446,491	23.8%	2.4%	536
Alabama	27,532	26,138	20,130	36.8	5.3	612
Arkansas	12,999	12,496	8,520	52.6	4.0	479
Delaware	3,659	4,033	3,014	21.4	−9.3	453
Florida	75,204	72,404	63,866	17.8	3.9	450
Georgia	47,424	45,904	34,168	38.8	3.3	552
Kentucky	15,572	15,104	12,060	29.1	3.1	380
Louisiana	35,736	35,810	25,195	41.8	−0.2	794
Maryland	23,274	22,842	20,450	13.8	1.9	425
Mississippi	21,397	20,476	12,251	74.7	4.5	743
North Carolina	28,772	27,628	27,914	3.1	4.1	345
Oklahoma[c]	23,385	22,780	18,151	28.8	2.7	667
South Carolina	22,837	21,606	19,015	20.1	5.7	555
Tennessee[c]	24,989	23,671	15,206	64.3	5.6	430
Texas[c]	151,782	153,056	127,766	18.8	−0.8	692
Virginia	33,729	31,662	27,260	23.7	6.5	460
West Virginia	4,504	4,164	2,483	81.4	8.2	250
West	274,526	265,351	207,661	32.2%	3.5%	415
Alaska	2,577	2,196	2,042	26.2	17.3	396
Arizona	28,008	26,463	20,291	38.0	5.8	513
California	160,329	157,295	131,745	21.7	1.9	452
Colorado	18,833	17,448	11,063	70.2	7.9	415
Hawaii	3,840	3,670	2,590	48.3	4.6	308
Idaho	6,204	5,984	3,328	86.4	3.7	461
Montana	3,290	3,328	1,999	64.6	−1.1	361
Nevada	10,478	10,233	7,713	35.8	2.4	483
New Mexico	5,772	5,408	3,925	47.1	6.7	309
Oregon	12,075	11,368	6,515	85.3	6.2	342
Utah	5,461	5,254	3,447	58.4	3.9	233
Washington	15,922	15,020	11,608	37.2	6.0	261
Wyoming	1,737	1,684	1,395	24.5	3.1	348

−Not calculated.

[a]Prisoners with sentences of more than 1 year per 100,000 residents.

[b]The incarceration rate includes an estimated 6,200 inmates sentenced to more than 1 year but held in local jails or houses of corrections.

[c]Includes some inmates sentenced to 1 year or less.

Source: Paige M. Harrison and Allen J. Beck, *Prisoners in 2002*. Washington, DC: U.S. Department of Justice, 2003:4.

of incarcerations for drug offenses for both men and women. Male drug offenders accounted for an increase of 15.2 percent during the period 1995–2002, while female drug offenders accounted for a 12.8 percent increase (Harrison and Beck, 2003:10). Table 6.2 shows the overall distribution of state and federal prisoners according to their respective jurisdictions for 2002, with contrasting information provided from 2001 and 1995. Table 6.3 shows a distribution of sentenced prisoners by offense according to their gender, race, Hispanic origin, and age for 2002.

TABLE 6.3

Number of Sentenced Prisoners Under State or Federal Jurisdiction, by Gender, Race, Hispanic Origin, and Age, 2002

| | Number of Sentenced Prisoners | | | | | | | |
| | Males | | | | Females | | | |
	Total[a]	White[b]	Black[b]	Hispanic	Total[a]	White[b]	Black[b]	Hispanic
Total	1,291,326	436,800	586,700	235,000	89,044	35,400	36,000	15,000
18–19	36,400	8,800	17,300	8,400	1,300	700	500	200
20–24	218,300	59,400	105,400	47,400	8,900	3,700	3,100	2,100
25–29	248,400	70,700	123,000	49,300	15,900	5,500	6,500	3,000
30–34	245,700	83,900	111,400	46,200	22,100	8,500	9,200	3,600
35–39	220,600	79,400	102,500	34,200	19,400	7,800	8,300	2,900
40–44	150,200	56,300	64,600	25,300	10,700	4,100	4,700	1,400
45–54	127,300	55,800	48,500	18,800	8,400	3,700	3,000	1,400
55 or older	38,900	21,500	10,800	4,800	1,900	1,200	500	200

Note: Based on custody counts from National Prisoners Statistics (NPS-1A) and updated from jurisdiction counts by gender at yearend. Estimates by age derived from the Surveys of Inmates in State and Federal Correctional facilities, 1997. Estimates were rounded to the nearest 100.
[a]Includes American Indians, Alaska Natives, Asians, Native Hawaiians, and other Pacific Islanders.
[b]Excludes Hispanics.
Source: Paige M. Harrison and Allen J. Beck, *Prisoners in 2002.* Washington, DC: U.S. Department of Justice, 2003:9.

SOME JAIL AND PRISON CONTRASTS

Prisons are constructed to house long-term offenders who are convicted of serious offenses compared with those housed in jails. Below are some of the contrasts between prisons and jails. Compared with prisons,

1. The physical plant of jails is poorer, with many jails under court order to improve their physical facilities to comply with minimum health and safety standards.

2. Jails usually do not have programs or facilities associated with long-term incarceration such as vocational, technical, or educational courses to be taken by inmates, jail industries, recreation yards, or psychological or social counseling or therapy.

3. Jails have a greater diversity of inmates, including witnesses for trials, suspects or detainees, defendants awaiting trial unable to post bail or whose bail was denied, juveniles awaiting transfer to juvenile facilities or detention, those serving short-term sentences for public drunkenness, driving while intoxicated, or city ordinance violations, mentally ill or disturbed persons awaiting hospitalization, and overflow from state and federal prison populations.

4. Jail inmate culture is less pronounced and persistent. There is a high inmate turnover in jails, with the exception of the state and federal convict population.

5. The quality of jail personnel is lower, with many jail personnel untrained, undertrained, or otherwise less qualified to guard prisoners compared with their counterparts, prison correctional officers. However, improvements in the quality of jail staff are being made annually in selected jurisdictions (Kiekbusch, 2000:19).

6. Jails are not usually partitioned into minimum-, medium-, or maximum-security areas. Control towers do not exist, where armed correctional officers patrol regularly. Jails are not surrounded by several perimeters, with barbed wire areas, sound-detection equipment, and other exotic electronic devices.

SELECTED JAIL AND PRISON ISSUES

This section examines briefly six major issues representing problems for both jails and prisons. These issues include: (1) jail and prison overcrowding; (2) violence and inmate discipline; (3) jail and prison design and control; (4) vocational/technical and educational programs in jails and prisons; (5) jail and prison privatization; and (6) gang formation and perpetuation.

Jail and Prison Overcrowding

Jails are expected to accommodate almost everyone brought to them for booking or processing. Murder suspects as well as public intoxication cases may be housed temporarily in the same tank or detention area to await further processing. The millions of admissions to and releases from jails annually only aggravate persistent jail overcrowding problems, despite the fact that most of those admitted to jails are not confined for lengthy periods. The volume of admissions and releases is severe enough and persistent enough to cause continuing jail overcrowding problems. Law enforcement arrest policies in many jurisdictions seriously aggravate jail overcrowding as well, as millions of arrestees occupy valuable jail space during booking and other perfunctory jail processing. The fact that numerous state and federal prisons contract with local jail authorities to house some of the prison inmate overflow suggests serious prison overcrowding as well.

Violent deaths, suicides, psychiatric commitments, and disciplinary infractions have been linked to jail and prison overcrowding (Camp et al., 2003). Some observers have argued that these results are very predictable. For instance, Wilkinson and Unwin (1999:98) have indicated, "Take a prison with inmates of many cultures, ethnic backgrounds and a basic tendency toward xenophobia: add a pinch of politically driven tightening of privileges; fold in a large dollop of life-long lessons in mistrust and hatred; cook at 170 percent of design capacity and top off with hot and humid summer months . . . even the most bucolic of communities would be hard-pressed to exist, much less thrive, in such an environment . . . Yet we ask this of prison inmates every day." These researchers also note that many inmates come from backgrounds that allow little exposure to people of different races, religions, behaviors, and attitudes, that this ignorance becomes the root of many street and prison gangs. However, the overcrowding problem and the many conditions it generates which are adverse for inmates has often been dealt with in a piecemeal fashion. For instance, Ohio conducts a Corrections Training Academy, where cultural diversity is taught to prospective correctional officer recruits. Thus, staff are sensitized to overcrowding and the multicultural blend of inmates, but the inmates themselves are not offered similar experiences.

An endless string of solutions have been suggested to ease jail and prison overcrowding. Some of these solutions are labeled as front-door solutions, because they pertain to policies and practices by criminal justice officials who deal with offenders before and during sentencing. Other solutions are back-door solutions, where strategies are suggested to reduce existing prison populations through early release or parole, furlough, administrative release, and several other options (Marion, 2002).

Typically, front-door solutions to prison overcrowding are frequently directed at prosecutors and judges, and the way they handle offenders. These include a greater use of diversion and/or assignment to community service agencies, where offenders circumvent the criminal justice system altogether and remain free within their communities. Greater use of probation by judges and recommendations of leniency from prosecutors have also been suggested, with an emphasis upon some form of restitution, community service, victim compensation, and/or fine as the primary punishment. Other solutions include greater plea bargaining where probation is included, selective incapacitation, where those offenders deemed most dangerous are considered for incarceration, assigning judges a fixed number of prison spaces so that they might rearrange their sentencing priorities and incarcerate only the most serious offenders, and decriminalization of offenses to narrow the range of crimes for which offenders can be incarcerated (Auerbahn, 2002).

Some of the back-door proposals by observers include easing the eligibility criteria for early release or parole, the administrative reduction of prison terms, where the governor or others shorten originally imposed sentences for certain offenders, modifying parole revocation criteria so as to encourage fewer parole violations, and expanding the number of community programs such as mediation and including the use of intensive supervised parole for more serious offender groups (Warwick, 2002). When offenders are released short of serving their full terms, public safety may be enhanced to the extent that there are collaborative efforts between jail officials and community agencies who can meet some or all of the needs of jail releasees (Lightfoot and Deluca, 2002).

Probably the most serious effect of prison overcrowding for inmates is upon their early-release chances. Parole-eligible inmates often find that because of prison overcrowding and the violence it generates, their parole chances are lessened. This is because there are far more inmates than self-help programs and prison labor can accommodate. Prisoners benefit if they can become involved in prison labor programs. However, only about 20 percent of all prisoners in the United States are included in such programs (Alarid, 2003). Many services, such as group or individual counseling, vocational/technical, and educational programs, are chronically understaffed and cannot be offered to all inmates who need or desire them. Even where inmates want to become involved in these programs, the mere fact that so many inmates must be accommodated means that some inmates will be excluded. As a result, some inmates will not receive the needed services or programs. If they do receive some of these services, the quality of services or programming will be adversely affected because of larger numbers of inmates who must be accommodated. Many parole-eligible inmates, therefore, will not have adequate opportunities to show parole boards what they have accomplished. This is one of the adverse consequences of ware-housing offenders under conditions of limited services and self-help programs (Bureau of Justice Assistance, 2000).

Violence and Inmate Discipline

Prisons and jails are breeding grounds for inmate violence (Fagan, 2003). Contributing to this potential for violence is the great mixture of races, ethnicities, and ages of inmates, together with chronic overcrowding. Prior drug/alcohol dependencies have also been associated with violence found in prisons, since often, these dependencies remain untreated following conviction and incarceration (Nielsen and Martinez, 2003). The increasingly visible presence of gangs has increased prison and jail violence as well, as inmates become affiliated with one gang or another, often for the purpose of self-protection (Straka, 2003). Every prison has screening mechanisms for new inmates according to standard criteria, but misclassifications frequently occur. Dangerous offenders and the mentally retarded or ill often commit aggressive acts against other inmates. But it is difficult to detect and distinguish between all offenders in terms of which ones pose the greatest risk to themselves or others. Placing inmates in solitary confinement for their own protection is most often not an option for the average prison. There is simply insufficient maximum-security space to accommodate all of those inmates who seek escape from other inmates who might wish to injure or exploit them. Also, there are limited policy provisions for insuring inmate safety from other violent inmates, although these provisions are not applied because of the exigencies of the situation. Drug abuse is also a contributing factor to inmate violence (Stohr et al., 2002).

Much prison violence goes undetected. Inmate-on-inmate assault is the most frequent type of violence, where one or more inmates physically or sexually assault another inmate. The assaulted inmate does not report the incident for fear of retaliation, which is highly foreseeable. Not all assaults are sex-oriented or initiated. Many assaults by inmates upon other inmates are started over something as trivial as disagreements over telephone use. Many prisoners suffer physical injuries, and these incidents are frequently unreported or unrecorded. Even when correctional officers suspect or observe rule-breaking and certain forms of inmate violence, this behavior is frequently ignored. Some researchers indicate that correctional officers often ignore this misconduct in order to obtain inmate cooperation and compliance with prison rules (Camp et al., 2003). This fact gives prisoners some degree of psychological control or power over those correctional officers who look the other way when they observe rule infractions.

Increasingly common are sexual assaults and psychological harassment in jails and prisons (Tartaro, 2002). These incidents of violence are often attributable to growing numbers of inmates with antisocial personality disorders in both prison and jail settings (Wogan and MacKenzie, 2002). Both male and female inmates are aggressors in such assaults (Struckman-Johnson and Struckman-Johnson, 2002). Widespread substance abuse among inmates has also contributed significantly to inmate violence (Stohr et al., 2002). Prison violence has been mitigated successfully in at least some state prisons. In the Washington State Penitentiary at Walla Walla, for example, administrators have trained staff to cope with inmate violence through an approach known as prevention and reaction (Buentello et al., 1992). With appropriate staff training,

Washington correctional officers are learning to prevent new prisoners from joining prison gangs through various intervention activities.

Probably the most visible form of prison violence is a riot. Rioting is on the rise in U.S. prisons as well as other countries, such as Germany (Kury and Smartt, 2002). Rioting among jail and prison inmates is not unique to the United States. Rioting occurs in virtually every prison in every country at one time or another. Even women's prisons have had higher levels of violence in recent years (Suter et al., 2002). Whenever prisoners riot, they cause considerable damage to prison property and inflict physical injuries on inmates and prison and/or jail staff. Between 1990 and 2002, for instance, there were over 2,000 incidents of inmate rioting in U.S. prisons and jails (Suter et al., 2002). Causes of these riots have been attributable to racial tension, changes in rules and regulations, mass escape attempts, gang conflicts, rumors, disputes among inmates and between inmates and staff members, drug and alcohol use, complaints about food, security procedures, and inmate overcrowding (Rolison et al., 2002; Tartaro, 2002).

It is difficult for jail and prison administrators to prepare effectively for riots. Sometimes informants from among the prisoners will give correctional officers some advance warning that a riot is about to occur (Bartollas and Ward, 2003). But most often, riots are spontaneous and unplanned, at least from an administrator's perspective. Therefore, administrators have devised various strategies for coping with, containing, and eliminating riot behavior when it erupts. Some of these strategies include control of the news media, which often plays into the hands of inmates who are seeking external recognition of their grievance or plight. Force, negotiations, and administrative concessions are other strategies that help to end rioting when it occurs. Whenever rioting ends, command and control structures are reexamined. Some reorganization occurs, where prison and jail administrators attempt to implement new policies and procedures that will minimize or even eliminate further rioting. One typical response by prison administrators is to impose greater restrictions and rule enforcement on inmates following rioting. However, this action often causes more disciplinary problems than it resolves. It has been recommended that an official nonviolent attitude should be adopted by prison administrators in high-custody facilities while using whatever force is necessary to confine and control high-risk inmates. Such a nonviolent stance from administrators helps to ease inmate tensions and reduce the level of prison violence (Camp et al., 2003).

Some observers note that we know far more about the causes of aggression and violence among inmates than we do about their treatment (Stohr et al., 2002). Aggressive behavior is typically the result of an interaction between personal characteristics and situational factors. Our technology is such that we have the capability of reasonably identifying the perceptual and cognitive patterns, coping skills, contingencies, and values of those most deserving of special attention from prison programs. However, those most likely to engage in violence and aggressive behavior or are at the greatest risk levels are often the same persons who are least amenable to treatment. Thus, some intervention programs offered in prisons fail because they target inmates who cannot benefit from the program. Or our intervention programs work for some offenders but not for others. Or the program was a true failure because it did not provide a specific service which targeted a factor unrelated to violent conduct (Lemieux, 2002).

One administrative change which has had somewhat positive results is the establishment of inmate councils. These councils, sometimes called inmate disciplinary councils, exist apart from administrative sanctioning mechanisms.

These councils are bodies that can hear and decide many low-level, nonserious inmate complaints against other inmates and even correctional officers or administrative policies. Usually, these councils can reach problem resolutions which satisfy most parties. All prisons at the state and federal levels currently have formal grievance procedures. These councils consist of inmates and a few prison correctional officers. Prisoners regard the addition of corrections officers as a way of provide these councils with some objectivity when hearing and deciding inmate grievances (Hasaballa, 2001).

Jail and Prison Design and Control

Some observers see a direct connection between new jail and prison design and a reduction in inmate violence (Sturges, 2002). Several proposals for resolving jail and prison problems are (1) to create new jails and prisons constructed in ways that will conserve scarce space and require fewer correctional officers; and (2) to reconstruct existing facilities to minimize prison violence and house more inmates. Prison construction in recent years has included increasingly popular modular designs. New modular designs also permit layouts and arrangements of cell blocks to enhance officer monitoring of inmates. But new prison construction is expensive, and many jurisdictions are either unwilling or unable to undertake new prison construction projects.

New jail and prison construction, the renovation or expansion of existing facilities, or the conversion of existing buildings previously used for other purposes take into account the matter of security and safety for both staff and inmates (Johnston, 2000). Stairwells and areas otherwise hidden from the view of correctional officers encourage inmate sexual or otherwise physical assaults. These areas can either be reduced or eliminated entirely with new architectural designs. It is generally conceded that reducing blind spots or areas not directly visible to officers and other corrections officials help to reduce the incidence of inmate assaults (Reisig, 2002). Further, institutional programming is enhanced, since there is better organization and planning through being able to anticipate the characteristics of future jail and prison clientele. If jail and prison officials have a better idea about the characteristics of those entering their facilities in future years, they can develop more effective programming to meet their needs. In the long run, inmates benefit from such planning (Prendergast et al., 2002).

Vocational/Technical and Educational Programs in Jails and Prisons

Most jails are not equipped to provide inmates with any vocational/technical and educational programs. Several reasons include the fact that most jails are not equipped with the space to offer such educational programming. Jail inmates do not have parole and good-time credit incentives compared with prison inmates. And jail inmates are usually serving short-term sentences that would interrupt any meaningful educational programming that might be contemplated. Even in those instances where jail educational programs have been devised and offered on a short-term basis to inmates, recidivism rates of graduates have not differed significantly from those who have not participated in educational programs offered at the jails (Sharp and Muraskin, 2003).

Many prisons lack a broad variety of programs geared to enhance inmate skills and education. This state of affairs seems consistent with the view that the rehabilitation orientation in American prisons is on the decline (Brewster and Sharp, 2002). However, there have been several successes among state and federal prison systems. For instance, drug offenders in the U.S. Bureau of Prison's Choice program, a drug treatment and intervention program, have for the most part been successfully treated. Inmates with drug dependencies are subjected to a ten-month program, including intake/evaluation/follow-up, drug education, skills development, lifestyle modification, wellness, responsibility, and individualized counseling/case supervision. The emphasis in the Choice program is upon education and the development of cognitive skills rather than on treatment and insight-oriented therapy (Walters et al., 1992).

In Washington, McNeil Island houses a portion of the state's serious offenders. In 1996 the prison facility, which houses 1,300 medium-security inmates, implemented an educational program known as the Work Ethic Camp (WEC) (Gianas, 1996). The camp recruits volunteers from among interested inmates who want to improve themselves. Designated correctional officers behave in ways that model demanding employers, although they develop a personally supportive relationship between themselves and participating inmates. Inmates, known as WECies, are expected to put in eight-hour workdays at different tasks. There is demanding work at the Island power station, motor pool, recycling plant, water-filtration plant, meat-packaging plant, and other facilities. Inmates learn boat repair and maintenance, road repair, building construction, facility maintenance, clerical work, farm work, and forest maintenance. WEC inmates are also taught basic work habits, including cleanliness, following instructions, planning tasks, teamwork, interpersonal skills, tool care, and supervisor–employee relationships. They also take courses in reading, writing, and math; adult basic education preparation; anger/stress management; victim awareness; community responsibility; dependable strengths articulation process; family dynamics; unlocking your potential; chemical dependency; health and wellness; job readiness; and transition planning. The WEC's objective is to produce productive, employable inmates who will leave McNeil Island ready to go to work for an employer on the outside. Evaluation of the program thus far has been favorable. Inmates are developing better self-images and self-respect. They are acquiring the skills necessary to make it more effectively on the outside when released. But much depends on whether inmates are motivated to become involved in programs such as the WEC (Garrity et al., 2002).

Some vocational/technical and educational programs are tailored to meet the needs of female inmates, including an emphasis on life skills (Schram and Morash, 2002). However, some evidence suggests that significant numbers of women have psychopathy, and that they may respond in different and sometimes unpredictable ways to vocational/technical programs or interventions (Jackson et al., 2002). In an Oregon prison, for example, a program was established in 1992 called the Women in Community Service program (WICS). This program was assessed during the period 1992–1995 and was determined to be effective for female offenders in different ways. The WICS was established to improve one's life skills, self-esteem, and motivation to change behavior. Vocational skills were emphasized, as well as drug- and alcohol-awareness courses and programs. The program's success has been determined by low recidivism rates among WICS participants in follow-up investigations (Day, Friedman, and Christophersen, 1998).

By the early 1990s, participation in jail or prison educational programs was mandatory in at least thirteen states (DiVito, 1991). Of those states making education mandatory, the primary inmate targets were those with obvious edu-

FIGURE 6.3   A female chain gang.
Courtesy of J. Peter Mortimer, Getty Images, Inc.

cational deficiencies who did not meet minimum educational criteria. Reduced sentence lengths were offered as incentives to participate in educational programs. The measure of success of these programs was whether inmates continue their education in jail or prison beyond the mandatory minimum. One of the more innovative inmate literacy programs is operated by the Virginia Department of Corrections. Commencing in 1986, the "no read, no release" program has emphasized literacy achievement at no lower than the sixth grade level and has made such an achievement part of the parole decision making process. Results have been favorably viewed by various states. However, compulsory educational programs in jails and prisons have been subjected to several constitutional challenges (DiVito, 1991).

In recent years, more than a few prison systems have gravitated toward offering life skills programs as a part of their educational services. The Delaware Department of Correction, for instance, established a life skills program in 1997. This program was offered in each of its four state prisons, where 5,000 inmates were housed. Participation in the program was voluntary, but each year approximately 300 inmates have enrolled. Nearly 85 percent have graduated from the program. The Delaware Life Skills Program, as it is called, runs three hours a day for four months. Each of five teachers conducts a morning and an afternoon course with 12 to 15 inmates in each course. The curriculum stresses three areas: academics; violence reduction; and applied life skills. Academics includes reading comprehension, mathematics, and language expression. The violence reduction component includes moral recognition therapy, anger management, and conflict resolution training. The applied life skills component includes credit and banking; job search; motor vehicle regulations; legal responsibilities and restitution; family responsibilities and child support; health issues; social services; educational services; cultural differences; and government and law (Finn, 1998:4-5). An evaluation of the life skills program offered by Delaware shows that the recidivism rate among program graduates was only 19 percent. This compares quite favorably with a control group where the recidivism rate was 27 percent. Thus, the objective of reducing recidivism among life skills participants was realized at all four Delaware institutions.

Parolees often benefit from the array of services extended to them in prison settings. Participating in educational programs, Alcoholics Anonymous, or some other educational or counseling is viewed as a desire to better oneself and indicative that rehabilitation may have occurred. Rehabilitation may or may not occur for particular inmates, depending upon whether they manipulate the system or use it for true self-improvement (Glick et al., 2001). In any case, parole boards seem impressed with whatever progress inmates manifest, regardless of an inmate's motives. Indeed, some research indicates that at least some parolees benefit in their postrelease after participating in correctional higher education programs (Batchelder and Pippert, 2002; Webster et al., 2001).

Jail and Prison Privatization

A proposal that has received mixed reactions in recent years is the privatization of jail and prison management by private interests. Legally, there is nothing to prevent private enterprises from operating prisons and jails as extensions of state and local governments and law enforcement agencies. Privatization has been most noticeable in the juvenile justice system. In fact, in 2002 over 30 percent of all incarcerated juveniles were being held in facilities owned and operated by private interests (Camp et al., 2002). Private interests argue that they can manage and operate jails and prisons more effectively and economically than many government agencies. Presently, this issue remains unresolved. However, there is no debating the fact that private sector proposals for the management of jails and other facilities have been increasing in recent years and result in considerable savings for the contracting local and state governments.

A significant hurdle is the political control issue. Who has control over offenders housed in and managed by persons in the private sector? Another issue is an administrative one. Should private enterprises be allowed to sanction convicted offenders? Will the current level of quality of inmate care be maintained when operated by private interests? Many government facilities are currently under court order to improve their living conditions for inmates. It is unlikely that the private sector would do a poorer managerial task relating to inmate management. But the accountability issue persists (Shichor and Sechrest, 2002).

Privatization has spread to probation and parole program operations. Private corporations can prepare presentence investigation reports or PSIs. They can also assist probation and parole departments in supervising probationer- or parolee-clients. In fact, guidelines are presently available to local and state governments about how private interests can interface with their own program operations and organization. In fact, the privatization phenomenon in corrections is not unique to the United States. Many other countries are currently experimenting with it (Camp et al., 2002).

A positive view of privatization in corrections is to view this phenomenon as an extension and a complement to existing public correctional programs. Private interests have been instrumental in devising many correctional innovations, including electronic monitoring and new technology for surveillance, control, and drug testing (Greene and Schiraldi, 2002; Wilson and Petersilia, 2002). Private innovators in corrections have made it possible for many convicted offenders to become enrolled in intermediate punishment programs and endure many sanctions imposed in lieu of traditional incarceration in a jail or prison.

Gang Formation and Perpetuation

One of the most serious problems in jails and prisons today is the prevalence and influence of gangs (Straka, 2003). A 2002 survey of all major U.S. prisons disclosed that although two-thirds had specific policies which prohibited gang recruitment, there was a gang presence in almost all facilities surveyed. About one sixth of all institutions reported that gang members had assaulted correctional staff. Two thirds of all institutions were providing some form of gang training for their correctional officers. Such training included recognition signs such as tattoos, clothing colors and trinkets, and hand gestures.

No one knows precisely how many gang members there are in U.S. prisons and jails today. And gangs are not exclusively a United States phenomenon. Gangs are found in virtually all prisons throughout the world (Straka, 2003). Estimates of 100,000 or more prison inmates involved in formal gang activity have been made, although that figure is probably much higher (Decker, 2001). Since many prison gang members were former street gang members, some idea of the prevalence of gangs in prisons can be gleaned by examining the prevalence and numbers of street gangs and their memberships. In 2002, for example, there were over 28,000 gangs and 780,000 gang members in the United States (Straka, 2003). Self-reports from a sample of gang members who were surveyed by researchers indicated that most of these gang members were involved in one or more illegal activities and were committing crimes. A sizeable portion of these gang members had served time in juvenile secure facilities, jails, or prisons.

Generally for prisons but also for jails, gang members are believed responsible for 50 percent or more of all institutional disturbances and problems. For this reason, several correctional systems have aggressively established programs designed to defeat gang influence and discourage gang recruitment and membership practices in a variety of ways. One effort is the Gang-Free Environment Program established in Illinois in 1996. The Taylorville Correctional Center (TCC) was created as a gang-free institution. Inmates were selected on the basis of their non-gang status. Programs were created to emphasize self-improvement, education, and employability, and to de-emphasize any need for gang affiliation. This meant that the institution had to create a safe environment for all inmates. Correctional officers received various types of training calculated to help them relate more effectively with inmates and to recognize any attempt at gang formation among the prisoners. One goal of the TCC is to encourage inmates to make general changes in their lifestyles. A Lifestyle Redirection Program has been initiated where various courses are offered to all inmates. Inmates are virtually free from any pressure to join gangs. The inmate selection process has been mostly successful (Alarid and Cromwell, 2002). Unfortunately, not all prisons are capable of offering such a luxury to their inmates. Prison gangs are not only pervasive but they are also powerful (Knox, 2000).

Prison gang development has been described. For instance, prospective recruits for existing prison gangs enter prison with feelings of fear of the new setting. They sense danger, feel isolated, and are lonely. There are virtually no rules for acceptance, no commitment to any group, no rules of conduct that are immediately apparent, and no formal leadership. Subsequently, many inmates gravitate toward one gang or another, often along racial or ethnic lines. The prison gang itself is characterized as having the following: (1) formal rules and constitution; (2) well-defined goals and philosophy; (3) hierarchy of formal leadership with clearly defined authority and responsibility; (4) membership for life; (5) members wear gang tattoos; (6) wholesale involvement in gang activities both inside and outside of the penal institution; and (7) ongoing criminal enterprise (Fong, Vogel, and Buentello, 1996:107).

In many instances, gangs have controlled prison culture and what transpires behind prison walls. They have intimidated prison staff. Furthermore, there is evidence that the same gangs have affiliate gangs in prisons in other states besides the ones where they originate (Straka, 2003). Beyond the disruptive effects of gangs on prison order and their influence over others within institutions, there are far-reaching effects that extend to those released from prison. Once someone has joined a prison gang, he or she is a part of that gang for life. Usually, the only way to leave a gang is by dying. The thought of betraying another gang member either within or without prison walls is reprehensible for most gang members (Rees, 1996). Therefore, when a gang member leaves prison either by serving his or her time or through parole, continuing allegiance to the gang is expected. If the gang member outside of prison can do one or more favors or perform services for other gang members inside prison, then he or she will perform these favors or services. In most instances, these favors involve criminal activity of one type or another (Valentine, 1995).

POs have a strong interest in determining whether their clients are affiliated with gangs. They learn gang recognition signals and familiarize themselves with gang territories in areas where their clients live. Gangs are considered community threat groups. Different states and the U.S. Probation Office have established specialized threat group programs where they attempt to coordinate their resources to combat those gang members on probation or parole who pose a serious threat to their communities (Sheehy and Rosario, 2003). Certain POs have special gang expertise and work with offenders who are gang members. It is their responsibility to identify tell-tale signs of gang activity and whether their clients are continuing their gang affiliations and traditions despite probation or parole program requirements to the contrary.

For probationers and parolees, gangs have a pervasive influence on whether these persons can remain law-abiding and conform with their different programs. There is ample evidence that prison and street gangs are closely intertwined. If gang membership requires probationers or parolees to commit new offenses, such as requisitioning drugs or money for currently incarcerated inmate-gang members, then this is a serious situation that POs must confront and resolve (Alarid and Cromwell, 2002).

Several methods are presently being employed to minimize the influence of gangs in both prisons and on the streets. Sophisticated tracking programs are being devised so that computer tracking of gang members can occur. Understanding the communication patterns of gang members both inside and outside of prison is crucial to effective PO work, especially for those POs who work closely with known gang members (Decker, 2001; Eckhart, 2001).

THE ROLE OF JAILS AND PRISONS IN PROBATION AND PAROLE DECISION MAKING

Whether inmates are in jails or prisons, they are obligated to comply with specific behavioral guidelines that will permit jail and prison officials to maintain order and discipline. Besides these requirements, many prisons and some jails have programs designed to assist inmates in different ways. Educational or vocational training are more readily available in prison settings, although some of the larger jails offer similar programs for long-term offenders. Remember that many jails have contracts with state and federal prison systems to house some of their inmate overflow. Thus, not every jail inmate is incarcerated for shorter intervals of a year or less. Counseling and other forms of assistance are available to inmates if these want such services (Eisenberg and Trusty, 2002).

Jail and prison officers and administrators submit written reports about inmate conduct, while confined. These reports may contain favorable or unfavorable information. Ultimately, this information is made available to paroling authorities so that a more informed parole decision can be made. If inmates cannot conduct themselves in a setting with explicit rules and regulations, then it is presumed that they cannot function well in their communities while on parole (Hemmens and Stohr, 2000).

The federal government and various states have experimented with various predictive classification systems used for pretrial detainees. Therefore, even in instances where one's guilt or innocence has not yet been established through trial, some preliminary screening mechanisms have already been implemented that may impact either favorably or unfavorably on a judge's sentencing decision later. In the Federal Bureau of Prisons, for instance, pretrial

FIGURE 6.4   Isolating inmates defeats prison gang formation.
Courtesy of John Chiasson, Getty Images, Inc.

detainees have been screened by various instruments and according to different predictive criteria to determine which alleged offenders would be good candidates for pretrial release. The results of such experimentation have been thus far inconclusive. Similar attempts to classify offenders have been made in other countries, such as Canada (Loza and Loza, 2002).

Attempts have also been made to forecast the successfulness of probationers based, in part, upon their incarcerative experiences (Newburn, 2002). In Eastern Pasco County, Florida, for example, a sample of 427 probationers sentenced to community supervision was examined between 1980 and 1982, with a follow-up investigation in 1987 (Liberton, Silverman, and Blount, 1992). Some of the probationers had been held in jails in pretrial detention until their trials. Others had been released on their own recognizance (ROR). Interestingly, researchers found that those offenders who had been incarcerated for periods exceeding two days had a much higher rate of recidivism compared with those offenders who were ROR. Specifically, the researchers found an inverse relationship between the length of pretrial commitment and the successful completion of probation. Factors relating to one's successful probation completion included being older, employed, married, and having some previous military service. We might speculate here that those offenders who were held in pretrial detention may have been more serious offenders compared with the ROR sample. Obviously, there were reasons for not allowing them to remain free in their communities pending their trial.

Some jails and most prisons attempt to screen incoming inmates according to their risk or dangerousness as well as their special needs (Lemieux, Dyeson, and Castiglione, 2002). Screening is also conducted to evaluate offenders and determine the most suitable level of custody for them. Since it becomes increasingly expensive to monitor offenders as the level of custody increases (e.g., from minimum-security to medium-security, from medium-security to maximum-security), it is in an institution's best interests economically to maintain prisoners at the least intense custody level while they are confined. This is why most prisons have reassessments of inmates periodically (e.g., every six months or a year) to determine whether their present level of custody should be increased or decreased.

For inmates in various state and federal prison systems, inmate classifications are very important in several respects. Imposing more stringent monitoring and closer custody on those prisoners who are considered most aggressive and violent will serve to protect less serious and nonviolent inmates (Schram and Morash, 2002). Beyond this, the lower one's classification level, the more the trust accorded that inmate. Parole boards consider one's present level of custody and whether one has behaved well while at that particular custody level. Again, it is in a prisoner's best interests to be confined at the lowest security level possible. Therefore, periodic reclassifications of offenders that tend to downgrade their present levels of custody are positive moves that influence one's parole chances accordingly (Petersilia, 2001). The prison system itself plays a crucial role in determining whether parole will be granted. Other relevant factors are the seriousness of the conviction offense, length of the original sentence, and the amount of time served in relation to that sentence length (Shichor and Sechrest, 2002).

In sum, jails and prisons are playing increasingly important roles in probation and parole decision making. Jails are devising more sophisticated classification procedures commensurate with those used in most prison systems.

These classification systems are helpful in separating offenders according to several criteria that optimize their safety and needs. As jails become more like prisons by establishing a broader array of inmate programs of an educational and vocational nature, inmates themselves will be able to do more to influence their chances of more favorable treatment (Levenson and Farrant, 2002). They can take affirmative steps to insure their involvement in community correctional programs where fewer restrictions exist.

SUMMARY

Jails were originally conceived as short-term facilities to house offenders charged with minor offenses, pretrial detainees, and those serving relatively short sentences. The American Jail Association considers a facility a jail if it houses inmates for periods of 72 hours or longer. Those facilities holding persons overnight are either lockups or holding tanks. In 2001, there were between 3,300 and 3,400 jails in the United States. In recent decades, jails have inadvertently assumed additional functions and responsibilities, including housing juvenile offenders for short periods; holding contract prisoners from federal and state prisons; housing witnesses; and providing a temporary haven for those suffering from psychological or mental problems. Jails also house probation and parole violators. Jails have little or no control over the types of inmates housed. About half of all jail inmates are unconvicted offenders, including drunks and vagrants. Shock probationers are also accommodated for short periods as a part of their split sentences. Most jails in the United States are old, many having been constructed prior to 1950.

Prisons are long-term facilities designed to hold more serious offenders. Early U.S. prisons were constructed in the late 1700s in Connecticut and Pennsylvania. Auburn (New York) State Penitentiary introduced several important innovations in U.S. corrections in the early 1800s, including the tier system, solitary confinement, and the congregate system. Striped uniforms also were pioneered by Auburn Penitentiary. Prisons are designed to provide societal protection, punish offenders, rehabilitate offenders, and assist in their eventual reintegration into society. Inmate classification is an important feature of prison systems. Prisons classify inmates into different security levels, such as minimum-, medium-, and maximum-security. Inmate housing costs rise as their custody level increases.

Jails are acquiring many of the characteristics of prisons, as officials acknowledge a growing jail population consisting of federal and state prisoners in need of rehabilitative services and other amenities. Jails and prisons share several problems, including chronic overcrowding, inmate violence, and various types of inmate programs. Prison and jail overcrowding is chronic and is a problem for most institutional administrators. Many other problems faced by prison and jail staffs are directly or indirectly influenced by overcrowding. Efforts to alleviate overcrowding have included innovations in building design and architectural rearrangements that permit more effective utilization of space and promote greater officer efficiency. Podular **direct supervision jails** and prisons are rapidly becoming popular as the most effective inmate management strategy. The private sector is gradually moving into jail and prison management and operations, effectively reducing inmate maintenance costs. Much privatization has thus far been restricted to juvenile facilities and aftercare, although more privately operated adult facilities are being established in different localities.

Prisons and jails also influence probationers and parolees by providing the courts and parole boards with feedback about inmate conduct while confined. Especially in prisons, an inmate's level of custody can be changed, either upward or downward, depending upon their bad or good conduct. Favorable behavioral reports encourage judges and parole boards to grant probationers and parolees greater benefits and freedoms.

Several issues affecting jails and prisons have been highlighted. Jails and prisons are chronically overcrowded. Overcrowding occurs because there is insufficient space to accommodate all persons who should be incarcerated and there are inadequate resources for new jail and prison construction. Jail and prison overcrowding contribute to and cause various problems for administrators and other inmates. One problem is increasing prison violence and inmate rioting for various reasons. Efforts have been made to reduce the amount of inmate violence. Changes in the architectural design and structuring of jails and prisons have lessened the incidence of violence in certain jurisdictions. Furthermore, the addition of helpful programs and services for inmate use have assisted many inmates to improve their personal skills and self-images. Thus, both jails and prisons today have made a concerted effort to furnish inmates with ample opportunities for self-improvement through vocational/technical and educational classes, group or individual counseling programs, and courses relating to anger management and improvement in social skills and interpersonal relations. Increasingly, the privatization of jails and prisons is occurring, although only a small fraction of the U.S. jail and prison inmate population today is under the control of private interests. Finally, gang presence in jails and prisons has increased over the past several decades. The formation and perpetuation of gangs in prison settings was examined, as well as the continuing effects of gang membership on parolees when they re-enter their communities.

QUESTIONS FOR REVIEW

1. What are some important events in the evolution of jails in the United States?

2. What are some general functions of jails? How do these contrast with the functions of prisons?

3. What were some of the innovations introduced by the Auburn State Penitentiary? Are any of these innovations still in evidence in modern-day prisons?

4. What are some major differences between jails and prisons?

5. What innovations did the Walnut Street Jail introduce? What was the influence of religion in correctional reforms during the 1700s and 1800s in the United States?

6. What are some major differences between minimum-security, medium-security, maximum-security, and admin max, super max, or maxi-maxi prison classifications? What are the implications of these different classification forms for inmates in correctional institutions?

7. What is the influence of prison and jail design and architecture on inmate management and control?

8. What are three major issues of relevance to both prisons and jails? How does jail or prison overcrowding contribute to inmate violence and discipline?

9. Do all prisoners have equal opportunity and access to vocational/educational programming in prisons? How does this access influence their potential for rehabilitation? How does prison privatization overcome services delivery problems associated with different types of vocational/educational programming and other amenities offered to inmates?

10. What is the role of prisons and jails in probation and parole decision making?

SUGGESTED READINGS

Bosworth, Mary (2002). *The U.S. Federal Prison System.* Thousand Oaks, CA: Sage.

Cunniff, Mark A. (2002). *Jail Crowding: Understanding Jail Population Dynamics.* Washington, DC: U.S. Department of Justice, National Institute of Corrections.

Gillespie, Wayne (2002). *Prisonization: Individual and Institutional Factors Affecting Inmate Conduct.* New York: LFB Scholarly Publishing.

Lerner, Jimmy A. (2002). *You Got Nothing Coming: Notes from a Prison Fish.* New York: Broadway Books.

Nichols, Mark et al. (2003). "Analysis of Mentally Retarded and Lower-Functioning Offender Correctional Programs." *Corrections Today* 65:119–121.

Sharp, Susan F. (2003). *The Incarcerated Woman: Rehabilitative Programming in Women's Prisons.* Upper Saddle River, NJ: Prentice Hall.

Urbina, Martin G. (2003). *Capital Punishment and Latino Offenders: Racial and Ethnic Differences in Death Sentences.* New York: LFB Scholarly Publishing.

INTERNET CONNECTIONS

American Correctional Health Services Association
http://www.corrections.com/achsa/indexl.html

American Jail Association
http://www.corrections.com/aja

American Civil Liberties Union
http://www.aclu.org

American Correctional Chaplains Association
http://www.correctionalchaplains.com/

American Service Group, Inc.
http://www.asgr.com/

Amnesty International
http://www.amnesty.org

Caged Kittens
http://www.cagedkittens.com

Citizens for Effective Justice
http://www.okplus.com/fedup/

Citizens for Legal Responsibility
http://www.clr.org/

Connections: A Correctional Education Program Serving Offenders with Special Learning Needs
http://www.theconnectionsprogram.com/MainPageText.htm

Cook County Boot Camp
http://www.cookcountysheriff.org/bootcamp/

Correctional Medical Services
http://www.cmsstl.com

Corrections resources
http://www.officer.com/correct

CounterPunch
http://www.counterpunch.org

CSS Special Supervision Services
http://www.csosa.gov/css_specialsupervision.htm

Death Row Speaks
http://www.deathrowspeaks.net/

Federal Bureau of Prisons
http://www.bop.gov/

Federal Bureau of Prisons Library
http://www.bop.library.net/

Federal Prison Consultants
http://www.federalprisonconsultants.com/

Female Special Needs Offenders
http://www.stars.csg.org/slc/special/2000/female_offenders.htm

Female Inmate Pen Pals
http://www.thepamperedprisoner.com

Gamblers Anonymous
http://www.gamblersanonymous.org/

George A. Keene, Inc.
http://www.keenejailequip.com/

International Association of Correctional
Training Personnel
http://www.iactp.org/

International Institute on Special Needs
Offenders
http://www.iisno.org.uk

Jail Management
http://www.mmmicro.com/jail_management.htm

Koch Crime Institute
http://www.kci.org/publications/bootcamp/docs/nij/Correctional_Boot+Camps/chpt17.htm

NaphCare, Inc.
http://www.naphcare.com/

Narcotics Anonymous
http://www.na.org

Narcotics Complete Recovery Center
http://www.drugrehab.net

National Institute of Corrections
http://www.nicic.org/

National Institute of Corrections Jail
Administration Training Program
http://www.nicic.org/services/training/programs/jails/jail-admin.htm

Objective Jail Classification
http://www.corrections.com/aja/training

Online Friends to Death Row Inmates
http://www.freeworldfriends.com

PRC Jail Record Management System
http://www.northrupgrummanit.com

PS.NET
http://www.ps.net/cms

Recovery Resources Online
http://www.soberrecovery.com

The Program for Female Offenders, Inc.
http://www.fcnetworks.org/Dir98/dir98front.html

Unauthorized Federal Prison Manual
http://www.bureauofprisons.com/

Very Special Women
http://www.vswomen.com

Women Behind Bars
http://www.womenbehindbars.com/

Women in Criminal Justice
http://www.wicj.com

Women's Prison Association
http://www.wpaonline.org/WEBSITE/home.htm

CHAPTER 7 | *Parole and Parolees*

Chapter Outline

Chapter Objectives

As the result of reading this chapter, the following objectives will be realized:

1. Describing the history and evolution of parole in the United States.
2. Identifying key figures who created or devised new early release systems.
3. Examining the relation between indeterminate sentencing and parole, as well as the subsequent shift among states to determinate and guidelines-based sentencing.
4. Understanding the philosophy of parole as well as highlighting some of the functions of parole.
5. Describing some of the major functions of parole programs.
6. Profiling parolees, including successful and unsuccessful ones.
7. Describing the growing gang presence throughout different U.S. cities and the influence of gangs on parolee successfulness and parole programs in general.
8. Examining whether parole is achieving its intended objectives or goals.

• *Reynolds was serving time in a Pennsylvania prison for murder. During Reynolds' imprisonment, Pennsylvania's parole eligibility policy was changed. The review process was revised so that it no longer began with the best interest of the convict, but rather with the safety of the public. At a subsequent parole hearing for Reynolds, he was denied parole. Reynolds appealed, alleging that the parole board had applied the new policy retroactively, and that* ex post facto *application of this policy violated his rights and jeopardized his opportunity to gain early release. A Pennsylvania appeals court disagreed with Reynolds. First, the court noted that Reynolds' punishment was not increased as the result of the new policy change. Further, the parole board declared that it did not apply the new policy in considering Reynolds' application for early release. Absent any proof of the application of the changed policy in Reynolds' case, the court could not say that* ex post facto *prohibitions were violated [*Reynolds v. Pa. Bd. of Probation & Parole, *2002].*

• *Kastman was a sex offender serving time in an Illinois prison. At his parole hearing, a psychologist testified that Kastman was still sexually dangerous and should not be released. Thus, the parole board denied his early release. Kastman appealed, challenging the credentials of the psychologist as well as the sociologist who prepared a socio-psychiatric report about Kastman for the parole board's review. Kastman contended that persons conducting psychiatric evaluations must be licensed under Illinois law for the proceedings in question. An appellate court rejected Kastman's appeal, saying that persons preparing socio-psychiatric reports do not have to be licensed under Illinois law, and that sociological professionals may properly participate in the preparation of such reports. The court noted, however, that any individual participating in such report preparation should be sufficiently qualified. In this case, the sociological professionals who assisted in the report preparation also engaged in social work, and thus they were qualified [*People v. Kastman, *2002].*

• *Layne was an Ohio inmate originally convicted of two counts of having a weapon while under a disability. Under a plea bargain agreement, several other crimes, including kidnapping and abduction were dropped. During Layne's incarceration, the Ohio Adult Parole Authority adopted new guidelines. These guidelines were intended to pro-*

mote a more consistent exercise of discretion and enable fair and more equitable decision making by the parole authority. Two factors to be considered were the seriousness of the offender's criminal offense as well as their risk of recidivism if released. Based on these factors, a criminal history/risk score can be calculated, together with an offense category score. These factors yield a range of months offenders must serve before they become eligible to be released. When the parole board considered Layne's parole eligibility, however, it used the originally charged offenses of kidnapping, abduction, and the two counts of having a weapon while under a disability for determining offense seriousness and criminal history/risk. Had these additional crimes, which were subsequently dropped, not been considered for calculating Layne's early release eligibility, he would have been released much earlier. In the present case, Layne was denied parole and he appealed, arguing that the parole board should not have considered these other crimes against him which had been dropped by the prosecutor. An appellate court agreed with Layne, holding that the Ohio Adult Parole Authority is bound to observe the state's plea agreement and must ignore the other offenses originally charged against Layne. Thus, Layne became immediately eligible for meaningful parole consideration. However, the court also held that the board continued to retain its discretion to consider any circumstances relating to the offense or offenses of conviction, including crimes that did not result in conviction, as well as any other factors they deemed relevant [Layne v. Ohio Adult Parole Authority, 2002].

• Pollock was a Maryland inmate convicted of murder. After serving 15 years in prison, Pollock was paroled. One parole condition was that Pollock must submit to a urinalysis once a year to determine whether he was in compliance with the "no drugs" and "obey all laws" requirements of his supervision. On one occasion, Pollock's urine tested positive for marijuana and his parole was revoked. Pollock appealed, citing improper labeling of his urine sample and other procedural irregularities which would invalidate the specimen tests and resulting punishment of parole revocation. In Pollock's case, a lab technician had placed an erroneous identification number next to Pollock's name on Pollock's urine specimen. The appellate court rejected Pollock's appeal, noting that although the government must follow its rules and regulations closely, one minor procedural irregularity does not nullify the final result of testing positive for marijuana use. Thus, the court held that the board had sufficient grounds to revoke Pollock's parole [Pollock v. Patuxent Institution Board of Review, 2002].

INTRODUCTION

This chapter looks at parole or early release from prison. A brief history of parole in the United States is provided. Included is a discussion of the philosophy of parole as well as several of its important functions. Parole has been criticized in recent years for various reasons. In some instances, dangerous persons have been paroled and they have committed serious crimes while under parole supervision. Some states have abolished parole outright. Thus, some consideration will be given to the positive and negative aspects of parole decision making. Alternatives to parole will also be examined. One consideration when contemplating parole for any particular offender is that offender's prior record. Thus, an examination of the types of persons who are paroled will be provided. Because many parolees have joined gangs while imprisoned, some attention will be given to the growing gang presence in communities and how parolees are affected by such gangs.

PAROLE DEFINED

Parole is the conditional release of a prisoner from incarceration (either from prison or jail) under supervision after a portion of the sentence has been served (McKean and Raphael, 2002). The major distinguishing feature between probation and parole is that parolees have served some time incarcerated in either jail or prison, while probationers have avoided incarceration. Some common characteristics shared by both parolees and probationers are that: (1) they have committed crimes, (2) they have been convicted of crimes, (3) they are under the supervision or control of probation or parole officers and (4) they are subject to one or more similar conditions accompanying their probation or parole programs. Some general differences are that generally, parolees have committed more serious offenses compared with probationers. Also, parolees have been incarcerated for a portion of their sentences while probationers are not generally incarcerated following their convictions for crimes. Furthermore, parolees may have more stringent conditions (e.g., curfew, participation in drug or alcohol rehabilitation, counseling, halfway house participation, more face-to-face contacts with their POs) accompanying their parole programs compared with probationers (Bickle et al., 2002).

THE HISTORICAL CONTEXT OF PAROLE

Parole existed in eighteenth century Spain, France, England and Wales (Bottomley, 1984). British convicts under sentence of death or convicted of other serious offenses created for England a problem currently confronting the United States: prison overcrowding. In the 18th century, Britain had no penitentiaries. But one option available was to export excess prisoners to the American colonies. After the Revolutionary War, this option no longer existed.

Seeking new locations for isolating its criminals from the rest of society, England selected Australia, one of several remote English colonies that had accommodated small numbers of offenders during the American colonial period when prisoner exportation was popular. The first large-scale **transportation** of convicts from England came to Australia in 1788. While many of these transportees were convicted of minor theft, it was intended by the English government that they should become builders and farmers. However, these were trades at which they were highly unsuccessful. It became apparent that officials needed to establish prisons to house some of their prisoner-transportees. One such outpost 1,000 miles off the coast of Australia was **Norfolk Island** where a penal colony was established. Another was **Van Dieman's Land** (Clay, 2001).

The private secretary to the lieutenant governor of Van Diemen's land in 1836 was a former Royal Navy officer and social reformer, Alexander Maconochie (1787–1860). In 1840, Maconochie was appointed superintendent of the penal colony at Norfolk Island. When he arrived to assume his new duties, he was appalled by what he found. Prisoners were lashed repeatedly and tortured frequently by other means. Maconochie had a penchant for humanitarianism, and his lenient administrative style toward prisoners was unpopular with his superiors as well as other penal officials. For instance, Maconochie believed that confinement ought to be rehabilitative, not punitive. Also, he felt that prisoners ought to be granted early release from custody if they behaved well and did good work while confined. Thus, Maconochie established the mark system whereby he gave prisoners **marks of commendation** and authorized the early release of certain inmates who demonstrated a willingness and ability to behave well in society on the outside. This action was the early manifestation of indeterminate sentencing that was subsequently established in the United States. Maconochie's termination as superintendent at Norfolk Island occurred largely because he filed a report that condemned the English penal system and the disciplinary measures used by the island penal colony. He was sent back to England in 1844.

Maconochie's prison reform work did not end with this dismissal. During the next five years, Maconochie was transferred from one desk job to another, although he continued to press for penal reforms. Eventually he was reassigned, probably as a probationary move by his superiors, to the governorship of the new Birmingham Borough Prison. His position there lasted less than two years. His superiors dismissed him for being too lenient with prisoners. In 1853, he successfully lobbied for the passage of the English Penal Servitude Act that established several rehabilitation programs for inmates and abolished transporting prisoners to Australia. Because of these significant improvements in British penal policy and the institutionalization of early-release provisions throughout England's prison system, Maconochie is credited as being the father of parole.

Sir Walter Crofton, a prison reformer and director of Ireland's prison system during the 1850s, was impressed by Maconochie's work and copied his three-stage intermediate system whereby Irish prisoners could earn their early conditional release. Crofton, also known as another father of parole in various European countries, modified Maconochie's plan whereby prisoners would be subject to:

1. strict imprisonment for a time;
2. transferred to an intermediate prison for a short period where they could participate in educational programs and perform useful and responsible tasks to earn **good marks;** and
3. given tickets-of-leave where they would be released from prison on license under the limited supervision of local police.

Under this third ticket-of-leave stage, released prisoners were required to submit monthly reports of their progress to police who assisted them in finding work. A study of 557 prisoners during that period showed only 17 had their tickets-of-leave revoked for various infractions. Thus, Walter Crofton pioneered what later came to be known as several major functions of parole officers: employment assistance to released prisoners, regular visits by officers to parolees, and the general supervision of their activities (Clay, 2001).

The United States connection with the European use of parole allegedly occurred in 1863 when Gaylord Hubbell, the warden at Sing Sing Prison, New York, visited Ireland and conferred with Crofton about his penal innovations and parole system. Subsequently, the National Prison Association convened in Cincinnati, Ohio, in 1870 and considered the Irish parole system as a primary portion of its agenda. Attending that meeting were Crofton, Hubbell, and other reformers and penologists. The meeting resulted in the establishment of a Declaration of Principles which promoted an indeterminate sentence and a classification system based largely on Crofton's work (Clay, 2001). Table 7.1 shows Crofton's mark system which functioned as a pattern for various states to follow after formally adopting versions of Crofton's scheme.

TABLE 7.1

Mark System Developed by Sir Walter Crofton

Class and Number of Marks to be Gained for Admission to the Intermediate Prisons for Different Sentences[a]	Sentences of Penal Servitude (Years)	Shortest Periods of Imprisonment				Periods of Remission on License
		In Ordinary Prisons		Shortest Period of Detention in Intermediate Prisons		
		Years	Months	Years	Months	
Class 1st $^{100}/_{90}$	3	2	2	0	4	
			2— —6			
Class 6 A, or 6 months in A class	4	2	10	0	5	
			3— —3			
Class 14 A, or 14 months in A class	5	3	6	0	6	The periods remitted on License will be proportionate to the length of sentences and will depend upon the fitness of each Convict for release after a careful consideration has been given to his case by the government.
			4— —0			
Class 17 A, or 17 months in A class	6	3	9	0	9	
			4— —6			
Class 20 A, or 20 months in A class	7	4	0	1	3	
			5— —3			
Class 28 A, or 28 months in A class	8	4	8	1	4	
			6— —0			
Class 44 A, or 44 months in A class	10	6	0	1	6	
			7— —6			
Class 59 A, or 59 months in A class	12	7	3	1	9	
			9— —0			
Class 68 A, or 68 months in A class	15	8	0	2	0	
			10— —0			

[a]The earliest possible periods of removal to Intermediate Prisons apply only to those of the most unexceptionable character, and no remission of the full sentence will take place unless the prisoner has qualified himself by carefully measured good conduct for passing the periods in the Intermediate Prisons prescribed by the Rules; and any delay in this qualification will have the effect of postponing his admission into the Intermediate Prisons, and thereby deferring to the same extent the remission of a portion of his sentence.
Source: Mary Carpenter, *Reformatory Prison Discipline as Developed by the Rt. Hon. Sir Walter Crofton in the Irish Convict Prison* (Montclair, NJ: Patterson-Smith, 1967, reprint of 1872 ed.).

Zebulon Brockway became the new superintendent of the New York State Reformatory at Elmira in 1876 and was instrumental in the passage of the first indeterminate sentencing law in the U.S. He is also credited with introducing the first **good-time system** where an inmate's sentence to be served is reduced by the number of good marks earned (Gransky and Patterson, 1999). Good time was given, which was credit applied to one's maximum sentence. If an inmate accumulated sufficient good-time credit, then he/she could be released short of serving the full sentence originally imposed by the judge (Payne and Gainey, 2000). Once this system was in operation and shown to be moderately effective, several other states patterned their own early-release standards after it in later years (Wang et al., 2000). Elmira Reformatory was important, in part, because it used the good-time release system for prisoners in 1876. Actually, the practice of using early release for inmates occurred in the United States much earlier. Parole was officially established in Boston by Samuel G. Howe in 1847. From 1790 to 1817, convicts were obligated to serve their entire sentences in prison (Clay, 2001).

In 1817, New York adopted a form of commutation or lessening of sentence which became known as good time. Through the accumulation of sufficient good time, an inmate could be granted early release through his good behavior. This good time early release was essentially a **pardon,** an executive device designed to absolve offenders of their crimes committed and release them, thus alleviating the prison overcrowding situation. The unofficial practice of parole, therefore, preceded the unofficial practice of probation by several decades. Officially, however, true parole resulted from the ticket-of-leave practice and was first adopted by Massachusetts in 1884, also the state first implementing officially the practice of probation in 1878 (Travis et al., 2002).

PAROLE AND ALTERNATIVE SENTENCING SYSTEMS

A general relation exists between indeterminate sentencing and parole. However, when jurisdictions adopt indeterminate sentencing schemes, this does not mean that either parole or parole boards are automatically established. Indeterminate sentencing indicates a minimum and a maximum term of years or months inmates may serve. Ordinarily, inmates must serve the minimum amount of time specified, but they may be released in different ways short of serving their full terms. Ordinarily, parole boards determine early-release dates for inmates under this type of sentencing system. But there are other early-release options besides parole board actions. For example, by 1911, nine states were using indeterminate sentencing. However, eleven years earlier in 1900, twenty states had established parole plans to effect the early release of prison inmates. Some of these jurisdictions had mandatory sentencing provisions, while others had determinate sentencing schemes. Early release short of serving one's full term could be administratively granted, from prison officials or the governor, or through the accumulation of good-time credits applied against the maximum time to be served. In short, it is not the case that indeterminate sentencing and parole boards must co-exist in any jurisdiction simultaneously (Munson and Reed, 2000).

Usually, a parole system in any state prison consisted of the warden and other local authorities including the prison physician, the superintendent of prisons, and certain community officials. The federal prison system had no formal parole board until 1910, and it was similarly comprised of officials making up state parole boards. Prior to the establishment of these boards and within the context of indeterminate sentencing, the discretion to release a prisoner short of serving his full term rested with the prison warden, superintendent, or state governor.

By 1944, all states had parole systems. The United States Congress formally established a United States Board of Parole in 1930. And by the 1960s, all states had some form of indeterminate sentencing. Apart from the obvious benefits of alleviating prison overcrowding, parole and indeterminate sentencing was perceived for nearly a century as a panacea for reforming criminals. The rehabilitative ideal dominated the structure and process of all phases of corrections as well as most corrections programs (Wilson and Petersilia, 2002).

Not all states used parole for rehabilitative purposes, however. In 1893, California adopted parole as (1) a way of minimizing the use of clemency by governors and (2) to correct and/or modify excessive prison sentences in relation to certain crimes committed. In fact, officials who favored parole in California were skeptical about its rehabilitative value. Parole was seen primarily as a period during which the end of a determinate sentence would occur that was originally imposed by the court (Petersilia, 2001). But a majority of the states stressed the rehabilitative value of indeterminate sentencing and parole generally. While the principle of deterrence dominated corrections philosophy for most of the period 1820–1900, from 1900–1960, the principle of rehabilitation was of primary importance. Indeterminate sentencing was largely in the hands of corrections "observers" such as social workers, wardens, and probation and parole officers (Burke, 2001).

One early criticism of parole was contained in a series of reports issued in 1931 by the **Wickersham Commission,** officially called the National Commission on Law Observance and Enforcement. The Wickersham Commission derived its name from its chairman, George W. Wickersham, a former United States Attorney General. Prepared shortly after the Prohibition Era and the Depression, the Wickersham reports were very critical of most criminal justice agencies and how they dealt with crime and criminals. Parole was not the sole target of criticism by the Wickersham Commission. However, it did receive many criticisms. Among the criticisms was that parole released many dangerous criminals into society, and these offenders were unsupervised and not rehabilitated. Also, the Wickersham Commission did not believe that a suitable system existed for determining which prisoners should be eligible for parole. While these reports caused considerable debate among corrections professionals for several years, nothing was done to alter the existing operations of state or federal parole systems. The rehabilitation or medical model became increasingly popular, together with social work and psychiatry, as members of these helping professions attempted to treat prisoner adjustment problems through therapy, medicine, and counseling.

Indeterminate Sentencing and Parole

Indeterminate sentencing is the only sentencing scheme which involves the intervention of parole boards. Because parole boards are vested with virtually absolute discretion concerning who does and doesn't get paroled, they are considered powerful entities. But because they have been responsible for the release of more than a few inmates who have subsequently committed violent crimes, they have attracted considerable adverse criticism. The major positive and negative aspects of indeterminate sentencing have been described. Some of the positive features of indeterminate sentencing include:

1. Allows for full implementation of rehabilitative ideal.
2. Offers best means of motivating involuntarily committed inmates to work for rehabilitation.
3. Offers maximum protection to society from hardcore recidivists and mentally defective offenders.
4. Helps maintain an orderly environment within the institution.

5. Prevents unnecessary incarceration of an offender and thus helps to prevent the correctional system from becoming a factory from which offenders emerge as hardened criminals.

6. Offers a feasible alternative to capital punishment.

7. Removes judgment as to length of incarceration from the trial court and puts it in the hands of a qualified panel of behavioral observers who make their final decision based on considerably more evidence than is available at the post-conviction stage of the trial.

8. Decision as to length of incarceration reflects the needs of the offender and not the gravity of the crime, in the best interests of both society and offender.

9. Prevents correctional authorities from being forced to release from custody an offender who is clearly not ready to rejoin society.

10. Prevents problem offender from retreating into a "sick" role during rehabilitation.

11. Acts as a deterrent to crime.

Some of the negative features of indeterminate sentences are:

1. Treatment is a myth, and vocational training is a fraud; inmates are neither treated, trained, nor rehabilitated.

2. Even if treatment were honestly attempted by staffs, psychotherapy with involuntarily committed patients are generally considered difficult; indeterminate sentencing supplies only negative motivation which will be insufficient for long-range results.

3. Even if effective therapy were plausible for some offenders, it is neither justified nor proper for all offenders, and there should be a right not to receive unwanted therapy.

4. Treatment is tokenism and rehabilitation is almost nonexistent; therefore, the indeterminate sentence is a device to hide society's dehumanizing treatment of criminals, particularly those who are poor or members of minority groups.

5. While taking criminals off the street, indeterminate sentencing makes it easy for society to ignore the underlying causes of crime.

6. The indeterminate sentence is most often used as an instrument of inmate control.

7. Psychiatrists become more jailers than healers; they know they will have to testify later in court about the patient and recommend or not recommend a prisoner's release.

8. Designations of some offenders as mentally ill is extremely arbitrary; therefore, single treatment approaches are impossible to devise.

9. There is great danger that indeterminate sentencing will be used to punish persons for unpopular political beliefs and views; religious and political nonconformists are ones most likely to rebel against a therapeutic system.

10. Indeterminate sentencing encourages the smart or cunning offender and is more favorable to him than to the less intelligent offender.

11. Despite the fact that courts are supposed to retain some measure of control, there is no adequate protection from life imprisonment under the guise of indeterminate sentencing (Fogel and Hudson, 1981:72–75).

Because of rising crime rates, unacceptable levels of recidivism among parolees, and general dissension among the ranks of corrections professionals about the most effective ways of dealing with offenders, the 1970s reflected a gradual decline in the significance and influence of the rehabilitation model. However, selected jurisdictions have reported success with parole programs where effective community supervision and offender management have been provided, or where POs have performed their supervisory roles properly (Whitehead and Blankenship, 2000). Whether parole rehabilitates is arguable. In any case, the rehabilitation model has been largely replaced by the justice model. The mission or perspective of the justice model is fairness, where prison is regarded as the instrument whereby sentences are implemented and is not to be held accountable for rehabilitating offenders. The justice model has assisted greatly in prompting most states as well as the federal government to undertake extensive revisions of their sentencing guidelines. The general thrust of these revisions is toward a get-tough-on-crime crusade that is replacing reform with retribution (Wilson and Petersilia, 2002).

Another goal of the justice model is to minimize if not eliminate entirely any sentencing disparities often associated with indeterminate sentencing schemes and the arbitrariness of parole board decisions. It is questionable, however, whether any sentencing scheme will achieve such desirable results. Some authorities suggest that there is every reason to believe that judges will continue to impose sentences according to previous discriminatory patterns where extra-legal factors are influential. These extra-legal factors include race, ethnicity, gender, age, and socioeconomic status.

The Shift to Determinate Sentencing

Nearly half of all states had shifted from indeterminate to determinate sentencing by 1995 (Petersilia, 2001). These sentencing shifts have resulted in the abolition of paroling authority in a few states for making early prisoner release decisions. An additional consequence has been to limit the discretionary sentencing power of judges. The remaining states and the District of Columbia have also instituted numerous sentencing reforms calculated to deal more harshly with offenders, to reduce or eliminate sentencing disparities attributable to race, ethnicity, or socioeconomic status, to increase prisoner release predictability as well as the certainty of incarceration, and/or to deter or control crime. In many of these states, the authority of parole boards to grant early release as well as the calculation of good-time credits have been restricted to varying degrees.

On November 1, 1987, the United States Sentencing Commission revamped entirely existing sentencing guidelines for federal district judges (U.S. Sentencing Commission, 2003). The long-range implications of these changes are unknown. However, some preliminary estimates have been projected. For instance, the average time served prior to November 1, 1987 for kidnapping was from 7.2 to 9 years. Under the new guidelines, they provide an incarcerative term for offenders of from 4.2 to 5.2 years. However, for first-degree murder convictions, the new guidelines prescribe 30 years to life for all offenders compared with 10 to 12.5 years time served, on the average, under old sentencing practices by federal judges. Therefore, more convicted felons will go to prison, but many of these offenses will carry shorter incarceration terms (U.S. Sentencing Commission, 2003).

While these sentencing guidelines are only applicable to United States district courts and federal judges and magistrates, some states have similar guidelines-based or presumptive sentencing schemes. Other states such as California, Minnesota, Pennsylvania, and Washington already have existing penalties for certain offenses which are similar in severity to those prescribed for the same offenses by the United States sentencing guidelines. By 2002, 26 states had established sentencing guidelines for their prison inmates (Camp and Camp, 2003).

Critics contend that while determinate sentencing may provide prisoners with release certainty and possibly result in more fairness in the sentencing process, there are several discretionary decisions at various stages in the adjudication and post-adjudication period uncontrolled by this sentencing form. Six decision-making stages and/or factors have been identified as critical to sentencing equity and predictability: (1) the decision to incarcerate; (2) the characteristics of the penalty scaling system, including the numbers of penalty ranges and offense categories; (3) presence or absence of aggravating or mitigating circumstances; (4) the parole review process; (5) the use of good time in calculating early release; and (6) revocation from supervised release (Cochran et al., 1997).

Additionally, prosecutorial discretion concerning which cases should be prosecuted, reports of arresting officers and circumstances surrounding arrests, evidentiary factors, and judicial idiosyncrasies figure prominently in many sentencing decisions at state and federal levels. Thus, regardless of the nature and scope of existing sentencing provisions, the prospects for the effective control over all of the relevant discretionary decisions which influence sentencing are not overwhelmingly favorable. Although parole boards in 36 states have continued to exercise discretion over the early release of prisoners, parole continues to draw criticism from both the public and corrections professionals (Wilson and Petersilia, 2002).

Good-Time Credits and Early Release.   Good-time credits may be called gain time, earned time, statutory time, meritorious time, commutation time, provisional credits, good conduct credits, or disciplinary credits (Wang et al., 2000). Whatever the term, good time is a reward for good behavior and a prevalent management tool in most U.S. prisons. For instance, Arkansas uses the good-time standard of 30 days of good time for every 30 days served. Thus, when offenders are sentenced to ten years in Arkansas, offenders know that for every month they serve, 30 days will be deducted from their ten-year maximum term. In Iowa, the standard of 15 days of good time for every 30 days served is used. Therefore, serving six years in an Iowa prison means that three years is deducted from one's original ten-year sentence. Accumulating good time and being released is not the same thing as being paroled. In the case of an Arkansas inmate who has served one half of his or her original sentence, he or she is free from prison without conditions. This is not absolute in all jurisdictions, however. In some states, inmates released as the result of good-time credit accumulation must serve some or all of their remaining time on supervised **mandatory release** (Munson and Reed, 2000). Table 7.2 shows various states with different good-time provisions.

A majority of states permit the accumulation of good-time credit at the rate of 15 days or more per month served. The Federal Bureau of Prisons permits 54 days per year as good-time credit to be earned by federal prisoners. Some states permit additional good-time credits to be accumulated for participation in

TABLE 7.2

Good-Time Credits for Different State Jurisdictions

More than 30 days per month:
Alabama, Oklahoma, South Carolina, Texas

30 days per month:
Arkansas, Florida, Illinois, Indiana, Kansas, Louisiana, Nevada, New Mexico, Virginia, West Virginia

20 days per month:
Maryland, Massachusetts

15 days per month:
Arizona, California, Connecticut, Kentucky, Maine, Nebraska, New Jersey, Rhode Island, South Dakota, Vermont, Washington, Wyoming

Less than 15 days per month:
Alaska, Colorado, Delaware, District of Columbia, Federal Bureau of Prisons, Iowa, Michigan, Mississippi, Missouri, New Hampshire, New York, North Carolina, North Dakota, Oregon, Tennessee

No good time given:
Georgia, Hawaii, Idaho, Minnesota, Ohio, Pennsylvania, Utah, Wisconsin

Adapted from James Ching, "Credits as Personal Property: Beware of the New *Ex Post Facto* Clause." *Corrections Compendium*, 22:1–16, 1997.

vocational or educational programs. A few states, such as New Hampshire, have an interesting variation on this theme. Instead of rewarding prisoners with good-time credits, New Hampshire authorities add 150 days to the minimum sentences imposed. These 150 days can be reduced at the rate of 12 1/2 days per month of good behavior or exemplary conduct, according to the New Hampshire prison system (Griset, 1996).

There are various motives behind different state provisions for good time. Prison overcrowding is perhaps the most frequently cited reason. However, good-time credit allowances can also encourage inmates to participate in useful vocational and educational programs. More than a few inmates abuse the good-time system by enrolling in these programs in a token fashion. But many inmates derive good benefits from them as well. Also, good-time credits influence one's security placement while institutionalized. Those inmates who behave well may be moved from maximum- to medium-, or from medium- to minimum-security custody levels over time. And we know that one's immediate classification level preceding a parole board hearing is taken into account as a factor influencing one's parole chances. Another reason for good-time allowances or credits is to maintain and improve inmate management by prison administrative staff. Well-behaved inmates make it easier for officials to administer prison affairs. Those who do not obey prison rules are subject to good-time credit deductions and are "written-up" by correctional officers for their misconduct. If inmates accumulate enough of these paper infractions, they may lose good-time credits or, as in New Hampshire, they may fail to reduce the extra time imposed above their minimum sentences.

THE PHILOSOPHY OF PAROLE

Like probation, parole has been established for the purpose of rehabilitating offenders and reintegrating them into society. Parole is a continuation of a parolee's punishment, under varying degrees of supervision by parole officers, ending when the originally imposed sentence has been served. Officials have noted that parole is earned rather than automatically granted after serving a fixed amount of one's sentence. The punitive nature of parole is inherent in the conditions and restrictions accompanying it which other community residents are not obligated to follow (Wilson and Petersilia, 2002).

Parole's 18th century origins suggest no philosophical foundation. In the 1700s, **penological pragmatism** permitted correctional officials to use parole to alleviate prison overcrowding. Roughly between 1850 and 1970, the influence of social reformers, religious leaders, and humanitarians upon parole as a rehabilitative medium was quite apparent (Bottomley, 1984). But as has been seen, the pendulum has shifted away from rehabilitation (not entirely) and toward societal retribution. The early California experience with parole was anything but rehabilitative. Rather, it was a bureaucratic tool to assist gubernatorial decision-making in clemency cases involving excessively long sentences (Messinger et al., 1985).

THE FUNCTIONS OF PAROLE

The functions of parole are probably best understood when couched in terms of **manifest** and **latent functions.** *Manifest functions* are intended or recognized, apparent to all. Latent functions are also important, but they are less visible. Two important manifest functions of parole are (1) to reintegrate parolees into society, and (2) to control and/or deter crime. Three latent functions of parole are (1) to ease prison and jail overcrowding, (2) to remedy sentencing disparities, and (3) to protect the public.

Offender Reintegration

Incarcerated offenders, especially those who have been incarcerated for long periods, often find it difficult to readjust to life in the community. Inmate idleness and a unique prison subculture, regimentation and strict conformity to numerous rules, and continuous exposure to a population of criminals who have committed every offense imaginable simply fail to prepare prisoners adequately for noncustodial living. Parole provides a means whereby an offender may make a smooth transition from prison life to living in a community with some degree of freedom under supervision. Parole functions as a reintegrative mechanism for both juveniles and adults (Petersilia, 2001).

Crime Deterrence and Control

It is believed by some correctional authorities that rewarding an inmate for good behavior while in prison through an early conditional release under supervision will promote respect for the law. Some persons believe that keeping an offender imprisoned for prolonged periods will increase the offender's bitterness toward society and result in the commission of new and more serious offenses. But there is some evidence to the contrary. For instance, a study of parole board decision making in Nebraska showed that parole-eligible inmates who were denied parole were more likely to comply with institutional rules and behave well following their parole denials. Institutional misconduct also decreased for offenders who were not granted parole hearings. This information suggests that once these inmates have been rejected for early release or denied a parole hearing, they may seek to conform with institutional rules to a greater degree than before they were granted hearings or were denied parole following hearings (Whitehead and Blankenship, 2000). Therefore, the prospect of parole provides a strong incentive for inmates to comply with institutional rules. While this doesn't mean that they will obey societal rules if released into their communities later, it is a good indication that they have the capacity to follow rules when they choose to do so, and if it is in their best interests. Parole boards are persuaded to grant early release to those offenders with good conduct records while incarcerated. They are deemed better risks than those who engage in institutional misconduct (Wilson and Petersilia, 2002).

 **BOX 7.1**

 **PERSONALITY HIGHLIGHT**

Robyn Schmalenberger
Drug Court Coordinator for the East Central Judicial District Drug Court, Fargo, North Dakota

Statistics:

A.A. (criminal justice), Bismarck State College; B.S. (social work and social and behavioral science), University of Mary; Licensed Correctional Officer; Licensed Peace Officer

Background:

I have worked for the North Dakota Department of Corrections and Rehabilitation, Division of Field Services for ten years. I presently work as the Drug Court Coordinator for the East Central Judicial District Drug Court in Fargo, North Dakota. Prior to my current position I worked as a parole officer in Fargo and Bismarck, North Dakota.

When I started college I was not sure of the field I wanted to go into. I gravitated toward criminal justice, as the classes appeared interesting. While attending school at the University of Mary and working on my degree in social work, I had the opportunity to complete two internships. My junior year I interned with the North Dakota Department of Corrections and Rehabilitation, Division of Field Services in Bismarck. The individual who supervised the internship made it interesting and exciting, taking me along on searches and arrests. For my senior internship I was at the North Dakota State Penitentiary in Bismarck working in the sex offender treatment program. During this placement, I learned tolerance for a population that many people do not want to deal with. After learning about the different areas of criminal justice, I knew that I wanted to work in parole/probation. This field appeared to combine law enforcement with social service-type work.

Work Experiences:

I began working with the Field Services Division in Fargo in 1993. Soon after I was hired,

BOX 7.1 (*Continued*)

I completed training at the North Dakota Law Enforcement Training Academy to become a licensed peace officer. During my first three years with the department, I supervised a special sex offender caseload. This may have been due to my experience at the penitentiary, but more than likely it was because it was not a popular caseload. I am grateful for the opportunity to supervise sex offenders. It enabled me to get involved with other agencies in the community and learn about a population that is difficult to manage. My biggest concern while supervising sex offenders was that they would commit another sex offense while on supervision. When a sex offender commits a crime there is almost always another person involved, often a child, who is being physically and emotionally harmed.

It is difficult to deal with deviant behavior for a long period of time. After working with this population for three years, I felt like I needed a change. I moved to Bismarck and supervised a regular caseload for the next six years. A majority of offenders on a regular caseload have alcohol and drug issues. Their addictions make it difficult for them to comply with probation, and they are frequently focused on getting more drugs. It is important to keep safety in mind when working with drug offenders, as they are unpredictable due to their drug use.

I have recently moved to Fargo and work as the East Central Judicial District Drug Court Coordinator. This position is a little different from regular probation/parole work as there is a team approach in dealing with drug court participants. In this position I have frequent contact with judges, attorneys, treatment staff, and law enforcement. There is a staffing each week that involves the judge, the probation officer, and the treatment provider. Decisions regarding the participants are made after the team discusses the case. Drug court meets once a week and the participants report their progress to the judge.

I enjoy my career in corrections an feel fortunate that I have been able to try different avenues while working as a parole/probation officer. I have been able to meet many interesting people at work. This includes both colleagues and clients. I have also been able to take part in numerous hours of continued education and training. The job is frustrating and stressful at times, as you are often working with people in crisis situations.

Advice to Students:

To work in parole/probation, you need to enjoy working with people, and it helps to be tolerant of different cultures, beliefs, and lifestyles. You need to be focused on helping people, but also you must be aware of safety and security issues. I have gotten into physical altercations with offenders and had to rely on my law enforcement training. You need to be able to use sound judgment skills to make decisions quickly. As there are constant deadlines to be aware of, such as completing pre-sentence investigations and parole investigations, good time management skills are helpful. There is also a large amount of documentation and paperwork that needs to be completed. Writing skills are a must in this career field. I recommend that as a student you take courses or become involved in activities that help you become comfortable with public speaking. I also recommend you take advantage of internships, as they give you an opportunity to get hands-on experience to see if you are suited for the job.

Early release from prison, under appropriate supervision, implies an agreement of trust between the state and offender (Josi and Sechrest, 1999). In many instances, this trust instills a degree of self-confidence in the offender which yields the desired law-abiding results. Then again, there are those who claim parole is a failure, although they cannot say for certain whether the problem rests with parole itself or with the abuse of discretion on the part of parole-granting bodies (Petersilia, 1999a). Deterrence and crime control actually extend beyond parole board decision making. PO supervisory practices within the community play an important part in controlling offender behaviors. Furthermore, POs can be of assistance in linking their clients with necessary community services, such as psychological counseling and programming, vocational/technical and educational programs, and other services (Burns et al., 1999).

Decreasing Prison and Jail Overcrowding

Another function of parole is to alleviate jail and prison overcrowding. Parole is a back-end solution, inasmuch as parole boards exercise considerable discretion about which offenders will be released short of serving their full terms, although more than a few parole board members in various jurisdictions do not perceive their decision making to be affected by prison overcrowding conditions. Every state has a paroling authority, although several states have eliminated parole as an early-release option. The fact that some states and the federal government have abolished parole and substituted other means whereby inmates may be freed short of serving their full sentences doesn't mean that those previously sentenced under an indeterminate sentencing scheme are no longer within the jurisdiction of parole boards (U.S. Sentencing Commission, 2003). For instance, Maine was the first state to abolish parole in 1976. However, its parole board continues to meet from time to time to hear early release petitions from inmates who were convicted prior to 1976. The old rules for early release still apply to these offenders. But their numbers are diminishing. In 1999, for instance, Maine had only 31 parolees, with two released from parole supervision. The Maine Parole Board will continue to exist as long as there are parolees in the state. If one or more parolees violate their parole conditions, the Maine Parole Board must determine whether such violations are sufficient to revoke their parole programs. If so, some Maine parolees may be returned to prison (Petersilia, 2001).

Most states have significant numbers of parolees and are quite different from Maine. In fact, in 2002 there were 753,141 persons on parole in the United States. This is a sizable number, since the total number of those incarcerated in jails and prisons in 2002 was about 2.1 million. Parole is definitely making a difference to jail and prison populations, since parolee numbers are about a third of the number of all incarcerated offenders. Also, there is a fairly brisk turnover among parolees annually, with slightly more parolees entering parole programs than are released from them. Although the number of parolees grew by 2.8 percent between 2001 and 2002 (732,333 and 753,141), parole is actually the slowest growing correctional population since 1995, averaging a growth of about 1.5 percent annually. This figure is the lowest compared with jail growth (4 percent annually), prison growth (3.5 percent annually), and probation growth (3.1 percent annually) for the same 1995–2002 period (Glaze, 2003).

The influence of parole boards on prison population sizes may be overstated. Some jurisdictions, such as Florida, report that following their abolition of parole in 1983 and a transformation from indeterminate to determinate sentencing, average prison sentences of convicted offenders were reduced to a greater degree through statutorily mandated earned good time credits. Thus, larger numbers of offenders were being released from Florida prisons earlier under determinate sentencing than under indeterminate sentencing where parole board discretion was exercised (Florida Department of Corrections, 2003).

BOX 7.2

Henry J. Atencio
Deputy Warden, Idaho Department of Corrections; formerly Manager, District 4 West Probation and Parole, Idaho Department of Corrections

Statistics:

B.A. (criminal justice, corrections, counseling), Boise State University; Certified Public Manager

Background and Experience:

Upon graduating from high school, I enrolled in Boise State University's Criminal Justice Program. For as long as I can remember, I wanted to work in the legal field. I believed that this was a noble profession where I would have the opportunity to positively impact my community. While I knew I belonged in the legal field, I really had no idea in what capacity I wanted to serve. Growing up I knew very little about probation and parole. All of my knowledge centered on police officers. They were (and remain today) the most visible personalities in law enforcement. How many movies or television shows do you see about probation and parole officers?

During the summer of my junior year in college, I had the opportunity to complete an internship with the Idaho Department of Correction, where I worked as a student intern in an adult probation and parole office. As an intern, I worked closely with senior probation officers, pre-sentence investigators, and probationers. In fact, at one point I supervised a caseload. I wrote pre-sentence investigation reports, and attended court. I learned the job responsibilities, pros and cons of the job, and how the criminal justice system worked. That was an eye-opening experience. Upon completing my internship, I knew that my calling was in corrections as a probation and parole officer.

In 1990 I was hired as a probation officer for the Idaho Department of Correction. For five years I directly supervised adult convicted felons who had been placed on probation by the courts or had earned early release on parole from the Idaho Commis-

sion for Pardons and Parole. I supervised the gamut of offenders from property and drug offenders to murderers and sex offenders. On the average, I supervised approximately 60 offenders at any given time with a high caseload of 105 offenders. I worked as the lead officer on our Intensive Supervision Program. As the name implies, this was an intense caseload; we supervised the most dangerous offenders and those who demonstrated the highest rehabilitative needs. With a partner, we provided around-the-clock supervision to 25 to 30 offenders.

As an officer I had the opportunity and responsibility to provide rehabilitation opportunities to criminal offenders. I took a humanistic approach to offender supervision. I treated each offender as an individual and with the dignity and respect that any human being deserves. I didn't browbeat the offenders; instead, I attempted to facilitate change with open and honest communication. This approach garnered a lot of success. In five years as a parole officer, I was never involved in a use-of-force incident, nor was I the subject of offender grievances. Don't misinterpret this! I enforced the terms and conditions of supervision and held offenders accountable for their behavior. But I did so in a low-key, non-threatening manner.

Supervising offenders in the community is difficult, challenging, and at times, a thankless profession. To a responsible and committed officer, this is not a job that is left at the office. I routinely worked evenings and weekends and was frequently awakened in the middle of the night to respond to out-of-control offenders.

(continued)

BOX 7.2 (*Continued*)

In 1995 I was promoted to our administrative office where I served as the department's Parole Coordinator. In this capacity, I worked with prison counselors, district offices, and the Parole Commission to ensure that parole plans were complete, investigated in a timely manner, and inmates were released accordingly. This was an administrative position and gave me the opportunity to see the big picture and the interconnectedness of our department. As a parole officer, my only concern was my caseload of offenders. I spent little time concerning myself with how my decisions impacted the rest of the department. As Parole Coordinator, I got my first taste of the complexity of our department.

Within a year I was promoted to Program Coordinator. I had a variety of responsibilities that ranged from implementing and managing federal grant-funded programs to auditing probation and parole officers around the state. In 2000, I accepted a lateral transfer to Probation and Parole Section Supervisor and in 2001, I became the District Manager of one of the largest districts in our state. As a manager I am responsible for setting the tone and direction of the district. A large part of my job is to coordinate with other criminal justice entities such as local law enforcement agencies, district judges, and prosecutors. I am the hiring authority, and I ensure that all staff receive proper training. I also have the unsavory task of staff accountability and discipline. Managing a

work unit and leading a group of individuals is both challenging and rewarding.

My career with the Idaho Department of Correction has been extremely varied and rewarding. I can tell you that I have enjoyed every day of my career and ended each day knowing that I had a positive impact in someone's life and contributed to my community. I got my start as an intern, and now I lead one of the largest districts in the state. Over the course of writing this biography, I accepted an interim assignment of Deputy Warden for our state's largest correctional institution. I recently accepted the position on a permanent basis starting a whole new chapter in my career.

Advice to Students:

Build your career on integrity! I have had the opportunity to work with people of great integrity. They are trusted and respected because they are people of their word. Unfortunately I have witnessed people destroy their careers because of poor decision making and a lack of honesty and integrity. Your character, honesty, and integrity are your most valuable tools in the corrections profession. Build, maintain, and protect your integrity at all costs. Remain open-minded and flexible to change and new challenges. Don't be afraid to step out of your comfort zone and challenge yourself. Stepping out of the box creates opportunities you may never have thought possible.

Compensating for Sentencing Disparities

One of the criticisms of sentencing practices in both the states and federal system is that judges impose disparate sentences on the basis of race/ethnicity, age, gender, and/or socioeconomic status. In an effort to remedy sentencing disparities, parole boards can exercise their discretion and adjust the sentences of those who appear to be unfairly penalized because of extra-legal factors. Evidence exists to suggest that some disparities in sentencing have been minimized through determinate sentencing in selected jurisdictions (Hofer et al., 1999).

Among the states to implement wholesale changes in their sentencing practices is Minnesota. Minnesota established sentencing guidelines in 1980, and officials noted substantial decreases in prior sentencing disparities attributable to race, ethnicity, age, gender, and socioeconomic status (Albonetti, 1999). Sentences were more uniform as to who goes to prison and how long they serve. Similar results have been found as the result of sentencing reforms in North Carolina and Georgia (Duncan, Speir, and Meredith, 1999).

An informed parole board is capable of making decisions about early releases of inmates that are fairer than otherwise calculated through determinate sentencing provisions. In more than a few jurisdictions, parole boards permit victims of crimes, the sentencing judge, prosecutor, and the media to be notified of and attend parole hearings, and they actively solicit essential documentation to support their subsequent parole decision (Burns et al., 1999). Inmates have an opportunity to present evidence of their progress while in prison as well as their constructive parole plans. If granted early release, they must sign an agreement to abide by the conditions required for successful parole supervision, and they are ultimately responsible for their own conduct while completing the term of their parole (Whitehead and Blankenship, 2000).

Public Safety and Protection

One of the primary areas of concern for citizens relating to parole is offender **risk.** There are no foolproof ways of forecasting an offender's future dangerousness. Yet, dangerous offenders are freed by parole boards daily throughout the United States (Greene and Schiraldi, 2002). Many of these offenders have demonstrated by their work in prison that they are potentially capable of leading law-abiding lives. Parole boards use different methods for determining which offenders should be released. Such forecasts of offender risk have been used since the 1920s. Predicting offender success on parole is a major policy issue in most jurisdictions. This issue has led to numerous reforms relating to sentencing and parole board decision making and the criteria used for risk forecasting (Auerbahn, 2002). Presently, there is no universal policy in effect throughout all U.S. jurisdictions. Each state and the federal government have independent criteria that are used for early-release decision making.

One critical issue is determining whose interests are more important—the public or the inmate. Parole offers inmates a chance to live reasonably normal lives in society. However, some risk is assumed by parole boards when parole is granted. No one knows for sure how each parolee will respond to his or her parole program. There are a certain proportion of parolee failures that cause people to view the whole idea of parole with skepticism (Finn and Muirhead-Steves, 2002). However, there are many other parolees who have successful experiences while on parole. They are able to readjust to community living and refrain from committing new offenses. For all practical purposes, they have become rehabilitated. In 2002 there were 447,991 parolees who were discharged from their parole programs, meaning that they endured their parole programs without incident and refrained from violating the law or their parole program conditions (Glaze, 2003). Proportionately, about a third of all parolees remain violation-free within their jurisdictions. This

FIGURE 7.1   Parole officer discusses parole plan with parolee.
Courtesy of James Shaffer, PhotoEdit.

doesn't mean that the other two-thirds commit new crimes, but they may violate one or more of their parole program conditions, such as curfew or failing an alcohol or drug test (Glaze, 2003).

Parole departments throughout the United States supervise their clients more or less intensively. Most departments have specialized units of parole officers to deal with parolees with particular problems, such as alcohol or substance abuse issues. Different types of community services are available to parolees with various problems to enable them to improve themselves in different ways. However, evidence suggests that some parole departments and POs have negative views toward their clients and are predisposed to view them unfavorably. Thus, the assistance parolees receive from their POs may not be entirely supportive (Petersilia, 2001).

The fact is that society must cope with eventual offender releases, since many offenders serve their time and are released unconditionally anyway. The early release of a portion of these offenders is based upon prior department practices and parole board dispositions. No offender who is seriously believed to pose a public risk is deliberately released short of serving his/her full term of confinement. Paroling authorities believe that they can predict with a reasonable degree of certainty that most of those who receive early release will be properly supervised and will live law-abiding lives, although no parole method is absolutely foolproof (Greene and Schiraldi, 2002). From the perspective of inmates, they believe that they deserve a chance to prove themselves capable of earning societal trust through their good works (Auerbahn, 2002). However, more than a few parolees are discharged who have various diagnosed or undiagnosed mental illnesses. It is often difficult to tell which of these parolees will reoffend or be unresponsive to community treatments. Thus, their risk posed to society is frequently indeterminate (Farabee, Shen, and Sanchez, 2002).

A PROFILE OF PAROLEES IN THE UNITED STATES

Numbers of Parolees Under Supervision

In 2002, 6.7 million persons were under some form of correctional supervision in the United States. Of these, 753,141 or about 11 percent were on parole. About 9 percent of these were federal parolees, while the remainder were from state prisons. The parole population grew in the United States by 2.8 percent between 2001–2002 (Glaze, 2003:1, 5). Twelve states reported parolee increases greater than 10 percent during 2001–2002. Among the largest increases were North Dakota (27.4 percent); New Mexico (25.6 percent); Kentucky (22.9 percent); and Oklahoma (21 percent) (Glaze, 2003:5). Substantial parolee decreases were reported by Washington (−38.7 percent), South Carolina (−14.4 percent), Florida (−12.8 percent), and Vermont (−11.4 percent). Overall there has been a sustained increase in parole since 1980 with no signs of declining (Hughes, Wilson, and Beck, 2003). Table 7.3 shows

TABLE 7.3

Adults on Parole, 2002

Region and Jurisdiction	Parole Population, 1/1/02	2002 Entries	2002 Exits	Parole Population, 12/31/02	Percent Change, 2002	Number on Parole per 100,000 Adult Residents, 12/31/02
U.S. total	732,333	468,506	447,991	753,141	2.8%	350
Federal	78,113	32,200	27,985	82,972	6.2%	39
State	654,220	436,306	420,006	670,169	2.4	311
Northeast	162,971	69,473	58,624	173,803	6.6%	421
Connecticut	2,126	2,060	1,931	2,255	6.1	86
Maine	31	1	0	32	3.2	3
Massachusetts[a]	3,718	3,715	3,698	3,718	–	–
New Hampshire[b]	953	480	470	963	1.0	101
New Jersey	11,931	10,812	10,829	11,914	−0.1	183
New York	56,719	24,416	25,145	55,990	−1.3	384
Pennsylvania[c]	86,238	27,245	15,771	97,712	13.3	1,037
Rhode Island	355	459	392	422	18.9	52
Vermont[b]	900	285	388	797	−11.4	171
Midwest	104,705	92,549	83,764	113,490	8.4%	234
Illinois[d]	30,148	33,498	28,188	35,458	17.6	377
Indiana	5,339	6,364	5,826	5,877	10.1	128
Iowa	2,614	2,574	2,278	2,910	11.3	131
Kansas[d]	3,991	4,528	4,529	3,990	0.0	199
Michigan	16,501	11,175	10,028	17,648	7.0	236
Minnesota	3,156	3,577	3,330	3,403	7.8	91
Missouri	12,864	10,515	9,846	13,533	5.2	320
Nebraska	530	763	719	574	8.3	45
North Dakota	117	373	341	149	27.4	31
Ohio	17,885	11,828	11,860	17,853	−0.2	209
South Dakota	1,437	1,131	896	1,672	16.4	299
Wisconsin*	10,123	6,223	5,923	10,423	3.0	256

(continued)

TABLE 7.3   (CONTINUED)

Region and Jurisdiction	Parole Population, 1/1/02	2002 Entries	2002 Exits	Parole Population, 12/31/02	Percent Change, 2002	Number on Parole per 100,000 Adult Residents, 12/31/02
South	224,269	94,772	97,917	220,409	−1.7%	285
Alabama[b]	5,663	2,162	2,516	5,309	−6.3	158
Arkansas	11,357	6,285	5,964	11,678	2.8	577
Delaware	530	262	241	551	4.0	91
District of Columbia[b]	4,506	2,668	1,877	5,297	−	1,147
Florida	5,891	4,369	4,732	5,138	−12.8	40
Georgia	20,809	10,376	9,948	20,912	0.5	331
Kentucky[d]	4,885	3,434	2,316	6,003	22.9	194
Louisiana	23,330	13,573	13,486	23,417	0.4	715
Maryland	13,415	7,478	7,622	13,271	−1.1	325
Mississippi[d]	1,788	912	884	1,816	1.6	87
North Carolina	2,954	3,341	3,490	2,805	−5.0	44
Oklahoma[b]	3,406	1,827	1,113	4,120	21.0	159
South Carolina	4,161	857	1,456	3,562	−14.4	116
Tennessee	8,074	3,023	3,164	7,933	−1.7	181
Texas[b]	107,688	30,506	35,126	103,068	−4.3	654
Virginia	4,873	3,006	3,349	4,530	−7.0	82
West Virginia	939	693	633	999	6.4	71
West	162,275	179,512	179,701	162,467	0.1%	336
Alaska	522	305	319	508	−2.7	112
Arizona[b]	5,143	6,928	4,130	7,941	−	198
California	117,903	149,234	154,335	113,185	−4.0	439
Colorado	5,733	4,738	4,256	6,215	8.4	184
Hawaii	2,608	1,065	1,148	2,525	−3.2	268
Idaho	1,657	1,274	968	1,961	18.3	204
Montana[d]	710	681	546	845	19.0	124
Nevada	4,025	2,203	2,257	3,971	−1.3	246
New Mexico	1,562	2,305	1,905	1,962	25.6	146
Oregon	18,290	8,233	7,216	19,307	5.6	727
Utah	3,410	2,245	2,273	3,382	−0.8	213
Washington[b]	155	10	70	95	−38.7	2
Wyoming	557	291	278	570	2.3	154

Note: Because of incomplete data, the population on December 31, 2002, does not equal the population on January 1, 2002, plus entries, minus exits.

—Not calculated.

[a]Data were not reported for 2002. All counts were based on data for 2001.

[b]All data were estimated.

[c]Data for entries and exits were estimated for nonreporting agencies.

[d]Excludes parolees in one of the following categories: absconder, out of State, or inactive.

[e]Data are for the year ending November 30, 2002.

Source: Lauren E. Glaze, *Probation and Parole in the United States, 2002.* Washington, DC: U.S. Department of Justice, 2003:5.

the number of state and federal offenders on parole for 2002, according to both state and U.S. region.

Methods of Release from Prison

Releases of large numbers of inmates on parole are the result of many factors. Some of these factors are prison overcrowding and good behavior of prisoners while confined. Also, prisons are attempting to manage their scarce space in order to accommodate the most dangerous offenders. Another major contributing factor is court-ordered prison population reductions because of health and safety regulations and cruel and unusual punishment conditions associated with some prison facilities that have been unable to comply with federally mandated guidelines under which inmates may be confined. Some of the older prisons in the United States are rat-infested, roach-ridden structures without proper heat or ventilation in winter or summer months. Coupled with chronic overcrowding, some of these institutions are simply inhumane. This is where courts draw the line and require minimal conditions under which human beings can be held in confinement.

A primary method of releasing inmates from prison is through parole board discretion. Parole board decision making accounts for approximately 42 percent of all inmate releases. For the federal government and those states that have abolished parole, usually the method of release has been designated as supervised mandatory release, where a parole board has not intervened. Approximately 50 percent of all inmate releases occur through this method. These types of releases are consistent with determinate sentencing, where inmates accrue sufficient good-time credits to apply against their maximum sentences to be released automatically. Thus, inmates serving determinate sentences of 10 years but who are accruing good-time at the rate of 30 days per month for every 30 days served will be released after serving five years. In many jurisdictions, these inmates are free from further supervision by corrections authorities. In other jurisdictions, these inmates must serve some time on parole under the supervision of POs. The remaining 8 percent of releases are parolees who have had their parole programs reinstated or they have been paroled for other reasons. Some inmates max out their sentences by serving them in their entirety or through administrative actions. In some instances, court-ordered reductions in inmate populations for a variety of reasons will cause administrators to release some inmates deemed to pose the least risk to society, regardless of the proportion of their sentences actually served (Kassebaum et al., 2001; Piquero et al., 2002).

Profiling Parolees

Table 7.4 shows some of the primary characteristics of parolees in the United States for 2002. These characteristics are compared with the parolee population from 1995. One of the most significant changes from 1995 to 2002 is that female parolees have increased from 10 percent to 14 percent of the parolee population. Along racial and ethnic lines, white parolees have increased proportionately from 34 to 39 percent, while black parolees have declined from 45 percent to 42 percent. The proportion of Hispanic parolees has decreased from 21 percent to 18 percent during the 1995–2002 period (Glaze, 2003).

Table 7.4

Characteristics of Adults on Parole, 1995, 2000, and 2002

Characteristic	1995	2000	2002
Total	100%	100%	100%
Gender			
Male	90%	88%	86%
Female	10	12	14
Race			
White	34%	38%	39%
Black	45	40	42
Hispanic	21	21	18
American Indian/Alaska Native	1	1	1
Asian/Pacific Islander[a]	–	–	–
Status of supervision			
Active	78%	83%	82%
Inactive	11	4	4
Absconded	6	7	8
Supervised out of State	4	5	5
Other	–	1	2
Sentence length			
Less than 1 year	6%	3%	4%
1 year or more	94	97	96
Type of offense			
Violent	**	**	24%
Property	**	**	26
Drug	**	**	40
Other	**	**	10
Adults entering parole			
Discretionary parole	50%	37%	39%
Mandatory parole	45	54	52
Reinstatement	4	6	7
Other	2	2	2
Adults leaving parole			
Successful completion	45%	43%	45%
Returned to incarceration	41	42	41
With new sentence	12	11	11
Other	29	31	30
Absconder[b]	**	9	9
Other unsuccessful[b]	**	2	2
Transferred	2	1	1
Death	1	1	1
Other	10	2	1

Note: For every characteristic there were persons of unknown status or type. Detail may not sum to total because of rounding.
**Not available.
–Less than 0.5%.
[a]Includes Native Hawaiians.
[b]In 1995 absconder and "other unsuccessful" statuses were reported among "other."
Source: Lauren E. Glaze, *Probation and Parole in the United States, 2002*. Washington, DC: U.S. Department of Justice, 2003:6.

Not much has changed between 1995 and 2002 regarding the status of supervision. Approximately 82 percent of all parolees were being actively supervised in 2002. About 8 percent of all parolees have absconded and are being hunted as fugitives. Another 5 percent have had their parole programs transferred to other states. It is not uncommon for some parolees to request that they be transferred to their home states for parole supervision if they have been convicted for a crime and are serving time in another state. This action is usually accomplished through interstate pacts or agreements among parole departments. Consent of both departments in the different jurisdictions is required.

Successful completion of parole has remained steady at 45 percent between 1995 and 2002. In 2002 about 41 percent of all parolees had been returned to incarceration, with 11 percent of these being returned to serve a new sentence and 30 percent for other reasons (e.g., technical parole violations). About 4 percent of all parolees had been serving sentences of less than one year, while 96 percent were serving sentences of one or more years. There are some preliminary observations about why parolees fail to complete their programs successfully. Parole revocations are highly correlated with excessive alcohol use and substance abuse. Furthermore, it would appear that at least for some samples of parolees studied, the greater the length of time spent in prison, the more they are likely to recidivate (Alarid and Cromwell, 2002). Of course, longer prison terms usually mean that more serious types of offenders are involved. Thus, it might be anticipated that more serious and/or violent offenders serving longer prison terms would be more likely to recidivate when paroled compared with less dangerous and nonviolent offenders serving shorter incarcerative terms.

Another factor relating to one's successfulness while on parole is whether offenders have been employed full- or part-time (Petersilia, 2001; Wilson and Petersilia, 2002). Those who are employed on a full-time basis are less likely to reoffend or violate their parole program conditions compared with those who are underemployed or unemployed while on parole.

THE GROWING GANG PRESENCE

Increasing numbers of parolees are affiliated with gangs. If convicted offenders are non-gang members when they enter prison, the likelihood is that when they leave prison on parole, they will be affiliated with a gang (Straka, 2003). Gang membership increases one's propensity to reoffend, since most gangs are involved in illicit criminal activities and induce their membership to engage in such criminal enterprises as drug trafficking.

Also, increasing numbers of offenders who enter jails and prisons are already affiliated with gangs. Most of these new inmates joined gangs as juveniles (Small et al., 2000). It is generally acknowledged that gangs exist in all states, that they are involved with drug sales and distribution, and that they are highly structured (Tonry, 1998). The variety and nature of gangs is explained by personal factors such as class, culture, race, and ethnicity, along with community factors such as poverty, social instability, and social isolation. Inter-gang violence is fairly common. Gang members are becoming older and remaining in gangs longer. Many of those entering prisons perpetuate their gang affiliations by joining existing gangs or forming their own groups for self-protection and other interests.

Parole officers have reported that one of their major problems in dealing with parolees is gang affiliation, which is not always apparent. Many parolees attempt to disguise their gang affiliation by removing recognizable gang tattoos or denying that they are gang members when visited by their POs. It is often difficult for POs to prescribe treatments or needed community services for those affiliated with gangs, since there is strong resistance from parolee–clients who are gang-affiliated to becoming meaningfully involved in helpful interventions. Parolee failure is strongly associated with prior records of delinquency and belonging to gangs prior to being arrested and convicted for present offenses (Eisenberg and Trusty, 2002).

Overcoming gang influence is difficult. POs may attempt to initiate contacts between parolees and their victims, where personal injuries or property losses were sustained as the result of crimes committed. Sometimes restorative justice methods are effective in increasing the likelihood that parolees will remain law-abiding while on parole (Seiter, 2000). But despite the best intentions of POs and their agencies, there will always be a hardcore contingent of parolees who will prove to be unstable and not abide by their parole program conditions. Some may even abscond from their jurisdictions (Williams, McShane, and Dolny, 2000). Greater police presence in gang-dominated neighborhoods assists POs in their attempts to keep parolees from engaging in further criminal activities as the result of gang influence (Grimes and Rogers, 1999). But the pervasiveness of gangs in areas where parolees are likely to reside, together with ready access to addictive substances and alcohol, mean that POs are fighting an uphill battle in their efforts to reform, rehabilitate, and reintegrate their parolee-clients (Gowen, 2001).

In many jurisdictions, parolee failures are drug-related (Dempster and Hart, 2002). Parolee failures attributable to substance abuse can sometimes be converted into positive experiences, however. In Kentucky, for example, a program known as the Halfway Back Program provides an alternative to incarceration for parolees with nonviolent technical violations that might otherwise trigger revocation proceedings. In the Halfway Back Program, parolees caught violating technical program conditions sign an agreement to complete their programs and refrain from committing future technical violations. These agreements between parolees and their POs seem to offer strong incentives to remain law-abiding, despite the adverse influence gangs in the area may have (Munden, Tewksbury, and Grossi, 1999). Other strategies, such as home confinement and electronic monitoring, may be necessary, however.

The Idea of Parole in Retrospect

It is evident that parole in the United States is increasing annually. This does not mean that the successfulness of parole is increasing to an equivalent degree. On the contrary. It would seem that much depends upon the nature of particular parole programs and the intensity of supervised release relating to how parolees are managed. The federal government has replaced parole with supervised release. Parole has already been abolished in Maine, and several other states have given serious consideration to proposals for its elimination. At one extreme, the "just-deserts" philosophy is that offenders should be punished for their crimes in accordance with whatever the law prescribes. However, the laws are not formulated with the right degree of precision. For example, most offenses prescribe a term of incarceration up to X years or months and/or a fine of not more than X dollars. Thus, important decisions must be made by prosecutors, judges, and other officials that attempt to match the severity of the punishment imposed with the seriousness of the crime committed. This is far from an exact science, although social scientists and others for centuries have wrestled with the problems of defining appropriate punishments that fit each crime. Scientific investigations have attempted to evolve ideal models or schemes that might fit neatly into a sentencing scheme that states or the federal government might adopt. In fact, there is little or nothing scientific about state and federal statutes and their accompanying sentencing patterns in any jurisdiction.

At the other extreme are those labeled as rehabilitation-oriented and/or who promote or endorse nonincarcerative, reintegrative programs or the early release of offenders so as to minimize the criminogenic effects of prisons and jails. It is unlikely that parole will be abolished on a national scale, at least for the next several decades. Methods for controlling or monitoring offenders while on probation or parole are constantly being improved, and new and better devices are being developed to insure greater supervisory effectiveness. Thus, better control of persons currently under PO supervision appears to be the most logical solution to present problems.

Prison overcrowding enters the picture as an extremely important intervening variable. Many state prison systems have contracts with local city or county jails to house some of their inmate overflow. Several state prison systems are currently under zero population growth court orders, where maximum prison capacities cannot be exceeded. A general shift in sentencing from indeterminate to determinate has eroded or eliminated parole board authority to grant prisoners early release. However, under determinate sentencing, considerable latitude in sentencing decisions and charging decisions exists for judges and prosecutors. One result of these sentencing reforms has been to increase the likelihood of being incarcerated for various offenses, although the length of incarceration has been significantly shortened.

And what happens to offenders who are incarcerated? Do they receive the rehabilitation they need? Do they received needed services, such as drug abuse counseling or other forms of assistance? Are they permitted to perform prison labor that prepares them for meaningful labor when they are eventually paroled? Presently, only about 22 to 25 percent of all inmates in state and federal prison systems have prison jobs (Camp and Camp, 2003). Thus, about 75 percent of all prison inmates do not have employment opportunities while confined in their prisons. Essentially, most prisoners are warehoused for their sentence durations, without benefit of vocational, educational, or other types of needed services. When parolees have recidivated and sued prison systems for their failure to rehabilitate them, the courts have been unsympathetic, declaring that prisoners do not have a right to be rehabilitated, unless otherwise provided by statute (Knight, 1992). Thus, if the courts do not recognize a prisoner's right to be rehabilitated, why should the public hold different expectations of correctional systems?

The just-deserts and rehabilitative philosophies present corrections officials with an unresolvable dilemma. No offender rehabilitation program is 100 percent recidivism-free. However, this fact does not mean that all rehabilitation-oriented parole programs ought to be scrapped. When particular parole programs have recidivism rates of 30 percent or less, this means they also have success rates of 70 percent or higher. Some offenders appear to be benefiting from program participation. One costly solution is to construct and staff more prisons to house more prisoners. But can the states and the federal government afford to do this? Consider California's dilemma. Presently, California places approximately 70 percent of its convicted felons on probation (Pastore and Maguire, 2003). What if these felons had been sentenced to incarceration, even for short terms? Where would California prison officials put them? Furthermore, it is difficult and costly to attract and hire educated and competent persons to work in correctional officer and PO positions to supervise and manage offenders in or out of prison.

However, communities are playing an increasingly important role in offender management. In fact, many organizations are being established in the private sector to assume roles and offender management functions originally performed by understaffed and underpaid government bureaucracies. Parolees are becoming involved in new and innovative community programs featuring useful activities, such as employment assistance, individual and group counseling, educational training, literacy services, and valuable networking with other community agencies and businesses (Eisenberg and Trusty, 2002). More dangerous offenders who are released on parole are often placed in electronic monitoring programs and/or subject to house arrest or home confinement.

Additionally, inmates who are within a few months of their prospective parole dates are being released, with or without supervision, for short periods through work or study release programs. Other inmates are permitted short leaves from prison through furloughs. Yet other inmates are housed temporarily in halfway houses in communities, where they can ease back into community life gradually. Halfway houses are facilities with some rules and regulations, including curfews and drug and alcohol checks. Some inmates have a particularly difficult time coping with the relatively new freedoms of community life after the strict discipline and regimentation they experienced while incarcerated. These halfway houses and community residential centers provide diverse functions for many recently paroled offenders (U.S. General Accounting Office, 2001).

Almost all of the programs available to probationers are also made available to parolees. While differences between probationers and parolees were more pronounced in past decades, it is becoming increasingly the case that they bear more similarities to one another than differences. One reason is that there is so little room available in prisons and jails that many felons cannot be accommodated. Some states, such as California, place as many as 70 percent of their convicted felons on probation annually, simply because there is no room for them in existing prison and jail facilities. Even the vast construction programs in California and other states are falling behind in attempting to keep pace with increasing numbers of offenders falling within some form of probation or parole supervision annually.

One prediction is that government will rely more heavily in future years on private interests for offender management responsibilities. Numerous experiments are underway to see which programs have the best results and minimize parolee failures. Failures most often occur because of the fact that many parolees are either unsupervised or undersupervised during their parole activity. Many of them lack the ability to fill out application forms for jobs. Also, many have drug- or alcohol-related problems that got them into trouble initially. Rapidly expanding community services are doing more to fill important parolee needs. Volunteers and paraprofessionals are becoming more valuable components of these growing community programs as well.

SUMMARY

Parole is early release from prison short of serving one's full sentence originally imposed by the court. Parole originated in the 18th century in Spain, France, and England, and became popular in the United States in the mid-1800s as a means of alleviating prison overcrowding. The father of parole, Alexander Maconochie, was an early prison reformer who sought to allow prisoners to earn early release through marks of commendation or good marks. These types of rewards have been continued in United States prisons as good time credits against time served.

United States sentencing reforms have resulted in the abolishment of parole boards in several states, although a majority of states continue to use indeterminate sentencing and parole boards as decision-making bodies to grant or refuse to grant prisoners early release. Parole boards have been criticized for their failure to recognize recidivists and/or dangerous prisoners who should be confined. However, no foolproof prediction tools presently exist to permit accurate predictions of dangerousness of prisoners or the risk to the public if offenders are released short of serving their full terms.

The philosophy of parole is prisoner rehabilitation through reintegrating offenders into society. The manifest and latent functions of parole include reintegrating offenders into society, controlling or deterring crime, alleviating prison overcrowding, remedying sentencing disparities attributable to race, ethnicity, or socioeconomic status, and public protection. No current profile of parolees exists other than selected characteristics of persons presently incarcerated in prisons. Few prisoners serve their full terms, and most are released either through parole board discretion or mandatorily after serving approximately one third of their sentences.

Shifts in the nature of sentencing have done much to influence how parole is treated. Many states continue to use parole boards with discretionary powers to release inmates short of serving their full terms. Other states utilize mandatory supervised release as a way of rewarding those who have accumulated sufficient good-time credits and show promise for successful adaptations to community life if released. Many states are currently reevaluating their sentencing provisions and standards. Presently, there is considerable controversy concerning the contrasting philosophies of rehabilitation and just-deserts, where some corrections professionals seriously question the rehabilitative value of parole programs. The United States Sentencing Commission implemented new guidelines for federal judges to follow in November of 1987, and the United States Parole Commission was greatly modified in 1992.

QUESTIONS FOR REVIEW

1. What is parole? What were some of the important historical events in England and the United States that significantly influenced the evolution of parole? What is the relation between indeterminate sentencing and parole?

2. What are some of the goals of parole? Do corrections professionals agree on these goals and the extent to which they are being achieved?

3. Why was there a shift to determinate sentencing and guidelines-based sentencing during the 1970s and 1980s? What is the significance of good-time credits for determinate sentencing and early release?

4. What is the primary philosophy of parole? What are two manifest functions and two latent functions of parole?

5. What are some general sociodemographic characteristics of parolees in the United States?

6. What is the significance of the growing gang presence and the effectiveness of parole programs?

7. What appears to be the future of parole in the United States?

8. How are the goals of offender reintegration and public safety relating to parolees potentially in conflict?

9. What is meant by penological pragmatism?

10. What was the Wickersham Commission and why was it critical of parole in the United States?

SUGGESTED READINGS

Cullen, Francis T., John E. Eck, and Christopher T. Lowenkamp (2002). "Environmental Corrections: A New Paradigm for Effective Probation and Parole Supervision." *Federal Probation* 66:28–37.

MacKenzie, Doris Layton and Robert Brame (2001). "Community Supervision, Prosocial Activities, and Recidivism." *Justice Quarterly* 18:429–448.

Messina, Nena, Eric Wish, and Susanna Nemes (2001). "Therapeutic Community Treatment May Reduce Future Incarceration: A Research Note." *Federal Probation* 65:40–45.

Quinn, James F., Larry Gould, and Linda Holloway (2001). "Community Partnership Councils: Meeting the Needs of Texas' Parole Officers." *Corrections Compendium* 26:1–5, 18–19.

Piehl, Anne Morrison (2002). *From Cell to Street: A Plan to Supervise Inmates After Release.* Boston: Massachusetts Institute for a New Commonwealth.

Shearer, Robert A. (2001). "Strategic Alignment in Community Supervision of Offenders." *APPA Perspectives* 25:18–21.

INTERNET CONNECTIONS

American Probation and Parole Association
http://www.appa-net.org/

Board of Prison Terms High Control Parolees
http://www.bpt.ca.gov/hcparolees.html

Crime Prevention Coalition of America
http://www.crimepreventioncoalition.org/

Federal Prison Consultants
http://www.federalprisonconsultants.com

Georgia Parolee Database
http://www.pap.state.ga.us/parolee_database.htm

International Corrections and Prisons Association
http://www.icpa.ca/related/parole

New Jersey State Parole Board
http://www.state.nj.us/parole

New York State Parole Department
http://www.parole.state.ny.us/specialrelease.html

Parole boards
http://crimelynx.com/stateparole

Parole links
http://www.tbcnet.com/~salsberry/Parole%20Sites

Parole Violators
http://www.bottomlinestudios.com/ParoleViolators.html

Parole Watch
http://www.parolewatch.org

Probation and parole sites
http://www.angelfire.com/md/ribit/states

Street Time
http://www.post-gazette.com/tv/20020623tvweek2p2.asp

U.S. Parole Commission
http://www.usdoj.gov/uspc/

CHAPTER 8 | *Early Release, Parole Programs, and Parole Revocation*

Chapter Outline

Chapter Objectives

As the result of reading this chapter, the following objectives will be realized:

1. Describing prerelease programs and how such programs are beneficial to prospective parole-eligible inmates.
2. Examining work and study release programs, their goals, functions, and effectivness as reintegrating mechanisms for parolees.
3. Describing furlough programs, their origins, functions, goals, and effectiveness.
4. Investigating halfway houses, their origins, functions, goals, and effectiveness.
5. Distinguishing between discretionary parole and mandatory parole and the jurisdictions that use these parole forms.
6. Examining various parole conditions imposed in different jurisdictions for offenders who are granted early release.
7. Describing intensive supervised parole programs and their conditions, as well as making comparisons with standard parole conditions.
8. Discussing parole officer responsibilities in relation to parolees under standard or intensive supervised parole.
9. Examining day reporting centers, fine programs, community service, and restitution as additional parole conditions.
10. Describing the composition and general orientations of parole boards as well as their functions.
11. Understanding the implementation of objective parole criteria and the politicalization of the parole-granting process.
12. Investigating circumstances and procedures whereby parole is revoked, including case law relative to the revocation process.
13. Describing landmark cases in parolee rights relative to parole actions, including revocations of parole.
14. Reviewing the rights of parolees in probation and parole revocation proceedings.

• *Glenn was a convicted Florida offender who was paroled. After being on parole for some time, Glenn violated one or more of his parole conditions. His parole officer sought a revocation action by the Florida Parole Board to revoke his parole program. Subsequently, Glenn's parole was revoked and he was returned to prison. Glenn requested authorities to count his time on parole as time served against his maximum prison sentence, but the request was denied. Glenn appealed the case and a Florida appeals court ruled that time served on parole does not count against one's maximum prison sentence. If a parolee violates his/her parole, he/she is returned to prison to serve out the remainder of the sentence [Glenn v. State, 2002].*

• *Mines was a Washington parolee whose parole was revoked following a parole board hearing. Mines was returned to prison and appealed the revocation action by the board. His attorney requested a taped transcript of the parole board proceedings in order to craft his appeal to an appellate court. However, the attorney was advised that the parole board hearing tape was blank. Thus, no written or tape-recorded record of the hearing existed. The attorney then sought to set aside the parole board action and reinstate*

Mine's parole pending a subsequent parole revocation hearing. The parole board refused and Mines appealed. A court of appeals denied Mines' petition to reinstate his parole program, holding in part that the failure of the parole board to record the proceedings was a minor procedural violation. Therefore, Mines appealed to the Washington Supreme Court. The court reversed the appellate court, holding that the parole board erred in failing to record the proceeding. A new parole revocation hearing was ordered for Mines [In re Mines, 2002].

- *An Oklahoma inmate serving a 30-year sentence for second-degree felony murder was advised by the parole board that he would soon be considered for pre-parole supervised release. Thereafter, the Oklahoma legislature eliminated the pre-parole supervised release program and replaced it with a Pre-parole Conditional Supervision Program. Under the new program, the inmate was no longer eligible for pre-parole release. He appealed, filing a habeas corpus action with a federal circuit court, claiming that he was entitled to consideration for the program. The 10th Circuit Court of Appeals heard the case and rejected the inmate's claim. It held that the elimination of the program did not increase the defendant's term of incarceration. Rather, the court held that pre-parole release eligibility is governed by the new statute. Because the parole board had not acted prior to the statute's enactment, it was essentially prevented from granting pre-parole release to the inmate on the basis of the new eligibility requirements [Powell v. Ray, 2002].*

- *Coleman was a Mississippi inmate who was serving a 20-year sentence for aggravated assault. Under Mississippi law, Coleman would become parole eligible after serving at least 50 percent of his sentence, or 10 years. Coleman served 10 years and was paroled. Subsequently, he was arrested for a firearm violation and his parole was revoked. A court imposed a new 3-year term on Coleman because of the firearms violation. Later Coleman wished to be given another chance on parole, but the parole board denied his request. He claimed that he was entitled to parole because of the 50 percent rule followed by Mississippi. He appealed the case and the appellate court ruled that since Coleman had been sentenced to 3 additional years for the firearms violation, the new calculation would be 10 years + 3 years (firearms violation) or 13 years. Thus, the recalculated sentence for Coleman to serve before becoming parole eligible again would be 13 years, not 10 years [Coleman v. State, 2001].*

INTRODUCTION

This chapter is about parole board early-release decision making. It examines the options and alternatives available to parolees when parole is granted. With the exception of life imprisonment and death penalty cases, most offenders sentenced to incarceration are eventually released back into their communities, either through the natural conclusion of their original sentences or through some alternative early release scheme such as parole. Parole is most frequently conditional, and parole programs involve filing reports with parole agencies, observing curfew, making restitution, performing community service, participating in individual or group counseling, or participating in educational or vocational/technical programs. There is considerable diversity among programs for parolees. Some of these programs will be described. Furthermore, some parolees may need to be supervised intensively, while other clients may simply be required to report in a manner similar to standard probation. Many parolees may only be required to make contact by letter or telephone with their POs, while others must make themselves accessible to random face-to-face visits at home or in the workplace.

Compared with programs designed for probationers such as pretrial diversion, shock probation, split sentencing, and various forms of intensive probation supervision, programs for parolees are rather unique in that they are, for the most part, transitional programs. Transitional programs are designed to assist recently imprisoned offenders in making any necessary psychological and social adjustments to become reintegrated into their communities. Parolees with special problems (e.g., mental illness, mental retardation, alcohol or drug dependencies, and sex offenders) may be required to participate in community activities and programs that deal directly with these problems. Sometimes parolees will be expected to make restitution to their victims or perform a limited amount of community service for the duration of their original sentences. These are additional conditions which parole boards may see fit to make a part of an offender's parole program.

The first section of this chapter describes several pre-release programs. These involve releases of inmates for limited purposes, such as short-term work assignments and for the purpose of taking academic courses at nearby schools. Some inmates take courses to complete their GEDs. Other clients take courses or participate in group or individual therapy not ordinarily offered in prison settings. Work and study release are defined and their advantages and disadvantages for participating offenders are described. Furlough programs are also examined. Furloughs are short leaves from prison and are usually limited to weekends and involve visits with family members. Some furloughs may serve other purposes, such as performing work or community service or making restitution to victims. The functions, goals, and advantages and disadvantages of furlough programs are discussed. Most parole program options are community-driven. This means that community-based corrections often manages or supervises parolees.

The parole-granting process is described. This includes a discussion of parole board conduct as it relates to early-release decision making for eligible jail or prison inmates. Parole board composition and diversity is also discussed. Parole boards exist in most states. However, numerous modifications in sentencing strategies among the states and federal government have greatly modified parole-granting practices in more than a few jurisdictions. In some instances, parole has been eliminated entirely as an early-release option for inmates. Parole boards orient themselves in various ways toward inmates. Some of these parole board orientations will be described. Parole boards also attempt to employ objective criteria when making parole decisions. Some of these criteria will be presented and critically examined.

Risk assessment instruments are also used and provide parole boards with important data about the future conduct of inmates. Parole boards are fallible entities, and their decision making is imperfect. But this fact does not deter them from attempting to make accurate forecasts of future parolee conduct. The final part of this chapter describes several landmark cases pertaining to parole revocation. Parolees are entitled to two-stage hearings before their parole boards and have minimum due-process rights. The chapter catalogues several important legal rights of parolees and presents various scenarios involving legal challenges to the different conditions of their parole programs.

PAROLE PROGRAMS

At one time or another in their lives, most inmates of prisons and jails will return to society. They will need to be supervised by POs to varying degrees of intensity, depending upon their needs and prior records (Cummings, 2003:9). This means that meaningful programs should be in place to receive and treat them, depending upon their individual circumstances. Most programs available to parolees are similar to those for probationers. In some states and the federal system, parolees and probationers report to the same persons or agencies. One distinction previously made between probationers and parolees is that parolees have served time in prison. For this reason alone, parolees are considered more dangerous than probationers. Parolees are granted early release from incarceration by parole boards or some other paroling authority. This does not mean that they will be removed entirely from supervision, however. Several different kinds of programs exist for particular types of parolees and require varying levels of parolee supervision and monitoring. This section examines six of these programs. These include (1) pre-release; (2) work/ study release; (3) furlough programs; (4) halfway houses and community residential centers; (5) standard parole with conditions; and (6) intensive supervised parole (ISP).

PRE-RELEASE

Pre-release is any action that results in a jail or prison inmate being granted a temporary leave from his/her institution for various purposes. Usually these purposes include meeting with prospective employers and working at jobs on a part-time basis until one's parole or early release is granted; studying or taking courses at nearby schools for the purpose of completing degrees; and visiting with families for the purpose of reuniting with them and establishing harmonious familial relations (Mellow and Ward, 2003:26-27). A **pre-release program** is any activity which enables inmates to leave their institutions on a temporary basis for purposes of employment, work, study, or familial contact. Pre-release programs are available to both male and female inmates. For example, the New Jersey State Parole Board recognizes that the successful reentry of prisoners into their communities is greatly enhanced whenever there are substantial social support services in place to assist them in the transition back to community living (Mellow and Ward, 2003:27). Sometimes pre-release programs are calculated to assist particular inmates with various addictions or dependencies. For instance, pre-release might enable some inmates with drug, alcohol, or gambling problems to receive needed assistance from community services through their temporary releases from custody.

Pre-release programs are transitional programs in that they enable inmates to make a smoother transition into their communities through gradual re-entry and temporary leaves from jail or prison. Sometimes these programs are called **pre-parole programs.** Oklahoma operates a Pre-Parole Conditional Supervision Program or PPCSP. PPCSP is a traditional exit from the prison system for many inmates. In Oklahoma, many prisoners who are about to be paroled are released under close supervision for limited periods. Commenced in 1988, the Oklahoma PPCSP requires inmates to submit a weekly parole plan to their POs, submit to drug and/or alcohol checks, observe curfew, maintain employment, and pay court costs. They must return to their prisons on weekends. If any inmate does not have a job, he/she must obtain one within 30 days following their pre-parole release. Over 80 percent of all PPCSP releasees have some sort of job lined up before being released. In order to qualify for inclusion in this program, inmates must have served at least 15 percent of their time and be within one year of their scheduled parole eligibility date. Any institutional infraction will delay an inmate's acceptance into the pre-parole program. PPCSP clients must pay a $20 monthly supervision fee, restitution, court costs, and child support.

Since the PPCSP was established in 1988, a 26 percent failure rate has been reported, meaning that few inmate-clients violated one or more of their pre-parole program conditions (Inciardi et al., 2002; Marion, 2002).

WORK/STUDY RELEASE

Work Release Programs

Work release, also called **work furlough, day parole, day pass,** and **community work,** refers to any program that provides for the labor of jail or prison inmates in the community under limited supervision. Sometimes, work release and work furlough are used interchangeably, referring to similar activities such as an inmate's participation in a job not ordinarily available to other prison inmates. Work release programs are also available to older youthful offenders (Stein-Lee, 2001). Work release is designed to ease inmates gradually back into their communities by permitting them short leaves from prison to perform jobs and assist in supporting their dependents. For instance, Illinois established a PreStart Program in 1991 which was intended to assist inmates who were about to be paroled in making easier transitions back into their communities. The program was implemented largely because the public was increasingly disenchanted with standard parole and the abrupt changes for inmates into society. More than a few parolees failed in their parole programs because of this abrupt transition. PreStart was designed to reintroduce inmates gradually back into their communities by providing temporary leaves for the purpose of locating employment and performing jobs on a part-time basis (Grant and Gillis, 1999).

Work release was unofficially condoned in the United States in 1906 when Vermont sheriffs assigned inmates to limited community work, this type of temporary release was actually an integral feature of Alexander Maconochie's plan for prison improvement in the 1840s and 1850s (Clay, 2001). The first formal acknowledgment of work release occurred in Wisconsin when the **Huber Law** was passed in 1913. Senator Huber of Wisconsin successfully secured the passage of a bill which permitted Wisconsin correctional institutions to grant temporary releases to low-risk misdemeanants. The first informal use of work release in the United States occurred in Vermont in 1906 where sheriffs, acting on their own authority, assigned inmates to work outside jail walls in the community. At that time, county sheriffs issued passes to certain low-risk inmates to work in the community during daytime hours, but they were obligated to return to jail at a particular curfew period. Most states have work release programs today, with over 40,000 inmates involved in such programs in 2002 (Camp and Camp, 2003). Work release was not popular and only sluggishly adopted on a large scale as an alternative to incarceration during the 1960s and 1970s. By the early 1980s, almost all states had work release programs (Stein-Lee, 2001).

The Goals and Functions of Work Release Programs.   The goals of work release programs are to:

1. Reintegrate offenders into the community.
2. Give offenders opportunities to learn and/or practice new skills.
3. Provide offenders with the means to make restitution to victims of crimes.

4. Give offenders a chance to assist in supporting themselves and their families.

5. Help authorities to more effectively predict the likelihood of offender success if paroled.

6. Foster improvements in self-images or self-concepts through working in a nonincarcerative environment and assuming full responsibility for their conduct.

Specific benefits accruing to offenders and the community are that at least some inmates are not idle and exposed to continuous moral decay associated with incarceration; prisoners pay confinement costs and can support their families; and prisoners can receive rehabilitative treatment and possibly make restitution to their victims (Leonardson, 1997).

The primary functions of work release for parolees are (1) community reintegration; (2) promotion of inmate self-respect; (3) repayment of debts to victims and society; and (4) provision of support for self and dependents.

Community Reintegration.   Work release enables the parolee to become reintegrated into the community. Even though parolees must return to their prisons or other places of confinement during nonworking hours, they enjoy temporary freedoms while performing useful work. Thus, when it comes time for them to be officially released through either a parole board decision, administrative action, or from the normal completion of their sentences, the adjustment to community life will not be abrupt and potentially upsetting psychologically or socially (Stein-Lee, 2001). It has been reported that for some inmates, at least, the transition to regular community living, which most citizens take for granted, can be traumatic and devastating (Carey, 2003:34–35).

Promotion of Self-Respect.   Plans for inmate labor in some jurisdictions are designed with rehabilitation in mind. Most work study programs attempt to instill self-esteem within those inmates originally untrained and incapable of performing even menial labor in the private sector. These work experiences are designed to equip inmates with skills useful to employers on the outside. Furthermore, inmates can earn sufficient income to offset some of their own housing expenses while in prison and provide supplementary amounts to their families (Stein-Lee, 2001).

Repayment of Debts to Victims and Society.   On October 12, 1984, President Reagan signed Public Law 98-473, which established the Comprehensive Crime Control Act. Also passed was the **Victims of Crime Act of 1984.** Currently, all states and the federal government have victim compensation programs. As a part of offender work release requirements, a certain amount of their earned wages may be allocated to restitution and to a general victim compensation fund. Thus, fines, restitution, and some form of community service have become common features of federal sentencing (18 U.S.C. Sec. 3563(a)(2), 2004). Almost every state has adopted some form of victim restitution program for offenders (Webster et al., 2001).

Provision of Support for Self and Dependents.   Those prisoners with wives and/or children ordinarily do not earn enough on work release to support their dependents totally. However, their income from work performed is helpful in providing for a portion of their dependents' necessities. It is also apparent that the potential for becoming involved in a work release program can function as an incentive for prisoners to comply with prison rules. Increasing numbers of states are obligating work releasees to contribute some of their earnings toward program costs as well as paying for some of their dependent support (Heymann and Brownsberger, 2001).

Determining Inmate Eligibility for Work Release Programs.   Not all inmates in prisons and jails are eligible for work release programs. Before an inmate may become eligible for such programs in some jurisdictions, they must serve a minimum portion of their originally prescribed sentences. Long-term inmates who have committed serious crimes are often automatically excluded from participation in work release because of their projected public risk if loosed in their communities. Statutory provisions in several states specify the minimum amount of time which must be served before inmates may make application to participate in work release. One advantage of being able to participate in work release is that it weighs heavily and favorably when inmates are eventually considered for parole. Those inmates who have completed work release programs successfully stand a much better chance of being paroled than those who have not been selected for participation. They have proven themselves capable of living and working with others on the outside and are not considered potentially troublesome.

Study Release Programs

Study release programs are essentially the same as work release programs, but for the express purpose of securing educational goals. Several types of **study release** have been identified: adult basic education, high school or high school equivalency (G.E.D.), technical or vocational education, and college. In 2002, there were over 1,000 inmates in study release programs (Camp and Camp, 2003). One reason for such low numbers of study releasees is that many educational programs are offered online by computer or are available through correspondence. Also, most prison systems have educational programs that enable inmates to receive degrees at various educational levels (Leonardson, 1997).

Determining Inmate Eligibility for Study Release.   An inmate's eligibility for study release involves several factors. First, inmates must be within a short time of being released anyway. For prospective parolees, study release may be granted to those within a year or less of being paroled. A second criterion is whether inmates have behaved well while institutionalized. Good behavior on the inside does not necessarily mean that inmates will behave well when on study release. However, compliance with institutional rules is generally a good indicator of compliance with program rules for study release. Few offenders wish to jeopardize their parole chances by violating program rules while on study release. Absconding or escaping while on work or study release will result in additional time to be served when these inmates are eventually apprehended. Usually, the time to be served becomes flat time that must be served if an inmate has previously absconded. Study release involves an element of trust on the part of the releasing institution. Violations of this trust by inmates are not favorably viewed by paroling authorities (Stein-Lee, 2001).

Inmates must also file a plan indicating the reasons for acquiring additional education and where their educational goals will lead them when released into the community. Educational training enhances an inmate's eligibility for particular kinds of work when parole is granted or whenever the offender is released from the system. More educated inmates are more employable. If restitution is a part of one's parole program, then acquiring greater amounts of education can assist in making restitution payments later (Leonardson, 1997).

Advantages and Disadvantages of Study Release Programs.   Study release programs prompt concern among community residents that some study releasees or other types of releasees will harm them or pose various threats to community safety. But the failure rate of study releasees is so low that program advantages far outweigh any of these disadvantages (Stiles, 1994). Study release helps to prepare inmates for different types of occupations or professions. The Tennessee Department of Corrections, for instance, has a study release program where selected inmates can learn data entry, building construction, welding, food services, industrial maintenance, surveying, and drafting. They become certified upon completing their study release programs. Many of their educational credits are transferrable to colleges and universities where they can undertake advanced graduate study, if interested (Tennessee Department of Corrections, 1994).

Some inmates do not actually utilize these study release programs for anything other than their cosmetic value for parole board appearances. For instance, a study of work and study release programs in two states, Oregon and California, shows that many prisoners believe that they are "under pressure" to participate in these types of prison programs. Many prisoners believe that such participation would look good to their parole boards. However, more than a few jurisdictions report that inmates have demonstrated remarkable progress related to greater knowledge about the harmful effects of drug abuse, greater discipline, and improved development in self-awareness and self-concept (Loza and Loza, 2002).

FURLOUGH PROGRAMS

Furloughs are authorized, unescorted leaves from confinement granted for specific purposes and for designated time periods, usually from 24 to 72 hours, although they may be as long as several weeks or as short as a few hours. The overall aim of **furlough programs** as a form of temporary release is to assist the offender in becoming reintegrated into society. Mississippi was the first state to use furloughs in 1918 on a limited basis for low-risk, minimum-security prison inmates who had served at least two or more years of their sentences and were regarded as good security risks (Heymann and Brownsberger, 2001). These furloughs usually involved conjugal visits with families or Christmas holiday activities for brief, 10-day periods and were believed valuable for preparing offenders for permanent reentry into their respective communities once parole had been granted. In 2002 there were approximately 10,000 inmates who participated in over 100,000 furloughs (Camp and Camp, 2003). Thirty states and the federal government used furloughs for eligible offenders. Florida granted the largest number of furloughs (68,000), followed by Rhode Island (5,000), Vermont (3,900), the federal system (3,400), and Nebraska (2,900). The fewest number of furloughs granted occurred in Arkansas, Tennessee, and Wisconsin, with 2 each. During 2002 nationally there were only about 100 inmates who absconded from their furlough programs. Mississippi has augmented its furlough program by providing conjugal visits as a part of inmate visitations. Such visits by spouses are believed to alleviate prison violence (Hensley, Koscheski, and Tewksbury, 2002).

Furloughs have many of the same characteristics as work release programs. There are about three times as many furloughs granted compared with work releases. The length of a furlough varies by jurisdiction. Most furlough programs tend to range from 24 to 72 hours throughout the United States, although some programs may offer inmates up to two weeks or more of freedom for special activities (Stein-Lee, 2001).

The Goals of Furlough Programs

The purposes of furloughs are several. Offenders are given a high degree of trust by prison officials and are permitted leaves to visit their homes and families. Interestingly, such furloughs are beneficial to both prisoners and to their families, because they permit family members to get used to the presence of the offender after a long incarcerative absence. Sometimes, prisoners may participate in educational programs (like study release) outside of prison. They can arrange for employment once paroled, or they can participate in vocational training for short periods. In Canada, for instance, furloughs may be granted to eligible inmates for the following reasons: to make contacts for employment; to visit close relatives; to obtain medical or psychiatric services; to visit seriously ill relatives or attend the funerals of close relatives; to appear before study groups; to make contacts for discharge; and to secure a residence upon release on parole or discharge. Such programs in Canada are called Temporary Absence Programs (Grant and Gillis, 1999).

Furloughs also provide officials with an opportunity to evaluate offenders and determine how they adapt to living with others in their community. Thus, the furlough is a type of test to determine, with some predictability, the likelihood that inmates will conform to society's rules if they are eventually released through parole. For some prisoners, furloughs function as incentives to conform to prison rules and regulations, because only prisoners who have demonstrated they can control their behaviors in prison will be considered by officials for temporary releases. Usually, though not always, prisoners selected for participation in furlough programs are nearing the end of their sentences and will eventually be paroled or released anyway. They are good risks because the likelihood they will abscond while on a furlough is quite remote (Webster et al., 2001).

The Functions of Furlough Programs.   Furloughs are intended to accomplish the following functions: (1) offender rehabilitation and reintegration; (2) the development of self-esteem and self-worth; (3) opportunities to pursue vocational/educational programs; and (4) aiding parole boards in determining when inmates are ready to be released.

Offender Rehabilitation and Reintegration.   The manifest intent of furloughs is to provide offenders with outside experiences to enable them to become accustomed to living with others in the community apart from the highly regulated life in prison or jail settings. Indications are that furloughs fulfill this objective in most instances. Furloughs assist inmates in making successful transitions from prison life to community living.

The Development of Self-Esteem and Self-Worth.   Furloughs instill within inmates feelings of self-esteem and self-worth. Again, the element of trust plays an important role in enabling those granted furloughs to acquire trust for those who place trust in them. The development of self-esteem and self-worth are unmeasurable. Yet, many of those granted furloughs report that they believe they have benefited from their temporary release experiences (Ryan, 1997).

Opportunities to Pursue Vocational/Educational Programs.   Another benefit of furlough programs for those in jurisdictions where furloughs are permitted and granted is that opportunities are available for inmates to participate in programs not available to them in prisons or jails. Thus, if inmates wish to take courses in typing, art, automobile repair, or philosophically oriented offerings in social science or related areas, furloughs permit them the time to pursue such courses. Sometimes, these furloughs are labeled as study release, because they involve a program of study designed for the offender's specific needs.

Aiding Parole Boards in Determining When Inmates Ought to Be Released.   A key function of furloughs as tests of inmate behavior are to alert parole boards which inmates are most eligible to be released and who will likely be successful while on parole (Travis et al., 2002). Indiana, for instance, has an 80 percent success rate with its furlough program as used for parole board decision making. In that jurisdiction, inmates are granted furloughs if they are within 60 days of being paroled. They are limited to 3-day furloughs, where they can make home visits, obtain required medical treatment or psychological counseling, participate in special training courses, and perform work or other duties (Indiana Department of Corrections, 2001).

Determining Inmate Eligibility for Furloughs.   In most jurisdictions, furloughs are granted only to inmates who meet special eligibility requirements. Usually, program participation is restricted to the following types of inmates: inmates must be at minimum-custody status; they must have served a fixed amount of their sentences and be within some fixed time of release; approval must be obtained from a committee that reviews all furlough applications; a clean institutional record is required; they must have a stable home environment; and they must not have prior records of violent offending (e.g., murder, aggravated assault, armed robbery, rape) (Stein-Lee, 2001).

Weaknesses and Strengths of Furlough Programs.   Not all states have furlough programs. One reason is that under certain types of sentencing systems, any **temporary release programs** are not permitted. Those offenders sentenced to mandatory prison terms cannot be released prior to serving their entire sentences, less the good time credits they may have acquired during the initial incarceration period. Under an indeterminate sentencing scheme, there is considerable latitude for paroling authorities to grant furloughs or work releases to those inmates who have shown they can conform their conduct to the institutional rules (Loza and Loza, 2002).

One possible consequence in the reduction of furlough programs nationally is that inmates in prisons and jails have less incentive to abide by institutional rules. In some jurisdictions that have abolished parole, furloughs and work release were considered incentives to comply with prison and jail regulations, since parole boards viewed favorably any offender who completed these programs successfully. But even though these programs have been terminated in some jurisdictions, there are still incentives to conform, such as the accumulation of good-time credits which may be applied against an offender's original sentence. The successfulness of furlough programs is demonstrated by the relatively low recidivism rates in certain jurisdictions using such programs on a limited basis (Meyer, 2001).

HALFWAY HOUSES AND COMMUNITY RESIDENTIAL CENTERS

Halfway Houses Defined

One of the most important components of transitional corrections is the **halfway house.** Halfway houses are either publicly or privately operated facilities staffed by professionals, paraprofessionals, and volunteers. They are designed to help parolees make the transition from prison to the community. They provide food, clothing, temporary living quarters, employment assistance, and limited counseling. Again, if the parolee has been confined for a long period, the transition can be difficult, possibly even traumatic (Marion, 2002). Sometimes these facilities are known as community residential centers.

In 2002, 32 states and the federal government operated halfway houses for parolees. There were over 24,000 halfway house clients (Camp and Camp, 2003). While the precise origin of halfway houses is unknown, some observers say evidence of halfway houses existed during the Middle Ages as a part of Christian charity (Marion, 2002). The Salvation Army is associated with halfway house operations in the United States in the early 1900s, although there were shelters such as the Philadelphia House of Industry in existence to serve the various needs of parolees as early as 1889. Much earlier in 1817, some reformist groups lobbied for halfway houses as a means of solving prison overcrowding problems. At that time, these proposals were rejected because the public feared **criminal contamination.** This was the belief that if ex-offenders lived together, they would spread their criminality like a disease. In time, the public warmed to the idea of halfway houses once it was learned that they exerted a high degree of supervision and control over halfway house clientele.

Sponsorship of halfway houses for the next 150 years stemmed primarily from private and/or religious sources. In 1845, the Quakers opened the **Isaac T. Hopper Home** in New York City, followed by the Temporary Asylum for Disadvantaged Female Prisoners established in Boston in 1864 by a reformist group. In 1889, the House of Industry was opened in Philadelphia, and in 1896, Hope House was established in New York City by Maud and Ballington Booth. Receiving considerable financial support from a missionary religious society called the Volunteers of America, the Boothes were able to open what became known as **Hope Houses** in Chicago, San Francisco, and New Orleans (Wilson, 1985:153).

State and federal governments during the 1800s and early 1900s continued to work toward the creation of halfway houses apart from those established in the private sector. In 1917, the Massachusetts Prison Commission recommended the establishment of houses to accommodate recently released offenders who were indigent. But this plan was rejected. Eventually in the 1960s, Attorney General Robert F. Kennedy recommended government sponsorship and funding for halfway house programs. In 1965, the Prisoner Rehabilitation Act was passed which authorized the establishment of community-based residential centers for both juvenile and adult pre-release offenders (Wilson, 1985:154).

One of the most significant events to spark the growth of state-operated halfway houses was the 1964 creation of the **International Halfway House Association (IHHA)** in Chicago. Although many of the halfway house programs continued to be privately operated after the formation of the IHHA, the growth in the numbers of halfway houses was phenomenal during the next decade. For instance, from 1966 to 1982, the number of halfway houses operating in the United States and Canada rose from 40 to 1,800 (Wilson, 1985:154). These figures are probably lower than the actual number of halfway houses in existence during those time periods, since these numbers were based on affiliation with the IHHA and the American Correctional Association. Other reports have stated as many as 2,500 halfway house facilities with over 150,000 beds existed in 2002 (Pastore and Maguire, 2003).

Halfway House Variations

Because there are so many different government-sponsored and private agencies claiming to be halfway houses, it is impossible to devise a consistent definition of one that fits all jurisdictions. There is extensive variation in the level of custody for clients ranging from providing simple shelter on a voluntary basis to mandatory confinement with curfew. There are also many different services provided by halfway houses. These might include alcohol or drug-related rehabilitation facilities with some hospitalization on premises, minimal or extensive counseling services, and/or employment assistance. Also, halfway house programs are designed for offenders ranging from probationers and prereleasees to parolees and others assigned to community service with special conditions (Bouffard, MacKenzie, and Hickman, 2000).

Halfway-In and Halfway-Out Houses

The concept of a halfway house is closely connected with the reintegrative aim of corrections. In recent years, at least two hyphenated versions of the term have emerged. First, **halfway-out houses** are facilities designed to serve the community needs of parolees. Second, **halfway-in houses** provide services for probationers in need of limited or somewhat restricted confinement (Bouffard, MacKenzie, and Hickman, 2000).

Halfway-in houses are deliberately intended to create uncomfortable atmospheres for them. Halfway-in houses structure the lives of probationers in various ways, mostly by making them comply with various program requirements (e.g., curfew, random drug and alcohol checks, and other technical details). In contrast, halfway-out houses, for parolees, are designed to provide homelike and supportive environments aimed at aiding the offender's readjustment to society. Like halfway-in houses, these homes also continue punishment through the high degree of supervision or offender control exerted by halfway-out house staff. But because their clientele are parolees and have served substantial time behind bars, their functions are more therapeutic, rehabilitative, and reintegrative rather than punishment-centered (Laufer and Arriola, 2002).

The Philosophy and Functions of Halfway Houses

More than any other parole program, the halfway house typifies the transition prisoners must make from the unique custodial world of prisons and jails to the outside community. Today, halfway houses furnish not only living accommodations and food, but also job placement services for parolees, group and/or individual counseling, medical assistance, placement assistance in vocational/technical training programs, as well as numerous other opportunities for self-development (Marion, 2002).

The major functions of halfway houses overlap some of those associated with other programs for parolees. These include (1) parolee rehabilitation and reintegration into the community; (2) provisions for food and shelter; (3) job placement, vocational guidance, and employment assistance; (4) client-specific treatments; (5) alleviating jail and prison overcrowding; (6) supplementing supervisory functions of probation and parole agencies; and (7) monitoring probationers, work/study releasees, and others with special program conditions.

Parole Rehabilitation and Reintegration into the Community.   The major function of halfway houses is to facilitate offender reintegration into the community. This is accomplished, in part, by providing necessities and making various services accessible to offenders. The administrative personnel of halfway houses, as well as the professional and paraprofessional staff members, assist in helping offenders with specific problems they might have such as alcohol or drug dependencies. Often, parolees have worked out a plan for themselves in advance of their parole date. This plan is subjected to scrutiny by parole board members, and the parolee often has the assistance of a PO in its preparation.

Provisions for Food and Shelter.   Some parolees have acquired savings from their work in prison industries, while other parolees have no operating capital. Thus, halfway houses furnish offenders with a place to stay and regular meals while they hunt for new occupations and participate in self-help programs. Furthermore, halfway house personnel help offenders locate apartments or more permanent private housing for themselves and their families.

Job Placement, Vocational Guidance, and Employment Assistance.   Almost every halfway house assists offenders by furnishing them job leads and negotiating contacts between them and prospective employers. Some halfway houses provide offenders with financial subsidization that must be repaid when the offender has successfully acquired employment and is relatively stable (Marion, 2002).

Client-Specific Treatments.   Offenders with special needs or problems, such as sex offenders, drug addicts or alcoholics, or mentally retarded clients, benefit from halfway houses by being permitted the freedom to take advantage of special treatment programs. They may receive counseling, medical treatment, or other services custom-designed for their particular needs. If these offenders were to be placed on the street on parole directly from a prison or jail, the transition for some would be too traumatic, and it is likely that they would revert to old habits or dependencies.

Alleviating Jail and Prison Overcrowding.   Any program that provides a safety valve for prison or jail populations contributes to alleviating overcrowding problems. Probably the major function of halfway houses is to assist offenders in becoming reintegrated into society after long periods in secure confinement. But the functions of such houses have become diversified over the years. In any case, the existence of halfway houses has contributed to some reduction in jail and prison overcrowding as both front-end and back-end solutions (Munden, Tewksbury, and Grossi, 1999).

Supplementing Supervisory Functions of Probation and Parole Agencies.
A latent function of halfway houses is to exercise some degree of supervision and control over both probationers and parolees. These supervisory functions

are ordinarily performed by probation or parole officers. However, when some inmates are released to halfway houses, halfway house staff assume considerable responsibility for client conduct (Bouffard, MacKenzie, and Hickman, 2000).

Monitoring Parolees, Work/Study Releasees, and Others with Special Program Conditions.   Many parolees have conditional parole programs which require their attendance at meetings and regular counseling. Thus, halfway houses can not only provide the basic necessities such as food, clothing, and shelter, but they can also offer assistance in transporting clients to and from their required meetings and counseling sessions (Pratt and Winston, 1999).

Strengths and Weaknesses of Halfway Houses

Blanket generalizations about halfway house effectiveness are difficult because there is so much diversity among halfway house programs (Bouffard, MacKenzie, and Hickman, 2000). Furthermore, these programs are often established on widely different philosophical bases or rehabilitative models. But several attempts to measure halfway house effectiveness have been observed. Effectiveness of halfway houses has been measured in three ways. First, are halfway houses more cost-effective compared with incarceration? Second, do halfway houses actually assist in reintegrating offenders into society? And third, do halfway houses reduce recidivism to a greater degree among parolees compared with other programs such as standard parole?

Some of the major strengths and weaknesses of halfway house programs are as follows:

1. Halfway houses are effective in preventing criminal behavior in the community as alternatives which involve community release.
2. The placement of halfway houses in communities neither increases nor decreases property values.
3. Halfway houses assist their clients in locating employment but not necessarily maintaining it.
4. Halfway houses are able to provide for the basic needs of their clients as well as other forms of release.
5. At full capacity, halfway houses cost no more, and probably less, than incarceration, although they cost more than straight parole or outright release from correctional systems (Marion, 2002).

STANDARD PAROLE WITH CONDITIONS

Discretionary Parole

Parole is both a guidelines process and a discretionary decision. **Discretionary parole** is a decision to release an offender from incarceration whose sentence has not expired, on condition of sustained lawful behavior that is subject to supervision and monitoring in the community by parole personnel who ensure compliance with the terms of release. Discretionary parole decisions are based on a number of factors that weigh the need for punishment, successful community reintegration, and victim and community restoration. It is rooted in the fundamental belief that offenders can be motivated to make positive changes in their lives (American Probation and Parole Association, 2003:10). A majority of jurisdictions use discretionary parole. If parole is granted to an inmate, but the inmate does not want to comply with one or more of the parole conditions, parole may be rejected. This scenario is unusual, although it does happen from time to time. The onerous conditions of parole are such that some inmates would rather finish the remainder of their sentences in prison than subject themselves to harsh parole conditions while living in their communities. Figure 8.1 is an example of a federal parole acknowledgement letter, and it shows where the inmate may either accept or reject parole release. A list of

PAROLE ACKNOWLEDGEMENT LETTER		REPORT DATE *(YYYYMMDD)*
1. INMATE NAME *(Last, First, Middle)*	**2. SSN**	**3. ID NUMBER**

4. CORRECTIONS FACILITY

5. ACKNOWLEDGEMENT

I have read and understand the attached notice of approval/disapproval of my parole.

6. PAROLE APPROVAL

☐ I accept parole release. I understand my release is conditional upon continued good behavior and acceptance for supervision by a US Probation/Parole Officer.

☐ I do not accept parole release.

7. PAROLE DENIAL

INSTRUCTIONS

You have the right to appeal the determination of the Service Clemency and Parole Board denying your release on parole. You may submit your appeal through the commanding officer of your confinement facility within 30 days of receipt of the attached denial letter. The appeal application may include any new or additional information which was not previously considered by the Service Clemency and Parole Board.

APPEAL SELECTION

☐ I desire to appeal the denial of my parole by the Service Secretary Clemency and Parole Board. I understand the decision on my appeal by the designee of the Service Secretary is final.

☐ I do not desire to appeal the denial of my parole by the Service Secretary Clemency and Parole Board.

PRIVACY ACT STATEMENT

AUTHORITY: 10 U.S.C. § 951, P.L. 90-377, and E.O. 9397.

PRINCIPAL PURPOSE(S): To notify an offender of approval for parole release and record the individual's acceptance or rejection of parole. This form is also used to notify an offender of a negative determination by the Service Clemency and Parole Board and to record an offender's decision to appeal or not appeal the decision denying parole.

ROUTINE USE(S): To the Department of Justice, in instances where the prisoner is incarcerated in a Federal Bureau of Prisons facility for incarceration.

DISCLOSURE: Voluntary; however, failure to provide the requested information may result in denial of parole or forfeiture of opportunity to elect appeal rights as to parole denial.

8. INMATE SIGNATURE		**9. DATE** *(YYYYMMDD)*
10. WITNESS NAME. GRADE AND TITLE *(Last, First, Middle)*	**11. SIGNATURE**	**12. DATE** *(YYYYMMDD)*

DD FORM 2716, NOV 1999

FIGURE 8.1   Federal Parole Acknowledgement Letter (public domain)

parole conditions is supplied with this form, although they are not shown here. In a few jurisdictions, parole may be mandatory and cannot be rejected for any reason.

Mandatory Parole

Some jurisdictions, such as Alaska, have **mandatory parole.** Under mandatory parole, parole-eligible inmates must accept parole whenever it is granted by the parole board. Figure 8.2 is an example of the Alaska Board of Parole

ALASKA BOARD OF PAROLE
ORDER OF MANDATORY PAROLE

Parolee _____ DOB _____ Released _____ Supv. Expires _____

The following terms and conditions are effective on the release date shown on the CERTIFICATE OF GOOD TIME AWARD (AS 33.20.030) for all prisoners released pursuant to AS 33.16.010(c) or AS 33.20.040. I understand I am required by law to abide by the conditions imposed, whether or not I sign these conditions. The Parole Board may have me returned to custody at any time when it determines a condition of parole has been violated.

CONDITIONS OF MANDATORY PAROLE

1. REPORT UPON RELEASE: I will report in person no later than the next working day after my release to the P.O. located at _____, and receive further reporting instructions. I will reside at: _____.

2. MAINTAIN EMPLOYMENT/TRAINING/TREATMENT: I will make a diligent effort to maintain steady employment and support my legal dependents. I will not voluntarily change or terminate employment without receiving permission from my Parole Officer (P.O.) to do so. If discharged or if employment is terminated (temporarily or permanently) for any reason, I will notify my P.O. the next working day. If I am involved in an education, training or treatment program, I will continue active participation in the program unless I receive permission from my P.O. to quit. If I am released, removed or terminated from the program for any reason, I will notify my P.O. the next working day.

3. REPORT MONTHLY: I will report to my P.O. at least monthly in the manner prescribed by my P.O. I will follow any other reporting instructions established by my P.O.

4. OBEY LAWS/ORDERS: I will obey all state, federal and local laws, ordinances, orders, and court orders.

5. PERMISSION BEFORE CHANGING RESIDENCE: I will obtain permission from my P.O. before changing my residence. Remaining away from my approved residence for 24 hours or more constitutes a change in residence for the purpose of this condition.

6. TRAVEL PERMIT BEFORE TRAVEL OUTSIDE ALASKA: I will obtain the prior written permission of my P.O. in the form of an interstate travel agreement before leaving the State of Alaska. Failure to abide by the conditions of the travel agreement is a violation of my order of parole.

7. NO FIREARMS/WEAPONS: I will not own, possess, have in my custody, handle, purchase or transport any firearm, ammunition or explosives. I may not carry any deadly weapon on my person except a pocket knife with a 3" or shorter blade. Carrying any other weapon on my person such as a hunting knife, axe, club, etc. is a violation of my order of parole. I will contact the Alaska Board of Parole if I have any questions about the use of firearms, ammunition or weapons.

8. NO DRUGS: I will not use, possess, handle, purchase, give or administer any narcotic, hallucinogenic (including marijuana/THC), stimulant, depressant, amphetamine, barbiturate or prescription drug not specifically prescribed by a licensed medical professional.

9. REPORT POLICE CONTACT: I will report to my P.O., not later than the next working day, any contact with a law enforcement officer.

10. DO NOT WORK AS AN INFORMANT: I will not enter into any agreement or other arrangement with any law enforcement agency which will place me in the position of violating any law or any condition of my parole. I understand that Department of Corrections and Parole Board policy prohibit me from working as an informant.

11. NO CONTACT WITH PRISONERS OR FELONS: I may not telephone, correspond with or visit any person confined in a prison, penitentiary, correctional institution or camp, jail, halfway house, work release center, community residential center, juvenile correctional center, etc. Contact with a felon during the course of employment or during Corrections-related treatment is not prohibited if approved by my P.O. Any other knowing contact with a felon is prohibited unless approved by my P.O. I will notify my P.O. the next working day if I have contact with a prisoner or felon.

12. CANNOT LEAVE AREA: I will receive permission from my P.O. before leaving the area of the state to which my case is assigned. My P.O. will advise me in writing of limits to the area to which I have been assigned.

13. OBEY ALL ORDERS / SPECIAL CONDITIONS: I will obey any special instructions, rules or orders given to me by the Board of Parole or by my P.O. and I will follow any special conditions imposed by the Board of Parole or my P.O.

14. WAIVE EXTRADITION: I will waive extradition to the State of Alaska from any state or territory of the United States, and I will not contest efforts to return me to Alaska by the Board of Parole or my P.O.

15. PROVIDE DNA SAMPLE: I will provide a blood and/or oral sample when requested by a health care professional acting on behalf of the State, if I am being released after a conviction of an offense requiring the State to collect the sample(s) for the DNA identification system under AS 44.41.035.

I have received a copy of these conditions of parole. I have had the opportunity to read these conditions or to have them read to me if I cannot read. My mandatory parole can be revoked and I can be required to serve the remainder of my sentence if I violate any parole conditions. I understand it is my responsibility to contact my P.O. if I have a question about the meaning or intent of any parole condition. I realize I can be arrested by a P.O. at any time with or without a warrant if my conduct so dictates.

_____   _____   _____   _____
Parolee signature   Date   Witness Signature   Title

DISTRIBUTION: WHITE - Board of Parole   YELLOW - Institution   PINK - Parolee   GOLD - Parole Officer

Alaska Board of Parole, P.O. Box 112000, Juneau, AK 99811-2000
Rev. 3/99; Alaska Board of Parole   [g:\parole\forms\Standard MR Cond.doc]

FIGURE 8.2   Alaska Board of Parole Order of Mandatory Parole (public domain)

Order of Mandatory Parole. It specifies most parole conditions, in that other special conditions of parole may be attached as ordered by the Alaska Parole Board. These conditions may include special individual or group counseling, participation in vocational/educational programming, or other community services. If the parolee has had problems with drugs or alcohol in past years, the parole board may direct that the parolee participate in appropriate treatments or programs suitable to these different forms of substance abuse. The parolee is given a six-page statement of supplemental conditions which may or may not be imposed by the Parole Board. The parolee does not have to sign the form, since parole granting in Alaska is mandatory. Parolees must accept these parole conditions, as well as any other special supplemental conditions the Alaska Parole Board sees fit to impose. Failure to comply with one or more of these conditions at any time may subject the parolee to parole revocation and a return to prison.

Interstate Parole Variations

In 2004, every state had parolees. Many of these offenders were granted early release by a parole board. There are some exceptions, however. In California, for example, most prison inmates receive a determinate sentence and are released on parole once they have served their prison terms, less any good-time credit which they have accumulated. Following their release from prison, the duration of their parole is 3 years. This involves PO supervision if these offenders choose to locate within the state. They must abide by the same types of conditions required of probationers. Once they have successfully completed their 3-year parole terms, they are officially released from the criminal justice system. For more serious California offenders who have been convicted of first- or second-degree murder, they have usually been sentenced to life terms with the possibility of parole. The California Board of Prison Terms meets and considers whether any of these offenders should be paroled. If they are eventually paroled, the length of their parole is for the rest of their lives. That is, they will be under PO supervision until they die. The records of both life and non-life parolees are reviewed periodically during their parole periods to determine if they are suitable for discharge from parole prior to their maximum discharge dates (Stephens, 2001:1).

Who Is Parole Eligible?

Since most states have revised or are revising their sentencing provisions, it is sometimes difficult to determine who is eligible for parole. Should parole be limited to nonviolent offenders, or should all types of offenders, even murderers and rapists, be paroled? Presently, all types of offenders may be considered for parole in those jurisdictions that use parole (Steiner, 2002). As we observed earlier, most states have modified or drastically altered their sentencing provisions so that today, it is not unusual for some states to have vestiges of several types of sentencing schemes that affect particular cohorts of prisoners differently. Mississippi is a case in point. Mississippi has identified several different classes offenders divided according to when they were convicted of crimes and sentenced. Mississippi uses the following scheme:

Parole Eligible/Earned Release Offenders:

1. Crimes committed on or before June 30, 1995.
2. Offenders required to serve 25 percent of their sentence.
3. Eligible for parole after 25 percent of time served.
4. Offender can "flat time" after serving only 50 percent of their sentence (offender is eligible for release).
5. Sex offenders, habitual offenders, or offenders with life sentences are not eligible.

Truth-In-Sentencing Offenders:

1. Crimes committed from July 1, 1995–December 31, 1999.
2. Every offender must serve 85 percent of his or her sentence in incarceration.
3. Remaining 15 percent of sentence served in Community Services under ERS supervision.

First-Time Nonviolent Offenders Eligibility (Mississippi Senate Bill 3028)

1. Crimes committed from January 1, 2000 to present.
2. Passed by Legislature on March 12, 2001.
3. Nonviolent first-time offenders must serve 25 percent of their sentence in incarceration, then eligible for parole consideration (Mississippi Parole Board, 2003:1-2).

It seems from this Mississippi example that the truth-in-sentencing provisions Mississippi introduced in 1995 caused their prison population to soar. In order to ease prison overcrowding, incarceration was re-evaluated for first-time offenders so that their parole eligibility was restored to 1995 standards. Mississippi has indicated that depending upon an inmate's sentence, some inmates are eligible to serve part of their sentence on parole. Although an inmate may be eligible for parole, it is not a guarantee that the inmate will be granted parole. A list of all inmates eligible for parole is generated by the Mississippi Department of Corrections and sent to the Mississippi Parole Board. The cases of the inmates on the list are reviewed by the parole board and a decision is made to grant or deny a parole hearing. At a parole hearing, the inmate's file is reviewed, including any rule violations during incarceration (Mississippi Parole Board, 2003:1).

The Mississippi example only pertains to changes in Mississippi sentencing practices from 1995 to the present. Other changes in sentencing laws in Mississippi were made prior to 1995. Thus, there are more than a few classes of inmates, depending upon what particular sentencing scheme pertained to them at the time they committed their crimes. Today, all inmate records are computerized in order to more easily determine who becomes parole eligible at any given time.

In a state such as Maine, for instance, parole was abolished in 1976 as an early-release mechanism. However, there were still several Maine inmates who were considered parole eligible in 2004. These were convicts who committed their crimes prior to the abolition of parole in 1976. Thus, Maine maintains a

BOX 8.1

Cheryl Green
Director, Baxter County, Arkansas Juvenile Services, Intake Officer

Statistics:

B.S. (psychology), Christian Heritage College; undergraduate work, Missouri Southern State College, Citadel Bible College; University of Arkansas.

Background:

I worked in youth camps when I was in high school and college. I was employed in management and as owner/operator in the business sector (food industry) prior to this public employment venture. My original interest was in youth and family counseling. After college and moving back to this geographical area with limited career choices, this job afforded me the opportunity to counsel without additional college degrees. I became invested in juvenile justice. Although always with the desire to pursue further education, program development has consumed my time up to this point. I feel that I am effective with my clientele. The system requires clients to maintain routine contact with their juvenile officers, whereas the mental health arena allows people to come in if and when they want help. Too often, because of their mental health issues, they cannot determine that they actually need counseling assistance. Therefore, I have been able to use counseling skills and see some good outcomes with an identified population. My determined (or as some would say, strong-willed/stubborn) personality has given me the tenacity to stay the course and jump through a lot of hoops to see our goals come to fruition. I am currently seeking to pursue further education. Distance learning has to be considered due to the 2 1/2 to 3-hour one-way drive time to any institution that offers this opportunity unless I relocate.

I have had extensive experience with various organizations. I have been a member of the Arkansas Volunteer Coordinator's As-

sociation, America's Promise, Baxter County Traditional Employment Assistance Coalition, Unified Community Resource Council, Twin Lakes Baptist Church, Protect Against Child Trauma (P.A.C.T.), Baxter County Multi-Disciplinary Team, Twin Lakes Literacy Council, Ozark Counseling Service, Arkansas Department of Human Services-Baxter County, Baxter County Single Parent Scholarship Board, and the Arkansas Department of Workforce Education. I'm currently an instructor for local law enforcement for their Part-Time II officer training; for the State of Arkansas, Administrative Office of the Courts for new juvenile officer certification; for public schools for conflict resolution through peer mediation programs; for local civic organizations regarding juvenile justice and our current programs; and most recently, a state representative for the National Juvenile Court Services Association, an affiliate of the National Council of Juvenile and Family Court Judges. My certifications include a Certified Volunteer Manager Certificate; Certified Juvenile Officer; Part Time II Law Enforcement Training; and Certified Trainer for Arkansas Juvenile Officer Association.

Experiences:

I began as a juvenile officer under a grant-funded pilot program in 1989 which was the same year Arkansas implemented a new juvenile justice system. As an intake officer, efforts to resolve matters without going to court are important. If a matter could be resolved through dispute resolution, parent-child mediation, implementation of boundaries iden-

BOX 8.1 (*Continued*)

tified in a contract, court intervention is suspended. If the matter is felony-related, violence-related, or "habitual in nature of commission," then court action is essential. A thorough social history, familial background, education assessment, prior legal matters, and mental health history are the baselines for a good intake interview. This information should be gathered from collateral sources and other persons/agencies in addition to the juvenile and parent. It is my opinion that the gestalt, holistic approach should always be maintained. Stepping outside of the box or looking for solutions that may not be identified as the norm should not be discounted. Even though law enforcement reads Miranda rights to juveniles, I feel that it is very important that these rights are reviewed at the intake session also for educational purposes to insure that the juvenile has clarity about their content. It's important to outline the due process procedures to the juvenile and parents during the intake interview as well. The juvenile officer is essentially a court investigator. Just because law enforcement has cited a juvenile, collection of all pertinent information is fundamental to the preparation of the case. While it is the prosecutor who legally files on matters, the work of the intake officer is often the backbone to the success of that role, and in the long run, the success of the juvenile. Currently the hours worked per week routinely exceed 50. My first 10 years, the hours consisted of 60 to 80 per week, just trying to maintain a caseload in a two-county area as well as develop and implement programs.

The Arkansas Juvenile Officer Association is not a division of the State of Arkansas. In Arkansas each respective judicial district is legislated to have a minimum number of staff. Then it is up to the individual juvenile court judge to negotiate with the counties of that judicial district to approve and budget for that minimum number plus any additional officers identified by the judge. Usually the judge settles for the number of officers the counties will fund rather than the number that is actually needed per work load. Many officers cover more than one county, which helps balance the pay scale for those officers. Baxter County is located in the 14th Judicial District, which comprises four counties in north central Arkansas. I am employed by two of the four counties.

Due to the rural setting, the services available to refer youth and families were essentially nonexistent or very limited in their scope prior to the 1990s. In 1994 when I became senior officer, I started developing programs for our local division. Since that time, we have grown from 3 employees with a budget of $75,000 to 21 employees and a budget of over $700,000. Only 7 of the employee positions are county-funded. The other 14 positions are funded by grants and contracts; therefore, it is a constant task seeking and writing proposals to secure funds to maintain these programs. I am privileged to work for a judge who is open to innovating programs and supportive of new ideas.

The programs developed are based on the needs of the population served by the court. This small rural setting of our area has afforded me an opportunity to network closely with community leaders. Baxter County has a program called the Host Home Program. This program has a twofold purpose. It acts as an emergency placement program for families in need of services allowing a brief respite or time-out period, or as an emergency shelter for runaways. Also, it serves as a supervised placement for youths who have committed crimes that aren't serious enough to get them locked up, but who would not receive the supervision at home to ensure their whereabouts until court proceedings. Youths are screened initially and may be held in a Host Home up to 30 days prior to returning home or to other suitable living arrangements. Many families enlist in this program as a ministry to their community. This program has allowed us to place children pending long-term living arrangements. I have had the occasion to place several children (who had already been in the social services system only to have been returned to a dysfunctional home and now involved in the juvenile justice system) in a warm, nurturing family that reared

(*continued*)

BOX 8.1 (*Continued*)

them beyond their eighteenth birthday. The youths that we were able to do this for continue on their life's journey as successful adults. I have been able to grow professionally and become diversified in many areas of juvenile justice. I have especially enjoyed implementing new programs for our community for the population we serve in the juvenile justice system.

Advice to Students:

I think too many people go into this line of work wanting to use their life experiences to help others. I find that those most effective in this field are the persons who know their boundaries, have integrity as a solid foundation, and have not necessarily had to go through everything imaginable to learn obedience and consequences. Those with too many life experiences often carry too much baggage from the past to endure the depth of problems of the population we serve in juvenile justice. They do not nor cannot maintain the long haul. Education is essential. Personal growth and expansion of skills are paramount. Many people entering this field of juvenile justice are

seeking a degree in criminal justice. I recommend that students seek classes in psychology as well. The legal aspect is much easier to lean than the mental health aspect necessary to know in dealing with the population we serve.

I also believe that it is essential to know now who you are and what God has called you to do with your life and go for it. Know why you desire a career in this field before you enter it. The needs are vast and dedicated workers are few, but the rewards can be indescribable. While I am committed to a personal relationship with God, knowledge of the Bible allows me to work within those precepts without proselytizing. It is essential to demonstrate your personal premise through actions rather than words. When I started my career in juvenile justice, my mentor advised me to take advantage of the educational opportunities that were available. He encouraged me to stay focused on the long-term vision and not the daily routine; that if you are doing what you are called upon to do, you will get tired but you will not burn out. I believe that advice, and I have experienced it and seen it.

part-time parole board that meets on occasion to decide parole for those few inmates who continue to be governed by the pre-1976 early-release standards under which they were sentenced. Regardless of how many sentencing changes have been implemented by any given state, for all parole-eligible inmates in all jurisdictions, there are several parole conditions that they must comply with if paroled.

Parole Conditions

All parole programs in all jurisdictions are conditional, in that they indicate what parolees must and must not do during their parole periods. For offenders with particular needs, such as alcohol or drug dependencies or gambling addictions, the conditions of their parole programs may include special provisions for community treatment on a regular basis. They may be required to attend Alcoholics Anonymous or Narcotics Anonymous meetings, or Gamblers Anonymous meetings. Parole boards usually determine whatever additional conditions should be included when paroling particular offenders.

Most parole agreements include standard conditions and a space for special conditions of parole, at the parole board's discretion. For instance, Ohio has the following types of provisions for its parolees. In order to be admitted to the Ohio parole program, parole-eligible inmates must sign the following document containing these provisions:

In consideration of having been granted supervision on December 1, 2001, I agree to report to my probation/parole officer within 48 hours or according to the written instructions I have received and to the following conditions:

1. I will obey federal, state, and local laws and ordinances, and all rules and regulations of the Fifth Common Pleas Court or the Department of Rehabilitation and Correction.
2. I will always keep my probation/parole officer informed of my residence and place of employment. I will obtain permission from my probation/parole officer before changing my residence or my employment.
3. I will not leave the state without written permission of the Adult Parole Authority.
4. I will not enter upon the grounds of any correctional facility nor attempt to visit any prisoner without the written permission of my probation/parole officer nor will I communicate with any prisoner without first informing my probation/parole officer of the reason for such communication.
5. I will comply with all orders given to me by my probation/parole officer or other authorized representative of the court, the Department of Rehabilitation and Correction or the Adult Parole Authority, including any written instructions issued at any time during the period of supervision.
6. I will not purchase, possess, own, use, or have under my control, any firearms, deadly weapons, ammunition, or dangerous ordnance.
7. I will not possess, use, purchase, or have under my control any narcotic drug or other controlled substance, including any instrument, device, or other object used to administer drugs or to prepare them for administration, unless it is lawfully prescribed for me by a licensed physician. I agree to inform my probation/parole officer promptly of any such prescription and I agree to submit to drug testing if required by the Adult Parole Authority.
8. I will report any arrest, citation of a violation of the law, conviction or any other contact with a law enforcement officer to my probation/parole officer no later than the next business day, and I will not enter into any agreement or other arrangement with any law enforcement agency which might place me in the position of violating any law or condition of my supervision unless I have obtained permission in writing from the Adult Parole Authority, or from the court if I am a probationer.
9. I agree to a search without warrant of my person, my motor vehicle, or my place of residence by a probation/parole officer at any time.
10. I agree to sign a release of confidential information from any public or private agency if requested to do so by a probation/parole officer.
11. I agree and understand that if I am arrested in any other state or territory of the United States or in any foreign country, my signature as witnessed at the end of the page will be deemed to be a waiver of extradition and that no other formalities will be required for authorized agents of the State of Ohio to bring about my return to this state for revocation proceedings.
12. I also agree to the following Special Conditions as imposed by the court or the Adult Parole Authority:

I have read or had read to me, the foregoing conditions of my parole. I fully understand these conditions, I agree to comply with them, and I understand that violation of any of these conditions may result in the revocation of my parole. In addition, I understand that I will be subject to the foregoing conditions until I have received a certificate from the Adult Parole Authority or a Journal Entry from the Court if I am a probationer, stating that I have been discharged from supervision.

The parolee signs this form and a witness also signs.

This agreement contains several important stipulations that are contained in virtually every parole agreement. First, the prospective parolee must agree to stay in continuous contact with his or her parole officer during the parole period, however long it may be. The offender may not possess firearms or dangerous weapons. The offender must remain in the state unless permission to leave it is obtained from the PO in advance. Drugs and alcohol are to be avoided, and drug and alcohol checks are to be permitted whenever the PO sees fit to administer them. In this particular form, the offender agrees to be extradited from external jurisdictions, even foreign countries, in the event that he or she absconds. And the prospective parolee agrees to warrantless searches at any time by his or her PO. If there are special conditions of parole, these must be complied with to the letter. If counseling or sex offender treatment is required, then the parolee must satisfy that condition. If attending Alcoholics Anonymous or some other group is required, this condition is mandatory. All conditions are mandatory.

The prospective parolee must agree to all of these conditions. Failure to agree to these conditions and sign the document will mean that parole will not be granted. While it may seem unusual for a prospective parolee not to sign this document and obtain early release, some inmates believe that the conditions are too stringent. They may exercise their right to remain in prison and serve out their sentences, particularly if they are within a few months or years of mandatory release anyway. And if the offender accepts these conditions and violates any one or more of them, he or she is liable of having his or her parole program revoked. A majority of parolees in the United States are currently under standard parole with conditions (Pastore and Maguire, 2003).

INTENSIVE SUPERVISED PAROLE (ISP)

Parolees are often subject to precisely the same kinds of behavioral requirements as probationers who are involved in intensive supervision programs. The New Jersey Intensive Probation Supervision Program is made up of inmates who have served at least three or four months of their prison terms (Ciancia and Talty, 1999). The use of house arrest, electronic monitoring, and several other programs may be a part of one's conditional early release from prison. The level of monitoring will vary according to the risk posed by the offender. But it is quite difficult to predict accurately one's risk to the public or general dangerousness (Getty, 2000).

Most parolees are **standard parolees,** in the sense that they are obligated to adhere to certain standard early release agreements formulated by paroling authorities. In 1987, the United States Sentencing Commission implemented new guidelines that included the following policy statement of recommended conditions of probation and **supervised release:**

1. The defendant shall not leave the judicial district or other specified geographical area without the permission of the court or PO.

2. The defendant shall report to the PO as directed by the court or PO and shall submit a truthful and complete written report within the first five days of each month.

3. The defendant shall answer truthfully all inquiries by the PO and follow the instructions of the PO.

4. The defendant shall support his dependents and meet other family responsibilities.

5. The defendant shall work regularly at a lawful occupation unless excused by the PO for schooling, training, or other acceptable reasons.

6. The defendant shall notify the PO within 72 hours of any change in residence or employment.

7. The defendant shall refrain from excessive use of alcohol and shall not purchase, possess, use, distribute, or administer any narcotic or other controlled substance, or any paraphernalia related to such substances, except as prescribed by a physician.

8. The defendant shall not frequent places where controlled substances are illegally sold, used, distributed, or administered, or other places specified by the court.

9. The defendant shall not associate with any persons engaged in criminal activity, and shall not associate with any person convicted of a felony, unless granted permission to do so by the PO.

10. The defendant shall permit a PO to visit him at any time at home or elsewhere and shall permit confiscation of any contraband observed in plain view by the PO.

11. The defendant shall notify the PO within 72 hours of being arrested or questioned by a law enforcement officer.

12. The defendant shall not enter into any agreement to act as an informer or a special agent of a law enforcement agency without the permission of the court.

13. As directed by the PO, the defendant shall notify third parties of risks that may be occasioned by the defendant's criminal record or personal history or characteristics, and shall permit the probation officer to make such notifications and to confirm the defendant's compliance with such notification requirement (U.S. Sentencing Commission, 2003).

Additional special provisions pertain to possession of weapons, restitution, fines, debt obligations, access to financial information, community confinement, home detention, community service, occupational restrictions, substance abuse program participation, and mental health program participation (U. S. Sentencing Commission, 2003:5.7-5.10).

The New Jersey Intensive Supervision Parole Program

One of the better **intensive supervised parole (ISP)** programs in the United States has been devised by New Jersey. The **New Jersey Intensive Supervision Program (NJISP)** was established June, 1983. Originally, the program was influenced by the traditional, treatment-oriented rehabilitation model and has been designed to target the least serious incarcerated offenders (Ciancia and Talty, 1999). Since 1983 the NJISP has become a model program which other states have emulated. Its program components are discussed at length in this section because of its successfulness.

Program Goals.   The goals of the NJISP are (1) to reduce the number of offenders serving state prison sentences by permitting them to be resentenced to an intermediate form of punishment; (2) to improve the utilization of correctional resources by making additional bed space available for violent criminals; and (3) to test whether supervising selected offenders in the community is less costly and more effective than incarceration.

Program Eligibility.   Who qualifies for the NJISP? First, anyone incarcerated in a New Jersey prison or county jail may apply for admission to the NJISP. However, there are mandatory exclusions consisting of the following:

1. Persons who have been convicted of homicide, a sex offense, a crime of the first degree, and robbery.
2. Persons who are serving sentences of life without the possibility of parole.
3. Persons who have convictions for organized crime activity.

For all other offenders, applications will be received and reviewed by an ISP Screening Panel. The ISP Screening Panel is comprised of three members drawn from 25 judges and citizen members. The Screening Panel screens applications received from eligible inmates. The screening standards are rigorous. Between 1983 and 1999, for instance, 38,000 applications from inmates were received. Only 19 percent (7,220) of these applications were approved and inmates were admitted into the NJISP.

The application process is more than merely rubber-stamping someone's application for inclusion. Applicants who are deemed eligible for the NJISP are interviewed by program staff. They must develop detailed case plans which set forth their goals and objectives for achieving program success. Participant goals include remaining free from illegal substances, strengthening relationships, maintaining steady employment, resolving legal problems, and paying required financial obligations. Applicants must also state that they will attend self-help sessions of Alcoholics Anonymous, take adult education courses, or receive family counseling, depending on individual offender circumstances. Applicants must indicate their willingness to abide by the NJISP conditions by signing their case plans.

Applicants must also obtain a sponsor within the community and they are encouraged to develop network teams. Community sponsors assist participants in complying with the NJISP conditions. They may provide participants with transportation to and from required meetings or to obtain employment. Community sponsors also sign an applicant's case plan and can offer suggestions about how to strengthen it. During the applicant investigation process, recommendations are solicited from the original sentencing judge, the prosecutor, previous probation and parole officers, victims, and the local police. This information is referred to as an assessment report and is forwarded to the ISP Screening Board for review. The Board deliberates in groups of three and decides whether to accept or reject particular applicants.

The Provisional Process.   An ISP Resentencing Panel receives recommendations from the ISP Screening Board and admits or denies program admission for each applicant. Accepted applicants are immediately released from prison or jail and placed into the NJISP. Those denied admission are returned to the New Jersey Department of Corrections.

The process is provisional, since all applicants must endure a 90-day trial period. The progress of each participant is tracked and reviewed by the Panel in 90-day intervals. Participants reappear before the Panel for formal resentencing into the program after they have been under supervision for 180 days. Prior to resentencing, participants are considered to be on conditional release from their prisons or jails.

The NJISP stresses that it does not overturn the original sentencing judge's decision; rather, the ISP Resentencing Panel merely changes the place of confinement. Further, the ISP Resentencing Panel does not declare that the original sentence was inappropriate. The Resentencing Panel stands by the original sentence imposed and deems it proper and justified. The NJISP is not a slap on the wrist. It is a demanding program requiring the participant to adhere to many stringent program requirements. Some applicants have been known to withdraw their applications once they learn that they will be under ISP supervision for 16 to 22 months. Finally, the NJISP is not a widening of the net of social control over offenders. Only those sentenced to serve incarcerative terms are considered eligible for program admission. Judges are prohibited from sentencing offenders directly into the NJISP.

Participants are advised that if they are admitted into the program, they can expect to be on the program for at least 16 months, and for a longer period if their original sentence was 5 or more years. If any program condition is violated while they are on the NJISP, then they may be expected to remain in the program for longer periods.

Program Requirements.   The NJISP requirements are among the most rigorous found in any state or federal ISP program. These are listed below.

Conditions of the Intensive Supervision Program (ISP)

You have been placed on the Intensive Supervision Program (ISP) by the ISP Resentencing Panel for a trial period of 90 days subject to your compliance with your case plan and the conditions listed below. If you are arrested for a new offense, the ISP Resentencing Panel may issue a warrant to detain you in custody, without bail, to await disposition on the new charges.

1. I will obey the laws of the United States, and the laws and ordinances of any jurisdiction in which I may be residing.
2. I am required to promptly notify my ISP Officer if I am arrested, questioned, or contacted by any law enforcement official whether summoned, indicted, or charged with any offense or violation.

3. I will report as directed to the Court or to my ISP Officer.

4. I will permit the ISP Officer to visit my home.

5. I will answer promptly, truthfully, and completely all inquiries made by my ISP Officer and must obtain approval prior to any residence change. If the change of address or residence is outside the region in which I am under supervision, I will request approval at least 30 days in advance.

6. I will participate in any medical and/or psychological examinations, tests, and/or counseling as directed.

7. I will support my dependents, meet my family responsibilities, and continue full time (35 hours or more per week), gainful employment. I will notify my ISP Officer prior to any change in my employment or if I become unemployed.

8. I will not leave the State of New Jersey without permission of my ISP Officer.

9. If I abscond from supervision (keep my whereabouts unknown to my ISP Officer), I may be charged with a new crime of Escape under 2C: 29-5, which may subject me to an additional sentence of up to five years consecutive to any ISP violation time.

10. I will not have in my possession any firearm or other dangerous weapon.

11. I will perform community service of at least 16 hours per month, unless modified by the ISP Resentencing Panel.

12. I will participate in ISP group activities as directed.

13. I will maintain a daily diary of my activities and a weekly budget while under supervision.

14. I will not borrow any money, loan any money, or make credit purchases without permission of my ISP Officer. I may be required to surrender any credit cards in my possession to my officer.

15. I will maintain weekly contact with my community sponsor and network team.

16. I will comply with the required curfew of 6 P.M. to 6 A.M. unless modified by my ISP Officer. If unemployed, I will abide by a 6 P.M. curfew unless modified by my ISP Officer.

17. I will submit at any time to a search of my person, places, or things under my immediate control by my ISP Officer.

18. I will abstain from all illegal drug use and consumption of alcohol (including nonalcoholic beer) and submit to drug and/or alcohol testing as directed. I also will not ingest any product containing poppy seeds. I will not use any medications, including over-the-counter medications, which contain alcohol.

19. I will notify my employer of my participation in ISP within 30 days after commencing employment.

20. I will not ingest any medication prescribed to someone else and will inform my ISP Officer of any medication prescribed to me by a physician or dentist.

21. I will file my Federal and State tax returns by the lawfully prescribed date and provide copies of the returns to my ISP Officer.

22. In accordance with State law, I cannot vote in any public election while under ISP supervision.

23. I will maintain telephone service at my approved residence. If the telephone service is discontinued, I will notify my ISP Officer immediately. I am not permitted to have a caller ID or call forwarding services on my telephone.

24. I cannot collect unemployment benefits, disability assistance, or welfare benefits without permission.

25. I cannot possess a pager (beeper) and/or cellular telephone unless approved by my ISP Officer.

26. I cannot visit inmates in county or state correctional facilities until I have completed 6 months of satisfactory ISP supervision and with the permission of the ISP Regional Supervisor.

27. I may not serve in the capacity of an informant for a law enforcement agency. If requested to do so, I must decline and inform my ISP Officer of the request.

28. I will not engage in any gambling including the purchase of lottery tickets. I will not enter a gambling establishment (casino) unless employed at such an establishment or given permission to visit such establishment by my ISP Officer.

29. I will turn in to my ISP Officer my driver's license (if driving privileges have been revoked), firearms ID card, and hunting license if any of them are in my possession.

30. I will comply with any and all directives from the ISP Resentencing Panel or my officer.

These are very rigorous conditions. All participants must agree to them in writing. A violation of any one or more of these conditions means that the Resentencing Panel will hear the charges and decide on the punishment. Program violations are cause for terminating one's involvement in the program and returning the offender to prison. The Resentencing Panel usually sits in parties of three and conducts hearings at least times per month. Hearings are held in various locations throughout New Jersey's 21 counties in an effort to acquaint judges and other judicial employees with the functions of the Resentencing Panel.

PO Responsibilities.   ISP officers spend about 80 percent of their time in direct field supervision. In 1998, for instance, officers conducted 556,202 participant contacts. Since 1984, POs have conducted almost 4 million contacts. Caseloads of POs are a maximum of 20 clients. Participants do not visit regional officers. Rather, POs visit participants at their work places, homes, and other places as deemed appropriate by the PO. Participants can reach their POs 24 hours a day. All POs are equipped with a message paging device which can be accessed through a toll-free 800 number. If any participant absconds from the program, the ISP arranges for and assists in the execution of arrest warrants. Violators will be tracked down by any and all means available to the State of New Jersey.

POs are unarmed. This is a concern for many POs involved in the NJISP. Strategies for working in unsafe areas have been devised. These include arranging meetings with community sponsors as escorts and the use of prearranged sites. All ISP officers and community development specialists are equipped with portable cellular telephones to assist in their monitoring and surveillance duties. ISP officers may search a participant's home, person, or vehicle without a warrant. Searches are conducted at random to determine whether participants are in possession of firearms or illegal contraband, or if they have any other prohibited items such as credit cards or cellular telephones or pagers.

Client Responsibilities. All ISP participants must maintain employment. They must be economically self-sufficient. During 1998 for instance, ISP participants had an average full-time income of $15,000. Participants are obligated to observe a curfew ranging from 6 P.M. to 6 A.M. These curfews may be changed with PO approval. Curfews are monitored through random visits, telephone calls, electronic surveillance, and by community sponsors, network team and family members. Participants can modify their curfews as they progress successfully through their programs. Participants must pay all court ordered financial obligations which may include restitution, child support, court mandated fines, drug penalties, Victim Crime Compensation Board fees, and other payments. Participants must perform at least 16 hours of community service each month. Projects may include maintenance work at hospitals, nursing homes, and geriatric institutes; cleaning municipal vehicles; picking up litter at parks and roadways; stuffing envelopes for nonprofit agencies; painting; carpentry; plumbing; tutoring; and clerical work for charitable organizations.

Clients must submit to urine monitoring to detect drug use. Alcohol ingestion is detected by using a Breathalyzer. The majority of participants have substance abuse problems. Participants are screened as often as three times a week. Positive tests are often confirmed by gas chromatography. Participants with positive tests are immediately confronted. Admission of drug use is considered to be a crucial element in the recovery process. Most participants admit to using drugs when confronted. ISP uses more than 100 outpatient and inpatient substance abuse, alcohol abuse, and psychological treatment providers. Educational seminars are held regularly for participants, and their attendance at these seminars is mandatory.

Sanctions are imposed for any program violation. The seriousness of the sanction depends upon the seriousness of the violation. The most commonly applied sanctions are increased curfew restrictions, additional community service hours, increased treatment requirements, home detention, and short-term incarceration.

The Successfulness of the NJISP. How does the NJISP measure the successfulness of its program? By March 1999, there were 7,154 participants, with about 44 percent of these (3,164) graduating. There were 2,774 (39 percent) participants returned to custody for violating program conditions. Of the program graduates, the recidivism figures have been most impressive. Using a 60-month followup of the NJISP graduates, only 7.5 percent had recidivated. This is a success rate of 92.5 percent. The cost of the NJISP is low compared with incarceration. In New Jersey, it costs $31,000 to house one offender in prison or jail for a year. The NJISP program costs for each participant per year were only $7,158.

A Profile of NJISP Clientele. In 1999 the active caseload of all NJISP clients was 1,133. Of these, 86 percent were male. The average sentence length for males was 51 months compared with 49 months for female offenders participating in the program. A majority of offenders were convicted for drug use and sales (63.7 percent for men and 73.1 percent for women). A majority of participants were never married. About 12 percent of all participants, both male and female, were married. The median educational level of all participants was 11

![gavel icon] **BOX 8.2**

Lisa Hutchinson Wallace
Assistant Professor of Justice, University of Alaska Fairbanks

Statistics:

B.S. (social and rehabilitative services), University of Southern Mississippi; M.S. (criminal justice with an emphasis in juvenile justice), University of Southern Mississippi; Ph.D. (urban and public affairs), University of New Orleans

Background:

I am an assistant professor in the Justice Department at the University of Alaska Fairbanks. After finishing my Ph.D. at the University of New Orleans, I moved to Fairbanks, Alaska, to teach at the university. Throughout my educational career, I have been employed in various positions within the juvenile and criminal justice systems.

Although I always knew that I wanted to work in the juvenile justice system, I never anticipated that I would be teaching in the university setting. During my studies and my practitioner experiences, however, my desire to teach juvenile justice became clearer. To excel in teaching, I felt it essential that I experience as many practitioner opportunities in the field as possible, which I did. I have worked in numerous aspects of the juvenile justice system. I have served as an advocate for abused and neglected children, both in paid and volunteer positions. I have worked in several delinquency prevention programs. I have been a juvenile probation officer, with primary duties including predispositional work. I have also worked on numerous grant-related projects that sought to increase the efficiency of various juvenile courts. I even served as a temporary correctional officer for a privately operated pretrial detention facility. To keep in touch with the juvenile justice system, I continue to work closely with several youth agencies on a volunteer basis.

Perhaps because of my educational pursuits or a natural curiosity, I have always been intrigued with the efficiency of our criminal and juvenile justice systems, as well as the motivations that propel changes in these systems. Naturally, this interest led to my focus on applied research. I have worked on several research projects that provided valuable baseline information on which citizens and officials could make sound decisions. I have conducted needs assessments for juveniles, court efficiency projects, as well as evaluations of various programs. The most interesting of my experiences in research was my tenure as the researcher coordinator for a nonprofit research agency. During the various research projects undertaken at this agency, I learned first-hand just how influential politics are in ultimately shaping the direction of our systems. That was a valuable lesson to be learned, for it taught me that practitioners must learn to adapt to the influence of politics while providing the best services possible for their clients.

Interesting Experiences:

My endeavors in the juvenile justice field have provided me with numerous exciting experiences. Perhaps the most interesting experience that I have had occurred while I was serving as a temporary correctional officer. Because of my educational pursuits, my colleagues at the juvenile court were convinced that I could not succeed as a practitioner. The test came within the first two days of my employment. I was trying to return a juvenile on administrative lockdown to the cell. The juvenile threatened me with bodily harm if she were returned to her cell. Realizing that I did not possess the physical strength necessary to win the battle, I used

(continued)

BOX 8.2 (Continued)

my wits. I began to talk calmly to the juvenile, asking her to tell me why she was angry and with whom she was angry. Rather quickly, the juvenile settled down and returned to her cell without incident. I learned a very valuable lesson that day: Always treat others with respect. Prior to that incident, I had been exposed to the belief that strength, rather than brains, is a more important employee characteristic for the correctional setting. Luckily, that belief was shattered after my experience. The juvenile later told me that I was one of the few people who had really taken the time to talk to her and treat her with respect. Since that experience, I have always tried to be as genuine and respectful as possible, no matter what the situation.

Insights Gained:

Working in the juvenile justice system can be both frustrating and rewarding. Every juvenile you meet is a unique individual. Remember their uniqueness and approach each juvenile as a new person and new case. Don't automatically assume the worst about a juvenile because of their behaviors or attitude. Often times, these juveniles have experienced many horrific events within their lifetimes. On the other hand, be firm in your response to delinquent behaviors. An effective practitioner in the delinquency field is one who identifies the needs of the juvenile, seeks to provide the appropriate services to meet these needs, helps the juvenile to recognize the inappropriateness of his or her behavior, as well as personal responsibility for such actions, all while treating the individual with respect.

Perhaps the saddest lesson I learned is that the link between child abuse and delinquency is all too real. Many of the children I came into contact with during my stint in the area of abuse and neglect became my clients when I was a probation officer. No matter what facet of the juvenile justice system you choose to work in, you will be faced with many horrendous accounts of abuse suffered by children. Be cognizant of this link. I truly believe that some kids rarely have a "fighting chance." Make sure that kids are given a fair chance to succeed. It is our jobs as juvenile justice practitioners to see that those children who want to succeed have the opportunity to do so.

Finally, prevention is an extremely important, but all too often forgotten, part of an appropriate response to juvenile delinquency. We can help children more by meeting their needs before they exhibit delinquent behavior, rather than trying to address their needs after they have committed a delinquent act. Whatever career path you choose, always remember that prevention is a valuable tool. Be supportive of prevention efforts.

Advice to Students:

The best advice I can give to students is to say that learning is a multifaceted process. Pay close attention to the vast theoretical knowledge you will gain throughout your educational career. Be sure, however, not to forget that practical knowledge is also an important part of your educational experience. Get as much practical experience as you can, either through internships, part-time employment, or volunteer work. In my opinion, an exceptional education is one that involves both the theoretical and practical worlds. Put forth your best efforts in both of these areas and you will succeed.

years. About 60 percent of all participants were high school graduates. A majority were employed (62 percent for men and 53 percent for women). About 38 percent of all male participants were first-offenders, while 49 percent of all female participants were first-offenders.

In New Jersey, at least, the public likes the NJISP. The media have given the NJISP very favorable coverage. There have been relatively few incidents involving victimizations through violent offending. One reason for this is that applicants are so rigorously screened before they are accepted into the program. ISP has had a very positive effect on most participants, by presenting educational seminars, offering courses in parenting skills, GED preparation, job searches and job application form assistance, and literacy courses.

The New Jersey Intensive Supervision Program is by no means the only program of its type in the United States. It has been widely copied in other jurisdictions. One common thread running through almost all of these ISP programs is the continuous monitoring and random checking of offenders (Marciniak, 2000; Maxwell and Gray, 2000). ISP means closer offender monitoring. This means that fewer clients will have a chance to use drugs or alcohol and avoid being detected through random checks. This constant monitoring seems to work in most ISP programs (Petersilia, 2001). Face-to-face contacts improve client compliance with program conditions. There is some variation among programs relating to client recidivism. Not all offenders are monitored as closely as they are in the New Jersey ISP. However, the two most important factors relating to program failure were drug/alcohol abuse and unemployment (New York State Division of Parole, 1998).

The Nevada Intensive Supervision Program

Nevada has established an intensive supervision program for both its probationers and parolees. The **Nevada Intensive Supervision Program (NISP)** program is one component of case management and a tool in assisting the Nevada Division of Parole and Probation in achieving its overall mission. It is also the ultimate level of supervision that the Nevada agency can provide for community safety and offender rehabilitation. The common elements of Nevada's ISP are as follows:

1. Frequent contacts with offenders
2. Smaller caseloads
3. A system of phases or levels
4. Curfews or electronic monitoring
5. Drug and alcohol testing
6. Graduated internal sanctions
7. Treatment and other interventions
8. Required employment
9. Employment seeking activities or schooling

All specialized caseloads are fielded to District IV (Las Vegas) which is the largest ISP unit within Nevada. These caseloads encompass residential confinement, mandatory parole release, offenders in need of true ISP monitoring, and the sex offender unit. These caseloads in 2001 totaled 1,044 offenders. The Nevada legislature authorized a 30:1 ratio for residential confinement and ISP offenders, and a 40:1 ratio for all others. The Division of Parole and Probation screens offenders for inclusion in its ISP program according to: (1) crimes of violence; (2) crimes involving drug trafficking or sales of controlled substances; (3) criminal activity of a sophisticated nature; (4) active gang affiliation; (5) sustained or chronic substance abuse history; (6) history of mental illness; and (7) court/board ordered. One or all of these criteria might function to deny admission to the ISP program for any particular offender.

The NISP encompasses two phases. The first phase consists of a 90-day period; during this time, the offender is placed either on court/board house arrest or curfew. The house arrest monitoring is provided by a contracted private company, who sets the fee for such service, and the offender is required to meet that financial obligation. Curfew can either be monitored by the appropriate officer or the offender may be referred to the private company offering that service (the offender is responsible for fee assessments when referred to the private company). During this initial 90-day period, the offender will be aggressively encouraged to enroll in and complete short-term goals such as outpatient substance abuse or alcohol counseling, employment counseling, and anger management.

The second phase of this program consists of either a 30- or 60-day period, during which time the offender is made ready to enter the general supervision population. During this time frame, the offender is taken off residential confinement or curfew and supervision requirements are greatly relaxed. If the offender relapses during this phase of supervision, then he or she is allowed one more opportunity to re-enter Phase I and try again to change his or her behavior to a positive vein, indicating that he or she can be managed in a general supervision population. Thus, the ISP was restructured with intent of providing an ultimate level of ISP and rehabilitation to promote long-term behavioral change that would eventually lead to enhanced public safety. If those efforts fail and result in a violation process, this Division could positively assure that there would be no other supervision strategies available to the offender.

The following are contract requirements for each phase or level of supervision:

Phase/Level I:

1 home contact

1 monthly report

2 field contacts or 2 surveillance contacts or 1 each

1 employment program/program verification

Special conditions as applicable

Phase/Level II:

1 home contact

1 monthly report

1 field contact or 1 surveillance

1 employment/program verification

Special conditions as applicable

Offenders on Residential Confinement:

2 home contacts

1 monthly report

1 residence verification

1 face-to-face contact

2 employment/program verifications

Special conditions as applicable

Surveillance of an offender may be considered to be a field contact with supervisory approval. All surveillance time shall be recorded in a surveillance log. The surveillance log is turned in to and maintained by the officer's immediate supervisor at the end of each month. At the beginning of 2001, the NISP unit worked a 7-day schedule, with a day and a swing shift. Caseloads were assigned according to geographic location. The team concept is utilized within this unit and generally the officers work with assigned partners when working the field. Most caseloads are integrated with both the residential confinement and NISP offenders and this was decided on because of two factors. First, the geographic location, and second, every officer cross-trains in all phases, therefore making it easier to have the same level of expertise throughout the 7-day period. The sex offender sub-unit presently has 10 officers, and at this time, their contact requirements are constantly changing. They generally work alone with the exception of a planned search/arrest. The program was implemented during the spring/summer of 2000. While success rates were not available at the time of this writing, to date (March 2001) 10 percent of all offenders were returned to either the court or parole board, which has resulted in a 3 percent revocation rate (Konopka, 2001:1–4).

OTHER PAROLE CONDITIONS

Parolees are subject to several different kinds of conditions while serving their parole terms. These conditions may be to attend Alcoholics Anonymous meetings, Narcotics Anonymous meetings, Gamblers Anonymous meetings, participate in individual or group counseling, take vocational/educational training, and seek and obtain continuous employment to support their dependents. Other conditions include (1) day reporting centers; (2) fines; (3) day fines; (4) community service orders; and (5) restitution.

Day Reporting Centers

For parolees, day treatment centers are operated primarily during daytime hours for the purpose of providing diverse services to offenders and their families. Day reporting centers are highly structured nonresidential programs utilizing supervision, sanctions, and services coordinated from a central focus. Offenders live at home and report to these centers regularly, and daily. As a part of community residential treatment centers, day treatment programs provide services according to offender needs (Illinois Department of Corrections, 2000). These services might include employment assistance, family counseling, and educational/vocational training. Day treatment centers can also be used for supervisory and/or monitoring purposes. Client behavior modification is a key goal of such centers. Limited supervisory functions can be performed by day treatment centers as well, such as employment verification and evidence of law-abiding conduct for probationers and parolees. These centers are also operated for the purpose of providing family counseling in **juvenile delinquency** cases through parent education and support groups (Brunet, 2002).

Fines

Fines and Criminal Statutes.   An integral part of sentencing in an increasing number of cases is the use of fines (Marion, 2002). The use of fines as sanctions can be traced to pre-industrialized and non-Western societies. Estimates suggest that over 14 million persons are arrested each year in the United States, and that a significant portion of these receive fines upon conviction. Ordinarily, state and federal criminal statutes provide for various incarcerative lengths upon conviction. Additionally, various fines are imposed as "and/or" conditions exercised at the discretion of sentencing judges. For instance, if law enforcement officers were to violate one's civil rights by the unlawful use of physical force or excessive force in making an arrest, they might be subject to penalties, including confinement in a state penitentiary up to 5 years and a fine of "not more than" $10,000. This means that if these law enforcement officers are convicted of violating one's civil rights, the judge can sentence them to prison for up to five years and impose a fine of $10,000. This would be within the judge's discretionary powers (Vigorita, 2002).

Types of Fines and Fine Collection Problems.   Different types of scenarios involving fines have been described. These include: (1) fines plus jail or prison terms; (2) fines plus probation; (3) fines plus suspended jail or prison terms; (4) fines or jail alternatives ($30 or 30 days); (5) fines alone, partially suspended; and (6) fines alone (Winterfield and Hillsman, 1993). The arguments for and against the use of fines as sanctions have also been clearly delineated. For instance, it has been claimed that (1) fines are logically suited for punishment because they are unambiguously punitive; (2) many offenders are poor and cannot afford fines; (3) because the poor cannot afford fines as easily as the rich, there is obvious discrimination in fine imposition; (4) someone else may pay the fine other than the offender; (5) often, fine payments are unenforceable because of offender absconding; (6) courts lack sufficient enforcement capability; and (7) fines may actually increase crime so that the poor can get enough money to pay previously imposed fines. The problems of fine collection are such that less than half of the fines imposed are ever collected in most U.S. courts. Billions of dollars are involved in fine nonpayment. In more than a few jurisdictions, fine payment rates at the time of conviction have only been 14 percent (McDonald, Greene, and Worzella, 1992:33).

Suspending Fines.   In many criminal cases, however, fines are suspended. This is because often, indigent or poor offenders cannot pay these fines or would have great difficulty paying them and supporting their families or fulfilling any of their other financial obligations. From our examination of probation and parole revocation, we know that one's probation or parole program cannot be revoked simply because of one's inability to pay program fees or fines. Thus, many judges do not impose fines because they will be uncollectible. Also, fines are not imposed in many cases because of certain jurisdictional precedents. In other instances, fines may be imposed but those obligated to pay fines will abscond. Even if those assessed fines do not abscond, the collection procedures in different jurisdictions are lax or unenforced (Illinois Department of Corrections, 2000).

Day Fines

Historically, the fine was not a prominent intermediate penalty in the United States because of deep skepticism among American criminal justice professionals. During the late 1970s and early 1980s, considerable effort was expended investigating alternative sentencing for offenders different from traditional indeterminate sentencing. Besides attempting to devise more equitable sentencing schemes through guidelines-based sentencing, determinate sentencing, and mandatory sentencing, offender accountability was heightened various ways (Turner and Greene, 1999). However, a key issue was how much should fines be in relation to an offender's ability to pay?

One solution is the use of **day fines,** an early European invention. Day fines are a two-step process whereby courts (1) use a unit scale or benchmark to sentence offenders to certain numbers of day-fine units (e.g., 15, 30, 120) according to **offense severity** and without regard to income; and (2) determine the value of each unit according to a percentage of the offender's daily income; total fine amounts are determined by multiplying this unit value by the number of units accompanying the offense (Winterfield and Hillsman, 1993:2). For instance, if Offender X were convicted of simple assault, this might have a unit value of 30. The offender may have a net daily income of $50. Suppose the percentage of net daily income to be assessed as a fine is 10 percent. This means that the offender's total fine would be $50 $\times$ 10% $\times$ 30 units (for simple assault), or $5 $\times$ 30 = $150. This $150 fine would be assessed an offender at the time of sentencing, and the method of fine payment would be determined as well. Fine payments may be in installments, usually over no longer than a 3-month period (McDonald, Greene, and Worzella, 1992:35–37).

The Staten Island Day Fine Experiment.   In August, 1988, judges in the New York City borough of Staten Island established a day-fine system similar to that developed earlier in Europe. This experiment was conducted because this jurisdiction and others like it in New York had considerable trouble collecting fines imposed when offenders were convicted of crimes. It was believed by Staten Island officials that day fines would actually increase the rate of fine payments, since day fines were determined in accordance with one's ability to pay. The project's planners had several goals in mind. These included:

1. A system of sentencing benchmarks proposing a specific number of day-fine units for each criminal offense.
2. A system for collecting necessary information about offenders concerning their ability to pay.
3. Policy guidelines and easy-to-use methods for establishing the value of each day-fine unit imposed for each offender.
4. Strategic improvements in the court's collection and enforcement mechanisms.
5. A microcomputer-based information system that automates and records collection and enforcement activities (McDonald, Green, and Worzella, 1992:19–22).

Establishing the amount of a day-fine unit involved determining one's net daily income expected as well as the number of one's dependents. Day-fine unit amounts would be scaled down according to increased numbers of dependents, for instance. Thus, every effort was made to distribute day fines equitably, according to one's ability to pay. This is in stark contrast with the idea of a fixed-fine system imposed on offenders, regardless of their earnings or numbers of dependents. The Staten Island experiment wanted to determine several things. First, were day fines higher or lower than fines previously assessed for similar offenses? Second, would the burden of calculating one's day fine amount deter fine collection? And third, would the new collection techniques used with day fines have any favorable impact on collection outcomes? The results were favorable. For instance, between April 1987 and March 1988, the total fine amounts imposed by the courts increased by 14 percent, while fines for average penal law offenses increased by 25 percent. Most important, collection rates under the new day-fine system rose to 85 percent. Capped collection amounts were those governed by statute. Thus, day-fine payments could not exceed statutory maximum fines for specific offenses, despite the fact that a day-fine amount may be generated in excess of this statutory maximum. An average of $440.83 was collected using uncapped day-fines compared with $205.66 collected under pre-day-fine traditional fine methods (Winterfield and Hillsman, 1993:3–5).

Winterfield and Hillsman (1993:5–6) say that the new collection techniques established by the Staten Island project has had the following advantages over traditional or more routine court procedures related to fine assessments and payment:

1. More extended terms for payment of the larger day fines
2. Fewer costly court appearances
3. Fewer warrants for nonappearance at postsentence hearings

Considered significant in the Staten Island experiments was the individualized nature of fine assessments and collection. Clearly, determining one's fine according to their ability to pay and arranging for installment payments of these fines is a more profitable way of court operation as well as a means of enhancing offender accountability. Similar experiments have been conducted in Milwaukee with consonant results.

Community Service Orders

Increasingly, conditions are imposed on parolees that provide for fines and some amount of community service. Community service sentencing is one of the best examples of the use of parole as a means of achieving offender accountability (Bickle et al., 2002). Under the **Victim and Witness Protection Act of 1982** (18 U.S.C. Sec. 3579-3580, 2004), community service orders were incorporated as an option in addition to incarceration at the federal level. One flaw of the Act was that it left unspecified when community service orders were to be imposed. Thus, judges could impose community service orders at the time of sentencing, or parole boards could make community service a provisional requirement for an inmate's early release. Victim advocates strongly urge that community service orders be an integral feature of the sentencing process. For instance, California has adopted community service orders as an integral part of their parole process (Stephens, 2001).

Community service means that parolees perform services for the state or community. The nature of community service to be performed is discretionary with the sentencing judge or paroling authority. In some jurisdictions, prisoners must perform a specified number of hours of community service such as lawn maintenance, plumbing and other similar repairs, or services that fit their particular skills. The philosophy underlying community service is more aligned with retribution than rehabilitation (Muiluvuori, 2001).

Forms of Community Service.   Community service is considered a punishment and is court-imposed. Many types of projects are undertaken by offenders as community service. Usually, these projects are supervised by POs or other officials, although reports are sometimes solicited from private individuals such as company managers or supervisors. A portion of offender earnings is allocated to victims as well as to the state or local public or private agencies overseeing the community services provided. In New Jersey, for example, community service orders include the following: assisting Community Food Banks throughout New Jersey with food drives; Adopt-a-Highway; the March of Dimes Walk-A-Thon; and assisting various Goodwill sites with sorting and cleaning donated items. Other community service projects include scraping, sanding, and digging; building renovations; maintenance of recreational areas and assistance in the operation of governmental facilities and nonprofit charitable events (Altschuler, 2001).

The Effectiveness of Community Service.   Serious questions are raised by authorities about the effectiveness of community service and restitution as sentencing options or parole program requirements. The fact that offenders are released into their communities for the purpose of performing community service raises a **public risk** issue for some people, although those offenders ordinarily selected for community service are low-risk and nonviolent. Other questions relate to the personal philosophies of judicial and correctional authorities, the offender eligibility and selection criteria used among jurisdictions, organizational arrangements, the nature of supervision over offenders performing community services, and how such services are evaluated. Community service is a just and fitting accompaniment to whatever sentence is imposed by judges or whatever conditions are established by paroling authorities when considering inmates for early release. The element of retribution is strong, and it is believed by some observers that offenders are better able to understand the significance of the harm they inflicted on others by their criminal acts (Bickle et al., 2002).

Restitution

An increasingly important feature of probation programs is restitution. Restitution is the practice of requiring offenders to compensate crime victims for damages offenders may have inflicted. Several models of restitution have been described. These include:

The Financial/Community Service Model.   The Financial/Community Service model stresses the offender's financial accountability and community service to pay for damages inflicted upon victims and to defray a portion of the expenses of court prosecutions. It is becoming more commonplace for probationers and divertees to be ordered to pay some restitution to victims and to perform some type of community service. Community service may involve cleanup activities in municipal parks, painting projects involving graffiti removal, cutting courthouse lawns, or any other constructive project that can benefit the community. These community service sentences are imposed by judges. Probation officers are largely responsible for overseeing the efforts of convicted offenders in fulfilling their community service obligations. These sentencing provisions are commonly called **community-service orders.**

Community-service orders are symbolic restitution, involving redress for victims, less severe sanctions for offenders, offender rehabilitation, reduction of demands on the criminal justice system, and a reduction of the need for vengeance in a society, or a combination of these factors. Community-service orders are found in many different countries and benefit the community directly. Further, where convicted offenders are indigent or unemployed, community service is a way of paying their fines and court costs. Donnelly (1980) summarizes some of the chief benefits of community service: (1) the community benefits because some form of restitution is paid; (2) offenders benefit because they are given an opportunity to rejoin their communities in law-abiding responsible roles; and (3) the courts benefit because sentencing alternatives are provided. Usually, between 50 and 200 hours of community service might be required for any particular convicted offender (Harris and Lo, 2002).

The Victim/Offender Mediation Model. The **victim/offender mediation model** is model focuses upon victim-offender reconciliation. Alternative dispute resolution is used as a mediating ground for resolving differences or disputes between victims and perpetrators. Usually, third-party arbiters, such as judges, lawyers, or public appointees, can meet with offenders and their victims and work out mutually satisfactory arrangements whereby victims can be compensated for their losses or injuries.

The Victim/Reparations Model. The **victim/reparations model** stresses that offenders should compensate their victims directly for their offenses. Many states have provisions that provide **reparations** or financial payments to victims under a Crime Victims Reparations Act. The Act establishes a state-financed program of reparations to persons who suffer personal injury and to dependents of persons killed as the result of certain criminal conduct. In many jurisdictions, a specially constituted board determines, independent of court adjudication, the existence of a crime, the damages caused, and other elements necessary for reparation. Reparations cover such economic losses as medical expenses, rehabilitative and occupational retraining expenses, loss of earnings, and the cost of actual substitute services. Restitution can heighten accountability and result in a reduction in recidivism among offenders. However, if restitution is not properly implemented by the court or carefully supervised, it serves little deterrent purpose (Altschuler, 2001; Bickle et al., 2002).

PAROLE BOARDS AND EARLY-RELEASE DECISION MAKING

Parole Boards, Sentencing Alternatives, and the Get-Tough Movement

By 1988, most states had changed their sentencing provisions. In many instances, these changes in sentencing provisions significantly limited the discretionary authority of parole boards to grant prisoners early release. By 2002 twelve states and the federal government had abolished parole in favor of determinate sentencing. Nevertheless, all states continue to use parole boards for those offenders sentenced under indeterminate sentencing and prior to parole's abolishment in specified jurisdictions (Camp and Camp, 2003).

Maine became the first state to abolish parole in 1976. The following states abolished parole in subsequent years: Minnesota (1982); Florida (1983); Washington and the Federal Bureau of Prisons (1984); Oregon (1989); Delaware (1990); Kansas (1993); Arizona and North Carolina (1994); Virginia (1995); Ohio (1996); and Wisconsin (1999) (Camp and Camp, 2003). By 1983, the Maine legislature enacted certain good-time provisions for the prison population. The primary reason given for abolishing parole in these jurisdictions was to remove early-release authority from parole boards which tended to exhibit discrimination and often used extralegal factors in the parole-granting process. Furthermore, concerned critics of the parole system believed that many offenders were being released too soon. That is, they weren't serving sufficient portions of their sentences. Thus, whenever parole boards released inmates short of serving their full sentences, these decisions inevitably drew criticism from those opposing parole. Ironically, since parole has been abolished in the states noted above, the amount of time actually served by state and federal inmates has decreased through the accumulation of good-time credits under substituted determinate and guidelines-based sentencing schemes. Thus, if critics worried about offenders being released too soon under their parole board systems, how must they feel now considering offenders are being released much earlier, unconditionally in fact, from their prison systems? Unfortunately, no sentencing scheme or reform has satisfied all critics (Steiner, 2002). The fact is that both violent and nonviolent offenders are being released daily from U.S. prisons, and many of those released are subject to little or no supervision or PO control (Travis et al., 2002).

The question of abolishing parole boards in any jurisdiction is a hotly contested issue and one not likely resolvable in the near future. Whenever persons currently on parole commit new offenses, angry community residents want to know why they were released short of serving their full terms in the first place. It is acknowledged that community corrections programs can greatly enhance a parolee's success chances by providing valuable employment assistance, food, clothing, counseling, and a host of other services. If parolees are released to some type of intensive parole supervision (ISP) program within their communities, it is not always the case that the ISP program will be beneficial to certain clients. Petersilia (2001) suggests that if jurisdictions are primarily interested in providing flexibility in sentencing decisions by imposing ISP that more closely fits the crimes of offenders, then ISP will likely be fruitful. But if jurisdictions are mainly concerned with reducing recidivism and system costs, then ISP programs, as they are currently structured, will focus more on surveillance as opposed to treatment, and thus they will have a greater failure rate, where failure is defined as greater parolee-client recidivism.

Parole Board Composition and Diversity

There is considerable diversity among parole boards in the United States. Most parole board members, whether full- or part-time, are governor-appointed. There are no special qualifications for parole board membership in most jurisdictions. Some parole board members might be former correctional officers or prison superintendents, while others may be retired judges, school teachers, or university professors.

Compared with other jurisdictions, Massachusetts probably has the most stringent criteria for parole board membership. Members of the Massachusetts Parole Board must possess a bachelor's degree and at five or more years of experience in corrections, law enforcement, social work, or other related field. One parole board member must be an attorney, while another must be a physician. States such as Texas, Oregon, and North Dakota do not require their parole board members to possess special qualifications. Since governors make parole board appointments in most jurisdictions, membership on these boards is largely political (Proctor, 1999).

Subtleties in Parole Name-Changing: Politically Correct and Client-Friendly Labels. In many jurisdictions, parole is a bad word. Simply using the word, parole, draws much criticism. But parole is indispensable. Without it, we would have to construct at least four, perhaps five times as many prisons and jails than presently exist, in order to accommodate all of those not granted this bad word. One way of living with this bad word without using it is to use a good word instead. This is like changing the name of insane asylum to mental hospital to the institute for the psychologically impaired. The diversity of labels applied to parole boards is evident in Table 8.1. Table 8.1 shows various state parole board labels for 2001.

TABLE 8.1

Parole Boards for Federal and State Jurisdictions, 2001

State	2001 Parole Board Name
Alabama	Board of Pardons and Paroles (3 full-time members; governor-appointed)
Alaska	Board of Parole (5 part-time members; governor-appointed)
Arizona	Board of Executive Clemency (5 full-time members; governor-appointed)
Arkansas	Post-Prison Transfer Board (7 members, 3 full-time, 4 part-time; independent)
California	Board of Prison Terms (7 full-time members; governor-appointed)
Colorado	Board of Parole (7 full-time members; governor-appointed)
Connecticut	Board of Parole (12 part-time members, chairman full-time; governor-appointed)
Delaware	Board of Parole (1 full-time, 4 part-time members; governor-appointed)
District of Columbia	U.S. Parole Commission (7 full-time members; appointed by U.S. Attorney General)
Florida	Parole Commission (3 full-time members; governor-appointed)
Georgia	Board of Pardons and Paroles (5 full-time members; autonomous)
Hawaii	Paroling Authority (3 full-time, 2 part-time, 1 full-time chairman; governor-appointed)
Idaho	Commission of Pardons and Parole (5 part-time members; appointed by Board of Corrections)
Illinois	Prisoner Review Board (12 full-time members; governor-appointed)
Indiana	Parole Board (5 full-time members; governor-appointed)
Iowa	Board of Parole (5 full-time members; governor-appointed)
Kansas	Parole Board (4 full-time members; governor-appointed)
Kentucky	Parole Board (8 full-time members; governor-appointed)
Louisiana	Board of Parole (7 full-time members; governor-appointed)
Maine	Parole Board (5 part-time members; governor-appointed; hears only cases pre-April 1976)
Maryland	Parole Commission (8 full-time members; appointed by Secretary of Public Safety and Correctional Services)

(continued)

TABLE 8.1 (CONTINUED)

State	2001 Parole Board Name
Massachusetts	Parole Board (6 full-time members; governor-appointed)
Michigan	Parole Board (10 full-time unclassified employees; appointed by Director of the Department of Corrections)
Minnesota	Board of Pardons (3 full-time members: governor, chief justice, attorney general) Hearings and Release Unit (8 full-time officers set terms of supervised release for adults and parole for juveniles)
Mississippi	Parole Board (5 full-time members; governor-appointed)
Missouri	Board of Probation and Parole (6 full-time members; governor-appointed)
Montana	Board of Pardons (3 part-time and 2 auxiliary members; governor-appointed)
Nebraska	Board of Parole (5 full-time members; governor-appointed)
Nevada	Board of Parole Commissioners (7 full-time members; governor-appointed)
New Hampshire	Board of Parole (7 part-time members; governor-appointed)
New Jersey	Parole Board (9 full-time members; governor-appointed)
New Mexico	Adult Parole Board (4 full-time members; governor-appointed)
New York	Board of Parole (19 full-time members; governor-appointed)
North Carolina	Post-Release Supervision and Parole Commission (5 full-time commissioners; governor-appointed)
North Dakota	Parole Board (3 part-time members; governor-appointed)
Ohio	Adult Parole Authority (12 full-time members; 3 chief hearing officers; 19 hearing officers; 24 parole board parole officers; appointed by Director of Department)
Oklahoma	Pardon and Parole Board (5 part-time, 3 appointed by governor, 1 by Court of Criminal Appeals, and 1 by Supreme Court)
Oregon	Board of Parole and Post-Prison Supervision (3 full-time members; governor-appointed)
Pennsylvania	Board of Probation and Parole (5 full-time members; governor-appointed)
Rhode Island	Parole Board (6 part-time members; governor-appointed)
South Carolina	Board of Paroles and Pardons (7 part-time members; governor-appointed)
South Dakota	Board of Pardons and Paroles (7 part-time members; independent and responsible to Department of Corrections)
Tennessee	Board of Paroles (7 full-time members; governor-appointed)
Texas	Board of Pardons and Paroles (18 full-time members; convene in 3-member panels, independent)
Utah	Board of Pardons and Parole (5 full-time members; governor-appointed)
Vermont	Board of Parole (5 part-time members; governor-appointed)
Virginia	Parole Board (5 full-time members; governor-appointed)
Washington	Indeterminate Sentence Review Board (3 part-time members, governor-appointed; determines parole for offenders sentenced prior to July 1984)
West Virginia	Parole Board (5 full-time members; governor-appointed)
Wisconsin	Parole Commission (5 full-time members; governor-appointed)
Wyoming	Board of Parole (7 full-time members; governor-appointed)
Federal	U.S. Parole Commission (7 full-time members; appointed by U.S. Attorney General)

Sources: Compiled by author from the American Correctional Association, *Probation and Parole Directory 2001–2003.* Lanham, MD: American Correctional Association, 2001.

Arkansas uses the name, "Post-Prison Transfer Board." Illinois uses "Prisoner Review Board." Maryland uses "Parole Commission." North Carolina uses "Post-Release Supervision and Parole Commission." Ohio uses "Adult Parole Authority." These creative names do not eliminate the fact that these are all parole boards. When these various bodies convene and hear inmate requests for early release, these release requests are either granted or denied. Regardless of the labels these jurisdictions choose to apply, these are parole functions being performed (Travis et al., 2002).

Functions of Parole Boards

Each parole board in the United States has different functions. No two parole boards are identical. However, a synthesis of functions is possible by comparing the goals and philosophical statements of various boards. A result of this synthesis includes the following major functions of parole boards:

1. To evaluate prison inmates who are eligible for parole and act on their application to approve or deny parole.
2. To convene to determine whether a parolee's parole should be revoked on the basis of alleged parole violations.
3. To evaluate juveniles to determine their eligibility for release from detention.
4. To grant pardons or a **commutation** of sentences to prisoners, where mitigating circumstances or new information is presented which was not considered at trial.
5. To make provisions for the supervision of adult offenders placed on parole; to establish supervisory agencies and select parole officers to monitor offender behavior.
6. To provide investigative and supervisory services to smaller jurisdictions within the state.
7. To grant reprieves in death sentence cases and to commute death penalties.
8. To restore full civil and political rights to parolees and others on **conditional release** including probationers.
9. To review disparate sentences and make recommendations to the governor for clemency.
10. To review the pardons and executive clemency decisions made by the governor (American Correctional Association, 2001).

Most parole boards make parole decisions exclusively. In a limited number of jurisdictions, these additional functions are performed, either according to statute or at the pleasure of the governor. In a limited number of jurisdictions, the paroling authority is vested in agencies independent of the governor.

Parole Board Standards.   Parole boards may evolve their own standards, subject to legislative approval. For instance, the Connecticut Parole Board has several standards that govern each early-release decision. These standards include:

1. The nature and circumstances of inmate offenses and their current attitudes toward them.
2. The inmate's prior record and parole adjustment if paroled previously.

3. Inmate's attitude toward family members, the victim, and authority in general.

4. The institutional adjustment of inmates, including their participation in vocational/educational programs while incarcerated.

5. Inmate's employment history and work skills.

6. Inmate's physical, mental, and emotional condition as determined from interviews and other diagnostic information available.

7. Inmate's insight into the causes of his/her own criminal behavior in the past.

8. Inmate's personal efforts to find solutions to personal problems such as alcoholism, drug dependency, and need for educational training or developing special skills.

9. The adequacy of the inmate's parole plan, including planned place of residence, social acquaintances, and employment program (Connecticut Board of Parole, 2001).

Parole boards in other jurisdictions have evolved elaborate operational rules for conducting their business. The Delaware Board of Parole, for example, has evolved a detailed set of rules and procedures for deciding individual cases of prospective parole-eligible offenders as well as for revoking the parole programs of those who have already been granted parole.

Parole Board Decision Making and Inmate Control

A major factor influencing parole board decision making is prison overcrowding. It is exerting a tremendous impact on how corrections professionals do their jobs. Dramatic increases in parole supervision have been observed, and the number of parole release and revocation hearings has grown markedly over the years (Pastore and Maguire, 2003). The aims of parole boards are similar to those of sentencing: treatment, incapacitation, deterrence, and deserts. However, parole boards appear to receive more criticism from the public about the decisions they make compared with earlier similar judicial decisions. The significant question for parole boards is *when* to release inmates, rather than whether to release them. Some states have attempted to adopt parole guidelines as a means of objectifying early-release decision making. However, parole boards in these jurisdictions have been hesitant, if not resistant, to adopting objective parole guidelines. One reason is that parole boards fear losing a certain amount of control over inmate releases. Also, parole boards do not know for sure which variables are most crucial in making these early-release decisions for particular parole-eligible inmates. The use of risk-screening instruments for determining which offenders should be paroled have exhibited results that are unimpressive (Zilkowsky et al., 2001).

Cases That Parole Boards Must Review. A majority of parole board decisions, however, involve property offenders, although persons convicted of murder, robbery, assault, rape, and other violent crimes face parole boards regularly as well. Examples include Sirhan Sirhan, convicted killer of Robert Kennedy; Charles Manson, Patricia Krenwinkle, and Leslie Van Houten, convicted murderers of several persons, including heiress Abigail Folger and actress Sharon Tate; James Richardson, who murdered his seven children by using a poison insecticide in Arcadia, Florida; and confessed serial killer Joel Rifkin, who murdered at least 13 prostitutes on Long Island and in upstate New York between 1990 and 1993.

Parole boards hear bizarre stories from various parole-eligible inmates. Not all parole-eligible inmates are celebrities. Some have achieved no notoriety at all. In some cases, the interval between the commission of a crime and one's conviction for it may span several decades. In November, 1990, for instance, Francis Malinosky, 45, entered into a plea agreement with city prosecutors about a murder committed eleven years earlier. Judith Leo-Coneys, a special education schoolteacher in Burlington, Vermont, was in love with the assistant director of special education, Francis Malinosky. Leo-Coneys, 32, decided to break off her romance with Malinosky. She disappeared shortly after going to Malinosky's home on November 5, 1979 to retrieve her personal belongings. Although Malinosky was a prime suspect, there was insufficient evidence to arrest or indict him for her murder, which was then unknown. As the investigation into Leo-Coneys's disappearance accelerated, Malinosky left Vermont in December 1979 and traveled to other cities, using assumed names and false identification. He was arrested in Los Angeles in April 1990. He agreed to confess to the murder of Leo-Coneys and show police where he had buried her body, provided that they charged him only with voluntary manslaughter rather than first-degree murder. He effectively avoided the death penalty. He led officers to her badly decomposed corpse in a shallow grave off of a logging road in Cabot, Vermont. His sentence: a 10- to 15-year term, with all but 5 years suspended. Malinosky would eventually become eligible for parole in 1993, but Vermont would have to release him unconditionally in 1995 anyway. Malinosky was subsequently freed unconditionally at the expiration of his sentence (adapted from Associated Press, Nov. 10, 1999:B2).

Cases That Parole Boards Do Not Have to Review. Sometimes, parole boards don't have to make difficult early-release decisions. They narrowly missed having to make a decision in the case of Dalton Prejean, however. Dalton Prejean was only 17 when he murdered Louisiana state trooper Donald Cleveland in 1977. He was convicted for shooting Cleveland, who had stopped Prejean and his brother for a routine traffic violation. Prejean fired two shots through Cleveland's head, killing him outright. Three years earlier when Prejean was only 14, he shot and killed a cab driver during an aborted robbery attempt. Subsequently, he was sentenced to the death penalty for the state trooper murder. After exhausting almost every appeal, his execution in the electric chair was scheduled for mid-May 1990.

Amnesty International and other capital punishment opponents appealed to the Governor of Louisiana, Buddy Roemer, to commute his sentence to life through executive clemency. Prejean was black, convicted by an all-white jury, suffered from partial brain damage, claimed he was remorseful, and had a history of abuse as a child. But Candy Cleveland, the widow of the murdered state trooper, made a judgment of her own: "There is always the possibility of good time, good behavior. . . . who knows, in 20 or 30 years, Prejean could be back on the street [to kill again]" (Shapiro, 1990:23). Governor Roemer denied Prejean's request for clemency and Prejean was electrocuted on schedule at Angola Prison. If Prejean's death sentence had been commuted to life-without-parole, it is possible that Candy Cleveland's prediction would have come true.

When offenders become eligible for parole, this does not mean parole will automatically be granted by the parole board. Parole boards have considerable discretionary power, and in many jurisdictions, they have absolute discretion over an inmate's early release potential. In fact, when federal courts have been petitioned to intervene and challenge parole board actions, the decisions of parole boards have prevailed (*Tarlton v. Clark,* 1971). It is helpful to review briefly some of the more important factors influencing parole board decision making. In deciding whether to grant parole for given inmates, the following factors are considered:

1. The commission of serious disciplinary infractions while confined.
2. The nature and pattern of previous convictions.
3. The adjustment to previous probation, parole, and/or incarceration.
4. The facts and circumstances of the offense.
5. The aggravating and mitigating factors surrounding the offense.
6. Participation in institutional programs that might have led to the improvement of problems diagnosed at admission or during incarceration.
7. Documented changes in attitude toward self or others.
8. Documentation of personal goals and strengths or motivation for law-abiding behavior.
9. Parole plans.
10. Inmate statements suggesting the likelihood that the inmate will not commit future offenses.
11. Court statements about the reasons for the sentence.

Developing and Implementing Objective Parole Criteria

Objective parole criteria have been compared with determinate sentencing policies, while traditional parole criteria have been equated with indeterminate sentencing systems. Among the advantages of objective parole criteria are: (1) inmates know their presumptive release dates within several months of their incarceration; (2) the paroling authority is bound or obligated to meet the presumptive release date; (3) the paroling authority uses scores consisting of an inmate's criminal history and offense severity to determine time ranges for parole release; and (4) the paroling authority uses a composite group score representing criminal histories of similar offenders to predict parole success (Petersilia, 2001).

Ironically, these objective parole criteria function to restrict the discretionary power and flexibility of parole boards. Therefore, while fairness to offenders and parole board accountability are increased by making the parole release decision-making process more explicit and consistent, there are some undesirable, unanticipated consequences. For example, the Florida Parole Commission implemented new objective parole criteria in 1980 (Camp and Camp, 2003). Prior to 1980, adult inmates of Florida's prisons had filed an average of 400 civil lawsuits annually. After the objective criteria went into effect, the number of lawsuits increased to more than 1,800 per year. The Florida Parole Commission's legal department had to increase its staff of attorneys from two to seven. Florida inmate lawsuits involved four primary issues directly related to the new objective parole criteria. First, inmates alleged that objective scoring system errors led to unfavorable classifications and unjustifiably longer incarceration terms. Second, inmates claimed they originally had been placed in the wrong level of offense severity, often stemming from an erroneous interpretation of their plea agreements. Third, the inmates claimed parole board members inconsistently extended or shortened their incarceration length by either considering or failing to consider certain aggravating circumstances such as using a weapon during the commission of the crime or causing serious injury to victims. The fourth issue alleged parole board failure to consider mitigating circumstances that would lessen the length of incarceration. All of these issues seemingly could be remedied by close monitoring of all parole board decision making and a demand for fairness and consistency in the application of objective parole criteria (Travis et al., 2002). Florida is not alone in facing costly inmate litigation and lawsuits. Other jurisdictions have been targeted by inmates who seek relief concerning their earned good-time credits, prison classification, and parole eligibility (*Corrections Compendium,* 2003:8).

Interest in devising consistent and objective early release criteria is probably as old as parole itself. Most of the popular and more scientific methods for devising predictive criteria have been developed since the late 1960s, however. In 1972, the United States Parole Commission started to use an actuarial device in predicting parole success of federal prisoners. By the early 1980s, every state had either devised a system or was using one originated by another jurisdiction whereby parole decision making could be objectified (Hoffman, 1994).

Corrections observers currently contend that the technology exists that can classify offenders accurately on the basis of their potential risk to public safety, social service, educational and vocational needs, and individual behavioral profiles. However, these observers also charge that many paroling bodies have not as yet fully exploited this technology in a cooperative and systematic manner (Petersilia, 2001). At the same time, other observers caution that the current state-of-the-art in statistical risk prediction is such that many developed models are unstable when applied to various prisoner populations from one state to the next. Furthermore, insufficient validation of prediction instruments has occurred. When a parole risk-assessment device was developed by Wisconsin officials for parole board decision making, for example, the device became popularly applied in several other states, especially after being recognized as a useful instrument by the National Institute of Corrections. However, the Wisconsin instrument appeared to lack validity when applied to a sample of New York parolees (U.S. Sentencing Commission, 2003). This strongly suggests the need to devise measures that are applicable for selected inmate populations on a state-by-state basis. For example, the Ohio Parole Board uses the following criteria as guidelines:

1. Current offense and details of the crime
2. Prior record: felonies-misdemeanors-juvenile
3. Supervision experiences: parole-furlough-probation
4. Institution adjustment: job assignment-work evaluation-rule infractions
5. Substance abuse program participation
6. Vocational or academic training
7. Personality evaluation: I.Q.-highest grade completed
8. Psychological reports
9. Psychiatric reports
10. Personal history factors: marital status-employment history-work skills-special problems

11. Parole plan: living arrangements-employment plans
12. Community attitude: prosecutor's recommendation-judge's recommendation-police or sheriff's recommendation-victim's statement
13. Detainers
14. Type and number of prior hearings
15. Results of prehearing conference with Case Manager or Unit Manager (Ohio Department of Correction and Rehabilitation, 2001).

These criteria are only guidelines, as noted by the Ohio Adult Parole Authority. Therefore, there may be departures which are based on the degree of aggravation or mitigation accompanying any eligible inmate's early-release request. It is Ohio's experience that using these criteria in conjunction with several other measures will increase its Adult Parole Authority effectiveness to about 75 percent. In short, Ohio authorities believe that 75 percent of their early-release decision making with these guidelines will result in successful decision making. Viewed another way, Ohio authorities expect no more than a 25 percent degree of recidivism among those paroled. Ohio bases their guidelines system on five major components. These components include:

1. Risk Instrument: The risk instrument is critical to the guidelines system. It looks at several factors dealing with an inmate's prior criminal history including the number of probations, paroles, and revocations. Age at first felony conviction and substance abuse history are also related to risk assessed points. The risk level totals equal 1, 2, or 3. The higher the number, the higher the risk.

2. Offense Score: Included in the guideline system are several offenses designated as "Endangering Offenses." If an inmate has ever been convicted of an Endangering Offense, either a juvenile or adult, one point is assessed towards the total score.

3. Institutional Score: The Parole Board will make a determination of the inmate's institutional adjustment at the time of the hearing. If the inmate is now serving or has recently served time in Disciplinary Control, Local Control, or Administrative Control, one (1) point will be assessed towards the total score.

4. Aggregate Score: The sum total of the Risk Score, the Offense Score, and the Institution Score equals the Aggregate Score.

5. Matrix: The Matrix is a grid containing twenty-four (24) cell divisions. Each cell contains the guidelines procedure into which an inmate is placed and a continuance range if the decision is not to release. The horizontal axis of the grid is the "Aggregate Score" 1–5. The vertical axis is the felony level reflecting the inmate's sentence. Sentences range from fourth degree to life (Ohio Department of Correction and Rehabilitation, 2001).

Each state has devised independent criteria governing early-release decision making for its parole board. All of these criteria are related to a degree, although there are significant variations. For example, Massachusetts has devised a parole risk instrument. For instance, the Massachusetts Parole Board uses a Release Risk Classification Instrument consisting of (1) number of returns to higher custody since Controlling Effective Date of Commitment; (2) custody standing prior to the Controlling Effective Date of Commitment; (3) total number of parole revocations; (4) number of adult convictions for property offenses; (5) number of charges for a person offense as a juvenile; (6) age at release hearing; and (7) evidence of heroin, opiate, or crack cocaine use. Both the number of returns to higher custody and age have maximum scores of "6" for four or more returns to higher custody and being 23 years of age or younger. One's custody standing and evidence of drug use each contribute 2 points, while the other factors are weighted by 1 point each. A high score of 19 points is possible. Such a person might be a 22-year-old cocaine addict who has prior offenses of burglary as an adult and robbery as a juvenile, who has been returned to a higher custody level on four previous occasions, has one previous parole revocation, and was incarcerated prior to the Controlling Effective Date. A three-part scale is used: 0–4 = low risk, 5–10 = moderate risk, and 11+ = high risk.

Utah uses the following factors to determine one's parole eligibility: (1) age at first arrest; (2) prior juvenile record; (3) prior adult arrests; (4) correctional supervision history; (5) supervision risk; (6) percentage of time employed in last 12 months, prior to incarceration; (7) alcohol usage problems; (8) drug usage problems; (9) attitude (motivation to change, willing to accept responsibility); (10) address changes during last 12 months (prior to incarceration); (11) family support; and (12) conviction or juvenile adjudication for assaultive offense in last five years.

Age, prior record, and drug/alcohol dependencies are obviously considered significant risk factors, at least for these instruments developed in these particular jurisdictions. In fact, these are critical components of most scales examined. Many jurisdictions believe that one's employment history and attitude (measured different ways) are also crucial to good parole decision making. The rationale for including these different components is grounded in considerable empirical research. We have already seen that many studies have focused upon recidivism and the characteristics of recidivists. Most of these studies have provided us with the bases for making actuarial predictions for various offender aggregates. Thus, younger offenders have higher recidivism rates than older offenders (Petersilia, 2001; Wilson and Petersilia, 2002). The age at which the onset of criminal behavior occurs is an important predictor. The earlier the onset of criminal conduct, the more likely recidivism will occur.

GRANTING OR DENYING PAROLE

Parole boards of all states using parole as an early-release mechanism always consider one's prior institutional behavior, the seriousness of the conviction offense, one's parole plan, the demeanor of the parole-eligible offender, and a host of other factors in making their decisions. Each case is different and requires differential consideration of various factors that may or may not influence one's successfulness on parole if that is the parole board's decision. Below are two examples taken from actual closed parole files from the Texas Department of Criminal Justice illustrating a parole denial in one instance and granting the offender's parole request in the other. The names of the inmates and other parties have been changed, as well as the dates and other specific identifying information for purposes of confidentiality.

Successful Parole Request
TEXAS DEPARTMENT OF CRIMINAL JUSTICE

INSTITUTIONAL DIVISION PAROLE CASE SUMMARY

UNIT: Ferguson   **PMA ( )**   **PPT ( )**   **PIA ( )**   **"3g"(N)**

NAME: OWENBY, Richard Allen   **TDC:** 68491936   **DATE:** 12-3-03   **CODE:** 12/00

MINIMUM EXPIRATION DATE: 1-13-05   **MAXIMUM EXPIRATION DATE:** 7-12-08

CALENDAR TIME SERVED: 10 YRS 8 MOS   **ON:** 20 YEARS   **DOCKET:** 5-04

PROPOSED RELEASE PLAN: **DISTRIBUTION:**   Central Office
(1) Grandmother and Sister: Region I
Matilda Cummings & Tanisha Jones,   Dallas District
4159 1st Avenue,   Huntsville IPO
Dallas, Dallas County, Texas 75210.
Telephone number: (214) 555-3111,
Sister: (214) 555-8645.
(2) None.

HALFWAY HOUSES: Dallas, Forth Worth, or Waco, Texas.

JOB/SKILLS: Will seek employment as a cook. Claims prior experience.

OTHER/COMMENTS: None.

RESTITUTION: None.

REPORTING INSTRUCTIONS: **IN PERSON:**   **TELEPHONE:**   **LETTER:**

DPO: **DISTRICT:**   **COUNTY:**   **APPROVED:**

COMMITMENT DATA INFORMATION

COUNTY	CAUSE #	OFFENSE:	SENTENCE:	DATE:
Dallas	F93-415-IU	AGG ROBBERY W/ DEADLY WPN (5-10-92)	20 YEARS	8-28-93

TOTAL SENTENCE: 20 YEARS   **SENTENCE BEGIN DATE:** 7-15-93

AGE: 31 (12-13-72)   **RACE:** Black   **SEX:** M   **HEIGHT:** 6'2"   **WEIGHT:** 210
EDUCATION: GED

DETAINERS: None.

PAROLE SUBJECT TO APPROVED RELEASE PLAN

This parole approval is not effective or final until a formal parole agreement is entered into and signed by the inmate and the State of Texas acting through the Board of Pardons and Paroles. The approval may be withdrawn by the Board or the Governor at any time prior to the acceptance and execution of the formal parole agreement.

PAROLE PANEL ACTION:

_____   _____
BOARD MEMBER'S INITIALS   **DATE**

PAROLE IS HEREBY ADOPTED AND APPROVED UPON ISSUANCE OF PAROLE CERTIFICATE AND EXECUTION OF PAROLE AGREEMENT.

CRIMINAL HISTORY: **TP:** 0;   **OP:** 0;   **TR:** 0;   **OR:** 0.

JUVENILE: None.

ADULT PROBATIONS: None.

ADULT INCARCERATIONS: None.

OTHER ARRESTS:
Attempt to Commit Capital Murder on a Police Officer (1), dismissed (1).

INSTANT OFFENSE SUMMARY:

Aggravated Robbery With A Deadly Weapon: On 5-10-92, in the daytime in Dallas, Texas the subject and Michael Wilson (Life sentence, TDC-ID, Coffield Unit) were allegedly walking down a bike trail in a city park. A statement from the victim states that Wilson pulled a knife and allegedly threatened the victim. The victim states that they became involved in a fight and Wilson cut the victim on the wrist and on the chin. The victim allegedly also pulled a knife but claims that he did not use the weapon. However, the subject states that he and codefendant were accused of allegedly hiding in bushes and then jumping out at the victim who was riding the bicycle and demanded his bicycle. According to the victim, he refused to give up is bicycle and Wilson became infuriated and tried to stab the victim. Wilson allegedly cut the victim's throat. When witnesses came on the scene, the subject and codefendant fled on foot. They then apparently threw the knives used in the offense in some bushes and officers recovered both knives, one of which had fresh blood on it. The subject states that he and the codefendant were arrested later that day hiding in some business near the scene. According to the subject, the victim was not injured that severely, however he did require treatment at an emergency room. The subject states that he was released on bond for approximately three weeks and claims he was never arrested during this time. Rationale of Present Offense: "I didn't know it was happening."

Substance Abuse History:

Drugs: From the age of 15 until this incarceration, the subject admits to smoking approximately two marijuana cigarettes every other day. He denies the use of any other narcotics. He denies the sale of narcotics. He reports no drug treatment. He claims he was not under the influence of any drugs at the time of the Present Offense.

Alcohol: The subject denies the use of alcohol.

Physical/Mental: None.

Social History:

The subject claims he completed the tenth grade in public school. His longest employment was for two years as a barbeque cook for his uncle's restaurant on weekends. He attended public school during the week. During the last two years in society, he was employed in this capacity and was employed in this capacity at the time of the Present Offense. He reports no military history.

Institutional Adjustment:

The subject is an SAT III status assigned as a Dryer Operator in the laundry. He presently does not participate in any self-improvement programs. The subject completed his GED certificate from Adams School District on 4-90 (verified). He has had the following disciplinary cases: Failure to Complete Work (1); Refusing to Obey an Order (1); Possession of Contraband (2); Trafficking and Trading (1); and Refusing to Work (2), all of which were minor cases and he has lost no good time. He has had no furlough.

Impression Section:

Mr. Owenby is a 31-year-old first-offender incarcerated for Aggravated Robbery with a Deadly Weapon sentenced to 20 years. Mr. Owenby initially was sentenced to 45 years; however, his case was overturned and the sentence was reduced from 45 years to 20. He reports no juvenile criminal history. He does report one other arrest for Capital Murder on a Police Officer; however, he claims this case was dismissed. Mr. Owenby admits to being involved in the Present Offense; however, he claims he was basically a bystander observing a fight. He claims that he was not involved in any robbery and there was no intention of robbing the victim. He claims that the codefendant and the victim just got into a fight. Mr. Owenby had a good attitude and cooperated in this interview. Positive factors affecting Mr. Owenby's release would be his limited criminal history, he completed his GED certificate, and he plans to reside with his grandmother and sister while returning to employment as a cook for his uncle's restaurant. Negative factors affecting Mr. Owenby's release would be the nature and seriousness of the present offense. In addition, he does not report any serious substance abuse history. Mr. Owenby has been incarcerated since 1993. It appears likely that he may encounter adjustment problems upon release due to his rather long incarceration. It would appear that a pre-parole transfer to a halfway house would benefit Mr. Owenby's adjustment upon release. However, his present aggravated offense excludes him from this program. Perhaps he could still be considered for PPT due to the fact that he has no history of other type of assaultive convictions and the fact that he was limitedly involved in the Present Offense. In addition, Mr. Owenby's sentence was reduced from 45 years to 20 years. Mr. Owenby was counseled regarding the services offered by the Project RIO Office that can assist him in job placement upon his release from prison.

SUBMITTED BY: Fred Drennon
Transitional case manager
DATE: 11-9-03

Result: Mr. Owenby was paroled subject to parole conditions.

TEXAS DEPARTMENT OF CRIMINAL JUSTICE
BOARD OF PARDONS AND PAROLES CASE SUMMARY

UNIT: Coffield

NAME: JACOBS, Norman Kingsley   **TDC NO:** 43218   **DATE:** 10-14-03

MINIMUM EXPIRATION DATE: 10-6-02   **MAXIMUM EXPIRATION DATE:** 1-4-05

CALENDAR TIME SERVED: 3 Years   **ON:** 5 Years   **DOCKET:** 9-03   **EMS DATE:** 10-03

PROPOSED RELEASE PLAN: **DISTRIBUTION:** Central Office
(1)   Mother, Mabel Jacobs   Region 1
         2222 2nd Avenue   Dallas District
         Dallas, Dallas County, Texas 75211   Huntsville IPO
                                                             Palestine IPO

HALFWAY HOUSES: Refused any choices as placement under any circumstances.

JOB/SKILLS: He will seek employment as a roofer.

OTHER/COMMENTS: None.

RESTITUTION: None.

REPORTING INSTRUCTIONS: **IN PERSON**   **TELEPHONE: LETTER:**

      DISTRICT: **COUNTY:**   **APPROVED**

COMMITMENT DATA INFORMATION

COUNTY:	CAUSE#:	OFFENSE:	SENTENCE:	Date:	TYPE:
Dallas	F02-33315	AGG ROBBERY/W DEADLY WPN (9-19-99)	5 Years	12-1-02	

TOTAL SENTENCE: 5 Years   **SENTENCE BEGIN DATE:** 6-14-00
AGE: 26 (7-14-77)   **RACE:** White   **SEX:** M   **HEIGHT:** 5'11"   **WEIGHT:** 160
EDUCATION: 9th Grade

DETAINERS: None.

PAROLE PANEL ACTION: _____   _____
                              BOARD MEMBER'S INITIALS   **DATE**

      PAROLE DENIED

CRIMINAL HISTORY: TF-0; **OP**-0; **TE**-0; **OR**-0

JUVENILE: Detailed 13-15, Riot, released to parents; Theft (2), released to parents.

ADULT INCARCERATIONS: None.

OTHER ARRESTS:

Mr. Jacobs admits to other arrests for: Unlawful Carrying Weapon and Violation of Controlled Substance Act, dismissed as part of plea bargain.

INSTANT OFFENSE SUMMARY:

AGGRAVATED ROBBERY WITH A DEADLY WEAPON: On 9-19-99, Mr. Jacobs is alleged to have taken the keys to the victim's vehicle by threatening him with a .38 caliber pistol. He fled the scene and was arrested approximately 6 hours later. Identification was made by the victim to the police and arrest was made by the license plate number. He was not released on bond. His rationale, "He loaned it to me."

SUBSTANCE ABUSE HISTORY:

DRUGS: Mr. Jacobs admits use of marijuana beginning at age 13 up to the time of incarceration and occasional basis of approximately once or twice monthly. He also states he began using cocaine by injection and smoking at age 21 for approximately 2 years up to the time of incarceration. This was on a once or twice monthly basis. He denies sale of drugs or treatment for substance abuse.

ALCOHOL: Mr. Jacobs admits consumption of beer beginning at age 13 up to the time of incarceration. At the time of the Instant Offense, he states he had consumed approximately one-fifth of whiskey by drinking it with water over the last 8 hours. He states he is not an alcoholic and also "I'm not going to stop drinking."

PHYSICAL/MENTAL:

PHYSICAL: TDC medical records and the inmate indicate he is diagnosed as having the following problems: high blood pressure, for which is prescribed Verapamil, 80 mg, once daily; a sinus condition, for which is prescribed pseudoephedrin (Actifed), one tablet twice daily; asthma condition, for which is prescribed Alupent Inhaler to be used as needed and Theador, 300 mg, twice daily; a heart condition, for which he is prescribed Capoten, 25 mg, twice daily; and an ulcer condition, for which is prescribed Tagamet, 400 mg, twice daily. It is apparent that employment possibilities will be severely restricted due to these conditions.

MENTAL: TDC medical records contain a Psychological Examination dated 1-16-01. At that time, he was diagnosed as Schizophrenia, Paranoid Chronic with accompanying Depression and Alcohol Dependency. In the past, he has been prescribed Valium, and while in county jail, he was prescribed Mellaril. This was due to feeling depressed off and on for several years. File material contains reports of two suicide attempts by overdosing on various types of pills. This was apparently done to gain attention but the inmate states "I didn't care about living no more." Collateral contact with unit psychological staff shows that he is currently undergoing therapy consisting of listening to relaxation tapes. The length of time necessary for maximum benefit was not determined. Evaluation at the time of release may be necessary to determine if MHMR services are necessary upon his return to society.

SOCIAL HISTORY:

Mr. Jacobs completed the 9th grade in regular education. He has received no vocational training. His longest prior employment was for two years as a roofer. At the time of the Instant Offense, he reports being unemployed for the previous one year and was a roofer prior to that. He has no military history.

INSTITUTIONAL ADJUSTMENT:

Mr. Jacobs is a Line Class II inmate assigned as a Clerk to the Records Conversion Area. He is not participating in any educational, vocational, or character development programs. He has received no furloughs. He has received three minor rule infraction violations in addition to the following ones: On 2-2-02, he was placed in solitary confinement for Refusing to Obey Orders; On 3-30-02, he was placed in solitary confinement and reduced to SAT IV for use of Indecent or Vulgar Language. On 5-7-02, he was again cited for Refusing to Obey Orders and Threatening an Officer, at which time he was reduced to Line Class II and forfeited 40 days of good conduct time. He states that he did not threaten the officer and that the officer lied concerning the circumstances of the case.

IMPRESSION SECTION:

Mr. Jacobs is a 26-year-old offender at TDC for his first incarceration. He has attempted supervised release on two occasions, one resulting in success. His current incarceration is due to a probation revocation due to Failure to Report and Failure to Pay Fees. His rationale for this felony conviction seems to be that he denies the seriousness of the circumstances and events that led to his conviction. It appears his assaultiveness should be of concern to decision makers when considering him for return to society. His conduct during this incarceration has not been satisfactory, which is reflected by his disciplinary record and being in a reduced time earning category with forfeited good conduct time. Additionally, he has been placed in solitary confinement on two occasions. He is not likely to complete a release without benefit of supervision and other programs. While incarcerated, Mr. Jacobs has not participated in unit programs. Major areas of concern are his deficiencies in educational achievements, vocational skills, control of drug and alcohol use and his apparent mental condition. Monitored abstinence from drug and alcohol use by urinalysis may be beneficial in determining relapse into past criminal behavioral activity. Supervision concerning completion of basic education and attaining vocational skills should be required during incarceration and after release until completion. Also compliance with treatment plans for psychiatric problems may be necessary. Attention to these areas after release could enhance his possibilities for remaining in society as a productive member.

Upon release Mr. Jacobs plans to reside with his family and seek employment as a roofer. Assistance from TEC or TRC could provide initial possibilities for gainful employment. Also inmate MHMR services may be necessary to assist his reintegration process. When asked concerning his thoughts about being paroled, he said, "I'm not going to stop drinking, regardless of the programs they send me to." This statement was reflective of his negative attitude concerning the criminal justice system, possible benefits from MHMR services, and substance abuse counseling. His poor physical and mental health conditions are negative factors toward an overall picture of his apparently poor chance for successful release.

Result: Mr. Jacobs was denied parole.

It is apparent from these cases that a great deal of information is compiled and factors into early-release decision making. The impressions and recommendations from parole officers who are assigned to make individual assessments of prospective parole-eligible offenders carry great weight with the parole board. In cases where inmates are subsequently paroled, their institutional conduct is generally satisfactory, with few writeups or incident reports. Further, they have participated in self-help groups and other programming offered by their prison. They acknowledge their problems and seek ways to remedy them. Less successful parole-eligible inmates deny they have problems, refuse to participate in prison programming, and may have poor attitudes concerning any assistance that may be offered. If they have alcohol or drug problems, they may deny the existence of such problems. If asked why they committed their conviction offenses, they are inclined to blame others for what happened, or they minimize their role in the crime.

These examples are only two such examples of thousands of reports filed each year in various jurisdictions where parole boards convene. Some parole boards append copies of presentence investigation reports to these documents to be used in support of any decision they might make. In many jurisdictions, victims are notified that particular offenders are being considered for parole. These victims may be offered an opportunity to attend their parole hearings and speak out against or in support of their parole, depending upon the attitudes and circumstances of the victims. Offenders themselves are usually permitted to address parole boards and make an argument for why they should be paroled. Although the process of parole granting is theoretically objective, it is clear from these particular reports that some subjectivity enters into parole decision making. In the next section, parole revocation will be examined.

THE PROCESS OF PAROLE REVOCATION

Parole **revocation** is a two-stage proceeding. Parolees who are in jeopardy of having their parole programs revoked through **revocation actions** are entitled to **minimum due process** rights. The governing case in all parole revocation proceedings is *Morrissey v. Brewer* (1972) discussed in the following section. The primary reason for extending minimum due-process rights to parolees is that they are in jeopardy of losing their liberty. They can be reincarcerated if the parole board determines that the nature of their parole program violation is sufficiently serious (Travis et al., 2002).

However, a majority of parolees are not returned to prison. Rather, they are placed under more restrictive supervision from their POs. Some parolees are electronically monitored and subjected to home confinement with strictly enforced curfews. Those who failed in their programs because of alcohol or substance abuse may be obligated to participate in counseling or group therapy. Self-help groups, such as Alcoholics Anonymous or Narcotics Anonymous, may be recommended as a part of their continuing parole program (Petersilia, 2001; Wilson and Petersilia, 2002).

 **BOX 8.3**

A PAROLE OFFICER LISTS EXCUSES GIVEN BY PAROLEES FOR PAROLE PROGRAM VIOLATIONS

Montie Guthrie, Dallas, Texas Parole Officer
During the 1990s, Montie Guthrie was employed with the Texas Department of Criminal Justice Parole Division. Guthrie supervised hundreds of parolees and prepared thousands of reports. He visited his parolee-clients in dangerous Dallas, Texas, neighborhoods, which were gang-infested and full of violence. On more than one occasion, his life was threatened by neighborhood toughs. Luckily for Guthrie, his parolee-clients always bailed him out. On one occasion, for example, Guthrie was visiting a dangerous parolee who had been convicted of aggravated assault and murder. The parolee was gigantic, with massive arms and chest. He was known to pummel his victims into submission or death. When Guthrie visited, another man, a gang member, was at the parolee's residence. The visitor didn't like Guthrie's inquiries of his parolee-client and the fact that Guthrie was looking around the apartment for possible illegal contraband. The visitor insulted Guthrie and invited him outside to fight. Instead, the parolee rose from his chair and advised his visiting friend that he, the parolee, would be stepping outside with his friend, not the parole officer. He advised his friend to "keep quiet" or suffer the consequences. He pointed his finger at his parole officer and said, "That's the man keeping me out of prison. Nobody lays a finger on him. Now sit down and keep quiet." Sometimes it pays to have friends in low places.

(continued)

BOX 8.3 (Continued)

As Guthrie reflects on his years with the Texas Department of Criminal Justice as a parole officer, he is amused at some of the incidents that involved some of his parolee-clients. In one particularly hilarious incident, Guthrie described a parolee who went hunting and shot an award-winning 18-point buck with a high-powered rifle. The shooting merited a visit from photographers and a reporter from a Dallas newspaper. The parolee's picture was printed in the paper, with the parolee holding the buck for everyone to see. The caption read, "Mr. _____ shot his trophy 18-point buck in northeast Coleman County just before Christmas. Mr. _____ said the buck would field dress about 150 pounds. The rack measured 18 inches. Mr. _____ was headed for the taxidermist and will probably soon have a fine trophy on the wall of his home." Ironically, Mr. _____ was a parolee. One of his parole program conditions was that he not possess or use firearms. This hunting antic came to Guthrie's attention when he read the morning newspaper. Mr. _____ had his parole revoked for the firearms violation and he was returned to prison.

Early in his career as a parole officer, Guthrie visited numerous clients. Some of them tested positive for drugs or alcohol. Others weren't home when they were supposed to be there. Some clients didn't report to his office when scheduled to do so at regular intervals. Still others absconded from the jurisdiction, only to be apprehended later. Each parolee had one or more excuses for violating his or her parole conditions. Guthrie catalogued these excuses:

- I didn't report because I was shot.
- I forgot.
- I don't know.
- My Corry (family member) died.
- I thought you said I didn't have to.
- I thought I was an annual (meaning once-a-year visit).
- I thought I would be arrested.
- I went to jail.
- I was sick.

- I came up here but you weren't here.
- My car broke down.
- I couldn't report because of my sister's drinking problem and I had to stay and watch her kids.
- I got married.
- My family said he (the parole officer) had homosexual tendencies and I was afraid he would come on to me.
- The reason I was positive (for cocaine) was my girlfriend put it on my _____ and then sucked it.
- You see, I'm always positive (for cocaine) because I go out to these clubs and these girls, man, they always want to get with me, right? So, when I'm not looking, they put coke in my drink to get me high so I'll get with them.
- Well, I didn't do no crack, man, I was just cookin' the stuff.
- I was just around a bunch of people smokin'.
- I didn't do no drugs! My girl, man, she smoked the stuff and it must have got on me when I went down on her.
- My neighbors sneaked into my house and put cocaine in my sugar.
- It was on the counter and when I brushed it off, it must have got in me.
- They do coke at this bar a lot on the table, and when I put the pretzels on the bar, some must a got on them and me when I ate them.
- I smoke weed because I'm trying to gain weight and I know I'll get the munchies if I don't.
- I was having sex with a guy who was high and he ejaculated in me.
- I was at a club and my friend saw a guy put something in my drink and didn't tell me.
- It's just weed!
- I'm taking vitamins and antibiotics.
- I smoke because I want to get with women.

BOX 8.3 (Continued)

- My girl was going back to school and I wanted to be sure to give it to her good before she went back so she'll think about me.

- I cut so much cocaine it must have absorbed into my skin.

- They're not as bad as they seem.

- My friends stole the car, and then they picked me up at the house in it.

- It wasn't crack—it was just a ball of soap.

- I don't remember.

- It was self-defense. He started calling my grandmother bad names, and so I stabbed him.

- I left because they were selling drugs where I lived. I didn't have time to tell you where I moved to.

- I didn't go to GED classes because someone is trying to kill me. They'll kill me if I go to that class.

As Guthrie says, once you think you've heard it all, you hear something new. There's never a dull moment in parole work!

***

Courtesy of Montie Guthrie. Compiled by author, February 2001.

The **parole revocation hearing** involves two stages. The first stage is when the offender appears before the parole board to answer the allegations relating to the parole program violation(s). If the parole board determines that the offender is guilty of one or more program rule infractions, then it must decide the punishment. This is the second stage. If a parolee's program is revoked, the parole board is obligated to furnish the parolee with its reasons in writing. Further, the parole board recommends what the parolee must do if reincarcerated in order to earn another chance at parole (Travis et al., 2002). Below are several cases involving parole revocation.

LANDMARK CASES AND SELECTED ISSUES

Morrissey v. Brewer (1972).   The first landmark case involving the constitutional rights of parolees was *Morrissey v. Brewer* (1972). In 1967, John Morrissey was convicted by an Iowa court for "falsely drawing checks" and sentenced to not more than seven years in the Iowa State Prison. He was eventually paroled from prison in June, 1968. However, seven months later, his parole officer learned that while on parole, Morrissey had bought a car under an assumed name and operated it without permission, obtained credit cards under a false name, and gave false information to an insurance company when he was involved in a minor automobile accident. Also, Morrissey had given his parole officer a false address for his residence.

The parole officer interviewed Morrissey and filed a report recommending that parole be revoked. The reasons given by the officer were that Morrissey admitted buying the car and obtaining false I.D., obtaining credit under false pretenses, and he also admitted being involved in the auto accident. Morrissey claimed he "was sick," and that this condition prevented him from maintaining continuous contact with his parole officer. The parole officer claimed that Morrissey's parole should be revoked because Morrissey had a habit of "continually violating the rules." The parole board revoked Morrissey's parole and he was returned to the Iowa State Prison to serve the remainder of his sentence. Morrissey was not represented by counsel at the revocation proceeding. Furthermore, he was not given the opportunity to crossexamine witnesses against him, he was not advised in writing of the charges against him, no disclosure of the evidence against him was provided, and reasons for the revocation were not given. Morrissey also was not permitted to offer evidence in his own behalf or give personal testimony.

Morrissey's appeal to the Iowa Supreme Court was rejected, but the U. S. Supreme Court heard his appeal. While the Court did not address directly the question of whether Morrissey should have had court-appointed counsel, it did make a landmark decision in his case. It overturned the Iowa Parole Board action and established a two-stage proceeding for determining whether parole ought to be revoked. The first or preliminary hearing is held at the time of arrest and detention, where it is determined whether probable cause exists that the parolee actually committed the alleged parole violation. The second hearing is more involved and establishes the guilt of the parolee relating to the violations. This proceeding must extend to the parolee certain minimum due process rights. These rights are:

1. The right to have written notice of the alleged violations of parole conditions.
2. The right to have disclosed to the parolee any evidence of the alleged violation.
3. The right of the parolee to be heard in person and to present **exculpatory evidence** as well as witnesses in his behalf.
4. The right to confront and crossexamine adverse witnesses, unless cause exists why they should not be crossexamined.
5. The right to a judgment by a neutral and detached body, such as the parole board itself.
6. The right to a written statement of the reasons for the parole revocation.

Thus, the significance of the Morrissey case is that it set forth minimum due process rights for all parolees, creating a two-stage proceeding whereby the alleged infractions of parole conditions could be examined and a full hearing conducted to determine the most appropriate disposition of the offender.

For several decades, interest in the rights of probationers and parolees has increased considerably (South Carolina Department of Probation, Parole and Pardon Services, 1993). Not only has more attention been devoted to this subject in the professional literature, but various courts in different jurisdictions, including the U.S. Supreme Court, have set forth landmark decisions that influence either positively or negatively the lives of those in probation or parole programs (Vigdal and Stadler, 1994:44).

Pennsylvania Board of Probation and Parole v. Scott (1998). Scott, a parolee, was suspected of possessing firearms in violation of his parole conditions. Parole officers conducted a warrantless search of his premises and discovered firearms. Scott's parole was revoked on the basis of the discovered evidence and he was recommitted to prison. Scott appealed, alleging that his

Fourth Amendment right against unreasonable searches and seizures had been violated and that evidence thus seized was not admissible in a parole revocation hearing. The U.S. Supreme Court held that a parolee's Fourth Amendment rights do not apply in parole revocation hearings, and that incriminating evidence discovered and seized in violation of a parolees' Fourth Amendment rights may be introduced at parole revocation proceedings.

Pennsylvania Department of Corrections v. Yeskey (1998). Yeskey was a Pennsylvania prison inmate who was sentenced to 18–36 months in a correctional facility, but was recommended for placement in a Motivational Boot Camp, which, if successfully completed, would have led to his parole in just 6 months. Yeskey was rejected by the boot camp officials because of a medical history of hypertension. Yeskey sued the Pennsylvania Department of Corrections, alleging that the exclusion violated the Americans with Disabilities Act (ADA), and the federal court rejected his claim, contending that the ADA was inapplicable to state prison inmates. The Third Circuit Court of Appeals reversed and remanded, and the government appealed to the U.S. Supreme Court who heard the case. The U.S. Supreme Court affirmed the appellate court, declaring that the ADA provision prohibiting a public entity from discriminating against qualified individuals with disabilities on account of that person's disability applied to inmates in state prisons.

Pardons

When the U.S. president or a state governor pardons someone who may or may not be on probation or parole, the effect of these pardons is different, depending upon the jurisdiction. Generally, a pardon is tantamount to absolution for a crime previously committed. Someone has been convicted of the crime, and the intent of a pardon is to terminate whatever punishment has been imposed. In *United States v. Noonan* (1990), for instance, Gregory Noonan was convicted and sentenced in 1969 for "failing to submit to induction into the armed forces." President Jimmy Carter granted a pardon to Noonan on January 21, 1977, wherein Carter declared a "full, complete and unconditional pardon" to persons convicted during the Vietnam War for refusing induction. Noonan sought to have his record of the original conviction expunged. An **expungement order** has the effect of wiping one's slate clean, as though the crime and the conviction had never occurred. Noonan believed that his conviction, which remained on his record, adversely affected his employment chances. Thus, he sought to expunge his record because of the pardon he had received from Carter. However, the Third Circuit Court of Appeals, a federal appellate court, refused to grant him this request. The Court declared that "a pardon does not blot out guilt nor does it restore the offender to a state of innocence in the eye of the law." In short, at least in Noonan's case, the presidential pardon was effective in removing the punishment but not the criminal record.

Not all courts agree with the Third Circuit Court of Appeals. In some state appellate courts, a different position has been taken regarding the influence of a pardon on one's criminal record. Following the lead of a Pennsylvania court of appeals, the Indiana Court of Appeals declared in the case of *State v. Bergman* (1990) that a pardon does expunge one's criminal record. The Governor of Indiana had pardoned a convict, Berman, for a crime he had previously committed. Bergman sought to have his record expunged, in much the same way as page 374, Chapter 8 Early Release, Parole Programs, and Parole Revocation

Noonan. The Indiana Court of Appeals declared that pardons "block out the very existence of the offender's guilt, so that, in the eye(s) of the law, he is thereafter as innocent as if he had never committed the offense." Subsequent state court decisions have concurred with both Pennsylvania and Indiana.

Despite the fact that some offenders have been pardoned, this does not always exempt them from having their pardoned offense used against them in subsequent court proceedings involving new crimes. For instance, Moore was pardoned for a crime he committed in Louisiana (*Moore v. State,* 2002). Moore eventually moved to Mississippi where he was arrested and charged with felony driving under the influence. He was convicted and his prior Louisiana criminal record was used against him in a Mississippi court to enhance his sentence. Moore appealed, alleging that his pardoned offense was in effect expunged and that it could no longer be considered of relevance in any future sentencing. The Mississippi appellate court disagreed, citing Louisiana law in defense of the enhanced Mississippi criminal court sentence. Under Louisiana law, automatic pardon provisions do not restore defendants to the status of innocence. Thus, the court held that Mississippi could utilize the "pardoned offense" to enhance Moore's sentence for a crime he committed in Mississippi.

Violating One or More Parole Program Conditions

When probationers or parolees are subject to having their programs revoked by respective authorities, what is the nature of evidence that can be used against them to support their program revocation? What are their rights concerning PO searches of their premises? What about the program conditions they have been obligated to follow? What about parole board recognition of and obligation to follow minimum-sentence provisions from sentencing judges? These issues and several others are discussed briefly below.

Parole Board Actions and Rights.   Parole boards have considerable discretionary powers. They may deny parole or grant it. They may revoke one's parole and return the offender to prison, or they may continue the offender's parole program, with additional supervision and other conditions (Archwamety and Katsiyannis, 2000). Below are listed a variety of cases dealing with numerous issues. Some of these issues may appear trivial, although their significance to affected probationers or parolees is profound.

Inmates who become eligible for parole are not automatically entitled to parole. Parole boards have considerable discretion whether to grant or deny parole to any inmate. Short of serving their full sentences or completing a portion of their term less any applicable good-time credit, inmates are not automatically entitled to be paroled (Mississippi Parole Board, 2003). In the case of *Williams v. Puckett* (1993), a Mississippi man convicted of armed robbery and forgery was sentenced to a mandatory sentence of 10 years plus a 5-year term for the forgery conviction. In Mississippi, inmates become eligible for parole after serving 10 years of terms imposed in excess of 10 years, by statute. However, since the armed robbery conviction involved a mandatory prison term of 10 years, this meant that the entire sentence of 10 years must be served. Thus, according to Mississippi law, the inmate must serve at least one-fourth of the 5-year term for the forgery conviction before actual parole eligibility occurred. Even then, the

Mississippi Parole Board would not be obligated to automatically grant his early release.

In a subsequent case in Pennsylvania, an inmate considered violent, Coady, challenged the Pennsylvania Parole Board regarding its 1996 decision to make it more difficult for violent offenders to be paroled (*Coady v. Pa.Bd. of Probation & Parole,* 2002). Coady petitioned the court and argued that since he had been convicted of a violent offense prior to 1996, the new parole guidelines implemented by the Pennsylvania Parole Board could not be applied retroactively to him. Thus, he believed, the parole board was obligated to consider him for early release, despite the fact that he was in a broad class of violent offenders. The Pennsylvania Parole Board sought the dismissal of Coady's petition, but the court refused to dismiss it. Even if the court were to rule in Coady's favor, the discretionary powers of the Pennsylvania Parole Board are such that it could continue to deny Coady early release for any number of reasons. In a worst-case scenario for Coady, he would serve his maximum sentence and Pennsylvania would have to free him from prison unconditionally. This holds true in other states, such as Georgia. Georgia implemented paroling guidelines in the late 1990s, although the guidelines themselves did not compel parole board members to parole any particular inmate. Rather, the guidelines merely established an initial date of eligibility for parole, and the ultimate granting or denial of parole to a prisoner remained discretionary with the parole board (*Daker v. Ray,* 2002).

Sometimes the sensationalism surrounding one's original conviction offense will influence parole boards to deny parole to otherwise parole-eligible inmates, regardless of their suitability for parole. In California, for example, Leslie Van Houten, 53, a former follower of Charles Manson, was convicted of murder in 1970 and sentenced to death. Subsequently, her sentence was commuted to life imprisonment, which made her parole eligible. As of 2002 she had made 14 visits to the California Board of Prison Terms for consideration for early release. On each of these occasions, her parole requests were denied. Prior to her 2002 parole hearing, Van Houten filed a suit requesting the court to order her release from prison. The court rejected her request. It is doubtful that Van Houten will ever be paroled. This is due primarily to the politically charged nature of her conviction offense and the unfavorable publicity for parole officials and the California governor that her parole would likely generate. In the meantime, the California Board of Prison Terms has paroled numerous murders who have committed far more heinous acts than Van Houten (Associated Press, June 12, 2002). Political pressures exerted on parole board members are found beyond California. In 2003 New Jersey Parole Board members admitted off the record that their parole decision making was strongly influenced by the New Jersey governor's office, and that if they failed to make decisions consistent with their governor's sentiments, their jobs would be in jeopardy (Baldwin and McClure, 2003).

Even under conditions of mandatory parole, offenders are not necessarily freed from prison. In the federal system, for instance, if an inmate is paroled as a mandatory parolee, he or she may serve some of his or her parole time on prison grounds in special housing units. This type of placement, outside the conventional prison itself but within the prison perimeter, is fairly common at both the state and federal levels. And if a mandatory parolee is subsequently sent to community corrections and violates one or more parole conditions, the parolee may be returned to prison to serve a term in prison up to the full length of the mandatory parole period, which is usually set at 180 days (*Gwinn v. Reid,* 2002).

Parole boards do not have to recognize explicit parole guidelines when determining an inmate's parole eligibility.   Blackburn was a parole-eligible inmate in a Missouri prison and became eligible for early release under paroling guidelines which had been previously established (*Blackburn v. Mo. Bd. of Probation & Parole,* 2002). Because of the violent nature of Blackburn's offense and other factors, the Missouri Parole Board elected not to follow its guidelines and denied early release to Blackburn. Blackburn appealed, arguing that the Missouri Parole Board failed to follow its own guidelines for determining whether he should be released. An appellate court disagreed and upheld the Missouri Parole Board decision, holding that various parole regulations are simply intended to provide guidelines, and this fact does not remove the board's discretion in relation to parole release decisions. As such, the regulations did not create a liberty interest for Blackburn which was protected by due process.

In another case involving a federal prisoner who was eligible for early release under the U.S. Sentencing Guidelines, the U.S. Parole Commission denied parole to Gometz (*Gometz v. U.S. Parole Commission,* 2002). Gometz became parole eligible after serving a significant portion of his sentence under the Sentencing Guidelines. However, he had engaged in at least six instances of misconduct during his confinement, including an attempted assault on another prison inmate, which had been classified by prison authorities as attempted murder. Gometz was never prosecuted for this assault or for the other misconduct. Nevertheless, the U.S. Parole Commission considered this information in determining its denial of parole to Gometz. Gometz appealed, contending that the U.S. Parole Commission had abused its authority by not following the guidelines articulating his early release. An appellate court upheld the U.S. Parole Commission action, noting that the Commission can make independent findings of criminal conduct and even consider unadjudicated offenses that are connected to the offense of conviction.

Inmates who serve some of their parole program time in a halfway house are entitled to credit equal to the time served in the halfway house applied against their maximum sentences.   In Ohio, a parolee, Fair, was placed in a halfway house, W.O.R.T.H. During the time Fair spent at the halfway house, Fair was closely supervised by halfway house staff. After several months of living in the halfway house, Fair violated one or more halfway house rules. His parole program was revoked. The parole board denied him credit against his maximum sentence for the time he spent in the halfway house facility. Fair appealed and an Ohio court of appeals ordered the parole board to give him the time he had served at the halfway house. The court reasoned that the halfway house was a "confinement facility" and thus Fair's time spent there should be credited toward his maximum prison sentence (*State v. Fair,* 2000).

But not all states follow Ohio. In Alaska, for example, a parolee, Fortuny, was in a community residential treatment facility for a period of time when he violated one or more conditions of his parole (*State v. Fortuny,* 2002). Fortuny asked that he be granted the amount of time spent in the community halfway house and that time should be applied against his maximum sentence. The parole board refused his request and he appealed. The Alaska appeals court upheld the parole board and declared that whether the time in a halfway house counts against one's maximum sentence depends on whether the parolee is in the halfway house voluntarily or by means of a parole condition. In Fortuny's case, Fortuny was in the residential facility voluntarily, and thus the time he had served in the halfway house could not be applied against his maximum time to be served.

In a third case, a Louisiana parolee committed a new offense and was jailed for a period of time. Subsequently, the parolee asked that his time in jail should be applied toward his maximum original sentence. The parole board denied the request and the parolee appealed. An appellate court set aside the parole board decision and declared that any jail time served by the parolee should count and be applied against his maximum sentence (*Perry v. Day*, 2001).

Inmates who have been sentenced under an indeterminate sentencing scheme and are subsequently paroled cannot change their sentence to a determinate sentence if their parole is revoked.   Perez was a Kansas parolee who had originally been sentenced under an indeterminate sentencing scheme (*State v. Perez*, 2000). Subsequently his parole was revoked because of one or more program violations. Perez sought to have his sentence changed to a determinate one, since under a determinate sentencing scheme, he would be eligible for release in a shorter time and without the restrictive conditions of a parole program. The parole board denied his request to change his sentence to a determinate one. Perez appealed, contending that the parole program violation amounted to a new crime and he should be sentenced under the new determinate sentencing scheme Kansas had adopted since he was originally incarcerated. The Kansas Supreme Court upheld the parole board action, saying that Perez's parole violation was not a crime in the same sense that an offender would be convicted of a crime. Thus, the appellate court distinguished between crimes and parole violations and held that Perez would continue to serve his indeterminate sentence subject to its original conditions.

Inmates who have been paroled and who subsequently commit a new violent act while on parole may have their parole programs revoked and be returned to prison to serve the remainder of their sentences in their entirety.   In New York, a parolee's program was revoked after it was alleged that he had assaulted his pregnant girlfriend by striking her about the head and threatening to kill her. At the revocation hearing the girlfriend affirmed her original statements given to investigating police officers, but she claimed that she had lied and that a female friend had assaulted her. The parole board gave no credence to her recantation and revoked the client's parole despite pending criminal charges against him in relation to the assault. An appeal of this revocation was unsuccessful, since the parole board may consider unadjudicated charges when making revocation decisions (*People ex rel. Fryer v. Beaver*, 2002).

If a paroling authority does not hold a revocation hearing for a parolee in a timely manner, it may not revoke his parole.   Wells was a Washington, D.C., parolee who had previously been convicted of several crimes. During his parole on one of these offenses, Wells went to a foreign country in violation of his parole and committed a new offense. He was sentenced to serve time in a foreign prison and eventually returned to the United States. Two years following his release from the foreign prison, paroling authorities in the District of Columbia sought to revoke his parole and return him to prison. Wells argued that the 2-year delay in bring charges against him for violating his parole barred the revocation action taken. An appeals court denied Wells' appeal, holding that the failure of District of Columbia authorities to file a detainer warrant with the foreign prison was mere negligence. Furthermore, a convicted person should not be excused from serving his sentence merely because someone in a ministerial capacity makes a mistake with respect to the execution of his sentence (*Wells v. United States, 2002*).

If a paroling authority imposes a special condition of parole, such as regulating financial disclosures, involvement in real estate activities, or psychiatric evaluations, these are not considered unusual and unconstitutional parole conditions. Benny was convicted of mail fraud and racketeering and sentenced to 30 years (*Benny v. U.S. Parole Commission, 2002*). After serving 10 years, Benny was paroled. Several special conditions of parole were imposed that regulated Benny's financial disclosures and his involvement in real estate activities. Subsequently Benny was charged with numerous parole violations, including failure to disclose personal income and loans made to a nephew. On the basis of these and other parole condition violations, Benny's parole was revoked. Benny appealed his revocation, contending among other things that these parole conditions were unreasonable. The appellate court disagreed and upheld Benny's parole revocation and return to prison.

In an Oregon case, a prospective parolee was required to undergo a psychiatric evaluation prior to being released on parole. The inmate objected to this pre-parole condition and appealed. The Oregon appellate court held that the Oregon Parole Board may require any prisoner being considered for parole to participate in a psychiatric or psychological examination prior to being released on parole. If the prisoner refuses to participate in such an examination, the board is not obligated to release him or her (*Gholston v. Palmateer, 2002*).

SUMMARY

The idea of pre-release was introduced, together with an examination of several pre-release programs. Pre-release programs are available to parole-eligible inmates who are within a short time of being released. These programs include work release, where inmates may be granted temporary leaves from their prisons to work at jobs in their communities. Other temporary leaves may be used for earning academic degrees. These programs are known as study release. Variations from standard parole include halfway houses and furloughs. These are community-based programs and provide offenders with opportunities for reintegration into the community. Halfway houses or community residential centers may be either publicly or privately operated. They exist to provide offenders with housing, food, counseling, and other services while on parole. These programs are considered transitional because they permit offenders to gradually reenter society and make an adjustment from highly structured and regulated prison life. Furloughs are temporary unescorted leaves designed to permit offenders to become reunited with families or to engage in employment. Most of the time, these programs are granted to low-risk, minimum-security offenders.

Other programs include standard parole with conditions. All parole programs are conditional, in that there are certain expectations made of all parolees. These conditions prohibit the use of alcohol or illegal drugs, ownership of firearms, and cellular telephones and beepers. Further, parolees must permit their supervising POs to visit their premises and conduct searches without warrant at any time. Parole is either discretionary or mandatory. Where parole is discretionary, a parole-eligible inmate may refuse parole and its accompanying conditions, if it is offered by a parole board. For mandatory parole, parole-eligible inmates must accept it regardless of their personal feelings about the accompanying program conditions. Some states and the federal government have abolished parole outright, since the legislatures of these jurisdictions have been displeased by parole board decision making. Other ways of gaining early release for inmates have been devised, such as the accumulation of good-time credits. No early-release program is perfect, however, and there are critics who complain about all parole or early-release systems. There are still parole boards in states that do not have parole anymore, since those offenders who were sentenced before parole was abolished are still entitled to parole hearings. In these jurisdictions, parole boards operate on a part-time basis.

Some parole programs involve intensive parolee supervision. One of these programs is the New Jersey Intensive Supervision Program. This program selects participants from numerous applicants annually. Any interested New Jersey jail or prison inmate may apply for entry into the New Jersey ISP. However, New Jersey authorities only accept about 19 percent of all applicants. Several types of inmates are automatically excluded, including those with violent criminal records, sex offenders, and those affiliated with organized crime. The New Jersey program boasts a recidivism rate of less than 10 percent and has successfully operated since 1983. Another ISP program is operated by Nevada. This program is different from New Jersey's ISP program. The Nevada ISP program emphasizes community safety and offender rehabilitation. It relies on frequent contact with probationers, frequent drug/alcohol checks and curfew monitoring, smaller caseloads, graduated sanctions for program violations, and legitimate employment or involvement in vocational/educational training for its participating probationers. Both the New Jersey and Nevada programs have modestly successful completion rates as well as low recidivism.

By 1988, all states had modified their existing sentencing provisions. Maine abolished parole in 1976, and the federal government technically abolished parole in 1992, although supervised early release procedures have been continued. Many states are moving toward some form of determinate sentencing or presumptive or guidelines-based sentencing schemes. A majority of states continue to use parole boards for granting early release to prisoners. Parole board composition varies among jurisdictions, and the criteria for granting parole vary considerably as well. In many jurisdictions, prisoners may acquire good-time credits that serve to reduce their sentences a certain number of days for each month served.

Several conditions may be imposed by a paroling authority, including day reporting, community service, and victim restitution. Together with fines and day fines, community service partially defrays the costs associated with the offender's crime, such as the victim's medical bills and property damage. There are many forms of community service and restitution. Not everyone agrees how or when these types of sanctions ought to be applied, however. Also, it is difficult to evaluate the effectiveness of these sanctions as deterrents to further criminal activity.

Parole boards vary in their composition. Most parole board appointments are political and made by the governors of states. Parole board members in most jurisdictions do not need to have any special training in corrections or law enforcement. Parole boards attempt to predict which inmates should receive early release. They also determine dates for first parole consideration, fix the minimum time to be served, and award good time credits to inmates who have earned them. Studies of parole board decision making reveal that predictions of one's successfulness on parole are imperfect. The primary criticisms of parole boards focus upon a lack of consistent parole criteria. Therefore, several objective parole criteria have been devised and implemented. But in the politically charged atmosphere of parole decision making, objective parole criteria are difficult to apply in all cases. Parole boards must meet and determine whether or not parole should be granted for any inmate who is considered parole-eligible. Also, some parole boards have the authority to reduce one's sentence from life without the possibility of parole to life, where parole becomes an option. Some parole boards are vested with pardon authority and can release certain inmates unconditionally. Some cases are not reviewable by parole boards. Inmates on death row are usually barred from parole board review and action. In most cases, however, parole is granted with numerous stringent behavioral conditions and program requirements.

If parolees violate one or more of their parole program conditions, they are subject to having their parole programs revoked. Parole revocation is the process of returning an inmate to prison for one or more technical violations or for committing new crimes. The revocation process has been examined by the United States Supreme Court, and several landmark cases have presented parolees with specific rights. Both parolees and probationers have been vested with several important constitutional rights in the last few decades, as the U. S. Supreme Court has extended due process and equal protection to encompass them. Before parolees can have their parole program revoked, a two-stage hearing is mandatory, where probable cause is first determined, and then an appropriate disposition of each case is made impartially by the parole board. Minimum due process rights and a two-stage revocation hearing were set forth in the U.S. Supreme Court case of *Morrissey v. Brewer.* It is likely that other significant rights will apply to parolees in future years as the U.S. Supreme Court faces new and different appeals from parolees and probationers.

QUESTIONS FOR REVIEW

1. What is pre-release? What are several types of pre-release programs? How is a pre-release program useful for reintegration purposes?

2. What are work release and study release? What are several functions and goals of these types of pre-release programs? Who qualifies for such programs?

3. What are furloughs? What are some functions of furloughs? What are some advantages of furloughs for prisoners?

4. What are halfway houses and their functions? How do halfway houses assist offenders in community reintegration? What are some arguments against halfway houses being located within communities?

5. What are some differences between discretionary and mandatory parole?

6. What are two programs that use intensive supervised parole? What are some of their program elements? How is program eligibility determined in each of these programs you have described?

7. What is a parole board? How is politics related to parole board composition? What kinds of objective criteria have been established for parole boards to follow? Under what circumstances might these objective criteria not be followed? Is any special training required of parole board members? Why or why not?

8. What is parole revocation? What are the general rights of parolees who are in jeopardy of having their parole programs revoked?

9. What is the significance of the case of *Morrissey v. Brewer* in parole revocation? What are two rights extended to parolees in this particular case? Must all states observe these rights?

10. What is a pardon? Under what circumstances might a parole board grant someone a pardon? What are the consequences for one's criminal record if a pardon is granted?

SUGGESTED READINGS

Harries, Keith (2002). "Applications of Geographical Analysis in Probation and Parole." *APPA Perspectives* 26:26–31.

Hughes, Timothy A., Doris James Wilson, and Allen J. Beck (2001). *Trends in State Parole, 1990–2000.* Washington, DC: U.S. Department of Justice, Bureau of Justice Statistics.

Morris, Norval (2002). *Maconochie's Gentlemen: The Story of Norfolk Island and the Roots of Modern Prison Reform.* New York: Oxford University Press.

Petersilia, Joan (2003). *Returning Home: Parole and Prisoner Reentry in the US.* New York: Oxford University Press.

Piehl, Anne Morrison (2002). "Inmate Reentry and Post-Release Supervision: The Case of Massachusetts." *APPA Perspectives* 26:32–38.

Taxman, Faye S. (2002). "Supervision—Exploring the Dimensions of Effectiveness." *Federal Probation* 66:14–27.

INTERNET CONNECTIONS

Administrative Office of the U.S. Courts
http://www.uncle-sam.com/uscourts.html,
http://www.uscourts.gov/

American Psychological Association
http://www.apa.org

Correctional Industries Association
http://www.corrections.com/industries/

Corrections Corporation of America
http://www.correctionscorp.com/

Faith to Faith Friends
http://www.f2ff.com

Furlough programs
http://www.xpay.net/SevFurloughPrograms
.htm

Gender Programming Training and Technical Assistance Initiative
http://www.girlspecificprogram.org

Glaser Institute on Reality Therapy
http://www.wglasserinst.com/whatisrt

Gurley House Women's Recovery Center
http://www.thegurleyhouse.org

ISCOS Halfway Houses
iscos.org.sq/halfway.shtml

National Association of Social Workers
http://www.naswdc.org

National Corrections Corporation
http://www.nationalcorrections.com

National State History of Halfway Houses
http://www.ni-cor.com/halfwayhouses
.html

North Carolina Study Release Program
http://www.doc.state.nc.us/DOP/Program/
studyrel.htm

PACER Service Center
http://www.pacer.psc.uscourts.gov/

Probation and Parole Compact Administrators Association
http://www.ppcaa.net/

Reynolds Work Release Second Chance Program
http://www.wa.gov/doc/
REYN02DSWRdescription.htm

Social work agencies
http://www.sc.edu/swan/national

Work furlough programs
http://www.dcn.davis.ca.us/YoloLINK/
services/S0026.html

Work release frequently asked questions
http://www.dc.state.fl.us/oth/inmates/
wr.htm

CHAPTER 9

*Probation/Parole Organization
and Operations: Recruitment, Training,
and Officer-Client Relations*

Chapter Outline

Chapter Objectives

As the result of reading this chapter, the following objectives will be realized:

1. Understanding the structure and function of probation and parole departments.
2. Distinguishing between correctional officers, probation officers, and parole officers, and examining how different jurisdictions view these work roles.
3. Profiling POs and describing their primary characteristics and training.
4. Describing the recruitment process and selection requirements for those performing PO functions.
5. Describing assessment centers and their role in the recruitment of POs.
6. Discussing the controversy over whether POs should carry firearms when performing their duties.
7. Describing different forms of negligence in the performance of PO tasks, as well as the liabilities associated with PO work.
8. Describing various caseload models used by probation/parole agencies and how caseloads are assigned.
9. Examining the code of ethics associated with PO work.
10. Describing the unionization and collective bargaining associated with probation and parole agencies.

• *Georgia bestowed the Governor's Public Safety Award on several parole officers. Parole Officers Tom Lord, Kris Stancil, and Tamara Stubbs were nominated for awards because of their extraordinary dedication and hard work on the job. Officer Lord was instrumental in getting duty ammunition upgraded to a better, effective load, saving the agency and taxpayers a lot of money. Officer Kris Stancil coordinated the first annual Brett Dickey Memorial Scholarship golf tournament, honoring a deputy who was killed in the line of duty in 1996. Officer Stubbs was nominated for her long hours and hard work at the Eatonton Parole Office. She has continuously provided a positive example, a positive attitude, and consistently high productivity. She is a role model for offenders and co-workers alike. Parole Officer Paul Parker received an award also for his work in locating and capturing a parolee who had removed his electronic monitor and left his residence. After the parolee was taken into custody, Parker discovered the man attempting suicide in his cell. Through Parker's quick thinking and assistance, authorities were able to revive the man and get him medical attention. Thanks to Officer Parker's courage and intelligence, the Bartow County community was protected from danger and the life of the parolee was saved [Source: Adapted from the Associated Press, "Governor's Public Safety Award." October 25, 2000].*

• *A Lowell County, Massachusetts probation officer, Richard J. Marcotte, 41, was charged with extorting quantities of Percocets and Percodans from a probationer he was supervising from February through March 2000. The indictment said that Officer Marcotte would be supplied Percocets and Percodans in exchange for favorable treatment toward the probationer. Marcotte was charged with two counts of possession of Schedule II controlled substances. [Source: Adapted from the Associated Press, "Probation Officer Charged with Extortion and Possession of Controlled Substances." November 10, 2000].*

• *North Carolina probation and parole officers received recognition for various acts of heroism. Bob Hogan, Chief Probation/Parole Officer in Burke County, helped coordinate and carry out searches of 15 offenders' residences where illegal drugs, firearms, and drug paraphernalia were found. Hogan's lead by example, work ethics, and dedication make him an outstanding role model for those he supervises. Carl Wayne Jewett is a probation/parole officer in Tarboro. On September 16, 2000, Jewett helped to rescue 20 stranded flood victims in the Dunbar community. The next day, Jewett reported for work and for the next 15 days, he averaged more than 11 hours a day in truck, boat, and helicopter rescue operations. Officer Laura Bowers Bame from Cabarrus County supervises sex offenders. At one time, she was supervising a sexual predator from Texas, who frequented bowling alleys in search of young people to molest. Bame visited area bowling alleys and advised employees to be on the lookout for the sexual predator. An owner of a bowling alley reported to Bame that the sexual predator had recently joined a bowling league to teach youngsters. Bame arrested the predator and he was extradited back to Texas. [Source: Adapted from the Associated Press, "Department of Correction Honors Officers of the Year." May 12, 2000].*

• *Randall Nester, 35, a Johnson County, Missouri probation officer, was charged with forcing or attempting to force four female probationers to engage in sexual acts. One probationer said, "He would tell me to meet him in another area of the building where he would force himself on me and lift up my shirt, violating me as a woman." The charges against Nester include rape, four counts of first-degree sexual misconduct, four counts of corruption by a public servant, and one count of sexual abuse. Another female probationer claims she was sent back to prison after she resisted Nester's advances. Another woman said she was told by Nester that he would recommend her for early release if the two of them could "hook up." [Source: Adapted from the Associated Press, "Police Charge Probation Officer with Rape." January 7, 2003].*

• *Idaho Probation Officer Tom Blewett was charged with planting false evidence in the file of probationer Fred Leas, 51, of Helmer. It is also alleged that Blewett arbitrarily imposed curfews on Leas without a valid court order to that effect. While Leas was away working, it is alleged that Blewett searched Leas' home thoroughly, looking for something that might lead to his arrest. Unable to find anything, it is alleged that Blewett composed a letter that claimed he had witnessed Leas take indecent liberties with his daughters the previous summer. It was subsequently revealed that Blewett and the sentencing Judge John Stegner are cousins who allegedly conspired to implicate Leas in various types of wrongdoing for the purpose of imprisoning him. [Adapted from* The Idaho Observer, *"Tom Blewett—Leas' Probation Officer—May Be in Serious Trouble." March 18, 2000].*

• *Michael Snowden, a former Cincinnati, Ohio police chief, was hired by the Hamilton County's Probation Department to reform the department in January 1999. Snowden soon became critical of the probation department for failing to conduct adequate urine tests on probationers; disparities in the numbers of probationers found in violation of their probation for failing to meet conditions; probation officers not meeting with probationers on their caseloads; and various forms of misconduct among probation officer staff. Subsequently, complaints against Snowden mounted from both within and without the probation department. These complaints were critical of his management style as well as excessive departmental changes. One charge was that Snowden had falsified his academic credentials. Snowden produced certified copies of his academic credentials to an investigative panel and submitted his resignation. He said, "I'm not going to stay around for a witch hunt. It's just not worth it to me." [Adapted from the* Cincinnati Inquirer, *"Snowden Quits Amid Dissension." April 5, 2000].*

• *Hal Chandler is a probation officer in Florida. He has lobbied for changes in his job, including more generous retirement packages, in view of the high-risk jobs performed by him and fellow officers. "There is a level of risk going out in the field," says Chandler.*

"Especially when the sun goes down, because some of these areas really change and become more dangerous after dark." Chandler has visited the homes of a transsexual forger, a teenager who almost killed his 2-week-old baby, and a man who can't keep his hands off of pre-teen girls. All the while, Chandler was armed only with a small canister of pepper spray as he made his way through some of Jacksonville's toughest neighborhoods. Most times Chandler doesn't run into too much trouble. But he has had his life threatened in person and by telephone. He's fought off angry pit bulls and has been offered drugs from people who see him in the neighborhood. Other drawbacks to visiting convicts' homes are that sometimes he has had to spray himself with insect repellent because fleas and roaches will climb on his legs and bite him. But Chandler does find some satisfaction once in a while, helping a convict dry out and stay out of prison. He says that it's kind of stressful, but he feels good when he sees someone turn things around and make it through their probation. [Adapted from The Correctional Compass, *"What Other People Are Saying: Jobs with Risks." June 1, 1999].*

INTRODUCTION

This chapter is about the recruitment, selection, and training of probation and parole officers. When a mandate was issued by the President's Commission of 1967, significant developments occurred in corrections and probation/parole which led to improvements in programs, personnel, and policies in almost every local, state, and federal jurisdiction. We will examine the contemporary condition of probation and parole services as well as the state of these services in previous years. While considerable improvements have been made in efforts to recruit and retain quality personnel and upgrade the quality of services provided offenders, much more needs to be done. This chapter will assess the progress made as well as highlight those areas in need of improvement.

Correctional officers are prison or jail staff and their supervisors who manage inmates, while probation and parole officers supervise and manage probationers and parolees in a variety of offender **aftercare** programs (American Correctional Association, 2003). Since the departments of correction in many states select POs as well as prison staff and conduct training programs for all of their correctional personnel, similar criteria are often used for selecting correctional officers as well as for POs. Thus, useful information will be gleaned from the general correctional literature which is applicable to POs as well as prison and jail personnel. This does not mean that prison and jail correctional officers necessarily share the same characteristics with POs. One major difference is that correctional officers manage and interact with incarcerated offenders, while POs manage and interact with non-incarcerated criminals. There are also differing pay scales, work requirements, and other important characteristics that serve to distinguish between these two officer populations that deal with offenders at different points in time.

There is been a substantial and continuing increase in the number of personnel working in the area of adult and juvenile corrections. In 2002 there were over 700,000 personnel in corrections for both adults and juveniles. This is an increase of nearly 350 percent compared with the 214,000 personnel reported in 1986 (American Correctional Association, 2004). There were 270,000 correctional officers in U.S. jails and prisons in 2002. Also, there were 420,000 personnel working in adult and juvenile probation and parole services for the same period (American Correctional Association, 2003). Thus, probation and parole personnel made up about 65 percent of all persons working with convicted offenders.

Probation officers are hired to manage probationers exclusively in many jurisdictions, while parole officers deal only with parolees. Some observers believe that probation officers deal with lower-risk and less dangerous offenders than parole officers. Parole officers are assigned ex-convicts who have already served a portion of their sentences in prisons or jails, usually because of felony convictions. Confinement implies a greater level of dangerousness than those who are selected to participate in probation programs. However, evidence suggests that probation officers are receiving more dangerous offenders into their charge annually through felony probation, as prison and jail overcrowding make it impossible to incarcerate all criminals who should be incarcerated.

In many jurisdictions, probation and parole officers supervise both types of offenders interchangeably (American Correctional Association, 2003). In many states, probation and parole officers are combined in official reports of statistical information to organizations such as the American Correctional Association. Within the adult category, states such as Alabama, Florida, Virginia, Washington, and Wyoming report total numbers of probation and parole aftercare personnel.

THE ORGANIZATION AND OPERATION OF PROBATION AND PAROLE AGENCIES

Different departments and agencies in each state administer probation and parole departments. Most states have departments of corrections that supervise both incarcerated and nonincarcerated offenders. In some jurisdictions these tasks are overseen by departments of human services, departments of youth services, or some other umbrella agency.

Functions and Goals of Probation and Parole Services

The following functions and goals of probation and parole services are to:

- supervise offenders
- ensure offender-client compliance with program conditions by conducting random searches of offender premises, maintaining contact with offender-client employers, and otherwise maintaining occasional face-to-face spot checks
- conduct routine and random drug/alcohol checks
- provide networking services for employment assistance
- direct offender-clients to proper treatment, counseling, and other forms of requested assistance
- protect the community and its residents by detecting program infractions and reporting infractions to judges and parole boards
- assist offenders in becoming reintegrated into their communities
- engage in any rehabilitative action that will improve offender-client skills and law-abiding behavior

Organization and Administration of Probation and Parole Departments

Each state and large city has its own organization for administering and supervising probationers and parolees. The volume of offenders makes a significant difference in how departments are managed and the sizes of PO caseloads

(Quinn, Gould, and Holloway, 2001:1). In some areas of the country, such as New York, PO caseloads for supervising probationers are as high as 400. In other parts of the country, caseloads for POs may be as low as 10. Obviously, in those areas where PO caseloads are sizable, the nature of supervision exercised over these offenders is different from the supervision received by clients when client caseloads are under 25 (Camp and Camp, 2003).

Some jurisdictions have drive-in windows established in shopping centers where clients may drive up to a window like they are going to withdraw cash from an automated teller machine. However, instead of withdrawing cash, they place their hands on a surface that reads their palm prints and verifies their where-abouts. In other locations, such as Long Beach, California, large numbers of proba-tioners and some parolees report to a central office monthly to verify that they are employed and are remaining law-abiding. These check-ins mean that numerous offenders can be supervised. However, the nature of the supervision is question-able. Without frequent, random, and direct face-to-face contact with offender-clients, POs have no way of knowing whether these clients are law-abiding or engaging in some illicit behavior. Only those brought to the attention of police come to the attention of POs. Also, POs may detect probation or parole program vi-olations during random visits to offender-clients' premises at odd hours.

Most states and the federal government attempt to divide clients according to the seriousness of their prior offending. Some offenders are deemed at greater risk of reoffending than others. Therefore, they are targeted for more intensive supervision. Lower-risk offenders are less likely to reoffend, and therefore their supervision does not need to be as intense.

One example of a probation and parole agency is the Field Services Divi-sion Central Office in North Dakota. Figure 9.1 shows a diagram of this office. There is a director, a program manager, business officer, release program man-ager, three community offender services program managers, and an institu-tional offender services manager.

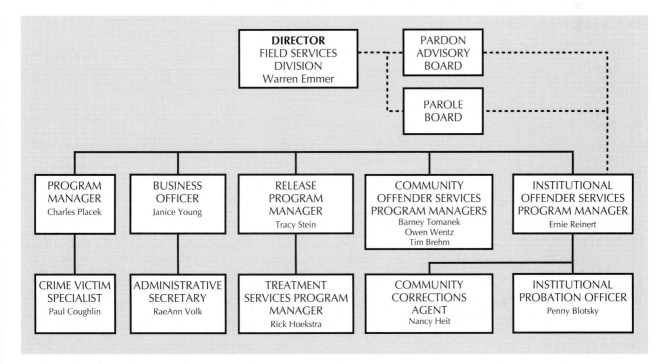

FIGURE 9.1 North Dakota Field Division Central Office.
Source: Courtesy of Elaine Little, Director, North Dakota Department of Corrections and Rehabilitation.)

One good feature of Figure 9.1 is that it is relatively simple. There simply aren't that many persons on probation or parole in North Dakota. For example, in 2002, there were 3,356 probationers and 268 parolees in North Dakota to be supervised (Camp and Camp, 2003). Despite these low numbers, even the North Dakota Probation and Parole Field Services division can be fairly complex. Figure 9.2 shows a diagram of the division of labor for Parole and Probation Field Services.

In Figure 9.1, there is a general manager over four major regions of North Dakota, together with a manager who supervises an intensive program for offenders who need to be more closely monitored. North Dakota is a large state geographically, and thus, it is imperative to divide it according to quadrants, with a West Region Supervisor, a Central Region Supervisor, a South Region Supervisor, and a North Region Supervisor. Notice in Figure 9.2 that there are 14 major cities and surrounding areas served by these four regions. Under the Intensive Program, there are four major intensive supervision supervisors and support staff to supervise offenders. These programs operate primarily out of Bismarck or Fargo.

The general mission of the Field Services Division overseeing probationers, parolees, and other community-based clients is to protect society by ensuring that the community-placed offenders are provided responsible supervision that requires them to be an active participant in their rehabilitation. Supervising offenders requires proactive intervention and case management strategies. The Field Services Division continuously reviews and modifies programs it provides to address community safety issues, prison overcrowding, and offender needs. The Intensive Supervision Program and comprehensive Day Reporting Program typify programming designed to facilitate the supervision of those offenders posing the greatest risks and needs. Halfway houses, home confinement programs, and curfews are some of the intermediate sanctions used to

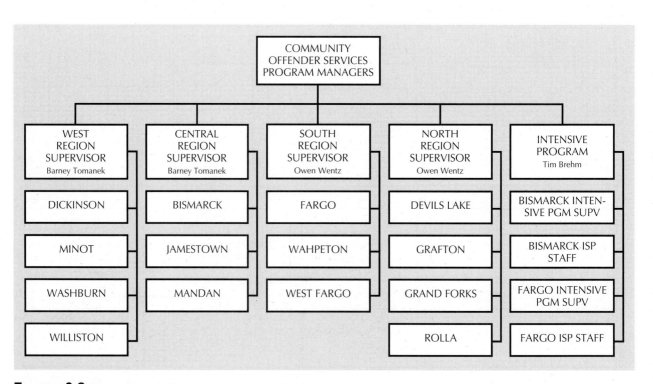

FIGURE 9.2 North Dakota Parole and Probation Field Services.
Source: Courtesy of Elaine Little, Director, North Dakota Department of Corrections and Rehabilitation.

verify compliance with supervision sanctions. Electronic monitoring and on-site drug testing are also tools used regularly by POs to supervise offenders.

A prototype of an intensive supervision program for community-based correctional services has been established by the American Probation and Parole Association. Figure 9.3 shows this prototypical intensive supervision program.

Figure 9.3 begins with the offender-client population to be served by different community agencies. These agencies devise mission statements that articulate clearly their goals and policies. Relations with local law enforcement agencies, parole boards, judges and courts are lumped under "Other CJS Components." The community where the agency is based is considered as another significant input that influences agency policy and protocol. One of the primary goals of these community-based agencies is to reduce offender recidivism (Albrecht and van Kalmthout, 2002). This goal is achieved in part through shifting from a custodial, incapacitative, and punitive mode to a more integrated approach of interventions and risk-control strategies. A

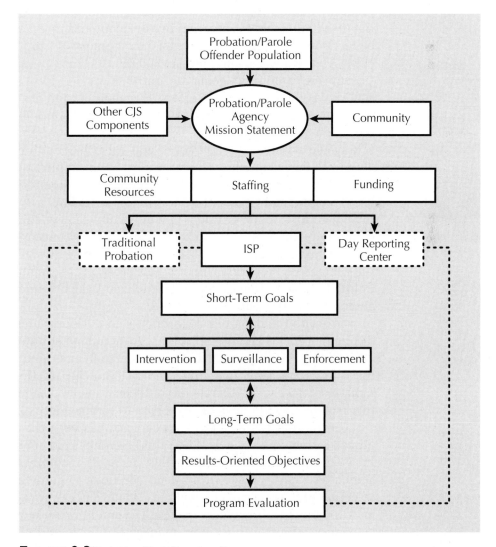

FIGURE 9.3 Program Development Process.
Source: From Fulton, Gendreau, and Paparozzi, 1995:26; reprinted with the permission of the American Probation and Parole Association.

balanced approach to offender supervision is stressed, where individual offender needs are prioritized and met. A balanced approach emphasizes three things: heightening offender accountability; concern for public safety; and maximizing offender rehabilitation. Prior agency goals were short-term ones; under future agency planning, goals are projected as long-range ones. Better risk control is both a short-term and long-term goal sought by all community-based agencies. Such risk control is achieved to a greater degree when agencies provide a greater range of assistance and offender services that meet offender needs, particularly in the areas of employment and substance abuse (Cepeda and Avelardo, 2003). The prototype also encourages focusing upon results of programs rather than program activities. It is accepted that the two primary missions of probation and parole are to protect society and rehabilitate offenders.

Critical factors in effective program development include (1) needs assessment; (2) adequate staffing; (3) proper and ample funding; (4) engaging stakeholders, including establishing working task forces and creating more effective public relations; (5) networking with community service providers; (6) close program monitoring and evaluation; (7) targeting greater numbers of high risk/need offenders for program involvement and treatment; and (8) developing better selection instruments for the inclusion of program participants (Matthews, Hubbard, and Latessa, 2001).

Several ambitious goals are outlined for the ideal community-based ISP agency: (1) increased public safety; (2) rehabilitation of offenders; (3) provision of intermediate punishments; (4) reduction in prison/jail overcrowding; and (5) reduction in operating costs. ISP objectives should be specific, measurable, achievable within a limited time, and identified with an actual result (Berg, 2001). Critical elements for successful program implementation include smaller PO caseloads; a greater range of correctional interventions; a more objectives-based management system; systematic case review; a system of positive reinforcement for clients; a system of control and accountability; victim restitution; community involvement; and aftercare. Several successful community-based ISP programs include New Jersey's ISP program devised in 1983; the Massachusetts Intensive Probation Supervision Program, implemented in 1985; and the Colorado Judicial Department's Specialized Drug Offender Program (SDOP) created in the early 1990s (Kerik, 2000).

Probation and parole departments in various states are administered by different agencies and organizations. Although most states have departments of corrections that supervise both incarcerated and nonincarcerated offenders, these tasks are sometimes overseen in other jurisdictions by departments of human services, departments of youth services, or some other umbrella agency that may or may not have the expertise to service these clients adequately.

During the 1990s, a growing concern has been the **professionalization** of all correctional personnel. When the President's Commission on Law Enforcement and Administration of Justice made its recommendations in 1967, few standards were in place in most jurisdictions to guide administrators in their selection of new recruits (Angelone, 2000). Thus, it was not unusual for critics of corrections to frequently make unfavorable remarks about and unflattering characterizations of those who manage criminals and oversee their behaviors. Because of the complexity of contemporary correctional roles, new pools from which to recruit, and greater social science training, different types of officers may be required to demonstrate a broader range of skills.

Selected Criticisms of Probation and Parole Programs

Probation and parole programs been viewed unfavorably over the years, both in the United States and in other countries (such as England). Efforts have been made to link the failure of rehabilitation in probation and parole with specific programs and personnel. The most common criticisms of rehabilitation programs are that they are disorganized, inadequately funded, and understaffed (Freeman, 1999). Few programs dependent upon public funds for their operation and continuation will acknowledge adequate staffing and funding. Thus, most programs are perpetually in a state of need, where requests are made annually for larger portions of public resources and budgets are stretched to justify greater allocations for agency funding.

What evidence suggests that enlarging correctional staffs and spending more money on correctional programs will necessarily result in lower recidivism rates? Interestingly, the enlargement of correctional staffs, especially in probation and parole, has made it possible in some jurisdictions for officers to supervise their clients more closely through lower offender caseloads. However, greater supervision of offenders has resulted occasionally in an increase in the number of reported technical violations of an offender's probation or parole program (Baumer et al., 2002). Technical violations do not mean that crime among probationers and parolees has increased, only that they are now more frequently observed and recorded. These offenders stand a good chance of having their probation or parole revoked because of such violations, thus giving the public the impression that their criminal activity is increasing.

Criticisms of POs generally have centered on the inadequacy of their training, lack of experience, and poor educational background. For example, studies of POs have shown that they are typically white, come from rural areas, are politically conservative, have mixed job histories, have entered corrections work at a turning point or after failure in another career, or are merely holding their present job while anticipating a career move to a more promising alternative. Many POs seem to lack professionalism (Giles and Mullineux, 2000).

Professionalization is often equated with acquiring more formal education rather than practical skills involving one-to-one human relationships with different types of offender-clients (Correctional Service of Canada, 2000). Educational programs for officers often overemphasize the laws and rules of institutions and the mechanics of enforcement. Often underemphasized are people skills and the ability to cope with human problems (e.g. physically or mentally impaired clients), those abilities required if the quality of officers is to be raised (Griffin, 2002). Although the following list is not exhaustive, it contains some of the more prevalent reasons for criticisms of probation and parole programs and personnel:

1. Probation and parole programs have historically been fragmented and independent of other criminal justice organizations and agencies. Without any centralized planning and coordinating, probation and parole programs have developed haphazardly in response to varying jurisdictional needs.

2. The general field of corrections has lacked professionalization associated with established fields with specialized bodies of knowledge. Often, corrections officers have secured their training through affiliation with an academic program in sociology, criminal justice, or political science. While these programs offer much relating to the correctional field, they are

not designed to give corrections-oriented students the practical exposure to real problems faced by officers on duty and dealing with real offenders.

3. Most jurisdictions have lacked licensing mechanisms whereby officers can become certified through proper in-service training and education. However, this situation has greatly improved during the last few decades. In 2002, probation and parole officers averaged 246 hours of training, including 38 hours of in-service training. Also in 2002, there were formal training programs in all U.S. jurisdictions (Camp and Camp, 2003).

4. Until the early 1980s, only one state required a college education of probation or parole officer applicants, and some states had as their only prerequisite the ability to read and write, presumably for the purpose of completing PSI reports. Despite the fact that the relation between a college education and probation or parole officer effectiveness has not been demonstrated conclusively, some evidence suggests that college training is particularly helpful in the preparation of presentence investigations and understanding criminal law and potential legal issues and liabilities which might arise in the officer–client relationship.

5. Past selection procedures for probation and parole officers have focused upon physical attributes and security consideration. An emphasis in recruitment upon physical attributes has historically operated to exclude women from probation and parole work, although there is evidence showing a greater infusion of women into correctional roles in recent years. For example, in 1986 only 12 percent of all POs in the United States were women. But by 2002, the proportion of female POs had risen to about 50 percent (Camp and Camp, 2003).

6. Probation and parole officer training has often been based upon the military model used for police training (Doerner and Dantzker, 2000). In those states with centralized corrections officer training and in-service programs for those preparing for careers in probation and parole work, a fundamental program flaw has been overreliance upon police training models whose relevance is frequently questioned by new recruits. Highly structured training programs frequently fail to provide prospective probation and parole officers with the sorts of practical experiences they will encounter face-to-face with offender-clients.

Experimental Proactive Probation/Parole Programs

In a concerted effort to improve the effectiveness of their roles in communities, probation and parole departments have taken steps to overcome some of the major criticisms directed against them and their performance. One means of addressing some or all of these criticisms without incurring substantial additional expenses has been for probation departments to locate some of their personnel in satellite offices throughout their communities as a means of becoming closer to the public and making it easier to provide client services from more centralized locations in areas where offenders live. One example is Maricopa County, Arizona, where the county's Adult Probation Department has located several satellite offices in selected neighborhoods. Probation officers assigned to these offices work near where probationers live. In many respects, these officers are like "beat cops," where the beats are several neighborhood blocks where POs can walk to and from client residences from their satellite locations. Initially neighborhood residents who knew about probationers living among them were terrified of the presence of these offenders. However, the beat probation officers soon became known to community residents, who accepted their presence. After four years, these community-based POs alleviated much community fear of offenders, as POs were able to more closely supervise and monitor them and their whereabouts (Campbell and Wolf, 2002:30).

Another instance of proactive probation officer action occurred in 1992 in Boston, where Operation Night Light was born. Probation officers began riding with police officers during evening hours in response to reports of crimes. POs quickly became aware that some of their clients, including gang members, were involved in some of these crimes. When some of these clients saw their POs interacting in concert with police officers during crime investigations, it gave them a new appreciation of the PO role. One of the more important outcomes of Operation Night Light was that it gave POs greater insight into the lifestyles of many of their clients and improved greatly their individual effectiveness in enforcing client program conditions. POs also began to network with community churches and civic organizations, gaining support for their proactive role in probationer program rule enforcement (Campbell and Wolf, 2002:31).

In Vermont between 1984–1994, there was a great deal of crime committed by probationers and parolees. The public wanted something done about it. The probation department eventually established a reparative program that brought together offenders and their victims. In 1994 Vermont overhauled its entire sentencing structure, giving probation departments more extensive powers to devise community solutions to problems posed by certain probationers. The Reparative Probation Program was established. This program sought to give low-risk probationers (e.g., check forgers, shoplifters, vandals, burglars) the option of meeting with reparative boards of community volunteers who devised 90-day probation sentences requiring offenders to make up for the harm their actions caused various victims. As a result of participating in and successfully completing the 90-day reparative conditions and doing what these boards ask them to do, probationers can avoid regular probation at the end of the 90-day program. The system seems to work thus far, especially with these low-risk offenders (Campbell and Wolf, 2002:31).

Another program targeting more youthful offenders was initiated in Deschutes County in Oregon in 1996. The juvenile probation division was drastically overhauled, and regular juvenile POs became known as community justice officers. These officers were now community problem solvers. Community-based probation was integrated throughout the new system in several ways. A Restoration Team was established that drafted agreements between offenders and victims requiring offenders to make up for their actions by working for their victims until any cost incurred from the offense had been reimbursed. Some youthful offenders were assigned to the Restorative Community Work Service, which required them to work on projects that a Community Outreach Team would develop with various community residents. Activities were created such as helping to build homes for low-income families, both to pay back the community and to give offenders a sense of accomplishment. Some offenders became eligible for a program called Fresh Start, which paid them a minimum wage until they could earn enough to repay their crime victims. Another team of POs was created and called the Accountability Team. This team liaisoned between probationers and the courts to devise service projects for at-risk youths. These and other back-to-the-community programs are just a few of the many attempts to bolster the image of POs in the eyes of community residents and to restore public confidence in PO work. The successfulness of these programs and their growing numbers throughout the United States suggests that probation departments are becoming more effective in promoting greater program compliance among their offender-clients. In time, the image of probation departments will improve measurably, although there are continuing problems of adequate funding that block or impede effective programming (Campbell and Wolf, 2002:33–34).

PROBATION AND PAROLE OFFICERS: A PROFILE

Characteristics of Probation and Parole Officers

Who are probation and parole officers? What are their characteristics? Although little comprehensive information about POs exists, surveys have been conducted in recent years which depict the characteristics of those performing various correctional roles. These surveys indicate a gradual move toward greater corrections officer professionalization. Historically, evidence of professionalizing probation work has been found in various cities, such as Chicago, during the period 1900–1935 (Sims, 2001). During World War II (1941–1945), federal probation officer professionalization was greatly improved, as the federal government moved to expand and extend its probation officer personpower to include military offenders as well as civil ones. In 1942, for instance, there were only 251 federal probation officers in the entire system (Oviedo, 2003:5). It was during this time interval that federal POs cultivated a more in-depth familiarity with presentence investigation reports, which had to be completed for military personnel in larger numbers. Federal POs, therefore, were obligated to take on additional responsibilities and develop greater flexibility and professionalism in the performance of their duties. One indication of greater professionalization of the corrections profession has been the movement toward accreditation and the establishment of accreditation programs through the American Correctional Association (ACA) and the American Probation and Parole Association (APPA) (American Correctional Association, 2004; Youngken, 2000).

A majority of PO staff are female (58 percent), white (78 percent), possess bachelor's degrees (76 percent), and have 9 to 12 years experience. Entry-level salaries for POs ranged in 2002 from a low of $18,200 in Kentucky to a high of $45,600 in California, with the average entry-level salary being about $26,000 (Camp and Camp, 2003). Maximum salaries among jurisdictions for POs ranged from a low of $30,000 in West Virginia to a high of $88,000 in Alaska (Camp and Camp, 2003), with the average highest salary at $56,000. The federal probation system had an entry-level salary of $28,000, with a high salary of $97,500, averaging $49,900. Most state systems presently require bachelor's degrees as the minimum education for entry-level parole officer positions. In a few states, the general entry-level requirements for PO positions are less stringent. In 1990, for instance, a few jurisdictions required a bachelor's degree or equivalent experience. By 2002, a majority of jurisdictions required bachelor's degrees for entry-level positions (Camp and Camp, 2003).

Considering the relatively low salaries of POs compared with those in other correctional positions and in the private sector, their higher median ages, and their comparatively lower educational levels, it is understandable that probation and parole have drawn criticism in the last few decades concerning the lack of professionalism POs seem to exhibit. This problem is explained, in part, by the

BOX 9.1

Bruno Mediate
Supervisor, Westmoreland County Adult Probation/Parole Greensburg, PA

Statistics:

M.S. (administration of justice), Shippensburg University of Pennsylvania; B.A. (criminology, security management)

Background:

I became interested in the criminal justice field at a very young age. I had a cousin working as a Pennsylvania State Trooper and another as a probation officer. The stories they told as well as watching the many police shows of the 60s and 70s really made a career in law enforcement seem glamorous. However, upon my graduation from college, I decided to utilize my minor and pursue a career in security management. Due to the declining steel industry in the Pittsburgh region at that time, most large corporations were either not hiring or laying off employees. I was able, however, to obtain employment for a private security company as an undercover investigator for a brief time and was eventually hired by a large retail store chain as a security manager trainee. The long hours and low pay did not seem very glamorous and prompted me to enroll in business classes at the local community college. I actually went into the sales field for approximately one year. As fate would have it, a fraternity brother of mine worked as a juvenile probation officer and notified me of some job openings. I applied and was eventually hired.

Work Experience:

I worked as a juvenile probation officer for three years and felt that I had a good rapport with juveniles and their families and appeared to make a difference in many of their lives. I also had the opportunity to receive my master's degree in the administration of justice while working in juvenile probation.

Shortly after obtaining my master's degree, an opportunity almost passed me by. Our county prison as well as other prisons throughout the mid to late 1980s was extremely overcrowded. The county created a prison population officer to work at the jail and act as a liaison between the jail and the courts. This person would be directly responsible to monitor the population on a daily basis, expedite any unnecessary delays involving hearings, parole releases, and nominal bond hearings. Even though I did not see the announcement until after the application deadline and also after several candidates had already been interviewed, I applied anyway and was hired. This position was a management-level position and gave me the opportunity to work closely with the prison board, county commissioners, judges, and all criminal justice departments in Westmoreland County. I also had the opportunity to recommend, create, and receive funding for alternative programs to incarceration such as electronic monitoring.

In 1992 Westmoreland County received state funding to create an intermediate punishment program, which utilizes electronic monitoring as an alternative to jail. I was selected as the program supervisor. In 1993 the program was transferred to the Adult Probation/Parole Department where I currently am still the program supervisor. Our program is currently the third largest electronic monitoring program in Pennsylvania. The Allegheny County (Pittsburgh) and Philadelphia programs are the only larger programs. We currently utilize active Radio Frequency (RF) electronic monitoring equipment as well as passive voice/breath

(*continued*)

BOX 9.1 (*Continued*)

testing equipment. The equipment works through the offender's telephone line. We also utilize a secure Internet connection to our electronic monitoring vendor to access offender files, change schedules, and other tasks. Technology has really changed over the past ten years. Global positioning satellite (GPS) systems, which utilize satellites to track an offender's movement, are the latest technology and are becoming popular with many criminal justice agencies. Westmoreland County is currently in the process of testing "passive" GPS equipment. The officers in my unit spend most of their time in the field and work a number of nontraditional hours, enabling them to have more contact with offenders. Also, I am currently a part of a statewide Integrated Information System in Pennsylvania called JNET (PA Justice Network). The concept is to integrate all criminal justice agencies throughout Pennsylvania by sharing information via a secured Internet connection.

Working with offenders and their families, both juvenile and adult, can be very frustrating at times. Juveniles are very unpredictable and can be doing good one day and end up in the detention center the next. One of the hardest things I ever had to deal with as a juvenile probation officer was watching a child being separated from his/her family and being placed into an institution. Even though it was in the child's and family's best interests, it was hard to get used to. Working with adult offenders who have been involved with the criminal justice system for many years and who also have serious drug and alcohol problems is equally as difficult. Approximately 75 percent of the offenders in our system have drug and alcohol problems, and 50 percent of those are dually diagnosed with mental health problems. In addition to the in-home breath alcohol testing mentioned earlier, we also conduct random urine screening for drugs. Offenders who test positive for drugs can face a wide range of sanctions, including temporary (shock) incarceration or going through the full revocation process. In many cases, a determination is made whether to have the offender assessed/reassessed for drug and alcohol issues and be placed into the appropriate level of drug and alcohol

treatment. I sometimes refer to our system as the revolving door, because we keep seeing many of the same offenders coming in and out over and over again.

Since 2001 our department has been trained to carry firearms. We have also received training in self-defense and O.C. (Oleoresin Capsicum) spray. I currently am involved with martial arts and hold a second degree black belt in Tae Kwon Do. Throughout the years, my officers and I have been involved in several dangerous situations. Being in an offender's environment and not being prepared or aware of your surroundings makes you very vulnerable. An officer's training, experience, ability to remain calm and to use his or her wits usually gets him or her out of most situations. Working in teams or with the police in dangerous areas has also proved to be beneficial. Unfortunately, many colleagues throughout Pennsylvania and the nation have not been as fortunate.

Advice to Students:

1. Learn to be open-minded and flexible; don't be one-dimensional.
2. Don't be afraid to think out of the box.
3. Be aware that offenders will try to manipulate you.
4. Don't be afraid of technology; it can only enhance your supervision abilities.
5. Don't forget about an offender's family and friends; they can be your best source of information.
6. Learn as much about your criminal justice system as possible and create a network with each agency.
7. Education is important; a four-year degree is usually required for probation/parole work, and a master's degree can only enhance your chances for advancement.
8. An internship in probation/parole or related criminal justice agency is very beneficial and can sometimes even lead to full-time employment.
9. Always be aware of your surroundings while working in the field; know your limitations; know how to use your wit as well as your brain; and work with a partner whenever possible.

lack of professional identity characterizing PO work, the fact that there is no recognized professional school to prepare leaders for probation, and no nationally recognized scholars or administrators who can be called eminent leaders in probation or parole. However, some evidence suggests that improvements are being made in selected jurisdictions to improve the professionalism of correctional officers generally, including POs and their administrations (Stinchcomb, 2000).

What Do POs Do?

Many different PO functions have been identified, reflecting considerable diversity associated with PO roles. These include supervision, surveillance, investigation of cases, assisting in rehabilitation, develop and discuss probation conditions, counsel, visit homes and work with clients, make arrests, make referrals, write PSI reports, keep records, perform court duties, collect fines, supervise restitution, serve warrants, maintain contracts with courts, recommend sentences, develop community service programs, assist law enforcement officers and agencies, assist courts in transferring cases, enforce criminal laws, locate employment for clients, and initiate program revocations.

POs spend much of their time preparing reports or PSIs for convicted offenders at the request of judges. They must maintain contact with all offenders assigned to their supervision. They must be aware of community agencies and employment opportunities so that their function as resource staff may be maximized. They must perform informal psychological counseling. They must enforce the laws and insure offender compliance with the requirements of the particular probation or parole program. When faced with dangerous or life-threatening situations in their contacts with offenders, they must be able to make decisions about how best to handle these situations. They must be familiar with their legal rights, the rights of offenders, and their own legal liabilities in relation to clients (del Carmen and Bonham, 2001). POs must be flexible enough to supervise a wide variety of offender-clients. Increasing numbers of PO clients are from different ethnicities and cultures. Thus, greater cultural awareness is required of today's POs.

A summary of the primary duties of probation and parole officers in North Dakota seems to typify this general work:

1. Supervise offenders to ensure compliance with parole, probation, or community placement agreements.
2. Perform scheduled and unscheduled home visits.
3. Conduct searches, with or without a warrant, of homes, vehicles, and possessions of criminal offenders to determine if they have dangerous, illegal, or stolen goods, or for any other evidence that might indicate criminal behavior.
4. Manage cases by means of direct contact with offenders; indirect contact through individuals who are acquainted with or have an impact on the offender's life, and the maintenance of records required by the Department of Corrections and Rehabilitation.
5. Conduct investigations, prepare reports, and make recommendations for the offender's placement and level of risk to the community.
6. Notify court-mandated sex offenders of their responsibility to register with local law enforcement and monitor their adherence to this statute.
7. Assist law enforcement in criminal investigations.

BOX 9.2

PERSONALITY HIGHLIGHT

Yoleeta C. Howell
Judicial District Manager 18th Judicial District, Guilford County, Greensboro, North Carolina

Statistics:

M.S. (education and guidance counseling), South Carolina State College; B.S. (health and physical education), North Carolina Central University; Professional Management course, North Carolina State Personnel; Staff Development and Training (2-year program); Governor's Award for Excellence.

Work Background:

When I was in graduate training at South Carolina State College, I completed a practicum in mental health. I worked with substance abusers, those with severe depression, and persons with diverse behavioral problems. Later I worked with Dr. Isaac Burnett at North Carolina A & T State University, where I continued my work with OSHA for nine months. Although fulfilling, I wanted to work in a field where I could apply my counseling skills. Following that experience in 1977, I applied for a probation and parole position with the North Carolina Department of Correction. I was hired with the state and began my work in Pre-Release and Aftercare Services, where I provided individual and group counseling to inmates. I assisted them in acquiring the skills they would need to become rehabilitated and subsequently reintegrated back into society. My inmate-clients consisted of a variety of offenders, including burglars, sex offenders, robbers, thieves, drug dealers—the full range of convicted felons. Almost all of these offenders being considered for parole were moved to a minimum-security unit prior to being released into their communities. I did a lot of counseling with them during the period 1977–1980.

In 1980 I became a parole officer. At that time, there were small numbers of parole officers in various jurisdictions throughout the state. My caseload ranged from 80 to 110 offenders. In 1989 I became a Unit Supervisor. This was a "first" for me in several respects. I was the first black female to be-

come a Unit Supervisor in the state. My responsibilities included supervising eight officers throughout a ten-county area. In 1991 I became Parole Services Manager. This was another "first" in that I was the first black female Parole Services Manager in the state, among five Parole Service Managers with the only other female manager being white. The third "first" occurred in 1993 when I became the first black female Judicial District Manager, a position I continue to hold today. My responsibilities include all aspects of personnel, fiscal and budgeting matters, and hiring entry-level POs. Presently I conduct internal investigations, initial orientations for all new PO hires, and Death Row Investigations for the Governor's Office.

Experiences:

During my years as a parole officer, I had many harrowing experiences involving my parolees. On one occasion when I was in my 20s, I went to do an investigation of one of my clients, a young man who had been convicted of a violent offense and was currently incarcerated. It was very early on a Saturday morning and no one was on the streets. I was unarmed, since parole officers were not authorized to carry firearms until 1978. I arrived at the inmate's father's house at 7:30 A.M. The man seemed cordial enough. He invited me in and showed me to a dining room table. Then he proceeded to lock the door. There were numerous locks on the door, and he locked every single one of them. Then he went into the kitchen nearby and rifled through one of the drawers. I

BOX 9.2 (*Continued*)

could observe him from where I was seated, and he was acting very agitated. He started pulling sharp knives out of the drawer and throwing them on the kitchen counter. The more knives he pulled from the drawer, the more agitated he became. I was unnerved by this whole experience. Not only had he locked me in his house, but now he was acting crazy, throwing knives around on his kitchen counter. I looked around the house for possible exits, and I spied an open rear kitchen door. If necessary, I thought, I could run past him and exit if he suddenly attacked me. Needless to say, he was making me more nervous by the minute. Suddenly, I had a thought. I yelled out to him, "Hey, where does your son's mother live, anyway? I need to talk to her a little." He stopped what he was doing with the knives and looked at me. "How do I get to your ex-wife's place?" I asked. He came out of the kitchen, went to the front door and unlocked all of the locks. "Come here," he said. "I'll show you." He led me outside and down to the sidewalk. He pointed out where the mother lived and I thanked him and left. Breathing easier now, I reflected on the fact that the man himself was mentally ill and could have done me some serious harm. Furthermore, I knew from the son's PSI report that he had mental health issues and was in prison for assaulting and stabbing a police officer as well as other innocent bystanders. His family had a variety of mental disorders, and they had a long history of violence. I never did find out what happened to the father. I'm just grateful that I was able to get away from him on that peculiar Saturday morning visit. My last thought was, "No one knows where I am, as I had not reported that I would be working on Saturday morning." Big mistake!

On another occasion, I contacted a parolee who had violated several of his parole conditions. The man was not living at his given address. He had moved to another location without informing our department. Also he had quit his job without notifying us. Like my earlier experience with the man with mental problems, this particular client

came from a family with problems, including his mother, who was "not all there." I advised the parolee that he needed to come to our office. Eventually he came to the office, whereupon we advised him that he had violated his parole and would have to reappear before the parole board. As soon as he heard this, he became extremely violent, jumping up and down, behaving irrationally. Several other officers came into the room, and it eventually took six officers to subdue him and place him in handcuffs. Even restrained like that, he was still trying to get free, kicking and yelling. It was our policy to take these alleged parole violators to a medium security prison unit for temporary detention pending a hearing. This was a 1 1/2 hour trip by car, where three people escorted him. I drove. When we got to the prison, the man was taken to a room. He was still very agitated. The prison officers removed his handcuffs and the man went crazy. He screamed and attempted to jump up from a sofa where he was placed. A correctional officer captain slapped him hard, knocking him to the other end of the sofa. He eventually became subdued, but later he filed a grievance against the officer who struck him. We were called as witnesses, but none of us "saw anything." We weren't about to testify against the correctional officer, who was merely acting to protect us from this man's violent conduct.

During my experience as a parole officer, I was often in dangerous circumstances and places, such as gang-controlled neighborhoods, drug hotspots, and lower class housing projects. Often, street lights in these areas were busted out, drug deals were going on, persons were lying around under stairwells, some doing drugs. These were areas that armed police officers sought to avoid. They were that dangerous. On one occasion, I recall two of my officers walking toward the apartment complex to interview one of their clients. Suddenly two pit bulls charged from an apartment, heading for the unsuspecting POs. But an unidentified male called the dogs back just in time, laughing the entire time. On another occasion, one of our young

(continued)

BOX 9.2 (Continued)

parolees went to see a woman in one of these housing projects. She was just a friend of our parolee, not a girlfriend. In reality she was the girlfriend of a notorious drug dealer from Jamaica. When the drug dealer found her talking with our parolee, he had some of his men capture the parolee. They kept him in the apartment, where they beat and tortured him. The drug dealer thought the parolee was coming on to his girlfriend. A total misunderstanding. Anyway, they eventually shot the parolee to death, dismembered his body, and wrapped the various parts in plastic trash bags. The bags were placed in a dumpster. Police never found the man's body, but other circumstantial evidence led to the drug dealer's arrest, and he was subsequently convicted of the parolee's murder. I came to realize that the level of drug dealing in the greater Greensboro area was due in large part to the fact that major interstate highways converge there (I-85 and I-40).

Although the PO caseloads for supervising such offenders should not exceed 30, in reality, these caseloads surge to over 45–50. With drug abuse comes HIV/AIDS, hepatitis, and tuberculosis. Whenever POs interact with such parolees with these diseases, they must wear protective gloves and other clothing whenever they must arrest them and take them into custody for one reason or another. Usually, these arrested persons have violated one or more conditions of their parole programs. When POs visit them, the POs are often accompanied by law enforcement officers, such as city police officers or county deputy sheriffs. It is a very dangerous business.

I don't want anyone to get the idea that all dangerous parolees are men. Women are just as dangerous. In one case, one female parolee in her early 20s convicted of heroin use and prostitution had violated some of her parole conditions. When our officers went to her location, which was on the third floor of an extended-stay hotel, the woman escaped by jumping out of the window. She broke her ankle when she hit the ground, but she got up and continued running away. She was apprehended in the lobby of the hotel. She still had some heroin residue dripping from her arm, where she had just injected herself. She was very violent and it took several officers to restrain her. In the 70s and 80s, female parolees were more passive, committing forgery, bad check writing, petty larceny, and other property offenses. However, during the last few decades, females have become as violent or more violent than men. Presently female violence in North Carolina is escalating at a more rapid rate, with much of this violence being drug-related.

When I became Judicial District Manager and moved into administration, my duties changed significantly. Now I conduct reviews of PO work. It is personally gratifying to me to be able to be in a position where I can assist POs in my jurisdiction improve themselves and their work quality and performance. I love investigations and investigative work. My supervisory duties include monitoring Chief Probation/Parole Officers and field staff. Do they show up for their appointments with parolees in a timely manner? Do they make it on time for their court appearances, which are frequent? I also do investigative background checks and reports relating to offenders on death row. If there are appeals, the governor and others need reports about these persons. My office has background paperwork on all of these offenders. I often prepare these reports and submit them to the proper persons so that informed decisions can be made about death row inmates. One of these reports involved a truck driver who killed numerous women in various states, including Texas, South Carolina, and North Carolina. The man would always strangle the women with an undergarment, have sex with them possibly after their deaths, and then dump them in various bodies of water, such as lakes or rivers. Since the man is wanted in several other states and must undergo trials, it will be a while before he is eventually executed for his crimes.

My jobs over the years have had their ups and downs. While more than a few POs dislike the paperwork associated with their

BOX 9.2 (*Continued*)

jobs, I happen to like it. I love to write. Also, I enjoy doing investigative work, compiling background information, criminal histories, interviewing family members, and obtaining information from victims about how their lives have been affected by certain offenders. Some of the rewarding experiences are the result of seeing certain offenders with whom I have worked actually go on to achieve college degrees or become successful in various businesses. In one case, a young man was convicted of kidnapping and assault together with another man. When the young man was paroled, I was instrumental in getting him into college. He was smart and had a lot of potential. Unfortunately, he became involved in various crimes and was rearrested and convicted. He is now serving 45 years in prison for these crimes. Most of those I work with who turn out to be successful are younger offenders in their 20s and 30s. Older offenders, in their 40s and 50s, seem more set in their criminal ways and are more difficult to change; they "age out." The chances of them changing their behaviors at these stages in their lives are very remote. I have not had many successful experiences with older repeat offenders. I would estimate that I have been successful in helping about a third of all of my clients. The rest either do well for a period of time and eventually recidivate, or they recidivate habitually and never become rehabilitated. The downside of being an administrator is the administration of personnel work. I don't especially like the routine paperwork of administration. I do it and do it well, but it is not the greatest selling feature for the job. Originally I got into this type of work to help people and utilize my counseling skills. I have found that no single counseling method works for all parolees. It is important to develop strategies for helping persons on a case-by-case basis, and hands-on training is vital in fulfilling this objective.

It has been fascinating for me over the years, seeing how our state has adopted various supervisory methods for our parolees and probationers. We now use global positioning satellite tracking for sex offender monitoring. We have developed drug courts, sex offender control programs, day reporting centers, and electronic monitoring programs as a part of our growing Special Operations Unit. We network with various schools to provide educational experiences for students in their early years, and we assist school resource officers in their duties. We have initiated DART, or a Drug Alcohol Recovery Treatment program, which provides 28-day and 90-day inpatient treatment for those with drug or alcohol abuse problems. We also have a Violent Crime Task Force and Community Policing. At the same time, we have lost several programs, such as boot camps, which have been discontinued due to budget cuts.

Advice to Students:

For those wishing to pursue a career in probation/parole, I would say, "Be prepared." We screen applicants through the administration of various tests and their responses to hypothetical scenarios, such as "What ifs....?" "What would you do if...?" Most applicant rejections involve poorly prepared persons who have inadequate writing skills and verbal abilities. Incredibly many of our applicants are college graduates who cannot think on their feet or who have poor writing skills. They can't put a coherent sentence together or explain what they would do in certain hypothetical scenarios. Successful applicants must "sell" themselves to us in interviews. What should you do to maximize your chances of getting a job with us? Take courses in speech and writing. Counseling skills are important, too. An exposure to social work courses is helpful. You definitely need exposure to cultural diversity. There are many good courses at universities today that deal with cultural diversity. You can learn about cultural diversity in criminal justice, sociology, and social work. These areas are very valuable in preparing you for probation/parole work. You must know how to talk to people. A special kind of attitude is required. You must deal with

(*continued*)

BOX 9.2 (Continued)

your clients on their level. This means that you need to understand them and where they are coming from. This doesn't mean simply learning how to talk like they do. This means understanding them in depth.

We offer four-week intensive training courses for all entry-level POs. On-the-job training involves pairing these entry-level people with some of our best, seasoned officers. If you're entering this area for the money, forget it. Probation/parole work doesn't pay that well. It is a labor of love. You have to love what you are doing. We find that most persons who leave probation/parole work shortly after entering it do so because of low pay. If you want to get into

this type of work to push people around and bully them, you will not be successful. There are always these types of persons in our field, but they are unpopular and have a string of unsuccessful experiences with their clients. Internships are very valuable. If you are at a school offering internships with probation/parole departments, by all means latch on to one of these internships. And I'm not talking about a one-day-per-week internship. I'm talking about those internships that involve 40-hour work weeks. I've got an intern now who I'd like to hire, because he has really developed a lot of valuable skills for doing this type of work. I can't recommend these types of experiences too much.

8. Collect, handle, and maintain evidence in accordance with evidentiary law.

9. Maintain necessary certifications and licensures (North Dakota Department of Corrections and Rehabilitation, 2004: 1–4).

Legally prescribed functions of POs have been articulated by others. In 2003 a study was conducted of all state probation agencies and the functions of POs described. Between 1992 and 2002, the number of different tasks to be performed by POs in various state and federal jurisdictions has increased. Explicit in this expansion of tasks is the growing influence of law enforcement-related functions. In 2002, 23 separate PO tasks were identified. These include supervision; surveillance; case investigations; assisting in rehabilitation; developing/discussing probation/parole conditions; counsel; visiting home/work; arrest; making referrals; writing PSI reports; keeping records; performing other court duties; collecting restitution; serving warrants; maintaining contact with the courts; recommending sentences; developing community service programming; assisting law enforcement agencies; enforcing criminal laws; assisting the court in transferring cases; locating employment for probationers/parolees; initiating revocation actions; and law-enforcement/peace officer functions (Purkiss et al., 2003:20).

Recruitment of POs

When POs are recruited, what type of training should they receive? How much education should be required, and what educational subjects have the greatest relevance for correctional careers? No immediate answers are available for these questions (Maund and Hammond, 2000). While most of us would agree that Ph.D. degrees are not essential for the effective performance of PO work, some educational training is desirable. Currently, observers disagree about how much education should be officially required as a part of the recruitment process.

BOX 9.3

**Deputy Probation Officer Trainee:
Open $12.54 hourly**

• *Description: Maintaining security and safety of juveniles incarcerated within county institutions and providing counseling on an occasional basis to juvenile wards.*

• *Minimum Qualifications: No experience is required.*

• *Training: Equivalent to completion of 60 units at an accredited college, with at least 9 units in the behavioral sciences (experience as a group or youth counselor, or other paid, full-time experience in related juvenile work may be substituted on a year-for-year basis for the required education). Applicants receiving their degree outside the United States must submit proof of accreditation by a recognized evaluation agency.*

• *License or Certificate: Possession of, or ability to obtain, a valid California state driver's license, proof of adequate vehicle insurance, and medical clearance will be required.*

• *Special Requirements: Prior to employment, candidates selected for appointment must complete and pass a background investigation and pre-employment psychological and medical examinations. Candidates will be notified as to when these examinations will take place.*

• *Examination: Written. The written examination may include multiple choice, true/false, fill-in, matching, and/or essay type questions directly related to the required* knowledge and abilities *for this classification.*

• *Tentative Test Date: A written examination is scheduled for Thursday, August 7, 200-. To be eligible for participation on this examination date, qualified applications must be received at the Placer County Personnel by 5:00 p.m. on Friday, July 18, 200-. You will be notified by U.S. mail of the time and location prior to the scheduled examination. Please notify the Personnel Department of any address change for all applications submitted.*

• *Knowledge and Ability to: Work effectively in stressful situations; learn to maintain security and safety of incarcerated juveniles within an institutional setting; observe wards under supervision; interpret and understand human behavior; identify potential problems; exercise good judgment and make sound decisions; understand the problems involved in handling juveniles under restraint; inspire confidence and gain the respect of juvenile wards, problem-solve situations by mediating disputes; learn to restrain physically aggressive juveniles; know routine safety and security measures; explain procedures and policies to inmates; be sensitive to various cultural and ethnic groups present in the community; establish and maintain effective working relationships, communicate clearly and concisely, both orally and in writing; on an intermittent basis, sit while preparing reports or counseling juveniles; walk to supervise wards within the institutions; stand, bend, and squat to book juveniles into the facility or perform searches; kneel to restrain a juvenile; climb in situations of pursuit; manage physical confrontations when individuals become physically abusive; fine hand manipulation for computer use; visual, auditory, and sense of smell needed for supervision of incarcerated juvenile; physically be able to restrain juvenile and adult inmates; and lift very heavy weight. [Source: Placer County, California Public Information Office, 2003].*

County Probation Officer, $29,343–$50,812

• *Kind of Examination: Applicants will be screened and qualified based on education and experience as shown on the application and attached supplemental questionnaire. For this reason, applicants are urged to fill in the application form and supplemental questionnaire completely providing detailed information concerning the kinds of jobs they have held, the dates they have held them, where and exactly what their duties were. If there are more than five or fewer qualified applicants, the supplemental questionnaire will be used to rank applicants and tied scores will not be*

(continued)

BOX 9.3 (Continued)

broken. If there are five or fever qualified applicants, they will be considered equally qualified and placed on the register in alphabetical order.

• *Purpose of Examination:* To establish an employment register to fill a vacancy and any vacancies that may occur in the future with the Montgomery County Community Corrections Department.

• *Closing Date:* Applications and supplemental questionnaire must be filed with the Montgomery City-County Personnel Department, 520 South Court Street, PO Box 1111, Montgomery, Alabama 36101-1111 (334) 241-2675. Applications and supplemental questionnaire must be completely filled out and received in the Personnel Office not later than 5:00 p.m. July 11, 200-.

• *Nature of Work:* The fundamental reason this position exists is to provide supervision of misdemeanants who are in need of stricter supervision than regular court supervised probation. This position is within a formal probationary program. The essential functions are to monitor offenders, serve as court liaison, perform law enforcement duties, and perform administrative duties. This position reports to the Community Corrections Executive Director.

• *Requirements of Work:* Ability to operate standard office equipment including word processors, computer terminals, typewriters, adding machines, calculators, dictaphones, copiers and transcribers. Ability to follow written and oral instructions. Ability to communicate in writing so that information flows logically and conveys the appropriate message. Ability to communicate verbally so that information flows logically and conveys the appropriate message. Ability to include the proper amount of detail in documentation as needed to ensure that all necessary information is provided to reader. Ability to read and comprehend materials such as memos, correspondence, and written orders as needed to ensure work activities are accomplished according to policy and procedure and exchange or acquire information. Ability to identify and choose appropriate decisions from a variety of alternate choices as needed to prioritize work duties and determine appropriate

actions to take in situations. Ability to determine whether sufficient facts are presented to support a recommended action. Ability to analyze situations thoroughly, identify potential problems, and find effective solutions. Ability to collect, evaluate, and analyze data and information as needed to conduct research and make determinations regarding client compliance. Ability to extract and summarize information from laws, ordinances, correspondence, etc. as needed to document findings and recommendations and prepare case plans. Ability to obtain facts and information by using interviewing skills and techniques. Ability to exhibit the appropriate level of fitness in dealing with clients. Ability to interact with others to include courtesy, tact, and diplomacy as needed to provide/gather information and establish effective working relationships. Ability to interact with individuals from varying socioeconomic and cultural backgrounds to include the ability to recognize commonly used slang terms as needed to explain information to clients or the general public and encourage or enforce client compliance with procedures. Ability to add and subtract as needed to process collected fees. Ability to establish priorities, set deadlines, and develop work schedules and guidelines for completion of projects. Knowledge of the operation of court and court processing activity. Knowledge of court practices and procedures and of the Alabama statutes, rules and regulations. Knowledge of legal terminology as needed to conduct research, interact with judges, officers of the court, clients, etc. and complete and interpret reports. Knowledge of the classification of crime such as felonies, misdemeanors, and violations as needed to conduct research for possible alternative release. Knowledge of caseload management procedures as needed to supervise clients.

• *Special Requirements:* Must possess and maintain a current Alabama driver's license. Must be willing to work nights, shifts, and weekends.

• *Minimum Qualifications:* Bachelor's degree in business administration, public administration, criminal justice, or a closely related field, and at least one year of probation caseload management experience or an equivalent com-

BOX 9.3 (Continued)

bination of education and experience. Must be currently certified as a police officer by the Alabama Peace Officers Standards and Training Commission (APOSTC). Applicants who have completed a Certified Police Academy from another state or a Military or Federal Law Enforcement Academy or currently have less than a two-year break in service must complete the POST Refresher Training Course in order to become a permanent law enforcement employee. [Supplemental Questionnaire is provided in actual application packet]. [Source: Montgomery County, Alabama City-County Personnel Department, 2003].

Juvenile Probation Officer I, Bilingual (Spanish/English)

• All persons are eligible to apply. No preference or priority given to City employees.

• Filing Period: Applications and supplemental form will be accepted until 5:00 p.m. Friday, May 23, 200-.

• Location: Murphy-Bernardini Regional Juvenile Justice Center.

• Salary: Approximately $33,478 to start with merit increases to $47,305 per year with paid retirement or $36,893 to start with merit increases to $52,130 with employee paid retirement. There is no Social Security, other than 1.45 percent for Medicare. No State income tax. The City offers a competitive health care program paid 100 percent for employee only, it is offered to the dependents, at a cost to the employee.

• The Job: This is an entrance level class requiring a minimum level of previous experience and training in the behavioral sciences, criminal justice, or other related field.

1. Under close supervision, investigates and supervises juvenile offenders or court wards.
2. Makes arrests in connection with suspected probation violators.
3. Makes recommendations to the court regarding detention and dispositional decisions.

4. Aids in the social rehabilitation of wards including compliance with court orders and conditions of probation.
5. Performs casework counseling; represents the Department in court, at institutions, foster homes and community agencies.
6. Assists in coordinating cooperative relationships with agencies and boards.
7. Assists in developing resources for youths; helps to promote greater understanding of local juvenile justice system with families and the community; and performs related work as required and in a manner consistent with policies, procedures, and practices of the Carson City Juvenile Probation Department.
8. The position will be required to perform the above listed duties with Hispanic families and youth.
9. The job requires the individual to interface with the general public and could require entering private dwellings which do not and are not required to meet handicapped accessibility standards.

• Minimum Qualifications: Any combination equivalent to experience and education that could likely provide the required knowledge and abilities. Preferred Graduation from an accredited college or university with major course work in criminal justice, sociology, psychology, social services, or a closely related field; or a two-year Associate degree in the above and two years of full-time paid experience, as listed below; or graduation from high school or equivalent, and four years of full-time paid experience conducting casework services and investigations, developing detailed reports, making program eligibility determinations, providing supervision services, conducting enforcement activities and preparing and presenting legal documents and/or reports in a court of law; qualifying experience may be obtained in a parole and probation, law enforcement, correctional casework or comparable setting. Applicants will need to demonstrate fluent bilingual (Spanish/English) skills, reading, writing, speaking.

(continued)

BOX 9.3 (Continued)

• *About the Exam: Examination will consist of an analysis of the applicant's training and experience based on the application. Written, reading, speaking, translation demonstration/assessment of Spanish and English skills. The assessment/interview date is pending. In order that a proper evaluation can be made, the application should be as complete and detailed as possible. Ranking will be based on scores given to training, education, and experience beyond the minimum qualifications. The Human Resource Department reserves the right to call only the highly qualified applicants to the interview.*

• *Supplemental Questionnaire: If you are interested in applying for this position, you must complete and return the Supplemental Questionnaire, which you can access for viewing/downloading here [on Internet]. The questionnaire is in PDF format so you'll need Adobe Acrobat, which you can download free here.*

• *Special Note: The list will remain in effect for one year. Employees must be willing to work overtime, shifts, weekends, and holidays. Position has a one-year probationary period. Must be able to respond within 30 minutes while on call. Must possess a valid Class C Nevada driver's license at the time of appointment. Must be P.O.S.T. certified or agree to complete P.O.S.T. training within one (1) year of the date of hire. Employment is contingent upon the results of a physical examination performed by a licensed physician and tuberculosis test at candidate's expense.*

• *Special Conditions: If offered employment, the candidate will be required to submit to a background investigation, which could include a drug test, voice stress test, DMV and criminal check plus employer and reference check. Persons rejected as result of the background check will be removed from the eligible list/job.*

• *Reasonable Accommodations: The Human Resources Department will make efforts to provide reasonable accommodations to disabled candidates in the examination process. If you have special needs, please notify the Human Resource Department when you turn in your application or at least three (3) days prior to the examination by calling (775) 887-2103. [Source: Carson City, Nevada Human Resources, 201 North Carson Street #4, Carson City, NV 89701, 2003].*

The selection requirements and recruitment procedures included in this section are not exhaustive. But they serve as a set of standards against which PO recruitment, selection, and training programs may be evaluated. Traditional PO selection procedures have tended to focus upon weeding out those unfit for PO work rather than upon selecting those possessing the skills needed for successful job performance. PO training in most states includes several weeks of class time (e.g., social sciences, humanities, and/or police sciences) and two or more weeks of in-service training (American Correctional Association, 2004; Camp and Camp, 2003). However, some states had no in-service or course requirements in place for those aspiring to PO roles. By 2002, most states had minimum numbers of introductory hours that ranged from 40 to 1,480, while in-service hours ranged from 20 to 160 (Camp and Camp, 2003).

Minimum Educational Requirements for POs. In 2003, minimum educational requirements of those entering the correctional field were a high school diploma or the GED for an entry-level PO position; community college (two years) diploma; or some college work. Because of the recent emphasis upon professionalization, increasing numbers of jurisdictions are requiring a bachelor's degree for entry-level PO jobs (American Correctional Association, 2004).

The Use of Written Examinations for Screening Applicants.   While over 80 percent of the programs required a written examination, only about 20 percent subjected recruits to psychological screening. The Minnesota Multiphasic Personality Inventory and Inwald Personality Inventory appear to be those most popularly applied, when any are used. Very few programs included physical examinations, medical checks, or FBI inquiries. Several programs had no formal testing or examination procedures as a means of screening PO candidates (American Correctional Association, 2003). By 2003, most jurisdictions had considerably more rigorous physical and psychological qualifications for starting positions (American Correctional Association, 2004).

PO TRAINING AND SPECIALIZATION

Assessment Centers and Staff Effectiveness

The focus upon behaviorally based methods for selecting and evaluating POs not only results in the hiring of better line personnel, but it also functions to identify those most able to perform managerial tasks. It is clear that a key element in the success of any probation program is the quality of line staff. A key element in maintaining line staff quality is managerial adequacy.

Assessment centers are useful for identifying potential chief probation officers and administrators for probation/parole programs. Personality tests are often used to identify those prospective officers who would have the right temperament for PO work. These assessment centers have often been patterned after those established for recruiting police officers in different jurisdictions (Coleman, 2002).

If the right kinds of managers can be selected and promoted, line staff can be molded into productive work units to better serve offender-clients. Managers can assist their probation/parole organizations to devise more clearly defined mission

FIGURE 9.4   Increasing numbers of jail officers are better trained and educated.

statements of goals and objectives and to establish greater uniformity of quality of performance among staff members. While assessment centers are not foolproof and should not be considered as cookbook methods for selecting "good managers," they are helpful by providing for specific tests and assessments of those desirable qualities of leadership and managerial effectiveness which should be seriously considered by administrators. Criminal justice generally has had a continuing need for better managers, and thus criminal justice professionals including corrections personnel should explore every management evaluation tool available, including assessment centers (Kirchhoff, Lansinger, and Burack, 1999).

The Florida Assessment Center

The Dade County, Florida, Department of Corrections and Rehabilitation was one of the first state corrections agencies to establish an assessment center for the selection of entry-level officers (Page, 1995). While using assessment centers to screen personnel for organizational positions is not a new concept, especially in private industry, the use of such centers in corrections recruitment and training is innovative. Currently, a large number of law enforcement agencies employ assessment centers or other pivotal screening facilities to separate the fit from the unfit among applicants for law enforcement positions.

The **Florida Assessment Center** moves beyond traditional selection mechanisms such as the use of paper-pencil measures, standard personality, interests, and aptitude/IQ tests or inventories by examining a candidate's potential on the basis of the full scope of the job. This is accomplished by a previously established job task analysis made of the different correctional chores to be performed by prospective applicants. The Dade County Assessment Center has identified the following skills associated with corrections work of any kind: (1) the ability to understand and implement policies and procedures; (2) the ability to be aware of all elements in a given situation, and to use sensitivity to others and good judgment in dealing with the situation; and (3) the ability to communicate effectively (Page, 1995).

On the basis of various measures designed to tap into each of these personal and social skills, the most qualified candidates are targeted for further testing and interviews. These tests include preparations of written reports, role-playing and acting out problem situations, and videotaped situational exercises. The Center strives to provide candidates with as much realism as possible concerning the kinds of situations they will encounter in dealing with criminals either inside or outside of prison. Also emphasized is an awareness of race, gender, and ethnicity in the social dimension of relating with offenders. Three-person teams of evaluators screen applicants on the basis of their objectivity and manner in responding to various job-related simulated challenges. A key objective is to assist prospective corrections personnel to avoid legal challenges and suits by clients and/or prisoners. Thus, when subsequent decisions are made by corrections officers and others and challenged in court, the basis for the challenges will be unlikely attributable to faults associated with the selection process (Metchik, 1999).

The evaluators in the Florida Assessment Center are themselves trained by other assessors or correctional officers so that they may more readily determine those most appropriate candidates for correctional posts. Observing, categorizing, and evaluating candidate skills are procedures requiring extensive training, and the Assessment Center continually subjects its own selection process to both internal and external scrutiny and evaluation. Assessment center officials in both Florida and other jurisdictions where such centers are used believe that the training their officers receive also helps to reduce their potential for lawsuits from clients (Dear et al., 2002).

The Use of Firearms in Probation and Parole Work

Because the idea of POs carrying firearms is fairly new, little information exists about it. Also, it is too early to evaluate the long-range implications of PO firearms use in the field. In 2000, there were 24 states which authorized the use of firearms for parole officers. Twenty-six states authorized firearms use for their probation officers (American Correctional Association, 2003). More probation and parole officer training programs are featuring topics related to PO safety, especially in view of the shift from the medical model toward more proactive, client-control officer orientations (Budd, 1999). Few professionals in criminology and criminal justice question that each generation of probationers and parolees includes more dangerous offenders. Largely because it is impossible at present to incarcerate everyone convicted of crimes, the use of probation and parole as front-end and back-end solutions to jail and prison overcrowding is increasing. Also increasing are reports of victimization from POs working with probationers and parolees in dangerous neighborhoods (Kassebaum et al., 2001). It is not necessarily the case that probationer-clients or parolee-clients are becoming more aggressive or violent toward their PO supervisors, although there have been reports of escalating client violence against their supervising POs (McGrath, Cumming, and Holt, 2002). The fact is that POs are obligated to conduct face-to-face visits with their clients, and that in many instances, these face-to-face visits involve potentially dangerous situations and/or scenarios. However, some evidence suggests a decline in the future of home visits as a standard PO function (Small and Torres, 2001).

Life-Threatening Situations and Assaults Against POs By Their Clients. Anonymous interviews with POs supervising both adults and juveniles give us some insight as to the potential hazards of PO work. One PO supervising juvenile offenders in Cincinnati, Ohio, for instance, reported that she was assaulted and physically beaten by youthful gang members associated with one of her juvenile clients. The juvenile client himself was apologetic and promised to advise his gang members to leave her alone the next time she appeared in his neighborhood. However, her broken arm, jaw, and lost teeth will be reminders of her neighborhood visit. In another situation, a male PO visited a parolee in a rundown section of Los Angeles. The parolee had been drinking excessively. When the PO entered the client's apartment, the parolee held a rifle to his own chin, threatening suicide. At one point, as the parolee continued to drink, he pointed the rifle at the PO and said, "You're the reason its come to this . . . I might as well blow your fuckin' head off too." After three hours of talking, the parolee was coaxed into surrendering his weapon with a promise from the PO "not to do anything." The PO left and never said a word about the incident. Within a month, the PO had resigned and became a postal worker. Increasingly, PO training involves understanding about how to deal with drug- or alcohol-dependent clients in productive ways (Read, 1992:4–6).

POs are increasingly leery of laws that make firearms easily available to dangerous persons, including their own clients (Florida Department of Law Enforcement, 1998; Maxey, 2002). The hazards of PO work are clearly portrayed in the results of a nationwide survey conducted by the Federal Probation and

Pretrial Officers Association in 1993 (Bigger, 1993:14–15). This study disclosed the following assaults or attempted assaults against officers nationwide since 1980:

Murders or attempted murders	16
Rapes or attempted rapes	7
Other sexual assaults or attempted sexual assaults	100
Shot and wounded or attempted shot and wounded	32
Uses or attempted use of blunt instrument or projectile	60
Slashed or stabbed or attempted slashed or stabbed	28
Car used as weapon or attempted use of car as weapon	12
Punched, kicked, choked or other use of body/attempted	1,396
Use or attempted use of caustic substance	3
Use or attempted use of incendiary device	9
Abducted or attempted abduction and held hostage	3
Attempted or actual unspecified assaults	944
TOTAL	2,610

A more recent survey of 1,120 state and county probation and parole officers in Minnesota raises several concerns about officer safety. Of the sample surveyed, 19 percent reported one or more physical assaults during their career, while 74 percent reported being verbally or physically threatened one or more times. About 4 percent actually were physically assaulted one or more times in the past year, while 37 percent reported being physically or verbally threatened one or more times during the past year (Arola and Lawrence, 1999:32).

Self-Protection of Provocation?   Whether POs should arm themselves during their visits to clients is often a moot question, since they arm themselves anyway, regardless of probation/parole office policy. When POs are put to a vote, however, the results are often divided 50–50. For instance, a study of 159 POs attending an in-service training session during 1990 at a state probation training academy investigated these POs' opinions about their right to carry firearms while on the job. A carefully worded question, "Should POs be given the legal option to carry a firearm while working?" was asked of these 159 POs. Responses indicated that 59 percent of the officers believed that they should have the legal option to carry a firearm. This doesn't mean that 59 percent of these officers would carry firearms on the job; rather, they supported the idea of one's choice to carry a firearm while working if such a choice were made available. In the same study, POs were asked whether they would endorse a requirement to carry a firearm as a part of one's PO work. Over 80 percent of the female POs interviewed opposed such a requirement, while about 69 percent of the male POs responded similarly. However, 80 percent of all officers interviewed said that they would carry a firearm if required to do so.

Opposition to POs carrying firearms is largely that this moves POs into a law enforcement function. Furthermore, if it becomes generally known that POs carry firearms, this may escalate a situation between a PO and an armed client to the point where injuries or deaths could occur. In contrast, other professionals argue that changing offender populations have transformed into successive generations of more dangerous, violent clientele (Brown, 1994). A fundamental issue at the center of this controversy is the amount and type of training POs receive who will carry these firearms (Arola and Lawrence, 1999). States, such as Florida, have authorized their POs to use firearms since 1992. Other jurisdictions have permitted this practice since the 1970s. However, all POs who are authorized to carry firearms receive extensive firearms training as well as psychological training so that the necessity of using a firearm will be for self-protection and a last resort.

Establishing Negligence in Training, Job Performance, and Retention

Not only is PO work increasingly hazardous, but POs are become increasingly liable for their actions taken in relation to the clients they supervise. Lawsuits against POs are becoming more commonplace. Many of these lawsuits are frivolous, but they consume much time and cause many job prospects to turn away from PO work (Jones and del Carmen, 1992). There are three basic forms of immunity: (1) absolute immunity, meaning that those acting on behalf of the state can suffer no liability from their actions taken while performing their state tasks (e.g., judges, prosecutors, and legislators); (2) qualified immunity, such as that enjoyed by probation officers if they are performing their tasks in good faith; and (3) quasi-judicial immunity, which generally refers to PO preparation of PSI reports at judicial request (Jones and del Carmen, 1992:36–37). In the general case, POs enjoy only qualified immunity, meaning that they are immune only when their actions were taken in good faith. However, there is some evidence that the rules are changing related to the types of defenses available to POs, although the limits of immunity continue to be vague and undefined. Jones and del Carmen (1992) have clarified at least two different conditions which seem to favor POs in the performance of their tasks and the immunity they derive from such conditions:

1. Probation officers are considered officers of the court and perform a valuable court function, namely the preparation of PSI reports.
2. Probation officers perform work intimately associated with court process, such as sentencing offenders.

Despite these conditions, Jones and del Carmen (1992) believe that it is unlikely that POs will ever be extended absolute immunity to all of their work functions. In some later and related research, del Carmen and Pilant (1994:14–15) have described judicial immunity and qualified immunity as two types of immunity that are generally available to public officials including POs. Judicial liability is like absolute immunity described earlier. Judges must perform their functions and make decisions that may be favorable or unfavorable to defendants. Lawsuits filed against judges are almost always routinely dismissed without trial on the merits. Parole boards also possess such judicial immunity in most cases. In contrast, qualified immunity ensues only if officials, including POs, did not violate some client's constitutional rights according to what a reasonable person would have known (Morgan, Belbot, and Clark, 1997).

Liability Issues Associated with PO Work

A summary of some of the key liability issues related to PO work is provided below.

1. Some information about a POs' clients is subject to public disclosure while some information isn't subject to public disclosure. POs must constantly reassess their working materials about specific clients and decide which

information is relevant under certain circumstances. It would be advisable, for instance, to inform prospective employers of certain probationers or parolees if the work involves custodial services in a large apartment complex and the particular probationers/parolees are convicted voyeurs, rapists, exhibitionists, or burglars. POs might also inform banks that particular probationers/parolees have been convicted of embezzlement if these clients are seeking work in a bank setting or any other business where they will be working around and handling money. But it may not be appropriate to advise an employer that the probationer/parolee is a convicted drug dealer if the client is seeking to become a car salesperson or factory worker. Also, in most states, if POs know that their clients have AIDS, it is improper for POs to report this fact to a client's employer. This is because there are statutory prohibitions against such disclosures except under certain circumstances. These circumstances vary considerably among state jurisdictions. Some states have no policy on this issue. Thus, it is up to individual agencies to adopt their own policies. A general rule within most PO agencies is that if a probationer or parolee obtains a job on his or her own, there is no officer or agency liability because reliance is absent. However, an agency's rules may require disclosure by the officer when he or she learns of the probationer or parolee's job, even if the job was obtained by the offender (Miller, Sluder, and Laster, 1999).

2. POs have a duty to protect the public. Their work in this regard may subject them to lawsuits. This issue relates closely to the first. If particular probationers or parolees have made threats to seek revenge against particular persons or organizations, it would be advisable for POs to report that these clients are in the community and may pose a risk to one or more former victims. There are some notable distinctions in degrees of liability, however. Del Carmen (1990:36) says that if a probationer says he is going to kill his wife and the PO does nothing about it, liability may attach and the PO may be liable for not warning the wife or notifying authorities. But if a parolee tells his PO that he feels like going out to commit armed robbery and actually carries it out, the liability of the PO is questionable, since it is unreasonable for us to assume that the PO knew where and when the client would commit the robbery. Furthermore, saying one may go out and commit armed robbery and actually committing the robbery are two different matters. The PO may conclude that her client is simply "blowing off steam," "getting emotions out in the open where they can be dealt with productively," or some other such similar interpretation.

3. PO use of firearms may create hazards for both POs and their clients. POs are increasingly carrying firearms for their personal protection when entering dangerous neighborhoods or housing projects where their clients reside. If they use their firearms, there is some likelihood that someone, possibly the probationer/parolee, the PO, or an innocent bystander or relative may be seriously or fatally injured. Liability of this sort is always possible. One way of minimizing such liability is to provide POs with proper firearms training prior to authorizing them to carry dangerous weapons. While this doesn't guarantee that they will avoid lawsuits and liability, it does minimize the risk of such legal actions by others. Often, when POs are sued by their clients or others, U.S.C., Title 42 Section 1983 (2004), which is the **Civil Rights Act,** civil rights actions are involved. These are usually tort actions and settled in civil courts rather than criminal courts (Moore, 2001). Also in

other countries, such as England, the Human Rights Act of 1999 was implemented in October 2000, which greatly expanded the powers of citizens to file lawsuits against police officers believed to be negligent (Falcao, 2000).

4. POs may supervise their clients in a negligent manner. Watkins (1989:30–31) describes an Arizona case where several POs were sued because of victim injuries sustained as the result of a failure to properly supervise a dangerous client. In the Arizona case (*Acevedo v. Pima County Adult Probation Department,* 1984), a convicted felon, a child sexual abuser, was placed on probation and subsequently sexually molested several children of the plaintiff. The POs supervising this offender knew of his sexual deviance and propensities. However, they allowed him to rent a room on premises where the plaintiff and her five children resided. The Arizona Supreme Court observed that while POs do many diverse tasks and have demanding responsibilities, they must not knowingly place clients in situations where their former conduct might create a hazard to the public. In this case, the lawsuit against the POs was successfully pursued. It may also be argued that these POs failed to warn the plaintiff of their clients' sexual propensities. This, too, could have warranted a lawsuit against these POs.

5. PO PSI report preparation may result in liability. One of the more important PO functions is the preparation of PSI reports at the request of judges prior to offender sentencing. Much information is contained in these PSI reports, some of which may not be directly relevant to sentencing. Thus, it may not be necessary to disclose the entire contents of PSIs at any particular time. At the federal level, at least, federal judges may disclose the contents of PSI reports except where (1) disclosure might disrupt rehabilitation of the defendant; (2) the information was obtained on a promise of confidentiality; and (3) harm may result to the defendant or to any other person. Subsequently, when inmates are about to be paroled, the PSI report may again be consulted. Obviously, the long-term impact of a PSI report is substantial. Errors of fact, unintentional or otherwise, may cause grievous harm to inmates and jeopardize seriously their chances for early release (Roberts et al., 1999). If the information barring them from early release is contained in the PSI document, and if the parole board relies heavily upon this information in their denial of parole to particular offenders, and if the information contained therein is inaccurate or false, a cause of action or lawsuit may be lodged against the original PO who prepared the PSI report.

6. Liabilities against POs and/or their agencies may ensue for negligent training, negligent retention, and deliberate indifference to client needs. POs may not have particular counseling skills when dealing with certain offenders who have psychological problems. They may give poor advice. Such advice may cause offenders to behave in ways that harm others. Also, POs may not be adequately prepared or trained to carry firearms. They may discharge their firearms under certain circumstances than can cause serious injury or death. These are examples of negligent training. Negligent retention might be a situation where certain POs are maintained by a probation agency after they have exhibited certain conduct or training deficiencies that they have failed to remedy. Failing to rid an organization of incompetent employees is negligent retention. Finally, when POs meet with their probationer/parolee/clients, they may believe particular offenders need certain community services or assistance. However, these POs may deliberately refrain from providing such assistance or making it possible for

their clients to receive such aid. If certain clients are drug-dependent and obviously in need of medical services, deliberate indifference on the part of the PO would be exhibited if the PO did nothing to assist the client in receiving the needed medical treatment. This would be an example of deliberate indifference. Deliberate indifference may be a vengeful act on the part of the PO, an omission, or simple failure to act promptly.

While the above list of PO legal liabilities is not exhaustive, it represents the major types of situations where POs incur potential problems from lawsuits. Jones and del Carmen (1992:36) suggest at least three different types of defenses used by POs when performing their work. These defenses are not perfect, but they do make it difficult for plaintiffs to prevail under a variety of scenarios. These defenses include the following: (1) POs were acting in good faith while performing the PO role; (2) POs have official immunity, since they are working for and on behalf of the state, which enjoys sovereign immunity; and (3) POs may not have a special relationship with their clients, thus absolving them of possible liability if their clients commit future offenses that result in injuries or deaths to themselves or others (Klotter and Edwards, 1998).

Probation and Parole Officer Labor Turnover

In 2002, there was a turnover among probation and parole officers of 16 percent. Among probation/parole officer recruits in training, the turnover rate was higher at 23 percent (Camp and Camp, 2003). In view of a number of continuing problems confronting those entering probation and parole service as a career, it is understandable why there is a high degree of **labor turnover** among POs. There are several explanations for this turnover. First, the rapid increase in the offender population managed by POs has created significant logistical problems. Some observers have indicated that POs must continue to maintain their current level of activity in an environment where the public demands greater punishment, incarceration, and a decrease in public expenditures (Camp and Camp, 2003). Furthermore, there is a lack of consensus among POs about their goals and professional objectives, as well as how these goals ought to be realized. Some POs see themselves as **brokers** who provide referral services to offender-clients or arrange offender contacts with community agencies that provide special services, including counseling and training. Other POs see themselves as **caseworkers** who attempt to change offender behavior through educating, enabling, or mediating whenever offender problems occur. Many POs have asked whether the public has come to expect too much from them, particularly in view of financial cutbacks and greatly increased offender caseloads.

PROBATION AND PAROLE OFFICER CASELOADS

The **caseload** of a probation or parole officer is considered by many authorities to be significant in affecting the quality of supervision POs can provide their clients. Caseloads refer to the number of offender-clients supervised by POs. Caseloads vary among jurisdictions (American Correctional Association, 2003). Theoretically, the larger the caseload, the poorer the quality of supervision and other services. Intensive probation supervision (IPS) is based on the premise that low offender caseloads maximize the attention POs can give their clients, including counseling, employment, social, and psychological assistance. The success of such IPS programs suggests that lower caseloads contribute to lower recidivism rates among parolees and probationers. It is also conceded that other program components such as fines, curfews, and community service may have some influence on the overall reduction of these rates (Wooldredge and Thistlewaite, 2002).

Ideal Caseloads

The earliest work outlining optimum caseloads for professionals was Chute (1922). Chute advocated caseloads for POs no larger than 50. Similar endorsements of a 50-caseload limit were made by Edwin Sutherland in 1934, the American Prison Association in 1946, the Manual of Correctional Standards in 1954, and the National Council of Crime and Delinquency in 1962 (Gottfredson and Gottfredson, 1988:182). The 1967 President's Commission on Law Enforcement and Administration of Justice lowered the optimum caseload figure to 35.

In 2002, actual caseloads of POs varied greatly, ranging from a low of 40 clients in Nebraska to a high of 81 clients in California (Camp and Camp, 2003). IPS had caseloads ranging from 9 per officer in Wyoming to a high of 51 in Rhode Island. Considerable jurisdictional variation exists regarding both regular and intensive supervision caseloads for POs.

Presently there is no agreement among professionals as to what is an ideal PO caseload (Riley, Ebener, and Chiesa, 2000). On the basis of evaluating caseloads of POs in a variety of jurisdictions, Gottfredson and Gottfredson (1988:182) have concluded that "it may be said with assurance . . . that (1) no optimal caseload size has been demonstrated, and (2) no clear evidence of reduced recidivism, simply by reduced caseload size, has been found." This declaration applies mainly to standard probation/parole supervision, and it is not intended to reflect on the quality of recent ISP programs established in many jurisdictions. Because the composition of parolees and probationers varies considerably among jurisdictions, it is difficult to develop clear-cut conclusions about the influence of supervision on recidivism and the delivery of other program services. An arbitrary caseload figure based upon current caseload sizes among state jurisdictions would be about 30 clients per PO. This is perhaps the closest number to an ideal caseload size. The average caseload for POs in 2002 was 124, while the average intensive supervision caseload was 25. These differences suggest that different jurisdictions have variable ideas about what is or isn't standard or intensive supervision (Camp and Camp, 2003).

Changing Caseloads and Officer Effectiveness

Do smaller PO caseloads mean greater effectiveness and quality of services provided clients by their supervising POs? It is assumed that if POs have fewer clients to supervise, then they will be able to supervise their clients more effectively. There is great variation among jurisdictions about how optimum caseloads, large or small, should be defined. If POs are asked, they will almost always say that the lower their caseload, the more effective they are at helping their probationers and parolees. If probationers and parolees are asked the same question, they will tell a similar story. Close supervision of their behaviors while on probation or parole is more often viewed as assistance rather than punishment. This is especially true for those clients with drug or alcohol dependencies.

As we have moved into the twenty-first century, the nature of PO client supervision is changing. We are increasingly relying upon technology in our relations with probationers and parolees. Electronic monitoring and home confinement, drive-by check-ins at probation department offices, and distance contacts between offenders and their supervisors by mail or other means suggests fewer face-to-face encounters. It is clear that officer safety is becoming increasingly crucial and presently a dominant issue in discussions of how best to supervise offenders.

PO jobs are becoming increasingly complex, and POs are learning to be more effective as service brokers. This means that they are networking their clients with more community services annually to provide improved treatments and other offender needs (Arthur, 2000). At the same time, some jurisdictions are experimenting with group reporting. In Anoka County, Minnesota, group reporting involves offender/clients reporting to their probation departments at particular times and meeting as a group with their assigned POs. Thus, this gives POs a chance to meet face-to-face with a large number of clients at any given time, rather than to hazard visits to dangerous neighborhoods for face-to-face visits on a one-on-one basis (Arola and Lawrence, 1999).

Technology is being incorporated into the PO–client relation in other ways as well. More probationers are having to undergo polygraph or lie detector testing as a condition of their probation or parole programs (Falkin, Strauss, and Bohen, 1999). If there is a criminal investigation, some clients on probation or parole may become suspects. Therefore, their submission to a polygraph test will either include or exclude them as suspects. Also, these clients can be asked about program infractions which are not easily detected, such as drug use or associating with known criminals. If the answers to these questions are incriminating, they may be the preliminary grounds to seek a revocation of one's program.

FIGURE 9.5   Office visits with POs increase caseload sizes.

Caseload Assignment and Management Models

The court sentences offenders to probation, while parole boards release many prisoners short of serving their full terms. POs must reckon with fluctuating numbers of offenders monthly, as new assignments are given them and some offenders complete their programs successfully. No particular caseload assignment method has been universally adopted by all jurisdictions. Rather, depending on the numbers of offenders assigned to probation and parole agencies, PO caseload assignment practices vary. Carlson and Parks (1979) have studied various caseload assignment schemes. Their investigation has led to the identification of four popular varieties of assignment methods. These include (1) the conventional model, (2) the numbers game model, (3) the conventional model with geographic considerations, and (4) specialized caseloads.

The Conventional Model.   The **conventional model** involves the random assignment of probationers or parolees to POs. Thus, any PO must be prepared to cope with extremely dangerous offenders released early from prison on parole, those with drug or alcohol dependencies or in need of special treatment programs, and those requiring little, if any, supervision. However, those convicted of violent offenses may no longer be violent. Spouses may kill in the heat of passion, but it is highly unlikely that they will kill again. By the same token, it is possible that low-risk, less dangerous property offenders may become violent through offense escalation.

The conventional model is the most frequently used caseload assignment method in probation and parole agencies throughout the United States. There are no specific logistical problems that need to be dealt with, and POs can be assigned offender-clients on an as-needed basis. The major drawback is that POs must be extremely flexible in their management options, because of the diversity of clientele they must supervise.

The Numbers Game Model.   The **numbers game model** is similar to the conventional model. In order to apply this model, the total number of clients is divided by the number of POs, and POs are given randomly the designated number. For instance, if there are 500 offenders and 10 POs, 500/10 = 50 offenders per PO. Another version of the numbers game model is to define an optimum caseload such as 40, and determine how many POs are required to supervise 40 offenders each. Thus, PO hiring is influenced directly by the numbers of offenders assigned to the jurisdiction and whatever is considered the optimum caseload. This type of caseload assignment method is arguably the least expensive and easiest to use.

The Conventional Model with Geographic Considerations.   The **conventional model with geographic considerations** is applied on the basis of the travel time required for POs to meet with their offender-clients regularly. Those POs who supervise offenders in predominantly rural regions are given lighter caseloads so that they may have the time to make reasonable numbers of contacts with offenders on a monthly or weekly basis. Those POs who supervise largely urban offenders are given heavier caseloads because less travel time between clients is required. POs are given clients who live in close proximity to one another in a particular geographical area, such as the northwest part of a city, to minimize the travel time to visit these clients. From a time management standpoint, this caseload assignment method is probably the most practical to use.

The Specialized Caseloads Model. Sometimes caseload assignments are made on the basis of PO specialties. The **specialized caseloads model** pertains to PO assignments to clients who share particular problems, such as drug or alcohol dependencies. The POs assigned to these clients have special skills relating to these dependencies. Often, these POs have developed liaisons with Alcoholics Anonymous or other organizations so that their service to clients can be enhanced (Falkin, Strauss, and Bohen, 1999). Perhaps certain POs have had extensive training and education in particular problem areas to better serve certain offender-clients who may be retarded or mentally ill. Some POs by virtue of their training may be assigned more dangerous offenders. Those POs with greater work experience and legal training can manage dangerous offenders more effectively compared with fresh new PO recruits. In some respects, this is close to **client-specific planning,** where individualization of cases is stressed. This is particularly true of domestic violence and sex offender cases, where special PO preparation and training is vital (Keilitz et al., 2000; Patrick et al., 2000). This caseload assignment model is the most expensive to use, because it relies on specialty areas or areas of expertise on the part of particular POs who are recruited specifically to work with probationers or parolees with certain types of problems.

BOX 9.4

PERSONALITY HIGHLIGHT

Monte Guthrie
Senior Patrol Agent, U.S. Border Patrol, Department of Justice, Immigration and Naturalization Service

Statistics:

B.S. (criminal justice), Tarlton State University; M.S. (criminal justice), Texas A & M International University

Interests and Experiences:

Currently I am a Senior Patrol Agent with the U.S. Border Patrol, having entered the Immigration and Naturalization Service in 1995. Prior to my tenure as a federal agent, I was a District Parole Officer with the State of Texas in Dallas, Texas for over three years, with the last two of these years concentrating mostly on street and prison gang members.

As a federal agent with the U.S. Border Patrol in Laredo, Texas, I have literally arrested thousands of individuals, ranging from honest workers trying to make a better life for themselves and their families to serious, hardened criminals convicted of crimes ranging from murder and rape to drug delivery

charges. In addition, I have seized tens of thousands of pounds of illegal drugs, with my largest single seizure being 1,800 pounds of marijuana. That is quite a sight to see. Many people do not realize that over half of the drugs reported as seized by the DEA every year in the U.S. come from the seizures made by the U.S. Border Patrol. I have traveled all over the country and have even been detailed to the South Pacific, in order to interdict illegal Chinese freighters bringing over 600 Chinese people into Guam. I've worked with practically every federal (FBI, DEA) and state (local police, DPS, Texas Rangers) agency that exists in the State of Texas. I have interdicted drugs along the banks of the Rio Grande River with

BOX 9.4 (Continued)

U.S. Special Forces members, including Army Rangers and Navy Seals, and I have executed warrants with U.S. Customs and U.S. Marshals agents. All in all, it's been quite a ride.

Before that, I was a District Parole Officer with the State of Texas for over three years. I concentrated and focused on gang members, and I served as one of the gang liaisons with the Dallas Police Department, Sheriff's Office, and various state, local, and federal agencies under my immediate supervisor, who was the primary liaison. I supervised prison as well as street gang members. Some of the more interesting prison gangs were the Mexican Mafia, Texas Mafia, Texas Syndicate, and the Aryan Brotherhood. The street gangs were the various Crip and Blood sets as well as several independent Mexican American gangs. I observed first-hand two gang drive-by shootings, one of which was directed at my parole office. The area of Dallas where I was assigned was the Fair Park area, which is generally considered to be one of the roughest ghetto areas in the entire state. The area was an excellent testing ground to study street gangs, with approximately 20 major street gang sets within a 5-square-mile area. I also spoke at several conferences about my insights and experiences with street gangs. It was a learning experience, working with so many highly trained and experienced veterans of the war against street gangs.

My work has given me a wide range of experience from which to draw. I have seen horrible sights, such as bodies I have personally discovered in the Rio Grande that were dumped there after prolonged torture, finally being executed by having their throats cut or being shot in the head, as well as incredibly humorous things. One of these was the illegal alien who was trying to get to San Antonio, Texas. He locked himself in a railroad boxcar full of Corona beer and started drinking. It took two hours and over twenty police officers, Border Patrol Agents, and firemen to secure this one extremely drunk, beer-bottle throwing Mexican who weighed about 110 pounds soaking wet. I have more amusing anecdotes than I can honestly remember, and many terrible experiences that I cannot forget.

Working in the field of criminal justice finds oneself in an almost continual state of change and flux, as the job is almost never the same. While there are, of course, the routine aspects of the job, something new always comes up. For those looking for a career free from the confines of the desk and office, it is unparalleled.

Advice to Students:

If you truly feel that this career is for you, then fully commit yourself and begin the process. Look into the agency of your choice and see what they require. A college degree, while not always a must, is very important for pay and advancement potential. Keep your nose clean and avoid those situations and people that will get you into legal trouble, which will certainly derail your career plans. Get yourself into sufficient physical shape to do the job. Bone up on your writing skills—they are extremely important regardless of which branch of criminal justice you wish to enter. Finally, one must have a serious mind set in this line of work. It is not for the slacker or the faint of heart. This is not to say that you must have zero sense of humor. On the contrary. It is, however, a difficult and demanding career that will test you every day and will take its toll, if you let it.

This type of work requires a person to be able to go from controlled destructiveness to sympathy and caring, sometimes in a matter of minutes. You must be willing to take a life as well as risk your own to save one. If you cannot use violence or if you have little compassion for others, then this career is not for you. Those are the two spectrums of the job. Usually it falls somewhere in between, but those two ends are always possibilities. It is neither a job for the meek nor the bully. It is for those who sincerely want to try to make their little piece of the world a better place and are willing to get dirty in order to do so. If, after investigating and thinking about this, you feel that you still want a career in this line of work, then go for it. Best of luck to you in whatever endeavor you choose.

OFFICER/CLIENT INTERACTIONS

Although recruitment for POs is designed to identify and select those most capable of performing increasingly demanding PO tasks, little uniformity exists among jurisdictions regarding the types of POs ultimately recruited. Each PO brings to the job a philosophy of supervision based, in part, on agency expectations. Furthermore, each PO has individual differences and attitudes toward work that influence their supervisory style. Some POs are more punitive than others, while some see themselves as rehabilitators or therapists.

In the course of interacting with different kinds of offenders, it is not unusual for POs to acquire a certain amount of cynicism about their jobs and those they supervise. If an offender recidivates by committing a new offense, some POs may take this new offense personally and consider it an indication of their failure at helping certain offender-clients. Read et al. (1997), Storm (1997) and others have examined the multi-faceted nature of PO work and identified a variety of roles performed by POs. Sometimes, these work roles come into conflict with one another.

These work roles include but are not limited to the following: (1) the **detector,** where the PO attempts to identify troublesome clients or those who have one or more problems which could present the community with some risk; (2) the broker, where the PO functions as a referral service and supplies the offender-client with contacts with agencies who provided needed services; (3) the **educator, enabler,** and **mediator,** where the PO seeks to instruct and assist offenders to deal with problems as they arise in the community; and (4) the **enforcer,** where POs perceive themselves as enforcement officers charged with regulating client behaviors (Strong, 1981).

Role conflict is inherent in the PO–offender relationship (Sims, 2001). It cannot be eliminated. The PO desires a successful outcome for the client, where the terms of the probation or parole are fulfilled, and where the client emerges from the program to lead a productive life. But often, the circumstances leading to an offender's original arrest and conviction continue to exist and influence offender behaviors. Old acquaintances, family circumstances, and the added pressures of maintaining a job and complying with stringent probation or parole program conditions cause problems for more than a few offenders. Many revert to their old ways by committing new crimes and/or violating one or more program requirements.

If a PO reports a parolee or probationer for violating a program rule, there is a possibility that the offender will eventually retaliate by either threatening the PO or carrying out aggressive acts. At the same time, the PO has considerable power and can influence significantly the life chances of those supervised. An unfavorable report may mean prison for probationers or a longer term in prison for parolees. Objectivity is required of all POs, although achieving objectivity and detachment in performing the PO role is difficult. Many POs take it personally whenever one of their offenders fails or is returned to prison. They regard offender failure as their own failure. After all, some of these POs entered their profession originally to help others. When their strategies for helping others are apparently ineffective, this failure reflects adversely on their own job performance. Seasoned POs recommend to those entering the field initially that they should not get too friendly with their offender-clients. They must constantly divorce their emotions from their work roles. There is some evidence, however, that POs find this difficult to do. POs attempt to perform helping functions while at the same time, they must be enforcers of legal conditions.

Women on probation or parole are considered troublesome by many POs (Stephen, 1993). Some POs feel women take up too much of their time with a variety of what agents consider minor problems. Additionally, female clients evidence problems of adjustment related to family, children, and employment. For these and related reasons, women are less likely than men to be reported for anything but the most serious kinds of rule infractions. Researchers suggest that POs treat female probationers and parolees differently because of their paternalistic beliefs that womens' family-based obligations are more important than mens' (Holgate and Clegg, 1991).

Many POs are frustrated because they lack the time and resources to do the kind of job they believe is maximally helpful to their clients. Because of their increasing caseload responsibilities, POs cannot possibly devote the proper amount of time to any given offender without interfering with their time allocations to other clients. The immense paperwork associated with the PO role has caused more than few POs to opt for alternative professions. The progress of offenders must be reported regularly to the courts, parole boards, and various agencies. These reports are tedious to complete. Increased caseloads and work pressures are not only stressful, they also lead to a reduction in the quality of general services and supervision extended to offender-clients (Read et al., 1997).

A CODE OF ETHICS

POs abide by a general code of ethics. Ethical codes have been developed for most professional organizations, such as law enforcement agencies (Baker, 2002). A **code of ethics** refers to regulations formulated by major professional societies that outline the specific problems and issues frequently encountered by persons who practice the profession. POs are in continuous contact with criminals who are either on probation or parole. Often, POs must make ethical choices that involve moral dilemmas. POs exercise considerable discretion over their clients, and they are expected to exercise their discretion wisely. Thus, POs have a responsibility to act properly in controlling individual clients. But at the same time, they must balance societal interests against the interests of their clients.

The American Probation an Parole Association has evolved a code of ethics for its membership. Below is the Code of Ethics:

1. I will render professional service to the justice system and the community at large in effecting the social adjustment of the offender.
2. I will uphold the law with dignity, displaying an awareness of my responsibility to offenders while recognizing the right of the public to be safeguarded from criminal activity.
3. I will strive to be objective in the performance of my duties, recognizing the inalienable right of all persons, appreciating the inherent worth of the individual, and respecting those confidences which can be reposed with me.
4. I will conduct my personal life with decorum, neither accepting nor granting favors in connection with my office.
5. I will cooperate with my co-workers and related agencies and will continually strive to improve my professional competence through the seeking and sharing of knowledge and understanding.

6. I will distinguish clearly, in public, between my statements and actions as an individual and as a representative of my profession.

7. I will encourage policy, procedures, and personnel practices which will enable others to conduct themselves in accordance with the values, goals, and objectives of the American Probation and Parole Association.

8. I recognize my office as a symbol of public faith and I accept it as a public trust to be held as long as I am true to the ethics of the American Probation and Parole Association.

9. I will constantly strive to achieve these objectives and ideals, dedicating myself to my chosen profession (American Probation and Parole Association, 1997).

Federal probation officers have also established an ethical code to abide by when supervising offenders. This code is as follows:

1. As a Federal Probation Officer, I am dedicated to rendering professional service to the courts, the parole authorities, and the community at large in effecting the social adjustment of the offender.

2. I will conduct my personal life with decorum, will neither accept nor grant favors in connection with my office, and will put loyalty to moral principles above personal consideration.

3. I will uphold the law with dignity and with complete awareness of the prestige and stature of the judicial system of which I am a part. I will be ever cognizant of my responsibility to the community which I serve.

4. I will strive to be objective in the performance of my duties; respect the inalienable rights of all persons; appreciate the inherent worth of the individual; and hold inviolate those confidences which can be reposed with me.

5. I will cooperate with my fellow workers and related agencies and will continually attempt to improve my professional standards through seeking of knowledge and understanding.

6. I recognize my office as a symbol of public faith and I accept it as a public trust to be held as long as I am true to the ethics of the Federal Probation Service. I will constantly strive to achieve these objectives and ideals, dedicating myself to my chosen profession (Administrative Office of U.S. Courts, 2001).

Jones and Lurigio (1997:29-32) have typified several different kinds of probation/parole officers. They have classified them into (1) punitive officers; (2) welfare officers; (3) passive officers; and (4) synthetic officers.

Punitive Officers

Punitive officers are very dogmatic and orient themselves toward their clients as law enforcement officers. They put societal interests above the interests of their clients. They file petitions to **violate** their clients' programs with great frequency. The punitive officer seeks to control offender behavior through threats and intimidation.

Welfare Officers

Welfare officers are like social workers in that they focus upon treatment and rehabilitation. Such officers focus their attention on advocating, brokering, education, enabling, and mediating. They assist their clients in finding employment and even help them fill out job applications. They consider their roles are largely therapeutic.

Passive Officers

Passive officers care little about the needs of society or their clients. They merely go through the day in a perfunctory way, performing their jobs in minimal ways. Their primary interest is getting through the day, the week, the month, and the year, and eventually retiring with full pension and benefits. They seek to advance their own positions within their agencies. They simply follow the rules set forth for them to follow, nothing more, nothing less.

Synthetic Officers

Synthetic officers are actually a blend of enforcers and social workers. They want very much to supervise their offenders so that they will remain law-abiding. They work closely with police departments. But at the same time, they understand the complexities of probationers' and parolees' problems and the limitations of working through those problems. These officers are both humanitarian and justice oriented (Farkas, 2000).

It is unknown how many officers of particular types there are throughout the different state and federal agencies and organizations. All officers share a common bond, however, in that they should be guided by the ethic of care, the central goal of which is to reintegrate offenders into their communities (Brodsky, Zapf, and Boccaccini, 2001; Sims, 2001). Thus, they must continually reevaluate their positions and how they relate with their clients. The PO–client relation is a dynamic and ever-changing one.

PO UNIONIZATION AND COLLECTIVE BARGAINING

Historically, American probation and parole officers have been among the last professional aggregates to organize for the purpose of forming unions and engaging in collective bargaining (U.S. Bureau of Justice Assistance, 1994). A survey of the professional literature found in the source files of *Criminal Justice Abstracts* during the period 1968 through 1999 reveals that 90 percent of all references to unions and collective bargaining relate primarily to police organizations (Champion, 2001). Most of the remaining articles and books on the subject of unions and collective bargaining pertain to correctional officers who are affiliated with prisons and jails. Several reasons for these early developments and the emphasis upon unionization for police officers and correctional staff are that criminal suspects and inmates have been the most volatile aggregates to file lawsuits against specific officers. Often these lawsuits have proved groundless. However, individual officers have had to hire their own defense counsels for the purpose of self-protection against frivolous suits. Through unionization, police officer and correctional officer unions now provide ample funds for defense work where individual officers are sued by citizens or inmates (Zhao and Lovrich, 1997). Another objective of these unions is to secure additional benefits pertaining to working conditions, officer safety, and retirement (Crawley, 2002).

But during the 1990s, POs have organized at local, state, and federal levels to establish collective bargaining mechanisms and unions for common purposes (Committee of Seventy, 1998). Virtually every major city and all states have probation and parole officer unions today that represent PO interests. One of the oldest unions is the L.A. County Probation Officers Union. This was an outgrowth of the American Federation of State, County, and Municipal Employees (AFSCME), one of the country's largest public employees' unions. AFSCME is affiliated with the AFL-CIO and began as a series of smaller unions during the 1930s. In 1955, the membership of AFSCME numbered 100,000 employees. In 1945, a group of World War II veterans who became employed as probation officers in Los Angeles County in California founded AFSCME Local 685. In 1969, Local 685, under the strong leadership of Henry Fiering, began to aggressively fight for the rights of its employees with the L.A. County Probation Department in all matters concerning wages, hours, benefits, and working conditions, including caseload assignments.

The L.A. County Probation Officers Union is only one of hundreds of local unions across the country today who lobby for the rights and entitlements of POs. In New York, for example, the New York State Probation Officers Association (NYSPOA) was formed during the late 1960s to represent the interests of line officers working in the field of probation. The preamble to the constitution of the NYSPOA says that the association, recognizing the need to preserve human dignity through acceptance, empathy, and understanding, advocates the use of those corrective facilities, professions, skills and rehabilitative procedures that will best protect society through the reduction of crime and **delinquency.** Over the years, the NYSPOA has strived to write, influence, and/or support legislative endeavors that would permit probation officers to perform their functions effectively, efficiently, and safely. The NYSPOA works with other professional organizations, such as the American Probation and Parole Association, to further its interests and objectives. The NYSPOA is continually striving to upgrade the quality of professional services rendered by its affiliate officers. In 1991, for instance, an annual conference was proposed that would provide low-cost training for interested POs and address their diverse needs.

Probation and parole officer unions also arbitrate and settle grievances, whether they are generated by probationers or parolees or by POs themselves. In some instances, grievances pertain to the pay POs should receive for overtime they engage in while supervising their clients. For instance, a New Jersey county settled a grievance originating from New Jersey PO supervisors who had been given additional supervisory responsibilities to supervise other POs. The pay differential was only 94 cents per hour, and the county balked at paying the additional hourly wage. But the union representing the POs arbitrated a settlement, with the county paying over $5,800 owed to PO supervisors.

Salary increases at fixed rates are also negotiated by unions through collective bargaining. In one county, for example, a cost-of-living pay raise was negotiated at 4 percent for January 1998, 3 percent for January 1999, 3 percent for January 2000, and 2 percent for January 2001. If POs in this particular county should be promoted, demoted, or transferred, there are contract provisions calling for salary adjustments to levels consistent with the salary range held prior to the promotion, transfer, or demotion.

At the city level, probation and parole unions are having a more significant voice and power over the lives of affiliate POs. In Portland, Oregon, for instance, the city council has recognized the Parole and Probation Employee's Association (PPEA) to represent its membership as a collective bargaining unit. Some of the issues negotiated include caseloads, working hours, compensation for overtime, confidentiality issues, PSI report preparation time, fringe benefits relating to vacations, and retirement. Regarding caseloads, the Department of Corrections has alleged that POs have caseloads of 8 under ISP and 50 cases per PO under standard supervision. However, the PPEA has alleged that standard caseloads are closer to 100 clients per PO. A PPEA representative said that because of the sheer volume of cases, "we've become a bunch of desk-bound pencil pushers" (Probation and Parole Employee's Association, 2001:2). One issue of importance to POs in the PPEA is whether POs should be permitted to possess and carry firearms during the performance of their PO tasks. This issue has not been resolved as of early 2001. A bill has been proposed and was before the Oregon legislature in early 2001 to authorize firearms use by POs, including an appropriate amount of firearms safety training. These are some of the types of issues unions attempt to resolve for their memberships.

Probation and parole officer unions are not unique to the United States. For instance, there are probation and parole officer unions in Canada and other countries. In Ontario, Canada, for instance, there is a Probation Officers Association of Ontario, Inc. (POAO). The POAO is committed to the following objectives:

1. To speak with credibility on issues in criminal justice.
2. Facilitate increased understanding of the specialized role of the Probation Officer.
3. Provide representative perspectives on legislative issues to policymakers.
4. Provide a forum for an exchange of professional experience and opinion.
5. Promote good fellowship and esprit de corps among members.
6. Foster good will, understanding, and cooperation with others working in the criminal justice system.
7. Educate and involve the community in corrections.

The POAO expects its membership to subscribe to the following values:

1. That Probation Officers achieve professional status and continue to receive an ongoing education.
2. That its members are fully committed to a Code of Ethics.
3. That community corrections programs retain their validity as an effective means of rehabilitation for offenders.
4. That autonomy be maintained, while at the same time the responsibilities of the Ministries, OPSEU, and other components of the criminal justice system be acknowledged.
5. That involvement in the decision-making process be democratic and participatory at all levels.

Over 1,000 probation and parole officers belong to the POAO and they supervise more than 80,000 offenders in the community. POs supervise probation orders, parole, conditional sentences and conditional supervision orders. They monitor and enforce compliance with these court orders and others such as restitution to victims and community service orders. These professionals prepare detailed and comprehensive presentence investigation reports and predispositional reports for juveniles. Pre-parole reports are also prepared for the Ontario Board of Parole.

SUMMARY

Both adult and juvenile corrections has escalated during the last few decades. POs have assumed increased responsibilities and supervisory tasks in dealing with an increasingly diverse and dangerous clientele. The functions of probation and parole services are to supervise offenders, ensure offender compliance with program goals and provisions, conduct routine alcohol/drug checks, provide networking services for employment assistance, direct offender-clients to proper treatment, counseling, and other forms of assistance, protect the community by detecting a client's program infractions and reporting them to judges or parole boards, assisting offenders in becoming integrated into their communities, and engaging in any useful rehabilitative enterprise that will improve offender-client skills.

The organization and administration of probation and parole services is most often within the scope of departments of corrections in most states. Services vary among the states, although there are common elements to all probation and parole services and programs. The complexity of organizational structure is highly dependent upon the nature of clientele supervised and their special needs. The rehabilitative aim of corrections has not been particularly successful. For this and other reasons, probation and parole departments have drawn extensive criticism from an increasingly discontent public. Criticisms have focused upon the lack of skills and training of POs and the ineffectiveness of their performance. Professionalization through organizations such as the American Correctional Association and the American Probation and Parole Association have attempted to raise standards relating to the selection, recruitment, and training of POs throughout the nation.

In 2003, relatively few jurisdictions required bachelor's degrees for PO work. However, a majority of POs had some college education or had completed college. Increased education is the primary means for improving one's professionalization. Observers suggest that there is a high correlation between higher education achieved and work effectiveness among POs. Because of an increasingly ethnically and racially diverse clientele, POs have received additional training in cultural diversity. Some POs are recruited for dealing with special offender populations where English is a second language. Assessment centers are used for PO training. One assessment center is the Florida Assessment Center, which focuses upon selecting and evaluating the best POs for supervising offenders in a Florida community control program.

One important issue being raised in greater numbers of jurisdictions is whether POs should carry firearms. About half the states authorized the use of firearms for POs in 2003. Other states without such provisions were considering legislation in 2003. There is a controversy over whether POs should be armed. Some persons feel that armed POs tend to provoke their clients, while others see being armed as a reasonable means of self-protection, particularly if POs must enter dangerous, gang-controlled neighborhoods to visit their clients. One of the hazards of PO work is the lawsuit syndrome, where clients sue POs for various reasons. Thus, a part of PO training is designed to acquaint them with the conditions and situations that are most likely to result in lawsuits. Thus, the potential for lawsuits can be avoided or minimized. POs are continually subjected to periodic evaluations to determine their competence in job performance. Labor turnover among POs averages about 15 percent per year. Most POs who leave the profession tend to seek better jobs in the private sector or graduate to federal employment where the pay and benefits are substantially greater than state compensation.

Another important issue is the matter of caseloads. Caseloads refer to the number of clients managed by POs in any state or federal agency. No one knows what is an ideal caseload, and there is considerable variation in caseloads among jurisdictions. POs supervise offenders either intensively or generally, depending upon the programs imposed by judges and parole boards. No precise figures have been agreed upon as to what constitutes an optimum caseload size for POs. There are different caseload assignment models. These include the conventional model (the most popular), the numbers-game model (the easiest and least expensive), the conventional model with geographic considerations (the most expedient in terms of PO time management), and the specialized caseloads model (the most expensive). Officer–client interactions are affected by different factors, including the orientations of POs toward offenders. Some of these orientations are detectors, enablers, educators, mediators, and enforcers. Depending upon a PO's orientation, interactions with clients are positively or negatively influenced. Some amount of role conflict therefore exists, as POs attempt to perform their jobs under different sets of circumstances established by each jurisdiction. Most POs belong to one or more organizations where codes of ethics have been promulgated. These codes of ethics obligate POs to adhere to stringent behavioral guidelines in the performance of their jobs. It is expected that PO adherence to these codes of ethics will eventually improve their effectiveness and job performance, and that ultimately, client recidivism will decline.

Probation and parole officers have formed unions and engage in collective bargaining in all states. Many of these unions are at local, county, and state levels, and all unionization is designed to achieve better conditions for POs. Issues involve pay, retirement benefits, caseloads and assignments, promotional opportunities, and various types of grievances about the job and its benefits. Each union has articulated objectives. Union representatives are authorized to negotiate contracts with city, county, state, and federal governments to determine pay scales, working hours and conditions, and other matters of relevance to their memberships. Unions also attempt to improve the quality of professionalism among their memberships by sponsoring annual conferences where workshops are conducted to learn various skills. All union members are encouraged to improve their skills on a regular basis to promote their own interests within their respective probation or parole agencies.

QUESTIONS FOR REVIEW

1. What are some general functions and goals of probation and parole services?
2. Are all probation and parole agencies organized in the same way? What are some of the reasons for different types of organizational arrangements?

3. What are several criticisms of probation and parole programs?

4. What is an assessment center? What are some characteristics of the Florida Assessment Center?

5. What are some of the chief characteristics of POs? Why is there high labor turnover among new POs?

6. What are some of the reasons for unionizing probation and parole departments and engaging in collective bargaining?

7. Under what circumstances should POs carry firearms during the performance of their work? In what ways would carrying firearms provoke incidents between POs and their clients?

8. Is there an ideal caseload for a PO? How are caseloads determined?

9. What are four different kinds of caseload assignment methods? What are some of their defining characteristics? Which one is the most expensive and why?

10. What are some of the negligence and liability issues associated with the performance of PO work?

SUGGESTED READINGS

Abadinsky, Howard (2003). *Probation and Parole: Theory and Practice 8/e.* Upper Saddle River, NJ: Prentice Hall.

Basile, Vincent D. (2003). "A Model for Developing a Reentry Program." *Federal Probation 66*:55–58.

Lambert, Eric G., Nancy Lynne Hogan, and Shannon M. Barton (2002). "Satisfied Correctional Staff: A Review of the Literature on the Correlates of Correctional Staff Job Satisfaction." *Criminal Justice and Behavior 29*:115–143.

Morgan, Robert D., Richard A. VanHaveren, and Christy A. Pearson (2002). "Correctional Officer Burnout: Further Analyses." *Criminal Justice and Behavior 29*:144–160.

Seiter, Richard P. (2002). *Correctional Administration: Integrating Theory and Practice.* Upper Saddle River, NJ: Prentice Hall.

Seiter, Richard P. (2003). "Prisoner Reentry and the Role of Probation Officers." *Federal Probation 66*:50–54.

INTERNET CONNECTIONS

American Correctional Association
http://www.corrections.com/aca/index

Burnout in Billings
http://www.cannabisnews.com/news/16/thread16603.shtml

Citizens for Legal Responsibility
http://www.clr.org

Corrections Industries Association
http://www.correctionalindustries.org

Corrections industries links
http://www.corrections.com/industries

Corrections news
http://www.newstopics.corrections.com

National Institute of Corrections
http://www.nicic.org

Intermediate Skills
http://www.ojdda.org/intlesplan.html

International Corrections and Prisons Association
http://www.icpa.ca/home.html

Naber Technical Enterprises: Correctional Training, Correctional Consulting, Jail Research for Criminal Justice and Public Safety
http://www.nteusa.orgflyers/08.html

Probation officer recruitment
http://www.wvmccd.cc.ca.us/wvmccd/police/officer_hire.html

Ventura County Probation Agency
http://www.ventura.org/vcap/recruitm.htm

CHAPTER 10 | Probation and Parole Professionals

Chapter Outline

Chapter Objectives

As the result of reading this chapter, the following objectives will be realized:

1. Examining different ways of assessing offender needs and risk.
2. Understanding dangerousness and different types of risk prediction, including anamnestic, actuarial, and clinical prediction.
3. Evaluating the effectiveness of risk/needs assessment instruments.
4. Describing selective incapacitation and understanding several criticisms of it.
5. Describing apprehension units who track down absconders.
6. Describing gang and research units that operate in probation and parole departments.
7. Understanding the relation between stress and burnout and the consequences of burnout for job performance and effectiveness.
8. Examining different sources of stress and ways of alleviating it.
9. Describing the role of volunteers in PO work and the functions and legal liabilities of using volunteers.
10. Examining the roles and legal liabilities of paraprofessionals in probation/parole and community-based corrections.

INTRODUCTION

This chapter examines the changing PO role. There are serious concerns throughout the correctional community about whether POs are peace officers or police officers. PO responsibilities include supervising dangerous clients and ensuring that they comply with their probation or parole program requirements. One of the first things POs attempt to do is ascertain the degree of risk posed by the offenders they supervise. The first part of this chapter examines the assessment of offender risk. Several risk measures are presented. Since POs are expected to assist their clients as well as monitor their behaviors, some of these instruments attempt to determine offender needs as well as their risk levels. Needs instruments will be described. It is very important to define an offender's needs in order for POs to network and coordinate the most appropriate community services as interventions in a client's behalf.

PO work is increasingly specialized. More offenders who are freed on probation or parole abscond or leave their jurisdictions without PO permission. They cannot be immediately located. Thus, many probation and parole agencies have established apprehension units to track down absconders and return them to their jurisdictions. If absconders are located and returned, they face possible probation or parole program revocation. Therefore, it is dangerous business to be a part of apprehension units and to hunt fugitives who want to avoid capture.

Gangs are a pervasive part of our society. Thousands of gangs exist throughout the United States. Gangs are commonplace in prisons and jails as well as on city streets. Therefore, it is essential that POs familiarize themselves with gang recognition signs and symbols. When POs enter particular neighborhoods where their clients reside, often these neighborhoods are gang-dominated. Thus, there is an element of danger that exists merely during the act of checking up on a POs' clients. The gang phenomenon will be examined to the extent that it influences PO work and how POs do their jobs, especially where a portion of one's probationer- or parolee-clients are gang members. Probation and parole agencies also have research units whose task it is to study client profiles and devise new and improved supervision procedures. Some of the activities of these research units will be described.

PO work is stressful. There are numerous demands on POs, including their work for criminal courts, their supervision of dangerous clientele, and other general occupational hazards. The stresses of PO work will be examined, including a discussion of possible sources of stress. Stress often leads to burnout, which in turn causes POs to become less effective in the performance of their work. Burnout is examined, including a discussion of how it is assessed. Several solutions are proposed to alleviate stresses and burnout associated with the PO role.

The final part of this chapter examines the roles of volunteers and paraprofessionals who often assist with offender management in a variety of ways. Volunteers are unsalaried workers. Often they are found working with offenders in halfway houses. They assist them with filling out job applications and perform teaching functions. Usually, volunteers have no legal training or qualifications that authorize them to direct probationers or parolees in their required programming by the court or parole board. Nevertheless, they do perform several valuable services for probation and parole departments and officers. Paraprofessionals have some amount of formal training working with offenders. Many paraprofessionals have college degrees in disciplines that complement probation and parole work, such as criminal justice, sociology, political science, psychology, or social work. Their roles will also be described. Finally, because volunteers and paraprofessionals are not as well-trained as regular POs, they are unusually vulnerable to legal liabilities of different kinds. They may give offenders the wrong type of advice. Or they may give illegal assistance to offenders without the knowledge that what they are doing is wrong or should not be done. Thus, the legal liabilities of these volunteers and paraprofessionals will be examined and discussed.

PROBATION AND PAROLE: RISK/NEEDS ASSESSMENTS

Assessing Offender Risk: A Brief History

Many **risk assessment** measures have been devised and are used largely for the purpose of determining probabilities that offender/clients will engage in dangerous or maladjusted behaviors (Nijboer et al., 2002). These probabilities are subsequently used for placement, program, and security decision making. Needs measures and instruments enable corrections personnel and administrative staffs to highlight client weaknesses or problems which may have led to their convictions or difficulties initially. Once problem areas have been targeted, specific services or treatments might be scheduled and provided. Various Christian Reform movements have been credited with establishing an early prisoner **classification system** in the eighteenth century (Kemshall and Maguire, 2001). Behavioral scientists, especially psychiatrists and psychologists, conducted research during the period 1910–1920 and found that custody-level placements of inmates as well as other program assignments could be made by using certain psychological characteristics as predictors (Virginia Criminal Sentencing Commission, 2001).

Criminologists and criminal justice scholars have become increasingly involved in devising risk assessment inventories and needs indices, using combinations of psychological, social, socioeconomic, and demographic factors and related criteria to make dangerousness forecasts and behavioral predictions (Patrick et al.,

2000). Formal, paper-pencil risk and needs instruments began to proliferate during the 1960s. Some of this instrumentation was used with juvenile offenders. Later, numerous behavioral and psychological instruments were devised and used for the purpose of assessing client risk or inmate dangerousness (Maguire et al., 2001). The **Minnesota Multiphasic Personality Inventory (MMPI),** consisting of 550 true-false items, was originally used in departments of corrections for personality assessments. While this instrument is still applied in many correctional settings, some researchers, such as Edwin Megargee, have extracted certain items from the MMPI for use as predictors of inmate violence and adjustment. The use of **classification** devices such as Megargee's are often designated as MMPI-based assessments or classifications. Applications of scales such as Megargee's have received mixed results and evaluations. In at least some studies, such scales have demonstrably low reliability (Wooldredge and Thistlewaite, 2002).

Herbert Quay's work preceded the work of Megargee (Quay and Parsons, 1971). Quay devised a relatively simple typology of delinquent behavior, classifying delinquents into four categories: Undersocialized Aggression, Socialized Aggression, Attention Deficit, and Anxiety-Withdrawal-Dysphoria. Juveniles would complete a self-administered questionnaire and their personality scores would be quickly tabulated. Depending upon how particular juveniles were depicted and classified, different treatments would be administered to help them. Later, Quay devised a scale which he called AIMS, or the Adult Internal Management System (Quay, 1984). Again, Quay used a self-administered inventory, the Correctional Adjustment Checklist and the Correctional Adjustment Life History. His adult typology consisted of five types of inmates: Aggressive Psychopathic, Manipulative, Situational, Inadequate-Dependent, and Neurotic-Anxious.

Another system is the I-Level Classification, referring to the Interpersonal Maturity Level Classification System. This system was originally devised by Sullivan, Grant, and Grant (1957). It is based on a mixture of developmental and psychoanalytic theories and is administered by psychologists or psychiatrists in lengthy clinical interviews. Clients are classified as being at particular "I-Levels," such as I-1, I-2, and so on, up to I-7. Each I-level is a developmental stage reflecting one's ability to cope with complex personal and interpersonal problems. The higher the I-level, the better adjusted the client. In recent years there have been scale improvements, including the Jesness Inventory (JI), which was devised by Carl Jesness (2003). The JI is a 155-item, true-false questionnaire with easy-to-understand items yielding 10 trait scores, an index of asocial tendencies, and nine personality subtype scales. The JI purportedly measures social maladjustment, value orientation, immaturity, autism, alienation, manifest aggression, withdrawal depression, social anxiety, repression, denial, and an asocial index (Jesness, 2003).

It was not until the 1980s, however, that state corrections departments began to create and apply risk assessment schemes with some regularity and in correctional areas beyond the institutional setting. For example, Arizona created its first Offender Classification System manual in 1986 (Arizona Department of Corrections, 1991). Instrumentation for risk assessment was established in Illinois in the mid-1980s. Tennessee sought requests for proposals in 1987 to devise risk measures for its inmate population. Missouri introduced a variation of AIMS for use in its Department of Corrections in 1988. Many jurisdictions are currently revising or have recently revised their risk and needs instruments (Campbell, 1995). Iowa's Risk/Needs Classification System was implemented in December, 1983 and revised extensively in 2001 (Iowa Department of Correctional Services, 2003). The Iowa Department of Corrections Reassessment of Client Risk is shown in Figure 10.1.

IOWA DEPARTMENT OF CORRECTIONS REASSESSMENT OF CLIENT RISK

Client Name_____ ICBC#_____
                    Last   First   Middle

Date of Reassessment_____ Officer's Name_____

Offense_____

INSTRUCTIONS: Score Items and add total score.   **SCORE**

1. Age at first Adult Conviction/Juvenile Adjudication (include deferreds)	24 or older	= −2	[ ]
	20 to 23	= 0	[ ]
	19 or younger	= 1	[ ]
2. Prior Juvenile Commitments	None	= 0	[ ]
3. Prior Probations/Parole Supervisions (Adult/Juvenile Adjudications)	One or more	= 2	[ ]
	None	= 0	[ ]
4. Number of Prior Probation/Parole Revocations (Adult/Juvenile Adjudications)	One or more	= 2	[ ]
	None	= 0	[ ]
	One or more	= 2	[ ]
5. Felony/Misdemeanor Convictions (include present offense, deferreds, juvenile adjudications); Circle applicable and add for score. Do not exceed a total of 3.	Burglary or Robbery	= 1	[ ]
	Theft, Forgery, FUFI, Fraudulent Practices	= 1	
	Assault, Weapons Public Order Offenses	= 1	
6. Misdemeanor Conviction History (Simple & Serious Misdemeanors Only); Include present offense, deferreds & Juvenile Adjudications.	None	= 0	[ ]
	None or one	= 0	
	Two or more	= 1	[ ]
7. Sex	Female	= 0	
	Male	= 1	[ ]
8. Alcohol Usage Problems	No interference	= 0	
	Occasional abuse	= 1	
	Frequent abuse	= 2	[ ]
9. Drug Usage Problems	No interference	= 0	
	Occasional abuse	= 1	
	Frequent abuse	= 2	[ ]

*10. **Employment** Satisfactory one year or longer	= −2		
Secure or not applicable	= 0		
Unsatisfactory or Unemployed, unemployable	= 2	[ ]	

(continued)

FIGURE 10.1   Iowa Department of Corrections Reassessment of Client Risk.

Source: Iowa Department of Correctional Services, 2003.

*11.	**Companions** No adverse relationships	=	0			
	Associations occasionally negative	=	1			
	Associations almost completely negative	=	2	[	]	
*12.	**Problems with Current Living Situation** Relatively stable relationships and/or address	=	0			
	Moderate disorganization or stress	=	1			
	Major disorganization/ stress	=	2	[	]	
*13.	**Response to Supervision Conditions** No problems of consequence	=	0			
	Moderate compliance problem	=	1			
	Frequently unwilling to comply	=	3	[	]	
*14.	**New Arrests** None	=	0			
	One or more arrests	=	3	[	]	
*15.	**Use of Community Resources**					
	Not needed	=	0			
	Productively utilized	=	0			
	Needed, but not available	=	1			
	Utilized, but not beneficial	=	2			
	Client rejected referral	=	3	[	]	

TOTAL SCORE   [   ]

Clients are assigned to the highest level of supervision indicated on the following scale:

Risk

31 to 15   Intensive
14 to 8   Normal
 7 to 2   Minimum
 1 to –5   Administrative

Levels of Supervision

1   Intensive
2   Normal
3   Minimum
4   Administrative

FIGURE 10.1   *(Continued)*

Reason for Override

0   Assaultive offense
1   Severity of offense
2   Special conditions set by parole board, court, or district
3   Client not available for active supervision
4   Force field indicates high needs

5   Other _____

_____

_____

_____

_____

_____

_____

Comments_____

_____

_____

_____

_____

Level   [   ]

Revised Level   [   ]

Override reason code   [   ]

_____

Override approval/date

FIGURE 10.1   *(Continued)*

1. Classification systems enable authorities to make decisions about appropriate offender program placements.

2. Classification systems help to identify one's needs and the provision of effective services in specialized treatment programs.

3. Classification assists in determining one's custody level if confined in either prisons or jails.

4. Classification helps to adjust one's custody level during confinement, considering behavioral improvement and evidence of rehabilitation.

5. While confined, inmates may be targeted for particular services and/or programs to meet their needs.

6. Classification may be used for offender management and deterrence relative to program or prison rules and requirements.

7. Classification schemes are useful for policy decision making and administrative planning relevant for jail and prison construction, the nature and number of facilities required, and the types of services to be made available within such facilities.

8. Classification systems enable parole boards to make better early-release decisions about eligible offenders.

9. Community corrections agencies can utilize classification schemes to determine those parolees who qualify for participation and those who don't qualify.

10. Classification systems enable assessments of risk and dangerousness to be made generally in anticipation of the type of supervision best-suited for particular offenders.

11. Classification schemes assist in decision making relevant for community crime control, the nature of penalties to be imposed, and the determination of punishment.

12. Classification may enable authorities to determine whether selective incapacitation is desirable for particular offenders or offender groupings.

Dangerousness and risk are often used interchangeably. Dangerousness and risk both convey propensities to cause harm to others or oneself. What is the likelihood that any particular offender will be violent toward others? Does an offender pose any risk to public safety? What is the likelihood that any particular offender will commit suicide or attempt it? Risk (or dangerousness) instruments are screening devices intended to distinguish between different types of offenders for purposes of determining initial institutional classification, security placement and inmate management, early release eligibility, the level of supervision required under conditions of probation or parole, and even whether the death penalty should be applied at the time of sentencing for capital offenses (Brock, Sorensen, and Marquart, 2000; Krauss et al., 2000). Most state jurisdictions and the federal government refer to these measures as risk instruments rather than dangerousness instruments. There is considerable variance among states regarding the format and content of such measures. An example of one of the less elaborate versions of a risk assessment instrument is one used by the Massachusetts Parole Board illustrated in Figure 10.2.

Additionally, a **needs assessment instrument** measures an offender's personal/social skills, health well-being and emotional stability, educational level and vocational strengths and weaknesses, alcohol/drug dependencies, mental ability, and other relevant life factors, and which highlight those areas for which services are available and could or should be provided. Needs assessment devices, measures, scales, or inventories identify the types of services offenders might require if incarcerated (Bickle et al., 2002). If some offenders are illiterate, they may be placed, either voluntarily or involuntarily, into an educational program at some level, depending upon the amount of remedial work deemed necessary. Psychologically disturbed or mentally ill offenders may require some type of counseling or therapy (Silver, 2000). Some offenders may require particular medications for illnesses or other maladies. Sometimes instruments are designed in such a way so as to assess both needs and risk (Holt, 1997). In Figure 10.3, the Kansas Department of Corrections has devised a risk and needs assessment coding form for assessing the future conduct and needs of parolees.

MASSACHUSETTS PAROLE BOARD
Release Risk Classification Instrument

Name: _____   MCI-Number: _____

SID: _____   Actual Release Date: _____

Hearing Location: _____   Hearing Date: _____

Completed By: _____   Completion Date: _____

Controlling Effective Date of Commitment: _____

1. Number of returns to higher custody since the Controlling Effective Date of Commitment (Count all revocations, returns from escape and probation surrenders):	0 = 0 points 1 = 2 points 2, 3 = 4 points 4 or more = 6 points [ ]
2. Custody standing prior to the Controlling Effective Date of Commitment:	Not under custody = 0 points On street supervision = 1 point Incarceration = 2 points [ ]
3. Total number of parole revocations on prior state sentences:	None = 0 points 1 or more = 1 point [ ]
4. Number of adult convictions for property offenses prior to the Controlling Effective Date of Commitment:	None = 0 points 1 or more = 1 point [ ]
5. Number of charges for a person offense as a juvenile:	None = 0 points 1 or more = 1 point [ ]
6. Age at release hearing:	34 or older = 0 points 28–33 = 2 points 24–27 = 4 points 23 or younger = 6 points [ ]
7. Evidence of heroin, cocaine, or crack cocaine use: Notes (verbal admission): _____	No = 0 points Yes = 2 points [ ]

_____

8. SCORE: Add the numerical scores of questions 1 through 7 and enter the total score in this box.   [ ]

SCORING: A score between 0–4 = Low Risk; 5–10 = Moderate Risk; 11 or more = High Risk

FIGURE 10.2   Massachusetts Parole Board Release Risk Classification Instrument.
Source: Massachusetts Parole Board, 2003.

Risk and need assessments may also be referred to jointly and contained in a longer inventory or measure, labeled a risk-need assessment. An inspection of these devices and the individual items included within them will indicate which factors seem to have the greatest priority and predictive utility. The offender need assessment inventory shown in Figure 10.4 also assigns greater or lesser weights to different items which focus upon various dimensions of one's

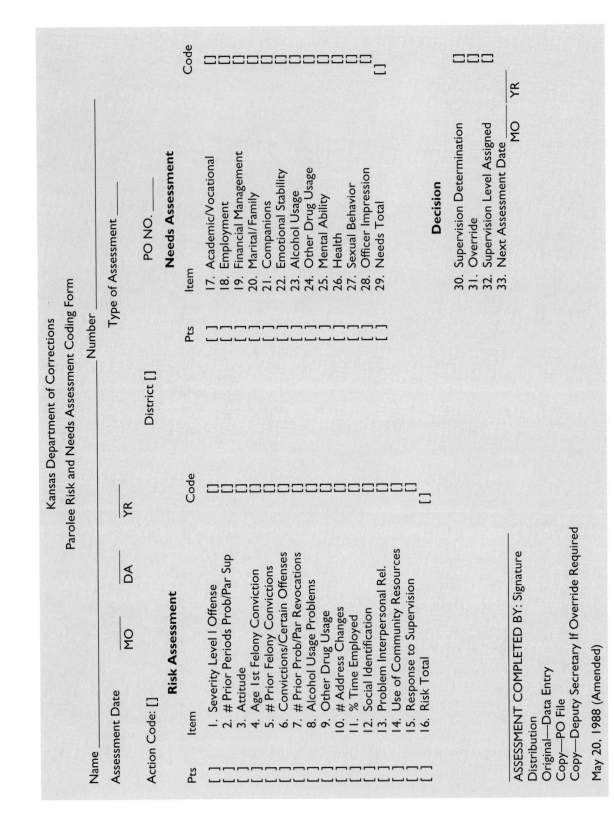

FIGURE 10.3 Kansas Department of Corrections Parolee Risk and Needs Assessment.

Source: Kansas Department of Corrections, 2003.

OFFENDER NEED ASSESSMENT

Client's Name_____ Officer's_____

Select the appropriate answer and enter the associated weight in the score column. Total all scores to arrive at the need assessment score.

SCORE

1. ACADEMIC/VOCATIONAL SKILLS:
   a. High school or above skill level.................................0   [   ]
   b. Has vocational training; additional not needed...................1   [   ]
   c. Has some skills; additional needed...............................2   [   ]
   d. No skills; training needed.......................................3   [   ]
2. EMPLOYMENT:
   a. Satisfactory employment for 1 year or longer.....................0
   b. Employed; no difficulties reported; or homemaker, student, retired or
      disabled and unable to work......................................2   [   ]
   c. Part-time, seasonal, unstable employment or needs additional employment;
      unemployed, but has a skill......................................3   [   ]
   d. Unemployed & virtually unemployable; needs training..............5   [   ]
3. FINANCIAL STATUS:
   a. Longstanding pattern of self-sufficiency.........................0   [   ]
   b. No current difficulties..1   [   ]
   c. Situational or minor difficulties................................2   [   ]
   d. Severe difficulties..4   [   ]
4. LIVING ARRANGEMENTS (Within last six months):
   a. Stable and supportive relationships with family or others in living group.0
   b. Client lives alone or independently within another household.....1
   c. Client experiencing occasional, moderate interpersonal problems
      within living group...2
   d. Client experiencing frequent and serious interpersonal problems within
      living group..4   [   ]
5. EMOTIONAL STABILITY:
   a. No symptoms of instability.......................................0
   b. Symptoms limit, but do not prohibit adequate functioning.........3
   c. Symptoms prohibit adequate functioning...........................5   [   ]
6. ALCOHOL USAGE (Current):
   a. No interference with functioning.................................0
   b. Occasional abuse; some disruption of functioning.................3
   c. Frequent abuse; serious disruption; needs treatment..............6   [   ]
7. OTHER SUBSTANCE USAGE (Current):
   a. No interference with functioning.................................0   [   ]
   b. Occasional substance abuse; some disruption of functioning; may need
      treatment...3
   c. Frequent substance abuse; serious disruption; needs treatment....5   [   ]
8. MENTAL ABILITY:
   a. Able to function independently...................................0
   b. Some need for assistance; potential for adequate adjustment;
      mild retardation..2
   c. Deficiencies suggest limited ability to function independently;
      moderate retardation..3   [   ]
9. HEALTH:
   a. Sound physical health; seldom ill................................0
   b. Handicap or illness interferes with functioning on a recurring basis......1
   c. Serious handicap or chronic illness; needs frequent medical care.........3   [   ]
10. SEXUAL BEHAVIOR:
   a. No apparent dysfunction..0
   b. Real or perceived situational or minor problems..................2
   c. Real or perceived chronic or severe problems.....................3   [   ]
11. OFFICER'S IMPRESSION OF CLIENT NEEDS:
   a. None...0
   b. Low..1
   c. Moderate...2
   d. High...4   [   ]

TOTAL SCORES 1 THROUGH 11   [   ]

FIGURE 10.4 Alaska Department of Corrections Offender Need Assessment Scale.

Source: Alaska Department of Corrections, 2003.

life. Those areas having the largest number of points potentially assigned include employment, emotional stability, and alcohol usage. These items have possible large scores of "5," "6," and "5" respectively. All other items, including academic/vocational skills, financial status, other substance abuse, mental ability, health, living arrangements, sexual behavior, and the officer's impression of a client's needs have a largest weight of "4" or less. Again, on the basis of one's cumulative score or raw point total, interpretive tables are consulted to determine one's level of needs and types of needs which should be addressed with one or more services. These services might include alcohol or drug abuse treatment programs, vocational/educational training, employment counseling, or individual/group therapy (Motiuk, Belcourt, and Bonta, 1995). Those areas most indicative of one's greatest weaknesses or needs are typically those with the largest score weights.

Types of Risk Assessment Instruments

Three basic categories of risk classifications have been identified. These include (1) anamnestic prediction; (2) actuarial prediction; and (3) clinical prediction.

Anamnestic Prediction.   **Anamnestic prediction** is the prediction of offender behavior according to past circumstances. If circumstances are similar now, it is likely they will behave the same way now. For example, a presentence investigation report may show that an offender was alcohol- and drug-dependent, unemployed, inclined toward violence because of previous assault incidents, and poorly educated. Recidivists convicted of new crimes may exhibit present circumstances similar to those which prevailed when they were convicted of their earlier offense. Thus, judges and others might rely heavily upon the situational similarity of past and present circumstances to measure offender risk. However, if some offenders have made a significant effort between convictions to obtain additional education or training for better job performance, or if they are no longer alcohol- or drug-dependent, other types of behavioral forecasts will have to be made. This is because different circumstances exist now compared with previous circumstances (Heyman et al., 2002).

Actuarial Prediction.   **Actuarial prediction** is based upon the characteristics of a class of offenders similar to offenders being considered for probation, parole, or inmate classification (Wollert, 2002). Considering others like them, situated as they are, this is how they behaved in the past. Therefore, it is likely that those persons who exhibit similar characteristics to the general class of offenders considered for these different sanctioning and classification options will behave in ways similar to that particular class (McGrath et al., 2003). In effect, this is an aggregate predictive tool. For instance, assume we have targeted a large sample of persons placed on probation and track them over a 2-year period. We determine that 65 percent of these probationers did not complete their probationary periods satisfactorily. We describe these failures as follows: they are predominantly young, black, unemployed or underemployed, lack a high school education, were victims of child abuse, and are drug-dependent. Now, whenever young, black, unemployed, less educated, drug-dependent, former child-abuse victims are considered for probation, parole, inmate classification, or some intermediate sanctioning option, their chances of being placed in one program or another, or of being classified one way or another, may be influenced greatly by the general characteristics of previous program failures. Interestingly, it seems that program failures are more often described and used to structure risk instruments than are program successes (Fields and McNamara, 2003).

Clinical Prediction.   **Clinical prediction** is based upon the predictor's professional training and experience working directly with the offender. Based upon extensive diagnostic examinations, the belief is that the offender will behave in a certain way (Witt et al., 1996). The subjectivity inherent in clinical prediction is apparent. The skills of the assessor are prominent. However, such prediction is more expensive, since each clinical prediction is individualized. Both anamnestic and actuarial prediction respectively utilize situational factors and general characteristics of offenders in forecasting their future risk. Interestingly, the highest degrees of validity are associated with actuarial and anamnestic predictions (for instance, those currently used by parole boards), and they are considered very reliable. Predictors in clinical predictions are usually psychiatrists or psychologists with extensive clinical training and experience with deviant conduct and criminal behavior (Prins, 1999). Some research has found that actuarial prediction is superior in its predictive utility compared with clinical prediction (Gardner et al., 1996).

Any prediction tools which are used, and any claims about their validity and reliability, and/or the recommendations concerning their applicability to specific offender situations, are subject to certain limitations (Dillingham et al., 1999). For instance, Morris and Miller (1985:35-37) have suggested three guiding principles for parole boards to consider when making early release decisions. These include:

1. Punishment should not be imposed, nor the term of punishment extended, by virtue of a prediction of dangerousness, beyond that which would be justified as a deserved punishment independently of that prediction.

2. Provided this limitation is respected, predictions of dangerousness may properly influence sentencing decisions and other decisions under criminal law.

3. The base expectancy rate of violence for the criminal predicted as dangerous must be shown by reliable evidence to be substantially higher than the base expectancy rate of another criminal with a closely similar criminal record and convicted of a closely similar crime but not predicted as unusually dangerous, before the greater dangerousness of the former may be relied on to intensify or extend his/her punishment.

Judges and especially probation officers are also interested in behavioral prediction. The PSI report prepared for any offender sometimes contains a recommendation for some form of probation or incarceration. This recommendation is based on the probation officer's belief that the offender will either be a good risk or a poor risk for probation. This is behavioral prediction. **Prediction** means an assessment of some expected future behavior of a person including criminal acts, arrests or convictions. Predictions of future criminal behavior date back to Biblical times although our concern here is with contemporary developments and the current state-of-the-art prediction and assessment devices. Assessments of offender risk have been devised by most departments of corrections throughout the United States. Iowa, Kansas, and Massachusetts are only a few of the states which have devised such instruments. Several important and desirable characteristics of these instruments have been outlined. These include:

1. The model should be predictively valid.
2. The model should reflect reality.

3. The model should be designed for a dynamic system and not remain fixed over time.

4. The model should serve practical purposes.

5. The model should not be a substitute for good thinking and responsible judgment.

6. The model should be both qualitative and quantitative (Rans, 1984:50).

The paroling authority next consults a table of offense characteristics consisting of categories varying in offense severity. Adult ranges in numbers of months served are provided for each category and are crosstabulated with the four-category parole prognosis above. Thus, a parole board can theoretically apply a consistent set of standards to prisoners committing similar offenses. When the board departs from these standards, especially when parole is possible for an offender but denied, a written rationale is provided for both the prisoner and appellate authorities. And an inmate has the right to appeal the decision of the parole board to a higher authority such as the National Appeals Board (18 U.S.C. Sec. 4215, 2004). Consistency is highly desirable in the application of any parole criteria. Many inmate lawsuits involve allegations of inconsistent application of parole eligibility guidelines.

The Effectiveness of Risk Assessment Devices

Present efforts to develop classification schemes to predict offender future behavior remain at best an unstable business. This criticism applies to both adult and juvenile risk assessment measures that are currently applied (Caldwell, 2002). Risk assessment devices developed and used in one state are often not applicable to offenders in other states. In some states such as Massachusetts, risk assessment instruments are used by probation officers to decide which probationers should be supervised with varying frequency. Results were favorable (i.e., lower recidivism rates were observed) where certain high-risk offenders received greater supervision by probation officers compared with high-risk offenders not receiving greater supervision.

Two important questions in designing any instrument to predict future criminal conduct are (1) which factors are most relevant in such predictions? and (2) what weight should be given each of these factors? We don't know for sure. One recurring criticism of prediction studies and the development of risk assessment instruments is that much work is needed on the definition and measurement of criteria (Harris, Rice, and Cormier, 2002). This does not mean that all of the instruments presently developed are worthless as predictors of success on probation or parole. But it does suggest these measures are imperfect (Buttell and Pike, 2002). Therefore, it may be premature to rely exclusively on instrument scores to decide who goes to prison and who receives probation. But in many jurisdictions, risk assessment scores are used precisely for this purpose (Robinson, 2002).

Some Applications of Risk/Needs Measures

We have already discussed several of the many potential applications of **risk/needs instruments** and measures. One convenient way of highlighting the most common applications of these instruments by the different states is to examine their own utilization criteria and objectives (Corrado et al., 2002). The following state utilization criteria are not intended to represent *all* other states or to typify them. Rather, they have been highlighted because of their diversity of objectives. For example, Iowa's Classification Risk Assessment Scale is used for the following purposes:

1. Program planning.
2. Budgeting and deployment of resources.
3. Evaluating services, programs, procedures, and performances.
4. Measuring the potential impact of legislative and policy changes.
5. Enhancing accountability through standardization.
6. Equitably distributing the workload.
7. Improving service delivery to clients. (Iowa Department of Correctional Services, 2003)

The above goals for Iowa are couched in the context of initial placement decisions and closely related to management objectives, including allocating scarce resources most profitably in view of system constraints. Theoretically, if the system's processual features are optimized, offender management is also. Presumably, the quality of services available to offender-clients would also be improved. But as we have seen, risk assessments serve several purposes. For instance, the Ohio Parole Board uses a guideline system for determining early releases of certain offenders through parole or furlough. This guideline system incorporates a risk assessment instrument and has the following objectives:

1. To provide for public protection by not releasing those inmates who represent a high risk of repeating violent or other serious crimes.
2. To provide an appropriate continuum of sanctions for crime.
3. To cooperate with correctional management in providing safe, secure, and humane conditions in state correctional institutions.
4. To recognize the achievement of those inmates with special identifiable problems relating to their criminal behavior who have participated in institutional programs designed to alleviate their problems.
5. To make the decision-making process of the Adult Parole Authority more open, equitable, and understandable both to the public and to the inmate. (Ohio Parole Board, 2003)

In Ohio, the parole board guideline system objectives differ substantially from those of Iowa. The Ohio risk assessment objectives are more offender-oriented, with emphases upon the appropriateness of sanctions and identifying offender-client needs which may be met by particular services. There are also greater concerns for public safety and greater community comprehension of the parole decision-making process. Most states distinguish between offender evaluations for the purpose of determining their institutional risk and their public risk. Again, the device contents are often identical or very similar. An examination of the utilization criteria for other state risk assessment devices yields similar diversity of instrument goals. It is possible to group these diverse objectives according to several general applications. Thus, we may conclude that for most states, the following general applications are made of risk assessment instruments at different client-processing stages:

1. To promote better program planning through optimum budgeting and deployment of resources.
2. To target high-risk and high-need offenders for particular custody levels, programs, and services without endangering the safety of others.
3. To apply the fair and appropriate sanctions to particular classes of offenders and raise their level of accountability.
4. To provide mechanisms for evaluating services and programs as well as service and program improvements over time.
5. To maximize public safety as well as public understanding of the diverse functions of corrections by making decision making more open and comprehensible to both citizens and offender-clients. (Champion, 1994)

Selective Incapacitation

Selective incapacitation is incarcerating certain offenders deemed high risks to public safety and not incarcerating other offenders determined to be low risks, given similar offenses. Selective incapacitation applies to certain high-risk offenders and is designed to reduce the crime rate by incapacitating only those most likely to recidivate (J. McGuire, 2002). Obviously, selective incapacitation is discriminatory in its application, and the ethics and fairness of predictive sentencing are frequently called into question. Professionals who deal with violent persons on a regular basis, mental health professionals and psychiatrists, also question the accuracy of dangerousness indices, especially when such devices are used for justifying preventive detention. There are too many variables that can interfere with proper prediction of individual behavior (Auerbahn, 2002).

In Washington, for instance, specific types of offenders have been targeted for special punishment following their conventional sentences. Washington State's legislature passed the Sexual Predator Act in 1990, which allows for the civil commitment of sex offenders in a mental health facility if they are deemed to pose a future danger to others. Identifying a specific offender aggregate for more extensive punishment when they have served their full terms raises questions about the fairness of their extended terms, even though these extended terms are mental hospitals and not prisons. Some critics label Washington's Sexual Predator Act as premature and unscientific (Brody and Green, 1994), since we currently lack the scientific skills to make precise predictions about one's future conduct. Similarities have been drawn between the treatment of habitual sex offenders and habitual drunk drivers, for example. One conclusion is that we have created a special category of offenders from which there is no escape. The only real predictor to be inferred based on current knowledge is that patients with a history of sexually violent behavior are in a high-risk group for committing future acts of this nature. Therefore, anyone treated for sexual deviance is at high risk for repeating such acts (McGrath, Cumming, and Holt, 2002). In many of these situations, the law selects poor candidates for more extensive treatment in mental hospitals. The use of preventive detention for such purposes raises both moral and legal questions for analysis.

THE CHANGING PROBATION/PAROLE OFFICER ROLE

The quality of PO personnel is increasing compared with past years (Kelly et al., 2001). The American Correctional Association and several other agencies are expanding their training options and arrangements to permit larger numbers of prospective corrections recruits to acquire skills and training. Raising the minimum standards and qualifications associated with corrections positions generally and PO work specifically will eventually spawn new generations of better-trained officers to managing growing offender populations. New generations of POs are also having to familiarize themselves with computers and computer software programs designed for offender control and surveillance (Renzema, 2000).

One belief is that more educated POs may be able to manage better the stress associated with PO work. But at the same time, there are indications that more educated POs and other corrections officers have higher levels of dissatisfaction with their work compared with less educated officers. Personality factors appear crucial for making successful adaptations to PO work. Also, there is high labor turnover among corrections personnel. This means that comparatively few officers remain in PO work long enough to acquire useful skills and abilities to assist their clients effectively (Cosgrove, 1994). While the composition of the PO work force is changing gradually each year, technological developments and changes in the laws governing PO/offender-client interactions and the rights of offenders are also occurring. For instance, the use of electronic monitoring of offenders is making it possible to increase officer caseloads dramatically without affecting seriously the amount of time officers spend monitoring offender whereabouts. This is especially applicable in the case of low-risk offenders sentenced to probation or paroled property offenders.

But electronic monitoring, together with home incarceration, is inadvertently changing the qualifications of those who supervise offenders with these electronic devices. Private enterprises are entering the correctional field in increasing numbers, and their involvement in probation or parole programs where electronic monitoring and house arrest are used as sanctions is apparent. What kinds of POs will be needed in future years to read computer printouts, drive by offender homes with electronic receiving devices, and conduct telephonic checks of offenders? Not all clients on probation or parole are nonviolent, low-risk offenders. Increasing numbers are dangerous felons who have committed violent crimes (Johnson and Jones, 1994). Therefore, POs are required who possess more than minimal qualifications in order to adequately supervise those uncharacteristic of the average probationer or parolee. While in-service training is desirable, not all states include in-service training in their recruitment process. Unless there are drastic changes in both the image and rewards associated with PO work in the near future, more offenders will receive increasingly inadequate services from probation and parole professionals as caseloads are enlarged. This circumstance will only serve to increase recidivism rates associated with various probation and parole programs (Camp and Camp, 2003).

Global Positioning Satellite Systems: Tracking Offenders from Outer Space

Technological advancements in offender monitoring also modify PO roles and how they do their jobs. One of the more recent developments is the **global positioning satellite system (GPS),** which is a method of locating an offender whereabouts by using satellites in outer space. Using space-age technology, the Florida Department of Corrections began a pilot project in 1997 to track the location and movements of offenders in real time, 24 hours a day, and notify probation officers of any violations as they occurred. The pilot program was conducted at probation offices in Tampa and Clearwater. GPS is a network of satellites, used by the U.S. Department of Defense, that pinpoints targets and guides bombs. It has been used for everything from helping hikers find their way through the woods to guiding law enforcement to locate stolen vehicles. With GPS, POs can track an offender on a computer screen and can tell what street the offender is on, anywhere in the state (Frost, 2002).

The GPS can actually customize equipment for particular offenders and create zones of inclusion or exclusion. Thus, POs can be warned if offenders approach their former victims in any way, or enter their neighborhoods. Some areas can simply be declared off limits, and these rules can be enforced easily through GPS. GPS offenders strap pager-size units to their ankles and carry lunchbox-size personal tracking devices (PTDs). POs can send instant messages to their clients through these PTDs and can warn offenders to leave particular locations immediately. One immediate benefit of such a system is to protect victims from various clients (Renzema, 2000).

A survey of Florida POs who have used GPS and PTD reveals mixed feelings. Some Florida POs say that the primary usefulness of GPS is to enforce curfews and whether offenders are present or absent in their homes or other places. The GPS system is not designed to show where offenders are during approved absence periods. Furthermore, the GPS system doesn't show what an offender is doing at any particular location. Most POs agreed that those offenders who could use GPS and PTDs the most were violent sex offenders and predators with prior criminal histories. According to some Florida POs, the technology is so new that some Florida judges don't know what they are dealing with. They sometimes assign traffic violators, bad check writers, and drug addicts to GPS and PTDs. These systems are not designed to deter traffic misconduct, bad check writing, or illegal use of drugs. Another problem is the technical failure of GPS or PTD devices, such as battery failure or system malfunctions. One skeptical judge, Judge John Kuder of Pensacola, decided to test the GPS system before sentencing convicted offenders to it. He wore the GPS and PTD devices for five days, doing everything he could to try and outsmart the system. Kuder went to a movie theater that had been designated as "off limits" for the test and left a note at the box office saying, "The mouse was here." Four minutes later, a Florida Department of Corrections PO signed the same note at the box office, saying "So was the smart cat. Busted!" Judge Kuder said, "This is one challenge I'm very glad I lost" (Mercer, Brooks, and Bryant, 2000:80).

Is technology going to replace PO surveillance functions? Probably not. At least it will probably operate similarly to electronic monitoring and home confinement programs that are a part of Florida's community control program. GPS and PTDs are simply alternative systems for tracking offenders' whereabouts. POs are still needed to conduct face-to-face visits with their clients, administer substance abuse kits and determine program violations related to illegal substances or alcohol, and determine other types of program violations (Kelly et al., 2001). But the system does seem to suggest that surveillance techniques in the future will become increasingly sophisticated and that perhaps POs can use the extra time saved to do other more important things to assist their clients in becoming reintegrated and rehabilitated.

APPREHENSION UNITS

One fact of life faced by all probation and parole agencies is that some proportion of their clients will abscond, or flee the jurisdiction. After all, probationers and parolees have the freedom and mobility to move about within their communities. If they choose to do so, they can flee the jurisdiction and attempt to elude their supervisors. Absconders also include a portion of jail and prison inmates who have been placed on work release, study release, or furloughs. However, these inmates are almost always within a few months of being released anyway. Thus, prisons and jails do not regard them as serious escape risks if they are entrusted not to abscond if given temporary leaves for various purposes. Fortunately, the proportion of absconders in probation and parole is quite low, less than 5 percent (Camp and Camp, 2003). The same is true for inmates of prisons and jails who abscond while on work and study release or are in furlough programs. The rate of apprehension of these fugitives is over 90 percent. Thus, most of these offenders are eventually apprehended.

All departments of correction throughout the United States have **apprehension units** to track **absconders** (Parent and Snyder, 1999). Apprehension units are dedicated departments consisting of specialists who engage in offender tracking and apprehension. Their business is to find absconders and bring them back to their jurisdictions for punishment. Absconders are subject to penalties such as five years' imprisonment for escape. This is an additional sentence in relation to the sentences they are serving for other crimes. For instance, when offenders sign intensive supervised probation documents, they often agree not to oppose extradition from another jurisdiction if they flee and are eventually apprehended. Probation and parole departments attempt to cover all contingencies relating to the retrieval of escapees from their various programs. Responses to absconders have included greater line officer responsibility; new information sources to locate absconders; expanded agency fugitive units; and tying sanctions for absconding to offender risk (Williams, McShane, and Dolny, 2000).

Locating absconders using case files for tracking purposes is not new. The U.S. Probation Office and U.S. Marshals Service have tracked offenders in this fashion for decades. Whenever offenders are processed during booking, they are fingerprinted, photographed, and interviewed by authorities. They are required to provide all relevant contact information, including names, addresses, and telephone numbers of family members and where they have lived during the most recent 10-year period. This information is cross-checked to determine its validity and reliability. If some of these offenders escape later, this case file information is consulted and greatly assists U.S. marshals in tracking down federal fugitives.

There have been numerous attempts to forecast potential absconders in advance. Using actuarial methods, potential Texas absconders seem to exhibit the following characteristics. They are often older, minorities, have fewer skills, outstanding debts, credit problems or bad credit, prior extensive unemployment, greater drug or alcohol abuse, had more unsavory friends with prior criminal records, and were serving longer sentences. Even absconders from halfway houses shared many of these same traits (White, 2000). More recent evidence about absconders from parole programs has shown that they tend to be less dangerous and pose less societal risk, although they do have extensive prior criminal records, are emotionally unstable, and have more parole supervisions and revocations (Williams, McShane, and Dolny, 2000).

One major issue that has arisen to confront probation and parole agencies is how to punish absconders. Before extensive prison and jail overcrowding, the simple solution and punishment was to reconfine these offenders for prolonged periods. However, with chronic prison and jail overcrowding, this option is rapidly diminishing. Also, more than a few probation and parole departments have oversized caseloads and cannot allocate sufficient resources to locate absconders. The reduced availability of prison sanctions whenever absconders are located underscores the need to highlight and target high-risk offenders as potential absconders and streamlining the procedures for apprehending them and returning them to custody. Those considered to be high-risk are clients who are serving longer prison terms and have previously been in prison or jail. However, no present methods are foolproof for identifying those most likely to abscond (White, 2000; Williams, McShane, and Dolny, 2000).

BOX 10.1

PERSONALITY HIGHLIGHT

Marcy M. Black
Senior Probation and Parole Officer
Close Community Supervision Unit
Self Defense and Arrest Techniques Instructor
Fugitive Recovery Team, Idaho Department of Correction

Statistics:

A.A. (communications, psychology) Highline Community College; Western Washington University; Idaho State Peace Officers Academy; Idaho Department of Correction Academy

Background:

I attended Western Washington University and majored in Communications and minored in Psychology. I originally planned on having a career in public relations or broadcast, but my interests changed. I had friends in the criminal justice program, and I became interested in pursuing a career in law enforcement. In 1996, I was in the process of becoming a Reserve Officer when I was hired by the Coeur d'Alene Police Department. I completed the Idaho State Peace Officers Academy, and was employed as a Patrol Officer for the Coeur d'Alene Police Department. In 1997, an outdoor program for troubled youths was hiring counselors, and I always had a desire to work with adolescents. I worked as a juvenile counselor at ASCENT, a rehabilitative outdoor program for youths located in Naples, Idaho. In 1998,

the Idaho Department of correction was hiring probation and parole officers. I thought this was a prime opportunity to combine my law enforcement experience and utilize my counseling skills. On November 1, 1998, I was hired as a probation and parole officer for the state of Idaho and have been with the department approximately five years.

Work Experiences:

There is rarely a dull moment in community corrections. Duties vary and that is what keeps this career from being monotonous. It is continually changing to meet the needs of the public and the offender. While working for the department, I have been lucky and had the opportunity to supervise a wide range of caseloads. I have worked in a satellite office on a regular caseload, supervised interstate offenders, and I am currently on the Close Com-

BOX 10.1 (*Continued*)

munity Supervision Unit. This unit focuses on the "high risk" offender and is a more intensive supervision level. The offenders are hooked up on electronic monitoring and adhere to a weekly schedule. Technology is changing rapidly, and we are currently using a GPS system to monitor our offenders. This is an excellent device to hold the offender accountable and maintain the safety of the community. The Idaho Department of Correction has implemented the "broken windows" philosophy, and the probation and parole officers are spending the majority of their time out in the community. Probation and parole officers are spending more time out in the field; conducting residence checks, contacting employers, and are working directly with substance abuse providers, job service, vocational rehabilitation, and other community resources.

Working in community corrections can be very satisfying, and at times can be extremely frustrating. There are the individuals who have made poor choices in the past, and probation gives them an opportunity to change their lifestyle. The individuals who are successful on probation and parole are the ones who sincerely want to make a change. Most just need guidance and resources to help them succeed. To be able to assist these individuals and help them achieve their goal is rewarding and fulfilling. I become frustrated with the individuals who use the system as a revolving door. They receive cognitive counseling, substance abuse treatment, and other programs designed to help them succeed and then they are back committing new crimes.

Being a probation and parole officer can be stressful and extremely dangerous. I supervise offenders who have been convicted of manufacturing methamphetamine, murder, rape, aggravated battery, forgery, burglary, and various other crimes. Residence checks on the offenders are high risk because you never know what you will encounter. I have entered residences containing methamphetamine labs, arrested out-of-control offenders because they are on illegal substances, found loaded weapons and contraband, and have had contact with violent fugitives. There was a drive-by shooting at one of the offices, and luckily no one was injured. Officer safety is a big issue. Training, communication, and good judgment are the key elements to getting out of sticky situations.

People who work in community corrections are invested in their careers. The majority of my co-workers are caring, hardworking team players, who are striving to make a difference in the community. I appreciate their knowledge, experience, dedication, enthusiasm and especially their sense of humor. It takes a special person to be successful in this field.

Advice to Students:

Make sure you are entering the corrections field for the right reasons. This is not a glamorous career and the pay is less than desirable. Working with people with different lifestyles and beliefs is a must in this field. Keep in mind that the offenders are people and should be treated fairly, in an unbiased manner, and with respect. I would recommend you obtain experience through an internship program, reserving, ride-along programs, or by volunteering. Hands-on experience can help you determine if this is the career of your choice.

GANG UNITS

In 2002 there were 29,000 known gangs in the United States (Thornberry et al., 2003). About 22,000 of these gangs were in large and small cities compared with suburban or rural counties. There was a total membership of over 800,000 **gang** members. Since gangs are a pervasive phenomenon in U.S. society, they have become a major problem for POs who have found that increasing numbers of their clients are current or former gang members. One response has been the formation of **gang units.** Gang units were created originally to identify gang presence in neighborhoods as well as gang influence. Gang membership was also indicative of likely criminality, since most gangs are involved in illicit activities, particularly drugs and drug trafficking. However, gangs have been increasingly linked with violent crimes including homicides. Gang units were originally formed by police departments to combat gang-related crime in larger cities where gangs were most visible (Katz, Maguire, and Roncek, 2002).

During the last few decades, both juvenile and adult probation and parole departments have established specialized gang units to learn more about their gang-affiliated clientele. One result has been that POs have learned a lot more in recent years about gang activities in neighborhoods where clients are supervised; gang member personal alcohol and drug use; and antisocial peer networks distinguishing between gang and non-gang members. What is even more compelling about the work of probation and parole agency gang units is that they are discovering a closer connection between prison and street gangs and their relation with organized crime on several levels. Examples of the interplay between prison and street gangs are Chicago's Gangster Disciples and Latin Kings. These are gangs who have moved from disorganized collectivities to smooth-running organized crime groups with corporate divisions of labor and contemporary conceptual frameworks for conducting illegal businesses (Finn, 1999).

But not all gang activity occurs in major cities in states with large populations. In Virginia, for instance, there are approximately 320 gangs. According to probation department personnel, many of these gang members are probationers or have previously been on probation. Assault, vandalism, and intimidation are most often linked with gang activities, although about half appear to be involved in drug trafficking and gun distribution. Gangs are not strictly a U.S. phenomena, but rather, they are found in other parts of the world. Often, gangs in other countries are loosely linked with their U.S. counterparts (Gordon, 2000).

Of particular concern to POs is the link between street gangs and prison gangs. Many inmates of prisons and jails are gang members. When they are eventually released on parole, they link up with their gang counterparts in cities where they become involved in their parole programs. PO concerns stem from the fact that when ex-convicts return to the streets and reinvolve themselves in gang activities, ex-convicts have a proclivity toward greater violence which spills over into street gang activities. Thus, the involvement of ex-convicts in youth gangs increases the life of the gangs and their level of violent crime (Wilson, 2000:35). Nearly half of all gangs report such increased violence as the result of ex-convicts returning to their gangs.

POs strive to enhance their knowledge of both street and prison gangs in order to more effectively supervise them. This means learning gang jargon and prison argot or the use of special phrases and hand gestures that are relevant only to gang members. Such argot, jargon, and hand signals are ways of communicating among gang members, even with prison staff or POs present, and without their awareness or knowledge. However, as POs become more aware of this new language, they can interdict at appropriate times and take the necessary steps to control their clients. Thus, an important training component for both POs and correctional officers in institutions is gang interpersonal communications skills to help prepare them to interact with offender populations whose speech is intended to manipulate or misdirect. Sometimes, POs work with tactical police officers, community youth workers, and neighborhood representatives to work toward reducing violent criminal activity. One project was known as the Little Village Gang Violence Reduction Project in Chicago, Illinois. POs were able to learn much about gang phenomena generally and become better at performing their supervisory responsibilities, particularly where gang members were involved (Spergel and Grossman, 1997). One outcome of such experiments has been more effective social intervention by POs of specific gang members as clients, greater crime prevention, and general gang suppression.

RESEARCH UNITS

An essential component of any probation or parole department is a **research unit.** Research units compile extensive information about probationer and parolee characteristics as well as information about inmate populations of jails and prisons. It is important for POs to have an accurate profile of the clients they are supervising or will eventually supervise. Research units are essential to effective probation and parole program planning. Networking with established community services can be achieved more effectively if offender needs can be anticipated.

Research units are also in the business of devising risk–needs instrumentation for use by judges and paroling authorities. Again, it is imperative for these persons and agencies to have indicators at their disposal concerning offender needs and the risks they might pose if granted probation or parole. Research units are also involved in departmental and organizational programming, both within their own agencies and throughout the community. They devise new and improved strategies for offender supervision and management, as well as better ways of administering agency resources. Several jurisdictions have devised research units for the purpose of compiling much valuable information about offenders and their risks and needs (Katz, Webb, and Schaefer, 2000).

Research units are also important in effective court management, which can eventually ease the problems of POs in their supervisory duties. Research units for the courts, probation and parole departments, and police agencies have existed for several decades, and they have proved instrumental at providing essential information for task coordination and crime reduction.

STRESS AND BURNOUT IN PROBATION/PAROLE OFFICER ROLE PERFORMANCE

The selection and recruitment of the right kinds of personnel to perform PO work roles is designed to identify those most able to handle the stresses and strains accompanying the job. The concern about occupational stress has been rising steadily in recent years (Calhoun, 2001). Virtually all occupations and professions have varying degrees of stress associated with them. Probation and parole work is not immune from stress and **burnout.** Whitehead and Lindquist (1992) studied 400 probation and parole officers in various states and found that they tended to offer more negative than positive comments about their work. In fact, these researchers reported that the POs studied had stress levels comparable to police officers as well as significant job burnout, stress levels, and **job dissatisfaction** (Whitehead, 1989). Similar findings have been reported by Finn (1999) and Sims (2001) relating to correctional officer stress levels and the reasons given for stress through self-reports.

Stress

Stress is a nonspecific response to a perceived threat to an individual's well-being or self-esteem (Sims, 2001). It is important that we recognize that these stress responses are not specific, and that each person reacts differently to the same situation triggering stress. Some people react to stress with somatic complaints of aches and pains, while others may exhibit irritability, loss of attention span, or fatigue. Furthermore, what is stressful for one person may not be stressful to another. Therefore, several factors including one's previous experiences with the event, constitutional factors, and personality may function to mediate the stress and one's reaction to the event. In-service training is regarded by many departments of correction as important, since the training exposes new recruits to different officer-offender relationships that generate stress. Becoming familiar with a variety of officer-offender interactions and recognizing potentially problematic interpersonal situations is one means of effectively combating stress or at least minimizing it. Although it is not known precisely how education relates to stress reduction, more educated POs probably are more aware of several behavioral or interactional options whenever problems arise between themselves and probationers or parolees (Simmons, Cochran, and Blount, 1997).

Some stress is good. A moderate amount of stress enhances the learning and creative processes, while too little stress may induce boredom or apathy. However, we don't know for sure how much stress is too much. We do know that correctional officers have twice the national average divorce rate. Also, they have the highest heart attack rates among all types of state employees, including police officers. These statistics appear to result directly from the stressful aspects of corrections work (Morgan, VanHaveren, and Pearson, 2002). However, a study by Patterson (1992) of 4,500 police, correctional, and probation/parole officers showed that there was a curvilinear relation between perceived stress and time on the job. This might be interpreted as follows: there is considerable stress among many of these officers in their early years on the job, followed by a stress decline. In turn, this stress increases as on-the-job experience increases. Obviously, blanket generalizations about stress and the amount of one's job experience are difficult to formulate (Sims, 2001).

Burnout

Burnout is one result of stress (Gershon et al., 2002). Burnout emerged as a popular term in the mid-1970s to describe work alienation, apathy, depersonalization, depression, and a host of other job-related complaints (Perez and Shtull, 2002). Not everyone agrees about how burnout ought to be defined. Maslach (1982:30–31) has identified at least fifteen different connotations of the term. These are:

1. A syndrome of emotional exhaustion, depersonalization, and reduced personal accomplishment that can occur among individuals who do people work of some kind.

2. A progressive loss of idealism, energy, and purpose experienced by people in the helping professions as a result of the conditions of their work.

3. A state of physical, emotional, and mental exhaustion marked by physical depletion and chronic fatigue, feelings of helplessness and hopelessness, and the development of a negative self-concept and negative attitudes toward work, life, and other people.

4. A syndrome of inappropriate attitudes toward clients and self, often associated with uncomfortable physical and emotional symptoms.

5. A state of exhaustion, irritability, and fatigue that markedly decreases the worker's effectiveness and capability.

6. To deplete oneself. To exhaust one's physical and mental resources. To wear oneself out by excessively striving to reach some unrealistic expectations imposed by oneself or by the values of society.

7. To wear oneself out doing what one has to do. An inability to cope adequately with the stresses of work or personal life.

8. A malaise of the spirit. A loss of will. An inability to mobilize interests and capabilities.

9. To become debilitated, weakened, because of extreme demands on one's physical and/or mental energy.

10. An accumulation of intense negative feelings that is so debilitating that a person withdraws from the situation in which those feelings are generated.

11. A pervasive mood of anxiety giving way to depression and despair.

12. A process in which a professional's attitudes and behavior change in negative ways in response to job strain.

13. An inadequate coping mechanism used consistently by an individual to reduce stress.

14. A condition produced by working too hard for too long in a high-pressure environment.

15. A debilitating psychological condition resulting from work-related frustrations, which results in lower employee productivity and morale.

The common elements of these definitions seem to be emotional, mental, and physical exhaustion that debilitates and weakens one's ability to cope with situations. Definitions 2, 3, and 4 above are particularly crucial for PO work, since as POs must maintain effective relations with their clients on a continuous basis and regularly evaluate their progress (Morgan, VanHaveren, and Pearson, 2002). When stress rises to the level where burnout is generated, offender-clients experience corresponding decreases in the quality of delivery services from probation/parole personnel (Boothby and Clements, 2000). The importance of burnout is that it signifies a reduction in the quality or effectiveness of an officer's job performance. Such debilitating reductions in effectiveness are often accompanied by higher recidivism rates among probationers and parolees, more legal problems and case filings from officer-client interactions, and greater labor turnover among POs (Sims, 2001).

Sources of Stress

Stress among POs and other professionals emanates from several sources. Stress researchers have targeted the following as the chief sources of stress among POs: (1) job dissatisfaction, (2) role conflict, (3) role ambiguity, (4) officer-client interactions, (5) excessive paperwork and performance pressures, (6) low self-esteem and public image, and (7) job risks and liabilities.

Job Dissatisfaction.   Job dissatisfaction is somewhat unwieldy, as it occurs as the result of a variety of factors. Some of these overlap those cited above which generate work-related stress. Low pay, burgeoning caseloads, and unchallenging work figure prominently in an officer's decision to leave PO work for better employment opportunities elsewhere (Patterson, 1992).

Role Conflict.   Role conflict occurs as the result of having to adhere to conflicting expectations. When POs collect supervision fees from their indigent clients, this often creates a type of conflict about their roles as rehabilitators and enforcers. The expectations of the probation officer role are unusual and sometimes conflicting. These expectations may be those of supervisors, and they sometimes are in conflict with a PO's concept of how the job ought to be performed. Sometimes role conflict occurs when the probation supervisor and administrator each expects the PO to complete different tasks at the same time. The logistical complications are apparent, and role conflict ensues (Clear and Latessa, 1993). Mills (1990) summarizes many of the feelings of POs who sense the frustrations of role conflict: "Nobody said it would be like this;" "Why do you think they call them [probationer/clients] cons?;" "If there is a problem, see the probation officer;" "How am I doing so far?;" "I never took this job to get rich;" and "Will this ever end?" Mills (1990:7) says that "for the probation officer, it is important to maintain a freshness and enthusiasm toward the career. In part this calls on the officer to establish and maintain a well-balanced life." Unfortunately, nobody ever explains to the average PO how this can all be accomplished.

Role Ambiguity.   Closely related to role conflict is **role ambiguity.** Role ambiguity occurs whenever POs have inadequate or even conflicting information about their work roles, the scope and responsibilities of the job, and the ethics of certain unwritten practices that are commonplace among many POs. Observers have long been critical of probation and parole agencies and other organizations for failing to make explicit program goals and mission statements (Hawkins, 2001). The fact that often, probation and parole program goals are diffuse or unspecified makes it difficult for POs working with those programs to focus their energies in productive directions consistent with program objectives (Johnson and Grant, 1999).

Officer-Client Interactions.   Work overload, inadequate agency resources, and problems related to client contact often contribute to job stress. In some instances, officers felt that their efforts in relating to offender-clients were frequently misunderstood and they were perceived as antagonistic toward those they were supposed to help. Mismatching of officers and their clients also accounts for a certain proportion of interpersonal problems that arise in various agencies. Workload deployment systems based upon a successful match between officer skills and clients to be supervised can make a significant difference in the day-to-day operation of probation/parole agencies.

Excessive Paperwork and Performance Measures.   The larger a PO's caseload, the more the paperwork associated with the clients supervised. A growing problem is increased caseloads in many jurisdictions without an accompanying increase in the numbers of POs to perform the greater amount of work. Officers working under increased work pressure must produce more work in the same amount of time. The preparation of PSIs takes time. During any given period, the amount of time devoted to report preparation accounts for almost three-fourths of the PO's 40-hour work week. Closely related to excessive paperwork and performance pressures is the fact of bureaucratization. Bureaucratization stresses adherence to abstract rules, a hierarchy of authority, task specialization, explicit spheres of competence, emotional neutrality, and promotion on the basis of merit and expertise (Champion, 2003). Probation departments have been depicted by various investigators as more or less bureaucratic. As a result of these variable bureaucratic features either present or absent in probation/parole agencies, POs acquire different orientations toward their work (Jurich, Casper, and Hull, 2001).

Low Self-Esteem and Public Image.   The low self-esteem and public image of POs is well known, and it invariably influences the quality of work they perform. There is little POs can do in the short range to modify significantly their low public image. However, as recruitment efforts are more successful in attracting better-qualified applicants for PO positions, it is likely that the quality of services delivered will improve. One result of improved delivery of services may be a better public image associated with PO work.

High Risks and Liabilities.   Those working with criminals incur several risks. Some risk may be associated with the type of offender clientele served. Parolees who have been formerly convicted of aggravated assault, murder, rape, or some other type of violent crime may pose a degree of risk to the personal safety of POs. There is also an element of risk incurred from a client's associates who may be violent criminals. These are unknown and incalculable hazards. In addition to these personal risks, however, are legal liabilities incurred by POs who must interact with their offender-clients. In the course of furnishing them with counseling, job assistance, and other services, POs risk giving them poor advice, violating their privacy, maligning them to others, and preventing them from participating in various programs. POs must be aware of their legal responsibilities (Sims, 2001). At the same time, they must be aware of those actions that may lead to lawsuits against them from dissatisfied offender clientele. Many POs say that their training may not be sufficient to equip them with the legal and practical expertise needed to do good jobs (Vohryzek-Bolden, Croisdale, and Barnes, 1999).

Mitigating Factors to Alleviate Stress and Burnout

It is believed by many authorities that probation and parole organizations and agencies are at fault in creating dangerously high stress and burnout levels among POs and other correctional officers. One theory is that organizational factors directly contribute to employee stress (Sims, 2001). When a calling becomes the job, one no longer lives to work but works to live. Thus, POs may lose enthusiasm, excitement, and a sense of mission about the work. While some observers say that it is virtually impossible to prevent burnout among POs, regardless of their coping strategies and mechanisms, it is possible for the organization to implement changes to minimize it. If organizational heads will recognize what causes stress and burnout, they have a better than even chance of dealing with it effectively (Wargent, 2002). One way of alleviating stress and burnout is to incorporate features into PO training programs to make them more streetwise so as to be safer when conducting face-to-face visits with their clients (Jurich, Casper, and Hull, 2001). This might encompass hand-to-hand combat training and other self-defense skills.

Participative Management.   **Participative management** is the philosophy of organizational administration where substantial input is solicited from the work staff and used for decision making purposes where one's work might be affected. Thus, subordinates' opinions become crucial to organizational decision making as lower-level participants are given a greater voice in how the organization is operated or administered. Organizational solutions stress greater employee involvement in the decision-making process relating to offender treatment and supervision (Champion, 2003). Generally, a lack of participation in decision-making is a key source of stress and burnout. Employee commitment to do better work can be enhanced through bringing a PO's goals into harmony with those of the organization. Management by Objectives or MBO has been suggested as one means of accomplishing participatory goal setting between organizational heads and agency personnel, although MBO has lost momentum as a goal-setting and motivating strategy in recent years.

The Kalamazoo, Michigan Probation Enhancement Program developed in 1981 utilized employment skills classes, a job club, peer support groups, basic life skills classes, and general equivalency diploma preparation to assist probationers and parolees. POs involved in this Kalamazoo project derived considerable satisfaction from this activity. The evaluation of the program by Kalamazoo probation office officials focused primarily on the success rates of program participants rather than on the POs who worked closely with them to achieve those success rates. This is one indication of the failure of agency leaders to reward their staffs properly for work they are "expected" to do anyway (Champion, 2003).

Possible Gender and Age Differences in Stress and Burnout Associated with PO Work.   Do female POs have more or less stress and burnout compared with their male PO counterparts? Not according to a review of research on the subject (Sims, 2001). Apparently, the problems of women officers are the problems of male officers, so that neither gender requires special attention. Both males and females who pursue PO careers may have similar personality backgrounds. The premise of personality as a determinant has not been systematically studied thus far. This applies similarly to studies of male and female police officer stress levels (Calhoun, 2001; Sims, 2001).

Age as a factor in burnout also seems to be a contributing factor. We might simplify such thinking by stating that as POs get older, the more burnout they experience. This postulation has little consistent empirical support. In short, some studies show this happens, while other studies show it doesn't happen. For instance, one study has reported that older POs (age 51 or older) tend to experience more emotional exhaustion and low feelings of personal accomplishment. In turn, this sensed lack of accomplishment has led to decreased client contact, which, in turn, has decreased PO work effectiveness (Simmons, Cochran, and Blount, 1997). In the same study, however, younger POs often exhibited greater role conflict and emotional exhaustion, accompanied by greater client contact. Apparently, in this study at least, younger officers are driven toward greater client contact to resolve role conflict situations and reduce emotional exhaustion, while older officers are driven away from clients because of feelings of depersonalization and a lack of accomplishment.

VOLUNTEERS IN PROBATION/PAROLE WORK

Who Are Volunteers?

A **corrections volunteer** is any unpaid person who performs auxiliary, supplemental, augmentative, or any other work or services for any law enforcement, court, or corrections agency (Evans, 2001:142). Corrections volunteers vary greatly in their characteristics and abilities, in their ages, and in their functions. For instance, Girl Scouts, ages 12 to 16, work closely with female inmates and their children at the Maryland Correctional Institution for Women in Jessup, Maryland (Moses, 1993:132). Girl Scouts play with the daughters of female inmates during twice monthly Girl Scout troop meetings. Troop projects are planned as well as future activities, where female inmates and their daughters may become involved and experience more intimate bonding not ordinarily possible under penal conditions (American Probation and Parole Association, 1996).

What Do Corrections Volunteers Do?

Some **volunteers** are retired school teachers who work with jail and prison inmates to assist them in various kinds of literacy programs (Sharp and Muraskin, 2003). The Gray Panthers, an organization of elderly volunteers, provide various services and programs targeting older inmates specifically (Long, Wells, and DeLeon-Granados, 2002; Zhao et al., 2002). Some volunteers, such as septuagenarian Brigitte Cooke in Huntington, Pennsylvania, work with death row inmates or those serving life sentences. Her services include spiritual guidance, support, and compassion (Love, 1993:76–78). Some volunteers are crime victims who confront criminals who have committed crimes suffered by victims. Yet, other volunteers provide religious training and conduct services for inmates and others. Other types of volunteers work as daycare service personnel to care for young children of female parolees and probationers who perform full-time work in connection with their probation or parole programs (Tomkins et al., 2002).

Some Examples of Correctional Volunteer Work.   One volunteer program designed for working with female offenders both in prison and in community-based programs is called The Program for Female Offenders. This program provides for volunteers who visit the Allegheny County, Pennsylvania Jail three times a week and the State Correctional Institution at Muncy on a less frequent but regular basis (Arnold, 1993:120). Incarcerated women are assisted by volunteers who help them adjust to prison life. Certain family and legal problems may be dealt with, using the volunteers as intermediaries. For those women who have been recently released, the agency operates a training center, two residential facilities and a day treatment program. All of these facilities are located in Pittsburgh (Arnold, 1993:120). One facility, the Program Center, is a work release facility that serves 34 female prisoners. Volunteers provide these women with job assistance, GED preparation, and life skills. Parenting programs and day care services are also provided largely through the use of volunteer services. Arnold (1993:120–122) says that volunteers deserve special recognition for the unpaid services. This Pennsylvania program has outlined some valuable types of functions performed by these volunteers. These functions include:

1. Serving as tutors at the skill training center and handling most GED preparation.
2. Providing transportation to parenting sessions at their residential centers.
3. Teaching women hobby skills such as knitting, sewing, and dressmaking.
4. Teaching computer and job search skills at the skill training center.
5. Providing gifts for women and their children every Christmas.

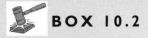

BOX 10.2

Elissa Rumsey
State Representative, U.S. Department of Justice, Office of Juvenile Justice and Delinquency Prevention

Statistics:

B.A. (psychology, public policy), University of California-Berkeley; M.S. (criminal justice), Northeastern University

Background:

Volunteering has always been an important part of my life. My parents strongly emphasized its virtues, and the expectation was clear that I'd begin volunteering early in life. At the age of 14, I began assisting at the county library in Davis, California, where I grew up. At the library, I was tasked with shelving books. My favorite section to shelve was the non-fiction 364.152s, also known as the true-crime section. I read books like *Fatal Vision, The Stranger Beside Me,* and *In Cold Blood* over and over again. Ultimately, the library hired me on a part-time basis to shelve books for pay. That lesson stuck with me (i.e., volunteer your time, and one day you might be paid for it) and would pave the way to future volunteer-to-paying jobs.

When I began college I wanted to continue to volunteer in some capacity. First, I was a crisis-intervention counselor on a suicide prevention hotline. For four hours each week, I would take calls and try to help people through different types of crises. That work showed me the clear intersect between mental health and criminal justice, since many of the callers had either been to jail, were calling from jail, or were soon headed for jail. In fact, I actually once met one of the callers in jail. This is because the second volunteer job I took was an internship at the Berkeley Own Recognizance Project. This work involved interviewing persons at the local police department lockup soon after they had been arrested. The idea was to ensure their right to bail, which the Eighth Amendment says should be afforded every

person, in an attempt to prevent cruel and unusual punishment. The Bail Reform Act of 1968 further emphasized that bail should not only be in the form of money, but additionally that a person's word would also suffice that they would make all scheduled court appearances.

My job was to interview persons in jail shortly after they had been arrested to determine their eligibility for an "own recognizance" or "OR" release. After spending about two hours in the jail doing interviews, I'd go back to the office and call the references the person had provided. The goal was to show that the person had enough ties to the community such that they had incentive to appear in court when the time came. And so I would call their relatives, ministers, neighbors, bosses (although this was rare, since who wants their boss to know they're in jail?; moreover, many of them were unemployed). The idea was to verify what these arrestees had told me about their ties with the community. Later in the day, a different set of interns would present the findings to the judge who would then decide if an OR release should be granted.

One time, I was interviewing an alleged arsonist. He was a fellow student accused of trying to burn down one of the dormitories. Fortunately, he did not succeed. After reading the arrest report (which I always did before commencing an interview), I remembered thinking that this sounded like a guy I was talking to on the crisis hotline a few weeks earlier. The arrest report was also somewhat unique in that it had a letter at-

BOX 10.2 (*Continued*)

tached from the city's fire chief saying that based on the defendant's alleged actions (and some previous arson attempts), he should not be granted bail or placed on OR release. When I went to interview him in his cell (I always sat in a chair just outside of the cell and talked with clients through the food pass-through), almost immediately I recognized his voice. Of course, I did not let on that we had spoken previously on the crisis hotline, and as he told me of his "ties to the community," he was delusional enough that I felt that it was highly unlikely that he would recognize me. Fortunately, he didn't, and I was able to complete the interview. Needless to say, as an accused arsonist, he was not granted OR release.

That internship also turned into a paid position, as I was promoted to Sunday Intern Supervisor. This meant that every Sunday morning, I'd arrive at the jail at 7:00 A.M., act as the lead interviewer, and then back at the office, I would be in charge of the volunteers who had also done interviews that morning. The caseload on Sundays was usually fairly large, since it included persons arrested over the weekend. Thus again, my volunteer efforts paid off, not only in terms of the vast amount of knowledge and experience gained working in the criminal justice system, but in terms of money to help pay my university tuition.

After completing my undergraduate and graduate degrees, I moved to Washington, DC, in the hope of working on criminal and juvenile justice policy. While it took a while to find a "real" job, I was immediately able to hook up with a volunteer organization called Offender Aid and Restoration (OAR). After completing 40 hours of training, I was certified to work in the Arlington County (Virginia) Jail. I was soon matched with another volunteer who wanted to teach Life Skills to inmates. We decided to teach stress management, and over the past 7 years, we have been going to the jail weekly to provide this instruction for inmates.

Initially, I was a little anxious while working in the Virginia jail, but only be-

cause I did not yet know how it operated. Those of you who have been in or worked in enough jails know that all have different rules, policies, procedures, and norms. My mother worked in a jail while I was growing up, and so I had some familiarity with her jail surroundings. I was familiar with the jail I worked in while at college; and I had been lucky enough to go on multiple tours of jails and prisons as a part of my undergraduate and graduate education. And so I had a general sense of how these jails operated. But all of that changes once you begin to work regularly in the same jail. You slowly begin to get to know the deputies, the support staff, the program staff, and the medical personnel. For the most part, they come to appreciate you and support you, but of course, there is always some resistance. You can always tell when a new group of deputies has been hired, as they are usually quite strict about enforcing each and every rule (which is not a bad thing). The more seasoned deputies are more likely to let certain rules slide, which also is not necessarily a bad thing. Overall, it does make for a stressful environment, as one never knows which deputies are going to be on duty, and certain deputies are known for making life difficult for volunteers. At the same time, though, there are deputies who truly appreciate the work volunteers do, as they realize that it might be less work for them in terms of dealing with unruly inmates.

And of course, I have faced some unruly inmates in jail. Because I am a volunteer though, most inmates are incredibly respectful of the work I am trying to do. Plus, when they attend my class, it is their choice to do so. It is not required. And so usually they have a positive incentive to attend, in that they are there because they want to learn how to relieve stress. The stories they tell about their stressors always drives home to me that regardless of whatever people say about "three squares and a roof over their head," incarceration can be a terrible situation. To have all of your basic freedoms and liberties taken away is something not many

(*continued*)

BOX 10.2 (Continued)

people can relate to. Now you may be thinking, "But all these people committed a crime and need to do the time." But you have to remember that this is a *jail,* and the majority of people in the jail I work at are pre-trial detainees and/or are awaiting sentencing (which could be probation). Technically, if they are pre-trial detainees, they are not guilty of anything, except not having enough money to post bail, not having the benefit of an OR program, or not having a good enough attorney to get them out pre-trial.

Even though I know that many of them are pre-trial detainees or awaiting sentence (because they are almost always stressing about court dates), it is rare in class that we actually talk about what a person did to end up in jail. I certainly don't ask. Sometimes, tough, an inmate will bring it up in relation to their individual stress. Obviously their case is what they are most stressed about. Hearing their stories always reaffirms why I feel that it is important to work in the jail. The pre-trial inmates are most striking, because remember, so far they have not been convicted of a crime. One man, a recent immigrant from Africa, had been in jail for nine months for driving on a suspended license. *Nine months!* Pre-trial! Many of them tell us that they are there for low-level drug offenses, and addiction is a common and recurring theme during our class discussions. Many also have serious health issues, such as diabetes and hypertension. One night class was particularly striking in that all of the inmates were terribly stressed out and all about the same thing: One of their fellow inmates, a man of 35, had died that morning. Everyone was having breakfast and during the meal, this inmate stood up, said he wasn't feeling very well, keeled over and began having seizures. The inmates implored the deputies to act, but they were told that there is a rule that says only the medical staff can do CPR. And so they all had to sit back and watch the man die.

Another time, a man in my class kept talking out of turn, didn't seem to be following the discussion very well, and kept wanting to tell his story. He was a city bus driver who decided that he didn't want to keep working one day because his head hurt. And so he told everyone to get off of the bus and he drove to a deserted spot and parked the bus there. He was arrested later and brought to jail. I'll never forget him because he came up to me after class to show me his head. He had a long scar where he had had surgery. It clearly messed with his mind. And instead of receiving mental health assistance, he went to jail.

After serving 5 years as a volunteer inside the jail, work that I continue to do, I was asked to serve on the board of directors for OAR. This was an honor because it allowed me to further volunteer my time in an effort to shape the direction of the agency that does far more than just place volunteers in jails. OAR also provides case management, community service opportunities and other reentry services to inmates both before and after their release. As a board member, I have learned how nonprofit agency budgets are planned and maintained while also helping to shape the direction and future of the agency.

Ultimately, the most important reason I do volunteer work in the jail is *race.* Because the most consistent and obvious thing I see every time I enter the jail (or any jail for that matter) is race. The vast majority of inmates are African American and Hispanic. This says to me that racism is alive and well in America. For we all know that white people commit crimes too, but they just don't go to jail for them. Income inequality certainly plays an important role, because people in jail are for the most part not wealthy, middle class, or even close to it. When asked by the inmates why I am there and what interest do I have in working them, this is what I tell them: That in fact we have something in common. If you look at how society views women, and blond women in particular, it is not terribly far from how African Americans are viewed. That is, if the media were to be believed, the only value of blonde women is physical. We do not have brains and we are best running around the beach a la *Baywatch.* The same thing is true about how many African Americans are portrayed. They are

BOX 10.2 (*Continued*)

stereotyped often as having no brains, but worse, they are portrayed as mostly criminals. The point is, though, that we are both misrepresented by society in negative ways such that achieving social and economic status equal to that of white men is that much more difficult. Not that it is impossible, but that there are simply more barriers. Certainly more so for African Americans, as they are more likely to be incarcerated more than blonde women. And so one reason I teach the class is to show them that not all blonde women are stupid, and that as an individual, I am willing to volunteer my free time to try and make things better for persons who are incarcerated. Moreover, in talking about positive role models like Nelson Mandela, Oprah Winfrey, as well as local people who have made positive contributions to society through their own intelligence, fortitude, and strength, the class affirms that there are people in society who have faced similar stress and still managed to emerge as positive, contributing members of society.

Arnold says that often, these tasks lead to friendships between volunteers and inmate/clients. Arnold also advises that it is important to place volunteers in positions where they will feel safe and comfortable. She suggests the following guidelines:

1. Don't take offenders home or lend them money.
2. Don't share your troubles with offenders.
3. Learn to listen effectively.
4. Don't try to solve offenders' problems.
5. Don't make judgments.
6. Report irregular behavior to the agency staff. This is not being disloyal.
7. Don't provide drugs or alcohol to offenders.
8. Don't always expect to be appreciated.
9. Do have empathy and patience.
10. Do care. (Arnold, 1993:122).

Criticisms of Volunteers in Correctional Work

There Is Pervasive Volunteer Naivete.   Not everyone is enthusiastic about volunteer involvement in law enforcement, the courts, or corrections. There arise unusual situations from time to time where inmates and other types of offenders might harm volunteers or be harmed by the very volunteers trying to help them. One problem that is cited frequently by critics of volunteerism is volunteer naivete (Salcido, Ornelas, and Garcia, 2002).

Volunteers Do Not Make Long-Term Commitments with Clients.   Because of the voluntary, unpaid nature of volunteer work, many volunteers may be in correctional settings for brief periods, tire of their activities, and leave. While POs generally held positive attitudes about the influence of volunteers in assisting them in their regular duties, the most frequent criticism was that a significant proportion of volunteers do not stay with their clients for adequate time periods. Often, clients are shuffled back and forth between volunteers and regular POs. As a result, clients feel manipulated or "let down" by the particular volunteer absence (Zhao et al., 2002).

Volunteers Often Do Not Want to Work Independently.   Some volunteers do not wish to work independently from POs in assisting their clients. This situation has necessitated a considerable and unnecessary expenditure of valuable time on the part of the supervising PO, who was often overworked with heavy caseloads and numerous other required duties.

Volunteers Often Lack Expertise and Experience.   Often a chief concern of POs is that volunteers lacked general knowledge about the specific rules and policies of their probation/parole offices (Sharp and Muraskin, 2003). Thus, if some offenders violate program rules, volunteers may experience difficulty reporting them for these infractions. Volunteers seem to be more easily manipulated compared with regular POs.

Law Enforcement Agencies and the Courts Are Reluctant to Share Information About Offenders with Volunteers Serving PO Functions.   It is probably natural for law enforcement organizations and the courts to take a dim view of disclosing confidential information about offender-clients to volunteers who are operating in unofficial capacities. Thus, the confidentiality issue continues to be pervasive among probation departments (Long, Wells, and DeLeon-Granados, 2002).

Volunteers Threaten Job Security.   It seems to follow that if a department or agency utilizes the services of volunteers to supplement the work performed by full-time staff, then some of those full-time staff may not be needed in future months or years. Some employees of corrections agencies have expressed this particular fear, regardless of its foundation in truth.

Since Volunteers Are Unpaid, They Don't Respond to Orders Like Regular Staff.   Unpaid personnel who work with corrections agencies on a voluntary basis are under no special obligation to adhere to specific working hours or schedules. Most volunteers wish to comply with the requirements of the tasks they are assigned. But volunteers may have a totally different type of commitment to work compared with paid staff members. If volunteers don't like certain tasks they are assigned, they don't have to reappear at work in the future.

Some Volunteers May be Aiders and Abetters.   Bayse (1993:16) describes a situation that occurred at a prison when a local pastor regularly brought church members into the prison for worship services together with inmates. He allowed a woman from a nearby church to join the group one Sunday at the last moment. The pastor did not know that the woman was wearing two dresses and a wig. When she excused herself to go to the bathroom, an inmate discretely followed her and outfitted himself in her extra dress and wig. Dressed as a woman, he returned with her to the church group and left with them when they exited the prison. He was apprehended a few days later. But this story indicates some of the potential harm volunteers can cause to corrections officials if they develop close relationships with prisoners or if their backgrounds are not carefully screened.

Because of the nonprofessional nature of volunteer work generally, questions often arise concerning the quality of work volunteers can perform (Tomkins et al., 2002). If volunteers are assigned case-sensitive work, such as working with probationers and/or parolees, they must necessarily become exposed to confidential materials or information about their clients. In fact, some volunteers in certain probation/parole agencies often act on instructions from these agencies to obtain such information from law enforcement sources or the courts. Should these volunteers be granted access to this information? Ogburn (1993:66) has provided the following admonitions to persons or organizations interested in establishing volunteer programs:

1. Evaluate the need.
2. Develop goals and job descriptions.
3. Involve staff.
4. Actively recruit volunteers.
5. Educate volunteers about inmates.
6. Explain security needs to volunteers.
7. Give volunteers the big picture.
8. Evaluate program effectiveness.
9. Recognize your volunteers' contributions.

Further, Bayse (1993:43–47) admonishes volunteers to be: (1) ethical; (2) good listeners; (3) empathetic, but not gullible; (4) respectful; (5) genuine; (6) patient; (7) trustworthy; (8) confrontive; (8) objective—don't take sides; (9) non-hostile; and (10) non-expectant of thanks.

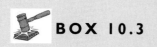 **BOX 10.3**

ON THE ETHICS OF USING VOLUNTEERS

D.J. Bayse (1993:48–50) also provides prospective volunteers with some suggestions and rules:

1. Use appropriate language. Don't pick up inmate slang or vulgarity. Using language that isn't a part of your style can label you a phony.
2. Do not volunteer if you are a relative or visitor of an inmate in that institution.
3. Do not engage in political activities during the time voluntary services are being performed.
4. Do not bring contraband into prison. If you are not sure what is contraband, ask the staff. People who bring in contraband are subject to permanent expulsion and/or arrest.

5. Do not bring anything into or out of a facility for an inmate at any time, no matter how innocent or trivial it may seem, unless with the written permission of the superintendent. Volunteers should adopt a policy of saying no to any request by an inmate to bring in cigarettes, money, magazines or letters. If in doubt, ask a staff member.
6. Keep everything in the open. Do not say or do anything with an inmate you would be embarrassed to share with your peers or supervisors.
7. Do not give up if you failed at your first try. Try again.
8. Don't overidentify. Be a friend, but let inmates carry their own problems. Be

(continued)

BOX 10.3 (Continued)

supportive without becoming like the inmates in viewpoint or attitude.

9. Do not take anything, including letters, in or out of a correctional facility without permission. Respect the confidentiality of records and other privileged information.

10. Do not bring unauthorized visitors or guests with you to the institution. They will be refused admission.

11. Do not give out your address or telephone number. If asked, you might say, "I'm sorry, but I was told that it was against the rules to do that."

12. Do not correspond with inmates in the facility in which you volunteer or accept collect telephone calls from them at your place of residence.

13. Be aware that the use of, or being under the influence of, alcohol or drugs while on institution grounds is prohibited.

14. Don't impose your values and beliefs on inmates. Do not let others impose a lower set of values on you.

15. Don't discuss the criminal justice system, the courts, inconsistency in sentencing or related topics. Although everyone is entitled to his or her own opinion, what volunteers say can have serious repercussions in the dorms or with staff.

16. Ask for help. If you are uncertain about what to do or say, be honest. It is always best to tell the inmate that you will have to seek assistance from your supervisor. Inmates don't expect you to have all the answers.

17. Know your personal and professional goals. Be firm, fair and consistent.

18. If you have done something inappropriate, tell your coordinator regardless of what happened. It is far better to be reprimanded than to become a criminal.

Source: Adapted from D.J. Bayse (1993). *Helping Hands: A Handbook for Volunteers in Prisons and Jails,* pp. 48–50. Laurel, MD: American Correctional Association.

PARAPROFESSIONALS IN PROBATION/PAROLE WORK

Paraprofessionals in virtually every field are salaried assistants who work with professionals. A corrections paraprofessional is a someone who possesses some formal training in a given correctional area, is salaried, works specified hours, has formal duties and responsibilities, is accountable to higher-level supervisors for work quality, and has limited immunity under the theory of agency. Agency is the special relation between an employer and an employee whereby the employee acts as an agent of the employer, able to make decisions and take actions on the employer's behalf (Black, 1990:62).

The Roles of Paraprofessionals

The quality of paraprofessional work reflects the amount of training these personnel receive (Loza and Loza, 2002). For instance, in various prisons, paraprofessionals are used to assist mental health professionals and psychiatrists. Some correctional staff may have demonstrable abilities as mental health caregivers. Other volunteers are especially good working with children (Connelly et al., 2000). In some jurisdictions, corrections personnel are given specialized mental health training and experience with mental health counseling. While the primary professional goals of clinical and correctional staff may conflict from time to time, it is apparent that the two professions share common functions. Actually, properly trained correctional staff as mental health paraprofessionals can supply quality mental health care compared with the work quality of many professionals who work with inmates (Lea, Auburn, and Kibblewhite, 1999).

Paraprofessionals working with family therapists in this fashion learn about family and juvenile laws and how youths should be counseled and treated (Dembo et al., 1999). Paraprofessionals may be of significant assistance when counseling family members with drug or alcohol abuse problems (Shearer, 2000). Paraprofessionals have also been used in mediation projects, such as alternative dispute resolution. As we have seen, alternative dispute resolution is a civil alternative to a criminal prosecution. Impartial arbiters reconcile differences between offenders and their victims and attempt to mediate these conflicts in an equitable manner.

Legal Liabilities of Volunteers and Paraprofessionals

The Case of Hyland v. Wonder (1992).   One of the few higher-profile legal cases involving volunteers was the case of *Hyland v. Wonder* (1992). This case involved a volunteer who had worked at a juvenile probation department for several years. After serving as a volunteer and working with juveniles during this period, the volunteer became critical of how the probation office was being managed. He wrote a letter to those overseeing the probation department where he was volunteering, outlining various complaints and asserting how certain improvements would benefit the office. His services as a volunteer were subsequently terminated. He sued, claiming that his criticisms of the probation department were protected by the free speech provision of the First Amendment. Furthermore, he contended that he had a protected liberty interest in his continued status as a volunteer, and that this liberty interest was protected by the "due process" clause of the Fourteenth Amendment. The federal Ninth Circuit Court of Appeals heard his appeal after his complaint was dismissed by a U.S. District Court earlier. The Appellate Court determined that the agency could not deprive the defendant of a valuable government benefit as punishment for speaking out on a matter of public concern. The nature of his public concern was government inefficiency, incompetence, and waste. But the Court declared that he was not vested with a property/liberty interest in his volunteer position, however. Thus, he was not in the position of being able to state or create a claim of entitlement for the purposes of the due process clause of the Fourteenth Amendment.

In the Hyland case, a volunteer had spent so much time in his volunteer work with the probation department that he came to regard his position and opinions as equivalent with regular full-time employees, or so it would appear. His lawsuit is evidence of his enthusiasm for the work and the seriousness he attached to it. However, the Court was unsympathetic to the extent that his volunteer time accrued did not vest him with any real standing regarding office policies. This is a good example of how some volunteers can lose their perspective of who they are and why they are there. It is also a good example of one pitfall of volunteer work.

As employees of various helping agencies associated with law enforcement, the courts, and corrections, paraprofessionals enjoy immunity from prosecution similar to that of regular law enforcement officers, corrections officers, and POs. This immunity is not absolute, but rather, it is limited to acts within the scope of one's duties and responsibilities. Thus, paraprofessionals act on behalf of the agencies employing them. Under certain conditions, organizations that employee staff who injure or cause harm to others may be liable under the theory of **respondeat superior.** This doctrine is based on the principle of master and servant. If the servant does something to harm others while performing work for the master, then the master might be liable. An example might be if a Los Angeles County Probation Officer shot and wounded a probationer during a confrontation, the Los Angeles County Probation Department might be liable under certain conditions. However, public agencies, such as the Los Angeles County Probation Department, enjoy some qualified immunity from lawsuits, many of which are often frivolous.

The liability coverage of paraprofessionals is very similar to that of volunteers. Organizations using both volunteers and paraprofessionals are subject to lawsuits in the event an action by a paraprofessional or volunteer results in damages to inmates or offender-clients. This is especially true if paraprofessionals are used in counseling and other programs involving sex offenders, where their potentially insufficient training may generate various liability issues (Lee, Auburn, and Kibblewhite, 1999). These damages may be monetary, physical, or intangible, such as psychological harm. Title 42, Section 1983 of the **U.S. Code Annotated** (U.S. Code Annotated, 2004) outlines various types of civil rights violations that might be used as bases for lawsuits. Among the bases for different lawsuits by offender-clients are allegations of **negligence.** Negligence may be:

1. Negligent hiring (e.g., organization failed to "weed out" unqualified employees who inflicted harm subsequently on an inmate or probationer/ parolee).

2. Negligent assignment (e.g., employee without firearms training is assigned to guard prisoners with a firearm; firearm discharges, wounding or killing an inmate).

3. Negligent retention (e.g., an employee with a known history of poor work and inefficiency is retained; subsequently, work of poor quality performed by that employee causes harm to an inmate or offender-client).

4. Negligent entrustment (e.g., employee may be given confidential records and may inadvertently furnish information to others that may be harmful to inmates or offender-clients).

5. Negligent direction (e.g., directions may be given to employees that are not consistent with their job description or work assignment; this may result in harm to inmates or offender-clients.

6. Negligent supervision (e.g., employee may supervise prisoners such that inmate problems are overlooked, causing serious harm and further injury or death to inmate or offender-client) (Barrineau, 1994:55–58).

One way of minimizing lawsuits against paraprofessionals and other employees of correctional agencies is to train them so that they can perform their jobs appropriately. Barrineau (1994:84) lists several criteria that are important to establish as a part of a training program for paraprofessionals and others in the event subsequent lawsuits are filed:

1. The training was necessary as validated by a task analysis.

2. The persons conducting the training were, in fact, qualified to conduct such training.

3. The training did, in fact, take place and was properly conducted and documented.

4. The training was "state-of-the-art" and up-to-date.

5. Adequate measures of mastery of the subject matter can be documented.

6. Those who did not satisfactorily "learn" in the training session have received additional training and now have mastery of the subject matter.

7. Close supervision exists to monitor and continually evaluate the trainee's progress.

Barrineau notes that these criteria alone are insufficient to insulate fully one's organization against lawsuits from offender-clients. Nevertheless, they provide some suitable criteria that can be cited in the event an organization or its employees are ever sued. The rule recommended by Barrineau is to document that such training is provided and has occurred (*Whitley v. Warden,* 1971). The theory is that if an event is not documented, it did not happen, as in training (Shearer, 2000).

SUMMARY

POs are supervising an increasingly dangerous clientele. Annually, the numbers of probationers and parolees is escalating. Many of these new entries in to probation and parole programs are gang members with prior histories of violence. Therefore, it is imperative for POs to have some detailed information about the clientele they will be supervising. One method of determining the risk posed by such clients is to develop and use risk assessment instruments. Probationers as well as parolees are administered risk assessment instruments, either by probation departments or by parole boards. The intent is to determine which certain offenders are most likely to reoffend and pose safety risks to the public and their supervising POs. Offenders considered more dangerous than others may be confined for longer periods under selective incapacitation, or they may be more intensively supervised by their probation or parole programs.

Assessing offender risk has been done for many decades. Classification is an attempt to place offenders in those programs that will enable them to maximize the program benefits. Some offenders have particular weaknesses or needs, such as low levels of education and a lack of work skills. Such offenders will need more assistance than others when networking with community agencies. Thus, one function of classification is to identify not only the level of risk posed by offenders, but also to indicate the types of needs which must be addressed. PO supervisory responsibilities can be enhanced to the extent that they can anticipate offender needs and match them with appropriate community agencies for counseling or treatment.

Risk assessments are classified according to whether they are actuarial, anamnestic, or clinical. Actuarial devices, the most popular, identify the characteristics of program failures. Thus the focus is upon which characteristics are associated with probationers and parolees who do not succeed in their programs. Thus, probation-eligible or parole-eligible offenders may either be granted or denied probation or parole on the basis of the extent to which they match the characteristics of program failures. Actuarial prediction is popular largely because anyone can administer a paper-pencil questionnaire delving into superficial details of one's background and prior criminal record. Anamnestic prediction is using one's past experiences and comparing them with one's anticipated future experiences.

Parole boards are especially adept at ascertaining whether one's parole plan is sufficiently unique to show them that the conditions under which a parolee will be living will be substantially different from the conditions that originally led to trouble with the law. Thus, anamnestic prediction compares past circumstances with future circumstances and predictions are made about how these changed circumstances will modify the future behaviors of prospective parolees. Clinical prediction is the least used of the three types of prediction. The main reason is that it is too costly to administer on a large-scale basis. Clinicians, psychologists, and psychiatrists must become involved with probationers or parolees, and this involvement is time-consuming and expensive. Few jurisdictions have the resources to apply clinical prediction. Ultimately, no single prediction method is foolproof, and virtually every method is flawed where future behaviors are predicted. Thus, one method is about as good as the others for predicting one's future risk or dangerousness, despite how much one prediction form is marketed or promoted over the others as the best method.

The roles of POs are gradually changing. One reason for such change is technological advancements relating to client supervision. Global satellite tracking systems are currently being used in growing numbers of jurisdictions to determine offender whereabouts. Further, like electronic monitoring, while such tracking systems cannot control behavior, they can offer probation agencies and POs an early warning of whether their clients are entering restricted areas where former victims of their crimes reside. Thus, there is a safety element introduced through such tracking systems, although there is presently some controversy among POs about the usefulness and applications of such technology.

In every probation and parole department, there are apprehension units, or special departments whose personnel have the responsibility of tracking down program absconders. Every year, there is a proportion of absconders who leave their jurisdictions without permission and attempt to elude capture. In 2002 about 5 percent of all clients under different forms of supervision in the community were absconders. These included some inmates who were granted temporarily releases, such as work release, study release, or furloughs. Even some halfway house residents have absconded from their parole programs. Several factors were identified with absconders. Most probation and parole departments in the larger cities have gang units, or special task forces who study gang formation and operations. More POs are interacting with gang members who not only are affiliated with street gangs but associated with other gang members while incarcerated in prisons and jails. Finally, most larger probation and parole departments have research units who compile valuable statistical information about those supervised and their characteristics.

PO work is stressful. Stress is a nonspecific response to a perceived threat to an individual's well-being or self-esteem. Stress may lead to burnout, which directly interferes with a PO's work performance. Some of the sources of stress include job dissatisfaction, role conflict, role ambiguity, excessive paperwork obligations, high caseloads, and high risks and liabilities which accompany supervising dangerous offenders. Assisting POs in their supervisory work are volunteers and paraprofessionals. Volunteers are unpaid, yet they perform valuable services such as teaching parolees and probationers how to read and fill out job applications. They perform other tasks as well, depending upon the particular jurisdiction and PO needs. Paraprofessionals have had some training related to the work they perform, although they do not have the requisite skills to be full-fledged POs. Their work is more advanced compared with volunteers, and they are paid for what services they render. Both volunteers and paraprofessionals are at risk regarding their legal liabilities. No one working with probationers or parolees is immune from lawsuits that might be filed. Usually, the least-experienced workers are most vulnerable to lawsuits from clients, since they may offer adverse advice unintentionally. The legal liabilities of volunteers and paraprofessionals were described and discussed.

QUESTIONS FOR REVIEW

1. What is risk assessment? What are risk assessment instruments?

2. What is meant by classification? What are some of its functions?

3. What are three kinds of risk prediction? Which one is best? What are the criteria for deciding whether a particular risk assessment instrument works?

4. What is selective incapacitation? Is it constitutional?

5. How is technology changing the PO role? How is global satellite tracking changing the offender monitoring and the nature of PO supervision?

6. What is stress? How does it differ from burnout? How can stress be mitigated? What are some job consequences of burnout?

7. What are apprehension units? What are gang units? Do many probation and parole departments have such units? What are their functions?

8. Who are correctional volunteers? What are some of the functions performed by volunteers for POs? What are some of the problems with using volunteers in relation to offender/clients? What legal liabilities are associated with volunteer work in probation or parole?

9. What is a corrections paraprofessional? What do paraprofessionals do? What are some general ethical considerations concerning the use of volunteers and paraprofessionals in the supervision and education of offender/clients on probation or parole?

10. What is negligence? What are several different types of negligence?

SUGGESTED READINGS

Alarid, Leanne Fiftal and Paul F. Cromwell (2002). *Correctional Perspectives: Views from Academics, Practitioners, and Prisoners.* Los Angeles: Roxbury.

Farrall, Stephen et al. (2002). "Long-Term Absences from Probation: Officers' and Probationers' Accounts." *Howard Journal of Criminal Justice* 41:263–278.

Silver, Eric and Lisa L. Miller (2002). "A Cautionary Note on the Use of Actuarial Risk Assessment Tools for Social Control." *Crime and Delinquency* 48:138–161.

Steiner, Benjamin D. (2002). "Keeping the Public in the Dark: The Unavailability of Public Information Concerning the Parole of Murderers." *Homicide Studies* 6:167–178.

INTERNET CONNECTIONS

Fugitive Apprehension Unit
*http://www.doc.missouri.gov/Horizon/
fugitive05_k03.htm*

Gang unit resources
*http://www.officer.com/special_ops/gang
.htm*

Paraprofessionals
*http://www.ptcwct.ptc.edu:8800/public/
CRJ244OSM/*

Parole officer stress
*http://www.enlightenedsentencing.org/
what-probation-officers-say.htm*

Probation in the New Century
*http://www.dcor.state.ga.us/pdf/proFY01
.pdf*

Support staff probation
*http://www.bvsd.k12.co.us/sb/policies/
GDM.htm*

Violent Fugitive Apprehension Section
*http://www.state.ma.us/msp/unitpage/
violent.htm*

Volunteers and paraprofessionals in
probation and parole
*http://www.copbiz.com/Products/Books/
corrections.htm*

Volunteers In Prevention, Probation, and
Prisons, Inc.
http://www.comnet.org/vip/

Volunteers of America
http://www.voa.org/

Worcester County Gang Unit
*http://www.worcester.da.com/daunits/
gangst.html*

CHAPTER 11 | *Theories of Offender Treatment*

Chapter Outline

> ## Chapter Objectives
>
> *As the result of reading this chapter, the following objectives will be realized:*
>
> 1. Determining what is meant by theories of criminal behavior and how theories are used to explain and predict such behavior.
> 2. Describing biological theories of criminal conduct, including abnormal physical structure, heredity, and biochemical disturbances.
> 3. Describing psychological theories, including psychoanalytic theory, cognitive development theory, and social learning theory.
> 4. Understanding sociological and/or sociocultural theories, including differential association, anomie theory, the subculture theory of delinquency, and social control theory.
> 5. Understanding conflict/Marxist theory.
> 6. Understanding reality therapy and social casework.
> 7. Understanding the differences between various theories and how they relate to and drive different offender programs.
> 8. Determining which theories are best for explaining offender behaviors and program development.

• *Jeff A. was sentenced to home confinement and electronic monitoring in Michigan for a burglary conviction. It was his first offense. He had no prior record. One evening he left his home, went to a convenience store, and encountered another man with a boom box. The other man was enjoying his music, carrying the boom box on his shoulder. Jeff A. approached the man and demanded his boom box. The man refused and attempted to leave the convenience store. Jeff A. took out a pistol and shot the man through the boom box into his head, killing him instantly. Jeff A. fled, but police had him on video and he was arrested for murder a few hours later. No one could explain why Jeff A., someone with no criminal record other than a property crime conviction and no history of violence, would commit murder.*

• *Chester V., an 11-year-old California juvenile, was a gang wanna-be. He wasn't doing well in school. He had a poor home life. He wanted to join a particular neighborhood gang, but so far, no one in the gang paid him any attention. One afternoon, Chester V. stole a .357 magnum revolver from a gun store and stalked two rival gang members. He caught up with them in a city park and shot both of them to death while they drank water from a fountain near a baseball field. Later he told certain gang members what he had done, and he asked them if that made him tough enough for gang membership. The result was the arrest of Chester V. after the gang members reported him to the police.*

INTRODUCTION

For several centuries, scientists have attempted to explain crime, what causes it to occur, and how it most effectively can be treated. This chapter describes several theories or explanations for committing crimes. Theories are explanatory schemes that attempt to link events with presumed causes of those events. Subsequent research attempts to show the predictive utility of theories and the events they are designed to explain.

There are important contrasts between how the criminal justice system handles a case like Jeff A. when determining his guilt or innocence and how criminologists might explain or account for the same behavior. The criminal justice system processed Jeff A. for his crime. The criminologist would attempt to account for Jeff A.'s actions by asking questions about Jeff A.'s sanity or mental capacity or condition. What was Jeff A.'s mental state when the crime was committed? While not all criminologists agree on which explanations are best under these circumstances, criminology does focus upon the forms of criminal behavior, the causes of crime, the definition of criminality, and societal reaction to crime. This chapter looks at several explanations for criminal behavior. Several of these explanations have influenced the criminal justice system in different ways.

The matter of Chester V. is somewhat different, primarily because Chester V. is a juvenile, not an adult. Criminologists might also conjecture about why Chester V. committed his crime. Chester V. will be processed by the juvenile justice system, and most certainly his defense counsel will focus upon his home, school circumstances, and peer group influences in an effort to mitigate the seriousness of what he did. There are many explanations for different forms of juvenile delinquency just as there are many alternative explanations for criminal conduct, regardless of how heinous or nonserious that conduct may be.

Because probationers and parolees have been convicted of crimes, they have often been studied by researchers who delve into their motives and intent. This inquiry has led to the formulation of various treatments designed to rehabilitate offenders or cause them to change their criminal ways. These treatments are also known as interventions. Interventions are experiences interjected into the lives of persons at different ages in order to cause changes in their future circumstances. For instance, in elementary schools, some students have been identified as being at risk of becoming delinquent. They may be socially isolated or exhibit psychological problems. They may be indifferent to authority or simply refuse to obey a teacher's instructions. Psychologists and others have devised terms to account for some of this behavior. Attention deficit disorder or ADD is used to explain why some students have difficulty staying "on task" in classroom situations. Some students are hyperactive, and they have medications prescribed for them to control their hyperactivity.

In short, interventions with at-risk youths or with adult probationers and parolees are intended to correct their current behaviors and cause them to become law-abiding. If we look hard enough at any particular intervention, we will usually find some criminological theory lurking in the background. There are those, for example, who believe that youthful offenders should not be exposed to the trappings of juvenile courts, which are increasingly like criminal courts in their appearance. Thus, it has been advocated that for many of these youths, they should be sheltered from these formal proceedings and diverted from the juvenile justice system if possible. In the interest of protecting or insulating certain youths from criminal court-like proceedings, therefore, it is believed that they will not define themselves as criminals or delinquents. And as a result, they may be saved from a life of crime by being treated in some way rather than punished through incarceration or probation. Labeling theory is the explanatory scheme behind this type of diversionary action. Youths can avoid the criminal taint or label of being criminal or delinquent. Thus, if they don't define themselves that way, they will have a better chance of becoming rehabilitated.

Interventions in preschool or in the early school years that target at-risk youths are designed to provide them with opportunities they might not otherwise have because of their socioeconomic circumstances. Being at risk doesn't always mean being socioeconomically deprived, however. There are risk factors such as family violence or instability, drug use, alcohol consumption, social isolation, bullying, and other circumstances that cause some youths to be identified by authorities as being at risk (Klein, Bartholomew, and Hibbert, 2002). What should be done to rescue these youths from the circumstances that are believed to contribute to their future potential criminal conduct? Various types of counseling and therapeutic interventions are attempted which target some of these at-risk youths. The idea is to help them understand themselves and acquire better self-concepts and self-esteem. Social isolates are drawn out and into school groups and activities. They are provided with social opportunities and learning experiences that they otherwise might not have. Behind these types of interventions are theories known as differential or limited opportunity.

For other youthful offenders in their teens, boot camps are used to instill discipline within them. We have examined boot camps earlier, and they are military-like interventions where self-esteem, self-respect, acceptance of responsibility, and respect for authority are heightened. Many juveniles are attracted to gangs and engage in delinquent or criminal conduct because they lack the resistance to avoid delinquent groups or criminal organizations. Boot camps are designed, in part, to assist participants in acting independently without having to rely on delinquent gangs for esteem and recognition. A theory of delinquent subcultures underlies many boot camp programs that are operating in the United States today.

This chapter describes different theories of criminal and delinquent behavior. Explored are biological theories, psychological theories, and sociological theories that have been used to explain deviant and criminal conduct. These theories are important to understand, since they are linked closely with the interventions used by POs in relation with their clients. Further, these theories are the basis for many of the experiences and programs to which probationer/parolee/clients are exposed. The chapter concludes by evaluating these theories in terms of their predictive utility. Which theory is best? No single theory is universally accepted by all criminologists. No single theory dominates PO policy and practice. Nevertheless, PO work is often couched in one type of theory or another. Thus, we can more effectively understand why POs orient themselves to clients in particular ways through a knowledge of the theories that drive their behaviors and the interventions they utilize.

THEORIES OF CRIMINAL BEHAVIOR

A **theory** is a set of assumptions that attempts to explain and predict relationships between phenomena. The primary functions of theories are to explain and predict. Regarding probationer recidivism, we are interested in explaining why certain probationers commit new offenses while on probation. We are also interested in predicting the occurrence of these crimes. Criminologists conduct statistical studies to identify circumstances of probationers who cannot remain law-abiding (Lattimer, Dowden, and Muise, 2001). They might suggest that such probationers were unemployed or underemployed, or that they were on drugs or under the influence of alcohol, or had associated with other known criminals prior to committing these new offenses. If adolescents join a delinquent gang and commit burglaries or engage in gang fights, the criminologist might say that these adolescents had unstable home environments, were not doing well in school, or needed peer companionship and esteem. Thus, several theories may be needed to account for one's criminal conduct.

Observers disagree about the objectives of probation and parole. Some see probation and parole as rehabilitative, while others see it as a deterrent to crime. Yet others see the objective of probation and parole as purely punitive. There are those who believe that probation and parole embraces all of these objectives. Understanding the causes of crime and criminal behavior is useful in designing effective treatment strategies that can be useful in the rehabilitative and reintegrative process. The criminal justice system, including the statutes applicable to sanctioning criminal offenders, has evolved over several centuries. The influence of various theories of criminal behavior on probationer and parolee conduct and the development of subsequent interventions used in their treatment are apparent. Many theories of criminal behavior can be grouped into three general categories that stress different causal factors: (1) biological theories; (2) psychological theories; and (3) sociological or sociocultural theories.

Between 1890 and 2000, there has been a major theoretical shift in the thinking of criminologists about why people commit crimes. Early theories of crime emphasized factors inside persons or internal to them. Bad blood, malfunctioning glands, physical deformities, having a criminal personality, having criminal drives or tendencies, possession by evil spirits, heredity, and mental illness are some of the many internal concepts advanced to explain deviant behavior generally and criminal behavior specifically (Walsh et al., 2002).

During the 1940s and 1950s, some criminologists changed their thinking about criminal behavior to those phenomena occurring externally, such as the person's social status or sociocultural position, group pressures and gang conformity, antisocial criminal patterns, associating with criminals, labeling one's self as a criminal, or learning to be a criminal (Piquero and Tibbetts, 2002). While this shift has not been overtly acknowledged, it is apparent that the emergence of violent delinquent gangs and social circumstances of adult offenders have undermined existing internal explanations of criminal behavior. Another indication of this shift is the subtle change in research literature that explains crime and describes criminality. Although interpretations of trends in the criminological research literature are largely impressionistic, explanations of crime today emphasize causal factors that differ from those emphasized in the 1920s and 1930s.

This shift does not mean that professionals have abandoned internal explanations for external ones. Rather, external theories are currently more popular than internal theories. This popularity may be seen in the treatment and rehabilitation of criminal offenders. Manipulating the external environment of criminals, their home life, or associates seems easier to accomplish than modifying their genetic structure, driving out evil spirits, or erasing criminal propensities, whatever they might be. Of course, there are other explanations for this shift. Recent theoretical developments in sociology and psychology have emphasized the importance of social or external factors in predicting criminal behavior. Also, criminologists have learned more about genetic make-up, the role of diet in altering personality characteristics, and the medical control of various psychological disorders. Interestingly, these and similar developments have recently renewed interest in some of the more popular internal explanations for criminal behavior.

For example, sociobiologists believe that body chemistry and genetic makeup are crucial in determining all human behavior, including deviance and criminal conduct. **Sociobiology** is the scientific study of the causal relation between genetic structure and social behavior. Some of the treatment programs currently used for offenders are based, in part, upon this biological explanation for criminal behavior (Paternoster and Bachman, 2001).

One important issue shared by all of these theories, regardless of their intuitive value, or innovativeness, or general interest, is whether they can be used to explain and predict criminal behavior. How can each theory be applied? Can effective rehabilitative programs be developed for probationers and parolees? Can any of these theories be used to control criminal behavior or prevent crime? These practical questions are often used to assess the adequacy of any of the theories described here.

Some of these theories of criminal behavior may seem archaic in view of our current state of scientific knowledge. But their impact may be measured or evaluated according to their influence on correctional policies and other criminal justice issues. Thus, while a theory of criminal behavior may be refuted and found to be false, it nevertheless may have important implications for the policies of various agencies within the criminal justice system. For instance, one theory of criminal behavior shown to be false was that heredity transmitted criminal characteristics genetically from one generation to the next. During the 1930s and 1940s, thousands of state and federal prisoners were sterilized, because it was believed that their sterilization would prevent the birth of new generations of criminal offspring.

But evaluations of these theories are not limited to strictly pragmatic criteria. Sometimes, explanations of criminal behavior are abstract and provide contextual backgrounds for other, more practical, theories. For instance, sociologists say that the social class structure of the United States explains certain kinds of crimes. Crime fluctuates among neighborhoods as well as among social classes. Evidently, there is some connection between the social class structure and crime. It is unlikely that major changes will soon occur in the social class structure of the United States that affect crime or crime rates. But this fact doesn't preclude criminologists from using social class as an explanation for crime and crime trends. And it probably encourages POs to orient themselves in particular ways toward probationers or parolees according to the nature of the neighborhoods where they live as well as their ethnic or racial backgrounds and general socioeconomic information.

Biological Theories

Biological theories of criminal behavior include (1) abnormal physical structure, (2) hereditary criminal behaviors, and (3) biochemical disturbances.

Abnormal Physical Structure.   One biologically based set of theories has attempted to link **abnormal physical structure** with criminal behaviors (Lynam et al., 2000). A pioneer of the school of thought that criminals may be identified by their abnormal or unusual physical characteristics was the Italian physician, Cesare Lombroso (1835–1909). He coined the expression, "born criminals." In fairness to Lombroso, his beliefs about the relation between physique and criminal propensities were developed during the period when Charles Darwin's theory of evolution was popular in science. Darwin argued that humans evolved from lower life forms and that some humans were more advanced in their biological development than others. Less advanced humans had visible physical characteristics closely associated with the physical features of criminals. Thus, Lombroso's explanation of crime made much more sense than it does today.

Lombroso said that (1) criminals are, by birth, a distinct type; (2) this type can be recognized by asymmetrical craniums, long lower jaws, flattened noses, scanty beards, and low sensitivity to pain; (3) these characteristics do not themselves cause crime but assist in our identification of personalities disposed toward criminal behavior; (4) such persons cannot refrain from criminal behavior except under unusual social circumstances; and (5) different physical features are associated with different kinds of crime (Wasserman and Wachbroit, 2001).

Originally, Lombroso argued that 100 percent of the prison population was comprised of born criminals, but in later years, he modified this figure to about 40 percent. His treatise on the subject was published in 1876 and was expanded into three volumes (Lombroso, 1918). His views later were known as "the Italian school" or the "positive school," because direct empirical indicators of criminal tendencies could be identified (i.e., cranium shape, jaw angles, body hair, etc.) compared with other speculation about criminal conduct.

Lombroso's studies of Italian prison inmates led him to observe that many had long, sloping foreheads, pointed ears, narrow or shifty eyes, receding chins, and overly long arms. Subsequent comparisons of other prisoners with the nonincarcerated population-at-large have revealed no significant differences in physical characteristics between criminals and noncriminals, however. One explanation for Lombroso's views about physique and criminal behavior is that often persons with odd appearances are rejected by others. This rejection might lead them to follow deviant or criminal paths. The labeling theory of deviant behavior described later in this chapter examines this phenomenon more fully.

Lombroso's views still enjoy popularity in the media whenever particularly bizarre events occur. For instance, the late Truman Capote wrote a nonfictional work entitled *In Cold Blood.* This book detailed the murder of an entire Kansas family by two drifters. These men were apprehended, tried and convicted of murder, and executed. At or about the time of their execution, their photographs appeared in *The Saturday Evening Post.* The writer of the article suggested that readers observe that one of the murderers had a face made up from two parts where the two parts did not quite match up with one another. Attention was drawn to portions of the murderer's photograph showing that one eye was not level or even with the other, the mouth curved down on one side and up on the other side, and that the ears were unevenly matched. This physical description was provided in a popular national magazine in the late 1960s.

A popular outgrowth of Lombroso's positivist thinking was the concept of various body types by Sheldon (1949). Sheldon classified persons into three distinct categories: (1) **endomorph** (fat, soft, plump, jolly); (2) **ectomorph** (thin, sensitive, delicate), and (3) **mesomorph** (strong, muscular, aggressive, tough). Sheldon wrote extensively about the behavioral characteristics of each body type. He devised a complex numerical system where persons possessed features of one body type to a greater degree than the other two types. He eventually developed crude indices from which generalizations about criminal behavior could be made. He said that ectomorphs tend to commit forgery, fraud, or burglary (passive, nonviolent crimes), while mesomorphs tend to commit robbery, rape, murder, assault and other physically demanding crimes. Sheldon believed that body type was a cause of particular types of criminal conduct. Subsequent studies and extensive research by criminologists and others have failed to support Sheldon's theory.

Hereditary Criminal Behaviors.   **Heredity** as a cause of criminal conduct suggested the inheritance of certain physical and behavioral characteristics from parents or ancestors. Whether people became criminals depended upon their lineage or hereditary background. If one's ancestors were cattle rustlers, thieves, or rapists, then the offspring would also tend to be cattle rustlers, thieves, or rapists. Little scientific evidence exists supporting this theory (Hodgins, 2001).

A more recent heredity-based theory of criminal behavior is the **XYY syndrome.** "X" and "Y" are labels assigned to the human sex chromosomes. Males are *XY,* while females are *XX.* These sex chromosomes, *X* and *Y,* are inherited from the mother and father. The father transmits the *Y* or "aggressive" chromosome, while the *X* or "passive" chromosome comes from the mother. Occasionally, infants are born with an *XYY* (doubly aggressive?) chromosomatic pattern.

In the 1960s, researchers were intrigued by the discovery that Richard Speck had an *XYY* chromosomatic pattern. At the time, Speck was in prison for the brutal murder of eight student nurses in Chicago. Could this extra *Y* chromosome have caused his violent behavior? Geneticists have investigated the *XYY* syndrome in selected, captive-audience situations: prisons. Their studies show that (1) there appears to be more *XYY* people in the criminal population compared with the general population, and that (2) less than 5 percent of the prison population has the *XYY* syndrome. Thus, the *XYY* syndrome is not a consistent cause of criminal behavior (Zonderman, 1999; Martens, 2002).

Biochemical Disturbances.   A third group of biologically based theories of criminal behavior focuses upon biochemical disturbances and glandular malfunctions as inducing criminal acts. The thyroid, adrenal, pituitary, and hypothalamus glands have been linked with different kinds of aggressive and antisocial behavior. Glands have been shown to control metabolism, growth, and activity levels. Hyperactivity, or abnormally active behavior, is often associated with oversecretions or undersecretions of various hormones. However, recent medical developments have led to a greater understanding of our biochemical functions and to the development of drugs and synthetic chemicals that can control abnormal behavior. Thorazine is administered to mental patients to control various psychotic disorders. Diazepam, an antidepressant, is used to treat severe alcohol withdrawal or to help patients manage severe anxiety or stress. These products alter hormonal states and permit some regulation of deviant and criminal behavior (Martens, 2002).

For more than a few probationers and parolees who are sex offenders, various drugs have been utilized to contain their sexual urges (Mears et al., 2003). Together with counseling and medicine, many sex offenders are leading normal lives today as probationers and parolees. This is because their problems are believed to be hormone related to a degree. And chemical imbalances can be regulated with proper drug therapies.

Psychological Theories

Another set of theories about criminal conduct is based in psychology, the study of individual behavior. By studying individual behavior, psychologists try to explain the inner workings of the mind. Since various components of the criminal justice system must determine criminal intent and the defendant's mental competence to stand trial, prosecutors and defense attorneys often turn to psychologists for help. Psychologists and psychiatrists, physicians who specialize in treating mental disorders, are often asked to examine defendants and give their expert testimony in court. Psychological theories of criminal behavior have also influenced correctional and rehabilitative programs. Psychological counselors and psychiatrists play key roles in contemporary criminal rehabilitative therapy. Three psychological theories are presented here. They include (1) psychoanalytic theory, (2) cognitive development theory, and (3) social learning theory.

Psychoanalytic Theory.   **Psychoanalytic theory** was created by the Austrian neurologist Sigmund Freud (1856–1939). Frustrated by the primitive technology of his day, Freud tried to explain the human personality and mental disorders through the interaction of the concepts of the **id,** the **ego,** the **superego,** and the **libido.** The id is the "I want" associated with the behavior of infants. Getting a 2-year-old to share his or her jellybeans or ice cream is nearly impossible. As children grow, they learn that the id cannot always be satisfied. The child cannot have everything he or she wants. Therefore, the id is eventually controlled by the ego, which embodies society's standards and conventional rules. As the child matures into adolescence, moral values are incorporated into the personality. Moral values are the domain of the superego. The libido is the sex urge or drive which Freud believed was inborn. Freud explained criminal behavior as a function of an inadequately developed ego, the controlling mechanism for the id. When persons fail to control their impulses and disregard the rights and feelings of others, their aggressive behaviors often follow deviant paths and criminal acts occur (Johansson-Love and Geer, 2003). Rape may be the result of an uncontrollable libido, and theft may be the result of a poorly developed ego, according to Freud. More than a few POs have bought into the idea that some of their clients have underdeveloped egos and psychological problems that must be resolved through some form of counseling or therapy. This type of approach is used by enablers, brokers, and educators, and it reflects a social work orientation toward the PO role. POs using this approach in dealing with their clients would be more inclined to recommend some form of counseling, individually or in a group, for offenders who violate one or more program conditions. They would be less likely to report program infractions compared with enforcers. (Kanazawa and Still, 2000).

Cognitive Development Theory.   **Cognitive development theory** stresses **cognitive development** through a learning process involving various stages. Jean Piaget (1896–1980) was one of the first to stress the importance of cognitive stages of development and the idea that all normal individuals pass through the same sequential periods in the growth or maturing of their ability to think or to gain knowledge and awareness of themselves and their environment (VanderZanden, 1984:116-117). As a child moves through various stages of development, he or she acquires an awareness of people, objects, and especially, standards of behavior or judgments of right and wrong (Gaarder and Belknap, 2002).

　　Piaget's notions about cognitive development have been modified and expanded by Kohlberg (1963). Kohlberg has described six stages in the development of a person's moral judgment. These levels, or stages, reflect a different type of relationship between the individual and his or her society. Kohlberg divides the six stages into three categories: (1) the preconventional level; (2) the conventional level; and (3) the postconventional level. Kohlberg says that very young children, some adolescents, and many criminals are in the preconventional stage of development. Thus, psychologists supporting this theory associate criminal behavior with inadequate moral development during childhood. Some gender bias is inherent in Kohlberg's scheme, because conventional role conformity traditionally encourages males in our culture to acquire protective/aggressive behaviors, while females are socialized to be more submissive and nurturing.

A contrary perspective has been devised by Yochelson and Samenow (1976). These researchers reject the notion that criminal behavior is the direct result of one's environment. Rather, they believe that those who become criminals do so because they want to. At a very early age, youths seek associations with others who may be delinquent. The excitement of committing delinquent acts becomes a self-perpetuating influence in their lives. As these youths graduate to more serious offenses as adults, the same excitement urges them to carry out criminal acts. Yochelson and Samenow believe that free will rather than one's environment determines whether a criminal career pattern will be pursued. Thus, if criminal behavior is to be decreased or eliminated by any conventional treatment program, it is imperative that psychologists and others try to dissuade these people from thinking about committing crimes. Changing their thoughts about crime will lead to a cessation of their criminal behaviors. But Yochelson and Samenow do not answer the question of why these people "think" about engaging in criminal acts. In short, little support exists for their position. However, their theorizing is an interesting contrast with the work of Kohlberg and others who stress environmental experiences as primary ingredients for stimulating criminal behavior.

Social Learning Theory.   Applied to criminology, **social learning theory** is that criminal behavior is learned by modeling the behaviors of others who are criminal. It does not propose that criminal conduct is copied or imitated. Rather, those who use others as models for their criminal behavior do so as the result of strong incentives to do so. Deviant and criminal conduct as well as conventional conduct stems from the process of reinforcement, whereby people perceive others who are rewarded (by goods, money, or social status) for conforming to conventional rules or are punished for deviating from those same rules. This type of reinforcement, called external reinforcement, is seen as a crucial social reinforcement mechanism that propels people toward conventional behavior. People also derive reinforcement from internal sources. Some people may engage in self-punishment when they perceive themselves behaving badly, or they may reward themselves for self-perceptions of conformity and appropriate behavior. Most important, reinforcement arises from observing others being rewarded for their conduct. Depending upon the environment in which people are socialized, reinforcement may stem from conventional sources or from unconventional ones. Those who observe a criminal being rewarded with goods, money, social status, or acclaim may be motivated to model or emulate this deviant or criminal behavior (Agnew et al., 2002).

In those instances where people do not fit in with certain social groups, or if they are unsuccessful in adapting to social situations and perceive little or no reward for their conventional behavior, they may learn other behaviors for which rewards of various kinds are forthcoming. Such conduct may be criminal conduct, and it can yield rewards from others who are criminal. This type of situation reinforces deviant conduct and dissuades people from adopting conventional modes of behavior.

Social learning theory fails to explain the roles played by close friends, family, and other agencies of socialization in modifying one's conventional or unconventional conduct (Rebellon, 2002). It stresses psychological factors and alludes to certain stimulus-response behavior patterns reflected by behaviorism. Its main value is that it focuses our attention upon the social contexts in which conventional or unconventional conduct is acquired. However, it does not adequately explain the process of acquiring these behaviors (Benda, 2002).

Sociological and/or Sociocultural Theories

Sociological and sociocultural theories are as equally diverse as psychological theories. There is considerable interplay between psychological and sociological perspectives. However, sociologists focus more closely upon the social processes involved in criminal conduct, as well as the importance of social structure. They believe that forces or processes in the external social environment lead people to commit criminal acts. **Social process theories** stress external forces as causes of criminal conduct, in contrast to the internal forces, emphasized by biological and psychological theories. Several popular sociological theories of criminal behavior are (1) differential association; (2) anomie theory; (3) strain theory; (4) labeling theory; (5) social control theory; and (6) conflict/Marxist theory.

Differential Association Theory.   The sociologist Edwin Sutherland (1893–1950) is credited with formulating perhaps the best-known sociological theory of crime. Sutherland's theory, known as **differential association theory,** was formally

FIGURE 11.1   Boys being questioned by the police.

presented in the 1920s, and a few researchers still use it to explain some forms of adult crime (Hochstetler, Copes, and DeLisi, 2002). Sutherland used the differential association concept to explain the process by which people became criminals. As the name implies, association with criminals is an important part of this process. However, it is an oversimplification of Sutherland's theory to state that simple association with criminals causes a person to become a criminal. The theory is more complex than that. In some respects, Sutherland's theory is an outgrowth of **cultural transmission theory** developed by Shaw and McKay (1929). These sociologists believed that criminal behavior patterns are transmitted in much the same manner as culture is transmitted through **socialization.** Socialization is learning through contact with others or social learning (Tilley, 2002).

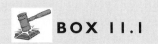

BOX 11.1

PERSONALITY HIGHLIGHT

David Shichor
Professor Emeritus, Department of Criminal Justice, California State University at San Bernardino

Statistics:

B.A. (sociology and history), Hebrew University, Jerusalem; M.A. (sociology), California State College Los Angeles; Ph.D. (sociology), University of Southern California

Background:

Dr. Shichor has written, edited, and co-edited 9 books and published over 70 articles and chapters in professional journals and academic books. The current professional interests of Dr. Shichor focus on theories of crime and delinquency, theories of punishment, privatization in criminal justice, victimology, and white-collar crime.

On Criminology Theories:

There is no one theory that could explain the whole volume and all forms of criminal and delinquent activity. However, there are several theoretical schemes that might be useful in explaining certain forms and patterns of crime and delinquency. Most theories available focus on patterns of law violations that are mostly committed by lower-class criminals and delinquents, mainly because they are the majority among those who are officially defined and handled as offenders.

Criminological theories are usually divided into three types: (1) biological theories that are based on the physiological or genetic factors leading certain individuals to become offenders; (2) psychological theories that see the root causes of criminal and delinquent behavior in personality traits, emotional maladjustment, and/or other psychological problems of offenders; and (3) sociological theories that focus on social factors that influence criminal and delinquent behavior.

Being trained as a sociologist, I am partial to sociological theories because they are the ones that can explain why one group is more criminal than another, or why one society has higher crime rates than others. I find that one of the older theories, forwarded by probably the most known U.S. criminologist, Edwin H. Sutherland, the differential association theory, provides one of the more feasible and useful explanations of crime and delinquency, but unlike some

⚖ BOX 11.1 (*Continued*)

others, it can have an explanatory value of middle-class and upper-class crime and delinquency as well.

Differential association theory emphasizes that human behavior is based on learning. It focuses upon the importance of the primary group (intimate groups characterized by face-to-face relations) influence and peer pressure among criminals and juveniles. The theory is stated in the form of nine points, suggesting that patterns of criminal behavior are learned like any other behavior patterns. This assumption negates to a large degree the biological and psychological explanations of crime and delinquency. Furthermore, it does emphasize the importance and influence of close, intimate groups in this learning process. This is especially relevant for teenagers who are very much open to peer group pressure. According to this theory, the learning process in this context involves both the techniques of committing actual criminal acts (how to do) and also the attitudes, motivations and justifications for committing criminal acts (why to do). Becoming a criminal or a delinquent depends very much on whether the close-knit primary group of an individual relates positively or negatively to the rules and norms of society. If there is a strong tendency in this group to relate negatively to conventional rules and norms, the likelihood that members of this group will become criminals or delinquent is high. The extent of this likelihood and readiness to get involved in crime and delinquency varies with the importance that individuals attach to their relationship with their primary group. It depends on how deeply they are committed to their group, how long is their association with the crimi-

nal or delinquent group, and how intense is the juvenile's involvement with the group.

By emphasizing the importance of differential association of individuals, Sutherland helped to explain why offenders growing up and living under similar conditions are involved to different degrees in criminal and delinquent behavior. He also extended his theory to explain the involvement of upper- and middle-class offenders in white-collar crime.

The differential association theory, like most theories in the social sciences, has had its critics, but still, it has held its ground quite well. Also, it has served as a catalyst for the development of other theoretical developments that were based on many of its premises or were the refinement of the differential association theory. These developments included among others the social learning, the differential opportunity, and the differential identification theories. I believe that the differential association theory is still relevant and has an important explanatory value of crime and juvenile delinquency.

Advice to Students:

Since differential association theory is almost a classic in criminology and juvenile delinquency, I would suggest that you read carefully Sutherland's nine points. They are relatively easy to understand and the points follow a logical sequence. After reading this theory, you can try to tie it to several other theories such as the other learning theories and strain theories, showing that theoretical explanations do not develop in a vacuum, but that science is a cumulative enterprise.

Expanding on the work of Shaw and McKay, Sutherland outlined a fairly elaborate multidimensional social interaction process that would induce a person to adopt criminal behaviors. The dimensions of differential association theory include (1) frequency, (2) duration, (3) priority, and (4) intensity. The transmission of deviant (and criminal) cultural values and behaviors occurs in a social learning context. In this context, the potential criminal has frequent contact with criminals. These frequent contacts are of some lasting duration. Priority and intensity are more elusive concepts in Sutherland's scheme. Priority refers to either the lawful or criminal behavior learned in early childhood. This persists throughout a person's life to reinforce criminal behaviors whenever associations with criminals occur. Intensity is the degree of emotional attachment to either conventional or criminal groups and the prestige allocated each. Thus, criminal behaviors acquired at an early age and reinforced through frequent and lengthy emotional attachments with one or more criminals are seen as primary contributing factors explaining why people become criminals.

Professionals involved in corrections programs have shown some respect for Sutherland's differential association ideas over the years. In some jurisdictions, first-offenders are not placed in the same cells with more seasoned repeat offenders. But this policy is a luxury. It is relinquished when incarceration rates are high and prison funding is low. Thus, because of overcrowding, penal authorities sometimes mix all inmates, regardless of the nature or seriousness of the crimes they have committed. This overcrowding situation has caused some observers to label prisons and jails as institutions of higher criminal learning, where more seasoned criminals teach first-offenders how to avoid being apprehended the next time.

Critics of differential association theory have said that Sutherland's terms are difficult to define and understand. What is meant by an intense relation? How frequent is frequent? Also, Sutherland's theory does not explain all types of criminal conduct. Although Sutherland intended his theory to account for most criminal behavior, numerous exceptions to his scheme over the years caused him to believe that additional factors such as opportunity and individual needs were equally important and ought to be considered (Walsh et al., 2002). Therefore, he eventually adopted multiple-factor theoretical explanations for criminal conduct in later years and gave less attention to differential association (Short, 2002).

Closely related to differential association theory and applied to juveniles is **neutralization theory** (Costello, 2000). POs who work with juveniles frequently encounter youths who deny responsibility for what they have done. They deny that they caused anyone injury or they claim that the victim deserved whatever injuries were received. These youths are living examples of what Gresham Sykes and David Matza (1957) called neutralization theory. Neutralization theory is the explanation of delinquency that holds that delinquents experience guilt whenever they commit crimes, although simultaneously, they respect the legitimacy of the social order of their community. Their delinquency is episodic rather than chronic. They are said to drift into delinquent conduct. Drifting means that they must first neutralize their legal and moral values with rationalizations of various kinds (Boehnke and Winkels, 2002).

Most juveniles spend their early years on a behavioral continuum ranging between unlimited freedom and total control or restraint. These persons drift toward one end of the continuum or the other, depending upon their social and psychological circumstances. If youths have strong attachments with those who are delinquent, then they "drift" toward the unlimited freedom end of the continuum and perhaps engage accordingly in delinquent activities. However, the behavioral issue is not clear-cut. Juveniles most likely have associations with normative culture as well as the delinquent subculture. Therefore, at least some delinquency results from rationalizations created by youths that render delinquent acts acceptable under the circumstances. Appropriate preventive therapy for such delinquents might be to undermine their rationales for delinquent behaviors through empathic means.

Rationalizations used by juveniles to account for their misconduct include that there is no real victim; that they believe their victim deserved to be injured; that they committed their crimes for family members or friends; that the police and others are out to get them; that no one actually was hurt by whatever they did; and that the delinquency was not really their fault. PO dealings with juveniles frequently disclose such rationalizations. Thus, they are able to understand why some delinquents do not accept any responsibility or exhibit remorse when they have done something wrong. But neutralization theory posits that delinquents do, indeed, feel guilt at some level (Alexander and Bernard, 2002). POs can use this guilt to their advantage when prescribing appropriate community therapies for juvenile offenders.

Anomie Theory or Innovative Adaptation. The use of anomie in **anomie theory** is a misnomer. **Anomie** literally means normlessness, or a condition when the norms or behavioral expectations are unknown, undefined, or in conflict. People seldom experience true normlessness. Robert King Merton (1938, 1957) is credited with developing anomie theory, which was originally proposed by the French sociologist, Emile Durkheim (1858–1917). Anomie theory states that all people in society are taught to pursue certain culturally approved goals. These people are also taught socially acceptable or approved institutionalized means by which these goals may be achieved. Merton's theory of anomie emphasized the ways that persons adapt to goal attainment and the means they use to achieve these goals. He referred to these as the **modes of adaptation.** Merton said that persons either accept or reject the goals of their society. Also, they either accept or reject the approved means to achieve those goals (Merton, 1938).

According to Merton, conformity is the most common adaptation. People accept the culturally approved goals and the socially approved means to achieve them. People might want a new car or a new home, and they will work patiently at socially acceptable jobs so that they may eventually acquire these possessions. However, some people accept the culturally approved goals, but they reject the means to achieve those goals. For instance, a trustee at a state prison once confided that he had been an "A" student at a large California university. He was majoring in business administration and planned a business career. At the end of his third year, however, he decided the educational process was too slow and that his calculations of future earnings were too low for his particular desires. He said, "I decided that to get what I want fast, I've got to have a lot of money. The best place to get a lot of money fast is a bank. So I started robbing banks." His adaptation to the goals/means relation was innovation. His criminal behaviors were the innovative means he substituted to achieve certain desired, culturally approved goals.

Much criminal behavior, according to Merton, is innovative behavior. And this mode of adaptation was the focus of his theory of anomie. Merton's theory also tried to explain drug abusers and alcohol users. These people have been labeled as retreatists because they withdraw from others and reject the culturally approved goals as well as the means to achieve them. Such people may be unemployed, vagrant, or otherwise indifferent about achieving the culturally approved goals sought by others. Other adaptation forms included in Merton's scheme are ritualism (rejecting the goals, accepting the means) and rebellion (accepting and rejecting some of the goals and means and substituting new goals and means). Ritualists might be people who conclude that they will never have the nice home and new car, but they will nevertheless work at their socially approved jobs until retirement. In contrast, rebels reject the goals and the means and are interested in creating new societal goals through revolution or rebellion (Bernburg, 2002).

Merton's theory of anomie is particularly relevant for explaining property crimes such as burglary and larceny. The people who commit these crimes may want material wealth or expensive possessions, but they are unwilling or unable to earn money through socially acceptable occupations. Thus, they will likely seek goal attainment through innovative means. Merton's theory is economically based and concerned with gaining access to certain success goals. Some critics say that Merton made an erroneous assumption that poor persons are more prone toward criminal behavior than rich persons. Furthermore, Merton has not explained the embezzlement or tax fraud of successful business executives (Pratt and Godsey, 2002). It might be, however, that such criminals are simply seeking a culturally approved goal through innovative means. Another criticism is that the theory does not explain noneconomic crimes such as aggravated assault or rape. However, anomie is not intended to explain these kinds of offenses. Finally, some critics have said that Merton's scheme does not deal with criminal behavior as a process (Walsh et al., 2002).

Merton's scheme presents several adaptations persons can make in attaining goals and choosing the means to achieve those goals. It is a static theory rather than a dynamic one. Merton's innovative mode is more or less an automatic response which is almost always regarded as deviant and/or criminal. By comparison, differential association theory analyzes such dynamic processes as the duration and intensity of social associations that encourage and condone criminal acts. Sutherland's differential association theory about white collar criminals and Merton's innovative modes of adaptation may be linked theoretically to the **theory of opportunity.** According to this theory, middle and upper class persons have more opportunities to gain access to and achieve success goals, whereas lower class persons lack these opportunities (Lester, 2000). Therefore, lower-class persons tend to achieve success by achieving certain deviant and/or criminal objectives which are respected by other criminals.

The Subculture Theory of Delinquency.   During the 1950s, sociologist Albert Cohen (1955) focused upon and described **delinquent subcultures.** Delinquent subcultures exist, according to Cohen, within the greater societal culture. But these **subcultures** contain value systems and modes of achievement and gaining status and recognition apart from the mainstream culture. Thus, if we are to understand why many juveniles behave as they do, we must pay attention to the patterns of their particular subculture.

The notion of a delinquent subculture is fairly easy to understand, especially in view of the earlier work of Shaw and McKay (1929). While middle- and upper-class children learn and aspire to achieve lofty ambitions and educational goals and receive support for these aspirations from their parents as well as predominantly middle-class teachers, lower-class youths are at a distinct disadvantage at the outset. They are born into families where these aspirations and attainments may be alien and rejected. Their primary familial role models have not attained these high aims themselves. At school, these youths are often isolated socially from upper- and middle-class juveniles, and therefore, social attachments are formed with others similar to themselves. Perhaps these youths dress differently from other students, wear their hair in a certain style, or use coded language when talking to peers in front of other students. They acquire a culture unto themselves and one that is largely unknown to other students. In a sense, much of this cultural isolation is self-imposed. But it functions to give them a sense of fulfillment, of reward, of self-esteem and recognition apart from other reward systems. If these students cannot achieve one or more of the various standards set by middle-class society, then they create their own standards and prescribe the means to achieve those standards.

Cohen is quick to point out that delinquency is not a product of lower socioeconomic status per se. Rather, children from lower socioeconomic statuses are at greater risk than others of being susceptible to the rewards and opportunities a subculture of delinquency might offer in contrast with the system's middle-class reward structure. Several experiments have subsequently been implemented with delinquents, where these subcultures have been targeted and described, and where the norms of these subcultures have been used as intervening mechanisms to modify delinquent behaviors toward nondelinquent modes of action. The Provo Experiment was influenced, to a degree, by the work of Cohen (Empey and Rabow, 1961). Samples of delinquent youths in Provo, Utah, were identified in the late 1950s and given an opportunity to participate in group therapy sessions at Pine Hills, a large home in Provo that had been converted to an experimental laboratory.

In cooperation with juvenile court judges and other authorities, Pine Hills investigators commenced their intervention strategies assuming that juvenile participants (l) had limited access to success goals, (2) performed many of their delinquent activities in groups rather than alone, and (3) committed their delinquent acts for nonutilitarian objectives rather than for money (Empey and Rabow, 1961). These investigators believed that since the delinquents had acquired their delinquent values and conduct through their subculture of delinquency, they could "unlearn" these values and learn new values by the same means. Thus, groups of delinquents participated extensively in therapy directed at changing their behaviors through group processes. The investigators believed that their intervention efforts were largely successful and that the subcultural approach to delinquency prevention and behavioral change was fruitful.

An interesting variation on the subcultural theme is the work of Wolfgang and Ferracuti (1967). Wolfgang and other associates investigated large numbers of Philadelphia, Pennsylvania, boys in a study of birth cohorts. In that study, he found that approximately 6 percent of all boys accounted for over 50 percent of all delinquent conduct from the entire cohort of over 9,000 boys (Wolfgang, Figlio, and Sellin, 1972). These were chronic recidivists who were also violent offenders. Wolfgang has theorized that in many communities, there are subcultural norms of violence that attract youthful males. They regard violence as a normal part of their environment, they use violence, and respect the use of violence by others. On the basis of evidence amassed by Wolfgang and Ferracuti, it appeared that predominantly lower-class and less-educated males formed a disproportionately large part of this **subculture of violence.** Where violence is accepted and respected, its use is considered normal and normative for the users. Remorse is an alien emotion to those using violence and who live with it constantly. Thus, it is socially ingrained as a subcultural value (Austin and Kim-Young, 2000).

The subcultural perspective toward delinquent conduct is indicative of a strain between the values of society and the values of a subgroup of delinquent youths (Grietens, Rink, and Hellinckx, 2003). Therefore, some researchers have labeled the subcultural perspective a **strain theory.** The strain component is apparent since although many lower SES youths have adopted middle-class goals and aspirations, they may be unable to attain these goals because of their individual economic and cultural circumstances. This is a frustrating experience for many of these youths, and such frustration is manifested by the strain to achieve difficult goals or objectives (Agnew et al., 2002). While middle-class youths also experience strain in their attempts to achieve middle-class goals, it is particularly aggravating for many lower-class youths, since they sometimes do not receive the necessary support from their families. Merton's anomie theory greatly influenced the development of strain theory.

Obviously, a myriad of other explanations for delinquent conduct have been advanced by various theorists. Those selected for more in-depth coverage above are by no means the best theories to account for delinquency. Their inclusion here is merely to describe some of the thinking about why juveniles might be attracted toward delinquent conduct. Some of the other approaches that have been advocated include **containment theory** and **differential reinforcement theory** (Lersch, 1999).

Containment theory is closely associated with the work of sociologist Walter Reckless (1967). Reckless outlined a theoretical model consisting of "pushes" and "pulls" in relation to delinquency. By pushes he referred to internal personal factors, including hostility, anxiety, and discontent. By pulls he meant external social forces, including delinquent subcultures and significant others. The containment dimension of his theoretical scheme consisted of both outer and inner containments. Outer containments, according to Reckless, are social norms, folkways, mores, laws and institutional arrangements that induce societal conformity. By inner containments, Reckless referred to individual or personal coping strategies to deal with stressful situations and conflict. These strategies might be a high tolerance for conflict or frustration and considerable ego strength. Thus, Reckless combined both psychological and social elements in referring to weak attachments of some youths to cultural norms, high anxiety levels, and low tolerance for personal stress. These persons are most inclined to delinquent conduct. A key factor in whether juveniles adopt delinquent behaviors is their level of self-esteem. Those with high levels of self-esteem seem most resistant to delinquent behaviors if they are exposed to such conduct while around their friends.

In 1966, Robert Burgess and Ronald Akers attempted to revise Sutherland's differential association theory and derived what they termed differential reinforcement theory. Differential reinforcement theory actually combines elements from labeling theory and a psychological phenomenon known as conditioning. Conditioning functions in the social learning process as persons are rewarded for engaging in certain desirable behaviors and refraining from certain undesirable behaviors. Juveniles perceive how others respond to their behaviors (negative reactions) and may be disposed to behave in ways that will maximize their rewards from others. Also, in some respects, Burgess and Akers have incorporated certain aspects of the "looking-glass self" concept originally devised by the theorist Charles Horton Cooley. Cooley theorized that people learned ways of conforming by paying attention to the reactions of others in response to their own behavior. Therefore, Cooley would argue that we imagine how others see us. We look for other's reactions to our behavior and make interpretations of these reactions as either good or bad reactions. If we define others' reactions as good, we will feel a degree of pride and likely persist in the behaviors. But, as Cooley indicated, if we interpret their reactions to our behaviors as bad, we might experience mortification. Given this latter reaction or at least our interpretation of it, we might change our behaviors to conform to what others might want and thereby elicit approval from them. While these ideas continue to interest us, they are difficult to conceptualize and investigate empirically. Akers and others have acknowledged such difficulties, although their work is insightful and underscores the reality of a multidimensional view of delinquent conduct.

Labeling Theory.   A third popular sociological theory of criminal behavior is **labeling theory.** Labeling theory is associated with the work of Edwin Lemert (1951), although Howard S. Becker (1963) and John Kitsuse (1962) have also been credited with being among its early advocates. Labeling theory is concerned with the social definitions of criminal acts rather than the criminal acts themselves. Labeling theory attempts to answer at least two questions: (1) What is the process whereby persons become labeled as criminals or deviants? and (2) How does such labeling influence the persons labeled as deviant?

The basic assumptions of labeling theory are: (1) no act is inherently criminal; (2) persons become criminals by social labeling or definition; (3) all persons at one time or another conform to and deviate from laws; (4) getting caught begins the labeling process; (5) the person defined as criminal will develop a criminal self-definition; and (6) the person will seek others similarly defined and develop a criminal subculture (Kenney, 2002).

According to Lemert (1951), there are two types of deviation: (1) primary and (2) secondary. A **primary deviation** involves violations of law that often can be and frequently are overlooked. College students who pull pranks such as disassembling the university president's car and reassembling it on the roof of the women's dormitory are mildly chided by police rather than arrested for criminal vehicular theft. A **secondary deviation** occurs when violations of the law have become incorporated into a person's lifestyle or behavior pattern. Usually, by the time secondary deviations have occurred, the offender has accepted the label of deviant or criminal and is on the road toward joining a criminal subculture.

Many labeling theorists say they are not interested in explaining criminal acts. Instead, they want to explain the social process of labeling and one's personal reaction to being labeled. Nevertheless, a strong explanatory element is prevalent. In effect, the labeling theorist is saying that persons who react to social labeling by defining themselves as deviant or criminal will not only engage in further criminal activity, they will also seek out others like themselves and form criminal subcultures. This subcultural development is the equivalent of rejecting the rejectors (Lilly, Cullen, and Ball, 2002).

Some evidence of the influence of labeling may be found by examining arrest rates by race and social class. Labeling theorists argue that the most likely targets of labeling are persons who are young, non-white, and of lower socioeconomic statuses. These persons are most likely to be labeled by police and others as deviant or inclined to be criminal.

More arrests tend to be made in high-crime areas. Coincidentally, high-crime areas tend to be low-rent districts that attract a disproportionately large number of the poor and ethnic and racial minorities. These are the same areas that tend to attract larger numbers of police such that arrest rates will be increased. Also, law enforcement officers may be more inclined to take advantage of persons of lower socioeconomic statuses. When compared with middle- or upper-class citizens, lower-class persons have fewer resources and lack the legal sophistication to resist or retaliate within the legal system. Again, deviance or criminal conduct is like a social status that, once assigned, changes the relationship the person has with others.

Labeling theory is an external explanation for criminal behavior. Criminal behavior is whatever lawmakers—an external source—say it is. A criminal is whomever a society labels as criminal. The offender's acceptance of the label criminal merely completes the process, and leads the offender to seek the companionship of others labeled as deviants. In some respects, labeling theory involves some interplay between the social and psychological realms. The offender reacts to social definitions, the offender interprets or defines himself/herself as deviant or criminal, and the offender forms subcultures with others in an effort to win acceptance and preserve self-worth (Li and Moore, 2001).

However, labeling theory fails to account for the people who either reject deviant labels or successfully unlabel themselves as criminals or deviants. It also inadequately explains occasional offenders or weekend deviants, persons leading two morally different lives by associating with diverse community elements. Finally, persons who engage in victimless crimes or crimes where the victim is a willing participant (e.g., gambling and prostitution) seem to escape the psychological effects of being labeled a deviant. The theory does not explain the mental compartmentalization these people seem to use in refusing to define themselves as deviants.

It is interesting to note that most probation and parole program agreements reflect critical elements of labeling theory. Among most provisions are that probationers and parolees are not to associate or have contact with any known criminals. Furthermore, visits to prisons or jails to visit incarcerated friends or relatives is strictly prohibited. PO approval is required for any contact to be made among offenders. What other reason would there be to deny one a chance to visit his/her friends acquired while incarcerated or to associate with friends in the community who also happen to have criminal records?

Social Control Theory.   Sometimes referred to as **bonding theory, social control theory** focuses upon the processual aspects of becoming bonded or attached to the norms and values of society (Hirschi, 1969). As the bonds between society and people become stronger, the possibility that people will engage in deviant or criminal behaviors becomes weaker. Bonding consists of several dimensions. These include (1) attachment, the emotional or affective dimension linking us with significant others whose opinions we respect and whose admonitions we follow; (2) commitment, the energy expended by an individual in particular activities, either conventional or unconventional; (3) belief, a person's moral definition of the propriety of particular conduct, that the laws and rules should be obeyed; and (4) involvement, the degree of intensity with which one is involved in conventional conduct or with which one espouses conventional values.

Persons who have strong attachments with conventional groups and their opinions, who manifest beliefs in the values of the group, who are intensely involved in these groups' activities, and who expend considerable energy in these activities will probably not become deviant or exhibit criminal conduct. But if one or more of these bonding dimensions are weakened, people stand a better chance of deviating from the expectations of conventional society. For instance,

BOX 11.2

Dennis Giever
Associate Professor and Chair, Department of Criminology, Indiana University of Pennsylvania

Statistics:

B.C.J., M.C.J., New Mexico State University; Ph.D. (criminology) Indiana University of Pennsylvania

Background:

I received both my bachelor's and master's degrees in criminal justice from New Mexico State University in Las Cruces, New Mexico, in 1990 and 1992 respectively. I continued my education at Indiana University of Pennsylvania and obtained my Ph.D. in 1995. When I started college it was never my intent to continue so far in academia as I did. My earlier goal was to join the U.S. Air Force, but certain events led me in another direction. Early in my college career I became fascinated by the criminal justice system and attempts to explain and, as such, control criminal behavior. I also found academia to be both challenging and rewarding. It afforded me the opportunity to stay involved in a number of areas that I was very interested in, including computers, history, biology and statistics. Academia is always challenging and always new. It is one field in which you continually have to stay ahead of the game. It also affords you the opportunity to work closely with individuals of all walks of life.

As criminologists are prone to do, I became fascinated in trying to understand criminal behavior among the many individuals I would meet either in court or in correctional settings. Our field offers so many possible explanations of crime, including biological, psychological, and social factors. And while most of these theories of criminal behavior were plausible to me, I was never fully intrigued by any one of them. It was more an exercise of understanding the different theoretical approaches in an effort to prepare for the many tests and written papers I was undertaking in school. It was not until the first year of my doctoral course work that I began to fully explore what was known as the control perspective in our field. The year was 1992 and Michael Gottfredson and Travis Hirschi had just published a new text entitled *A General Theory of Crime.* My first exposure to this work was during a lecture in one of the classes I was taking in my first semester as a doctoral student. I became intrigued by what I heard and went over to the college bookstore and ordered a copy of this new book. Once I began to read it, I became very excited about this new approach to explaining criminal behavior. In fact, I devoted the next two or three years of my life to carefully exploring this theory and conducting research to test a number of propositions developed by the authors.

To understand Gottfredson's and Hirschi's general theory of crime, one should do as the authors did and start with the event and work backwards to the causes of such acts. One of the most intriguing aspects of the theory was the fact that the authors did not claim that their theory was just an explanation of criminal acts, but rather, it looked first at criminal acts and found many similarities between them and other types of noncriminal activities. This point just plain stuck with me. It made sense that many acts that are criminal are such just because society has chosen to label them as such. Their definition of crime did not limit itself to just those

(continued)

BOX 11.2 (*Continued*)

events that society had deemed illegal. They looked at acts that were criminal and found similarities with many other types of activities which they referred to as analogous acts. All such acts shared something in common; they tended to be short-lived, immediately gratifying, easy, simple, and exciting. In a sense, the authors were claiming that criminal acts were similar to many other activities that one could undertake. Thus, their theory did not really look at criminal activity, but rather at acts that were short-lived, immediately gratifying, easy, simple, and exciting.

Once they had established the event, the authors moved next to the characteristics of the actor. Not everyone chooses to become involved in acts that meet the above criteria. According to Gottfredson and Hirschi, crime and analogous acts appeal to persons who are unrestrained by concerns for the long-term consequences of their behavior. Individuals who are conscious of the long-term consequences of their behavior, according to the authors, possess a personality trait that they refer to as self-control. Those lacking in self-control, according to Gottfredson and Hirschi, are likely to be impulsive, insensitive, physical (as opposed to verbal), risk taking, short sighted, and nonverbal. These individuals who lack self-control are the very same individuals who are more likely to become involved in the types of behaviors mentioned above. What is important here is the fact that not all such acts are criminal. There are many manifestations of low self-control that are not criminal. Some examples given by Gottfredson and Hirschi include many types of risk-taking activities such as sky diving, smoking, promiscuous sex, and such. Once again, I found this argument very intriguing. In fact, many of the experiences I had with friends or acquaintances while growing up supported this argument.

Another way one might look at this aspect of the theory is to understand that not everyone has access to the same opportunities. Those who have money and a more affluent lifestyle can often act out their personalities in areas such as car racing, sky diving, or white-water rafting. Those who do not have such opportunities and are seeking the same risk-taking rush may find themselves involved in criminal activity, since no other legal outlet exists. These events are known as manifestations of low self-control. As one can see, in some cases these manifestations are legal but risk-taking activities; in other instances they are illegal, and as such, risky.

Another point that really struck home for me was how this line of thinking did a really good job of explaining upper-world crime. While many of the criminological theories I was studying did a very poor job of explaining corporate crime, Gottfredson's and Hirschi's theory just seemed to fit. Those corporate individuals who were involved in inappropriate corporate activity lacked self-control, just like their street crime counterparts. The only difference was their standing in the community. The acts are just differing manifestations of the same problem: a lack of self-control.

The final piece that is missing is what contributes to a person's level of self-control. According to Gottfredson and Hirschi, self-control is a trait or enduring personality characteristic that is established early in a person's life (the first five to eight years). In order for a person to develop higher levels of self-control, three conditions of child rearing or parental management must be present. These include monitoring of the child; recognition of deviant behavior whenever it occurs; and an appropriate punishment for inappropriate behavior. In short, Gottfredson's and Hirschi's theory claims that inadequate parental management results in a person who is low in self-control, which, in turn, influences this person's choice when faced with any number of opportunities for immediate gain or pleasure. Often these opportunities are illegal in nature. It is important to point out that as a control theory, we must remember that low self-control is not a result of parenting, but rather, it is a consequence of a lack of proper parental management. Gottfredson and Hirschi would argue that, left to their own devices, everyone would lack self-control, and the role of par-

BOX 11.2 (Continued)

ents is to properly socialize their children. This is in stark contrast to social learning theories that claim that individuals learn how to become criminal.

While the number of studies addressing this theory is growing, few studies focus on the key element of parental management and how it can be empirically tested. If the theory has merit, one can see the obvious policy implications. As a society, we must do everything possible to help parents more effectively socialize their young children. According to this theory, we only have the first five to eight years of a child's life to do this, and the onus is on the parents rather than the schools or other social agencies. It is by no stretch of the imagination an easy undertaking but once again, one of the appealing aspects is that even if the theory is not found to be effective in predicting future criminal activity, anything done to strengthen the ability of parents to better socialize their young children can be seen as a positive social change.

Advice to Students:

I hope all students in our field are just as enthusiastic as I am about addressing the causes of criminal behavior. If you are truly interested in doing something about this problem, then it is imperative that you first have a deep understanding of the possible causes of such behavior. The many differing theoretical perspectives in our discipline are an attempt to do just that. They must be studied, scrutinized, analyzed, and further refined if our efforts are ever going to be successful. As an added benefit, anyone taking a careful look at these theories will gain a much better understanding of the differing social backgrounds of persons living in our complex society. We all naturally see things from our own perspective. To be effective at promoting change, we must, to coin a phrase, see the world through someone else's eyes to fully understand what their lives are like. We cannot just pass judgment and expect everyone to act as we might.

when people cease to believe that the group they associate with is important and/or exhibits the right values or standards, a weakening of the bond occurs (Le, 2002). It may be that a delinquent gang can lure youths away from conventional groups by permitting them to develop close attachments and involvements in delinquent gang activity. A type of rivalry occurs between one's conventional bonds and the developing bonds of less conventional social groups.

Hirschi's social control theory builds upon the differential association theory developed by Sutherland. Sutherland's dimensions of intensity and priority appear closely related to Hirschi's notions of attachment, commitment, and involvement (Chung et al., 2002). While Sutherland attempted to account for white-collar crime, Hirschi has used his bonding theory to explain juvenile delinquency. In Hirschi's investigation of a sample of junior and senior high school youth in California, he found that those students who exhibited strong attitudes and attachments to teachers and school officials were less inclined to engage in delinquent activity. These were also those earning higher grades and making a more successful adjustment to the rigors of school work than students with weaker bonds. As for youths engaged in delinquent activity, Hirschi found that they were frequently the poor performers academically, disliked school, and had few positive experiences with school faculty and officials (Hirschi, 1969).

Hirschi's theory has been criticized for several reasons. First, it fails to specify the precise relation between these bonding dimensions and conventional and non-conventional conduct. Many youths have attachments to both conventional and nonconventional groups, and yet, no clear pattern of delinquency or nondelinquency emerges as a result. Which dimensions have the greatest weight in predicting deviant conduct? What are the roles of parents and church officials in the lives of these youths? How does social class function as an explanatory variable?

Social control theory is strongly psychological, since it holds that one's mental attachments and beliefs are critical in linking the individual to society's conventional norms (Heubner and Betts, 2002). This theory may explain why certain individuals reject conventional behavior for deviant conduct, but it cannot be used to predict which youths among large groups will turn to crime (Unnever, Cullen, and Pratt, 2003). Hirschi's emphasis on school experiences is an inherent weakness, since it does not account for bonding processes that take place outside of school settings (Stewart, 2003). Its application is restricted to explaining deviance among adolescents who are in school.

Conflict/Marxist Theory. Sometimes called **Marxist criminology, conflict criminology, conflict theory, critical criminology,** or **radical criminology, conflict/Marxist theory** explains criminal conduct by focusing our attention on the people who have the political power to define crime for the rest of society. According to this theory, the masses can be divided into the have-nots, the poor people who are manipulated and controlled by the haves, the rich and powerful people who have vested interests in capital, industry, and business.

Statistically, persons in the lower socioeconomic strata are arrested more frequently than those in the upper socioeconomic strata. These facts do not mean that those in the lower socioeconomic categories commit more crime. Instead, these statistics show that the ruling elite has targeted these poor people for harassment. This harassment is a strategy for maintaining the status quo and preserving existing societal arrangements that perpetuate and legitimize the power of the "haves". This theory also asserts that one reason for the formal creation of the police in 1829 was to protect the interests of those in power. These interests exert considerable influence on how crime is defined. Vagrancy and loitering laws were created, in part, as a means for keeping people from wandering about, looking for better jobs and work (Lilly, Cullen, and Ball, 2002).

Conflict/Marxist theory is a general scheme to account for societal characteristics. It does not explain individual behaviors or the behavior of small groups. It is not linked with any particular social process of acquiring criminal behaviors, and it defines criminal behavior as the result of legislative definitions created by the rich and powerful (Pratt and Lowenkamp, 2002). To use this theory for creating a specific plan to deal with crime and influence the lives of probationers and parolees, we would have to change our basic social and economic structure.

Reality Therapy

Reality therapy was created by William Glasser (1976). Glasser was a psychiatrist by training and accepted developmental theory as an explanation of deviant conduct up to a point. Glasser rejected the developmental theoretical explanation that once a cause is known for a particular criminal behavior, the problem can be dealt with by having the probationer/parolee/client understand the problem's origins. Reality therapy is a confrontational method of behavior modification where one's criminality is simply unacceptable to a PO. Glasser contends that all persons are born with two primary psychological needs. There is a need for love and a need for acceptance, self-worth, or recognition. Those POs who practice reality therapy must acquire the trust of their clients and get close to them emotionally. POs must therefore cultivate a tentative friendship between themselves and their clients, so that their clients can feel free to disclose things about themselves.

POs using reality therapy must get emotionally involved with their clients. The PO is not interested in trying to understand one's prior circumstances and what led to their present circumstances. The focus is upon the present, and the intent of the PO is to assist clients in evaluating their behavior and why it is unacceptable. Thus, it is unimportant to know the etiology of one's criminality. All too often, this is used as a crutch by the client. Many clients love to rationalize their conduct as being the product of a miserable childhood or poor upbringing or bad social circumstances in their school years.

Reality therapy works best if the PO is able to establish a support group of several clients. Sympathy and excuses are rejected. The PO does not label the client as sick or disturbed. Rather, there are problems that are unacceptable and they need to be dealt with and resolved. The PO is an enabler in this regard. Glasser says the POs can assist their clients by helping them devise better plans for the future. Where appropriate, the PO should lavish the client with praise for acceptable, law-abiding conduct as a reinforcement.

Reality therapy has been criticized because some clients feel uncomfortable disclosing things about themselves on an intimate level (Marsh and Walsh, 1995). For some clients, they prefer rejecting a PO's help rather than risk accepting it, because they expect to be disappointed when the therapy doesn't work. POs who work hard to cultivate close relationships with clients may actually drive them away emotionally. Therefore, reality therapy is an intervention that should be used only by selected POs who are qualified and disposed to working with hard-to-manage offenders.

SOCIAL CASEWORK

Social casework is an intervention technique that is service-oriented. It is the development of a relation between the PO and his or her clients with a problem-solving context, and coordinated with the appropriate use of community resources. Social casework rests on three basic tenets: (1) assessment, or gathering and analyzing relevant information on which to base a plan for one's client; (2) planning, or thinking about and organizing facts into a meaningful, goal-oriented explanation; and (3) intervention, or implementation of the plan.

Social casework is a product of social work, which emerged as an intervention strategy during the 1920s. Important to social workers are human relations skills and the capacity to mobilize community resources to assist clients. POs who use the social casework method for assisting their clients attempt to find solutions for their problems that interfere with or minimize their effectiveness as persons. If parolees or probationers have difficulty seeking and maintaining continuous employment, social caseworker-POs can assist them in resolving problems that may be inhibiting them from being successful in this regard.

Good social caseworkers acquire understandings of their clients and attempt to assist them in developing constructive solutions to their problems. They are concerned with client self-esteem and feelings of self-worth. They want clients to be able to function apart from the caseworker. Thus, they provide clients with encouragement and moral support, together with necessary training from community resources. They are reassuring and believe strongly in counseling and guidance as strategies for coping and behavioral changes.

WHICH THEORY IS BEST? AN EVALUATION

Theories about Adult Offenders

There is no single theory to explain crime or criminal conduct that is universally accepted by all researchers as the best one. Each theory has strengths and weaknesses and has exerted varying degrees of influence on the criminal justice system in processing offenders. Two important criteria for evaluating theories of criminal behavior are the extent to which they enable us to explain and predict that behavior. An evaluation of these theories suggests that creating a satisfactory theory stringently meeting these criteria is quite difficult.

Most of the theories presented, regardless of whether they were biological, psychological, or sociological, emphasized single-factor causation. One factor (e.g., glands, genes, improper or inadequate ego development, or anomie) was usually featured as the chief cause of criminal behavior, and all other factors were either subordinated or ignored.

One problem with evaluating these theories is that, often, the historical context in which they were generated is overlooked. As we have already seen, Cesare Lombroso's work on the relation between physique and criminal behavior was devised during the time when Charles Darwin's *Origin of the Species* was popular. Biological evolution was considered to be an important explanation for certain kinds of social behaviors in the 1870s as well as for the next several decades. Assessing Lombroso's work in view of our current knowledge makes his theorizing seem comical. In contrast, psychologists investigated the influence of an air pollutant, ozone, on criminal behavior in 1987. James Rotton, a psychologist at Florida International University has estimated that every year, ozone provokes hundreds of cases of family violence in large cities with bad air (Londer, 1987:6). How will this theory be viewed by criminologists and others 100 years from now?

In all likelihood, criminal behavior is the result of a combination of these factors. It is insufficient to rely entirely upon a single cause for such a complex phenomenon. There are criminals of every size and shape and variety. The same crimes such as murder or robbery are committed by many different kinds of people for a variety of reasons. It may be that in time of war, murdering the enemy will cause someone to be a hero, whereas murder in other contexts and at other times would be punished severely. However, there is a problem with developing conglomerate or "holistic" theories, because they may not be theories at all in the formal sense.

Obviously, explanations advanced by Lombroso and Sheldon attaching significance to one's body structure have little or no predictive value. We cannot look at someone and determine from their physical features whether they are criminals or will become criminals. Also, genetic structure fails to explain and predict criminal behavior. Theories emphasizing the id, ego, and superego as crucial determinants of social conduct are very difficult to test empirically. Such phenomena cannot be extracted from persons and dissected and examined microscopically. If we rigorously apply the standards of science and empiricism and subject all explanations advanced to the most scrupulous experiments and tests, all theories of criminal behavior presented in this chapter fail such tests.

Theories about Delinquency

Assessing the importance or significance of theories of delinquency is difficult. First, almost all causes of delinquent conduct that have been advocated by experts during the past century continue to interest contemporary investigators (Garbarino et al., 2002). The most frequently discounted and consistently criticized views are the biological ones, although as we have seen, sociobiology and genetic concomitants of delinquent conduct persist to raise unanswered questions about the role of heredity in the delinquency equation. Psychological explanations seem more plausible than biological ones, although the precise relation between the psyche and biological factors remains unknown. If we focus upon psychological explanations of delinquency as important in fostering delinquent conduct, almost invariably we involve certain elements of one's social world in such explanations. Thus, one's mental processes are influenced in various ways by one's social experiences. Self-definitions, important to psychologists and learning theorists, are conceived largely in social contexts, in the presence of and through contact with others. It is not surprising, therefore, that the most fruitful explanations for delinquency are those that seek to blend the best parts of different theories that assess different dimensions of youths, their physique and intellectual abilities, personalities, and social experiences. Intellectual isolationism or complete reliance on either biological factors exclusively or psychological factors exclusively or sociological factors exclusively may simplify theory construction, but in the final analysis, such isolationism is unproductive. Certainly, each field has importance and makes a contribution toward explaining why some youths exhibit delinquent conduct and why others do not. Applying a purely pragmatic approach in assessing the predictive and/or explanatory utility of each of these theories, we may examine contemporary interventionist efforts that seek to curb delinquency or prevent its resurgence.

FIGURE 11.2   Teen boys shoplifting.
Courtesy of Jim Smith, Photo Researchers, Inc.

Program successes are often used as gauges of the successfulness of their underlying theoretical schemes (Stouthamer-Loeber and Loeber, 2002). Since no program is 100 percent effective at preventing delinquency, it follows that no theoretical scheme devised thus far is fully effective. Yet, the wide variety of programs that are applied today to deal with different kinds of juvenile offenders indicates that most psychological and sociological approaches have some merit and contribute differentially to delinquency reduction. As we will see in subsequent chapters, policy decisions are made throughout the juvenile justice system and are often contingent upon the theoretical views adopted by politicians, law enforcement personnel, prosecutors and judges, and correctional officials at every stage of the justice process. For the present, we may appreciate most views because of their varying intuitive value and selectively apply particular approaches to accommodate different types of juvenile offenders.

A bottom line concerning theories of delinquency generally is that their impact has been felt most strongly in the area of policy making rather than in behavioral change or modification. Virtually every theory is connected in some respect to various types of experimental programs in different jurisdictions. The intent of most programs has been to change behaviors of participants. However, high rates of recidivism characterize all delinquency prevention innovations, regardless of their intensity or ingenuity. Policy decisions implemented at earlier points have long-range implications for present policies in correctional work. Probationers and parolees as well as inmates and divertees, adults and juveniles alike, are recipients or inheritors of previous policies laid in place by theorists who have attempted to convert their theories into practical experiences and action.

Current policy in juvenile justice favors the "get-tough" orientation, and programs are increasingly sponsored that heavily incorporate accountability and individual responsibility elements. In the past, projects emphasizing rehabilitation and reintegration were rewarded more heavily through private grants and various types of government funding. No particular prevention or intervention or supervision program works best. Numerous contrasting perspectives about how policy should be shaped continue to vie for recognition among professionals and politicians. The theories that have been described here are indicative of the many factors that have shaped our present policies and practices.

TREATMENT PROGRAMS AND THEORIES

One way of evaluating these theories is to examine the successes that have resulted when these theories have been applied at various stages of the criminal justice process (Burke, Loeber, and Mutchka, 2002). Which theories seem to be most influential in formulating policies in our various correctional institutions? Which theories receive the most consistent emphasis and support from foundations that underwrite research projects examining the causes of criminal behavior? To identify which theories seem most popular, it might be helpful to study parole board hearings. Parole boards determine whether incarcerated prisoners should be released before serving their full sentences. Parole boards consider many factors in deciding whether an offender should be released. Did the inmate behave properly in prison? Did they exhibit any unusual behavioral disorders? What is the likelihood that these offenders will be able to cope effectively with life on the "outside"? Halfway houses, places where parolees can stay temporarily in the community until they can find appropriate employment and housing, were created to help offenders adjust to life outside prison.

Have inmates had vocational training or group therapy or rehabilitative counseling? What are the reports of the counselors who interacted with these inmates and listened to their problems? All answers to these questions combine to form a release quotient or **salient factor score.** This is a numerical value that predicts an inmate's chances of living on the outside in the community with others and not committing new crimes (Wolf, 2002).

Differential association theory seems influential in parole decisions and the conditions prescribed for parolees. For instance, persons who are paroled are required not to associate with other known criminals as one of several parole conditions. But many parolees violate this condition because the community has labeled them as ex-convicts. This community rejection makes it difficult for these former criminals to obtain employment. Thus, in a sense, society compels these persons to seek social attachments with other criminals. This frustrates their efforts to go straight and refrain from further criminal activity (Hammett, Roberts, and Kennedy, 2001).

One way of determining which delinquency theories are most popular and/or influence policy and administrative decision making relative to juveniles is to catalog the ways offenders are treated by the juvenile justice system after their apprehension by police or others. A preliminary screening of juvenile offenders may result in some being diverted from the juvenile justice system. One manifest purpose of such diversionary action is to reduce the potentially adverse influence of labeling on these youths. A long-term objective of diversion is to minimize recidivism among divertees. While some experts contend that the intended effects of diversion, such as a reduction in the degree of social stigmatization toward status offenders, are presently unclear, inconsistent, and insufficiently documented, other professionals endorse diversion programs and regard them as effective in preventing further delinquent conduct among first-offenders. In fact, the preponderance of evidence from a survey of available literature is that diversion, while not fully effective at preventing delinquent recidivism, nevertheless tends to reduce it substantially (Hubner and Wolfson, 2000).

Besides using diversion per se with or without various programs, there are elements or overtones of other theoretical schemes that may be present in the particular treatments or experiences juveniles receive as they continue to be processed throughout the juvenile justice system. At the time of adjudication, for example, juvenile judges may or may not impose special conditions to accompany a sentence of probation. Special conditions may refer to obligating juveniles to make restitution to victims, to perform public services, to participate in group or individual therapy, or to undergo medical treatment in cases of drug addiction or alcohol abuse. Some investigators have suggested that those youths who receive probation accompanied by special conditions are less likely to recidivate compared with those youths who receive probation unconditionally (Wilson and Petersilia, 2002).

Learning to accept responsibility for one's actions, acquiring new coping skills to face crises and personal tragedy, improving one's educational attainment, and improving one's ego strength to resist the influence of one's delinquent peers are individually or collectively integral parts of various delinquency treatment programs, particularly where the psychological approach is strong.

Several psychologists have conducted an extensive review of group therapy literature as applied to the treatment of juvenile delinquents (McKean and Raphael, 2002). They conclude that group therapy is particularly effective for more aggressive adolescents. They also report that much of the research surveyed is conducted in residential settings, such as group homes. In these less traditional, nonthreatening circumstances, juveniles seem to be more amenable to behavioral change and improved conduct.

During the late 1970s, a program known as "Getting It Together" was established in a large city juvenile court jurisdiction (Carpenter and Sugrue, 1984). The program emphasized a combination of affective (emotional) and social skills training designed to assist those with immature personalities and who exhibited neurotic behaviors. Over the next several years, many delinquent youths participated in this program. A majority reported improved self-esteem and socially mature behavior, better communication skills with authorities and parents, greater self-control, more positive values, and more adequate job skills. Ego strength levels for most participating youths improved, as did the quality of peer relationships and a reduction of various sexual problems. This program, in addition to other similar enterprises, has been guided to a great degree by social learning theory (Benda, 2002).

SUMMARY

Theories explain and predict relationships between various phenomena. Criminologists theorize about criminal behavior and describe the characteristics of persons convicted of crimes as well as their motives. Efforts are made to determine whether criminals have the necessary *mens rea* or guilty mind or criminal disposition in the crimes they commit. Nineteenth century biological theories of criminal behavior stressed the importance of physical characteristics as indicators of criminal propensities. One biological theory determined that criminal behavior was hereditary. Other biological explanations focused upon body type as a predictor. These theories have been discounted. Biochemical imbalance or glandular problems were also believed linked with criminal conduct, although no consistent evidence exists to support such beliefs.

Psychoanalytic theory developed by Freud emphasizes early selfish behaviors of infants that sometimes remain uncontrolled as children grow older. The id, or "I want" part of the personality remains unchecked by the ego, or that part of the personality that includes the standards and conventional rules of society. Again, criminal behavior is one predictable result. The psychological theory of moral development emphasizes developmental stages in the lives of children. As they grow and mature, they incorporate into their personality systems certain socially acceptable behavior patterns. Sometimes, disruptions occur in these stages, and criminal conduct results.

Sociological or sociocultural theories of criminal behavior stress social and environmental factors as influential in promoting criminal conduct. One sociological theory, anomie, is that people experience a conflict between aspiring to achieve socially acceptable goals and the culturally approved means to achieve those goals. People adapt to this conflict in different ways. Some persons engage in innovative or unconventional behavior to achieve desired objectives. Another sociological theory is labeling. According to this theory, deviance is whatever a group says it is. Labeling theory involves no moral judgments of criminal actions. Rather, attention is directed at social definitions of criminal behavior and a person's responses to being labeled as criminal.

An evaluation of these theories may be made according to several criteria. Can we predict criminal behavior by using them? Which are most useful for helping us to understand why people commit crimes? In addition to evaluating their usefulness in predicting crime, these theories can be evaluated by considering the importance each is given in various sectors of the criminal justice system. Counseling programs and group therapy and rehabilitative practices in prison settings are strongly influenced by psychological theories. Correctional institutional policies and guidelines are influenced strongly by differential association theory and the labeling perspective. Finally, single-factor explanations of criminal behavior have inherent weaknesses, because they highlight one variable or circumstance and ignore others. The best explanations are those that combine the best elements of several theoretical schemes.

There are several theories of delinquency. Similar to theories about adult criminality, theories of delinquency may be grouped into biological, psychological, and sociological explanations. Biological theories strongly imply a causal relation between physique and other genetic phenomena and delinquent behaviors. Psychological theories include psychoanalytic theory devised by Sigmund Freud and promoted by others. Social learning theory is similar to psychoanalytic theory, although it stresses imitation of significant others.

A popular sociological view of delinquency is labeling theory. Those who engage in wrongdoing may come to adopt self-definitions as delinquents, particularly if significant others and the police define them as delinquents. Having frequent contact with the juvenile justice system enhances such labeling for many youths. Labeling theorists often argue that delinquents are acting out the behaviors others expect from them. Closely related to labeling theory is bonding theory, where juveniles develop either close or distant attachments to schools, teachers, and peers. Delinquency is regarded as a function of inadequate bonding or a weakening of social attachments. Other theories include containment theory, neutralization or drift theory, and differential association. Each of these views suggests the power or attraction of group processes in the onset of delinquent conduct.

Theories of delinquency are often evaluated according to how they influence public policy relating to juvenile conduct and its prevention or treatment. Diversionary programs that prevent further juvenile contact with the juvenile justice system are influenced largely by labeling theory, since it is believed that youths will become more deeply entrenched in juvenile conduct to the extent that they are exposed to the formal system and juvenile courts. Individual and group therapy, often a part of treatment programs for errant juveniles, seek to use ego development strategies coupled with various learning methods to improve self-definitions, reduce antisocial behaviors, and promote more healthy attitudes toward others. Programs that emphasize personal responsibility for one's actions or encourage youths to become more active in decision making seem to make a difference in reducing recidivism among program participants. No theory is universally accepted, however.

QUESTIONS FOR REVIEW

1. What is theory? What is the importance of prediction and explanation as critical components of theory in explaining criminal or delinquent conduct?

2. What are some differences between labeling theory and differential association theory? Which theory directs attention to the nature of the crime committed? Which theory directs attention to the societal reaction toward the offender? Which theory do you feel is the more "sociological" of the two?

3. What evidence exists to support the idea that body type has something to do with the causes of criminal behavior? What evidence has been provided to show support for the relation between body types and criminal behavior?

4. How do biochemical disturbances relate to criminal conduct?

5. What is meant by psychoanalytic theory? How do the id, ego, superego, and libido influence criminal conduct?

6. What is a delinquent subculture? How does a delinquent subculture explain how delinquency originates and is perpetuated over time?

7. What is differential association theory? What are several key components of it?

8. What is meant by anomie theory? What are the modes of adaptation? How does the innovative mode relate to crime and criminal conduct?

9. What is the labeling process whereby someone becomes deviant? What factors seem to be most important in this theoretical explanation of criminal behavior? What are the basic assumptions or principles of labeling theory?

10. How do we know which theories of crime and delinquency are best and which ones should be used to explain criminal or delinquent conduct? What is the relation between different treatment programs for delinquents and adult offenders and theories that explain delinquent or criminal conduct?

SUGGESTED READINGS

Hunter, Ronald D. and Mark L. Dantzker (2002). *Crime and Criminality: Causes and Consequences.* Upper Saddle River, NJ: Prentice Hall.

Lilly, J. Robert, Francis T. Cullen, and Richard Ball (2002). *Criminological Theory: Context and Consequences.* Thousand Oaks, CA: Sage.

Maguire, Mike, Rod Morgan, and Robert Reiner (2002). *The Oxford Handbook of Criminology.* New York: Oxford University Press.

Rowe, David C. (2002). *Biology and Crime.* Los Angeles: Roxbury.

Schmalleger, Frank (2002). *Criminology Today* (3rd ed.). Upper Saddle River, NJ: Prentice Hall.

INTERNET CONNECTIONS

Advances in Criminological Theory
http://www.newark.rutgers.edu/rscj/journals/advances.htm

Criminological Theory on the Web
http://www.home.attbi.com/~ddemelo/crime/crimetheory.html

Criminology theory
http://www.roxbury.net/crimtheorypast2.html

North Carolina Department of Corrections Offender Treatment Programs
http://www.doc.state.nc.us/Substance/Treatmen.htm

Offender treatment programs
http://www.house.state.mo.us/bills/HB407.htm

Sex Offenders Treatment Program
http://www.auditor.leg.state.mn.us/sexoff.htm

Understanding Criminological theory
http://www.faculty.ncwc.edu/toconnor/301/crimtheo.htm

CHAPTER 12 | *Offender Supervision: Types of Offenders and Special Supervisory Considerations*

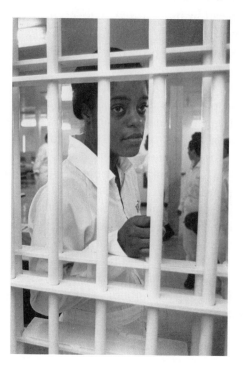

Chapter Outline

Chapter Objectives
Introduction
Special-Needs Offenders:
   An Overview
Mentally Ill Offenders
Gang Members

Sex Offenders
Offenders with HIV/AIDS
Substance-Abusing Offenders
Community Programs for
   Special-Needs Offenders

Summary
Questions for Review
Suggested Readings
Internet Connections

Chapter Objectives

As the result of reading this chapter, the following objectives will be realized:

1. Understanding the general nature and composition of the special-needs offender population.
2. Understanding the problems of mentally ill offenders on probation and parole.
3. Describing HIV/AIDS and drug/alcohol dependent offenders and the supervisory problems they pose for POs.
4. Describing gang members and how POs supervise them.
5. Understanding sex offenders and other special-needs offenders and the various programs used to treat them.
6. Understanding therapeutic communities and their relevance for special-needs offenders.
7. Describing drug courts and the drug court movement.
8. Describing various interventions, including the idea of the therapeutic community.
9. Understanding the functions of Alcoholics Anonymous, Narcotics Anonymous, and Gamblers Anonymous.
10. Describing gang members, their characteristics, and tattoo removal programs.

• *Rick H. is an alcoholic in Philadelphia, Pennsylvania. He began drinking when he was 12. He stole liquor from the liquor cabinet of his parents' bar at home, and he carefully refilled the liquor bottle with water after drinking alcohol from it. He was drunk a lot of the time while he was in high school. When he graduated from high school, he went to college where he continued to drink. After his freshman year in college, he returned home and went out with some boyhood friends. He went to a bar with them, used a false ID to gain entry, and got drunk. At some point during the evening, one of the young men said something about robbing a liquor store, getting some booze and money. Rick H. went along. One of Rick H.'s friends had a .45 caliber automatic pistol that belonged to his father. Rick H. was too drunk to drive and simply sat in the car, while two of his friends went into a liquor store at 11:00 P.M. and robbed it. The liquor store owner was a little slow opening the cash drawer and Rick's friend with the gun shot the store clerk in the chest, killing him instantly. As they drove away from the scene, they crossed over the double line on a nearby highway and had a head-on collision with another car. Although no one was seriously injured in the potentially serious accident, the youths were captured by police and linked to the liquor store shooting, which had just been reported. The .45 automatic was recovered from the wrecked car, including the cash stolen. Rick H. was charged with felony murder. In a plea bargain, he pleaded guilty to involuntary manslaughter and received a prison sentence of 10 years. While in prison, he has participated in Alcoholics Anonymous meetings, received substance-abuse counseling, and other treatment. He is now on parole attending community-based centers for his problems. Rick H. admits that he is powerless when it comes to alcohol. He needs a strong support system to keep him from drinking. Rick is a special-needs offender.*

• *Tyrone R. is a drug dealer in Detroit, Michigan. Tyrone R. began his career in drugs by being a lookout for a gang when he was 7 years of age. Now he is 22 and a full-fledged drug dealer. He makes about $3,000 a day in drug sales. On occasion he has used force,* *including knives and guns, to make his different clients pay for their drugs. Tyrone R. is still a gang member. He continues to associate with many of his old gang friends, some of whom use his drugs. Tyrone sells ecstasy, marijuana, crack cocaine, and heroin. Tyrone uses heroin himself and is addicted to this substance. Recently, Tyrone R. was arrested by Detroit police on a drug possession charge. He was convicted and is now serving a 5-year sentence in the state penitentiary. Tyrone R. is a special-needs offender.*

* *Abraham G. is a paraplegic. He was wounded in the back during the Gulf War in the early 1990s and is very bitter about his disability and the meager benefits he receives from the government. Confined to a wheelchair, Abraham G. decided to rob a bank to get the kind of money he thinks he needs to live comfortably. One afternoon he wheeled himself into a local bank branch and handed the teller a note, telling her that he had a gun and wanted all of the money in her cash drawer. He collected about $3,500 and wheeled himself out of the bank. A few blocks later, he was stopped by a passing cruiser and arrested for the bank robbery. He was found to be unarmed. The money was recovered. His case was turned over to the FBI. Under a federal plea bargain with the U.S. Attorney's Office, Abraham G. pled guilty to simple robbery. Under the U.S. Sentencing Guidelines, Abraham G. was given a sentence of 36 to 48 months. He is now serving his second year in a federal prison. Abraham G., who has no substance-abuse problems, is not affiliated with any gang, and is not mentally disabled, is a special-needs offender.*

INTRODUCTION

This chapter is about special-needs offenders, the types of problems they create for those who house them in prisons or jails or supervise them in communities on probation or parole, and the programs designed to assist them to live reasonably normal lives. POs supervise an increasingly diverse clientele. In the 1950s and 1960s, POs enjoyed far greater predictability in their work than today. Conventional distinctions were made between property offenders (e.g., burglars, thieves, those convicted of vehicular theft) and violent offenders, or those who committed crimes against the person (e.g., homicide, aggravated assault, forcible rape, and robbery). Although there always have been offenders with problems, substance abuse, mental illness, and communicable diseases have become pervasive in American society, especially since the 1970s (Hammett, Harmon, and Rhodes, 2002). Contemporary probationers and parolees as clients have special problems and are in need of unconventional services and resources.

In 2002, for instance, an estimated 283,800 mentally ill offenders were incarcerated in U.S. prisons and jails. Among probationers that same year, 570,000 were identified as mentally ill, while 475,000 reported a mental or emotional condition, and 285,000 had been admitted overnight to a mental hospital for treatment (Glaze, 2003). Over half of all mentally ill clients have prior histories in jails and prisons of institutional violence. It is not unexpected, therefore, that such violence will carry over into their probation and parole programs as a part of a continuing pattern. Relatively little has been done to intervene and assist mentally ill inmates and PO clients. They continue to pose supervisory hazards for their POs, largely because of their unpredictability. Thus, the first part of this chapter examines mentally ill offenders who are under PO supervision.

A growing segment of the offender population both within and without the prison setting are gang members. Gang members present supervision problems for POs for a variety of reasons. One of these reasons is that gangs tend to form subcultures with strong group norms. In turn, these norms create a substantial resistance to change. Thus, when POs attempt to intervene in the lives of gang members and help them become more law-abiding, they often encounter subcultural barriers that are gang-generated. Thus, the process of coping with gang-affiliated clients will be discussed. Some of the strategies for overcoming resistance to change will be highlighted, including recently developed tattoo removal programs.

A third type of criminal POs supervise is the sex offender. Some of these sex offenders are child sexual abusers. They may be required to avoid frequenting areas where small children are located, such as schools and parks. While sex offenders are not especially abundant, there are sufficient numbers such that POs assigned to supervise them must pay particular attention to their whereabouts and activities. Many sex offenders are obligated to attend individual and group counseling and participate in sex offender programs as a part of their special parole and probation program conditions. These activities require continuous monitoring by attentive POs. Also, these offenders cannot be monitored on a 24/7 basis, and thus their freedom to roam about in their communities means that they may be able to reoffend without their PO's knowledge at different times. Problems of monitoring sex offenders will also be examined.

A fourth type of offender is one infected with the HIV virus, which may lead to AIDS. Increased numbers of AIDS/HIV cases have occurred, largely because of indiscriminate drug use, needle-sharing, and/or unprotected sex. Prisons and jails are optimum breeding grounds for the transmission of AIDS/HIV, since they place offenders in close proximity with one another where stronger offenders can sexually exploit the weaker ones (although some same-sex relations are consensual). Furthermore, AIDS/HIV is not restricted to the male inmate population. Female inmates are exhibiting increased rates of AIDS/HIV in recent years. Therefore, POs are supervising increased numbers of clients with such communicable diseases as AIDS/HIV. However, tuberculosis among offenders has increased in the United States in recent years as well. This is a highly contagious disease and presents greater dangers for POs, since it can be transmitted more easily than AIDS/HIV. For POs, supervising POs with tuberculosis places them at far greater risk. AIDS/HIV offender-clients will be described, as well as the special supervisory provisions for POs who must monitor them.

Another category of offender is developmentally disabled. Persons who are developmentally disabled have physical impairments that impede their normal functioning. The wheelchair bank robber described in one of this chapter's opening scenarios is such an offender. These offenders have disabilities that require special care and handling on the part of those who supervise them. Other types of disabilities may include heart disease, diabetes, high blood pressure, and other related ailments. Special provisions must be made for such offenders, regardless of whether they are in prisons or jails or in their communities under the supervision of POs.

By far the largest category of offenders in need of close supervision are substance abusers. Substance abuse is considered the single most important problem among probation and parole offenders. It has been estimated that between 55 and 80 percent of all probationers and parolees have been involved with drugs or alcohol, and that illicit substances were involved in their original offenses. The incidence of relapse is especially high for substance-abusing offenders, and POs must devise innovative strategies for the supervision. Because substance-abusing offenders are so prevalent within the probationer and parolee community, and because of the unique problems they pose for their supervising POs, improved screening mechanisms have been devised to detect illegal drug use of offenders under supervision. POs have had to work harder to link these offenders with necessary community services so that they can receive appropriate therapy and treatment. Furthermore, they are inclined to relapse at high rates. This means that POs must be more vigilant at detecting relapses and rapidly moving to control such behavior when it occurs.

One response to greater drug use among offenders has been the development of specialized courts to deal only with drug abusers. These are drug courts, and they provide therapies and recommended programs to involve those most in need of treatment and community services. They also make provisions for followup monitoring by POs as well as appropriate sanctions if their relapses are chronic or repetitive over time. These drug courts will be described, including their operations and services. POs increasingly rely on therapeutic communities, or treatment models which emphasize integrated community services at several different levels to meet the complex needs of substance-abusing offenders and others. Therapeutic communities and their functions will be described. A part of the therapeutic community are interventions such as Alcoholics Anonymous for those with alcohol addictions; Narcotics Anonymous for those with drug dependencies; and Gambler's Anonymous for those addicted to gambling. Therapeutic communities also exist for developmentally disabled, handicapped, and/or mentally retarded offenders. These programs will be described.

SPECIAL-NEEDS OFFENDERS: AN OVERVIEW

In this section, an overview of **special-needs offenders** is presented. This overview is intended to describe the various types of offender populations that POs supervise. When certain probationers and parolees have serious needs and dependencies, this requires special services from POs and an extraordinary amount of care and supervision. In some probation and parole agencies, special assignments are made to certain POs with skills relevant for those clients with particular disabilities or problems. These are referred to as specialized caseloads. Many probation and parole departments do not have the resources or personpower to allocate POs for specialized services. Thus, POs must supervise all offenders, regardless of whether they have special problems requiring unconventional community intervention, assistance, or programming.

The first part of this section will describe problems of coping with special-needs offenders. What must POs do to manage or supervise offenders with serious dependencies and other problems? What are the pressures on POs to monitor these offenders closely? What should POs do when they detect program violations among those most likely to relapse and commit program violations? There are no easy answers to these questions. As each offender aggregate is described, some idea of the magnitude of the problem is also presented. Thus, we are sensitized to just how significant a problem these offenders pose for their supervising POs. In subsequent sections of this chapter, these different types of special-needs offenders are examined in closer detail. In these latter sections, several interventions and community programs are also presented that are used in conjunction with their supervision.

Coping with Special-Needs Offenders

Any correctional program, whether it is institutional corrections or community-based corrections, will inevitably have to deal with and make provisions for special-needs offenders. Special-needs offenders include physically, mentally, psychologically, or socially impaired or handicapped offenders who require extraordinary care and supervision. Sometimes, elderly offenders are classified as special-needs offenders to the extent that they might require special diets, medicines, or environments. Mental retardation, illiteracy, and physical disabilities are some of the many kinds of problems associated with special-needs offenders. Some definitions of special-needs offenders include women, although female offenders and their problems and programs are treated elsewhere (Gowdy et al., 1998). Operators of community-based correctional facilities face continual dilemmas over the need to accommodate these offenders in special facilities and the need to move offender-clients generally into mainstream society and assist them to live independently.

Regarding the provisions for special-needs offenders in many community corrections programs, major problems have been identified, including lack of access to adequate mental health services, inadequate information and training among court and corrections personnel, and insufficient interagency coordination and cooperation (Bowen et al., 2002). In more than a few instances, some of these inmates have attempted suicide or have assaulted other inmates. Some suicide attempts have been successful, and some inmate assaults have been fatal (Canada Solicitor General, 1998; Victoria Department of Criminal Justice Services, 1998). Some community corrections facilities are linked closely with other close-custody prisons, such as the Massachusetts Correctional Institution (MCI) for women at Framingham. The Framingham institution, which houses 530 female convicts, offers assistance in the following areas: (1) mental health counseling; (2) substance abuse treatment; (3) parenting and family services; (4) employment planning, education, and vocational counseling; and (5) health screenings, treatment and referrals (American Correctional Association, 1994). These services seem offender-relevant, since a lack of education and drug abuse are two of the major obstacles to finding employment.

In Texas, for example, a Special Needs Parole Program has been established to provide for an early parole review for special health needs offenders who require 24-hour skilled nursing care. Between 1995 and 1999, for instance, the number of cases screened for the program declined markedly by 54 percent, as did those referred to the parole board for early release. Those released on Special Needs Parole declined by 67 percent. These declines were attributable to ineffective and inadequate screening procedures as well as tougher parole criteria. It was found that over 50 percent of all referred cases in 1999 were simply ineligible for parole because of Texas statutes. However, 38 percent were referred for parole anyway, and of these, 22 percent were granted early release (Texas Criminal Justice Policy Council, 2000).

Almost contemporaneously with the Texas Special Needs Program, an independent survey was undertaken of U.S. state prisons from 1991 to 1997. It was found that the number of inmates aged 50 and over increased by 115 percent during this period, while the overall prison population grew by almost 84 percent. It was also found that increasing numbers of prisons were housing special-needs offenders, older offenders with health problems, and disabled inmates in special prison areas or including them in programs specifically designed for their conditions (Edwards, 1998). This means that Texas and perhaps other jurisdictions are retaining more special-needs offenders for longer prison terms, although corrections officials are having to make special (and more expensive) arrangements for their care and treatment. Eventually, a portion of these offenders will be released on parole, and the problems of the institution will be passed along to paroling authorities.

Community corrections may not provide the degree of protection that needs to be extended to persons with one or more disabilities or handicaps. Those who are mentally ill may not be able to function normally in their communities. Some offenders who are mentally impaired may require constant monitoring and supervision, primarily for their own protection (Silver, 2000). Some observers believe that it will be necessary for entire Departments of Correction in each state to address the problems of special-needs offenders from a total systems approach. A comprehensive corrections plan can be effective at maximizing the cost-efficiency of correctional construction. The growing number of special-needs populations will require new thinking by architects and administrators to meet inmates' and clients' special health, program, and management needs (Anderson, Sestoft, and Lilleback, 2000).

Sex offenders often pose special problems for community corrections staff. Sex offenders may have committed rape, incest, voyeurism, or any of several other sexual behaviors and/or perversions. Treatments of sex offenders sometimes involve the hormonal drug, Depo-Provera, and some patients may be monitored by a penile plethysmograph, a device that measures the significance of various sexual stimuli relating to one's arousal (Dutton, 2000; Johnson and Knight, 2000).

Many offenders involved in community-based corrections programs have learning disabilities. Special education courses and services are needed to meet their needs more effectively (Eisenberg, Arrigona, and Kofowit, 1999). Several components of successful correctional special educational programs have been identified. These include functional assessments of the skills and learning needs of handicapped offenders, a curriculum that teaches functional academic and living skills, vocational special education, and transitional programs that facilitate moving from correctional systems to community living. In more than a few instances, inmate mothers about to be released may have previously been addicted to crack cocaine or other drugs. It is imperative that they should be put in contact with appropriate agencies or community centers upon their release so that they can continue to receive information and education about the dangers of drug use and how such use might imperil their children (Humphries, 1999).

Correctional agencies must manage a wide range of offenders including those with special problems. These offenders or clients present unusual challenges for probation and parole officers as well as program administrators who must adjust their supervisory methods and program components accordingly. Special types of offenders may have deep-seated psychological problems that are not immediately diagnosed. They may react in unpredictable ways to various types of treatments or therapy. Because their behaviors may be unexpected or unanticipated, they may become violent and harm themselves or others. Persons who are abnormal in some respects behave in abnormal ways. Probation and parole personnel are not always prepared for each and every contingency that may arise. It is a good idea to know about these special types of offenders, their needs, behavior patterns, and what, if anything, of an unusual nature might be expected from them.

Unfortunately, there is often inadequate communication between institutional staff and community services or institutional care officials who can intercede and recommend appropriate treatment for inmates who misbehave or exhibit unconventional behaviors. For example, front-line correctional staff of prisons may not deem it necessary to report to mental health officials that certain inmates are cutting themselves, masturbating publicly, or smearing feces on their cell walls. One reason for not reporting such incidents is that some correctional staff have acquired cynical attitudes about inmates and their attempts to seek recognition from others. Attracting officer and medical attention by engaging in unconventional behaviors are sometimes used to manipulate staff. Thus, correctional officers may dismiss such behaviors as unimportant when they may, indeed, be indicative of deep-seated personality disturbances in need of attention or treatment (Lovell and Rhodes, 1997:40).

This overview encompasses the following offender aggregates: (1) mentally ill offenders, (2) sex offenders and child sexual abusers, (3) drug/alcohol dependent offenders (3) AIDS/HIV offenders, (4) gang members, and (5) developmentally disabled offenders.

Mentally Ill Offenders

No one knows how many mentally ill inmates there are in prisons and jails throughout the United States (Cornelius, 1996). Estimates suggest that as many as 600,000 mentally ill offenders are currently incarcerated (Pastore and Maguire, 2003). Mentally ill or retarded inmates present correctional officials with problems similar to those who have drug/alcohol dependencies. Frequently, inadequate staffing makes diagnoses of inmates and their problems difficult. Because of the short-term confinement purpose of jails, these facilities are not prepared to adequately treat those inmates with serious mental disturbances or deficiencies. Suicides in jails and prisons are frequently linked with the mental condition of inmates unable to cope with confinement. Mentally ill inmates also exhibit a high degree of socially disruptive behavior. This disruptive behavior occurs not only during confinement but later, when these inmates are discharged. In many jurisdictions, treatment services for mentally retarded offenders receive a low budgetary and program priority (Paradis et al., 2000).

Offenders who are mentally ill are incarcerated disproportionately in relation to other offenders (Mastrofski et al., 2000). Mentally ill inmates tend to mask their limitations and are highly susceptible to prison culture and inmate manipulation. Also, these offenders are often unresponsive to traditional rehabilitation programs available to other inmates. They present correctional officers with unusual discipline problems unlike other inmates. Corrections officers often are high-school educated with little, if any, training in dealing with mentally ill individuals. Obviously, proper classification systems should be devised to identify different types of disabled inmates. Evidence indicates that such classification systems are currently being devised in many jail settings and that corrections generally is becoming more responsive to the needs of these types of offenders (California Board of Corrections, 2000).

A deinstitutionalization movement commenced in 1968 in the United States, where mentally ill offenders were increasingly shifted from institutional to community care. This movement has not been uniform throughout all jurisdictions, however. One aim of deinstitutionalization has been to reduce jail and prison populations by diverting the mentally ill or retarded to nonincarcerative surroundings such as hospitals. However, deinstitutionalization has not been entirely successful in this respect One unintended consequence of deinstitutionalization has been to discharge large numbers of mentally disturbed offenders back into the community prematurely after a short hospitalization. Police once again encounter these offenders because of their inability to cope with the rigors of the street. In fact, the police bring these same individuals back into jails and prisons through "mercy bookings," where they mistakenly believe correctional personnel can take care of them more effectively. Thus, the cycle is repeated, where the stresses of jail or prison exacerbate latent psychotic, convulsive, and behavioral factors (California Board of Corrections, 2000).

Of course, deinstitutionalization of mentally ill offenders does not significantly alleviate the burden on probation and parole departments who must supervise these clients. POs and their agencies have had to make significant adjustments and programmatic changes to accommodate mentally ill offenders. One of the greatest areas of concern, from the standpoint of agency personnel, relates to supervising those who are learning disabled or mentally retarded. Often, because these offenders cannot express themselves or indicate their needs, it is difficult to identify the most appropriate services or legal assistance they might require. Many POs lack skills in dealing with these clients, although many agencies throughout the United States are improving their services delivery (Corrado et al., 2000).

Gang Members

In 2002 there were over 800,000 active gang members in 29,000 youth gangs throughout the United States, both on the streets and in U.S. prisons and jails (Pastore and Maguire, 2003). Virtually every city with a population of 250,000 or greater reported the presence of gangs. Furthermore, there were significant gang increases in suburban and rural areas of the United States, as the number of gang members in these areas increased by 50 percent from 1996 to 2002.

It is difficult to understand why youth gangs form and perpetuate themselves over long periods of time. Gangs emerge, grow, dissolve, and disappear for reasons that are poorly understood. Gangs are defined as self-formed associations of peers, united by mutual interests, with identifiable leadership and internal organization, who act collectively or as individuals to achieve specific purposes, including the conduct of illegal activity and control of a particular territory, facility, or enterprise. They may include either adults or juveniles (Wilson, 2000:1).

Several problems confront POs who must supervise gang members. When gang members have been incarcerated for a period of time, they emerge from prisons or jails and seem to increase the level of violence among their street gang affiliate memberships (Wilson, 2000:35–36). POs must interact with these gang members, often on their own turfs, where gang members utilize hand signs and special language to deceive POs and mislead them. There are also dangers whenever POs enter known gang-controlled neighborhoods for the purpose of visiting other gang-member clients (Knox, 2000). It has been reported that over 50 percent of all gang members in the United States have used firearms at one time or another during the commission of a violent crime (Wilson, 2000:28–29). This is one of the reasons many POs have sought to carry firearms when they make house visits to their clients. About half of all states have approved firearms use for their POs, in part because of these potential dangers to PO lives and security.

Gangs are prevalent in schools throughout the United States (Howell and Lynch, 2000). In fact, the number of students reporting the presence of gangs in schools doubled between 1989 and 1995. A high percentage of students reported that gang members brought firearms to their schools at different times. Many students also reported a high degree of illicit drug use among gang members on school property. When students were interviewed in a 1998 survey about gang presence in their schools, 80 percent replied that they knew of the presence of specific gangs by their names. About 80 percent also said that they recognized gang associations through particular student groupings during the school day. About 56 percent reported tagging or the presence of gang graffiti on their school property, and 71 percent said that gang members usually wore identifying clothing to set themselves apart from other students to be recognized more easily (Howell and Lynch, 2000).

Gangs also create a pattern of resistance to change. Thus, when POs attempt to intervene and intercede with any particular offender, there is an overpowering sense of betrayal on the part of the gang member-client if he or she accepts the PO's suggested intervention. This does not always occur. But POs encounter resistance from more than a few gang member-clients nevertheless (Kelly, 2000).

Many gangs are involved in illicit activities, such as dealing drugs or transporting firearms (Decker, 2000). When POs supervise gang members, there is always the possibility that they are continuing their involvement in these illicit activities. However, actual drug use by probationers or parolees can easily be checked with various devices at random times. Thus, many gang members are smart enough not to get caught doing drugs while serving time in probation or parole programs. Despite these checks, POs often regard their interventions with gang members as unproductive, since it is difficult to overcome the influence of gang membership. Self-definitions of gang membership and involvement in delinquent activities are strong (Bjerregaard, 2002).

Sex Offenders and Child Sexual Abusers

Another category of offenders receiving special emphasis from corrections are sex offenders including child sexual abusers. Sometimes these offenders are grouped with criminals who are mentally ill and deserve special services, while others feel they should receive no unique consideration. Since many sex offenses are committed against victims known by the offender as a friend or family member, a large number of these incidents are not reported to the police. Thus, no one really knows how many sex offenders there are in the United States at any given time.

It has been estimated that convicted rapists made up about 2 percent of the prison population in the United States in 1998 (Beck, 2000b:10). About 234,000 sex offenders were under some form of correctional supervision during the same period (Robinson, 1998). Sex offenders are persons who commit a sexual act prohibited by law. Fairly common types of sex offenders include rapists and prostitutes, although sex offenses may include voyeurism (peeping toms), exhibitionism, child sexual molestation, incest, date rape, and marital rape. This list is not exhaustive. **Child sexual abusers** are adults who involve minors in virtually any kind of sexual activity ranging from intercourse with children to photographing them in lewd poses. Although the exact figure is unknown, it is believed that approximately 2 million children are sexually victimized annually. It is also estimated that 90 percent of all child sexual abuse cases are never prosecuted, although this situation appears to be changing (Kruttschnitt, Uggen, and Shelton, 2000).

Public interest in and awareness of sex offenders is based on the belief that most convicted sex offenders will commit new sex offenses when released. Regardless of the diverse motives of sex offenders, there is general agreement among professionals that these offenders usually need some form of counseling or therapy. Many jurisdictions currently operate sex therapy programs designed to rehabilitate sex offenders, depending upon the nature of their sex crime (Marshall and Serran, 2000).

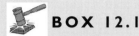 **BOX 12.1**

PERSONALITY HIGHLIGHT

Nina Juarez
Webb County, Texas Juvenile Detention Center

Statistics:

M.A., B.S. (criminal justice, psychology), Texas A & M International University

Background:

I was born and raised in Laredo, Texas. I attended local public schools and graduated from J.W. Nixon High School in 1985. I became interested in law enforcement when I was a senior in high school. I briefly joined the Laredo Police Department. Later I enrolled at the Laredo Community College and attained an Associate's Degree in law enforcement in 1987. In my sophomore year, I worked part-time at the local college in security. I issued parking violations within the campus area. After graduation I joined the U.S. Coast Guard Reserves. I received basic training at Cape May, New Jersey; drill weekends once a month were done with the San Antonio group at Brooks Air Force Base. We traveled to and from Corpus Christi, Texas, Naval Air Station for our drill training, conducted port security duties, and law enforcement training. Law enforcement was my interest up until I did my internship in my senior year at Texas A & M International University, and that experience helped reassure me that this was the career I wanted to pursue. I volunteered with the local Texas Youth Commission (TYC) Parole Office located at the

Webb County Detention Center. The parole officer provided me with extensive knowledge, experience, and skills to perform the duties of a parole officer supervising young offenders released from TYC facilities. I attained new skills and experience, and I felt great once I had accomplished the duties of a parole officer. Since then, I decided that I wanted to pursue a job in that area and realized my passion for this field of study. First, I worked at a local shelter with at-risk youths. The youths placed at the shelter were probationers, parolees, and homeless youths. I obtained my one experience and later applied for a PO position. In 1997 I was hired as a Webb County Juvenile Probation Officer. I have worked in different units within the department. I love my job and I pray that I will continue to work with at-risk youths for a long time. I learn much from my co-workers, clients, and their families, and all of the people who are involved in guiding these young individuals to a better path in life.

Experiences:

POs go from wearing one title to the next on any given day. The duties of a PO are not stable. I have gone through a crisis with a
(continued)

BOX 12.1 (*Continued*)

home-related problem at the beginning of my shift and ended with a suicidal crisis that goes beyond my 8-hour day. One time I had a juvenile in my office who was reporting for the first time. I had not met him before and had no idea who I was dealing with. I did not have the file, and I had only read briefly that the child was placed on ISP with me. It was already 5:00 P.M. and only one PO and myself were left in the office. I conducted the office visit and escorted the juvenile out the front door. I gave the juvenile enough time to exit the parking lot and then advised the other PO that I was off for the rest of the day. I went to my truck and drove off. Well, before I exited the parking lot, I noticed that the juvenile who had been in my office was in the vehicle parked on the street by the stop sign and several other individuals were exiting the truck to check out something. I had noticed another car on the street but didn't pay much attention to it. And so I continued to drive. While driving, I looked in my rear view mirror and noticed that the truck was following me. Once the truck got too close to my car and I noticed that one passenger was leaning forward and grabbing something. I noticed that it was a handgun and that the passenger was waiving it out the window. The next thing I remember was driving away and leaving the scene as fast as I possibly could. I told myself that I didn't want to be either a victim or witness—I just wanted to get home. I knew that the passenger in the truck was my client. The next day I asked the boy about following me and waiving the gun. He claimed to have no idea what I was talking about.

On another occasion I visited a child victim of one of my clients, who was a sex offender. After reading the police report of the incident, I didn't want to see the sex offender client. I was very upset and angry with that person. But then I had second thoughts. If I wanted to make something positive happen from that experience, I would have to set aside my feelings and do my job to the best of my ability. I visited with the victim and watched the victim at play. I spoke also with the sex offender. Subsequently, I recommended a psychiatric evaluation for the sex offender as well as confinement. The sex offender remained incarcerated for several years. In a followup, I determined that the victim was recovering well, and the parents were learning to cope with what had happened to the child. As a court officer, I frequently have been assigned sex offender cases. Now that I am in the ISP unit, these types of offenders are my key priorities in my caseload.

Advice to Students:

My advice to students thinking about working as a probation officer is as follows. You will not get rich and earn a lot of money. Your life is always in danger. You need to have the patience and love working with young offenders, and you must interact with their immediate and/or extended families from all ethnic and socioeconomic groups, including the victims, who may be young or old. It is best to volunteer or complete an internship at your local probation department in order to see if that is what you really wish to pursue. Remember to pursue and research whatever you love doing, because it is going to be a job you might be performing for the rest of your career. I thank God that I was able to do an internship with a parole officer who did a great job teaching me and allowing me to work with the parolees as though I was their PO. When interns volunteer at our department and are assigned to work with me, I provide them with a variety of tasks and teach them what a PO's duties are all about. I have seen interns apply and have seen new POs quit on their first day. And so if you volunteer at the local detention center, it is probably best to start at the intake unit where juveniles are being processed, because that is where the whole procedure starts and the action begins.

Sex offenders offer POs a unique challenge. First, sex offenders expect some amount of assistance from community programs designed to counsel and treat them. Thus, they believe they are in a therapeutic milieu whenever they are freed on probation or parole with conditions. In accordance with their program expectations, they obtain honest employment and attempt to lead law-abiding lives. Most sex offenders do not have lengthy criminal records, nor do they have moderate or severe substance-abuse problems or dependencies or unstable lifestyles. But the media and public have quite a different view of sex offenders. They are viewed as unstable predators who seek to repeat their victimizations whenever possible (Firestone et al., 2000). Reports of escapes of violent sexual predators from treatment centers and mental hospitals do little to dispel public sentiment against sex offenders (Dolan, Harckness, and McGuire, 2000). In support of this belief, 48 states had passed community notification legislation by 1998 so that sex offenders would be required to register whenever they relocated to different communities to start new lives. Obviously, the public regards sex offending as a most egregious activity and desires to punish it most severely. Thus, the dilemma arises about how POs can effectively supervise these offenders without posing a risk to public safety, and at the same time avoid undercutting the offender's ability to get back on to a crime-free path (Robinson, 1998:18). There are no easy answers to this dilemma.

AIDS/HIV Offenders

A growing problem in corrections is AIDS/HIV or **Acquired Immune Deficiency Syndrome (AIDS)/Human Immunodeficiency Virus (HIV).** Estimates are that by 1997, there were over 3 million AIDS/HIV cases in the United States, and that the number of AIDS cases was doubling about every 8 to 10 months (Office of Justice Programs, 2001). AIDS is particularly prevalent among jail and prison inmates (Correctional Association of New York, 2000; Shewan and Davies, 2000). Prisoners living in close quarters are highly susceptible to the AIDS virus because of the likelihood of anal-genital or oral-genital contact. Although there has been much improvement in creating greater AIDS awareness among inmates through educational programs, the fact is that AIDS education in incarcerative settings has not slowed the spread of this disease appreciably (Marcus, Amen, and Bibace, 1992). By the beginning of 1998, for instance, there were 22,548 AIDS-infected inmates in state prisons and 1,030 AIDS-infected inmates in federal penitentiaries (Office of Justice Programs, 2001:1). Interestingly, female inmates in state and federal prisons had a higher AIDS infection rate compared with men. For male prisoners, about 2.2 percent were AIDS-infected compared with 3.5 percent of all female inmates.

It follows that if AIDS is prevalent and increasing among jail and prison inmates, then it is prevalent and increasing among probationers and parolees as well. Thus, AIDS has become a primary topic of concern among POs and their agencies (Lurigio, Bensinger, and Laszlo, 1990). In view of the various circumstances under which AIDS has been transmitted in recent years, from saliva or blood residue from dentists and others working in different health professions, POs have perceived that their risk of being infected with the AIDS virus has increased greatly. Many probationers and parolees are former drug offenders. Drug-dependent clients represent a special danger, since AIDS is known to be easily transmitted when drug addicts share their needles used to inject heroin and other substances. It is widely known from media reports that some crimes have been perpetrated by some offenders wielding needles and other objects they say have been infected with AIDS. Thus, these actions pose additional risks for supervising POs who must be on their guard and protect themselves from becoming infected.

Indirectly related to the rise in AIDS/HIV in prisons, jails, and probation and parole programs is the rise in tuberculosis. Between 1976 and 1996, for instance, there was a 50 percent increase in the number of New York State prison inmates infected with tuberculosis. Much of this tuberculosis is untreatable and fatal. It is more easily transmitted than AIDS/HIV, although AIDS/HIV inmates and clients seem at greater risk of contracting tuberculosis than other inmates who are AIDS/HIV-free. Today, virtually every prison conducts a routine tuberculosis skin test to determine whether particular inmates are infected. If they are infected, then they are almost always isolated from the general inmate population in an effort to control the spread of this disease. Some of the nation's larger jails, such as the Los Angeles County Jail, conducts routine mini chest films, which are single view, low-dose, screening radiographs to detect active pulmonary disease. Thus, early detection of this disease can be immediately isolated and treated (Andrus, Fleming, and Knox, 1999).

Drug/Alcohol Dependent Offenders

Drug and alcohol abuse are highly correlated with criminal conduct (Taxman and Bouffard, 2003). Large numbers of pretrial detainees are characterized as having drug and/or alcohol dependencies. Furthermore, there is evidence that many offenders suffer from polysubstance abuse (Litt and Mallon, 2003). Offenders with drug or alcohol dependencies present several problems for correctional personnel (Leukefield et al., 2003). Often, jails are not equipped to handle their withdrawal symptoms, especially if they are confined for long periods. Also, the symptoms themselves are frequently dealt with rather than the social and psychological causes for these dependencies. Thus, when offenders go through alcohol detoxification programs or are treated for drug addiction, they leave these programs and are placed back into the same circumstances that caused the drug or alcohol dependencies originally.

A fairly common offender category under PO supervision is the DWI or DUI offender. These are persons who have been convicted of drunk driving or driving under the influence of alcohol or drugs (U.S. Department of Justice, 1999:1). It has been estimated that 513,200 persons convicted of drunk driving were under correctional supervision during 1999. Of these, about 454,500 were on probation, while 41,100 were in local jails, and another 17,600 were in prisons. For POs, it is important to note that during the 1990s, the correctional supervision rate for drunk drivers rose from 151 for every 1,000 DWI arrests to 347 for every 1,000 DWI arrests (U.S. Department of Justice, 1999:1). DWI or DUI offenders must complete special conditions of probation relating to attending Alcoholics Anonymous meetings, Mothers Against Drunk Drivers meetings, and driving schools in various jurisdictions. All of this information must be documented and filed with the probation office. POs must keep track of all of these offenders in order ensure program compliance.

Prisons and jails do not always insulate inmates from continued drug or alcohol abuses. Illegal substance abuse is prevalent among inmates in state and federal prisons (Straub, 1997). Corrections employees are often about as likely as prisoners to abuse drugs, since the employees themselves are frequently the major conduits for smuggling drugs into prison settings. Currently, many state, local, and federal agencies conduct routine urinalyses of their employees to detect and/or deter drug abuse among them as well as inmates (Ellsworth, 1996).

Pretrial detainees have often been involved in additional criminality while awaiting trial. Even samples of pretrial detainees who were subjected to periodic drug tests as a specific deterrent were found to have high failure-to-appear rates and rearrests (Britt, Gottfredson, and Goldkamp, 1992). Drug dependencies also account for greater numbers of dropouts and failures among those involved in both juvenile and adult intervention programs. For those on either probation or parole, drug and/or alcohol dependencies present various problems and account for program infractions, rearrests, and general adjustment and reintegration problems.

Those re-entering the community on parole after years of incarceration are especially vulnerable to drug dependencies during the first six months following their release (Nurco, Hanlon, and Bateman, 1992). Individual or group counseling and other forms of therapy are recommended for drug- or alcohol-dependent clients, although many clients are considered as treatment-resistant (Dawson, 1992). Since 1972, various community-based treatment programs have been implemented to treat and counsel drug-dependent clients. These community-based programs have been collectively labeled **Treatment Alternatives to Street Crime (TASC)** and currently are being operated in numerous jurisdictions throughout the United States to improve client abstinence from drugs, increase their employment potential, and improve their social/personal functioning.

Developmentally Disabled Offenders

A growing but neglected population of offenders are those with physical handicaps. Some offenders are confined to wheelchairs, and therefore, special facilities must be constructed to accommodate their access to probation or parole offices or community-based sites. Other offenders have hearing or speech impairments that limit them in various ways. For instance, Counselor Kay McGill, of the Rehabilitation Services Division of the Georgia Department of Human Resources, has described her role in dealing with certain handicapped parolees (*Georgia Parole Review,* 1990). One of her parolee-clients was described as suffering from tinnitus, an inherited condition involving a constant roaring in one's head and where sound is amplified and unfiltered. The client had difficulty holding a job and suffered from depression and insecurity stemming from his tinnitus condition. McGill arranged for her client to acquire a job involving working with an electronics program with low noise levels and some isolation. In the general case, the Georgia Rehabilitation Services Division is an agency whose mission is to get their clients functioning at an optimal level, so that they may adjust more normally within their communities (*Georgia Parole Review,* 1990:176).

Physically challenged offenders often require greater attention from their POs. Acquiring and maintaining employment is sometimes difficult for persons with different types of physical handicaps, such as the parolee-client managed by Kay McGill. Many POs become brokers between their own agencies and community businesses, which are encouraged to employ certain of these clients with special problems. Community volunteers are increasingly helpful in assisting probation and parole agencies with physically handicapped clients.

MENTALLY ILL OFFENDERS

Thousands of mentally ill individuals pass through local correctional facilities annually. One-quarter of all inmates in prisons and jails in 1996 reported that they had been diagnosed or treated for one type of mental illness or another (Conly, 1999:3). Nearly 89,000 of these inmates said that they were on some form of prescription medication for a mental illness, while another 51,000 reported that they had been admitted to a mental health program at one time or another during their commission of crimes.

For institutional corrections, the problems of mentally ill are manifold. Many mentally ill offenders are violent, and they are recidivists (Grisso et al., 2000). A study of mentally ill patients was conducted in 1998, known as the MacArthur Violence Risk Assessment Study. The sample investigated consisted of 1,136 persons who had been hospitalized for mental disorders. Many of these persons had criminal records, and self-disclosures by these patients were that about a third had violent thoughts. Many patients were self-proclaimed substance abusers, and they predicted that they would leave their institutions and commit violent acts if given the opportunity. A correlation was demonstrated between their psychopathy, anger, and impulsiveness (Grisso et al., 2000). The disturbing fact is that many of these patients, when released, will actually carry out their violent thoughts and act accordingly. Therefore, many new commitments to jails and prisons are former mental patients with histories of violence. A sample of New York inmates revealed that a high percentage of detainees age 62 or older were charged with violent felonies and had previously been hospitalized in New York or elsewhere (Paradis et al., 2000). Many of those committed to jails reported that they previously had been diagnosed with mental problems and reportedly had paranoid delusions that were known to psychiatric staff. However, little or no attempt was made to detain them beyond short-term observation periods in the facilities where they were confined.

Many mentally ill inmates of prisons and jails slip through the cracks and are not diagnosed as mentally ill. Rather, they are simply regarded as violent inmates by correctional officers. Thus, they avoid treatment for their mental problems altogether. Some prisoners develop psychoses of one type or another as the result of confinement. For instance, prisoners placed in solitary confinement seem to have a higher incidence of onset of psychiatric disorders compared with those not placed in solitary confinement (Anderson, Sestoft, and Lilleback, 2000).

Most prisons in the United States and in other English-speaking countries such as England and Canada attempt to screen incoming inmates for mental disorders. For instance, at the Durham Prison in England, new inmates undergo health assessments designed to determine their mental conditions. Many of these inmates are improperly diagnosed, however, and almost all of them are placed in the general population with other inmates. Researchers who investigated this situation have concluded that these misclassifications and misdiagnoses were attributable to inappropriate staff training and experience. Furthermore, when incoming prisoners were screened, they were discouraged by staff from carrying on conversations where their mental illnesses might become more apparent (Birmingham et al., 2000). Even when mentally ill offenders are processed or screened properly, they may not receive the appropriate therapy. In some instances, they may receive no therapy at all (Hodgins and Muller-Isberner, 2000; Timonen et al., 2000).

Court intervention has not always been helpful. During the 1980s and 1990s, increasingly used was the verdict of guilty-but-mentally-ill. This verdict enabled juries to convict mentally ill offenders of crimes that resulted in their hospitalization rather than incarceration. Supposedly, these offenders would receive appropriate treatment and then be released into the general inmate population of the nearest prison. However, many of these offenders have escaped incarceration when civil authorities have authorized their release from hospital custody (Palmer and Hazelrigg, 2000; Sreenivasan et al., 2000).

When these offenders are eventually transferred to parole services, their mental problems accompany them. In more than a few instances, POs do not know that these persons are mentally disturbed. But increasing numbers of states are devising risk/needs assessment devices that permit POs the opportunity of detecting some of the more mentally disordered clients (Simourd and Hoge, 2000). Despite these advancements in technology and test improvements, it is still difficult for many authorities to detect antisocial personalities and those most likely to become violent and reoffend (Rogers et al., 2000). The most direct indicators of problem parolees is through contacts with prison officials who have supposedly had an opportunity to examine these parole-eligible inmates and determine their psychopathy. However, all too often, inmates with serious psychological problems are improperly diagnosed or not diagnosed at all. Therefore, it is unexpected whenever POs discover mentally unstable clients among their caseloads where no prior warning had been given from institutional officials. Again, the problem was often attributable to a lack of properly trained jail or prison staff who either didn't take the time to diagnose certain inmates properly or failed to recognize the signs of mental illness whenever they were prevalent (Borum, 1999).

One attempt to aggressively deal with the mentally ill population was implemented in Maryland in 1994 following a pilot study of assessing mental illness among inmates in jails and prisons and how communities and institutions were coping with it. In the early 1990s, it was estimated that approximately 700 inmates were being confined in local facilities in Maryland. However, Maryland, not unlike other jurisdictions, lacked sufficient and adequately trained staff to properly screen and treat the mentally ill who were processed by local jails. Often, mentally ill individuals were simply ignored, unless they proved disruptive or attempted suicide. Early in the development of the program, some Maryland officials asked if "we could shoot them up with something to calm them down and just let them sleep while they are here" (Conly, 1999:5). After several pilot projects, Maryland officials created the Community Criminal Justice Treatment Program or MCCJTP. This program was founded on two principles: (1) The target population requires a continuum of care provided by a variety of service professionals in jail and in the community that is coordinated at both the State and local levels; and (2) local communities are in the best position to plan and implement responses to meet the needs of the mentally ill offenders in their jurisdictions.

The goals of the MCCJTP are to improve the identification and treatment of mentally ill offenders and increase their chances of successful independent living, thereby preventing their swift return to jail, mental hospitals, homelessness, or hospital emergency rooms. In some locations, MCCJTP also aims to reduce to period of incarceration, through postbooking diversion, and even reduce the likelihood of incarceration altogether.

The MCCJTP works as follows:

1. Preliminary identification of candidates for program services is made following arrest, after self-referral by the defendant, or as the result of referrals by the arresting officer, the classification officer, jail medical staff, the substance abuse counselor, or other jail personnel.

2. The MCCJTP case manager meets with candidates to conduct an in-jail diagnostic interview and an individual needs assessment.

3. While in jail, the inmate meets with the case manager for counseling and the development of an aftercare plan. A typical plan will include substance abuse counseling, educational services, recreational services, employment training, and eventually, suitable housing.

4. MCCJTP case mangers help link clients to specified services, such as psychiatric day treatment, substance abuse treatment, vocational rehabilitation, and educational services.

5. Case managers were responsible for monitoring offenders for program compliance and to ensure their compliance with housing agreements and participation in daily activities and treatment plans.

6. The length of stay in the MCCJTP depends upon client progress, which monitored daily. Judicial approval is required. The case is left open for one year. At the end of the year, the judge either closes the case or reopens it.

The probation department actively assists the MCCJTP in a variety of ways, usually through networking with community agencies to provide clients with needed services and programs. Between 1994 and 1998, the program has been highly successful. While persons with mental illnesses have not been cured outright, most have been brought to a level where they can function fairly normally with assistance from caregivers provided through the MCCJTP.

State and federal probation and parole services have gradually increased their roles in assessing the prevalence of mental illness among their clientele. In 1995, 41 states indicated that mental health agencies, private practitioners, or the courts were the primary determinants of one's mental condition. Only nine states had provisions for and kept records of the prevalence of mental illness among their probation and parole populations (Boone, 1995:34). While these figures have improved somewhat since 1995, there are still inadequate assessments of mentally ill clients among a majority of state probation and parole agencies (Camp and Camp, 2003; Pastore and Maguire, 2003).

GANG MEMBERS

The National Youth Gang Survey is disturbing in a number of respects. First, it demonstrates the pervasiveness of gangs in American society. Second, it shows the strength gangs have in virtually every locality where they exist. Third, it demonstrates the interaction between prison/jail inmates and street gangs. And fourth, it illustrates the diverse forms of criminal activities associated with gang membership (Wilson, 2000). As we have seen, in 2000 there were at least 800,000 known gang members in 29,000 gangs in the United States.

What is even more disturbing is that during the last half century since the 1950s, there have been numerous changes in the structure, organization, and activities of gangs. Gangs are increasingly lethal in their choice of weaponry, which often includes automatic weapons used in conventional warfare between nations. Other changes include the fact that no longer are gangs confined to large urban centers. They have branched out into smaller communities and towns. Further, more gang members are remaining in their gangs well into their adult years. More gangs are graduating into large-scale drug trafficking and gun sales both nationally and internationally (Elder, 1996). Gangs are big business, and many gangs are increasingly organized according to corporate structural models, complete with executive boards and chairmen (Triplet and Ross, 1998:29–30).

The public is more frequently aware of gang presence by the incidence of drive-by shootings that occur in larger cities, such as Los Angeles, New York, and Chicago. Often, these drive-by shootings involve deaths of innocent bystanders who are standing in close proximity to rival gang members who are the intended targets (Levine and Parra, 2000). Relatively little is known by the public about gang involvement in large-scale drug trafficking and other criminal enterprises.

Considerable investigation has been conducted concerning why persons become affiliated with gangs initially. Psychological and social maladjustments are often cited, such as low self-esteem and being an isolate in schools and other social settings (Sutherland and Shepherd, 2002). Both male and female gang members appear to have joined gangs for essentially the same reasons (Miller and Brunson, 2000). Yet other persons join gangs for mutual protection. They feel safe where there is strength in numbers (Aguirre and Baker, 2000).

POs have an uneasy relation with clients who are affiliated with gangs. We have already examined some of these reasons earlier in this chapter. Gangs exert considerable social and psychological influence over their memberships, and this influence often undermines PO attempts to change the attitudes of gang member-clients. Further, there is the possibility and likelihood that gang member-clients will continue to engage in illicit activities of their gangs without PO knowledge.

Community and PO response to gangs and gang interventions have usually broken down into the following categories:

1. Community organization or neighborhood mobilization.
2. Social intervention, which involves youth outreach and street work counseling.
3. Opportunities provision, which involves jobs, job training, and education.
4. Suppression, which involves arrest, incarceration, and supervision.
5. Organizational development, which involves adapting organizations to facilitate dealing with gangs, such as the development of gang units in police departments (Triplet and Ross, 1998:30).

Increasingly, gang intervention programs are emphasizing partnerships with different agencies, including schools (Shelden, Tracy, and Brown, 2004). The GREAT (Gang Resistance Education and Training) program involves school resource officers and works in conjunction with gang units from police departments to educate nongang members in schools to avoid gangs. Other programs are geared toward younger youths. For instance, the Montreal Preventive Treatment Program is a multicomponent prevention program designed to prevent antisocial behavior among boys of lower socioeconomic statuses who display disruptive problem behavior in kindergarten (Howell, 2000:7). Parent training was combined with individual social skills for boys ages 7 to 9. Parents received an average of 17 training sessions to improve social skills and self-control. The training was implemented in small groups containing both disruptive and nondisruptive boys and used coaching, peer modeling, self-instruction, reinforcement contingencies, and role-playing to build skills (Tremblay et al., 1996). Followup evaluations of this research showed less delinquency, substance abuse, and gang involvement by age 15 among those studied.

In order for early childhood or adolescent programs to maximize their effectiveness, they must target those persons most susceptible to gang membership.

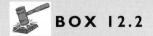

BOX 12.2

Pat Campos
Case Management Director, Webb County Juvenile Department, Laredo, Texas

Statistics:

B.S. (criminal justice), Laredo State University; paralegal certificate, Texas A & M International University

Background:

I was born in Laredo, Texas and graduated from Martin High School in 1977. As a senior I took a criminal justice class, which was being offered for the first time in our high school. It was a very interesting class and it provided the students with the opportunity to work side by side with different law enforcement officers and agents. I knew immediately that I wanted to pursue a career in criminal justice and work as a law enforcement officer. However, I knew that I would have trouble trying to convince my parents of my career choice. Upon graduating from high school, I enrolled at Laredo Community College and began my work in business administration. It was my mother's dream to have one of her eight children pursue a career in business. My older siblings were already in educational careers, and as the middle child, I decided to accept the challenge. I did very well in my business courses and really enjoyed them; however, my heart was not in business administration. I sat with my parents and advised them I could no longer continue pursuing a career as a business major and explained to them that I wanted to start my criminal justice career immediately.

While working in criminal justice, I was employed as a substitute teacher at a local high school. It was a wonderful experience, but I knew that a professional career in teaching was not something I wanted to pursue either. It was during my last semester at the university that one of my friends from middle school told me that there was a position available in the Juvenile Department. He explained

to me what the duties were but I told him I wasn't interested in working with delinquent children. I wanted to be a patrol officer, to be out on the streets and not sitting in an office. However, God had other plans for me.

I began working at the Webb County Juvenile Department in 1981 as a Juvenile Detention Officer. Since then I have been an Intake Officer/Program Coordinator, Community Service Coordinator, Field Probation Officer, Intensive Supervision Officer, and presently I serve as Case Management Director supervising 20 probation officers, one program coordinator, and one victim's coordinator.

Experiences:

Prior to working for the Juvenile Department, my experience in working with youth was as a youth minister at church and as a substitute teacher. However, nothing I had learned in school or as a volunteer worker with youth prepared me sufficiently for what I subsequently encountered at the Juvenile Department. I was saddened to see so many children wasting their lives. I was determined to do whatever it took to help these children. I knew that these children could do well; therefore, I would challenge them to achieve and perform to their highest potential and provide them with incentives whenever they succeeded at anything.

In 1982 I was named Detention Officer of the Year, and in 1990, the Webb County Juvenile Board of Judges honored me with a resolution for introducing the first Operation Kick-It program to all middle and high schools

BOX 12.2 (Continued)

in the United and Laredo Independent School Districts. This program was funded by Texas and run by the Texas Department of Criminal Justice. They would have young prisoners go to the schools and talk to students about their experiences which led them to be incarcerated in the state penitentiary.

During my 22 years in the Juvenile Department, I have had many memorable experiences working with delinquent children. I remember having to go to the hospital with one of my female clients because her 5-month-old baby had to be admitted to the hospital due to dehydration. Once the baby was admitted to the hospital, this female juvenile offender never went back to see her baby. The hospital staff called and advised me that the mother had abandoned her baby; therefore, I would go to the hospital every four hours to feed the baby myself.

I also recall when I took one of my male offenders to lunch at a restaurant of his choice for accomplishing some goals I had set for him. He chose to eat at the Sirloin Stockade because he said that some friends had always talked about all the food they had there. It was a heartbreaking experience for me especially because this child had never eaten a meal in a restaurant. He did not know how or what to order. I placed the order for him, and while we were waiting, he ate salad, soup, and a lot of desserts. When they finally brought his plate, he asked me if he could take it home so that his brothers could eat food from a restaurant.

I also remember those children who for unknown reasons were involved in Satanic cults. I remember having in my caseload one male and female who claimed to be the high priest and priestess in their cults. To this date I remember the day I conducted my first home visit to the male juvenile's house. The stepmother invited me in and led me to the child's bedroom. As I was going into the room, I noticed that everything was dark, and so I asked him to turn on the lights. There was not much light in the room even after the lights were turned on, because the light bulb

was purple, the windows were covered with black blankets, and the walls were plastered with posters of demons and beasts. On one side of the bed, he had a small altar with an animal skull, some black candles, and other items he used during his rituals. He was always amazed because I was not afraid of him like everyone else was and I knew a lot about what they did. Honestly, he was not the first child I supervised who was in a Satanic cult. I would always get invitations to their parties. The majority of these times, the parents were unaware of what their children were doing.

Some of the saddest and most difficult moments of my professional career have been the times I have attended the funerals of many of these children who have lost their lives to drug overdoses, car wrecks, gang-related shootings, and suicides. It is at these times that we find out how many of these children were well-liked and admired by their peers. I worry about these young children attending the funerals because they are going through the pain of losing a friend and there is no parent with them to give them emotional support. I must say that there are some of our children who have been successful and are now married and/or gainfully employed. There is one particular female who encountered many problems as a child. She is now married and is teaching in one of our local schools. Then there is a male who kept running away from home because he had major problems with his parents. He is also married now and practices law. There are others who are still enrolled in institutions of higher learning. I am very proud of them because they have overcome major obstacles in an effort to succeed.

In my 22 years of working with the Juvenile Department, I have noticed that about 90 percent of the children referred to our department were not functioning at grade level. I also noticed that the majority of these troubled kids could not read or write; therefore, they would become discipline problems at school. Frustrated with the fact that the educational system was failing the children, and gangs, drugs, and

(*continued*)

BOX 12.2 (*Continued*)

violence were infesting the schools, I decided to run for the school board. I was elected to the United Independent School District Board in May 2003. I had two prior unsuccessful attempts, but that did not stop me from accomplishing my goal. My mother was a champion for education and she instilled the value of an education to her children. She would tell us, "Whatever your dream is, set some goals, have a strong determination, and persevere to accomplish it." That is exactly what I did. One of the most rewarding events that I, as a school board member, have attended is the graduation ceremonies of our three high schools. It is very emotional for me to hand diplomas to many of our Laredo youth and I am particularly moved upon handing these to some of our probationers who overcame so many obstacles in order to reach such heights.

Advice to Students:

My advice to my staff has always been to be honest with these children and show them respect and genuine care and concern for their needs. This is the same advice I will give to those students who wish to pursue a career in juvenile probation. It is not easy working with troubled children, especially because many of them have gone through so much pain, hurt, abuse, and violence. Many have experienced rejection from parents, family, teachers, and even friends. You will experience very trying times with these children, but never give up on them. These are human lives you are dealing with, and any decision or recommendation you make will greatly impact their lives. These children will immediately know if you truly care for them or are there just to get a paycheck. Another bit of advice for students is the same I got from my mother. That is, "Whatever your dream is, set some goals, have a strong determination, and persevere to accomplish it." Follow your heart; believe in yourself, and work to make this world a better place to live in. The pay as a probation officer will never be the greatest, but the rewards of seeing these children succeed despite all of the obstacles in their lives is priceless.

These are known as at-risk children. One way of identifying at-risk factors is to study the characteristics and background of known gang members and work backwards to nongang adolescents with those same characteristics. For example, gang members exhibit the following characteristics: They are largely male, socially inept, maladjusted, sexually promiscuous, suffering from low self-esteem, ethnic minorities, exhibiting sociopathic personalities, and are closely associated with antisocial peers (Frankfort-Howard and Romm, 2002). Geographically, areas characterized with high unemployment, poverty, the absence of meaningful jobs, and economically distressed neighborhoods seemed to be breeding grounds for prospective gang members. Clearly, the identification of at-risk youths is at best diffuse. Given this diffuseness, a comprehensive gang model has been recommended that provides a multifaceted approach targeting individual youths, peer groups, families, and the community (Brownfield and Thompson, 2002).

What can POs do to intervene where gang members form a portion of their clientele? One program which was initiated in Boston, Massachusetts is Operation Night Light. Commenced in 1992, Operation Night Light is a specialized unit with two goals: (1) curbing gang violence; and (2) enforcing court-ordered conditions of probation. The program involves teams of police officers and probation officers who visit the homes of probationers who are known gang members. The objective of these visits is to ensure program compliance with curfews and to conduct visual inspections of one's premises for illegal contraband, cellular telephones, illegal beepers, and other items that might be used for illicit purposes. Operation Night Light, which eventually became Operation Tracker, has been successful enough to eliminate the blind spots of communication between the police and POs (Triplet and Ross, 1998:31).

What seems to have emerged from Operation Tracker and similar programs is that in order to maximize their effectiveness, POs need to be in greater contact with police organizations and communicate with them. Probation officers need to equip themselves with the knowledge and techniques to recognize the presence of gang activity. One method of obtaining such knowledge is increased communication with various criminal justice agencies, primarily police departments. It is the case that whenever police officers stop a person on the street for investigation, they may not know that the person is a parolee or probationer. With more frequent communication between POs and police officers, these communication gaps can be narrowed such that offender accountability can be improved (Triplet and Ross, 1998:34).

Tattoo Removal Programs

Whenever gang members wish to leave gangs, they often find it hard to do so. If they relocate to other regions of the country, chances are there will be affiliate gangs in those new territories who will recognize those who recently moved there. One of the telltale signs of gang membership is a gang **tattoo.** Gang members place tattoos on their hands, arms, feet, faces, and other places on their bodies as symbols of their gang affiliation. If these tattoos are in conspicuous places, then it attracts the attention of affiliate gang members. One of the most frequent locations where tattoos are given to new gang members is in prisons and jails. Other inmates use crude instruments to install permanent tattoos on their new members. The tattoo is seemingly a symbol of ownership, implying that the gang owns the gang member forever. Once a gang member, always a gang member, or so some gang members would like their membership to believe. Some gangs are so deeply entrenched in one's social and personal world that they will not let anyone leave their gang under penalty of death. Gang membership is often taken that seriously. More than a few deaths have been the result of persons attempting to leave their gangs.

Increasingly, POs and police agencies are offering to remove these symbols of gang membership for those desiring to detach themselves from gangs. The Ventura County, California Sheriff's Department has a **tattoo removal program,** where gang members can have their tattoos removed at no charge through laser surgery. According to this program, whenever a gang member wants to get out of the gang and find employment, it is almost impossible to do so. This is because employers fear gang members and can easily recognize them through the tattoos they wear. Tattoos are essentially a stigma that follows them through life. They cannot get a job, nor can they have lasting relationships with anyone. Thus, they cannot become productive members of society.

The tattoo removal program operated by the Ventura County Sheriff's Department consists of the following process. First, gang members must attend a tattoo removal screening. They are interviewed about why they want their tattoos removed. They are asked about where they plan to relocate to escape contact with their former gang associates. They must perform a certain number of community service hours in order to pay for the removal of their tattoos. Once they have been interviewed and performed the necessary hours of community service, which may include graffiti removal of their own gangs' symbols, they will have their tattoos removed free of charge. Thus, they can detach themselves from gang membership by having the most visible signs of gangs removed from their bodies. Once these tattoos are removed, these persons can leave their communities and establish new lives elsewhere where others do not know about their prior affiliation with gangs (Ventura County Sheriff's Department, 2001). Tattoo removal programs similar to the one operated by the Ventura County Sheriff's Department are operated in other parts of the country with positive results.

SEX OFFENDERS

The **Missouri Sexual Offender Program (MOSOP)** is targeted to serve the needs of incarcerated, nonpsychotic sexual offenders. The program can supervise effectively over 700 offenders who are required to complete the program before becoming eligible for parole. MOSOP approaches sex offenders on the assumption that their sex offenses resulted from learned patterns of behavior associated with anxious, angry, and impulsive individuals. The three-phase program obligates offenders to attend ten weeks of courses in abnormal psychology and the psychology of sexual offending. In other phases, inmates meet in group therapy sessions to talk out their problems with counselors and other inmates. MOSOP officials believe that if the program can reduce sex offender recidivism by only 3 percent, it will pay for itself from the savings of court costs and inmate processing and confinement (Kuznestov, Pierson, and Harry, 1992).

The Minnesota Department of Corrections operates a project known as **180 Degrees, Inc.** This is similar to a halfway house for parolees, but it is designed for those who have received no previous treatment for their sex offenses (Driggs and Zoet, 1987). Participation in 180 Degrees, Inc. is limited only to those offenders willing to admit they have committed one or more sex offenses and who can function as group members. Offenders form men's sexuality groups that meet for 90-minute meetings over a 13-week period. All participants contract with officials to write an autobiography of their offense, a description of the victim, a listing of sexual abuse cues, the development of a control plan, and personal affirmations (Driggs and Zoet, 1987:126). While this program is not fully effective, it does seem to help some offenders understand their behavior.

Sex offenders, especially child sexual abusers, pose significant problems for both jail and prison authorities as well as community-based corrections personnel. Child sexual abusers are often abused themselves by other inmates when their crimes become known to others. Other sex offenders become the prey of stronger inmates who use these offenders for their own sexual gratification. Many sex offenders request that they be segregated from other prisoners because of danger to themselves. But because of limited resources and space, jail and prison officials cannot often segregate these offenders effectively from other inmates.

Within communities, many sex offenders and child sexual abusers are placed in community-based facilities for treatment and counseling (Wilson et al., 2000). A survey of 2,961 juvenile and adult sex offender treatment programs has indicated an increase of 133 percent in the number of these providers between 1986 and 1990 (Knopp, Freeman-Longo, and Stevenson, 1992). The most frequently used treatment method in sex offender treatment agencies is peer group counseling. For example, the State of Washington operates the Special Sex Offender Sentencing Alternative (SSOSA), which permits community treatment in lieu of determinate sentences for adult, felony sex offenders (Washington State Department of Social and Mental Health Services, 1991). The Washington program has found that intensive counseling and therapy for many of these clients has substantially reduced their recidivism within the community.

Various models of PO training and caseload assignments have been described that include sex offender specialization. Some officers are specialists in that they have received unique training in counseling sex offenders. Some POs have acquired M.S.W. degrees and are certified counselors for those with sex or alcohol problems. One of these PO training models is the specialized caseloads model, where clients are assigned according to their particular offenses and/or psychological problems (Firestone et al., 2000). Sex offenders and child sexual abusers are among those clients receiving particular supervision from PO specialists, just as chemically dependent persons might be supervised by special POs who have acquired additional chemical dependency training (Fisher, Beech, and Browne, 2000; Marshall and Serran, 2000).

OFFENDERS WITH HIV/AIDS

Inmates, probationers, and parolees with AIDS/HIV are at risk of transmitting their disease to others. While institutionalized, inmates with AIDS/HIV are often isolated physically from the general inmate population to prevent the spread of their disease to other inmates (Shewan and Davies, 2000). However, their isolation cannot be continued indefinitely. Some authorities believe that institutionalization is the last chance many of these persons will have to receive appropriate treatment under any type of meaningful supervision (Marquart et al., 1999). Even while some prisoners with AIDS/HIV are confined, particularly in local jails, sometimes they are ill-treated or denied treatment by insensitive jail personnel as a punishment for their condition (Vaughn and Smith, 1999). At some point, most of these offenders will be paroled. When they come under the supervision of paroling authorities, they are often assigned to a PO trained in sexually transmitted diseases. These are specialized caseloads. POs with special knowledge can be more effective in the management and supervision of AIDS/HIV-infected clients.

It is often the case that AIDS/HIV-infected inmates are known to POs before their arrival. This way, POs can arrange appropriate community services and treatment so that when their clients arrive, their therapy can continue without interruption (Anno, 1998). Often, new clients with AIDS/HIV have other problems, such as drug dependencies. POs must also plan to address these types of problems as well. Increasing numbers of AIDS/HIV-infected clients are women. If some of these women are pregnant or have borne children prior to their earlier confinement, then POs must arrange to educate them concerning how to prevent the spread of AIDS/HIV. Some investigations have revealed that the knowledge among women with AIDS/HIV, how it was acquired, and how it can be transmitted is extremely low. Thus, it is critical that these persons receive special education courses or a general exposure to knowledge about AIDS/HIV and its transmission (Brewer, Marquart, and Mullings, 1998). Usually, a community agency can assist in this regard (Maxwell and Wallisch, 1998).

Some inmates with AIDS/HIV who are within a short time of early release may be granted work or study release from their confinement. There are obvious risk factors associated with permitting these persons to work for limited periods outside of prison walls. However, it has been found that if these persons are properly supervised within a supportive community environment, then their transition back into their communities later goes more smoothly (Harrison et al., 1998).

SUBSTANCE-ABUSING OFFENDERS

Offenders who are arrested and convicted for substance abuse are increasing compared with other offender groups. It is estimated that when alcohol abusers are combined with drug abusers within the offender population, between 80 and 90 percent of them have some type of addiction or problem (Shearer and Carter, 1999:30). Between 1980 and 1994, for instance, the number of state and local arrests for drug offenses rose from 581,000 to 1,350,000 (Corbett and Harris, 1999:67). The population of chronic illicit drug users consists largely of poor, undereducated, unemployed, and uninsured persons. These persons commit crimes at disproportionately higher rates than other criminals and they pose substantial health risks to their associates (Lurigio and Swartz, 1999:67). Furthermore, they comprise the population of probationers and parolees most likely to relapse while free within their communities under PO supervision. Thus, they present fairly serious monitoring problems for POs in all jurisdictions. And this problem is increasing rather than diminishing.

For POs, an effective supervision strategy requires a reliable drug-testing program as well as a consistent and well-formulated policy that holds offenders accountable for their decision to use drugs or otherwise violate the special drug aftercare consideration. The range of consequences for drug aftercare violations must be clearly spelled out in the office policy manual and overseen by unit supervisors; the expectations of abstinence and possible sanctions must be carefully reviewed with the offender during the initial interview; and, most essential, the threatened sanctions must be imposed when and if violations occur if we are to be effective in controlling and treating drug offenders (Torres, 1998:36).

In the early 1990s, the typical response whenever drug or alcohol abusers were encountered in courts was to place them under intensive probation or parole supervision, with considerable monitoring and randomized drug and alcohol checks. While these types of checks are still conducted in most if not all state and federal jurisdictions, they do not appear to be working to decrease the extent of substance abuse (Martin and Lurigio, 1994:25). What does seem to work is combining prevention and education programs for non-drug users with treatment programs for users. This is acknowledged as the most effective strategy for reducing drug demand. Treatment for incarcerated and nonincarcerated offenders not only reduces drug use but also suppresses the criminal activity associated with it. Moreover, offenders who are forced into drug treatment by legal mandates are just as successful in recovery as those who voluntarily enter treatment programs, and they often remain in their programs for longer periods (Martin and Lurigio, 1994:25).

In Cook County, Illinois during 1989, an Evening Narcotics Court was established due to the high volume of felony drug cases that were appearing before judges. Between 1989 and 1993, the Evening Narcotics Court had handled 19,485 probation cases and conducted 3,900 presentence and pretrial investigations. Contemporaneous with the Evening Narcotics Court, an Illinois Drug Offender Specialized Supervision Program was established as well as a Home Confinement Unit. These additional programs enabled Cook County authorities the opportunity of providing larger numbers of drug offenders with nonincarcerative options. The Cook County Jail inmate population was greatly alleviated as a result. However, what did the program accomplish since its inception?

The first major hurdle was to screen prospective applicants for inclusion. Probation officers conducted interviews with likely candidates and selected from them approximately 600 offenders who were considered eligible. Subsequently, more offenders became involved in the program as resources and personnel expanded. Courts ordered these offenders to maintain employment, complete their education, participate in outpatient treatment, and remain at home with their families under mild supervision from the probation department. During 1992 for instance, home confinement officers made approximately 122,000 face-to-face visits and 77,700 telephone contacts with program participants. Drug tests and urinalyses were conducted thousands of times for these offenders. Initially, about 46 percent of all participants tested positive for at least one illegal drug. However, they were permitted to remain in their programs. But their supervision was intensified. After a while, only 33 percent tested positive for one or more illegal drugs, mostly cocaine. Offenders who continued to test positive for illegal drugs were referred to drug treatment programs for additional assistance. Although the program was not 100 percent effective in eliminating illicit drug use, it did divert a substantial number of drug abusers to a therapeutic environment where they could withdraw from drugs over time and remain connected with their families (Martin and Lurigio, 1994:26–27).

In other jurisdictions, more aggressive offender monitoring and supervision has been proposed. For instance, some observers contend that the traditional medical model, which considers drug and alcohol dependence as a disease which can be cured with some type of long-term therapy and treatment, is not suitable for criminal offenders who have serious addictions (Torres, 1998:36). The medical model is closely associated with the social work approach and places POs in positions to be manipulated by their addicted clients. Few offenders are willing to oblige their supervising POs or anyone else to give up their drugs or alcohol voluntarily. What usually happens is that there are frequent relapses where POs merely suggest starting over or trying again with a particular therapy. Also, many addicted clients are master manipulators and design various methods to beat the systems that are designed to test whether they are using specific drugs. It is not unusual for POs to give offenders chance after chance following drug tests which are "dirty" or disclose the use of one or more drugs within the past 24 or 48 hours (Torres, 1997:17). For many POs, this is part of establishing rapport with their clients and earning their trust. Some clients, for instance, object to being ordered to refrain from using alcohol, if their addiction happens to be cocaine. Why should they be expected to refrain from alcohol use if they have another type of addiction? One answer is that alcohol consumption is associated with a higher rate of relapse involving their drug of choice, whether it is cocaine, heroin, or some other addictive substance. The most common positives for drugs include cocaine, amphetamines, morphine, and marijuana. Other drugs include anabolic steroids, barbiturates, phencyclidine (PCP), and prescription medications such as diazepam (Valium), codeine, and methadone (Curtis, 2003).

Many offenders attempt to beat the tests administered by POs or private contractors by doing different things to contaminate their urine or blood specimens. Some of the techniques offenders use include using a rubber penis filled with clean urine; attaching to the unobserved side of the penis a tube leading to a container under the armpit; inserting a small bottle of clean urine into the vagina; pouring clean urine into a specimen bottle; dipping the bottle into the urinal or toilet and filling it with water; or contaminating the urine sample with various foreign substances, such as Drano, chlorine, or bleach. Other clients flush their specimens. This is one of the more common ways of trying to beat the tests. Flushing means to consume large quantities of water, coffee, or other liquids to dilute the concentration of drugs in the body and accelerate the excretion. The greater the liquid intake, the lower the concentration of the drug and the quicker the excretion rate. Some offenders simply fail to show up for their counseling sessions or treatment. Skipping meetings means no test and no detection (Torres, 1996:18–23). For many POs, a "no show" at a counseling session is "less serious" than testing positive for drugs.

Sam Torres, a former federal probation officer, believes that a continuum of sanctions should be imposed instead of the usual course of treatment prescribed by the medical model. The sanctions are as follows:

1. Admonishment, which is a verbal warning that the test was positive, or that the offender failed to report for testing.

2. Verbal admonishment by a probation officer, which is a verbal warning issued to the offender that further drug use will have consequences, such as mandatory participation in a 12-step program or other activities.

3. Written admonishment by the probation officer, which is a formal letter to the offender advising him/her of consequences for continuing to test positive for drug use.

4. Verbal admonishment by the probation officer and supervisor, which adds weight to the admonishment.

5. Written admonishment by the U.S. Parole Commission, if the client is a federal probationer or parolee.

6. Verbal admonishment by the court.

7. Lengthen the time in the current phase, or simply extending the time period of their current phase level.

8. Increase the client's phase level to closer supervision and testing.

9. Increase the level of supervision, including more frequent offender monitoring.

10. Community service as a punishment.

11. Alcoholics Anonymous or Narcotics Anonymous mandatory meetings; offenders must sign cards at these meetings to signify they attended.

12. Outpatient counseling.

13. Electronic monitoring.

14. Community correctional center participation.

15. Reside and participate in a sober-living program.

16. Arrest, short-term custody, and reinstatement to supervision.

17. Intermittent incarceration.

18. Therapeutic community (residential drug treatment).

19. Arrest, custody, and recommendation for program revocation (Torres, 1998:38–44).

The importance of these different stages of increasing sanctions is to make it clear to offenders that their relapses will have specific consequences. It is insufficient to merely threaten to do something. The PO actually has to follow through and do it. Torres recommends a zero tolerance policy, and he believes that offenders should be held accountable for their decision to use drugs. They are engaging in a rational choice to violate program requirements. Clients are given numerous opportunities to overcome their addictions. Complete abstinence is the recommended therapy according to this model (Torres, 1997).

Unfortunately, it is a fact that if drug-abusing offenders are eventually incarcerated, they will easily acquire drugs in their institutions from other inmates. There is about as much drug use, if not more, in prisons and jails than there is on city streets. Inmates use a multitude of methods to smuggle drugs into their institutions. And there are many creative ways of paying for these drugs in order to continue their addictions (Lurigio and Swartz, 1999:67–70).

Drug Screening and Methadone Treatment

Detecting drug abuse is most often accomplished through clinical screenings performed by addiction counselors or others. A clinical screening is an initial gathering and compiling of information to determine if an offender has a problem with alcohol or drug abuse (AOD) and if so, whether a comprehensive clinical assessment is warranted. Screening is accomplished through a structured interview or instruments designed to get offenders to self-report information. Screening also filters out individuals who have medical, legal, or psychological problems that must be addressed before they can fully participate in treatment (Shearer and Carter, 1999:30).

Some agencies use the Psychopathic Personality Inventory (PPI), which is a 56-item, self-report inventory that provides a total score on psychopathy and factor scores on eight dimensions of psychopathy: Machiavellian egocentricity; social potency; cold-heartedness; carefree nonplanfulness; fearlessness; blame externalization; impulsive nonconformity; and stress nonimmunity. The major screening and assessment is a standardized set of procedures designed to: (1) establish baseline information about AOD dependence; (2) assess client readiness for counseling; and (3) serve as treatment planning tools for counseling by identifying (a) the client's high-risk situations for AOD use and (b) the client's coping strengths and weaknesses (Brody and Rosenfeld, 2002).

Clients are considered ready for treatment when they perceive and accept that they have a problem or "own" the problem. In many instances, however, clients do not appear ready for treatment. They tend to minimize, deny, or reject and resist any attempt to help them from counselors. Certainly a part of this resistance or denial is related to their present addictive state, since they are not rational enough to appreciate the logical curative consequences of withdrawal (Shearer and Carter, 1999:32).

Perhaps the most serious problem associated with deterring substance abusers from persisting in their addictions is the physical reactions offenders experience during the withdrawal period. In instances of heroin addiction, for instance, complete and immediate abstinence from heroin causes intense pain throughout the body, complete with nausea, vomiting, and cramping. These symptoms continue for several days. Withdrawal from drugs is not a pleasant experience. Additionally, there is always the possibility that because of one's bodily condition and weakness, the physical stress of withdrawal can be debilitating, causing permanent nerve damage, even death. Therefore, in certain cases where serious addictions to drugs exist, the withdrawal treatment is gradual. Several drugs are used in the withdrawal process. These drugs, such as methadone, are also narcotics, but they cause fewer violent withdrawal symptoms. For instance, methadone is a synthetic narcotic used to treat morphine and heroin addiction. Actually, it is more powerful than morphine, but it has fewer debilitating side effects and the body can withstand adverse withdrawal reactions more easily. In short, drug withdrawal with the assistance of other drugs is more easily tolerated by the body. Many treatment programs, conducted under controlled hospital conditions, utilize methadone and other substances to treat serious addictions.

Some observers believe that the use of methadone in treating heroin and morphine addiction is merely substituting one narcotic for another and that one can become addicted to methadone. However, this observation neglects the fact that there are other dimensions to one's overall treatment program, including chemical dependency education, counseling, and other nondrug therapies. Furthermore, offenders receive continuous monitoring and are medically evaluated on a regular basis to determine how their body is responding to treatment. With the volume of drug-abusing offenders entering the criminal justice system, one increasingly used response is the drug court.

COMMUNITY PROGRAMS FOR SPECIAL-NEEDS OFFENDERS

Therapeutic Communities

A **therapeutic community** is a treatment model in which all activities, both formal and informal, are viewed as interrelated interventions that address the multidimensional disorder of the whole person. These activities include educational and therapeutic meetings and groups, as well as interpersonal and social activities of the community. Within this theoretical framework, social and psychological change evolves as a dynamic interaction between the individual and the peer community, its context of activities, and expectations for participation (Deitsch et al., 2001:26). Therapeutic communities are often mandated by the courts or parole boards for persons with particular substance-abuse problems or chemical dependencies. For instance, 720 offenders were mandated by the court for drug treatment into three highly structured therapeutic communities in the northeastern United States during the period from 1990 to 1993. They were subjected to a battery of tests, including the Circumstances, Motivation, Readiness, and Suitability attitudinal scale. In the cases of these court-placed offenders, the periods of their detention were unspecified. It remained at the discretion of program authorities to determine when they had successfully completed their programs by participating in community programming as outlined by their therapeutic community plan (Maxwell, 2000).

Many therapeutic community models are commenced in prison or jail settings and subsequently continued in an offender's city or town (Burdon et al., 2003). Therefore, therapeutic community clientele have the benefit of continuing their treatment and programming under limited supervision following their release from incarceration. Often, these therapeutic community programs are designed for offenders with chemical dependencies rather than for mentally ill patients (Stohr et al., 2002). Programs have been established in Texas, Washington, DC, and Delaware.

A Delaware-based therapeutic community, known as CREST, is prison-based and is applied to females who are encouraged to form networks of support for one another. During an experimental period in the mid-1990s, 41 female participants were involved in CREST, including a control group of 39 female work releasees. Both groups were compared while in prison, as well as in 6- and 18-month followups after they were released from incarceration. Women participating in the CREST program were more successful in remaining law-abiding, with a 39 percent recidivism rate. However, those who were on standard work release had a recidivism rate of 50 percent. Thus, the likelihood of relapse was greater for those who were not a part of the CREST program (Farrell, 2000). A similar study of substance-abusing clients was conducted in Washington, DC. Two therapeutic communities were studied and involved 412 randomly drawn drug-abusing clients (Nemes, Wish, and Messina, 1999). The program lasted 12 months and involved numerous community interventions and experiences. Subsequently, the clients were placed on outpatient services. Marked reductions in illicit drug use and crime were found among the clients who completed the program.

For POs, therapeutic community involvement of parolees alleviates some of their pressure to locate and integrate offender programming. It is already in place for some of these offenders. Thus, a PO's job is made much easier by simply having to supervise offenders already networked within their therapeutic community environments. A PO's work might consist primarily of performing periodic and random drug or curfew checks. The concept of therapeutic community is being considered and applied in countries outside of the United States. It appears to be gaining in popularity as an intervention for persons with serious addiction problems (Thomas, Holzer, and Wall, 2002).

Alcoholics Anonymous, Narcotics Anonymous, and Gamblers Anonymous Programs

As we have seen in therapeutic community and drug court interventions, **Alcoholics Anonymous** and **Narcotics Anonymous** programs have played major roles as community support mechanisms in order to provide social support for recovering alcohol and drug abusers (Cunningham et al., 1998). Alcoholics Anonymous and Narcotics Anonymous programs are designed to provide information and guidance for those with alcohol and drug dependencies. They are offered to inmates in prisons and jails as well as in their communities. They both involve a series of steps where participants admit that they are powerless to control their cravings for alcohol or drugs. These programs are frequently linked with probation and parole programs. Other programs deal with offenders who have been convicted of domestic violence-related offenses (Decker et al., 2002). Judges and parole boards often require probationers and parolees to attend their meetings as one of their special conditions of probation or parole.

Similar to the twelve-step program used by Alcoholics Anonymous, the twelve-step program for Narcotics Anonymous is as follows:

1. We admitted that we were powerless over our addiction, that our lives had become unmanageable.

2. We came to believe that a Power greater than ourselves could restore us to sanity.

3. We made a decision to turn our will and our lives over to the care of God as we understood Him.

4. We made a searching and fearless moral inventory of ourselves.

5. We admitted to God, to ourselves, and to another human being the exact nature of our wrongs.

6. We were entirely ready to have God remove all these defects of character.

7. We humbly asked Him to remove our shortcomings.

8. We made a list of all persons we had harmed, and became willing to make amends to them all.

9. We made direct amends to such people whenever possible, except when to do so would injure them or others.

10. We continue to take personal inventory and when we were wrong promptly admitted it.

11. We sought through prayer and meditation to improve our conscious contact with God as we understood Him, praying only for knowledge of His will for us and the power to carry that out.

12. Having had a spiritual awakening as a result of these steps, we tried to carry this message to addicts, and practice these principles in all our affairs (Narcotics Anonymous, 1999).

Meetings of these groups are usually announced in local newspapers daily throughout the nation. Persons are advised of their street locations and times. Some meetings are "closed," meaning that they are not open to the general public. These are occasions where permanent membership can band together and discuss intimate details of their alcohol and narcotics addictions with one another. Other meetings are open, and the public is invited. Only those with drug or alcohol dependencies are encouraged to attend these open meetings, although it is unlikely that someone wishing to see what goes on at these meetings would be barred from participating. During the meetings, which usually last one hour, each person is given an opportunity to stand, identify him- or herself by first name only, and indicate the nature of his or her addiction. Some attendees take this opportunity to apologize to the group for their addictions. They elicit acceptance and empathy from other attendees. At the end of the meeting, a prayer is uttered, with all of those willing to do so linking hands in a large circle.

The religious components in both Alcoholics Anonymous and Narcotics Anonymous have alienated certain drug abusers who are atheists and do not believe in God. Several options have been made available to them, including various secular organizations that are organized along lines similar to those of AA and NA. In some areas of the country, such as Tampa, Florida, groups of substance-abusing adult probationers have been encouraged to form associations and hold meetings that emphasize positive behaviors (Peters et al., 1993).

Some observers question the value of AA and NA as viable interventions. Where convicted offenders are required to attend such meetings as a part of

their probation programs, there is no way that they can be induced to participate actively in these meetings once there. They sign a card signifying their attendance. There is no pressure on them to become actively involved in
discussions. No one can compel them to say anything about themselves
(O'Callaghan, Gagnon, and Brochu, 1990). Nevertheless, POs continue to encourage those with alcohol and drug dependencies to attend these meetings,
and attend them with great frequency (Read, 1990).

Increasingly recognized as a serious addiction is gambling. Where it is permitted, gambling is not illegal. Nevertheless, it is addictive in much the same
sense that alcohol and drugs are addictive. In many areas of the country, organizations have been established to treat gambling addiction, especially where it
has been related to criminal activity. Persons who gamble may lose a lot of
money. They may resort to crime to obtain additional money to pursue their
gambling addiction. Usually, Gamblers Anonymous organizations have included
twelve-step programs similar to AA and NA, although they also include educational programming emphasizing personal financial counseling. Individual and
group therapy also accompany Gamblers Anonymous programming, depending
upon the jurisdiction (Gowen and Speyerer, 1995). Gamblers Anonymous organizations have been in existence for several decades (Livingston, 1974).

Drug Courts and the Drug Court Movement

Drug Courts Defined.   **Drug courts** are special courts that are dedicated exclusively to the needs of drug-abusing offenders. They work with prosecutors, defense
counsels, treatment professionals, probation officers, and other community agencies to achieve case outcomes for drug abusers that will maximize their successful
treatment. Drug courts were established in 1989 in Dade County, Florida (Goldkamp, 2000). Since 1989 and through 2001, drug courts have been implemented in
over 600 jurisdictions. More than 150,000 drug-using offenders have participated
in drug court programs. Of these, about 70 percent have successfully completed
their programs or are actively participating in them (Peters and Murrin, 2000).

One unique feature of drug courts is the specialization they exhibit toward
drug-abusing offenders. Most other courts are courts of general criminal jurisdiction, where drug offenders are combined with other types of criminals and punished similarly. However, drug courts recognize the atypicality of drug abusers
and their need for special services provided only through an integrated community program involving several helping agencies. Although drug courts are currently enjoying a remarkable degree of success in the treatment of drug-abusing
offenders, not everyone is enthusiastic about their emergence and persistence.
One criticism is that for some drug abusers, being sent to a drug court for processing is more stigmatizing than therapeutic. Thus, the reintegrative intentions
of drug courts may be defeated in part because of their specialization in dealing
exclusively with drug offenders. Thus, diversion to drug court may be regarded
as discriminatory by some drug abusers, who in turn, will reject the reintegrative
efforts of those seeking to assist them (Miethe, Lu, and Reese, 2000).

Despite this criticism, drug courts show no signs of abating in the near future. If anything, they are being expanded in more diverse areas of the country
annually, and at a phenomenal growth rate (Goldkamp, 2000). Furthermore,
drug courts are not exclusively focused on drugs. There are drug courts that
address alcohol dependency as well as hard drugs. A unique DWI drug court
has been established in Las Cruces, New Mexico, for example, where specially

trained court personnel assess first- and second-time DWI offenders for symptoms of alcoholism. A subsequent treatment program is prescribed by the judge, which includes individual, group, and family counseling sessions. Results from a 24-month followup suggest that the DWI drug court in New Mexico is having a substantial impact on decreasing the recidivism rates of DWI offenders who participate in the program compared with nonparticipants (Breckenridge et al., 2000).

One feature of drug courts is that they provide for more consistent and frequent monitoring of participating offenders who are ordered into particular therapies (Belenko, 1999). Not only is the supervision more comprehensive, but there are increased rates of retention in treatment and reduced drug use and criminal behavior while participants are in these programs. Drug courts are designed to handle more serious offenders, many of whom have prior criminal histories with a myriad of physical and mental health needs. Recidivism rates almost always decline following one's participation in such programs (Belenko, 1999; National Drug Court Institute, 1999a, 1999b).

The Drug Court Model. There is a model typically followed by drug courts. This model entails the following characteristics:

1. A single drug court judge and staff who provide leadership and focus.
2. Expedited adjudication through early identification of appropriate program participants and referral to treatment as soon as possible after arrest.
3. Intensive long-term treatment and aftercare for appropriate drug-using offenders.
4. Comprehensive and well-coordinated supervision through regular status hearings before a single drug court judge to monitor treatment progress through program compliance.
5. Increased defendant accountability through a series of graduated sanctions and rewards.
6. Mandatory and frequent drug testing (Huddleston, 1998:98).

A study of 24 drug courts by Columbia University's National Center on Addiction and Substance Abuse (CASA) has provided one of the first major academic reviews and analyses of drug court effectiveness. How has the model worked with offenders? Essentially, the study found that drug courts provide closer, more comprehensive supervision and much more frequent drug testing and monitoring than conventional forms of community supervision, such as probation or parole. More important, drug use and criminal behavior are substantially reduced while offenders are participating in drug court programs. The CASA study further summarizes findings from older and newer drug courts. The results are fairly consistent in that:

- Drug courts have been successful in engaging and retaining felony offenders in programmatic and treatment services who have substantial substance abuse and criminal histories but little prior treatment engagement.
- Drug courts provide more comprehensive and closer supervision of the drug-using offender than other forms of community supervision.
- Drug use and criminal behavior are substantially reduced while clients are participating in drug court.

- Criminal behavior is lower after program participation, especially for graduates, although few studies have tracked recidivism for more than one year post-program.
- Drug courts generate cost savings, at least in the short term, from reduced jail/prison use, reduced criminality and lower criminal justice system costs.
- Drug courts have been successful in bridging the gap between the court and the treatment/public health systems and spurring greater cooperation among the various agencies and personnel within the criminal justice system, as well as between the criminal justice system and the community (Belenko, 1999; Huddleston, 1998:99–100).

The cost-effectiveness of drug courts has been assessed. In Multnomah County, Oregon, a program known as the STOP Drug Court Diversion Program was evaluated. A sample of 150 participants was compared with three other groups, including STOP non-completers (persons who failed drug tests or did not appear at their status hearings). For every taxpayer dollar spent on programming costs of STOP, a $2.50 savings to taxpayers was realized. If victimization costs are factored in, then the cost savings rises to about $10 for every dollar spent on programming (Finigan, 1999). Similar savings have been reported by other jurisdictions (Peters and Murrin, 2000; Winfree and Giever, 2000).

The Jefferson County (Kentucky) Drug Court Program.   An example of one drug court in action is the Jefferson County Drug Court Program in Kentucky. Based on the Dade County, Florida, model, this model diverts first-time, drug possession offenders into a 12-month community treatment program that includes acupuncture and the development of social and educational skills (Vito and Tewksbury, 1998:46). It is monitored directly by the drug court judge, who helps to supervise the offenders' treatment programs. The model breaks down the traditional adversarial roles of prosecutors and defense attorneys. If the judge believes that offenders are trying to break the pattern of addiction, then the offenders remain in treatment even after they test positive for drugs several times. Therefore, the treatment program may be continued indefinitely until the offender successfully completes the program.

The drug court judge extends judicial oversight throughout all phases of the program. Clients are required to attend sessions of drug court on a schedule set by the judge. Before weekly sessions of drug court, the judge is provided with individualized progress reports for all participants. During these court sessions, the judge reviews the program progress of each client. Upon review, the judge may (1) continue client participation; (2) permanently remove the client from the program; or (3) remand the client to a term of jail incarceration for failure to meet program requirements.

Participation in drug court is voluntary. Referrals are made to the drug court from prosecutors, or public or private attorneys. Clients must be 18 years of age and meet the following criteria established by the prosecutor:

1. Possession versus trafficking cases: Preference is given to cocaine possession cases; trafficking cases are considered after a review of possession cases.
2. Prior drug arrests: Defendants with multiple trafficking arrests in their history are not considered.
3. No history of violent offenses: Offenders with a history of violent crimes are not eligible for inclusion in the program.
4. Eligibility: Only Jefferson County cases are eligible for inclusion.

5. Police approval: The lead officer in the case is consulted in the decision to recommend a client for diversion into the drug court program.

6. Quantity of cocaine: Any offender in possession of 1 or more ounces of cocaine is not eligible for drug court; any offender with 5 or more grams of cocaine is presumed to be trafficking in drugs and is placed on the trafficking list of offenders eligible for program review (Vito and Tewksbury, 1998:46).

After all applicants are screened and meet the initial screening criteria, they must undergo a psychological assessment. The purpose of the assessment is to determine whether the client is amenable to treatment and does not pose a risk to the community. Drug court participants must abide by all program conditions. All drug court participants must be punctual, attend all required program sessions, be nonviolent, refrain from attending treatment sessions while under the influence of drugs, and behave lawfully. The aim is to create and maintain a receptive treatment environment, promote prosocial behavior, and establish a sense of individual accountability among clients. The various treatment programs offered through the drug court include acupuncture; meditation; individual counseling; group therapy; Alcoholics Anonymous (AA); Narcotics Anonymous (NA); and chemical dependency education (Vito and Tewksbury, 1998:46–47).

There are three treatment phases:

Phase I: Detoxification (10 days)

1. Four random drug tests

2. Attendance at a minimum of five weekly meetings of AA/NA

3. Participation in all individual and group counseling sessions as determined by program staff

4. Optional acupuncture and/or meditation sessions

In order to move to phase II, the client must receive a maximum of four negative drug screens, attend all assigned individual and group therapy sessions, and attend all weekly AA/NA meetings.

Phase II: Stabilization (108 days)

1. Acupuncture and/or meditation sessions as needed/requested

2. Two weekly drug tests (a minimum number of positive drug screenings during each of the first four weeks and no positive drug screens by the sixth week of this phase are necessary to move to phase III)

3. Attendance at a minimum of four AA/NA meetings as prescribed by the treatment plan; clients must obtain an AA/NA sponsor.

4. Attendance at all individual and group counseling sessions as prescribed by the treatment plan.

5. Significant progress toward meeting treatment plan goals as determined by treatment program staff and the drug court judge.

Phase III: Aftercare (6 months)

1. Acupuncture and/or meditation sessions as requested by the client.

2. Random drug tests.

3. Participation in educational, vocational, remedial, and other training programs as specified in the individual treatment plan.

4. Individual and group counseling as needed.

5. Attendance at a minimum of three AA/NA meetings per week.

6. Maintenance of and regular contact with a full-time AA/NA sponsor.

In order to graduate from the drug court program, clients must meet the following requirements: (1) remaining drug-free as shown by the results of their drug tests in the last two months of this phase; (2) securing or maintaining employment or enrolling or maintaining enrollment in an educational program; and/or engaging in full-time parenting responsibilities. Only those clients who have paid all accrued fees will be permitted to graduate from drug court (Vito and Tewksbury, 1998:47–48).

Results from the Jefferson County Drug Court Program were based on an analysis of 237 clients who were screened and included in the program. They were compared with a sample of 76 persons who were screened but not included in the program. Reconviction was used as the recidivism measure and indicator of program failure. There were significant differences in failure rates of graduates compared with nonparticipants. Graduates of drug court had a reconviction rate of 13 percent, while the reconviction rate of the comparison group was 55 percent. This finding suggests that the Jefferson County Drug Court treatment program has been successful. However, the graduates were also compared according to whether they were subsequently charged with a drug/alcohol-related offense. This time, about 43 percent of the graduates had been charged during the followup period, however, these figures are slightly lower than the nongraduates, of whom 46 percent were charged with new drug offenses. Thus, nearly half of all drug court graduates were unable to avoid relapses back to drugs. One recommendation was that drug court graduates should continue to receive regular drug testing and monitoring in order to maintain their resistance to drugs (Vito and Tewksbury, 1998:50–51).

Drug court programs in other jurisdictions have had similar success rates. The Brooklyn, NY Treatment Court was commenced in 1996. Over 1,000 drug abusers were placed in treatment programs by this drug court during the interval 1996–1999. Two-thirds were still actively involved in the program, and about one-third had completed 180 days of treatment. While there were relapses, relapse rates were similar to the Jefferson County, Kentucky, rates of about 50 percent (Harrell and Roman, 1999). And in Riverside, California, a drug court operated a Recovery Opportunity Center (ROC), which was a drug treatment day program. There were 103 ROC clients who were followed up after 20 months from program admission. Of the graduates, 58 percent showed no signs of substance abuse. Recidivism rates for graduates were about 15 percent, again comparable with the Jefferson County, Kentucky, program (Sechrest et al., 1998).

SUMMARY

Special-needs offenders present diverse problems for probation agencies and paroling authorities throughout the United States. Special-needs offenders include those who are drug- or alcohol-dependent, the mentally ill, sex offenders and child sexual abusers, developmentally disabled offenders, and offenders with AIDS/HIV or other communicable diseases such as tuberculosis. POs have increasing responsibilities for networking among various community-based agencies that offer diverse services for offender-clients. Many communities do not have adequate services that coincide with some of the problems manifested by offenders. Attempts are being made to individualize offender treatments, to provide family counseling and parenting education as a means of preventing family violence, and to provide offenders with parenting skills so that better childhood interventions can be employed. Supervising offenders is hazardous work. POs need to acquire greater training to anticipate the types of offenders they will supervise and how different psychological and social offender problems should be resolved whenever they arise.

Mentally ill offenders are abundant in our prisons and jails. Many of these persons become clients of POs, and POs must learn different ways of supervising these clients whose behaviors are often violent and unpredictable. Another class of special-needs offender is the sex offender. While sex offenders make up only a small proportion of jail and prison inmates as well as clients of POs, they are regarded as a most heinous aggregate by citizens generally. Thus, POs have increased responsibilities to monitor sex offenders of different types very closely as a way of protecting the community from them. Most, however, have no prior criminal histories, are nonviolent, and pose little or no danger to others.

Drug and/or alcohol dependent offenders are associated with over 80 percent of all criminal activity and arrests. The likelihood of relapse is greatest among this offender aggregate. Therefore, POs must monitor their progress closely, often by administering urinalyses and other types of tests to determine the presence of illegal substances. Another class of offender is the client with AIDS/HIV and/or tuberculosis. Tuberculosis cases have been rising in the United States at an alarming rate. While POs have a low likelihood of contracting AIDS/HIV from their clients, they are at far greater risk when interacting with tuberculosis-infected clients.

Gang members comprise another offender category that requires special treatment and supervision. POs must be cognizant of gang signs and symbols as well as the dangers of entering gang territories for the purpose of visiting their gang member clientele. Developmentally disabled offenders must be accommodated as well. While there aren't many of these offenders in the population, their numbers are growing. POs must increasingly network with various community agencies to see that these persons have their needs met appropriately.

Various types of interventions have been recommended for each of these offender groupings. For sex offenders, community treatment programs and sex therapy classes are often required as a part of their probation or parole programs. Offenders with AIDS/HIV or tuberculosis must be linked with appropriate agencies so that they can learn how to avoid transmitting their diseases to others. Thus, educational courses of various kinds are recommended or required as a part of their therapeutic treatment. The largest aggregate of offenders under PO supervision have drug or alcohol dependencies. In recent years, drug courts have been established in most jurisdictions. These drug courts are specialized courts that hear only DWI or drug cases. Appropriate treatments are recommended or required. Drug courts work closely with a network of persons and agencies to ensure that drug dependent offenders receive appropriate instruction and treatment as needed. Often, counseling on an individual or group basis is recommended. Several drug court programs in different parts of the United States were described.

Increasingly, therapeutic communities are being established in different communities as treatment models for persons with different types of addictions or dependencies. Therapeutic community refers to multiple interventions and agencies networked in such a way so as to achieve a positive result for participating clients. Therapeutic communities are often instituted in prisons and jails, although they continue once offenders leave incarceration on probation or parole. Assisting offenders in their rehabilitation are private self-help organizations, such as Alcoholics Anonymous, Narcotics Anonymous, and Gamblers Anonymous. Often, attendance at these meetings is compulsory for probationers or parolees with drug or alcohol or gambling addictions.

Gangs are pervasive in U.S. society. Numbers of members, organizational structure, and operational sophistication are such that many POs find it difficult to relate to them. Learning programs are established to inform and advise POs about the latest advancements in gang psychology and methodology. Police agencies and parole/probation departments are working closer together in those areas where gang presence is especially strong. Greater communication between these agencies assists POs in heightening offender accountability. If gang members want to leave their gangs, there are tattoo removal programs to assist them free of charge in ridding themselves of telltale tattoos that often are used to control and manipulate them. Without identifying tattoos, such persons can move to other parts of the country and start new lives without the fear of being recognized by other gang members and enlisted involuntarily into illicit gang activities.

QUESTIONS FOR REVIEW

1. Who are special-needs offenders? What problems do they pose for supervising POs?

2. How do probationers and parolees with AIDS/HIV or tuberculosis pose special supervisory problems for POs?

3. Who are developmentally disabled offenders? What special provisions for these offenders must be made by supervising POs?

4. How many mentally ill offenders are under the supervision of POs throughout the United States? In what ways do mentally ill offenders pose a danger to POs during their supervision?

5. Why are sex offenders, who are relatively few in number compared with other offender groups, given so much attention by the media and public? How does this attention affect how POs supervise them?

6. What are some of the special programs that have been created for sex offenders and are a mandatory part of their probation or parole programs?

7. Why are substance-abusing offenders so troublesome for their supervising POs? What is the rate of relapse among drug- and alcohol-dependent offenders? How can relapse be prevented?

8. What are drug courts? What are some characteristics of drug courts that distinguish them from other types of courts? To what extent do drug courts interact with various community agencies to assist offenders on probation or parole?

9. What are Alcoholics Anonymous, Narcotics Anonymous, and Gamblers Anonymous? What is their relation to religion, if any? How do they operate in relation to various offender treatment programs?

10. What is a tattoo removal program and what are its objectives?

SUGGESTED READINGS

Holmes, Ronald M. and Stephen T. Holmes (eds.) (2002). *Current Perspectives on Sex Crimes.* Thousand Oaks, CA: Sage.

Johnstone, Gerry (2002). *Restorative Justice: Ideas, Values, and Debates.* London: Willan.

Jordan, B. Kathleen et al. (2002). "Lifetime Use of Mental Health and Substance Abuse Treatment Services by Incarcerated Women Felons." *Psychiatric Services* 53: 317–325.

Krebs, Christopher P. (2002). "High-Risk HIV Transmission Behavior in Prison and the Prison Subculture." *Prison Journal* 82: 19–49.

Thornton, David (2002). "Constructing and Testing a Framework for Dynamic Risk Assessment." *Sexual Abuse: A Journal of Research and Treatment* 14: 139–153.

INTERNET CONNECTIONS

Adcare Correctional Drug and Alcohol Treatment Programs
http://www.adcare.com/correc/

Addictions page
http://www.well.com/user/woa

Alcoholics Anonymous
http://www.alcoholics-anomymous.org

International Institute on Special Needs Offenders
http://www.iisno.org.uk/

MAN Domestic Violence Offender Treatment Program
http://www.themangroup.org/downloads/Offender_Treat_Recs4-17.pdf

Shadow Track Technologies
http://www.shadowtrack.com/?sources=Overture

Smart Recovery
http://www.smartrecovery.org

Special Offenders and Special Needs Offenders
http://www.shsu.edu/~icc_rjh/364f00.htm

Texas Council on Offenders with Mental Impairments
http://www.tdcj.state.tx.us/tcomi-contcare.htm

2003 International Conference on Special Needs Offenders
http://www.specialneedsoffenders.org/aboutus.html

CHAPTER 13 | *Juvenile Probation and Parole*

Chapter Outline

Chapter Objectives

As the result of reading this chapter, the following objectives will be realized:

1. Defining and describing juveniles and juvenile delinquency, including its various forms.
2. Identifying status offenses and the process of deinstitutionalization of status offenses.
3. Examining the juvenile justice system, including its historical evolution, the various components of it, and various dispositional alternatives.
4. Describing the waiver or transfer process for certifying juveniles as adults so that they may be prosecuted in criminal courts as adults.
5. Highlighting several landmark juvenile cases involving U.S. Supreme Court decisions extending various rights to juveniles.
6. Describing the nature of juvenile offenses and offense seriousness.
7. Describing various probation programs for juveniles, including diversion and probation.
8. Describing the process of predispositional report preparation and the contents of such reports.
7. Identifying various detention and parole programs available for juveniles.
8. Highlighting several important trends in juvenile probation and parole and program revocation.

• *M.E.B. was a North Carolina juvenile adjudicated delinquent and placed on probation. One condition of his probation was that he must wear a sign around his neck which read, "I AM A JUVENILE CRIMINAL." M.E.B. appealed, contending that this condition was unreasonable. An appeals court agreed and overturned the judge's decision regarding that specific probation requirement. The court said that the condition imposed by the judge violated North Carolina law. There were specific statutory provisions which protected the confidentiality of juvenile offenders. Moreover, the focus under the juvenile justice system is not punishment, but promoting the best interests of the child. The condition imposed in the present case unnecessarily subjected the juvenile to public humiliation and embarrassment. [Matter of M.E.B., 2002]*

• *D.W.L. was an Alabama juvenile who was adjudicated delinquent for a property offense. As a part of his probation orders, the judge ordered D.W.L. to pay restitution to the victim for the damage he had caused to the victim's property. D.W.L. failed to make restitution, at which time the juvenile court judge ordered D.W.L.'s father to pay the restitution. The father objected and appealed. The appellate court upheld the right of the juvenile court judge to hold D.W.L.'s father accountable for paying the restitution. Although a rule exists to make a parent a party to a juvenile court proceeding, this was not followed in the present case. However, the father had not objected to the restitution order when it was originally imposed, which included the provision that if the juvenile failed to pay the restitution, the parent would be liable for it. Thus, parents may be held liable for the delinquent acts of their children, including the responsibility to pay restitution if required. [D.W.L. v. State, 2001]*

• *J.R.M. was a juvenile who was brought before the juvenile court in Minnesota on three different occasions. Following one of these appearances, J.R.M. was granted diversion, which he completed successfully. On his third appearance before the juvenile court judge, he was adjudicated delinquent on a drug charge. The judge ordered J.R.M. to undergo an inpatient treatment as a part of his rehabilitation. J.R.M. objected and appealed. The appel-*

late court ruled that inpatient commitments of juveniles can only be made for juveniles if their present offense is their third offense, and if it involves a controlled substance. In this case, J.R.M.'s requirement by the juvenile court judge to undergo inpatient treatment was overturned by the appellate court. It held that the prior judgment of diversion should not have been counted against J.R.M. as one of three drug-related offenses. [In re J.R.M., *2002*]

• *Adrian R. was a California juvenile charged with misdemeanor assault and battery in connection with his activities with a criminal street gang. The court placed Adrian R. on a 5-year probationary term under the supervision of his grandparents. Under the conditions of Adrian R.'s probation, he was not to have any contact with the other two juveniles involved in the attack on the assault victim; he was not to be present at any known gang gatherings; and he was not to be around anyone he knew to be a gang member. Adrian R. was also required to register under California's Penal Code as a gang-affiliated individual. Adrian R. appealed, alleging these conditions were unconstitutionally vague, violated his rights of free speech and association, and that registering as a gang member was tantamount to an unreasonable search and seizure. A California appellate court rejected all of Adrian R.'s arguments, declaring all of these conditions reasonable and in the furtherance of governmental interests. For instance, under California law, the term gang had a specific and limited meaning. The registration requirement was not unreasonable, since the juvenile on probation has a reduced expectation of privacy. The court ruled that the government interest in detecting and preventing crime outweighed this narrow intrusion on the defendant's speech and association rights.* [In re Adrian R., *2002*]

• *N.D.F. was a Indiana juvenile adjudicated delinquent following a hearing where evidence was presented of two prior delinquency adjudications on unrelated felony charges in other jurisdictions. N.D.F. appealed, contending that his prior adjudications were irrelevant to the present hearing, since they involved adjudications from other jurisdictions. The Indiana appellate court disagreed and held that it was proper for the juvenile court to consider prior adjudications in other jurisdictions when deciding the nature of the disposition for N.D.F. for his current adjudication offense.* [N.D.F. v. State, *2002*]

INTRODUCTION

This chapter is about juvenile probation and parole. There is little consistency among jurisdictions throughout the United States about how juvenile probation and parole are handled. No national policies exist that apply to every jurisdiction. Thus, it is impossible to make blanket generalizations about the juvenile probation and parole process, except in the broadest of terms. The first section describes juveniles and juvenile delinquency. How are juvenile delinquents defined? Another class of juvenile is the status offender. Status offenders differ in several significant ways from juvenile delinquents. These differences will be described. The deinstitutionalization of status offenders is a movement that commenced in the 1970s to remove status offenders from incarcerative settings normally used for more serious juveniles. While many states have implemented the deinstitutionalization of status offenders, other states are either undecided on the issue or are moving slowly toward such a policy. This policy will be described and its significance and relevance for affected juveniles will be explained.

The second section presents an overview of the juvenile justice system, describing briefly the origins and functions of juvenile courts. The doctrine of *parens patriae,* inherited from England, has had a profound influence on juvenile courts in the United States. This doctrine will be described. The juvenile justice system or process, as some professionals prefer to label it, will be presented from the point of juvenile arrests, intake, petitions and adjudicatory proceedings, and judicial dispositions. Various dispositional options available to juvenile court judges will be listed and described. These include nominal, conditional, and **custodial disposition** options. The next section of the chapter examines various juvenile probation and parole programs. It is not intended to be comprehensive, since juvenile justice textbooks cover this information in far greater detail. Nevertheless, several key programs will be described that provide the reader with a broad perspective of available juvenile probation and parole programs.

The final section describes the **juvenile** probation and parole revocation process. Almost no U.S. Supreme Court action has been taken regarding revocations of juvenile probation and parole. Often, state and local jurisdictions have followed the guidelines of probation and parole revocations set forth by various precedent-setting landmark cases for adult criminals. They included *Mempa v. Rhay* (1967), *Gagnon v. Scarpelli* (1973), and *Morrissey v. Brewer* (1972). Juvenile courts and revocation proceedings are not bound by these adult cases, however. But the cases do serve as guidelines for juvenile courts to follow at their option. Several state cases involving juvenile probation and parole revocation will be presented, however, in order to illustrate how different jurisdictions deal with juvenile probation or parole program violations.

JUVENILES AND JUVENILE DELINQUENCY

Juvenile Offenders

Juvenile offenders or **juvenile delinquents** are classified and defined according to several different criteria. For instance, the 1899 Illinois **Juvenile Court Act** that created juvenile courts determined that the jurisdiction of juvenile courts extended to all juveniles under the age of 16 who were found to be in violation of any state or local laws (Grietens, Rink, and Hellinckx, 2003). About a fifth of all states, including Illinois, currently place the upper age limit for juveniles at either 15 or 16. In the remaining states, the upper limit for juveniles is 17 (except for Wyoming, where it is 18). Ordinarily, the jurisdiction of juvenile courts includes all young persons who have not yet attained the age at which they should be treated as adults for purposes of criminal law (Black, 1990:867). At the federal level, juveniles are considered to be persons who have not yet attained their eighteenth birthday (18 U.S.C., Sec. 5031, 2004).

Upper and Lower Jurisdictional Age Limits.   While fairly uniform upper age limits for juveniles have been established in all U.S. jurisdictions (either under 16, under 17, or under 18 years of age), there is no uniformity concerning applicable lower age limits. English common law placed juveniles under age 7 beyond the reach of criminal courts, since it was believed that those under age 7 were incapable of formulating criminal intent or *mens rea*. However, many juvenile courts throughout the United States have no specified lower age limits for those juveniles within their purview. Few, if any, juvenile courts will process three-year-olds who kill others through the juvenile court, although these courts technically can do so in some jurisdictions.

Treatment and Punishment Functions of Juvenile Courts.   The idea that in order for juvenile courts to exercise jurisdiction over juveniles, these youths must be offenders and have committed criminal acts is misleading. Many youths who appear before juvenile court judges have not violated any criminal laws. Rather, their status as juveniles renders them subject to juvenile court control, provided certain circumstances exist. These circumstances may be the quality of their adult supervision, if any. Other circumstances may be that they run away from home, are truant from school, or loiter on certain city streets during evening hours. **Runaways,** truants, or curfew violators are considered **status offenders,** since their actions would not be criminal ones if committed by adults. Additionally, children who are physically, psychologically, or sexually abused by parents or other adults in their homes are brought within the scope of juvenile court authority. Some of these children are PINS, or persons in need of supervision. These youths are often supervised and treated by community social welfare agencies (Tracy, 2002).

Delinquency and Juvenile Delinquents

The majority of youthful offenders who appear before juvenile courts are those who have violated state or local laws or ordinances. The jurisdiction of juvenile courts depends upon the established legislative definitions of juveniles among the different states. The federal government has no juvenile court. Rather, federal cases involving juveniles infrequently are heard in federal district courts, but adjudicated juveniles are housed in state or local facilities if the sentences involve commitment to secure youth facilities. Ordinarily, upper and lower age limits are prescribed. In reality, the most liberal definition of juvenile delinquency is whatever the juvenile court believes should be brought within its jurisdiction (Flowers, 2002). This definition vests juvenile judges and other juvenile authorities with broad discretionary powers to define almost any juvenile conduct as delinquent conduct. Today, the majority of U.S. jurisdictions restrict their definitions of juvenile delinquency to any act committed by a juvenile that, if committed by an adult, would be considered a crime (Tracy, 2002).

Status Offenders

Status offenses are any acts committed by juveniles that would (1) bring the juveniles to the attention of juvenile courts and (2) not be crimes if committed by adults. Common juvenile status offenses include running away from home, truancy, and curfew violations. Many of the youths who engage in this conduct are incorrigible, habitually disobedient, and beyond parental control. Truants and liquor law violators may be more inclined to become chronic offenders and to engage in more serious, possibly criminal, behaviors (Bond-Maupin and Maupin, 2002). An influential factor contributing to juvenile offender chronicity and persistence is contact with juvenile courts. Contact with juvenile courts, especially frequent contact, is believed by some researchers to stigmatize youths and cause them either to be labeled or acquire self-concepts as delinquents or deviants (Chesney-Lind and Okamoto, 2001). Therefore, diversion of certain types of juvenile offenders from the juvenile justice system has been advocated and recommended to minimize these potentially adverse consequences of systemic contact.

AN OVERVIEW OF THE JUVENILE JUSTICE SYSTEM

The **juvenile justice system** consists of a more or less integrated network of agencies, institutions, organizations, and personnel that process juvenile offenders. This network is made up of law enforcement agencies, prosecutors and courts;

corrections, probation, and parole services; and public and private community-based treatment programs that provide youths with diverse services. The definition is intentionally qualified by the phrase more or less integrated because the concept of juvenile justice means different things for the states and to the federal government. Also, in some jurisdictions, the diverse components of the juvenile justice system are closely coordinated, while in other jurisdictions, these components are at best loosely coordinated, if they are coordinated at all (Felson and Haynie, 2002).

The Origins and Purposes of Juvenile Courts

Juvenile Courts as an American Creation.   Juvenile courts are a relatively recent American creation. However, modern U.S. juvenile courts have various less formal European antecedents. While the origin of this cutting point is unknown, the age of 7 was used in Roman times to separate **infants** from those older children who were accountable to the law for their actions. During the Middle Ages, English common law established under the monarchy adhered to the same standard. In the United States, several state jurisdictions currently apply this distinction and consider all children below the age of 7 not accountable for any criminal acts they may commit. This is a **common law** practice.

Early Juvenile Reforms.   Reforms in the American colonies relating to the treatment and/or punishment of juvenile offenders occurred slowly. Shortly after the Revolutionary War, religious interests in the United States moved forward with various proposals designed to improve the plight of the oppressed, particularly those who were incarcerated in prisons and jails. In 1787, the Quakers in Pennsylvania established the Philadelphia Society for Alleviating the Miseries of Public Prisons. This largely philanthropic society comprised of prominent citizens, religious leaders, and philanthropists was appalled by existing prison and jail conditions. Male, female, and juvenile offenders alike were housed in common quarters and treated poorly. In 1790, the Society's efforts were rewarded. The Philadelphia Walnut Street Jail described in Chapter 5 had considerable historical significance for corrections as well as for juvenile offenders. One of its major innovations was that women and children were maintained in separate rooms apart from adult male offenders during evening hours.

The **New York House of Refuge** was established in New York City in 1825 by the Society for the Prevention of Pauperism. This was an institution largely devoted to managing status offenders, such as runaways or incorrigible children. Compulsory education and other forms of training and assistance were provided to these children. However, the strict, prison-like regimen of this organization was not entirely therapeutic for its clientele. Many of the youthful offenders who were sent to such institutions, including the House of Reformation in Boston, were offspring of immigrants (Hess and Clement, 1993).

The Case of Ex parte Crouse.   Until the late 1830s, little consistency was apparent related to the division of labor between parental, religious, and state authority over juveniles. In 1839, a decision in a state case invested juvenile authorities with considerable parental power. The case of *Ex parte Crouse* (1839) involved a father who sought custody of his daughter from the Philadelphia House of Refuge. The girl had been committed to that facility by the court because she was declared unmanageable. She was not given a jury trial. Rather, the judge arbitrarily committed her. A higher court rejected the father's claim that parental control of children is exclusive, natural, and proper. It upheld the power of the state to exercise necessary reforms and restraints to protect children from themselves and their environments. While this decision was only applicable to Pennsylvania citizens and their children, other states took note of it and sought to invoke similar controls over errant children in their jurisdictions. In effect, children (at least in Pennsylvania) were temporarily deprived of any legal standing to challenge decisions made by the state in their behalf. This was the general state of juvenile affairs until the post–Civil War period known as reconstruction.

Extensive family migration toward large cities occurred after the Civil War. New York, Philadelphia, Boston, and Chicago were centers where fragmented families attempted to find work. Often, both parents had to work, and such work involved extended working hours (e.g., 16-hour work periods). This meant that while parents worked, increasing numbers of children roamed city streets unsupervised. Religious organizations subsequently intervened as a way of protecting unsupervised youths from the perils of life in the streets. Believing that these youths would subsequently turn to lives of crime as adults, many reformers and philanthropists sought to save them from their plight. Thus, in different cities throughout the United States, various groups were formed to find and control these youths by offering them constructive work programs, healthful living conditions, and above all, adult supervision. Collectively, these efforts became widely known as the **child-saver movement. Child-savers** came largely from the middle and upper classes, and their assistance to youths took many forms. Food and shelter were provided to children who were in trouble with the law or who were simply idle. Private homes were converted into settlements where social, educational, and other important activities could be provided for needy youths.

Reform Schools.   In a period prior to the Civil War, **reform schools** were established and proliferated. One of the first state-operated reform schools was established in Westboro, Massachusetts, in 1848 (Myers and Sangster, 2001). By the end of the nineteenth century, all states had reform schools (Harlan, 1998). All of these institutions were characterized by strict discipline, absolute control over juvenile behavior, and compulsory work at various trades. Another common feature was that they were controversial. In the mid-1900s almost every reform school was renamed. The most common name attributed to such facilities in later years was industrial schools, to emphasize their vocational and educational components rather than punishment-centered ones (Knupfer, 1997).

Children's Tribunals.   While Illinois is credited with establishing the first juvenile court system in the United States, an earlier juvenile justice apparatus was created in Massachusetts in 1874. This was known as a **children's tribunal,** and it was used exclusively as a mechanism for dealing with children charged with crimes; it was kept separate from the system of criminal courts for adults. These tribunals lasted for several decades until they were eventually replaced with more formal juvenile court systems.

Dependent and Neglected Children.   Few legal challenges of state authority over juveniles were lodged by parents during the 1800s. But in 1870, an Illinois case made it possible for special courts to be established to dispose of juvenile matters and represented an early recognition of certain minimal rights they might have. Daniel O'Connell, a youth who was declared vagrant and in need of supervision, was committed to the Chicago Reform School for an unspecified period.

O'Connell's parents challenged this court action, claiming that his confinement for vagrancy was unjust and untenable. Existing Illinois law vested state authorities with the power to commit any juvenile to a state reform school as long as a reasonable justification could be provided. In this instance, vagrancy was a reasonable justification. The Illinois Supreme Court distinguished between misfortune (vagrancy) and criminal acts in arriving at its decision to reverse Daniel O'Connell's commitment (*People ex rel. O'Connell v. Turner,* 1870). In effect, the court nullified the law by declaring that reform school commitments of youths could not be made by the state if the "offense" was simple misfortune. They reasoned that state's interests would be better served if commitments of juveniles to reform schools were limited to those committing more serious criminal offenses rather than those who were victims of misfortune. Those who were considered victims of misfortune were called **dependent and neglected children** (McGloin and Widom, 2001).

The First Juvenile Court.   Three decades later, the Illinois legislature established the first juvenile court on July 1, 1899, by passing the Act to Regulate the Treatment and Control of Dependent, Neglected, and Delinquent Children, or the Juvenile Court Act. This act provided for limited courts of record, where notes might be taken by judges or their assistants, to reflect judicial actions against juveniles (Buel, 2002). The jurisdiction of these courts, subsequently designated as "juvenile courts," would include all juveniles under the age of 16 who were found in violation of any state or local law or ordinance. Also, provision was made for the care of dependent and/or neglected children who had been abandoned or who otherwise lacked proper parental care, support, or guardianship. No minimum age was specified that would limit the jurisdiction of juvenile court judges. However, the act provided that judges could impose secure confinement on juveniles 10 years of age or over by placing them in state-regulated juvenile facilities such as the state reformatory or the State Home for Juvenile Female Offenders. Judges were expressly prohibited from confining any juvenile under 12 years of age in a jail or police station. Extremely young juveniles would be assigned POs who would look after their needs and placement on a temporary basis. Between 1900 and 1920, 20 states passed similar acts to establish juvenile courts. By the end of World War II, all states had created juvenile court systems. However, considerable variation existed among these court systems, depending on the jurisdiction.

Major Differences between Criminal and Juvenile Courts.   The intent of this section is not to describe either criminal or juvenile courts in depth, but rather, to show several major similarities and differences between them. Also, the diversity among juvenile courts in every jurisdiction is such that it precludes blanket generalizations about them. Generally, the following statements about these different courts are accurate.

1. Juvenile courts are civil proceedings exclusively designed for juveniles, whereas criminal courts are proceedings designed for alleged violators of criminal laws. In criminal courts, alleged criminal law violators are primarily adults, although selected juveniles may be tried as adults in these same courts.

2. Juvenile proceedings are informal, whereas criminal proceedings are formal. Attempts are made in many juvenile courts to avoid the formal trappings that characterize criminal proceedings.

3. In most states, juveniles are not entitled to a trial by jury, unless the juvenile judge approves.

4. Both juvenile and criminal proceedings are adversarial. Juveniles may or may not wish to retain or be represented by counsel. Today, most states make provisions in their juvenile codes for public defenders for juveniles if they are indigent and cannot afford to hire private counsel.

5. Criminal courts are courts of record, whereas juvenile proceedings may or may not maintain a running transcript of proceedings.

6. The standard of proof used for determining one's guilt in criminal proceedings is beyond a reasonable doubt. In juvenile courts, judges use the same standard for juvenile delinquents who face possible commitment to secure juvenile facilities. In other court matters leading to non-commitment alternatives, the court uses the civil standard of preponderance of the evidence.

7. The range of penalties juvenile judges may impose is more limited than criminal courts. Both juvenile and criminal courts can impose fines, restitution, community service, probation, and other forms of conditional discharge. Juvenile courts can also impose residential secure or nonsecure placement, group homes, and camp/ranch experiences. Long terms of commitment to secure facilities are also within the purview of juvenile court judges. In most criminal courts, however, the range of penalties may include life imprisonment or the death penalty in those jurisdictions where the death penalty is used.

This comparison indicates that criminal court actions are more serious and have more significant long-term consequences for offenders compared with actions taken by juvenile courts (*Judicature,* 2001). However, juvenile courts do have sanctioning power to place juveniles in secure confinement for lengthy periods, if circumstances warrant. We should not discount this type of court power just because the court deals with juvenile matters and not criminal cases. Juvenile courts are guided by strong rehabilitative orientations in most jurisdictions, despite a general get-tough movement that has occurred during the 1980s and 1990s, whereas criminal courts are seemingly adopting more punitive sanctions for adult offenders (M. McGuire, 2002). While many critics see juvenile courts moving toward a just-deserts philosophy in the treatment and **adjudication** of juveniles, many youths are still subject to treatment-oriented nonsecure alternatives rather than custodial options. Furthermore, overcrowding is a chronic problem in many juvenile facilities. Thus, correctional agencies for juveniles mirror many of the same problems of adult corrections. Thus, it is in the best interests of the state to provide alternatives to incarceration for both adult and juvenile offenders. This "best interests" philosophy of juvenile courts is based on an early doctrine known as *parens patriae.*

Parens Patriae

Juvenile courts have always had considerable latitude in regulating the affairs of juveniles. This freedom to act in a child's behalf was rooted in the largely unchallenged doctrine of **parens patriae** (Sanborn, 2001). The *parens patriae* doctrine received formal recognition in U.S. courts in the case of *Ex parte Crouse* (1838). This case involved the commitment of an unruly and incorrigible female child to a state agency. When the parents of the child attempted to regain custody over her later, their request was denied. She remained a ward of the state by virtue of the power of the state agency charged with her supervision. This case set a precedent in that the state established almost absolute control over juvenile custody matters.

The primary elements of *parens patriae* that have contributed to its persistence as a dominant philosophical perspective in the juvenile justice system are summarized as follows:

1. *Parens patriae* encourages informal handling of juvenile matters as opposed to more formal and criminalizing procedures.
2. *Parens patriae* vests juvenile courts with absolute authority to provide what is best for youthful offenders (e.g., support services and other forms of care).
3. *Parens patriae* strongly encourages benevolent and rehabilitative treatments to assist youths in overcoming their personal and social problems.
4. *Parens patriae* avoids the adverse labeling effects that formal court proceedings might create.
5. *Parens patriae* means state control over juvenile life chances.

One early example of *parens patriae* is when police officers interacted with juveniles during the 1940s, 1950s, and 1960s. Whenever juveniles were apprehended by police officers for alleged infractions of the law, they were eventually turned over to juvenile authorities or taken to juvenile halls for further processing. Juveniles were not advised of their rights to an attorney, to have an attorney present during any interrogation, and to remain silent. They were subject to lengthy interrogations by police, without parental notification and consent or legal counsel. Juveniles had virtually no protection against adult constitutional rights violations by law enforcement officers and/or juvenile court judges. Due process simply did not apply to juveniles.

Because of the informality of juvenile proceedings in most jurisdictions, there were frequent and obvious abuses of judicial discretion. These abuses occurred because of the absence of consistent guidelines whereby cases could be adjudicated. Juvenile POs might casually recommend to judges that particular juveniles ought to do a few months in an industrial school or other secure detention facility, and the judge might be persuaded to adjudicate these cases accordingly. However, several forces were at work simultaneously during the 1950s and 1960s that would eventually have the conjoint consequence of making juvenile courts more accountable for specific adjudications of youthful offenders. One of these forces was increased parental and general public recognition of and concern for the liberal license taken by juvenile courts in administering the affairs of juveniles. The abuse of judicial discretion was becoming increasingly apparent and widely known. Additionally, there was a growing disenchantment with and apathy for the rehabilitation ideal, although this disenchantment was not directed solely at juvenile courts.

It has been said that the juvenile court as originally envisioned by Progressives was procedurally informal, characterized by individualized, offender-oriented dispositional practices. However, the contemporary juvenile court has departed markedly from this Progressive ideal. Today, juvenile courts are increasingly criminalized, featuring an adversarial system and greater procedural formality. This formality effectively inhibits any individualized treatment these courts might contemplate, and it has increased the perfunctory nature of sentencing juveniles adjudicated as delinquent (Fader et al., 2001; Kempf-Leonard and Peterson, 2000).

The major shift from *parens patriae,* state-based interests to a due process juvenile justice model gradually occurred during the 1970s. This shift signified a general abandonment of most of these parens patriae elements. Decision making relative to youthful offenders became more rationalized, and the philosophy of "just-deserts" became more dominant as a way of disposing of juvenile cases. Thus, this shift meant less discretionary authority among juvenile judges, since they began to decide each case more on the basis of offense seriousness and prescribed punishments rather than disposing of such cases on the basis of individual characteristics of youthful offenders (Kirkish et al., 2000).

Arrests and Other Options

Figure 13.1 is a generic diagram of the juvenile justice process, commencing with an arrest. Generally, police officers need little justification to apprehend juveniles or take them into custody. Little uniformity exists among jurisdictions about how an "arrest" is defined. There is even greater ambiguity about what constitutes a juvenile arrest (Wolcott et al., 2001).

Technically, an arrest is the legal detainment of a person to answer for criminal charges or (infrequently at present) civil demands. By degree, arrests of juveniles are more serious than taking them into custody. Since any juvenile may be taken into custody for suspicious behavior or on any other pretext, all types of juveniles may be temporarily detained at police headquarters or at a sheriff's station, department, or jail. Suspected runaways, truants, or curfew violators may be taken into custody for their own welfare or protection, not necessarily for the purpose of facing subsequent offenses. It is standard police policy in most jurisdictions, considering the sophistication of available social services, for officers and jailers to turn over juveniles to the appropriate agencies as soon as possible after these youths have been apprehended and taken into custody. At this stage of juvenile processing, the juvenile is in jeopardy of losing his or her liberty, especially if there are subsequent proceedings in more serious juvenile cases. The Baxter County Juvenile Services in Mountain Home, Arkansas, for instance, provides juvenile arrestees with a written Miranda warning, which they must sign, together with their parents, an attorney, and the juvenile officer. Figure 13.2 is an example of this warning. The first screening of juveniles before further proceedings occur is intake.

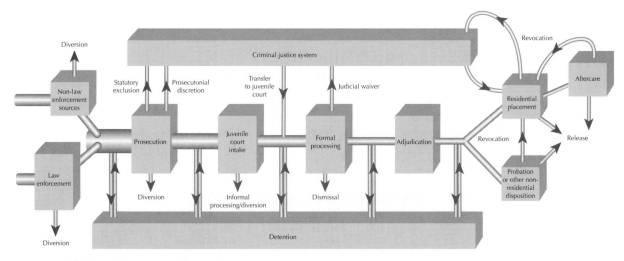

FIGURE 13.1   The Juvenile Justice System.
Source: Office of Juvenile Justice and Delinquency Prevention (2003).

MIRANDA WARNING

1. You have the right to remain silent. *(You do not need to say anything).*

   _____

2. Anything you say can and will be used against you in a court of law. *(Anyone you say anything to, i.e.: neighbor, friend, police officer, teacher or anyone else, can come to court and repeat what you told them).*

   _____

3. You have the right to talk to a lawyer, one will be appointed, free of charge, to represent you before any questioning, if you wish.

   _____

4. If you cannot afford to hire a lawyer, one will be appointed, free of charge, to represent you before any questioning, if you wish. *(This is a decision you have to make. It does not depend upon whether you or your parents have the money to hire an attorney).*

   _____

5. You can decide at anytime to exercise these rights and not answer any questions or make any statements, or have a lawyer present. *(If you decide to answer questions, you may, or you can stop the questioning anytime you want. It is your decision if you want to have an attorney present at this time).*

   _____

6. Do you understand each of these rights I have explained to you?

   _____

7. Having these rights in mind, do you wish to talk to us now? *(Remember, you have the right to talk with an attorney before you make any statements. If you wish to do so, we will provide you with the name and telephone number of the Public Defender. The Public Defender is an attorney provided by Baxter County to speak on your behalf to the court or any authorities you want him to).*

   _____

Public Defender: KENFORD CARTER, P.O. BOX 1438, FLIPPIN, AR 72634 - 870/453-1462

Juvenile	Date	Parent/Guardian	Date
Attorney	Date	Juvenile Officer	Date

FIGURE 13.2   Miranda warning used by Baxter County Juvenile Services, Mountain Home, Arkansas, 2003.
Source: Baxter County Juvenile Services.

Intake Screenings and Detention Hearings

Intake or an **intake screening** is the second major step in the juvenile justice process. It is a more or less informally conducted screening procedure whereby intake POs or other juvenile court functionaries decide whether detained juveniles should be (1) unconditionally released from the juvenile justice system, (2) released to parents or guardians subject to a subsequent juvenile court appearance,

(3) released or referred to one or more community-based services or resources, (4) placed in secure detention subject to a subsequent juvenile court appearance, or (5) waived or transferred to the jurisdiction of criminal courts (Glaser et al., 2001).

Preceding an intake hearing, juveniles are advised of their right to be represented by counsel. They are given an opportunity to request counsel or waive their right to counsel. Figure 13.3 is a waiver of right to counsel form used by the Baxter County Juvenile Services in Mountain Home, Arkansas. Depending upon what the juvenile and his or her parents wish, they must indicate at which stages, if any, counsel is requested, and they must sign this form.

WAIVER OF RIGHT OF COUNSEL

Case No:_____

IN THE MATTER OF _____ **, A JUVENILE**

NOW COMES _____ **, the juvenile**

respondent, in the above titled and numbered case, in person and together with his/her

parent(s) in writing and in the presence of _____

and after having been informed of his/her right to an attorney, and that the court would

appoint counsel to represent him/her at no cost, nevertheless knowledgeable and willfully

waives his right to be represented by legal counsel during the following stages of the

proceedings in this case:

_____   **Intake Interview**

_____   **Plea and Arraignment**

_____   **Adjudication and Disposition**

No promises or threats have been made to me; and no pressure or coercion of any kind has been used against me.

_____   _____
Juvenile Officer   **Juvenile Respondent**

_____   _____
Date   **Date**

_____   _____
Parent   **Parent**

_____   _____
Date   **Date**

FIGURE 13.3   Waiver of Right to Counsel Form Used by Baxter County Juvenile Services, Mountain Home, Arkansas.

During intake hearings, intake POs have virtually unbridled discretion regarding a youth's chances in the system. Apart from certain state-mandated hearings that must precede formal adjudicatory proceedings by juvenile judges, no constitutional provisions require states to conduct such hearings. Intake officers seldom hear legal arguments or evaluate the sufficiency of evidence on behalf of or against youths sitting before them. These proceedings, which most often are informally conducted, usually result in adjustments, where intake officers adjust the particular matter informally to most everyone's satisfaction. A more formal proceeding, a **detention hearing,** is held for the purpose of determining whether a juvenile ought to be held in **detention** until his/her case can be heard by a juvenile court judge.

Petitions and Adjudicatory Proceedings

Jurisdictional Variations in Juvenile Processing.   There is considerable variation in different jurisdictions about how juvenile courts are conducted. Increasingly, juvenile courts are emulating criminal courts in many respects. Most of the physical trappings are present, including the judge's bench, tables for the prosecution and defense, and a witness stand. In some jurisdictions such as Ocean County, New Jersey, however, these facilities are being redesigned to appear less courtlike and threatening. Manuals are currently available that catalog various pleadings defense attorneys may enter in juvenile courtrooms, and there is growing interest in the rules of juvenile court procedure. Further, there appears widespread interest in holding juveniles more accountable for their actions than was the case in past years (Feld, 2000).

Petitions.   Either prosecutors file **petitions** or act on the petitions filed by others. Petitions are official documents filed in juvenile courts on the juvenile's behalf, specifying reasons for the youth's court appearance. These documents assert that juveniles fall within the categories of dependent or neglected, status offender, or delinquent, and the reasons for such assertions are usually provided. Filing a petition formally places the juvenile before the juvenile judge in many jurisdictions. But juveniles may come before juvenile judges in less formal ways. Those able to file petitions against juveniles include their parents, school officials, neighbors, or any other interested party. The legitimacy and factual accuracy of petitions are evaluated by juvenile court judges (Applegate et al., 2000).

Juvenile Court Judicial Discretion.   In most jurisdictions, juvenile judges have almost absolute discretion in how their courts are conducted. Juvenile defendants alleged to have committed various crimes may or may not be granted a trial by jury, if one is requested. Few states permit jury trials for juveniles in juvenile courts, according to legislative mandates. After hearing the evidence presented by both sides in any juvenile proceeding, the judge decides or adjudicates the matter. An adjudication is a judgment or action on the petition filed with the court by others. If the petition alleges delinquency on the part of certain juveniles, the judge determines whether the juveniles are delinquent or not delinquent. If the petition alleges that the juveniles involved are dependent, neglected, or otherwise in need of care by agencies or others, the judge decides the matter.

If the adjudicatory proceeding fails to support the facts alleged in the petition filed with the court, the case is dismissed and the youth is freed. If the adjudicatory proceeding supports the allegations, then the judge must adjudicate the youth as either a delinquent, a status offender, or a youth in need of special treatment or supervision. Then, the juvenile court judge must dispose of the case according to several options. The judge may order a predispositional report to be prepared by a juvenile probation officer. Another option is for the judge to declare the juvenile to be an adult and transfer or waive the youth to a criminal court for processing. An underlying concern of most juvenile court judges is heightening the juvenile offender's accountability, regardless of the disposition imposed (Andrews and Marble, 2003).

Youth Courts as an Informal Alternative to Formal Juvenile Court Action. In a growing number of jurisdictions, less serious juvenile offenders are being diverted from formal juvenile court processing and sent to **youth courts** or **teen courts** or **peer courts** where they are judged by other teenagers. Such courts were started in the early 1990s, and Orange County, California, was one of the first youth courts to be established (Gray, 2003:31). Actually, youth courts are diversion programs for certain juvenile offenders who are carefully screened by the juvenile probation authorities. The purposes of youth courts are to provide an institutional means for young offenders to focus upon ethics, individual responsibilities, the long-range importance in their lives of getting accurate information and making intelligent decisions, and the fact that they are important role models for other teens, especially their younger siblings.

The Orange County Youth Court (OCYC), for instance, accepts low-level juvenile offenders who must admit to the charges against them and waive their rights confidentially. They personally appear at a high school outside of their own school district, so that no one present knows their identity. Both the juvenile and his or her parents are sworn in and a jury of students at the host high school is impaneled to hear these cases. The teen jurors are questioned about whether they can be fair and impartial. Then a probation officer reads a statement of charges against the juvenile. The juvenile and his or her parents are given an opportunity to make statements about the situation and to provide any useful background information about the offense that might be helpful to jury members. When the jury feels that it has sufficient information to render a verdict, it retires and deliberates. When the jury returns, the judge (who is a sitting county judge) reviews the jury's recommendations and tries to incorporate them into the youth's sentence. If the juvenile completes the sentence within four months, the offense is officially dismissed and the juvenile record is expunged.

The types of sentences imposed by youth courts include fine payments, community service, picking up trash in a city park, graffiti removal, and/or working with the sick, injured, or elderly at local medical institutions; individual or family counseling is sometimes recommended; restitution to victims may be required; completion of drug/alcohol treatment programs may be required; school attendance is mandatory; and writing letters of apology to victims is recommended. Subsequently, youthful offenders themselves may be called upon to become jurors in later cases involving other juveniles accused of crimes.

Obviously, it is crucial to screen carefully those juveniles who are most amenable to youth court influence. More than a few juveniles are manipulative and calculating, and they may take advantage of the leniency of the youth court system. Also, adult influence is minimized. It is important to stress that the sanctions imposed originate from teens against other teens. Certain cases are automatically excluded. These include cases involving dangerous weapons and violent crimes. Youth courts have no jurisdiction to impose or recommend incarceration, even if for brief periods. Their sanctions are exclusively nominal and conditional. By July 2003, there were 900 youth court programs operating in 46 states and the District of Columbia. Youth courts have a high degree of success, with recidivism rates lower than 20 percent. It is difficult to calculate exactly how many youths have been assisted by peer courts since the early 1990s, but there are several thousand successfully diverted youths who have benefitted from this experience thus far (Gray, 2003:33).

The Holland, Michigan, Teen Court.   An example of a teen court in action is found in Holland, Michigan. The Holland Teen Court (HTC) is based on the philosophy that a youthful law violator does not continue to be an offender when a peer jury decides the punishment. The HTC is a way for youths to keep their records clean. The jury, which consists of other teens, does not decide innocence or guilt. Rather, it only assesses sentences. Youths going before the HTC plead guilty and agree to accept whatever sentence the HTC imposes. Once the sentence is fully satisfied, all charges against the juvenile are dismissed. The offender pays no fine and there are no fees involved in HTC participation.

Most referrals to the HTC are by police. Figure 13.4 is a referral form used by the HTC. Usually, first offenders are those most likely referred. Cases that normally come before the HTC include misdemeanors, such as malicious destruction, underage smoking, and curfew violations. All youths who appear before the HTC must sign a consent form to participate. Or any referred youth may refuse to participate. These respective forms are shown in Figures 13.5 and 13.6.

Youths, who must be between the ages of 10 and 17, must have a parent or guardian present. All persons who give testimony are sworn in and must tell the truth. After jurors have questioned the defendant and witnesses, it retires to a jury room and decides the sentence to be imposed. The decision is written down and handed to the judge who reconvenes the court, calls the defendant before the bench, and reads the sentence. A form showing the jury verdict is illustrated in Figure 13.7.

Sentences need not be unique and should fit the offense. Some possible sentences might include completing community service hours for nonprofit organizations, assisting with community clean-up projects, making a written/oral apology, writing an essay, and paying damages to a victim. Defendants are permitted to reject sentences imposed by the HTC and go before the juvenile court. This is rare, however. Usually the judge will not alter the sentence meted out by the HTC, but the judge may alter the sentence if it results in undue degradation or humiliation, or if the sentence is too severe. If the teen court imposes restitution orders, a contract is issued between the teen court coordinator, the youth, and his/her parents. This form is shown in Figure 13.8. Sometimes a letter of apology is required. An example of such a letter is shown in Figure 13.9. Finally, if community service is ordered, a record or log is maintained of this service and when it is completed. An example of such a log is shown in Figure 13.10.

The HTC coordinator meets in advance with the youth and the youth's parents and explains the youth's rights and the HTC program. Volunteers from the local high school serve on the jury. Orientation sessions are conducted to acquaint new jurors with some of the rudimentary elements of court procedure and jury deliberations.

REFERRAL TO TEEN COURT

Date of Referral:_____

Referral Source:_____

Contact Person:_____

Telephone No.:_AM_____   PM_____

Type of Offense: (Check one)

Retail Fraud:_____   Malicious Destruction of Property:_____   Other:_____

_____

Location of Offense:_____

_____

Name of Offender:_____

Address of Offender:_____

Telephone No.:_AM_____   PM_____

Name of Parent or Guardian:_____

Address:_____

Telephone No.:_AM_____   PM_____

Statement of Offense:

_____

_____

_____

_____

Return to: Joyce Barkel
                                  Administrator of Volunteer Services
                                  Attention: Teen Court
                                  City Hall
                                  Holland, MI 49423
                                  616/355-1324

Date received:_____

Date processed:_____

Date Completed:_____

FIGURE 13.4   Referral to Teen Court, Holland, Michigan.

The hope of the HTC is that developing patterns of criminal behavior will be interrupted through promoting self-esteem, providing motivation for self-improvement, and the development of a healthy attitude toward authority. The HTC challenges youths to perform at their highest level of ability and places a high priority on educating youths about the responsibilities of individuals, family members, and citizens (Holland Teen Court, 2003:2–3).

HOLLAND TEEN COURT
CONSENT FORM

JUVENILE NAME:_____

ADDRESS:_____

CHARGE:_____

HOLLAND TEEN COURT IS A VOLUNTARY PROGRAM THAT HAS BEEN EXPLAINED TO ME. I ADMIT THAT I AM GUILTY OF THE OFFENSE THAT I HAVE BEEN CHARGED WITH. I UNDERSTAND THAT I HAVE A RIGHT TO SEEK LEGAL COUNSEL. I UNDERSTAND THAT A JURY OF MY PEERS WILL HEAR MY CASE AND ASSIGN THE CONSEQUENCES THEY DEEM APPROPRIATE. THE CONSEQUENCES MAY INCLUDE, BUT ARE NOT LIMITED TO, COMMUNITY SERVICE, RESTITUTION, AN APOLOGY, COUNSELING, OR OTHER ALTERNATIVE OPPORTUNITIES PROGRAM. I UNDERSTAND THAT IF I FAIL TO APPEAR OR COMPLETE THE ASSIGNED CONSEQUENCES WITHIN A SPECIFIED TIME, MY CASE WILL BE REFERRED TO THE OTTAWA COUNTY PROBATE DEPARTMENT FOR CRIMINAL PROSECUTION. I UNDERSTAND THAT IF I SUCCESSFULLY COMPLETE THE CONSEQUENCES THAT THE TEEN COURT JURY ASSIGNS, THIS CHARGE WILL NOT BE HELD AGAINST ME IN ANY FUTURE PROCEEDINGS.

I AGREE TO THESE TERMS:_____   _____
                                        NAME   DATE

PARENT/GUARDIAN CONSENT

THE HOLLAND TEEN COURT PROGRAM, AND THE CHARGE AGAINST MY CHILD HAVE BEEN EXPLAINED TO ME. I UNDERSTAND THAT THIS IS A VOLUNTARY PROGRAM AND I HEREBY AUTHORIZE MY CHILD TO PARTICIPATE.

PARENT/GUARDIAN_____

FIGURE 13.5   Holland Teen Court Consent Form, and "Refusal to Participate" Form.

REFUSAL TO PARTICIPATE

After being informed of my rights and the requirements of this program, I hereby refuse the services of this court, and ask that my case be referred back to the referring agency. I understand that by this act my case enters into the judicial system and may result in a court hearing.

Date: _____

_____
Signature of Juvenile

_____
Signature of Parent or Guardian

_____
Referring Officer

_____
Teen Court Coordinator/Staff

FIGURE 13.6   Holland Teen Court Consent Form, and "Refusal to Participate" Form.

HOLLAND TEEN COURT
SENTENCING GUIDELINES
JURY VERDICT

DEFENDANT: _____

1. _____ Community Service (specify in hours) _____
   (Consider 8 hours to 24 hours as a range)

   Level 1 – 8-12 hours (curfew violation; smoking/possessing cigarettes; trespassing; littering; fireworks possession; city ordinance violation; retail fraud <$25; loud music)

   Level 2 – 12-24 hours (retail fraud >$25, MDP <$100; larceny <$200, disorderly conduct; R & C <$200)

   To be completed by (specify date) _____

2. _____ Restitution (specify amount) $_____

   To be completed by (specify date) _____

3. _____ Essay (specify number of words) _____

   Topic: _____

   To be completed by (specify date) _____

4. _____ Apologize to victim with written proof to the court within 2 weeks

5. _____ Other (specify) _____

Date: _____   Jury Foreperson: _____

FIGURE 13.7   Holland Teen Court Sentencing Guidelines Verdict.
Source: Holland Teen Court, Holland, Michigan.

Transfers, Waivers, or Certifications

Transfers refer to changing the jurisdiction over certain juvenile offenders to another jurisdiction, usually from juvenile court jurisdiction to criminal court jurisdiction (Flowers, 2002). Transfers are also known as waivers, referring to a **waiver** or change of jurisdiction from the authority of juvenile court judges to criminal court judges (Salekin, 2002). Prosecutors or juvenile court judges decide that in some cases, juveniles should be waived or transferred to the jurisdiction of criminal courts. Presumably, those cases that are waived or transferred are the most serious cases, involving violent or serious offenses, such as homicide, aggravated assault, forcible rape, robbery, or drug-dealing activities.

TEEN COURT RESTITUTION CONTRACT

Date of Referral_____   Case No. _____

Juvenile Name _____

Address _____ Phone _____

Victim _____

Address _____ Phone_____

Offense & Date of Offense

_____
_____
_____
_____

Type of Restitution (Include Specific Amount & Time)

_____
_____
_____
_____

I agree that the above information is acceptable to me and will comply to the best of my ability

_____   _____
Juvenile   Teen Court Coordinator

_____   _____
Juvenile's Parent or Guardian   Juvenile's Parent or Guardian

FIGURE 13.8   Teen Court Restitution Contract.
Source: Holland Teen Court, Holland, Michigan.

In some jurisdictions, such as Utah, juveniles are waived or transferred to criminal courts through a process known as **certification.** A certification is a formal procedure whereby the state declares the juvenile to be an adult for the purpose of a criminal prosecution in a criminal court. The results of certifications are the same as for waivers or transfers. Thus, certifications, waivers, and transfers result in juvenile offenders being subject to the jurisdiction of criminal courts where they can be prosecuted as though they were adult offenders. A 14-year-old murderer, for instance, might be transferred to criminal court for a criminal prosecution on the

TEEN COURT

LETTER OF APOLOGY

Dear Teen Court Defendant,

An apology is a part of the recommended sentence of City of Holland Teen Court. Nearly every minor who comes before Teen Court is required to apologize either orally, in writing, or both. The sentencing report that was given to you after the Teen Court hearing will indicate your apology sentence. Completed letters should be sealed, addressed, stamped and given to the Teen Court Coordinator to be mailed. IMPORTANT: If it is unclear to whom the letter should be sent, please send it to your parent(s) or guardian.

If you choose, you can use the following worksheet to help you organize the information to express your thoughts and feelings. Please call Teen Court Coordinator _____ with any questions at _____

A letter of apology should include the following:

Date_____

Name of person or organization _____

Street Address _____

City, State, Zip Code _____

Dear _____,

I was responsible for (doing what)

_____

_____(when)_____

_____

_____

I am sorry because (why) _____

_____

Since the offense I have taken responsibility by (doing what)

_____

_____

The experience of my arrest, court hearing, and consequences has taught me that

_____

I realize now that my offense hurt (who)_____

_____

and I regret (what) _____

_____

Sincerely,

_____

FIGURE 13.9   Teen Court Letter of Apology.

Source: Holland Teen Court, Holland, Michigan.

Community Service Work Log

Community Service Location:

Participant's Name:

Community Service Due Date:

Date	Project	Hours	Signature of Supervisor
_____	_____	_____	_____
_____	_____	_____	_____
_____	_____	_____	_____
_____	_____	_____	_____
_____	_____	_____	_____
_____	_____	_____	_____
_____	_____	_____	_____
_____	_____	_____	_____

Total Hours: _____

Supervisor's Comments:

Supervisor's Signature: _____ Date: _____

Participant's Signature: _____ Date: _____

It is the participant's responsibility to get this work log to Teen Court.
Fax 616.355.1490 Mail:Teen Court, 270 S. River Ave, Holland, MI 49423

Holland Teen Court
www.teen-court.org
Revised 9/00

FIGURE 13.10   Community Service Work Log.
Source: Holland Teen Court, Holland, Michigan.

murder charge. In criminal court, the juvenile, now being treated as though he were an adult, can be convicted of the murder and sentenced to a prison term for one or more years. If the juvenile is charged with capital murder, is 16 or older, and lives in a state where the death penalty is administered to those convicted of capital murder, then he or she can potentially receive the death penalty as the maximum punishment for that offense, provided there is a capital murder conviction. Or criminal court judges might impose life-without-parole sentences on these convicted 16- or 17-year-olds. Imposing life-without-parole sentences or the death penalty are *not* within the jurisdiction of juvenile court judges. Their jurisdiction ends when an offender becomes an adult. Thus, a delinquency adjudication on capital murder charges in juvenile court might result in a juvenile being placed in the state industrial school until he is 18 or 21, depending upon whichever is the age of majority or adulthood. In all cases, juveniles are entitled to an attorney to represent them as a matter of right (Burruss and Kempf-Leonard, 2002).

TYPES OF WAIVERS

There are four types of waiver actions: (1) judicial waivers, (2) direct file, (3) statutory exclusion, and (4) demand waivers. In the discussion of these waivers below, it is important to note that some jurisdictions use several different types of waivers simultaneously. Thus, if a state uses a judicial waiver, it may also use statutory exclusion, direct file, and/or demand waivers as well. Legislative provisions dictate the nature and types of waivers approved for juvenile court use.

Judicial Waivers

The largest numbers of waivers from juvenile to criminal court annually come about as the result of direct judicial action. **Judicial waivers** give the juvenile court judge the authority to decide whether to waive jurisdiction and transfer the case to criminal court (Sickmund, 2003). In 1999 judicial waivers were used in 47 states. Three states, Massachusetts, Nebraska, and New York, did not use judicial waivers (Sickmund, 2003:8).

There are three kinds of judicial waivers. The first type, **discretionary waivers,** empower the judge to waive jurisdiction over the juvenile and transfer the case to criminal court. Because of this type of waiver, judicial waivers are sometimes known as discretionary waivers. The second type of judicial waiver is the **mandatory waiver.** In the case of a mandatory waiver, the juvenile court judge *must* waive jurisdiction over the juvenile if probable cause exists that the juvenile committed the alleged offense. The third type of judicial waiver is called a **presumptive waiver.** Under the presumptive waiver scenario, the burden of proof concerning a transfer decision is shifted from the state to the juvenile (Myers, 2001). It requires that certain juveniles be waived to criminal court unless they can prove that they are suited to juvenile rehabilitation.

Judicial waivers are often criticized because of their subjectivity. Two different youths charged with identical offenses may appear at different times before the same judge. On the basis of impressions formed about the youths, the judge may decide to transfer one youth to criminal court and adjudicate the other youth in juvenile court. Obviously, the intrusion of extralegal factors into this important action generates a degree of unfairness and inequality (Podkopacz and Feld, 2002). A youth's appearance and attitude emerge as significant factors that will either make or break the offender in the eyes of the judge. These socioeconomic and behavioral criteria often overshadow the seriousness or pettiness of offenses alleged. In the context of this particular type of transfer, it is easy to see how some persistent, nonviolent offenders may suffer waiver to criminal court. This is an easy way for the judge to get rid of them (Sickmund, 2003).

 **BOX 13.1**

Rick Sandoval

Executive Director, New Mexico Juvenile Parole Board, Albuquerque, New Mexico

Statistics:

B.A. (criminal justice), University of New Mexico

Background:

Well, I would have to say that my experience with juvenile corrections began at a very early age. I am a native New Mexican from the small village of Springer in northeastern New Mexico. The reason I say "at an early age" is because Springer is the home of the New Mexico Boy's School, the state's largest institution for male juveniles. My father worked as a correctional officer at the facility prior to my birth, and my mother started as an administrative secretary when I was 2 or 3 years old. I guess you could say that I was predisposed to juvenile corrections even before birth.

Although my father only worked at the school for a short time, my mother was in the business for the long haul. She continued her education, while serving as the administrative secretary to the superintendent for about 15 years. Eventually, she became the Deputy Superintendent of Administration. This allowed me the opportunity to spend countless hours at the facility throughout my entire childhood. Little did I know that I would follow in mom's footsteps many years later!

I graduated from Springer High School in 1987 and was awarded an academic scholarship to the University of New Mexico (UNM) in Albuquerque. At the time, I was planning to pursue a degree in business and/or pre-law, with the intent of becoming an attorney. After my freshman year at UNM, I hit a small stumbling block towards my declared major. Little did I know that this major was going to require a plethora of math courses, which turned out to be my biggest weakness throughout my academic life. I was then forced to look at other options, and I remembered an intriguing soci-

ology class from the prior semester. I spoke with my advisor and she sold me on the "no math" requirements for either the sociology of criminal justice degrees. I then began to take juvenile delinquency and related sociology/criminal justice courses, and I was surprisingly drawn back to juveniles that I had virtually grown up with all of my life.

During my third year at UNM, I was able to land a job with the District Attorney's Office. I was fortunate to have a close family friend from my hometown who was a metro judge and a district attorney prior to that. He was able to assist me with obtaining a DWI clerk position, which included managing all of the records for the metropolitan division. This was an exciting yet tiresome position that virtually did not allow me to enjoy many of the social luxuries that other college students had. I wasn't able to take all of those fun spring breaks or long holiday vacations during my last four years at the university. I worked 35 to 40 hours a week and averaged five classes a semester. Again, these were sacrifices that I never knew would benefit my career to the fullest extent.

During my senior year at UNM and working now two years for the D.A.'s office, I did my criminal justice internship with the Juvenile Probation and Parole Office. I served as a Preliminary Hearing Officer, which allowed me to familiarize myself with the juvenile justice system to a great extent. It also gave me the opportunity to work "hands-on" with first-time offenders and their families. I enjoyed this so much that I continued in this position for 6 to 8 months after my semester-long internship was completed. It obviously paid off as I received the

BOX 13.1 (*Continued*)

Outstanding Volunteer-Hearing Officer for 1992, an award that I was very proud of.

In June 1992 I left the D.A.'s office to take an administrative assistant position at the Youth Diagnostic & Development Center/New Mexico Girl's School. This was like returning home as once again I was in a secure juvenile facility. This experience was invaluable as I really started to grasp the overall functions of a large facility. Learning the administrative functions really brought to light the big picture of working with juveniles. I only served in this position for about 8 months before I was hired as an Adolescent Support staff, assigned to the Gang Intervention Unit within the Juvenile Probation and Parole Office. I really believe that this job was my first wake-up call in this field of work. I was amazed to see and work with the dozens of gang members and their respective families in Albuquerque. Many of the families were as dysfunctional as the clients we served, and it was quite discouraging to see the sense of hopelessness that many of these young people and their families had. During my time in this position, I began the first Adolescent Support Program that was based in a public school setting and directed by a Children, Youth, and Families Department (CYFD) employee. I was tasked with supervising and counseling between 15 and 25 sixth- through eighth-grade at-risk youth. This proved to be another wonderful challenge that I really took a great deal of pride in. After only about a year or so in this position, the program's funding was cut and then I pursued a more early-intervention approach to juveniles.

Based on my successful work at the middle school as a CYFD employee/contractor, I was able to land a position as the Assistant Director of After School Programs for the middle school and its four elementary feeder schools. I directly oversaw about 40 programs at the middle school and over 50 programs in the elementary schools. At the same time, since this position was only part-time, I was also directing the Adolescent Substance Abuse Program (ASAP) for the UNM Department of Family and Community Medicine. Fortunately for me, both of these jobs were housed at one school and really allowed me the opportunity to create and facilitate some strong programming for my clients. It also gave me invaluable experience in the areas of program development, implementation, and facilitation. The ASAP initiative I directed was recognized on a national level and I was able to take five students to Boston, Massachusetts. We gave presentations to the Community Fellowships and the graduate-level students at M.I.T. and Harvard University respectively. The ASAP initiative was only a 10-month contract, so upon completing this obligation, I was picked up full-time by New Day Shelters in Albuquerque. I was to be the Assistant Director of the Choices Program, another adolescent outreach program sponsored by a well-known child advocacy group.

It was during my time in these two positions that I came across two gentlemen who were interested in the School-to-Work initiative. I really felt that this was an area that was in dire need of addressing. After working with hundreds of young people from impoverished neighborhoods throughout Albuquerque, I could see the value that good job training and job placement could have on young teenagers and their self-esteem. I took it upon myself to develop (in five unpaid months) and prepare for the implementation of one of the state's first School-to-Work programs. The two other cofounders of this initiative and I came up with the name, Youth Opportunities in Retaining, Inc. (YOR)—a private, nonprofit organization. I served as the Program Director for less than six months before the program's president, Mr. Steve Beffort, was asked by the Governor of New Mexico to become his Cabinet Secretary of General Services. This catapulted me into the President position in just a matter of months.

We started the YOR program in August 1994, with 3 high schools in 2 different communities. By the fourth year we were serving approximately 18 high schools in 7 New Mexico communities. By year five, we were selected by the National Retail Federation in Washington, DC, as the pilot program for the

(continued)

BOX 13.1 (*Continued*)

retail School-to-Work programs for the entire United States. In 2002 our YOR program was in 13 states and serving thousands of youths throughout the country.

Currently, I serve at the pleasure of Governor Bill Richardson as his Executive Director of the New Mexico Juvenile Parole Board. I feel that I was blessed with this job because I am a strong advocate for youth and I do not believe in the institutionalization of juveniles. The parole board is the releasing authority for the State of New Mexico, and my office is tasked with ensuring that the juveniles, who are committed to the custody of the state, are appropriately rehabilitated and returned back to their respective communities. This while assuring that the community itself is safe from the delinquent behaviors that are attributed to the juveniles being committed to the custody of CYFD.

Advice to Students:

As you can see, I have spent a great deal of time discussing my background with young people and juveniles. I could share countless stories of the many youth that I have had to deal with during my professional career, and trust me, I have worked with almost every type of juvenile and youth during my 11+

years in this field. These experiences have enlightened me with the realities that not only our children face, but also our communities and society as a whole. I would encourage anyone who is looking to enter this field of work to be resilient! You are going to see firsthand the many ills that affect our families and the destructive behaviors that are spawned by abuse (physical and sexual), neglect, substance abuse, and domestic violence, to name a few. Remember, it indeed does take a village to raise a child, and we are only as good as those who we have touched and left behind long after we leave this earth. When developing programs for youth, what I have always tried to advocate for is to never forget the family unit itself. Our society is generally more reactive than proactive. We tend to develop initiatives that are the result of inappropriate or illegal behaviors, while we rarely address the real problem itself. We need to take on the root of the disease and not just the symptoms of it. Humans are creatures of habit, and learned behaviors are often developed from our parents. When you begin to work with troubled juveniles in the field, you can and should always evaluate the family by which the child is reared. Best of luck to all of you and please go out and make a difference in your community!

Although judges have this discretionary power in most jurisdictions, youths are still entitled to a hearing where they can protest the waiver action. While it is true that the criminal court poses risks to juveniles in terms of potentially harsher penalties, it is also true that being tried as an adult entitles youths to all of the adult constitutional safeguards, including the right to a trial by jury. In a later section of this chapter, we will examine closely this and other options that may be of benefit to certain juveniles. Thus, some juveniles may not want to fight waiver or transfer actions, largely because they may be treated more leniently by criminal courts.

Direct File

Whenever offenders are screened at intake and referred to the juvenile court for possible prosecution, prosecutors in various jurisdictions will conduct further screenings of these youths. They determine which cases merit further action and formal adjudication by judges. Not all cases sent to prosecutors by intake officers automatically result in subsequent formal juvenile court action. Prosecutors may decline to prosecute certain cases, particularly if there are problems with witnesses who are either missing or who refuse to testify, if there are evidentiary issues, or if there are overloaded juvenile court dockets. A relatively small proportion of cases may warrant waivers to criminal courts.

Under **direct file,** the prosecutor has the sole authority to decide whether any given juvenile case will be heard in criminal court or juvenile court (Feld, 2000). Essentially, the prosecutor decides which court should have jurisdiction over the juvenile. Prosecutors with direct file power are said to have **concurrent jurisdiction.** This is another name for direct file. In Florida, for example, prosecutors have concurrent jurisdiction. They may file extremely serious charges (e.g., murder, rape, aggravated assault, robbery) against youths in criminal courts and present cases to grand juries for indictment action. Or prosecutors may decide to file the same cases in the juvenile court. In 2002, prosecutors in 14 states and the District of Columbia had concurrent jurisdiction and could file charges against juveniles in either criminal or juvenile court. These jurisdictions included Arizona, Arkansas, Colorado, the District of Columbia, Florida, Georgia, Louisiana, Massachusetts, Michigan, Montana, Nebraska, Oklahoma, Vermont, Virginia, and Wyoming (Sickmund, 2003:9).

Statutory Exclusion

Statutory exclusion means that certain juvenile offenders are automatically excluded from the juvenile court's original jurisdiction. Legislatures of various states declare a particular list of offenses to be excluded from the jurisdiction of juvenile courts (Snyder, Sickmund, and Poe-Yamagata, 2000). Added to this list of excluded offenses is a particular age range. Thus, in Illinois, if a 16-year-old juvenile is charged with murder, rape, or aggravated assault, this particular juvenile is automatically excluded from the jurisdiction of the juvenile court. Instead, the case will be heard in criminal court. In 1999, 29 states had statutory exclusion provisions and excluded certain types of offenders from juvenile court jurisdiction. Minimum age ranges for statutory exclusion ranged from 13 to 17. These states included Alabama, Alaska, Arizona, California, Delaware, Florida, Georgia, Idaho, Illinois, Indiana, Iowa, Louisiana, Maryland, Massachusetts, Minnesota, Mississippi, Montana, Nevada, New Mexico, New York, Oklahoma, Oregon, Pennsylvania, South Carolina, South Dakota, Utah, Vermont, Washington, and Wisconsin (Sickmund, 2003:10). Because state legislatures created statutory exclusion provisions, this waiver action is sometimes known as a **legislative waiver.** And because these provisions mandate the automatic waiver of juveniles to criminal court, they are also known as **automatic waivers.**

Demand Waivers

Under certain conditions and in selected jurisdictions, juveniles may submit motions for **demand waivers.** Demand waiver actions are requests or motions filed by juveniles and their attorneys to have their cases transferred from juvenile courts to criminal courts. Why would juveniles want to have their cases transferred to criminal courts? One reason is that most U.S. jurisdictions do not provide jury trials for juveniles in juvenile courts as a matter of right (*McKeiver v. Pennsylvania,* 1971). However, about a fifth of the states have established provisions for jury trials for juveniles at their request and depending upon the nature of the charges against them. In the remainder of the states, jury trials for juveniles are granted only at the discretion of the juvenile court judge. Most juvenile court judges are not inclined to grant jury trials to juveniles. Thus, if juveniles are (1) in a jurisdiction where they are not entitled to a jury trial even if they request one from the juvenile court judge; (2) face serious charges; and (3) believe that their cases would receive greater impartiality from a jury in a criminal courtroom, they may seek a demand waiver in order to have their cases transferred to criminal court. Florida permits demand waivers as one of several waiver options (Bilchik, 1996:3).

Other Types of Waivers

Reverse Waivers.   **Reverse waivers** are actions by the criminal court to transfer direct file or statutory exclusion cases from criminal court back to juvenile court, usually at the recommendation of the prosecutor. Typically, juveniles who would be involved in these reverse waiver hearings would be those who were automatically sent to criminal court because of statutory exclusion. Thus, criminal court judges can send at least some of these juveniles back to the jurisdiction of the juvenile court. Reverse waiver actions may also be instigated by defense counsels on behalf of their clients. **Reverse waiver hearings** are held in these matters.

Once an Adult/Always an Adult.   The **once an adult/always an adult provision** is perhaps the most serious and long-lasting for affected juvenile offenders. This provision means that once juveniles have been convicted in criminal court, they are forever after considered adults for the purpose of criminal prosecutions. For instance, suppose a 12-year-old is transferred to criminal court in Vermont and subsequently convicted of a crime. Then, at age 15, if the same juvenile commits another crime, such as vehicular theft, he would be subject to prosecution in criminal court. Thus, the fact of a criminal court conviction means that the juvenile permanently loses access to the juvenile court. In 2002, 34 states had once an adult/always an adult provisions (Sickmund, 2003:7).

The once an adult/always an adult provision is not as ominous as it appears. It requires that particular jurisdictions keep track of each juvenile offender previously convicted of a crime. This record-keeping is not particularly sophisticated in different jurisdictions. Some juveniles may simply move away from the jurisdiction where they were originally convicted. Fourteen-year-old juveniles who are convicted of a crime in California may move to North Dakota or Vermont, where they may be treated as first-offenders in those juvenile courts. How are North Dakota and Vermont juvenile courts supposed to know that a particular 14-year-old has a criminal conviction in California? Information sharing among juvenile courts throughout the United States is extremely limited or nonexistent. Thus, often the intent of the once an adult/always an adult provision can be defeated simply by relocating to another jurisdiction.

Blended Sentencing Statutes.   In slightly less than half of all states (22) in 2002, new laws were adopted that created **blended sentencing statutes.** Blended sentencing statutes are provisions that permit either juvenile or criminal courts to impose both juvenile and adult punishments on juveniles who are convicted of serious offenses. For example, a juvenile court in Alaska or Michigan may be able to impose both a juvenile and adult punishment on a juvenile adjudicated delinquent by a jury. If a 15-year-old juvenile is found guilty of a crime by a Michigan juvenile court, the juvenile court judge, at his or her discretion, may impose both a juvenile penalty (e.g., incarceration in secure juvenile facility until the juvenile reaches the age of his or her majority or adulthood) as well as a criminal one (e.g., a sentence of 20 years to be served in a Michigan penitentiary for adults). Juvenile courts with blended sentencing statutes may have either a **juvenile exclusive blended sentence,** where the judge may impose either a juvenile punishment or an adult punishment, *but not both,* or a **juvenile inclusive blended sentence,** where the judge may impose *both* a juvenile punishment and an adult punishment.

Criminal courts in some jurisdictions are also vested with blended sentencing statutes. Thus, if a 16-year-old juvenile offender were to be convicted of a serious offense, the criminal court judge could impose both a juvenile punishment and an adult punishment. Criminal courts with blended sentencing statutes may have either the **criminal exclusive blended sentence,** where the judge may impose either a juvenile punishment or an adult punishment, *but not both,* or the **criminal inclusive blended sentence,** where the judge may impose *both* a juvenile punishment and an adult punishment. Usually, in most jurisdictions with such statutes, panels of experts are convened 6 months prior to the juvenile's age of majority or adulthood to review the juvenile's prior institutional conduct. If the juvenile's conduct has been favorable (e.g., attainment of a GED, participation in anger management training, participation in individual or group counseling, law-abiding behavior, conformity to institutional rules), the committee has the discretionary power to waive the adult portion of the originally imposed sentence by either the juvenile or criminal court judge. Thus, blended sentencing statutes are intended to provide strong incentives for juveniles to behave well while confined and participate in self-improvement programs and activities. They are considered a juvenile's last chance to avoid adult sanctions. Waivers, transfers, and/or certifications are thus avoided in those jurisdictions with such blended sentencing statutes (Sickmund, 2003:7).

In 2002, juvenile court jurisdictions with either exclusive or inclusive blended sentencing statutes include Alaska, Colorado, Connecticut, Illinois, Kansas, Massachusetts, Michigan, Minnesota, New Mexico, Rhode Island, South Carolina, and Texas. Criminal court jurisdictions with either exclusive or inclusive blended sentencing statutes included Arkansas, California, Colorado, Florida, Idaho, Iowa, Michigan, Missouri, Oklahoma, Vermont, Virginia, and West Virginia (Sickmund, 2003:7).

The Rationale for the Use of Transfers or Waivers

The basic rationale underlying the use of waivers is that the most serious juvenile offenders will be transferred to the jurisdiction of criminal courts where the harshest punishments, including capital punishment, may be imposed as sanctions. Since juvenile courts lack the jurisdiction and decision making power to impose anything harsher than secure confinement dispositions of limited duration in industrial or reform schools, it would seem that the waiver would be an ideal way to impose the most severe punishments on those juveniles who commit the most violent acts. All states have provisions that allow juveniles under certain conditions to be tried as if they were adults in criminal court by one or more transfer or waiver provisions (Salekin, Rogers, and Ustad, 2001). Several reasons for the use of transfers, waivers or certifications include the following:

1. To make it possible for harsher punishments to be imposed.
2. To provide just-deserts and proportionately severe punishments on those juveniles who deserve such punishments by their more violent actions.

3. To foster fairness in administering punishments according to one's serious offending.

4. To hold serious or violent offenders more accountable for what they have done.

5. To show other juveniles who contemplate committing serious offenses that the system works and that harsh punishments can be expected if serious offenses are committed.

6. To provide a deterrent to decrease juvenile violence.

7. To overcome the traditional leniency of juvenile courts and provide more realistic sanctions.

8. To make youths realize the seriousness of their offending and induce remorse and acceptance of responsibility.

Youths designated for transfer or waiver by various participants in the juvenile justice process should exhibit certain consistent characteristics. Age, offense seriousness, and prior record (including previous referrals to juvenile court, intake proceedings and dispositions, or juvenile court delinquency adjudications) are some of these characteristics. For example, Grisso, Tomkins, and Casey (1988) indicate that several extralegal factors function to enhance the likelihood that a juvenile will be waived to criminal court. These researchers gathered data from fifty state juvenile codes. Using content analysis, they searched court records and read decisions involving transferred juveniles, appeals of these transfers to appellate courts, and various law review articles pertaining to transfers. They supplemented their analysis with interviews of 85 court personnel and a survey of 1,423 representatives from 127 courts in 34 states. They concluded several things about the juveniles who were subjects of transfers. First, those with extensive prior records or involvement with the juvenile justice system were more frequently detained and subjected to transfer.

Second, many of these youths exhibited emotional disturbances of various kinds. Such emotional disturbance seemed to promote self-destructive behavior and poor school adjustment. These youths were most unwilling to accept interventions suggested by juvenile courts and intake officers. Thus, unwillingness to accept intervention became an important extralegal factor that adversely influenced the transfer decision. Third, the researchers found that those transferred tended to lack self-discipline and failed to comply with rules or court orders and conditional sanctions imposed by juvenile court judges. Therefore, a youth's unwillingness to comply with institutional rules became another extralegal factor impinging upon the waiver decision (Stewart, 2003).

In 1998, 1.8 million cases were referred U.S. juvenile courts, where about half (962,000) were heard (Flores, 2003:12; Puzzanchera, 2003). Of those cases formally heard by juvenile courts, 23 percent were person offenses, 45 percent were property offenses, 11 percent were drug law violations, and 22 percent were public order offenses and other miscellaneous crimes. Most of these cases were referred to juvenile court by law enforcement officers. During the period 1989–1998, the greatest increase in referrals to juvenile court were for drug offenses (148 percent), followed by person offenses (88 percent). There was only an 11 percent increase in juvenile case filings with juvenile courts for property offenses (Sickmund, 2003:12). Approximately 8,100 youths were transferred to criminal court in 1998 compared with 12,100 cases waived in 1994 (Sickmund, 2003:26). This represents less than 1 percent of all youths who were formally processed by juvenile courts. Most juveniles transferred were male (93 percent) and 55 percent were black.

About 36 percent of all transferred cases were person or violent offenses, while 40 percent consisted of property offenses. Drug and public order offenses made up the remainder of the 24 percent of transferred cases (Sickmund, 2003:26).

Youngest Ages for Transfers to Criminal Court

In 1998, 24 state jurisdictions and the District of Columbia indicated no specified age for transferring juveniles to criminal courts for processing. Two states, Kansas and Vermont, specified age 10 as the minimum age at which a juvenile could be waived. Colorado and Missouri established age 12 as the earliest age for a juvenile waiver. Table 13.1 shows the minimum transfer age specified by statute for all U.S. jurisdictions.

Waiver Decision Making

Organizational and political factors are at work to influence the upward trend in the use of transfers. Politicians wish to present a get-tough facade to the public by citing waiver statistics and showing their increased use is the political response to the rise in serious youth crime. Despite political rhetoric, there has been a decrease in the use of waivers. Between 1994 and 1998, for instance, the use of transfers decreased by 50 percent. A majority of those transferred were charged with felonies (Sickmund, 2003:28).

Several types of waivers can be used to negotiate transfers of jurisdiction from juvenile to criminal courts. One of these is the automatic transfer or automatic waiver which several jurisdictions currently employ. This means that if youthful offenders are within a particular age range, such as ages 16 or 17, and if they are charged with specific types of offenses (usually murder, robbery, rape, aggravated assault and other violent crimes), they will be transferred automatically to criminal courts. These types of waivers, also known as legislative

TABLE 13.1

Minimum Transfer Age Specified by Statute

Age	State
None	Alaska, Arizona, Delaware, District of Columbia, Florida, Georgia, Hawaii, Idaho, Indiana, Maine, Maryland, Montana, Nebraska, Oklahoma, Oregon, Pennsylvania, Rhode Island, South Carolina, South Dakota, Tennessee, Texas, Washington, West Virginia, and Wisconsin
10	Kansas, Vermont
12	Colorado, Missouri
13	Illinois, Mississippi, New Hampshire, New York, North Carolina, and Wyoming
14	Alabama, Arkansas, California, Connecticut, Iowa, Kentucky, Louisiana, Massachusetts, Michigan, Minnesota, Nevada, New Jersey, North Dakota, Ohio, Utah, and Virginia
15	New Mexico

Source: Melissa Sickmund, *Juveniles in Court.* Washington, DC: Office of Juvenile Justice and Delinquency Prevention, 2003:9.

waivers because they were mandated by legislative bodies in various states and carry the weight of statutory authority, involve no discretionary action by juvenile court actors. For other types of waivers, the decision making process is largely discretionary by either prosecutors or judges (Puzzanchera et al., 2003).

Because of the discretionary nature of the waiver process, large numbers of the wrong types of juveniles are transferred to criminal courts. The wrong types of juveniles are wrong because they are not those originally targeted by juvenile justice professionals and reformers to be the primary candidates for transfers. The primary targets of waivers are intended to be the most serious, violent, and dangerous juveniles who are also the most likely to deserve more serious sanctions that criminal courts can impose. But there is a serious credibility gap between the types of juveniles who are actually transferred each year and those who should be transferred (Massachusetts Statistical Analysis Center, 2001; Salekin, 2002). In 1999, for instance, we have already seen that 64 percent of all youths transferred to criminal court were charged with nonviolent (e.g., property, drug, or public order) offenses. Only 36 percent of those transferred in 1999 were charged with person offenses or violent crimes (Sickmund, 2003:26–29). If transfers, waivers or certifications were applied as they were intended to be applied, 100 percent of those transferred annually would be serious, violent offenders. Juvenile courts would handle all of the other cases (Salekin, Rogers, and Ustad, 2001).

Waiver Hearings

All juveniles who are waived to criminal court for processing are entitled to a hearing on the waiver if they request one (Sickmund, 2003). Thus, a **waiver hearing** is a formal proceeding designed to determine whether the waiver action taken by the judge or prosecutor is the correct action, and that the juvenile should be transferred to criminal court. Waiver hearings are normally conducted before the juvenile court judge. Waiver hearings are initiated through a **waiver motion,** where the prosecutor usually requests the judge to send the case to criminal court. These hearings are to some extent evidentiary, since a case must be made for why criminal courts should have jurisdiction in any specific instance. Usually, juveniles with lengthy prior records, several previous referrals, and/or one or more previous adjudications as delinquent are more susceptible to being transferred. While the offenses alleged are most often crimes, it is not always the case that the crimes are the most serious ones. Depending upon the jurisdiction, the seriousness of crimes associated with transferred cases varies. Disproportionately large numbers of cases involving property crimes are transferred to criminal courts for processing. In some instances, chronic, persistent, or habitual status offenders have been transferred, particularly if they have violated specific court orders to attend school, participate in therapeutic programs, perform community service work, make restitution, or engage in some other constructive enterprise. If waivers are to be fully effective, then only the most serious offenders should be targeted for transfer. Transferring less serious and petty offenders accomplishes little in the way of enhanced punishments for these offenders.

Reverse Waiver Hearings

In those jurisdictions with direct file or statutory exclusion provisions, juveniles and their attorneys may contest these waiver actions through reverse waiver hearings. Reverse waiver hearings are conducted before criminal court judges to determine whether to send the juvenile's case back to juvenile court. For both waiver and reverse waiver hearings, defense counsel and the prosecution attempt to make a case for their desired action. In many respects, these hearings are similar to preliminary hearings or preliminary examinations conducted within the criminal justice framework. Some evidence and testimony are permitted, and arguments for both sides are heard. Once all arguments have been presented and each side has had a chance to rebut the opponents' arguments, the judge decides the matter.

Time Standards Governing Waiver Decisions

Although only less than 1 percent of all juveniles processed by the juvenile justice system annually are transferred to criminal courts for processing as adults, most states had time limits governing transfer provisions for juveniles as of 1999 (Flores, 2003). In Maryland, for example, a 30-day maximum time limit existed between one's detention and the **transfer hearing.** If the transfer hearing results in a denial of the transfer, then there is a 30-day maximum between the denial of the transfer and the juvenile court adjudication. In contrast, Minnesota provides only a 1-day maximum between placing youths in adult jails and filing transfer motions by juvenile court prosecutors. New Mexico's provisions are similar to those of Maryland.

IMPLICATIONS OF WAIVER HEARINGS FOR JUVENILES

Those juveniles who contest or fight their transfers to criminal courts or attempt to obtain a reverse waiver wish to remain within the juvenile justice system, be treated as juveniles, and be adjudicated by juvenile court judges. But not all juveniles who are the subject of transfer are eager to contest the transfer. There are several important implications for youths, depending upon the nature of their offenses, their prior records, and the potential penalties the respective courts may impose (Feld, 2000). Under the right circumstances, having one's case transferred to criminal court may offer juvenile defendants considerable advantages not normally enjoyed if their cases were to remain in the juvenile court. In the following discussion, some of the major advantages of disadvantages of being transferred will be examined.

Positive Benefits Resulting from Juvenile Court Adjudications

Among the positive benefits of having one's case heard in juvenile court are that:

1. Juvenile court proceedings are civil, not criminal; thus, juveniles do not acquire criminal records.
2. Juveniles are less likely to receive sentences of incarceration.
3. Compared with criminal court judges, juvenile court judges have considerably more discretion in influencing a youth's life chances prior to or at the time of adjudication.
4. Juvenile courts are traditionally more lenient than criminal courts.
5. There is considerably more public sympathy extended to those who are processed in the juvenile justice system, despite the general public advocacy for a greater get-tough policy.
6. Compared with criminal courts, juvenile courts do not have as elaborate an information-exchange apparatus to determine whether certain juveniles have been adjudicated delinquent by juvenile courts in other jurisdictions.

7. Life imprisonment and the death penalty lie beyond the jurisdiction of juvenile judges, and they cannot impose these harsh sentences.

Adverse Implications of Juvenile Court Adjudications

Juvenile courts are not perfect, however, and they may be disadvantageous to youthful many offenders. Some of their major limitations are that:

1. Juvenile court judges have the power to administer lengthy sentences of incarceration, not only for serious and dangerous offenders, but for status offenders as well.
2. In most states, juvenile courts are not required to provide juveniles with a trial by jury.
3. Because of their wide discretion in handling juveniles, judges may underpenalize a large number of those appearing before them on various charges.
4. Juveniles do not enjoy the same range of constitutional rights as adults in criminal courts.

JUVENILE RIGHTS

During the mid-1960s and for the next twenty years, significant achievements were made in the area of juvenile rights. Although the *parens patriae* philosophy continues to be somewhat influential in juvenile proceedings, the U.S. Supreme Court has vested youths with certain constitutional rights. These rights do not encompass all of the rights extended to adults who are charged with crimes. But those rights conveyed to juveniles thus far have had far-reaching implications for how juveniles are processed from arrest through probation and parole.

Landmark Cases in Juvenile Justice

Kent v. United States *(1966).* The first major juvenile rights case to preface further juvenile court reforms, *Kent v. United States* (1966) established the universal precedents of (1) requiring waiver hearings before juveniles can be transferred to the jurisdiction of a criminal court [excepting legislative or automatic waivers, although reverse waiver hearings must be conducted at the juvenile's request], and (2) juveniles are entitled to consult with counsel prior to and during such hearings. In 1959, Morris A. Kent, Jr., a 14-year-old in the District of Columbia, was apprehended and charged with several housebreakings and attempted purse snatchings. He was adjudicated delinquent and placed on probation. Subsequently in 1961, an intruder entered the apartment of a woman, took her wallet, and raped her. Fingerprints at the crime scene were later identified as those of Morris Kent, who had been fingerprinted in connection with his delinquency case in 1959. On September 5, 1961, Kent admitted the offense as well as other crimes, and the juvenile court judge advised of his intent to waive Kent to criminal court. Kent's mother had obtained an attorney in the meantime, and Kent's attorney advised the court that he intended to oppose the waiver. The judge ignored the attorney's motion and transferred Kent to the U.S. District Court for the District of Columbia where Kent was tried and convicted of six counts of housebreaking by a federal jury, although the jury found him "not guilty by reason of insanity" on the rape charge. Kent's conviction was reversed by the U.S. Supreme Court. The majority held that Kent's rights to due process and to the effective assistance of counsel were violated when he was denied a formal hearing on the waiver and his attorney's motions were ignored. The U.S. Supreme Court said that the matter of a waiver to criminal court was a "critical stage" and thus, attorney representation was fundamental to due process. In adult cases, for instance, critical stages are those that relate to the defendant's potential loss of freedoms (i.e., incarceration). Because of the Kent decision, waiver hearings are now considered critical stages.

In re Gault (1967).   The Gault case is the most significant of all landmark juvenile rights cases. Certainly, it is considered the most ambitious. In a 7-2 vote, the U.S. Supreme Court articulated the following rights for all juveniles: (1) the right to a notice of charges; (2) the right to counsel; (3) the right to confront and cross-examine witnesses; and (4) the right to invoke the privilege against self-incrimination. The petitioner, Gault, requested the Court to rule favorably on two additional rights sought: (1) the right to a transcript of proceedings; and (2) the right to an appellate review. The Court did not rule on either of these additional rights. The facts are that Gerald Francis Gault, a 15-year-old, and a friend, Ronald Lewis, were taken into custody by the Sheriff of Gila County, Arizona, in the morning of June 8, 1964, for allegedly making an obscene telephone call to a female neighbor. At the time, Gault was on probation because of purse snatching. A verbal complaint was filed by the neighbor of Gault, Mrs. Cook, alleging that Gault had called her and made lewd and indecent remarks. When Gault was taken into custody by police, his mother and father were at work. Indeed, they did not learn where their son was until much later that evening. A subsequent informal adjudication hearing of Gault was held, where a one-sided presentation was given about Gault's alleged obscene conduct. The witness against him, Mrs. Cook, did not appear or offer testimony. Thus, she was not available for cross-examination by Gault or his attorney. A court probation officer gave the basically one-sided account incriminating Gault. Subsequently, the judge ordered Gault to the Arizona State Industrial School until he became 21. [If an adult had made an obscene telephone call, he would have received a $50 fine and no more than 60 days in jail. In Gerald Gault's case, he was facing nearly 6 years in a juvenile prison for the same offense]. After exhausting their appeals in Arizona state courts, the Gaults appealed to the U.S. Supreme Court. The U.S. Supreme Court reversed the Arizona Supreme Court, holding that Gault did, indeed, have the right to an attorney, the right to confront his accuser (Mrs. Cook) and to cross-examine her, the right against self-incrimination, and the right to have notice of the charges filed against him. All of these rights had been violated by the original juvenile court judge during the adjudicatory proceedings.

In re Winship (1970).   Winship established an important precedent in juvenile courts relating to the standard of proof used in established defendant guilt. The U.S. Supreme Court held that "beyond a reasonable doubt," a standard ordinarily used in adult criminal courts, was henceforth to be used by juvenile court judges and others in establishing a youth's delinquency. Formerly, the standard used was the civil application of "preponderance of the evidence." The facts in the Winship case are that Samuel Winship was a 12-year-old charged with larceny in New York City. He purportedly entered a locker and stole $112 from a woman's pocketbook. Under Section 712 of the New York Family Court Act, a juvenile delinquent was defined as "a person over seven and less than sixteen years of age who does any act, which, if done by an adult, would constitute a crime." Interestingly, the juvenile judge in the case acknowledged that the proof to be presented by the prosecution might be insufficient to establish the guilt of Winship beyond a reasonable doubt, although he did indicate that the New York Family Court Act provided that "any determination at the conclusion of an **adjudicatory hearing** that a juvenile did an act or acts must be based on a preponderance of the evidence" standard (397 U.S. at 360). Winship was adjudicated as a delinquent and ordered to a training school for 18 months, subject to annual extensions of his commitment until his eighteenth birthday. Appeals to New York courts were unsuccessful. The U.S. Supreme Court subsequently heard Winship's appeal and reversed the New York Family Court ruling because the "beyond a reasonable doubt" standard had not been used in a case where incarceration or loss of freedom was likely.

McKeiver v. Pennsylvania *(1971)*. The McKeiver case was important because the U.S. Supreme Court held that juveniles are not entitled to a jury trial as a matter of right. The facts are that in May 1968, Joseph McKeiver, age 16, was charged with robbery, larceny, and receiving stolen goods. McKeiver was represented by counsel who asked the court for a jury trial "as a matter of right." This request was denied. McKeiver was subsequently adjudicated delinquent. On appeal to the U.S. Supreme Court later, McKeiver's adjudication was upheld. The U.S. Supreme Court said that jury trials for juveniles are not a matter of right but rather at the discretion of the juvenile court judge. In about a fifth of the states today, jury trials for juveniles in juvenile courts are held under certain conditions.

Breed v. Jones *(1975)*. This case raised the significant constitutional issue of **double jeopardy.** The U.S. Supreme Court concluded that after a juvenile has been adjudicated as delinquent on specific charges, those same charges may not be alleged against those juveniles subsequently in criminal courts through transfers or waivers. The facts are that on February 8, 1971 in Los Angeles, California, Gary Steven Jones, was 17 years old, was armed with a deadly weapon and allegedly committed robbery. Jones was subsequently apprehended and an adjudicatory hearing was held on March l. Jones was adjudicated delinquent on these robbery charges. Following this delinquency adjudication, the juvenile court judge transferred Jones to criminal court to stand trial on these same charges. Jones was subsequently convicted of robbery. Jones appealed the decision and the U.S. Supreme Court reversed the robbery conviction, concluding that the robbery adjudication was considered the equivalent of a criminal trial on the same charges. This constituted double jeopardy. The juvenile court judge should have disposed Jones to secure confinement following his adjudication on the robbery charges or simply waived jurisdiction over Jones initially to criminal court. Dual court actions on the same charges were unconstitutional because they represented double jeopardy for Jones.

Schall v. Martin *(1984)*. In this case, the U.S. Supreme Court issued juveniles a minor setback regarding the state's right to hold them in preventive detention pending a subsequent adjudication. The Court said that the preventive detention of juveniles by states is constitutional, if judges perceive these youths to pose a danger to the community or an otherwise serious risk if released short of an adjudicatory hearing. This decision was significant, in part, because many observers advocated the separation of juveniles and adults in jails, those facilities most often used for preventive detention. Also, the preventive detention of adults was not ordinarily practiced at that time. [Since then, the preventive detention of adults who are deemed to pose societal risks has been upheld by the U.S. Supreme Court (*United States v. Salerno,* 1987). The facts are that 14-year-old Gregory Martin was arrested at 11:30 P.M. on December 13, 1977 in New

York City. He was charged with first-degree robbery, second-degree assault, and criminal possession of a weapon. Martin lied to police at the time, giving a false name and address. Between the time of his arrest and December 29 when a fact-finding hearing was held, Martin was detained a total of 15 days. His detention was based largely on the false information he had supplied to police and the seriousness of the charges pending against him. Subsequently, he was adjudicated a delinquent and placed on 2 years' probation. Later, his attorney filed an appeal, contesting his preventive detention as violative of the Due Process Clause of the Fourteenth Amendment. The U.S. Supreme Court eventually heard the case and upheld the detention as constitutional.

OFFENSE SERIOUSNESS AND DISPOSITIONS: AGGRAVATING AND MITIGATING CIRCUMSTANCES

In 2002, an estimated 2 million delinquency cases were disposed of in the juvenile justice system. About 12,000 cases were transferred to criminal court, and less than 10 percent of these cases resulted in incarceration. Most were either downgraded, dismissed, or sentences of probation were imposed (Puzzanchera et al., 2003; Sickmund, 2003). In fact, the use of probation for both male and female juvenile offenders in juvenile courts increased dramatically between 1989 and 1999, with over 60 percent of all adjudicated cases receiving probation (Sickmund, 2003). Whether juveniles are first-offenders or have prior juvenile records is crucial to many prosecutorial decisions. The overwhelming tendency among prosecutors is to divert petty first-offenders to some conditional program. Influencing prosecutorial decision making is the presence of aggravating and/or mitigating factors.

Aggravating and Mitigating Circumstances

Aggravating Circumstances.   Aggravating circumstances are those that enhance penalties imposed by juvenile court and criminal court judges (Coyne and Entzeroth, 2001; Sorensen and Wallace, 1999). Key aggravating factors include the following:

1. Death or serious bodily injury to one or more victims.
2. An offense committed while an offender is awaiting resolution of other delinquency charges.
3. An offense committed while the offender is on probation, parole, or work release.
4. Previous offenses for which the offender has been punished.
5. Leadership in the commission of a delinquent act involving two or more offenders.
6. A violent offense involving more than one victim.
7. Extreme cruelty during the commission of the offense.
8. The use of a dangerous weapon in the commission of the offense, with high risk to human life.

Mitigating Circumstances.   Mitigating factors are those that lessen penalties imposed by these respective courts (Schwartz and Isser, 2001). Key mitigating factors include the following:

1. No serious bodily injury resulting from the offense.
2. No attempt to inflict serious bodily injury on anyone.
3. Duress or extreme provocation.
4. Circumstances that justify the conduct.
5. Mental incapacitation or physical condition that significantly reduced the offender's culpability in the offense.
6. Cooperation with authorities in apprehending other participants, or making restitution to the victims for losses they suffered.
7. No previous record of delinquent activity.

Judicial Dispositional Options

Juvenile judges may exercise several options when deciding specific cases. These judges may adjudicate youths as delinquent and do no more other than to record the event. If the juvenile appears again before the same judge, harsher sentencing measures may be taken. The judge might divert juveniles to community-based services or agencies for special treatment. Those youths with psychological problems or who are emotionally disturbed, sex offenders, or those with drug and/or alcohol dependencies may be targeted for special community treatments (Delaware Office of the Budget, 2002). Various conditions as punishments such as fines, restitution, or some form of community service may also be imposed by judges. The more drastic alternatives are varying degrees of custodial sentences, ranging from the placement of juveniles in foster homes, camp ranches, reform schools, or industrial schools. These nonsecure and secure forms of placement and/or detention are usually reserved for the most serious offenders (Goldson and Jamieson, 2002). Below is a summary of judicial options. One or more of the following eleven options may be exercised in any delinquency adjudication:

Nominal Sanctions:
1. A stern reprimand may be given.
2. A verbal warning may be issued.

Conditional Sanctions:
3. An order may be given to make restitution to victims.
4. An order may given to pay a fine.
5. An order may be given to perform some public service.
6. An order may be given to submit to the supervisory control of some community-based corrections agency on a probationary basis.
7. A sentence may be imposed, but the sentence may be suspended for a fixed term of probation.

Custodial Sanctions (Nonsecure and Secure):
8. An order may be issued for the placement of the juvenile in a foster home.
9. An order may be issued for the placement of the juvenile in a residential center or group home.
10. An order may be given to participate under supervision at a camp ranch or special school (either nonsecure or secure detention).

11. An order may be given to be confined in a secure facility for a specified period.

Nominal and Conditional Sanctions

Nominal dispositions are verbal and/or written warnings issued to low-risk juvenile offenders, often first-offenders, for the purpose of alerting them to the seriousness of their acts and their potential for receiving severe conditional punishments if they ever should re-offend. These sanctions are the least punitive alternatives.

Youth Diversion and Community-Based Programs.   One of the earliest delinquency prevention strategies that can be implemented by juvenile court judges and other actors throughout the juvenile justice system is diversion. Diversion is the temporary directing of youths from the juvenile justice system, where they can remain with their families or guardians, attend school, and be subject to limited supervision on a regular basis by a juvenile PO.

Youth Service Bureaus (YSBs).   Diversion programs have operated in the United States for many years. In the early 1960s, **Youth Service Bureaus (YSBs)** were established in numerous jurisdictions in order to accomplish diversion's several objectives. While we still cannot identify precisely those youths considered delinquency-prone or youths at risk, YSBs were created, in part, as places within communities where delinquent-prone youths could be referred by parents, schools, and law enforcement agencies. Actually, YSBs were forerunners of our contemporary community-based correctional programs, since they were intended to solicit volunteers from among community residents and to mobilize a variety of resources that could assist in a youth's treatment. The nature of treatments for youths, within the YSB concept, originally included referrals to a variety of community services, educational experiences, and individual or group counseling. YSB organizers attempted to compile lists of existing community services, agencies, organizations, and sponsors who could cooperatively coordinate these resources in the most productive ways to benefit affected juveniles (Romig, 1978). Many youths were victims of adult domestic violence, which caused increasingly serious adjustment problems (Edleson et al., 2003).

Diversion may be either unconditional or conditional. Unconditional diversion simply means that the divertee will attend school, behave, and not reappear before the juvenile court for a specified period. Conditional diversion may require juveniles to attend lectures, individual or group psychotherapy, drug or alcohol treatment centers, police department-conducted DUI classes, and/or vocational or educational classes or programs. Successful completion of the diversion program likely means dismissal of the case. These programs are of variable lengths, but most run for periods of 6 months to 1 year.

See Our Side Program.   In Prince George's County, Maryland, a program was established in 1983 called **See Our Side (SOS)** (Mitchell and Williams, 1986:70). SOS is referred to by its directors as a "juvenile aversion" program, and dissociates itself from "scare" programs such as Scared Straight. Basically, SOS seeks to educate juveniles about the realities of life in prison through discussions and hands-on experience and attempts to show them the types of behaviors that can lead to incarceration (Mitchell and Williams, 1986:70). Clients coming to SOS are referrals from various sources, including juvenile court, public and private schools, churches, professional counseling agencies, and police and fire departments. Youths served by SOS range in age from 12 to 18, and they do not have be adjudicated as delinquent in order to be eligible for participation. SOS consists of four 3-hour phases. These are described below.

Phase I: Staff orientation and group counseling session where staff attempt to facilitate discussion and ease tension among the youthful clients; characteristics of jails are discussed, including age and gender breakdowns, race, and types of juvenile behavior that might result in jailing for short periods.

Phase II: A tour of a prison facility.

Phase III: Three inmates discuss with youths what life is like behind bars; inmates who assist in the program are selected on the basis of their emotional maturity, communications skills, and warden recommendations.

Phase IV. Two evaluations are made—the first is an evaluation of SOS sessions by the juveniles; a recidivism evaluation is also conducted for each youth after a one-year lapse from the time they participated in SOS; relative program successfulness can therefore be gauged.

SOS officials conducted an evaluation of the program in September 1985. It was found that SOS served 327 youths during the first year of operation, and that a total of 38 sessions were held. Recidivism of program participants was about 22 percent. Again, this low recidivism rate is favorable. Subsequent evaluations of the SOS program showed that the average rate of client recidivism dropped to only 16 percent. The cost of the program was negligible. During the first year, the program cost was only $280, or about 86 cents per youth served.

Custodial Sanctions

The custodial options available to juvenile court judges are of two general types: (1) nonsecure facilities, and (2) secure facilities (Giovanni, 2002). Nonsecure custodial facilities are those that permit youths freedom of movement within the community. Youths are generally free to leave the premises of their facilities, although they are compelled to observe various rules, such as curfew, avoidance of alcoholic beverages and drugs, and participation in specific programs that are tailored to their particular needs (Schaps and Solomon, 2003). These types of nonsecure facilities include foster homes, group homes and halfway houses, camps, ranches, experience programs, and wilderness projects.

Non-Secure Facilities

Foster Homes.   If the juvenile's natural parents are considered unfit, or if the juvenile is abandoned or orphaned, **foster homes** are often used for temporary placement. Those youths placed in foster homes are not necessarily law violators. They may be **children in need of supervision (CHINS)** or **persons in need of supervision (PINS)** (*Matter of Zachary "I",* 1993). Foster home placement provides youths with a substitute family. A stable family environment is believed by the courts to be beneficial in many cases where youths have no consistent adult supervision or are unmanageable or unruly in their own households (Kivett et al., 2002).

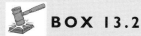

BOX 13.2

David Melville
Treatment Supervisor, Department of Human Services Division of Youth Correction, Intensive Community Aftercare Program (ICAP), Salt Lake City, Utah

Statistics:

B.A. (sociology), University of Utah; M.S. (mental health counseling), University of Phoenix

Experience:

I am currently the treatment supervisor for a community-based aftercare program based in Salt Lake City. The program provides halfway house-type programming and supervision for young men released from one of the state's secure facilities. Utah has five secure facilities for the state's most violent and chronic juvenile offenders. Adolescents in Utah can be under the jurisdiction of Youth Corrections until their twenty-first birthday. I began my career with Youth Corrections as a part-time counselor in one of the secure facilities while I was still working on my bachelor's degree. I have held the position of Senior Treatment Counselor in a facility; parole officer, working with adolescent parolees after their release; hearing officer for the Youth Parole Authority; and currently, the supervisor for the Intensive Community Aftercare Program (ICAP). As a nontraditional college student (i.e., taking more than 10 years to finish my degree), I have continued my education throughout my career. I received a master's degree in mental health counseling in 2003.

Background:

I began working with kids when I was still an adolescent. I was born in New York and started working for the Village of Hempstead Recreation Department as a seasonal employee when I was 16 years old. I enjoyed working with underprivileged or at-risk youths from the very beginning. I felt a sense of personal accomplishment when I could help a child deal with a difficult situation or learn a new skill. My first college experience was at St. John's University. I tried various majors, but with little commitment. I was probably more committed to dating and partying. I began working full time and taking classes as I could. I took a job in Texas with the Missouri-Pacific Railroad and worked on a line gang for almost two years before deciding I should return to school. I soon moved to Utah and began attending the University of Utah, but still without enough commitment. While in Utah I worked as a roughneck for various oil well-drilling companies. There I experienced adequate financial rewards but less than adequate working and living conditions. Again I realized that a college education was the key to success. I began to take my studies more seriously and took a job with the Salt Lake County Recreation Department, again working with kids in one of the more economically depressed areas of Salt Lake. I became the informal crisis intervention specialist at the recreation center, and I believe that this played a part in rekindling my interest in working with at-risk youth. As I continued in school, I pursued my interest in working with kids and applied for a job with the State Division of Youth Corrections. I could only find part-time employment, but I started working at Decker Lake Youth Center and going to school with renewed enthusiasm.

The youth that are placed in secure care in Utah have an average of 5 felony and 14 misdemeanor convictions. On average, they spend between 9 and 12 months in the facility before they are released to an aftercare program. Those convicted of capital offenses serve closer to 40 months. In working with such severely delinquent youth, you

(continued)

BOX 13.2 (*Continued*)

really get a chance to see the factors that contribute to the formation of a career criminal. You also get to see the resilience of some individuals who surprise everyone by turning their lives around and becoming productive citizens. Personally, I found the work to be very rewarding, always a challenge, and never boring.

Due to my work experience and continued schooling, I was able to get hired as a full-time counselor for the state and continued to work while I pursued my degree–not the easiest way to finish school, but persistence pays off. I was able to advance to the position of a Senior Counselor, with a little more responsibility, and soon after that, I finished my undergraduate work. As I continued to advance within Youth Corrections, my next position as a parole officer. This is a much more diverse and challenging position, as you work with and supervise youth on parole who have been released from one of the state's secure facilities. This is where the rubber hits the road. At this point, the youth either succeed in fulfilling the obligation of their Parole Agreement, commit another crime for which they will be tried as an adult (even if they are still under 18), or their parole can be violated and they can be returned to the secure facility. I also held the position of Hearing Officer for the Youth Parole Authority, which is an administrative position processing youth through the system. But the cubicle got to me and I found that I missed direct service with the youth.

I continued in school after graduation and earned a master's degree in counseling in 2003. I am now the Treatment Supervisor of the Intensive Community Aftercare Program, which is a residential program for the youth after they are released from a secure facility. The work is still challenging, and if it is boring, we are doing something wrong. Recidivism rates are difficult to measure, but in the first seven months of this new program, we have not had any youth go AWOL from the facility. Prior to that period, the facilities averaged two AWOL youths per month. I continue to be a realistic optimist and try to impress upon the youth that "you are free to make your own choices, but you are not free from the consequences of those choices." This is often a difficult concept for adolescents to grasp. It is also one of life's more important lessons.

Interesting Experiences:

Working with teens, interesting and unbelievable experiences are frequent. In my first week as a parole officer, I had a parolee I was meeting for the first time attempt to hit me with a chair (he was quickly restrained and returned to secure care, soon to graduate to prison). I have had a 17-year-old parolee give birth to her first child, and boy, did I get some dirty looks in the store when I would take her shopping for groceries and diapers. I have attended funerals and weddings of parolees. I have worked with youth who have been convicted of murder, rape, robbery, and almost every other crime imaginable. I have seen youth who I thought did not have a chance become successful, be terminated from parole and then go on to college. There are both tragic cases and comical cases. One of the best was a youth that had violated parole and was AWOL. He had an active warrant out for his arrest when we located him. As my partner and I entered the apartment where he was located, his eyes widened and without missing a beat, he said, "I was just about to call you guys. I want to turn myself in." After suppressing our laughter, we told him that that wouldn't work because we found him first. He smiled, turned, and placed his hands behind his back. As I said, when working with youth, it is never boring and always a challenge.

Advice to Students:

If you are going into this line of work to become rich and famous, you may be on the wrong track. If you want to make a difference in the lives of others, you are on the right one. I would encourage students to get a variety of experiences working with different populations. Even part-time experience or volunteering will give you an idea of what you are in for. Talk to people who have experiences in that field. Always look for ways to improve your skills and look for opportunities to learn where you least expect them.

Foster home placements are useful in many cases where youths have been apprehended for status offenses. Most families who accept youths into their homes have been investigated by state or local authorities in advance to determine their fitness as foster parents. Socioeconomic factors and home stability are considered important for child placements. Foster parents often typify middle-aged, middle-class citizens with above-average educational backgrounds. Despite these positive features, it is unlikely that foster homes are able to provide the high intensity of adult supervision required by more hard-core juvenile offenders. Further, it is unlikely that these parents can furnish the quality of special treatments that might prove effective in the youth's possible rehabilitation or societal reintegration. Most foster parents simply are not trained as counselors, social workers, or psychologists. For many nonserious youths, however, a home environment, particularly a stable one, has certain therapeutic benefits.

Group Homes.   Another nonsecure option for juvenile judges is the assignment of juveniles to **group homes.** Placing youths in group homes is considered an intermediate option available to juvenile court judges. Group homes are community-based operations that may be either publicly or privately administered. Usually, group homes will have counselors or residents to act as parental figures for youths in groups of 10 to 20. Certain group homes, referred to as family group homes, are actually family-operated, and thus, they are in a sense an extension of foster homes for larger numbers of youths. In group homes, nonsecure supervision of juvenile clients is practiced (Kivett et al., 2002). Privately or publicly operated, group homes require juvenile clients to observe the rights of others, participate in various vocational or educational training programs, attend school, participate in therapy or receive prescribed medical treatment, and observe curfew. Urinalyses or other tests may be conducted randomly as checks to see whether juveniles are taking drugs or consuming alcohol contrary to group home policy (Parker, 2001). If one or more program violations occur, group home officials may report these infractions to juvenile judges who retain dispositional control over the youths. Assignment to a group home is usually for a determinate period (Collins, Schwartz, and Epstein, 2001).

Positively, group homes provide youths with the companionship of other juveniles. Problem-sharing often occurs through planned group discussions. Staff are available to assist youths to secure employment, work certain difficult school problems, and absorb emotional burdens arising from difficult interpersonal relationships. However, these homes are sometimes staffed by community volunteers with little training or experience with a youth's problems. There are certain risks and legal liabilities that may be incurred as the result of well-intentioned but bad advice or inadequate assistance. Currently, there are limited regulations among states for how group homes are established and operated. Training programs for group home staff are scarce in most jurisdictions, and few standards exist relating to staff preparation and qualifications. Therefore, considerable variation exists among group homes relating to the quality of services they can extend to the juveniles they serve.

Camps, Ranches, Experience Programs, and Wilderness Projects.   **Camps** and **ranches** are nonsecure facilities that are sometimes referred to as **wilderness programs** or experience programs. A less expensive alternative to the detention of juvenile offenders, even those considered chronic, is participation in experience programs. **Experience programs** include a wide array of outdoor programs designed to improve a juvenile's self-worth, self-concept, pride, and trust in others (Wilson and Lipsey, 2000).

Hope Center and Responsible Living Skills Program.   An example of a fairly successful wilderness experiment is the Hope Center and Responsible Living Skills Program or the **Hope Center Wilderness Camp** in Washington state (McLain, 2001). This camp has an organized network of several interdependent, small living groups who live outdoors for up to 30 days. The camp's goals are to provide quality care and treatment in a nonpunitive environment, with frequent evaluations of appropriate placement, education and treatment, and possible return to the youths' families. Youths range in age from 16 to 18. Participants are involved in various special events and learn to cook meals outdoors, camp, and other survival skills. The aim of the program is for youth to work toward independent living. The program is regarded as transitional.

Secure Confinement

Short-Term and Long-Term Facilities.   **Secure confinement** for juveniles in the United States emulate adult prisons or penitentiaries in several of their characteristics. There is considerable peer violence in many juvenile institutions, similar to violence in adult settings (Peterson-Badali and Koegl, 2002). They are also either short-term or long-term. These terms are ambiguous as they pertain to juvenile secure custody facilities. Short-term confinement facilities, sometimes referred to as detention, are designed to accommodate juveniles on a temporary basis. These juveniles are either awaiting a later juvenile court adjudication, subsequent foster home or group home placement, or a transfer to criminal court. Sometimes youths will be placed in short-term confinement because their identity is unknown, and it is desirable that they should not be confined in adult lockups or jails (Neustatter, 2002). When juveniles are placed in these short-term facilities, they are considered held in detention. Opposed to detention, juveniles placed in long-term facilities may be confined for several days or years, although the average duration of juvenile incarceration across all offender categories nationally is about 6 or 7 months (Altschuler and Armstrong, 2002). The average short-term incarceration in public facilities for juveniles is about 30 days. Most juvenile court judges use incarceration as a last-resort disposition, if the circumstances merit incarceration. By far the most frequently used sanction against juveniles is probation (Podkopacz and Feld, 2002).

One persistent question is which juvenile offenders are most deserving of detention or secure confinement? This question has never been answered to everyone's satisfaction. There are instances of status offenders being locked up for lengthy periods, together with juvenile delinquents. Some delinquents who have committed serious offenses are not locked up at all; rather, they receive probation. The increased use of risk-assessment instruments by different juvenile courts has attempted to remedy problems of fairness in terms of who should or should not be confined. But much work remains to be done on perfecting such instruments (Withrow, 2003).

JUVENILE POS AND PREDISPOSITIONAL REPORTS

Juvenile Probation Officers

Many probation officers who work with juveniles report that their work is satisfying (Harry, 2000). Many of these juvenile POs are expanding their fundamental skills training in dealing with troubled youths (Reddington and Kreisel,

2003:41). Many of them see themselves as playing an important part in shaping a youth's future by the nature of the relationship they can establish between themselves and the juveniles with whom they work. James R. Davis, a probation officer with the Department of Probation in New York City for 22 years, has supervised both adults and juvenile offenders. Usually, the juveniles he supervises are those age 16 and over who have been transferred to criminal courts because of more serious offenses they have committed. He shares his experiences by noting:

> Generally, I supervise adults from the age of 16 and over who are placed on probation by the court. Sometimes, I have supervised juveniles under age 16 who are tried in adult courts under the New York State Juvenile Laws. Although I have had only a few cases of juveniles who are tried as adults, they present the worst cases to me, and I am sure, to other probation officers. This is logical, since they are accused of violent crimes. Now there is a special worker who handles these [kinds of] cases. I remember a case of a juvenile who was 15 and tried as an adult. He was charged with felonious assault. He was hostile and noncooperative when supervised by me. For example, he didn't report on time, he was verbally abusive to me, and he was loud and hostile. He was arrested while on probation for another felony assault charge. He was known to have beaten up his grandmother. When I initiated a violation of probation for the new arrest, he became quite hostile and wanted to know why I did this. He even followed me one night into the street, and I had to get into a cab to escape him. He beat up another probationer in the waiting area of the office and was finally transferred to an intensive probation caseload.
>
> I was supervising another juvenile who was placed on adult probation at the age of 15 for robbery. He had an arrest prior to being placed on probation for robbery and was arrested again during supervision for another robbery. He always tried to work, and at first he was cooperative. However, during supervision he became hostile, noncooperative, failing to keep appointments, and failing to wait for his turn in the office. He was black and insisted that he wanted a black probation officer, since I was white. However, the judge incarcerated him for a few weeks because of this new robbery charge. He is now awaiting the disposition of his new robbery case. Although I am still supervising him, the relationship between him and me is tense and fragile; he is still nervous and impatient, and he doesn't keep appointments on time. He minimizes his arrest record. He claims that blacks do not receive justice with white agents of the criminal justice system. His mother absconded from the home, and he is now supervised by his grandmother.
>
> Although I [now] supervise [primarily] adults, anyone from the age of 16 to 19 is given a youthful offender status except for a few violent offenders. However, I believe that juveniles under 16 who are tried as adults present some special problems and do need supervision in a special caseload by experienced probation officers who are trained for this type of experience [Interview with James R. Davis, January, 1999].

Probation Work and Professionalism

There is a keen sense of professionalism among most probation and parole officers (Brumbaugh and Birkbeck, 2000). The American Correctional Association and the American Probation and Parole Association are two of the most important professional organizations today that disseminate information about corrections and probation and parole programs and provide workshops and various forms of professional training (Reddington and Kreisel, 2000). Many probation and parole officers attend the meetings of these and other professional organizations to learn about the latest innovations and probation programs. Sweet (1985) views probation work with juveniles as a timely opportunity to intervene and make a difference in their lives. Thus, he sees probation as a type of therapy. He divides the therapy function that probation officers can perform into five simple steps:

1. Case review—probation counselors need skills to read the behaviors of the youths they supervise and their probable antecedents.

2. Self-awareness—probation counselors need to inspect their own reactions to youths; are they too impatient or overly sensitive? Traditional transference and countertransference issues must be addressed.

3. Development of a relationship—great patience is required; children are often rejected, and probation officers must learn to accept them and demonstrate a faith in their ability to achieve personal goals.

4. The critical incident—the testing phase of the relationship, where juveniles may deliberately act up to test honesty and sincerity of PO.

5. Following through—successive tests will be made by juveniles as they continue to verify the PO's honesty and sincerity; POs do much of the parenting that their clients' parents failed to do.

Sweet considers these stages integral features of action therapy that can often be more effective than insight-oriented therapy (Sweet, 1985:90).

Because of their diverse training, POs often orient themselves toward juvenile clients in particular ways that may be more or less effective. Because many juvenile offenders are considered manipulators who might take advantage of a PO's sympathies, some POs have devised interpersonal barriers between themselves and their youthful clients. Other POs have adopted more productive interpersonal strategies. In most juvenile cases, POs seek to instruct and assist offenders to deal with their personal and social problems in order to fit better into their community environments. If POs continuously check up on their youthful clients or regard them with suspicion, they inhibit the growth of productive interpersonal relations that might be helpful in facilitating a youth's reentry into society (Hassell and Maguire, 2001). Enforcement-oriented officers and those who attempt to detect rule infractions almost always create a hostile working relationship with their clients, and communication barriers are often erected that inhibit a PO's effectiveness.

In recent years, the National Center for Juvenile Justice (NCJJ) has established a recommended curriculum and course of training of up to 200 hours for juvenile POs. The fundamental skills training curriculum outlined by the NCJJ has incorporated the following elements as essential components in one's training to deal effectively with juvenile probationers/parolees:

1. Probation officer safety

2. Supervision skills

3. Courtroom presentations

4. Juvenile justice system overview

5. Enhancing the profession

6. Special problems and appropriate responses

7. Writing the recommendation
8. Appreciating cultural diversity
9. Assessment skills
10. The probation profession
11. Adolescence and delinquency
12. Interpersonal communications skills
13. Predispositional report recommendations
14. Managing resources and time

Suggested meeting topics of groups of juvenile POs undergoing training have included training in general; national standards; specialized topics (e.g., victims, female offenders, gangs, firearms); safety; best practices; certification of officers; outcome measures and competencies; financial resources, and caseload management (Reddington and Kreisel, 2003:44).

Juvenile Probation Officer Functions

The functions of juvenile POs are diverse, and they include such tasks as report preparation, home and school visits, and a variety of other client contacts. They often arrange contacts between their clients and various community-based corrections agencies who provide services and specific types of psychological and social treatments (Beymer and Hutchinson, 2002). POs themselves perform counseling tasks with their clients. They also must enforce laws associated with probation or parole program conditions. Thus, if offenders have been ordered to comply with a specific curfew and/or reimburse victims for their financial losses, POs must monitor them to ensure that these program conditions have been fulfilled.

Some of the major PO dimensions that are deemed most important are:

1. Problem-solving (problem analysis—the ability to grasp the source, nature, and key elements of problems; judgment—recognition of the significant factors to arrive at sound and practical decisions)
2. Communication (dialogue skills—effectiveness of one-on-one contacts with youthful clients, small group interactions; writing skills—expression of ideas clearly and concisely)
3. Emotional and motivational (reactions to reassure—functioning in a controlled, effective manner under conditions of stress; keeping one's head; drive—the amount of directed and sustained energy to accomplish one's objectives)
4. Interpersonal (insight into others—the ability to proceed, giving due consideration to the needs and feelings of others; leadership—the direction of behavior of others toward the achievement of goals)
5. Administrative (planning—forward thinking, anticipating situations and problems, and preparation in advance to cope with these problems; commitment to excellence—determination that the task will be well-done).

In 2002 it was estimated that there were 25,000 juvenile probation officers in the United States (Pastore and Maguire, 2003). These officers provided intake services for nearly 2 million juveniles, predispositional studies of over 800,000 cases, and received over 800,000 cases for supervision (American Correctional

Association, 2003). These cases are not distributed evenly throughout the various juvenile probation departments in the United States. Thus, caseloads for some POs are considerably larger than they are for others. A high caseload is arbitrarily defined as 50 or more juvenile clients, although caseloads as high as 300 or more have been reported in some jurisdictions. When caseloads are particularly high, this places an even greater burden on the shoulders of juvenile POs who must often prepare predispositional reports for youths at the juvenile court judge's direction.

The Predispositional Report and Its Preparation

Juvenile court judges in many jurisdictions order the preparation of **predispositional reports,** which are the functional equivalent of presentence investigation reports for adults. Predispositional reports are intended to furnish judges with background information about juveniles to make a more informed sentencing decision. They also function to assist probation officers and others to target high-need areas for youths and specific services or agencies for individualized referrals. This information is often channeled to information agencies such as the National Center for Juvenile Justice in Pittsburgh, Pennsylvania, so that researchers may benefit in their juvenile justice investigations. They may analyze the information compiled from various jurisdictions for their own research investigations (Rogers and Williams, 1995).

Predispositional reports are completed for more serious juveniles and function like presentence investigation reports prepared by POs for adults. Juvenile court judges order these prepared in most cases, unless there are statutory provisions in certain jurisdictions that govern their automatic preparation. These predispositional reports contain much of the same information as PSI reports. Sometimes, juveniles whose families can afford them have private predispositional reports prepared to influence judges to exert leniency on the juvenile offender (Rogers and Williams, 1995). In fact, that is precisely what Peter Greenwood and Susan Turner found when they compared case dispositions of youths where private predispositional reports had been prepared against those cases where standard reports had been compiled by juvenile POs. Greenwood and Turner described client-specific planning as the name given by the National Center on Institutions and Alternatives to its process of developing alternative sentencing plans designed to minimize the incarceration of its clients (Greenwood and Turner, 1993:232).

Trester (1981:89–90) has summarized four important reasons for why predisposition reports should be prepared:

1. These reports provide juvenile court judges with a more complete picture of juvenile offenders and their offenses, including the existence of any aggravating or mitigating circumstances.
2. These reports can assist the court in tailoring the disposition of the case to an offender's needs.
3. These reports may lead to the identification of positive factors that would indicate the likelihood of rehabilitation.
4. These reports provide judges with the offender's treatment history, which might indicate the effectiveness or ineffectiveness of previous dispositions and suggest the need for alternative dispositions.

It is important to recognize that predispositional reports are not required by judges in all jurisdictions. By the same token, legislative mandates obligate officials in other jurisdictions to prepare them for all juveniles to be adjudicated. Also, there are no specific formats universally acceptable in these report preparations. Figure 13.11 is an example of a predisposition report.

Rogers (1990:44) indicates that predisposition reports contain insightful information about youths that can be helpful to juvenile court judges prior to

THE PREDISPOSITION REPORT

**A Model Set of Field Notes to Guide Preparation of
Juvenile Court Predisposition Reports**

COURT REPORT OUTLINE

CASE NO:_____ HEARING DATE:_____

ADDRESS:_____PHONE:_____

1.	REASON FOR HEARING:	PETITION NO.:	PETITION DATE:	W&I	SUB:	
	NAME: (AKA):			AGE:		
	ALLEGATION AND REFERENCE TO P.D. REPORT OR COMPLAINT:					
2.	PRESENT SITUATION	FIRST COURT WARD		REFERRAL DATE AND AGENCY:		
	PLACE AND DATE OF DETENTION OR CUSTODY:			RELEASED TO:	DATE:	
3.	CITATION	SERVED MAILED	TO:			
	SERVED BY:		LOCATION		DATE:	
4.	LEGAL RESIDENCE	DETERMINING PARENT:		ARRIVED IN SAN DIEGO COUNTY:		
	VERIFICATION:			RESIDENCE OF CHILD:		
5.	PREVIOUS HISTORY:					
6.	STATEMENT OF CHILD (Description, attitude, and statements re: allegation and home):					
	RACE:	HAIR:	EYES:	HT:	WT:	MARKS:

FIGURE 13.11 A Predispositional Report.

Source: Joseph W. Rogers, "The Predisposition Report: Maintaining the Promise of Individual and Juvenile Justice." *Federal Probation* 54:51–52, 1990.

7. STATEMENT OF PARENTS (Description, attitude, and statement re: allegation and child):

8. STATEMENT OF VICTIM, WITNESSES, RELATIVES OR OTHERS (Name, Address, Date and Relation to Case):

9. FAMILY HISTORY

| FAMILY HISTORY | MARRIAGE OF NATURAL PARENTS, DATE AND PLACE: |

CHILDREN AND ORDER OF BIRTH

AGE, EDUCATIONAL LEVEL AND BACKGROUND OF NATURAL PARENTS

DATE, PLACE, REASON AND EFFECTS OF SEPARATION, DIVORCE, REMARRIAGE (CUSTODY):

PREVIOUS RESIDENCE; EMPLOYMENT; DATE ARRIVED S. D. CO.; PRESENT FAMILY UNIT:

| DESCRIPTION OF HOME AND FURNISHINGS: | OWNED | | $ |
| | RENTED | | $ |

COMMUNITY RELATIONSHIP AND ENVIRONMENTAL FACTORS: POLICE RECORD OF PARENT AND/OR SIBLINGS:

DISEASES IN HISTORY OF EITHER PARENT: HANDICAPS, MENTAL DISORDERS, ALCOHOLISM, SUICIDE; HEALTH INSURANCE AND HOSPITAL ELIGIBILITY:

RELIGION AND ATTENDANCE:

PARENT - CHILD RELATIONSHIP:

FIGURE 13.11   (Continued).

sentencing. Six social aspects of a person's life are crucial for investigations, analysis, and treatment. These include: (1) personal health, physical and emotional; (2) family and home situation; (3) recreational activities and use of leisure time; (4) peer group relationships (types of companions); (5) education; and (6) work experience. According to the National Advisory Commission on

Criminal Justice Standards and Goals as outlined in 1973, predispositional reports have been recommended in all cases where the offenders are minors. In actual practice, however, predisposition reports are only prepared at the request of juvenile court judges. No systematic pattern typifies such report preparation in most U.S. jurisdictions. Table 13.2 shows the type of information reported in a sample of 162 predisposition reports.

Rogers (1990:46) says that the following characteristics were included in 100 percent of all of the cases: (1) gender, (2) ethnic status, (3) age at first juvenile court appearance, (4) source of first referral to juvenile court, (5) reason(s) for referral; (6) formal court disposition; (7) youth's initial placement by court; (8) miscellaneous court orders and conditions, (9) type of counsel retained, (10) initial

TABLE 13.2

Percentage of Juvenile Case Records in Which Line Item Information Was Located

Variable Identification	Item Number	Percentage
Case code number	1–3	
Sex	4	100
Ethnic status	5	100
Age, 1st juv. ct. appearance	6	100
Source of 1st referral	7	100
Reason for 1st referral/ct. hearing	8–9	100
Recoding of prior item	10	100
Formal court disposition	11	100
Youth's initial placement by court	12	100
Miscellaneous court orders	13	100
Detention prior to 1st hearing	14	100
Type of counsel retained	15	100
Initial plea	16	100
Presiding, initial ct. hearing	17	99
Number of prior offenses	18	100
Age, time of initial offense	19	100
Number of off. after 1st hearing	20	100
Youth's total offense number	21	100
Number companions, 1st offense	22	100
Usual companionship portrait	23	92
Living arrangements 1st ct. hearing	24	99
Parents' marital status	25	99
Youth's age at divorce/death	26	93
Household economic status	27	95
Public assistance recipient?	28	88
Income dependence number	29	96
Type of neighborhood	30	60
Home assessment	31	85
Parental work situation	32	94
Parental education background	33	19
Father's health	34	78
Mother's health	35	85

(continued)

TABLE 13.2   (CONTINUED)

Variable Identification	Item Number	Percentage
Youth's school academic standing	36	94
Youth's school attendance	37	94
Youth's att./perception:sch.	38	83
Parents' att. toward youth's educ.	39	59
Child's birth	40	72
Organic/emotional dysfunctions	41	85
Other educational problems	42	80
Youth's church attendance	43	28
Youth's job record	44	73
Leisure-time interests	45	64
Youth's mental health portrait	46	86
Highest IQ recorded	47	45
Psychological intervention	48	85
Community outpatient care	49	35
Residential inpatient care	50	43
Statement of juvenile	51	92
Statement of mother	52	83
Statement of father	53	56
Youth's generalized explanation	54	95
Parent's generalized explanation	55	88
JPO's generalized explanation	56	93
Alienation	57	96
Childhood rejection	58	88
Child's concept of self	59	90
Dominant manifest personality	60	97
Personality direction	61	93
Usual peer group relationship	62	89
Achievement orientation	63	77
Siblings relationships	64	74
Mother/child relationship	65	93
Father/child relationship	66	84
Principal discipline source	67	85
Quality of discipline	68	77
Family difficulty with police	69	76
Last known offense	70–71	99
Decoding of prior item	72	99
Time under JPO supervision	73	93
Number of detentions	74	100
Number of out-of-home placements	75	100
Dominant form of JPO contact	76	83
JPO home visit frequency	77	67
Overall frequency of contact	78	78
Final status of case	79	95
Judge, last court hearing	80	99

Source: Joseph W. Rogers, "The Predisposition Report," *Federal Probation* 54:48 (1990).

plea; (11) number of prior offenses; (12) age and time of initial offense; (13) number of offenses after first hearing; (14) youth's total offense number; (15) number of companions, first offense, (16) number of detentions, and (17) number of out-of-home placements. These predisposition reports may or may not contain victim impact statements. Presentence investigation reports or PSIs prepared for adults convicted of crimes are the equivalent of predispositional reports. It is more common to see such victim impact statements in adult PSI reports, although some predispositional reports contain them in certain jurisdictions. These statements are often prepared by victims themselves and appended to the report before the judge sees it. They are intended to provide judges with a sense of the physical harm and monetary damage victims have sustained, and thus, they are often aggravating factors that weigh heavily against the juvenile to be sentenced.

JUVENILE PROBATION AND PAROLE PROGRAMS

About 2 million juvenile cases are processed annually by juvenile courts. About 800,000 of these are assigned to POs for predispositional study, while 600,000 cases are assigned for supervision (Pastore and Maguire, 2003). The most common form of probation is standard probation. Standard juvenile probation is more or less elaborate, depending upon the jurisdiction. Of all sentencing options available to juvenile court judges, standard probation is the most commonly used. Standard probation programs are either a conditional or unconditional nonincarcerative sentence of a specified period following an adjudication of delinquency.

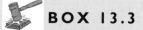 **BOX 13.3**    **PERSONALITY HIGHLIGHT**

Maria Stops
State of New Mexico Juvenile Parole Board, Clinical Social Worker, and President of Youth Advocates Alliance

Statistics:

M.A. (counseling and educational psychology), B.A. (sociology), New Mexico State University; licensed M.S.W. and Professional Clinical Counselor

Background:

I was born and raised in Southwest Philadelphia, Pennsylvania, and came to Las Cruces, New Mexico, at 17 years of age to attend New Mexico State University (NMSU). At the time, I was seeking adventure, wanted to be more than 2,000 miles away from my parents, and convinced myself and my family that I needed to come to NMSU because I wanted to pursue a degree in horticulture and animal science.

Approximately a year after I began at NMSU, I changed my major to sociology and criminal justice. I had always been fascinated with the study of people from other cultures, human behavior in its many forms, and the
(continued)

BOX 13.3 (*Continued*)

juvenile/criminal justice systems. However, I still had not conquered my feelings of wanderlust and left NMSU to attend the University of Montana in Missoula as an exchange student. I returned in 1978 and completed my sociology degree. In 1979 I began a master's in counseling and educational psychology (CEP) at NMSU, and I was funded through a research fellowship for minority women. I graduated with my M.A. in 1981 and began to pursue a Ph.D. the following semester. I completed the majority of my doctoral work in CEP and then decided to leave the university and work for a nonprofit community mental health center for several years.

In 1990 New Mexico created the New Mexico Youth Authority. I was employed as one of four clinical social workers to work with regional juvenile probation officers. I completed home studies, clinical assessments, and made recommendations to the courts regarding the child's need for treatment services. I also made recommendations to the presiding Children's Court Judge regarding the need for out-of-home placements, including commitments to the state's juvenile correctional facilities. In the early 1990s, the New Mexico Youth Authority was dismantled and a new department was created. This was called the Children, Youth and Families Department, which combined children's social and protective services along with juvenile correctional/facilities/juvenile parole offices all under one cabinet secretary.

Working with young people in the juvenile justice system was one of the most rewarding jobs I have ever had. I stayed in this capacity until 1999 when I left to work for the Las Cruces Public Schools. I am currently employed as a Special Education Social Worker to approximately 80 students who have been placed in an alternative school setting due to weapons, drugs, or safety violations on their main high school campus. I provide individual and group counseling related to a students Individual Education Plan (IEP). In 2000 several other individuals and I formed a nonprofit organization called Youth Advocates Alliance. Our nonprofit organization is dedicated to creating and fostering humane conditions of confinement for children

who are incarcerated throughout juvenile correctional facilities in our state. We are very much concerned about the lack of bona fide vocational, educational, and treatment services for incarcerated youth and seek to hold the Children, Youth and Families Department accountable for the services that our youth are currently receiving. Most, recently I was appointed to the State of New Mexico Juvenile Parole Board in January 2003. I am deeply honored to have been selected by Governor Bill Richardson for the position and am hopeful that the new board along with the director of the Parole Board can facilitate meaningful transitions and aftercare discharge planning for our youths returning back to their home communities.

Work Experience:

In 1996 there was a small disturbance involving approximately 5 to 7 young boys at one of the state's northern juvenile correctional facilities. Because of this, over 80 young boys were transported to the adult county facility in the community where I reside. I was asked by the department that I worked for to be the clinical treatment coordinator for these young boys and to develop a program of service that would be provided *pro bono* by community members. The youths were detained at this facility for almost 2 1/2 months. My community rallied to the needs of these youths and provided a number of creative programs and innovative services. The boys were eventually taken back to their originating facility in the middle of the night without any notice to the youths or their counselors, teachers, and artists who had developed a therapeutic relationship with each of them. A month later when we were finally granted permission to visit them, we were appalled and completely disheartened at their conditions of confinement.

The juvenile facility was beyond overcrowding and all programs (mental health, educational vocational, recreational) had been completely suspended. The boys were locked in their cells, sometimes up to three youths in a single-person cell, for 23 hours a day. These conditions lasted for several

BOX 13.3 (Continued)

months before they were again transferred to another adult correctional facility due to overcrowding.

No other event in my clinical career has had such a profound effect on me and altered my way of "seeing." As a result, I have come to believe that we are doing a complete disservice to young juveniles who are incarcerated by simply modeling our youth programs after an adult corrections model and warehousing them in facilities that closely resemble their adult counterparts. If we don't provide our incarcerated youths with the best practices known in rehabilitating delinquent youth and give them all of the skills and knowledge that they need to succeed, we are simply committing them to a life of poverty and hopelessness, not to mention the adult correctional system.

Advice to Students:

My views on working with difficult or delinquent youths have changed over the years as the result of some of the struggles I have personally experienced in the juvenile justice system. The following principles and beliefs have served me well. Hopefully they will be of some value to you and assist you in this awesome task of helping young persons find their path once again:

- View the incarcerated deliquent youths that you work with as stu-

dents, not "inmates." If you want them to behave like students who have hope and a future, then treat them that way.

- Delinquent youth are not intrinsically "bad youth." They may have done bad things but they have the capability to change their behavior from antisocial to prosocial.

- It is not enough for you to care for the delinquent youths that you work with; they must be taught and empowered to care and contribute to a cause greater than themselves.

- You can place a youth in the best program or facility, but it will be the *relationship* that you develop and sustain with that child that will make the difference. Don't be afraid to care for that child beyond the length of the probationary agreement or commitment.

"To be reclaimed is to be restored to value, to experience attachment, achievement, autonomy, and altruism—the four well-springs of courage" (Dr. Janusz Korcyak).

Unconditional and Conditional Probation

How Many Juveniles Are There on Probation?   As of this writing, there were no official statistics available that indicated for sure how many juveniles were on probation in the United States at any given time. Of all of the populations and agencies in the justice system, the one that is the least studied is juvenile probation (Hancock, 2003:22). We know that over 2 million juveniles come to the attention of police annually and that about half of these offenders are referred to juvenile authorities for some type of action. We also know that the sanction of choice imposed on juveniles who are adjudicated delinquent is probation, and that most adjudicated juveniles receive it. It would be nothing more than an educated guess to estimate the number of juveniles on probation at any given time would be somewhere between 500,000 and 1 million, although we don't know for sure.

Therefore, in late 2003 the Office of Juvenile Justice and Delinquency Prevention (OJJDP) initiated a census of juveniles on probation. The census, conducted in conjunction with researchers at George Mason University in Virginia, planned to develop the Census of Juvenile Probation Supervision Offices and the Census of Juveniles on Probation (Hancock, 2003:24). Currently we do not have the data to provide a national description of juvenile probation, to properly account for the size of the juvenile probation population, or to make comparisons from one probation office to another. The results of these censuses will provide information about and insight into the types of services that are available across the country to juveniles on probation, the processing options that are available for certain types of crimes, the size of caseloads and how they differ from one jurisdiction to another, the types of juveniles in the system, and the community partnerships and prevention programming that are offered by probation agencies (Hancock, 2003:22). The initial data set was to be gathered from a random number of juvenile probation agencies by mid-2004. All probation agencies were to be contacted and data collected by 2006. Given the time lag between data collection and information dissemination, it is likely that this information will become available to general practitioners in the criminal justice field by 2007–2008.

Probation Programs for Juveniles. Probation programs for juveniles are either unconditional or conditional and exhibit many similarities with adult probation programs. Unconditional standard probation basically involves complete freedom of movement within the juvenile's community, perhaps accompanied by periodic reports by telephone or mail with a PO or the probation department. Because a PO's caseload is often high, with several hundred juvenile clients that must be managed, individualized attention cannot be given to most juveniles on standard probation. Sometimes police officers are called upon to assist POs in their supervisory tasks (Giblin, 2002). The period of unsupervised probation varies among jurisdictions depending upon offense seriousness and other circumstances.

Conditional probation programs may include optional conditions and program requirements, such as performing a certain number of hours of public or community service, providing restitution to victims, payment of fines, employment, and/or participation in specific vocational, educational, or therapeutic programs. It is crucial to any probation program that an effective classification system is in place so that juvenile judges can sentence offenders accordingly. Baird (1985:32–34) suggests that a variation of the National Institute of Corrections' (NIC) Model Classification Project scheme be used for juvenile classifications, where both risk and needs are assessed. General terms of standard probation usually include the following:

1. To obey one's parents or guardians.
2. To obey all laws of the community, including curfew and school laws.
3. To follow the school or work program approved by the PO.
4. To follow instructions of the PO.
5. To report in person to the PO or court at such times designated by the PO.
6. To comply with any special conditions of probation.
7. To consult with the PO when in need of further advice.

Juveniles sentenced to standard probation experience little change in their social routines. Whenever special conditions of probation are included, these special conditions usually mean more work for POs. Some of these conditions might include medical treatments for drug or alcohol dependencies, individual or group therapy or counseling, or participation in a driver's safety course. In some instances involving theft, burglary, or vandalism, restitution provisions may be included, where youths must repay victims for their financial losses. Most standard probation programs in the United States require little, if any, direct contact with the probation office. Logistically, this works out well for POs, who are frequently overworked and have enormous client caseloads of 300 or more youths. However, greater caseloads mean less individualized attention devoted to youths by POs, and some of these youths require more supervision than others while on standard probation (Cohn et al., 2002).

Standard probation exhibits relatively high rates of recidivism, ranging from 40 to 75 percent. Even certain youth camps operated in various California counties have reported recidivism rates as high as 76 percent (Levin, Langan, and Brown, 2000). Therefore, it is often difficult to forecast which juveniles will have the greatest likelihood of reoffending, regardless of the program we are examining.

According to Baird (1985:36), the following elements appear to be predictive of future criminal activity and reoffending by juveniles: (1) one's age at first adjudication; (2) a prior criminal record (a combined measure of the number and severity of priors); (3) the number of prior commitments to juvenile facilities; (4) drug/chemical abuse; (5) alcohol abuse; (6) family relationships (parental control); (7) school problems; and (8) peer relationships. An additional factor not cited by Baird but may have significant predictive value is whether youths who are currently on probation violate one or more conditions of their probation programs. Needs assessments should be individualized, based upon the juvenile's past record and other pertinent characteristics, including the present adjudication offense (Baird, 1985:36). The level of supervision should vary according to the degree of risk posed to the public by the juvenile. While Baird does not provide a weighting procedure for the different risk factors listed above, he does describe a supervisory scheme that acts as a guide for juvenile probation and aftercare. This scheme would be applied based on the perceived risk of each juvenile offender. His scheme would include the following:

Regular or Differential Supervision
1. Four face-to-face contacts per month with youth.
2. Two face-to-face contacts per month with parents.
3. One face-to-face contact per month with placement staff.
4. One contact with school officials.

Intensive Supervision
1. Six face-to-face contacts per month with youth.
2. Three face-to-face contacts per month with parents.
3. One face-to-face contact per month with placement staff.
4. Two contacts with school officials.

Alternative Care Cases
1. One face-to-face contact per month with youth.
2. Four contacts with agency staff (one must be face-to-face).
3. One contact every two months with parents.

An assignment to any one of these supervision levels, including **alternative care cases,** should be based on both risk and needs assessments. Baird says that often, agencies make categorical assignments of juveniles to one level of supervision or another, primarily by referring to the highest level of supervision suggested by two or more scales used (Baird 1985:38). Each juvenile probation agency prefers specific predictive devices, and some agencies use a combination of them. Again, no scale is foolproof, and the matter of false positives and false negatives arises, as some juveniles receive more supervision than they really require, while others receive less than they need.

Not all probation orders involving juveniles are lenient. In the *Matter of Jessie GG* (1993), for instance, a New York high school student was placed on a 2-year probationary term and ordered to pay $1,500 restitution for damages to a victim's property. The 2-year probationary period coincided with his ability to pay. Further, it was the harshest disposition the juvenile court judge could impose.

Juvenile probationers do not have the same rights as adult probationers. For instance, a California juvenile probationer, Michael T., was placed on probation with the provision that supervising POs and police could conduct warrantless searches of his premises at any time (*In re Michael T.,* 1993). A similar provision for warrantless searches and seizures on a juvenile probationer's premises has been made in the case of *In re Bounmy V.* (1993), where the offender was a known cocaine dealer and was suspected of secreting cocaine on his premises at different times.

Juvenile Intensive Supervised Probation (JISP) Programs

Juvenile intensive supervised probation (JISP) programs, alternatively known as intensive probation supervision (IPS) programs, have become increasingly popular for managing nonincarcerated offender populations. Since the mid-1960s, these programs have been aimed primarily at supervising adult offenders closely, and in recent years, IPS programs have been designed for juvenile offenders as well. Intensive supervised probation is a highly structured and conditional supervision program for either adult or juvenile offenders that serves as an alternative to incarceration and provides for an acceptable level of public safety. Some researchers argue that the effectiveness of IPS is how well certain risk control factors are managed by supervising POs rather than the sheer intensity of their supervision over clients (Cohn et al., 2002; Tracy, 2002).

Characteristics of JISP Programs.   JISP programs for juveniles have been developed and are currently operating in about one half of all U.S. jurisdictions (Cohn et al., 2002). Similar to their adult ISP program counterparts, JISPs are ideally designed for secure detention-bound youths and are considered as acceptable alternatives to incarceration. This is what JISP programs were always meant to be. JISPs are differentiated from other forms of standard probation by citing obvious differences in the amount of officer/client contact during the course of the probationary period. For example, standard probation is considered no more than two face-to-face officer/client contacts per month. JISP programs might differ from standard probation according to the following face-to-face criteria: (1) two or three times per week versus once per month, (2) once per week versus twice per month, or (3) four times per week versus once per week (the latter figure being unusually high for standard probation contact) (Armstrong, 1988:346).

Different types of PO dispositions toward their work are evident in descriptions of the various services provided by the different JISP programs investigated by Armstrong. For example, of the 55 programs he examined (92 percent of his total program sample), he found that the following range of services, skills, and resources were mentioned as being brokered by POs in different jurisdictions:

1. Mental health counseling
2. Drug and alcohol counseling
3. Academic achievement and aptitude testing
4. Vocational and employment training
5. Individual, group, and family counseling
6. Job search and placement programs
7. Alternative education programs
8. Foster grandparents programs
9. Big Brother/Big Sister programs

Not all IPS programs are alike, however (Wiebush, 1990:26). Nevertheless, many juvenile IPS programs share similarities, including the following:

1. Recognition of the shortcomings of traditional responses to serious and/or chronic offenders (e.g., incarceration or out-of-home placement).
2. Severe resource constraints within jurisdictions that compel many probation departments to adopt agency-wide classification and workload deployment systems for targeting a disproportionate share of resources for the most problematic juvenile offenders.
3. Program hopes to reduce the incidence of incarceration in juvenile secure detention facilities and reduce overcrowding.
4. Programs tend to include aggressive supervision and control elements as a part of the "get-tough" movement.
5. All programs have a vested interest in rehabilitation of youthful offenders.

From these analyses of IPS program content generally, we can glean the following as basic characteristics of IPS programs:

1. Low officer/client caseloads (i.e., 30 or fewer probationers)
2. High levels of offender accountability (e.g., victim restitution, community service, payment of fines, partial defrayment of program expenses)
3. High levels of offender responsibility
4. High levels of offender control (home confinement, electronic monitoring, frequent face-to-face visits by POs)
5. Frequent checks for arrests, drug and/or alcohol use, and employment/school attendance (drug/alcohol screening, coordination with police departments and juvenile halls, teachers, family) (Wiebush, 1990).

Other Juvenile Probation and Parole Programs

Electronic Monitoring for Juvenile Offenders.   Charles (1989a) describes the implementation of an electronic monitoring (EM) program for juvenile offenders in Allen County, Indiana. Known as the Allen County, Indiana, Juvenile

Electronic Monitoring Program Pilot Project or EMP, this program was commenced as an experimental study in October, 1987 and was conducted for 9 months through May 1988. At the time the study started, the probation department had 25 POs who were appointed by the court and certified by the Indiana Judicial Conference. During 1987, 2,404 juveniles were referred to the probation department by the court. About 34 percent of these were female offenders. During that same year, 167 youths were incarcerated in secure facilities for delinquents at a total cost of $1.5 million. Charles (1989b:152–153) indicates that because of fiscal constraints, Allen County agreed to place only six juveniles in the EM program. However, two of these youths recidivated and were dropped from it shortly after it started. The remaining four youths remained in the program. The juvenile judge in these cases sentenced each youth to a 6 month probationary period with EM. Each youth wore a conspicuous wristlet that eventually became a symbol of court sanctions. Like the proverbial string tied around one's finger, the wristlet was a constant reminder that these juveniles were "on probation." Further, others who became aware of these EM devices became of assistance in helping these youths to avoid activities that might be considered in violation of probation program conditions.

Despite the small number of participants in Charles' research, his findings are of interest and suggest similar successful applications on larger offender aggregates. Each juvenile was interviewed at the conclusion of the program. They reported that their wristlets were continuous reminders of their involvement in the probation program. However, they didn't feel as though program officials were spying on them. In fact, one of the youths compared his experience with EM with his previous experience of being supervised by a PO. He remarked that whenever he was under the supervision of the PO, he could do whatever he wished, and there was little likelihood that his PO would ever find out about it. However, he was always under the threat of being discovered by the computer or by the surveillance officer.

Another interesting phenomenon was the fact that the wristlet enabled certain offenders to avoid peer pressure and "hanging out" with their friends. Since they had wristlets, they had good excuses to return home and not violate their curfews. Also, the families of these juveniles took a greater interest in them and their program. In short, at least for these four youths, the program was viewed very favorably and considered successful. Parents who were also interviewed at the conclusion of the program agreed that the program and monitoring system had been quite beneficial for their sons. While EM for juveniles is still in its early stages of experimentation in various jurisdictions, Charles (1989b) believes that it is a cost-effective alternative to incarceration.

Subsequent investigations into the use of EM for juvenile offenders have been promising. For instance, EM has been used effectively as a gang intervention tool in jurisdictions such as Suffolk County, New York. The Gang Reduction and Intervention Program (GRIP) has utilized EM for monitoring gang members who have been adjudicated delinquent and placed on probation (Iaria, 2000). The mission of GRIP is to identify and minimize illegal gang activity in the probation population by networking with police officers and probation officers to conduct searches, enforce curfews, initiate home inspections, and conduct surveillance. All juveniles involved in GRIP are issued ID cards that contain information about their program requirements, including curfew restrictions and other conditions. EM technology is used in conjunction with this program to verify a probationer's geographical whereabouts (Iaria, 2000).

EM is increasingly used in other countries such as England, with positive results reported (Richardson, 1999).

Home Confinement and Juveniles.   In many jurisdictions, home confinement is supplemented with electronic monitoring (Schlatter, 1989). Relatively little is known about the extent to which home confinement is used as a sentencing alternative for juvenile offenders. Since probation is so widely used as the sanction of choice except for the most chronic recidivists, home confinement is most often applied as an accompanying condition of electronic monitoring. However, this type of sentencing may be redundant, since curfew for juvenile offenders means home confinement anyway, especially during evening hours. As a day sentence, home confinement for juveniles would probably be counterproductive, since juveniles are often obligated to finish their schooling as a probation program condition. Again, since school hours are during the daytime, it would not make sense to deprive juveniles of school opportunities through some type of home detention.

Shock Probation and Boot Camps.   Shock probation has sometimes been compared erroneously with **Scared Straight,** a New Jersey program implemented in the late 1970s. Scared Straight sought to frighten samples of hard-core delinquent youths by having them confront inmates in a Rahway, New Jersey, prison (Petrosino, Turpin-Petrosino, and Finckenauer, 2000). Inmates would yell at and belittle them, calling them names, cursing, and yelling. Inmates would tell them about sexual assaults and other prison unpleasantries in an attempt to get them to refrain from reoffending. However, the program was unsuccessful. Despite early favorable reports of recidivism rates of less than 20 percent, the actual rate of recidivism among these participating youths was considerably higher. Furthermore, another control group not exposed to Scared Straight had a lower recidivism rate (Feder and Boruch, 2000).

The juvenile version of shock probation or shock incarceration is perhaps best exemplified by juvenile boot camps (MacKenzie and Wilson, 2001). Also known as the Army Model, boot camp programs are patterned after basic training for new military recruits. Juvenile offenders are given a taste of hard military life, and such regimented activities and structure for up to 180 days are often sufficient to "shock" them into giving up their lives of delinquency or crime and staying out of jail. Boot camp programs in various states have been established, including the Regimented Inmate Discipline program in Mississippi, the About Face program in Louisiana, and the shock incarceration program in Georgia.

Two good examples of boot camp programs are the U.S. Army Correctional Activity (USACA) in Fort Riley, Kansas, established in 1968, and the Butler (New York) Shock Incarceration Correctional Facility (Styve et al., 2000). In both programs, inmates wear army uniforms, learn basic army drills, salute, and participate in a rigorous correctional treatment program. Ordinarily, youthful first-offender felons are targeted for involvement in these programs. The Butler Shock program, for instance, involves young offenders ranging in age from 16 to 29. They must stay in the camp for 6 months and comply with all program rules. About 88 percent of all boot camp trainees are successful and win a parole later. The Butler facility has inmates who have been heavily involved in drug-dealing. About 90 percent of all participants have been convicted of drug offenses. They have rigorous work details, must complete school work, and adhere to a highly disciplined regimen. They are given 8 minutes for meals, and they must carry their leftovers in their pockets.

Their days begin at 5:30 A.M., with reveille blaring over the intercom. Immediately, drill instructors start screaming at them. Besides military drilling, all inmates must experience drug counseling and study. At the Fort Riley facility, inmates may learn vocational skills and crafts. They also receive counseling and other therapy and treatment. At both camps, physicians and other support staff are ready to furnish any needed medical treatment. When they eventually leave the facility, most have changed their outlook on life and have acquired new lifestyles not associated with crime. Again, recidivism rates among these inmates are under 30 percent, which is considered an indication of program success.

REVOKING JUVENILE PROBATION AND PAROLE

Parole for juveniles is similar to parole for adult offenders (del Carmen, Parker, and Reddington, 1998). Those juveniles who have been detained in various institutions for long periods may be released prior to serving their full sentences.

Purposes of Juvenile Parole

The general purposes of parole for juveniles are:

1. To reward good behavior while youths have been detained.
2. To alleviate overcrowding.
3. To permit youths to become reintegrated back into their communities and enhance their rehabilitation potential.
4. To deter youths from future offending by insuring their continued supervision under juvenile parole officers.

Numbers of Juveniles on Parole

Estimates vary about how many juvenile offenders are on parole at any given time. The present lack of coordination among jurisdictions relating to juvenile offender record-keeping makes it difficult to determine actual numbers of juvenile parolees or probationers at any given time. Further, some jurisdictions continue to prevent public scrutiny of juvenile court adjudicatory proceedings or their results. Since one's juvenile record is expunged or sealed upon reaching adulthood, even historical research on this subject is limited by various systemic constraints. About 24,000 youths were involved in some form of juvenile parole program in 2002 (American Correctional Association, 2003).

Juvenile parolees share many of the same programs used to supervise youthful probationers. Intensive supervised probation programs are used for both probationers and parolees in many jurisdictions. Further, juvenile POs often perform dual roles as juvenile parole officers as they supervise both types of offenders. Studies of juvenile parolees tend to show that the greater the intensity of parole, the lower the recidivism (Altschuler, Armstrong, and MacKenzie, 1999; Lewis and Howard, 2000). Influencing the successfulness of juvenile parole is whether juveniles are successfully employed or actively involved in development or counseling programs. For most juveniles who spend time behind bars or reform school walls, this experience is traumatic. About 65 percent of the juveniles on parole refrain from committing new offenses (American Correctional Association, 2003).

Juvenile Parole Decision Making

The decision to parole particular juveniles is left to different agencies and bodies, depending upon the jurisdiction. Studies of imposing secure confinement upon juvenile delinquents indicate that in 45 state jurisdictions, the lengths of secure confinement are indeterminate. In 32 states, early-release decisions are left up to the particular juvenile correction agency, whereas 6 states use parole boards exclusively, and 5 other states depend upon the original juvenile court judge's decision. Only a few states had determinate schemes for youthful offenders, and therefore, their early release from secure custody would be established by statute in much the same way as it is for adult offenders (American Correctional Association, 2003).

A 7-member parole board in New Jersey is appointed by the governor and grants early release to both adult and juvenile inmates. Utah uses a Youth Parole Authority, a part-time board consisting of 3 citizens and 4 staff members from the Utah Division of Youth Corrections. This board employs objective decision-making criteria to determine which juveniles should be paroled. However, sometimes discrepancies exist between what the Authority actually does and what it is supposed to do. Some criticisms have been that the primary parole criteria are related to one's former institutional behavior rather than to other factors, such as one's prospects for successful adaptation to community life, employment, and participation in educational or vocational programs (Norman and Wadman, 2000).

Similar criticisms have been made about youth parole boards in other states. Many of these juvenile parole boards consist of persons who make subjective judgments about youths on the basis of extralegal and subjective criteria. Predispositional reports prepared by juvenile POs, records of institutional behavior, a youth's appearance and demeanor during the parole hearing, and the presence of witnesses or victims have unknown effects on individual parole board members. Parole decision making is not an exact science. Subjectivity is endemic to this process. When subjective criteria impact this decision making process, a juvenile's parole chances are significantly subverted. Thus, parole board decision making profiles in various jurisdictions may show evidence of early-release disparities attributable to racial, ethnic, gender, or socioeconomic factors (Norman and Wadman, 2000).

Juvenile Parole Policy

Ashford and LeCroy (1993:186) undertook an investigation of the various state juvenile parole programs and provisions. They sent letters and questionnaires to all state juvenile jurisdictions, soliciting any available information on their juvenile paroling policies. Their response rate was 94 percent, with 47 of the 50 states responding. One interesting result of their survey was the development of a typology of juvenile parole. Ashford and LeCroy discovered eight different kinds of juvenile parole used more or less frequently among the states. These were listed as follows:

1. Determinate parole (length of parole is linked closely with the period of commitment specified by the court; paroling authorities cannot extend confinement period of juvenile beyond original commitment length prescribed by judge; juvenile can be released short of serving the full sentence).

2. Determinate parole set by administrative agency (parole release date is set immediately following youth's arrival at secure facility).

3. Presumptive minimum with limits on the extension of the supervision period for a fixed or determinate length of time (minimum confinement period is specified, and youth must be paroled after that date unless there is a showing of bad conduct).

4. Presumptive minimum with limits on the extension of supervision for an indeterminate period (parole should terminate after fixed period of time; parole period is indeterminate, where PO has discretion to extend parole period with justification; parole length can extend until youth reaches age of majority and leaves juvenile court jurisdiction).

5. Presumptive minimum with discretionary extension of supervision for an indeterminate period (same as 4 except PO has discretion to extend parole length of juvenile with no explicit upper age limit; lacks explicit standards limiting the extension of parole).

6. Indeterminate parole with a specified maximum and a discretionary minimum length of supervision.

7. Indeterminate parole with legal minimum and maximum periods of supervision.

8. Indeterminate or purely discretionary parole. (Ashford and LeCroy, 1993:187–191).

Juvenile Probation and Parole Revocation

Probation and parole revocations are the termination of one's probation or parole program (PPP), usually for one or more program violations. Drug violations are common among juveniles on parole (Haapanen and Britton, 2002). When one's PPP is terminated, regardless of who does the terminating, there are several possible outcomes. One is that the offender will be returned to secure detention. This is the most severe result. A less harsh alternative is that offenders will be shifted to a different kind of PPP. For instance, if a juvenile is assigned to a halfway house as a part of a parole program, the rules of the halfway house must be observed. If one or more rules are violated, such as failing to observe curfew, failing drug or alcohol urinalyses, or committing new offenses, a report is filed with the court or the juvenile corrections authority for possible revocation action. If it is decided later that one's PPP should be terminated, the result may be to place the offender under house arrest or home confinement, coupled with electronic monitoring (Archwamety and Katsiyannis, 2000). Thus, the juvenile would be required to wear an electronic wristlet or anklet and remain on the premises for specified periods. Other program conditions would be applied as well. The fact is that one is not automatically returned to detention following a parole revocation.

Usually, if a return to incarceration or detention is not indicated, the options available to judges, parole boards, or others are limited only by the array of supervisory resources in the given jurisdiction. These options ordinarily involve more intensive supervision or monitoring of offender behaviors. Severe overcrowding in many juvenile detention facilities discourages revocation action that would return large numbers of offenders to industrial schools or youth centers. Intermediate punishments, therefore, function well to accommodate larger numbers of serious offenders, including those who have their parole revoked (Lewis and Howard, 2000). Keeping juveniles in their communities contributes significantly to the reintegrative efforts of community services and paroling agencies (Altschuler and Armstrong, 1999).

The process of PPP revocation for juveniles is not as clear-cut as it is for adult offenders (Travis et al., 2002). The U.S. Supreme Court has not ruled decisively thus far about how juvenile PPP revocation actions should handled. Prior to several significant U.S. Supreme Court decisions, either PPP revocation could be accomplished for adult offenders on the basis of reports filed by POs that offenders were in violation of one or more conditions of their PPPs. Criminal court judges, those ordinarily in charge of determining whether to terminate one's probationary status, could decide this issue on the basis of available evidence against offenders (Josi and Sechrest, 1999). For adult parolees, former decision making relative to terminating their parole could be made by parole boards without much fanfare from offenders. In short, parole officers and others might simply present evidence that one or more infractions or violations of PPP conditions had been committed. These infractions, then, could form the basis for revoking PPPs as well as a justification for these decisions.

Juvenile Case Law on Probation Revocations

When youths are placed on probation, the most frequently used dispositional option by juvenile court judges, they are subject to having their program revoked for one or more violations of program conditions (Shapiro et al., 2001; Ulmer, 2001). Several cases are presented below to show how different juvenile courts handle probation revocations.

The Case of In re Kentron D. *(2002).*   Kentron D. was a California juvenile adjudicated for a delinquent offense and placed on probation. At a later date, two probation officers allegedly witnessed Kentron D. violate two different probation conditions and wrote a probation report of what they had observed. Subsequently, a probation revocation hearing was held for Kentron D., but the probation officers were absent from the hearing. Nevertheless, the juvenile court judge relied on the written report and summarily revoked Kentron D.'s probation. Kentron D. appealed this decision, which was heard by the California Court of Appeals. The appellate court overturned the revocation action, holding that the mere submission of a report of bad conduct is inadmissible hearsay. Furthermore, Kentron D. was not permitted the opportunity to confront and cross-examine the probation officers, who were absent. Their unavailability was never explained. Additionally, there was no good cause showing as to why these officers were absent from the hearing. Good cause normally exists when the declarants (the probation officers) are unavailable; when the declarants, although not legally unavailable, can be brought to the hearing only through great difficulty and expense; or when the declarant's presence would pose a risk of harm, mental or emotional, to the declarants. Kentron D.'s probation program was therefore reinstated [*In re Kentron D.,* 2002].

The Case of In re Oscar R. *(2002).*   Oscar R. was a California juvenile adjudicated delinquent on serious charges but placed Oscar R. on probation. Subsequently, Oscar R. allegedly threatened and harassed another juvenile at school, as well as calling another juvenile and telling him to "watch his back." The juveniles were so afraid of Oscar R. that they withdrew from school and enrolled in home study courses. Also they reported these incidents to Oscar R.'s probation officer, who recommended probation revocation to the juvenile court judge. At a later revocation hearing, Oscar R.'s probation was revoked, largely on the testimony of the probation officer. The other juvenile victims did not attend nor did they testify. Oscar R. appealed, contending that he was not permitted the right of confronting and cross-examining his accusers. Further, Oscar R. contended that the probation officer's testimony was hearsay and thus inadmissible against him. However, a California appeals court upheld the revocation action, holding that hearsay is admissible in a probation revocation hearing, especially when reported by the probation officer as well as documented carefully in a probation report about Oscar R.'s threats. Furthermore, the fact that the juvenile victims did not attend did not prejudice the hearing, since their presence would have posed a risk of harm to them, in the sincere opinion of the probation officer. Under these circumstances, it was not an abuse of judicial discretion to consider the hearsay evidence presented in court by the probation officer [*In re Oscar R.,* 2002].

The Case of In re Eddie M. *(2002).*   Eddie M. was a California juvenile adjudicated delinquent and placed in a camp for 1 year. However, Eddie M. misbehaved at the camp and violated various camp rules, which were noncriminal in nature. The juvenile probation officer supervising Eddie M. recommended that a modification in placement be made and that Eddie M. should be placed under the supervision of the California Youth Authority and institutionalized. The juvenile court judge modified Eddie M.'s program and committed him to the California Youth Authority. Eddie M. objected, contending that the standard of proof, beyond a reasonable doubt, had not been used in the modification hearing. The appellate court upheld Eddie M.'s program modification, holding that because noncriminal conduct had been alleged, the standard of proof required was relaxed for such a program modification hearing [*In re Eddie M.,* 2002].

The Case of In re Eldridge T. *(2002).*   Eldridge T. was a California juvenile adjudicated delinquent and placed on probation, including several special conditions of probation. Subsequently, Eldridge T. allegedly committed various acts that were violations of his special probation program conditions. However, the court was not furnished any direct evidence of such violations. Nevertheless, the juvenile court judge ordered Eldridge T. committed to the California Youth Authority as a more restrictive disposition, and Eldridge T. appealed. An appellate court reversed the juvenile court judge's order, holding that absent any evidence that Eldridge T. had violated a previous court order for a condition of probation, the juvenile court could not impose a more restrictive placement of the juvenile in the California Youth Authority [*In re Eldridge T.,* 2002].

The Case of In re Cross *(2002)*.   Cross was an Ohio juvenile adjudicated delinquent for a serious offense. The judge placed him on probation, which was one of the least serious dispositions available. Cross could have been placed in the temporary custody of an institution for the care of delinquent children, or the judge could have imposed institutionalization until Cross was 21, and the time would have been served at an institution operated by the Department of Youth Services. Later, Cross completed his probation. Following his probation, Cross committed what amounted to a probation program violation, but not a delinquent offense. The juvenile court judge ordered Cross to the custody of the Department of Youth Services to be institutionalized until age 21. Cross objected, and an appellate court heard his appeal. The court reversed the juvenile court judge, holding that the judge lost jurisdiction over Cross when Cross had completed his probationary term. Thus, there was no authority for continuing jurisdiction over the juvenile [*In re Cross,* 2002].

The Case of J.P. v. State *(2002)*.   J.P. was an Indiana juvenile adjudicated delinquent and ordered to enroll in an educational program as a part of his probation program conditions. Furthermore, J.P. was required to report at least monthly and have at least telephonic contact with his probation officer. J.P. was subsequently accepted into the CAMP Program, which was technically an educational program although different from the one ordered by the juvenile court judge. Later, the J.P.'s supervising probation officer reported to the court that J.P. had failed to enroll in the proper educational program and that he also had failed to report to the probation office as directed. An order was issued revoking J.P.'s probation and J.P. appealed. While the appellate court found that there was no set time limit imposed by the juvenile court for J.P. to enroll in the directed educational program, and that the CAMP Program was considered an educational program, it did find that sufficient evidence existed to show that J.P. had failed to abide by the probation condition of contacting his probation officer on a regular basis. Thus, his revocation was upheld [*J.P. v. State,* 2002].

The Case of In re Emiliano M. *(2002)*.   Emiliano M. was a California juvenile adjudicated delinquent and placed on probation. At a later point, Emiliano M. was found to be in possession of an air pistol by his probation officer, and an order revoking his probation was issued. He was granted a new term of probation, but with the additional condition that he register as a gang member. Emiliano M. appealed and the appellate court overturned the new probation condition. The California appellate court held that the requirement of registration as a gang member could only be imposed if the juvenile had been convicted of a crime in a criminal court or has had a petition sustained in a juvenile court for certain enumerated offenses. In the present case, the requirement of registration as a gang member could not be imposed for the juvenile's possession of air pistols because such activity was not charged as a crime, but was treated only as a probation violation. Moreover, the juvenile's willful violation of probation did not constitute the crime of contempt under the general contempt statute for which gang registration could be imposed [*In re Emiliano M.,* 2002].

The Case of In re D.S.S. *(2002)*.   D.S.S. was a Texas juvenile adjudicated delinquent and placed on probation. Among the conditions of D.S.S.'s probation was that he refrain from using drugs or alcohol. Periodic urinalyses were required, and on one occasion, D.S.S. tested positive for drug use. A urinalysis report was used in an initial hearing to determine whether D.S.S. had indeed violated one of his probation conditions. Later, the juvenile court modified D.S.S.'s probation. D.S.S. demanded to see the urinalysis test results but the court refused to disclose the report or its contents to D.S.S. D.S.S. appealed, alleging it was court error to refuse to allow him to see the urinalysis results. An appellate court upheld the juvenile court decision, holding that under a bifurcated probation revocation scheme (where the first stage simply establishes the violation in question and the second stage determines the disposition), no rule exists obligating the juvenile court to provide such urinalysis results to juvenile defendants in dispositional proceedings [*In re D.S.S.,* 2002].

Juvenile Case Law on Parole Revocations

There is very little current information about juvenile parole revocation (del Carmen, Parker, and Reddington, 1998; Travis et al., 2002). A few of the more recent cases involving parole eligibility and/or revocation involving juveniles are reported below.

In re Richard Mills, Minor Child *(2002).*   Richard Mills was an Ohio juvenile adjudicated delinquent for several misdemeanor offenses and placed on probation. Subsequently, Mills violated one or more probation program conditions, including several additional misdemeanor charges and failing to report to his probation officer, and he was committed to the Ohio Department of Youth Services (ODYS). After a short interval, Mills was paroled. While on parole, Mills committed new parole program violations, including three misdemeanors and failing to report to his parole officer. An order revoking Mills' parole was entered but he was ordered to serve 60 days in a juvenile detention center following a suspension of the parole revocation. After nearly eight weeks, Mills was charged with felony robbery and one count of felony failure to comply with the orders of a police officer. The court adjudicated Mills delinquent on these charges and ordered him to the ODYS for a period of 1 year to age 21 on the robbery charge and 3 months to age 21 on the failure to comply charge, the dispositions to run consecutively. Mills was given zero amount of time off of these dispositions for the time he had spent in detention, which was 51 days. Mills appealed, alleging that judicial error occurred when he was denied credit for the time served in detention. An appellate court heard the case and ruled that the trial court had erred when it failed to give Mills 51 days' credit toward his dispositions and the total length of his new commitment. Mills was subsequently awarded the 51 detention days to be counted against his recent commitment to ODYS for the two felony adjudications [*In re Richard Mills, Minor Child,* 2002].

Matter of Jamie D. *(2002).*   Jamie D. was a New York juvenile adjudicated delinquent and placed on probation. Later he violated the terms of his probation and was placed in a nonsecure facility for a period of time. Jamie D. was subsequently paroled but continued to violate his program conditions for various reasons. His parole program was later revoked and he was institutionalized for a period of time. Jamie D. appealed this revocation action, contending that he should be given another opportunity to function in a less restrictive alternative such as the nonsecure facility. The appellate court rejected Jamie D.'s appeal, noting that evaluation reports indicated that Jamie D. required a more structured environment and intense supervision than he could obtain through community-based services, that his mother could not control his behavior, and that he had threatened school staff [*Matter of Jamie D.,* 2002].

In re Terry T. *(2002)*.   Terry T. was a 12-year-old Wisconsin juvenile adjudicated delinquent and placed in a residential home for one year. Later, on parole, Terry T. violated one or more technical program conditions and his parole was revoked. His original dispositional order was revised and he was ordered to a Serious Juvenile Offender Program for a 1- to 5-year term. Terry T. appealed, contending that authorities could not extend his original 1-year term because of technical program violations. The appellate court agreed, holding that any extension of an order may not exceed 1 year, and no revision or change of placement may extend the expiration date of the original order. Thus, the order extending the juvenile's commitment had to be reversed [*In re Terry T.,* 2002].

Prospective juvenile parolees are entitled to certain minimum due-process rights in various states similar to those articulated in the adult case of *Morrissey v. Brewer* (1972). Similar procedures are followed in several other states (Cohn et al., 2002). Despite these procedural safeguards, parole revocation hearings for juveniles are often scripted in advance (Cavender and Knepper, 1992).

Because the literature on juvenile parole violators is scant, it is difficult to profile them. Early research has shown, however, that those parolees who have had the longest institutional commitment lengths are also the more likely to have their parole revoked (Haapanen and Britton, 2002). However, this may be a somewhat self-fulfilling observation, since the most serious offenders are given the longest sentences anyway, and they are more likely to recidivate.

A study of some magnitude was conducted by Visher, Lattimore, and Linster (1991). This study involved 1,949 juveniles paroled from the California Youth Authority between July 1, 1981 and June 30, 1982. An 88 percent failure rate was reported by these researchers. This is somewhat misleading, however, since a failure was any rearrest or parole revocation following parole. Only 14 percent failed because of a parole revocation. This means that there were many rearrests, but apparently these rearrests were unsubstantiated subsequently and these parolees were released or had their cases dismissed if charges had been filed against them. The 14 percent failure figure is impressive. At least for this sample of juvenile offenders, parole seemed to work for 86 percent of them, despite the failures observed by these researchers. The average length of time between one's parole and rearrest was 10 months. Considering what we know about juvenile offending, most juvenile delinquents eventually grow out of delinquent conduct anyway as they mature. This is also known as the aging out process.

SUMMARY

Juvenile delinquents commit acts that would be crimes if committed by adults. Status offenders commit acts that would not be crimes if committed by adults. Considerable variation exists among juvenile court jurisdictions. Most juvenile court jurisdictions throughout the United States deal with juveniles charged with delinquent offenses. A majority of jurisdictions use age 18 as one's age of adulthood. In a minority of jurisdictions, status offenders are processed in the same manner as delinquent offenders. The juvenile court is a civil court. Thus, when juvenile cases are presented and decided, the results are a civil adjudication or judgment. This adjudication is not the same as a criminal conviction. Juveniles do not acquire criminal records from juvenile court adjudications of any kind.

The juvenile justice process commences with an arrest, or with a youth being taken into custody. A screening process known as intake occurs, where an intake officer decides whether the case merits further review from a juvenile court prosecutor. More serious cases are petitioned to the juvenile court, where a hearing is held. The outcome of the hearing is an adjudication or judgment. In some instances, less serious offenders are diverted to teen courts or youth courts, where juries of one's teen peers decide punishments to be imposed. These youth courts are increasingly popular, inasmuch as other youths sanction delinquent offenders rather than adults. The punished youths seem to have more respect for punishments administered by other youths like them.

Sometimes, if the offense warrants, juveniles may be waived, certified, or transferred to criminal courts and tried as if they were adults. A greater range of severe penalties may be imposed on those convicted of crimes in criminal courts. When youths are transferred to criminal court for prosecution, the intent of the transfer or waiver is to make it possible to impose more severe penalties on the transferred juveniles. However, this outcome doesn't always occur. Different types of transfers include judicial waivers, prosecutorial waivers, direct file, statutory exclusion, or demand waivers. Youths may protest these transfers or waivers through waiver hearings, although a juvenile court judge's ruling is usually final in the matter. In recent years, blended sentencing statutes have been passed by various states enabling both juvenile court and criminal court judges to impose both juvenile and adult penalties on convicted offenders. Many states have lowered the age at which juveniles may be considered adults for the purpose of a criminal prosecution. Less than 1 percent of all juvenile offenders are transferred to criminal courts each year.

However, most cases commenced in the juvenile justice system remain within it, where juvenile court judges have various options if offenders are adjudicated delinquent. These options include nominal, conditional, and custodial dispositions. The most frequently used option by juvenile court judges is probation. Frequently, juveniles who have been adjudicated delinquent and have recidivated at a later date will be placed on probation again. In fact, secure confinement of juveniles is considered a last resort in most juvenile court jurisdictions.

Since 1966 juveniles have acquired various rights commensurate with those enjoyed by adult offenders who face criminal charges in adult courts. Juveniles have the right to an attorney, the right to cross-examine their accusers, the right to give testimony in their own behalf, the right to a jury trial in a few states, the right against double jeopardy, and the right to be found guilty beyond a reasonable doubt if their liberty is in jeopardy. In those cases where one's liberty is not in jeopardy, the juvenile court continues to use the civil standard of "preponderance of the evidence." Judges rely on the presence of various aggravating or mitigating circumstances when adjudicating juveniles appearing before them. These circumstances are similar to the ones considered by criminal court judges when sentencing adult offenders. Juvenile court judges may impose nominal sanctions or verbal warnings, conditional dispositions such as probation, or custodial sanctions, which may include incarceration in a juvenile institution. The most frequently used punishment by juvenile court judges is probation, however.

Many of the probation and parole programs for adults are also found in the juvenile justice system. Juveniles may be placed on unconditional or conditional diversion, unconditional or conditional probation, intensive supervised probation, and with or without conditions, including victim compensation or restitution, fines, community service, electronic monitoring, home confinement, and/or suggested psychological treatments or counseling. In many instances, juvenile court judges require juvenile POs to prepare predispositional reports to assist judges in the dispositions they impose for adjudicated juveniles. These predispositional reports are similar to PSI reports prepared for adult offenders by their POs at the direction of the criminal court.

No one knows how many juveniles there are on probation or parole at any given time, although there are efforts underway to conduct a census of juvenile probationers and parolees sometime before 2010. The most successful probation and parole programs for juveniles involve activities that improve their coping skills, self-images, and self-respect. Accountability is an important component of these programs, as well. Boot camps and shock probation or incarceration seem useful as well for instilling youths with greater individual responsibility and accountability.

Juveniles are subject to having their probation or parole programs revoked if they violate one or more program rules or requirements. States vary considerably in terms of the criteria applied to determine whether one's program should be revoked. Juveniles do not enjoy the same range of rights in their own probation and parole revocation hearings compared with adult probationers or parolees. However, each jurisdiction is guided by the U.S. Supreme Court cases that have been decided for adult offenders. But no state is obligated to follow the rulings set forth in these cases. Thus, there is a great deal of individuality in applying different rules for each juvenile's revocation case.

QUESTIONS FOR REVIEW

1. What are some major differences between delinquents and status offenders? What is meant by the deinstitutionalization of status offenses?

2. What is meant by the doctrine of *parens patriae?* What are its origins and how does common law relate to juvenile offender processing?

3. What is the significance of *Ex parte Crouse* and *People ex rel. O'Connell v. Turner?*

4. What are some of the key differences between juvenile courts and criminal courts?

5. What are four types of waiver or transfer actions? What are the goals of transfers? Are these goals being achieved? What are blended sentencing statutes and why are they increasingly important in juvenile offender processing?

6. What were five rights conveyed to juveniles by the U.S. Supreme Court between 1966 and 1980?

7. What are three types of dispositions that juvenile court judges can impose? Which disposition is used most frequently?

8. What is a youth court or teen court? What are some characteristics of a youth court? How effective are youth courts in dealing with minor juvenile offenders?

9. What is a predispositional report and what is its importance in juvenile court proceedings? Who prepares such reports? What are some of the contents of these reports?

10. What is the probation and parole revocation process like for juvenile offenders? What are some of the reasons given by juvenile courts for revoking a juvenile's probation program? Are all states consistent in revoking a juvenile's probation or parole? Why or why not?

SUGGESTED READINGS

Braithwaite, John (2002). *Restorative Justice and Responsive Regulation.* Oxford, UK: Oxford University Press.

Brownfield, David and Kevin Thompson (2002). "Distinguishing the Effects of Peer Delinquency and Gang Membership on Self-Reported Delinquency."*Journal of Gang Research* 9:1–10.

Gaarder, Emily and Joanne Belknap (2002). "Tenuous Borders: Girls Transferred to Adult Court."*Criminology* 40:481–518.

Glaser, Brian A., Georgia B. Calhoun, and John V. Petrocelli (2002). "Personality Characteristics of Male Juvenile Offenders by Adjudicated Offenses as Indicated by the MMPI-A." *Criminal Justice and Behavior* 29:183–201.

Huff, C. Ronald (2002). *Gangs in America III.* Thousand Oaks, CA: Sage.

Peterson, Badali Michele and Christopher J. Koegl (2002). "Juveniles' Experiences of Incarceration: The Role of Correctional Staff in Peer Violence."*Journal of Criminal Justice* 30:41–49.

Podkopacz, Marcy R. and Barry C. Feld (2002). "The Back Door to Prison: Waiver Reform, 'Blended Sentencing,' and the Law of Unintended Consequences." *Journal of Criminal Law and Criminology* 91:997–1071.

Potter, Roberto Hugh and Suman Kakar (2002). "The Diversion Decision-Making Process from the Juvenile Court Practitioners' Perspective: Results of a Survey." *Journal of Contemporary Criminal Justice* 18:20–36.

INTERNET CONNECTIONS

ABA Juvenile Justice Center
http://www.abanet.org/crimjust/juvjus/home.html

Building Blocks for Youth
http://www.buildingblocksforyouth.org/issues/girls/resources.html

Center for Court Innovation
http://www.courtinnovation.org/

Communication Works
http://www.communicationworks.org

Council of Juvenile Correctional Administrators
http://www.corrections.com/cjca

Juvenile Boot Camp Directory
http://www.kci.org/publication/bootcamp/prerelease.htm

Juvenile Intensive Probation Supervision
http://www.nal.usda.gov/pavnet/yf/yfjuvpro.htm

Juvenile Justice Reform Initiatives
http://www.ojjdp.ncjrs.org/pubs/reform/ch2_k.html

National Council of Juvenile and Family Court Judges
http://www.ncjfcj.unr.edu/

National Girls' Caucus
http://www.pacecenter.org

National Youth Court Center
http://www.youthcourt.net

North Carolina IMPACT Boot Camps
http://www.doc.state.nc.us/impact/

Office of Juvenile Justice and Delinquency Prevention
http://www.ojjdp.ncjrs.org

PACE Center for Girls, Inc.
http://www.pacecenter.org

Rights for All
http://www.amnesty-usa.org/rightsforall/juvenile/dp/section2.html

Riker's Island High Impact Incarceration Program
http://www.correctionhistory.org/html/chronicl/nycdoc/html/hiip.html

Teen Boot Camp
http://www.teenbootcamps.com

Teen Court
http://www.teen-court.org

Texas Juvenile Probation Commission
http://www.tjpc.state.tx.us/

Wilderness Programs, Inc.
http://www.wildernessprogramsetc.com

Youth Alternatives, Inc.
http://www.volunteersolutions.org/volunteer/agency/one_177937.html

Youthful Offenders Parole Board
http://www.yopb.ca.gov/

Chapter Outline

Chapter Objectives
Introduction
Program Evaluation: How Do We
   Know Programs Are Effective?
Balancing Program Objectives
   and Offender Needs

Recidivism
Recidivists and Their Character-
   istics
Probationers, Parolees, and
   Recidivism

Summary
Questions for Review
Suggested Readings
Internet Connections

Chapter Objectives

As the result of reading this chapter, the following objectives will be realized:

1. Examining what is meant by program evaluation and some of the ways programs are assessed.
2. Describing various outcome measures used to determine whether community-based corrections programs are effective.
3. Determining the balance between community-based correctional programming and offender needs.
4. Defining recidivism and examining several popular meanings of term as pertaining to probation and parole.
5. Examining recidivism and parole and probation revocation.
6. Describing characteristics of recidivists, including their offenses and other pertinent traits.
7. Comparing and contrasting recidivism between parolees and probationers.
8. Examining the views of probationers and parolees and the reports they make about those factors most influential in curbing their own recidivism.

• *In order to more effectively monitor its probationers and parolees, Georgia established a statewide networked computer application known as FLOID (Field Log of Interaction Data). This application was believed significant in swiftly tracking offenders' participation in community programs and compliance with other program rules. Under previous procedures, Georgia POs relied primarily on direct contacts with their clients and personalized reports of their progress. FLOID refocuses a PO's energy and attention toward whether offenders are participating in required programs and whether they are employed. Also, field drug and alcohol checks are performed at random times, and immediate sanctions are invoked if clients fail these tests. Georgia believes that FLOID is a significant deterrent to criminal activity among its probationer and parolee populations (Bralley and Provost, 2001:120–121).*

• *Sex offender registries enable various jurisdictions to track the movements of convicted offenders who are among the most despised and feared criminals. Registration and notification laws are intended to reduce recidivism among these offenders. However, is this information always up-to-date and accurate? A study was conducted of the Kentucky State Police Sex Offender Registry as well as the Internet website for the registry, and 537 sex offender records were examined for accuracy. It was found that in a majority of cases, photographs were missing from the website and address information was either incorrect or nonexistent. The findings reported by this research raise serious concerns about the effectiveness of sex registries to fulfill their mission of promoting public safety and awareness (Tewksbury, 2002:25).*

• *The Virginia Department of Corrections has been concerned about the burgeoning problem of illegal drug use among probationers and parolees throughout the state. In May 2001 Virginia implemented Operation Consequences at a district probation and parole office, which involved the random testing of offenders for illegal drug use. Offenders who tested positive for drugs were immediately detained. A continuum of sanctions was employed, ranging from warnings, substance abuse treatment, detoxification, outpatient treatment, inpatient (30-day) treatment, and/or detention. Subsequently, there have been few positive drug outcomes among probationers and parolees who understand that immediate sanctions will be implemented. Operation Consequences has been judged as successful at reducing illegal drug use and recidivism (Rasmussen, 2003:31).*

INTRODUCTION

How do we know if community-based correctional programs for probationers and parolees work? Because there are so many programs out there, which ones are most effective? Do these programs achieve their objectives, and to what degree? This chapter is about program evaluation and recidivism. Every intervention program applied to both juveniles and adults is subject to evaluation at one time or another. Investigators want to know whether a particular program is cost-effective and whether it accomplishes its stated goals. Programs are either successful or unsuccessful. Offender-clients either "fail" or "succeed." How is the successfulness or unsuccessfulness of programs and offender-clients measured? The first part of this chapter examines the criteria conventionally used to evaluate program effectiveness. Both objective and subjective criteria are considered in this discussion.

Because there are so many different kinds of offenders of various ages, there are numerous intervention, rehabilitation, and reintegration programs designed to assist them in meeting their diverse needs. We will find that program success is subject to widely different interpretations, and many professionals use diffuse and even inconsistent criteria to evaluate whether a program's goals are attained. Because the successfulness of programs often depends on the nature of the program clientele, some attention will be given to how clients are selected for inclusion in particular programs. Some programs engage in creaming, where only the most low-risk and eligible offenders are included. Thus, some bias exists at the outset favoring program successfulness. If only the most desirable clients are included, more favorable results will be expected, compared with those programs that include more dangerous and higher risk clientele.

Recidivism is an important measure of program success or failure. Therefore, considerable attention will be devoted to describing recidivism and its many varieties. Recidivism is examined in the context of both juvenile and adult probationers and parolees. Probationer recidivism will be compared with parolee recidivism to determine any significant differences, if any (Cohn et al., 2002). What kinds of offenders are more likely to recidivate, and under what types of conditions? What factors are useful in decreasing recidivism? Recidivism seems to fluctuate among probationers and parolees according to various program conditions. Which program conditions seem most likely to reduce recidivism? The chapter concludes with an examination of attitudes expressed by probationers and parolees themselves about their reasons for recidivating.

PROGRAM EVALUATION: HOW DO WE KNOW PROGRAMS ARE EFFECTIVE?

Program evaluation is the process of assessing any corrections intervention or program for the purpose of determining its effectiveness in achieving manifest goals (Southern Methodist University, 2002). Program evaluation investigates the nature of organizational intervention strategies, counseling, interpersonal interactions, staff quality, expertise, and education, and the success or failure experiences of clients served by any program. Several examples below illustrate what is meant by program evaluation.

Example 1.   *Day reporting centers have become a popular mode of intermediate sanction in many communities in the United States. They permit probationers and parolees to check in on a regular basis. They provide various services related to employment placement, counseling, and other forms of assistance. Also, such centers enable personnel to administer drug/alcohol checks to clients on a routine basis as a check to see if they are complying with their program requirements. In Utah, it is believed that day reporting centers have a crime deterrent effect on those clients who report to these centers on a regular basis.* Whether we agree or disagree with this statement is irrelevant. The fact is, some researchers believe this. A study was conducted of two day reporting centers. One is located in Ogden, Utah. It is the Northern Utah Day Reporting Center, which opened in 1996. The other is the Valley Mental Health Center in Salt Lake City. The Utah Department of Corrections operates and administers the Ogden program, while a private contractor operates the Salt Lake City program under Utah Department of Corrections auspices. Offenders are referred to these programs by probation and parole officers. The Valley Mental Health Center employs two full-time and two part-time therapists to provide treatment. Department of Corrections staff include a program specialist, two probation/parole agents, and two correctional officers. A psychiatrist and a registered nurse are also available one day per week to provide psychotropic medication evaluation and management.

Offenders are referred to these programs by probation or parole officers. Most clients in these programs are parolees. After acceptance into the program, clients meet with a therapist for a psychosocial assessment and then are prescribed appropriate treatment programming based on the assessment as well as the conditions of the probation or parole agreements. Treatment options include classes or group meetings for substance abuse, cognitive restructuring, anger management, domestic violence, mental health and parenting skills. Treatment is cognitive-behavioral and is focused upon relapse prevention. Successful program completion normally occurs after 18 weeks. There are 100 to 200 participants in these programs at any given time.

A random sample of 92 participants was obtained who had been successfully discharged. Offenders were classified according to gender, race, marital status, number of children, education, probation/parole status, current offense(s) and psychiatric diagnoses. The evaluation was the rate of post-discharge problems observed among those who had successfully completed the program. The results of the study showed that 62 offenders (67 percent) had no post-discharge problems within at least one year of completing the programs. Thirty offenders had new offenses which resulted in 20 reincarcerations. The program was considered successful, particularly since a majority of the participants were parolees with concurrent mental disorders and a higher propensity to reoffend. In the opinions of the researchers, the goals of these centers, to provide accessible offender services and reduce jail and prison crowding, are being accomplished (Williams and Turnage, 2001:1–3).

Example 2. *In 1998 there were 178 hazardous incident reports involving assaults on corrections personnel, including probation and parole officers, in the United States. In early 2000, the Missouri Department of Corrections commenced an officer training program in its probation and pretrial offices, using interactive video or the Firearms Training System (FATS), to enhance their officers' ability to win violent clashes in hazardous incidents with clients. It was believed that such training would increase officer mental preparedness when faced with critical incidents involving dangerous and violent probationers and parolees.* Again, whatever we believe is irrelevant. The Missouri Department of Corrections believes such training is valuable and will have positive consequences for its officers. A study was conducted wherein four firearms instructors conducted a 3-day firearms training program with 36 probation officers using an interactive video machine. Teams of two officers each completed 1.5 hours on the FATS machine. The FATS machine projects a video image onto a screen. The screen is connected to two speakers, and two model 66 Smith & Wesson-like pistols, exact replicas of what the officers carry on duty, are used. The officers were required to wear clothes that they normally wear on duty, including holsters for street work.

Each officer was provided with an inert cap-stun canister, which actually sprayed a harmless peppermint concoction when the pistol triggers were pulled. Different hazardous scenarios were projected on the wall like a life-sized movie, and the speakers helped to augment the atmosphere, making the officers feel that they were actually within the screened scenarios. The officers were confronted with criminals with pistols or knives, under different environmental circumstances, such as homes, alleyways, and other places. Under the different hazardous conditions, officers responded with differing types of force, including deadly force, by firing their pistols at the perpetrators on-screen. Later, officers broke down each scenario and explained their actions taken. The machine replayed the scenario and officers were able to judge the accuracy of their shooting. Immediately following their training, officers completed an exit questionnaire that assessed their impressions of the training effectiveness as well as their confidence levels regarding future hazardous situations. The evaluation was the degree to which opinions among participating officers changed more favorably to firearms use for self-defense purposes. It was found that 79 percent of these officers changed their perceptions regarding the value of a firearm for self-defense to a great extent. Although the sample size used in this study was small, the Missouri Department of Corrections believes the FATS program has demonstrated positive results and has encouraged its implementation throughout the state (Scharr, 2001:45–47).

Example 3.   *In 1999 Janet Reno announced a new initiative to promote community safety and reduce recidivism among recently released prison inmates called a felony reentry court. Felony re-entry courts are designed similar to drug courts in that judges retain control over offenders who either receive split sentences of jail followed by probation or probation exclusively. These courts are designed to empower judges to aggressively monitor offenders released into the community while providing them with a variety of services that facilitate their community reintegration. Ohio established one of these felony re-entry courts in Richland County in November 2000. It was believed that the felony re-entry court would reduce recidivism among sentenced offenders.* Again, whether we agree with this belief is irrelevant. When Ohio established its re-entry felony court, it targeted almost exclusively offenders who had been granted judicial release and/or given a split sentence, as well as selected parolees and post-release control offenders. Excluded were sex offenders and those subject to post-release control supervision. Many of these offenders fall within a non-reporting status category and are subject to periodic checks every six months. Thus they were excluded.

Once cases were accepted for the felony reentry court, the presiding judge decided the conditions that would apply in each offender's case. Treatment alternatives included drug/alcohol counseling and individual or group therapy; vocational and educational assistance; and family counseling and guidance. Offenders were subject to intensive supervision while in their communities. The length of programming varied according to each offender, but it ranged from 1 to 10 months for all participants. In the event of program infractions, judges were authorized to graduate sanctions to include more intensive monitoring and more frequent drug/alcohol screens or checks. Other sanctions included community service, fines, additional counseling, and 2- to 3-day punitive jail incarceration. For those released from incarceration, a transition plan was required to ensure a smooth re-entry into the community. These offenders were also subject to intensive supervision while in the program. Offender compliance with program rules resulted in diminishing sanctions, positive reinforcement, and formal acknowledgment of the offender's efforts leading to the successful completion of the re-entry court program. The evaluation was the amount of recidivism observed during a 1-year period following the program's implementation. In January 2002, 115 clients had gone through the felony re-entry court program. Of these, 19 clients (16.5 percent) had failed and were returned to incarceration. On the basis of this evidence, the felony re-entry court program has been judged successful in reducing recidivism (Spelman, 2003:25–26).

Example 4.   In recent years restorative justice circles have become increasingly popular as alternative civil means of resolving victim-offender matters in lieu of criminal prosecutions. The City of South St. Paul, Minnesota, has established a restorative justice circle program as an alternative to criminal prosecutions. Researchers believe that restorative justice circles can repair harm to victims, promote offender accountability and acceptance of responsibility, and have a positive impact of victim-offender mediation. Whether we believe that restorative justice circles can do these things is irrelevant. Between January 1997 and June 2000, 35 cases were referred by the courts to a restorative justice circle program in South St. Paul. These referrals were mostly at the pre-charge status. Circle participants included the family members of victims, victims, offenders and their families, community representatives, and other individuals. Although both offenders and victims felt uneasy about participating in these circles, they nevertheless chose to participate in order to express their feelings about the incident (crime), their desire for the offender to take responsibility for his or her actions, and the future relationship between the victim and offender. All persons, including offenders, were encouraged to express their views and opinions. Suggested solutions or remedies were considered and discussed. Subsequently, an agreement would be made between victims and offenders, and a period of time would elapse while healing occurred. The evaluation was whether the restorative justice circles had a positive impact on participants. All participants were interviewed during a followup period. Most victims felt supported by the community and welcomed the opportunity to participate meaningfully in the justice process. Offenders' feelings were mixed, although most were encouraged by their acceptance from others and were pleased that they could repair the harm they had caused. The South St. Paul authorities concluded that while restorative justice circles are not necessarily intended to operate on a large-scale basis, they do provide positive experiences for most participants, including the offenders (Umbreit, Coates, and Vos, 2002a).

Some Recommended Outcome Measures

The American Probation and Parole Association (APPA) has been involved in a longitudinal investigation and survey to determine various alternative outcome measures for assessing intermediate punishment program effectiveness. The

APPA Board of Directors consists of probation and parole administrators, probation and parole line staff, and representatives from various affiliate organizations (American Correctional Association, American Jail Association) throughout the United States and Canada. The APPA distributed a survey instrument to all APPA board members and prefaced their questionnaire with the following:

> Assume that your department is going to be evaluated by an outside evaluator. The results of the evaluation will determine the level of funding for the next fiscal year. What outcome measure(s) would you want the evaluator to use in "measuring" the success of your program(s)? What outcome measure(s) would you not want the evaluator to use in the evaluation?

The survey yielded a response from 30 different board members. This was a response rate of 31 percent, since survey instruments were originally sent to over 90 persons. Table 14.1 shows the relative rankings and ratings of the top 23 criteria cited by these board members as alternative outcome measures they would like to see used.

TABLE 14.1

Alternative Outcome Measures from APPA Board of Directors Survey: Top 23

Measure	No. of Board Members Selecting Measure
Amount of restitution collected	10
Number of offenders employed	10
Technical violations	9
Alcohol/drug test results	9
New arrests	8
Fines/fees collected	7
Number completed supervision	6
Hours community service	6
Number sessions of treatment	5
Number/ratio revocations	5
Percent financial obligations collected	5
Employment stability/days employed	5
New arrests: crime type/seriousness	4
Meeting needs of offenders	4
Family stability	4
Education attainment	4
Costs/benefits/services/savings	4
Days alcohol/drug free	4
Number of treatment referrals	3
Time between technical violations	3
Marital stability	3
Wages/taxes paid	3
Compliance with court orders	3

Source: Harry N. Boone, Jr. (1994b). "Recommended Outcome Measures for Program Evaluation: APPA's Board of Directors Survey Results." *APPA Perspectives 18*:19.

An inspection of Table 14.1 shows that the amount of restitution collected tops the list of criteria preferred by these board members. Logically, this would be a direct empirical, tangible indicator of agency effectiveness. As we have seen in previous chapters, community-based programs are increasingly incorporating elements that heighten offender accountability. Making restitution to victims or to the community is an increasingly common program element. Employment is also a key agency goal of many community-based agencies. Thus, many board members selected number of offenders employed as another preferred indicator of agency effectiveness. Other criteria in the top five included technical violations, alcohol/drug test results, and new arrests. Possibly because agencies have more effective monitoring mechanisms in place and improved supervision styles, it is less likely for program clients to engage in technical program violations, fail in drug/alcohol test results, and be rearrested for new offenses. When asked which measures were not preferred for program evaluation, the responding board members cited twelve program components. These are shown in Table 14.2.

Table 14.2 shows that board members at least would downplay recidivism rates, revocation rates, technical violations, and new arrests as outcome measures of program effectiveness. Boone (1994b:20) said that "there was considerable confusion among the 30 respondents as to exactly what outcome measures should or should not be used to evaluate their respective programs." Ideally, more effective programs have lower recidivism rates than less effective programs. All agencies want to exhibit low rates of recidivism among their clientele. Any agency disclosing a recidivism rate of 10 percent or less would most certainly be considered for federal or private funding, since the program would be demonstrably successful. But such low recidivism rates are hard to obtain in most agencies. Again, an informal standard of 30 percent has existed for several decades. This 30 percent standard suggests that programs with recidivism rates 30 percent or less are successful programs, while those with rates above

TABLE 14.2

Outcome Measures Not to Use to Measure Program Success

Measure	No. of Board Members Selecting Measure
Recidivism	8
Revocation rates	6
Technical violations	5
New arrests	4
Single measure	2
Public/media perception	2
New conviction	2
Number of positive drug tests	2
Cost of services/efficiency	2
Number of contacts	2
Number of clients	2
Client evaluation	2

Source: Harry N. Boone, Jr. (1994b). "Recommended Outcome Measures for Program Evaluation: APPA's Board of Directors Survey Results." *APPA Perspectives* 18:20.

30 percent are not successful. Some observers use the word *failure* to describe such programs.

In many respects, it is unfair to label any particular program as a failure or a success on the basis of demonstrated client recidivism rates (Seiter, 2000). Every agency deals with a different breed of offender—sex offenders, property offenders, spouse batterers, chronic delinquents, persistent property offenders, shoplifters, robbers, and thieves (Gregory and Erez, 2002). Designing intervention programs that will decrease the chronicity of such offenders is probably an impossible task, since certain types of offenders persist in their offending, no matter what types of intervention strategies are applied. Also, different time lengths are used to gauge recidivism. Some standards are a year following one's program commencement, while other standards are two or three years. Some standards are even shorter, as short as three or six months. With such different time dimensions over which to determine recidivism of clientele, a meaningful discussion of recidivism in any general sense is of little or no consequence when assessing the merits and weaknesses of particular programs.

Another factor is that many program and agency personnel wish to include those offenders most likely to succeed in those programs. However, these clientele may not be the ones who need the particular program intervention. Ideally, if jail- or prison-bound offenders, and both high- and low-risk types, are program targets, then any program that reduces recidivism among these offenders will deserve more careful consideration and should be given greater funding priority. But many community-based intervention programs are designed to work with low-risk offenders as a means of keeping them integrated in their communities. These persons are usually first-offenders with little likelihood of reoffending. Unfortunately, there is a net-widening effect that occurs with the establishment of such programs. In restorative justice, for instance, perpetrators are often selected on the basis of their first-offender status and the nonseriousness of their crimes against one or more victims. Not everyone qualifies for victim-offender mediation, thus, selectivity tends to bias the results of such interventions (Presser and VanVoorhis, 2002).

Probably every community-based corrections program has eligibility criteria used for selection prospective clientele from among the offender population. Many programs regarded as successful in fulfilling their objectives and aims are guilty of selecting only the most success-prone clients. These include low-risk offenders and first-offenders. Particular types of offenders are deliberately excluded. For instance, some programs may declare that if offenders have a history of violent conduct, are mentally ill or psychologically disturbed, or are sex offenders, then they will be ineligible for inclusion in those programs. If only the most problem-free offenders are selected from the jail- or prison-bound offender population for probation or placement in a community-based correctional program, then the program effectiveness will be enhanced simply because a higher quality of clientele is being included. Those who are unlikely to succeed in these programs are systematically excluded. This is called creaming.

The term no doubt derives from dairying, where the cream is skimmed from fresh milk. In a sense, the "cream of the crop" of eligible offenders is herded into intervention programs. Agency heads can later say, "See—we have a successful program . . . look at our low rates of recidivism among our clients." Certainly they have low recidivism rates. They have excluded those least likely to succeed— probably the very offenders that need the intervention programs they are capable of providing. The New Jersey IPS program for parolees is an example of creaming.

By way of brief review, the New Jersey IPS program had a strict client selection process. For instance, it consists of several screening stages. Final decisions on which applicants would be accepted were made by a resentencing panel of Superior Court judges. Reasons for rejecting applicants included first- and second-degree felonies, too many prior felony convictions, prior crimes of violence, and applicant reluctance to comply with IPS provisions. Thus, the New Jersey program was targeted for low-risk offenders with the least likelihood of recidivating. Not unexpectedly, the New Jersey ISP program reported recidivism rates of less than 20 percent. Thus, a type of self-fulfilling prophecy is created, where the program will succeed because we have done everything in our power to enhance the success of the program, including a careful screening of program applicants. The true test of any intervention program is whether it can make a difference for the hard-core offender aggregate. Short of permanently incarcerating all of our hard-core offenders, one important goal of community-based intervention programs should be to reintegrate unreintegratable offenders into their communities with some measure of success. Not many community-based corrections organizations are willing to implement programs that cater to the least successful clientele pool.

In recent years there has been a greater effort among researchers to experiment with offenders who are more violent or are at greater risk of reoffending. Drug abusers have historically had high relapse rates, no matter how much intervention and assistance they receive from different social services. But there are exceptions. In Oklahoma, for example, drug courts have been established to focus on providing support services for many of those convicted of drug offenses. Substantial numbers of offenders were referred to drug courts during the period 1997 to 2000. Over 1,000 participant/clients became involved in the Oklahoma drug court program, which provided systematic drug abuse treatment, aftercare services, prerelease planning, and postprogram supervision. For samples of 749 and 325 clients who were described as nonviolent felony offenders with a history of substance abuse, they were studied over time to determine their degree of relapse. A large sample of these persons became designated as drug court graduates and were compared with non-drug court probationers with prior histories of drug abuse. In a 2-year followup, only 14 percent of the drug court graduates recidivated or relapsed compared with 22 percent of the non-drug court probationers. This difference was considered significant and indicative of a successful intervention (Wright et al., 2000).

But there are also project failures. In a study of the effectiveness of a sexual assault education program that focused on psychological barriers to resistance, 117 female students at a large, midwestern university were randomly assigned to treatment and control groups to acquaint them with the specifics of sexual assault. Eighty percent of the women participated in a 7-month followup session designed to heighten their level of awareness concerning sexual assault. A comparison of the treatment and control groups after the study was completed showed that the program was unsuccessful in influencing any of the outcome variables, including dating behaviors, knowledge of sexual assault, sexual communication, resistance strategy, self-blame, perception of risk to self, disclosure of the experience, and reporting assaults to police. Researchers did not regard this failure experience as an indication that rape education efforts ought to be abandoned. Rather, they believed that their programming should be reexamined and modified so that effective program elements could be identified and used successfully with subsequent samples of university women (Breitenbecher and Scarce, 2001).

BALANCING PROGRAM OBJECTIVES AND OFFENDER NEEDS

The major objectives of community-based probation and parole programs for juveniles and adults are summarized as follows:

1. Facilitating offender reintegration
2. Continuing offender punishment
3. Heightening offender accountability
4. Ensuring community protection or safety
5. Promoting offender rehabilitation
6. Improving offender skills and coping mechanisms
7. Resolving offender social and psychological problems
8. Alleviating jail and prison overcrowding
9. Monitoring offender behaviors
10. Reducing offender chemical dependencies
11. Collecting fines, restitution payments, and other fees
12. Enforcing the law, including community service orders
13. Employing support personnel, corrections workers, and professionals/paraprofessionals
14. Producing low rates of recidivism among agency clientele
15. Coordinating and networking agency tasks and functions with other community agencies
16. Justifying agency budget

This list is not exhaustive. Many functions or objectives above overlap with one another. The fact is that agencies are multifaceted, striving to achieve diverse goals or aims. Many of these organizational aims are mentioned by Petersilia and Turner (1993). They note the following agency goals with accompanying performance indicators:

1. Assessing offender's suitability for placement (performance indicators = accuracy and completeness of PSIs; timeliness of revocation and termination hearings; validity of classification/prediction instrument; percent of offenders receiving recommended sentence or violation action; and percent of offenders recommended for community who violate)
2. Enforcing court-ordered sanctions (performance indicators = number of arrests and technical violations during supervision; percent of ordered payments collected; number of hours/days performed community service; number of favorable discharges; numbers of days employed, in vocational education or school; and drug-free and/or alcohol-free days during supervision)
3. Protecting the community (performance indicators = number and type of supervision contacts; number and type of arrests during supervision; number and type of technical violations during supervision; number of absconders during supervision)
4. Assisting offenders to change (performance indicators = number of times attending treatment/work programming; employment during supervision;

number of arrests and/or technical violations during supervision; number drug-free and/or alcohol free days during supervision; and attitude change)

5. Restoring crime victims (performance indicators = payment of restitution; extent of victim satisfaction with service and department)

Thus, these programs exist for a variety of reasons. Some of these reasons are totally unrelated to offender needs, such as employment of agency personnel and justifying the agency budget. It is important to coincide agency processes with offender needs as a way of demonstrating program effectiveness. Petersilia and Turner (1993) have reduced almost all of these agency functions to things that can be counted. We can count the amount of collected fine payments and restitution. We can count numbers of days alcohol-free or drug-free. We can count numbers of rearrests, numbers of favorable discharges, numbers of days employed. However, there are many intangibles that cannot be counted. We do not know, for instance, whether offender familial relations are actually improving. We might count the number of 911 calls for reports of spousal abuse or other forms of familial conflict for various offender-clients. This might be a negative gauge of positive family functioning. Also, we do not know whether true psychological changes are occurring within any particular offender-client (White et al., 2002). We only know that these offender-clients have been provided with the means for change. We don't know for sure whether changes actually occur in designated or targeted program areas.

During the 1990s, Arizona officials decided to evaluate the effectiveness of their probation services, since probation is the most common way for Arizona's offenders to serve their sentences. Although over 35,000 probationers were being supervised by county-level probation services, a study was conducted of a sample of 845 probationers during the period 1994 to 1998. Most offenders had concurrent substance abuse problems. It was subsequently learned that three major factors were associated with probationer success. These included maintaining employment, completing community service requirements, and completing a drug treatment program. The overall success rate for completing the probation program for those offenders studied was 63 percent. About 85 percent of all offenders who consistently participated in drug abuse counseling completed their probation program successfully. And there was a 90 percent success rate for those who maintained employment during their probationary period (Norton, 1999).

When PSI reports are prepared for any offender, POs make a point of identifying problem areas that could or should be addressed by subsequent programming. These are identified as offender needs. We have an array of risk-needs instruments that assess both an offender's dangerousness and the special needs they might exhibit. When inmates are classified upon entry into jails or prisons, they are usually assessed with either self-administered or other types of paper-pencil tests or devices that seek to determine their most appropriate placement, whether it is a particular custody level or rehabilitation/educational/vocational/counseling program. In Virginia, for instance, inmates with low reading levels are tracked to special educational classes designed to improve their literacy levels (Hawk et al., 1993). It is logical to assume that if the literacy levels of inmates can be improved, then their chances for employment are also improved. Completing job application forms requires a minimum amount of literacy, for example. Offenders with psychological or social adjustment problems may benefit from individual or group therapy or various forms of sensitivity training.

What about alcohol or drug usage? In prisons, there is a low likelihood that alcoholism or drug dependency will continue to be problematic for offenders. We know that inmates have access to drugs in most prisons or jails. But what can we do now that will help offenders cope with their community environment when they are subsequently released from prison? If alcohol or drug dependencies contributed to their crimes, then what coping mechanisms can be provided these offenders while they are institutionalized? Drug and alcohol dependency classes are provided inmates with these kinds of problems (identifiable need areas). But do these classes prevent subsequent recurrences of alcohol and drug dependency?

Parole boards in most jurisdictions face offenders every day, both adults and juveniles, who are chronic recidivists with drug and alcohol dependencies (Parker, 2001). They ask prospective parolees, "Did you participate in Alcoholics Anonymous while in prison?" Prospective parolee: "Yes." Parole board: "But you have been convicted of a new crime, and when you were caught, you were drunk. What happened?" Prospective parolee: "I got in with the wrong crowd," "I had a setback," "I had some personal problems," "I just couldn't pass up a drink," or "I went along with the crowd for old time's sake." Some offenders never escape the problems that contributed to their criminal activity, no matter how much training, coursework, therapy, or counseling they receive.

Any community-based corrections program attempts to provide useful interventions that will assist offender-clients in various ways. Some of these interventions include the use of injectable methadone administered to drug addicts on an outpatient basis (Beaumont, 2001). Assisting former gang members in avoiding subsequent renewed contact with their gang associates is also important (Curry and Decker, 2003). Volunteers and paraprofessionals assist offender-clients in filling out job application forms, in reading programs, or in other reintegrative or rehabilitative activities. Meeting diverse offender needs is viewed as a primary way of reducing or eliminating recidivism (Osgood, McMorris, and Potenza, 2002). And recidivism is probably the most direct way of measuring program effectiveness, despite other program components, aims, or alternative outcome measures.

RECIDIVISM

Recidivism Defined

A conceptual Tower of Babel exists regarding recidivism. Numerous investigations of this phenomenon have been conducted, although no consensus exists about the meaning of the term (Minor, Wells, and Sims, 2003). Criminologists and other observers can recite lengthy lists of characteristics that describe recidivists. But describing recidivists and using those characteristics as effective predictors of recidivism are two different matters. For example, if a parole board uses a salient factor score to predict an offender's degree of success on parole, some inmates will be refused parole because their scores suggest they are poor risks. At the same time, other inmate scores may indicate good risks. The poor risks are denied parole, while the good risks are granted it. However, among the poor risks are inmates who will never recidivate (false positives), while among the good risks (who eventually become parolees) are serious recidivists (false negatives). Parole boards are interested in minimizing the frequency of both false positives and false negatives.

When a false positive is denied parole, certain moral, ethical, and legal issues are raised about continuing to confine otherwise harmless persons. When a false negative is granted parole and commits a new, serious offense, the public is outraged, the parole board is embarrassed, and the integrity of test developers and the validity of prediction instruments are called into question. Judges who impose probation instead of incarceration or incarceration instead of probation are subject to similar attacks on similar grounds. Numerical scales are often used as more objective criteria for probation or parole decision making. It is not necessarily the case that these scales are superior to personal judgments by judges or parole boards. But references to numbers seem to objectify early release or probation-granting decisions compared with visual appraisals of offenders and subjective interpretations of their backgrounds contained in PSIs. Several problems have been identified relating to recidivism and its measurement (Buttell, 2002; Friendship, Beech, and Browne, 2002). A brief listing of some of the more common problems is provided below:

1. The time interval between commencing a probation or parole program and recidivating is different from one study to the next. Some studies use 6 months, while others use 1 year, 2 years, or 5 years.

2. There are many different meanings of recidivism. Comparing one definition of recidivism with another is like comparing apples with oranges.

3. Recidivism is often dichotomized rather than graduated. Thus, people either recidivate or they don't recidivate. No variation exists to allow for degrees of seriousness of reoffending of any type.

4. Recidivism rates are influenced by multiple factors, such as the intensity of supervised probation or parole, the numbers of face-to-face visits between POs and their clients, and even the rate of prison construction.

5. Recidivism rates may be indicative of program failures rather than client failures.

6. Recidivism only accounts for official rule or law violations; self-reported information indicates that higher rates of recidivism may actually exist compared with those that are subsequently reported and recorded.

7. Considerable client variation exists, as well as numerous programmatic variations. Depending on the client population under investigation, recidivism is more or less significant.

8. Policy shifts in local and state governments may change how recidivism is used or defined as well as the amount of recidivism observed in given jurisdictions.

We know, or at least we think we know, that recidivists tend to be male, black, younger, less educated, and have lengthy prior records. In fact, having a lengthy prior record appears to be most consistently related to recidivism. Therefore, should we make it official judicial or parole board policy not to grant probation or parole to younger, less educated, black males with lengthy prior records? No. These are aggregate characteristics and do not easily lend themselves to individualized probation or parole decision making (Cohn et al., 2002).

One continuing problem is that while these and other characteristics describe the general category of recidivists (whomever they may be), these characteristics are also found among many non-recidivists. Thus, based upon relevant information about offenders, prediction measures must be devised and tested to improve their validity. A related problem is determining whether recidivism has occurred. This means some degree of agreement needs to be established concerning what does and does not mean recidivism.

Existing measures of recidivism complicate rather than simplify its definition. It is important to pay attention to how recidivism is conceptualized in the research literature, since probation or parole program failures or successes are measured by recidivism rates (Buttell, 2002; Southern Methodist University, 2002). And a general standard has emerged among professionals that a failure rate above 30 percent means that a probation or parole program is ineffective. Ineffective in what sense? Reducing crime? Rehabilitating offenders? Both?

BOX 14.1

PERSONALITY HIGHLIGHT

Eli B. Silverman
Professor of Police Studies and Criminal Justice Administration, John Jay College of Criminal Justice, City University of New York

Statistics:

B.A. (political science), Allegheny College; M.A. (political science), Pennsylvania State University; Ph.D. (public management), Pennsylvania State University

Background and Observations:

The winding path sometimes unexpectedly provides a better route to a fresher view of new places than does the main highway. In retrospect, my interest, involvement, and research in criminal justice management and reform falls into this category. After receiving undergraduate and master's degrees in political science and a Ph.D. in public management, I found myself as an American Society of Public Administration Fellow assigned as Special Assistant to the Assistant Attorney General for Administration in the U.S. Department of Justice (DOJ) in Washington, DC. At the DOJ my responsibilities covered a wide range of newly established Law Enforcement Assistance Administration, analysis, and recommendations regarding staffing and relationship of the Community Relations Service, and evaluations of reporting procedures for federal prisoners in nonfederal institutions.

The following year I continued my interest in governmental management issues and reform when I served as a Research Associate at the National Academy of Public Administration in Washington, DC. We evaluated federal programs including four Department of Housing and Urban Development Assistance Programs in eight cities and NASA space projects. While in Washington, I was offered a position at John Jay College of Criminal Justice, City University of New York, where I have served as chair of the department of government and management, associated dean of social sciences, and then professor in the department of law, police studies, and criminal justice administration. Developing and teaching community policing, police management, policy analysis, and other courses with a very diverse student body, including those employed in the criminal justice system, has been very exciting, opening me up to new perspectives and insights.

My association with New York's criminal justice system led to involvement in program design and instruction in training programs for many agencies such as the New York City Police Department, the New York

(continued)

BOX 14.1 (Continued)

State Division of Parole, the New York State Department of Corrections, the New York Housing Authority, and the New York City Health and Hospital Corporation. I helped design a degree program for training in alcohol and drug treatment for criminal justice professionals. Although not planned, my criminal justice interests broadened as I also researched and wrote about policing in other countries. I was a Visiting Professor at the British Police Staff College in the United Kingdom and the University of Toulouse in France. I lectured in Spain, Portugal, Finland, Germany, France, Canada, Russia, Australia, England, Scotland, and Ireland. My travels in these and other countries exposed me to criminal justice professionals and practitioners with exciting ideas and perspectives.

In all of these activities, I now find a common thread of which I was not always aware. This pertains to an interest in improving the effectiveness of criminal justice organizations. For example, when I first began the research for my book, *NYPD Battle Crime: Innovative Strategies in Policing,* most of the literature believed policing made little difference to crime rates compared with social and economic factors. In addition, the prevailing view was that contemporary policing required radical reforms, from reactive, incident-driven responses to crimes already committed to more coherent, information-driven, problem- and community-oriented policing strategies. Yet these types of police reforms have historically been frustrated by bureaucratic resistance, insularity, defensiveness, and organizational rigidity.

My interest in the New York City and other police departments demonstrated the value of situational and information-driven crime prevention tactics (in terms of opportunities, victims, nature, and patterns of times, places, and choices). Police departments can and have enhanced their organizational and managerial effectiveness geared to information-driven strategies, which indeed can have a substantial impact on crime rates.

Advice to Students:

By all means pursue your interests and career goals, and if you find that they meet your expectations, then do everything within your power to excel in your chosen field. At the same time, however, be open to the unforeseen opportunities that may unfold. You may find in the course of your career, as I did, that the field may change or other related or even unrelated opportunities may present themselves. Your work supervisor may ask you to tackle an assignment that feels uncomfortable and may seem abstract or unrelated to your training or experience. Yet you may bring a fresh perspective to it that others who are daily embedded in the work may not. Moreover, you may find that you even enjoy the assignment and find that you are good at it. Remember that the criminal justice field contains many aspects and dimensions. The profession relies on numerous disciplines including sociology, criminology, economics, political science, anthropology, and other related fields. Practitioners who possess clear and communicable writing and speaking skills have distinct advantages. The criminal justice field is a big wheel with many spokes. And so be open to the countless roads that lead to work, career, and personal satisfaction.

Recidivism means program failure. Or does it? There is a wide variety of probation and parole programs available to the courts and corrections officials for many different kinds of offenders. One common problem faced by all programs is that observers have trouble matching the right programs with the right clientele (Bickle et al., 2002; Truitt et al., 2002). We have much descriptive information about recidivists. Numerous evaluation studies are conducted annually of various offender programs and virtually all strategies for dealing with offenders are examined and reexamined. For instance, Minor, Wells, and Sims

(2003:32) studied 200 federal prisoners in Kentucky from 1996 through 1999. They found that six variables were predictors of recidivism: (1) Younger persons recidivated more than older persons; (2) those with prior records recidivated more than first-offenders; (3) those ordered to complete substance abuse treatment had higher recidivism rates; (4) those ordered to undergo mental health treatment had higher recidivism rates; (5) those not ordered to do community service had higher rates of recidivism; and (6) a majority of nonwhites had higher recidivism rates. While these findings are not generalizable to recidivists in general, they do coincide with what others have found about recidivist characteristics. But no matter the cure proposed, the illness remains. Treatments are rarely pure, however, and therefore, their evaluations are necessarily complicated. Probationers or parolees who violate one or more terms of their probation or parole, regardless of the type of program examined, are considered recidivists.

Recidivism seems relevant when we are interested in the rehabilitative value of programs, but many programs involving intensive supervision of parolees and probationers seem focused primarily on crime control (Kronick, Lambert, and Lambert, (1998). Some of the different ways of operationalizing recidivism are:

1. Rearrest
2. Parole or probation revocation or unsatisfactory termination
3. Technical parole or probation rule violations
4. Conviction for a new offense while on parole or probation
5. Return to prison
6. Having a prior record and being rearrested for a new offense
7. Having a prior record and being convicted for a new offense
8. Any new commitment to a jail or prison for 60 days or more
9. Presence of a new sentence exceeding 1 year for any offense committed during a 5-year parole followup
10. Return of released offenders to custody of state correctional authorities
11. Return to jail
12. Reincarceration
13. The use of drugs or alcohol by former drug or alcohol abusers
14. Failure to complete educational or vocational/technical course or courses in or out of prison/jail custody.

The most commonly used conceptualizations include rearrests, reconvictions, revocations of parole or probation, reincarcerations, and technical program violations (Cohn et al., 2002; Fabelo, 2002).

Types of Recidivism

Rearrests.   As a measure of recidivism, **rearrest** is frequently used in evaluation studies of parole/probation program effectiveness, although rearrests are highly misleading (Marciniak, 2000). The most obvious flaw is that it is uncertain whether offenders have actually committed new offenses. Sometimes, if a crime has been committed in the neighborhood where particular clients are residing in a halfway house, *and* if the crime is similar in nature to the crime(s) for which the ex-offenders were previously convicted, detectives and police may look up the offenders and interview them. Since offender associations with police authorities are inherently strained anyway, it is likely that police would interpret an offender's nervousness as a sign of guilt (Steiner, Cauffman, and Duxbury, 1999). Thus, the offender might be subject to rearrest based upon the suspicions of officers. The crucial element is whether the officers have probable cause to justify the client's arrest. Constitutional safeguards exist, of course, to protect all citizens from unreasonable arrests by police. However, law enforcement officers find it relatively easy to justify their actions to the court when dealing with former offenders and parolees, even where the Constitutional rights of ex-offenders have been infringed (Stanz and Tewksbury, 2000).

However, a rearrest is interpreted as recidivism by some researchers, and this means program failure. Rearrested offenders are not necessarily taken to jail or returned to prison; they may continue in their present probation or parole programs. Of course, it is also possible that the ex-offender did, indeed, commit a new crime. But this must be proved, beyond a reasonable doubt, in a court of law. Some jurisdictions use the preponderance of evidence standard for probation/parole revocations. This standard is less stringent than the beyond-a-reasonable-doubt standard.

In New York, for instance, many probationers/parolees adjourn their revocation hearings pending the outcome of their court cases. If they are acquitted of criminal charges, this obviously impacts their probation/parole revocation process favorably. If the result of a trial is a conviction for the probationer/parolee, then a revocation hearing on the violation will not be conducted. A certificate of disposition would suffice as evidence of a conviction and sentence. However, not all parolees or probationers who are rearrested for new crimes are prosecuted for those crimes. They may instead be sent to prison. Due to the *Morrissey v. Brewer* (1972) decision, however, two hearings (i.e., one to determine probable cause and the other an actual revocation proceeding) are required before the paroling authority can summarily revoke parole.

Reconvictions.   **Reconviction** for a new offense is probably the most reliable indicator of recidivism as well as the most valid definition of it (Breckenridge et al., 2000). This represents that at least one new crime has been committed by an offender while on probation or parole, and the court has determined offender guilt beyond a reasonable doubt. Arguably, some observers may counter by saying that any failure to observe probation or parole conditions or placing oneself in a position to increase the likelihood of arrest (e.g., violating curfew or associating with other offenders) is evidence that offender rehabilitation has not occurred. However, if crime control is of primary importance to those involved with probationers and parolees, then this argument fails to hold (Pratt, 2000).

Revocations of Parole or Probation.   A revocation of parole or probation means that parolees or probationers have violated one or more of the conditions associated with their supervision status (Fabelo, 2002). These conditions may be as harmless as missing a 10:00 P.M. curfew by five minutes or as serious as committing and being convicted of a new felony. Parole and probation officers have some discretionary authority where technical program violations are involved. They may overlook these incidents or report them. If the incident is a rearrest, the discretion passes to others such as arresting officers and prosecutors or is at least shared. If interpersonal relations between clients and POs have become strained, the PO may exaggerate the violation, regardless of how minor it may be.

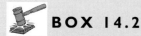

Cathy Fulda
Business Development Executive, Behavioral Interventions
Boulder, Colorado

Statistics:

B.S. (physical education), University of Cincinnati

Background and Work Experience:

I began my professional career in teaching aerobics and physical fitness classes at a local YMCA. I then transitioned to selling advertising for a regional newspaper. I quickly realized that sales was where I wanted to spend the rest of my professional life. I then embarked on a 7-year sales career selling radio advertising for three local radio stations.

I remarried in 1983 and continued my sales career in radio, while raising a blended family of two girls and a boy. In 1986, my husband and a business associate embarked on a business venture that resulted in one of the first electronic monitoring service programs in the United States. My husband asked me to give up my job in radio advertising to head up operations for this new company, since he was unable to leave his college teaching position at a local university. I accepted the challenge and began using my sales skills to promote this new technology/service to judges, sheriffs, probation officers, and corrections officials throughout the Midwest.

The company grew from single-digit monitoring to over 450 being monitored in 1990. It was at that time that BI Incorporated acquired our company, and both my husband and I joined the new company as vice presidents. Although my husband has left the company, I have stayed with the company and now have 13 years of experience in a variety of areas within the criminal justice system. My current position is that of a regional salesperson, with responsibilities for developing business and program solutions for criminal justice agencies in three Mid-

western states. I have developed many long-standing relationships over the last 17 years and can attest to the importance of having and developing interpersonal skills to be successful in this or any other career choice.

While with BI, I had the opportunity to introduce a new technology designed to enforce protective orders for victims of domestic abuse. I became very involved in promoting this new program throughout the United States and seeing the need for more accountability in domestic violence situations. In addition to my work at BI, I have also found ways to continue my love of teaching physical exercise by offering aerobics classes to female inmates at the local jail. I have also become a volunteer at a local women's shelter and regularly provide them with meals and exercise programs.

Advice to Students:

The move from an advertising career to one in criminal justice has been extremely rewarding, especially since I have been able to combine my love of selling with my love for people. I have thoroughly enjoyed working with my customers through my sales position. In the years before joining BI Incorporated, I was able to work one-on-one with those placed on electronic home detention, as well with those charged with supervising those individuals.

I have found that a servant heart and strong communication skills go a long way in defining and creating a successful career. The technical skills can generally be learned in a short period of time, but the interpersonal

(continued)

BOX 14.2 (*Continued*)

skills have to be present to achieve success. Work on these skills as you contemplate a career in criminal justice. Use internships and other field experiences to hone these skills and prepare for your eventual entry into your chosen career area. Keep your options open. You may want to consider a career with one of the many private companies providing services to offenders. This is an option that many graduates did not have in the past, but it does provide another option to the traditional public service careers that characterized criminal justice in the past. In whatever you do, know that you are entering a field that requires the best talent available in order to solve the pressing problems of our complex society.

Many factors influence a parole or probation revocation decision. Prison or jail overcrowding is one of them. The seriousness of the violation is also considered. A third factor is the recommendation of the PO. The main problem with a technical violation of parole or probation, however, is that often it is not related to crime of any kind. Therefore, a revocation based solely on technical criteria is irrelevant as a crime control strategy, unless it can be demonstrated empirically that failure to revoke would have resulted in a new crime being committed. And most, if not all, observers are not prepared to make such assertions at present. A revocation of probation or parole does not necessarily mean a return to prison or jail, however. Depending upon the grounds for the revocation and other factors, an offender may be placed on a probation or parole program with a higher control level. This is one reason why revocations of probation and parole cannot be equated directly with reincarceration.

Reincarcerations.   The use of **reincarceration** as a measure of recidivism is as misleading as counting the numbers of rearrests and revocations among probationers and parolees (Joo, 1993). Reincarceration does not specify the type of incarceration. After probation is revoked, a probationer may be placed in a state or federal prison. After a federal parolee's status has been revoked, the parolee may be placed in a city or county jail for a short period rather than returned to the original federal prison. The most frequent usages of recidivism include rearrests, reconvictions, and reincarcerations, although many other meanings have been given it. Arguably, it seems that the most relevant connotation applied to recidivism is a new conviction for a criminal offense as opposed to a simple rearrest or parole revocation for a technical program violation, both of which might be grounds for reincarceration. Reincarceration as a measure of recidivism is unreliable as well because it fails to distinguish between the true law breaker and the technical rule violator.

Technical Program Violations.   **Technical program violations** might include curfew violation, failing a drug or alcohol urinalysis, failing to report employment or unemployment, failing to check in with the PO, failing to file a monthly status report in a timely way, or missing a group therapy meeting. Technical program violations are not crimes. However, they are legitimate conditions of probation or parole that are enforceable. Failure to comply with any one more of these program requirements (e.g., making restitution to victims, performing so many hours of community service) may be the basis for a possible probation or parole revocation action. Technical program violations have been used in more than a few studies as a measure of recidivism (Stanz and Tewksbury, 2000). While technical program violations have been used as recidivism measures, they are not particularly the best indicators (Brunet, 2002). Prioritizing the most frequently used measures of recidivism, we might list reconvictions, reincarcerations, rearrests, and probation/parole revocations, in that order. Boone (1994a) has offered some suggestions to clarify the use of recidivism in program evaluation and research. He says that we ought to:

1. Standardize the definition of recidivism.
2. Discourage the use of recidivism as the only outcome measure for community corrections programs.
3. Define alternative outcome measures for the evaluation of community corrections programs.
4. Educate interested stakeholders, including the general public, on alternative measures.
5. Encourage researchers, evaluators, and agency personnel to use appropriate outcome measures to evaluate program success/failure (Boone, 1994a:17).

It is unlikely that Boone's first two suggestions will ever be implemented. There is simply too much variety among community corrections programs presently. Too many different vested interests have a stake in seeing recidivism conceptualized in different ways to fit neatly into particular funding priorities by showing program "successes." The public as well as stakeholders definitely need to be educated concerning various ways of measuring agency success or effectiveness. True, recidivism is not the only way successfulness or effectiveness should be measured. The last three of Boone's suggestions suggest both short- and long-range planning to allow for testing alternative outcome measures of program accomplishments.

Factors Associated with Lower Recidivism Rates

Researchers have identified several important factors that seem to correlate more or less highly with lower rates of recidivism. These factors vary in importance among studies, but there does appear to be some consistency in study findings regarding them. These factors include:

1. Treatment is based on behavioral strategies influenced by empirically valid theories of criminal behavior.
2. Treatment is delivered in the offender's natural environment.
3. A variety of intervention strategies are employed to respond to a wide range of offender needs, particularly criminogenic needs.
4. The program is intensive (100+; hours over a course of three to four months).
5. The emphasis is upon positive reinforcement and prosocial behavior.
6. There is an attempt to match client needs and learning styles.
7. Aftercare is provided.

8. Administrators and faculty are trained, qualified, and well-supervised.

9. There is organizational support (Withrow, 2002).

RECIDIVISTS AND THEIR CHARACTERISTICS

Avertable and Nonavertable Recidivists

One of most innovative aspects of the study was the classification of recidivists with prior records of incarceration into avertable recidivists and nonavertable recidivists. **Avertable recidivists** are those offenders who would have still been in prison serving their original sentences in full at the time they were confined for committing new offenses. **Nonavertable recidivists** are those offenders whose prior sentences would not have affected the commission of new crimes. Examples of avertable and nonavertable recidivists using more recent sentencing periods are as follows. Suppose John Doe is a new 1995 prison admission. Doe was previously incarcerated in 1990 for armed robbery and given a 2- to 15-year sentence in a state prison. The parole board released Doe in 1993, whereupon Doe committed several burglaries. He was apprehended by police and eventually convicted of burglary in 1995. Had he still been in prison serving his entire 15-year sentence, those burglaries he committed never would have occurred. Doe is called an avertable recidivist, because his crimes occurred within the maximum range of his original sentence (e.g., 1990–2005).

John Doe's sister, Jane, was convicted in 1991 of vehicular theft. Jane was sentenced to 3 years. Jane served her time and was eventually released. Jane obeyed the law for several years, but in 1999 she was arrested for and convicted of stealing another automobile. Since she had already served the maximum sentence of 3 years for vehicular theft from 1991 to 1994, the maximum range of her original sentence no longer applied. Jane is classified as a nonavertable recidivist. Both she and her brother, John, are recidivists, because they are criminal offenders who have been convicted of previous crimes. But John's new crimes may have been averted had John been forced to serve his maximum sentence. This doesn't rule out the possibility that when John finally served the maximum 15-year sentence for armed robbery, he could commit new crimes and therefore be classified as a nonavertable recidivist like his sister.

Nonavertable recidivists tend to account for substantially higher percentages of crimes compared with avertable recidivists in virtually every crime category. Second, nonavertable recidivists compared with first-timers account for substantially smaller percentages of violent crimes and drug offenses but somewhat higher percentages of property crimes, with few exceptions. The percent of offenses under the avertable recidivists category theoretically represents the proportion of crimes that would not have been committed by these offenders had they been obligated to serve out their entire sentences.

The work of Miranne and Geerken (1991) is significant here. These investigators tested a 7-item scale devised by Peter Greenwood at the **Rand Corporation** (Greenwood, 1982). This scale purportedly differentiated between high- and low-rate offenders on the basis of their responses to seven items on a self-report instrument. The Miranne-Geerken study utilized a similar, but more elaborate, form of the original Greenwood instrument and obtained self-reports from 200 convicted inmates at facilities operated by the Orleans (Louisiana) Parish Criminal Sheriff in New Orleans. Essentially, their findings were similar to those of the Greenwood study. High-rate and low-rate offenders could be identified, although the findings were inconclusive to the extent that a change in public policy about selective incapacitation could not be substantiated. Miranne and Geerken do highlight an important consideration, however. They note that "if high-rate offenders could be accurately identified and distinguished from low-rate offenders, sentencing the former to a longer period of incarceration than the latter could possibly increase cost-effectiveness" [and conceivably lower the crime rate by incarcerating the high-rate offenders for longer periods] (Miranne and Geerken, 1991:514).

Public Policy and Recidivism

State legislators and policy makers have seized results such as these as foundations for arguments that mandatory and/or determinate sentencing and more rigorous parole criteria ought to be employed. In view of the sentencing reforms enacted by various states and current trends, these figures have apparently been persuasive or at least influential in changing sentencing policies and parole criteria.

The study conducted by the Bureau of Justice Statistics (BJS) is one of the larger surveys of recidivists and their characteristics. But each year, new waves of offenders enter jails and prisons. The profile changes, probably daily. But there are some general patterns that emerge, not only from this analysis but from other research as well. According to the BJS survey, using reconviction as an indicator of an adult recidivist, recidivists appear to share the following characteristics:

1. Recidivists tend to be male.
2. Recidivists tend to be younger (under 30), and recidivism declines with advancing age.
3. Recidivists tend to have an educational level equivalent to high school or less.
4. Recidivists tend to have lengthy records of arrests and/or convictions.
5. Recidivists tend to be under no correctional supervision when committing new offenses.
6. Recidivists tend to have a record of juvenile offenses.
7. Recidivists tend to commit crimes similar to those for which they were convicted previously.
8. Recidivists tend to have alcohol or drug dependency problems associated with the commission of new offenses.
9. Recidivists tend not to commit progressively serious offenses compared with their prior records.
10. Recidivists tend to be unmarried, widowed, or divorced.
11. Recidivists tend to be employed, either full-time or part-time, when committing new offenses (Bureau of Justice Statistics, 2002).

Again, these characteristics considered singly or in any combination make predictions of dangerousness or public risk difficult at best. Parole boards might use such information as supplemental when interviewing prospective parolees. Judges might consider such information when deciding the appropriate sentence for a convicted offender. The odds favor future offender behaviors consistent with previous offender behaviors (Petersilia, 2001). The odds increase as the number of characteristics associated with recidivists increases. But the certainty of recidivism for any specific offender can never be predicted in any absolute sense. Prediction schemes seem more effective when large numbers of offenders sharing similar characteristics are aggregated, but parole boards and judges make decisions about individual offenders, not groups of them (Wilson and Petersilia, 2002).

PROBATIONERS, PAROLEES, AND RECIDIVISM

The immense interest of states in sentencing reforms directed away from rehabilitation and toward justice with greater certainty of punishment stems, in part, from public dissatisfaction with how the courts and corrections have dealt with offenders in recent decades. Recidivism spells failure to many citizens, and judicial leniency in sentencing, real or imagined, has contributed to a backlash of sorts. This backlash is similar to the public reaction to John Hinckley's acquittal on charges that he attempted to assassinate President Reagan, on the grounds that he was insane at the time the offense was committed. The insanity defense was quickly abolished in several states and vastly overhauled in others. This occurred despite the fact that the insanity defense is used in fewer than 1 percent of all criminal prosecutions and is successfully used in only a small fraction of those cases.

Alarming statistics stimulate public concern about parole and probation programs. The United States Department of Justice says that 65 percent of released prisoners will return to prison within two years, and most of these will occur within one year from one's release. Parole may hold down prison populations, but there may be a tradeoff through increased street crime (Petersilia, 2001). Greater certainty of incarceration coupled with longer terms of confinement for law violators are advanced by reformers as solutions for reducing and controlling crime. However, research has never demonstrated conclusively that longer prison sentences make ex-offenders less likely to commit new crimes.

Curbing Recidivism

Strategies for decreasing recidivism rates include incarceration, intensive supervised probation/parole, and a wide range of intermediate punishments already discussed including electronic monitoring, house arrest, and community-based treatment programs (Bloom et al., 2002). The more intensive monitoring an offender receives, the less the recidivism, although some intensively supervised offenders recidivate. The treatment or rehabilitation orientation is not a bad one, although many observers feel that many established treatment programs do not fulfill their stated goals. The fact that 50 percent or more of all offenders, incarcerated or on probation, will recidivate in the future at some unspecified time is evidence of the rehabilitative failure of any program, including incarceration. However, one influential but conservative voice favoring incapacitation is James Q. Wilson, who argues that while imprisonment may not rehabilitate offenders, it does keep them off the streets away from the general public. And this may be the most effective means of crime control. Another controversial solution recommended by some observers is selective incapacitation (Auerbahn, 2002).

A report prepared by the National Council on Crime and Delinquency (NCCD) has examined parolee recidivism in California and has found that parolee failures have increased from 23 percent in 1975 to 53 percent in 1983 (Austin, 1987). This report yields findings similar to those presented by Rand researchers. Administrative parole revocations have jumped from 5 to 35 percent since 1975, but the proportion of parolees being returned for new felonies committed while on parole increased by only 5 percent. Parolee failures do not seem related to program failures, however. Rather, external and administrative factors appear largely to blame for many of these. The following factors contribute significantly to the growing numbers of administrative parole revocations:

1. Declining levels of financial assistance and narcotic treatment resources for parolees.
2. Increases in parole supervision caseloads.
3. A shift in public and law enforcement attitudes regarding parolees and law violators in general.
4. Jail overcrowding.
5. A more efficient law enforcement/parole supervision system (Austin, 1987).

Thus, curbing recidivism rates might be achieved by more effective implementation of probation/parole program goals, smaller caseloads for POs (probably resulting in more frequent contact with probationer or parolee clients), and increasing the capacity of delivery systems (i.e., greater funding) to meet the specialized needs of offenders such as those with drug dependency problems or alcoholism (Cohn et al., 2002). The NCCD findings and corresponding recommendations are shared by other researchers as well. Paradoxically, more frequent contact between POs and their clients may make POs more aware of client technical violations of their program requirements. This doesn't mean that PO clients are committing more program violations, but rather, that POs are in the position of observing their clients more frequently and the likelihood of observing program infractions is increased.

SUMMARY

Program evaluation is the process of assessing any corrections intervention or program for the purpose of determining its effectiveness in achieving manifest goals. Program evaluation almost always involves recidivism as an indicator of program goal attainment. However, other alternative outcome measures are used, including costs, benefits, and savings to communities, wages and taxes paid, and compliance with court orders. Recidivism refers to repeat offending, although it has no universally applicable definition. It applies to criminals who commit or are suspected of committing new offenses, and connotations of the term are associated with rearrests, reconvictions, reincarcerations, parole/probation revocations, and technical program violations.

Parole boards and judges are interested in minimizing recidivism in their parole-granting and sentencing capacities. Often, salient factor scores are useful in forecasting one's potential successfulness as a parolee, and judges rely on pre-sentence investigations of offenders when deciding the correct sentence to impose. No technique or measure accurately forecasts recidivism, however. False positives and false negatives attest to the low predictive power of instruments purportedly designed to measure dangerousness or public risk. Recidivists tend to be younger males with lengthy prior records of convictions. They usually, though not always, have less education, are from lower socioeconomic statuses, and tend to commit new offenses similar to their prior offense convictions. Recidivism declines with advancing age.

Factors influencing recidivism appear to be probation or parole status, length of prison term, and type of offense. Property offenders tend to recidivate more than violent offenders. Parolees tend to recidivate more than probationers. The greater the level of probation/parole supervision, the less the recidivism while on probation/parole. The length of incarceration appears to have little influence on recidivism. This finding undermines arguments advanced by observers that longer prison terms will reduce crime and recidivism.

Probation and parole programs and their administration can be improved. Many programs are either new or in early experimental stages so that definite conclusions about their effectiveness cannot be drawn. Probationers themselves believe increased contact with probation officers and program incentives and rewards for compliance ought to be incorporated as a means of increasing program effectiveness and reducing recidivism. Differential supervision may actually be an incentive for many probationers/parolees. The longer one remains violation-free while under supervision, the less intense will be the supervision. Some states have automatic probation/parole program discharges, where probationers/parolees will automatically be released from the criminal justice system after successfully completing a 3-year term of supervision with incurring revocations or program violations.

QUESTIONS FOR REVIEW

1. What is meant by creaming? How does creaming influence program effectiveness?

2. What is a "needs instrument"? What types of items are included on needs instruments?

3. Differentiate between avertable recidivists and nonavertable recidivists. Give some examples.

4. Identify at least six different connotations of recidivism. Which recidivism measures are most popular?

5. Which recidivism measure seems most realistic and why?

6. What are some general characteristics of recidivists? Is there agreement about these characteristics? Why or why not?

7. How can recidivist characteristics be used to predict offender risk or dangerousness?

8. Should technical program violations be used as a measure of program failure? Which program violations do you believe are most important, given your exposure to standard probation and parole programming?

9. Does the amount of time an offender spends in a probation or parole program influence his or her recidivism potential? Why or why not?

10. Some researchers believe that recidivists tend to commit more serious offenses. Is this true? Why or why not?

11. In what respect(s) is/are reincarcerations misleading as evidence of parole program failure?

12. How can recidivism be decreased? What are some strategies experts have proposed for reducing recidivism among probationers and parolees?

SUGGESTED READINGS

Bloom, Barbara et al. (2002). "Moving Toward Justice for Female Juvenile Offenders in the New Millennium: Modeling Gender-Specific Policies and Programs." *Journal of Contemporary Criminal Justice 18:*37–56.

Dowdy, Eric R., Michael G. Lacy, and N. Probha Unnithan (2002). "Correctional Prediction and the Level of Supervision Inventory." *Journal of Criminal Justice 30:*29–39.

Friendship, Caroline, Anthony R. Beech, and Kevin D. Browne (2002). "Reconviction as an Outcome Measure in Research." *British Journal of Criminology 42:*442–444.

Jackson, Yo (2002). "Mentoring for Delinquent Children: An Outcome Study with Young Adolescent Children." *Journal of Youth and Adolescence 31:*115–122.

Laycock, Gloria et al. (2003). "Methodological Issues in Working with Policy Advisors and Practitioners." In Nick Tilley, *Analysis for Crime Prevention.* Monsey, NY: Criminal Justice Press.

Mosher, Clayton J., Terence D. Miethe, and Dretha M. Phillips (2002). *The Mismeasure of Crime.* Thousand Oaks, CA: Sage.

Presser, Lois and Patricia Van Voorhis (2002). "Values and Evaluation: Assessing Processes and Outcomes of Restorative Justice Programs." *Crime and Delinquency 48:*162–188.

Zimring, Franklin (2003). *The Contradictions of American Capital Punishment.* New York: Oxford University Press.

INTERNET CONNECTIONS

Abstract on Recidivism
http://www.hare.org/abstracts/loza1.html

Basic Guide to Program Evaluation
http://www.eval.org/EvaluationDocuments/ progeval.html

Bureau of Data and Research Program Accountability Measures
http://www.djj.state.fl.us/RnD/r_digest/ issue37/issue37.pdf

Expert Program Evaluation Services
http://www.statistics-talk.com

Guidelines for State Parole Program Evaluation
http://www.csulb.edu/~ddowell/guidelines .htm

The NIJ Research Review
http://www.ncjrs.org/rr/vol1_1/17.html

Oregon Department of Corrections Recidivism of New Parolees
http://www.doc.state.or.us/research/Recid .pdf

Recidivism of Adult Felons
http://www.auditor.leg.state.mn.us/ped/ pedrep/9701-sum.pdf

Recidivism of Adult Probationers
http://www.co.hennepin.mn.us/commcorr/ reports/RecidivismofAdultProbationers.htm

Glossary

Abnormal physical structure Explanation of criminal conduct using physical indicators such as the shape of earlobes, head shapes and contours, and body deformities that are viewed as contributory to deviance or crime.

Absconders Persons who flee their jurisdictions while on probation, parole, work release, study release, or furloughs without permission.

Acceptance of responsibility Acknowledg-ment by convicted offenders that they are responsible for their actions and have rendered themselves totally and absolutely accountable for the injuries or damages they may have caused; used by judges to mitigate sentences during sentencing hearings; an integral factor in U.S. sentencing guidelines offense severity calculations, influencing numbers of months of confinement offenders may receive.

Acquired Immune Deficiency Syndrome (AIDS)/Human Immunodeficiency Virus (HIV) A condition in which the body's immune system is unable to fight illness and disease, making sufferers susceptible to a host of infections that otherwise do not affect healthy people; a possible consequence of HIV infection.

Actuarial prediction Anticipation of future inmate behavior based on a class of offenders similar to those considered for parole.

Adjudication Decision by juvenile court judge deciding whether juvenile is delinquent, status offender, or dependent/neglected; finding may be "not delinquent."

Adjudicatory hearing Formal proceeding involving a prosecutor and defense attorney where evidence is presented and the juvenile's guilt or innocence is determined by the juvenile court judge.

Admin max Level of security designation to denote a penitentiary that holds only prisoners with extensive criminal histories who are escape-prone or especially violent. The highest security level exists at such facilities.

Aftercare General term to describe a wide variety of programs and services available to both adult and juvenile probationers and parolees; includes halfway houses, psychological counseling services, community-based correctional agencies, employment assistance, and medical treatment for offenders or ex-offenders.

Agency The special relation between an employer and an employee whereby the employee acts as an agent of the employer, able to make decisions and take actions on the employer's behalf.

Aggravating circumstances Factors that enhance one's sentence; these include whether serious bodily injury or death occurred to a victim during crime commission and whether offender was on parole at time of crime.

Alcoholics Anonymous Voluntary organization originating in 1935. Membership consists of people who are either addicted to alcohol or wish to avoid becoming addicted to alcohol. Group meets informally, discusses family, personal and social problems that contributed to alcohol abuse and ways of overcoming such problems. Employs a multistep program with social support to avoid alcohol on a day-to-day basis. Occasionally used in conjunction with state sanctions for individuals convicted of driving while intoxicated.

Alternative care cases Borderline cases where judges may sentence offenders to either incarceration or probation subject to compliance with various conditions.

Alternative dispute resolution (ADR) Proce-dure whereby a criminal case is redefined as a civil one and the case is decided by an impartial arbiter, where both parties agree to amicable settlement; criminal court is not used for resolving such matters; usually reserved for minor offenses.

Alternative sentencing Also creative sentencing where judge imposes sentence other than incarceration; often involves good works such as community service, restitution to victims, and other public service activity.

American Correctional Association (ACA) Established in 1870 to disseminate information about correctional programs and correctional training; designed to foster professionalism throughout correctional community.

Anamnestic prediction Anticipation of inmate behavior according to past circumstances.

Anomie Condition of normlessness as set forth in Robert K. Merton's theory of anomie.

Anomie theory Robert Merton's theory, alleging persons acquire desires for culturally approved goals to strive to achieve, but they adopt innovative, sometimes deviant, means to achieve these goals; anomie implies normlessness; innovators accept societal goals but reject institutionalized means to achieve them.

Apprehension units Specific departments within correctional services that pursue those who leave their jurisdictions without permission or abscond; probation and parole departments have apprehension units dedicated to hunting down absconders.

Arraignment Proceeding following an indictment by a grand jury or a finding of probable cause from a preliminary hearing; determines (1) plea; (2) specification of final charges against defendant(s); and (3) trial date.

Arrest Taking persons into custody and restraining them until they can be brought before court to answer the charges against them.

Assessment centers Agencies designed for selecting entry-level officers for correctional work; assessment centers hire correctional officers and probation or parole officers.

Auburn State Penitentiary Prison constructed in New York in 1816; known for its creation of tiers, or different levels of custody for different types of offenders; also known for use of striped clothing for prisoners to distinguish them from the general population if prisoners escape confinement; also known for congregate system, where offenders could dine in large eating areas; also used solitary confinement; custody levels are medium and maximum.

Augustus, John Private citizen acknowledged as formulator of probation in U.S. in Boston, Massachusetts, 1841.

Automatic waivers (also **Legislative waivers**) Actions initiated by state legislatures where-by certain juvenile offenders are sent to criminal courts for processing rather than to juvenile courts; usually requires a certain age range (16–17) and prescribed list of offenses (e.g., rape, homicide, armed robbery, arson); a type of certification or waiver or transfer.

Avertable recidivists Offenders who would still have been in prison serving a sentence at a time when new offense was committed.

Bail A surety to procure the release of those under arrest and to assure that they will appear later to face criminal charges in court; also known as a bailbond.

Balanced approach View of offender rehabilitation that stresses heightening offender accountability, individualizing sanctions or punishments, and promoting community safety.

Banishment Punishment form used for many centuries as a sanction for violations of the law or religious beliefs. Those found guilty of crimes or other infractions were ordered to leave their communities and never return; in many instances, this was the equivalent of the death penalty, since communities were often isolated and no food or water were available within distances of hundreds of miles from these communities (see also Transport).

Behavioral reform John Augustus's attempt to change behaviors of persons charged with crimes in early 1840s; Augustus believed that changes in one's behaviors could be influenced by periods of probation, contrition, and abstinence (e.g., from alcohol).

Beyond a reasonable doubt Standard used in criminal courts to establish guilt or innocence of criminal defendant.

Biological theories Explanations of criminal conduct which emphasize the genetic transmission of traits that figure prominently in deviant behavior; any explanation that focuses upon biology and heredity as sources of criminal behavior.

Blended sentencing statutes Provisions adopted by 22 states in 1999 that permit juvenile or criminal court judges to impose either juvenile or adult punishments or both upon juveniles convicted of crimes.

Bonding theory A key concept in a number of theoretical formulations. Emile Durkheim's notion that deviant behavior is controlled to the degree that group members feel morally bound to one another, are committed to common goals, and share a collective conscience. In social control theory, the elements of attachment, commitment, involvement, and belief; explanation of criminal behavior implying that criminality is the result of a loosening of bonds or attachments with society; builds on differential association theory. Primarily designed to account for juvenile delinquency.

Booking An administrative procedure designed to furnish personal background information to a bonding company and law enforcement officials. Booking includes compiling a file for defendants, including their name, address, telephone number, age, place of work, relatives, and other personal data.

Boot camps Highly regimented, military-like, short-term correctional programs (90–180 days) where offenders are provided with strict discipline, physical training, and hard labor resembling some aspects of military basic training; when successfully completed, boot camps provide for transfers of participants to community-based facilities for nonsecure supervision.

Boston House of Corrections Jail where convicted offenders were confined for various offenses, including drunkenness and disorderly behavior; operated during 1830s and 1840s.

Bridewell Workhouse Established in 1557 in London, England; designed to house vagrants and general riffraff; noted for exploitation of inmate labor by private mercantile interests.

Brockway, Zebulon First superintendent of New York State Reformatory at Elmira in 1876; arguably credited with introducing first "good-time" system whereby inmates could have their sentences reduced or shortened by the number of good marks earned through good behavior.

Broker PO work role orientation where PO functions as a referral service and supplies offender-client with contacts at agencies who provide needed services.

Bureau of Justice Statistics Bureau created in 1979 to distribute statistical information concerning crime, criminals, and crime trends.

Burnout Psychological equivalent of physical stress, characterized by a loss of motivation and commitment related to task performance.

Camps Nonsecure youth programs, usually located in rural settings, designed to instill self-confidence and interpersonal skills for juvenile offenders; also known as Wilderness Programs.

Career criminals Those offenders who earn their living through crime; they go about their criminal activity in much the same way workers or professional individuals engage in their daily work activities; career criminals often consider their work as a "craft," since they acquire considerable technical skills and competence in the performance of crimes.

Caseload Number of clients or offenders probation or parole officers must supervise during any given time period, such as one week or one month.

Caseworker Any probation or parole officer who works with probationers or parolees as clients; term originates from social work where caseworkers attempt to educate, train, or rehabilitate those lacking coping skills.

Cellular telephone devices Electronic monitoring equipment worn by offenders that emits radio signal received by local area monitor.

Certification (see **Transfers**)

Charge reduction plea bargaining Type of plea bargaining where the inducement from the prosecutor is a reduction in the seriousness of charge or number of charges against a defendant in exchange for a guilty plea.

Children in need of supervision (CHINS) Any youth who has no responsible parent or guardian and needs one.

Children's tribunal Early form of court dealing with juvenile offending; 1850s through 1890s; informal judicial mechanisms for evaluating seriousness of juvenile offenders and prescribing punishments for them.

Child-saver movement Largely religious in origin, loosely organized attempt to deal with unsupervised youth following the Civil War; child-savers were interested in the welfare of youths who roamed city streets unsupervised.

Child-savers Philanthropists who believed that children ought to be protected; originated following the Civil War.

Child sexual abusers Adults who involve minors in virtually any kind of sexual activity ranging from intercourse with children to photographing them in lewd poses.

Chronic offenders Repeat offenders who continually reoffend; repeat offenses and new convictions may be for misdemeanors or felonies, but there is a continuation of offending over a period of years; persistent offenders.

Civil Rights Act Title 42, Section 1983 of the U. S. Code permitting inmates of prisons and jails as well as probationers and parolees the right to sue their administrators and/or supervisors under the "due process" and "equal protection" clauses of the Fourteenth Amendment.

Clark, Benjamin C. Philanthropist and "volunteer" probation officer who assisted courts with limited probation work during 1860s; carried on John Augustus's work commenced in early 1840s.

Classification Attempts to categorize offenders according to type of offense, dangerousness, public risk, special needs, and other relevant criteria; used in institutional settings (prisons) for purposes of placing inmates in more or less close custody and supervision.

Classification system Means used by prisons and probation/parole agencies to separate offenders according to offense seriousness, type of offense, and other criteria; no classification system has been demonstrably successful at effective prisoner or client placements; any means of determining the dangerousness or risk of offenders in order to place them in either specific community programs or appropriate custody levels while confined.

Client-specific planning Caseload assignment method where individualization of caseload assignments is stressed, depending upon particular offender needs and certain PO skills useful in fulfilling those needs.

Clinical prediction Anticipation of inmate behavior based upon professional's expert training and working directly with offenders.

Code of ethics Regulations formulated by major professional societies that outline the specific problems and issues that are frequently encountered in the types of research carried out within a particular profession. Serves as a guide to ethical research practices.

Cognitive development Stages in the learning process where a person acquires abilities to think and express him- or herself; thoughts about the feelings of others are acquired.

Cognitive development theory Also called developmental theory, stresses stages of learning process whereby persons acquire abilities to think and express themselves, respect the property and rights of others, and cultivate a set of moral values.

Combination sentence (see **Split sentencing**)

Common law Authority based on court decrees and judgments that recognize, affirm, and enforce certain usages and customs of the people. Laws determined by judges in accordance with their rulings.

Community-based corrections Several types of programs that manage offenders within the community instead of prison or jail; includes electronic monitoring, day-fine programs, home confinement, intensive supervised probation/parole.

Community-based supervision Reintegrative programs operated publicly or privately to assist offenders by providing therapeutic, support, and supervision programs for criminals; may include furloughs, probation, parole, community service, and restitution.

Community control A Florida community-based correctional program involving home confinement and electronic monitoring for offender supervision.

Community control house arrest Florida program where offenders are confined to their own homes, instead of prison, where they are allowed to serve their sentences.

Community corrections Any one of several different types of programs designed to supervise probationers and parolees; includes but not limited to home confinement, electronic monitoring, day reporting centers, probation, parole, intensive supervised probation, intensive supervised parole, furloughs, halfway houses, work release, and study release.

Community corrections act Statewide mechanism included in legislation whereby funds are granted to local units of government and community agencies to develop and deliver "front end" alternative sanctions in lieu of state incarceration.

Community Education Centers (CEC) Estab-lished in Denver, Colorado, and Newark, New Jersey, includes several programs aimed at incarcerated women with substance abuse problems; includes educational instruction on relapse prevention, vocational and educational guidance, individual and group counseling, and equipping women with productive life skills.

Community model Relatively new concept based on the correctional goal of offender reintegration into the community; stresses offender adaptation to the community by participating in one or more programs that are a part of community-based corrections.

Community reintegration Process whereby offender who has been incarcerated is able to live in community under some supervision and gradually adjust to life outside of prison or jail; theory is that transition to community life from regimentation of prison life can be eased through community-based correctional program and limited community supervision.

Community residential centers Transitional agencies located in neighborhoods where offenders may obtain employment counseling, food and shelter, and limited supervision pertaining to one or more conditions of probation or parole; an example might be day reporting/treatment program.

Community service Sentence imposed by judges in lieu of incarceration where offenders are obligated to perform various tasks that assist the community and help to offset the losses suffered by victims or the community at large.

Community service orders Symbolic restitution, involving redress for victims, less severe sanctions for offenders, offender rehabilitation, reduction of demands on the criminal justice system, and a reduction of the need for vengeance in a society, or a combination of these factors.

Community work (see **Work release**)

Commutation Administratively authorized early release from custody; e.g., prisoners serving life terms may have their sentences commuted to 10 years.

Concurrent jurisdiction (see **Direct file**)

Conditional diversion program Plan where divertees is involved in some degree of local monitoring by probation officers or personnel affiliated with local probation departments.

Conditional release Any release of inmates from custody with various conditions or program requirements; parole is a conditional release; any release to a community-based corrections program is a conditional release.

Conflict criminology (see **Radical criminology**)

Conflict/Marxist theory (see **Radical criminology**)

Conflict theory (see **Radical criminology**)

Congregate system A prison management system that allows inmates to work together and eat their meals with one another during daylight hours.

Containment theory Explanation elaborated by Walter Reckless and others that positive self-image enables persons otherwise disposed toward criminal behavior to avoid criminal conduct and conform to societal values. Every person is a part of an external structure and has a protective internal structure providing defense, protection, and/or insulation against one's peers, such as delinquents.

Continuous signalling devices Electronic monitoring devices that broadcast an encoded signal that is received by a receiver-dialer in the offender's home (see **Electronic monitoring**).

Continuous signalling transmitters Appara-tuses worn around the ankle or wrist that emit continuous electronic signals that may be received by POs who drive by an offender's dwelling with a reception device.

Contract prisoners Inmates from state or federal prison systems who are accommodated in local jails for designated periods such as one or more years at reduced rates in order to reduce prison overcrowding.

Conventional model Caseload assignment model where probation or parole officers are assigned clients randomly.

Conventional model with geographic considerations Similar to conventional model; caseload assignment model is based upon the travel time required for POs to meet with offender-clients regularly.

Cook, Rufus R. Philanthropist who continued John Augustus's work, particularly assisting juvenile offenders through the Boston Children's Aid Society in 1860.

Corrections The aggregate of programs, services, facilities, and organizations responsible for the management of people who have been accused or convicted of criminal offenses.

Corrections officers Personnel who work in any correctional institution, such as a jail, prison, or penitentiary; formerly known as "guards"; preferred term currently as per American Correctional Association and American Jail Association resolutions.

Corrections volunteer Any unpaid person who performs auxiliary, supplemental, or any other work or services for any law enforcement, court, or corrections agency.

Courts Public judiciary bodies that apply the law to controversies and oversee the administration of justice.

Creaming Term to denote admitting only the most qualified offenders to a rehabilitative program; these offenders are low-risk, unlikely to reoffend, and very likely to succeed.

Creative sentencing Name applied to a broad class of punishments that offer alternatives to incarceration and that are designed to fit a particular crime.

Crime classification index Selected list of offenses that are used to portray crime trends; index offenses are usually divided into Type I or more serious offenses, and Type II offenses or less serious offenses; compiled by Federal Bureau of Investigation and Department of Justice.

Crime control A model of criminal justice that emphasizes containment of dangerous offenders and societal protection.

Crimes Violations of the law by persons held accountable under the law; must involve *mens rea* and *actus reus* as two primary components.

Crimes against the person Less frequently used term to describe a criminal act involving direct contact with another person and/or injury to that person, usually where a dangerous weapon is used; person crimes include aggravated assault, rape, homicide, robbery, more recently designated as violent crime; presently such crimes are considered violent crimes or crimes of violence.

Crimes against property Any criminal act not directly involving a victim; e.g., burglary, vehicular theft (not carjacking); larceny; arson (of an unoccupied dwelling); more recently designated as property crime.

Crimes of violence Any crime involving potential or actual injury to a victim, where a weapon is used to facilitate the offense; usually includes homicide, rape, or aggravated assault.

Criminal contamination Belief that if ex-offenders live together or associate closely with one another, they would spread their criminality like a disease; fear originally aroused from construction of halfway houses for parolees.

Criminal exclusive blended sentence Statute providing that criminal court judges may impose either a juvenile punishment or an adult punishment on juveniles convicted of one or more crimes, but both juvenile and adult punishments shall not be imposed simultaneously.

Criminal inclusive blended sentence Statute providing that criminal court judges may impose both juvenile and adult punishments on juveniles convicted of one or more crimes.

Criminal justice system Integrated network of law enforcement, prosecution and courts, and corrections designed to process criminal offenders from detection to trial and punishment; interrelated set of agencies and organizations designed to control criminal behavior, detect crime, and apprehend, process, prosecute, rehabilitate, and/or punish criminals.

Criminal trial An adversarial proceeding within a particular jurisdiction, where a judicial determination of issues can be made, and where a defendant's guilt or innocence can be decided impartially.

Criminogenic environment Typically, prisons are viewed as "colleges of crime" where inmates are not rehabilitated but rather learn more effective criminal techniques; any interpersonal situation where the likelihood of acquiring criminal behaviors is enhanced.

Critical criminology A school of criminology that holds that criminal law and the criminal justice system have been created to control the poor and have-nots of society. Crimes are defined depending upon how much power is wielded in society by those defining crime.

Crofton, Sir Walter Director of Ireland's prison system during 1850s; considered "father of parole" in various European countries; established system of early release for prisoners; issued "tickets of leave" as an early version of parole.

Cultural transmission theory Explanation emphasizing transmission of criminal behavior through socialization. Views delinquency as socially learned behavior transmitted from one generation to the next in disorganized urban areas.

Custodial disposition Punishment imposed by juvenile courts that may involve either secure or nonsecure confinement in a detention facility or group home.

Dangerousness Defined differently in several jurisdictions: prior record of violent offenses; potential to commit future violent crimes if released; propensity to inflict injury.

Day fines A two-step process whereby courts (1) use a unit scale or benchmark to sentence offenders to certain numbers of day-fine units (e.g., 15, 30, 120) according to offense severity and without regard to income; and (2) determine the value of each unit according to a percentage of the offender's daily income; total fine amounts are determined by multiplying this unit value by the number of units accompanying the offense.

Day parole (see **Work release**)

Day pass (see **Work release**)

Day reporting centers Operated primarily during daytime hours for the purpose of providing diverse services to offenders and their families; defined as a highly structured non-residential program utilizing supervision, sanctions, and services coordinated from a central focus; offenders live at home and report to these centers regularly; provides services according to offender needs; these services might include employment assistance, family counseling, and educational/vocational training; may be used for supervisory and/or monitoring purposes; client behavior modification is a key goal of such centers.

Defendants Persons who have been charged with one or more crimes.

Defendant's sentencing memorandum Version of events leading to conviction offense in the words of the convicted offender; version may be submitted together with victim impact statement.

Defense counsel Any lawyer who represents and defends someone accused of a crime in court.

Delinquency Any act committed by an infant of not more than a specified age who has violated criminal laws or engages in disobedient, indecent, or immoral conduct and is in need of treatment, rehabilitation, or supervision; status acquired through an adjudicatory proceeding by juvenile court.

Delinquent A juvenile who commits an offense that would be a crime if committed by an adult.

Delinquent subcultures Close associations formed between youths who have committed crimes; bonds formed and patterns of behavior closely resemble societal rules such that these groupings are referred to as subcultures; characteristics include ways of gaining status and recognition or promotion.

Demand waivers Actions filed by juveniles and their attorneys to have a case in juvenile court transferred to the jurisdiction of criminal courts.

Department of Justice Organization headed by Attorney General of United States; responsible for prosecuting federal law violators; oversees Federal Bureau of Investigation and the Drug Enforcement Administration.

Dependent and neglected children Official category used by juvenile court judges to determine whether juveniles should be placed in foster homes and taken away from parents or guardians who may be deemed unfit; children who have no or little familial support or supervision.

Deserts model Way of viewing punishment in proportion to offense seriousness; the punishment should fit the crime.

Detainer warrants Notices of criminal charges or unserved sentences pending against prisoners in the same or other jurisdictions.

Detector PO work role orientation where PO attempts to identify troublesome clients or those who are most likely to pose high community risk.

Detention Any holding of a juvenile for a specified period to await an adjudicatory proceeding.

Detention hearing Judicial or quasi-judicial proceeding held to determine whether it is appropriate to continue to hold or detain a juvenile in a shelter facility.

Determinate sentencing Sentence involving confinement for a fixed period of time and which must be served in full and without parole board intervention, less any good time earned in prison.

Deterrence Actions that are designed to prevent crime before it occurs by threatening severe criminal penalties or sanctions; may include safety measures to discourage potential lawbreakers such as elaborate security systems, electronic monitoring, and greater police officer visibility.

Differential association theory Edwin Sutherland's theory of deviance and criminality through associations with others who are deviant or criminal. Theory includes dimensions of frequency, duration, priority, and intensity; persons become criminal or delinquent because of a preponderance of learned definitions that are favorable to violating the law over learned definitions unfavorable to it.

Differential reinforcement theory In social learning theory, strengthening or increasing the likelihood of the future occurrence of some voluntary act. Positive reinforcement is produced by rewarding behavior, negative reinforcement by an unpleasant or punishing stimulus. Differential reinforcement is produced when a person comes to prefer one behavior over another as the result of more rewards and less punishment. Self-reinforcement refers to self-imposed positive or negative sanctions.

Direct file Condition where prosecutor has sole authority to determine whether juvenile will be prosecuted in juvenile or criminal court.

Direct supervision jails Constructed so as to provide officers with 180-degree lines of sight to monitor inmates; employ a podular design; modern facilities also combine closed-circuit cameras to continuously observe inmates while celled.

Discretionary parole Condition to release offender from incarceration whose sentence has not expired, on condition of sustained lawful behavior that is subject to supervision and monitoring by parole personnel who ensure compliance with terms of release.

Discretionary waivers (see **Judicial waivers**)

Diversion The official halting or suspension of legal proceedings against criminal defendants after a recorded justice system entry, and possible referral of those persons to treatment or care programs administered by a nonjustice or private agency (See also Pretrial release).

Diversion programs (see **also Diversion**) Several types of programs preceding formal court adjudication of charges against defendants; defendants participate in therapeutic, educational, or other helping programs; may result in expungement of criminal charges originally filed against defendant; may include participation in Alcoholics Anonymous or driver's training programs.

Divertees Persons who participate in a diversion program or are otherwise granted diversion.

Double jeopardy Fifth Amendment guarantee that protects against a second prosecution for the same offense following acquittal or conviction for the offense and against multiple punishments for the same offense.

Drug courts Special courts that handle only drug cases and are designed to work with prosecutors, defense counsels, treatment professionals, and probation officers to achieve a case outcome that is in the best interests of drug-involved offenders; established in 1989.

Due process model (see **Justice model**) Emphasizes one's constitutional right to a fair trial and consistent treatment under the law; the "equal protection" clause of the Fourteenth Amendment is also stressed; sentencing disparities attributable to race, ethnic origin, gender, or socioeconomic status should not to be tolerated.

Early Head Start Program Provides intensive parenting classes for imprisoned pregnant women; enables incarcerated women to keep their babies for up to 18 months before being released to prerelease centers, where they may be placed for an additional 18 months; a reintegrative process.

Early release (see **Parole**)

Earned good time Credit earned and applied against one's maximum sentence through participation in GED programs, vocational/technical programs, counseling, and self-help groups while in prison.

Ectomorph Body type described by Sheldon; person is thin, sensitive, delicate.

Educator (see **Enabler**)

Ego Sigmund Freud's term describing the embodiment of society's standards, values, and conventional rules.

Electronic monitoring Use of telemetry devices to verify that an offender is at a specified location at specified times.

Elmira Reformatory Institution constructed in Elmira, New York, in 1876; experimented with certain new rehabilitative philosophies espoused by various penologists including its first superintendent, Zebulon Brockway (1827–1920); considered the new penology and used the latest scientific information in its correctional methods; used a military model comparable to contemporary boot camps; prisoners performed useful labor and participated in educational or vocational activities, where their productivity and good conduct could earn them shorter sentences; inmates were trained in close-order drill, wore military uniforms, and paraded about with wooden rifles; authorities regarded this as a way of instilling discipline in inmates and reforming them; Elmira Reformatory credited with individualizing prisoner treatment and the use of indeterminate sentencing directly suited for parole actions; widely imitated by other state prison systems subsequently.

Enabler PO work role orientation where PO seeks to instruct and assist offenders in dealing with problems as they arise.

Endomorph Body type described by Sheldon; person is fat, soft, plump, jolly.

Enforcer PO work role orientation where POs see themselves as enforcement officers charged with regulating client behaviors.

Exculpatory evidence Any evidence or material that shows or supports a defendant's innocence.

Experience programs (see **Wilderness programs**)

Expungement The act of removing one or more records of an arrest or conviction from an offender's court files and other legal documents; usually ordered by the court following a successful diversion program.

Expungement order (see **also Sealing of record**) Act of removing a juvenile's record from public view; issued by juvenile court judges, order instructs police and juvenile agencies to destroy any file material related to juvenile's conduct.

False negatives Offenders predicted not to be dangerous but who turn out to be dangerous.

False positives Offenders predicted to be dangerous but who turn out not to be dangerous.

Federal Bureau of Investigation (FBI) Investigative agency that is the enforcement arm of the Department of Justice; investigates over 200 different kinds of federal law violations; maintains extensive files on criminals; assists other law agencies.

Felony Crime punishable by imprisonment in prison for a term of one or more years; a major crime; an index crime.

Felony probation Procedure of granting convicted felons probation in lieu of incarceration, usually justified because of prison overcrowding; involves conditional sentence in lieu of incarceration.

Female Offender Regimented Treatment Program (FORT) Oklahoma program for incarcerated women, especially first offenders, with disciplinary problems and substance-abuse issues; aims are to reduce prison over-crowding and recidivism; program elements include substance-abuse counseling, strict military discipline, and self-esteem enhancing experiences.

Fines Financial penalties imposed at time of sentencing convicted offenders; most criminal statutes contain provisions for the imposition of monetary penalties as sentencing options.

First-offenders Criminals who have no prior record of criminal activity.

First-time offenders Criminals who have no previous criminal records; these persons may have committed crimes, but they have only been caught for their current offense.

Flat time Actual amount of incarceration inmates must serve before becoming eligible for parole or early release.

Florida Assessment Center One of the first state corrections agencies to establish center for selection of entry-level correctional officers; uses intensive screening procedures for selecting applicants for officer positions.

Foster homes Temporary placements in a home where family setting is regarded as vital; children in need of supervision targeted for out-of-own-home placement.

Freedom of Information Act (FOIA) Act that makes it possible for private citizens to examine certain public documents containing information about them, including IRS information or information compiled by any other government agency, criminal or otherwise.

Front-end solution Any solution for jail and prison overcrowding prior to placement of convicted offenders in jail or prison settings; programs include diversion, probation, and any community-based correctional program.

Furlough programs Authorized, unescorted leaves for inmates; designed to permit incarcerated offenders opportunity of leaving prison temporarily to visit their homes with promise to return to facility at expiration of furlough.

Furloughs Authorized, unescorted leaves from confinement granted for specific purposes and for designated time periods.

Gang Self-formed associations of peers, united by mutual interests, with identifiable leadership and organization, who act collectively or as individuals to achieve specific purposes, including the conduct of illegal activity, or the control of a particular territory, facility, or enterprise.

Gang units Special departments in police, probation, or parole agencies dedicated to identifying and supervising the activities of gang members.

Gaol Early English term for a contemporary jail (pronounced "jail").

Georgia Intensive Supervision Probation Program (GISPP) Program begun in 1982 that established three phases of punitive probation conditions for probationers; phases moved probationers through extensive monitoring and control to less extensive monitoring, ranging from 6 to 12 months; program has demonstrated low rates of recidivism among participants.

Get-tough movement General trend among sentencing reformers and others to toughen current sentencing laws and punishments to require offenders to serve more time; philosophy of punishment advocating less use of probation and more use of incarceration.

Global positioning satellite system (GPS) Network of satellites, built by the U.S. Department of Defense, that pinpoints targets and guides bombs. Currently used by some jurisdictions for the purpose of tracking probationers and parolees and their whereabouts.

Good marks Credits obtained by prisoners in nineteenth century England where prisoners were given credit for participating in educational programs and other self-improvement activities.

Good time Credit applied to a convicted offender's sentence based upon the amount of time served; states vary in allowable "good time"; average is 15 days off of maximum sentence for every 30 days served in prison or jail; incentive for good behavior, thus called "good time"; the amount of time deducted from the period of incarceration of a convicted offender; calculated as so many days per month on the basis of good behavior while incarcerated.

Good-time system Method introduced by Elmira Reformatory in 1876 where an inmate's sentence to be served is reduced by the number of good marks earned; once this system was in operation and shown to be moderately effective, several other states patterned their own early-release standards after it in later years.

Grand jury Special jury convened in about one half of all states; comprised of various citizens; numbers vary among states; purposes are to investigate criminal activity or determine probable cause that a crime has been committed and a designated suspect probably committed it; yields "true bill" or indictment or presentment, or "no true bill," finding insufficient probable cause to merit indictment.

Group homes Also known as group centers or foster homes, these are facilities for juveniles that provide limited supervision and support; juveniles live in home-like environment with other juveniles and participate in therapeutic programs and counseling; considered nonsecure custodial.

Guidelines-based sentencing Also known as presumptive sentencing, this form of sentencing specifies ranges of months or years for different degrees of offense seriousness or severity and one's record of prior offending; the greater the severity of conduct and the more prior offending, the more incarceration time is imposed; originally used to create objectivity in sentencing and reduce sentencing disparities attributable to gender, race, ethnicity, or socioeconomic status.

Habeas corpus Writ meaning "produce the body"; used by prisoners to challenge the nature and length of their confinement.

Habitual offenders Criminals who engage in continuous criminal activity during their lives; recidivists who continually commit and are convicted of new crimes.

Halfway house Any nonconfining residential facility intended to provide alternative to incarceration as a period of readjustment of offenders to the community after confinement.

Halfway-in houses Dwellings that provide services catering to those probationers in need of limited or somewhat restricted confinement apart from complete freedom of movement in the community.

Halfway-out houses Facilities designed to serve the immediate needs of parolees from those established to accommodate probationers in the community.

Heredity Theory that behaviors are result of characteristics genetically transmitted; criminal behaviors would be explained according to inherited genes from parents or ancestors who are criminal or who have criminal propensities.

Home confinement Called house arrest, home incarceration, intended to house offenders in their own homes with or without electronic devices; reduces prison overcrowding and prisoner costs; intermediate punishment involving the use of offender residences for mandatory incarceration during evening hours after a curfew and on weekends.

Home incarceration (see **Home confinement**)

Hope Center Wilderness Camp Organized network of four interdependent, small living groups of twelve teenagers each; goals are to provide quality care and treatment in a nonpunitive environment, with specific emphases on health, safety, education, and therapy; emotionally disturbed youths whose offenses range from truancy to murder are selected for program participation; informal techniques used, including "aftertalk" (informal discussing during meals), "huddle up" (a group discussion technique), and "powwow" (a nightly fire gathering); special nondenominational religious services are conducted; participants involved in various special events and learn to cook meals outdoors, camp, and other survival skills.

Hope Houses In 1896, Hope House was established in New York City by Maud and Ballington Booth; receiving considerable financial support from a missionary religious society called the Volunteers of America, the Boothes were able to open additional Hope houses in future years in Chicago, San Francisco, and New Orleans.

House arrest (see **Home confinement**)

Howard, John (1726–1790) English prison reformer who influenced upgrading prison conditions throughout England and United States.

Huber Law Legislation passed in Wisconsin in 1913 authorizing the establishment of work release programs.

Id The "I want" part of a person, formed in one's early years; Sigmund Freud's term to depict that part of personality concerned with individual gratification.

Idaho Intensive Supervised Probation Program Launched as a pilot project in 1982; a team consisting of one PO and two surveillance officers closely supervised a small group of low-risk offenders who normally would have been sent to prison; the program was quite successful; in October, 1984, Idaho established a statewide ISP program with legislative approval; this step was seen as a major element in the "get tough on crime" posture taken by the state.

Implicit plea bargaining Entry of guilty plea by defendant with the expectation of receiving a more lenient sentence from authorities.

Incidents A specific criminal act involving one or more victims.

Indeterminate sentencing Sentences of imprisonment by the court for either specified or unspecified durations, with the final release date determined by a parole board.

Index offenses Includes eight serious types of crime used by the FBI to measure crime trends; information is also compiled about twenty-one less serious offenses ranging from forgery and counterfeiting to curfew violations and runaways; index offense information is presented in the UCR for each state, city, county, and township that has submitted crime information during the most recent year.

Indictment A charge against a criminal defendant issued by a grand jury at the request of the prosecutor; the establishment of probable cause by a grand jury that a crime has been committed and a specific named individual committed it.

Infants Legal term applicable to juveniles who have not attained the age of majority; in most states, age of majority is 18.

Information Prosecutor-initiated charge against criminal defendant; a charge against a criminal defendant issued by a prosecutor and based upon a finding of probable cause.

Initial appearance First formal appearance of criminal suspect before a judicial magistrate, usually for the purpose of determining the nature of criminal charges and whether bail should be set.

Intake Process of screening juvenile offenders for further processing within the juvenile justice system.

Intake screening Critical phase where determination is made by probation officer to release juvenile, to detain juvenile, or to release juvenile to parents pending subsequent court appearance.

Intensive probation supervision (IPS) Any program designed to supervise probationers closely, with increased numbers of face-to-face visits by POs and more frequent drug and alcohol checks.

Intensive supervised parole (ISP) Intensified monitoring by POs where more face-to-face visits and drug/alcohol testing are conducted; seems to have a lower amount of recidivism compared with more standardized parole programs.

Intensive supervised probation programs (ISP) Supervised probation under probation officer; involves close monitoring of offender activities by various means (also known as "Intensive Probation Supervision" or IPS).

Intermediate punishments Sanctions involving punishments existing somewhere between incarceration and probation on a continuum of criminal penalties; may include home incarceration and electronic monitoring.

Intermittent confinement Sentence where offender must serve a portion of sentence in jail, perhaps on weekends or specific evenings; considered similar to probation with limited incarceration (see also **Split sentence**).

International Halfway House Association (IHHA) State-operated halfway houses was the creation of the IHHA in Chicago, 1964; although many of the halfway house programs continued to be privately operated after the formation of the IHHA, the growth in the numbers of halfway houses was phenomenal during the next decade; for instance, from 1966 to 1982, the number of halfway houses operating in the United States and Canada rose from 40 to 1,800.

Isaac T. Hopper Home In 1845, the Quakers opened the **Isaac T. Hopper Home** in New York City, followed by the Temporary Asylum for Disadvantaged Female Prisoners established in Boston in 1864 by a reformist group.

Jail A facility built to house short-term offenders serving sentences of less than one year.

Jail as a condition of probation Sentence where judge imposes limited jail time to be served before commencement of probation (See also Split sentence).

Jail boot camps Short-term programs for offenders in a wide age range; those in New York and New Orleans have age limits of 39 years and 45 years respectively; many of the existing jail boot camps target probation or parole violators who may face revocation and imprisonment.

Jail overcrowding Condition that exists whenever the number of inmates in a jail exceeds the number designated as the operating capacity for the jail.

Jail removal initiative Movement to remove juveniles from adult jails.

Job dissatisfaction Lack of interest in work performed by correctional officers; apathy or discontentment with tasks or assignments.

Judicial plea bargaining Type of plea bargaining where judge offers a specific sentence.

Judicial reprieves Temporary relief or postponement of the imposition of a sentence; commenced during Middle Ages at the discretion of judges to permit defendants more time to gather evidence of their innocence or to allow them to demonstrate that they had reformed their behavior.

Judicial waivers (also **Discretionary waivers**) Transfer of jurisdiction over juvenile offenders to criminal court, where judges initiate such action.

Jurisdiction Power of a court to hear and determine a particular case.

Jury trial An entitlement of being charged with a crime carrying a penalty of incarceration of six months or more; an adversarial proceeding involving either a civil or criminal matter that is resolved by a vote of a designated number of one's peers, usually 12 members; as opposed to a "bench trial," where a judge hears a case and decides guilt or innocence of defendants or whether plaintiffs have prevailed against defendants in civil cases.

Just-deserts model (see also **Deserts model**)

Justice model Punishment orientation or philosophy that emphasizes punishment as a primary objective of sentencing; fixed sentences, an abolition of parole, and an abandonment of the rehabilitative ideal.

Juvenile Also known as an infant legally; a person who has not attained his or her eighteenth birthday.

Juvenile Court Act Provided for limited courts of record in 1899 in Illinois, where notes might be taken by judges or their assistants, to reflect judicial actions against juveniles; the jurisdiction of these courts, subsequently designated as "juvenile courts," would include all juveniles under the age of 16 who were found in violation of any state or local law or ordinance; also, provision was made for the care of dependent and/or neglected children who had been abandoned or who otherwise lacked proper parental care, support, or guardianship.

Juvenile delinquency Violation of the law by a person prior to his or her eighteenth birthday; any illegal behavior committed by someone within a given age range punishable by juvenile court jurisdiction.

Juvenile delinquents Any minor who commits an act that would be a crime if committed by an adult.

Juvenile exclusive blended sentence Statute providing that juvenile court judges may impose either a juvenile punishment or an adult punishment on a juvenile convicted of a crime, but a juvenile and an adult punishment may not be imposed simultaneously.

Juvenile inclusive blended sentence Statute providing that juvenile court judges may impose both a juvenile punishment and an adult punishment simultaneously on a juvenile convicted of a crime.

Juvenile intensive supervised probation programs (JISPs) Intensive supervision programs for youthful offenders possessing many of the same features as programs for adults, including more frequent face-to-face visits, curfews, drug and alcohol checks, electronic monitoring, and home confinement.

Juvenile justice system The process through which juveniles are processed, sentenced, and corrected after arrests for juvenile delinquency.

Juvenile offenders (see **Juvenile delinquents**)

Labeling theory Explanation of crime attributed to Edwin Lemert whereby persons acquire self-definitions that are deviant or criminal; persons perceive themselves as deviant or criminal through labels applied to them by others; the more people are involved in the criminal justice system, the more they acquire self-definitions consistent with the criminal label.

Labor turnover The degree to which new POs and correctional officers replace those who quit, die, or retire.

Latent functions Unrecognized, unintended functions; associated with probation or parole, latent functions might be to alleviate prison or jail overcrowding.

Law enforcement The activities of various public and private agencies at local, state, and federal levels that are designed to ensure compliance with formal rules of society that regulate social conduct.

Law Enforcement Assistance Administration (LEAA) Program commenced in 1968 and terminated in 1984, designed to provide financial and technical assistance to local and state police agencies to combat crime in various ways.

Legislative waiver (see **Statutory exclusion**)

Level of custody Degree of supervision and confinement for inmates, depending upon their type of crime committed, whether they pose a danger to themselves or other prisoners, and their past institutional history; varies from minimum-security, medium-security, to maximum-security conditions.

Libido Sigmund Freud's term describing the sex drive believed innate in everyone.

Limited risk control model Method of supervising offenders based on anticipated future criminal conduct; uses risk assessment devices to place offenders in an effective control range.

Lockdown Security measure implemented in prisons that have undergone rioting; usually involves solitary confinement of prisoners for undetermined period; removal of amenities, such as televisions, store privileges.

Lock-ups Short-term facilities to hold minor offenders; include drunk tanks, holding tanks; while these facilities are counted as jails, they exist primarily to hold those charged with public drunkenness or other minor offenses for up to 48 hours; the American Jail Association suggests that to qualify as a true jail, the facility must hold inmates for 72 hours or longer, not 48 hours.

Maconochie, Captain Alexander (1797–1860) Prison reformer and former superintendent of the British penal colony at Norfolk Island and governor of Birmingham Borough Prison; known for humanitarian treatment of prisoners and issuance of "marks of commendation" to prisoners that led to their early release; considered the forerunner of indeterminate sentencing in the United States.

Mandatory parole Type of early release that must be accepted by parole-eligible inmates regardless of whether they do or do not wish to be paroled.

Mandatory release Type of release from jail or prison where inmates have served their full terms or when they have fulfilled sentences specified according to particular sentencing scheme, such as guidelines-based sentencing or determinate sentencing; mandatory releasees would be subject to automatic release upon serving some portion of their incarcerative terms less good-time credits applied for so many months or days served.

Mandatory sentencing Court is required to impose an incarcerative sentence of a specified length, without the option for probation, suspended sentence, or immediate parole eligibility.

Mandatory waiver Transfer initiated by judges who are required to waive jurisdiction over a juvenile to criminal court.

Manifest functions Intended or recognized functions; associated with probation and parole, manifest functions are to permit offender reintegration into society.

Marks of commendation Points accrued by convicts for good behavior under Alexander Maconochie's (1840s) term of leadership at Norfolk Island; authorized early release of some inmates who demonstrated a willingness and ability to behave well in society on the outside; this action was forerunner of indeterminate sentencing subsequently practiced in the United States.

Mark system (see **Tickets of leave**)

Marxist criminology (see **Radical criminology**)

Maxi-maxi (see **Maximum-security**) Level of custody that accommodates the most violence-prone inmates who are inclined to escape whenever the opportunity arises and who are considered extremely dangerous; in many cases, maxi-maxi prison inmates are placed in solitary confinement and severe restrictions are imposed; confinement in isolation for 23 1/2 hours per day with 1/2 hour for exercise is not uncommon; privileges are extremely limited.

Maximum-security Level of custody where prisoners are closely supervised and given little freedom; subject to constant surveillance, often solitary confinement; limited privileges.

Mediation The process of working out mutually satisfactory agreements between victims and offenders; an integral part of alternative dispute resolution.

Mediator (see **Enabler**)

Medical model Also known as "treatment model," this model considers criminal behavior as an illness to be treated.

Medium-security Level of custody in a prison where inmates are given more freedoms compared with maximum-security facilities; their movements are monitored; often, these facilities are dormitory-like, and prisoners are eligible for privileges.

Mens rea Criminal mind or guilty mind; one component of a crime.

Meritorious good time Credit earned and applied against one's maximum sentence to be served in prison for engaging in acts of heroism or other feats that should be recognized for their merit; used in conjunction with determinate sentencing schemes.

Mesomorph Body type described by Sheldon; person is strong, muscular, aggressive, tough.

Minimum due process (see **also Due process**) Rights accorded parolees resulting from *Morrissey v. Brewer* (1972) landmark case; two hearings are required: (a) The first is a preliminary hearing to determine whether probable cause exists that a parolee has violated any specific parole condition; (b) the second is a general revocation proceeding; written notice must be given to the parolee prior to the general revocation proceeding; disclosure must be made to the parolee concerning the nature of parole violation(s) and evidence obtained; parolees must be given the right to confront and cross-examine their accusers unless adequate cause can be given for prohibiting such a cross-examination; a written statement must be provided containing the reasons for revoking the parole and the evidence used in making that decision; the parolee is entitled to have the facts judged by a detached and neutral hearing committee.

Minimum-security Level of custody in a prison that is designated for nonviolent, low-risk offenders; housed in efficiency apartments; inmates permitted family visits, considerable inmate privileges.

Minnesota Multiphasic Personality Inventory (MMPI) Personality assessment measure purportedly measuring several personality traits, such as anxiety, authoritarianism, and sociability.

Minnesota sentencing grid Sentencing guidelines established by Minnesota legislature in 1980 and used by judges to sentence offenders; grid contains criminal history score, offense seriousness, and presumptive sentences to be imposed; judges may depart from guidelines upward or downward depending upon aggravating or mitigating circumstances.

Misdemeanant One who commits a misdemeanor.

Misdemeanor Crime punishable by confinement in city or county jail for a period of less than one year; a lesser offense.

Missouri Sexual Offender Program (MOSOP) Program targeted to serve the needs of incarcerated, nonpsychotic sexual offenders; the program can supervise effectively over 700 offenders who are required to complete the program before becoming eligible for parole; approach is that sex offenders behaviors resulted from learned patterns of behavior associated with anxious, angry, and impulsive individuals; the three-phase program obligates offenders to attend 10 weeks of courses in abnormal psychology and the psychology of sexual offending. In other phases, inmates meet in group therapy sessions to talk out their problems with counselors and other inmates.

Mitigating circumstances Factors that lessen the severity of the crime and/or sentence; such factors include old age, cooperation with police in apprehending other offenders, and lack of intent to inflict injury.

Mixed sentence (see also **Split sentence**) Two or more separate sentences imposed where offenders have been convicted of two or more crimes in the same adjudication proceeding.

Modes of adaptation Robert Merton's typology of how persons orient themselves to societal goals and the means used to achieve those goals.

Narcotics Anonymous. Similar to Alcoholics Anonymous, members band together to avoid the use of narcotics and other drugs.

Narrative Portion of presentence investigation report prepared by probation officer or private agency where description of offense and offender are provided; culminates in and justifies a recommendation for a specific sentence to be imposed on the offender by judges.

National Crime Victimization Survey (NCVS) A random survey of approximately 60,000 dwellings, about 127,000 persons age 12 and over, and approximately 50,000 businesses; smaller samples of persons from these original figures form the database from which crime figures are compiled; carefully worded questions lead people to report incidents that can be classified as crimes. This material is statistically manipulated in such a way so as to make it comparable with *Uniform Crime Report* statistics; this material is usually referred to as victimization data.

National Incident-Based Reporting System (NIBRS) A compendium of incident-level data for a broad range of offenses; all incidents involving crimes are counted, even if they arise out of an ongoing sequence of criminal events (e.g., a suspect robs a liquor store, shoots the clerk, assaults customers, steals a car, and commits vehicular homicide before being arrested by police).

Needs assessment instrument Any questionnaire device that is designed to forecast an offender's problems and required community services (e.g., physical and/or mental health, education, counseling).

Negligence Liability accruing to prison or correctional program administrators and POs as the result of a failure to perform a duty owed clients or inmates or the improper or inadequate performance of that duty; may include negligent entrustment, negligent training, negligent assignment, negligent retention, or negligent supervision (e.g., providing POs with revolvers and not providing them with firearms training).

Net-widening Pulling juveniles into juvenile justice system who would not otherwise be involved in delinquent activity; applies to many status offenders (also known as "widening the net").

Neutralization theory Explanation holds that delinquents experience guilt when involved in delinquent activities and that they respect leaders of the legitimate social order. Their delinquency is episodic rather than chronic, and they adhere to conventional values while drifting into periods of illegal behavior. In order to drift, the delinquent must first neutralize legal and moral values.

Nevada Intensive Supervision Program (NISP) Parole program operated in Nevada that heightens supervision over parolees through more frequent face-to-face contacts, smaller caseloads, more curfew and drug/alcohol checks, graduated internal sanctions, treatment, and other interventions.

New Jersey Intensive Supervision Program (NJISP) Program commenced in 1983 to serve low-risk incarcerated offenders and draws clients from inmate volunteers; program selectivity limits participants through a 7-stage selection process; participants must serve at least 4 months in prison or jail before being admitted to program that monitors their progress extensively; similar to Georgia Intensive Probation Supervision Program in successfulness and low recidivism scores among participants.

New York House of Refuge Established in New York City in 1825 by the Society for the Prevention of Pauperism; an institution largely devoted to managing status offenders, such as runaways or incorrigible children; compulsory education and other forms of training and assistance were provided to these children; the strict, prison-like regimen of this organization was not entirely therapeutic for its clientele; any of the youthful offenders who were sent to such institutions, including the House of Reformation in Boston, were offspring of immigrants.

NIMBY syndrome Meaning "not in my back yard"; refers to attitudes of property owners who live near where community-based correctional facilities are planned for construction; property owners believe they will suffer declined property values and will be at risk because of felons roaming freely near their homes; opposition opinion toward construction of community-based correctional facilities.

No bill, no true bill Finding of a grand jury that insufficient evidence exists to find probable cause against a criminal defendant that a crime was committed and that the suspect committed it.

Nonavertable recidivists Offenders whose prior sentence would not have affected the commission of new crimes.

Norfolk Island Penal colony established on this island in 1840s supervised by Alexander Maconochie; noted for establishment of mark system and marks of commendation leading to contemporary use of good-time credits in U.S. prisons and jails.

Numbers game model Caseload assignment model for probation or parole officers where total number of offender/clients is divided by number of officers.

Objective parole criteria General qualifying conditions that permit parole boards to make nonsubjective parole decisions without regard to an inmate's race, religion, gender, age, or socioeconomic status.

Offender control Philosophy that says if we can't rehabilitate offenders, we can control their behavior while on probation; priority shift in probationer management toward greater use of intermediate punishments designed for better offender monitoring.

Offender rehabilitation Condition achieved when criminals are reintegrated into their communities and refrain from further criminal activity (see **Rehabilitation**).

Offenders Persons convicted of a crime.

Offense seriousness score Indicator based upon criminal offense severity; often used in guidelines-based sentencing schemes such as are used in Minnesota; U.S. sentencing guidelines uses offense seriousness scores to calculate numbers of months of incarceration for convicted offenders, together with one's criminal history score.

Offense severity Seriousness of offense, according to monetary amount involved in theft, embezzlement; degree of injuries inflicted on one or more victims; amount of drugs involved in drug transactions; other alternative measures of crime seriousness.

Once an adult/always an adult provision When juveniles are transferred to criminal court for processing in particular jurisdictions, they will forever after be treated as adults if they commit new offenses, regardless of whether they are still juveniles.

180 Degrees, Inc. Similar to a halfway house for parolees, but it is designed for those who have received no previous treatment for their sex offenses; participation is limited only to those offenders willing to admit they have committed one or more sex offenses and who can function as group members; offenders form men's sexuality groups that meet for 90-minute meetings over a 13-week period; all participants contract with officials to write autobiographies of their offenses, descriptions of the victims, listing of sexual abuse cues, the development of control plans, and personal affirmations.

Overcharging Action by prosecutors of charging a defendant with more crimes than are reasonable under the circumstances; raising the charge to a more serious level, expecting a conviction of lesser crime.

Overcrowding Condition that exists when numbers of prisoners exceed the space allocations for which the jail or prison is designed; often associated with double-bunking or putting two prisoners per cell.

Paraprofessionals Persons who possess some formal training in a given correctional area, are salaried, work specified hours, have formal duties and responsibilities, are accountable to higher-level supervisors for work quality, and have limited immunity under the theory of agency.

Pardon An executive device designed to absolve offenders of their crimes committed and release them, thus alleviating the prison overcrowding situation.

Parens patriae Literally "parent of the country"; refers to doctrine where state oversees the welfare of youth; originally established by King of England and administered through chancellors.

Parole Status of offenders conditionally released from a confinement facility prior to expiration of their sentences, placed under supervision of a parole agency.

Parole board Body of governor-appointed or elected persons who decide whether eligible inmates may be granted early release from incarceration.

Parolees Offenders who have served some time in jail or prison, but have been released prior to serving their entire sentences imposed upon conviction.

Parole officers (POs) Corrections officers who supervise and counsel parolees and perform numerous other duties associated with parolee management.

Parole revocation Two-stage proceeding that may result from a parolee's reincarceration in jail or prison; first stage is a preliminary hearing to determine whether parolee violated any specific parole condition; second stage is to determine whether parole should be cancelled and the offender reincarcerated.

Parole revocation hearing A formal meeting of a parolee with a parole board, where the parole board determines whether a parolee is guilty or innocent of a parole program infraction or rule violation; if guilt is established, then parole board must determine punishment to be imposed, which may include intensification of supervision in present parole program or return to prison; two-stage proceeding to determine (1) whether parolee has committed offense or offenses requiring revocation of parole and (2) what punishment should be imposed; a critical stage.

Participative management Theory of organizations in which employees have some input regarding departmental operations.

Passive officers POs who care little about their clients or societal needs; these persons perform their jobs in a perfunctory manner, going through the motions, doing their jobs and fulfilling minimal job requirements.

Peer courts (see **Youth courts**)

Penitentiary Facility generally designed to be self-contained and to house large numbers of serious offenders for periods of one year or longer; characterized by manned perimeters, walls, electronic security devices, and high custody levels.

Pennsylvania System Devised and used in Walnut Street Jail in 1790 to place prisoners in solitary confinement; predecessor to modern prisons; used solitude to increase penitence and prevent cross-infection of prisoners; encouraged behavioral improvements.

Penological pragmatism Use of early form of parole to release prisoners from prisons to reduce overcrowding; originally used in 1700s, used increasingly in 1800s.

Persistent felony offenders Persons who continually commit new felonies and are convicted of them; repeat offenders.

Persistent offenders Persons who are convicted multiple times for crimes during their lives.

Persons in need of supervision (PINS) Youths who need the supervision and management of an adult guardian or parent.

Petition Official document filed in juvenile court on the juvenile's behalf specifying reasons for court appearance.

Philadelphia Society for Alleviating the Miseries of Public Prisons Established in 1787, Quaker society devoted to improving jail conditions in Philadelphia; consisted of philanthropists and religionists.

Plea bargaining A preconviction agreement between the defendant and the state whereby the defendant pleads guilty with the expectation of either a reduction in the charges, a promise of sentencing leniency, or some other government concession short of the maximum penalties that could be imposed under the law.

Prediction An assessment of some expected future behavior of a person including criminal acts, arrests, or convictions.

Predispositional reports Document prepared by juvenile intake officer for juvenile judge; purpose of report is to furnish the judge with background about juveniles to make a more informed sentencing decision; similar to PSI report.

Preliminary hearing, preliminary examination Hearing by magistrate or other judicial officer to determine if person charged with a crime should be held for trial; proceeding to establish probable cause; does not determine guilt or innocence.

Pre-parole programs Any transitional programs, including work release, study release, furloughs, or other temporary leaves for various purposes; inmates are usually within several months of being granted early release; the intent of such programs is to reintegrate these offenders into their communities gradually and avoid the shock of shifting from highly structured and regulated prison life into community living without prison restrictions and regulations.

Preponderance of evidence Standard used in civil courts to determine defendant or plaintiff liability.

Pre-release Any transitional program that assists inmates in prisons or jails in adapting or adjusting to life in their communities by offering them temporary leaves from their institutions.

Pre-release program Prior to granting parole, inmates may be placed on furloughs or work or study release to reintegrate them gradually back into their communities.

Presentence investigation Activities performed either by a probation officer or private organization to assist judges in sentencing convicted offenders; includes a description of the offense, work background and social history of offender, victim impact statement, educational attainment, work record, and other important details.

Presentence investigation report (PSI) Document prepared by a probation officer, usually at the request of a judge, wherein a background profile of a convicted offender is compiled; includes PO's version of crime committed, convicted offender's statement, victim impact statement, and other relevant data compiled from court records and interviews with persons who know offender and victim.

Presentment A charge issued by a grand jury upon its own authority against a specific criminal defendant; a finding of probable cause against a criminal suspect that a crime has been committed and the named suspect committed it.

President's Commission on Law Enforcement and the Administration of Justice 1967 panel empowered to investigate the state of training and standards used for police officer selection; made recommendations to President of United States to authorize funds to improve officer selection and training methods for general improvement of law enforcement effectiveness.

Presumptive sentencing Punishment prescribed by statute for each offense or class of offense; the sentence must be imposed in all unexceptional circumstances, but where there are mitigating or aggravating circumstances, the judge is permitted some latitude in shortening or lengthening the sentence within specific boundaries, usually with written justification.

Presumptive waiver A transfer in which a juvenile must be waived to criminal court for processing unless he or she can prove he or she is suitable for rehabilitation.

Pretrial detainees Persons charged with crimes and who are placed in custody, usually a jail, prior to their trial.

Pretrial detention Order by court for defendant (juvenile or adult) to be confined prior to adjudicatory proceeding; usually reserved for defendants considered dangerous or likely to flee the jurisdiction if released temporarily.

Pretrial diversion Act of deferring prosecution of a criminal case by permitting defendant to complete a specified period of months or years, usually with conditions; usually persons who comply with behavioral requirements of diversion may have their original charges dismissed, reduced, or expunged.

Pretrial release Freedom from incarceration prior to trial granted to defendants (see **ROR**).

Pretrial services Various duties performed by probation officers for either state or federal courts; may include investigations of persons charged with crimes and bail recommendations.

Preventive detention Constitutional right of police to detain suspects prior to trial without bail, where suspects are likely to flee from the jurisdiction or pose serious risks to others.

Primary deviation Minor violations of the law that are frequently overlooked by police (including "streaking" or swimming in a public pool after hours).

Prison overcrowding Condition resulting whenever inmate population exceeds rated or design capacity.

Prisons Facilities designed to house long-term serious offenders; operated by state or federal government; houses inmates for terms longer than one year.

Privatization General movement in corrections and law enforcement to supplement existing law enforcement agencies and correctional facilities with privately owned and operated institutions, organizations, and personnel; theory is that private management of such organizations can be more cost-effective and reduce capital outlays (taxation) associated with public expenditures for similar functions.

Probable cause Reasonable belief that a crime has been committed and that a specified person accused of the crime committed it.

Probatio A period of proving or trial or forgiveness.

Probation Sentence not involving confinement that imposes conditions and retains authority in sentencing court to modify conditions of sentence or resentence offender for probation violations.

Probationers Persons who do not go to jail or prison, but rather serve a term outside of prison subject to certain behavioral conditions.

Probation officer (PO) Corrections official who functions to monitor convict's progress outside of prison.

Probation officer caseload The number of probationer/clients supervised by probation officer; caseload is determined in different ways, depending upon particular probation agency policies.

Probation revocation The process whereby a judge conducts a two-stage proceeding to determine whether a probationer's probation program should be revoked or terminated; such terminations are based on one or more program infractions, which may include curfew violation, use of illegal drugs, possession of illegal contraband, of commission of a new offense.

Probation Subsidy Program California program implemented in 1965 and providing for local communities with supplemental resources to manage larger numbers of probationers more closely; a part of this subsidization provided for community residential centers where probationers could "check in" and receive counseling, employment assistance, and other forms of guidance or supervision.

Professionalization Equated with acquiring more formal education rather than practical skills involving one-to-one human relationships with different types of offender-clients; more recently associated with improvements in officer selection, training, and education; accreditation measures are implemented to standardize curricula and acquisition of skills that improve one's work proficiency.

Professionals Persons who are members of a learned profession or have achieved a high level of proficiency, competency, and training.

Program evaluation The process of assessing any corrections intervention or program for the purpose of determining its effectiveness in achieving manifest goals; investigates the nature of organizational intervention strategies, counseling, interpersonal interactions, staff quality, expertise, and education, and the success or failure experiences of clients served by any program.

Program for Female Offenders, Inc. (PFO) Pennsylvania program established in 1974, guided by two goals: reforming female offenders and creating economically dependent women; started with a job placement service; training centers were eventually created and operated by different counties on a nonprofit basis; center offerings have included remedial math instruction, English instruction, and clerical classes such as word processing, data entry, and telecommunications skill training; counseling has also been provided for those women with social and psychological problems; currently serves 300 women per year, and the community facilities have a low recidivism rate of only 3.5 percent.

Programmed contact devices Electronic mon-itoring devices; similar to the continuous signal units, except that a central computer calls at random hours being monitored to verify that offenders are where they are supposed to be; offenders answer the telephone and their voices are verified by computer.

Progressive Era 1960s and 1970s time period where liberals stressed rehabilitation for convicted offenders rather than lengthy prison sentences.

Property crimes Felonies or misdemeanors that do not involve direct contact with specific victims; examples include theft, burglary of unoccupied dwellings, vehicular theft (not car-jacking), embezzlement; fraud.

Prosecutions Carrying forth of criminal proceedings against a person culminating in a trial or other final disposition such as a plea of guilty in lieu of trial.

Prosecutors Court officials who commence criminal proceedings against defendants; represents state interests or government interest; prosecutes defendants on behalf of state or government.

Public defender Court-appointed attorney for indigent defendants who cannot afford private counsel.

Public risk A subjective gauge of an offender's perceived dangerousness to the community if released, either on probation or parole; sometimes assessed through risk assessment instruments.

Punitive officers POs who seek to catch their offender-clients in program rule violations by checking up on them more frequently than usual; those POs aggressively seeking to enforce program rules and violate officers.

Radical criminology Stresses control of the poor by the wealthy and powerful. Crime is defined by those in political and economic power in such a way so as to control lower socioeconomic classes (e.g., vagrancy statutes are manifestations of control by wealthy over the poor).

Ranches (see also **Wilderness programs**) Nonsecure facilities for juvenile delinquents designed to promote self-confidence and self-reliance; located in rural settings; involve camping out and other survival activities for confidence building.

Rand Corporation Private institution that conducts investigations and surveys of criminals and examines a wide variety of social issues; located in Santa Monica, California; distributes literature to many criminal justice agencies; contracts with and conducts research for other institutions.

Reality therapy Behavior modification method focusing upon the collaborative relation between a PO and a client; client is accepted for what he or she is, but where behavior is unacceptable; rationalization for behavior is rejected; an outgrowth of developmental theory.

Rearrest One indicator of recidivism; consists of taking parolee or probationer into custody for investigation in relation to crimes committed; not necessarily indicative of new crimes committed by probationers or parolees; may be the result of police officer suspicion.

Recidivism New crime committed by an offender who has served time or was placed on probation for previous offense; tendency to repeat crimes.

Recidivism rates Proportion of offenders who, when released from probation or parole, commit further crimes; measured several different ways, including probation revocation, parole revocation, violating curfew, testing positive for drugs or alcohol, or failing to appear for weekly or monthly meetings with POs.

Recidivists Offenders who have committed previous offenses and are convicted of new crimes.

Reconviction Measure of recidivism where former convicted offenders are found guilty of new crimes by a judge or jury.

Reform schools Early establishments providing secure confinement for more serious types of juvenile offenders; juvenile equivalent to prisons; taught youths various crafts and trade skills; intended to reform youth's behavior; unsuccessful at behavior modification.

Rehabilitation Correcting criminal behavior through educational and other means, usually associated with prisons.

Rehabilitation model Orientation toward offenders that stresses reintegration into society through counseling, education, and learning new ways of relating to others.

Rehabilitative ideal (see **Rehabilitation**)

Reincarceration Return to prison or jail for one or more reasons including parole or probation violations and revocations, rearrests, and reconvictions.

Released on their own recognizance (ROR) Act of releasing defendants charged with crimes into the community prior to trial, without bail or other restrictions; usually ROR defendants have strong community ties and have committed minor or non-violent offenses.

Reparations Damages paid an offender to victims for injuries and property loss because of a crime.

Repeat offenders Habitual offenders who continually reoffend and are convicted of new offenses during a span of years.

Research unit Component of any probation or parole department that compiles extensive information about probationer and parolee characteristics as well as information about prison and jail populations; assists in program planning and developing risk assessment instrumentation and other tasks.

Respondeat superior Doctrine that holds master (supervisor, administrator) liable for actions of slave (employees).

Restitution Stipulation by court that offenders must compensate victims for their financial losses resulting from crime; compensation for psychological, physical, or financial loss by victim; may be imposed as a part of an incarcerative sentence.

Restorative justice Every action that is primarily oriented toward doing justice by repairing the harm that has been caused by a crime.

Reverse waiver hearings Formal meetings with juvenile court judge and criminal court to determine whether youths who have been transferred to criminal court for processing as the result of an automatic waiver or legislative waiver can have this waiver set aside so that the case may be heard in juvenile court.

Reverse waivers Actions filed by juveniles to have their transferred cases waived from criminal court back to juvenile court.

Revocation Action taken by parole board or judge to revoke or rescind the parolee's or probationer's program because of one or more program violations.

Revocation actions Any decision by a judge or parole board to consider revoking a probationer's or parolee's program based upon one or more reasons related to program violations.

Reynolds, James Bronson Early prison reformer, established The University Settlement in 1893 in New York; settlement project ultimately abandoned after Reynolds and others could not demonstrate its effectiveness at reform to politicians and the public generally.

Risk Danger or potential harm posed by an offender, convicted or otherwise; likelihood of being successful if placed in a probation or parole program intended to reintegrate or rehabilitate through community involvement.

Risk assessment Any attempt to characterize the future behaviors of persons charged with or convicted of crimes; involves behavioral forecasts of one's propensity to pose harm or a danger to themselves or to others; usually paper-pencil devices that yield scores of one's potential dangerousness; used for probation and parole decision making.

Risk assessment instruments Predictive device intended to forecast offender propensity to commit new offenses or recidivate.

Risk/needs instruments The same type of device as a risk-assessment instrument, with the exception that items are included that attempt to determine or define necessary services, counseling, education, or any other helpful strategy that will deter offenders from future offending.

Role ambiguity Lack of clarity about work expectations; unfamiliarity with correctional tasks.

Role conflict Clash between personal feelings and beliefs and job duties as probation, parole, or correctional officer.

Rules of Criminal Procedure Formal rules followed by state and federal governments in processing defendants from arrest through trial; these vary from state to state.

Runaways Juveniles who leave their home for long periods without parental consent or supervision; unruly youths who cannot be controlled or managed by parents or guardians.

Salient factor score Numerical value that is used by parole boards and agencies to forecast an offender's risk to the public and future dangerousness; numerical classification that predicts the probability of a parolee's success if parole is granted; different numerical designations indicate years when scoring devices were created.

Scared Straight New Jersey program devised in 1980s where juveniles visit inmates in prisons; inmates talk to youths and scare them with stories of their prison experiences; intended as a delinquency deterrent.

Screening cases Procedure used by prosecutor to define which cases have prosecutive merit and which do not; some screening bureaus are made up of police and lawyers with trial experience.

Secondary deviation Law violations that have become incorporated into person's lifestyle or behavior pattern.

Secure confinement Placement of juvenile offender in facility that restricts movement in community; similar to adult penal facility involving total incarceration.

See Our Side (SOS) Program Prince George's County, Maryland, program established in 1983; SOS is referred to by its directors as a "juvenile aversion" program and dissociates itself from "scare" programs such as Scared Straight; seeks to educate juveniles about the realities of life in prison through discussions and hands-on experience and attempts to show them the types of behaviors that can lead to incarceration; clients coming to SOS are referrals from various sources, including juvenile court, public and private schools, churches, professional counseling agencies, and police and fire departments; youths served by SOS range in age from 12 to 18, and they do not have be adjudicated as delinquent in order to be eligible for participation. SOS consists of four, three-hour phases.

Selective incapacitation Selectively incarcerating individuals who show a high likelihood of repeating their previous offenses; based on forecasts of potential for recidivism; includes but not limited to dangerousness.

Self-reported information Any data about one's personal criminal offending disclosed by the offender other than by official recordings of arrests; any disclosures of crimes committed by offenders which are otherwise unknown to police.

Sentence recommendation plea bargaining Agreement between defense counsel and prosecutor where prosecutor recommends a specific sentence to the judge in exchange for a defendant's guilty plea.

Sentencing Phase of criminal justice process where judge imposes a penalty for a criminal conviction; penalty may include a fine and/or incarceration in a jail or prison for a period of months or years; may also include numerous nonincarcerative punishments, such as community-based corrections.

Sentencing hearing A formal procedure following one's criminal conviction where judge hears evidence from convicted offender and others concerning crime seriousness and impact; PSI report introduced as evidence to influence judicial decision making; additional testimony heard to either mitigate or aggravate sentence imposed.

Sentencing memorandum Core element of pre-sentence investigation report where an offender provides his or her version of the offense and the nature of his or her involvement in that offense; may include mitigating factors that might lessen sentencing severity.

Sentencing Reform Act of 1984 Act that provided federal judges and others with considerable discretionary powers to provide alternative sentencing and other provisions in their sentencing of various offenders.

Sex offenders Persons who commit a sexual act prohibited by law; common types of sex offenders include rapists and prostitutes, although sex offenses may include voyeurism ("peeping toms"), exhibitionism, child sexual molestation, incest, date rape, and marital rape.

Shire-reeves The early English term used to refer to the chief law enforcement officer of counties (shires) who was known as a reeve. Contemporary usage of the term has been abbreviated to "sheriff," who is the chief law enforcement officer of U.S. counties.

Shock incarceration (see **Shock probation**)

Shock parole (see **Shock probation**)

Shock probation (see also **Shock probation programs**) Placing an offender in prison for a brief period, primarily to give him or her a taste of prison life (for "shock value") and then releasing the person into the custody of a probation/parole officer.

Shock probationers Any convicted offenders sentenced to a shock probation program.

Shock probation programs Derived from the fact that judges initially sentence offenders to terms of incarceration, usually in a jail; after offenders have been in jail for a brief period (e.g., 30, 60, 90, or 120 days), they are brought back to reappear before their original sentencing judges; these judges reconsider the original sentences they imposed on these offenders; provided that these offenders behaved well while incarcerated, judges resentence them to probation for specified terms; first used in Ohio in 1964.

Situational offenders First-offenders who commit only the offense for which they were apprehended and prosecuted and are unlikely to commit future crimes.

Social casework An approach to modifying the behavior of criminals by developing a close relation between the PO and client, within a problem-solving context, and coordinated with the appropriate use of community resources.

Social control theory Explanation of criminal behavior that focuses upon control mechanisms, techniques and strategies for regulating human behavior, leading to conformity or obedience to society's rules, and that posits that deviance results when social controls are weakened or break down, so that individuals are not motivated to conform to them.

Socialization Learning through contact with others.

Social learning theory Applied to criminal behavior, theory stressing importance of learning through modeling others who are criminal; criminal behavior is a function of copying or learning criminal conduct from others.

Social process theories Explanations of criminal conduct that arise from one's social environment and close associations with others.

Sociobiology Scientific study of causal relation between genetic structure and social behavior.

Solitary confinement Technically originated with Walnut Street Jail; used subsequently and originally attributed to the Auburn (New York) State Penitentiary in 1820s, where prisoners were housed individually in separate cells during evening hours.

South Carolina Intensive Supervised Probation Program Plan implemented in 1984; primary aims of the ISP program were to heighten surveillance of participants, increase PO/client contact, and increase offender accountability; started ISP program as a pilot or experimental project.

Specialized caseloads model PO caseload model based on POs' unique skills and knowledge relative to offender drug or alcohol problems; some POs are assigned particular clients with unique problems that require more than average PO expertise.

Special-needs offenders Inmates, probationers, and parolees with unique problems, such as drug or alcohol dependencies, communicable diseases such as tuberculosis or AIDS/HIV, mental illness, or developmental disabilities and mental retardation; may include gang members who require unconventional interventions.

Split sentencing Procedure whereby judge imposes a sentence of incarceration for a fixed period, followed by a probationary period a fixed duration; similar to shock probation.

Standard parolees Anyone on parole who must comply with the basic parole program conditions; as opposed to someone who is intensively supervised by POs with frequent face-to-face visits and random drug and alcohol checks.

Standard probation programs Probationers conform to all terms of their probation program, but their contact with probation officers is minimal; often, their contact is by telephone or letter once or twice a month.

Status offenders Any juveniles who commit offenses that would not be crimes if committed by adults (e.g., runaway behavior, truancy, curfew violation).

Status offenses Violations of statutes or ordinances by minors that, if committed by adult, would not be considered either felonies or misdemeanors.

Statutory exclusion Certain juveniles, largely because of their age and offense committed, are automatically excluded from juvenile court jurisdiction.

Statutory good time Credit prescribed by the U.S. Congress and state legislatures that prisoners may apply toward their maximum sentences; a method of obtaining early release under determinate sentencing schemes.

Stigmatization Social process whereby offenders acquire undesirable characteristics as the result of imprisonment or court appearances; undesirable criminal or delinquent labels are assigned those who are processed through the criminal and juvenile justice systems.

Strain theory A criminological theory positing that a gap between culturally approved goals and legitimate means of achieving them causes frustration which leads to criminal behavior.

Stress Negative anxiety that is accompanied by an alarm reaction, resistance, and exhaustion; such anxiety contributes to heart disease, headaches, high blood pressure, and ulcers.

Study release Essentially the same as work release programs, but study release is for the express purpose of securing educational goals; several types of study release have been identified: adult basic education, high school or high school equivalency (GED), technical or vocational education, and college.

Study release programs (see **Study release**)

Subculture of violence Subculture with values that demand the overt use of violence in certain social situations. Marvin Wolfgang and Franco Ferracuti devised this concept to depict a set of norms apart from mainstream conventional society, in which the theme of violence is pervasive and dominant. Learned through socialization with others as an alternative lifestyle.

Subcultures Social cliques and behavior patterns of selected groups, such as gangs.

Summary offense Any petty crime punishable by a fine only.

Superego Sigmund Freud's term describing that part of personality concerned with moral values.

Supervised release Any type of offender management program where clients must be supervised by probation/parole officers more or less intensively.

Synthetic officers POs who are actually a blend of enforcers and social workers, wanting to ensure that their clients are obeying program rules but at the same time wanting to rehabilitate them.

Tattoo Symbol of gang membership that are placed on the body in different locations to signify one's gang affiliation.

Tattoo removal program Any process whereby gang members can have their gang tattoos removed in order to escape gang control.

Technical program violations Any infractions by probationers or parolees of the terms of their probation or parole agreements; some violations may include failing drug or alcohol checks, violating curfew, associating with known felons, possessing firearms or cellular telephones or pagers.

Teen courts (see **Youth courts**)

Temporary release programs Any type of program for jail or prison inmates designed to permit them absence from confinement, either escorted or unescorted, for short-term periods; work release, study release, and furloughs are most common types of temporary release.

Theory An integrated body of propositions, definitions, and assumptions that are related in such a way so as to explain and predict the relation between two or more variables.

Theory of opportunity Explanation of deviant behavior and criminality that is class-based and suggests that persons in the lower socioeconomic classes have less opportunity to acquire scarce goods; therefore, they obtain these goods by illegal means.

Therapeutic community A treatment model in which all activities, both formal and informal, are viewed as interrelated interventions that address the multidimensional disorder of the whole person. These activities include educational and therapeutic meetings and groups, as well as interpersonal and social activities of the community; within this theoretical framework, social and psychological change evolves as a dynamic interaction between the individual and the peer community, its context of activities, and expectations for participation.

Therapeutic jurisprudence View of judges that attempts to combine a "rights" perspective—focusing on justice, rights, and equality issues—with an "ethic of care" perspective—focusing on care, interdependence, and response to need.

Tickets-of-leave Document given to a prisoner as the result of accumulating good-time marks that obligate the prisoner to remain under limited jurisdiction and supervision of local police.

Tiers Different floors of a prison or penal institution designed to hold prisoners who have committed various types of offenses.

Tier system Auburn (New York) State Penitentiary innovation in 1820s designed to established multiple levels of inmate housing, probably according to type of conviction offense and institutional conduct.

Torts Civil wrongs, omissions where plaintiff seeks monetary damages; as distinguished from crimes, where incarceration and fines may be imposed.

Total institution Erving Goffman's term describing self-contained nature of prisons; depicts all community functions inside prison walls, including social exchange, living.

Totality of circumstances Sometimes used as the standard whereby offender guilt is determined or where search and seizure warrants may be obtained; officers consider entire set of circumstances surrounding apparently illegal event and act accordingly.

Traditional treatment-oriented model Stresses traditional rehabilitative measures that seek to reintegrate the offender into the community through extensive assistance; may include elements of the justice and limited risk control models, its primary aim is "long-term change in offender behavior"; includes strategies, such as (a) developing individual offender plans for life in the community such as work, study, or community service, (b) full-time employment and/or vocational training, and/or (c) using community sponsors or other support personnel to provide assistance and direction for offenders.

Transfer hearing Also known as certification or waiver, this is a proceeding to determine whether juveniles should be certified as adults for purposes of being subjected to jurisdiction of adult criminal courts where more severe penalties may be imposed.

Transfers Proceedings where juveniles are remanded to the jurisdiction of criminal courts to be processed as though they were adults; also known as certification and waiver.

Transportation This form of punishment was banishment to remote territories or islands where law violators would work at hard labor in penal colonies isolated from society.

Treatment Alternatives to Street Crime (TASC) Since 1972, various community-based treatment programs have been implemented to treat and counsel drug-dependent clients; collectively labeled Treatment Alternatives to Street Crime (TASC) and currently are being operated in numerous jurisdictions throughout the United States to improve client abstinence from drugs, increase their employment potential, and improve their social/personal functioning.

Treatment model (see **Medical model**)

True bill Finding by grand jury that probable cause exists that a crime was committed and a specific person or persons committed it; an indictment; a presentment.

Truth-in-sentencing provisions Legislatively mandated proportionately longer incarcerative terms that must be served by inmates before they become parole-eligible; the federal government requires that its inmates must serve at least 85 percent of their imposed sentences before they are eligible for supervised release.

Unconditional diversion program No restrictions are placed on offender's behavior; no formal controls operate to control or monitor divertee's behavior.

Uniform Crime Reports (UCR) Published annually by the Federal Bureau of Investigation; include statistics about the number and kinds of crimes reported in the United States annually by over 15,000 law enforcement agencies; the major sourcebook of crime statistics in the United States; compiled by gathering information on 29 types of crime from participating law enforcement agencies; crime information is requested from all rural and urban law enforcement agencies and reported to the FBI.

User fees Monthly fees paid by divertees or probationers during the diversion or probationary period to help defray expenses incurred by the public or private agencies that monitor them.

U.S. Code Annotated Comprehensive compendium of federal laws and statutes, including landmark cases and discussions of law applications.

U.S. sentencing guidelines Standards of punishment implemented by federal courts in November 1987 obligating federal judges to impose presumptive sentences on all convicted offenders; guidelines exist based upon offense seriousness and offender characteristics; judges may depart from guidelines only by justifying their departures in writing.

University Settlement Privately operated facility in New York commenced in 1893 by James Bronson Reynolds to provide assistance and job referral services to community residents; settlement involved in probation work in 1901; eventually abandoned after considerable public skepticism, and when political opponents withdrew their support.

Van Dieman's Land 1780s English island penal colony established off the coast of Australia; used to accommodate dangerous prisoners convicted of crimes in England.

Victim and Witness Protection Act of 1982 Federal act designed to require criminals to provide restitution to victims; provides a sentencing option that judges may impose.

Victim compensation Any financial restitution payable to victims by either the state or convicted offenders.

Victim impact statement (VIS) Statement filed voluntarily by victim of crime, appended to the presentence investigation report as a supplement for judicial consideration in sentencing offender; describes injuries to victims resulting from convicted offender's actions.

Victimization data Carefully worded questions lead people to report incidents that can be classified as crimes; this material is statistically manipulated in such a way so as to make it comparable with UCR statistics; this material is usually referred to as victimization data.

Victimizations The basic measure of the occurrence of a crime and is a specific criminal act that affects a single victim.

Victim-offender mediation model Third-party arbiters meet with victims and their victimizers to work out mutually agreeable solutions to problems with aim of compensating victims for their losses.

Victim-offender reconciliation Any mediated or arbitrated civil proceeding or meeting between offender and victim where mutually satisfactory solution is agreed upon and criminal proceedings are avoided.

Victim-Offender Reconciliation Project (VORP) A specific form of conflict resolution between the victim and the offender; face-to-face encounter is the essence of this process; Elkhart County, Indiana, has been the site of VORP since 1987; primary aims of VORP are to (1) make offenders accountable for their wrongs against victims, (2) reduce recidivism among participating offenders, and (3) heighten responsibility of offenders through victim compensation and repayment for damages inflicted.

Victim-reparations model Third-party arbitration mechanism where compensation to victims is negotiated and perpetrators reimburse victims directly by paying reparations.

Victims of Crime Act of 1984 Under Public Law 98-473 the Comprehensive Crime Control Act was established; Chapter 14 of this act is known as the Victims of Crime Act of 1984; as a part of all state and federal government victim compensation programs, work release requirements, a certain amount of earned wages of work releasees may be allocated to restitution and to a general victim compensation fund.

Violate To engage in revocation actions or take steps to revoke a client's probation or parole program because of one or more rule infractions.

Violent crimes Any criminal act involving direct confrontation of one or more victims; may or may not involve injury or death; examples are aggravated assault, robbery, forcible rape, homicide.

Volunteers Hardworking, unpaid, dedicated individuals who fill in the gaps for correctional agencies and provide much-needed services that victims, inmates, parolees, probationers, and their families might otherwise not receive because of limited funding for programs.

Waivers (see **Transfers**)

Waiver hearing Motion by prosecutor to transfer juvenile charged with various offenses to a criminal or adult court for prosecution; waiver motions make it possible to sustain adult criminal penalties.

Waiver motion Move by defense or prosecution to transfer juvenile to jurisdiction of criminal court.

Walnut Street Jail Pennsylvania legislature authorized in 1790 the renovation of a facility originally constructed on Walnut Street in 1776, to house the overflow resulting from overcrowding of the High Street Jail; used as both a workhouse and a place of incarceration for all types of offenders; 1790 renovation was the first of several innovations in U.S. corrections, including (1) separating the most serious prisoners from others in 16 large solitary cells; (2) separating other prisoners according to their offense seriousness; and (3) separating prisoners according to gender.

Welfare officers POs who are like social workers in that they focus on rehabilitation and treatment when working with their probationer- or parolee-clients.

White-collar crime Offenses committed by people in the course of performing their jobs or occupations; embezzlement and fraud are examples of white-collar crime.

Wickersham Commission A National Commission on Law Observance and Enforcement established in 1931 and chaired by George W. Wickersham; evaluated and critiqued parole as well as the practices of various criminal justice agencies in managing the criminal population.

Wilderness program Any nonsecure outdoors program that enables juvenile delinquents to learn survival skills, self-confidence, self-reliance, and self-esteem; used for secure-confinement bound offenders.

Women in Community Services Lifeskills Program (WICS) Woman-centered model to promote self-sufficiency and independence; oriented toward female inmates with histories of sexual and physical abuse; teaches job readiness, personal empowerment, and life management skills; used in Oregon, Tennessee, and Texas.

Women's Network (WN) Maricopa County, Arizona, program focusing upon female probationers with substance abuse problems; primary goal is to educate female offenders about drug and alcohol abuses and acquiring coping strategies.

Work furlough (see **Work release**)

Workhouse Incarcerative facilities in England in 1700s where sheriffs and other officials "hired out" their inmates to perform skilled and semi-skilled tasks for various merchants; the manifest functions of workhouses and prisoner labor were supposed to improve the moral and social fiber of prisoners and train them to perform useful skills when they were eventually released; however, profits from inmate labor were often pocketed by corrupt jail and workhouse officials.

Work release Any program where inmates in jails or prisons are permitted to work in their communities with minimal restrictions and supervision, are compensated at the prevailing minimum wage, and must serve their nonworking hours housed in a secure facility.

XYY syndrome. Theory of criminal behavior suggesting that some criminals are born with extra "Y" chromosome, characterized as the "aggressive" chromosome compared with the "passive X" chromosome. The extra Y chromosome produces greater agitation, greater aggressiveness, and criminal propensities.

Youth courts Adjudicatory proceedings where teen juries decide minor juvenile offender cases and impose nonincarcerative punishments, such as community service or restitution; also known as peer courts and teen courts.

Youth Service Bureaus (YSBs) Established in numerous jurisdictions in order to accomplish diversions several objectives; places within communities where "delinquent-prone" youths could be referred by parents, schools, and law enforcement agencies; forerunners of contemporary community-based correctional programs, since they were intended to solicit volunteers from among community residents and to mobilize a variety of resources that could assist in a youth's treatment; the nature of treatments for youths, within the YSB concept, originally included referrals to a variety of community services, educational experiences, and individual or group counseling; original YSBs attempted to compile lists of existing community services, agencies, organizations, and sponsors who could cooperatively coordinate these resources in the most productive ways to benefit affected juveniles.

Internet Addresses for Professional Organizations and Probation/ Parole Agencies

Academy of Criminal Justice Sciences
www.acjs.org

Administrative Office of U.S. Courts
www.uscourts.gov

American Academy of Forensic Sciences
aafs.org

American Bar Association
www.abanet.org

American Correctional Association
corrections.com/aca/

American Judges Association
aja.ncsc.dni.us

American Probation and Parole Association
www.appa-net.org

American Society of Criminology
asc41@infinet.com

also   bsos.umd.edu/asc/

American Sociological Association
asanet.org

Bureau of Justice Statistics
www.ojp.usdoj.gov/bjs/

Bureau of Prisons
www.bop.gov

Department of Justice
usdoj.gov

FBI Academy
fbi.gov/academy/academy.htm

FBI Laboratory
fbi.gov/lab/report/labhome.com

FBI Law Enforcement Bulletin
leb@fbiacademy.edu

Federal Bureau of Investigation
fbi.gov

Federal Judicial Center
www.fjc.gov

Federation of Law Societies of Canada
flsc.ca

Freedom of Information Act
citizen.org

Immigration and Naturalization Service
ins.usdoj.gov/

Law and Society Association
webmaster@lawandsociety.org

National Association of Counsel for Children
naccchildlaw.org

National Association for Court Management
nacm.ncsc.dni.us/

National Association of Drug Court Professionals
www.drugcourt.org

National Association of Pretrial Services Agencies
napsa.org

National Association of State Judicial Educators
www.nasje.org

National Center for State Courts
www.ncsc.dni.us

National Center for Youth Law
www.youthlaw.org

National Clearinghouse for Judicial Educational Information
jeritt.msu.edu

National Council of Juvenile and Family Court Judges
www.ncjfcj.unr.edu

National Criminal Justice Reference Service
www.ncjrs.org

National District Attorneys Association
www.ndaa.org

National Institute of Corrections
nicic.org/inst/

National Institute of Justice
www.ojp.usdoj.gov/nij

National Institute of Justice Data Resources Program
nacjd@icpsr.umich.edu

National Law Enforcement and Corrections Technology Center
www.nlectc.org/

Office of Justice Programs
ojp.usdoj.gov/

Office of Juvenile Justice and Delinquency Prevention (OJJDP)
www.ojjdp.ncjrs.org

OJP Drug Court Clearinghouse and Technical Assistance
Project
www.american.edu/academic.depts/spa/justice/dcclear.htm

Pacific Sociological Association
psa@csus.edu

Sentencing Project
www.sentencingproject.org

Sex Offender Awareness Page
www.sharlow.com/

Sourcebook of Criminal Justice Statistics
albany.edu/sourcebook/

Southern Sociological Society
levin@soc.msstate.edu

State Judicial Institute
www.statejustice.org

Uniform Crime Reports
fbi.gov/ucr

U.S. Customs Service
customs.ustreas.gov

U.S. Federal Judiciary
www.uscourts.gov/

U.S. Government Printing Office
access.gpo.gov

U.S. Marshals Service
us.marshals@usdoj.gov

U.S. Parole Commission
usdoj.gov/parole.htm

U.S. Sentencing Commission
www.usscr.gov

U.S. Supreme Court
supct.law.cornell.edu/supct/

Vera Institute of Justice
broadway.vera.org

Victim-Offender Reconciliation Project (VORP)
vorp.com

Western and Pacific Association of Criminal Justice Educators
WPACJE@boisestate.edu

References

ABRAMSKY, SASHA (2002). *Hard Time Blues: How Politics Built a Prison Nation.* New York: St. Martin's.

ADAIR, JR., DAVID N. (2000). "Revocation Sentences: A Practical Guide." *Federal Probation* 64:67–73.

ADMINISTRATIVE OFFICE OF U.S. COURTS (1997). *PSI Reports: Preparation and Examples.* Washington, DC: Administrative Office of U.S. Courts.

ADMINISTRATIVE OFFICE OF U.S. COURTS (2001). *Federal Probation Officer Code of Ethics.* Washington, DC: Administrative Office of U.S. Courts.

AGNEW, ROBERT, et al. (2002). "Strain, Personality Traits, and Delinquency: Extending General Strain Theory." *Criminology: An Interdisciplinary Journal* 40:43–72.

AGUIRRE, ADALBERTO JR. and DAVID BAKER (eds.) (2000). "Latinos and the Criminal Justice System." *Justice Professional* 13:3–102.

AIM, INC. (2003). *About Inmate Mothers: AIM Overview.* Montgomery, AL: AIM, Inc.

ALARID, LEANNE FIFTAL (2003). "A Gender Comparison of Prisoner Selection for Job Assignments While Incarcerated." *Journal of Crime and Justice* 26:95–116.

ALARID, LEANNE FIFTAL and PAUL F. CROMWELL (2002). *Correctional Perspectives: Views from Academics, Practitioners, and Prisoners.* Los Angeles: Roxbury.

ALASKA DEPARTMENT OF CORRECTIONS (2003). *Alaska Long-Term Prisoner Classification Form.* Anchorage, AK: Alaska Department of Corrections.

ALBONETTI, CELESTA A. (1999). "The Avoidance of Punishment: A Legal-Bureaucratic Model of Suspended Sentences in Federal White-Collar Cases Prior to the Federal Sentencing Guidelines." *Social Forces* 78:303–329.

ALBONETTI, CELESTA A. and JOHN R. HEPBURN (1997). "Probation Revocation: A Proportional Hazards Model of the Conditional Effects of Social Disadvantage." *Social Problems* 44:124–138.

ALBRECHT, HANS JOERG (2002). "Electronic Monitoring." *MonatSchrift fuer Kriminologie und Strafrechtsreform* 85:84–104.

ALBRECHT, HANS JEORG and ANTON VAN KALMTHOUT (2002). *Community Sanctions and Measures in Europe and North America.* Frieburg, Germany: Max Planck Institut fur Auslandisches und Internationls Strafrecht.

ALBRIGHT, KATHLEEN et al. (1996). *Evaluation of the Impact of Boot Camps for Juvenile Offenders.* Washington, DC: U.S. Department of Justice.

ALEXANDER, A. DAKTARI and THOMAS J. BERNARD (2002). "A Critique of Mark Colvin's Crime and Coercion: An Integrated Theory of Chronic Criminology." *Crime, Law, and Social Change* 38:389–398.

ALLEN, HARRY E. et al. (2002). *Risk Reduction: Interventions for Special Needs Offenders.* Belmont, CA: Wadsworth.

ALTSCHULER, DAVID M. (2001). "Community Justice Initiatives: Issues and Challenges." *Federal Probation* 65: 28–32.

ALTSCHULER, DAVID M. and TROY L. ARMSTRONG (1999). *Reintegration, Supervised Release, and Intensive Aftercare.* Washington, DC: U.S. Office of Juvenile Justice and Delinquency Prevention.

ALTSCHULER, DAVID M. and TROY L. ARMSTRONG (2002). "Juvenile Corrections and Continuity of Care in Community Context." *Federal Probation* 66:72–77.

ALTSCHULER, DAVID M., TROY L. ARMSTRONG, and DORIS LAYTON MACKENZIE (1999). *Reintegration, Supervised Release, and Intensive Aftercare.* Washington, DC: U.S. Office of Juvenile Justice and Delinquency Prevention.

AMERICAN CORRECTIONAL ASSOCIATION (1983). *The American Prison: From the Beginning . . . A Pictorial History.* College Park, MD: American Correctional Association.

AMERICAN CORRECTIONAL ASSOCIATION (1993). *Female Offenders: Meeting Needs of a Neglected Population.* Laurel, MD: American Correctional Association.

AMERICAN CORRECTIONAL ASSOCIATION (1994). *Field Officer and Resource Guide.* Laurel, MD.

AMERICAN CORRECTIONAL ASSOCIATION (2000). *Juvenile and Adult Directory.* Lanham, MD: American Correctional Association.

AMERICAN CORRECTIONAL ASSOCIATION (2001). *Probation and Parole Directory 2001–2004.* Lanham, MD: American Correctional Association.

AMERICAN CORRECTIONAL ASSOCIATION (2003). *Probation and Parole Directory 2003–2005.* Lanham, MD: American Correctional Association.

AMERICAN CORRECTIONAL ASSOCIATION (2004). *2003 Directory, Adult and Juvenile.* Lanham, MD: American Correctional Association.

AMERICAN PROBATION AND PAROLE ASSOCIATION (1996). *Restoring Hope Through Community Partnerships: The Real Deal in Crime Control—A Handbook for Community Corrections.* Lexington, KY: American Probation and Parole Association.

AMERICAN PROBATION AND PAROLE ASSOCIATION (1997). *The American Probation and Parole Association Code of Ethics.* Lexington, KY: American Probation and Parole Association.

AMERICAN PROBATION AND PAROLE ASSOCIATION (2003). "Discretionary Parole." *APPA Perspectives* 26:19.

AMES, LYNDA J. and KATHERINE T. DUNHAM (2002). "Asymptotic Justice: Probation As a Criminal Justice Response to Intimate Partner Violence." *Violence Against Women* 8:6–34.

ANDERSON, H.S., D. SESTOFT, and T. LILLEBACK (2000). "A Longitudinal Study of Prisoners on Remand: Psychiatric Prevalence, Incidence and Psychopathology in Solitary vs. Non-Solitary Confinement." *Acta Psychiatrica Scandinavica* 102:19–25.

ANDREWS, CHYRL and LYNN MARBLE (2003). *Changes to OJJDP's Juvenile Accountability Program.* Washington, DC: U.S. Department of Justice.

ANDRUS, J.K., D.W. FLEMING, and C. KNOX (1999). "HIV Testing in Prisoners: Is Mandatory Testing Mandatory?" *American Journal of Public Health* 79:40–42.

ANGELONE, RON (2000). "Standards: What Good Are They, Anyway?" *Corrections Today* 62:62–64.

ANNO, B. JAYE (ed.) (1998). "HIV Infection among Incarcerated Women." *Journal of Correctional Health Care* 5:123–254.

ANSAY, SYLVIA J. and Deena Benveneste (1999). "Equal Application of Unequal Treatment: Practical Outcomes for Women on Community Control in Florida." *Women and Criminal Justice* 10:121–135.

APPLEGATE, BRANDON K. et al. (2000). "Individualization, Criminalization, or Problem Resolution: A Factorial Survey of Juvenile Court Judges' Decisions to Incarcerate Youthful Felony Offenders." *Justice Quarterly* 17:310–331.

ARCHAMBEAULT, WILLIAM G. and DONALD R. DEIS JR. (1996). *Cost Effectiveness Comparisons of Private Versus Public Prisons in Louisiana.* Baton Rouge, LA: School of Social Work, Louisiana State University.

ARCHWAMETY, TEARA and ANTONIS KATSIYANNIS (2000). "Academic Remediation, Parole Violations, and Recidivism Rates." *Remedial and Special Education* 21:161–170.

ARIZONA DEPARTMENT OF CORRECTIONS (1991). *Offender Classification System (OCS): Classification Operating Manual.* Phoenix, AZ: Arizona Department of Corrections.

ARIZONA DEPARTMENT OF CORRECTIONS (2004). *Intensive Probation Teams.* Phoenix, AZ: Arizona Department of Corrections.

ARMSTRONG, TROY L. (1988). "National Survey of Juvenile Intensive Probation Supervision, Part I." *Criminal Justice Abstracts* 20:342–348.

ARNOLD, CHARLOTTE S. (1992). "The Program for Female Offenders, Inc.—a Community Corrections Answer to Jail Overcrowding." *American Jails* 5:36–40.

ARNOLD, CHARLOTTE S. (1993). "Respect, Recognition are Keys to Effective Volunteer Programs." *Corrections Today* 55:118–122.

AROLA, TERRYL and RICHARD LAWRENCE (1999). "Assessing Probation Officer Assaults and Responding to Officer Safety Concerns." *APPA Perspectives* 22:32–35.

AROLA, TERRYL and RICHARD LAWRENCE (2000). "'Broken Windows' Probation: The Next Step in Fighting Crime." *APPA Perspectives* 24:26–33.

ARTHUR, LINDSAY G. (2000). "Punishment Doesn't Work!" *Juvenile and Family Court Journal* 51:37–42.

ASHFORD, JOSE B. and CRAIG WINSTON LeCROY (1993). "Juvenile Parole Policy in the United States: Determinate Versus Indeterminate Models." *Justice Quarterly* 10:179–195.

ASSOCIATED PRESS (1999). "Convicted Murderer Freed in Vermont Under" *Long Beach Press-Telegram,* November 10, 1999:B2.

ASSOCIATED PRESS (2002). "Van Houten Turned Down Again By California Parole Board." *Long Beach Press-Telegram,* June 12, 2002:A3.

ATKINS, ELLIOT (1996). "Post-Verdict Psychological Consultation in the Federal Courts." *American Journal of Forensic Psychology* 14:25–335.

AUERBAHN, KATHLEEN (2002). "Selective Incapacitation, Three Strikes, and the Problem of Aging Prison Populations: Using Simulation Modeling to See the Future." *Criminology and Public Policy* 1:353–388.

AUGUSTUS, JOHN (1852). *A Report of the Labors of John Augustus for the Last Ten Years: In Aid of the Unfortunate.* New York: Wright and Hasty.

AUSTIN, JAMES (1987). *Success and Failure on Parole in California: A Preliminary Evaluation.* San Francisco, CA: National Council on Crime and Delinquency.

AUSTIN, JAMES, KELLY DEDEL JOHNSON, and MARCIA GREGORIOU. (2000). *Juveniles in Adult Prisons and Jails: A National Assessment.* Washington, DC: U.S. Bureau of Justice Assistance.

AUSTIN, JAMES, MICHAEL JONES, and MELISSA BOLYARD (1993). *The Growing Use of Jail Boot Camps: The Current State of the Art.* Washington, DC: U.S. Department of Justice, Office of Justice Programs.

AUSTIN, ROY L. and S. KIM-YOUNG (2000). "A Cross-National Examination of the Relationship between Gender Equality and Official Rape Rates." *International Journal of Offender Therapy and Comparative Criminology* 44:204–221.

BAIRD, S. CHRISTOPHER (1985). "Classifying Juveniles: Making the Most of an Important Management Tool." *Corrections Today* 47:32–38.

BAKER, THOMAS E. (2002). *Effective Police Leadership: Moving Beyond Management.* Englewood Cliffs, NJ: Prentice Hall.

BALDWIN, TOM and SANDY McCLURE (2003). "Parole Board Officials Cite Pressures." Trenton, NJ: Gannett State Bureau.

BALBONI, JENNIFER M. and JACK McDEVITT (2001). "Hate Crime Reporting: Understanding Police Officer Perceptions, Department Protocol, and the Role of the Victim." *Justice Research and Policy* 3:1–28.

BARBEE, ANDY, MIKE EOSEMBERG, and ANGIE GUNTER (2002). *Trends, Profiles, and Policy Issues Related to Felony Probation Revocations in Texas.* Austin, TX: Texas Criminal Justice Policy Council.

BARRINEAU, H.E. III (1994). *Civil Liability in Criminal Justice* (2nd ed.). Cincinnati, OH: Anderson.

BARTOLLAS, CLEMENS and DAVID WARD (2003). *Becoming a Model Warden: Striving for Excellence.* Lanham, MD: American Correctional Association.

BATCHELDER, JOHN STUART and J. MARVIN PIPPERT (2002). "Hard Time or Idle Time: Factors Affecting Inmate Choices Between Participation in Prison Work and Education Programs." *Prison Journal* 82:269–280.

BAUMER, ERIC P. et al. (2002). "Crime, Shame, and Recidivism." *The British Journal of Criminology* 42:40–59.

BAYSE, D.J. (1993). *Helping Hands: A Handbook for Volunteers in Prisons and Jails.* Laurel, MD: American Correctional Association.

BEAUMONT, BETTY (2001). "Survey of Injectable Methadone Prescribing in General Practice in England and Wales." *International Journal of Drug Policy* 12:91–101.

BECK, ALLEN J. (2000). *Prisoners in 1999.* Washington, DC: U.S. Department of Justice.

BECKER, HOWARD S. (1963). *Outsiders: Studies in the Sociology of Deviance.* New York: Free Press.

BEDNAR, SUSAN G. (2003). "Substance Abuse and Woman Abuse: A Proposal for Integrated Treatment." *Federal Probation* 67:52–57.

BEHR, EDWARD (1996). *Prohibition: Thirteen Years that Changed America.* New York: Arcade.

BELENKO, STEVEN R. (1999). "Research on Drug Courts: A Critical Review 1999 Update." *National Drug Court Institute Review* 2:1–58.

BENDA, BRENT B. (2002). "Religion and Violent Offenders in Boot Camp: A Structural Equation Model." *Journal of Research in Crime and Delinquency* 39:91–121

BENDA, BRENT B., NANCY J. TOOMBS, and MARK PEACOCK (2002). "Ecological Factors in Recidivism: A Survival Analysis of Boot Camp Graduates After Three Years." *Journal of Offender Rehabilitation* 35:63–85.

BENZVY-MILLER, SHEREEN (1990). "Community Corrections and the NIMBY Syndrome." *Forum on Corrections Research* 2:18–22.

BERG, JULIE (2001). "Accountability in Private Corrections: Monitoring the Performance of Private Prisons in South Africa." *South African Journal of Criminal Justice* 14:327–343.

BERNBURG, JON GUNNAR (2002). "Anomie, Social Change, and Crime: A Theoretical Examination of Institutional-Anomie Theory." *British Journal of Criminology* 42:729–742.

BEYMER, JUDITH K. and ROGER L. HUTCHINSON (2002). "Profile of Problem Children from a Rural County in Indiana." *Adolescence* 37:183–208.

BICKLE, GAYLE et al. (2002). *Ohio Corrections Research Compendium*. Columbus, OH: Ohio Department of Rehabilitation and Correction.

BIGGER, PHILLIP J. (1993). "Officers in Danger: Results of the Federal Probation and Pretrial Officers Association's National Study on Serious Assaults." *APPA Perspectives* 17:14–20.

BILCHIK, SHAY (1996). *State Responses to Serious and Violent Juvenile Crime*. Pittsburgh, PA: National Center for Juvenile Justice.

BIRMINGHAM, LUKE et al. (2000). "Mental Illness At Reception Into Prison." *Criminal Behaviour and Mental Health* 10:77–87.

BJERREGAARD, BETH (2002). "Self-Definitions of Gang Membership and Involvement in Delinquent Activities." *Youth and Society* 34:31–54.

BLACK, HENRY CAMPBELL (1990). *Black's Law Dictionary (6th Ed.)*. St. Paul, MN: West.

BLOCK, DIANA (2003). *Making the Transition Work: Women's Prison Association and Home*. New York, NY: Women's Prison Association.

BLOMBERG, THOMAS G. and GORDON P. WALDO (eds.) (2002). "Implementing an Evaluation Research and Accountability-Driven System for Juvenile Justice Education in Florida." *Evaluation Review* 26:239–351.

BLOOM, BARBARA et al. (2002). "Moving Toward Justice for Female Juvenile Offenders in the New Millennium: Modeling Gender-Specific Policies and Programs." *Journal of Contemporary Criminal Justice* 18:37–56.

BOEHNKE, KLAUS and DAGMAR WINKELS (2002). "Juvenile Delinquency Under Conditions of Rapid Social Change." *Sociological Forum* 17:57–79.

BOND-MAUPIN, LISA J. and JAMES R. MAUPIN (2002). "The (Mis)uses of Detention and the Impact of Bed Space in One Jurisdiction." *Juvenile and Family Court Journal* 53:21–31.

BONTA, JAMES, SUZANNE CAPRETTA-WALLACE, and JENNIFER ROONEY (1999). *Electronic Monitoring in Canada*. Ottawa, CAN: Solicitor General Canada.

BONTA, JAMES, SUZANNE CAPRETTA-WALLACE, and JENNIFER ROONEY (2000). "Can Electronic Monitoring Make a Difference?" *Crime and Delinquency* 46:61–75.

BOONE, JR., HARRY N. (1994a). "An Examination of Recidivism and Other Outcome Measures: A Review of the Literature." *APPA Perspectives,* 18:12–18.

BOONE, JR., HARRY N. (1994b). "Recommended Outcome Measures for Program Evaluation: APPAs Board of Directors Survey Results." *APPA Perspectives,* 18:19–20.

BOONE, HARRY N. JR. (1995). "Mental Illness in Probation and Parole Populations: Results from a National Survey." *APPA Perspectives* 19:32–44.

BOOTHBY, JENNIFER L. and CARL B. CLEMENTS (2000). "A National Survey of Correctional Psychologists." *Criminal Justice and Behavior* 27:716–732.

BORUM, RANDY (1999). *Misdemeanor Offenders with Mental Illness in Florida: Examining Police Response, Court Jurisdiction, and Jail Mental Health Service*. Tallahassee, FL: Florida Department of Children and Families.

BOSWELL, GWYNETH and PETER WEDGE (2002). *Imprisoned Fathers and Their Children*. Belmont, CA: Wadsworth.

BOTTOMLEY, A. KEITH (1984). "Dilemmas of Parole in a Penal Crisis." *The Howard Journal of Criminal Justice* 23:24–40.

BOTTOMS, ANTHONY, LORAINE GELSTHORPE, and SUE REX (eds.) (2001). *Community Penalties: Change and Challenges*. Devon, UK: Willan.

BOUFFARD, JEFFREY A., DORIS LAYTON MACKENZIE, and LAURA J. HICKMAN (2000). "Effectiveness of Vocational Education and Employment Programs for Adult Offenders: A Methodology-Based Analysis of the Literature." *Journal of Offender Rehabilitation* 31:1–42.

BOWEN, ERICA et al. (2002). "Evaluating Probation Based Offender Programs for Domestic Violence Perpetrators: A Pro-Feminist Approach." *The Howard Journal of Criminal Justice* 41:221–236.

BOWERS, DAN M. (2000). "Home Detention Systems." *Corrections Today* 62:102–106.

BRAITHWAITE, JOHN (2001). "Crime in a Convict Republic." *Modern Law Review* 64:11–50.

BRAITHWAITE, JOHN (2002). *Restorative Justice and Responsive Regulation*. Oxford, UK: Oxford University Press.

BRALLEY, JAMES and JOHN PROVOST (2001). "Reinventing Supervision: Georgia Parole's Results-Driven Supervision." *Corrections Today* 63:120–123.

BRECKENRIDGE, JAMES F. et al. (2000). "Drunk Drivers, DWI 'Drug Court' Treatment, and Recidivism: Who Fails?" *Justice Research and Policy* 2:87–105.

BREITENBECHER, KIMBERLY HANSON and MICHAEL SCARCE (2001). "An Evaluation of the Effectiveness of a Sexual Assault Education Program Focusing on Psychological Barriers to Resistance." *Journal of Interpersonal Violence* 18:387–407.

BREWER, VICTORIA E., JAMES W. MARQUART, and JANET L. MULLINGS (1998). "Female Drug Offenders: HIV-Related Risk Behavior, Self Perceptions, and Public Health Interpretations." *Criminal Justice Policy Review* 9:185–208.

BREWSTER, DENNIS R. and SUSAN F. SHARP (2002). "Educational Programs and Recidivism in Oklahoma: Another Look." *Prison Journal* 82:314–334.

BRITT, CHESTER L. III, MICHAEL R. GOTTFREDSON, and JOHN S. GOLDKAMP (1992). "Drug Testing and Pretrial Misconduct: An Experiment on the Specific Deterrent Effects of Drug Monitoring Defendants on Pretrial Release." *Journal of Research in Crime and Delinquency* 29:62–78.

BROCK, DEON E., JON SORENSEN, and JAMES W. MARQUART (2000). "Tinkering with the Machinery of Death: An Analysis of the Impact of Legislative Reform on the Sentencing of Capital Murderers in Texas." *Journal of Criminal Justice* 28:343–349.

BRODSKY, STANLEY L., PATRICIA A. ZAPF, and MARCUS T. BOCCACCINI (2001). "The Last Competency: An Examination of Legal, Ethical, and Professional Ambiguities Regarding Evaluations of Competence for Execution." *Journal of Forensic Psychology Practice* 1:1–25.

BRODY, ARTHUR L. and RICHARD GREEN (1994). "Washington State's Unscientific Approach to the Problem of Repeat Offenders." *Bulletin of the American Academy of Psychiatry and the Law* 22:343–356.

BRODY, YOSEF and BARRY ROSENFELD (2002). "Object Relations in Criminal Psychopaths." *International Journal of Offender Therapy and Comparative Criminology* 46:400–411.

BROWN, PAUL W. (1994). "Mental Preparedness: Probation Officers Need to Rely on More Than Luck to Ensure Safety." *Corrections Today* 56:180–187.

BROWN, SAMMIE (2000). "Into the Millennium with Comprehensive Objective Prison Classification Systems." *Corrections Today* 62:138–139.

BROWN, VALERIE (1992). "Idaho's Intensive Supervision Program." *Corrections Compendium* 17:7–8.

BROWNFIELD, DAVID and KEVIN THOMPSON (2002). "Distinguishing the Effects of Peer Delinquency and Gang Membership on Self-Reported Delinquency." *Journal of Gang Research* 9:1–10.

BRUMBAUGH, SUSAN and CHRISTOPHER BIRKBECK (2000). *Juvenile Referrals and Dispositions in New Mexico, 1998.* Albuquerque, NM: New Mexico Criminal and Juvenile Justice Coordinating Council.

BRUNET, JAMES R. (2002). "Day Reporting Centers in North Carolina: Implementation Lessons for Policymakers." *Justice System Journal* 23:135–156.

BUDD, TRACEY (1999). *Violence at Work: Findings from the British Crime Survey.* London, UK: U.K. Home Office.

BUEL, SARAH M. (2002). "Why Juvenile Courts Should Address Family Violence: Promising Practices to Improve Intervention Outcomes." *Juvenile and Family Court Journal* 53:1–16.

BUENTELLO, SALVADOR et al. (1992). "Gangs: A Growing Menace on the Streets and in Our Prisons." *Corrections Today* 54:58–97.

BURDON, WILLIAM M. et al. (2003). "Sanctions and Rewards in Prison-Based Therapeutic Community Treatment." *Federal Probation* 67:47–52.

BUREAU OF JUSTICE ASSISTANCE (2000). *A Second Look at Alleviating Jail Crowding: A Systems Perspective.* Washington, DC: U.S. Department of Justice, Office of Justice Programs.

BUREAU OF JUSTICE STATISTICS (2002). *Recidivism.* Washington, DC: U.S. Government Printing Office.

BURGESS, ROBERT and RONALD AKERS (1966). "Differential Association-Reinforcement Theory of Criminal Behavior." *Social Problems* 14:128–147.

BURKE, PEGGY B. (2001). "Collaboration for Successful Prisoner Reentry: The Role of Parole and the Courts." *Corrections Management Quarterly* 5:11–22.

BURKE, JEFFREY D., ROLF LOEBER, and JOHN S. MUTCHKA (2002). "A Question for DSM-V: Which Better Predicts Persistent Conduct Disorder: Delinquent Acts or Conduct Symptoms?" *Criminal Behavior and Mental Health* 12:37–52.

BURNS, JERALD C. and GENNARO F. VITO (1995). "An Impact Analysis of the Alabama Boot Camp Program." *Federal Probation* 59:63–67.

BURNS, RONALD et al. (1999). "Perspectives on Parole: The Board Members' Viewpoint." *Federal Probation* 63:16–22.

BURRUSS, GEORGE W. and KIMBERLY KEMPF-LEONARD (2002). "The Questionable Advantage of Defense Counsel in Juvenile Court." *Justice Quarterly* 19:37–67.

BURT, GRANT N. et al. (2000). "Three Strikes and You're Out: An Investigation of False Positive Rates Using a Canadian Sample." *Federal Probation* 64:3–6.

BUTTELL, FREDERICK P. (2002). "Exploring Levels of Moral Development among Sex Offenders Participating in Community-Based Treatment." *Journal of Offender Rehabilitation* 34:85–95.

BUTTELL, FREDERICK P. and CATHY K. PIKE (2002). "Investigating Predictors of Treatment Attrition among Court-Ordered Batterers." *Journal of Social Service Research* 28:53–68.

BYRNE, JAMES M. (1986). "The Control Controversy: A Preliminary Examination of Intensive Probation Supervision Programs in the United States." *Federal Probation* 50:4–16.

BYRNE, STUART, MITCHELL K. BYRNE, and KEVIN HOWELLS (2001). "Defining the Needs in a Contemporary Correctional Environment: The Contribution of Psychology." *Psychiatry, Psychology, and the Law* 8:97–104.

CAHALAN, MARGARET WERNER and LEE ANNE PARSONS (1986). *Historical Corrections in the United States, 1850–1984.* Washington, DC: Bureau of Justice Statistics.

CALDWELL, MICHAEL F. (2002). "How Do We Know About Juvenile Sexual Reoffense Risk?" *Child Maltreatment* 7:291–302.

CALHOUN, GEORGIA B. (2001). "Differences Between Male and Female Juvenile Offenders as Measured by the BASC." *Journal of Offender Rehabilitation* 33:87–96.

CALIFORNIA BOARD OF CORRECTIONS (2000). *Improving California's Response to Mentally Ill Offenders: An Analysis of County-Level Needs.* Sacramento, CA: California Board of Corrections.

CALIFORNIA DEPARTMENT OF ALCOHOL AND DRUG PROGRAMS (2003). *Female Offender Treatment Program (FOTP).* Sacramento, CA: California Department of Alcohol and Drug Programs.

CALIFORNIA DEPARTMENT OF CORRECTIONS (1998). *Historical Trends: Institution and Parole Population, 1976–1996.* Sacramento, CA: California Department of Corrections.

CALIFORNIA DEPARTMENT OF CORRECTIONS (2003). *Elkhorn Correctional Facility Boot Camp.* Sacramento, CA: California Department of Corrections.

CAMP, CAMILLE GRAHAM and GEORGE M. CAMP (2003). *The Corrections Yearbook 2002.* Middletown, CT: Criminal Justice Institute, Inc.

CAMP, DAVID A. and HARJIT S. SANDHU (2003). *Evaluation of Female Offender Regimented Treatment Program (FORT).* Oklahoma City, OK: Oklahoma Department of Corrections.

CAMP, SCOTT D. et al. (2002). "Using Inmate Survey Data in Assessing Prison Performance: A Case Study Comparing Private and Public Prisons." *Criminal Justice Review* 27:26–51.

CAMP, SCOTT D. et al. (2003). "The Influence of Prisons on Inmate Misconduct: A Multilevel Investigation." *Justice Quarterly* 20:501–533.

CAMPBELL, JACQUELYN C. (ed.) (1995). *Assessing Dangerousness: Violence by Sexual Offenders, Batterers, and Child Abusers.* Thousand Oaks, CA: Sage.

CAMPBELL, ROBIN and ROBERT VICTOR WOLF (2002). "Problem Solving Probation: An Overview of Four Community-Based Experiments." *APPA Perspectives* 26:26–34.

CANADA SOLICITOR GENERAL (1998). *Towards a Just, Peaceful and Safe Society: The Corrections and Conditional Release Act Five Years Later.* Ottawa, CAN: Public Works and Government Services of Canada.

CAREY, MARK (2003). "The Metamorphosis of an Inmate." *APPA Perspectives* 27:34–37.

CARLSON, ERIC W. and EVALYN PARKS (1979). *Critical Issues in Adult Probation: Issues in Probation Management.* Washington, DC: U.S. Department of Justice.

CARPENTER, MARY (1967). *Reformatory Prison Discipline as Developed by the Rt. Hon. Sir Walter Crofton in the Irish Convict Prison.* Montclair, NJ: Patterson-Smith (reprint of 1872 ed.).

CARPENTER, PATRICIA and DENNIS P. SUGRUE (1984). "Psychoeducation in an Outpatient Setting: Designing a Heterogeneous Population of Juvenile Delinquents." *Adolescence* 19:113–122.

CAVANAUGH, MICHAEL J. (1992). "Intensive Supervision in South Carolina: Accountability and Assistance." *Corrections Compendium* 17:1–6.

CAVENDER, GRAY and PAUL KNEPPER (1992). "Strange Interlude: An Analysis of Juvenile Parole Revocation Decision Making." *Social Problems* 39:387–399.

CEPEDA, ALICE and VALDEZ AVELARDO (2003). "Risk Behaviors Among Young Mexican-American Gang-Associated Females: Sexual Relations, Partying, Substance Abuse, and Crime." *Journal of Adolescent Research* 18:90–106.

CHAMPION, DEAN J. (1994). *Measuring Offender Risk: A Criminal Justice Sourcebook.* Westport, CT: Greenwood.

CHAMPION, DEAN J. (2001). *Review of Literature Relating to Collective Bargaining and Probation and Parole Officers.* Laredo, TX: Texas A & M International University.

CHAMPION, DEAN J. (2003). *Administration of Criminal Justice: Structure, Function, and Process.* Englewood Cliffs, NJ: Prentice Hall.

CHANG, TRACY P.H. and DOUGLAS E. THOMPKINS (2002). "Corporations Go to Prisons: The Expansion of Corporate Power in the Correctional Industry." *Labor Studies Journal* 27:45–69.

CHARLES, MICHAEL T. (1989a). "The Development of a Juvenile Electronic Monitoring Program." *Federal Probation* 53:3–12.

CHARLES, MICHAEL T. (1989b). "Electronic Monitoring for Juveniles." *Journal of Crime and Justice* 12:147–169.

CHESNEY-LIND, MEDA and SCOTT K. OKAMOTO (2001). "Gender Matters: Patterns in Girls' Delinquency and Gender Responsive Programming." *Journal of Forensic Psychology Practice* 1:1–28.

CHUNG, ICK JOONG et al. (2002). "Childhood Predictors of Offense Trajectories." *Journal of Research in Crime and Delinquency* 39:60–90.

CHUTE, C.L. (1922). "Probation and Suspended Sentence." *Journal of the American Institute of Criminal Law and Criminology* 12:558.

CIANCIA, JAMES J. and RICHARD B. TALTY (1999). *New Jersey Intensive Supervision Program.* Trenton, NJ: Division of Parole and Community Programs.

CLARK, PATRICIA M. (1995). "The Evolution of Michigan's Community Corrections Act." *Corrections Today* 57:38–39, 68.

CLAY, JOHN (2001). *Maconochie's Experiment.* London, UK: John Murray.

CLAYTON, SUSAN L. (2003). "Bureau of Justice Statistics Releases New Findings on Correctional Populations." *On the Line* 26:1–2.

CLEAR, TODD R. and HARRY R. DAMMER (2000). *The Offender in the Community.* Belmont, CA: Wadsworth.

CLEAR, TODD R. and EDWARD J. LATESSA (1993). "Probation Officers' Roles in Intensive Supervision: Surveillance Versus Treatment." *Justice Quarterly* 10:441–462.

COCHRAN, JOHN K. et al. (1997). "Assessing Sentencing Reform: An *Ex Ante* Impact Assessment of the Oklahoma Truth-in-Sentencing Act." *Journal of Crime and Justice* 20:107–130.

COCOZZA, JOSEPH J. and KRISTIN A. STAINBROOK (1998). *The Ohio Linkages Project: Final Evaluation Report.* Delmar, NY: Policy Research Associates.

COHEN, ALBERT K. (1955). *Delinquent Boys.* Glencoe, IL: Free Press.

COHN, ALVIN W. et al. (2002). "What Works in Corrections?" *Federal Probation* 66:4–83.

COID, JEREMY W. (2001). "The Federal Administrative Maximum Penitentiary, Florence, Colorado." *Medicine, Science, and the Law* 41:287–297.

COLEMAN, JOHN L. (2002). *Police Assessment Testing: An Assessment Center Handbook for Law Enforcement Personnel, 3/e.* Springfield, IL: Charles C. Thomas.

COLLINS, MARY ELIZABETH, IRA M. SCHWARTZ, and IRWIN EPSTEIN (2001). "Risk Factors for Adult Imprisonment in a Sample of Youth Released from Residential Child Care." *Children and Youth Services Review* 23:203–225.

COMMITTEE OF SEVENTY (1998). *Philadelphia Police Department Governance Study.* Philadelphia: Morrison.

COMMUNITY EDUCATION CENTERS (2003). *CEC Programs Target Women's Needs.* Roseland, NJ: Community Education Centers.

CONABOY, RICHARD P. (1997). "The United States Sentencing Commission: A New Component in the Federal Criminal Justice System." *Federal Probation* 61:58–62.

CONLY, CATHERINE (1999). *Coordinating Community Services for Mentally Ill Offenders: Maryland's Community Criminal Justice Treatment Program.* Washington, DC: National Institute of Justice.

CONNECTICUT BOARD OF PAROLE (2001). *Mission, Functions, and Procedures.* Hartford, CT: Connecticut Board of Parole.

CONNELLY, CLARE and SHANTI WILLIAMS (2000). *Review of the Research Literature on Serious Violent and Sexual Offenders.* Glasgow: Scottish Executive Central Research Unit.

CONNELLY, CYNTHIA D. et al. (2000). "Assessment of Intimate Partner Violence among High-Risk Postpartum Mothers: Concordance with Clinical Measures." *Women and Health* 31:21–37.

CONRAD, JOHN P. (1987). "Return to John Augustus." *Federal Probation* 51:22–27.

COOK COUNTY CIRCUIT COURT (2003). *Court Programs.* Chicago: Cook County Circuit Court.

CORBETT, RONALD P. JR. and M. KAY HARRIS (1999). "Up to Speed: A Review of Research for Practitioners." *Federal Probation* 63:67–71.

CORNELIUS, GARY F. (1996). *Jails in America: An Overview of Issues (2/e).* Laurel, MD: American Correctional Association.

CORRADO, RAYMOND R. et al. (2000). "Diagnosing Mental Disorders in Offenders: Conceptual and Methodological Issues." *Criminal Behaviour and Mental Health* 10:29–39.

CORRECTIONAL ASSOCIATION OF NEW YORK (2000). *Health Care in New York State Prisons: A Report of Findings and Recommendations By the Visiting Committee on Correctional Association of New York.* New York: Correctional Association of New York Prison Visiting Committee.

CORRECTIONAL SERVICE OF CANADA (2000). *Reflections of a Canadian Prison Warden: The Visionary Legacy of Ron Wiebe.* Ottawa, ON: Correctional Service of Canada.

CORRECTIONS COMPENDIUM (2003). "Inmate Lawsuits and Grievances." *Corrections Compendium* 28:8.

COSGROVE, EDWARD J. (1994). "ROBO-PO: The Life and Times of a Federal Probation Officer." *Federal Probation* 58:29–30.

COSTELLO, BARBARA J. (2000). "Techniques of Neutralization and Self-Esteem: A Critical Test of Social Control and Neutralization Theory." *Deviant Behavior* 21:307–329.

COUNTY OF STEARNS (2003). *The Stearns County, Minnesota ISP Program.* Stearns County, MN: County of Stearns, Minnesota.

COURTRIGHT, KEVIN E., BRUCE L. BERG, and ROBERT J. MUTCHNICK (1997). "The Cost Effectiveness of Using House Arrest with Electronic Monitoring for Drunk Drivers." *Federal Probation* 61:19–22.

COYNE, RANDALL and LYN ENTZEROTH (2001). *Capital Punishment and the Judicial Process, 2/e.* Englewood Cliffs, NJ: Prentice Hall.

CRAISSATI, JACKIE, GRACE McCLURG, and KEVIN D. BROWNE (2002). "The Parental Bonding Experiences of Sex Offenders: A Comparison Between Child Molesters and Rapists." *Child Abuse and Neglect* 26:909–921.

CRAWLEY, ELAINE (2002). "Bringing It All Back Home? The Impact of Prison Officers' Work on Their Families." *Probation Journal* 49:277–286.

CROWLEY, PATRICK (2003). "Shock Probation Requested in Auto Death Case." *Cincinnati Inquirer,* March 4, 2003:1–3.

CULLEN, FRANCIS T. (1986). "The Privatization of Treatment: Prison Reform in the 1980's." *Federal Probation* 50:8–16.

CULLIVER, CONCETTA C. (1993). *Female Criminality: The State of the Art.* New York: Garland.

CUMMINGS, HOMER (2003). "They All Come Out." *Federal Probation* 67:9–11.

CUNNINGHAM, JOHN A. et al. (1998). "Current Research and Clinical Practice." *Journal of Offender Rehabilitation* 27:167–208.

CURRY, G. DAVID and SCOTT H. DECKER (2003). *Confronting Gangs: Crime and Community 2/e.* Belmont, CA: Wadsworth.

CURTIS, RIC (2003). "Crack, Cocaine, and Heroin: Drug Eras in Williamsburg, Brooklyn, 1960–2000." *Addiction Research and Theory* 11:47–63.

DALLEY, LANETTE P. (2002). "Policy Implications Relating to Inmate Mothers and Their Children: Will the Past Be Prologue?" *Prison Journal* 82:234–268.

D'ANCA, ALFRED R. (2001). "The Role of the Federal Probation Officer in the Guidelines Sentencing System." *Federal Probation* 63:20–23.

DAWSON, ROGER E. (1992). "Opponent Process Theory for Substance Abuse Treatment." *Juvenile and Family Court Journal,* 43:51–59.

DAY, MICHAEL, SHARON FRIEDMAN, and KRISTIN CHRISTOPHERSEN (1998). *A Women-Centered Approach to Correctional Programming: The WICS Lifeskills Program in Portland, OR.* Portland, OR: Portland State University.

DEAR, GREG E. et al. (2002). "Prisoners' Willingness to Approach Prison Officers for Support: The Officer's Views." *Journal of Offender Rehabilitation* 34:33–46.

DECKER, SCOTT H. (2000). "Legitimating Drug Use: A Note on the Impact of Gang Membership and Drug Sales on the Use of Illicit Drugs." *Justice Quarterly 17:* 393–410.

DECKER, SCOTT H. (2001). *From the Streets to Prison: Understanding and Responding to Gangs.* Indianapolis, IN: National Major Gang Task Force.

DECKER, SCOTT H. et al. (2002). *An Implementation Assessment of the Domestic Violence Projects in Lake Winnebago and Kankakee Counties.* Washington, DC: National Institute of Justice.

DEITCH, DAVID A. et al. (2001). "Does In-Custody Therapeutic Community Substance Abuse Treatment Impact Custody Personnel?" *Corrections Compendium* 26:1–24.

DEL CARMEN, ROLANDO V. (1990). "Probation and Parole: Facing Today's Tough Liability Issues." *Corrections Today* 52:34–42.

DEL CARMEN, ROLANDO V. and JAMES ALAN PILANT (1994). "The Scope of Judicial Immunity for Probation and Parole Officers." *APPA Perspectives* 18:14–21.

DELAWARE DEPARTMENT OF CORRECTIONS (2003). *Bureau of Community Corrections.* Dover: Delaware Department of Corrections.

DELAWARE OFFICE OF THE BUDGET (2002). *Delaware Juvenile Recidivism: 1994-2000 Level III, IV, and V Recidivism Study.* Dover, DE: Delaware Office of the Budget, Statistical Analysis Center.

DEL CARMEN, ROLANDO V. and GENE BONHAM (2001). "Overview of Legal Liabilities." *APPA Perspectives* 25:28–33.

DEL CARMEN, ROLANDO V., MARY PARKER, and FRANCES P. REDDINGTON (1998). *Briefs of Leading Cases in Juvenile Justice.* Cincinnati, OH: Anderson.

DEL CARMEN, ROLANDO V. et al. (2000). *Civil Liabilities and Other Legal Issues for Probation/Parole Officers and Supervisors 3/e.* Washington, DC: U.S. National Institute of Corrections.

DEMBO, RICHARD et al. (1999). "Engaging High Risk Families in Community Based Intervention Services." *Aggression and Violent Behavior* 4:41–58.

DEMPSTER, REBECCA J. and STEPHEN D. HART (2002). "The Relative Utility of Fixed and Variable Risk Factors in Discriminating Sexual Recidivists and Nonrecidivists." *Sexual Abuse: A Journal of Research and Treatment* 14:121–138.

DICKEY, WALTER J. and DENNIS WAGNER (1990). *From the Bottom Up: The High Risk Offender Intensive Supervision Program.* Madison, WI: Continuing Education and Outreach, University of Wisconsin Law School.

DILLINGHAM, DAVID D. et al. (1999). *Annual Issue 1999: Classification and Risk Assessment.* Longmont, CO: U.S. National Institute of Corrections.

DiVITO, ROBERT J. (1991). "Survey of Mandatory Education Policies in State Penal Institutions." *Journal of Correctional Education* 42:126–132.

DOELLING, DIETER, ARTHUR HARTMANN, and MONIKA TRAULSEN (2002). "Legalbewachrung Nach Tacter-Opfer-Ausgleich im Jugendstrafrecht." *Monatsschrift fuer Krimmologie und Strafrechtsreform* 85:185–193.

DOLAN, RICHARD, MARTI HARKNESS, and KATHY McGUIRE (2000). *Special Preview: Escape from Martin Treatment Center for Sexually Violent Predators.* Tallahassee, FL: Office of Program Policy Analysis and Government Accountability, Florida Legislature.

DOEREN, STEPHEN E. and MARY J. HAGEMAN (1982). *Community Corrections.* Cincinnati, OH: Anderson.

DOERNER, WILLIAM G. and MARK L. DANTZKER (eds.) (2000). *Contemporary Police Organization and Management: Issues and Trends.* Boston: Butterworth-Heinemann.

DONNELLY, S.M. (1980). *Community Service Orders in Federal Probation.* Washington, DC: National Institute of Justice.

DOUGLAS COUNTY COURT (2003). *Programs and Services.* Douglas County, KS: Douglas County Court.

DOWDY, ERIC R., MICHAEL G. LACY, and N. PRABHA UNNITHAN (2002). "Correctional Prediction and the Level of Supervision Inventory." *Journal of Criminal Justice* 30:29–39.

DRIGGS, JOHN and THOMAS H. ZOET (1987). "Breaking the Cycle: Sex Offenders on Parole." *Corrections Today* 49:124–129.

DUNBABIN, JEAN (ed.) (2002). *Captivity and Imprisonment in Medieval Europe.* Basingstoke, UK: Palgrave Macmillan.

DUNCAN, RANDALL W., JOHN C. SPEIR, and TAMMY MEREDITH (1999). "An Overlay of the North Carolina Structured Sentencing Guidelines on the 1996 Georgia

Felony Offender Population." *Justice Research and Policy* 1:43–59.

DUTTON, DONNIE W. (ed.) (2000). "Post-Conviction Sex Offender Testing." *Polygraph* 29:1–115.

DZUR, ALBERT W. and ALAN WERTHEIMER (2002). "Forgiveness and Public Deliberation: The Practice of Restorative Justice." *Criminal Justice Ethics* 21:3–20.

ECKHART, DAN (2001). "Civil Actions Related to Gangs: A Survey of Federal Cases." *Corrections Management Quarterly* 5:23–36.

EDLESON, JEFFREY L. et al. (2003). "How Children are Involved in Adult Domestic Violence: Results from a Four-City Telephone Survey." *Journal of Interpersonal Violence* 18:18–32.

EDWARDS, TODD (1998). *The Aging Inmate Population.* Atlanta, GA: Southern Legislative Conference, Council of State Governments.

EDWARDS, WILLIAM and CHRISTOPHER HENSLEY (2001). "Restructuring Sex Offender Sentencing: A Therapeutic Jurisprudence Approach to the Criminal Justice Process." *International Journal of Offender Therapy and Comparative Criminology* 43:646–662.

EGGLESTON, CAROLYN REBECCA (1989). *Zebulon Brockway and Elmira Reformatory: A Study of Correctional/Special Education.* Richmond, VA: Virginia Commonwealth University.

EGGLESTON, ELAINE P. and JOHN H. LAUB (2002). "The Onset of Adult Offending: A Neglected Dimension of the Criminal Career." *Journal of Criminal Justice* 30:603–622.

EISENBERG, MICHAEL, NANCY ARRIGONA, and DEE KOFOWIT (1999). *Overview of Special Needs Parole Policy.* Austin, TX: Texas Criminal Justice Policy Council.

EISENBERG, MICHAEL and BRITTANI TRUSTY (2002). *Overview of the Inner Change Freedom Initiative: The Faith-Based Prison Program within the Texas Department of Criminal Justice.* Austin, TX: Texas Criminal Justice Policy Council.

ELDER, ALICE P. FRANKLIN (1996). "Inside Gang Society: How Gang Members Imitate Legitimate Social Forms." *Journal of Gang Research* 3:1–12.

ELLSWORTH, THOMAS (ed.) (1996). *Contemporary Community Corrections.* Prospect Heights, IL: Waveland.

EMPEY, LAMAR T. and JEROME RABOW (1961). "The Provo Experiment in Delinquency Rehabilitation." *American Sociological Review* 26:679–695.

ENOS, RICHARD, JOHN E. HOLMAN, and MARNIE E. CARROLL (1999). *Alternative Sentencing: Electronically Monitored Correctional Supervision, 2/e.* Bristol, IN: Wyndham Hall.

EREZ, EDNA and KATHY LASTER (eds.) (2000). "Special Issue on Domestic Violence." *International Review of Victimology* 7:1–242.

ERWIN, BILLIE S. (1986). "Turning Up the Heat on Probationers in Georgia." *Federal Probation* 50:17–24.

EVANS, DONALD G. (1999). "Broken Windows: Fixing Probation." *Corrections Today* 61:30–31.

EVANS, DONALD G. (2001). "Volunteer Program Aids Released Offender Supervision." *Corrections Today* 63:142–144.

FABELO, TONY (2002). "The Impact of Prison Education on Community Reintegration of Inmates: The Texas Case." *Journal of Correctional Education* 53:106–110.

FADER, JAMIE J. et al. (2001). "Factors Involved in Decisions on Commitment to Delinquency Programs for First-Time Juvenile Offenders." *Justice Quarterly* 18:323–341.

FAGAN, THOMAS J. (2003). *Negotiating Correctional Incidents.* Lanham, MD: American Correctional Association.

FALCAO, TERRY (2000). "The Human Rights Act of 1999: Opening the Door to Negligence Actions Against the Police." *The Police Journal* 73:61–68.

FALKIN, GREGORY P., SHIELA STRAUSS, and TIMOTHY BOHEN (1999). "Matching Drug-Involved Probationers to Appropriate Drug Interventions." *Federal Probation* 63:3–8.

FALS, STEWART WILLIAM (2003). "The Occurrence of Partner Physical Aggression on Days of Alcohol Consumption: A Longitudinal Diary Study." *Journal of Counseling and Clinical Psychology* 71:41–52.

FARABEE, DAVID, HAIKANG SHEN, and SYLVIA SANCHEZ (2002). "Perceived Coercion and Treatment Need Among Mentally Ill Parolees." *Criminal Justice and Behavior* 29:76–86.

FARKAS, MARY ANN (2000). "A Typology of Correctional Officers." *International Journal of Offender Therapy and Comparative Criminology* 44:431–449.

FARRALL, STEPHEN et al. (2002). "Long-Term Absences from Probation: Officers' and Probationers' Accounts." *The Howard Journal of Criminal Justice* 41:263–278.

FARRELL, AMY (2000). "Women, Crime, and Drugs: Testing the Effect of Therapeutic Communities." *Women and Criminal Justice* 11:21–48.

FARRELL, PENNIE and CHARLES EDSON (2003). "Identification and Management of Psychopaths in Court-Mandated Treatment Programs." *Corrections Compendium* 28:6–7, 25–29.

FAULKNER, DAVID (2002). "Prisoners as Citizens." *British Journal of Community Justice* 1:11–19.

FEATHER, N.T. and JACQUELINE SOUTER (2002). "Reactions to Mandatory Sentences in Relation to the Ethnic Identity and Criminal History of the Offender." *Law and Human Behavior* 26:417–438.

FEDER, LYNETTE and ROBERT F. BORUCH (eds.) (2000). "The Need for Experimental Research in Criminal Justice Settings." *Crime and Delinquency* 46:291–334.

FELD, BARRY C. (2000). *Cases and Materials on Juvenile Justice Administration.* St. Paul, MN: West Group.

FELSON, RICHARD B. and DANA L. HAYNIE (2002). "Pubertal Development, Social Factors, and Delinquency among Adolescent Boys." *Criminology* 40:967–988.

FERRARO, KATHLEEN J. (2003). "The Words Change, But the Melody Lingers: The Persistence of Battered Woman Syndrome in Criminal Cases Involving Battered Women." *Violence Against Women* 9:110–129.

FESTERVAN, EARLENE (2003). *Women Probationers: Supervision and Success.* Lanham, MD: American Correctional Association.

FIELDS, SCOTT A. and JOHN R. McNAMARA (eds.). (2003) "The Prevention of Child and Adolescent Violence: A Review." *Aggression and Violent Behavior* 8: 61–91.

FIGUEIRA-McDONOUGH, JOSEFINA et al. (2002). *Women at the Margins: Neglect, Punishment, and Resistance.* Binghamton, NY: Haworth.

FINIGAN, MICHAEL W. (1999). "Assessing Cost Off-Sets in a Drug Court Setting." *National Drug Court Institute Review* 2:59–91.

FINN, MARY A. and Suzanne Muirhead-Steves (2002). "The Effectiveness of Electronic Monitoring with Violent Male Parolees." *Justice Quarterly* 19:293–312.

FINN, PETER (1999). "Correctional Officer Stress: A Cause for Concern and Additional Help." *Federal Probation* 62:65–74.

FIRESTONE, PHILIP et al. (2000). "Prediction of Recidivism in Extrafamilial Child Molesters Based on Court-Related Assessments." *Sexual Abuse: A Journal of Research and Treatment* 12:203–221.

FISHER, DAWN, ANTHONY BEECH, and KEVIN BROWNE, (2000). "The Effectiveness of Relapse Prevention Training in a Group of Incarcerated Child Molesters." *Psychology, Crime, and Law* 6:181–195.

FLANAGAN, LAMONT W. (1997). "Prison Is a Luxury We Can No Longer Afford." *Corrections Management Quarterly* 1:60–63.

FLORES, J. ROBERT (2003). *Juveniles in Court.* Washington, DC: Office of Juvenile Justice and Delinquency Prevention Programs.

FLORIDA ADVISORY COUNCIL (1994). *Local Government and the State-Level Partnership.* Tallahassee, FL: Florida Advisory Council on Intergovernmental Relations.

FLORIDA DEPARTMENT OF CORRECTIONS (1999). *Time Served By Criminals Sentenced to Florida's Prisons: The Impact of Punishment Policies from 1979–1999.* Tallahassee, FL: Florida Department of Corrections Bureau of Research and Data Analysis.

FLORIDA DEPARTMENT OF CORRECTIONS (2000). *Education and Programs: Operational Plan for Female Offenders.* Tallahassee, FL: Florida Department of Corrections.

FLORIDA DEPARTMENT OF CORRECTIONS (2003). *Florida's Community Supervision Population Monthly Status Report.* Tallahassee, FL: Florida Department of Corrections, Bureau of Research and Data Analysis, Community Supervision Section.

FLORIDA DEPARTMENT OF LAW ENFORCEMENT (1998). *Buying Guns in Florida.* Tallahassee, FL: Florida Department of Law Enforcement Statistical Analysis Center.

FLOWERS, R. BARRI (2002). *Kids Who Commit Adult Crimes: Serious Criminality by Juvenile Offenders.* Binghamton, NY: Haworth.

FOGEL, DAVID and JOE HUDSON (1981). *Justice as Fairness: Perspectives on the Justice Model.* Cincinnati, OH: Anderson.

FONG, ROBERT S., RONALD E. VOGEL, and SALVADOR BUENTELLO (1996). "Prison Gang Dynamics: A Research Update." In J. Mitchell Miller and Jeffrey P. Rush (eds.), *Gangs: A Criminal Justice Approach.* Cincinnati, OH: Anderson.

FRANKFORT-HOWARD, ROBYNE and STEPHAN ROMM. (2002). "Outcomes of a Residential Treatment of Antisocial Youth: Development of or Cessation from Adult Antisocial Behavior." *Residential Treatment for Children and Youth* 19:53–70.

FREEMAN, ROBERT M. (1999). *Correctional Organization and Management: Public Safety, Policy Challenges, Behavior, and Structure.* Boston: Butterworth-Heinemann.

FRIENDSHIP, CAROLINE, ANTHONY R. BEECH, and KEVIN D. BROWNE. (2002). "Reconviction as an Outcome Measure in Research." *The British Journal of Criminology* 42:442–444.

FROST, GREGORY A. (2002). "Florida's Innovative Use of GPS for Community Corrections." *Journal of Offender Monitoring* 15:6.

GAARDER, EMILY and JOANNE BELKNAP (2002). "Tenuous Borders: Girls Transferred to Adult Court." *Criminology: An Interdisciplinary Science* 40:481–518.

GARBARINO, JAMES et al. (2002). "Trauma and Juvenile Delinquency: Theory, Research, and Interventions." *Journal of Aggression, Maltreatment, and Trauma* 6:1–264.

GARDNER, WILLIAM et al. (1996). "Clinical Versus Actuarial Predictions of Violence in Patients with Mental Illnesses." *Journal of Counseling and Clinical Psychology* 64:602–609.

GARRITY, THOMAS F. et al. (2002). "Factors Predicting Illness and Health Services Use Among Male Kentucky Prisoners with a History of Drug Abuse." *Prison Journal* 82:295–313.

GEER, TRACEY M. et al. (2001). "Predictors of Treatment Completion in a Correctional Sex Offender Treatment Program." *International Journal of Offender Therapy and Comparative Criminology* 45:302–313.

GEORGIA PAROLE REVIEW (1990). "Georgia Rehabilitation Program Helps Disabled Parolees." *Corrections Today* 52:174–176.

GERSHON, ROBYN R.M. et al. (2002). "Work Stress in Aging Police Officers." *Journal of Occupational and Environmental Medicine* 44:160–167.

GETTY, CAROL P. (2000). *Supervised Release Matters: A Study of Post Incarceration in the Federal System, 1994–1998.* Ann Arbor, MI: University Microfilms Services.

GIANAS, GREG. (1996). "Washington's McNeil Island Work Ethic Camp: An Evolution in Corrections?" *Corrections Compendium* 21:1–9.

GIBLIN, MATTHEW J. (2002). "Using Police Officers to Enhance the Supervision of Juvenile Probationers: An Evaluation of the Anchorage CAN Program." *Crime and Delinquency* 48:116–137.

GIDO, ROSEMARY L. (ed.) (1998). "Evolution of the Concepts Correctional Organization and Organizational Change." *Criminal Justice Policy Review* 9:5–139.

GILES, MELANIE and JUDITH MULLINEUX. (2000). "Assessment and Decision-Making: Probation Officers' Construing of Factors Relevant to Risk." *Legal and Criminological Psychology* 5:165–185.

GILLIS, JOHN W. (2002a). *Restitution: Making It Work.* Washington, DC: U.S. Department of Justice.

GILLIS, JOHN W. (2002b). *Victim Input into Plea Agreements.* Washington, DC: U.S. Department of Justice.

GIOVANNI, ERIC. (2002). "Perceived Needs and Interests of Juveniles Held in Preventive Detention." *Juvenile and Family Court Journal* 53:51–63.

GLAESER, EDWARD L. and BRUCE SACERDOTE. (2000). *The Determinants of Punishment: Deterrence, Incapacitation, and Vengeance.* Cambridge, MA: National Bureau of Economic Research.

GLASER, BRIAN A. et al. (2001). "Multi-Observer Assessment of Problem Behavior in Adjudicated Youths: Patterns of Discrepancies." *Child and Family Behavior Therapy* 23:33–45.

GLASSER, WILLIAM. (1976). *The Identity Society.* New York: Harper and Row.

GLAZE, LAUREN E. (2003). *Probation and Parole in the United States, 2002.* Washington, DC: Bureau of Justice Statistics.

GLICK, BARRY et al. (2001). *Recess Is Over: A Handbook for Managing Youthful Offender in Adult Systems.* Lanham, MD: American Correctional Association.

GLOVER, WILLIAM V. (2002). "Successfully Implementing a Full Mandatory Attendance Policy in the Arkansas Department of Correction School District." *Journal of Correctional Education* 53:101–105.

GOFFMAN, ERVING. (1961). *Asylums.* Garden City, NY: Anchor.

GOLDKAMP, JOHN S. (2000). "The Drug Court Response: Issues and Implications for Justice Change." *Albany Law Review* 63:923–961.

GOLDSON, BARRY and JANET JAMIESON. (2002). "Community Bail or Penal Remand? A Critical Analysis of Recent Policy Developments in Relation to Unconvicted and/or Unsentenced Juveniles." *British Journal of Community Justice* 1:63–76.

GOODING, VIRGIL A. SR. (2001). "Family Therapy in Community-Based Corrections: A Promising Trend." *APPA Perspectives* 25:38–41.

GORDON, ROBERT M. (2000). "Criminal Business Organizations: Street Gangs and 'Wanna-Be' Groups: A

Vancouver Perspective." *Canadian Journal of Criminology* 42:39–60.

GOTTFREDSON, MICHAEL R. and DON M. GOTTFREDSON. (1988). *Decision Making in Criminal Justice: Toward the Rational Exercise of Discretion (2nd ed.).* New York: Plenum.

GOVER, ANGELA R., DORIS LAYTON MACKENZIE, and GAYLENE J. STYVE (2000). "Boot Camps and Traditional Correctional Facilities for Juveniles: A Comparison of the Participants, Daily Activities, and Environments." *Journal of Criminal Justice* 28:53–68.

GOWDY, VONCILE B. et al. (1998). *Women in Criminal Justice: A Twenty-Year Update.* Rockville, MD: U.S. National Criminal Justice Reference Service.

GOWEN, DARREN. (1995). "Electronic Monitoring in the Southern District of Mississippi." *Federal Probation* 59:10–13.

GOWEN, DARREN. (2000). "Overview of the Federal Home Confinement Program, 1988–1996." *Federal Probation* 64:11–18.

GOWEN, DARREN. (2001). "Analysis of Competing Risks in the Federal Home Confinement Program." *The Journal of Offender Monitoring* 14:5–9, 11.

GOWEN, DARREN and JERRI B. SPEYERER. (1995). "Compulsive Gambling and the Criminal Offender: A Treatment and Supervision Approach." *Federal Probation* 59:36–39.

GRABAREK, JOANNA K., MICHAEL L. BOURKE, and VINCENT VAN HASSELT. (2002). "Empirically Derived MCMI-III Personality Profiles of Incarcerated Female Substance Abusers." *Journal of Offender Rehabilitation* 35:19–29.

GRANSKY, LAURA A. and MARISA E. PATTERSON. (1999). "A Discussion of Illinois' Gang-Free Prison: Evaluation Results." *Corrections Management Quarterly* 3:30–42.

GRANT, BRIAN A. and CHRISTA A. GILLIS. (1999). *Day Parole Outcome, Criminal History, and Other Predictors of Successful Sentence Completion.* Ottawa, ON: Research Branch, Correctional Service of Canada.

GRAY, JAMES P. (2003). "The Peer Court Experience." *APPA Perspectives* 27:30–33.

GRAY, RICHARD M. (2001). "Addictions and the Self: A Self-Enhancement Model for Drug Treatment in the Criminal Justice System." *Journal of Social Work Practice in the Addictions* 1:75–91.

GREENE, JUDITH and VINCENT SCHIRALDI. (2002). *Cutting Correctly: New Prison Policies for Times of Fiscal Crisis.* Washington, DC: Justice Policy Institute.

GREENE COUNTY CRIMINAL COURT. (2003). *The Greene County Intensive Supervision Probation Program.* Greene County, OH: Greene County Criminal Court.

GREENWOOD, PETER W. (1982). *Selective Incapacitation.* Santa Monica, CA: Rand.

GREENWOOD, PETER W. and SUSAN TURNER. (1993). "Private Presentence Reports for Serious Juvenile Offenders: Implementation Issues and Impacts." *Justice Quarterly* 10:229–243.

GREENWOOD PRESS. (ed.) (2002). *Fair Trial Rights of the Accused: A Documentary History.* Westport, CT: Greenwood.

GREGORY, CAROL and EDNA EREZ. (2002). "The Effects of Batterer Intervention Programs: The Battered Women's Perspectives." *Violence Against Women* 8:206–232.

GRIETENS, HANS, JACOBUS RINK, and WALTER HELLINCKX. (2003). "Nonbehavioral Correlates of Juvenile Delinquency: Communications of Detained and Nondetained Young People About Social Limits." *Journal of Adolescent Research* 18:68–89.

GRIFFIN, MARIE L. (2002). "The Influence of Professional Orientation on Detention Officers' Attitudes Toward the Use of Force." *Criminal Justice and Behavior* 29:250–277.

GRIFFIN, MARIE L. and GAYLENE S. ARMSTRONG. (2003). "The Effect of Local Life Circumstances on Female Probationers' Offending." *Justice Quarterly* 20:213–239.

GRIMES, PAUL W. and KEVIN E. ROGERS. (1999). "Truth-in-Sentencing, Law Enforcement, and Inmate Population Growth." *Journal of Socio-Economics* 28:745–757.

GRISET, PAMALA L. (1996). "Determinate Sentencing and Administrative Discretion over Time Served in Prison: A Case Study of Florida." *Crime and Delinquency* 42:127–143.

GRISSO, THOMAS, ALAN TOMKINS, and PAMELA CASEY. (1988). "Psychosocial Concepts in Juvenile Law." *Law and Human Behavior* 12:403–438.

GRISSO, THOMAS et al. (2000). "Violent Thoughts and Violent Behavior Following Hospitalization for Mental Disorder." *Journal of Counseling and Clinical Psychology* 68:388–398.

GROSSI, ELIZABETH L. (ed.) (1997). "Prison and Jail Boot Camps." *Journal of Contemporary Criminal Justice* 13:93–205.

HAAPANEN, RUDY and LEE BRITTON. (2002). "Drug Testing for Youthful Offenders on Parole: An Experimental Evaluation." *Criminology and Public Policy* 1:217–244.

HALE, TESSA. (2001). "Creating Visions and Achieving Goals: The Women in Community Service's Lifeskills Program." *Corrections Today* 63:33–37.

HAMMETT, THEODORE M., MARY PATRICIA HARMON, and WILLIAM RHODES. (2002). "The Burden of Infectious Disease among Inmates of and Releasees from United States Correctional Facilities." *American Journal of Public Health* 92:1789–1794.

HAMMETT, THEODORE M., CHERYL ROBERTS, and SOFIA KENNEDY. (2001). "Health-Related Issues in Prison Reentry." *Crime and Delinquency* 47:390–409.

HANCOCK, STEPHANIE. (2003). "The First National Census on Juvenile Probation." 27:22–23.

HARLAN, VERNON T. (1998). *Urban Decay: Adolescent Separatism, Rap Culture, and Mainstream America.* Bethesda, MD: Austin & Winfield.

HARRELL, ADELE and JOHN ROMAN. (1999). *Process Evaluation of the Brooklyn Treatment Court and Network of Services: The First Three Years.* Washington, DC: The Urban Institute.

HARRELL, ADELE et al. (2002). "Breaking the Cycle of Drugs and Crime: Findings from the Birmingham BTC Demonstration." *Criminology and Public Policy* 1:189–216.

HARRIS, GRANT T., MARNIE E. RICE, and CATHERINE A. CORMIER. (2002). "Prospective Replication of the Violence Risk Appraisal Guide in Predicting Violent Recidivism among Forensic Patients." *Law and Human Behavior* 26:377–394.

HARRIS, PATRICIA M., REBECCA D. PETERSEN, and SAMANTHA RAPOZA. (2001). *Journal of Criminal Justice* 29:307–318.

HARRIS, ROBERT J. and T. WING LO. (2002). "Community Service: Its Use in Criminal Justice." *International Journal of Offender Therapy and Comparative Criminology* 46:427–444.

HARRISON, LANA D. et al. (1998). "Integrating HIV-Prevention Strategies in a Therapeutic Community Work-Release Program for Criminal Offenders." *Prison Journal* 78:232–243.

HARRISON, PAIGE M. and ALLEN J. BECK (2003). *Prisoners in 2002.* Washington, DC: Bureau of Justice Statistics.

HARRISON, PAIGE M. and JENNIFER C. KARBERG. (2003). *Prison and Jail Inmates at Midyear 2002.* Washington, DC: U.S. Department of Justice.

HARRY, JENNIFER L. (2000). "ACA's New President Focuses on Employees." *On the Line* 23:1, 3.

HASABALLA, AIDA Y. (2001). *The Social Organization of the Modern Prison.* Lewiston, NY: Edwin Mellen.

HASSELL, KIMBERLY and EDWARD R. MAGUIRE. (2001). *The Colorado Springs Juvenile Offender Unit: A Process and Impact Evaluation.* Silver Spring, MD: 21st Century Solutions.

HAULARD, EDGAR R. (2001). "Adult Education: A Must for Our Incarcerated Population." *The Journal of Correctional Education* 52:157–159.

HAWK, KATHLEEN et al. (1993). "Volunteers: Corrections' Unsung Heroes." *Corrections Today* 55:63–139.

HAWKINS, HOMER C. (2001). "Police Officer Burnout: A Partial Replication of Maslach's Burnout Inventory." *Police Quarterly* 4:343–360.

HEMMENS, CRAIG. (1999). "Legal Issues in Probation and Parole." *APPA Perspectives* 23:16–17.

HEMMENS, CRAIG and MARY K. STOHR (eds.) (2000). "Ethics in Corrections." *Prison Journal* 80:123–222.

HENNING, KRIS R. and LISA M. KLESGES. (2002). "Utilization of Counseling and Supportive Services By Female Victims of Domestic Violence." *Violence and Victims* 17:623–636.

HENSLEY, CHRISTOPHER, MARY KOSCHESKI, and RICHARD TEWKSBURY. (2002). "Does Participation in Conjugal Visitations Reduce Prison Violence in Mississippi? An Exploratory Study." *Criminal Justice Review* 27:52–65.

HESS, ALBERT G. and PRISCILLA F. CLEMENT. (eds.) (1993). *History of Juvenile Delinquency.* Aalen, Germany: Scientia Verlag.

HEUBNER, ANGELA J. and SHERRY C. BETTS. (2002). "Exploring the Utility of Social Control Theory for Youth Development: Issues in Attachment, Involvement, and Gender." *Youth and Society* 34:123–145.

HEYMAN, BOB et al. (2002). "Risk Management in the Rehabilitation of Offenders with Learning Disabilities: A Qualitative Study." *Risk Management: An International Journal* 4:33–45.

HEYMAN, PHILIP B. and WILLIAM N. BROWNSBERGER. (eds.) (2001). *Drug Addiction and Drug Policy: The Struggle to Control Dependence.* Cambridge, MA: Harvard University Press.

HIRSCHI, TRAVIS. (1969). *Causes of Delinquency.* Berkeley: University of California Press.

HOCHSTETLER, ANDY, HEITH COPES, and MATT DELISI (2002). "Differential Association in Group and Solo Offending." *Journal of Criminal Justice* 30:559–566.

HODGINS, SHEILAGH. (2001). "The Major Mental Disorders and Crime: Stop Debating and Start Treating and Preventing." *International Journal of Law and Psychiatry* 24:427–446.

HODGINS, SHEILAGH and RUDIGER MULLER-ISBERNER. (eds.) (2000). *Violence, Crime, and Mentally Disordered Offenders: Concepts and Methods for Effective Treatment and Prevention.* Chichester, UK: Wiley.

HOFER, PAUL J. et al. (1999). "The Effect of the Federal Sentencing Guidelines on Inter-Judge Disparity." *Journal of Criminal Law and Criminology* 90:239–321.

HOFFMAN, PETER B. (1994). "Twenty Years of Operational Use of a Risk Prediction Instrument: The United States Parole Commission's Salient Factor Score." *Journal of Criminal Justice* 22:477–494.

HOLGATE, ALINA M. and IAN J. CLEGG. (1991). "The Path to Probation Officer Burnout: New Dogs, Old Tricks." *Journal of Criminal Justice* 19:325–337.

HOLLAND TEEN COURT. (2003). *The Holland Teen Court Program.* Holland, MI: City of Holland Volunteer Services.

HOLT, NORMAN. (1996). *Inmate Classification: A Validation Study of the California System.* Sacramento: California Department of Corrections.

HOLT, NORMAN. (1997). *A New Risk Assessment Model for Parolees: Combining Risk and Stakes.* Sacramento, CA: California Department of Corrections.

HOLT, VICTORIA L. et al. (2003). "Do Protection Orders Affect the Likelihood of Future Partner Violence and Injury?" *American Journal of Preventive Medicine* 24:16–21.

HOLTERMAN, THOM. (2001). "Neighborhood-Centered Conflict Mediation in the Netherlands." *Contemporary Justice Review* 4:41–48.

HOUK, JULIE M. (1984). "Electronic Monitoring of Probationers: A Step Toward Big Brother?" *Golden Gate University Law Review* 14:431–436.

HOWELL, JAMES C. (2000). *Youth Gang Programs and Strategies.* Washington, DC: U.S. Department of Justice.

HOWELL, JAMES C. and JAMES P. LYNCH (2000). *Youth Gangs in Schools.* Washington, DC: U.S. Department of Justice.

HUBBARD, PHIL. (1998). "Community Action and the Displacement of Street Prostitution: Evidence from British Cities." *Geoforum* 29:269–286.

HUBNER, JOHN and JILL WOLFSON. (2000). *Handle with Care: Serving the Mental Health Needs of Young Offenders.* Washington, DC: Coalition for Juvenile Justice, U.S. Office of Juvenile Justice and Delinquency Prevention.

HUDDLESTON, C. WEST. (1998). "Drug Courts as Jail-Based Treatment." *Corrections Today* 60:98–101.

HUGHES, HERBERT. (1987). *The Fatal Shore.* New York: Alfred Knopf.

HUGHES, TIMOTHY A., DORIS JAMES WILSON, and ALAN J. BECK. (2003). "Trends in State Parole: The More Things Change, the More They Stay the Same." *APPA Perspectives* 26:26–33.

HUMPHRIES, DREW (1999). *Crack Mothers: Pregnancy, Drugs, and the Media.* Columbus, OH: Ohio State University Press.

HUNT, KIM S. et al. (2001). "Toward a Continuous Learning System: Restructuring Sentencing and Supervision Practice in the District of Columbia." *Justice Research and Policy* 3:35–55.

HYDE, ROBERTA, BEVERLY BRUMFIELD, and JUDITH NAGEL. (2000). "Female Inmate Health Care Requests." *Journal of Correctional Health Care* 7:91–103.

IARIA, VINCENT J. (2000). "The Use of Technology and ID Cards in Suffolk County's Gang Reduction and Intervention Program (GRIP)." *The Journal of Offender Monitoring* 13:16–17.

ILLINOIS DEPARTMENT OF CORRECTIONS. (2000). *Two-Year Report on Illinois Department of Corrections' Chicago Southside Day Reporting Center.* Springfield, IL: Illinois Department of Corrections.

INCIARDI, JAMES A. et al. (2002). "Evaluating Component Effects of a Prison-Based Treatment Continuum." *Journal of Substance Abuse Treatment* 23:63–69.

INDIANA DEPARTMENT OF CORRECTIONS. (2001). *An Assessment of Furlough Programs: Preliminary Report.* Indianapolis: Indiana Department of Corrections.

IOWA DEPARTMENT OF CORRECTIONAL SERVICES. (2003). *Iowa Classification System: Assessment & Reassessment of Client Risk Instructions & Scoring Guide.* Davenport, IA: Iowa Department of Correctional Services.

IRWIN, JOHN. (1985). *The Jail: Managing the Underclass in American Society.* Berkeley: University of California Press.

ISRAEL, MARK and JOHN DAWES. (2002). "'Something from Nothing': Shifting Credibility in Community Correctional Programs in Australia." *Criminal Justice: The International Journal of Policy and Practice* 2:5–25.

JACKSON, REBECCA L. et al. (2002). "Psychopathy in Female Offenders: An Investigation of Its Underlying Dimensions." *Criminal Justice and Behavior* 29:692–704.

JACOBY, JOSEPH E. (2002). "The Endurance of Failing Correctional Institutions: A Worst Case Study." *Prison Journal* 82:168–188.

JERMSTAD, TODD and ROLANDO V. DEL CARMEN. (2002). "Constitutionality of Probation and Parole Conditions." *APPA Perspectives* 26:36–45.

JESNESS, CARL F. (2003). *The Jesness Inventory Manual.* North Tonawanda, NY: MHS.

JOHANSSON-LOVE, JILL and JAMES H. GEER. (2003). "Investigation of Attitude Change in a Rape Prevention Program." *Journal of Interpersonal Violence* 18:84–89.

JOHNSON, CINDY. (2000). "For Better or Worse: Alternatives to Jail Time for Environmental Crimes." *New England Journal on Criminal and Civil Confinement* 26:265–297.

JOHNSON, GRANT M. and RAYMOND A. KNIGHT. (2000). "Developmental Antecedents of Sexual Coercion in Juvenile Sexual Offenders." *Sexual Abuse: A Journal of Research and Treatment* 12:165–178.

JOHNSON, RICHARD R. (2001). "Intensive Probation for Domestic Violence Offenders." *Federal Probation* 65:36–39.

JOHNSON, SARA L. and BRIAN A. GRANT. (1999). *Review of Issues Associated with Serious Spouse Abuse among Federally Sentenced Male Offenders.* Ottawa, ON: Research Branch, Correction Service of Canada.

JOHNSON, W. WESLEY and MARK JONES. (1994). "The Increased Felonization of Probation and Its Impact on the Function of Probation: A Descriptive Look at County Level Data from the 1980s and 1990s." *APPA Perspectives* 18:42–46.

JOHNSTON, NORMAN. (1973). *The Human Cage: A Brief History of Prison Architecture.* New York: Walker.

JOHNSTON, NORMAN. (2000). *Forms of Constraint: A History of Prison Architecture.* Urbana, IL: University of Illinois Press.

JOHNSTON, WENDY. (2001). "Boston Area Program Integrates Electronic Monitoring with Substance Abuse Treatment for Women." *The Journal of Offender Monitoring* 14:20–21.

JONES, MARK and ROLANDO V. DEL CARMEN. (1992). "When Do Probation and Parole Officers Enjoy the Same Immunity as Judges?" *Federal Probation* 56:36–41.

JONES, MARYLOUISE E. and ARTHUR J. LURIGIO (1997). "Ethical Considerations in Probation Practice." *APPA Perspectives* 20:26–32.

JOO, HEE JONG. (1993). *Parole Release and Recidivism: Comparative Three-Year Survival Analysis of Four Successive Release Cohorts of Property Offenders in Texas.* Ann Arbor, MI: University Microfilms International.

JOSI, DON A. and DALE K. SECHREST. (1999). "A Pragmatic Approach to Parole Aftercare: Evaluation of a Community Reintegration Program for High-Risk Youthful Offenders." *Justice Quarterly* 16:51–80.

JUDICATURE (2001). "Victims' Rights in Juvenile Court: Has the Pendulum Swung Too Far?" *Judicature* 85: 140–146.

JURICH, SONJA, MARTA CASPER, and KIM A. HULL. (2001). "Training Correctional Educators: A Needs Assessment Study." *The Journal of Correctional Education* 52:23–27.

KANAZAWA, SATOSHI and MARY C. STILL (2000). "Why Men Commit Crimes (and Why They Desist)." *Sociological Theory* 18:434–447.

KANSAS DEPARTMENT OF CORRECTIONS (2003). *Risk Assessment Instrumentation.* Topeka, KS: Kansas Department of Corrections.

KARP, DAVID R. (2001). "Harm and Repair: Observing Restorative Justice in Vermont." *Justice Quarterly* 18:727–757.

KARP, DAVID R. (2003). "Does Community Justice Work? Evaluating Vermont's Reparative Probation." *APPA Perspectives* 27:32–37.

KASSEBAUM, GENE et al. (2001). *Parole Decision Making in Hawaii: Setting Minimum Terms, Approving Release, Deciding on Revocation, and Predicting Success and Failure on Parole.* Washington, DC: U.S. Government Printing Office.

KATZ, CHARLES M., EDWARD R. MAGUIRE, and DENNIS W. RONCEK (2002). "The Creation of Specialized Police Gang Units: A Micro-Level Analysis of Contingency, Social Threat, and Resource Dependency Explanations." *Policing: An International Journal of Police Strategies and Management* 25:472–506.

KATZ, CHARLES M., VINCENT J. WEBB, and DAVID R. SCHAEFER (2000). "The Validity of Police Gang Intelligence Lists: Examining the Differences in Delinquency Between Documented Gang Members and Nondocumented Delinquents." *Police Quarterly* 3:413–437.

KAUFFMAN, KELSEY (2001). "Mothers in Prison." *Corrections Today* 63:62–65.

KAUTT, PAULA M. (2002). "Location, Location, Location: Interdistrict and Intercircuit Variation in Sentencing Outcomes for Federal Drug-Trafficking Offenses." *Justice Quarterly* 19:633–671.

KEILITZ, SUSAN et al. (2000). *Specialization of Domestic Violence Case Management in the Courts: A National Survey.* Washington, DC: National Center for State Courts.

KELLY, BRIAN J. et al. (2001). "Technology and Corrections." *Federal Probation* 65:1–70.

KELLY, ROBERT J. (2000). *Encyclopedia of Organized Crime in the United States: From Capone's Chicago to the New Urban Underworld.* Westport, CT: Greenwood.

KEMPF-LEONARD, KIMBERLY and ELICKA PETERSON (2000). "Expanding Realms of the New Penology: The Advent of Actuarial Justice for Juveniles." *Punishment and Society* 2:66–97.

KEMPKER, ERICIA (2003). "The Graying of American Prisons: Addressing the Continued Increase of Geriatric Inmates." *Corrections Compendium* 28:1–4, 22–26.

KEMSHALL, HAZEL and MIKE MAGUIRE (2001). "Public Protection, Partnership, and Risk Penalty: The Multi-Agency Risk Management of Sexual and Violent Offenders." *Punishment and Society: The International Journal of Penology* 3:237–264.

KENNEY, J. SCOTT (2002). "Victims of Crime and Labeling Theory: A Parallel Process?" *Deviant Behavior* 23:235–265.

KERIK, BERNARD B. (2000). "Accountability: The Key to Staff Safety." *Corrections Today* 62:124–126, 147.

KERLE, KENNETH E. (1998). *American Jails: Looking to the Future.* Boston: Butterworth-Heinemann.

KIEKBUSCH, RICHARD G. (2000). "Professionalizing Our Jails: The Academic Connection." *American Jails* 14: 19–24.

KING, RYAN S. et al. (2002). *Distorted Priorities: Drug Offenders in State Prisons.* Washington, DC: The Sentencing Project.

KINGSNORTH, RODNEY et al. (1999). "Criminal Sentencing and the Court Probation Officer: The Myth of Individualized Justice Revisited." *Justice System Journal* 20:255–273.

KIRKISH, PATRICIA et al. (2000). "The Future of Criminal Violence: Juveniles Tried As Adults." *Journal of the American Academy of Psychiatry and the Law* 28:38–46.

KITSUSE, J.I. (1962). "Societal Reaction to Deviant Behavior: Problems of Theory and Method." *Social Problems* 9:247–256.

KIVETT, DOUGLAS D. et al. (2002). "Social Control in a Group Home for Delinquent Boys." *Journal of Contemporary Ethnography* 31:3–32.

KLEIN, SHIRLEY R., GEANNINA S. BARTHOLOMEW, and JEFF HIBBERT (2002). "Inmate Family Functioning." *International Journal of Offender Therapy and Comparative Criminology* 46:95–111.

KLEINIG, JOHN and MARGARET LELAND SMITH (2002). *Discretion, Community, and Correctional Ethics.* Lanham, MD: Rowan and Littlefield.

KLINENBERG, ERIC (2001). "Bowling Alone, Policing Together." *Social Justice* 28:75–80.

KLOTTER, JOHN C. and TERRY D. EDWARDS (1998). *Criminal Law,* (5th ed.). Cincinnati, OH: Anderson.

KNIGHT, BARBARA B. (1992). "Women in Prison as Litigants: Prospects for Post-Prison Futures. *Women and Criminal Justice* 4:91–116.

KNOPP, FAY H., ROBERT FREEMAN-LONGO and WILLIAM FERREE STEVENSON (1992). *Nationwide Survey of Juvenile and Adult Sex-Offender Treatment Programs and Models.* Orwell, VT: Safer Society Program.

KNOX, GEORGE W. (2000). "A National Assessment of Gangs and Security Threat Groups (STGs) in Adult Correctional Institutions." *Journal of Gang Research* 7:1–45.

KNUPFER, ANNE MEIS (1997). "African-American Facilities for Dependent and Delinquent Children in Chicago, 1900–1920: The Louise Juvenile School and the Amanda Smith School." *Journal of Sociology and Social Welfare* 24:193–209.

KOHLBERG, L. (1963). "The Development of Children's Orientations Toward a Moral Order: Sequence in the Development of Human Thought." *Vita Humana* 6:11–33.

KONOPKA, AL (2001). *Nevada ISP Program.* Las Vegas, NV: Division of Parole and Probation. (personal communication, March 8, 2001)

KOONS-WITT, BARBARA A. (2002). "The Effect of Gender on the Decision to Incarcerate Before and After the Introduction of Sentencing Guidelines." *Criminology* 40:297–328.

KOVANDZIC, TOMISLAV V. (2001). "The Impact of Florida's Habitual Offender Law on Crime." *Criminology* 39: 179–203.

KRAMER, JOHN H. and JEFFREY T. ULMER (2002). "Downward Departures for Serious Violent Offenders: Local Court Corrections to Pennsylvania's Sentencing Guidelines." *Criminology* 40:897–932.

KRAUSS, DANIEL A. et al. (2000). "Beyond Prediction to Explanation in Risk Assessment Research: A Comparison of Two Explanatory Theories of Criminality and Recidivism." *International Journal of Law and Psychiatry* 23:91–112.

KREBS, CHRISTOPHER P. (2002). "High-Risk HIV Transmission Behavior in Prison and the Prison Subculture." *Prison Journal* 82:19–49.

KRONICK, ROBERT F., DOROTHY E. LAMBERT, and E. WARREN LAMBERT (1998). "Recidivism Among Adult Parolees: What Makes the Difference?" *Journal of Offender Rehabilitation* 28:61–69.

KRUTTSCHNITT, CANDACE, CHRISTOPHER UGGEN, and KELLY SHELTON (2000). "Predictors of Desistance Among Sex Offenders: The Interaction of Formal and Informal Social Controls." *Justice Quarterly* 17:61–87.

KULIS, CHESTER J. (1983). "Profit in the Private Presentence Report." *Federal Probation* 47:11–16.

KURKI, LEENA and NORVAL MORRIS (2001). "The Purposes, Practices, and Problems of Supermax Prisons." In *Crime and Justice: A Review of Research, Vol. 28,* Michael Tonry (ed.). Chicago: The University of Chicago Press.

KURY, HELMUT and URSULA SMARTT (2002). "Prisoner-on-Prisoner Violence: Victimization of Young Offenders in Prison." *Criminal Justice: The International Journal of Policy and Practice* 2:411–437.

KUZNESTOV, ANDREI, TIMOTHY A. PIERSON, and BRUCE HARRY (1992). "Victim Age Basis for Profiling Sex Offenders." *Federal Probation* 56:34–38.

LANDRY, WENDY (2001). "Female Offenders: Walking Through Enhanced Supervision." *Federal Probation* 65:46–48.

LATESSA, EDWARD J., LAWRENCE F. TRAVIS, and ALEXANDER HOLSINGER (1997). *Evaluation of Ohio's Community Corrections Act Programs and Community-Based Correctional Facilities.* Cincinnati, OH: Division of Criminal Justice, University of Cincinnati.

LATIMER, H.D., J.C. CURRAN, and B.D. TEPPER (1992). *Home Detention Electronic Monitoring Program.* Nevada City, NV: Nevada County Probation Department Second Floor Courthouse.

LATTIMER, JEFF, CRAIG DOWDEN, and DANIELLE MUISE (2001). *The Effectiveness of Restorative Justice Practices: A Meta-Analysis.* Ottawa, ON: Department of Justice Canada.

LAUEN, ROGER J. (1997). *Positive Approaches to Corrections: Research, Policy, and Practice.* Lanham, MD: American Correctional Association.

LAUFER, FRANKLIN N. and KIMBERLY R. ARRIOLA (2002). "From Jail to Community: Innovative Strategies to Enhance Continuity of HIV/AIDS Care." *Prison Journal* 82:84–100.

LE, THAO (2002). "Delinquency among Asian/Pacific Islanders: Review of Literature and Research." *Justice Professional* 15:57–70.

LEA, SUSAN, TIM AUBURN, and KAREN KIBBLEWHITE (1999). "Working with Sex Offenders: The Perceptions and Experiences of Professionals and Paraprofessionals." *International Journal of Offender Therapy and Comparative Criminology* 43:103–119.

LEHMAN, JOSEPH D. (2001). "Reinventing Community Corrections in Washington State." *Corrections Management Quarterly* 5:41–45.

LEMERT, EDWIN M. (1951). *Social Pathology.* New York: McGraw-Hill.

LEMIEUX, CATHERINE M. (2002). "Social Support among Offenders with Substance Abuse Problems: Overlooked and Underused?" *Journal of Addictions and Offender Counseling* 23:41–57.

LEMIEUX, CATHERINE M., TIMOTHY B. DYESON, and BRANDI CASTIGLIONE (2002). "Revisiting the Literature on Prisoners Who Are Older: Are We Wiser?" *Prison Journal* 82:440–458.

LEMON, NANCY K.D. (2001). *Domestic Violence Law.* St. Paul, MN: West Group.

LEMOV, PENELOPE (1992). "The Next Best Thing to Prison." *Corrections Today* 54:134–136.

LEONARDSON, GARY (1997). *Results of Early Release: Study Prompted by Passage of HB 685.* Helena, MT: Montana Board of Crime Control.

LERSCH, KIM MICHELLE (1999). "Social Learning Theory and Academic Dishonesty." *International Journal of Comparative and Applied Criminal Justice* 23:103–114.

LESTER, DAVID (2000). "Armed Robbery and the Availability of Firearms in Canada." *EuroCriminology* 14: 113–115.

LEUKEFELD, CARL et al. (2003). "An Employment Intervention for Drug Abusing Offenders." *Federal Probation* 67:27–31.

LEVENSON, JOE and FINOLA FARRANT (2002). "Unlocking Potential: Active Citizenship and Volunteering by Prisoners." *Probation Journal* 49:195–204.

LEVIN, DAVID J., PATRICK A. LANGAN, and JODI M. BROWN (2000). *State Court Sentencing of Convicted Felons, 1996.* Washington, DC: U.S. Bureau of Justice Statistics.

LEVINE, GENE N. and FERANDO PARRA (2000). "The Gangbangers of East Los Angeles: Sociopsycho-Analytic Considerations." *Journal of Gang Research* 7:9–12.

LEWIS, ALAN DANA and TIMOTHY J. HOWARD (2000). "Parole Officers' Perceptions of Juvenile Offenders Within a Balanced and Restorative Model of Justice." *Federal Probation* 64:40–45.

LI, LI and DENNIS MOORE (2001). "Disability and Illicit Drug Use: An Application of Labeling Theory." *Deviant Behavior* 22:1–21.

LIBERTON, MICHAEL, MITCHELL SILVERMAN, and WILLIAM R. BLOUNT (1992). "Predicting Probation Success for the First-Time Offender." *International Journal of Offender Therapy and Comparative Criminology* 36:335–347.

LIGHTFOOT, CALVIN and LAUREN DELUCA (2002). "From Prerelease to Postrelease: A Public Safety Collaborative Effort." *American Jails* 16:17–20.

LILLY, J. ROBERT, FRANCIS T. CULLEN, and RICHARD A. BALL (2002). *Criminological Theory: Context and Consequences,* (3rd ed.). Thousand Oaks, CA: Sage.

LIN-RUEY, LIN (1997). *Community Corrections: Study Prompted by Passage of HB685.* Helena, MT: Montana Board of Crime Control.

LINDNER, CHARLES (1992a). "The Probation Field Visit and Office Report in New York State: Yesterday, Today, and Tomorrow." *Criminal Justice Review* 17:44–60.

LINDNER, CHARLES (1992b). "Probation Officer Victimization: An Emerging Concern." *Journal of Criminal Justice* 20:53–62.

LINDNER, CHARLES (1992c). "The Refocused Probation Home Visit: A Subtle But Revolutionary Change." *Federal Probation* 56:16–21.

LINDNER, CHARLES and MARGARET R. SAVARESE (1984). "The Evolution of Probation: University Settlement and the Beginning of Statutory Probation in New York City." *Federal Probation* 48:3–12.

LISTUG, DAVID (1996). "Wisconsin Sheriff's Office Saves Money and Resources." *American Jails* 10:85–86.

LITT, MARK D. and SHARON D. MALLON (2003). "The Design of Social Support Networks for Offenders in Outpatient Drug Treatment." *Federal Probation* 67:15–20.

LIVINGSTON, JAY (1974). *Compulsive Gamblers: Observation on Action and Abstinence.* New York: Harper Torchbooks.

LOGAN, T.K., KATIE WILLIAMS, and CARL LEUKEFELD (2001). "A Statewide Drug Court Needs Assessment: Identifying Target Counties, Assessing Readiness." *Journal of Offender Rehabilitation* 33:1–25.

LOMBROSO, CESARE (1918). *Crime: Its Causes and Remedies.* Boston: Little, Brown.

LONDER, RANDI (1987). "Can Bad Air Make Bad Things Happen?" *Parade Magazine* August 9, 1987:6.

LONG, JENNIE, WILLIAM WELLS, and WILLIAM DeLEON-GRANADOS (2002). "Implementation Issues as a Community and Police Partnership in Law Enforcement Space: Lessons from a Case Study of a Community Policing Approach to Domestic Violence." *Police Practice and Research: An International Journal* 3:231–246.

LOVE, BILL (1993). "Volunteers Make a Big Difference Inside a Maximum Security Prison." *Corrections Today* 55:76–78.

LOZA, WAGDY and AMEL FANOUS LOZA (2002). "The Effectiveness of the Self-Appraisal Questionnaire as an Offender's Classification Measure." *Journal of Interpersonal Violence* 17:3–13.

LUCKEN, KAROL (1997). "Privatizating Discretion: 'Rehabilitating' Treatment in Community Corrections." *Crime and Delinquency* 43:243–259.

LURIGIO, ARTHUR J. (2000). "Persons with Serious Mental Illness in the Criminal Justice System: Background, Prevalence, and Principles of Care." *Criminal Justice Policy Review* 11:312–325.

LURIGIO, ARTHUR J., GAD J. BENSINGER, and ANNA T. LASZLO (eds.) (1990). *AIDS and Community Corrections: The Development of Effective Policies.* Chicago: Loyola University Chicago.

LURIGIO, ARTHUR J. and JAMES A. SWARTZ (1999). "The Nexus Between Drugs and Crime: Theory, Research, and Practice." *Federal Probation* 63:67–71.

LUTZE, FAITH E. and DAVID W. MURPHY (1999). "Ultramasculine Prison Environments and Inmates' Adjustment: It's Time to Move Beyond the 'Boys Will Be Boys' Paradigm." *Justice Quarterly* 16:709–733.

LYNAM, DONALD R. et al. (2000). "The Interaction Between Impulsivity and Neighborhood Context on Offending: The Effects of Impulsivity Are Stronger in Poorer Neighborhoods." *Journal of Abnormal Psychology* 109:563–574.

LYNCH, JAMES P. (2002). "Using Citizen Surveys to Produce Information on the Police: The Present and Potential Uses of the National Crime Victimization Survey." *Justice Research and Policy* 4:61–70.

LYNETT, ELIZABETH and RICHARD ROGERS (2000). "Emotions Overriding Forensic Opinions: The Potentially Biasing Effects of Victim Statements." *Journal of Psychiatry and Law* 28:449–457.

MA, YUE (2002). "Prosecutorial Discretion and Plea Bargaining in the United States, France, Germany, and Italy: A Comparative Perspective." *International Criminal Justice Review* 12:22–52.

MACKENZIE, DORIS LAYTON and DAVID B. WILSON (2001). "The Impact of Boot Camps and Traditional Institutions on Juvenile Residents: Perceptions, Adjustment, and Change." *Journal of Research on Crime and Delinquency* 38:279–313.

MAGUIRE, MIKE et al. (2001). *Risk Management of Sexual and Violent Offenders: The Work of Public Protection Panels.* London, UK: U.K. Home Office.

MALONEY, DENNIS, GORDON BAZEMORE, and JOE HUDSON (2001). "The End of Probation and the Beginning of Community Corrections." *APPA Perspectives* 25: 22–30.

MARCINIAK, LIZ MARIE (2000). "The Addition of Day Reporting to Intensive Supervision Probation: A Comparison of Recidivism Rates." *Federal Probation* 64:34–39.

MARCUS, DAVID K., THEODORE M. AMEN, and ROGER BIBACE (1992). "A Developmental Analysis of Prisoners' Conceptions of AIDS." *Criminal Justice and Behavior* 19:174–188.

MARION, NANCY (2002). "Effectiveness of Community-Based Correctional Programs: A Case Study." *Prison Journal* 82:478–497.

MARQUART, JAMES W. et al. (1999). "The Implications of Crime Control Policy on HIV/AIDS-Related Risk Among Women Prisoners." *Crime and Delinquency* 45:82–98.

MARSH, ROBERT L. and ANTHONY WALSH (1995). "Physiological and Psychosocial Assessment and Treatment of Sex Offenders: A Comprehensive Victim-Oriented Program." *Journal of Offender Rehabilitation* 22: 77–96.

MARSHALL, FRANKLIN H. (1989). "Diversion and Probation." In *The U.S. Sentencing Guidelines: Implications for Criminal Justice,* Dean J. Champion (ed.). New York: Praeger.

MARSHALL, WILLIAM L. and GERIS A. SERRAN (2000). "Improving the Effectiveness of Sexual Offender Treatment." *Trauma and Violence and Abuse: A Review Journal* 1:203–222.

MARTENS, WILLEM H.J. (2002). "Criminality and Moral Dysfunctions: Neurological, Biochemical, and Genetic Dimensions." *International Journal of Offender Therapy and Comparative Criminology* 46:170–182.

MARTIN, CHRISTINE, ARTHUR J. LURIGIO, and DAVID E. OLSON (2003). "An Examination of Rearrests and Reincarcerations among Discharged Day Reporting Center Clients." *Federal Probation* 67:24–30.

MARTIN, NANCY L. and ARTHUR J. LURIGIO (1994). "Special Probation Programs for Drug Offenders." *APPA Perspectives* 18:24–27.

MASLACH, CHRISTINA (1982). *Burnout: The Cost of Caring.* Englewood Cliffs, NJ: Prentice-Hall.

MASSACHUSETTS PAROLE BOARD (2003). *Risk Assessment.* Boston: Massachusetts Parole Board.

MASSACHUSETTS STATISTICAL ANALYSIS CENTER (2001). *Implementation of the Juvenile Justice Reform Act: Youthful Offenders in Massachusetts.* Boston: Massachusetts Statistical Analysis Center.

MASTROFSKI, STEPHEN D. et al. (2000). "The Helping Hand of the Law: Police Control of Citizens on Request." *Criminology* 38:307–342.

MATTHEWS, BETSY, DANA JONES HUBBARD, and EDWARD LATESSA (2001). "Making the Next Step: Using Evaluability Assessment to Improve Correctional Programming." *Prison Journal* 81:454–472.

MAUND, NATALIE AYE and NICOLA HAMMOND (2000). *Risk of Re-Offending and Needs Assessments: The User's Perspective.* London, UK: Research and Statistics Directorate.

MAXEY, WAYNE (2002). "The San Diego Stalking Strike Force: A Multi-Disciplinary Approach to Assessing and Managing Stalking and Threat Cases." *Journal of Threat Assessment* 2:549–558.

MAXWELL, GABRIELLE and ALLISON MORRIS (2002). "Restorative Justice and Reconviction." *Contemporary Justice Review: Issues in Criminal, Social, and Restorative Justice* 5:133–146.

MAXWELL, JANE CARLISLE and LYNN S. WALLISCH (1998). *Substance Abuse and Crime among Probationers in Three Texas Counties: 1994–1995.* Austin, TX: Texas Commission on Alcohol and Drug Abuse.

MAXWELL, SHEILA ROYO (2000). "Sanction Threats in Court-Ordered Programs: Examining Their Effects on Offenders Mandated into Drug Treatment." *Crime and Delinquency* 46:542–563.

MAXWELL, SHEILA ROYO and KEVIN M. GRAY (2000). "Deterrence: Testing the Effects of Perceived Sanction Certainty on Probation Violation." *Sociological Inquiry* 70:117–136.

MCDONALD, DOUGLAS C., JUDITH GREENE, and CHARLES WORZELLA (1992). *Day Fines in American Courts: The Staten Island and Milwaukee Experiments.* Washington, DC: U.S. Department of Justice, Office of Justice Programs.

MCDONALD, PHYLLIS PARSHALL (2002). *Managing Police Operations: Implementing the New York Crime Control Model.* New York: New York Police Department.

MCGILLIS, DANIEL (1998). *Resolving Community Conflict: The Dispute Settlement Center of Durham, North Carolina.* Washington, DC: U.S. Department of Justice.

MCGLOIN, JEAN MARIE and CATHY SPATZ WIDOM (2001). "Resilience among Abused and Neglected Children Grown Up." *Development and Psychotherapy* 13: 1021–1038.

MCGRATH, ROBERT J., GEORGIA CUMMING, and JOHN HOLT (2002). "Collaboration among Sex Offender Treatment Providers and Probation and Parole Officers: The Beliefs and Behaviors of Treatment Providers." *Sexual Abuse: A Journal of Research and Treatment* 14:49–65.

MCGRATH, ROBERT J. et al. (2003). "Outcome of a Treatment Program for Adult Sex Offenders: From Prison to Community." *Journal of Interpersonal Violence* 18:3–17.

MCGUIRE, JAMES (2002). "Criminal Sanctions Versus Psychologically Based Interventions with Offenders: A Comparative Empirical Analysis." *Psychology, Crime, and Law* 8:183–208.

MCGUIRE, M. DYAN (2002). "Cumulative Disadvantage as an Explanation for Observed Disproportionality within the Juvenile Justice System: An Empirical Test." *Juvenile and Family Court Journal* 53:1–17.

MCKAY, BRIAN (2002). "The State of Sex Offender Probation Supervision in Texas." *Federal Probation* 66:16–20.

MCKEAN, LISE and JODY RAPHAEL (2002). *Drugs, Crime and Consequences: Arrests and Incarceration in North Lawndale.* Chicago: Center for Impact Research.

MCLAIN, BARBARA (2001). *Evaluation of the HOPE Act: New State Services for Street Youth.* Olympia, WA: Washington Department of Youth Services.

MCLENNAN, REBECCA MARY (1999). *Citizens and Criminals: The Rise of the American Carceral State.* Ann Arbor, MI: University Microfilms International.

MCMAHON, MARTHA and ELLEN PENCE (2003). "Making Social Change: Reflections on Individual and Institutional Advocacy with Women Arrested for Domestic Violence." *Violence Against Women* 9:47–74.

MEACHUM, LARRY R. (1986). "House Arrest: The Oklahoma Experience." *Corrections Today* 48:102–110.

MEARS, DANIEL P. and SAMUEL H. FIELD (2000). "Theorizing Sanctioning in a Criminalized Juvenile Court." *Criminology* 38:983–1019.

MEARS, DANIEL P. et al. (2003). *Drug Treatment in the Criminal Justice System: The Current State of Knowledge.* Washington, DC: Urban Institute Series on Drug Treatment in the Criminal Justice System.

MEGARGEE, EDWIN I. and JOYCE CARBONELL (1985). "Predicting Prison Adjustment with MMPI Correctional Scales." *Journal of Consulting and Clinical Psychology* 53:874–883.

MELLOW, JEFF and LENNY WARD (2003). "Community Strategies for Successful Reentry." *APPA Perspectives* 27:26–28.

MERCER, RON, MURRAY BROOKS, and PAULA TULLY BRYANT (2000). "Global Positioning Satellite System: Tracking Offenders in Real Time." *Corrections Today* 62:76–80.

MEREDITH, COLIN and CHANTAL PAQUETTE (2001). *Victims of Crime Research Series: Summary Report on Victim Impact Statement Groups.* Belmont, CA: Wadsworth.

MERTON, ROBERT KING (1938). "Social Structure and Anomie." *American Sociological Review* 3:672–682.

MERTON, ROBERT KING (1957). *Social Theory and Social Structure.* New York: Free Press.

MESSINGER, SHELDON L. et al. (1985). "The Foundations of Parole in California." *Law and Society Review* 19: 69–106.

METCHIK, ERIC (1999). "An Analysis of the 'Screening Out' Model of Police Officer Selection." *Police Quarterly* 2:79–95.

MEYER, JON'A F. (2001). "Strange Science: Subjective Criteria in Parole Decisions." *Journal of Crime and Justice* 24:43–70.

MIDKIFF, BILL (2000). "Collaborative Jail Mental Health Services." *American Jails* 14:49–53.

MIETHE, TERANCE D., HONG LU, and ERIN REESE (2000). "Reintegrative Shaming and Recidivism Risks in Drug Court: Explanations for Some Unexpected Findings." *Crime and Delinquency* 46:522–541.

MILLER, ARTHUR F. (2001). "Substance Abuse Treatment for Women with Children." *Corrections Today Magazine* 63:88–91.

MILLER, DANE C., RICHARD D. SLUDER, and DENNIS J. LASTER (1999). "Can Probation Be Revoked When Probationers Do Not Wilfully Violate the Terms or Conditions of Probation?" *Federal Probation* 63:23–29.

MILLER, JEROME G. (1996). *Search and Destroy: African-American Males in the Criminal Justice System.* New York: Cambridge University Press.

MILLER, JODY and ROD K. BRUNSON (2000). "Gender Dynamics in Youth Gangs: A Comparison of Males' and Females' Accounts." *Justice Quarterly* 17:419–448.

MILLS, DARRELL K. (1990). "Career Issues for Probation Officers." *Federal Probation* 54:3–7.

MILLS, JIM (1992). "Supervision Fees: APPA Issues Committee Report." *APPA Perspectives* 16:10–12.

MINOR, KEVIN I., JAMES B. WELLS, and CRISSY SIMS (2003). "Recidivism among Federal Probationers: Predicting Sentencing Violations." *Federal Probation* 67:31–36.

MIRANNE, ALFRED C. and MICHAEL R. GEERKEN (1991). "The New Orleans Inmate Survey: A Test of Greenwood's Predictive Scale." *Criminology* 29:497–518.

MISSISSIPPI PAROLE BOARD (2003). *Parole.* Jackson, MS: Mississippi Parole Board.

MITCHELL, GEORGE A. (1999). *Privatizing Parole and Probation in Wisconsin: The Path to Fewer Prisons.* Thiensville, WI: Wisconsin Policy Research Institute.

MITCHELL, JOHN J. and SHARON A. WILLIAMS (1986). "SOS: Reducing Juvenile Recidivism." *Corrections Today* 48:70–71.

MOORE, ERIC WILLIAM (2001). "Emerging Legal Constraints on Affirmative Action in Police Agencies and How to Adapt to Them." *Journal of Criminal Justice* 29:11–19.

MORGAN, KATHRYN D., BARBARA A. BELBOT, and JOHN CLARK (1997). "Liability Issues Affecting Probation and Parole Supervision." *Journal of Criminal Justice* 25:211–222.

MORGAN, ROBERT D., RICHARD A. VANHAVEREN, and CHRISTY A. PEARSON (2002). "Correctional Officer Burnout: Further Analysis." *Criminal Justice and Behavior* 29:144–160.

MORRIS, NORVAL and MARC MILLER (1985). "Predictions of Dangerousness." In *Crime and Justice: An Annual Review of Research, Vol. 6.* Michael Tonry and Norval Morris (eds). Chicago: University of Chicago Press.

MORTIMER, ED and CHRIS MAY (1997). *Electronic Monitoring in Practice: The Second Year of the Trials of Curfew Orders.* London, UK: U.K. Home Office.

MOSES, MARILYN C. (1993). "Girl Scouts Behind Bars: New Program at Women's Prisons Benefits Mothers and Children." *Corrections Today* 55:132–134.

MOTIUK, LAURENCE L., RAYMOND L. BELCOURT, and JAMES BONTA (1995). *Managing High-Risk Offenders: A Post-Detention Follow-Up.* Ottawa, ON: Correctional Service Canada, Communications and Corporate Development Branch.

MOUNT CARMEL YOUTH RANCH (2003). *Mount Carmel Youth Ranch.* Powell, WY: Mount Carmel Youth Ranch.

MUILUVUORI, MARJA LIISA (2001). "Recidivism among People Sentenced to Community Service in Finland." *Journal of Scandanavian Studies in Criminology and Crime Prevention* 2:72–82.

MUNDEN, DAVID P., RICHARD TEWKSBURY, and ELIZABETH L. GROSSI (1999). "Intermediate Sanctions and the Halfway Back Program in Kentucky." *Criminal Justice Policy Review* 9:431–449.

MUNSON, MICHELLE and TOM REED (2000). *Goal Met: Violent Offenders in Texas are Serving a Higher Percentage of Their Prison Sentences.* Austin: Texas Criminal Justice Policy Council.

MUNSON, MICHELLE and REGINA E. YGNACIO (2000). *The State Jail System Today: An Update.* Austin: Texas Criminal Justice Policy Council.

MYERS, BRYAN and JACK ARBUTHNOT (1999). "The Effects of Victim Impact Evidence on the Verdicts and Sentencing Judgments of Mock Jurors." *Journal of Offender Rehabilitation* 29:95–112.

MYERS, DAVID L. (2001). *Excluding Violent Youths from Juvenile Court: The Effectiveness of Legislative Waiver.* New York: LFB Scholarly.

MYERS, TAMARA and JOAN SANGSTER (2001). "Retorts, Runaways, and Riots: Patterns of Resistance in Canadian Reform Schools for Girls, 1930–1960." *Journal of Social History* 34:669–697.

NARCOTICS ANONYMOUS (1999). *The NA Way.* Van Nuys, CA: Narcotics Anonymous World Service Office.

NATIONAL COMMISSION ON LAW OBSERVANCE AND ENFORCEMENT (1931). *Wickersham Commission Reports.* Washington, DC: U.S. Government Printing Office.

NATIONAL DRUG COURT INSTITUTE (1999a). *DUI/Drug Courts: Defining a National Strategy.* Washington, DC: National Drug Court Institute.

NATIONAL DRUG COURT INSTITUTE (1999b). *Reentry Drug Courts.* Alexandria, VA: National Drug Court Institute.

NATIONAL LAW ENFORCEMENT AND CORRECTIONS TECHNOLOGY CENTER (1999). *Keeping Track of Electronic Monitoring.* Washington, DC: National Law Enforcement and Corrections Technology Center.

NELLIS, MIKE (2002). "Community Justice, Time, and the New National Probation Service." *Howard Journal of Criminal Justice* 41:59–86.

NEMES, SUSANNA, ERIC D. WISH, and NENA MESSINA (1999). "Comparing the Impact of Standard and Abbreviated Treatment in a Therapeutic Community." *Journal of Substance Abuse Treatment* 17:339–347.

NEUSTATTER, ANGELA (2002). *Locked In-Locked Out: The Experience of Young Offenders Out of Society and in Prison.* Washington, DC: U.S. Government Printing Office.

NEWBURN, TIM (2002). "Atlantic Crossings: Policy Transfer and Crime Control in the U.S.A. and Great Britain." *Punishment and Society* 4:165–194.

NEW YORK STATE DIVISION OF CRIMINAL JUSTICE SERVICES (2002). *Office of Justice Systems Analysis Research Report.* New York: New York State Division of Criminal Justice Services.

NEW YORK STATE DIVISION OF PAROLE (1998). *The Ninth Annual Shock Legislative Report.* Albany: New York State Division of Parole.

NEW ZEALAND DEPARTMENT OF CORRECTIONS (2001). *About Time: Turning People Away from a Life of Crime and Reducing Re-Offending.* Auckland, NZ: New Zealand Department of Corrections.

NIELSEN, AMIE L. and RAMIRO MARTINEZ, JR. (2003). "Reassessing the Alcohol-Violence Linkage: Results from a Multiethnic City." *Justice Quarterly* 20:445–469.

NIJBOER, JAN et al. (2002). "Recidivism." *Justiele Verkenningen* 8:9–107.

NORMAN, MICHAEL D. and ROBERT C. WADMAN (2000). "Utah Presentence Investigation Reports: User Group Perceptions of Quality and Effectiveness." *Federal Probation* 64:7–12.

NORTH DAKOTA DEPARTMENT OF CORRECTIONS AND REHABILITATION (2004). *Probation and Parole Officers: Duties and Responsibilities.* Bismarck: North Dakota Department of Corrections and Rehabilitation.

NORTH DAKOTA PAROLE BOARD (2003). *Parole Denials.* Bismarck: North Dakota Parole Board.

NORTON, DOUGLAS R. (1999). *Adult Probation Programs: Program Evaluation.* Phoenix: Arizona Office of the Auditor General.

NURCO, DAVID, THOMAS E. HANLON, and RICHARD W. BATE-MAN (1992, November). "Correlates of Parole Outcome among Drug Abusers." Unpublished paper presented at the annual meetings of the American Society of Criminology, New Orleans, LA.

NURSE, ANNE M. (2002). *Fatherhood Arrested: Parenting from Within the Juvenile Justice System.* Nashville, TN: Vanderbilt University Press.

O'CALLAGHAN, JEROME, ALAN D. GAGNON, and SERVE BROCHU (1990). "Alcohol and Legal Issues." *Alcoholism Treatment Quarterly* 7:87–146.

O'CONNOR, PATRICIA E. (2000). *Speaking of Crime: Narratives of Prisoners.* Lincoln: University of Nebraska Press.

OFFICE OF JUSTICE PROGRAMS (2001). *Rates of HIV Infection and AIDS-Related Deaths.* Washington, DC: Office of Justice Programs.

OGBURN, KEVIN R. (1993). "Volunteer Program Guide." *Corrections Today* 55:66–70.

OHIO DEPARTMENT OF CORRECTION AND REHABILITATION (2001). *Guidelines for Paroling Offenders: Working Draft.* Columbus: Ohio Department of Correction and Rehabilitation.

OHIO PAROLE BOARD (2003). *The Parole Board Guidelines.* Columbus: Ohio Parole Board.

OKUN, PETER (1997). *Crime and the Nation: Prison Reform and Popular Fiction in Philadelphia: 1786–1800.* Ann Arbor, MI: University Microfilms International.

OLDFIELD, MARK and M. OLDFIELD (2002). "What Works and the Conjunctural Politics of Probation: Effectiveness, Managerialism, and Neo-Liberalism." *British Journal of Community Justice* 1:79–97.

OSGOOD, D. WAYNE, BARBARA J. MCMORRIS, and MARIA T. POTENZA (2002). "Analyzing Multiple-Item Measures of Crime and Deviance: Item Response Theory Scaling." *Journal of Quantitative Criminology* 18:267–296.

OVIEDO, MIGUEL A. (2003). "Federal Probation During the Second World War." *Federal Probation* 67:3–8.

PAGE, BRIAN (1995). *Assessment Center Handbook.* Longwood, FL: Gould.

PALMER, CARLETON A. and MARK HAZELRIGG (2000). "The Guilty But Mentally Ill Verdict: A Review and Conceptual Analysis of Intent and Impact." *Journal of the American Academy of Psychiatry and the Law* 28:47–54.

PALMER, EMMA J., ANGELA HOLMES, and CLIVE R. HOLLIN (2002). "Investigating Burglars' Decisions: Factors Influencing Target Choice, Method of Entry, Reasons for Offending, and Victimization of a Property." *Security Journal* 15:7–18.

PARADIS, CHERYL et al. (2000). "Mentally Ill Elderly Jail Detainees: Psychiatric, Psychosocial, and Legal Factors." *Journal of Offender Rehabilitation* 31:77–86.

PARENT, DALE G. and BRAD SNYDER (1999). *Police-Corrections Partnerships.* Washington, DC: U.S. National Institute of Justice.

PARKER, HOWARD (2001). "Drug Interventions in the Youth Justice System." *Probation Journal* 48:110–118.

PARKER, MIKE (2002). "The Creation and Implementation of the Community Transition Unit." *American Jails* 15:37–43.

PASTORE, ANN L. and MAGUIRE, KATHLEEN (eds.) (2003). *Sourcebook of Criminal Justice Statistics, 2002.* Albany, NY: Hindelang Criminal Justice Research Center.

PATERNOSTER, RAYMOND and RONET BACHMAN (2001). *Explaining Criminals and Crime.* Los Angeles: Roxbury.

PATTERSON, BERNIE L. (1992). "Job Experience and Perceived Stress among Police, Correctional, and Probation/Parole Officers." *Criminal Justice and Behavior* 19:260–285.

PATRICK, DIANE et al. (2000). *How Is the Post Conviction Polygraph Examination Used in Adult Sex Offender Management Activities?* Denver, CO: Division of Criminal Justice, Colorado Department of Public Safety.

PAULSEN, DEREK and ROLANDO V. DEL CARMEN (2000). "Legal Issues in Police-Corrections Partnerships: Can the Police and Corrections Officers Work Together Without Violating Offenders' Constitutional Rights?" *Criminal Law Bulletin* 36:493–508.

PAYNE, BRIAN K. and RANDY R. GAINEY (1999). "Attitudes Toward Electronic Monitoring among Monitored Offenders and Criminal Justice Students." *Journal of Offender Rehabilitation* 29:195–208.

PAYNE, BRIAN K. and RANDY R. GAINEY (2000). "Is Good Time Appropriate for Offenders on Electronic Monitoring? Attitudes of Electronic Monitoring Directors." *Journal of Criminal Justice* 28:497–506.

PAYNE, BRIAN K. and RANDY R. GAINEY (2003). "Electronic Monitoring and Newspaper Coverage in the Press." *Journal of Crime and Justice* 26:133–160.

PECK, RAYMOND and ROBERT R. VOAS (2002). "Forfeiture Programs in California: Why So Few?" *Journal of Safety Research* 33:245–258.

PEREZ, DOUGLAS W. and PENNY R. SHTULL (2002). "Police Research and Practice: An American Perspective." *Police Practice and Research: An International Journal* 3:169–187.

PETERS, ROGER H. and MARY R. MURRIN (2000). "Effectiveness of Treatment-Based Drug Courts in Reducing Criminal Recidivism." *Criminal Justice and Behavior* 27:72–96.

PETERS, ROGER H. et al. (1993). "Alcohol and Drug Rehabilitation." *Journal of Offender Rehabilitation* 19: 1–79.

PETERSILIA, JOAN (ed.) (1998). *Community Corrections: Probation, Parole, and Intermediate Sanctions.* New York: Oxford University Press.

PETERSILIA, JOAN (1999a). "A Decade of Experimenting with Intermediate Sanctions: What Have We Learned?" *Justice Research and Policy* 1:9–23.

PETERSILIA, JOAN (1999b). "Parole and Prisoner Reentry in the United States." In *Prisons,* Michael Tonry and Joan Petersilia (eds.). Chicago: University of Chicago Press.

PETERSILIA, JOAN (2001). "When Prisoners Return to Communities: Political, Economic, and Social Consequences." *Federal Probation* 65:3–8.

PETERSILIA, JOAN M. and SUSAN TURNER (1993). *Evaluating Intensive Supervision Probation/Parole: Results of a Nationwide Experiment.* Washington, DC: U.S. Department of Justice, Office of Justice Programs.

PETERSON-BADALI, MICHELE and CHRISTOPHER J. KOEGL (2002). "Juveniles' Experiences of Incarceration: The Role of Correctional Staff in Peer Violence." *Journal of Criminal Justice* 30:41–49.

PETROSINO, ANTHONY, CAROLYN TURPIN-PETROSINO, and JAMES O. FINCKENAUER (2000). "Well-Meaning Programs Can Have Harmful Effects! Lessons from Experiments of Programs Such as Scared Straight." *Crime and Delinquency* 46:354–379.

PIQUERO, ALEX R. and STEPHEN G. TIBBETTS (eds.) (2002). *Rational Choice and Criminal Behavior: Recent Research and Future Challenges.* Belmont, CA: Wadsworth.

PIQUERO, ALEX R. et al. (2002). "Crime in Emerging Adulthood." *Criminology* 40:137–170.

PODKOPACZ, MARCY R. and BARRY C. FELD (2002). "The Back-Door to Prison: Waiver Reform, 'Blended Sentencing,' and the Law of Unintended Consequences." *Journal of Criminal Law and Criminology* 91:997–1071.

POGREBIN, MARK R. and MARY DODGE (2001). "Women's Accounts of Their Prison Experiences: A Retrospective View of Their Subjective Realities." *Journal of Criminal Justice* 29:531–541.

POLETIEK, FENNA H. (2002). "How Psychiatrists and Judges Assess the Dangerousness of Persons with Mental Illness." *Behavioral Sciences and the Law* 20:19–29.

POOLE, LINDSEY, STEPHEN WHITTLE, and PAULA STEPHENS (2002). "Working with Transgendered and Transsexual People as Offenders in the Probation Service." *Probation Journal* 49:227–338.

POULSON, BARTON and KATHY ELTON (2002). "Participants' Attitudes in the Utah Juvenile Victim-Offender Mediation Program." *Juvenile and Family Court Journal* 33:37–45.

PRATT, JOHN (2000). "The Return of the Wheelbarrow Man: The Arrival of Postmodern Penalty?" *British Journal of Criminology* 40:127–145.

PRATT, TRAVIS C. and TIMOTHY W. GODSEY (2002). "Social Support and Homicide: A Cross-National Test of an Emerging Criminological Theory." *Journal of Criminal Justice* 30:589–601.

PRATT, TRAVIS C. and CHRISTOPHER T. LOWENKAMP (2002). "Conflict Theory, Economic Conditions, and Homicide." *Homicide Studies* 6:61–83.

PRATT, TRAVIS C. and MELISSA R. WINSTON (1999). "The Search for the Frugal Grail: An Empirical Assessment of the Cost-Effectiveness of Public vs. Private Correctional Facilities." *Criminal Justice Policy Review* 10:447–471.

PRENDERGAST, MICHAEL L. et al. (2002). "Involuntary Treatment within a Prison Setting: Impact on Psychosocial Change During Treatment." *Criminal Justice and Behavior* 29:5–26.

PRESSER, LOIS and PATRICIA VANVOORHIS (2002). "Values and Evaluation: Assessing Procedures and Outcomes of Restorative Justice Programs." *Crime and Delinquency* 48:162–188.

PRINS, HERSCHEL (1999). *Will They Do It Again? Risk Management In Criminal Justice and Psychiatry.* New York: Routledge.

PROBATION AND PAROLE EMPLOYEES' ASSOCIATION (2001). *Minutes of January 2001.* Portland, OR: Probation and Parole Employees' Association.

PROBATION ASSOCIATION (1939). *John Augustus: The First Probation Officer.* New York: Probation Association.

PROCTOR, JON L. (1999). "The 'New Parole': An Analysis of Parole Board Decision Making as a Function of Eligibility." *Journal of Crime and Justice* 22:193–217.

PROCTOR, JON L. and MICHAEL PEASE (2000). "Parole as Institutional Control: A Test of Specific Deterrence and Offender Misconduct." *Prison Journal* 80:39–55.

PURKISS, MARCUS et al. (2003). "Probation Officer Functions: A Statutory Analysis." *Federal Probation* 67:12–23.

PUZZANCHERA, CHARLES et al. (2003). *Juvenile Court Statistics 1998.* Washington, DC: Office of Juvenile Justice and Delinquency Prevention.

QUAY, HERBERT C. (1984). *Managing Adult Inmates.* College Park, MD: American Correctional Association.

QUAY, HERBERT C. and L.B. PARSONS (1971). *The Differential Behavioral Classification of the Adult Male Offender.* Philadelphia, PA: Temple University [Technical report prepared for the U.S. Department of Justice Bureau of Prisons, Contract J-1C-22, 253].

QUINN, JAMES F., LARRY GOULD, and LINDA HOLLOWAY (2001). "Community Partnership Councils: Meeting the Needs of Texas' Parole Officers." *Corrections Compendium* 26:1–5, 18–19.

RADLI, ERIC R. (1997). "Boot Camps: A 'Highly Intensive Supervision, Training, and Education Program.'" *American Jails* 11:85–90.

RAFTER, NICOLE HAHN (1997). *Creating Born Criminals.* Urbana: University of Illinois Press.

RANS, LAUREL L. (1984). "The Validity of Models to Predict Violence in Community and Prison Settings." *Corrections Today* 46:50–63.

RASMUSSEN, ALAN C. (2003). "Successful Supervision System for the Substance Abuser." *APPA Perspectives* 27:30–31.

RASMUSSEN, DAVID W. and BRUCE L. BENSON (1994). *Intermediate Sanctions: A Policy Analysis Based on Program Evaluations.* Tallahassee, FL: Report prepared for the Collins Center for Public Policy.

RAYNOR, PETER and TERRY HONESS (1998). *Drugs and Alcohol Related Offenders Project: An Evaluation of the West Glamorgan Partnership.* London, UK: Drugs Prevention Initiative, UK Home Office.

READ, EDWARD M. (1990). "Twelve Steps to Sobriety: Probation Officers 'Working the Program.'" *Federal Probation* 54:34–42.

READ, EDWARD M. (1992). "Euphoria on the Rocks: Understanding Crack Addiction." *Federal Probation* 56:3–11.

READ, EDWARD M. et al. (1997). "Variety of On-the-Job Special Skills, Special Duties in Federal Probation." *Federal Probation* 61:25–37.

REBELLON, CESAR J. (2002). "Reconsidering the Broken Homes/Delinquency Relationship and Exploring Its Mediating Mechanisms." *Criminology: An Interdisciplinary Journal* 40:103–136.

RECKLESS, WALTER C. (1967). *The Crime Problem* (2nd ed.). New York: Appleton-Century-Crofts.

REDDINGTON, FRANCES P. and BETSY WRIGHT KREISEL (2000). "Training Juvenile Probation Officers: National Trends and Practice." *Federal Probation* 64:28–32.

REDDINGTON, FRANCES P. and BETSY WRIGHT KREISEL (2003). "Basic Fundamental Skills Training for Juvenile Probation Officers: Results of a Nationwide Survey of Curriculum Content." *Federal Probation* 67:41–45.

REES, THOMAS A. JR. (1996). "Joining the Gang: A Look at Youth Gang Recruitment." *Journal of Gang Research* 4:19–25.

REISIG, MICHAEL D. (2002). "Administrative Control and Inmate Suicide." *Homicide Studies* 6:84–103.

RENZEMA, MARC (2000). "Tracking GPS: A Third Look." *The Journal of Offender Monitoring* 13:6–8, 27.

RICHARDSON, FRANCOISE (1999). "Electronic Tagging of Offenders: Trials in England." *Howard Journal of Criminal Justice* 38:158–172.

RICHARDSON, GORD and BURT GALAWAY (1995). *Evaluation of the Restorative Resolutions Project of the John Howard Society of Manitoba.* Winnipeg, MB: Faculty of Social Work, University of Manitoba.

RILEY, K. JACK, PATRICIA A. EBENER, and JAMES CHIESA (2000). *Drug Offenders and the Criminal Justice System.* Santa Monica, CA: Rand Corporation.

ROBBERS, MONICA L.P. (2003). "Reconnecting, Rebuilding, Re-Educating: Evaluating a Responsible Fatherhood Program for Incarcerated 'Deadbeat' Dads." *Corrections Compendium* 28:1–4, 29–31.

ROBERTS, DOROTHY E. et al. (1999). "Supreme Court Review." *Journal of Criminal Law and Criminology* 89:775–1140.

ROBERTS, JOHN W. (1997). "The Federal Bureau of Prisons: Its Mission, Its History, and Its Partnership with Probation and Pretrial Services." *Federal Probation* 11:53–57.

ROBERTS, JULIAN V. (2002). "Alchemy in Sentencing: An Analysis of Sentencing Reform Proposals in England and Wales." *Punishment and Society* 4:425–442.

ROBERTS, JULIAN V., JOAN NUFFIELD, and ROBERT HANN (2000). "Parole and the Public: Attitudinal and Behavioral Responses." *Empirical and Applied Criminal Justice Research Journal* 1:1–25.

ROBINSON, GWEN (2002). "Exploring Risk Management in Probation Practice: Contemporary Developments in England and Wales." *Punishment and Society* 4:5–25.

ROBINSON, LAURIE (1998). "Managing Sex Offenders in the Community: Challenges and Progress." *APPA Perspectives* 22:18.

ROGERS, JOSEPH W. (1990). "The Predisposition Report: Maintaining the Promise of Individualized Juvenile Justice." *Federal Probation* 54:43–57.

ROGERS, JOSEPH W. and JAMES D. WILLIAMS (1995). "The Predispositional Report, Decision Making, and Juvenile Court Policy." *Juvenile and Family Court Journal* 45:47–57.

ROGERS, RICHARD et al. (2000). "Prototypical Analysis of Antisocial Personality Disorder: A Study of Inmate Samples." *Criminal Justice and Behavior* 27:234–255.

ROLISON, GARRY L. et al. (2002). "Prisoners of War: Black Female Incarceration at the End of the 1980s." *Social Justice* 29:131–143.

ROMIG, DENNIS A. (1978). *Justice for Our Children.* Lexington, MA: Lexington Books.

ROTTMAN, DAVID and PAMELA CASEY (1999). "Therapeutic Jurisprudence and the Emergence of Problem-Solving Courts." *National Institute of Justice Journal* July:12–19.

ROWE, G.S. (1989). "Black Offenders, Criminal Courts, and Philadelphia Society in the Eighteenth Century." *Journal of Social History* 22:685–712.

ROY, SUDIPTO and JENNIFER N. GRIMES (2002). "Adult Offenders in a Day Reporting Center: A Preliminary Study." *Federal Probation* 66:44–50.

RUEFLE, WILLIAM and KENNETH MIKE REYNOLDS (1995). "Curfews and Delinquency in Major Cities." *Crime and Delinquency* 41:347–363.

RYAN, JAMES E. (1997). "Who Gets Revoked? A Comparison of Intensive Supervision Successes and Failures in Vermont." *Crime and Delinquency* 43:104–118.

RYAN, JOSEPH P., RANDY K. DAVIS, and HUILAN YANG (2001). "Reintegration Services and the Likelihood of Adult Imprisonment: A Longitudinal Study of Adjudicated Delinquents." *Research on Social Work Practice* 11:321–337.

SALCIDO, RAMON M., VINCENT ORNELAS, and JOHN A. GARCIA (2002). "A Neighborhood Watch Program for Inner-City School Children." *Children and Schools* 24:175–187.

SALEKIN, RANDALL T. (2002). "Clinical Evaluation of Youth Considered for Transfer to Adult Criminal Court: Refining Practice and Directions for Science." *Journal of Forensic Psychology Practice* 2:55–72.

SALEKIN, RANDALL T., RICHARD ROGERS, and KAREN L. USTAD (2001). "Juvenile Waiver to Adult Criminal Courts: Prototypes for Dangerousness, Sophistication-Maturity, and Amenability to Treatment." *Psychology Public Policy Review* 7:381–408.

SANBORN, JOSEPH B. (2001). "A *Parens Patriae* Figure or Impartial Fact Finder: Policy Questions and Conflicts for the Juvenile Court Judge." *Criminal Justice Policy Review* 12:311–332.

SCHAPS, ERIC and DANIEL SOLOMON (2003). "The Role of the School's Social Environment in Preventing Student Drug Use." *Journal of Primary Prevention* 23:299–328.

SCHARR, TIMOTHY M. (2001). "Interactive Video Training for Firearms Safety." *Federal Probation* 65:45–51.

SCHLATTER, GARY (1989). "Electronic Monitoring: Hidden Costs of Home Arresdt Programs." *Corrections Today* 51:94–95.

SCHMIDT, ANNESLEY K. (1998). "Electronic Monitoring: What Does the Literature Tell Us?" *Federal Probation* 62:10–19.

SCHMITZ, RICHARD J., PINKY S. WASSENBERG, and MARISA E. PATTERSON (2000). *Evaluations of the Christian County Extended Day Program, Peoria County Anti-Gang and Drug Abuse Unit, and Winnebago Day Reporting and Assessment Centers.* Chicago: Illinois Criminal Justice Information Authority.

SCHRAM, PAMELA J. and MERRY MORASH (2002). "Evaluation of a Life Skills Program for Women Inmates in Michigan." *Journal of Offender Rehabilitation* 34:47–70.

SCHWARTZ, IRA M. (ed.) (1999). "Will the Juvenile Court System Survive?" *Annals of the American Academy of Political and Social Science* 56:8–184.

SCHWARTZ, LISTA LINZER and NATALIE K. ISSER (2001). "Neonaticide: An Appropriate Application for Therapeutic Jurisprudence?" *Behavioral Sciences and the Law* 19:703–718.

SECHREST, DALE K. et al. (1998). *The Riverside County Drug Court: Final Research Report.* San Bernardino, CA: Criminal Justice Department, California State University-San Bernardino.

SEITER, RICHARD P. (ed.) (2000). "Restorative Justice: A Concept Whose Time Has Come." *Corrections Management Quarterly* 4:74–85.

SENJO, SCOTT R. (2001). "Drug Court Implementation: An Empirical Assessment of Court Procedure on Offender Program Completion." *Justice Professional* 14:239–267.

SENJO, SCOTT R. and LESLIE A. LEIP (2001). "Testing and Developing Theory in Drug Court: A Four-Part Logit Model to Predict Program Completion." *Criminal Justice Policy Review* 12:66–87.

SHAPIRO, EMILY F. et al. (2001). *Extended Jurisdiction Juvenile (EJJ) Offenders: A Study of Revocations.* Minneapolis: Institute on Criminal Justice, University of Minnesota Law School.

SHAPIRO, WALTER (1990). "A Life in His Hands." *Time,* May 28, 1990:23–24.

SHARP, SUSAN F. and ROSLYN MURASKIN (2003). *The Incarcerated Woman: Rehabilitative Programming in Women's Prisons.* Upper Saddle River, NJ: Prentice Hall.

SHAW, CLIFFORD R. and HENRY D. MCKAY (1929). *Juvenile Delinquency and Urban Areas.* Chicago: University of Chicago Press.

SHEARER, ROBERT A. (2000). "Coerced Substance Abuse Counseling Revisited." *Journal of Offender Rehabilitation* 30:153–171.

SHEARER, ROBERT A. (2003). "Identifying the Special Needs of Female Offenders." *Federal Probation* 67:46–51.

SHEARER, ROBERT A. and CHRIS R. CARTER (1999). "Screening and Assessing Substance-Abusing Offenders: Quantity and Quality." *Federal Probation* 63:30–33.

SHEEHY, ROBERT D. and EFRAIN A. ROSARIO (2003). "Connecting Drug Paraphernalia to Drug Gangs." *FBI Law Enforcement Bulletin* 72:1–6.

SHELDON, WILLIAM H. (1949). *Varieties of Delinquent Youth.* New York: Harper and Row.

SHELDEN, RANDALL G., SHARON K. TRACY, and WILLIAM B. BROWN (2004). *Youth Gangs in American Society.* Belmont, CA: Wadsworth/Thomson.

SHEWAN, DAVID and JOHN B. DAVIES (eds.) (2000). *Drug Use and Prisons: An International Perspective.* Amsterdam, Netherlands: Harwood.

SHICHOR, DAVID and DALE K. SECHREST (1998). "A Comparison of Mediated and Non-Mediated Juvenile Offender Cases in California." *Juvenile and Family Court Journal* 49:27–39.

SHICHOR, DAVID and DALE K. SECHREST (2002). "Privatization and Flexibility: Legal and Practical Aspects of Interjurisdictional Transfer to Prisons." *Prison Journal* 82:386–407.

SHORT, JAMES F. (2002). "Criminology: The Chicago School and Sociological Theory." *Crime, Law, and Social Change* 37:107–115.

SICKMUND, MELISSA (2003). *Juveniles in Court.* Washington, DC: Office of Juvenile Justice and Delinquency Prevention.

SIGLER, ROBERT T. and DAVID LAMB (1995). "Community-Based Alternatives to Prison: How the Public and Court Personnel View Them." *Federal Probation* 59: 3–9.

SILVER, ERIC (2000). "Race, Neighborhood Disadvantage, and Violence among Persons with Mental Disorders: The Importance of Contextual Measurement." *Law and Human Behavior* 24:449–456.

SIMMONS, CALVIN, JOHN K. COCHRAN, and WILLIAM R. BLOUNT (1997). "The Effects of Job-Related Stress and Job Satisfaction on Probation Officers' Inclinations to Quit." *American Journal of Criminal Justice* 21: 213–229.

SIMONS, DOMINIQUE, SANDY K. WERTELE, and PEGGY HEIL (2002). "Childhood Victimization and Lack of Empathy as Predictors of Sexual Offending Against Women and Children." *Journal of Interpersonal Violence* 17:1291–1307.

SIMOURD, DAVID J. and ROBERT D. HOGE (2000). "Criminal Psychopathy: A Risk-and-Need Perspective." *Criminal Justice and Behavior* 27:256–272.

SIMS, BARBARA (2001). "Surveying the Correctional Environment: A Review of the Literature." *Corrections Management Quarterly* 5:1–12.

SKOTNICKI, ANDREW (2000). *Religion and the Development of the American Penal System.* Lanham, MD: University Press of America.

SMALL, MARK A. et al. (2000). *Gangs in South Carolina: An Exploratory Study.* Washington, DC: U.S. Government Printing Office.

SMALL, SHAWN E. and SAM TORRES (2001). "Arming Probation Officers: Enhancing Public Confidence and Officer Safety." *Federal Probation* 65:24–28.

SNYDER, HOWARD N., MELISSA SICKMUND, and EILEEN POE-YAMAGATA (2000). *Juvenile Transfers to Criminal Court in the 1990s: Lessons Learned from Four Studies.* Washington, DC: U.S. Office of Juvenile Justice and Delinquency Prevention.

SONTHEIMER, HENRY and TRACI DUNCAN (1997). *Assessment of County Intermediate Punishment Programs.* Harrisburg: Pennsylvania Commission on Crime and Delinquency.

SORENSEN, JON and DONALD H. WALLACE (1999). "Prosecutorial Discretion in Seeking Death: An Analysis of Racial Disparity in the Pretrial Stages of Case Processing in a Midwestern County." *Justice Quarterly* 16: 559–578.

SOUTH CAROLINA DEPARTMENT OF CORRECTIONS (2003). *ISP Programs and Their Effectiveness.* Columbia: South Carolina Department of Corrections.

SOUTH CAROLINA DEPARTMENT OF PROBATION, PAROLE, AND PARDON SERVICES (1993). *Violations Guidelines and Administrative Hearings.* Columbia: South Carolina Department of Probation, Parole, and Pardon Services, Unpublished report.

SOUTH CAROLINA STATE REORGANIZATION COMMISSION (1991). *Prison Crowding in South Carolina: Is There a Solution?* Columbia, SC: South Carolina State Reorganization Commission.

SOUTH CAROLINA STATE REORGANIZATION COMMISSION (1992). *An Evaluation of the Implementation of the South Carolina Department of Corrections.* Columbia, SC: South Carolina State Reorganization Commission, A Jail and Prison Overcrowding Project Report.

SOUTHERN METHODIST UNIVERSITY (2002). *Evaluation of the DIVERT Court, Dallas County, Texas.* Dallas, TX: Southern Methodist University.

SPAANS, E.C. and C. VERWERS (1997). *Electronic Monitoring in the Netherlands: Results of the Experiment.* The Hague, Netherlands: Netherlands Ministry of Justice.

SPANGENBERG, ROBERT L. et al. (1987). *Assessment of the Massachusetts Probation System.* West Newton, MA: Spangenberg.

SPELMAN, JEFF (2003). *Felony Reentry Courts and Recidivism.* Richland County, OH: United Way NAPAC.

SPERGEL, IRVING A. and SUSAN F. GROSSMAN (1997). "The Little Village Project: A Community Approach to the Gang Problem." *Social Work* 42:456–470.

SPIEGEL, ALLEN D. and MARC B. SPIEGEL (1998). "The Insanity Plea in Early Nineteenth Century America." *Journal of Community Health* 23:227–247.

SPOHN, CASSIA and DAVID HOLLERAN (2002). "The Effect of Imprisonment on Recidivism Rates of Felony Offenders: A Focus on Drug Offenders." *Criminology* 40:329–358.

SPOONER, CATHERINE et al. (2001). "An Overview of Diversion Strategies for Australian Drug-Related Offenders." *Drug and Alcohol Review* 20:281–294.

SPRUIT, J.E. et al. (1998). "Special Issue: Forensic History." *International Journal of Law and Psychiatry* 21:315–446.

SREENIVASAN, SHOBA et al. (2000). "Neuropsychological and Diagnostic Differences Between Recidivistically Violent Not Criminally Responsible and Mentally Ill Prisoners." *International Journal of Law and Psychiatry* 23:161–172.

STALANS, LORETTA J., MAGNUS SENG, and PAUL YARNOLD (2001). *An Implementation and Initial Impact Evaluation of the Adult Sex Offender Probation Project in Cook County.* Chicago: Criminal Justice Information Authority.

STALANS, LORETTA J. et al. (2001). *Adult Sex Offender Program in Cook County.* Chicago: Illinois Criminal Justice Information Authority.

STANZ, ROBERT and RICHARD TEWKSBURY (2000). "Predictors of Success and Recidivism in a Home Incarceration Program." *Prison Journal* 80:326–344.

STARZYK, KATHERINE B. and WILLIAM L. MARSHALL (2003). "Childhood Family and Personological Risk Factors for Sexual Offending." *Aggression and Violent Behavior* 8:93–105.

STASTNY, CHARLES and GABRIELLE TYRNAUER (1982). *Who Rules the Joint? The Changing Political Culture of Maximum-Security Prisons in America.* Lexington, MA: Lexington Books.

STECK, PETER et al. (2002). "Killing of Sexual Partners By Women." *Monatsschrift fuer Kriminologie und Strafrechtsreform* 85:341–348.

STEFFENSMEIER, DARRELL J. et al. (2001). "Ethnicity and Judges' Sentencing Decisions: Hispanic-Black-White Comparisons." *Criminology* 39:145–178.

STEINER, HANS, ELIZABETH CAUFFMAN, and ELAINE DUXBURY (1999). "Personality Traits in Juvenile Delinquents: Relation to Criminal Behavior and Recidivism." *Journal of the American Academy of Child and Adolescent Psychiatry* 38:256–262.

STEIN-LEE, YETTA (2001). "The Psychosocial Needs of Hawaiian Women Incarcerated for Drug-Related Crimes." *Journal of Social Work Practice in the Addictions* 1:47–69.

STEPHEN, JACKIE (1993). *The Misrepresentation of Women Offenders: Gender Differences in Explanations of Crime in Probation Officers' Reports.* Norwich: UK: University of East Anglia, Social Work.

STEPHENS, MIKE (2002). "Community Safety and the Mentally Ill: How to Improve Community Care." *Community Safety Journal* 1:31–36.

STEPHENS, REGINA (2001). Personal letter. Sacramento, CA: Department of Corrections; Regina Stephens, Deputy Director, Parole and Community Services Division.

STEURY, ELLEN HOCHSTEDLER (1989). "Prosecutorial and Judicial Discretion." In *The U.S. Sentencing Guidelines: Implications for Criminal Justice,* Dean J. Champion (ed.). New York: Praeger.

STEVENS, DENNIS J. et al. (2002). "Case Study of Three Generations of Incarcerated Sexual Offenders." *Journal of Police and Criminal Psychology* 17:65–83.

STEWART, ERIC A. (2003). "School, Social Bonds, School Climate, and School Misbehavior: A Multilevel Analysis." *Justice Quarterly* 20:575–604.

STILES, DON R. (1994). "A Partnership for Safe Communities: Courts, Education and Literacy." *APPA Perspectives* 18:8–9.

STINCHCOMB, JEANNE B. (2000). "Developing Correctional Officer Professionalism: A Work in Progress." *Corrections Compendium* 25:1–4, 18–19.

STINCHCOMB, JEANNE B. and DARYL HIPPENSTEEL (2001). "Presentence Investigation Reports: A Relevant Justice Model Tool or a Medical Model Relic?" *Criminal Justice Policy Review* 12:164–177.

STOHR, MARY K. et al. (2002). "Inmate Perceptions of Residential Substance Abuse Treatment Programming." *Journal of Offender Rehabilitation* 34:1–32.

STOUTHAMER-LOEBER, MAGDA and ROLF LOEBER (2002). "Lost Opportunities for Intervention: Undetected Markers for the Development of Serious Juvenile Delinquency." *Criminal Behavior and Mental Health* 12: 69–82.

STORM, JOHN P. (1997). "What United States Probation Officers Do." *Federal Probation* 61:13–18.

STRAKA, RICHARD (2003). "The Violence of Hmong Gangs and the Crime of Rape." *FBI Law Enforcement Bulletin* 72:12–16.

STRANG, HEATHER (ed.) (2002). *Repair or Revenge: Victims and Restorative Justice.* Oxford, UK: Clarendon.

STRAUB, FRANK (1997). *Controlling Corruption in a Prison System: The New York State Department of Correctional Services, 1970–1990.* Ann Arbor, MI: University Microfilms International.

STRICKLAND, TED (2002). "Prison Bars Cannot Stop Disease." *Corrections Today* 64:108–110.

STRONG, ANN (1981). *Case Classification Manual, Module One: Technical Aspects of Interviewing.* Austin: Texas Adult Probation Commission.

STRUCKMAN-JOHNSON, CINDY and DAVID STRUCKMAN-JOHNSON (2002). "Sexual Coercion Reported by Women in Three Midwestern Prisons." *Journal of Sex Research* 39:217–227.

STURGES, JUDITH E. (2002). "Visitation at County Jails: Potential Policy Implications." *Criminal Justice Policy Review* 13:32–45.

STYVE, GAYLENE J. et al. (2000). "Perceived Conditions of Confinement: A National Evaluation of Juvenile Boot Camps and Traditional Facilities." *Law and Human Behavior* 24:297–308.

SULLIVAN, C., M.Q. GRANT, and J.D. GRANT (1957). "The Development of Interpersonal Maturity: Applications to Delinquency." *Psychiatry* 23:373–385.

SUNDT, JODY et al. (1998). "What Will the Public Tolerate?" *APPA Perspectives* 22:20–26.

SUTER, JENNIFER M. et al. (2002). "Anger in Prisoners: Women Are Different from Men." *Personality and Individual Differences* 32:1087–1100.

SWAMINATH, R.S. et al. (2002). "Experiments in Change: Pretrial Diversion of Offenders with Mental Illness." *Canadian Journal of Psychiatry* 47:430–458.

SWEET, JOSEPH (1985). "Probation as Therapy." *Corrections Today* 47:89–90.

SYKES, GRESHAM M. and DAVID MATZA (1957). "Techniques of Neutralization: A Theory of Delinquency?" *American Sociological Review* 22:664–670.

TAHA, AHMED E. (2001). "The Equilibrium Effect of Legal Role Changes: Are the Federal Sentencing Guidelines Being Circumvented?" *International Review of Law and Economics* 21:251–269.

TARTARO, CHRISTINE (1999). "Reduction of Suicides in Jails and Lockups through Situational Crime Prevention: Addressing the Needs of a Transient Population." *Journal of Correctional Health Care* 6: 235–263.

TARTARO, CHRISTINE (2002). "The Impact of Density on Jail Violence." *Journal of Criminal Justice* 30:499–510.

TAXMAN, FAYE S. and JEFFREY A. BOUFFARD (2003). "Drug Treatment in the Community: A Case Study of System Integration Issues." *Federal Probation* 67:4–14.

TAYCHEEDAH CORRECTIONAL INSTITUTION (2003). *Badger State Industries.* Fond du Lac, WI: Taycheedah Correctional Institution.

TENNESSEE DEPARTMENT OF CORRECTIONS (1994). *Tennessee Project CERCE (Comprehensive Education and Rehabilitation in a Correctional Environment) Resident Manual.* Nashville: Tennessee Department of Corrections.

TEWKSBURY, RICHARD (2002). "Validity and Utility of the Kentucky Sex Offender Registry." *Federal Probation* 66:21–26.

TEXAS CRIMINAL JUSTICE POLICY COUNCIL (2000). *Overview of Special Needs Parole Policy and Recommendations.* Austin: Texas Criminal Justice Policy Council.

TEXAS DEPARTMENT OF CRIMINAL JUSTICE (2003). *Texas Department of Criminal Justice Annual Report 2002.* Austin: Texas Department of Criminal Justice.

TEXAS YOUTH COMMISSION (2003). *Sheffield Boot Camp.* Austin: Texas Youth Commission.

THOMAS, CHRISTOPHER R., CHARLES E. HOLZER, and JULIE WALL (2002). "The Island Youth Programs: Community Interventions for Reducing Youth Crime and Violence." *Adolescent Psychiatry* 26:125–143.

THORNBERRY, TERENCE P. et al. (2003). *Gangs and Delinquency in Developmental Perspective.* Cambridge, UK: Cambridge University Press.

THURSTON COUNTY CORRECTIONS FACILITY (2003). *Turning Point Female Offender Program (TPFOP).* Thurston County, WA: Thurston County Sheriff's Office Corrections Facility.

TILLEY, NICK (ed.) (2002). *Analysis of Crime Prevention.* New York: Criminal Justice Press.

TIMASHEFF, NICHOLAS S. (1941). *One Hundred Years of Probation, 1841–1941.* New York: Fordham University Press.

TIMONEN, M. et al. (2000). "Psychiatric Admissions at Different Levels of the National Health Care Services and Male Criminality: The Northern Finland 1966 Birth Cohort Study." *Social Psychiatry and Psychiatry Epidemiology* 35:198–201.

TOMKINS, ALAN J. et al. (2002). "International Perspectives on Restorative and Community Justice." *Behavioral Sciences and the Law* 20:307–436.

TONRY, MICHAEL (ed.) (1998). *The Handbook of Crime and Punishment.* New York: Oxford University Press.

TONRY, MICHAEL (1999). *Fragmentation of Sentencing and Corrections in America.* Washington, DC: U.S. National Institute of Justice.

TONRY, MICHAEL (2001). *Penal Reform in Overcrowded Times.* Oxford, UK: Oxford University Press.

TORRES, SAM (1996). "The Use of a Credible Drug Testing Program for Accountability and Intervention." *Federal Probation* 60:18–23.

TORRES, SAM (1997). "The Substance-Abusing Offender and the Initial Interview." *Federal Probation* 61:11–17.

TORRES, SAM (1998). "A Continuum of Sanctions for Substance-Abusing Offenders." *Federal Probation* 62:36–45.

TORREY, E. FULLER (1999). "How Did So Many Mentally Ill Persons Get Into America's Jails and Prisons?" *American Jails* 13:9–13.

TRACY, PAUL E. (2002). *Decision Making and Juvenile Justice: An Analysis of Bias in Case Processing.* Belmont, CA: Wadsworth.

TRAVIS, JEREMY et al. (2002). *Beyond the Prison Gates: The State of Parole in America.* Washington, DC: Urban Institute Justice Policy Center.

TREMBLAY, PIERRE et al. (1996). "From Childhood Physical Aggression to Adolescent Maladjustment: The Montreal Prevention Experiment." In *Preventing Childhood Disorders, Substance Abuse, and Delinquency* R.D. Peters and R.J. McMahon (eds.). Thousand Oaks, CA: Sage.

TRESTER, HAROLD B. (1981). *Supervision of the Offender.* Englewood Cliffs, NJ: Prentice-Hall.

TRIPLET, RUSH and TOBY ROSS (1998). "Developing Partnership for Gang Intervention: The Role of Community Corrections." *APPA Perspectives* 22:29–35.

TROTTER, CHRISTOPHER (1996). "The Impact of Different Supervision Practices in Community Corrections: Cause for Optimism." *Australian and New Zealand Journal of Criminology* 29:29–46.

TRUITT, L. et al. (2002). *Evaluating Treatment Drug Courts in Kansas City, Missouri and Pensacola, Florida.* Cambridge, MA: Abt.

TURNER, SUSAN and JUDITH GREENE (1999). "The FARE Probation Experiment: Implementation and Outcomes of Day Fines for Felony Offenders in Maricopa County." *Justice System Journal* 21:1–22.

ULMER, JEFFREY T. (2001). "Intermediate Sanctions: A Comparative Analysis of the Probability and Severity of Recidivism." *Sociological Inquiry* 71:164–193.

UMBREIT, MARK S., ROBERT B. COATES, and BETTY VOS (2002a). "The Impact of Restorative Justice Conferencing: A Multi-National Perspective." *British Journal of Community Service* 1:21–48.

UMBREIT, MARK S., ROBERT B. COATES, and BETTY VOS (2002b). "Restorative Justice Circles: The Impact of Community Involvement." *APPA Perspectives* 26:36–40.

U.S. BUREAU OF JUSTICE ASSISTANCE (1994). *Drug Night Courts: The Cook County Experience.* Washington, DC: U.S. Bureau of Justice Assistance.

U.S. CODE ANNOTATED (2004). *United States Code Annotated.* St. Paul, MN: West.

U.S. DEPARTMENT OF JUSTICE (1999). *More Than 500,000 Drunk Drivers on Probation or Incarcerated.* Washington, DC: U.S. Department of Justice.

U.S. DEPARTMENT OF JUSTICE (2001). *Census of U.S. Jails, 1999.* Washington, DC: U.S. Department of Justice.

U.S. DEPARTMENT OF JUSTICE (2003). *Probation and Parole, 2002.* Washington, DC: U.S. Department of Justice.

U.S. GENERAL ACCOUNTING OFFICE (1998). *Fines and Restitution: Improvement Needed in How Offender's Payment Schedules Are Determined.* Washington, DC: U.S. General Accounting Office.

U.S. GENERAL ACCOUNTING OFFICE (2001). *Prisoner Releases: Trends and Information on Reintegration Programs.* Washington, DC: U.S. General Accounting Office.

U.S. OFFICE OF JUSTICE PROGRAMS (1998). *Rethinking Probation: Community Supervision, Community Safety.* Washington, DC: U.S. Office of Justice Programs.

U.S. SENTENCING COMMISSION (2003). *United States Sentencing Commission Guidelines Manual.* Washington, DC: U.S. Sentencing Commission.

UNNEVER, JAMES D., FRANCIS T. CULLEN, and TRAVIS C. PRATT (2003). "Parental Management, ADHD, and Delinquent Involvement: Reassessing Gottfredson and Hirschi's General Strain Theory." *Justice Quarterly* 20:471–500.

UTTING, DAVID and JULIE VENNARD (2000). *What Works with Young Offenders in the Community?* Essex, UK: Barnardo's.

VALENTINE, BILL (1995). *Gang Intelligence Manual: Identifying and Understanding Modern-Day Violent Gangs in the United States.* Boulder, CO: Paladin.

VALETTE, DELPHINE (2002). "AIDS Behind Bars: Prisoners' Rights Guillotined." *Howard Journal of Criminal Justice* 41:107–122.

VANDERZANDEN, JAMES W. (1984). *Social Psychology.* New York: Random House.

VAUGHN, MICHAEL S. and LINDA G. SMITH (1999). "Practicing Penal Harm Medicine in the United States: Prisoners' Voices from Jail." *Justice Quarterly* 16:175–231.

VENTURA COUNTY SHERIFF'S DEPARTMENT (2001). *Tattoo Removal Program.* Ventura, CA: Ventura County Sheriff's Department.

VICTORIA DEPARTMENT OF CRIMINAL JUSTICE SERVICES (1998). *Review of Suicides and Self-Harm in Victorian Prisons.* Melbourne, AUS: Victoria Department of Justice Correctional Services Task Force.

VIGDAL, GERALD L. and DONALD W. STADLER (1994). "Alternative to Revocation Program Offers Offenders a Second Chance." *Corrections Today* 56:44–47.

VIGORITA, MICHAEL S. (2002). "Fining Practices in Felony Courts: An Analysis of Offender, Offense, and Systemic Factors." *Corrections Compendium* 27:1–5, 26–27.

VIRGINIA CRIMINAL SENTENCING COMMISSION (2001). *Assessing Risk Among Sex Offenders in Virginia.* Richmond: Virginia Criminal Sentencing Commission.

VIRGINIA DEPARTMENT OF CORRECTIONS (2002). *Criminal Justice: 'MILK' Prison Program Provides Deeper Mother-Child Bond.* Richmond, VA: Virginia Department of Corrections.

VIRGINIA DEPARTMENT OF CORRECTIONS (2003). *Probation and Parole: Frequently Asked Questions.* Richmond: Virginia Department of Corrections.

VIRGINIA DEPARTMENT OF CORRECTIONS (2004). *Intensive Supervised Probation.* Richmond: Virginia Department of Corrections, Community Corrections.

VISHER, CHRISTY A., PAMELA K. LATTIMORE, and RICHARD L. LINSTER (1991). "Predicting the Recidivism of Serious Youthful Offenders Using Survival Models." *Criminology* 29:329–366.

VITO, GENNARO F., RONALD M. HOLMES, and DEBORAH G. WILSON (1985). "The Effect of Shock and Regular Probation upon Recidivism: A Comparative Analysis." *American Journal of Criminal Justice* 9:152–162.

VITO, GENNARO F. and RICHARD TEWKSBURY (1998). "The Impact of Treatment: The Jefferson County (Kentucky) Drug Court Program." *Federal Probation* 62:46–51.

VOHRYZEK-BOLDEN, MIKI, TIM CROISDALE, and CAROLE BARNES (1999). *Overview of Selected States' Academy and In-Service Training for Adult and Juvenile Correctional Employees.* Sacramento: California Commission on Correctional Peace Officer Standards and Training.

VOLLUM, SCOTT and CHRIS HALE (2002). "Electronic Monitoring: A Research Review." *Corrections Compendium* 27:1–4, 23–27.

VON HIRSCH, ANDREW (1992). "Proportionality in the Philosophy of Punishment." In *Crime and Justice: A Review of Research, Volume 16,* Michael Tonry (ed.). Chicago and London: University of Chicago Press.

VOSS, ROBERT B. et al. (2002). "Evaluation of a Program to Motivate Impaired Driving Offenders to Install Ignition Interlocks." *Accident Analysis and Prevention* 34:449–455.

WALKLATE, SANDRA (2002). "So Who Are the Victims Now?" *British Journal of Community Justice* 1:47–63.

WALSH, ANTHONY et al. (2002). *Biosocial Criminology: Introduction and Integration.* Lanham, MD: American Correctional Association.

WALSH, THOMAS C. et al. (1997). "Current Research and Clinical Practices." *Journal of Offender Rehabilitation* 26:125–203.

WALTERS, GLENN D. et al. (1992). "The Choice Program: A Comprehensive Residential Treatment Program for Drug Involved Offenders." *International Journal of Offender Therapy and Comparative Criminology* 36:21–29.

WALTERS, GLENN D. et al. (2002). "Assessing Change with the Psychological Inventory of Criminal Thinking Styles: A Controlled Analysis and Multisite Cross-Validation." *Criminal Justice and Behavior* 29:308–331.

WANG, EUGENE W. et al. (2000). "The Effectiveness of Rehabilitation with Persistently Violent Male Prisoners." *International Journal of Offender Therapy and Comparative Criminology* 44:505–514.

WARGENT, MARTIN (2002). "The New Government of Probation." *Howard Journal of Criminal Justice* 41:182–200.

WARREN, ROGER K. (1998). *Reengineering the Court Process.* Madison, WI: Presentation to Great Lakes Court Summit, September 24–25, 1998.

WARWICK, KEVIN (2002). "Intermediate Sanction Options Help Alleviate Jail Overcrowding." *American Jails* 16:21–24.

WASHINGTON STATE DEPARTMENT OF SOCIAL AND MENTAL HEALTH SERVICES (1991). *SSOSA Blue Ribbon Panel Final Report to the Legislature.* Olympia, WA: Washington State Department of Social and Mental Health Services.

WASSERMAN, DAVID and ROBERT WACHBROIT (eds.) (2001). *Genetics and Criminal Behavior.* Cambridge, UK: Cambridge University Press.

WATERS, J. EUGENE and WILLIAM L. MEGATHLIN (2002). "Evaluating Change in Social Climate in a Close Security State Correctional Facility." *Journal of Offender Rehabilitation* 34:71–84.

WATKINS, JOHN C. JR. (1989). "Probation and Parole Malpractice in a Noninstitutional Setting: A Contemporary Analysis." *Federal Probation* 53:29–34.

WEBSTER, RUSSELL et al. (2001). *Building Bridges to Employment for Prisoners.* Lanham, MD: American Correctional Association.

WHITE, JEAN M. (2000). *Outstanding Warrants in Milwaukee County: Fugitives from the Justice System.* Thiensville, WI: Wisconsin Policy Research Institute.

WHITE, ROBERT J. et al. (2002). "Extent and Characteristics of Woman Batterers among Federal Inmates." *International Journal of Offender Therapy and Comparative Criminology* 46:412–426.

WHITEHEAD, JOHN T. (1989). *Burnout in Probation and Parole.* New York: Praeger.

WHITEHEAD, JOHN T. and MICHAEL B. BLANKENSHIP (2000). "The Gender Gap in Capital Punishment Attitudes: An Analysis of Support and Opposition." *American Journal of Criminal Justice* 25:1–13.

WHITEHEAD, JOHN T. and CHARLES A. LINDQUIST (1992). "Determinants of Probation and Parole Officer Professional Orientation." *Journal of Criminal Justice* 20: 13–24.

WHITFIELD, DICK (1997). *Tackling the Tag: The Electronic Monitoring of Offenders.* Winchester, UK: Waterside.

WIEBUSH, RICHARD G. (1990). "The Ohio Experience: Programmatic Variations in Intensive Supervision for Juveniles." *Perspectives* 14:26–35.

WILKINSON, REGINALD A. and TESSA UNWIN (1999). "In Prison: A Recipe for Disaster." *Corrections Today* 60: 98–102.

WILLIAMS, D.J. and TIFFANEY AMBER TURNAGE (2001). "Success of a Day Reporting Center Program." *Corrections Compendium* 26:1–3, 26.

WILLIAMS, FRANK P. III, MARILYN D. McSHANE, and H. MICHAEL DOLNY (2000). "Predicting Parole Absconders." *Prison Journal* 80:24–38.

WILSON, GEORGE P. (1985). "Halfway House Programs for Offenders." In *Probation, Parole, and Community Corrections,* Lawrence Travis III (ed.). Prospect Heights, IL: Waveland.

WILSON, JAMES Q. (1997). *Moral Judgment: Does the Abuse Excuse Threaten Our Legal System?* New York: HarperCollins.

WILSON, JAMES Q. and JOAN PETERSILIA (2002). *Crime: Public Policies for Crime Control.* Oakland, CA: Institute for Contemporary Studies Press.

WILSON, JOHN J. (2000). *1998 National Youth Gang Survey.* Washington, DC: National Youth Gang Center.

WILSON, ROBIN J. et al. (2000). "Community-Based Sexual Offender Management: Combining Parole Supervision and Treatment to Reduce Recidivism." *Canadian Journal of Criminology* 42:177–188.

WILSON, SANDRA JO and MARK W. LIPSEY (2000). "Wilderness Challenge Programs for Delinquent Youth: A Meta-Analysis of Outcome Evaluations." *Evaluation and Program Planning* 23:1–12.

WINFREE, L. THOMAS JR. and DENNIS M. GIEVER (2000). "On Classifying Driving-While-Intoxicated Offenders: The Experiences of a Citywide DWI Drug Court." *Journal of Criminal Justice* 28:13–21.

WINFREE, L. THOMAS JR., GREG NEWBOLD, and S. HOUSTON TUBB (2002). "Prisoner Perspectives on Inmate Culture in New Mexico and New Zealand: A Descriptive Case Study." *Prison Journal* 82:213–233.

WINTERFIELD, LAURA A. and SALLY T. HILLSMAN (1993). *The Staten Island Day-Fine Project.* Washington, DC: U.S. Department of Justice.

WITHROW, BRIAN (2003). "Juvenile Detention Risk Assessment: An Evaluation of the Sedgwick County Instrument." *Corrections Compendium* 28:1–4, 31.

WITT, PHILIP H. et al. (1996). "Sex Offender Risk and the Law." *Journal of Psychiatry and the Law* 24:343–377.

WITTENAUER, CHERYL (2003). *C.H.A.M.P. Assistance Dogs, Inc.* Florissant, MO: C.H.A.M.P. Assistance Dogs, Inc.

WOGAN, MICHAEL and MARCI MACKENZIE (2002). "Antisocial Personality Disorder in a Sample of Imprisoned Non-Sex, Non-Arson Adult Male Offenders." *Journal of Offender Rehabilitation* 35:31–49.

WOLCOTT, DAVID et al. (2001). "'The Cop Will Get You': The Police and Discretionary Juvenile Justice, 1890–1940." *Child and Family Behavior Therapy* 23:33–43.

WOLF, YVAL (2002). "Violations of Out-Group and In-Group Regulations in the Eyes of Ordinary and Protected Prisoners: An Instance of Judgmental Modularity." *International Journal of Offender Therapy and Comparative Criminology* 46:206–219.

WOLFGANG, MARVIN E. and FRANCO FERRACUTI (1967). *The Subculture of Violence.* London: Tavistock.

WOLFGANG, MARVIN E., ROBERT M. FIGLIO, and THORSTEN SELLIN (1972). *Delinquency in a Birth Cohort.* Chicago, IL: University of Chicago Press.

WOLLERT, RICHARD (2002). "The Importance of Cross-Validation in Actuarial Test Construction: Shrinkage in the Risk Estimates for the Minnesota Sex Offender Screening Tool Revisited." *Journal of Threat Assessment* 2:87–102.

WOOD, PETER B. and HAROLD G. GRASMICK (1999). "Toward the Development of Punishment Equivalencies: Male and Female Inmates Rate the Severity of Alternative Sanctions Compared to Prison." *Justice Quarterly* 16:19–50.

WOOD, PETER B. and DAVID C. MAY (2003). "Racial Differences in Perceptions of the Severity of Sanctions: A Comparison of Prison with Alternatives." *Justice Quarterly* 20:605–631.

WOOLDREDGE, JOHN D. and AMY THISTLEWAITE (2002). "Reconsidering Domestic Violence Recidivism: Conditioned Effects of Legal Controls by Individual and Aggregate Levels of Stake in Conformity." *Journal of Quantitative Criminology* 18:45–70.

WORTLEY, RICHARD et al. (2002). *Situational Prison Control: Crime Prevention in Correctional Institutions.* Lanham, MD: American Correctional Association.

WRIGHT, DAVID et al. (2000). *Evaluation of Oklahoma Drug Courts, 1997–2000.* Oklahoma City, OK: Oklahoma Criminal Justice Resource Center.

YOCHELSON, SAMUEL and STANTON E. SAMENOW (1976). *The Criminal Personality.* New York: Jason Aronson.

YOUNGKEN, MICHAEL J. (2000). "The Commission on Accreditation for Corrections: Raising the Bar of Excellence." *Corrections Today* 62:98–112.

ZHAO, JIHONG and NICHOLAS LOVRICH (1997). "Collective Bargaining and the Police: The Consequences for Supplemental Compensation Policies in Large Societies." *Policing*

ZHAO, JIHONG et al. (2002). "Participation in Community Crime Prevention: Are Volunteers More or Less Fearful of Crime Than Other Citizens?" *Journal of Crime and Justice* 25:41–61.

ZHANG, SHELDON X. (2000). *Evaluation of the Los Angeles County Juvenile Drug Treatment Boot Camp.* Los Angeles: Los Angeles County Sheriff's Department.

ZILKOWSKY, DIANE et al. (2001). "Focusing on Alcohol and Drugs: Perspectives, Profiles, Programs." *Forum on Corrections Research* 13:1–60.

ZONDERMAN, JON (1999). *Beyond the Crime Lab: The New Science of Investigation* (rev. ed.). New York: Wiley.

Cases Cited

Name Index

Subject Index